THE VICTORIA HISTORY OF THE COUNTIES OF ENGLAND

A HISTORY OF

SHROPSHIRE

VOLUME X

THE VICTORIA HISTORY OF THE COUNTIES OF ENGLAND

EDITED BY C. R. J. CURRIE

THE UNIVERSITY OF LONDON
INSTITUTE OF
HISTORICAL RESEARCH

Oxford University Press, Great Clarendon Street, Oxford OX2 6DP
Oxford New York
Athens Auckland Bangkok Bogotá
Buenos Aires Calcutta Cape Town Chennai
Dar es Salaam Delhi Florence Hong Kong
Istanbul Karachi Kuala Lumpur
Madrid Melbourne Mexico City Mumbai
Nairobi Paris São Paolo Singapore
Taipei Tokyo Toronto Warsaw

and associated companies in
Berlin Ibadan

Oxford is a registered trade mark of Oxford University Press

Published in the United States
by Oxford University Press Inc., New York

British Library Cataloguing in Publication Data
Data available

ISBN 0 19 722789 9

Printed by H Charlesworth & Co Ltd
Huddersfield, England

INSCRIBED TO THE

MEMORY OF HER LATE MAJESTY

QUEEN VICTORIA

WHO GRACIOUSLY GAVE THE TITLE TO

AND ACCEPTED THE DEDICATION

OF THIS HISTORY

Acton Scott Hall from the south-west.
The main entrance, originally central, was moved to one side in the early 19th century.

A HISTORY OF
SHROPSHIRE

EDITED BY G. C. BAUGH

VOLUME X

WENLOCK, UPPER CORVE DALE, AND THE STRETTON HILLS

PUBLISHED FOR
THE INSTITUTE OF HISTORICAL RESEARCH
BY
OXFORD UNIVERSITY PRESS
1998

CONTENTS OF VOLUME TEN

LIST OF PLATES

For permission to reproduce material in their copyright, custody, or possession, thanks are offered to the Birmingham and Warwickshire Archaeological Society (plate 10), the Board of Trustees of the Victoria and Albert Museum (plate 27), the Bodleian Library (plate 20), the Hulton Deutsch Collection Ltd. (plate 35), Hunting Aerofilms Ltd. (plates 2, 4), the Ironbridge Gorge Museum Trust (plates 25–6, 30, 32–3), Much Wenlock Town Council (plate 36), the Revd. Canon M. H. Ridgway (plate 8), the Royal Commission on the Historical Monuments of England (frontispiece and plates 13–15, 17–18), Shropshire Archaeological and Historical Society (plate 19), Shropshire County Museum Service (plates 37, 40), the *Shropshire Magazine* (plates 5–6), Shropshire Newspapers Ltd. (plates 24, 31), Shropshire Records and Research Centre (plates 7, 9, 16, 21–3, 28–9, 34, 38–9, 41), and the University of Cambridge Committee for Aerial Photography (plates 1, 3).

Frontispiece

Acton Scott Hall. Photograph, 1962, by R.C.H.M.E. in N.M.R., neg. AA62/6857: Crown copyright

Plates between pages 232 and 233

1 Wenlock Edge. Photograph, 1965, in Cambridge University Collection of Air Photographs, neg. AMS 78: copyright reserved

2 Much Wenlock. Photograph, *c.* 1973, by Aerofilms Ltd., neg. A 219676

3 The Stretton Gap. Photograph, 1947, in Cambridge University Collection of Air Photographs, neg. Y 85: copyright reserved

4 Church Stretton. Photograph *c.* 1962 by Aerofilms Ltd., neg. A 96258

5 Shipton church. Photograph *c.* 1968 by Carl & Pat Jameson in S.P.L.

6 Tugford church. Photograph in S.P.L.

7 Eaton-under-Heywood church. Photograph by James Mallinson in S.P.L., neg. Mallinson 917

8 Hughley chancel screen. Photograph by Fred H. Crossley in Conway Library, Courtauld Institute of Art, neg. B47/6568

9 Heath chapel. Photograph *c.* 1900 in S.P.L.

10 Holdgate: Hall Farm. Photograph, 1949, by S. A. Jeavons in S.P.L.

11 Plaish Hall. Photograph, 1987, by P. A. Stamper

12 Wilderhope Manor. Photograph, 1993, by D. C. Cox

13 Larden Hall. Photograph, 1967, by R.C.H.M.E. in N.M.R., neg. BB67/4543: Crown copyright

14 Lutwyche Hall. Photograph, 1974, by R.C.H.M.E. in N.M.R., neg. BB74/3808: Crown copyright

15 Lutwyche Hall: the entrance hall. Photograph, 1974, by R.C.H.M.E. in N.M.R., neg. BB74/3819: Crown copyright

16 Upper Millichope: the Lodge. Photograph by James Mallinson in S.P.L., neg. Mallinson 716

17 Acton Scott Hall: the dining room. Photograph, 1962, by G. B. Mason in N.M.R., neg. AA62/6863: Crown copyright

18 Badger Hall: the museum. Photograph, 1888, in N.M.R., neg. BB74/2928

19 Badger Hall. Watercolour, 1824, by J. Homes Smith in S.P.L., J. H. Smith colln. no. 235

20 Lower Millichope: the old and new halls. Drawing, *c.* 1840, in Bodl. MS. Top. Salop. c. 2, f. 377

21 Broseley: the Square and High Street. Postcard by R. Mansell & Sons in S.P.L.

LIST OF MAPS AND OTHER FIGURES

The maps were drawn by K. J. Wass from drafts by G. C. Baugh (figs. 1, 3, 9, 16–17, 34), D. C. Cox (figs. 10–13, 15, 36, 38, 43), and P. A. Stamper (figs. 2, 4, 6–8, 14, 18–22, 24–6, 31, 33, 41, 46). Unless it is stated otherwise below, the maps are based on the tithe plans; it should be understood that the tithe plans and the other primary sources specified below are supplemented by sources cited in the text. Figs. 32, 39, and 44 were drawn by A. P. Baggs. For permission to reproduce material in their copyright, custody, or possession, thanks are offered to Birmingham University Library (fig. 37), the British Library Board (figs. 42, 45), the Rt. Hon. the Lord Forester (fig. 47), and the Ironbridge Gorge Museum Trust (fig. 28).

EDITORIAL NOTE

VOLUME X is the seventh volume of the *Victoria History of Shropshire* to be published, and the sixth since the revival of the project outlined in the Editorial Note to Volume VIII (1968). The partnership between the Shropshire County Council (with the continued support of the Walker Trust) and the University of London continued until 1994, local supervision of the *History*'s work being devolved by the Council's Leisure Services Committee on the Victoria County History Advisory Board. Mr. N. L. Pickering chaired the Committee and the Board from 1985 to 1993 when he was succeeded in both capacities by Mr. R. K. Austin, chairman of the Board 1993–4.

In 1994, a new partnership was formed to manage the Shropshire *History*: the University of Keele agreed to employ the local editorial staff with financial assistance from the Shropshire County Council, editorial control and other responsibilities remaining, as before, with the University of London. In 1994 the University of Keele formed a new Advisory Board on which the three partners were represented, and Mr. J. H. Y. Briggs became its chairman, Mr. Austin its vice-chairman. In 1997 Dr. J. R. Studd succeeded Professor Briggs. For thus securing a continuance of work on the Shropshire *History* for a further period of years the University of London records its gratitude to the University of Keele and the Shropshire County Council and also to Professor B. E. F. Fender, C.M.G., then Vice-Chancellor of Keele, and Mr. J. L. Hirst, then County Leisure Services Officer, for their successful endeavours to this end. Work on the present volume has also received the generous support of Bridgnorth District Council and Mr. T. S. Acton.

Of the local staff mentioned in the Editorial Note to Volume IV (1989) Mr. G. C. Baugh, County Editor, and Dr. D. C. Cox, Assistant County Editor, have continued in post. Dr. P. A. Stamper, Assistant County Editor since 1981, took up a new appointment in 1992. Mrs. J. M. Day continued until 1995 as part-time secretary, also undertaking some research. Her predecessor, Mrs M. B. Key, typed the index. Mr. P. B. Hewitt began to work voluntarily for the *History* in 1992.

For help given during the preparation of this volume thanks are offered to the Hereford Diocesan Registrar and to the staffs of the Hereford and Worcester Record Office, Hereford, under Miss D. S. Hubbard; the Natural and Historic Environment Group (Shropshire County Council Environment Department) under Mr. H. O. Thomas, especially Miss P. A. Ward; the Local Studies Library, Shrewsbury, under Mr. A. M. Carr; the Royal Commission on the Historical Monuments of England at Keele, under Mr. P. Everson; Shropshire Libraries, especially the Information Service under Elaine Moss and those at headquarters; the Shropshire Record Office successively under Mrs. L. B. Halford (now Mrs. K. Roberts) and Miss R. E. Bagley; the Staffordshire Record Office and William Salt Library, Stafford, successively under Dr. D. V. Fowkes and Mrs. D. M. A. Randall; and the Department of Manuscripts and Records of the National Library of Wales. Special mention too must be made of the invaluable practical assistance afforded over several years by Mrs. P. A. Downes, town clerk of Much Wenlock, and by the town council's archivists, the late Mr. V. H. Deacon and his joint successors Miss M. Furbank and Mr. O. G. McDonald. As so often in the past Mr. J. B. Lawson, Shrewsbury School Librarian, and Dr. B. S. Trinder have given much generous help, as has Mrs. M. Moran. Mr. M. W. Greenslade and Mr. D. A. Johnson are thanked for their help in checking materials in Stafford at a late stage in the preparation of the volume. Thanks are also owed to Professor C. R. Elrington, who after his retirement as General Editor of the Victoria History in 1994 continued to help with the editing of the volume, and to those landowners (in particular Lord Forester and Sir Michael Leighton) and private householders who have courteously given access to their property and muniments. Many others who have helped with particular articles or sources of information are named in appropriate footnotes.

Lines by Louis MacNeice on page 5 are quoted (from his *Collected Poems*, published by Faber & Faber, 1966) by permission of David Higham Associates.

The *General Introduction* to the *History* (1970) and its *Supplement 1970–90* (1990) outline the structure, aims, and progress of the series as a whole.

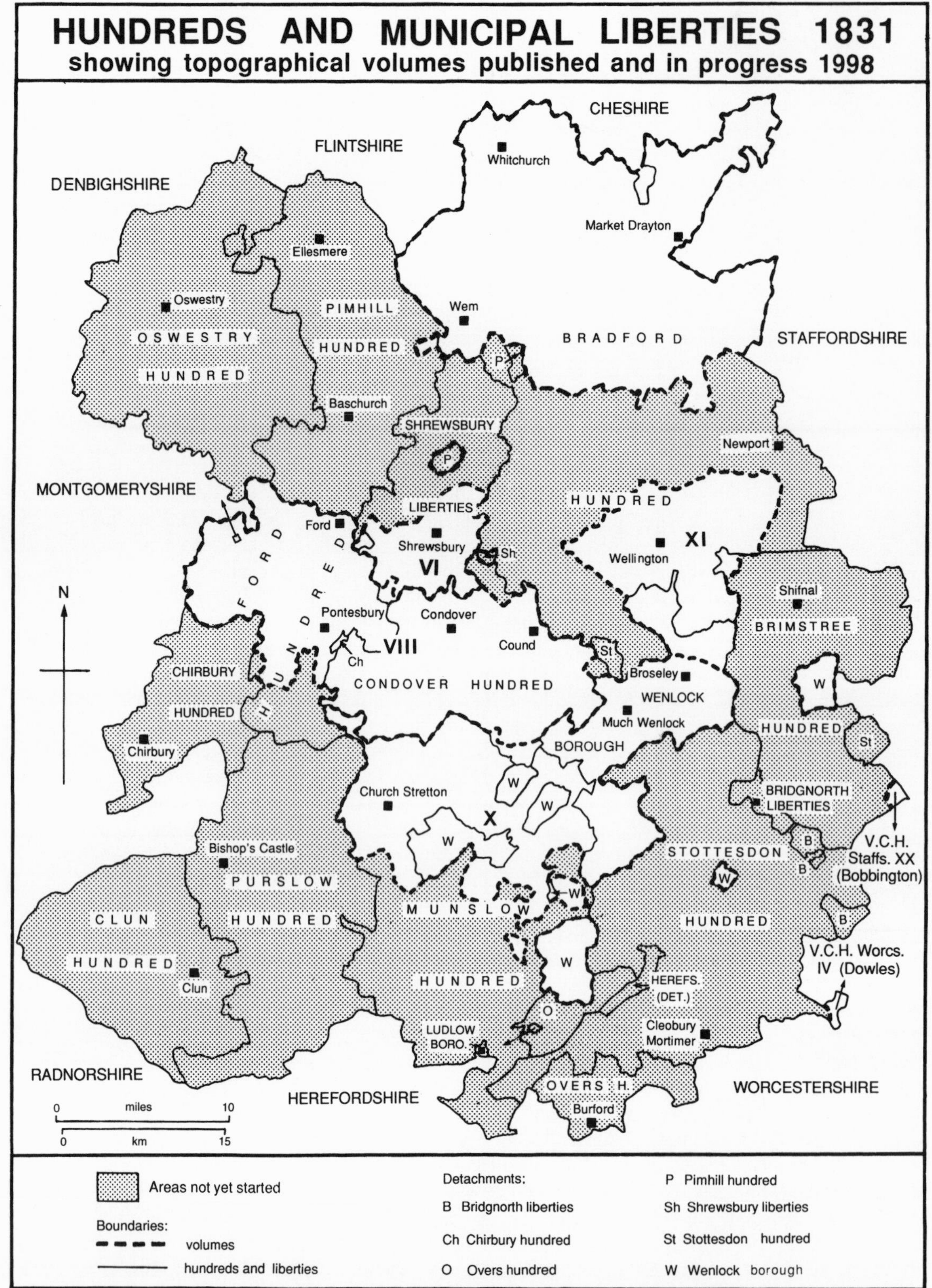

Fig. 1

In addition to the topographical volumes shown above as published and in progress, four general volumes have appeared: I (Natural History, Early Man, Romano-British Shropshire, Domesday, Ancient Earthworks, Industries, Forestry; 1908), II (Ecclesiastical Organization, Religious Houses, Schools, Sport, Population Table; 1973), III (County Government, Parliamentary Representation; 1979), and IV (Agriculture; 1989). A fifth general volume, V (Architecture), is in progress.

LIST OF CLASSES OF DOCUMENTS IN THE PUBLIC RECORD OFFICE

USED IN THIS VOLUME WITH THEIR CLASS NUMBERS

Board of Trade, Companies Registration Office

BT 31	Files of Dissolved Companies

Chancery

	Proceedings
C 1	Early
C 2	Series I
C 3	Series II
C 54	Close Rolls
C 60	Fine Rolls
C 66	Patent Rolls
C 78	Decree Rolls
C 93	Proceedings of Commissioners for Charitable Uses, Inquisitions and Decrees
	Masters' Exhibits
C 103	Blunt
C 104	Tinney
C 107	Senior
C 116	Court Rolls
	Inquisitions post mortem
C 132	Series I, Hen. III
C 133	Edw. I
C 134	Edw. II
C 135	Edw. III
C 136	Ric. II
C 138	Hen. V
C 139	Hen. VI
C 140	Edw. IV and V
C 141	Ric. III
C 142	Series II
C 143	Inquisitions ad quod damnum
C 145	Miscellaneous Inquisitions
C 148	Ancient Deeds, Series CS

Court of Common Pleas

CP 25	Feet of Fines
CP 40	Plea Rolls
CP 43	Recovery Rolls

Duchy of Lancaster

DL 7	Inquisitions post mortem

Exchequer, Treasury of the Receipt

E 32	Forest Proceedings
E 36	Miscellaneous Books

Exchequer, King's Remembrancer

E 142	Ancient Extents
E 150	Inquisitions post mortem, Series I
E 178	Special Commissions of Inquiry
E 179	Subsidy Rolls, etc.

Exchequer, Augmentation Office

E 302	Particulars of Concealments
E 303	Conventual Leases
E 315	Miscellaneous Books
E 326	Ancient Deeds, Series B

Exchequer, First Fruits and Tenths Office

E 339	Returns of Benefices

Exchequer, Pipe Office

E 358	Miscellaneous Accounts

Ministry of Education

ED 7	Public Elementary Schools, Preliminary Statements

Home Office

HO 67	Acreage Returns
	Various, Census Papers
HO 107	Population Returns
HO 129	Ecclesiastical Returns
HO 144	Correspondence and Papers, Domestic and General, Registered Papers, Supplementary
HO 334	Immigration and Nationality Department, Duplicate Certificates of Naturalization

Tithe Redemption Commission

IR 18	Tithe Files
IR 29	Tithe Apportionments
IR 30	Tithe Maps

Justices Itinerant, Assize and Gaol Delivery Justices, etc.

JUST 1	Eyre Rolls, Assize Rolls, etc.

Exchequer, Office of the Auditors of Land Revenue

LR 2	Miscellaneous Books

Ministry of Agriculture, Fisheries and Food

MAF 68	Various, Agricultural Returns, Parish Summaries

PUBLIC RECORD OFFICE CLASS NUMBERS

Maps and Plans

MPA	Maps and Plans from Chancery classes

Prerogative Court of Canterbury

PROB 4	Inventories post-1660, parchment

British Transport Historical Records

RAIL 502	Much Wenlock & Severn Junction Railway Co.

Court of Requests

REQ 2	Proceedings

Registrar General

RG 6	Society of Friends Registers and Certificates of Births, Marriages, and Deaths
	Census Records
RG 9	1861 Census Returns
RG 10	1871 Census Returns
RG 11	1881 Census Returns
RG 12	1891 Census Returns

Special Collections

SC 2	Court Rolls
SC 6	Ministers' and Receivers' Accounts
SC 12	Rentals and Surveys, Portfolios

State Paper Office

SP 1	State Papers, Hen. VIII, General Series
	State Papers Domestic
SP 16	Chas. I
SP 23	Interregnum
SP 44	Entry Books

Court of Star Chamber

	Proceedings
STAC 2	Hen. VIII
STAC 8	Jas. I

SELECT LIST OF ACCUMULATIONS AND COLLECTIONS IN THE SHROPSHIRE RECORD OFFICE

USED IN THIS VOLUME

Official Archives

	Shropshire (formerly Salop) County Council
119	Miscellanea
262, 1334, 2979	Education Department
3763	Victoria History of Shropshire
4873	County Secretary
293	Acton Scott parish
294, 3898	Much Wenlock parish
560	Shropshire quarter sessions
990	Ditton Priors parish
1564	Department of Education and Science
1565	Diddlebury parish
1705, 2788	Munslow parish
2005	Acton Scott parish
2079, 4011, 4044	Board of Inland Revenue
2251	Stoke St. Milborough school
2283, 3903	Hughley parish
2519, 3571	Cardington parish
2991	Broseley parish
2992	Barrow parish
2993	Benthall parish
3315	Eaton-under-Heywood parish
3365	Shrewsbury Corporation (pre-1836)
3568	Willey parish
3573	Rushbury parish
3894	Monkhopton parish
3900	Easthope parish
3901	Stanton Long parish
3902	Shipton parish
4131	Holdgate parish
4132	Tugford parish
4190	Church Commissioners
4323	Hope Bowdler parish
4366	Stoke St. Milborough parish
4367	Clee St. Margaret parish
4427	Linley parish
4480	Badger parish
4481	Beckbury parish
4526	Jackfield school
4598	Monkhopton school
4644	Abdon parish
4693	Charity Commissioners

Official Archives (*cont.*)

DA 3	Ludlow Corporation (post 1835)
DA 5	Shrewsbury Corporation (post 1835)
DA 6	Wenlock Corporation (post 1835)
DA 17	Bridgnorth Rural District Council
DA 18	Church Stretton Rural District Council
DA 19	Clun Rural District Council

Family and Estate Archives

2	Sandford of Sandford
20	Oakly Park estate
165	Dunne of Gatley Park
168	Lord Barnard
498	The Earl of Shrewsbury and Waterford
513	Cure of Badger
515	Vickers of Cranmere
567, 1066, 2557	Corbett of Longnor
757	Viscount Boyne
809	Benson of Lutwyche
840	Tyrwhitt-Jones of Stanley Hall
999	Orleton estate (*withdrawn*)
1037, 4572	More of Linley
1093, 2228	Aldenham Park estate
1224	Lord Forester
1514	Bruce-Smythe of Acton Burnell
1842, 2563, 3925	Acton of Acton Scott
1952	Kenyon-Slaney of Hatton Grange
2089	Moseley of Buildwas Abbey
2922	Lady Labouchere
3320	Childe of Kinlet
3385	Bishop of Shipton
3614	Haslewood of Bridgnorth
3657	Weston Park estate
4825, 5001	Corfield of Chatwall
5460	Cressett of Cound
5735	Brooke of Haughton

Other Archives

2138	Bishop's Castle Methodist circuit
2334	Wenlock Agricultural Reading Society
2533	Methodist records, various
2612, 2941, 3544	Ludlow Methodist circuit

Other Archives (*cont.*)

3212	South Shropshire Methodist circuit
3219	Church Stretton Methodist church
4791	Sun Alliance Insurance Group

Solicitors' Accumulations

314, 604	Potts & Potts of Broseley
783, 5236	G. H. Morgan & Sons of Ludlow
802, 1011, 3288, 3651	Salt & Sons (later Wace, Morgan & Salt) of Shrewsbury
924	R. J. R. Haslewood of Bridgnorth
933, 1135	Peele & Aris of Shrewsbury
1141	Clark & Co. of Ludlow
1150	Farrer & Co. of Lincoln's Inn Fields
1190	Pitt & Cooksey of Bridgnorth
1242	Cooper & Co. of Much Wenlock
1313	Balfour & Cooke of Shrewsbury
1359	Cooper & Co. of Bridgnorth
1634	G. R. & C. E. Wace of Shrewsbury
1670	Norris & Miles of Tenbury
1671	Marcy, Hemingway & Sons of Bewdley
1681	Cooper & Co. of Broseley
1709	Sprott, Stokes & Turnbull of Shrewsbury
2030	Salwey & Rickards of Ludlow
2664	Smith of Bridgnorth
3887	Warren, Upton & Garside of Market Drayton
4654	Wace, Morgan & Salt of Shrewsbury
5321	Bannister & King of Stourbridge

Artificial Collections

160	The Revd. R. C. Purton
163	Mr. M. S. Stobbs
171	Mr. N. G. Hyde
298	Mr. W. Baxter
536	Mr. D. Cole
563	Mr. P. M. E. Erwood
566, 637	Coalbrookdale Archives Association
775, 836	Mr. S. Raine
837, 1005, 1238, 2482, 2623, 2872, 4055, 4260	British Records Association
1146	Miss A. K. Head
1175	Dr. W. Watkins-Pitchford
1865, 3195	Sir Thomas Phillipps
1931, 4597	Mr. E. H. Pee
2024	Shrewsbury Borough Library
2906	Hereford City Library
3375, 3765	Mr. H. D. G. Foxall
3419	Mrs. A. N. Rowlands
3756	Mr. L. C. Lloyd
3931	Mr. T. H. Trowsdale
3956	Mr. N. J. Britnell
4175	Mr. P. Grinke
4208	Shropshire Family History Society
4774	Mr. T. H. Thompson
4792	Mr. G. F. Walker
4835	Mr. H. R. Pyper
4890	Dr. P. A. Stamper
5403	Dr. N. Mutton
5518	Mr. J. F. Henderson

NOTE ON ABBREVIATIONS

Among the abbreviations and short titles used the following may require elucidation:

Ag. Hist. Eng.	*Agrarian History of England and Wales*, i–vi, viii, ed. H. P. R. Finberg and J. Thirsk (1967–91)
Agric. H.R.	*Agricultural History Review*
Alum. Cantab.	J. and J. A. Venn, *Alumni Cantabrigienses* (1922–54)
Alum. Oxon.	J. Foster, *Alumni Oxonienses* (1887–92)
Arch. Jnl.	*Archaeological Journal*
B.A.A.	Birmingham Archidiocesan Archives
B.L.	British Library, London
B.M.	British Museum, London
B.R.L.	Birmingham Central Library, Reference Library Archives Department
Bk. of Fees	*Book of Fees* (H.M.S.O. 1920–31)
Bodl.	Bodleian Library, Oxford
Bull. Inst. Hist. Res.	*Bulletin of the Institute of Historical Research*
Burke, *Land. Gent.*	J. and J. B. Burke and others, *Genealogical and Heraldic Dictionary* [later *History*] *of the Landed Gentry* (1843–1972)
Burke, *Peerage*	J. Burke and others, *General* [later *Genealogical*] *and Heraldic Dictionary* [later *History*] *of the Peerage* (1826–1975)
Bye-Gones	*Bye-Gones relating to Wales and the Border Counties* (1871–1940)
C.S.	Cantilupe Society
Cal. Chart. R.	*Calendar of the Charter Rolls* (H.M.S.O. 1903–27)
Cal. Close	*Calendar of the Close Rolls* (H.M.S.O. 1892–1963)
Cal. Inq. Misc.	*Calendar of Inquisitions Miscellaneous (Chancery)* (H.M.S.O. 1916–69)
Cal. Inq. p.m.	*Calendar of Inquisitions post mortem* (H.M.S.O. 1904–in progress)
Cal. Pat.	*Calendar of the Patent Rolls* (H.M.S.O. 1891–in progress)
Camd. 3rd [etc.] ser.	R.H.S., Camden 3rd [etc.] series
Camd. Soc.	Camden Society
Camden, *Brit.*	W. Camden, *Britannia*
Cart. Sax. ed. Birch	*Cartularium Saxonicum*, ed. W. de G. Birch (1885–99)
Census	Census report (printed)
Ch. Cal. Dioc. Heref.	*Church Calendar and Clergy List for the Diocese of Hereford*
Close R.	*Close Rolls of the Reign of Henry III* (H.M.S.O. 1902–75)
Complete Peerage	G. E. C[okayne] and others, *Complete Peerage* (2nd edn. 1910–59)
Compton Census, ed. Whiteman	*Compton Census of 1676: a critical edition*, ed. A. Whiteman (British Academy Records of Social and Economic History, N.S. x, 1986)
Cranage	D. H. S. Cranage, *An Architectural Account of the Churches of Shropshire* (Wellington; 2 vols. 1901 and 1912, published in 10 parts 1894–1912). Cited by part number.
D.N.B.	*Dictionary of National Biography* (1885–in progress)
Dict. Welsh Biog.	*Dictionary of Welsh Biography down to 1940* (Honourable Society of Cymmrodorion; 1959 edn.)
E.H.R.	*English Historical Review*
E.P.N.S.	English Place-Name Society
Econ. H.R.	*Economic History Review*
Eng. P.N. Elements	A. H. Smith, *English Place-Name Elements* (E.P.N.S. 1970)
Eyton	R. W. Eyton, *Antiquities of Shropshire* (1854–60)
G.E.C. *Baronetage*	G. E. C[okayne], *Complete Baronetage* (1900–9)
Gent. Mag.	*Gentleman's Magazine* (1731–1867)
H.L.R.O.	House of Lords Record Office, Westminster
H.W.R.O.(H.)	Hereford and Worcester Record Office (Hereford)
H.W.R.O.(W.)	Hereford and Worcester Record Office (Worcester)

NOTE ON ABBREVIATIONS

Heref. D. & C. mun.	Hereford Dean and Chapter Muniments
Hist. Parl., Commons	*The History of Parliament: The House of Commons* (History of Parliament Trust, 1964–in progress)
Hist. Research	*Historical Research: The Bulletin of the Institute of Historical Research*
I.G.M.T.	Ironbridge Gorge Museum Trust
Inq. Non. (Rec. Com.)	*Nonarum Inquisitiones in Curia Scaccarii,* ed. G. Vanderzee (Record Commission, 1807)
Jnl. Brit. Arch. Assoc.	*Journal of the British Archaeological Association*
L. & P. Hen. VIII	*Letters and Papers, Foreign and Domestic, of the Reign of Henry VIII* (H.M.S.O. 1864–1932)
L.J.	*Journals of the House of Lords*
Leland, *Itin.* ed. Toulmin Smith	*Itinerary of John Leland*, ed. L. Toulmin Smith (1906–8)
Lond. Gaz.	*London Gazette*
M.U.L.	John Rylands University Library of Manchester
Med. Arch.	*Medieval Archaeology*
Mont. Colln.	*Montgomeryshire Collections: Journal of the Powysland Club*
N.L.W.	National Library of Wales, Aberystwyth
N.M.R.	R.C.H.M.E., National Monuments Record Centre, Swindon
O.N.S.	Office of National Statistics
O.S.	Ordnance Survey
O.S. *Area Bk.*	O.S. *Book of Reference to the Plan of the Parish of . . .*
Orders of Q. Sess.	*Abstract of the Orders made by the Court of Quarter Sessions,* ed. R. Ll. Kenyon and Sir Offley Wakeman (Shropshire County Records nos. 2–5, 7, 9, 11–17 [Shrewsbury, 1901–16])
P.N. Salop.	M. Gelling with H. D. G. Foxall, *Place-Names of Shropshire* (1990–in progress)
P.R.O.	Public Record Office, Kew. See pp. xvii–xviii
P.R.S.	Pipe Roll Society
Pevsner, *Salop.*	N. Pevsner, *Shropshire* (The Buildings of England, 1958)
Pipe R.	*Pipe Rolls*
Q. Sess. Rolls	*Full List and Partial Abstract of . . . the Quarter Sessions Rolls*, 1696–1820, ed. L. J. Lee and R. G. Venables (Shropshire County Records nos. 6, 10 [Shrewsbury, 1901–5]
R.C.H.M.E.	Royal Commission on the Historical Monuments of England
R.H.S.	Royal Historical Society
R.O.	Record Office
Rot. Hund. (Rec. Com.)	*Rotuli Hundredorum temp. Hen. III et Edw. I*, ed. W. Illingworth and J. Caley (Record Commission, 1812–18)
S.C.C.	Shropshire (formerly Salop) County Council
S.C.C. Mins.	*Shropshire* [formerly *Salop*] *County Council Reports and Minutes*
S.M.R.	Shropshire Sites and Monuments Record, S.C.C. Environment Department. Information cited by primary record number prefixed with SA
S.P.L.	Local Studies Library, Shrewsbury (formerly Shrewsbury Public Library; in 1995 amalgamated with S.R.O. to form Shropshire Records and Research Centre)
S.P.R.	*Shropshire Parish Registers* (Shropshire Parish Register Society, incorporated in the Shropshire Archaeological and Historical Society)
S.R.O.	Shropshire Record Office (in 1995 amalgamated with S.P.L. to form Shropshire Records and Research Centre). See pp. xix–xx
SA	See above, S.M.R.
Salop. Agric. Returns, 1905	Board of Agriculture Returns for Shropshire 1905, copy in possession of editor, *V.C.H. Salop.*
Salop. N. & Q.	*Shropshire Notes & Queries* (1884–1942)
Salop. (R.E.E.D.)	*Shropshire*, ed. J. A. B. Somerset (Records of Early English Drama, 1994)
Stat. Instr.	Statutory Instrument(s)
T.C.S.V.F.C.	*Transactions of the Caradoc and Severn Valley Field Club*
T.S.A.S.	*Transactions of the Shropshire Archaeological and Historical Society*

NOTE ON ABBREVIATIONS

Tax. Eccl. (Rec Com.)	*Taxatio Ecclesiastica Angliae et Walliae auctoritate P. Nicholai IV, circa A.D. 1291*, ed. T. Astle, S. Ayscough and J. Caley (Record Commission, 1802)
Trinder, *Ind. Rev. Salop.*	B. Trinder, *The Industrial Revolution in Shropshire* (1981)
V.C.H.	*Victoria County History*
Visit. Salop. 1623	*Visitation of Shropshire, taken in the Year 1623* (Harleian Society, xxviii–xxix, 1889)
W.A.A.	Archives of the Archbishop of Westminster
W.B.R.	Wenlock borough records
W.S.L.	William Salt Library, Stafford
Woolhope Trans.	*Transactions of the Woolhope Naturalists' Field Club*
Yr. Bk.	*Year Book*

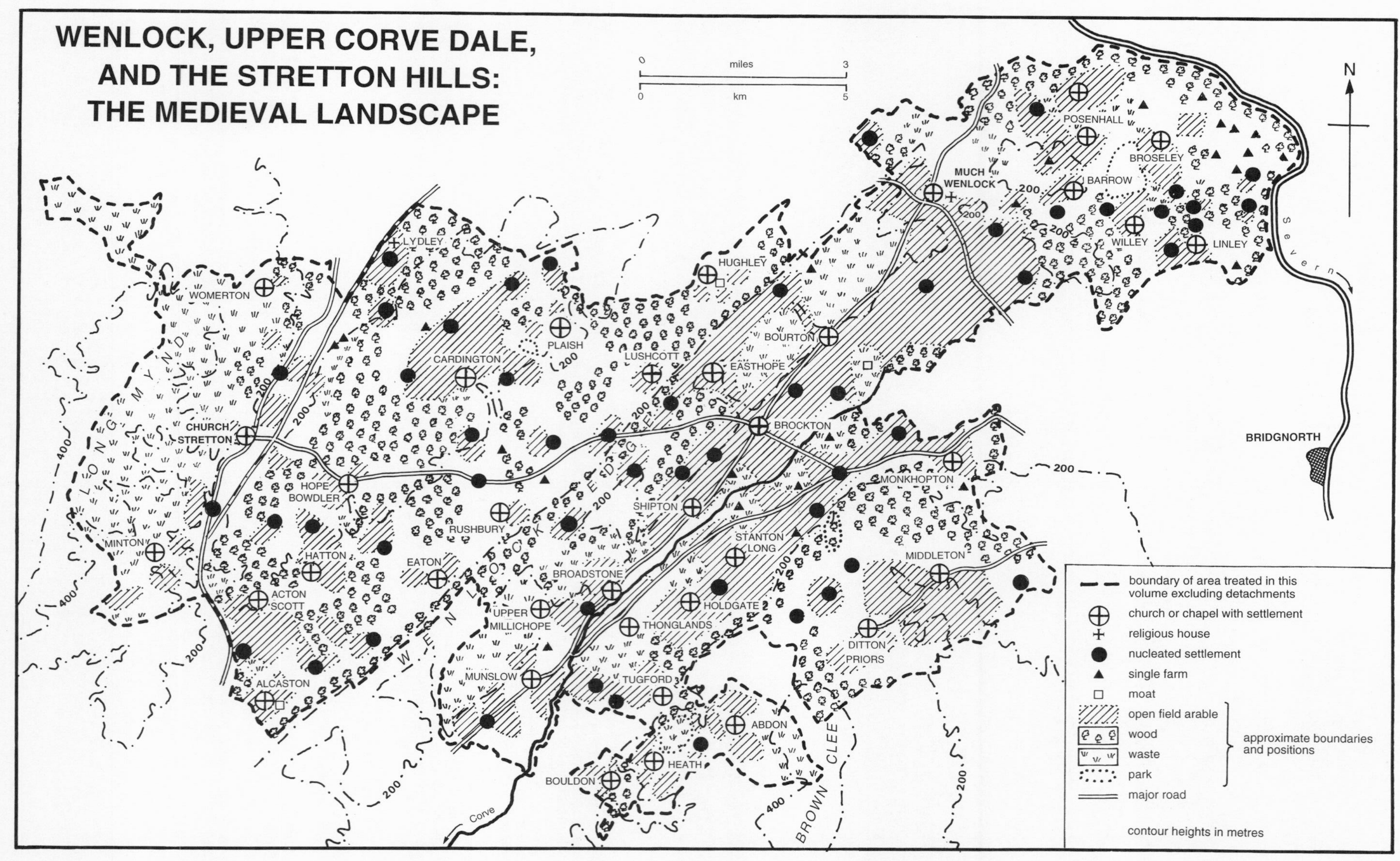

WENLOCK, UPPER CORVE DALE, AND THE STRETTON HILLS: THE MEDIEVAL LANDSCAPE
0
miles
3
0
km
5
N
MUCH WENLOCK
POSENHALL
BROSELEY
BARROW
WILLEY
LINLEY
Severn
BRIDGNORTH
HUGHLEY
BOURTON
EASTHOPE
LUSHCOTT
BROCKTON
MONKHOPTON
MIDDLETON
DITTON PRIORS
STANTON LONG
HOLDGATE
SHIPTON
THONGLANDS
TUGFORD
ABDON
HEATH
BOULDON
BROWN CLEE
BROADSTONE
UPPER MILLICHOPE
MUNSLOW
Corve
PLAISH
CARDINGTON
LYDLEY
WOMERTON
LONG MYND
CHURCH STRETTON
HOPE BOWDLER
RUSHBURY
EATON
HATTON
ACTON SCOTT
ALCASTON
MINTON
WENLOCK EDGE
200
400
boundary of area treated in this volume excluding detachments
church or chapel with settlement
religious house
nucleated settlement
single farm
moat
open field arable
wood
waste
park
approximate boundaries and positions
major road
contour heights in metres

Fig. 2

INTRODUCTION

THAT CENTRAL part of south Shropshire which includes the parishes treated in this volume[1] is a region traversed by ridges and dales and bounded by the vast upland commons of the Clee Hills on the south-east and the Long Mynd on the west.[2] On the south-eastern edge of the area Abdon, Ditton Priors, and the Heath lie on the north-western edge of the Old Red Sandstone plateau around the Clees, Abdon and Ditton sloping up towards the Brown Clee itself, Shropshire's highest summit at 540 m.[3] Monkhopton, below the plateau's northern scarp, drains towards the Mor brook. West of the plateau's escarpment the land falls sharply[4] into upper Corve Dale, with Weston, Oxenbold, Stanton Long, Holdgate, the shrunken settlement of Thonglands, Tugford, and Bouldon on its broader side, south-east of the Corve; opposite, on the right bank of the Corve and higher up from the river on a ridge of sand and gravel marked by the principal highway along the Dale, stand the settlements of Aston Munslow, Munslow, Hungerford, Broadstone, Shipton, Brockton, Patton, and (at the head of the dale) Bourton. Through most of those villages flow small tributary streams of the Corve draining steeply down from the ridge of Aymestry Limestone that bounds Corve Dale on its north-western side. Folded between the Aymestry Limestone and the harder unbroken limestone ridge of Wenlock Edge beyond is a line of small remote upland valleys or 'hopes', smaller-scale repetitions of Hope Dale (in Diddlebury);[5] they drain into Corve Dale by streams cutting through the softer Aymestry stone at Millichope, Lower Stanway (down from Wilderhope), Easthope, and Bourton (down from Presthope). The Edge continues west of Much Wenlock to end at Gleedon Hill north of the town; the hollow in which Much Wenlock lies would thus be another, though much larger and lower, 'hope', had not the Aymestry Limestone ridge disappeared south of the town. Instead east of Much Wenlock the land rises gradually to Barrow parish and Shirlett, beyond which are the Severnside parishes and townships in and below the Gorge, drained by short streams running swiftly to the river. Shirlett and the north end of the Aymestry Limestone ridge form the high ground, east and south of Much Wenlock, where the Mor brook's headwaters rise.

Wenlock Edge, wooded along its whole length,[6] is the most dramatically beautiful[7] feature of the region, made memorable by Housman even for those who have never seen it. To him also the area was unfamiliar, a country of the heart:[8]

On Wenlock Edge the wood's in trouble;
His forest fleece the Wrekin heaves;
The gale, it plies the saplings double,
And thick on Severn snow the leaves.

1 The following remarks generally exclude Badger, Beckbury, Deuxhill, Lesser Poston, and the main part of Stoke St. Milborough par.—places detached from the main area treated in the vol.

2 Cf. *V.C.H. Salop.* iv. 4, 7–9, 11–13.

3 At O.S. Nat. Grid SO 5936 8656.

4 Esp. noticeable at the Leath and Upper Netchwood on the roads from Ditton Priors to Stanton Long and Brockton.

5 *P.N. Salop.* i (E.P.N.S.), 113–14, 156.

6 From 1981 the Nat. Trust acquired *c.* 550 a. of the Edge, incl. some notable woods: *Nat. Trust Handbk.* (1993), 185.

7 As part of the area of outstanding natural beauty designated in 1959 (*V.C.H. Salop.* iii. 220) it connected the Wrekin with the S. Salop. hills.

8 *A Shropshire Lad* (1896), no. 31; R. P. Graves, *A. E. Housman, the Scholar Poet* (1980), 105–6; N. Page, *A. E. Housman: a Critical Biog.* (1983), 187–8.

Below the Edge's scarp lie Ape Dale (containing Acton Scott, Eaton-under-Heywood, and Rushbury) and, head to head with it, the Plaish brook valley (containing Hughley, Harley, and Wigwig).

Cardington village is enfolded on the west and south by the hills separating it from Hope Bowdler and Rushbury, and there at least relief may suggest the course of an early boundary between peoples, crossing the northern edge of the region. Most of Cardington parish drains east and then (like the places in the Plaish brook valley) north to the Severn at Sheinton. Plaish, and so perhaps other northern parts of Cardington parish, belonged to the territory of the Wreocensaete in the mid 10th century,[9] while further down the Plaish brook valley, beneath Wenlock Edge, Hughley and Wigwig (to judge from their membership of Condover hundred in 1086)[10] must also have been in the territory of the Wreocensaete and so have belonged to the diocese of Lichfield. Eventually all those places (like all the others treated in this volume)[11] were incorporated in Hereford diocese, which had generally been formed from the territory of the Magonsaete.

The great whale-backed hills around Hope Bowdler, made of older rocks than the dales and ridges to the south-east,[12] form one side of the narrow dale in which Church Stretton lies, on the eastern flank of the Long Mynd. There is evidence of prehistoric cultivation and settlement, notably on the high land around Church Stretton on the Long Mynd, Caer Caradoc, and Cardington Hill. Woodland clearance of lower ground was undertaken in the Iron Age, and there are forts and other enclosures of the period on the Clees, around Mogg Forest on the Aymestry Limestone ridge, and on the Long Mynd, Caer Caradoc, and the Lawley. The Roman road known as Watling Street West ran through the dale in which Church Stretton stands; another probably ran along Corve Dale, part of a road from Ashwood (in Kingswinford, Staffs.) to mid Wales and coinciding with the medieval Bridgnorth–Munslow road.[13] There are indications of Roman presence in the neighbourhood of those roads, in Ape Dale (with villas at Acton Scott and Hatton), and at Much Wenlock.[14]

The archaeological invisibility of the sub-Roman Celtic farmer and the absence of pagan Saxon remains combine to dissolve the picture until the arrival of the Mercian Angles in the area. They came perhaps relatively late as a ruling élite rather than early as farmer settlers:[15] certainly the first substantial evidence for English settlement in what was to become Shropshire is that of a dynasty reinforcing its local power and influence by the foundation of a monastery at Much Wenlock at the end of the 7th century. Wenlock abbey's earliest estates were concentrated in what became Much Wenlock parish, extending down into upper Corve Dale.[16] Some higher land occupied in early times, such as Mogg Forest, reverted to woodland in the Dark Ages. Elsewhere, however, as in Corve Dale, the most extensive areas of arable cultivation and the relatively large medieval open fields may indicate long established settlement, as seems also to be the case in Ape Dale (settled in Roman times and 'long open land' in the 13th century),[17] at

[9] To whose territory Plaish (in Cardington) belonged in the 10th cent.: C. Hart, 'The Tribal Hidage', *Trans. R.H.S.* 5th ser. xxi. 139 (wrongly stating that it is in Ape Dale), 141.

[10] *V.C.H. Salop.* viii. 1 (corr. below, Corrigenda).

[11] Most of them (but not Deuxhill, Ditton Priors, or Stoke St. Milborough) in the medieval rural deanery of Wenlock: *V.C.H. Salop.* ii. 3 (corr. below, Corrigenda), 24.

[12] Ibid. i, map facing p. 1.

[13] *V.C.H. Staffs.* xx. 197.

[14] Cf. O.S. *Map of Roman Brit.* (1978), S. sheet.

[15] M. Gelling, *W. Midlands in Early Middle Ages* (1992), 29, 53–4, 66–71, 122–3; *P.N. Salop.* i, pp. xii–xvii.

[16] Below, Lib. and Boro. of Wenlock.

[17] 'Longef[el]dsdale' (1272): cf. Eyton, xi. 377; *P.N. Salop.* i. 6–7.

Cardington,[18] and possibly at Ditton Priors. In those long-cultivated open dales Henley (in Acton Scott) and Topley (in Munslow) were probably woods named from their prominent isolation[19] on rising ground; by the mid 13th century Henley had become a small hamlet and probably an open common, but Topley remained a wood. In such long-settled valleys some of the two dozen or so places whose names include the element *tun* may be older than their English names.[20]

The western end and north-eastern corner of the area were well wooded at the end of the 11th century. Domesday Book records woodland belonging to Cardington, Hope Bowdler, Rushbury, Church Stretton, Ticklerton, and Much Wenlock; elsewhere, however, none was recorded.[21] Also confined to the west and north-east, with the significant exceptions of Henley and Topley, are places with names that include the element *leah*, indicating settlements in woodland clearings named probably not earlier than the mid 8th century.[22] The north-eastern settlements[23] are on the high land east and south-east of Much Wenlock, centred on Shirlett and continuous with similar settlements in the forest of the Wrekin beyond the Severn;[24] the north-western settlements[25] adjoin similar ones in the Long forest.[26] In the Norman period almost the whole area was afforested in Clee forest (from 1175 a private chase), Shirlett, and the Long forest; most of Shirlett and almost the whole of the Long forest were disafforested in 1301.[27]

In a few places[28] earthworks testify to Norman castle building, but only at Holdgate, *caput* of a feudal barony, is there any standing masonry.[29] Church Stretton had a royal castle in the 12th and early 13th century. More obvious are some of the Saxon and Norman churches so distinctively concentrated in south-east Shropshire, outstanding examples being those at Barrow, the Heath, Linley, and Much Wenlock.

Much of the area has always been remote from major roads, though that from Bridgnorth by Much Wenlock and over Wenlock Edge was once an important route from Worcester, and so ultimately from London and Bristol, to Shrewsbury and beyond.[30] The two roads most important to the region connect Ludlow with Shrewsbury and Much Wenlock, the former running through the Stretton gap on the western edge of the area, the latter along Corve Dale. The Ludlow–Shrewsbury road through the Strettons formed part of a more direct Bristol–Chester route certainly by the mid 17th century[31] and probably a century or more earlier, for Leland apparently travelled that way from the forest of Dean to Shrewsbury.[32]

In the region, as elsewhere in Shropshire,[33] the open fields and the woodlands shrank as pastoral farming and separate fields expanded from the late Middle Ages: save on a few estates belonging to absentee landlords or a multiplicity of owners[34]

[18] Well settled by the 10th cent. to judge from the existence of a royal est. at Plaish.

[19] M. Gelling, *Place-Names in the Landscape* (1984), 199.

[20] *P.N. Salop.* i, pp. xiii–xiv.

[21] Dom. Bk. records woodland belonging to Cardington, Hope Bowdler, Rushbury, Ch. Stretton, Ticklerton, and Much Wenlock but to no other place (except Badger) treated in this vol.: *Dom. Geog. of Midland Eng.* ed. H. C. Darby and I. B. Terrett (1971), 138–9 (where 'Corfe' should read 'Worfe').

[22] Gelling, *Place-Names in Landscape*, 198 sqq.

[23] Atterley, Bradeley, Bradley, Farley, and Perkley (in M. Wenlock), Bently (in Benthall), Broseley, Caughley (in Barrow), Hughley, Linley, and Willey.

[24] *V.C.H. Salop.* xi. 1, 3.

[25] Comley and Lydley (in Cardington).

[26] i.e. Frodesley, Leebotwood, etc.: *V.C.H. Salop.* iv. 45; viii. 79–80, 98–9, and map facing p. 1.

[27] Ibid. i. 485–6 (corr. ibid. ii. 319); iv. 45–6.

[28] Brockton, Rushbury, and Stretton.

[29] But the masonry is *c.* 1300.

[30] *V.C.H. Salop.* iv. 71; viii. 86.

[31] Ogilby, *Britannia* (1675), pl. 57.

[32] Leland, *Itin.* ed. Toulmin Smith, ii. 64–81 and map III.

[33] *V.C.H. Salop.* iv. 80–5, 119–22.

[34] Broadstone (in Munslow), Ditton Priors, Henley (in Acton Scott), Holdgate, Stanton Long, and M. Wenlock (cf. ibid. 173).

open fields had gone by the end of the 17th century. Extensive commons remained until the early 19th century,[35] and some were never inclosed.[36]

The area contains some notable medieval houses[37] but is more obviously characterized by a rich array of 16th- and early 17th-century manor houses. In the late 18th and earlier 19th century there were some notable estate improvements—by the Stackhouses at Acton Scott, the Myttons at Shipton, and (on a larger scale) the Lawleys in Much Wenlock parish. Lord Forester, however, owner of the largest landed estate in the area in the 19th century, spent on the extension of his property rather than its improvement:[38] hence the survival of many substantial 17th-century farmhouses in the north-eastern part of the area. Corve Dale farming was prosperous by the early 19th century[39] and the adoption of high feeding and manuring techniques[40] on different estates is attested by a striking chain of upland barns[41]—with cattle sheds, yards, and sometimes a cottage[42]—built along the north-western side of the Dale.[43]

From the 17th century limestone, coal, ironstone, clays, and good wood supplies gave rise to scattered quarrying, mining, iron, and ceramic industries. Only near the Severn Gorge, however, where some of England's first mineral railways were laid in the early 17th century, were such resources sufficiently large and close to long-distance transport to give rise to concentrations of industrial settlement.[44] The area and its river-borne coal trade were of some strategic importance during the early years of the Civil War. Broseley became the urban focus of the straggling Severnside industrial settlements, growing rapidly during the 17th and 18th centuries to become one of the county's most populous towns, famed for its clay tobacco pipes. By *c.* 1800, however, as local mines were worked out, it had begun to stagnate. Even so, the opening of the Severn Valley Railway in 1862 gave new life to the area, enabling the products of the big new brick and tile works at Benthall and Jackfield to become internationally renowned.

The area's only towns besides Broseley are Much Wenlock and Church Stretton. They have little in common with Broseley or each other. Much Wenlock, where there seems to have been some kind of settlement in Roman times, developed during the Middle Ages as a market town in the shadow of Wenlock priory; other local markets, however, were more successful, and it was as the centre of a large and eccentrically organized borough (containing also Broseley)[45] that the town was chiefly remarkable from the late Middle Ages. Church Stretton was long one of the county's smallest towns, without even a market until the earlier 17th century. Set, however, amid the scenery of the Long Mynd and the opposing line of hills between Ragleth and Caer Caradoc, Stretton became Shropshire's most notable resort. That role was developed from the 1860s, perhaps always with rather more

35 When parliamentary inclosure in S. Salop. accelerated: *V.C.H. Salop.* iv. 173–4.

36 Ibid. 256.

37 e.g. Gt. Oxenbold and Wenlock Abbey.

38 *T.S.A.S.* lix. 145–6; *V.C.H. Salop.* iv. 205.

39 *V.C.H. Salop.* iv. 9.

40 Principal elements in the development of high farming: *V.C.H. Salop.* iv. 177, 185.

41 Analogous to the outfarms, field barns, and high barns of Yorks. and other upland parts of Eng. and Wales: R. W. Brunskill, *Traditional Fm. Bldgs. of Brit.* (1987), 117–22; E. William, *Traditional Fm. Bldgs. in N.E. Wales 1550–1900* (1982), 31–2; C. Hayfield, 'Manure Factories? The post-enclosure high barns of the Yorks. Wolds', *Landscape Hist.* xiii. 33–45. Dr. P. A. Stamper is thanked for these refs. and for a sight of his unpublished survey of these bldgs.

42 e.g. at Whitbach (O.S. Nat. Grid SO 5316 9020).

43 The line continues lower down Corve Dale than the pars. treated in this vol., and there are isolated ones elsewhere, e.g. near Patton (Corve Barn) and Tugford.

44 Published after *V.C.H. Salop.* xi (see pp. 21–77) and the writing of histories of Benthall and Broseley (see below), C. Clark, *Eng. Heritage Bk. of Ironbridge Gorge* (1993), and J. Alfrey and C. Clark, *Landscape of Industry: Patterns of Change in the Ironbridge Gorge* (1993), provide useful surveys of the Severn Gorge's history and landscape.

45 And Madeley and Ironbridge. Municipal and cultural institutions were dispersed between the boro.'s various towns: cf. *V.C.H. Salop.* xi. 30, 58.

optimism about the future than was justified in the immediate event. In the 20th century growth was swifter as the town became a popular retirement place. It did not cease to be a resort; the hills and dales were too attractive to remain unvisited in the age of the motor car:[46]

And on the bare and high
Places of England, the Wiltshire Downs and the
Long Mynd
Let the balls of my feet bounce on the turf, my face
burn in the wind
My eyelashes stinging in the wind, and the sheep
like grey stones
Humble my human pretensions—

[46] Louis MacNeice, 'An Eclogue for Christmas' (1933), *Coll. Poems*, ed. E. R. Dodds (1966), 36. Unlike Housman MacNeice knew the area well from driving 'round Shropshire in a bijou car' (Baby Austin) while at Birm. univ. 1930–6: 'Autumn Journal' (1938), ibid. 115; MacNeice, *The Strings are False* (1965), 133; cf. J. Stallworthy, *Louis MacNeice* (1995), 141–2, 144–5, 185, 191, 226, 247, 252.

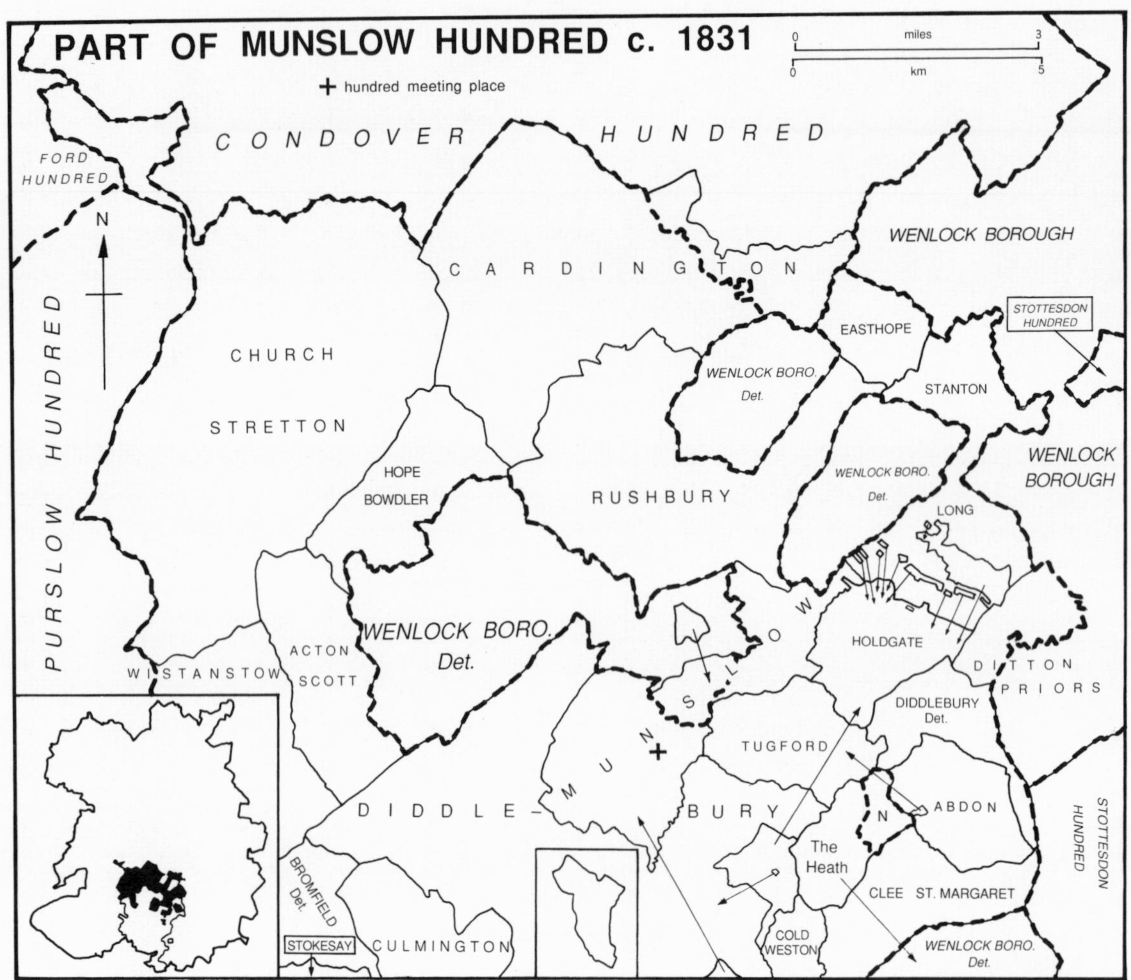

Fig. 3

The inset to the left shows in black only that part of the hundred treated in the present volume, which does not include the parishes of Wistanstow, Bromfield, Stokesay, Culmington, Diddlebury, Cold Weston, or Clee St. Margaret. The other inset map shows the shape of Lesser Poston, a detachment of Munslow parish whose distance from the main part of the parish is indicated by its northern tip shown on the main map. The Heath and Norncott (N), the former in Munslow hundred the latter in the borough of Wenlock, lay detached from the main part of Stoke St. Milborough parish (in Wenlock borough).

MUNSLOW HUNDRED
(part)

ABOUT 1831 the eleven parishes whose histories follow this article lay wholly or mainly in the northern part of Munslow hundred.[1] They comprise five of the seven parishes then wholly or partly in the hundred's Upper division[2] and six of the fourteen wholly or partly in the Lower division.[3]

For some three centuries, beginning in 1198, an extensive north-eastern part of the large county division based on Munslow hundred was occupied by the manors and townships that formed a hundredal liberty, or leet, subject to the privileged jurisdiction of Wenlock priory. In 1468 a quarter sessions borough of Wenlock was incorporated, and, in ways that seem to have been unintended (at least by the Crown), the new corporation's municipal privileges were extended to the whole of the priory liberty. That seems to have happened fairly promptly, otherwise such an odd borough could never have been conceived. More gradually, in the late 15th and earlier 16th centuries, the borough or liberty—eventually known as the Franchise—of Wenlock became a new division of the county.[4]

Distinct as the Munslow hundred and Wenlock Franchise county divisions thus became, in the area treated in this volume their parishes and townships interlocked in a way that was more complicated than in any other part of Shropshire.[5] Moreover the same area of Shropshire that became so oddly arranged after 1468 was also virtually the only area of the county described in 1086 which had complicated hundred territories:[6] then a detachment of Leintwardine hundred met the western end of Patton hundred and thus made the northern part of Culvestan hundred a detachment.[7] The later territorial complexity of the area can be attributed to the local interpretation of the 1468 charter (tolerated by the Crown), and the earlier situation too requires explanation. That would necessarily be more speculative, and here it can only be indicated that suggestions towards simplifying the Shropshire hundred boundaries as they are revealed in Domesday Book[8] have made it easier to detect pairings of eight of the nine south Shropshire hundreds; some pairs coincided with rural deaneries. Culvestan and Patton indeed were paired formally, having a common *caput*.[9] They coincided with two deaneries (Ludlow and Wenlock) rather than one.[10] A big break in that pattern, and prime cause of the complexity of hundred territories in the area treated in this volume, is the northern detachment of Leintwardine hundred comprising nine estates amounting to 21½ hides;[11] the detachment does not correspond with the medieval ruridecanal boundaries, and if, as along the Shropshire–Staffordshire border, ecclesiastical

1 The hist. of Munslow hund. as a whole is reserved for treatment in a future vol. of this *Hist*. Cf. *V.C.H. Salop*. iii. 45; iv. 205.

2 The other two were Culmington (a detached part of the divn.) and Wistanstow (half of which lay in Purslow hund.).

3 S.R.O., q. sess. order bk. 1828–31, p. 214; *V.C.H. Salop*. ii. 209.

4 Below, Lib. and Boro. of Wenlock.

5 Cf. figs 3, 16.

6 The apparently much greater complications in Alnodestreu have now been convincingly explained away: sources cited below, n. 8.

7 *V.C.H. Salop*. iii. 8 (including Stretton-en-le-Dale, perhaps wrongly, in Leintwardine hund.); *Dom. Bk.: Salop*. ed F. and C. Thorn (1986); *Salop. acc. to Dom. Bk*. (map, 1990) in *Salop. Domesday: Folios and Maps*, ed. R. W. H. Erskine (1988).

8 Arguing editorial mistakes during the writing of Great Domesday: C. P. Lewis, 'Intro. to Salop. Domesday', *Salop. Domesday*, ed. A. Williams and R. W. H. Erskine (1990), 4–6; F. R. Thorn, 'Hundreds and Wapentakes', ibid. 28–39.

9 *V.C.H. Salop*. i. 293, 316; iii. 6, 9.

10 Cf. maps ibid. ii. 24; iii. 8.

11 Consisting of Acton Scott and Alcaston; Chelmick; Minton; Wistanstow, Strefford, Whittingslow, and Woolston; and Cheney Longville.

boundaries long survived to represent ancient secular boundaries, then the Leintwardine detachment may not have been ancient. It may have resulted from a reorganization of hundreds in south-west Shropshire by Earl Roger, who certainly altered them in the south-east.[12]

Leintwardine hundred disappeared after 1086, and the estates in its northern detachment were distributed to other hundreds, some to Munslow, thus introducing (or restoring) a simpler pattern of hundred territories in the area.[13]

Munslow was a new hundred formed by amalgamating Patton and Culvestan hundreds. Eyton considered that there was a wholesale reorganization of the Shropshire hundreds in Henry I's reign, but that seems unlikely: changes may have been spread over the 12th century,[14] the union of Patton and Culvestan perhaps achieved a century earlier than that of Hodnet and Wrockwardine.[15] The Domesday hundreds that went to form Bradford hundred had not had a common *caput*. Patton and Culvestan, however, had one, at Corfham, and a degree of union—the transaction of the business of two hundreds in the same place and on the same occasions—may be assumed to be implicit in the possession of a single *caput*. The process of union, however, may have been pushed towards completion by the choice of a new *caput*. At first glance the likeliest time for the abandonment of Corfham may seem to be the moment when the manor was alienated by the Crown in 1155,[16] but the choice of Munslow as the new meeting place at that date seems inexplicable, for Munslow was in Aston manor, which had probably been held in chief since *c.* 1115 or earlier by the Banastre family,[17] prominent landowners outside Shropshire;[18] it was certainly not a royal estate in 1155. For a dozen or more years after 1086, on the other hand, Corfham was held in chief by the earl of Shrewsbury[19] while Aston was held of him by his sheriff.[20] The routine of hundred business fell to the sheriff and his officers; it thus seems reasonable to suppose that it was at some time between 1086 and the destruction of the earl's power in 1102 that the sheriff, doubtless with his overlord's acquiescence, shifted the hundred meeting place just across the river: removing it from Corfham (on a by-road from Diddlebury to Peaton) to his own manor of Aston, where a more eligible situation on the principal highway along Corve Dale was marked out by a well known tumulus—Munslow.[21]

The relocation of hundred business at Munslow was doubtless a real convenience for the sheriff and the many suitors and others concerned in it, for the road past Munslow ran from Much Wenlock to Ludlow and was thus the quickest route through the two hundreds. The change may not, however, have struck contemporaries as of great import, for as late as 1233 the name Culvestan was still in at least occasional use to indicate lower Corve Dale.[22] Thus the term Munslow hundred may have gained currency as gradually as the use of Culvestan declined.

[12] *V.C.H. Salop.* iii. 43. Cf. C. P. Lewis, 'Eng. and Norman govt. and lordship in Welsh borders 1039–87' (Oxf. Univ. D.Phil. thesis, 1985), 222–3, 238–49.

[13] *V.C.H. Salop.* iii. 34, 36, 40.

[14] Ibid. 11; Eyton, v. 145.

[15] *V.C.H. Salop.* xi. 93, 95.

[16] Eyton, iii. 330; v. 146. It was briefly in the Crown's hands again 1175–7.

[17] Ibid. v. 130–1.

[18] *V.C.H. Lancs.* i. 366 sqq.

[19] Eyton, v. 145; *V.C.H. Salop.* iii. 10.

[20] Below, Munslow, manor; for the relationship betw. earl and sheriff cf. *T.S.A.S.* lvi. 247.

[21] *P.N. Salop.* i (E.P.N.S.), 219–16.

[22] *V.C.H. Salop.* iii. 11 n. 60.

ACTON SCOTT

ACTON SCOTT parish (1,934 a., 783 ha.)[1] is a long, roughly rectangular tract of countryside running down from the south-facing slopes below Ragleth Hill across Ape Dale and rising up again to the crest of Wenlock Edge, which makes the south-eastern boundary of the parish. The parish has always been entirely rural and, despite the proximity of the county's main north–south route through the Stretton gap, fairly isolated and lightly populated. None of its three settlements, Acton Scott, Alcaston, and Henley, was ever more than a small village or hamlet.

Quinny or Marsh brook marks the central part of the parish's north-western boundary where the land falls steeply down from Castle Hill to the Stretton gap, drained by the brook. The southern part of the parish's north-eastern boundary is defined by Mar or Marsh[2] brook. Both brooks were mentioned in 1695 when the bounds of Acton Scott manor, occupying the north-western two thirds of the parish, were recorded.[3] The manor is drained by their tributaries, descending north-east and south-west from a central watershed. The south-eastern third of the parish, beneath the escarpment of Wenlock Edge, comprised Alcaston manor. The stream running along the foot of the Edge is there known as Byne brook,[4] and Alcaston drains south-eastwards into it.

The central and south-eastern parts of the parish are largely covered by glacial drift producing cold heavy soils.[5] The north-western part of the parish, once occupied by Oakwood common, is higher ground, mostly over 213 m. and lying on Ordovician mudstones of the Harnage Shales and the Acton Scott Group. There too soils are often heavy, though there are areas of easier worked loam like that east of Acton Scott Farm. Limestone occurs along Wenlock Edge and in the outcrop on which Acton Scott village stands.[6]

Running along or close to the parish's south-western boundary is the Church Stretton to Ludlow road, turnpiked in 1756.[7] It was perhaps then that a new section of road was made in Acton Scott parish along the foot of Castle Hill, *c.* 200 m. east of the old line in Wistanstow parish.[8] Before the 19th century roads led east from the Stretton–Ludlow road into the parish, to run south of Acton Scott village and north of Henley. From Acton Scott roads ran east and south-east to Hatton and Wolverton (in Eaton-under-Heywood).[9] Alcaston lay on a minor route along the foot of Wenlock Edge, midway between Upper Affcot (in Wistanstow) and Wolverton.[10] After T. P. Stackhouse went to live at Acton Scott in 1807[11] roads through that manor were much improved. Apart from numerous minor works,[12] in 1808–9 Welsh navvies built new roads from the Ludlow turnpike up Castle Hill to Acton Scott village and thence north across the common to meet a bridleway called Smallsty (OE. *smael* 'narrow', *stig* 'path')[13] between Little Stretton and Ragdon,[14] and *c.* 1817 a more northerly route from Acton Scott to Hatton was made.[15] Between 1812 and 1820 the road from Acton Scott to Wolverton, passing close to Acton Scott Hall, was closed.[16] The Marshbrook to Wall's Bank road, via Acton Scott and Hatton, was turnpiked under an Act of 1822.[17] The Stretton–Ludlow road was disturnpiked in 1873[18] and that from Marshbrook to Wall's Bank in 1878.[19]

The Buildwas to Craven Arms railway line of 1867, eventually part of the G.W.R., crossed the parish north of Henley; it was lifted soon after 1951.[20]

Enclosures west of Acton Scott village[21] and artefacts[22] indicate settlement and cultivation before the Roman conquest. East of Acton Scott Farm, within a sub- rectangular ditched enclosure,[23] is the site of a Roman villa, excavated in 1844 by Mrs. Frances Stackhouse Acton.[24]

The names of both manors in the parish contain the *-tun* element, with Alcaston meaning 'Alhmund's estate' and Acton perhaps a settlement with some specialized function in regard to oak timber. Acton Scott's suffix (sometimes a prefix, Scott's Acton) derives from one of the medieval families holding a share of the manor.[25] Henley hamlet, mentioned in 1255,[26] lies in the southern part of Acton Scott manor; its name may indicate an origin as a wood[27] where birds were kept.[28]

Neither manor was populous in 1086, with four recorded inhabitants at Acton and seven at Alcaston.[29] Alcaston may have been no larger in 1327 when three paid the subsidy. Six paid in 1327 from Acton Scott manor,[30] including Robert de la Wode who, like John *de quercubus* (fl. 1287),[31] perhaps lived in the Oakwood area.[32] Twenty-five men were mustered from Acton

1 O.S. *Area Bk.* (1884). This article was written 1991–2.
2 S.P.L., Deeds 1647.
3 S.R.O. 3925, box 12, ct. r. 11 Oct. 1695.
4 O.S. Map 1", index to tithe survey, sheet LXI. SW. [*c.* 1851].
5 Para. based on Geol. Surv. Map 1", drift, sheet 166 (1967 edn.), and inf. from Mr. T. S. Acton, who is thanked for his help.
6 Below, econ. hist.
7 Under 29 Geo. II, c. 59.
8 Plan of Castle Hill est. (in Mr. T. S. Acton's possession).
9 S.R.O. 3925, Acton Scott map of 1776.
10 S.R.O. 298/1; O.S. Map 1", index to tithe survey, sheet LXI. SW. [*c.* 1851].
11 Below, manors.
12 S.R.O. 3925, Acton Scott maps of 1776, 1820.
13 S.R.O. 3925, box 12, ct. r. 11 Oct. 1695; cf. *Eng. P.N. Elements* (E.P.N.S.), ii. 130, 152.
14 T. P. Stackhouse's diary (in Mrs. R. C. Acton's possession).
15 *Archaeologia*, xxxi. 339–45.
16 Cf. S.R.O. 2906/1, p. 27; 3925, maps of 1776, 1820.
17 3 Geo. IV, c. 49.
18 Ann. Turnpike Acts Continuance Act, 1872, 35 & 36 Vic. c. 85.
19 Ann. Turnpike Acts Continuance Act, 1877, 40 & 41 Vic. c. 64.
20 *Railway Mag.* cxi. 440–4.
21 Visible as crop marks: SA 1421, 2057.
22 *V.C.H. Salop.* i. 202; S.P.L., Chitty Files 31/13, 147/2–5; *Proc. Prehist. Soc.* xvii. 159–67.
23 SA 4419.
24 *Archaeologia*, xxxi. 339–45; *V.C.H. Salop.* i. 259–61; S.P.L., MS. 6007.
25 *P.N. Salop.* (E.P.N.S.), i. 1–4, 6–9, 15; below, manors.
26 *Rot. Hund.* (Rec. Com.), ii. 70.
27 Rather than a clearing: M. Gelling, *Place-Names in the Landscape* (1984), 199.
28 *P.N. Salop.* i. 150–1.
29 *V.C.H. Salop.* i. 338, 343.
30 *T.S.A.S.* 2nd ser. iv. 312–13.
31 *Cal. Inq. Misc.* i, p. 617.
32 *T.S.A.S.* 2nd ser. iv. 312.

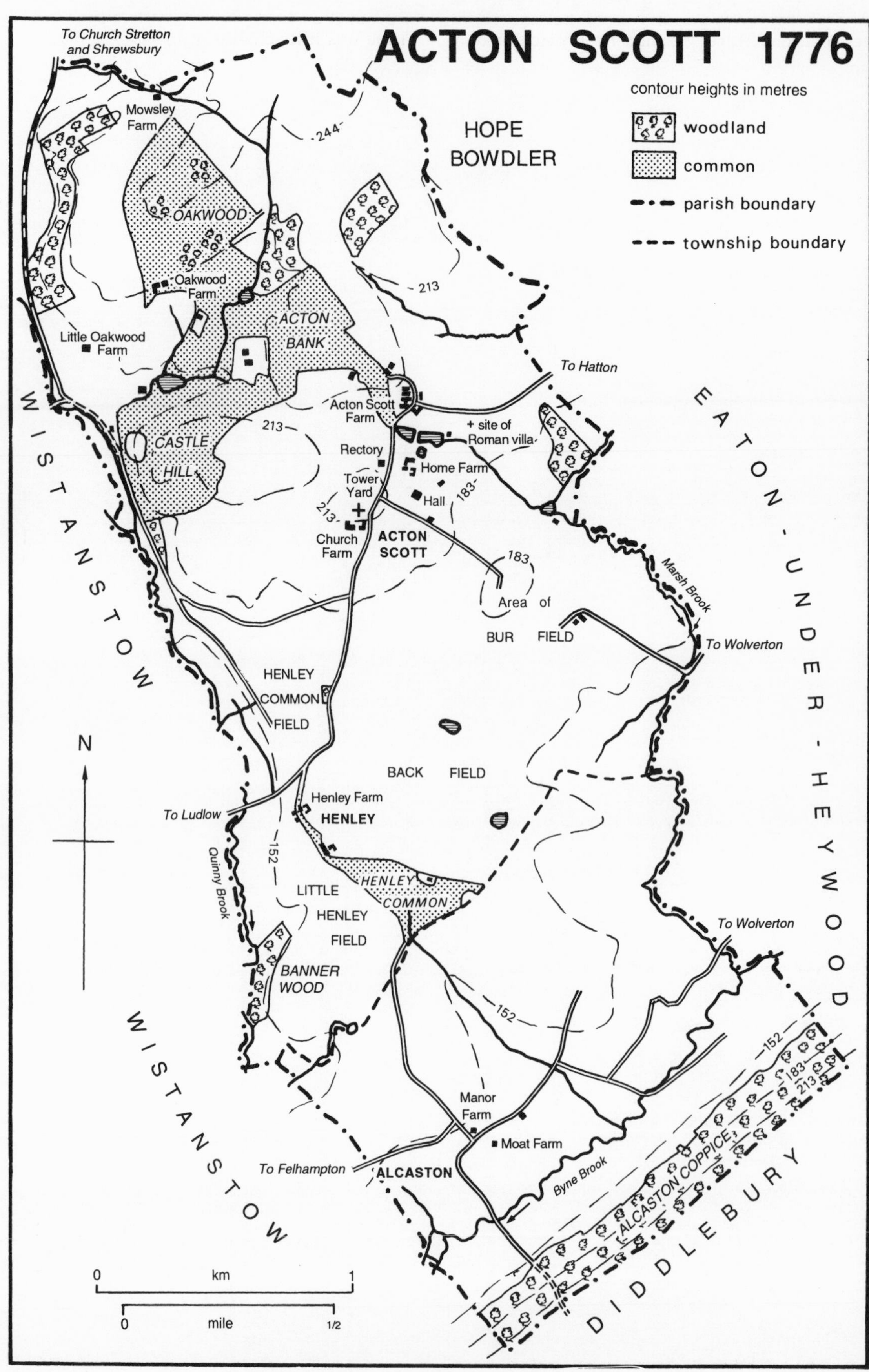
ACTON SCOTT 1776
contour heights in metres
woodland
common
parish boundary
township boundary
To Church Stretton and Shrewsbury
Mowsley Farm
OAKWOOD
Oakwood Farm
Little Oakwood Farm
ACTON BANK
CASTLE HILL
HOPE BOWDLER
244
213
To Hatton
Acton Scott Farm
+ site of Roman villa
Rectory
Home Farm
Tower Yard
Hall
183
Church Farm
ACTON SCOTT
Area of
BUR FIELD
Marsh Brook
To Wolverton
EATON-UNDER-HEYWOOD
WISTANSTOW
HENLEY COMMON FIELD
BACK FIELD
N
To Ludlow
Henley Farm
HENLEY
152
Quinny Brook
LITTLE HENLEY FIELD
HENLEY COMMON
BANNER WOOD
To Wolverton
Manor Farm
Moat Farm
To Felhampton
ALCASTON
Byne Brook
ALCASTON COPPICE
DIDDLEBURY
0 km 1
0 mile 1/2

Fig. 4

Scott in 1542 and 9 from Alcaston.[33] In 1676 there were 72 adults in the parish.[34] Four years earlier hearth tax had been paid for only 3 houses at Alcaston but for 15 at Acton Scott, where 8 were single-hearth houses,[35] several of them presumably squatter cottages in Oakwood, where a cottage had been licensed in 1667.[36] In the earlier 18th century the Oakwood cottages were probably known collectively as Woodhouses,[37] perhaps from Acton Woodhouse (mentioned in the 16th and 17th centuries),[38] a name later disused.

In the later 18th century the population may have increased a little, as it did in the early 19th, from 164 in 1801 to 215 in 1851.[39] A few more cottages were built, and in one or two cases farmhouses whose lands had been re-allotted were divided into labourers' dwellings: the former farmhouse at the north end of Henley common, for instance, housed four families in 1820.[40] Although the farmhouses were probably in a reasonable state of repair, some having been refurbished in the 1780s,[41] many cottages in 1810 were poor. Those on the common were mostly timber framed, two-roomed, and thatched, their windows rarely glazed; two farmhouses in Acton Scott manor then also remained thatched.[42] Many were much improved later, Frances Stackhouse Acton, the lord of the manor's widow, giving help with finance and design;[43] the cottages grouped at the south end of the former Oakwood common, for instance, were largely rebuilt in stone with elaborately glazed windows, and one became known as Swiss Cottage. An elaborate display of pierced barge boards and new casements was employed in the refurbishment of the 17th-century cottage at the bottom of Castle Hill, overlooking the Church Stretton to Ludlow road; it was later the post office.[44] Other projects influenced by Mrs. Stackhouse Acton (d. 1881)[45] probably included the construction of new lodges on the north, south, and west approaches to the Hall in the mid 19th century[46] and the building of a school, again in ornate timber framing, in 1866.[47]

In the 20th century the population continued its gradual decline in numbers, to 115 in 1991.[48] There was little change in settlement, though a few cottages were abandoned. Wood Acton, designed in the Cotswold style by P. R. M. Horder, was built in 1925 for Mrs. Laura Charlotte Wood Acton,[49] and in the late 1940s Ludlow rural district council built two pairs of farm workers' houses north of Acton Scott village.[50]

There was an alehouse at Acton Scott in the later 13th century[51] but no later public house is known. About 1730 the parish wake was said to be on Holy Cross day (14 September),[52] a century later on the Sunday before St. Matthew's day (21 September).[53] A library fund, raised 1829–33, was used to buy books of an improving character.[54] The village hall, designed by Horder, was built in 1926 at Mrs. Wood Acton's expense.[55] She had earlier started a nursing association which employed a village nurse and was financed by farmers' and cottagers' subscriptions.[56]

MANORS AND OTHER ESTATES. Eadric (Edric) held *ACTON*, later *ACTON SCOTT*, in 1066.[57] If, as seems probable, he was Edric the wild,[58] he may have forfeited the manor *c.* 1070 for his rebellious attack on Shrewsbury,[59] though he was soon reconciled with the king and is last definitely heard of in 1072 but may have survived as late as 1086; by then, however, Acton had passed to a kinsman.[60]

Roger of Montgomery, created earl of Shrewsbury in 1068, held Acton in chief in 1086, but in 1102 his son Earl Robert forfeited all his English lands and titles.[61] Later in the 12th century the FitzAlans became overlords of Acton Scott, and they were recorded as such until 1574.[62]

Probably in the 1150s William FitzAlan granted a mesne lordship over Acton to John le Strange who held it of William's barony of Oswestry in 1165.[63] The Stranges' mesne lordship was recorded until *c.* 1284.[64]

The terre tenancy was evidently divided be-

33 *L. & P. Hen. VIII*, xvii, p. 508.
34 *Compton Census*, ed. Whiteman, 259.
35 *Hearth Tax 1672* (Salop. Arch. Soc. 1949), 181, 183.
36 *Orders of Q. Sess.* i. 98.
37 Birm. Univ. Libr., Mytton Papers, i. 30.
38 S.R.O. 1093/2/522; 3925, box 12, ct. r. 6 July 1629.
39 *V.C.H. Salop.* ii. 219.
40 S.R.O. 3925, maps of 1776, 1820; S.P.L., MS. 6865, p. 16.
41 Below, econ. hist.
42 S.R.O. 2906/1, p. 27.
43 Talented artist, she illustrated her own bks.: *D.N.B.* s.v. Knight, T. A.; B.M. *Gen. Cat. of Printed Bks. to 1955* (photolithographic edn. 1959–66), i, col. 828; *Bye-Gones, 1880–1*, 188–9. For drawings elsewhere see e.g. *Trans. Caradoc Field Club* (1869), 6–24.
44 Mrs. Laura Charlotte Wood Acton's notes and drawings of Acton Scott est. and village (in Mrs. R. C. Acton's possession); O.S. Map 6", Salop. LXIV. NW. (1891 edn.).
45 *Bye-Gones, 1880–1*, 188–9; below, manors, for work on gardens at Acton Scott Hall.
46 West lodge existed by 1833: O.S. map 1", index to tithe survey, sheet LXI. SW. [*c.* 1851]; others built after 1839: S.R.O. 298/1.
47 Below, educ.
48 *Census* 1991.
49 S.P.L., SC19/93; A. Stuart Gray, *Edwardian Archit.: Biog. Dict.* (1985), 214–16. The ho. was extended in the 1970s.
50 Inf. from Mr. T. S. Acton.
51 *Salop.* (R.E.E.D.), i. 10.
52 Birm. Univ. Libr., Mytton Papers, i. 30.
53 W.S.L. 350/5/40, Acton Scott p. 23.
54 S.R.O. 2563/76.
55 Mrs. Wood Acton's notes, etc.
56 Notes at Acton Scott Historic Working Fm.
57 *V.C.H. Salop.* i. 343.
58 C. P. Lewis, 'Eng. and Norman Govt. and Lordship in Welsh Borders, 1039–1087' (Oxf. Univ. D.Phil. thesis, 1985), 82–3, 105–6, 364 (map 13). *Sylvaticus* or *salvage* would probably be better rendered 'outcast [in the woods]' than 'wild': *Ang.-Norm. Dict.* (Modern Humanities Research Assoc. 1977–92), 673; S. Reynolds, 'Eadric Silvaticus and the Eng. Resistance', *Bull. Inst. Hist. Res.* liv. 102–5.
59 Lewis, op. cit. 170–6; *V.C.H. Salop.* iii. 7.
60 A. Williams, *The English and the Norman Conquest* (1995), 92; below, this section.
61 *V.C.H. Salop.* i. 343; iii. 10.
62 *Rolls of Justices in Eyre, 1221–2* (Selden Soc. lix), p. 468; *Cal. Inq. Misc.* vi, p. 111; *Feud. Aids*, iv. 229; *Cal. Inq. p.m.* (Rec. Com.), iv. 199; *Cal. Inq. p.m. Hen. VII*, ii, p. 392; P.R.O., C 142/172, no. 119.
63 Eyton, xi. 375–6; H. le Strange, *Le Strange Records* (1916), 32–3.
64 *Rot. Hund.* ii. 70; *Feud. Aids*, iv. 222.

tween coheirs during King John's reign and, as no tenant in chief held any of the shares, some of which were further divided, subinfeudated, and probably sold, a connected history of the divided manor, reunited in 1587–8, must to some extent be speculative.[65]

Ealdraed (Eldred) held Acton of the earl of Shrewsbury in 1086.[66] Brother of the rich thegn Siward and so second cousin of Edric the wild, Ealdraed had held three Shropshire manors in 1066; he retained none of them in 1086[67] but besides Acton he held two manors, Smethcott and part of Aldon (in Stokesay), whose histories[68] throw light on Acton Scott's. Ealdraed's tenure of Acton may not have lapsed,[69] for its continuance seems the best explanation of the common elements in the 13th-century histories of the three manors, which had long been held of different lords. Ealdraed's part of Aldon was held of the Lacys by 1086,[70] Smethcott of the honor of Montgomery formed by Henry I.[71] Three sisters inherited thirds of the three manors in King John's reign and their father, dead by 1203, was William Leyngleys (the Englishman),[72] likely to have been Ealdraed's descendant.

The sisters were Christine, Maud, and Margery.[73] The shares of Christine and Maud in Acton manor were subdivided into sixths, probably by 1255 when four coparceners (probably representing five) were mentioned.[74] Christine's share of Acton may have passed by 1240, like her share of Aldon, to Roger le Poer, her son by her first husband, John le Poer. If so, by 1252 Roger's share of Acton may have passed (as his share of Smethcott did) to Roger Pichard.[75] Sir Roger Pichard (fl. 1278), of Staunton on Wye (Herefs.),[76] probably relinquished his interest in Acton before 1255. The owners of his share of Acton were then evidently Walter le Secular, husband of Christine's granddaughter Cecily, and Cecily's sister Joan.[77] Cecily and Joan were the daughters of Roger,[78] either Roger le Poer or Roger Pichard.

Soon after *c.* 1284 Cecily, as widow of Walter (fl. 1277), subinfeudated her share of Acton to John, son of Richard of Hatton, and John sold it to Alice, daughter of Hugh of Newton, inducted as rector of Acton Scott in 1278.[79] That share cannot be separately identified with later shares but is likely to have been one of those which Roger and Catherine Devereux and William of Ludlow may be presumed (from their interests in the advowson) to have held in 1305.[80] From William, son of the great wool merchant Lawrence, his share seems to have descended with Stokesay to his son Sir Lawrence, owner in the later 1340s,[81] to Sir Lawrence's descendant William Ludlow, one of three coparceners in the manor in 1428,[82] and to Maurice Ludlow, owner of the share in 1497;[83] nothing more is known of it.

In 1278 Cecily le Secular's sister Joan, perhaps a minor in 1255 when unmentioned as a coparcener,[84] and her husband Nicholas of Stafford subinfeudated her sixth of Acton manor and advowson to Robert of Stretton, clerk;[85] it was probably the share held by Robert of Munslow *c.* 1284 and, with a share of the advowson, by Stephen, a minor and son of Robert of Henley, in 1305.[86] Robert of Henley was the beneficiary of the subinfeudation of 1278:[87] Robert of Stretton was either the same man,[88] for whose son Robert of Munslow acted as guardian, or was a trustee for Robert of Henley, who was identical with Robert of Munslow. The use of the surname Henley suggests that the family was resident in the parish. Stephen of Henley, still alive in 1346,[89] was perhaps an ancestor of William of Henley, one of three coparceners of Acton manor in 1428 and presumably the same as the franklin William Minton of Henley, a coparcener in 1431.[90] The Henleys' share was probably that united with the larger part of the manor by Richard Acton's purchase in 1553 of a moiety of Oakwood common and a chief house at Henley.[91]

William Leyngleys's daughter Margery of Smethcott (fl. 1252) was succeeded in her third of Acton by her younger son Stephen of Smethcott (fl. 1255).[92] Stephen's son Roger held it *c.* 1284,[93] but Stephen's share of Acton was evidently soon afterwards given to his cousin's

65 But not so 'impossible' as alleged by Eyton (xi. 376, 380), who complicated matters further by introducing (ibid. 377) a 1272 deed relating to Hatton: cf. below, Eaton, manors.

66 *V.C.H. Salop.* i. 343.

67 Ibid. i. 320, 346–7; iv. 27; viii. 109; Lewis, 'Eng. and Norman Govt. and Lordship', 83–4, 104, 112–13, 365 (map 14); Williams, *English and Norman Conquest*, 91, 93–5; Eyton, xi. 375. Eyton, rather than Lewis, is followed on the 1066 ownership of Smethcott (unmentioned in *V.C.H. Salop.* viii. 151); Tumberland (adjoining Siward's est. at Letton: *Woolhope Trans.* xlvi. 86) is assumed to belong to this Ealdraed.

68 Eyton, v. 26–8; vi. 250–5; *V.C.H. Salop.* viii. 151–2.

69 As supposed by Eyton, v. 27.

70 *V.C.H. Salop.* i. 347.

71 Ibid. iii. 35, 38; viii. 151.

72 *V.C.H. Salop.* viii. 151; *Pedigrees from the Plea Rolls*, ed. G. Wrottesley (1905), 552.

73 Eyton, vi. 250.

74 Below, this section.

75 Eyton, v. 27; vi. 251; xi. 376; *V.C.H. Salop.* viii. 151. Pichard's share of Acton has to be surmised from his being a defendant to a suit of *darrein presentment*.

76 For Sir Rog. see Eyton, vi. 252–3; xi. 200; *Cartulary of Haughmond Abbey*, ed. U. Rees (1985), p. 144. W. H. Cooke, *Collns. towards Hist. and Antiquities of Co. of Heref. in continuation of Duncumb's Hist.: Hund. of Grimsworth* (1892), 155–9, states that Sir Rog., who had a son Rog. (fl. 1279), d. 1294.

77 *Rot. Hund.* ii. 70; below, this section.

78 Wrottesley, *Pedigrees from Plea Rolls*, 552.

79 Eyton, xi. 378, 382; *Reg. Cantilupe*, (C.S.), 81; below, church.

80 Eyton, xi. 378.

81 Ibid. 379. For Lawr. (d. 1294) see *V.C.H. Salop.* iv. 60; for his descendants and Stokesay cf. *Visit. Salop. 1623*, ii (Harl. Soc. xxix), 342; Eyton, ix. 334; S.P.L., MS. 2792, p. 77.

82 *Feud. Aids*, iv. 251.

83 S.R.O. 3365/165.

84 *Rot. Hund.* ii. 70.

85 P.R.O., CP 25/1/193/5, no. 33.

86 Eyton, xi. 378.

87 Wrottesley, *Pedigrees from Plea Rolls*, 552.

88 As perh. the existence of Rob. Clerk of Henley (fl. 1273: Eyton, xi. 377; xii. 3) suggests.

89 Ibid. xi. 379.

90 *Feud. Aids*, iv. 251, 269.

91 But see below, this section, for Ric. Acton's purchase (1553) of what was probably Henley fm. and one of the medieval man. shares.

92 Eyton, xi. 376–7; *Rot. Hund.* ii. 70. Steph. acted as ld. of Smethcott perhaps *c.* 1253 (S.R.O. 2922/11/1/1), but by 1255 that part of Smethcott was held by his neph. Phil., to whose heirs it descended: *V.C.H. Salop.* viii. 152 (corr. below, Corrigenda).

93 Eyton, xi. 378.

daughter Emme Purcell, heir to half of the third share of Margery's sister Maud.[94]

Maud[95] (d. by 1231)[96] seems to have left two daughters: by 1255 her share was divided between Thomas Purcell, husband of her granddaughter Emme, and Reynold le Scot, probably her grandson.[97]

Purcell's sixth share, to which Margery of Smethcott's third share was later added, belonged *c.* 1284 to John Purcell,[98] still the owner (of half of the manor) in 1320.[99] William Purcell, of Norbury, owned it in 1346 and 1349 and probably Hugh Purcell in 1400[1] and 1408.[2] During the 15th century the share passed to the Wynnesbury family: in 1473 Hamlet Wynnesbury, presumably descended from Alice Purcell, cousin of William Wynnesbury of Norbury and wife of Sir William Wynnesbury,[3] died seised of lands in Acton Scott and Henley.[4] For over a century the share followed the descent of Pillaton (Staffs.).[5] Hamlet was succeeded by his son William[6] (d. 1502), whose daughter and heir Alice, wife of Richard Littleton,[7] died seised of a moiety of the manor in 1529.[8] Alice's son Sir Edward Littleton died in 1558. His son, another Sir Edward, died in 1574,[9] Acton Scott having been settled in 1573 on his wife Alice for life.[10] In 1587 their son Edward sold that share of the manor to Richard Acton of Acton Scott and his son Edward,[11] reuniting the manor; in 1588, presumably on Alice Littleton's death, the Actons were enfeoffed in that share of the manor.[12]

Reynold le Scot, lord of part of the manor in 1255 and probably Maud's grandson, was alive in 1259, but by 1263 his son Walter had succeeded him. Walter's son Reynold le Scot (fl. *v.p.* 1263) held the share in 1272 and *c.* 1284. He was dead by 1305 when his widow Isabel le Scot was joint patron of the church. Reynold's son Walter (born *c.* 1268, fl. 1328)[13] was succeeded by his son John (fl. 1332–8) le Scot *alias* of Acton. John's son Roger Acton (fl. 1369)[14] was lord in 1397 of ½ knight's fee in Acton Scott.[15] He was apparently succeeded by Walter Acton, and Walter by his son Edmund. By 1425 Edmund's son William was lord[16] and was listed as a coparcener in 1428 and 1431.[17] William's son William was succeeded by his son Richard (d. by 1488),[18] who married Eleanor, daughter of Hamlet Wynnesbury, another coparcener in the manor.[19] Their son Thomas Acton, probably still a minor in 1497,[20] died in 1537. His son[21] Thomas (d. by 1553) was succeeded by his son Richard, then a minor,[22] under whom the manor was reunited in 1587–8.[23]

In 1553 a property that probably represented at least one of the medieval shares in the manor was sold by John Stringfellow to Richard Acton of Acton Scott. It comprised a moiety of Oakwood common, and a moiety of a capital messuage at Henley.[24] The Henley property was probably Henley farm, which remained part of the Acton Scott estate in 1991.[25] Henley Farm is an early 17th-century baffle-entry house, originally timber framed. It was largely clad in stone in the 18th century, when it was turned to face away from the farmyard.[26] The farm buildings were rebuilt in 1768.[27]

Richard Acton died in 1590 and was succeeded by his son Edward[28] (fl. 1621),[29] whose daughter and heir Frances (d. 1632) married Walter Acton of Aldenham (d. 1641). Their son and heir was Edward Acton of Aldenham (cr. bt. 1644, d. 1659) who compounded for his estates in 1646.[30] Sir Edward's son Sir Walter (d. 1665) was followed by his son Sir Edward (d. 1716).[31] Under a settlement of 1710[32] Acton Scott passed to Sir Edward's second son Edward Acton, of Acton Scott (d. 1747), whose heir was his nephew Edward Acton (d. 1775), also of Acton Scott. The younger Edward's wife Anne (d. 1780)[33] had a life interest in all his Shropshire estates.[34] In 1773 their daughter and heir Susanna married John Stackhouse[35] (d. 1819), the botanist.[36]

94 Wrottesley, *Pedigrees from Plea Rolls*, 552.
95 Called 'Cecily' ibid. This pedigree, made in 1320, seems inaccurate in some of the early generations (see next note), and 'Cecily' (not otherwise recorded as a dau. of Wm. Leyngleys) is here assumed to be an error for Maud, for whose existence Eyton marshals the contemporary evidence.
96 *V.C.H. Salop.* viii. 152 (corr. below, Corrigenda).
97 *Rot. Hund.* ii. 70; Wrottesley, *Pedigrees from Plea Rolls*, 552. Christine, ancestress of the Scotts (Wrottesley, op. cit. 552), is assumed to be Maud's elder dau., but the 1320 pedigree (ibid.) must err in making Reynold le Scot (fl. *c.* 1284) Christine's grandson through a supposed father Thos. Almost certainly two generations came betw. Christine and Reynold (fl. *c.* 1284) and Reynold's father was Wal., son of Reynold (fl. 1255–9): below. The Scotts were successors, but not heirs, of the Purcells at Smethcott: Eyton, vi. 253; *V.C.H. Salop.* viii. 152.
98 Eyton, xi. 378.
99 Wrottesley, *Pedigrees from Plea Rolls*, 552.
1 Eyton, xi. 378–80; *Reg. Trillek* (C.S.), 41.
2 *Reg. Mascall* (C.S.), 174.
3 *Visit. Salop. 1623*, ii. 411; cf. S.P.L., MSS. 2138, f. 231v.; 2795, p. 199; 4079, pp. 1388–99; *V.C.H. Staffs.* v. 119. There is no satisfactory acct. of the Wynnesburys before 1473: S.P.L., MS. 2788, p. 257.
4 P.R.O., C 140/45, no. 36.
5 *V.C.H. Staffs.* v. 119.
6 S.R.O. 1842/1; 3365/165.
7 *Cal. Inq. p.m. Hen. VII*, ii, p. 392.
8 S.R.O. 1842/1.
9 *V.C.H. Staffs.* v. 119.
10 P.R.O., C 142/172, no. 119.
11 S.R.O. 3925, box 9, deed, 24 Apr. 1587.
12 S.R.O. 1842/1.
13 Wrottesley, *Pedigrees from Plea Rolls*, 552; Eyton, xi. 376–9; *Feud. Aids*, iv. 222; above, n. 97.
14 W.S.L. 350/5/40, Acton Scott pp. 2–3; Eyton, xi. 379 (sources preferred to the pedigree in S.R.O. 3925, bdle. 11).
15 *Cal. Inq. Misc.* vi, p. 111.
16 W.S.L. 350/5/40, Acton Scott p. 3.
17 *Feud. Aids*, iv. 251, 269.
18 W.S.L. 350/5/40, Acton Scott pp. 3–4.
19 S.R.O. 1842/1.
20 S.R.O. 3365/165; *L. & P. Hen. VIII*, i, p. 438.
21 P.R.O., E 150/1220/11, naming Thos.'s son and heir as John.
22 W.S.L. 350/5/40, Acton Scott pp. 3–4; below, Henley fm.
23 Above, this section [Purcell share].
24 S.R.O. 1093/2/534; cf. below, this section (Alcaston).
25 Inf. from Mr. T. S. Acton.
26 SA 17308.
27 Below, econ. hist.
28 P.R.O., C 142/228, no. 7.
29 H.W.R.O.(H.), Heref. dioc. rec. AL 19/16, f. 285.
30 P. Gunn, *The Actons* (1978), 31; *T.S.A.S.* 4th ser. v. 58; *Cal. Cttee. for Compounding*, iii. 1541.
31 W.S.L. 350/5/40, Acton Scott pp. 5–6; Burke, *Peerage* (1908), 77–8.
32 S.R.O. 3925, box 8, deeds 19–20 Mar. 1709/10.
33 Ibid. bdle. 11, pedigree.
34 Historic Working Fm., Edw. Acton's will (transcript).
35 S.R.O. 2005/2, 18 Apr. 1754; MRg/1, 20 Apr. 1773.
36 *D.N.B.* s.v. Stackhouse, John; Burke, *Peerage* (1908), 77–8; *T.S.A.S.* lv, pedigree facing p. 82; W.S.L. 350/5/40, Acton Scott pp. 6–8; F. A. Stafleu and R. S. Cowan, *Taxonomic Literature*, v (Utrecht, 1985), 824–5.

Stackhouse's widow[37] owned Acton Scott until her death in 1834.[38] The next lord was their younger son Thomas Pendarves Stackhouse who assumed the additional name of Acton in 1834 and died without surviving issue in 1835.[39] T. P. Stackhouse Acton had lived at the Hall and in effect been the resident squire since 1807. A life interest in the Hall was left to his widow Frances (d. 1881), a writer on local history and archaeology,[40] but he was succeeded in the estate by his elder brother Edward William[41] (d. 1853), who had assumed the names Wynne-Pendarves in 1815. Perhaps after the expiry of an interest in the manor belonging to Wynne-Pendarves's sister Mrs. Holt[42] (d. 1873) his heir and great-nephew Augustus Wood came into the estate, assuming the additional name of Acton in 1874.

Augustus Wood Acton, honorary chief constable of Shropshire during the First World War,[43] died in 1918 and was succeeded by his daughter Joyce Stackhouse who, in 1923, married R. C. Fullerton-Smith (d. 1970);[44] in 1941 they assumed the name Acton in lieu of Fullerton-Smith. In 1966 Mrs. Acton passed the lordship of the manor to their son T. S. Acton,[45] the lord in 1991.

Thomas Acton (d. 1537) had a chief house at Acton Scott[46] which was probably the predecessor of Acton Scott Hall, standing north-east of the church. The Hall is a double- pile brick house of two and a half storeys built *c.* 1600. The entrance front on the south was of three bays and symmetrical, with a central door flanked by broad bay windows rising through two storeys. Service rooms occupied a rear basement. In 1672 it was taxed on 10 hearths.[47] Between 1807 and *c.* 1820, after having long been occupied by tenant farmers, the Hall was repaired and modernized, at least partly to plans by Joseph Bromfield. Blue roofing slates replaced the old stone ones, the chimneys were rebuilt, and stone was used in place of brick in replacement windows and for coping around the top of the building. Re-ordering of the rooms necessitated the removal of the main entrance to a porch built on the west side of the Hall, the creation of a new main staircase and the insertion of back stairs, the addition of a dining room on the east side of the Hall, and the construction of new service rooms.[48] Some of those service rooms were removed *c.* 1961–2.[49]

In the 18th century there was a bowling green to the south, a formal garden to the east, and the kitchen garden and Edward Acton's orchard to the north.[50] Between 1807 and *c.* 1820 new gardens were laid out and the Hall's surrounds were planted up with thousands of evergreens.[51] 'American' plants were introduced in 1811–12,[52] and by 1820 there was a rock garden[53] in an old quarry 300 m. south-west of the Hall, where Frances Stackhouse Acton later reconstructed part of the hypocaust from the Roman villa which she excavated in 1844.[54]

George Hill sold a freehold called *THE TOWER* to Charles Foxe (d. 1590) of Bromfield; Foxe left it to his youngest son Henry,[55] who in 1631 sold it to the tenant Richard Baldwin.[56] Baldwin mortgaged it in 1635 to Thomas Higgins,[57] whose son Thomas (kt. 1663)[58] became owner *c.* 1655.[59] Sir Thomas died *c.* 1685[60] and in 1694 his children sold the Tower to Sir Edward Acton, lord of the manor.[61]

The field called the Tower Yard is just north of the church.[62] The Tower was apparently occupied in the mid 17th century by the Baldwins[63] but later abandoned, and its ruins were quarried in 1790.[64] It was a stone building *c.* 17 ft. square internally with projections, one of them a fireplace, on three sides. Its walls were *c.* 3 ft. thick.[65] Presumably it was either the chamber end of a disappeared hall or, less probably, a tower house. Parallels, especially in Shropshire, are hard to find.[66]

The farm later known as *OAKWOOD* was identified in the 19th century with property sold in the 1590s by Thomas Rawlins to William Littleton of Little Stretton.[67] On Littleton's death in 1605 his estate included a cottage and 85 a. in Acton Scott, Oakwood, and Mowsley.[68] Before 1629 his nephew William Littleton had sold the farm to John Thynne (d. *c.* 1648),[69] whose family sold it in 1684 to Samuel Powell of Church Stretton.[70] By 1776 Oakwood farm was part of the manorial estate[71] and the farmhouse had probably been rebuilt in brick.[72]

By *c.* 1600 the Lewis family owned two free-

37 Rest of descent based on Burke, *Land. Gent.* (1952), 3, 2005.
38 Notes at Historic Working Fm.
39 M.I. in ch.; *D.N.B.* s.v. Stackhouse, John.
40 T. P. Stackhouse's diary; S.R.O. 2906/1, pp. 19, 37; *Salopian Shreds & Patches*, iv. 140, 142–3.
41 S.R.O. 2906/1, p. 37.
42 *P.O. Dir. Salop.* (1870), 8, gives John Stackhouse's dau. Katherine, the Revd. W. F. Holt's wife, as lady of the man.
43 *V.C.H. Salop.* iii. 228.
44 Inf. from Mr. T. S. Acton.
45 S.R.O., archivist's office file 'Mrs. Acton', letter, Joyce S. Acton to co. archivist 12 Aug. 1966.
46 P.R.O., E 150/1220/11.
47 *Hearth Tax 1672*, 181; cf. pl. 17; illus. of ho. in Bodl. MS. Top. c. 2, f. 46.
48 S.R.O. 2563/16; 2906/1, pp. 19–22, 24; T. P. Stackhouse's diary, s.a. 1811 (for Bromfield); W.S.L. 350/5/40, Acton Scott pp. 9, 14; above, frontispiece.
49 Historic Working Fm., notes of conversation with Mrs. R. C. Acton 1981.
50 S.R.O. 3925, map of 1776; 3925, box 10, surv. of Acton Scott *c.* 1776, fields A 2–8.
51 S.R.O. 2563/50; T. P. Stackhouse's diary.
52 T. P. Stackhouse's diary, s.a.
53 S.R.O. 3925, box 10, surv. of Acton Scott *c.* 1820, field A 7.
54 Inf. from Mr. R. S. Acton.
55 *T.S.A.S.* 2nd ser. xii. 141–2; P.R.O., C 142/235, no. 111.
56 S.R.O. 3925, box 8, deed 17 Oct. 1631.
57 Ibid. deed 29 Sept. 1635.
58 W. A. Shaw, *Kts. of Eng.* (1906), ii. 238.
59 S.R.O. 3925, box 8, deed 18 Aug. 1656.
60 Ibid. will (copy).
61 Ibid. deed 1 Mar. 1693/4.
62 S.R.O. 3925, maps of 1776, 1820; 3925, box 10, surv. *c.* 1776, field A 1; ibid. surv. of 1820, field A 5a.
63 S.R.O. 3925, box 8, deed 18 Aug. 1656.
64 W.S.L. 350/5/40, Acton Scott p. 15; S.P.L., MS. 6007, f. [18v.].
65 S.P.L., MS. 6007, f. [18v.]; above, fig. 5.
66 Dr. R. A. Higham and Messrs. J. R. Kenyon and P. Smith are thanked for their thoughts on the bldg.
67 W.S.L. 350/5/40, Acton Scott p. 19; S.R.O. 3320/1/1.
68 P.R.O., C 142/291, no. 91.
69 W.S.L. 350/5/40, Acton Scott p. 19.
70 S.R.O. 3320/1/2–5.
71 S.R.O. 3925, map of 1776.
72 Date stone illegible but in same style as those (of 1760s) on Acton Scott demesne bldgs. and Henley Fm. bldgs.

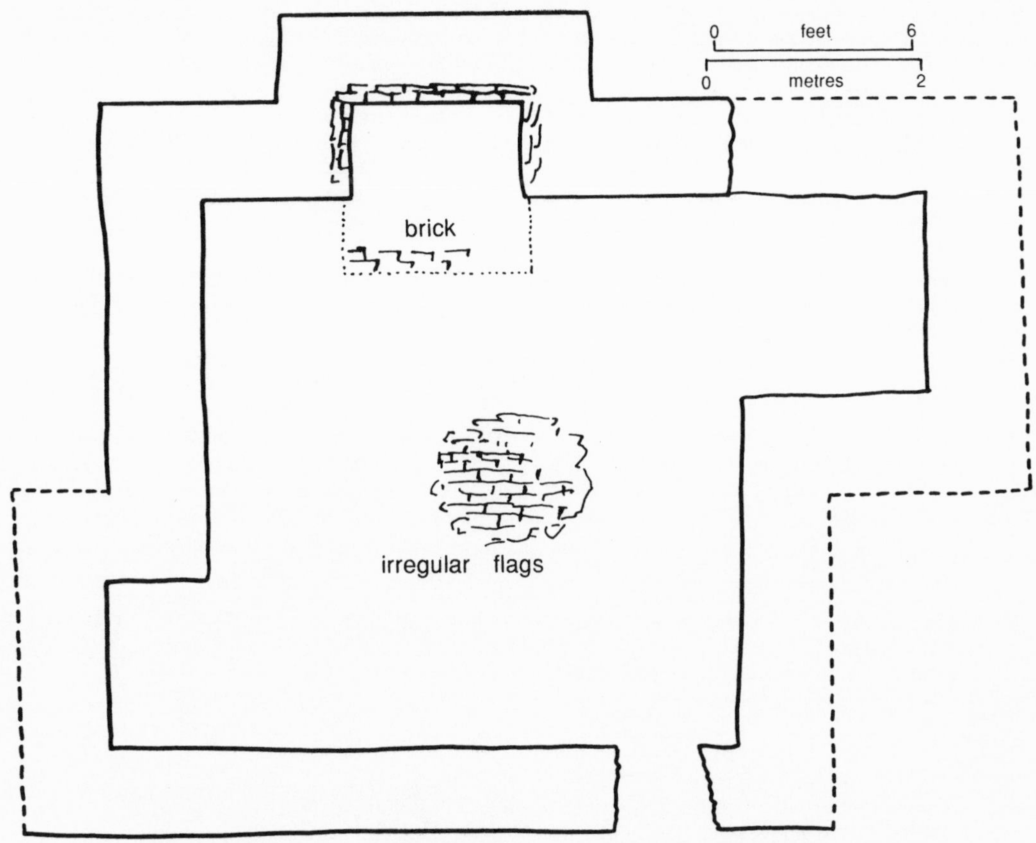

THE TOWER, ACTON SCOTT. GROUND PLAN c. 1790

Fig. 5

holds in the parish: a farm known later as Little Oakwood, and a farm at Henley, whose house (a stone building partly of 1719)[73] was known in the 20th century as Henley Cottages.[74] In 1743 those properties passed to Penryn Lewis's nephew Edmund Breeze (d. *c.* 1772), who left the Henley farm to his daughter Margaret, wife of Thomas Marson, and Little Oakwood to his grandson Samuel Thomas. Samuel's brother John sold both farms to John Stackhouse in 1808. Thereafter they descended with the manorial estate.[75] Little Oakwood Farm, a small 16th- or 17th-century building refronted in the mid 19th century, was sold without farm land in 1983 and much extended in 1985.[76]

Eadric (Edric) held *ALCASTON* in 1066. In 1086 Roger of Montgomery, earl of Shrewsbury, held the manor in chief and Helgot held it of him.[77] After Earl Robert's forfeiture in 1102[78] Helgot's heirs may have held the manor in chief.[79]

Alcaston was among the manors once Helgot's which passed by inheritance or enfeoffment to the Girros family, and Robert de Girros (d. *c.* 1190) was recorded as lord of Alcaston.[80] When, *c.* 1251, the Girros estate was divided between coheirs, Alcaston passed to Walter of Hopton.[81] By then, however, that was a mesne lordship, and in 1255 Vivian of Rossall was the terre tenant, holding Alcaston of his father Thomas of Rossall.[82] After 1259 Vivian apparently sold the manor to John FitzAlan (II) who died holding Alcaston under Sir Walter of Hopton in 1267. By 1272, however, while a third of the manor was claimed in dower by Isabel FitzAlan, Vivian's son Raymond was lord, apparently having been re-enfeoffed therein.[83] About 1284 Raymond 'of Alcaston' held Alcaston as ½ knight's fee under Richard FitzAlan, called tenant in chief.[84] The Rossalls' terre tenancy had apparently lapsed by 1302 when Richard, earl of Arundel, was found to have held Alcaston of Walter of Hopton.[85] The manor remained in the FitzAlans' hands until the earl of Arundel's forfeiture in 1397.[86] In 1398 it was granted for life to the king's harbinger Thomas Sy,[87] but was later restored to the FitzAlans: Beatrice, countess of Arundel, died seised of it in 1439.[88]

73 Date stone 'PL 1719'.
74 Shrews. Sch. Libr., James Deed 47; S.P.L., Deeds 12974; P.R.O., C 142/298, no. 38; C 142/505, no. 121.
75 S.R.O. 3925, box 3, abstr. of title; S.R.O. 3925, map of 1776.
76 Inf. from Mr. J. R. Ockenden.
77 *V.C.H. Salop.* i. 338; cf. above, this section (Acton).
78 *V.C.H. Salop.* iii. 10.
79 Cf. below, Holdgate, manors.
80 Eyton, xii. 1.
81 Ibid. x. 147; xii. 1.
82 Ibid. xii. 1; *Rot. Hund.* ii. 70.
83 Eyton, xii. 1–2.
84 Ibid. 3; *Feud. Aids*, iv. 224.
85 *Cal. Inq. p.m.* iii, p. 52.
86 *Cal. Fine R.* 1272–1307, 518; *Cal. Pat.* 1301–7, 545–6; *Cal. Close*, 1346–9, 244.
87 *Cal. Pat.* 1396–9, 278.
88 *Cal. Inq. p.m.* (Rec. Com.), iv. 199; *Complete Peerage*, i. 246.

By 1453 Alcaston was held by William Burley of Broncroft,[89] and it probably descended thereafter with the share of Munslow held from 1470 by the Lytteltons: in 1504 Joan Lyttelton was said to hold Alcaston of the earl of Shrewsbury.[90]

John Lyttelton may have sold Alcaston manor between 1507 and 1532 to Humphrey Ludlow,[91] although an interest in Alcaston and Henley was sold in 1552 by the earl of Oxford to John Stringfellow.[92] Ludlow's daughter and heir Elizabeth (d. 1575) married Humphrey Hill (d. 1585) of Court of Hill (in Burford), from whom Alcaston passed to their third son George. George Hill's son and heir Thomas died young and Alcaston passed to Thomas's cousin[93] Thomas Hill (d. 1656) of Court of Hill, who married Mary, daughter and heir of William Nesse of Acton Woodhouse. Their son Thomas Hill (d. 1702) was succeeded by his son the Revd. Nesse Hill (d. 1715), probably followed by Nesse's son Thomas (d.s.p. 1720). Thomas's brother Nesse was in possession by 1721 and died in 1732, being followed by his son Thomas (d. 1780) and grandson George Nesse Hill (d. 1830). G. N. Hill was succeeded by his brother William Nesse Hill, lord in 1846. Hill may have been succeeded by his younger brother the Revd. Thomas Hill,[94] but in 1853 a trustee for Joseph Loxdale Warren (d. 1888) bought the manor from mortgagees.[95] No mention of manorial rights was made when the estate was broken up and offered for sale after the death of J. L. Warren's son and namesake in 1909.[96]

Manor Farm incorporates part of a large and complex timber framed house, perhaps partly of *c.* 1580[97] and taxed on six hearths in 1672;[98] the eastern part was removed *c.* 1840.[99]

MOAT FARM, reputedly a home of Reynold Grey, earl of Kent (d. 1573), was later owned by John Baldwin (fl. 1642–54).[1] About 1655 it passed to Edward Baugh[2] (fl. 1672).[3] Lancelot Baugh (fl. 1757), perhaps Edward's son and heir,[4] left as heir a daughter Harriet, wife of the Revd. Lewis Maxey, whose trustees sold the farm to the trustees of Ralph Benson of Lutwyche (in Rushbury).[5] The farm, 205 a. in 1839,[6] was sold in the later 19th century by the Bensons and was part of the Warren estate offered for sale in 1913.[7]

Moat Farm stands on a platform *c.* 50 m. in diameter within a medieval moat, probably once square.[8] The house, principally of brick and including some diaper work on the front of the former northern wing, is probably later 17th-century and may be that taxed on eight hearths in 1672.[9] It was much altered in the 19th and 20th centuries.[10]

In 1553 John Stringfellow sold his moiety of a farm to John James, who in 1556 bought the other half from John Lyttelton. John James the younger was of Alcaston in 1623. William James owned the farm in 1644 and 1675, perhaps being succeeded by his son William and he, perhaps, by John James (fl. 1711). In 1714 John James sold his Alcaston property to Benjamin James,[11] who in turn sold it to Richard Ward of Harton in 1726.[12] The farm, like the Wards' Harton property,[13] was owned in the mid 19th century by Thomas Dunne.[14] The Dunnes sold it (*c.* 115 a.) in 1854 to J. L. Warren's trustee and it was incorporated in Alcaston Manor farm.[15]

William James's house, taxed on four hearths in 1672,[16] was timber framed and had a jettied first floor.[17] It stood on the east side of Alcaston.[18] It was demolished in the 1930s and farm workers' houses were built on the site.[19]

ECONOMIC HISTORY. In 1086 Acton was rated at 3 hides, Alcaston at one. Both manors had enough land for four ploughs: at Acton there were three, worked by tenants; at Alcaston there were two, one in demesne and one worked by the tenants.[20]

In the Middle Ages there were probably three sets of fields in the parish, for Acton Scott, Alcaston, and Henley. At Acton Scott where, in 1278, a sixth of the manor had included 2½ virgates of land, 6 a. of meadow, and 60 a. of wood,[21] extensive open-field land survived in three fields in the early 17th century.[22] South-east of the village Burr or Burgh field extended to Moor brook, while south-west of the village was Church field, perhaps also known as the field towards Henley.[23] The third field, Ryall field,

89 P.R.O., CP 25/1/195/22, no. 9.

90 *Cal. Inq. p.m. Hen. VII*, ii, pp. 577–8; below, Munslow, manors. Hardwicke claimed that Alcaston, forfeited by Vct. Lovel in 1485, was granted to the 4th earl of Shrews.: W.S.L. 350/5/40, Acton Scott p. 20.

91 For what follows (to the Revd. Nesse Hill's time) see *Cal. Inq. p.m. Hen. VII*, iii, pp. 331–2; W.S.L. 350/5/40, Acton Scott pp. 20–1.

92 S.R.O. 20/23/13; cf. above, this section (Acton Scott).

93 *Visit. Salop. 1623*, i (Harl. Soc. xxviii), 244.

94 S.P.L., MS. 4360, p. 241; *T.S.A.S.* 4th ser. viii. 247, 250, 252–3; S.P.L., Deeds 17067; S. Bagshaw, *Dir. Salop.* (1851), 519.

95 S.R.O. 3993/1–2; *Shrews. Chron.* 23 Mar. 1888, p. 5.

96 *Shrews. Chron.* 23 and 30 Apr. 1909; S.P.L., SC1/77.

97 Illus. on front of S.P.L., SC1/77; SA 171.

98 *Hearth Tax 1672*, 183.

99 SA 171; S. Bagshaw, *Dir. Salop.* (1851), 519.

1 W.S.L. 350/5/40, Acton Scott pp. 19–20; cf. L. Stone, *Crisis of the Aristocracy 1558–1641* (1965), 99 n. 1, 760–1; *Complete Peerage*, vii. 170–1. For Baldwin pedigree see S.P.L., MS. 4645, p. 203.

2 W.S.L. 350/5/40, Acton Scott p. 20; S.P.L., Deeds 18091C.

3 *Hearth Tax 1672*, 183.

4 But acc. to W.S.L. 350/5/40, Acton Scott p. 20, the owner 1660–95 was Ric. Baugh.

5 Ibid.

6 S.R.O. 298/1.

7 S. Bagshaw *Dir. Salop.* (1851), 519; S.P.L., SC1/77; above, this section (Alcaston), for Jos. Loxdale Warren.

8 S.R.O. 298/1; O.S. Map 1/2,500, Salop. LXIV. 9 (1903 edn.); SA 172.

9 *Hearth Tax 1672*, 183.

10 SA 172; S.P.L., SC1/77 (photo.); S. Bagshaw, *Dir. Salop.* (1851), 519.

11 S.R.O. 3887, box 50, partic. of deeds; P.R.O., C 3/338/24.

12 S.R.O. 3887, box 50, deed 24 June 1726.

13 Below, Eaton, manors.

14 S.R.O. 3887, box 50, abstr. of deeds; S. Bagshaw, *Dir. Salop.* (1851), 519.

15 S.R.O. 3993/2.

16 *Hearth Tax 1672*, 183.

17 W.S.L. 350/5/40, Acton Scott p. 21; Mrs. Wood Acton's notes.

18 S.R.O. 298/1, field 300.

19 Inf. from Mr. C. H. Hand.

20 *V.C.H. Salop.* i. 338, 343.

21 Eyton, xi. 377.

22 S.R.O. 2228/1, ff. 3–12; 3925, box 12, demesne surv. 1615.

23 H.W.R.O.(H.), HD 2/14/5.

adjoined the church, perhaps to the north-west. Inclosure, probably piecemeal, was occurring in the mid 17th century,[24] although one or two quillets in Burr field still survived in 1808.[25] The names and locations of Alcaston's fields[26] are unknown; inclosure there was probably 150 years earlier than at Acton Scott.[27] Open fields survived longest at Henley. In 1776 Back field lay north-east of Henley, Little Henley field abutted the south-west side of Henley common, and Henley Common field was north of Henley with Lower field beyond it.[28] All were inclosed between 1792 and 1820.[29]

Acton Scott, Henley, and Alcaston were all in the Long forest until 1301.[30] Acton Scott manor had a hay in 1086.[31] It probably lay in the northern half of the manor, which in the Middle Ages and later was occupied by an extensive common wood, probably alluded to in the manor's name.[32] In the Middle Ages the wood was usually referred to as Oakwood,[33] though by 1589[34] its southern part was sometimes distinguished as Castle Hill. It may have been those woods which in 1578 supplied 1,500 oaks to build Whitehall in Shrewsbury.[35] In 1811 the eastern portion of the common was called Acton Bank.[36] Cattle and sheep were pastured in the woods in the later 16th century,[37] and as late as 1657 mast was gathered in Oakwood.[38] By 1776, however, few trees remained,[39] and Oakwood was probably much reduced from its original extent.[40] The remaining common, *c.* 185 a. then called Hawkwood rather than Oakwood,[41] was inclosed in 1811.[42]

A second common, the triangular Henley common, lay on the southern boundary of Acton Scott manor.[43] It, like the adjoining hamlet, probably took its name from a former wood.[44] The common was noticed as Henley heath in 1695.[45] In the later 18th century it was intercommoned by Henley and Alcaston.[46] Proposals before 1821 to inclose it were opposed by the lord of Alcaston manor,[47] and it survives as a 16-a. common.[48]

Banner wood, first mentioned in 1589[49] and not subject to common rights, lies on the parish boundary near the southernmost tip of the manor.[50]

Alcaston's wood, mentioned in 1235,[51] covered the scarp of Wenlock Edge along the manor's south-eastern boundary. There was assarting in the manor in the Middle Ages.[52] Some time before 1692[53] the wood was inclosed and in 1839 the three principal Alcaston landowners each had a share of it.[54] In the early 19th century some at least was coppiced, with cordwood being coaled for the Bringewood (Herefs.) ironworks.[55]

The parish was well supplied with meadow along its streams.[56] Some, in the 17th century and later, was doled.[57]

When Nesse Hill died at Alcaston in the spring of 1676 he had corn (worth £5 17*s.* 6*d.*), wheat (£2 5*s.*), barley (£2), oats (£5 1*s.* 8*d.*), and peas (£1 16*s.*). Stock comprised 6 oxen, 25 cattle, a horse, *c.* 57 sheep, and a few pigs.[58]

Clover, vetches, and turnips were all grown on the Acton Scott demesne by 1753,[59] together with wheat, grey peas, and especially muncorn.[60] Hops too may have been tried at some stage.[61] In the 1750s, as later, lime (at least some coming from Blackwood in Eaton-under-Heywood) was used and allowances made to tenants for its use.[62] Demesne livestock in 1755 included enough sheep to supply 26 st. of wool, sent to Shrewsbury,[63] although in 1775 Home farm had just 22 sheep, together with 34 cattle (including a milking herd of 8), 20 pigs, 3 yoke of working oxen, and 6 wagon horses.[64] Its land in 1776[65] comprised 86 a. arable, 139 a. pasture, and 44 a. meadow. Whether at that date demesne stock was ever put on Oakwood common, which began 100 m. north of Home farm, is unknown. In 1776 in Acton Scott manor as a whole, excluding commons and woods, 37 per cent of the land was arable, 48 per cent pasture, and 15 per cent meadow. Most farms were fairly large: the Home farm and Acton Scott and Church farms were 220–270 a., Henley farm 164 a., and Oakwood (or Hawkwood) farm 76 a.

Lords of Acton Scott manor invested in improved farm buildings in the 18th century. Edward Acton built Church Farm in coursed stone in 1732 and John Stackhouse built a barn there in 1798.[66] In the 1760s Edward Acton's nephew and namesake, lord 1747–75, was probably much involved in the running of his estate. In the 1760s the Home farm buildings were largely rebuilt in brick with elaborate stone

24 S.R.O. 3925, box 12, note of lands exchanged 1649.
25 S.R.O. 2563/1, f. 16.
26 *Roll of Salop. Eyre 1256* (Selden Soc. xcvi), p. 221.
27 B.L. Lansd. MS. 1, f. 192v.
28 S.R.O. 3925, box 10, surv. *c.* 1776; 3925, map of 1776.
29 Cf. S.R.O. 3925, box 12, surv. bk. 1792; 3925, map of 1820.
30 *Cartulary of Shrews. Abbey*, ed. U. Rees (1975), ii, p. 250.
31 *V.C.H. Salop.* i. 343.
32 Above, this article, intro.
33 Mentioned 1235: Eyton, vi. 338.
34 H.W.R.O.(H.), HD 2/14/5.
35 F. Leach, *Co. Seats of Salop.* (1891), 215.
36 S.R.O. 3925, box 12, incl. award (copy).
37 H.W.R.O.(H.), HD 2/14/5.
38 S.R.O. 3925, box 12, ct. r. 1657.
39 S.R.O. 3925, map of 1776.
40 Map and other evid. suggests Oakwood and Lit. Oakwood fms. (est. by later 16th cent.: above, manors) were early inclosures from W. side of common. Earthwks. suggest original E. bdy. of common ran along hedge betw. fields numbered 82 and 83 in 1839 (S.R.O. 298/1).
41 e.g. S.R.O. 2563/1 *passim.*
42 S.R.O. 3925, box 12, incl. award (copy).
43 S.R.O. 3925, map of 1776.
44 Above, this article, intro.
45 S.R.O. 3925, box 10, Acton Scott man. bounds, 1695.
46 Ibid. box 10, surv. *c.* 1776.
47 S.R.O. 2563/14.
48 S.C.C. Ch. Exec.'s Dept., commons reg.
49 H.W.R.O.(H.), HD 2/14/5.
50 S.R.O. 298/1, fields 232–3.
51 Eyton, vi. 338.
52 S.P.L., Deeds 1633.
53 P.R.O., C 104/23, pt. 2, deed 18 Jan. 1691/2.
54 S.R.O. 298/1.
55 S.R.O. 165/99, 104, 112; P.R.O., IR 18/7921.
56 Field names: S.R.O. 298/1.
57 S.R.O. 2228/1, f. 6; 3925, box 12, demesne surv. 1615 and note of lands exchanged 1649.
58 H.W.R.O.(H.), Heref. dioc. rec., inv. 1 May 1676.
59 S.R.O. 3925, box 12, acct. bk. 1753–7, 27 Feb. 1753.
60 S.R.O. 2563/32, s.a. 1753, 1755–7, 1762.
61 W.S.L. 350/5/40, Acton Scott p. 15.
62 S.R.O. 2563/32, at end (Widow Parker's rental); /33, e.g. 21 June, 9 July, 29 Dec. 1757; 4–5 Jan., 30 Dec. 1758; 20 Jan. 1759.
63 S.R.O. 2563/32, s.a. 1755.
64 Ibid. val. of livestock by Moses Luther [1775].
65 Rest of para. based on S.R.O. 3925, box 10, surv., etc., of Acton Scott [*c.* 1776].
66 Barn demolished *c.* 1980.

details including quoins, coping stones, and kneelers with finials, and the farmyard at Henley was also rebuilt but with local stone. At the end of his life Acton may also have built Oakwood Farm.[67] He had a keen practical interest in arboriculture, especially in apple trees,[68] and between 1755 (when he began grafting experiments) and 1775 hundreds of apple, and some pear, trees were grafted (many apparently by Acton himself) and planted in closes, hedgerows, and cottage gardens. He gave dozens of others to relations, friends, and tenants. Large numbers of ash, poplar, and willow were raised from sets ('pitchers'), and in 1775 Acton gave *c.* 6,000 willow sets of different sorts to his neighbour Richard Wilding, of Ragdon. Acton also planted fir, larch, Spanish chestnut, elm, beech, walnut, and lime around the manor, and established a plantation of Scots fir on Oakwood common in 1771.

About 1792 the demesne was reduced to 28 a. and the manor's farms reorganized,[69] the first of many improvements undertaken in John Stackhouse's time and more especially after 1807, when his son T. P. Stackhouse took over the estate, until the later 1820s.[70] Much of the new land inclosed from Oakwood common in 1811[71] was put into Oakwood farm, which also absorbed Mowsley farm (23 a.) on the northern edge of the parish.[72] By 1820 Henley's open fields had been inclosed and the owners of freehold strips remaining in them bought out. The only other sizeable freehold in 1776, Little Oakwood farm, was also bought.[73] Field boundaries were altered throughout the parish to form more regular closes, drainage was undertaken, meadows floated, and a field barn[74] built in the northern part of Acton Scott farm. Extensive improvements were made to farmhouses, cottages, and roads.[75] Finally, in conjunction with work on the Hall and grounds,[76] all woodland in the parish, previously let with the individual farms, was brought into demesne. Much replanting was done especially on Castle Hill and around the Hall, 20,500 seedlings, including larch and fir, being bought 1812–14.[77]

From *c.* 1807, when T. P. Stackhouse went to live at Acton Scott,[78] oxen ceased to be used.[79] Over the next two decades new stock was introduced, presumably at least in part owing to the influence of Stackhouse's father-in-law T. A. Knight, the celebrated Herefordshire breeder of Hereford cattle.[80] New breeds and types included a Merino ram (1810), twelve Merino-Ryeland ewes (1812), and ten Hereford ewes (1810); a Hereford bull and two half-bred Herefords (1812); three Welsh heifers and a Welsh ox (1813); a Chinese sow and boar (1815); and an Indian heifer in 1829.[81] By 1810 a winnowing machine had been bought,[82] and by 1815 a turnip cutter and a straw cutter.[83] Corn was perhaps threshed at Church Farm, where the tenant William Parker had a threshing machine by 1811.[84] Cereals in hand in 1813 were 150 bu. of oats (worth £37), 125 bu. of barley (£44), and 80 bu. of wheat (£48). There were also 45 tons of hay (£135).[85] Trefoil, clover, and turnips were fodder crops.[86] The ground was limed,[87] and pasture was pared and burnt,[88] and in 1818 an area of peat near Henley common was set on fire and allowed to burn for several months to provide potash-rich ash.[89] In 1821 the Acton Scott estate reduced rents by as much as 25 per cent because of the agricultural depression,[90] and later in the decade allowances were made for drainage.

In 1793 labourers in the parish[91] earned 5*s.* a week in summer and 3*s.* in winter, at all times with meat and drink. Most kept pigs, and many or all of the farmers supplied them with milk. They bought cheese, but butter, meat, and beer were beyond them. Hemp may still have been spun and woven, as it had been in the 1750s.[92] Half a dozen of the cottagers had a field or two, others just a garden; they paid up to £2 a year, though some owed only an amercement of 2*s.* 6*d.* In the early 19th century the Acton Scott estate prepared ground for tree planting by letting the poor grow potatoes on it.[93]

In 1838 arable occupied 635 a. (36 per cent of the parish), pasture 725 a. (41 per cent), meadow 200 a. (12 per cent), and woodland 180 a. (11 per cent). About half of the arable, on heavy soil, was worked on a five-course fallow–wheat–oats–clover–clover rotation; the rest, on the shales and gravels in the north, was turnip soil used in a four-course wheat–turnips–barley–clover tillage reminiscent of Norfolk husbandry.[94]

The amount of arable, declining by 1838, continued to fall over the next 130 years, especially at the expense of grass for sheep.[95] The late 20th century saw a modest resurgence in cereal cultivation. Past farming practices were revived on a small scale when, in 1975, the county council took a lease of the Home farm buildings and 23 a. and opened Acton Scott Working Farm Museum (from 1990 the Acton Scott Historic Working Farm).[96]

67 Above, manors; date stones; *V.C.H. Salop.* iv. 185.
68 Para. based on S.R.O. 2563/35.
69 Cf. S.R.O. 3925, map of 1776; 3925, box 12, surv. bk. 1792.
70 Improvements included fms. in Wistanstow: S.R.O. 2563/15; cf. ibid. /16. Cf. above, manors; S.R.O. 1066/71, f. 42.
71 Above, this section.
72 Rest of para. based on S.R.O. 2563/1, e.g. ff. 8, 9; /13, 15–16; 3925, map of 1776; 3925, box 10, survs.; box 12, surv. bk. 1792.
73 Above, manors.
74 SA 17172.
75 Above, this article, intro.
76 Above, manors.
77 S.R.O. 2563/50, garden expenses, s.a.; T. P. Stackhouse's diary *passim.*
78 S.R.O. 1066/71, ff. 21–2.
79 Cf. S.R.O. 2563/32, val. of livestock by Moses Luther; /36, stock val. 1810.
80 *T.S.A.S.* lv, pedigree facing p. 82; S.R.O. 2563/36, livestock val. 1813, includes a cow supplied by 'Mr. Knight'.
81 S.R.O. 2563/36, s.a.
82 Ibid. stock val. 1810.
83 Ibid. deadstock val. 1816.
84 S.R.O. 4791/1/8, p. 600. For identification of Parker's fm. S.R.O. 3925, box 10, surv. of 1820.
85 S.R.O. 2563/36, deadstock val. 1813.
86 Ibid. vals. 1813–15.
87 Ibid. s.a. 1813, 1829.
88 Ibid. s.a. 1812.
89 T. P. Stackhouse's diary.
90 S.R.O. 2563/6.
91 S.P.L., MS. 6865, p. 18.
92 S.R.O. 2563/33, 28 May, 3 June 1757; cf. 3925, box 10, surv. *c.* 1776, fields D 13, E 11.
93 T. P. Stackhouse's diary, s.a. 1810–20.
94 P.R.O., IR 18/7921.
95 Table I and sources there cited.
96 *V.C.H. Salop.* iv. 269; inf. from Mr. N. C. Nixon.

Acton Scott manor had a mill in 1278.[97] It may have stood north or east of the hall where, in the 18th century and later, there was a chain of fish ponds between the village and Hatton pool.[98] Alcaston had a water mill in 1302.[99]

TABLE I

ACTON SCOTT: LAND USE, LIVESTOCK, AND CROPS

	1867	*1891*	*1938*	*1965*
Percentage of grassland	70	81	91	92
arable	30	19	9	8
Percentage of cattle	22	20	21	14
sheep	69	77	75	85
pigs	9	3	4	1
Percentage of wheat	52	34	28	27
barley	25	40	5	60
oats	23	26	67	0
mixed corn & rye	0	0	0	13
Percentage of agricultural land growing roots and vegetables	8	5	2	2

Sources: P.R.O., MAF 68/143, no. 20; /1340, no. 6; /3880, Salop. no. 216; /4945, no. 216.

Limestone was increasingly quarried for building stone in the 18th century, for instance from Oxstile quarry 0.5 km. west of the church and from near Church Farm for Wood Acton.[1] Stone may also have been got for slates in the later 18th century.[2] Bricks were burnt in the parish in 1758,[3] as they probably had been 150 years earlier for Acton Scott Hall.[4]

A smithy north of Acton Scott village, open by 1766, closed *c.* 1966.[5]

The parish clerk Edwin Bore (fl. 1812–25) was a well known maker of spinning wheels.[6]

LOCAL GOVERNMENT. Records of eleven sessions of Acton Scott court baron survive from between 1634 and 1695,[7] and a court was supposedly still held *c.* 1730.[8] A court baron for Alcaston was occasionally held at Alcaston Manor between 1793 and 1846.[9]

In 1709–10 there was a poor's stock of £20 10*s*., and £4 5*s*. was disbursed during the year to three people and an apprentice. Over the next 30 years the stock and expenditure gradually rose. A cottage was built for Frances Warde in 1738–9, and a nurse was paid in 1740–1.[10] By the end of the century £30–£40 was spent annually, and the farmers took in children.[11] Expenditure rose to £115 in 1802–3; it was used to give out relief to 21 adults and 6 children.[12] Expenditure reached a peak of £172 in 1818–19.[13]

There were two parish constables in 1793.[14]

The parish was in Church Stretton poor-law union 1836–1930,[15] Church Stretton rural sanitary district 1872–94, Church Stretton rural district 1894–1934, Ludlow R.D. 1934–74, and South Shropshire district from 1974.[16]

CHURCH. The church existed by 1252. The living was a rectory in the patronage of the lords of Acton Scott, rights being disputed between coparceners from time to time. Disputes and uncertainties occasionally caused their rights to lapse:[17] Hugh of Newton, presented by three patrons evidently towards the end of 1277, was actually collated to the rectory by lapse in 1278.[18] In later centuries turns were occasionally conveyed[19] and in 1934 the lady of the manor conveyed the advowson to the diocesan patronage board.[20] The living was held in plurality with Hope Bowdler 1939–46[21] and was then vacant, local retired clergy serving the cure,[22] until 1951 when the king presented through lapse.[23] From 1961 the patronage was suspended and the cure served by

97 Eyton, xi. 377.
98 S.R.O. 3925, maps of 1776, 1820; 2563/33, e.g. workmen's acct. at end, 19 Apr. 1760.
99 *Cal. Inq. p.m.* iii, p. 52.
1 Inf. from Mr. T. S. Acton.
2 S.R.O. 2563/32, s.a. 1770.
3 Ibid. /33, 16 Dec. 1757; 28 July 1758.
4 Above, manors.
5 S.R.O. 3925, maps of 1776, 1820; 3925, box 10, survs.; notes at Acton Scott Historic Working Fm.
6 S.R.O. 2906/1, pp. 32–4.
7 In S.R.O. 3925, box 12.
8 Birm. Univ. Libr., Mytton Papers, i. 30.
9 *T.S.A.S.* 4th ser. viii. 248–52.
10 S.R.O. 2563/67.
11 S.P.L., MS. 6865, p. 18.
12 *Poor Law Abstract*, H.C. 98, pp. 416–17 (1803–4), xiii.
13 *Poor Rate Returns*, H.C. 556, suppl. app. p. 142 (1822), v.
14 S.P.L., MS. 6865, p. 18.
15 V. J. Walsh, 'Admin. of Poor Laws in Salop. 1820–55' (Pennsylvania Univ. Ph.D. thesis, 1970), 148–50; *Kelly's Dir. Salop.* (1929), 22.
16 *V.C.H. Salop.* ii. 215, 217; iii. 178, and sources cited ibid. 169 n. 29.
17 Eyton, xi. 376–80, 382; *Reg. Orleton* (C.S.), 145; *Reg. Trillek* (C.S.), 41, 381; *Dioc. of Heref. Institutions (1539–1900)*, ed. A. T. Bannister (Heref. 1923), *passim.*
18 *Reg. Cantilupe*, pp. xxxviii, 81–2. Newton's collation in June 1278 (yr. deduced from what follows: cf. ibid. pp. xlii, lxv–lxvi) implies that the patrons' presentation (presumably at least 6 months earlier) was ineffective, perhaps because one of them, Rob. of Stretton, was not then seised: above, manors.
19 In 1547, 1679, and 1856: Bannister, op. cit. 5, 43, 171.
20 Heref. Dioc. Regy., reg. 1926–38, p. 429.
21 Ibid. reg. 1938–53, pp. 34, 314.
22 S.R.O. 2564/2; *Crockford* (1947), 1074; (1953–4), 233, 1086.
23 Heref. Dioc. Regy., reg. 1938–53, p. 501.

curates (or priests) in charge, some of them incumbents of nearby parishes.[24]

In the Middle Ages the living was worth *c.* £5.[25] In 1589 the glebe comprised a house, *c.* 35 a. of grassland, and rights of common.[26] The living was worth £42 *c.* 1708,[27] and £210 in 1825,[28] the tithes in the later 18th and earlier 19th century usually being let to the farmers, although a modus in lieu of hay tithes was paid from Alcaston.[29] In 1840 the tithes were commuted to £238 a year.[30] The living was worth £233 gross in 1885.[31] The 61-a. Glebe farm lay west of the rectory and by 1776 was enclosed by a ring fence.[32] The farm was sold in 1947.[33] The stone farmhouse, perhaps created in the early 19th century from 18th- century farm buildings, was probaby embellished by Mrs. Stackhouse Acton in the mid 19th century.[34]

In 1589 the parsonage comprised a 'mansion house' and outbuildings.[35] John Glascott, curate from 1772 and, after an interval away, rector 1781–1825, improved both the house—'very substantial, but small'—and the glebe before 1793.[36] In 1826 the patron paid £700 virtually to 're-erect' the house 'in the English style of ancient cottage architecture' to plans by John Carline.[37] The parsonage was sold with two acres in 1966.[38]

The names of known 13th- and 14th-century rectors suggest that most were local men;[39] none is known to have been a graduate. No institutions are recorded between 1408[40] and 1547,[41] during which time the cure was perhaps served from surrounding parishes. To the church's two bells of the 1350s a third was added in the 15th century; they form one of only two (complete) medieval rings in the county.[42] A light in the church was endowed before the Reformation.[43]

A chapel at Alcaston was recorded in 1256 when its chaplain was outlawed for murder.[44] The chapel escaped subjection to Acton Scott church after an inquiry into its status in 1318[45] and was a 'free chapel' in 1350 and when last mentioned in 1399. The advowson belonged to the terre tenant of Alcaston in 1259 and still in 1399 when, after the earl of Arundel's forfeiture, the chapel was in the hands of a royal warden.[46] The living was a rectory in 1285 and still in 1350.[47] The chapel's site is unknown.

Several post-Reformation rectors were pluralists, including Roger Norncott, rector from 1567[48] and also rector of Munslow and Hughley and prebendary of Hampton Bishop.[49] William Fosbrook, 1679–1726, the first known graduate rector of Acton Scott,[50] was vicar of Diddlebury 1676–1726[51] and in 1716 lived at Corfton with his son Edward (not yet in holy orders) as his curate, catechizing and baptizing. There were then two Sunday services, one with a sermon, and communion was celebrated thrice yearly.[52]

John Fleming, rector from 1745,[53] employed a curate.[54] It was probably his son and namesake who obtained the living in 1756 after he resigned.[55] Dr. John Fleming, rector (d. 1780), was also vicar of Highley 1756–77 and a county magistrate from 1762.[56] In 1779, to escape creditors whose demands had already placed him in Shrewsbury gaol, he went as chaplain on the 74-gun *Ajax*.[57] By 1793 his successor John Glascott was preaching to a moderately sized congregation each Sunday and celebrating communion for *c.* 40 six times a year.[58] Townley Clarkson, 1825–33, had livings in Cambridgeshire, where he lived, and Suffolk.[59] Waties Corbett, rector 1833–*c.* 1856, was also an absentee, being perpetual curate of Longnor and Leebotwood and Hereford diocesan chancellor.[60] An organ was bought *c.* 1849,[61] and in 1851 there were usually 140 at morning service, 50 in the afternoon.[62] Corbett's curate in 1851, G. A. Magee, was himself rector from 1856 to *c.* 1896.[63]

The church of *ST. MARGARET*, so dedicated by the later 18th century,[64] comprises chancel, nave, north chapel, south porch, and west tower. The rubble stone fabric of chancel, nave, and tower is probably medieval, and features such as the south nave window, lights in

24 *Crockford* (1969–70), 236; (1970–1), 66; (1987–8), 230, 299, 621; (1989–90), 480.
25 *Tax. Eccl.* (Rec. Com.), 167; *Valor Eccl.* (Rec. Com.), iii. 209; P.R.O., E 315/489, f. 13v.
26 H.W.R.O.(H.), HD 2/14/5.
27 J. Ecton, *Liber Valorum et Decimarum* (1711), 147.
28 H.W.R.O.(H.), HD 9, 'Notitia', f. 1.
29 S.P.L., MS. 6865, p. 21; W.S.L. 350/5/40, Acton Scott p. 27.
30 S.R.O. 293/1.
31 *Kelly's Dir. Salop.* (1885), 790.
32 S.R.O. 293/1; 3925, map of 1776; 4044/39, pp. 1–2; S.P.L., MS. 6865, p. 21.
33 Inf. from Mr. T. S. Acton.
34 Mrs. Wood Acton's notes.
35 H.W.R.O.(H.), HD 2/14/5.
36 S.P.L., MS. 6865, p. 20; Bannister, *Heref. Institutions*, 113; for illus. of ho. in 1794, Bodl. MS. Top. Salop. c. 2, f. 45.
37 W.S.L. 350/5/40, Acton Scott p. 27; S.P.L., MS. 6865, p. 24; H.W.R.O.(H.), HD 8, box 31, plan, specification, etc. For illus. see S.R.O. 4319/10.
38 Inf. from Heref. dioc. sec.
39 Eyton, xi. 382.
40 *Reg. Mascall* (C.S.), 174.
41 Bannister, *Heref. Institutions*, 5.
42 H. B. Walters, *Ch. Bells of Salop.* (Oswestry, 1915), 83–4.
43 *T.S.A.S.* 3rd ser. x. 373; *Cal. Pat.* 1572–5, pp. 220–1.
44 *Roll of Salop. Eyre 1256*, p. 222.
45 *Reg. Swinfield* (C.S.), 541; *Reg. Orleton*, 61–2.
46 Eyton, xii. 3; *Reg. Swinfield*, 526; *Reg. Trillek*, 389, 394; *Cal. Pat.* 1396–9, 482; 1399–1401, 101; cf. above, manors.
47 *Reg. Swinfield*, 545; *Reg. Orleton*, 61; P.R.O., CP 40/247, m. 165d. (ref. supplied by Mr. M. A. Faraday); Eyton, vii. 61.
48 Bannister, *Heref. Institutions*, 18.
49 Ibid. 9, 14, 16, 20; *T.S.A.S.* 4th ser. xi. 185–6; cf. Bannister, op. cit. 17, for other possible preferment.
50 Bannister, op. cit. 43, 72; S.R.O. 2005/2, s.a. 1726.
51 *T.S.A.S.* 4th ser. ii. 67; vii. 163.
52 H.W.R.O.(H.)., HD 5/14/1/3.
53 Bannister, *Heref. Institutions*, 85.
54 S.P.L., Deeds 979.
55 Bannister, op. cit. 92.
56 *V.C.H. Salop.* iii. 117 and n.
57 S.R.O. 796/237–46.
58 S.P.L., MS. 6865, pp. 20–2; for him see also S.R.O. 2906/1, pp. 28–31.
59 Bannister, *Heref. Institutions*, 146, 151; S.P.L., MS. 6865, pp. 23–4; W.S.L. 350/5/40, Acton Scott p. 23; *Alum. Cantab. 1752–1900*, ii. 58.
60 Bannister, op. cit. 151, 171; W.S.L. 350/5/40, Acton Scott p. 23; S.P.L., MS. 6865, p. 24; *S.P.R. Lich.* v (2), p. vi.
61 S.R.O. 2563/8, p. 153.
62 P.R.O., HO 129/354, no. 5.
63 S. Bagshaw, *Dir. Salop.* (1851), 518; Bannister, *Heref. Institutions*, 171, 211.
64 S.P.L., MS. 6865, p. 20. Dedication to St. Mary (B.L. Add. MS. 30316, f. 30v.) was perh. recorded erroneously *c.* 1740.

the tower, and some bench ends may be late medieval, as may have been the former south door in the chancel. The nave roof is perhaps 16th- or early 17th-century, the chancel roof mid 17th-century. The altar table too is 17th- century. The porch and probably the south door are of 1722;[65] other work of that date probably included the insertion of new windows in the nave and chancel and the renewal of the south chancel door. The altar rails too may be *c.* 1722.[66]

In 1793 the chancel, separated from the nave by a timber and lath-and-plaster screen, contained five pews, some benches, and a psalm singers' table. The nave had 18 pews; one, perhaps that built by Edward Baugh *c.* 1665, was canopied.[67]

John Stackhouse (d. 1819), lord of Acton Scott, left £500 for a family pew, built in 1820 as a north aisle.[68] Also about then a new east window was put in the chancel, the tower was repaired and a vestry made in it, and the the church was ceiled.[69] Font, pulpit, reading desk, and screen may also be early 19th-century; there is a bier of 1825; and the west organ gallery is presumably of *c.* 1849.[70] The seating was increased in 1876, when the 'clerical seats' were carved by the rector and their finials by Mr. Hill.[71]

About 1897 the box pews were replaced by new benches and prayer desks; 17th- and 18th-century panelling from the pews was re-used as a dado. The pulpit was moved from the north side of the nave to the south, and the font to near the south door.[72] Later changes were minor apart from the replacement of the south chancel door by a window *c.* 1929[73] and the complete rebuilding of the gallery (to take a second-hand organ) in 1968.[74]

In 1717 a silver chalice and paten were given by the new squire and patron Edward Acton (d. 1747),[75] to whom there is a large wall monument, designed by William Baker, in the chancel.[76]

The registers are substantially complete from 1690.[77]

NONCONFORMITY. None known.

EDUCATION. In 1793 children went to school in Hatton, Church Stretton, and Wistanstow,[78] but by 1819 the lord of Acton Scott was supporting a school for 25–30 pupils in a stone schoolhouse near Acton Scott Farm.[79]

In 1866 Mrs. Stackhouse Acton built an ornate timber framed school and teacher's house; she and her successors at the Hall supported it until 1949.[80] In 1873, attendance averaged 50, and the schoolroom accommodated 60,[81] later restricted to 50;[82] there was occasional overcrowding.[83] Government grant, earned by 1880, was reduced 1893–1900 owing to inadequate staffing.[84] The building was improved in the 1890s[85] and 1900s[86] and in 1921 and 1944.[87] From 1904 the county council paid the staff, renting the school and house from the managers.[88] The rector visited regularly and the annual diocesan scripture examinations were taken,[89] but only *c.* 1944 was the school designated a church school.[90] Briefly in 1941, when Liverpool evacuees came, infants were taught in the village hall kitchen. From 1936, except during the war, senior pupils attended Church Stretton woodwork and domestic science centres; in 1948 they transferred to Church Stretton Modern school[91] and in 1949 Acton Scott school became a county primary school.[92] There were 52 pupils in 1932 but only 27 by 1951 when the school closed, pupils going to Church Stretton or Wistanstow C.E. primary schools.[93]

In the early 1890s county council cookery classes were popular but horticulture classes were not.[94]

CHARITIES FOR THE POOR. John Mousell[95] left 5*s.* a year for the Acton Scott poor; in the late 18th century, as in the early 20th,

65 S.P.L., MS. 6865, p. 22; W.S.L. 350/5/40, Acton Scott p. 23.

66 S.P.L., Watton press cuttings, i. 383; MS. 372, vol. ii, f. 49.

67 S.P.L., MS. 6865, pp. 22–3; cf. S.P.L., MS. 6865, p. 23; below, Abdon, church (for the screen).

68 T. P. Stackhouse's diary, s.a. 1820. For Owen as designer of eccl. monuments, *Gent. Mag.* xcviii (1), 89.

69 T. P. Stackhouse's diary, s.a. 1821; S.P.L., MS. 6865, p. 23; W.S.L. 350/5/40, Acton Scott p. 23.

70 Above. For an illus. of ch. interior 1844 see print in S.P.L.

71 Mrs. Wood Acton's notes.

72 Heref. Dioc. Regy., reg. 1883–1901, pp. 585–7.

73 Ibid. reg. 1926–38, p. 202.

74 Inf. from Mr. T. S. Acton.

75 D. L. Arkwright and B. W. Bourne, *Ch. Plate Archd. Ludlow* (Shrews. 1961), 2.

76 Pevsner, *Salop.* 52; H. Colvin, *Biog. Dict. Brit. Architects, 1600–1840* (1978), 84.

77 S.R.O. 2005/1–2; /Rg/3; /MRg/1–2; regs. at ch.; cf. H.W.R.O.(H.), bp.'s transcripts for 1638 and from 1660; *S.P.R. Heref.* xxiii.

78 S.P.L., MS. 6865, p. 16. This section was written in 1982 and later revised.

79 *Digest Educ. Poor*, H.C. 224, p. 745 (1819), ix (2); S.R.O. 2563/5–8, s.a. 1831–3; S. Lough, *Acton Scott Sch.* (Salop. Co. Mus. Service, 1981), 3 (copy in S.R.O. 4252).

80 P.R.O., ED 7/102, ff. 21–2; S.R.O. 1334/1, p. 38; *Kelly's Dir. Salop.* (1885), 790; (1891), 254; (1905), 18; sch. managers' min. bk. 1903–49 (at Acton Scott Hall 1982; kindly made available by Miss S. Lough of the Working Fm. Mus.).

81 P.R.O., ED 7/102, ff. 21–2.

82 S.R.O. 1334/1, p. 112; *Kelly's Dir. Salop.* (1909), 20.

83 S.R.O. 1334/1, pp. 31, 36, 134–5; managers' min. bk. 1919 a.g.m.

84 S.R.O. 1334/1 *passim*, esp. pp. 112–14, 116, 122, 130, 135, 142, 147–8, 152; 3925, box 10, J. Williams to A. Wood Acton 25 June 1881.

85 S.R.O. 1334/1, pp. 109, 141; cf. p. 113.

86 Ibid. pp. 163, 179 (infants' rm.); managers' min. bk. 1904 a.g.m.

87 S.R.O. 1334/1, pp. 303–4; /2, pp. 101–3; cf. /1, pp. 113, 246.

88 Managers' min. bk. 1904 a.g.m.; inf. from Miss L. Stubbs, headmistress 1933–46.

89 S.R.O. 1334/1 *passim.*

90 S.R.O. 2782/39.

91 Inf. from Miss Stubbs; S.R.O. 1334/1, p. 483; /2, pp. 67–9, 132.

92 Managers' min. bk. 1949 a.g.m.

93 S.R.O. 1334/1, p. 434; 2782/46; inf. (1980, at Working Fm. Mus.) from the Revd. F. T. Rumball.

94 *S.C.C. Mins.* Intermediate Educ. Cttee. reps. 1891–3.

95 Prob. of Wistanstow: *S.P.R. Heref.* xvii (4), s.v. Mausall.

income was accumulated until it sufficed to buy them bibles or prayer books.[96] By 1975 the charity had lapsed.[97]

In 1786 and later income from £56, of which £20 had been given by one Edward Acton, was used to buy coal.[98] In 1975 income was £3.[99] The charity may include proceeds of the sale of a cottage left to the parish in 1827.[1]

CARDINGTON

ABOUT 1831 Cardington parish comprised the townships of Broome, Cardington, Chatwall and parts of Frodesley and Langley, Comley and part of Botvyle, Enchmarsh, part of Gretton, Lydley Hayes, Plaish, Holt Preen, and Willstone.[2] Part of Botvyle (a township in Lydley and Cardington manor) lay in Church Stretton parish by the 18th century,[3] and Gretton township lay partly in Cardington but mainly in Rushbury parish.[4] In 1883 the parish bounds, unchanged since the 1830s, contained 6,685 a. (2,705 ha.).[5]

The parish so defined was probably formed in the later 12th century when the manors of Lydley (including 'Botley', Botvyle, and Comley) and Cardington (including Chatwall, Enchmarsh, and Willstone) were united in the Templars' hands with a pension from Cardington church. The Templars combined the manors[6] and may also have acquired an overlordship of Plaish.[7] Lydley's early connexions were with Condover hundred[8] and so probably with Lichfield diocese,[9] as were Plaish's, which, in the later 10th century (when it included Broome and Chatwall), belonged to the territory of the Wreocensaete[10] and not to that of the people to the south for whom Hereford diocese had been created *c.* 690.[11] Thus the early Hereford–Lichfield diocesan boundary, probably marked at one point by the prominent escarpment at the south-western end of Hoar Edge, may have cut across what became the medieval parish of Cardington, approximating, from north of Caer Caradoc as far as the Gretton–Chatwall road east of Leyhill Farm, to its principal watershed until it joined the headwaters of Hughley brook, following that until it ran up to Wenlock Edge somewhere between Lushcott and Hughley.[12] Holt Preen did not form part of the parish until the late 16th century,[13] and the parts of the parish in Frodesley and Langley manors in the 19th century may have been incorporated later still.[14]

Small adjustments of Cardington parish bounds (especially on the north and west) were made between the 13th and the early 19th centuries. Pingleys Heys, north of Chatwall, seems to have been an area where the boundaries of Cardington, Acton Burnell, and Frodesley parishes were uncertain in the early 17th century.[15] Henry Leighton sold most of it to the lord of Langley (in Acton Burnell parish) in 1615 when the area already lay outside Cardington,[16] though part of it was regained for the parish between 1794 and 1841. Adjoining the southern part of Pingleys Heys to the north-west was another area which was lost to the parish, apparently because it was part of Frodesley manor; it too was regained between 1794 and 1841.[17] The inclosure of Caer Caradoc redefined the boundary with Church Stretton parish in 1822.[18]

The parish bounds of *c.* 1841 were not altered[19] until, in 1934, the part of the civil parish north-west of Hoar Edge was transferred to Longnor C.P.[20] In 1967 the north-western part of that area, including Penkridge Hall and Lydley Hayes, was transferred to Leebotwood C.P. Also in 1967 part of Gretton and land at Hill End was transferred from Rushbury to Cardington C.P.[21] The area treated here is that of the parish in the 1830s, though Gretton is treated with Rushbury parish, where most of it then lay.

For almost 1½ km. the north-western boundary of the parish followed Watling Street (West) through the Church Stretton valley. Parallel to, and ½ km. from, that road the ground rises

96 S.P.L., MS. 6865, p. 19; *24th Rep. Com. Char.* H.C. 231, p. 397 (1831), xi; S.R.O. 4693/4.

97 *Review of Local Chars.* (S.C.C. 1975), 52.

98 S.P.L., MS. 6865, p. 19; *24th Rep. Com. Char.* p. 397.

99 *Review of Local Chars.* 52.

1 S.R.O. 2563/6, Mich. 1827.

2 S. Bagshaw, *Dir. Salop.* (1851), 521–4; S.P.L., MS. 6741, p. 3; below (manors; econ. hist.) for parts of Frodesley and Langley. This article was written in 1986.

3 S.R.O. 567/1/64; 3288/2/2; fig. 6; below, Ch. Stretton, intro.

4 S.R.O. 3573/T/3; below, Rushbury, intro.

5 Cf. P.R.O., IR 30/29/65; O.S. *Area Bk.* (1883).

6 Below, manors (Lydley and Cardington).

7 The 13th-cent. chief and mesne ldships. did not include the Templars but in 1533 Plaish was said to be held of the Hospitallers: ibid. (Plaish).

8 *V.C.H. Salop.* viii. 1.

9 In which, almost certainly, all Condover hundred's parishes and manors originally lay: S. Bassett, 'Medieval Ecclesiastical Organisation in Vicinity of Wroxeter and its Brit. Antecedents', *Jnl. Brit. Arch. Assoc.* cxlv. 14–17.

10 Acc. to Dom. Bk. a detachment of Leintwardine hund.: *V.C.H. Salop.* i. 328; iii. 8; but cf. F. R. Thorn, 'Hundreds', *Salop. Domesday* [Intro. and Translation], ed. A. Williams and R. W. H. Erskine (1990), 33.

11 Cf. *Woolhope Trans.* xlii. 33, 36–45; *Origins of A.-S. Kgms.* ed. S. Bassett (1989), 181–2.

12 *V.C.H. Salop.* ii. 1. P. Sims-Williams, *Religion and Literature in W. Eng. 600–800* (1990), 44 n. 143, argues against this, though implausibly, for no one has ever supposed that the whole length of Wenlock Edge marked the Wreocensaete–Magonsaete boundary. That, like the dioc. boundary (see e.g. *Jnl. Brit. Arch. Assoc.* cxlv. 15 (fig. 4)—inconsistent, as far as Wigwig is concerned, with what is argued ibid. 8, and as far as Hughley is concerned with what is argued below, Hughley, intro.), probably left Wenlock Edge to cut across (as argued here) what became Cardington par.

13 *T.S.A.S.* lxx. 194, 197.

14 Next para.

15 S.R.O. 1514/297.

16 Below, manors; econ. hist.

17 S.R.O. 3651, plans of Rob. Corbett's est. 1794, map of Lydley and Cardington man. n.d.; P.R.O., IR 29/29/70; IR 30/29/70; below, manors (Leahills).

18 Below, Ch. Stretton, intro.

19 Cf. P.R.O., IR 30/29/54, 65, 70, 137, 162, 253; O.S. *Area Bk.* (1883).

20 *V.C.H. Salop.* viii. 107; O.S. Map 6", Salop. XLIX. SE. (1954 edn.).

21 By the *Salop (No. 2) Order 1966* (Stat. Instr. 1966, no. 1529): *V.C.H. Salop.* ii. 235–6; S.R.O., DA 19/701/6, maps 34–5, 39.

sharply from less than 183 m. to Little Caradoc (the lower part of Caer Caradoc hill) and the Lawley (377 m.).[22] South-east of the Lawley are the high parallel ridges of Hoar Edge (312 m.) and Yell Bank (321 m.),[23] while south-east of Caradoc rise Willstone hill, the parish's highest point (403 m.), and Cardington hill. Eastwards thence the land falls to *c.* 122 m. at the Hughley boundary.

Caradoc and the Lawley are formed by Pre-Cambrian tuffs, felstones, and greenstones, some of the oldest rock in the county, while around Hoar Edge and Comley are Cambrian grits and limestones, sources of building stone.[24] Robert Townson (1762–1827), geologist and traveller, lived at Lydley Hayes intermittently from 1788 with his brother-in-law John Witts, vicar of Cardington.[25] Comley quarry's geological interest led to its designation as a site of special scientific interest in 1953, and a small adjoining area became a nature reserve in 1976.[26] Over most of the eastern half of the parish the subsoil is boulder clay. The parish is drained by four systems: Comley, Lydley Hayes, and the north-eastern part of Chatwall drain north-west, eventually into Cound brook and so into the Severn at Cound; the central part of Chatwall drains north to Bullhill brook which empties into Cound brook at Cound; Broome, the south-eastern part of Chatwall, part of Plaish, and Holt Preen drain by Plaish (or Hughley) brook into the Severn near Sheinton; Cardington, Enchmarsh, Willstone, and part of Plaish drain south into Lakehouse (or Eaton) brook and so down Ape Dale into the Onny near Wistanstow.

Apart from Watling Street (West) there are few distinctive features marking the parish boundary, although it does follow watercourses here and there. The easternmost part of the parish lies in an angle formed by Hughley brook (known in 1331 and 1640 as Plaish river or brook)[27] and a tributary. Elsewhere short stretches of the boundary follow Dudley brook (so called in 1757),[28] Cardington brook, and streams flowing off Cardington hill and from between Hope Bowdler and Willstone hills; the last mentioned stream was known as Stank Stone gutter or brook in 1757 and later.[29]

The Roman road from Wroxeter to Caerleon, bounding the parish and known since *c.* 1700 as Watling Street, was called Botte Street in the Middle Ages.[30] The track that included the causeway which gave its name to Causeway wood (in Frodesley) has also been supposed, though with little good reason, to be Roman;[31] in the Middle Ages it was called Mershall's way.[32]

Generally it seems likely that the medieval road system was that in use in the 1980s. Known ancient roads named are Church Lane, in Plaish (1553);[33] Church Way, in Chatwall (1751);[34] the Lane Head, being the road west from Willstone up to the Cwms (1611);[35] Lea Lane, running north from Gretton to Leahills (1648);[36] and the way from Holt Preen to Shrewsbury across Bowman hill (1541).[37] The 'cross' at Enchmarsh in 1697 was presumably the crossroads there.[38] In the 1790s the roads of the parish were bad; none had been turnpiked.[39] The only known alteration occurred in the 1860s when a new road was made between Comley and Cardington to replace the old road slightly to the south.[40]

Since 1663 when Dugdale visited Caer Caradoc, named after and linked with the British chief Caratacus, the area's prehistoric remains have interested antiquaries.[41] Much flint work of Mesolithic to Bronze Age date has been found on Cardington hill, and there are other probable occupation sites, including a circular double-ditched enclosure perhaps of the Iron Age.[42] A cross dyke on the Lawley hints at prehistoric exploitation of the uplands.[43] North-east of the Lawley is a possible round barrow, while on the hill itself are two enclosures of probably later prehistoric date and military function.[44] No definite Roman occupation site is known in the parish,[45] but a hoard of Roman coins was found at the Holt *c.* 1802, probably near the 'Roman well', so called in 1898.[46] The 19th-century supposition that Battlestones (so called by 1623)[47] on Willstone hill was the site of an engagement between Romans and Britons in A.D. 51[48] can be dismissed.

Cardington and Willstone, each with the *tun* element, were presumably so named in the late Saxon period. Plaish too was a distinct estate by then.[49] The settlement at Lydley existed by 1066 as, probably, did those at 'Botley' and Botvyle, Chatwall, Comley, and Enchmarsh,[50] some of whose names point to their having been settled

22 O.S. Maps 1/25,000, SO 49, 59 (1956 edn.).

23 D. Mackney and C. P. Burnham, *Soils of Ch. Stretton Dist.* (Mem. Soil Surv. of Gt. Brit.; Harpenden, 1966), 11 and pl. IIa facing p. 57.

24 Para. based on *Salop.* [co. guide] (S.C.C. 1980), 47–8; below, econ. hist.; Geol. Surv. Map 1", drift, sheet 166 (1967 edn.).

25 S.R.O. 1066/39–40; Burke, *Land. Gent.* (1952), 2766; T. G. Vallance and H. S. Torrens, 'Rob. Townson', *Contributions to Hist. of Geol. Mapping*, ed. E. Dudich (Akadémiai Kiadó, Budapest, 1984), 391–8; *D.N.B.* (inadequate and partly erroneous acct.). Dr. Torrens is thanked for help with Townson.

26 Inf. from S.C.C. Planning Dept.; *Shrews. Chron.* 28 Nov. 1975, p. 1; S.R.O. 3496/1.

27 S.R.O. 1224/2/13; P.R.O., MPA 100. Cf. fig. 6 for modern names.

28 S.R.O. 567/1/64.

29 Ibid.; S.R.O. 3651, plan of Rob. Corbett's est. 1794.

30 *V.C.H. Salop.* i. 271; viii. 98.

31 Ibid. i. 273–4; viii. 142; SA 1918; *T.S.A.S.* lv. 43–4; S.P.L., MS. 6741, pp. 49, 51.

32 *V.C.H. Salop.* viii. 142.

33 S.P.L., Deeds 17424.

34 S.R.O. 5001/1/2/8, Churchway field.

35 S.R.O. 1359, box 28, abstr. of title to Mr. Russell's est.

36 S.R.O. 5001/1/1/1.

37 P.R.O., C 116/214, Holt Preen ct. r. 1541.

38 H.W.R.O.(H.), HD 2/14/6.

39 S.P.L., MS. 6741, p. 13.

40 P.R.O., IR 30/29/65; O.S. Map 6", SO 49 NE. (1954 edn.); S.R.O. 3571/Ve/1, 30 Oct. 1863, 16 Nov. 1864.

41 *T.S.A.S.* 3rd ser. viii, pp. vii–xii; below, this section (for Caractusians).

42 SA 556, 1906, 2064; S.P.L., Chitty 6" map LVI. NE.

43 *Bull. Bd. of Celtic Studies*, xxvi. 371.

44 SA 1256, 2541. See also SA 176.

45 But cf. S.P.L., Chitty File 275/10–15; SA 1907.

46 A. Sparrow, *Hist. Ch. Preen* (priv. print. 1898), 4; W.S.L. 350/5/40, Cardington p. 11.

47 S.R.O. 567, box 10, deed 6 May 1623.

48 W.S.L. 350/5/40, Cardington p. 5.

49 Below, manors.

50 Ibid.

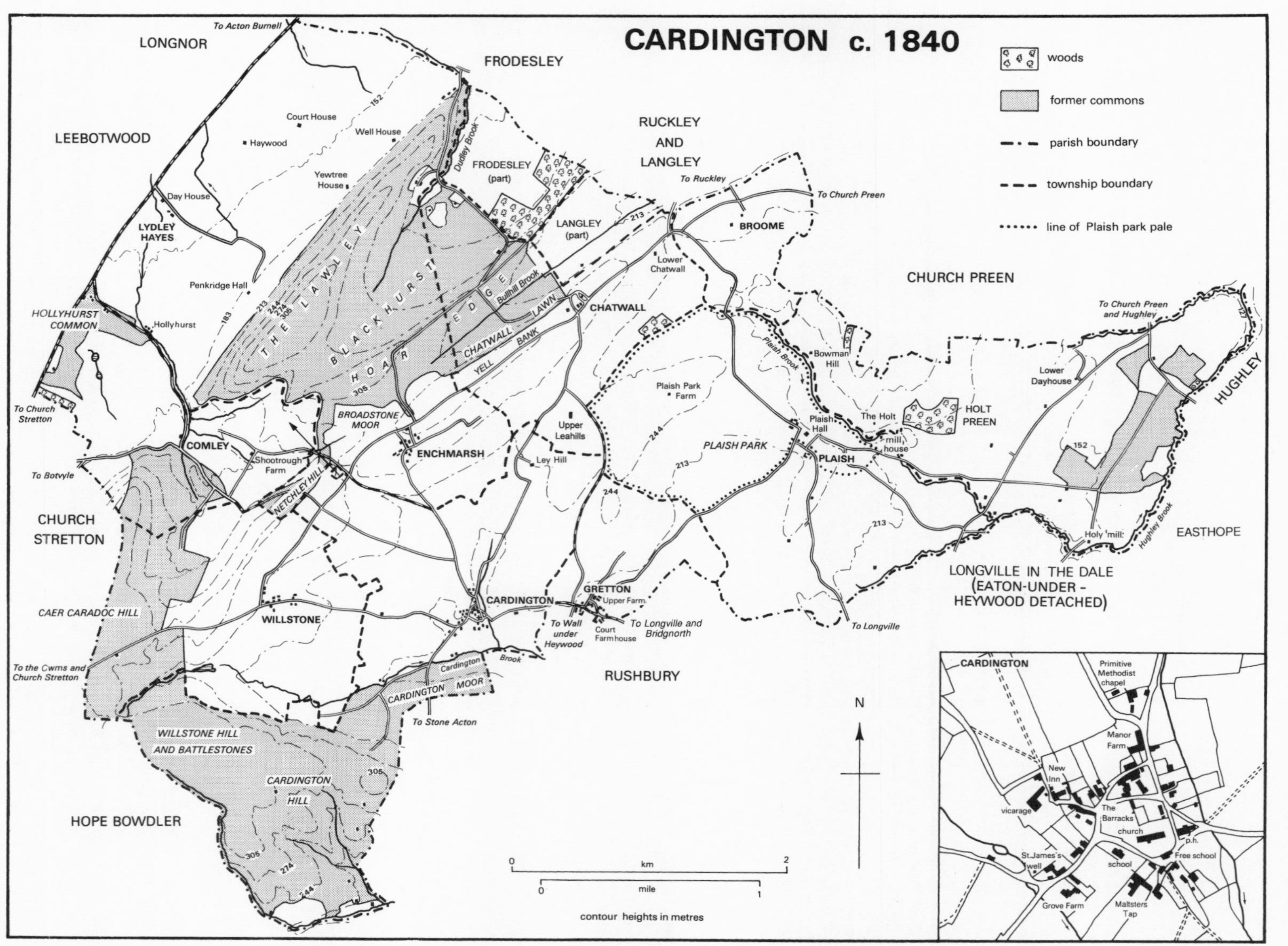
CARDINGTON c. 1840
woods
former commons
parish boundary
township boundary
line of Plaish park pale
To Acton Burnell
LONGNOR
FRODESLEY
LEEBOTWOOD
Court House
Haywood
Well House
Yewtree House
Day House
LYDLEY HAYES
Penkridge Hall
HOLLYHURST COMMON
Hollyhurst
To Church Stretton
COMLEY
Shootrough Farm
NETCHLEY HILL
To Botvyle
CHURCH STRETTON
THE LAWLEY
BLACKHURST
HOAR EDGE
BROADSTONE MOOR
ENCHMARSH
Dudley Brook
FRODESLEY (part)
LANGLEY (part)
Bullhill Brook
CHATWALL LAWN
YELL BANK
CHATWALL
RUCKLEY AND LANGLEY
To Ruckley
To Church Preen
BROOME
Lower Chatwall
CHURCH PREEN
Plaish Brook
Bowman Hill
Plaish Park Farm
Upper Leahills
Ley Hill
PLAISH PARK
Plaish Hall
The Holt
mill house
HOLT PREEN
PLAISH
Lower Dayhouse
To Church Preen and Hughley
HUGHLEY
Hughley Brook
Holy 'mill'
EASTHOPE
LONGVILLE IN THE DALE (EATON-UNDER-HEYWOOD DETACHED)
To Longville
CARDINGTON
GRETTON
Upper Farm
Court Farmhouse
To Longville and Bridgnorth
To Wall under Heywood
CAER CARADOC HILL
WILLSTONE
To the Cwms and Church Stretton
Cardington Brook
CARDINGTON MOOR
To Stone Acton
RUSHBURY
WILLSTONE HILL AND BATTLESTONES
CARDINGTON HILL
HOPE BOWDLER
N
0
km
2
0
mile
1
contour heights in metres
CARDINGTON
Primitive Methodist chapel
Manor Farm
New Inn
vicarage
The Barracks
church
p.h.
Free school
school
St. James's well
Grove Farm
Maltsters Tap

in woodland clearances. In Domesday Book those places were subsumed under others, principally Cardington which had a recorded population of 16. Plaish and Lydley had recorded populations of two each.[51]

In 1185 the Templars, who had an estate in the parish administered from a preceptory at Lydley,[52] had 36 tenants at Cardington, 10 at Enchmarsh, 8 at Chatwall, 5 at 'Botelegee', and 2 at Lydley.[53] How many brethren then lived at the preceptory is unknown; a century later three, with perhaps a couple of retired ones, seems to have been usual. It was presumably also at Lydley that the preceptory's farm servants lived; in 1308 there were 16 of them.[54]

In 1327 there were eight taxpayers in Cardington and whatever other places were taxed with it, five at Lydley, four each at Chatwall and Plaish, and three at Enchmarsh[55] which in 1256 had had a tavern.[56] Perhaps already the local population was falling.[57]

The earliest surviving secular buildings in the parish are the Barracks in Cardington village and Shootrough Farm, both of which have late medieval ranges. The Barracks, apparently a substantial residence, had a timber framed open hall with a crown-post roof and cusped laterals. Shootrough hall (1422) was cruck framed.[58] Two other cruck-built halls partly survive: Comley Cottage[59] and the Dayhouse at Lydley Hayes.[60] Both are probably late 15th- or early 16th-century but nothing is known of the holdings attached to them when built.

The medieval landscape was typical of upland wood–pasture. At least seven settlements in the parish had some sort of open-field system, and all had easy access to extensive common woods and pastures, especially those covering the western and northern hills.[61] In 1559–60 there were dwellings on the Lawley,[62] presumably those of the squatters or cottagers who often appeared in court in the following century charged with woodland clearances on the commons.[63] There were squatters elsewhere too: in 1640, for instance, there were five or six cottages in Holt Preen wood,[64] and by the early 19th century there was squatting on Cardington hill.[65]

In 1622 nine tenements at Lydley Hayes were listed and one at Nether Lydley.[66] Hearth tax was paid in 1672 on 18 houses in Cardington, 12 in Comley and Botvyle, 12 in Chatwall and Enchmarsh, 11 in Lydley Hayes, 9 in Holt Preen, and 6 in Willstone. Broome was taxed with Ruckley and Langley and some of the 18 houses taxed there were also presumably in the parish.[67] In 1676 there were 243 adults in the parish.[68]

Plaish Hall was built in brick *c.* 1580 for William Leighton,[69] but the great majority of buildings in the parish in the late 16th and early 17th century were timber framed. In Cardington village surviving examples include Chapel House, the Maltster's Tap, the Royal Oak, cross wings at the Barracks and at Manor Farm, and a barn adjoining Rose Cottage;[70] elsewhere they include Penkridge Hall,[71] Broome Hall Farm, a cross wing and barn at Shootrough Farm,[72] three bays of the Dayhouse at Lydley Hayes,[73] the east range of Chatwall Hall,[74] the core of Chatwall Home Farm,[75] and a barn at Dayhouse Farm in Holt Preen.[76] The demolished Court House at Lydley Hayes was another example and is well documented.[77] The larger farms, mostly late 16th- to 18th-century, exhibit a wide variety of plans and added wings. In the early 17th century, as can be seen in the Barracks,[78] stone chimneys began to be added to existing houses and open halls had upper floors inserted.

Soon afterwards local stone (available on Hoar Edge) began to be used more widely in the parish, at least in chief houses. One of the first such buildings, probably built by the Leightons of Plaish, was Holt Farm, also original for the adoption of the **E** plan and the reception hall. Other 17th-century stone buildings include the hall and west range of Chatwall Hall (probably 1659); Chatwall Home Farm and Bowman Hill Farm (both mid to late 17th-century);[79] Enchmarsh Lower Farm (1677); Grove Farm, Cardington (1683); Broome Farm and its buildings (*c.* 1700);[80] Chatwall Home Farm (*c.* 1700); and the hall range of Manor Farm, Cardington (*c.* 1700). Notable later examples include Willstone Lower Farm (1738);[81] Cardington vicarage (*c.* 1819); and the schoolmaster's house in Cardington (mid 18th-century).[82] By the later 18th century the parish had many substantial farmhouses; the residents of some aspired to gentility, and between 1681 and 1775[83] there were at least 12 families[84] of parish gentlemen. 'Very many of

51 Ibid.; *V.C.H. Salop.* i. 319, 322, 328, 342–3.
52 Below, manors.
53 *Rec. of Templars in Eng.* ed. B. A. Lees (1935), 37–41.
54 *V.C.H. Salop.* ii. 86.
55 *T.S.A.S.* 2nd ser. iv. 314–17.
56 *Roll of Salop Eyre 1256* (Selden Soc. xcvi), p. 226.
57 Below, econ. hist.
58 TS. reps., with drawings, by Mrs. M. Moran; Dept. of Environment, *List of Bldgs.: Shrews. and Atcham (pars. of All Stretton* [etc.]*)* (1986), 4, 16.
59 Mrs. Moran's rep.; *List of Bldgs.* 21; below, manors.
60 S.R.O. 3763/78/4/9; *List of Bldgs.* 32.
61 Below, econ. hist.
62 S.R.O. 2557/37.
63 Below, econ. hist.; local govt.
64 P.R.O., MPA 100.
65 P.R.O., IR 29/29/65; IR 30/29/65; S.P.L., MS. 6741, p. 11.
66 S.R.O. 567, box 3, rental; for Nether Lydley see also S.R.O. 567, box 11, deeds 1 and 4 Dec. 1576.
67 *Hearth Tax 1672* (Salop. Arch. Soc. 1949), 132, 135, 184–6.
68 *T.S.A.S.* 2nd ser. i. 90.
69 For Leighton, below, manors.
70 *List of Bldgs.* 10, 13–14, 16–18; Mrs. Moran's reps. on the Barracks and the Maltster's Tap (also known as Honeysuckle Ho.); M. R. Bismanis, 'Minor domestic archit. of the Middle Ages in cos. of Heref. and Salop.' (Nott. Univ. Ph.D. thesis, 1975), i. 168–70; ii. 18, 31.
71 Below, manors.
72 *List of Bldgs.* 4, 6; Mrs. Moran's rep. on Shootrough Fm.
73 S.R.O. 3763/78/4/9; *List of Bldgs.* 32.
74 Below, manors.
75 Inf. from Mr. Eric Mercer; *List of Bldgs.* 20.
76 *List of Bldgs.* 3.
77 S.R.O. 3763/78/4/2.
78 Mrs. Moran's rep.
79 Below, manors.
80 Date stones of 1698 and 1699 on ho., 1706 on barn.
81 *List of Bldgs.* 15, 17, 20–1, 30; inf. from Mr. Mercer on Chatwall Home Fm.
82 Below, church; educ.
83 S.R.O. 3288/2/1–2.
84 Baker, Corfield, Flavel, Maunsell, Norris, Perry, Rawlins, Russell, Sankey, Sheppard, Tipton, and Watkies: in all *c.* 26 individuals.

the county gentlemen of small fortunes', it was noted in 1793, 'lived in sufficient houses of their own within this parish till of late years, the sons of whom are removed to towns for the benefit of trade or have run through their property.'[85] Between 1750 and 1841[86] Chatwall shrank from four substantial houses to the two surviving in the late 1980s.[87]

In 1801 the parish's population was 623. It peaked at 768 in 1861 and then fell steadily to 352 in 1981.[88]

By the later 18th century even cottages and minor agricultural buildings were built in stone. Brick was rarely used until the later 20th century. Of the few new houses built then, most were single dwellings, and Manor Paddock, a group of five detached houses built on the northern edge of Cardington village *c.* 1986–7, was exceptional. Cardington, containing perhaps a third (*c.* 250) of the parish's inhabitants in 1841, remained the only populous village in what was otherwise a landscape of hamlets, farms, and squatter cottages. A picturesque stone-built village, loosely grouped around the church, Cardington was designated a conservation area in 1977,[89] and in the late 1980s many of its residents commuted elsewhere to work or were retired.

In the mid 18th century the Caractusian Society was founded to celebrate the legendary virtues of the British chief Caratacus. The society, meeting annually by 1755 (perhaps mainly in August),[90] may have been founded by William Russell of Lydley Hayes, later curate of Overton (Flints.). His kinsman John Russell (d. 1814) of Enchmarsh,[91] high constable of Munslow hundred, had earlier entertained ten petty constables to a meal on top of Caer Caradoc. At first the society enjoyed a cold collation on the hill, sometimes accompanied by orations lauding Caratacus and composed by members such as F. W. Read, rector of Munslow. By *c.* 1756 the party still ascended the hill but ate afterwards at the Bowling Green in Longnor. From 1757 a poem composed specially by Dr. Sneyd Davies was read annually at the dinner, to which 77 sat down in 1770. In the 1760s and 1770s Caractusians seem to have been drawn from good county society. They probably last met in 1777.

About 1740 Cardington wake was held on the Sunday after St. James's day (25 July).[92] In the 1760s and 1770s Chatwall wake was held on the morrow of Cardington wake.[93]

In the early 17th century there were alesellers at Cardington, Lydley Hayes, Plaish, and Willstone.[94] From the mid 18th century only Cardington had alesellers or beer houses. The New Inn, next to Cardington vicarage, was open between *c.* 1800 and the 1930s,[95] while the Royal Oak, also licensed *c.* 1800, still flourished in the 1980s.[96] A branch of the Shropshire Provident Society was formed in 1867 and by the 1890s there were also friendly and other societies for girls and women.[97]

A parish institute was founded in 1914 by Capt. S. H. Christy of Plaish. Killed in action later that year, he left £500 (to which his mother added £200) to Cardington District Nursing Association, which was connected with the institute. Thomas Cooke further endowed the association in 1932. By the 1970s Christy's and Cooke's endowments comprised a reading room, caretaker's cottage, and nurse's house and funds for their maintenance and for the relief of sick people[98] in Cardington and neighbouring parishes.[99]

The county library opened a 'book centre' in Cardington in 1926.[1]

MANORS AND OTHER ESTATES. Two men called Austin held *CARDINGTON* as two manors in 1066.[2]

In 1086 Roger of Montgomery, earl of Shrewsbury, held Cardington in chief, a lordship which Earl Robert's forfeiture ended in 1102. The sheriff Reynold of Bailleul held Cardington of the earl in 1086, and it presumably passed, probably by 1114, with most of the rest of Reynold's estates to Alan son of Flaald, ancestor of the FitzAlans.[3] Cardington manor probably comprised Cardington, Chatwall, Enchmarsh, and Willstone townships in 1086. In the later 1150s William FitzAlan granted Cardington and Enchmarsh townships, half of Chatwall, and pensions of 3 marks from Cardington church and 5*s.* from Cardington mill, to the Knights Templar.[4] The property, apparently held of the FitzAlans,[5] thus became part of the endowment of the preceptory then being established at Lydley,[6] and Cardington then descended with Lydley.

85 S.P.L., MS. 6741, p. 7.

86 S.R.O. 5001/1/2/8; P.R.O., IR 29/29/70; IR 30/29/70.

87 Chatwall Hall and Home Fm.

88 *V.C.H. Salop.* ii. 221; *Census*, 1981, Small Area Statistics: Salop.

89 Inf. from S.C.C. Planning Dept.; pl. 24.

90 Acct. based on *Gent. Mag.* xci (2), 421–2, 512–13; *Tours in Wales by Thos. Pennant*, ed. J. Rhys (1883), i, p. xxxii (for dates of tours, etc.); iii. 256–9; G. Hardinge, *Biog. Memoirs of Revd. Sneyd Davies* (1816), 186–8; Bodl. MS. Top. Salop. c. 1, ff. 363–5; S.R.O. 567/5/3/1/1, 23 Aug.; /5/3/1/3, 16 Aug.; /5/3/1/5, 10 Aug.; /5/3/1/6, 19 Aug.; /5/3/1/7, 21 July; /5/3/1/8, 28 Aug.; /5/3/1/10, 18 Aug.; /5/3/1/11, 10 Aug.; /5/3/1/12, 1 Aug.; /5/3/1/13, 8 Aug.; /5/3/1/14, 26 July; /5/3/1/15, 8 Sept.; *Shrews. Chron.* 31 July, 7 Aug. 1773; S. Bagshaw, *Dir. Salop.* (1851), 525.

91 S.R.O. 1439, bdle. 11, Russell pedigree.

92 B.L. Add. MS. 30316, f. 6v.

93 S.R.O. 567/5/3/1/6, 24–5 July; /5/3/1/8, 29–30 July; /5/3/1/10, 27 July.

94 S.R.O., q. sess. rec. parcel 254, badgers', drovers', and alesellers' licensing bk.

95 Ibid. parcels 255–6, regs. of alesellers' recognizances 1753–81; S. Bagshaw, *Dir. Salop.* (1851), 523–4; *P.O.* and *Kelly's Dir. Salop.* (1856–1941); O.S. Map 1/2,500, Salop. LVI. 3 (1927 edn.); Co. of Salop, *Return of Licensed Hos. 1901* (copy in S.P.L., accession 6117), 95. For soc. life in village in 1930s, J. A. Boulton, 'Transformed Idyll', *Orbis*, vii. 70–2.

96 S.R.O., archivist's office, Cardington (Royal Oak) file, corresp. *re* deeds; *Return of Licensed Hos. 1901*, 94.

97 S.R.O. 3571/Ce/Vis (1911); 3571/Gen/Misc/1, 4; 3571/Reg. (for 1890s).

98 Under a 1976 scheme: S.C.C. Ch. Exec.'s Dept., chars. index.

99 Hughley, Kenley, Ch. Preen, and Rushbury.

1 R. C. Elliott, 'Development of Public Libraries in Salop.' (Loughborough Univ. M.A. thesis, 1970; copy in co. libr.), 125; cf. *V.C.H. Salop.* iii. 206–7.

2 *V.C.H. Salop.* i. 322.

3 Ibid.; ibid. iii. 9–11.

4 Eyton, v. 122–3.

5 Ibid. 124; *Feud. Aids*, iv. 225.

6 *V.C.H. Salop.* ii. 85.

In 1066 *LYDLEY*, later *LYDLEY HAYES*, belonged to Auti who, in 1086, held it of Earl Roger, the tenant in chief. In 1086, besides Lydley, the manor probably included 'Botley', Botvyle, and Comley. Auti's estates, including Lydley, were probably forfeited soon after 1086, and if so may then have been held in chief and in demesne by the earl. The earl's tenancy in chief was forfeited in 1102.[7]

It seems likely that Henry I later granted Lydley to the lord of Pulverbatch for in the later 1150s Reynold of Pulverbatch's daughter Emme and her husband Herbert of Castle Holdgate ('de castello') granted 1 carucate at Lydley and 2 virgates in 'Botley' or Botvyle, part of Emme's inheritance, to the Templars;[8] it seems possible that 'Botley' and Botvyle are names representing the tenanted and demesne portions respectively[9] of the 2 virgates (½ hide) given by Herbert and Emme.[10] Their gift formed the basis of Lydley preceptory's endowment.[11]

By 1314, after the Templars' suppression, Lydley and Cardington were in the hands of Edmund FitzAlan, earl of Arundel, who, as heir of one of the preceptory's earliest benefactors, had a claim on them; the Hospitallers confirmed Arundel's title in 1324[12] and Lydley and Cardington then descended with Stretton-en-le-Dale manor until 1560.[13]

In 1559–60 Lydley and Cardington was among the manors sold by Henry, earl of Arundel, to Rowland Hayward (kt. 1570).[14] After Hayward's death in 1593[15] it was held by his widow Catherine who married Sir John Scott *c.* 1599 and was still alive in 1617. In 1623 her son Sir John Hayward sold Lydley and Cardington to Edward Corbett (d. 1653) of Longnor.[16] Lydley and Cardington then descended with Longnor,[17] and when Capt. R. W. Corbett died in 1987 the manor was part of his residuary estate.[18]

The preceptory demesne included a new dovecot in 1308–9 and was later known as Lydley Hayes farm.[19] A house *c.* 200 m. south-east of Watling Street, was perhaps early 17th-century; it was a 'handsome mansion' with a fishpond when demolished after 1817.[20]

Rowland Whitbrooke, a Bridgnorth wool merchant whose family came from Lydley Hayes, was Rowland Hayward's bailiff at Lydley Hayes in 1569. In 1586 Whitbrooke took a 21-year lease (renegotiated in 1592) of the demesnes at Lydley Hayes, and apparently *c.* 1590 he built Penkridge Hall at the foot of the Lawley, perhaps as a hunting box. It was presumably so called because Whitbrooke's wife Elizabeth (*née* Careswell) came from Penkridge (Staffs.).[21] In 1910 the Corbetts' *PENKRIDGE* estate comprised 244 a. In 1971 the Hall was bought by Lt.-Col. N. C. Faithfull.[22]

Built on earlier masonry (now a basement) the timber framed Penkridge Hall, jettied and elaborately decorated, had a large and a small room on each of its two main floors, the lower ones probably being service rooms. A staircase connected the floors, but the first-floor reception room had its own grand entrance from outside. Later 17th-century alterations, including truncation of the main upper room, made Penkridge a more typical country residence.[23]

Fulk Watkies had land at Comley in 1497.[24] William Watkies was succeeded in his tenement there by his son John in 1687. John Watkies the younger (fl. 1737), of Comley, was perhaps the latter's son. It was presumably his son, also John Watkies, who was dead by 1772 when his son William, gentleman,[25] held the *SHOOTROUGH* estate at Comley. In 1779 William passed it to his son William who added land bought from Robert Hawkins in 1812. Watkies (d. 1826) was succeeded by Thomas Galliers who, in 1852, sold Shootrough to Panton Corbett, lord of Lydley and Cardington.[26] It remained part of the Corbett estate in 1910.[27]

Shootrough Farm has a two bayed hall of *c.* 1422 framed by three full crucks. About 1609 a central stack and first floor were inserted in the hall, and a cross wing was added, perhaps on the site of a solar. The cross-wing parlour contains

7 Ibid. i. 342; Eyton, vi. 237–8; above, this section.

8 Eyton, vi. 237–9.

9 For the tenants in 1185 on the 2 'Botley' virgates given to the Templars by Herb. see Lees, *Templars in Eng.* 37; for the Templars' demesne in 1185 (incl. their mill) on the 2 Botvyle virgates given to them by Herb. see ibid. 41; Eyton, vi. 239–40.

10 Cf. *Rot. Cur. Reg.* (Rec. Com.), ii. 205.

11 *V.C.H. Salop.* ii. 85 (corr. below, Corrigenda).

12 Ibid. 86; Eyton, v. 124–5; vi. 242–3; *Feud. Aids*, iv. 229.

13 *Cal. Pat.* 1343–5, 488; 1345–8, 328; 1350–4, 524; 1354–8, 131; 1396–9, 213, 248, 250; 1461–7, 443–4; *Cal. Close*, 1346–9, 244; *Cal. Fine R.* 1413–22, 165–6; *L. & P. Hen. VIII*, xx (2), p. 414; S.R.O. 552, box 92, valor for Clun ldship. 1403–4; 2557/34–5; P.R.O., C 138/23, no. 54; C 138/59, no. 51; C 139/71, no. 37; C 139/98, no. 28; below, Ch. Stretton, manors.

14 P.R.O., CP 25/2/200/2 Eliz. I East. [no. 13]; *Cal. Pat.* 1558–60, 368; S.R.O. 567/2C/2–3; W. A. Shaw, *Kts. of Eng.* (1906), ii. 75.

15 P.R.O., C 142/241, no. 125; *T.S.A.S.* li. 131.

16 S.R.O. 567/1/54–61; /2C/6–16; box 11, deed 6 May 1623; *V.C.H. Salop.* viii. 63; P.R.O., C 142/363, no. 194; ibid. CP 25/2/344/21 Jas. I East. [no. 41]; *T.S.A.S.* li. 132.

17 S.R.O. 165/11–28; 567/1/64–70, 206; 567/3/23, 30–1; 802/29; q. sess. rec. box 260, reg. of gamekeepers 1711–42, 21 Nov. 1724; 1742–79, 9 Oct. 1762, 9 Apr. 1763, 1 May 1764, 18 July 1767; parcel 261, reg. of gamekeepers 1799–1807, ff. 12, 126; W.S.L. 350/5/40, Cardington p. 3; *P.O. Dir. Salop.* (1879), 293; *Kelly's Dir. Salop.* (1885–1941); *V.C.H. Salop.* viii. 110 (corr. below, Corrigenda).

18 *Shropshire Star*, 10 Dec. 1987, p. 23; inf. from Mr. D. H. G. Salt (1987).

19 P.R.O., E 358/18, m. 4; *V.C.H. Salop.* ii. 86.

20 S.R.O. 1066/115, ff. 46–8; 3651, plan of Rob. Corbett's est. 1794; *Salop. N. & Q.* N.S. i. 28, 32; R. Baugh, *Map of Salop.* (1808); S.P.L., MS. 6741, p. 15; below, church. Masonry at Lydley Hayes fm. site and Penkridge Hall basement make them possible preceptory sites: A. Evason, 'Leebotwood' (Lond. Inst. Educ. thesis, 1958), 18; below.

21 Inf. from Lt.-Col. N. C. Faithfull; S.R.O. 567, box 11, leases and arts. of agreement, 1586, 1592; box 30, ministers' accts. 1569; *Visit. Salop. 1623*, ii (Harl. Soc. xxix), 497–9; *T.S.A.S.* li. 132; *V.C.H. Staffs.* v. 125.

22 S.R.O. 1011, box 172, draft abstr. of claims to rt. of common; 4044/91, p. 11; W.S.L. 350/5/40, Cardington p. 10.

23 *V.C.H. Salop.* v (forthcoming); Bodl. MS. Top. Salop. c. 2, f. 414.

24 S.R.O. 3365/165.

25 S.R.O. 3288/2/1, 14 Apr. 1687, 28 Mar. 1737; /2/2, 4 Sept. 1772.

26 S.R.O. 1011, box 345, sched. of deeds *re* Shootrough est.; W.S.L. 350/5/40, Cardington p. 13.

27 S.R.O. 4044/91, p. 8.

original wall paintings, and the hall has early or mid 16th-century panelling.[28]

WILLSTONE, probably part of the Domesday manor of Cardington,[29] was later subinfeudated, and Miles of Hope's son Adam of Minton held Willstone as ¼ or ½ knight's fee of John FitzAlan (II) in 1242–3 and *c.* 1260.[30] Adam's brother Peter of Minton apparently succeeded him at Willstone.[31] John Willstone and Richard Cotes held ¼ knight's fee there of the earl of Arundel in 1431.[32]

In 1483 John Leighton of Church Stretton acquired property in the parish,[33] perhaps some of the land which his son Thomas had in Willstone by 1497[34] and in Lydley Hayes by 1501. Thomas acquired more in Willstone in 1498, and in 1501 he gave Stephen Kemsey four Willstone tenements in part exchange for the manor of Alberbury, but a few days later Kemsey returned the Willstone property to Leighton in exchange for land in Lydley Hayes. Leighton (kt. 1513)[35] died in 1519,[36] and his son John (d. 1532), cousin of the lord of Plaish,[37] owned 'three houses' in Willstone, which passed to his son Edward, not the only landowner in Willstone in 1583 as there was at least one other, Thomas Pinches. Edward Leighton (kt. 1591)[38] sold the 'three houses' in 1586 to Thomas More of Millichope, who later sold at least two, one to Thomas Churchman of Shipton in 1598, another to Richard Palmer in 1602.[39]

Farms in Willstone seem to have been owned separately in the 17th century and for most of the 18th, but in the later 18th century the Bakers were aggregating properties through marriage and purchase.[40] Probably the largest property, later known as Willstone farm, was owned by the Ruckleys in 1603. Francis Ruckley and his son Edward sold parts of their lands in Willstone to William Pigge of Plaish in 1603 and 1605. In 1662 that property was settled on Pigge's granddaughter Elizabeth on her marriage to Thomas Russell (d. 1687) of Willstone and Hollyhurst. Their great-grandson, the Revd. William Russell, sold it to John Baker in 1766.[41] About then Baker also acquired Uppingtons tenement and its tithes from the Russells.[42] Thomas Baker, gentleman, was probably John's brother and heir.[43]

Sarah, a daughter of Richard Roberts (d. 1745),[44] brought Willstone property to Thomas Baker when they married in 1758.[45] Both Thomas and his son Richard added to their Willstone property, and by 1794 Richard Baker and John Sheppard owned much of Willstone, where their properties were intermixed. Richard Baker died in 1811, and in 1822 the devisees of his son Richard (d. 1821) exchanged much land with the Ven. Joseph Corbett, by then the owner of John Sheppard's property[46] and probably of other land which he had bought since succeeding to the family estates in 1804.[47] The exchange produced two large consolidated farms. Lower farm, south of the road from Church Stretton to Cardington, passed to Elizabeth, sister of Richard Baker (d. 1821) and wife of Thomas Boulton (d. 1861). Upper farm, north of the road, belonged to the Corbetts. In 1910 virtually the whole township belonged to W. B. Boulton (320 a.) and Edward Corbett (400 a.), but the Boulton property was sold in 1922.[48]

Lower Farm, five bays and 2½ storeys over a basement, was built in 1738 for John (d. 1765) and Elizabeth (*née* Ambler; d. 1779) Sheppard following their marriage. It is a stylish building[49] of dressed grey sandstone, with a central doorway approached by five steps and surmounted by a cartouche containing a (damaged) version of the Ambler arms. The plan is four-square, and the south-west quarter has back stairs to the attics, apparently for servants or labourers. The front windows have moulded stone sills and fluted keystones, the gable ends coping stones and kneelers.[50] Outbuildings include a barn with cruck-derived principal rafters, perhaps 17th-century.

ENCHMARSH was part of Lydley and Cardington manor, and most of the township was owned by the Templars and their successors in the Middle Ages and by the Corbetts of Longnor later.[51]

Sir Edward Leighton (d. 1593) of Wattlesborough and his son Thomas (d. 1600) had property at Enchmarsh.[52]

28 SA 17217; Dept. of Environment, *List of Bldgs.: Wrekin* (1983), 4; *Vernacular Archit.* xxvii. 103, 105.
29 Above, this section.
30 *Cartulary of Haughmond Abbey*, ed. U. Rees (1985), p. 241; *Bk. of Fees*, iii. 962, 971.
31 *Cart. Haughmond*, p. 241.
32 *Feud. Aids*, iv. 267.
33 Loton Hall MSS., folio vol. 'Copies of Deeds', p. 31.
34 S.R.O. 3365/165.
35 W. A. Shaw, *Kts. of Eng.* (1906), ii. 36; Burke, *Peerage* (1967), 1482.
36 Loton Hall MSS., folio vol. 'Copies of Deeds', pp. 42–3, 59–60; cf. *V.C.H. Salop.* viii. 196–7, 266; *Visit. Salop. 1623*, ii. 324.
37 Botfield, *Stemmata Botevilliana*, 184, 186, omits a generation (Wm., d. 1533) of the Leightons of Plaish: cf. below, this section (Plaish).
38 Shaw, *Kts.* i. 123.
39 *L. & P. Hen. VIII*, xv, p. 406; S.R.O. 516/1/217; 3320/7 B/1–3; *Visit. Salop. 1623*, ii. 324; *V.C.H. Salop.* viii. 196.
40 S.R.O. 1359, box 28, abstrs. of title of Ric. Baker, Mr. Ric. Taylor, Mr. Russell; box 32, sched. of title deeds.
41 S.R.O. 1359, box 28, abstr. of title to Mr. Russell's est.; box 29, deeds 1606–62; box 30, deeds 1699–1766; S.P.L., MS. 4647, f. 58.
42 S.R.O. 1359, box 29, deeds 1724–75.
43 S.R.O. 3288/2/2, 21 Apr. 1758.
44 S.R.O. 1359, box 31, Ric. Roberts's will; 3571/Rg/3, bur. 15 Feb. 1744/5.
45 S.R.O. 1359, box 29, deed 14 Dec. 1758.
46 Ibid. box 28, abstr. of title of Ric. Baker; box 32, sched. of title deeds; 1643/146; 3651, maps of Rob. Corbett's est. 1794, map of Lydley and Cardington man. n.d.; S.R.O., incl. award C 4/36.
47 Perhaps former Roberts property: cf. *24th Rep. Com. Char.* H.C. 231, p. 401 (1831), xi.
48 S.R.O. 1359, box 34, Ric. Baker's will, deeds 29 June 1882 and 20 Nov. 1922, succession acct. on Revd. Wm. Boulton's d.; 4044/91, pp. 10–11; W.S.L. 350/5/40, Cardington p. 13.
49 Called Willstone Manor *c.* 1910 when W. B. Boulton farmed there: S.R.O. 4044/91, p. 10; *Kelly's Dir. Salop.* (1909), 56.
50 *List of Bldgs. (All Stretton* [etc]., p. 30; L. Ambler, *Ambler Fam.* [1924], 75 and pedigree facing p. 76; S.P.L., MS. 2793, pp. 291–2; *S.P.R. Heref.* iii (1), 34; S.R.O. 3571/Rg/3, bur. 23 Nov. 1765, 12 May 1779.
51 Eyton, v. 122–3; W.S.L. 350/5/40, Cardington p. 10; S.R.O. 516/1/217, 229; 4044/91, pp. 14–15.
52 S.R.O. 165/10, 150; *Visit. Salop. 1623*, ii. 324–5 (S.R.O. copy with MS. addns.).

In the 17th and 18th centuries various Russells, parish gentry, held tenements in Enchmarsh, where they lived;[53] their holdings probably included *LOWER HOUSE FARM*, which Richard Evason perhaps owned and occupied in the 1830s.[54] It was later owned by William Wall (d. 1881) and his son-in-law Thomas Woodcock (d. 1911) who also owned Enchmarsh Villa. Woodcock's son S. W. Woodcock probably sold Enchmarsh Villa in 1918 but kept Lower House farm until 1936.[55] In 1966 J. B. Dale sold Lower House to Col. K. M. Stuckey, the owner in 1986.[56]

Lower House Farm was probably extended *c.* 1677 to form a sandstone **H** plan house. The central ground-floor room has a large fireplace with flanking cupboards; a cupboard marked '16:W:R:E:77' probably refers to William (d. 1686) and Elizabeth (d. 1713) Russell. One of the cross wings was partly demolished *c.* 1810, when the eaves of the rest of the house were raised.[57]

CHATWALL, perhaps part of the Plaish estate in 963,[58] was probably part of Cardington manor in 1086. The half of Chatwall given by William FitzAlan to Lydley preceptory in the later 1150s probably reverted in or after 1308 to Edmund FitzAlan, earl of Arundel,[59] and the FitzAlans' overlordship of Chatwall remained in 1363.[60]

In 1255 their tenant of the other moiety was Gilbert de Buckenhull.[61] That mesne lordship had disappeared by 1363.[62]

Gilbert's tenant in 1255 was William, son of Alan of Drayton.[63] William's mesne lordship of the moiety seems to have descended with his portion of Berrington manor until 1315 or later,[64] but had disappeared by 1363.[65]

The terre tenant of that moiety by 1281 was Robert Burnell, bishop of Bath and Wells.[66] Thereafter, until at least 1587, that half of Chatwall descended with Acton Burnell manor.[67] Its later descent has not been traced.

The Corfields lived at Chatwall by the later 16th century, and in the later 17th century they built up a considerable estate there.[68] Thomas Corfield (d. 1657), a Wenlock bailiff and borough magistrate, is said to have enlarged Chatwall Hall.[69] His son Richard (d. 1680), of Chatwall, bought the adjoining Leahills property in 1648 and was described in 1656, like his successors in the estate down to the late 18th century,[70] as a gentleman.[71] In 1659 he remodelled his house, perhaps known as Chatwall Hall thereafter, and in 1676 he bought the Chatwall rectorial tithes; he may also have made a park.[72] In 1696 his son and namesake bought three messuages in Chatwall, formerly Henry Leighton's property, from Deborah, Lady Hopton, relict of Isaac Jones (d. 1652) of Ham (Surr.).[73] Corfield died in 1710 and his Chatwall estate went to his son and heir Thomas, except for what he had bought from Lady Hopton, which went to two other sons Walthall (d. 1727) and William. William (d. 1759) inherited Walthall's share and lived many years at Gretton.[74]

Thomas Corfield (d. 1732) greatly reduced the family estates[75] and in 1710 sold part of his interest in Chatwall to his brother Richard.[76] Richard Corfield settled his copyhold property in 1745 on his daughter Ann and her husband Robert Rawlins,[77] and in 1753 he left them his freehold in trust for their son R. C. Rawlins, a minor, who had come into possession by 1773. Ann conveyed the copyhold property to him in 1783,[78] just before he died[79] leaving all his estate to his son Thomas.[80] The chief house and its lands, which Thomas Corfield had settled on his son Edward in 1728, seem to have come to Thomas Rawlins after 1783.[81]

Rawlins, a Liverpool merchant, was bankrupt by 1798 and next year emigrated to America after the Chatwall estate (386 a.) was sold to Cornelius Bourne (d. 1804), another Liverpool merchant. Bourne's son Peter, also of Liverpool, died *c.* 1843 and his widow Margaret died in 1865.[82] In 1872 their son, the Revd. G. Drinkwater Bourne, sold his Chatwall estate (247 a.) to Richard Butcher,[83] whose family had an estate by 1808.[84]

In 1895 Butcher sold his Chatwall estate (388 a.) to Joseph Edge and E. B. Potts who, in 1899, sold it to Col. F. C. Corfield[85] (d. 1904), descendant of the earlier owners of much of the the estate. His widow (d. 1941) left it to their grandson F. V. Corfield, who sold the 540-a. estate in 1951.[86]

53 S.R.O. 1439, bdle. 11, Russell pedigrees; 3288/1/1–2; above, this article, intro.
54 W.S.L. 350/5/40, Cardington p. 10.
55 E. Cassey & Co. *Dir. Salop.* (1871), 102; S.R.O. 2947/53/55–63, 67–8, 77–85, 98; 3288/2/10.
56 Inf. from Col. Stuckey.
57 *List of Bldgs. (All Stretton* [etc.]*)*, p. 21; S.R.O. 1439, bdle. 11, Russell pedigrees.
58 *Landscape Hist.* x. 15–24.
59 Eyton, v. 122, 124–5; above, this section.
60 *Cal. Inq. p.m.* xi, p. 373.
61 *Rot. Hund.* (Rec. Com.), ii. 71.
62 *Cal. Inq. p.m.* xi, p. 373; Eyton, xi. 320.
63 *Rot. Hund.* ii. 71.
64 Eyton, v. 125; *Cal. Inq. p.m.* v, p. 392. Cf. *V.C.H. Salop.* viii. 18.
65 *Cal. Inq. p.m.* xi, p. 373.
66 *Cal. Chart. R.* 1257–1300, 249.
67 *Cat. Anct. D.* ii, C 2398; *Cal. Inq. p.m.* v, p. 392; xi, p. 373; *Cal. Inq. p.m.* (Rec. Com.), iv. 56, 265, 325; *L. & P. Hen. VIII*, vi, p. 89; xvi, p. 240; xvii, p. 28; *Cal. Pat.* 1547–8, p. 280; P.R.O., C 142/213, no. 149; cf. *V.C.H. Salop.* viii. 7--8; below, Rushbury, manors.
68 For the Corfields see J. Corfield, *The Corfields* (Rosanna, 1993); Sparrow, *Ch. Preen*, 47–54; S.R.O. 567/1/217; 4825.
69 S.R.O. 4825.
70 S.R.O. 3288/2/1–2; below, this section (Leahills).
71 S.P.L., Deeds 3090; MS. 4360, p. 128.
72 *V.C.H. Salop.* v (forthcoming); below, this section (rectory); S.R.O. 4597/32.
73 S.R.O. 5001/1/2/2–3; Northants. R.O., WC 52, 54.
74 S.R.O. 4825; 5001/1/2/30.
75 S.R.O. 4825.
76 S.R.O. 3288/2/1, p. 64; cf. 4825, giving 1720 as date of sale.
77 S.R.O. 3288/2/1, pp. 171–3.
78 S.R.O. 5001/1/2/9–11, 30.
79 S.R.O. 3571/Rg/3, bur. 11 Aug. 1783.
80 S.R.O. 5001/1/2/19.
81 S.R.O. 3288/2/1, pp. 110–12, 177, 188–9, 318; 4825.
82 S.R.O. 3288/2/1, pp. 354, 437–41; /2/6, pp. 309–11, 362; /2/7, pp. 205–7; 4825; 5001/1/2/27–42, 46.
83 S.R.O. 1681/250/15, 18.
84 Ibid. /250/10; 3288/2/4, pp. 35–6, 73–4; /2/5, pp. 250–60, 263, 266; /2/7, pp. 32, 34; below, this section (Leahills).
85 S.R.O. 1681/250/15, 18, 20.
86 S.R.O. 4044/91, p. 12; 4654/4; 5001/3/1/8; *Kelly's Dir. Salop.* (1905–41); Corfield, *Corfields*, 68, 84, 94, 107–15, 118.

Chatwall Hall is said to have been enlarged by Thomas Corfield in 1613. He may have been responsible for the timber framed east (probably parlour) range, which once extended further south. That house was supposedly fortified by Thomas's son Richard and attacked by Parliamentarians in the Civil War.[87] Richard probably built the present hall range and west range in 1659, of two storeys and an attic in dressed Hoar Edge grit sandstone. The hall was entered by a central doorway and had a corner fireplace. The house was taxed on four hearths in 1672.[88] Later additions include two late 19th-century gabled rear wings, and *c.* 1920 the original door to the hall was blocked and a new porch made.[89]

The nuns of Brewood (White Ladies) had a small property in Chatwall in 1535.[90]

In 1583 William Leighton held 4 a. of waste newly inclosed from the manorial demesne and Edward Leighton held three customary messuages in Chatwall[91] which later passed to William (d. 1607) and William's son Henry.[92] Pingleys Heys, *c.* 220 a. of wood and waste north of Chatwall, also passed from William to Henry. In 1615, when the property evidently formed part of Langley manor,[93] Henry sold Pingleys Heys to Humphrey Lee of Langley,[94] and it formed part of the Acton Burnell estate in 1910.[95] Henry's three customary messuages were bought by Richard Corfield in 1696.[96]

In the early 17th century the Briggses of Haughton (in Shifnal) had an estate at *LOWER CHATWALL.*[97] By 1751 Lower Chatwall (60 a.) belonged to the Corfields.[98] In 1751 the main house stood 200 m. north-east of the property that later bore that name, then only a cottage.[99]

LEAHILLS, later Upper Leahills, farm was sold in 1648 by the regicide Robert Wallop to Richard Corfield (d. 1680) of Chatwall, who had acquired the tenancy of the property from his father Thomas (d. 1657).[1] Leahills then descended, with the rectorial tithes of Chatwall and part of Frodesley, in the Corfield family until 1748 when John Corfield's mortgagee Thomas Lee, of Wroxeter, obtained both. On Lee's death the properties passed in moieties to his daughters. One had married the Shrewsbury draper Edward Blakeway and on his bankruptcy in 1760 her half was bought by her sister who, in 1763, married Blakeway's associate John Wilkinson, the ironmaster. In 1807 Wilkinson sold the property, mortgaged since 1765, to Elizabeth Clayton of Wroxeter.[2] The Revd. Roger Clayton sold the tithes, with some land, to John and Richard Stanier in 1832, and in 1841 John and Edward Stanier conveyed them to John Butcher, already the owner of an estate in Chatwall. In 1840 Clayton's trustees sold Upper Leahills to Samuel Jones and in 1897 it was acquired by Col. F. C. Corfield and soon united with the Chatwall estate and tithes which he bought in 1899 from the Butchers' successors.[3] Upper Leahills Farm, a 1½ storeyed stone house, has on it the dates 1647, with the initials of Richard and Sarah Corfield,[4] and 1897 with those of Frederick and Augusta Corfield.

In 963 King Edgar gave his thegn Wulfric an estate at *PLAISH* whose bounds suggest that it was mainly conterminous with the 19th-century manor, though in the north it extended into the valley beneath Hoar Edge and so included Chatwall and Broome.[5] Godwine held it in 1066.[6]

Earl Roger held the manor in chief in 1086. The tenancy in chief was presumably forfeited in 1102 by Robert of Bellême.[7] Roger de Lacy had held Plaish of Earl Roger in 1086, and *c.* 1175 the Lacys' interest (presumably then a tenancy in chief) passed to the FitzAlans. Richard FitzAlan was tenant in chief *c.* 1284.[8]

In 1086 Berner held Plaish of Roger de Lacy. In the 12th century the Higford family, possibly Berner's descendants, held Plaish of the Lacys, and *c.* 1284 William of Higford held it of Richard FitzAlan as ¼ knight's fee.[9]

Peter of Greete, of Greete (in Burford), held Plaish of the Higfords in 1255 as did Geoffrey of Greete, probably his son, *c.* 1284. The Greetes in turn subinfeudated the manor, and *c.* 1284 Roger de Lee appeared as their tenant there.[10]

The Hospitallers, having perhaps succeeded in the early 14th century to some interest of the Templars, were said to be the terre tenant's overlords in 1533.[11]

From the 13th century the actual terre tenants, with four levels of feudal lordship between them and the Crown *c.* 1284, appear to have been the Sprenchose family:[12] Richard in 1255 and 1272; Walter *c.* 1284 and in 1297; Richard in 1316–17; William in 1361; and Fulk and his wife Margaret from 1376.[13] In 1410–11 Edward Sprenchose was sheriff, as was Sir Fulk Sprenchose of Plaish in 1447.[14]

87 S.R.O. 4825; inf. from Mr. Eric Mercer; Hall shown on S.R.O. 5001/1/2/8.
88 *Hearth Tax 1672*, 185.
89 *V.C.H. Salop.* v (forthcoming); *List of Bldgs.: Shrews. and Atcham (All Stretton [etc.])*, 19.
90 *V.C.H. Salop.* ii. 83.
91 S.R.O. 567/1/217.
92 Ibid. /1/220.
93 Hen. Leighton had sold 'all' his Cardington property in 1614: S.R.O. 1104, box 26, deed 24 Oct. 1614; cf. S.R.O. 3651, plans of Rob. Corbett's est. 1794 and n.d. (marked 'par. of Acton Burnell').
94 S.R.O. 1514/111, 297.
95 S.R.O. 4044/91, pp. 13–14.
96 S.R.O. 567/1/225; above, this section.
97 *Visit. Salop. 1623*, i (Harl. Soc. xxviii), 69; P.R.O., CP 25/2/343/9 Jas. I Mich. [no. 51]; CP 25/2/477/13 Chas. I Trin. [no. 18].
98 Cf. S.R.O. 5001/1/2/8; /1/5/4, plan.
99 Fig. 6 shows the latter's position.
1 S.R.O. 5001/1/1/1–2; above, this section. For Wallop see *D.N.B.*
2 S.R.O. 4044/91, p. 13; 4825; 5001/1/1/4–9, 11–15, 17–22, 44–5; Trinder, *Ind. Rev. Salop.* 24, 29, 107, 110, 123, 126–7; above, this section (Chatwall); below, this section (rectory).
3 S.R.O. 5001/1/1/37–8; /1/5/8, 10; above, this section (Chatwall).
4 Cf. S.R.O. 4597/31.
5 H. P. R. Finberg, *Early Charters of W. Midlands* (1972), p. 149; P. H. Sawyer, *A.-S. Charters* (1968), no. 723; *T.S.A.S.* lvi. 30–1; *Landscape Hist.* x. 18–23.
6 *V.C.H. Salop.* i. 328.
7 Ibid.; iii. 7, 9–10.
8 Eyton, xi. 353–4.
9 Ibid.
10 Ibid.; ibid. iv. 335–6; *Feud. Aids*, iv. 222.
11 P.R.O., E 150/584, no. 3.
12 Incomplete and erroneous pedigrees of fam. appear in S.P.L., MS. 2788, pp. 252–3; *T.S.A.S.* vi. 92.
13 Eyton, vi. 299–300; xi. 354–5; *Feud. Aids*, iv. 222; *Rot. Hund.* ii. 71; S.R.O. 1037/3/54; S.P.L., Deeds 17741, ct. r. of 1376; 17744–5.
14 J. B. Blakeway, *Sheriffs of Salop.* (Shrews. 1831), 14, 70.

Sir Fulk's daughter and coheir Margery took Plaish to her husband Sir William Leighton (d. 1520).[15] Their son William (d. 1533) held the manor[16] and his widow Dorothy apparently held it during the minority of their son William.[17] From the 1560s that William (d. 1607) was active in county and regional government.[18] His son and successor William (fl. 1614), author of a verse eulogy of the king, *Vertue Triumphant* (1603), was imprisoned for debt *c.* 1610. His son and heir Harcourt Leighton held a commission for Parliament at Naseby (1645) and was an active county magistrate.[19] He died childless in 1658 leaving the manor, heavily mortgaged, to his brother-in-law Henry Goodricke of Ely (Cambs.). In 1670 Goodricke sold Plaish, still encumbered, to Rowland Hunt of Boreatton.[20]

Hunt, sheriff in 1672, died in 1699 and the manor then descended from father to son for six generations: Thomas (sheriff 1718, d. 1753),[21] Thomas (d. 1777),[22] Rowland (d. 1811), Rowland (sheriff 1830, d. 1835), and Rowland (d. 1878).[23] In 1884 Rowland's widow and son, Rowland, sold the Plaish estate to Edward Sayer (d. 1897), of Finchley (Mdx.), whose trustees still owned it in 1899.[24]

By 1903 James Dun-Waters owned Plaish. He sold it in 1911 to Capt. S. H. Christy (d. 1914) who left it in trust for W. E. B. Porter (d. unmarried 1934).[25] The Holt was sold in 1921,[26] and in 1934 the Plaish Hall estate (almost 950 a.), including the manor of Plaish, was put up for sale. Plaish Park farm (330 a.) was bought by the Joneses, who farmed it;[27] some of the rest, including the manor and the Hall, went to G. S. M. Warlow. Maj. M. S. Vaughan owned the Hall and Lower Home farm in the 1940s and bought the Holt and other nearby farms, keeping them after he sold the Hall to Capt. Walter Horridge[28] in 1953. Vaughan (d. 1967) sold the remaining estate (520 a., mainly four farms) in 1962. Probably *c.* 1966 the Hall was bought by D. F. Vosper, Lord Runcorn, on whose death in 1968 only 43 a. went with it.[29]

Parts of an earlier stone house were incorporated in Plaish Hall when it was rebuilt imposingly in brick.[30] Rebuilding may have happened *c.* 1580, when the earliest evidence for its surrounding park is found.[31] As rebuilt Plaish is an **H** shaped building of 2½ storeys, facing south-east (for descriptive purposes taken as east) to a courtyard. It was taxed on 22 hearths in 1672.[32] The great open hall, entered from outside by a south-east door, had an elaborate screen surmounted by a gallery at its south end and a fireplace in the west wall. Its roof, while apparently supported by hammer beams decorated with Anglo-Flemish ornament, in fact had an arch-braced tie beam carrying queen struts. At either end of the hall's west wall newel stairs rose in external octagonal stair turrets to the upper floors of the north and south ranges. The northern, residential, range had two main ground-floor rooms above a cellar: to the east a room (called the great parlour in 1670)[33] with a decorated plaster ceiling, and to the west the star parlour where the elaborately painted decoration of the wainscot included gold stars. On the great parlour's north wall a newel stair rose to the upper chamber. The ground floor of the south range comprised kitchen, larder, and butteries. Both ranges had garderobe towers. Externally the main stylistic elements were the symmetry of the east front, its diaper-patterned brickwork, and the tall brick chimneys resembling those of Compton Wynyates (Warws.) and Hampton Court.

Between the 1670s and 1884, when Edward Sayer bought it, Plaish Hall was usually let, in the later 18th and 19th centuries as a farmhouse.[34] In 1780 it was thought unsuited to that purpose and demolition was suggested.[35] Under Sayer's son C. E. Sayer, an architect,[36] the dilapidated building was extensively restored.[37] The octagonal stair turrets were rebuilt from first-floor level, to which they had been reduced at some time. On the west side a new single storeyed range containing scullery, larder, and gun room linked the two ranges. Inside a new screen was made for the hall, the original one having been moved since 1868 into the star, or oak, parlour for use as wainscot around the

15 Ibid. 70; Loton Hall MSS., folio vol. 'Copies of Deeds', common recovery of Donnington, Plaish, etc., 1524; H. E. Forrest, *Old Hos. of Wenlock* (Shrews. 1914), 48; for Leighton pedigree, S.P.L., MS. 4360, p. 786.

16 P.R.O., E 150/854, no. 3.

17 S.P.L., Deeds 17743, ct. of Dorothy Leighton.

18 *V.C.H. Salop.* iii. 60 n.; *T.S.A.S.* ii. 289–93; P. Williams, *Council in Marches of Wales* (1958), 89, 140, 143, 173, 190, 292, 350–1; *V.C.H. Salop.* viii. 60; S.R.O. 3905/4.

19 *T.S.A.S.* 3rd ser. ii. 320–1; *D.N.B.* s.v. Sir Wm. Leighton; *V.C.H. Salop.* iii. 96, 113; below, church.

20 S.P.L., Deeds 17654, 17685, 17739, 17765; Botfield, *Stemmata Botevilliana*, 186; *Hist. of Goodricke Fam.* ed. C. A. Goodricke (1897), 10 (grangerized copy in B.L., K.T.C. 104.a.8).

21 Blakeway, *Sheriffs*, 140, 171; S.P.L., MS. 4081, pp. 2231–3; S.P.L., Deeds 17016; S.R.O., q. sess. rec. box 260, reg. of gamekeepers 1711–42, 11 Jan. 1720/1.

22 S.R.O., q. sess. rec. box 260, reg. of gamekeepers 1742–79, 21 Oct. 1749; S.R.O., archivist's office, pedigree in 'Hunt of Boreatton' file.

23 Blakeway, op. cit. 244; S.P.L., MS. 4081, pp. 2231–3.

24 S.P.L., Deeds 17588, 17590; *Evening Standard*, 22 Nov. 1897; S.R.O. 5001/1/5/8 (plan).

25 S.R.O., reg. of electors, S. or Ludlow divn. (1904), p. 427; S.R.O. 3931/1/1, 2nd sched. mentioning deed 17 Nov. 1911; Heref. Dioc. Regy., reg. 1902–19, p. 488; S.R.O. 4044/91, p. 10; *T.S.A.S.* xlviii, pp. *iii–iv*; H. A. Tipping, *Eng. Homes, Period III*, i. 20; Burke, *Land. Gent.* (1937), 1596, 1833; *Shrews. Chron.* 23 Feb. 1934, p. 11 (perh. wrongly calling Porter Christy's neph.).

26 Below, this section. Rest of para. based on sale cats. and partics. in S.P.L.; S.R.O. 4654/5; inf. from Cmdr. and Mrs. J. D. Sayer, Easterton Ho., Mkt. Lavington (Wilts.).

27 S.R.O. 3913/1/3.

28 Burke, *Land. Gent.* (1952), 1286–7.

29 *The Times*, 22 Jan. 1968, p. 10; *Who Was Who, 1961–70*, 986; *Shropshire Mag.* Dec. 1968, p. 9; inf. from Mr. R. H. Merley.

30 Descr. based on *V.C.H. Salop.* v (forthcoming); Tipping, *Eng. Homes, Period III*, i. 14–21; *T.S.A.S.* lxvi. 90–6; S.P.L., MS. 6741, pp. 39–41; Victoria and Albert Mus., Nat. Art Libr., MSS. English *c.* 1930–64, Mrs. Bardswell's notebks., Salop. and Ches. (MS. L. 4855), Plaish.

31 Below, econ. hist.

32 *Hearth Tax 1672*, 184.

33 S.P.L., Deeds 17731.

34 Ibid. 17425, 17727; F. Stackhouse Acton, *Castles and Old Mansions of Salop.* (1868), 31.

35 S.P.L., Deeds 17746, esp. f. [1].

36 A. Felstead, J. Franklin, and L. Pinfield, *Dir. Brit. Architects 1834–1900* (1993), 806.

37 For restoration wk. see *T.S.A.S.* xlviii, pp. *iii–iv*; lxvi. 90–6; Tipping, *Eng. Homes, Period III*, i. 20–1; Forrest, *Old Hos. of Wenlock*, 48–9 and pl. facing p. 48; *Building News*, 14 Aug. 1891, p. 216; S.P.L., MS. 6741, p. 38.

fireplace.[38] At the same time panelling was moved from the north-west bedroom to the hall. Perhaps then, perhaps later, the ceiling of the south-east ground-floor room was painted in an early 16th-century style incorporating the monogram 'HR'. About 1905 a new entrance was made on the centre of the south side and the ground floor of that range was re-ordered. The western extension was perhaps also altered then;[39] as it certainly was during ruthless alterations made in the later 1930s, which involved the insertion of a floor across the central hall and demolition of the octagonal stair turrets. At the same time many of the hall's original roof timbers, including the so-called hammer posts, were removed and used in a new staircase.[40]

BROOME, perhaps part of the Plaish estate in 963,[41] later became a separate manor, held in 1066 by Thorsten (Turstin) and Austin and in 1086 by Earl Roger. In 1086 the earl held ¾ of the manor in demesne, Reynold the sheriff the rest.

The later medieval owners of Broome are unknown,[42] but *c.* 1630 Francis Wilkes held land there of Harcourt Leighton 'as of his manor of Plaish'[43] and the Leightons' interest in Broome passed with Plaish to the Hunts. Rowland Hunt was said to be lord of Broome *c.* 1840,[44] but in 1844 he owned no land in the township, which then consisted of two farms, Broome farm (131 a.) occupied by its owner Richard Woodcock, and Broome Hall farm (57 a.) owned by Joseph Gitton. By 1910 Woodcock's property belonged to Mrs. Corfield's Chatwall estate. Broome Hall farm then belonged mostly to James Preen (d. 1911), farmer and builder, though some of it had been absorbed into Bowman Hill farm on the Sparrows' Holt Preen estate[45] and James Preen's part seems later to have been acquired by the Chatwall estate.[46] Broome farm, bought by Maj. M. S. Vaughan probably in 1951 and sold by him in 1962, was acquired by R. H. Barbour, and the Fildes family bought it, with the Holt, in 1987.[47]

The Lees of Langley owned land in Broome in the 16th and 17th centuries.[48]

In 1086 1 hide at Preen, assumed to be what became the manor of *HOLT PREEN*, was held, like the rest of Preen, by Helgot, who held it of Earl Roger, the tenant in chief. The hide was held of Helgot by Godebold,[49] Earl Roger's clerk and probably a chaplain in St. Michael's chapel in the earl's castle in Shrewsbury.[50] Earl Roger's overlordship was presumably forfeited by his son Earl Robert in 1102,[51] but Holt Preen probably continued, like Church Preen, to form part of the barony of Castle Holdgate, though perhaps not for as long.[52]

By 1194 Holt Preen belonged to Robert de Girros. Robert divided 'Preen Girros' by subinfeudating part of it, and *c.* 1220 he sold that part to Haughmond abbey with the obligation, perhaps imposed by Godebold, to pay 5*s.* a year to St. Michael's chapel in Shrewsbury castle.[53] The canons of Haughmond acknowledged their liability to pay the 5*s.* a year in 1462[54] and retained their interest in Holt Preen, probably never amounting to much more than a rent of 17*s.* a year in lieu of all services,[55] until the abbey's surrender in 1539.[56]

The 17*s.* rent acquired by Haughmond *c.* 1220 was that which had been due from Adam de Girros for the part of Holt Preen in which Robert de Girros had enfeoffed him. Adam's successor by 1255 was Henry de Girros (fl. 1247) who held two thirds of 'Little Preen'. About 1260 Henry sold his Holt Preen property to Roger Sprenchose,[57] and in 1377 it belonged to Fulk Sprenchose, lord of Plaish.[58] Nothing more is known of the Sprenchose estate in Holt Preen.

Evidently before *c.* 1220 Adam de Girros had alienated part of his portion of Holt Preen, charged with the 17*s.* a year due since Adam's own enfeoffment. In 1234 Peter the mason and his wife Maud sold 1 carucate (which seems to have included at least 20 a. of wood in 1255) in Holt Preen to the Templars of Lydley,[59] who then became responsible for the 17*s.* a year due to Haughmond. After the Templars' suppression their Holt Preen property passed to the Hospitallers of Dinmore who retained it until the dissolution of their order in England and Wales in 1540.[60]

In 1552 the Crown sold the former Hospitaller manor to Lord Clinton and Say and Henry Herdson.[61] By 1557 it belonged to Thomas Lodge, a London alderman, and his wife Anne, who then sold it to William Leighton[62] of Plaish. It descended with Plaish until 1655 or later.[63]

The Savery (or Sabery) family seems to have

38 Cf. Stackhouse Acton, *Castles and Old Mansions*, pl. facing p. 31; Bodl. MS. Top. Salop. c. 2, f. 401; Tipping, op. cit. 20.

39 *T.S.A.S.* xlviii, p. *iv*; but cf. Tipping, op. cit. 18, based on *Country Life*, 26 May 1917, 520.

40 S.R.O. 1848/SP15; S.P.L., SC14/12a (plan); *List of Bldgs. (All Stretton* [etc.]*)*, 27–8.

41 *Landscape Hist.* x. 15–24.

42 *V.C.H. Salop.* i. 343; Eyton, vi. 244; *Domesday Bk.: Salop.* ed. F. and C. Thorn (1986), n. 4.28.1.

43 P.R.O., C 142/457, no. 87; S.P.L., Deeds 17654–5.

44 W.S.L. 350/5/40, Cardington p. 11.

45 P.R.O., IR 29/29/54; S.R.O. 2079/XLIX. 12, 16; 4044/91, p. 7; S. Laflin, *The Preens of Cardington* (priv. print. Birm. 1989), 36–7 (copy in S.P.L.); idem, 'Fam. of Jas. and Priscilla Preen' (TS. 1992; copy in S.P.L.); above, this section (Chatwall); below, this section (Holt Preen).

46 S.R.O. 5001/3/1/3.

47 Inf. from Mr. and Mrs. R. F. Fildes; above, this section (Chatwall; Plaish); below, this section (the Holt).

48 W.S.L. 350/5/40, Cardington p. 5.

49 *V.C.H. Salop.* i. 337. For the descent of the rest of the Domesday man. of Preen, ibid. viii. 125–6.

50 *T.S.A.S.* lvi. 252–3.

51 *V.C.H. Salop.* iii. 10.

52 Cf. ibid. viii. 125 (and sources there cited); Eyton, vi. 225–6; *T.S.A.S.* lxx. 195.

53 *Cart. Haughmond*, p. 178; Eyton, vi. 224–5.

54 By then to Battlefield coll., owner of St. Mic.'s: *Cart. Haughmond*, pp. 71–2.

55 Ibid. p. 178.

56 *V.C.H. Salop.* ii. 68.

57 *Cart. Haughmond*, p. 178; Eyton, vi. 224–5; *Rot. Hund.* ii. 62.

58 Eyton, xi. 354–5.

59 *T.S.A.S.* 4th ser. i. 394; *Rot. Hund.* ii. 63.

60 *Cart. Haughmond*, p. 178; L. B. Larking, *Kts. Hospitallers in Eng.* (Camd. Soc. [1st ser.], lxv), 199; P.R.O., SC 6/Hen. VIII/7263, m. 18; 32 Hen. VIII, c. 24.

61 *Cal. Pat.* 1550–3, 365; cf. *V.C.H. Salop.* iv. 129.

62 P.R.O., CP 25/2/77/655/4 & 5 Phil. & Mary Mich. no. 11.

63 S.P.L., Deeds 17685, 17739; P.R.O., CP 25/2/343/10 Jas. I East. [no. 48]; CP 25/2/591/1655 Trin. [no. 15].

had an interest in Holt Preen by 1707[64] but was hard up,[65] and Samuel Edwards, a London merchant, was interested in the property as early as 1718 and bought the manor in 1729 from Charles Savery and his son Charles.[66] Edwards, of West Coppice (in Buildwas), died in 1738,[67] and the manor was presumably sold to pay his debts.[68]

By 1767 the manor belonged to Elizabeth Cressett (d. 1792) of Cound.[69] She was succeeded by her cousin Henry Cressett Pelham (d. 1803),[70] followed by his widow Jane[71] who had 424 a. in 1803.[72] By 1820 the estate, to which by 1843 was added Dayhouse, later Lower Dayhouse, farm (owned in 1803 by Thomas Corfield and in 1823 and 1830 by Thomas Jones, a Shrewsbury grocer),[73] belonged to their daughter Frances Thursby (d. 1852).[74] By 1879 it had passed to Arthur Sparrow[75] of Church Preen (d. 1898), whose son Cecil B. Sparrow (d. 1905) succeeded. His son Arthur (of age 1913, d.s.p. 1921) was said to be lord of Holt Preen manor in 1918, but the title has not been traced thereafter. Arthur Sparrow sold most of his Holt Preen and Church Preen estates in 1918, though the land around Church Preen Manor was retained, including 46 a. in Holt Preen, and in 1934 Arthur's uncle, A. B. H. Hanbury-Sparrow (d. 1936), was described as a principal landowner in the parish.[76]

It seems likely that the manor's chief house was *THE HOLT*. If so, it was separately owned by the mid 18th century for it belonged to Thomas Norris (d. 1753)[77] and remained in his family in the 1830s;[78] it was reckoned 131 a. in 1803.[79] Rowland Hunt added it to the Plaish estate before 1855.[80] The description of Hunt as lord of Holt Preen manor in 1851[81] presumably derives from a belief that the Holt had been its chief house. In 1921 Jesse Jones bought the Holt from Capt. S. H. Christy's trustees,[82] and it later passed through the Vaughan (of Plaish), Barbour, and Fildes families.[83]

The Holt (later Holt Farm) is a small stone house of the mid 17th century built on an **E** plan; the full-height gabled porch is the central feature of the south front which, though only *c.* 15 m. long, is impressive by its symmetry. There are two storeys and an attic. It has perhaps the earliest example in the county of a fully developed reception hall; the hall, with a central stack at the north end, may also have served, as in the 19th century, as a kitchen. The projecting bays are less than 2 m. wide internally; behind the western one were two service rooms, behind the eastern one an unheated parlour. It was probably *c.* 1800 that the parlour was given a fireplace and stairs and that other rooms were altered and refurbished.[84]

Between *c.* 1220 and 1255 the rest of Preen Girros, about a third of the manor, passed to Preen priory[85] (in Church Preen). Its later descent has not been traced.

In 1542 the Crown leased a farm and a close called Bowmans Hill, said to have belonged to Haughmond abbey, to Richard Lee for 17*s.* a year.[86] In the 20th century Bowman Hill farm formed part of the Holt Preen estate and later of the Plaish estate.[87] The house, north-west of the Holt, is an **L** plan, baffle-entry sandstone building, perhaps mid to late 17th-century but extensively remodelled *c.* 1800.[88]

The appropriated *RECTORY*, worth £13 6*s.* 8*d.* in 1291 and £20 in 1338,[89] belonged to the Templars of Lydley, later to the Hospitallers of Dinmore, and passed to the Crown[90] presumably in 1540.[91] Some, if not all, of the rectorial tithes were probably acquired by Giles Covert, the purchaser (in 1534) of Preen priory, or his son, also Giles (d. 1557),[92] for in 1560 the younger Giles's brother and sister-in-law Richard and Catherine Covert sold the tithes of Cardington, Broome, and Plaish, with their Church Preen estate, to Humphrey Dickens.[93]

The rectorial tithes were acquired by the Leightons of Plaish (purchasers of the advowson and Holt Preen manor in 1556–7) who owned them by 1591.[94] In 1670 the Leightons' successor Henry Goodricke sold what was described as the Cardington rectorial estate, i.e. the tithes

64 S.R.O. 3571/Rg/2, s.a. 1731, memo. of agreement (8 May 1707) appropriating seat in ch. to Upper Dayho., Holt Preen.
65 S.P.L., Deeds 6232, p. 2.
66 S.R.O. 4572/6/2/55, 57; P.R.O., CP 25/2/1191/3 Geo. II Hil. [no. 4].
67 *V.C.H. Salop.* iii. 294; *Hist. Parl., Commons,* 1715–54, ii. 5.
68 Cf. below, M. Wenlock, manors (Presthope); S.R.O. 4572/6/2/60.
69 S.R.O., q. sess. rec. box 260, reg. of gamekeepers 1742–79, 28 Nov. 1767; *V.C.H. Salop.* viii. 63.
70 S.R.O., q. sess. rec. parcel 261, reg. of gamekeepers 1799–1807, f. 5; *V.C.H. Salop.* viii. 63.
71 S.R.O., q. sess. rec. parcel 261, reg of gamekeepers 1799–1807, f. 110; Burke, *Land. Gent.* (1952), 2002.
72 S.R.O., 515/5, pp. 106–10.
73 Ibid. p. 104; *24th Rep. Com. Char.* H.C. 231, pp. 401, 412 (1831), xi.
74 *4th Rep. Com. Char.* H.C. 312, p. 268 (1820), v; P.R.O., IR 29/29/162; *V.C.H. Salop.* viii. 64.
75 *P.O. Dir. Salop.* (1879), 293; cf. *V.C.H. Salop.* iv. 211.
76 S.R.O. 4044/91, pp. 16–17; S.P.L., SC2/39; Burke, *Land. Gent.* (1952), 2367; *Kelly's Dir. Salop.* (1922), 55; (1934), 58.
77 M.I. in Cardington ch.
78 W.S.L. 350/5/40, Cardington p. 11.
79 S.R.O. 515/5, p. 105.
80 S.P.L., Deeds 17267.
81 S. Bagshaw, *Dir. Salop.* (1851), 524.
82 S.R.O. 3931/1/1.
83 S.R.O. 4654/5; inf. from Mr. and Mrs. R. F. Fildes.
84 *V.C.H. Salop.* v (forthcoming); W.S.L. 350/5/40, Cardington p. 11; *List of Bldgs. (All Stretton* [etc.]*)*, 3; Forrest, *Old Hos. of Wenlock*, pl. facing p. 49.
85 *Rot. Hund.* ii. 62. In 1590 one 'Geerse' was locally reputed to have been a benefactor of the priory: Sparrow, *Ch. Preen*, 88.
86 P.R.O., E 315/214, f. 177.
87 S.R.O. 4654/5; S.P.L., SC2/39.
88 *List of Bldgs. (All Stretton* [etc.]*)*, 2; inf. from Mr. Eric Mercer.
89 *Tax. Eccl.* (Rec. Com.), 167; Larking, *Hospitallers in Eng.* 199; below, church.
90 P.R.O., C 1/132/11; SC 6/Hen. VIII/7263, m. 18.
91 32 Hen. VIII, c. 24. Dinmore preceptory seems not to have been suppressed before 1535 (as implied in D. Knowles and R. N. Hadcock, *Med. Religious Hos.: Eng. and Wales* (1971), 300, 303) but to have been by then without resident religious, and the property let to lay people.
92 Cf. *T.S.A.S.* lxx. 191–3, 196.
93 P.R.O., CP 25/2/200/2 Eliz. I Hil. [no. 3]; *V.C.H. Salop.* viii. 126.
94 P.R.O., CP 25/2/202/33 & 34 Eliz. I Mich. [no. 20]; above, this section (Holt Preen; Plaish); below, church.

of Cardington, Broome, and Plaish, to Rowland Hunt with Plaish manor.[95] Hunt kept the Plaish tithes, which descended with the Plaish estate until they were merged with it in 1841,[96] but he evidently soon sold the others.[97]

In the 1840s, when the parish's impropriate rectorial tithes were variously owned, some were merged in the freeholds and the rest were commuted to £231 9*s*. 9*d*.[98]

ECONOMIC HISTORY. In 1086 there were 11½ ploughteams in the four manors that lay wholly or mainly in the medieval parish. In Cardington there were 5 *servi* and 1 team on the demesne, and 15 *villani* and a radman held 7 more teams. In Lydley two radmen had 2 teams. In Plaish there was 1 team on the demesne, and a *villanus* and a *servus* had ½ team. There was no team at Broome,[99] and most, if not all, of the arable in the Domesday manor of Preen lay in what was to become Church Preen.[1] There was enough land for 10 more teams: 8 at Cardington, already by 1086 the most extensive and valuable (40*s*.) of the four manors, and 2 at Broome.[2]

In 1086 Cardington had 2 leagues of wood, Lydley had wood for 30 swine,[3] and most of Preen's wood for 100 swine was probably in Holt Preen, eventually part of Cardington parish.[4] No wood was recorded at Broome or Plaish,[5] though it is uncertain whether the 'common lea' on the border of Plaish and Preen a century earlier[6] was open or wooded pasture.[7] Nevertheless most land north and east of the parish's principal watershed (just above the road from Church Stretton to Church Preen as far as Yell Bank) was probably then wooded, while most of the Domesday ploughteams worked south of that road. The parish's ample medieval woodland was probably extensively intercommoned,[8] and by the late 14th century there may have been inclosed coppices for growing underwood.[9] Along with many other surrounding townships Botvyle, Cardington, Chatwall, Enchmarsh, Willstone, Plaish, and Preen seem to have intercommoned Haywood (in Eaton-under-Heywood and Rushbury) as an addition to the valuable commoning which they enjoyed in their own manorial woods.[10]

After Auti's forfeiture of Lydley and Botwood manors *c*. 1090, Botwood forest extended across Botte (later Watling) Street into the area north of Comley and west of the Lawley.[11] Just north of that area the Templars established a preceptory, settling, as so often, in a country requiring clearance and offering opportunities for agricultural exploitation.[12] Before 1200 they had assarted 40 a. in Botwood[13] and they evidently strengthened their claim to at least a part of the wood in the following half century.[14] Haughmond abbey had also gained rights in Botwood since the 1160s, and in 1273 the abbey and the Templars agreed to intercommon there outside the pannage month.[15] Botwood was mentioned in court records as late as 1462, but whether then still as a wood or just as open common is unknown.[16] Further north the wood of Lydley was divided in 1222 between the Templars, who received just over two thirds, and the lord of Longnor.[17] The name Lydley Hayes suggests that East Hay and West Hay woods were there.[18] There was assarting in East Hay in the early 14th century, and later only the Hay or Haywood were mentioned.[19] In the 1790s Haywood Farm stood *c*. 800 m. north-east of Lydley Hayes Farm.[20]

The hillside woods of Caradoc ('Cordok'), Blackhurst, and the Lawley ('la lyth', 'Lalleigh', or 'Lalleth') belonged to Lydley and Cardington manor. References to Cardington's wood in the 14th and 15th centuries may have been to a wood on Cardington Hill. Willstone too had its own wood in the Middle Ages.[21]

The Templars attempted to claim 100 a. of wood in Chatwall, which in 1276 was adjudged to the lord of that part of Chatwall which was not the Templars'.[22] Some woodland in Chatwall, however, was in Langley manor.[23]

Plaish had its own wood or woods; in 1235 its Small wood had a few oaks,[24] and pigs were pannaged in the lord's wood in 1506–7.[25]

Holt Preen presumably comprised the largest part of Preen's wood for 100 swine in 1086.[26] In 1235 that wood, then called the wood of Preen Girros, was reported to be reasonably well stocked with oak and underwood, although it had formerly been much felled. The wood had few animals except those passing through.[27] Within the next 20 years the Templars felled 20 a.,[28] and by 1338 the Hospitallers had 100 a. of arable there.[29]

At least seven settlements had one or more

95 S.P.L., Deeds 17685; Keele Univ. Libr. (Archives), M72/36/3.
96 S.P.L., Deeds 17692; MS. 6741, pp. 3–5; P.R.O., IR 29/29/253.
97 S.R.O. 1011, box 172, incl. bk. p. 60; 5001/1/1/3; S.P.L., Deeds 17687, 17740.
98 P.R.O., IR 29/29/54, 65, 70, 137, 162, 253.
99 *V.C.H. Salop*. i. 322, 328, 342–3.
1 Ibid. 337; viii. 126; Eyton, vi. 221; below, this section.
2 *V.C.H. Salop*. i. 322, 343.
3 Cf. ibid. iv. 40.
4 Below, this section.
5 *V.C.H. Salop*. i. 322, 328, 342–3.
6 *T.S.A.S*. lvi. 31.
7 M. Gelling, *Place-Names in the Landscape* (1984), 198–207 (on the varying significance of 'leah' names).
8 Lydley and Cardington man. officials included a woodward: below, local govt.
9 S.R.O. 2557/15 (mention of 'lez coupies' and underwood sales).
10 P.R.O., C 1/808, no. 47; below, Eaton-under-Heywood.
11 *V.C.H. Salop*. viii. 98, 101; Eyton, vi. 244–5.
12 *Hist. Keele*, ed. C. Harrison (1986), 6.
13 Eyton, vi. 247.
14 *Rot. Hund*. ii. 84.
15 Eyton, vi. 247; *Cart. Haughmond*, p. 143.
16 S.R.O. 2557/18, 20.
17 *V.C.H. Salop*. viii. 111; *T.S.A.S*. 3rd ser. vii. 380.
18 S.R.O. 2557/2; P.R.O., E 358/18, m. 4.
19 S.R.O. 2557/15, 19–20.
20 At O.S. Nat. Grid SO 490 987: S.R.O. 3651, plan of Rob. Corbett's est. 1794.
21 S.R.O. 2557/2–3, 7–8, 15, 18, 20–1; S.P.L., MS. 6741, p. 29.
22 Eyton, v. 125; *V.C.H. Salop*. ii. 85.
23 *V.C.H. Salop*. viii. 141; below, this section.
24 *V.C.H. Salop*. i. 485.
25 S.P.L., Deeds 17743, ct. r.
26 *V.C.H. Salop*. i. 337; viii. 125; Eyton, vi. 221.
27 Eyton, vi. 225; *T.S.A.S*. 4th ser. i. 394.
28 Eyton, vi. 225–6.
29 Larking, *Hospitallers in Eng*. 199.

open fields, mostly south of the road from Church Stretton to Church Preen in a stretch of country 5½ km. by 1½ km. between Comley and Plaish.[30] Fields included 'le Woluefeld' in Comley;[31] the field of Enchmarsh,[32] possibly known as Butt field;[33] Clayhill, Crosshill, and the Thornes (near Netchley) in Cardington; and Washfurlong in Chatwall.[34] North of Plaish traces of ridge and furrow indicate former open-field land on the east-facing slopes of the Plaish brook valley, and there was probably more lying west of the hamlet and later taken into the park.[35] Most evidence, however, is from the late 16th and early 17th century, when much of the open arable land was inclosed.[36] Cardington village then had three fields, probably called Standill field, Wythibutt Stile, and Crow Hill field;[37] the last named[38] is possibly to be identified with the earlier Crosshill field and the contemporary 'field towards Willstone', while one of the others may be the contemporary 'field towards Gretton'.[39] Willstone probably had three open fields, the Lower field or field towards Cardington, Sheppards or Shipholders field, and the field towards Enchmarsh. There were also arable lands at the Heald and in 'le cross', possibly subdivisions of the other fields.[40] That other places then had single areas of open-field land is suggested by references to Enchmarsh field,[41] probably south-east of the hamlet;[42] to the common field of Broome; and to the common field of Chatwall,[43] south of Chatwall and Lower Chatwall.[44]

In 1185 the Templars' tenants held 17¾ virgates: between them the 33 half-virgaters and 5 quarter-virgaters also held 173½ a. of assarts. There were 10 virgates in Cardington, 3½ in Enchmarsh, 2¼ in Chatwall, and 2 in 'Botley'. The rental value of the virgate holdings varied widely from place to place. Each ½ virgate was worth 60*d.* in 'Botley', 48*d.* in Enchmarsh, 27½*d.* in Chatwall, and either 40*d.*, 36*d.*, or 24*d.* in Cardington.[45]

The Templars' demesne was at Lydley, and in the late 12th and earlier 13th century its upland economy may have been complemented by the knights' cereal-growing estates in Corve Dale. Nevertheless marl was dug there in the early 13th century[46] and by the early 14th century oats, and to a lesser extent wheat, were grown, together with some peas, vetches, and rye.[47] In 1302, the year following the area's disafforestation, the Templars were granted free warren on their Lydley demesnes.[48] The surrounding woods and commons enabled them to keep a large flock whose wool provided an important cash crop; it comprised 376 sheep and lambs in 1308.

In 1308 the Lydley demesne also had *c.* 50 pigs, and its draught animals were 26 oxen and 12 horses.[49] About 1324 the demesne lands were let with 240 sheep, 22 oxen, and 22 cows.[50] The balance of the estate was probably typical of the area, with sheep and pigs well represented in a mixed farming regime.[51] Sheep remained particularly important throughout the parish and beyond the Middle Ages[52] and the Washing brook mentioned in 1541[53] was perhaps Plaish brook.

The parish may have suffered considerably in the agricultural setbacks of the early 14th century: the value of Cardington tithes was alleged to have fallen from £17 6*s.* 8*d.* in 1291 and £20 (the appropriated rectory) in 1338 to £5 in 1341, owing largely to the destruction of corn, to sheep murrain, and to the departure of 20 tenants.[54]

As the number of tenants fell in the later Middle Ages holdings were concentrated in fewer hands. By 1583, of the 22 customary messuages in Lydley and Cardington, the same number of virgate-based holdings as were listed under Cardington in 1185, one man held seven, one held three, and three others two. There were also four 'customary cottages'. Each customary tenant paid a small sum, usually about ten per cent of his rent, for the commutation of labour services.[55] Elsewhere in the parish the picture was similar. In 1635 the largest holding was 104 a., and there were others of 82 a. and 73 a.; three holdings were *c.* 50 a., nine were *c.* 20–*c.* 30 a., and there were ten of *c.* 12 a.; there were also a few cottagers.[56]

Besides entry fines, fare fees were recorded occasionally for customary holdings in Lydley and Cardington manor between the 15th and 18th centuries.[57] In the late 18th century copyholders' heriots were generally commuted to ½ or ⅔ their value. Estates were then mostly copyhold, descending according to the usual rules of inheritance, with no widow's freebench; entry fines amounted to a year's chief rent.[58] At

30 Fig. 6.
31 S.R.O. 2557/10.
32 Ibid. /2.
33 *T.S.A.S.* 2nd ser. iv. 315.
34 S.R.O. 2557/9–10; cf. S.R.O. 165/153, for location of the Thornes.
35 *Landscape Hist.* x. 21; P.R.O., IR 29/29/253; IR 30/29/253, fields 62, 83–4; below, this section.
36 Below, this section.
37 S.R.O. 567/1/229, ff. [14v., 17]; H.W.R.O.(H.), HD 2/14/15.
38 Cf. P.R.O., IR 29/29/65; IR 30/29/65, fields 164, 184; S.R.O., incl. award C 4/36, map of exchanges.
39 S.R.O. 567/1/255; 567, box 11, deed 10 Oct. 1618; H.W.R.O.(H.), HD 2/14/16.
40 S.R.O. 567/1/103; 1359, box 29, abstr. of title of Mr. Russell and deed 7 May 1700; S.P.L., MS. 6741, p. 31.
41 S.R.O. 567/1/110.
42 As field boundaries suggest.
43 S.R.O. 567/1/46.
44 S.R.O. 5001/1/2/8.
45 *Records of Templars in Eng.* 37–9; cf. *V.C.H. Salop.* ii. 85–6, on which the next 2 paras. are based.
46 *Rolls of Justices in Eyre, 1221–2* (Selden Soc. lix), pp. 447–8.
47 S.P.L., Deeds 7531; P.R.O., E 142/68, f. 7.
48 *Cartulary of Shrews. Abbey*, ed. U. Rees (1975), ii, p. 250; *Cal. Chart. R.* 1300–26, 33.
49 P.R.O., E 358/18, m. 4.
50 Cf. S.R.O. 567, box 10, deeds 8 Nov. [1323 x 1326], 29 Oct. 1324.
51 Cf. *Cal. Pat.* 1327–30, 79, 85, for a local grazier.
52 Below, this section.
53 P.R.O., C 116/214, Holt Preen ct. r. 1541.
54 *Tax. Eccl.* 167; above, manors (rectory); *Inq. Non.* (Rec. Com.), 187.
55 S.R.O. 567/1/217.
56 Ibid. /1/229; 567, box 11, deed 2 June 1632.
57 S.R.O. 165/11, 28, 153, 157; 567/1/255, 323; Loton Hall MSS., ct. r. 1481–3.
58 J. Plymley, *Gen. View of Agric. of Salop.* (1803), 93; S.P.L., MS. 6741, p. 9; S.R.O. 3288/2/8, loose 'Precedent for copyhold bill, customs, etc.'

the abolition of the tenure in 1926[59] there were still 25 copyhold tenants, and the last compensation for extinguishment of manorial incidents was paid to the lord in 1937.[60]

Chattel leases (99 years) for lives were granted on the Plaish estate by the mid 16th century.[61] In Lydley and Cardington manor 21-year leases were perhaps usual in the 1570s and 1580s,[62] chattel leases (80 years) for three lives in the late 1580s,[63] and freehold leases for three lives in the early 17th century.[64] Chattel leases (99 years) for three lives were introduced *c.* 1618,[65] and that remained the usual tenure in the manor at the end of the 17th century.[66] In Plaish in the late 17th and early 18th century leases for one and seven years were granted.[67] In the 1730s several chattel leases (99 years) for three lives were granted, heavy entry fines[68] probably indicating the lord's need of capital. There were several tenancies at will from 1777.[69]

Most recorded inclosure of open fields in the parish occurred piecemeal in the 17th century, and there are glimpses of the social tensions involved in the operation of the old open-field system at that time. In 1612, for instance, three men were fined 6*d.* each for breaching Enchmarsh's ringfield hedge while 15 men were fined 12*d.* each for tearing up Cardington's ringfield hedge.[70] Chatwall's open-field land had been completely inclosed by 1751, probably by Richard Corfield (d. 1680) or his son Richard (d. 1710), both of whom had enlarged and improved their Chatwall estate.[71] Nevertheless individual strips did survive around Cardington, Enchmarsh, and Willstone until the late 18th or early 19th century.[72]

Common woods and wastes were progressively reduced between the late Middle Ages and the early 19th century, partly to create parks. In 1445 Lee park belonged to the lord of Plaish; it was close to the Plaish–Gretton manorial boundary, probably near the later Ley Hill Farm.[73] About 1577 an enlarged park was created for the newly rebuilt Plaish Hall[74] which stood in its south-east corner; the park had a central lodge and included deer among its stock.[75] In 1671 it was used as horse pasture: 52 owners kept 119 animals there, over 100 being yearlings or 2-year-olds.[76] The park was split into farms in 1675–6,[77] when extensive felling took place and carpenters worked in the park squaring the timber and producing shingles and sawn 'panels and bottoms'.[78] In the later 1670s 'the park', presumably Park farm, was used to pasture sheep and cattle.[79] There may also have been a short-lived park at Chatwall in the later 17th and early 18th century,[80] and several 'park' field names adjoined Yewtree House in Lydley Hayes in the 18th century.[81]

It was probably in the 17th century that, as in neighbouring parishes like Longnor and Woolstaston,[82] much of the remaining woodland was cleared. Certainly it was believed in the early 19th century that it was in Charles I's reign that the trees on Caer Caradoc 'fell victim to the axe of the peasantry'.[83] In 1635, however, 300 a. of the Lydley and Cardington commons were well planted with oak, ash, and elm, and some tenants were setting saplings in plantations of 33 a., 23 a. (two plantations, of which at least one was of oak), and 4 a.[84] Much common pasture long survived the felling of the trees on it. Belonging to the manor of Lydley and Cardington in the early 17th century[85] were the commons, woods, and coppices of Caradoc and Lawley hills, Earls wood (probably near Comley and Botvyle),[86] Blackhurst (or Black Meres)[87], Hoar Edge (on which in 1757 lay Causeway wood),[88] Comley moor, Willstone green, Chatwall lawn, Cardington hills, Cardington wood, Cardington moor, the Netchleys, Broadstones moor, the Battlestones, Evenwood, the Pikes (on Cardington hill),[89] and Swynneyhurst. The lord and, under the bailiff's supervision, his tenants enjoyed all estovers and had unlimited common pasture 'for all manner of cattle' over at least 2,000 a.[90]

Although the Corbetts were considering inclosure and improvement as early as 1628,[91] extensive commons and wastes survived in Lydley and Cardington manor until 1822, when 1,879 a. (including *c.* 300 a. in Church Stretton parish) were inclosed and allotted. The main awards were 940 a. to the Ven. Joseph Corbett, which included 167 a. in respect of his rights as lord of the manor; 385 a. to the vicar, of which 33 a. were for his glebe and 352 a. in lieu of his tithes from the manor; 104 a. to Richard Barker's testamentary trustees; 68 a. to Samuel Wilding of All Stretton; and 62 a. to Peter Bourne. There were 28 other allotments all under 50 a., and many exchanges were made.[92]

59 Under 12 & 13 Geo. V, c. 16, ss. 128, 191; 15 & 16 Geo. V, c. 4.
60 S.R.O. 3288/2/8, table at end of bk.
61 S.P.L., Deeds 17424, 17814.
62 S.R.O. 567, box 11, deeds 9 June 1571, 3 Dec. 1573, 1 Dec. 1586.
63 Ibid. deed 3 July 1588; 567/2C/16, sched. of leases.
64 Ibid. /2C/16, sched. of leases. 65 Ibid.; ibid. /3/10.
66 S.R.O. 567, box 31, partic. of real est. of Sir U. Corbett.
67 S.P.L., Deeds 17719, 17728–9.
68 Ibid. 17682–3, 17689–91.
69 Ibid. 17755–7, 17759; S.P.L., MS. 4850.
70 S.R.O. 567/1/110; for ring hedges see G. Elliott, 'Field Systems in NW. Eng.' *Studies in Field Systems in Brit. Isles*, ed. A. R. H. Baker and R. A. Butlin (1973), 47–9.
71 S.R.O. 5001/1/2/8; above, manors.
72 S.R.O., incl. award C 4/36, map of exchanges; 3651, plans of Rob. Corbett's est. 1794. 73 S.R.O. 840/2/3/29.
74 C. Saxton, *Map of Salop.* (1577). For bounds cf. ibid.; P.R.O., IR 29/29/253; IR 30/29/253; S.P.L., Deeds 17746–7; for the Hall see above, manors.
75 S.P.L., Deeds 17726, 17746–7; N.L.W., Pitchford Hall 1561, 1598.
76 S.P.L., Deeds 17684.
77 Ibid. 17659, 17692, 17746–7.
78 Ibid. 17668–72, 17721.
79 Ibid. 17671; 17724, corresp. 30 June 1679.
80 S.R.O. 4597/32; 4825; above, manors (Chatwall).
81 N.L.W., MS. 18453C, fields F 84–6, 88.
82 *V.C.H. Salop.* viii. 107, 170.
83 W.S.L. 350/5/40, Cardington p. 6.
84 S.R.O. 567/1/229, ff. [3, 6–7, 22].
85 Ibid. /2C/11.
86 Ibid. /1/152.
87 Ibid. /2A/9b.
88 Ibid. /1/64.
89 P.R.O., IR 29/29/65; IR 30/29/65, fields 308–9.
90 S.R.O. 567/1/229, f. [22].
91 S.R.O. 567, box 29, deed 16 Oct. 1628.
92 Under 54 Geo. III, c. 189 (Local and Personal): S.R.O., incl. award C 4/36; S.R.O. 4835/98; fig. 6.

Before 1615 wood and waste near Chatwall lay in Langley manor. It was called 'Harlithe' or 'Pynleshai',[93] later Pingleys Heys. In 1615 Humphrey Lee, lord of Langley, bought most of it (*c.* 220 a.) from Henry Leighton, who was allowed to cut and coal the timber and underwood there for 12 years. Intercommoning of the area by Chatwall and Langley ended, but some properties in Broome had common rights there until 1799 when they were bought up by Lee's successor Sir Edward Smythe.[94]

In the 1560s Holt Preen wood, said to comprise 500 a., probably extended over most of the parish east of the Holt. It abutted the common woods of Hughley and Kenley, and the three woods seem to have been intercommoned. About then, soon after his purchase of the manor and perhaps when inclosure was beginning in Hughley and Kenley, William Leighton inclosed, subdivided, and let out *c.* 100 a. from Holt Preen wood. About 1610 Hughley men, instigated by Francis Wolryche who had recently bought Hughley manor, broke Leighton's inclosures claiming that the wood had formerly been commoned by Hughley.[95] In 1639 Harcourt Leighton renewed the attack on Holt Preen wood when he inclosed, with the Holt Preen commoners' consent, 55 of the remaining 272 a. The wood then seems to have been typical wood–pasture, with widely spaced oak and ash standards among grassland and holly and gorse scrub. Leighton felled the timber in his inclosure, *c.* 100 oaks and ashes 90 years old. He apparently intended to make a coppice, wood for charcoal having already been sold from Holt Preen to Kenley forge in the 1620s. Hughley men soon broke the inclosure, but a subsequent lawsuit established Leighton's rights.[96] Samuel Edwards, lord of Holt Preen 1729–38, inclosed all or most of the remaining common.[97] Common east of the road to Kenley in 1762[98] had been inclosed by 1843.[99]

Pastoral farming prevailed in the parish in the early 17th century, and some holdings seem to have been entirely pastoral.[1] In 1621 people from Comley were presented for washing sheep skins in Long pool, presumably the pool north of Battlestones.[2] As earlier, the extensive commons facilitated the keeping of sheep, goats, pigs, cattle, and horses, not only by providing open grazing land but also because browse, especially holly, could be cut in winter.[3] The local economy had a pastoral bias, cattle being particularly important.[4] Such a bias gave rise to small rural trades based on leather and wool: there were glovers among the Blackhurst cottagers[5] and in the 1660s at least one weaver and one dyer in Cardington; the dyer perhaps built a fulling mill at Harley.[6]

Of arable crops, hemp and flax were widely grown in the parish by the early 17th century: 17 people were presented for watering hemp and flax in Moor brook in 1610, and 14 in 1612. A watering pit near the brook was mentioned in 1630.[7] Flax and hemp were probably processed locally although the two spinning wheels owned by Edward Griffiths of Enchmarsh in 1693 might have been used to work wool.[8] Flax and hemp were probably still grown, although perhaps less widely, in the 18th and 19th centuries;[9] in 1814 the vicar claimed tithe of 1*d.* an acre on flax and 5*s.* an acre on hemp.[10]

On the Plaish estate great improvements were made in 1828 by Thomas Eaton, the new tenant of Hall and Plaish farms. Rowland Hunt's agent William Story contrasted the local farmers ('oafs') with Eaton. Sheaves farm was 'nearly in the state Adam would have found it', whereas Eaton had introduced barley and turnips, milked 20 cows, bred horses, and had so many cattle and sheep that he had to rent extra pasture. Moreover he had better equipment than Story had seen since leaving Holderness (Yorks. E.R.).[11]

By 1843 in most of the parish a four-course rotation was followed and turnips were grown where suitable, 200–300 a. of them in the later 19th century.[12] Sheep had long been the commonest livestock,[13] and *c.* 1840 both the Lawley and Caer Caradoc were described as high sheep pastures.[14] When sheep were sold at East Wall (in Rushbury) in 1853 the auctioneer made special mention of their having been bred on Cardington and Willstone hills.[15] In 1891 there were over 7,700 sheep in the parish.[16] Cows were the other main livestock, kept for milk and rearing.[17] In the early and mid 19th century *c.* 1,000 a. of the lower land were usually under the plough,[18] but the amount of arable fell markedly in the late 19th and early 20th century. In fact

93 So in the 1280s (P.R.O., C 143/6, no. 10), 'Pymleies heys' in the 1630s (C 142/477, no. 189). The 1274 'Tywleshey' (*Cal. Inq. Misc.* i, p. 290) is presumably a misreading.

94 S.R.O. 1514/111, 297 (giving bounds of Pingleys Heys), 299; *V.C.H. Salop.* viii. 141 (corr. below, Corrigenda).

95 S.R.O. 2922/1/1/1–2; *V.C.H. Salop.* viii. 93; below, Hughley, econ. hist.

96 S.R.O. 2922/1/1/2–17.

97 S.P.L., Deeds 6232, p. 6; cf. above, manors (Holt Preen).

98 S.R.O. 283/1–2.

99 P.R.O., IR 29/29/162; IR 30/29/162.

1 Ibid.; S.R.O. 567/1/229.

2 S.R.O. 567/1/110; fig. 6.

3 S.R.O. 567/1/46–63, 83–127 *passim.*

4 H.W.R.O.(H.), Heref. dioc. rec., invs. of Eliz. Harris, 1691; Edw. Harris, 1692; Ric. Yates, 1692; Edw. Griffiths, 1692; Wm. Pinches, 1693; Elinor Whittley, 1698; Fra. Whicke, 1700.

5 S.R.O. 567, box 11, deed 2 June 1632.

6 *V.C.H. Salop.* viii. 89; S.R.O. 3571/P/5/1.

7 S.R.O. 567/1/106, 109, 126; see also /1/100, 112.

8 H.W.R.O.(H.), Heref. dioc. rec., inv. of Edw. Griffiths 1692.

9 S.R.O. 567/1/262, 336 (mentioning hemp butts); 5001/1/2/8; N.L.W., MS. 18453C, field names on pp. 5, 7–8, 10.

10 S.R.O. 1011, box 172, draft abstr. of claims to rt. of common in Cardington and Ch. Stretton, f. [2].

11 S.P.L., Deeds 19508; W.S.L. 350/5/40, Cardington p. 12.

12 S.R.O. 3651/T/II, Cardington, rep. on agreement for commutation, p. 6; P.R.O., MAF 68/3880, Salop. no. 222; MAF 68/4945, no. 222.

13 H.W.R.O.(H.), Heref. dioc. rec., invs. of Ric. Smythe, 1700; Rog. Davies, 1700; Ric. Flavell, 1701; Wm. Blakeway, 1703; Ric. Hooper, 1705; Daniel Bee, 1705.

14 W.S.L. 350/5/40, Cardington pp. 6, 10.

15 *Eddowes's Jnl.* 16 Mar. 1853, p. 3.

16 P.R.O., MAF 68/1340, no. 6.

17 Table II; S.R.O. 3651/T/II, Cardington, rep. on agreement for commutation, p. 6; *Kelly's Dir. Salop.* (1909–41), for cow keepers.

18 Sources cited in Table II; P.R.O., HO 67/12/56.

Table II

Cardington: Land use, livestock, and crops

		1867	*1891*	*1938*	*1965*
Percentage of	grassland	69	76	87	82
	arable	31	24	13	18
Percentage of	cattle	16	10	43	28
	sheep	77	85	52	61
	pigs	7	5	5	11
Percentage of	wheat	41	30	27	30
	barley	32	36	11	58
	oats	27	34	60	8
	mixed corn & rye	0	0	2	3
Percentage of agricultural land growing roots and vegetables		9	8	3	2

Sources: P.R.O., MAF 68/143, no. 15; /1340, no. 6; /3880, Salop. no. 222; /4945, no. 222.

after 1700 the parish's economy remained predominantly pastoral. Cattle increased in importance in the 20th century, and barley had become the chief arable crop by the 1960s.[19]

There was a mill at Cardington by the 1150s,[20] and in the late 14th and early 15th century there were two.[21] The Upper mill stood south-east of Cardington village in 1757.[22] Later usually known simply as Cardington mill, it probably closed in the mid 19th century.[23]

The Templars' demesne mill at Lydley in the late 12th century[24] was mentioned *c.* 1346[25] and perhaps in 1529.[26] It presumably stood on the stream at Lydley Hayes,[27] on which also stood Hollyhurst, or Comley, mill, mentioned in 1529. Milling at the Templars' mill probably ceased in the early 19th century.[28] A mill place and mill pool were noted at Nether Comley in 1583.[29] The Templars built a new mill at Botvyle *c.* 1190,[30] but its exact location is unknown.

There was a water mill at Plaish in the 16th century.[31] Mentioned in the 17th century[32] and repaired in the early 18th,[33] the mill, which stood 200 m. south-east of the Holt, had been demolished by 1843.[34]

Holy mill, recorded in 1516, stood on Hughley brook in Holt Preen. It was probably the mill said in 1803 to have an overshot wheel which occasionally drove two pairs of stones. Milling ended in the later 19th century.[35]

Stone from Hoar Edge, Causeway wood, and Chatwall may have been used at *Viroconium*,[36] and a quarry apparently marked the 10th-century bounds of Plaish.[37] Stone was quarried in Lydley in the 14th century[38] and on Blackhurst in the 17th,[39] and by the 19th century many quarries were worked in the parish.[40]

Bricks were made near Penkridge Hall before 1628 and perhaps later.[41]

There was a clay pit in Plaish in the 15th century.[42] Steatite (soapstone) and quartz from the parish were used by the pottery industries, locally and in Staffordshire, in the 18th and 19th centuries.[43]

There was some prospecting for minerals in the parish in the mid 18th century. Several people were 'trying for coal' on Cardington moor in 1757,[44] and in 1764 the ironmaster John Wilkinson took a 21-year lease from Sir Richard Corbett to prospect for copper, lead, and tin on Lydley and Cardington commons.[45] In the earlier 19th century copper was mined on Cardington hill.[46]

In the 1850s Cardington village had two shops and several tradesmen: two stonemasons, two carpenters, a blacksmith, a wheelwright, a tailor, a shoemaker, and a butcher. In addition Comley had a wheelwright and Enchmarsh a blacksmith.[47] During the First World War the number of tradesmen declined, and thereafter none resided outside Cardington village.[48]

LOCAL GOVERNMENT. Rolls of the court known after the earlier 16th century as the court of Lydley and Cardington survive for various years from the 14th to the 18th century,[49] and

19 P.R.O., HO 67/12/56; Table II.
20 Eyton, v. 122.
21 S.R.O. 2557/14, 19.
22 S.R.O. 567/1/64; /1/337; /3/10, 1 Apr. 1635; cf. S.R.O. 165/31, 159–60.
23 S.R.O. 567/3/101–2; mill not mentioned in trade dir.
24 Larking, *Hospitallers in Eng.* 40.
25 S.R.O. 2557/4.
26 S.R.O. 567, box 30, ministers' accts., Lydley man.
27 SA 551.
28 S.R.O. 516/1/217; 567, box 29, deed 10 Feb. 1726/7; box 30, ministers' accts., Lydley man.; 1011, box 172, draft abstr. of claims to rt. of common 1814.
29 S.R.O. 516/1/217.
30 Eyton, vi. 240; *Pipe R.* 1190 (P.R.S. N.S. i), 127.
31 S.P.L., Deeds 17741, ct. r.; P.R.O., C 116/214, Holt Preen ct. r. of 1541.
32 S.P.L., Deeds 17663.
33 Ibid. 17711–12, 17726; cf. ibid. 17618.
34 P.R.O., IR 29/29/253; IR 30/29/253, field 72.
35 S.R.O. 515/5, p. 107; 1224, box 342, Prior Gosnell's reg. f. 32.
36 *T.S.A.S.* lv. 43–4.
37 Ibid. lvi. 31; *Landscape Hist.* x. 19, 23 n.; above, this article, intro.
38 P.R.O., E 358/18, m. 4; S.P.L., Deeds 7531.
39 S.R.O. 567/1/208.
40 S.R.O., incl. award C 4/36.
41 S.R.O. 567, box 29, deed 16 Oct. 1628 (field name); names of fields B 48–9, 53–4 in N.L.W., MS. 18453C and of corresponding fields on plan (1794) of Rob. Corbett's est. in S.R.O. 3651.
42 S.P.L., Deeds 17743, ct. r. 1412.
43 Below, Caughley, econ. hist.; T. Gregory, *Salop. Gaz.* (1824), 79; C. Hulbert, *Hist. and Descr. of Salop.* ii (1837), 197; P.R.O., IR 29/29/253; IR 30/29/253, fields 24, 27; S.R.O. 840, box 117, Notes on Manors and Livings 1812, p. 1.
44 S.R.O. 567/1/66.
45 S.R.O. 802, box 29, deed 24 June 1764.
46 O.S. Map 1", sheet LXI. SW. (1833 edn.).
47 *P.O. Dir. Salop.* (1856), 27–8.
48 *Kelly's Dir. Salop.* (1885–1941).
49 S.R.O. 567/1/46–67; 2557/1–41; Loton Hall MSS., ct. r. 1481–2.

there is an unbroken series of court books 1681–1937,[50] besides other, less formal, court papers and records.[51]

Some medieval court records distinguish between great and little courts, showing that the great court was held twice yearly in March, April, or May and in September, October, or November.[52] The little court may have been held monthly, bi-monthly, or even less regularly. In 1338 the pleas and perquisites of court were worth £1;[53] then, as later, much of the business concerned regulation of the manor's extensive woods and commons, and the manor had a woodward as well as a bailiff.[54] In 1481, besides offences against the commons and open fields, there were cases of pound breach, malting, and bloodshed; two merchet fines of 2*s*. were paid.[55]

In the early 17th century most business at the twice yearly great court concerned the agricultural round or transfer of copyholds, although there were occasional presentments of cottage building, the sale of bad meat, and breaches of the assize of ale (1600); of assault, eavesdropping, and keeping inmates (1609); of barratry and keeping a hound (1610); and of drunkenness (1612). In terms of the numbers of presentments the court was most active in the mid 17th century, and in the 1650s there were complaints against an oppressive manorial bailiff, Richard Flavell, who on one occasion had a man's ears cropped for his having cropped the 'wash oak' at Comley. By the early 18th century the court did little but regulate cottage building and encroachments and transfer copyholds; the last surviving estreat roll dates from 1794.[56] In the 1930s the court dealt with the lord's compensation for the abolition of copyhold tenure.

Between the 1760s and the 1790s the court met at John Russell's house, west of the Lawley, gaining it the name Court House;[57] in 1815 the Ven. Joseph Corbett claimed to have fitted it up for the purpose.[58]

There was a pound at the west end of Cardington village and one at Comley.[59]

Rolls of Plaish manor court survive from 1376 to the earlier 17th century, with some concentrations in the mid 15th and early 16th centuries. Some estreats survive from 1620–37. Where distinguished, courts were usually described as courts baron, though in 1420–1, 1509, and 1517 so-called great courts were held.[60] Occasionally in the late 16th and early 17th century tenants of the Leightons in Broome and Chatwall were separately presented.[61]

In 1421–2 Broome presented at the great court of the baron of Castle Holdgate.[62]

Richard, earl of Cornwall and king of the Romans (d. 1272), withdrew the suit of Holt Preen from Condover hundred to his liberty of Castle Holdgate.[63] Records of Holt Preen manor court survive from the 1540s and 1550s, 1598, the 1620s and 1630s, and 1708. Courts were mainly concerned with offences in Preen wood.[64] In 1557 and *c*. 1740 it was claimed that Holt Preen had a court leet as well as court baron.[65]

There were four parish constables in 1848 and usually six in the 1850s and 1860s, though in 1856 nine were appointed. In the years before the general abolition of parish constables in 1895 Cardington usually had two,[66] though the parish had been allocated one of the county constabulary's first police officers in 1840.[67]

The parish had two overseers in the later 17th century[68] and later. In the 1740s and 1750s the parish subscribed to Cleobury Mortimer workhouse, where it seems usually to have had two or three paupers.[69] Poor-rate expenditure rose from £58 15*s*. in 1756 to £143 8*s*. 11*d*. in 1783 and £160 10*s*. 8*d*. in 1791. In the later 18th century poor children were apprenticed, and the parish farmed its poor to neighbouring parishes, though in the end that 'did not answer'. In the 1790s the parish built a poor-house, the £40 debt on which was repaid in 1799;[70] it probably stood south-west of the village.[71] There were five inmates in 1802–3, three of them aged over 60 and disabled. About 1818 some 28 adults received permanent out-relief and *c*. 30 occasional relief.[72] Expenditure on the poor in the post-war depression probably peaked in 1816 at £494 6*s*. In the 1820s expenditure was usually *c*. £350, and in the early 1830s *c*. £300 or less.[73] About 1830 those receiving out-relief were considered eligible also to receive gifts of coal at Christmas from a parish charity. The cottages owned by parish charities[74] may also have allowed the parish to house paupers at low rents. A salaried

50 S.R.O. 3288/2/1–8; 3651/1/1–11.
51 S.R.O. 567/1/68–206, 255–388; 2557, box 4.
52 But once in June (1505) and once in Jan. (1533): S.R.O. 567/1/46–63; 2557/1–40.
53 Larking, *Hospitallers in Eng.* 199.
54 e.g. S.R.O. 2557/3, 5.
55 Loton Hall MSS., ct. r.
56 S.R.O. 567/1/9, 88, 105, 112, 204, 207–15.
57 Ibid. /1/73–8; 1011, box 172, draft abstr. of claims to rt. of common (mention of 'old ct. ho.'). The Ct. Ho. was later Lawley Fm., the name Ct. Ho. passing to the former Yewtree Ho.: cf. S.R.O. 3651, plan of Rob. Corbett's est. 1794; O.S. Map 6", SO 49 NE. (1954 edn.).
58 *Gent. Mag.* xci (2), 421.
59 S.R.O. 567/1/349; 3651, map of Lydley and Cardington man., pencilled addn.; P.R.O., IR 29/29/65; IR 30/29/65, field 168.
60 S.P.L., Deeds 17741–3; P.R.O., C 104/22, pt. 1, estreats; C 116/215–17.
61 P.R.O., C 116/215–16.
62 S.P.L., MS. 2, f. 146.
63 *Rot. Hund.* ii. 91; cf. below, Holdgate, local govt.
64 P.R.O., C 116/214-18; C 104/22, pt. 1; ibid. SC 2/197/113.
65 P.R.O., CP 25/2/77/655/4 & 5 Phil. & Mary Mich. no. 11; S.R.O. 4572/6/2/56; cf. *T.S.A.S.* lxx. 195 (ibid. 200 nn. 107–8, cites the foregoing sources incorrectly).
66 S.R.O. 3571/Ve/1–2; q. sess. min. bk. 1889–98, 9 Apr. 1895.
67 S.R.O., q. sess. Const. Cttee. rep. bk. 1839–53, p. 77.
68 S.R.O. 3571/P/5/1–2.
69 S.R.O. 2519/8–13; 3571/P/10a/1–6; /P/10b/1; /P/10c/1--12; /P/10d/1; S.P.L., MS. 6741, p. 11.
70 S.R.O. 3571/Ve/1 *passim*; /Ce/D/7; S.P.L., MS. 6741, pp. 11, 13; below, charities.
71 P.R.O., IR 29/29/65; IR 30/29/65, field 174.
72 *Poor Law Abstract*, H.C. 98, pp. 416–17 (1803–4), xiii; H.C. 82, pp. 370–1 (1818), xix.
73 *Poor Rate Returns*, H.C. 556, suppl. app. p. 142 (1822), v; H.C. 334, p. 177 (1825), iv; H.C. 219, p. 165 (1830–1), xi; H.C. 444, p. 160 (1835), xlvii.
74 Below, charities.

assistant overseer, perhaps the first such, was appointed in 1857.[75]

The vestry formed a burial board in 1876 and next year a garden adjoining the churchyard was bought as a new burial ground.[76]

The parish was in Church Stretton poor-law union 1836–1930,[77] Church Stretton highway district 1863–95,[78] Church Stretton rural sanitary district 1872–94, Church Stretton rural district 1894–1934, Atcham R.D. 1934–74, and Shrewsbury and Atcham borough from 1974.[79]

CHURCH. Parts of the church may be 12th-century.[80]

In 1185 Cardington was evidently a rectory in the patronage of the Templars, though the parson, Arnulf, rendered 3 marks a year to them for the church and 12*d*. *pro fraternitate*.[81] Bishop Vere (1186–98) appropriated the church[82] to the Templars of Lydley who evidently became patrons of the vicarage. When a vicarage was ordained is unknown, but there was one by 1291[83] and Ralph de Turneye, instituted 1334, is the first vicar known by name.[84] The king presented to the living in 1308 following the Templars' suppression that year.[85] When, in 1324, the Hospitallers confirmed the earl of Arundel as owner of the former Templar estate in Lydley and Cardington, they reserved the church and all its rights, with the priest's house.[86] Thereafter, until their suppression in 1536, the Hospitallers presented to the living.[87]

In 1553 the Crown sold the advowson to George Cotton and Thomas Reve, London speculators,[88] and in 1556 Thomas Lodge, a London alderman, and his wife sold it to William Leighton of Plaish,[89] who presented to the living in 1566.[90] In 1624 and 1633, when Harcourt Leighton was outlawed for debt, the Crown presented.[91] By the 1630s the Leightons were exercising the patronage again.[92] In 1670 Rowland Hunt bought the advowson and Plaish,[93] which then descended together until 1934.[94] On at least one occasion before 1819 a turn was sold.[95] In 1934, when the Plaish estate was sold, the advowson was bought by R. G. Barker, a Shrewsbury timber merchant, but it was reunited with the estate and manor of Plaish (in the Warlows' hands) 1937–9. In 1939 it passed to Frederick V. Corfield (kt. 1972), soon to become owner of the Chatwall estate.[96] From 1969 the benefice was left vacant and the patronage suspended, the rector of Hope Bowdler with Eaton-under-Heywood and Rushbury being appointed priest in charge in 1971. From 1980 Cardington was held in plurality with those benefices, with residence at Hope Bowdler Rectory; their patrons, including Sir Frederick Corfield for Cardington, were to present jointly.[97]

In 1291 the vicarage was worth £4,[98] but when Philip Halghton resigned it in 1418 he was given a pension of £4 6*s*. 8*d*., 3 a. of glebe with meadow, and the hay tithe of 'Wysmedewe'.[99] In 1535 the vicarage was worth £6 2*s*. 4*d*. net.[1] There were 30 a. of glebe in 1589, and 52½ a. in 1607, comprising *c*. 14 pieces of land, mainly grassland, scattered around the parish.[2] Then or earlier there was a tithe barn.[3]

In 1793 the vicar collected a quarter of his tithes and let the rest.[4] In Lydley and Cardington manor *c*. 1814 he tithed a wide range of produce in kind: wool and lambs, the agistment of unprofitable cattle, pigs and geese, orchards, roots, clover and grass seeds, coppice wood, and honey; two eggs were due on a hen, three on a cock. Moduses were 1*d*. a cow, 6*d*. a calf, 1*d*. a colt, the statutory 5*s*. an acre on hemp and flax, and a hay modus from each farm. The vicar also claimed smoke penny, garden penny, and 4*d*. from each tradesman.[5] In the townships outside that manor, to judge from statements *c*. 1842, the vicar had similar tithe claims.[6] At least 35 a. of his 51-a. glebe were let in 1814,[7] and in 1817 the living was worth £200.[8] The vicar's tithes in Lydley and Cardington manor were extinguished in 1822 when its commons were inclosed: he was allotted 33½ a. in respect of his glebe and 352 a. on Cardington and Caradoc hills in lieu of all his tithes from Botvyle, Cardington, Chatwall, Comley, Enchmarsh, Lydley Hayes, and Willstone townships.[9] During the earlier 1840s his tithes in the other manors, including

75 S.R.O. 3571/Ve/1, 18 Mar. 1857.

76 Ibid. /BB/17–18; /Ve/2, 16 June and 15 Sept. 1876, 27 Apr. and 13 July 1877.

77 V. J. Walsh, 'Admin. of Poor Laws in Salop. 1820–55' (Pennsylvania Univ. Ph.D. thesis, 1970), 150; *Kelly's Dir. Salop.* (1929), 57.

78 *Lond. Gaz.* 27 Mar. 1863, p. 1767; S.R.O., S.C.C. Local Govt., etc., Cttee. min. bk. 1894–1903, p. 29.

79 *Rural District Councillors Electn. Order, 1894* (Local Govt. Bd. order no. 31847); *V.C.H. Salop.* ii. 212, 217; iii. 178 and sources cited ibid. 169 n. 29.

80 Below, this section.

81 Lees, *Rec. of Templars in Eng.* pp. cvii, 40; Eyton, v. 123.

82 *Reg Swinfield* (C.S.), 396.

83 *Tax. Eccl.* (Rec. Com.), 167.

84 S.R.O. 2557/6; Eyton, v. 128.

85 Eyton, v. 128; *Cal. Pat.* 1307–13, 57; *V.C.H. Salop.* ii. 86.

86 S.R.O. 567, box 9, deed 29 Oct. 1324.

87 Knowles and Hadcock, *Med. Religious Hos.* 290; P.R.O., SC 6/Hen. VIII/7262, m. 17d.; Eyton, v. 128; *Reg. Stanway* (C.S.), 186; *Reg. Mayew* (C.S.), 186; *Reg. Bothe* (C.S.), 448.

88 *Cal. Pat.* 1547–53, 295, 297.

89 P.R.O., CP 25/2/654/3 & 4 Phil. & Mary Mich. no. 47.

90 *Dioc. of Heref. Institutions (1539–1900)*, ed. A. T. Bannister (Heref. 1923), 17.

91 Ibid. 30; *T.S.A.S.* 3rd ser. v. 363; S.P.L., MS. 6741, p. 41; above, manors (Plaish).

92 *T.S.A.S.* 3rd ser. v. 363; 4th ser. ii. 57.

93 S.P.L., Deeds 17685, 17739; above, manors.

94 Bannister, *Heref. Institutions*, 59–60, 71, 73–4, 109, 140, 142; Hulbert, *Hist. Salop.* ii. 197.

95 S.P.L., MS. 6741, p. 17.

96 Heref. Dioc. Regy., reg. 1926–38, p. 452; 1938–53, pp. 54, 61, 273, 544; 1953–68, pp. 86, 234; S.R.O. 5001/2/1–2; *Heref. Dioc. Yr. Bk.* (1985), 42; *Who's Who* (1988), 378; above, manors.

97 Heref. Dioc. Regy., reg. 1969– (in use), pp. 15, 73, 354–5.

98 *Tax. Eccl.* 167.

99 *Reg. Lacy* (C.S.), 114.

1 *Valor Eccl.* (Rec. Com.), iii. 210.

2 H.W.R.O.(H.), HD 2/14/15–16.

3 S.R.O. 567, box 11, deeds 1 June 1608, 10 Oct. 1618.

4 H.W.R.O.(H.), HD 9, 'Notitia', f. 14.

5 S.R.O. 1011, box 172, draft abstr. of claims to rt. of common in Cardington and Ch. Stretton, f. [2]; above, econ. hist.

6 P.R.O., IR 29/29/54, 65, 70, 137, 162, 253; S.R.O. 3573/T/3B.

7 S.P.L., MS. 6741, p. 15.

8 H.W.R.O.(H.), HD 9, 'Notitia', f. 14.

9 S.R.O., incl. award C 4/36; P.R.O., IR 29/29/65, 70.

Frodesley and Langley, were commuted to a total of £47 a year; in Frodesley and Langley the rent charges in lieu of the vicar's tithe (principally of hay) were apportioned to the land then meadow, pasture, or wood while the impropriate (principally grain) tithes were apportioned to the arable land.[10] In the mid 19th century the living was worth *c.* £290 but by 1900 only £210.[11] The greater part of the glebe, 376 a. in the late 19th century, comprised Middle Hill, North Hill, and the Gutter farms on Cardington Hill. Most of it was sold in 1920, only 29 a. remaining in 1929.[12]

In 1716 the vicarage house, probably near the church,[13] was in good repair.[14] By the late 18th century it was considered small, badly situated, and 'infirm from its antiquity', and John Witts, vicar 1777–1816, lived in the mansion at Lydley Hayes.[15] Early in W. J. Hughes's long incumbency (1819–65) he and his father built a new vicarage:[16] of coursed grey sandstone rubble, the south-west or garden front is of five bays, the central three projecting slightly and surmounted by a triangular pediment. A coach house and stable block stand north-east.[17]

In 1185 Arnulf, the parson, may have employed Inard, a married priest, as curate.[18] There was a 'literate' deacon *c.* 1300,[19] but no pre-Reformation vicar is known to have graduated. In 1524 a Cambridge student, Richard Farley, was instituted; he resigned *c.* 1526 and William Hall became vicar.[20] Hall (d. 1560) was employing a stipendiary priest in 1542.[21] Before the Reformation there was a light in the church endowed with lands at Botvyle.[22]

In 1542 there was a chapel at Plaish dedicated to St. Margaret;[23] it probably stood in Chapel Yard just south-west of the Hall,[24] and its ruins survived until the early 19th century.[25] Allusion was made about then to a former chapel at Penkridge[26] not otherwise known.

William Leighton (d. 1607) of Plaish left land to endow church repairs and £50 for the making of his tomb in the chancel.[27] Roger Maunsell (d. 1651) also endowed church adornments and repair.[28]

The first known graduate vicar was Adam Griffiths (1610–?1612), who probably came straight from university.[29] His successor Edward Wotton, also a graduate, employed a curate in 1623 but in 1624 was deprived for adultery.[30] John Cuffyn was 'put in by the ruling powers' in 1657–8 but soon replaced by Daniel Bee (d. 1705), vicar for 47 years;[31] in 1668 Bee preached twice each Sunday.[32] Thomas Corfield, member of a prominent local family, was vicar 1705–7.[33] His successor William Painter (1708–?24) conducted two Sunday services and communion was celebrated four times a year.[34] During the last years of their long incumbencies Francis Southern (1730–77), who left money for an annual New Year's day sermon, and John Witts (1777–1816) employed curates;[35] from 1809 Witts was also Archdeacon Corbett's curate at Church Preen.[36] In 1793 there were two Sunday services (one with a sermon), monthly communion, and a service each holy day. On average *c.* 200 attended church, the farmers being better attenders than the poor. There were 44 pews in the nave, 8 in the gallery, and 3 in the chancel; men and women sat on different sides of the church 'and different families have sittings in the same and different pews'. There were then usually *c.* 40 communicants, whereas *c.* 200 communicated at Easter; the communion offertory, *c.* £3 a year, was given to the poor at Christmas and Easter.[37] Curates served the cure 1816–19 as the vicar, George Hunt, the patron's brother, was non-resident.[38]

On Census Sunday 1851 morning service was attended by 69 adults and 26 children, the afternoon one by 8 adults and 18 children. None of the 170 seats was free,[39] but by 1867 all 212 seats were free.[40] Soon after the restoration of 1867–8 the psalm singers and band were replaced by a choir and harmonium.[41] In the late 19th and early 20th century there were usually two Sunday services and *c.* 80 Easter communicants.[42] In 1889 a lay reader led mission services at Comley, and in 1910–11 the vicar conducted weekly and occasional services around the parish.[43]

The church of *ST. JAMES*, so dedicated by 1542,[44] has a chancel, nave, west tower, and

10 P.R.O., IR 29/29/54, 70, 137, 162, 253; S.R.O. 3573/T/3B.

11 P.R.O., HO 129/354, no. 21; *Rep. Com. Eccl. Revenues* [67], pp. 434–5, H.C. (1835), xxii; *P.O. Dir. Salop.* (1856–79); *Kelly's Dir. Salop.* (1885–1900).

12 *Kelly's Dir. Salop.* (1891), 283; (1922), 55; (1929), 57; S.R.O. 3571/Cl/Gl/30–1. *Return of Glebe Land, 1887*, H.C. 307, p. 58 (1887), lxiv, records the glebe as 352 a., i.e. the 1822 allotment in lieu of tithe.

13 S.P.L., MS. 6741, p. 19.

14 H.W.R.O.(H.), HD 5/14/1/10.

15 S.R.O. 4791/1/8, p. 114; S.P.L., MS. 6741, p. 15; Dudich, *Contributions to Hist. of Geol. Mapping*, 391–2; above, manors.

16 Bannister, *Heref. Institutions*, 142, 178; S.R.O. 3571/Rg/6, p. 91; S.P.L., MS. 6741, pp. 17, 19.

17 *List of Bldgs. (All Stretton* [etc.]*)*, 15.

18 Eyton, v. 123.

19 Loton Hall MSS., vol. of 23 deeds, p. 5 (deed of *c.* 1300).

20 *Reg. Bothe*, 338–9; cf. *Alum. Cantab. to 1751*, ii. 121.

21 *T.S.A.S.* vi. 115–16, 130.

22 *Cal. Pat.* 1569–72, p. 345.

23 *T.S.A.S.* vi. 115–16.

24 S.P.L., Deeds 17673; 17746–7, field A12; P.R.O., IR 29/29/253; IR 30/29/253, field 66.

25 *Woolhope Trans.* 1886–9, 238.

26 S.P.L., MS. 6741, p. 15.

27 *T.S.A.S.* ii. 291–2.

28 Ibid. iv. 317–18; below, charities.

29 *Alum. Oxon. 1500–1714*, ii. 607; *T.S.A.S.* 3rd ser. viii. 44–5.

30 *T.S.A.S.* 3rd ser. viii. 45; *Cal. S.P. Dom.* 1603–25, 160.

31 W.S.L. 350/3/40, Cardington p. 18.

32 H.W.R.O., HD 7, 1668/410.

33 S.R.O. 4597/32; Bannister, *Heref. Institutions*, 59–60; Corfield, *Corfields*, 52, 54; above, manors (Chatwall).

34 Bannister, op. cit. 60, 71; H.W.R.O.(H.), HD 5/14/1/10.

35 Bannister, op. cit. 74, 109, 140; S.R.O. 3571/Rg/2, note on back endpaper; *24th Rep. Com. Char.* H.C. 231, p. 401 (1831), xi.

36 Sparrow, *Ch. Preen*, 27.

37 S.P.L., MS. 6865, pp. 75–6; cf. G. W. O. Addleshaw and F. Etchells, *Archit. Setting of Anglican Worship* (1948), 90.

38 W.S.L. 350/3/40, Cardington pp. 18, 20; S.R.O. 3571/Rg/2, note on back endpaper.

39 P.R.O., HO 129/354, no. 21.

40 *Rep. of Heref. Dioc. Ch. Bldg. Soc., Archd. of Salop 1869* (Ludlow, 1870; copy in S.P.L.), 19.

41 S.R.O. 3571/ChW/1, s.a. 1849–50, 1852, 1866, 1870.

42 Ibid. /Reg, p. 15 and *passim*; /Ce/Vis (1909).

43 Ibid. /Ce/Vis (1910–11); *Ch. Cal. Dioc. Heref.* (1890), 139.

44 *T.S.A.S.* vi. 115–16.

south porch and is mostly built of coursed rubble.[45] The eastern part of the nave is probably early 12th-century and one window and a blocked doorway survive in each side wall. The south doorway may have been enlarged in the later 12th century. Late in the 12th century the nave was extended west and new north and south doorways were made in the extension; the north doorway re-uses what is probably an older tympanum reversed. A Norman tub font with arcaded decoration was perhaps turned out in the 1820s.[46] In the 13th century a west tower and a long chancel, both externally as wide as the nave, were added. The chancel has plain single- and two-light windows in the side walls and a much restored triple lancet in the east wall. In the 14th century three two-light windows were inserted in the nave, one on the north side, two on the south. In the 15th or early 16th century an upper stage and battlements were added to the tower. Of similar date are the nave and chancel roofs.

The present porch and south door are of 1639 and 1648.[47] In 1685 the pulpit and 'reading pew' on the north side were said to be poorly lit.[48] In 1703 Maunsell's charity[49] was spent on a new window in the south wall of the nave west of the porch.[50] A west gallery was inserted in 1741–2.[51] There was a dormer window on the south side of the east end of the nave in the late 18th century.[52]

The chancel was modestly restored in 1863,[53] and the porch received attention *c.* 1865.[54] In 1867–8 the church was restored to a scheme by Henry Curzon of London. Little structural work was necessary, but the church was refitted and reseated throughout and generally made good, some windows being renewed. Individuals' and townships' names and initials carved on the old pews were incorporated in the new benches. The west gallery was probably removed then, as was a stone wall or screen between nave and chancel; the screen, said in 1857 to be 'almost of recent erection', had had a tall round-headed central arch and smaller side openings.[55] The tower was restored in 1882,[56] a reredos with Minton tiles introduced in 1885, a new clock fitted in 1889, and a new tower arch screen introduced in 1894.[57]

In 1553 the church had three bells and a silver chalice and paten.[58] New bells were cast in 1626, 1630 or 1639, and 1740; the oldest one survives with another of 1752 and two of 1887.[59] A silver chalice and cover paten were acquired *c.* 1700.[60]

The registers are mainly complete from 1598.[61]

NONCONFORMITY. There were three protestant dissenters in 1676, apparently all members of one 'Anabaptist' family.[62] In 1716 there were said to be a papist at Chatwall and an Independent at Broome.[63]

Meeting houses were licensed at Cardington in 1817 and 1828 and at Enchmarsh in 1831, but there was said to be none in the parish in 1851.[64] Between the later 1830s and the 1860s the Enchmarsh society, with a membership of 12 in 1860 which doubled in the later 1860s, was the largest of the parish's Primitive Methodist societies; a meeting place was registered in 1861. Meetings, camps, and revivals were also held at Blackhurst, Cardington, and Dayhouse.[65] A short-lived (1862–6) society at Cardington ceased when turned out of its meeting place, but in 1869 the Enchmarsh society opened a brick chapel at the north end of Cardington village and became known as the Cardington society. It had 24 members in 1872,[66] the year the chapel was registered for marriages[67] and probably the zenith of Methodism in the parish.[68] The Blackhurst society ceased in 1906. In 1912 the Cardington society had 12 members, and there were then perhaps three or four nonconformist families in the parish.[69] The chapel was sold in 1951.[70]

EDUCATION. William Pool kept school in 1676,[71] George Lowe and John Ketley in 1694, Thomas Langford in 1701, and Francis Southern in 1716, 1719, and 1734.[72]

Under the will (proved in 1721) of Serjeant William Hall, of London, trustees built and

45 For descr. see Cranage, ii. 77–9; St. Deiniol's Libr., Hawarden, Sir Steph. Glynne's ch. notes, xcvii, ff. 83–4; Pevsner, *Salop.* 93–4. Mr. Eric Mercer provided comments on the ch.

46 Bodl. MS. Top. Salop. c. 2, f. 163; S.P.L., MS. 6741, pp. 17, 21.

47 Cranage, ii. 78.

48 H.W.R.O.(H.), HD 7, faculty petition (perh. not proceeded with) 16 Sept. 1685. 49 Above, this section.

50 *T.S.A.S.* iv. 317; S.P.L., J. H. Smith colln. no. 40.

51 S.R.O. 3489/1–2; 3571/Fa/int/2/1–2.

52 S.P.L., MS. 372, vol. i, f. 36; MS. 6741, p. 23; B.L. Add. MS. 21010, f. 22.

53 S.R.O. 3571/Ve/1, 11 May 1863; Cranage, ii. 79.

54 *Salopian Shreds & Patches*, v. 74.

55 S.R.O. 3571/Fa/Rest/1/1, 4–5; *Rep. of Heref. Dioc. Ch. Bldg. Soc., Archd. of Salop 1869*; *Salopian Shreds & Patches*, v. 74; *Ch. Cal. Dioc. Heref.* (1870), 136; St. Deiniol's Libr., Glynne's ch. notes, xcvii, f. 83; A. J. C. Hare, *Salop.* (1898), 89–90.

56 *Salopian Shreds & Patches*, v. 74.

57 *Ch. Cal. Dioc. Heref.* (1886), 138; (1890), 139; (1895), 143.

58 *T.S.A.S.* 2nd ser. xii. 308, 326.

59 H. B. Walters, *Ch. Bells of Salop.* (Oswestry, 1915), 85.

60 D. L. Arkwright and B. W. Bourne, *Ch. Plate Archd. Ludlow* (Shrews. 1961), 15.

61 S.R.O. 3571/Rg/1–9; regs. at ch.; cf. H.W.R.O.(H.), bp.'s transcripts from 1660. 62 *Compton Census*, ed. Whiteman, 259.

63 H.W.R.O.(H.), HD 5/14/1/10.

64 Heref. Dioc. Regy., reg. 1791–1821, p. 183; 1822–42, p. 161; *Orders of Q. Sess.* iii. 271; P.R.O., HO 129/354, no. 21.

65 S.R.O. 2138/48–9; 3219/3; O.N.S. (Birkdale), Worship Reg. no. 12939.

66 S.R.O. 1242, box 12, abstr. of title (1877) of Job Wall to freehold messuage in Cardington, p. 6; 3212/5/1, p. 12; 3219/1 (3 Sept. 1866, 7 Dec. 1868, 7 June, 6 Sept. 1869), 3, 71; O.N.S. (Birkdale), Worship Reg. no. 19353.

67 *Lond. Gaz.* 29 Mar. 1872, p. 1685.

68 Membership declined from 1872: S.R.O. 3219/3.

69 Ibid. /4, s.a. 1906; /5, s.a. 1912; 3571/Ce/Vis (1904, 1912).

70 S.R.O. 3212/5/2–9.

71 R. Hume, 'Changing Patterns of Educ. Devt. in Salop. 1660–1833' (Keele Univ. Ph.D. (Educ.) thesis, 1982), 311. This section (a longer version of which is in S.R.O. 3763) was written *c.* 1982.

72 H.W.R.O.(H.), HD 5/14/1/10; HD 5/15, Cardington; HD 7, chwdns.' presentments 5–7 Nov. 1694 (refs. provided by Dr. Hume); *Woolhope Trans.* xxxiv. 135–6.

endowed a free school, opened in 1723 for pupils aged 4–14 years. The two storeyed school, three bays of brick with sandstone details, stood at the churchyard edge. Each pupil paid 1*s*. admission fee and a yearly 'coal shilling'. The master, paid £12 a year in 1793, supervised his pupils in church and taught the catechism, reading, writing, and arithmetic.[73] In 1819 there were 25–30 pupils, only those who could read the psalter being admitted.[74]

From *c*. 1783 children of the Corbetts' tenants could attend Longnor charity school,[75] and by 1793 a Sunday school was held in church in warm weather.[76] In 1814 John Russell left £5 a year towards the Sunday school,[77] which had *c*. 30 pupils in 1819.[78] He also left £10 a year for a schoolmistress to teach 12 poor girls to read, knit, and sew;[79] the endowments were later transferred to the free school.[80]

In the early 1830s there were probably 50–60 pupils at the free school, 12 girls at Russell's school, and 35 fee-paying pupils at three other day schools, one of which was perhaps in Holt Preen near Hughley brook. The free school and Russell's school sent pupils to the Sunday school and they made up the 32 children usually at morning service *c*. 1851.[81]

The free school building was condemned in 1871[82] and in 1876 Cardington C.E. Free school was built opposite; schoolroom and classroom accommodated 120 pupils, later reduced to 100.[83] Government grant was earned by 1877.[84] Inadequate staffing periodically limited the school's efficiency,[85] but in the 1890s retention of pupils in the upper standards was commended.[86] Attendance, however, was often poor,[87] the classroom was small,[88] and the cold stuffy building was improved only gradually.[89] Gardening was taught from 1915 and senior pupils attended Church Stretton woodwork or domestic science centres from 1936.[90] Liverpool evacuees were accommodated 1939–42.[91] When senior pupils left for Church Stretton Modern school in 1948 the school became a C.E. primary school,[92] aided from 1955.[93] The roll was 58 in 1922, 37 in 1975, and 18 in 1981, when 16 pupils transferred to Rushbury C.E. (Controlled) Primary school, thus in effect closing the school.[94]

County-council classes in stock management (1898-1902) and poultry keeping (1899-1901) were well attended.[95]

CHARITIES FOR THE POOR. By will proved 1608 William Leighton of Plaish left pieces of land called Church Land which he had bought *c*. 1595 from William Tipper and Robert Dawe, speculators in concealed lands; the income was to be divided equally between the poor and church repairs.[96] Those pieces were evidently the Church Estate[97] scattered in relics of the open fields of Enchmarsh and Willstone: in 1817, during the inclosure of Lydley and Cardington, the parish exchanged them with the Ven. Joseph Corbett for *c*. 15 a. lying together along the way from Cardington to Cardington Hill[98] and eventually known as the Moor farm.[99] From the 17th century the rent (£28 a year by 1838) was divided between the church and the poor;[1] in 1830 the poor received money and coal at Christmas, and the estate also included cottages, mainly occupied by paupers. The charity, half for the poor and half for church purposes, was combined with Roger Maunsell's charity in 1895.

Roger Maunsell (d. 1651)[2] left 26*s*. 8*d*. a year charged on land in Stanton Long: for the first three years of each septennium it was to provide bread for six people on Sunday, men one week and women the next, for the next three years sacramental bread and wine, and in the seventh year an adornment of the church. The charity was used thus in 1830. In 1895 it was combined with the Chapel Lands charity, 3/7 of Maunsell's legacy to be used for the poor, 4/7 for church purposes. In 1975 the combined charities' income was £221.

About 1700 Dinah Roberts left £1 6*s*. a year charged on a farm at Willstone for weekly bread doles in the parishes of Cardington and St. Julian's, Shrewsbury,[3] in alternate years. In 1975 income was £1 a year.

Cardington had an interest in the charity of Sir Richard Corbett (d. 1774) for clothing children, still given in the 1860s.[4]

Francis Southern (d. 1777), vicar, left the interest on £32 10*s*. for bread to be given to widows or old men when they attended divine worship. In 1814

73 *24th Rep. Com. Char.* H.C. 231, pp. 398–400 (1831), ix; S.C.C. *Salop. Char. for Elem. Educ.* (1906), 12; S.R.O. 2519/1; 3489/4–5; S.P.L., MS. 6741, p. 13.
74 *Digest Educ. Poor*, H.C. 224, p. 747 (1819), ix (2).
75 *V.C.H. Salop*. viii. 114–15.
76 S.P.L., MS 6741, p. 13.
77 *Salop. Char. for Elem. Educ.* 12–13.
78 *Digest Educ. Poor*, 747.
79 *Salop. Char. for Elem. Educ.* 12–13.
80 *Kelly's Dir. Salop*. (1885), 819.
81 Cf. *24th Rep. Com. Char.* 400; *Educ. Enq. Abstr.* H.C. 62, p. 771 (1835), xlii; P.R.O., HO 129/354, no. 21; O.S. Map 1/2,500, Salop. LVII. 1 (1883 edn.).
82 *Salop. Char. for Elem. Educ.* 12.
83 P.R.O., ED 7/102, ff. 134–5; S.R.O. 3571/Sch/Fa, corresp., estimates, etc.; 3571/Sch/LB/2, note at beginning of index; *Kelly's Dir. Salop*. (1885), 819.
84 S.R.O. 3571/Sch/LB/1, pp. 1, 126, 136, 171.
85 Ibid. pp. 12, 22, 56, 280; /2, pp. 4, 20, 32–3, 52–3, 114, 124, 127–8, 152–3, 162.
86 Ibid. /1, p. 234.
87 See e.g. ibid. pp. 23, 123, 183; /2, pp. 24, 117, 124; /3, p. 194.
88 Ibid. /1, pp. 171–3, 183–5.
89 Ibid. pp. 214, 227, 231; /2, pp. 132–3, 260; /3, p. 250; *S.C.C. Mins. (Educ.)* 1954–5, 120.
90 S.R.O. 3571/Sch/LB/2, pp. 138–9; /3, pp. 105, 107.
91 Ibid. /3, pp. 132, 138, 148.
92 Ibid. pp. 187, 194–5; *S.C.C. Mins. (Educ.)* 1949–50, 18.
93 *S.C.C. Mins. (Educ.)* 1953–4, 172; 1954–5, 128.
94 S.R.O. 3571/Sch/LB/2, p. 229; /3, p. 292; /4, Dec. 1981–Jan. 1982; *Shropshire Star*, 23 Dec. 1981, p. 9.
95 *S.C.C. Mins.* Intermediate Educ. Cttee. reps. 1897–1902.
96 *T.S.A.S.* ii. 292; for Tipper and Dawe see *An Essex Tribute: Essays presented to F. G. Emmison*, ed. K. Neale (1987), 153, 158–61.
97 Rest of section based on *24th Rep. Com. Char.* H.C. 231, pp. 400–2 (1831), xi; *Review of Local Chars.* (S.C.C. 1975), 43; S.C.C. Ch. Exec.'s Dept., chars. index.
98 Cf. S.R.O., incl. award C 4/36, pp. 32–4 and map of lands exchanged.
99 S.R.O. 3571/Cy/C/2.
1 S.R.O. 19/2/1, f. 78.
2 M.I. in ch.
3 *T.S.A.S.* x. 201.
4 *V.C.H. Salop*. viii. 110, 115.

the legacy was used to buy a cottage at the east end of the village; the parish put paupers in it and the churchwardens then spent £1 6s. a year on the Sunday bread doles. The charity had two cottages in 1929,5 and in 1975 its income was £104.

In 1786 interest on a stock of £45 was paid to the poor, but in 1799 the parish used the stock (apart from £5 lost) to repay £40 borrowed to build a poorhouse.[6]

Anne Tipton (d. 1788)[7] left £1 10s. a year charged on the Lower Day House property to be given weekly in bread to twelve poor. In 1975 income was £2.

John Russell (d. 1814),[8] of Enchmarsh, left the interest on £570 for educational and church purposes and for bread on four feast days and woollen gowns at Christmas for six widows and six girls. By 1905 gowns were no longer given. That year part of the stock was assigned to a separate educational charity;[9] the income from Russell's eleemosynary legacy was £6 in 1975.

Capt. S. H. Christy (d. 1914), of Plaish, left £2,500, the interest to be divided between four widows of Cardington and neighbouring parishes.[10] In 1975 income was £118.

HOPE BOWDLER

COMPRISING the manors and townships of Hope Bowdler, Chelmick, and Ragdon, Hope Bowdler parish (1,730 a., 700 ha.)[11] lies 3 km. east-south-east of Little Stretton, mainly on the south-facing slopes of the south-western end of Ape Dale. On the west and north the boundary, defined by *c.* 1600, runs along the foot of Ragleth hill (in Little Stretton), over the crest of Hazler hill, along the foot of Helmeth hill, and around the back of Hope Bowdler hill. It was marked across Hazler by a ditch, and in the Cwms below Hope Bowdler hill by Cowbatch (perhaps a corruption of Cwmbatch) cross, gone before 1622.[12] Elsewhere the boundary follows field edges and streams. Its course up the east side of Chelmick valley and north of Soudley (in Eaton-under-Heywood) may have been defined in the earlier 13th century.[13]

The civil parish was slightly enlarged in 1967, when Dryhill Farm and *c.* 24 a. (*c.* 10 ha.) were transferred from Church Stretton urban district and C.P.,[14] and again in 1987 when Stone House farm and adjoining fields at Soudley were transferred from Eaton-under-Heywood C.P.[15]

Hazler and Hope Bowdler hills (the latter an upland mass rising to three distinct crowns) are among the Uriconian volcanic outcrops which are a prominent feature of Shropshire's central uplands and variously consist of tuffs, basalt, andesites, and dacites. The rest of the parish lies upon Ordovician flags, siltstones, and sandstones.[16] Small streams rising in the parish drain south or south-east, some down short steep valleys or 'batches'. Notable are Rag batch south of Ragdon, the Chelmick valley, and Hope batch (presumably the How batch of 1616) which gave access from east of Hope Bowdler village to Hope Bowdler hill.[17]

The principal road through the parish is that from Church Stretton, via Hope gate (mentioned 1601)[18] on the western parish boundary and Hope Bowdler village, to Wall under Heywood (in Rushbury) and Much Wenlock; it was turnpiked in 1765 with a toll gate at Hope gate[19] and disturnpiked in 1875.[20] From it, in Hope Bowdler village, a road branches south to Ticklerton. Some ancient routes survived in the 20th century as footpaths, notably that from Chelmick to Acton Scott, mentioned in 1616.[21] The road running north-east from Hope gate, called the Cwms lane in 1622,[22] was probably that called Bentley lane in 1769.[23]

A circular enclosure[24] and traces of fields above the modern limit of cultivation,[25] all on Hope Bowdler hill, are probably prehistoric.

'Hope' describes the small upland valley enclosed between Hope Bowdler and Hazler hills to the north and west and the highest parts of Haywood common (in Eaton-under-Heywood) to the south-east. There are many such hopes in south Shropshire and before 1066 the vill was distinguished (presumably by the name of an otherwise unrecorded Saxon) as Fordritishope. Probably during the 12th century it was renamed Hope Bollers or Buthlers from the family name (Boullers) of the lords of the honor of Montgomery.[26]

Chelmick, 'Ceolmund's dairy farm',[27] was a separate manor in the 11th century; it had a berewick[28] whose whereabouts are unknown. Ragdon's status is less certain, but it was prob-

5 *Kelly's Dir. Salop.* (1929), 57.
6 Cf. above, local govt.
7 S.R.O. 3571/Rg/3, bur. 11 Aug. 1788.
8 Ibid. /Rg/6, p. 2 no. 10.
9 S.C.C. *Salop. Char. for Elem. Educ.* (1906), 13.
10 *Kelly's Dir. Salop.* (1929), 57.
11 O.S. *Area Bk.* (1885). This article was written in 1991. Messrs. A. B. Dakers and P. Morgan are thanked for inf. and access to records.
12 *T.S.A.S.* xlix. 250; *Ch. Stretton*, ed. C. W. Campbell-Hyslop and E. S. Cobbold, ii (1904), 195; S.P.L., Deeds 2599, ct. r. of 1623; fig. 7. S.R.O., incl. award C 4/36, marks the cross site erroneously; it is at O.S. Nat. Grid SO 472 942.
13 Eyton, v. 116; xi. 350.
14 *Salop (No.2) Order 1966* (Stat. Instr. 1966, no. 1529); *V.C.H. Salop.* ii. 235–6; S.R.O., DA 19/701/6, map 38.
15 *S. Salop. (Pars.) Order 1987* (Stat. Instr. 1987, no. 496).
16 *V.C.H. Salop.* iv. 11–12; Geol. Surv. Map 1", drift, sheet 166 (1967 edn.).
17 H.W.R.O. (H.), HD 2/14/28.
18 Campbell-Hyslop and Cobbold, *Ch. Stretton*, ii. 195.
19 5 Geo. III, c. 86; A. Dakers, *Fordritishope: Hist. of a Salop. Par.* (Ragdon, 1986), 67–70; P.R.O., IR 29/29/165; IR 30/29/165, field 24.
20 Ann. Turnpike Acts Continuance Act, 1873, 36 & 37 Vic. c. 90.
21 H.W.R.O.(H.), HD 2/14/28.
22 *T.S.A.S.* xlix. 250.
23 S.R.O., QR 70/4. Cf. Campbell-Hyslop and Cobbold, *Ch. Stretton*, ii. 195, for location of 'Bentle's green'.
24 SA 4089.
25 Below, econ. hist.
26 *P.N. Salop.* (E.P.N.S.), i. 156–7; below, manors.
27 *P.N. Salop.* i. 75.
28 Below, manors.

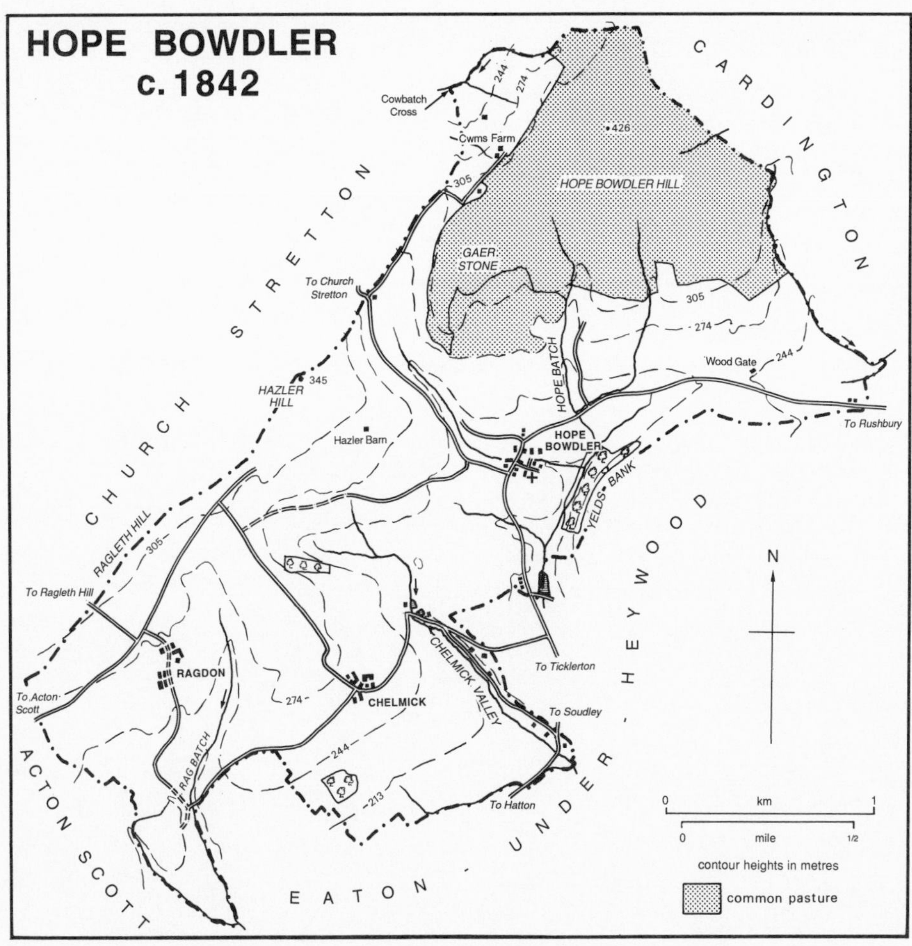

Fig. 7

ably subsumed under Hope Bowdler in 1086.[29] It shares the first element of its name (perhaps ME. *ragge,* 'mass of coarse stone') with Ragleth hill to the north-west[30] but the hill is in Church Stretton[31] and there is no evidence that Ragdon commoned it.[32]

In 1086 there were 2 *villani*, 4 *servi*, and 2 bondwomen in Hope Bowdler manor, and 9 *villani* at Chelmick.[33] Nine people paid subsidy in 1327.[34] In 1672 hearth tax was paid on 12 houses in Hope Bowdler and 11 in Chelmick and Ragdon,[35] and in 1676 there were 80 adults in the parish.[36] By 1811 the villages had grown little, if at all: Hope Bowdler township had 101 people in 17 houses, and Chelmick and Ragdon 71 in 15.[37] The population, however, had started to rise, from 130 in 1801 to a peak of 202 in 1831. Thereafter it fell, reaching its lowest point, 121, in 1921.[38] In 1991 the population was 181, the highest figure for over 100 years.[39]

Few details of the medieval settlement pattern are known. Hope Bowdler town end was mentioned in 1285[40] and 1616.[41] Each of the three villages, the only known medieval settlements, had its own open fields, and there were extensive upland commons, probably still largely wooded.[42]

The few survivals suggest that the principal medieval farmhouses were timber framed.[43] In 1672 the only substantial building, Ragdon manor house, was taxed on eight hearths. Two houses were taxed on four hearths, 3 on three, 3 on two, and 14 on one.[44] By the 18th century at the latest new buildings, with the possible exception of some cottages, were almost wholly of stone.[45] In 1832[46] house walls were mainly stone, with a little timber framing. Some agricultural buildings were weather-boarded. A wheelwright's cottage, brick with a tiled roof, was unusual, the only other notable use of brick before the 20th century being the refronting of Hope Bowdler Hall.[47] The wheelwright also occupied a carpenter's shop built by the rector on waste in the village centre in 1821.[48] Some

29 Ibid.; Eyton, v. 118. Eyton rejected the possibility that Ragdon was Chelmick's berewick.
30 Dr. Margaret Gelling is thanked for comment.
31 Above.
32 Cf. below, econ. hist.
33 *V.C.H. Salop.* i. 338.
34 *T.S.A.S.* 2nd ser. iv. 311.
35 *Hearth Tax 1672* (Salop. Arch. Soc. 1949), 183.
36 *Compton Census*, ed. Whiteman, 259.
37 S.R.O. 4323/Rg/3, copy census ret. 1811.
38 *V.C.H. Salop.* ii. 223.
39 S.C.C. Property and Planning Services Dept. inf. rep. C91/103.
40 *Cal. Inq. Misc.* i, p. 609.
41 H.W.R.O.(H.), HD 2/14/28.
42 Below, econ. hist.
43 e.g. Upper Ho., Hope Bowdler, and Lower Fm., Ragdon: below, manors.
44 *Hearth Tax 1672*, 183.
45 Timber framing may have persisted longer for internal walls.
46 S.R.O. 809, box 9, valn. of Hope Bowdler est. 1832. See also S.R.O. 4791/1/2, p. 23; /1/6, p. 180; /1/9, p. 379.
47 Below, manors.
48 Still standing. See Dakers, *Fordritishope*, 96–7.

buildings were covered with clay tiles or stone slates, and the rectory (1809) was probably roofed in blue slate;[49] thatch, however, was still common in 1832, especially on cottages and agricultural buildings.

Squatters' cottages, some perhaps as late as the 19th century,[50] were built mainly down the north-east side of the Chelmick valley, where there were eight cottages in the mid 19th century, and at the north end of Soudley where there were three, just inside the parish. Some survived, much modernized, in 1991; the sites of others were occupied by 20th-century houses and bungalows.[51] In the 19th century Cwms Farm (in existence by 1804)[52] and a cottage stood on the west side of Hope Bowdler hill, and two cottages at Woodgate (where people were living by 1724)[53] on the south side.[54]

In the late 19th and the 20th century many new houses were built on the sites of derelict ones,[55] a significant exception being the council housing north-east of Hope Bowdler village: four houses built in the 1930s, two during the Second World War, and six in the 1950s. In 1984–5 three houses were formed by barn conversions at Manor Farm, Hope Bowdler.[56]

In the 1730s Hope Bowdler wake was kept on the Sunday after midsummer day.[57] There seem to have been very few alesellers in the parish during the 17th and 18th centuries, often none;[58] in 1793 there had been no alehouse within memory.[59] An inn opened in Hope Bowdler village in the early 19th century but had little custom in 1832 and probably closed soon after.[60] Between at least 1899 and 1901 there was a reading room in the village,[61] and in 1908 R. B. Benson provided a church room there[62] which was used for social functions.

MANORS AND OTHER ESTATES. In 1066 Edric the wild held *FORDRITISHOPE*, later *HOPE BOWDLER*. Presumably after his rebellion in 1069–70 the manor passed to Roger of Montgomery, earl of Shrewsbury, tenant in chief in 1086.[63] The earl's chief lordship was presumably forfeited in 1102 by his son Robert of Bellême.[64] By 1201 the manor (with two others which had been held by the same Domesday undertenant) formed part of Robert de Boullers's honor of Montgomery[65] and successive lords of that honor remained overlords until 1425 or later.[66] In 1465 and 1466 the manor was held of Thomas Preston.[67]

Hugh fitz Turgis held the manor of Earl Roger in 1086.[68] Yvette of Wilderley claimed the vill of Hope in 1195.[69] In 1201 Roger de Say was superseded as tenant in fee by Richard of Wilderley.[70] Probably from that time until the late 13th century or later Hope Bowdler and Wilderley (in Church Pulverbatch) together were reckoned, as the 'fee of Hope Bowdler', to comprise 1 knight's fee, ⅘ of that service being due from Hope Bowdler.[71] Richard of Wilderley's son, Stephen of Hope,[72] was lord in 1240. Before 1255 the manor passed to Otes of Hodnet, seneschal of Montgomery.[73] Before his death in 1284 Otes apparently enfeoffed Robert Burnell, bishop of Bath and Wells, in the manor, for by 1285 Burnell was said to hold the manor of Otes's heir William of Hodnet.[74] The Hodnets' interest is not recorded later. Thenceforward until the attainder of Francis, Lord Lovel, in 1485 Hope Bowdler descended with Acton Burnell,[75] although held in dower by Edward Burnell's widow Aline 1315–63.[76]

In 1486 Henry VII granted the manor to Sir John Savage of Clifton (Ches.).[77] It descended in that family until 1600[78] when Sir John Savage sold it to Edward and John Lutwyche.[79] The manor then descended with Lutwyche (in Rushbury) until the partial dispersal of the Lutwyche estate in 1785[80] when Hope Bowdler manor and *c.* 244 a. were bought by William Cheney Hart, a barrister.[81] After Hart's death in 1819 the manor and *c.* 1,000 a. were put up for sale, being bought by Ralph Benson's trustees in 1828.[82] The lordship and estate descended with the Bensons' Lutwyche property until 1921 when the 1,370-a. Hope Bowdler estate was put up for sale. Manorial rights were not mentioned in the particulars of 1921,[83] and no later reference to the lordship has been noticed.

There was a manor house in 1294,[84] but in

49 Below, church. Cf. Dakers, op. cit. 76.
50 Above, this section [pop.]; Dakers, op. cit. 139; A. Dakers, *Ticklerton Tales* (Ragdon, 1991), 174–5.
51 Dakers, *Fordritishope*, 104–9, 130–49.
52 Below, econ. hist. 53 S.R.O. 4323/Rg/1, s.a. 1724.
54 Dakers, *Fordritishope*, 71, 88–90.
55 Ibid. *passim.* 56 Ibid. 151.
57 Birm. Univ. Libr., Mytton Papers, iv. 756.
58 S.R.O. q. sess. rec. parcel 254, badgers', drovers', and alesellers' licensing bk.; parcels 255–9, regs. of alesellers' recognizances 1753–1828. 59 S.P.L., MS. 6865, p. 106.
60 S.R.O. 809, box 9, valn. of Hope Bowdler est. 1832; 2563/103–4; Dakers, *Fordritishope*, 81–3; S. Bagshaw, *Dir. Salop.* (1851), 539 (no mention).
61 Subscription bk. in possession of Mr. P. Morgan.
62 S.R.O. 809, box 9, bdle. of corresp.; *Kelly's Dir. Salop.* (1937), 119. 63 *V.C.H. Salop.* i. 338.
64 Ibid. iii. 9; Eyton, v. 144.
65 Eyton, iv. 114; *Cur. Reg. R.* ii. 19.
66 e.g. *Rot. Hund.* (Rec. Com.) ii. 70; *Cal. Inq. p.m.* ii, p. 18; iii, p. 122; v, p. 392; xi, p. 373; xiv, pp. 349–50; xv, p. 259; xvii, pp. 268, 449; *Feud. Aids*, iv. 222, 246; *Cal. Pat.* 1374–7, 278; P.R.O., C 139/19, no. 32.
67 P.R.O., C 140/13, no. 27; C 140/497, no. 20.
68 *V.C.H. Salop.* i. 338 69 Eyton, vi. 258.
70 *Cur. Reg. R.* ii. 19; Eyton, v. 115.
71 Eyton, v. 116–17; vi. 259–60; *Cartulary of Haughmond Abbey*, ed. U. Rees (1985), p. 238.
72 *Cart. Haughmond*, p. 237.
73 *Rot. Hund.* ii. 70; Eyton, v. 116.
74 Eyton, v. 117; ix. 331–2; *Feud. Aids*, iv. 222.
75 *Cal. Inq. Misc.* i. 469–70; *Cal. Inq. p.m.* iii, p. 122; v, p. 392; *Feud. Aids*, iv. 269; P.R.O., C 138/54, no. 116; C 140/13, no. 27; C 148/45; cf. *V.C.H. Salop.* viii. 7.
76 *Feud. Aids*, iv. 246; *Cal. Inq. p.m.* xi, pp. 371–3.
77 *Cal. Pat.* 1485–94, 101–2; *D.N.B.*
78 G. Ormerod, *Hist. Co. Chester* (1882), i. 713–16; *L. & P. Hen. VIII*, x, p. 365; xii (2), pp. 352–3; P.R.O., E 150/849, no. 2. 79 P.R.O., CP 25/2/203/42 Eliz. Hil. [no. 3].
80 P.R.O., C 142/381, no. 160; Glam. R.O., CL/Deeds I, Salop. 2 Feb. 1638/9; S.R.O., q. sess. rec. box 260, reg. of gamekeepers 1711–42, 25 Oct. 1734, 25 Apr. 1735; 1742–79, 7 Oct. 1761, 7 Sept. 1765; S.R.O. 4835/2; B.R.L., MS. 577365; cf. below, Rushbury, manors (Lutwyche).
81 S.P.L., MS. 6865, p. 104; S.R.O. 4791/1/2; Dakers, *Fordritishope*, 2.
82 W.S.L. 350/5/40, Hope Bowdler p. 6; *Shrews. Chron.* 9 July 1819, p. 2; Dakers, op. cit. 2, 93.
83 S. Bagshaw, *Dir. Salop.* (1851), 539; S.P.L., SC3/25; S.R.O. 1313/184. 84 *Cal. Inq. p.m.* iii, p. 122.

1315 there were said to be no buildings.[85] William Cheney Hart was probably the first resident lord since Stephen of Hope in the mid 13th century; Hart lived in the village in a large stone farmhouse which he was probably responsible for enlarging and refronting in brick. By 1819 it was known as Hope Bowdler Hall. Outbuildings include an early 19th-century pigeon house. The farm was bought in 1921 by George Preece, whose family owned it until 1972 when the house was sold with 22 a.[86]

Buildwas abbey was given ½ virgate in Hope Bowdler in the later 1240s by William, son of William of Chelmick (also called William Erdulf).[87] If the abbey retained that land until its suppression in 1536, it was subsumed under Ragdon.[88]

LOWER HOUSE farm was probably part of the property owned in the late 16th and early 17th century by William Preen, who was succeeded by his son William. Then, as later, it was known as Stile, or Church Stile, House.[89] Sir Edward Lutwyche, lord of the manor, owned it by 1692,[90] and it descended with the manor until 1921 when George Preece bought it. His family had the farm, 216 a. and grazing rights, until 1972. The stone and timber framed house, reckoned inferior in 1838, was extensively remodelled in the later 19th century.[91]

UPPER HOUSE farm, reputedly owned or occupied by Edwin Phipps (fl. 1485),[92] may have been the Phillipses' home in the later 16th century.[93] In 1674 the Baxters of Earnstrey Park (in Diddlebury) owned it.[94] Part of the Lutwyche estate in 1785,[95] it descended with Hope Bowdler manorial estate[96] until George Preece bought it in 1921. The belief that Edwin Phipps built the house in 1485[97] may refer to the hall range, whose rear wall is close studded. The house was largely remodelled in stone early in the 19th century

Edric the wild owned *CHELMICK*, including an unnamed berewick, in 1066.[98] From 1086 the overlordship[99] and the mesne lordship (the latter last recorded in 1541)[1] seem to have descended with those of Hope Bowdler.[2]

In 1255 Baldwin of Montgomery, provost of Montgomery, was Otes of Hodnet's tenant at Chelmick.[3] His son William probably sold Chelmick to Hugh of Wotherton (fl. 1272–85). Hugh's daughter and coheir Eve predeceased her husband Richard Hord, who died in 1325 seised of the hamlet and court of Chelmick for life in right of his wife.[4] The next lord was perhaps Roger Hord; his son John died in possession in 1398, when his heirs were Fulk Sprenchose and John Gotmond.[5]

Sir Thomas Leighton, whose family had links with the Hords and the Sprenchoses,[6] was evidently lord in 1497.[7] In 1500 the manor was among property he exchanged with Stephen Kemsey.[8] On Kemsey's death in 1540 the manor passed to his son Robert,[9] who in 1559 sold it to Thomas Phillips.[10] Francis Phillips of Chelmick (d. 1657)[11] was perhaps the father of Philip Phillips,[12] who in 1666 sold the manor to Thomas Russell. Russell was succeeded by his son William (d. 1727), who in 1721 settled the manor on his son and daughter-in-law Thomas (d. 1746) and Elizabeth (d. 1753). On Elizabeth's death, or perhaps earlier, Chelmick passed to their son William, a Worcester surgeon,[13] who is said to have sold the manor to Thomas More of Millichope.[14]

Thomas More died in 1767,[15] and Chelmick passed to his son-in-law Dudley Ackland.[16] In 1782 Ackland sold the lordship to Edward Lloyd (d. 1790) of Shrewsbury, who left it to his kinsman, the Revd. William Calcott.[17] Calcott (d. 1820) was probably succeeded by Charles Morrall (d. 1822), whose son William owned it in 1825. The Hon. M. W. B. Nugent, evidently in right of his wife, William's niece (d. 1856), owned 146 a. in the parish in 1843.[18] In 1874 the Revd. Cyrus Morrall and the Revd. John Morrall sold the manor and Manor farm to Job Taylor (d. *c.* 1886). Taylor's trustees conveyed Chelmick to Thomas Berks Turner, on whose death the manor and farm were sold in 1907 to Miss Lilian Holland Buddicom.[19] She sold them in 1918 to George Davies (d. 1932), whose son Fred sold them in 1963 to John Davies,[20] the owner in 1991.

Chelmick Manor Farm, described in 1793 as 'an old mansion now a farmhouse', is a mid 17th-century hall and cross wing. The 1½ storeyed stone and timber framed hall range may be slightly later than a substantial two storeyed

85 P.R.O., C 134/48, no. 9.
86 Dakers, *Fordritishope*, 91–5; S.R.O. 4791/1/6, p. 180.
87 Eyton, v. 117; xi. 351.
88 Below, this section.
89 S.R.O. 1146/28, 29a; Bodl. MS. Blakeway 8, f. 365; Dakers, *Fordritishope*, 102.
90 S.R.O. 179/5.
91 Dakers, op. cit. 102–4.
92 Ibid. 84.
93 S.R.O. 1146/26, 28; Bodl. MS. Blakeway 8, f. 365.
94 S.P.L., Deeds 1364.
95 S.R.O. 4835/2, p. 22 (Thomas's fm.).
96 P.R.O., IR 29/29/165; S.P.L., SC3/25; W.S.L. 350/5/40, Hope Bowdler p. 6; S.R.O. 4791/1/2, p. 23; 4044/40, p. 22.
97 Dakers, *Fordritishope*, 61, 84–5 for illustr.
98 *V.C.H. Salop.* i. 338.
99 Eyton, xi. 349–51.
1 *Rot. Hund.* ii. 70; Eyton, xi. 349–51; P.R.O., C 134/96, no. 6; C 142/63, no. 41.
2 Above, this section.
3 *Rot. Hund.* ii. 70; Eyton, xi. 170.
4 Eyton, xi. 351–2; P.R.O., C 134/96, no. 6.
5 *Cal. Inq. p.m.* xvii, p. 423.
6 *Visit. Salop.* i. 252; above, Cardington, manors (Plaish).
7 S.R.O. 3365/165.
8 Loton Hall MSS., brown folio vol. 'copies of deeds', p. 42.
9 P.R.O., C 142/63, no. 41.
10 P.R.O., CP 40/1184, rot. 352.
11 W.S.L. 350/5/40, Hope Bowdler p. 6.
12 H.W.R.O.(H.), HD 7, 1668/231.
13 W.S.L. 350/5/40, Hope Bowdler p. 6; S.R.O. 1011, box 166, abstr. of title; q. sess. rec. box 260, reg. of gamekeepers 1742–79, 17 May 1748 (Wm. called ld.).
14 J. Chambers, *Biog. Illustr. of Worcs.* (1820), 449.
15 Below, Munslow, manors (Lr. Millichope).
16 S.R.O. 1224, box 101, abstr. of title of Dudley Ackland 1790; S.R.O., q. sess. rec. box 260, reg. of gamekeepers 1742– 79, 1 Nov. 1775.
17 S.P.L., Deeds 1701; N.L.W., Plas Yolyn, no. 367.
18 S.R.O. 2024/1; P.R.O., IR 29/29/165; CP 43/967, rot. 218; Burke, *Peerage* (1949), 2110; Burke, *Land. Gent.* (1937), 1632.
19 S.R.O. 2024/9, 12–13.
20 Dakers, *Fordritishope*, 128; S.P.L., SC2/32–3.

stone range built end-on to the road and with mullioned and transomed windows and star shaped brick stacks.[21]

Wenlock priory may have had land in Chelmick in the earlier 13th century.[22]

In 1635 Henry Smith's trustees bought four properties in Chelmick from Thomas and Frances Chelmick for the poor of Shrewsbury. Soon after 1906 the premises, then Upper Farm (139 a.), were sold to William Davies, who sold them in 1942 to Ellis Jones.[23] His son David Jones was owner in 1991.[24] Upper Farm was rebuilt in stone with brick details, probably soon after 1805. The buildings, of good quality, form a three-sided courtyard open to the road, with the house, probably retained from the pre-1805 arrangement, as part of the long back range.[25]

Between the later 11th and the 13th century *RAGDON* was probably reckoned a member of Hope Bowdler manor, and in 1255 Otes of Hodnet did suit for it to county and hundred.[26]

In the 1220s the terre tenant was Robert de Lee. Between 1245 and 1255 his son Robert Acton, a clerk and in 1236–7 deputy under-sheriff, gave all his Ragdon land to Buildwas abbey (which already owned land in the parish) subject to the service, due from a portion of the estate, of providing a foot soldier to do ward at Montgomery castle for 15 days a year.[27]

Buildwas retained its land in Ragdon until the abbey was dissolved in 1536.[28] In 1537 Ragdon, like most of the former abbey lands, was sold to Edward, Lord Grey of Powis.[29] In 1598 Grey's natural son Edward Grey sold Ragdon, then termed a manor, to Thomas Chelmick,[30] who remained in possession in 1623.[31] John Chelmick had succeeded by 1644. By 1671 the manor belonged to Thomas Davies, (d. 1679),[32] and by 1694 to Richard Davies[33] (d. 1708) of Hope Bowdler. Richard was succeeded by his son-in-law, the Revd. Thomas Adney (d. 1735), Adney by his son Richard (d. 1739), and Richard in turn by his son Richard.[34] In 1761 Richard Adney sold the manor to John Stanier.[35] Stanier (d. 1782)[36] was succeeded by his son Charles (d. 1789),[37] and Charles by his son Charles Price Stanier, lord in 1807.[38] C. P. Stanier's cousin[39] John Stanier owned it by 1839. He died in 1867, leaving it to his widow Eleonora (d. 1868); their son J. P. Stanier sold Ragdon Manor farm (154 a.) in 1920, no mention then being made of manorial rights.[40] The farm changed hands several times in the next 70 years, the house being separated from its land in 1987.[41]

Ragdon Manor Farm is a three bayed, two storeyed early 19th-century stone building, stuccoed.[42] A new farmhouse was being built in 1991.[43]

The other farm in Ragdon township in the 19th century, 165 a. in 1843, was Lower, or Ragdon, farm.[44] Thomas Smith owned it *c.* 1793.[45] It remained in his family until the earlier 20th century.[46] In 1947 it was bought by Jack Wilding whose family had been tenants since the late 18th century.[47] Wilding's son Richard was owner in 1991. Ragdon Farm is basically **T** shaped. The hall range, originally of base-cruck construction, had a ceiling and first floor inserted in the 17th century. Part of one cruck blade survived in 1992, in the parlour. The hall range, externally of stone, was of 1½ storey; in 1900 brick was used to give two full storeys and to extend the house north. A stone cross wing is probably mid 19th-century and presumably replaced an earlier range.

ECONOMIC HISTORY. In the 19th and 20th centuries the upper limit of enclosed fields around Hope Bowdler hill was at *c.* 300 m. Above that, up to *c.* 350 m., are the scarped and banked remains of fields;[48] older than inclosure ditches probably of the 18th century,[49] they are likely to be prehistoric or early medieval.

In 1086 it was reckoned that Hope Bowdler and Chelmick each had land enough for six ploughteams. At Hope Bowdler there were two teams in demesne and one worked by *villani* and at Chelmick three worked by *villani*.[50] In 1239 a tenant held a nook and 3 a. at Hope Bowdler for 2*s.* a year and two days' harvesting.[51] There were 67 a. of demesne in the late 13th century.[52] By 1292 Philip Burnell had been granted a market and fair,[53] not heard of later.

In 1341 the mountainous terrain, tenants' poverty, and sheep murrain were among reasons

21 S.P.L., MS. 6865, p. 104; Dakers, op. cit. 125–6, for illustr. Mrs. M. Moran is thanked for her remarks on ho.

22 Eyton, xi. 350; *T.S.A.S.* 4th ser. vi. 178.

23 *24th Rep. Com. Char.* H.C. 231, p. 234 (1831), xi; Dakers, op. cit. 122–5.

24 Local inf.

25 Dakers, op. cit. 123, for illustr.; *24th Rep. Com. Char.* 234; Char. Com. scheme 3 Aug. 1906 (copy in S.P.L., D 37.2 v.f.).

26 Eyton, v. 118–20; *Rot. Hund.* ii. 70.

27 Eyton, v. 118–20; *Cal. Chart. R.* 1257–1300, 418, 420; above, this section.

28 Eyton, v. 119–20; *V.C.H. Salop.* ii. 58; S.R.O. 3365/165.

29 *V.C.H. Salop.* ii. 58 (incorrectly dated 1539); iv. 129; *L. & P. Hen. VIII*, xii (2), p. 166; S.R.O. 212, box 452, grant of 1537.

30 P.R.O., CP 25/2/203/40 Eliz. I East. no. 10; Barnard MSS., Raby Castle, box 1, bdle. 27, no. 60; *V.C.H. Salop.* xi. 187.

31 S.R.O. 1011, box 166, deed 30 Jan. 1622/3.

32 P.R.O., CP 25/2/478/18 Chas. I East. [no. 21]; CP 25/2/713/23 Chas. II Trin. [no. 7]; S.R.O. 4323/Rg/1, bur. 16 Nov. 1679.

33 P.R.O., CP 25/2/867/6 Wm. & Mary Mich. [no. 15].

34 S.P.L., MS. 4646, p. 110; Birm. Univ. Libr., Mytton Papers, iv. 756.

35 P.R.O., CP 25/2/1393/2 Geo. III Mich. [no. 10]; S.P.L., MS. 6865, p. 105; S.R.O. 1135/2.

36 *S.P.R. Lich.* iv (3), 20.

37 Ibid. 27; doc. formerly S.R.O. 999/Pp (2) 8, now at Orleton Hall.

38 S.R.O., q. sess. rec. parcel 261, reg. of gamekeepers 1799–1807, f. 158.

39 S.R.O. 1135/2.

40 S.R.O. 2947/76/1-17; /100/1; S. Bagshaw, *Dir. Salop.* (1851), 539; S.P.L., SC1/25; Dakers, *Fordritishope*, 112.

41 Dakers, op. cit. 115; local inf.

42 Dakers, op. cit. 111, for illustr.

43 Local inf.

44 P.R.O., IR 29/29/165; IR 30/29/165.

45 S.P.L., MS. 6865, p. 104; below, Eaton-under-Heywood, manors (Harton).

46 P.R.O., IR 29/29/165; S.R.O. 4044/40.

47 Rest of para. based on Dakers, *Fordritishope*, 115–18 (incl. illustr.); local inf.

48 SA 1908.

49 Below, this section.

50 *V.C.H. Salop.* i. 338.

51 *T.S.A.S.* 4th ser. iv. 176.

52 *Cal. Inq. p.m.* iii, p. 122.

53 T. F. Dukes, *Antiquities of Salop.* (1844), 221.

given for a fall in the value of tithes.[54] Holdings probably began to be engrossed in the following decades. At Chelmick *c.* 1480 there were two virgate holdings and nine ½-virgate holdings, some held for rent and others for rent and unspecified services; there were also *c.* 48 a. of assarts. All were held for various rents and unspecified services by four men with roughly equal holdings.[55]

Each township had its own open fields, partly inclosed by the early 17th century.[56] Chelmick's were perhaps the most extensive: Lower field lay south of the village, Cross field north of it, and Ditch Cop field beyond that; the Feggy field lay east of Ditch Cop field.

There were extensive grazing lands in the parish, not only on Hope Bowdler hill: in the Middle Ages and later the three vills intercommoned Hay wood (in Eaton-under-Heywood and Rushbury), and Chelmick men had rights on Soudley common (in Eaton-under-Heywood),[57] although disputes over inclosures there are recorded as early as 1226.[58] In the early Middle Ages much woodland remained. Hope Bowdler had 2 leagues of woodland in 1086,[59] a high figure[60] which suggests that all the hills forming the western and northern third of the vill were wooded. In 1235 oak and hazel in Hope wood were said to be well warded, but underwood was not increasing.[61] In 1286 Hope Bowdler was among the places in the Long forest where Bishop Burnell was to be allowed to take timber for Acton Burnell castle.[62] Hope Bowdler, Chelmick, and Ragdon were disafforested in 1301.[63]

In the mid 16th century Ragdon men were being excluded from the lord's wood at Hope; pigs were still feeding there, and the vert included holly. Wood gate, 1 mile east of Hope Bowdler village, was probably the main way in to the wood. In 1623 the lord's wood was called 'the coomes', and presumably stood on the western side of Hope Bowdler hill in the area of the later Cwms farm and perhaps along the northern flank of the hill too. The central and southern parts of the hill were probably cleared of trees by that time since furze and gorse were collected. In the early 17th century Hope Bowdler commoners also had rights in Helmeth wood (in Church Stretton), and encroachments and inclosures in the wood were presented at Hope Bowdler manor court.[64]

In 1736 the commons in the parish were said to be Hope Bowdler hill and part of Hazler hill.[65] The latter lay mostly in Church Stretton parish,[66] and probably the parts in both parishes were inclosed in 1790.[67] Cottagers profited from the remaining commons, and in 1793 the poor were said to be relatively well off: most had pigs, some a cow, and some a few sheep.[68] As late as 1829, however, landowners were suppressing inclosures on the waste in Chelmick.[69]

At an unknown date, but probably in the later 18th century, Hope Bowdler hill was divided up by banks and ditches.[70] By 1828, it seems, those divisions had broken down, and a re-apportionment of common rights was talked of,[71] while in 1832 a valuation of the Hope Bowdler estate recommended division of the hill, then reckoned a good dry sheepwalk, into allotments.[72] By then Cwms wood was probably long gone, and in 1843 there were only 20 a. of woodland in the parish.[73]

In the early 20th century six farms had sheep stints on Hope Bowdler hill, in all for 810 animals, regulated by the Church Stretton Commoners' Association. The common rights had lapsed by the early 1970s. In 1991 the hill was owned by G. F. W. Preece whose grandfather George Preece had bought it from G. R. Benson in 1921.[74]

At his death in 1673 Henry Preen of Hope Bowdler had corn growing and in store worth £9 0*s.* 8*d.*; stock included a yoke of oxen, 21 other cattle, 4 horses, 5 pigs, and 250 sheep, presumably run on Hope Bowdler hill. Richard Eaton (d. 1674), also of Hope Bowdler, farmed with a similar balance, though his cereals were worth £60: he had 6 oxen, 28 other cattle, horses worth £5 (thrice the value of Preen's), 5 pigs, and 120 sheep; in store was hay worth £10. Mary Richards (d. 1668) of Chelmick, a widow, farmed in a small way with 4 cows and 2 horses and had corn worth £3. She also spun and wove and owned linen yarn (10*s.*), hemp and flax (£1 10*s.*), and woollen cloth and yarn (10*s.*).[75] Flax and hemp had been grown in the parish in 1567,[76] and cottagers wove in the 18th century.[77]

Potatoes were grown at Ragdon in the 1750s.[78] Some attempts were made *c.* 1800 to improve farming methods. In 1793[79] the four-course Norfolk rotation may have been in use in the parish, and the amount of arable was perhaps close to that in 1843,[80] 57 per cent of agricultural land (excluding Hope Bowdler hill). Agricultural prosperity in the war years around 1800 encouraged landlords to invest in farm buildings. At the Cwms the landlord built outhouses

54 *Inq. Non.* (Rec. Com.), 186.
55 Loton Hall MSS., Chelmick ct. r. 1479–82.
56 Para. based on H.W.R.O.(H.), HD 2/14/28; field names in P.R.O., IR 29/29/165; IR 30/29/165.
57 Below, Eaton-under-Heywood, econ. hist.; Rushbury, econ. hist.
58 Eyton, v. 116; xi. 350; above, this article, intro.
59 *V.C.H. Salop.* i. 338.
60 Equivalent to *c.* 5 km. (O. Rackham, *Ancient Woodland* (1980), 113, 115), roughly the distance from S. end of Ragleth to N. end of Hope Bowdler hill.
61 Eyton, vi. 338.
62 *Cal. Pat.* 1281–92, 228; *V.C.H. Salop.* viii. 8; iv. 45.
63 *Cartulary of Shrews. Abbey*, ed. U. Rees (1975), ii, p. 250.
64 S.P.L., Deeds 2599, ct. r. 1567, 1569, 1612, 1623.
65 Birm. Univ. Libr., Mytton Papers, iv. 756.
66 Below, Ch. Stretton, econ. hist.
67 P.R.O., IR 29/29/165; IR 30/29/165, fields 128–9, 153.
68 S.P.L., MS 6865, p. 106.
69 S.R.O. 2563/42, n. at end of bk.
70 Marked on O.S. Map 1/10,000, SO 49 SE. (1980 edn.).
71 S.R.O. 5652/1.
72 S.R.O. 809, box 9.
73 P.R.O., IR 29/29/165.
74 S.P.L., SC3/25; S.C.C. Ch. Exec.'s Dept., commons reg., reg. unit no. CL 89; inf. from Miss M. Preece.
75 H.W.R.O.(H.), Heref. dioc. rec., invs. of 1667, 1673.
76 S.P.L., Deeds 2599, ct. r. 1567.
77 Weaving pattern bk. in possession of Mr. P. Morgan; inf. from Mr. Morgan; Dakers, *Fordritishope*, 21.
78 S.R.O. 2563/33, 30 Apr. 1757.
79 S.P.L., MS. 6865, p. 105; *V.C.H. Salop.* iv. 178.
80 P.R.O., IR 29/29/165.

in 1804[81] and probably the farmhouse too; a fold yard and barn *c.* 200 m. north-west of the farm are probably also of that date.[82] At Chelmick Shrewsbury corporation remodelled the buildings of Upper farm soon after 1805, the work probably financed by the sale of newly inclosed common.[83] Hazler Barn (demolished *c.* 1980), a field barn with cottage for Lower House farm, was probably built 1817 × 1828.[84] Nevertheless in 1832 several farms on the Hope Bowdler estate were reported to be ill drained and poorly or over cropped.[85]

After the mid 19th century[86] grassland increased, to 92 per cent in 1938. Over three quarters of Hope Bowdler remained pasture in 1965. Sheep continued the main stock in what was essentially an upland parish, although the number of cattle increased substantially after the Second World War.

A water mill stood at the north end of the Chelmick valley by the early 17th century,[87] and the name Walkers close next to a pool at Soudley may indicate the site of a fulling mill.[88]

TABLE III

HOPE BOWDLER: LAND USE, LIVESTOCK, AND CROPS

		1867	*1891*	*1938*	*1965*
Percentage of	grassland	70	74	92	79
	arable	30	26	8	21
Percentage of	cattle	10	10	14	15
	sheep	86	86	81	83
	pigs	4	4	5	2
Percentage of	wheat	51	27	31	23
	barley	38	48	3	60
	oats	11	25	66	17
	mixed corn & rye	0	0	0	0
Percentage of agricultural land growing roots and vegetables		9	9	2	4

Sources: P.R.O., MAF 68/143, no. 20; /1340, no. 6; /3880, Salop. no. 271; /4945, no. 271.

Some of the pools at Soudley and Chelmick, used in the 19th and 20th centuries as fishponds, probably began as quarries. Many local buildings are of Soudley sandstone including Hope Bowdler church (1862–3).[89] Stone was also got elsewhere in the parish.[90] Bricks were made west of Woodgate Farm.[91] Copper was mined at the north end of Hazler hill before the mid 19th century.[92]

In the late 19th and early 20th century Hope Bowdler enjoyed a little of the prosperity brought to the area by visitors to Church Stretton. Between 1902 and 1905 tenants ran the Rectory as Hope Bowdler Pension, and paying guests were also accommodated there during the incumbency of A. P. Matthews, 1905–50.[93] Local attractions included Chelmick pools and the nearby cottage tea rooms.[94]

LOCAL GOVERNMENT. Two dozen court rolls for Hope Bowdler survive for years between 1497 and 1662.[95] Chelmick had a court by 1326[96] and rolls survive for 1479 and 1482.[97]

In the late 18th century there was one constable for Hope Bowdler and one for Chelmick and Ragdon.[98] Then, as in the 19th century, Chelmick and Ragdon were usually reckoned one township.[99]

The poor rate amounted to *c.* £3 a year *c.* 1750. In 1792 it was *c.* £58, mostly to relieve old men and an increasing number of bastard children.[1] In the early 19th century expenditure several times exceeded £90, and in 1832 reached £119 16*s.* There seems never to have been a poorhouse. Nine adults and four children received permanent relief in 1802–3 and 12 people occasional relief, probably typical early 19th-century figures for the parish.[2] Children were apprenticed to farmers.[3]

The parish was in Church Stretton union 1836–1930,[4] Church Stretton highway district 1863–95,[5] Church Stretton rural sanitary district 1872–94, Church Stretton rural district 1894–1934, Ludlow R.D. 1934–74, and South Shropshire district from 1974.[6] The civil parish had a joint council with Eaton-under-Heywood C.P. from *c.* 1967.[7]

CHURCH. A church was probably built in the 12th century. The living was a rectory by *c.*

81 Date stone.
82 P.R.O., IR 30/29/165, field 6; *T.C.S.V.F.C.* xi. 195–6.
83 Above, manors.
84 Cf. B.L. Maps, O.S.D. 217; Dakers, *Fordritishope*, 75–6.
85 S.R.O. 809, box 9, valn. of Hope Bowdler est. 1832.
86 Para. based on Table III.
87 SA 4426; H.W.R.O.(H.), HD 2/14/28; P.R.O., IR 29/29/165; IR 30/29/165, fields 201–2.
88 P.R.O., IR 29/29/165; IR 30/29/165, field 111.
89 Below, church.
90 e.g. P.R.O., IR 29/29/165; IR 30/29/165; O.S. Maps 6", Salop. LVI. NW. (1883 edn.); LVI. SW. (1889 edn.).
91 P.R.O., IR 29/29/165; IR 30/29/165, fields 68, 68a.
92 O.S. Map 6", Salop. LVI. SW. (1889 edn.); Dakers, *Fordritishope*, 49–52.
93 Dakers, op. cit. 79–81; Heref. Dioc. Regy., reg. 1902–19, p. 157; 1938–53, p. 499.
94 Dakers, op. cit. 131–4; S.P.L., SC2/32.
95 S.P.L., Deeds 2599.
96 P.R.O., C 134/96, no. 6.
97 Loton Hall MSS., Chelmick ct. r. 1479–82.
98 S.P.L., MS. 6865, p. 106.
99 Ibid. p. 103; S.R.O. 4323/Rg/3, copy census ret. 1811.
1 S.P.L., MS. 6865, p. 107.
2 *Poor Law Abstract*, H.C. 98, pp. 418–19 (1803–4), xiii; H.C. 82, pp. 372–3 (1818), xix; *Poor Rate Returns*, H.C. 556, suppl. app. p. 142 (1822), v; H.C. 334, p. 177 (1825), iv; H.C. 219, p. 165 (1830–1), xi; H.C. 444, p. 160 (1835), xlvii.
3 S.P.L., MS. 6865, p. 106.
4 V. J. Walsh, 'Admin. of Poor Laws in Salop. 1820–55' (Pennsylvania Univ. Ph.D. thesis, 1970), 150; *Kelly's Dir. Salop.* (1929), 117.
5 *Lond. Gaz.* 27 Mar. 1863, p. 1767; S.R.O., S.C.C. Local Govt., etc., Cttee. min. bk. 1894–1903, p. 29.
6 *Rural Dist. Councillors Electn. Order, 1894* (Local Govt. Bd. order no. 31847); *V.C.H. Salop.* ii. 215, 217; iii. 179, and sources cited ibid. 169 n. 29.
7 Inf. from the clk.

1231, when Stephen of Hope, probably by then lord of the manor, was patron.[8] Until 1466 or later the overlords of Hope Bowdler were patrons and usually presented.[9] Nevertheless the Burnells, lords of the manor, may have claimed an interest: in 1296 the king presented as guardian of Philip Burnell's heir,[10] and later the advowson was said to be held by Hugh, Lord Burnell (d. 1420).[11]

In 1564 and 1569 Simon Kemsey had the advowson;[12] the Kemseys had been lords of Chelmick until Simon's brother Robert sold the manor in 1559.[13] By 1621 William Chelmick of Chelmick was patron.[14] Sampson Lure exercised a turn in 1640.[15] Between the 1690s and the earlier 19th century the advowson descended with the manor of Ragdon;[16] a turn was apparently bought *c.* 1699.[17]

Some time after 1806[18] the Staniers, lords of Ragdon, disposed of the advowson to William Cheney Hart, lord of Hope Bowdler, with whose property Ralph Benson's trustees bought it in 1828.[19] The Bensons kept it until 1950 when Maj. G. R. Benson gave it to the Hereford diocesan patronage board.[20] It was held in plurality with Acton Scott 1951–*c.* 1966.[21] In 1966 the united benefice of Hope Bowdler with Eaton-under-Heywood was created; from later that year it was held in plurality with Rushbury. In 1970 the newly built rectory at Hope Bowdler became the benefice house[22] and in 1971 the incumbent became also priest in charge of Cardington. From 1980 the three benefices were held in plurality.[23]

In 1291 the rectory was worth £4 13*s.* 4*d.*, out of which the rector of Rushbury had a portion of 2*s.*[24] In 1341 glebe, hay tithes, small tithes and offerings were valued at £2 13*s.* 4*d.*[25] In the 14th century the rectory was reckoned to be worth £8 13*s.* 4*d.*; the rector of Rushbury still had a portion.[26] In 1535 the living was worth £6 12*s.* 10*d.* net.[27] The glebe was *c.* 60 a. in 1616, mainly scattered parcels and strips.[28]

The living's value rose to £44 *c.* 1708,[29] to £50 or £60 *c.* 1730,[30] and to £300 by 1823.[31] In 1832 the house and 45 a. were reckoned to be worth £55 a year and the tithes £255 10*s.*; the total net value was £280 10*s.*[32] In 1843 the tithes, mainly collected in kind, were commuted to £237 17*s.* 6*d.*[33] The living was worth £240 in 1885.[34] By 1887 there were only 20a. of glebe, the same amount as in 1989.[35]

In 1616 the parsonage was of four bays and had a four bayed barn.[36] G.W. Marsh built a new stone rectory in 1809.[37] In 1862 a second floor was added and the house was modernized and enlarged to plans by F. P. Cockerell.[38] A new rectory was built on a new site in 1970.[39]

Two rectors were licensed to study in the 14th century.[40] John Pryce, the first known graduate rector (1567–*c.* 1569), lived at Pontesbury, where he was a portioner.[41] Eighteenth- and 19th-century rectors often employed curates.[42] Several rectors, notably Henry Newnam (1699–1743), Richard Adney (1748–68), John Stanier (1771–1806), and R. G. Benson (1860–96), were presented by kinsmen.[43] G. W. Marsh was imprisoned for debt and so by *c.* 1828 had been absent several years.[44]

In 1716 communion was celebrated five times a year.[45] In 1805 violin, cello, and oboe were played in church.[46] In 1851 the church had 90 seats, all owned or rented; 35–40 people usually attended morning service and 15 the afternoon service.[47]

The old church of *ST. ANDREW*, so dedicated by *c.* 1740,[48] comprised chancel, nave with south porch, and west tower.[49] An 'image' of St. John the Baptist from Hope Bowdler was burnt in Much Wenlock market place in 1547.[50] A west gallery was installed in 1777.[51]

In 1862–3 a new church, of Soudley stone with Grinshill stone dressings, was built to a design by S. Pountney Smith,[52] the cost being met by subscriptions, sales of work, and a mortgage of the church rate. It comprises chancel

8 *Roll of Salop. Eyre 1256* (Selden Soc. xcvi), p. 95; above, manors (Hope Bowdler).

9 *Cal. Pat.* 1272–81, 6; 1374–7, 278; *Cal. Inq. p.m.* xv, p. 262; *Reg. Cantilupe* (C.S.), 16, 28, 185, 235; *Reg. Swinfield* (C.S.), 527–8, 535; *Reg. Trillek* (C.S.), 380; *Reg. Mascall* (C.S.), 174; *Reg. Stanbury* (C.S.), 182; P.R.O., C 138/54, no. 116; cf. above, manors (Hope Bowdler).

10 *Cal. Pat.* 1292–1301, 185.

11 P.R.O., C 138/54, no. 116.

12 *Dioc. of Hereford Institutions (1539–1900)*, ed. A. T. Bannister (Heref. 1923), 16, 19.

13 Above, manors; *V.C.H. Salop.* viii. 266.

14 H.W.R.O.(H.), Heref. dioc. rec., AL 19/16, f. 291; W.S.L. 350/5/40, Hope Bowdler p. 1.

15 *T.S.A.S.* 4th ser. ii. 58.

16 S.P.L., MS. 6865, p. 105; W.S.L. 350/5/40, Hope Bowdler p. 3; Bannister, *Heref. Institutions*, 54, 83, 86, 100, 104, 133; above, manors.

17 *T.S.A.S.* 4th ser. ii. 80.

18 Ibid. 4th ser. vii. 169.

19 S.R.O. 5652/1; above, manors.

20 Heref. Dioc. Regy., reg. 1938–53, p. 496.

21 Ibid. p. 531; inf. from Heref. dioc. sec.

22 Heref. Dioc. Regy., reg. 1953–68, pp. 513, 527, 563; 1969– (in use), p. 50; below, this section.

23 Heref. Dioc. Regy., reg. 1969– (in use), pp. 354–5; above, Cardington, church.

24 *Tax. Eccl.* (Rec. Com.), 167.

25 *Inq. Non.* 186.

26 P.R.O., E 315/489, f. 13v.

27 *Valor Eccl.* (Rec. Com.), iii. 208.

28 H.W.R.O.(H.), HD 2/14/28.

29 J. Ecton, *Liber Valorum et Decimarum* (1711), 147.

30 Birm. Univ. Libr., Mytton Papers, iv. 756.

31 H.W.R.O.(H.), HD 9, 'Notitia', f. 32.

32 S.R.O. 809, box 9, valn. of Hope Bowdler est. 1832.

33 P.R.O., IR 29/29/165; Dakers, *Ticklerton Tales*, 173.

34 *Kelly's Dir. Salop.* (1885), 863.

35 *Return of Glebe Land, 1887*, H.C. 307, p. 59 (1887), lxiv; inf. from Heref. dioc. sec.

36 H.W.R.O.(H.), HD 2/14/28.

37 W.S.L. 350/5/40, Hope Bowdler p. 3; S.R.O. 809, box 9, valn. of Hope Bowdler est. 1832.

38 Heref. Dioc. Regy., reg. 1857–69, pp. 203–4, 336; S.R.O. 4323/Pge/1; Dakers, *Fordritishope*, 76–7.

39 Dakers, op. cit. 81.

40 *Reg. Swinfield*, 545; *Reg. Trillek*, 396.

41 Bannister, *Heref. Institutions*, 18–19; *T.S.A.S.* 4th ser. xi. 185, 193.

42 e.g. S.R.O. 4323/Rg/1–3; /MRg/1–2.

43 Bannister, op. cit. 56, 83, 86, 100, 104, 133, 175, 211; S.R.O. 3963/Chyd/2; 4323/Rg/1, bur. 24 May 1743; *S.P.R. Lich.* iv (3), 28; Dakers, *Fordritishope*, 78.

44 S.R.O. 3489/5, p. 5.

45 H.W.R.O.(H.), HD 5/14/1/14.

46 *Par. Mag.* Oct. 1973 (copy in S.P.L).

47 P.R.O., HO 129/354, no. 22.

48 B.L. Add. MS. 30316, f. 30.

49 S.P.L., MS. 372, vol. i, f. 93; J. H. Smith colln. no. 106; St. Deiniol's Libr., Hawarden, Sir Steph. Glynne's ch. notes, xcvii, f. 123; Birm. Univ. Libr., Mytton Papers, iv. 756.

50 *T.S.A.S.* vi. 106, 120.

51 *Par. Mag.* Oct. 1973.

52 Heref. Dioc. Regy., reg. 1857–69, pp. 369–70; S.R.O. 4323/Ch/1–28.

with south vestry, nave with south porch, and west tower. Several windows have late 19th- and early 20th-century glass by C. E. Kempe.[53] The east window, *c.* 1870, is by Done & Davies of Shrewsbury.[54]

Only the pulpit, of 1639 but probably rebuilt, survives from the old furnishings. The plate includes an Elizabethan chalice and a cover paten of 1572.[55] One bell is medieval, another is by Thomas Roberts, 1681; one of two others is dated 1887, and two more were added when the bells were rehung in 1929.[56]

The registers survive from 1564 but with gaps in the later 18th century.[57]

The churchyard was extended in 1923.[58]

NONCONFORMITY. None known.

EDUCATION. Hope Bowdler children could attend Cardington free school established in 1723.[59]

In 1819 three private schools had 20 pupils in all; none existed by 1833.[60] A National school opened with 40 places in 1857;[61] it and the adjacent teacher's house were built of stone.[62] Besides weekly fees pupils paid for books and coal. The mistress was certificated and the school was probably soon under inspection and earning government grant.[63] Attendance averaged 30 1885–1913.[64] In 1927 a few pupils from the closed Eaton-under-Heywood C.E. school were admitted.[65] From 1936 seniors attended Church Stretton domestic science[66] and woodwork centres.[67] At the managers' request the school closed in 1948, pupils going to Church Stretton Modern and C.E. Primary schools.[68]

CHARITIES FOR THE POOR. Members of the Adney, Russell, and Phillips families each left £2 to the poor. In the late 18th century the stock produced an income of 6*s.*, distributed on St. Thomas's day.[69] By the early 19th century 12*s.* worth of bread was distributed yearly in addition to the cash doles on St. Thomas's day. G. W. Marsh, rector, then added £4 to the £18 stock, and the St. Thomas's day doles were thereby increased to 10*s.* a year by *c.* 1830.[70] Those charities were afterwards lost.[71]

RUSHBURY

UNTIL 1883 Rushbury parish comprised 4,808 a. (1,946 ha.).[72] It contained the townships of Rushbury, Stone Acton, Wall under Heywood, and Wilderhope and Stanway (including Lutwyche). It also included part of East Wall (the rest being in a detached part of Eaton-under-Heywood parish), and most (647 a., 262 ha.) of Gretton township, the remainder (161 a., 65 ha.) being in Cardington parish. The Rushbury part of Gretton included 176 a. in detached portions, once commons, at the Gilberries and west of Wall under Heywood.[73]

If suggestions made about the late definition of Cardington parish[74] are correct, the parish centred on Rushbury in Anglo-Saxon times[75] may have been larger than it was later in the Middle Ages: if Rushbury did lose territory, at least some of the loss was probably in the north, where Gretton township lay across the medieval boundary between Cardington and Rushbury parishes.[76] Whenever it was that Rushbury parish bounds were defined, in woodland areas there may have been no precise boundary for centuries. On the east, where a wooded ridge divides Lutwyche, Wilderhope, and Stanway from Shipton parish, the boundary was probably defined in the earlier 16th century,[77] though it is there that an Iron Age hill fort,[78] above Lutwyche on one of several knolls along the limestone ridge, stands athwart the parish boundary; ¾ km. to the south-west the boundary touches another prehistoric, or Roman, enclosure.[79]

In 1883 the civil parish was enlarged by the transfer to it of the detached part of Eaton-under-Heywood parish: Longville and Lushcott townships and part of East Wall.[80] In 1967 the greater part of Gretton township in Rushbury C.P. and land at Hill End were transferred to Cardington C.P. At the same time boundary adjustments added small areas, anciently parts

53 *Par. Mag.* Sept. 1973.
54 *Ch. Cal. Dioc. Heref.* (1870), 137; *P.O. Dir. Salop.* (1870), 239.
55 D. L. Arkwright and B. W. Bourne, *Ch. Plate Archd. Ludlow* (Shrews. 1961), 33–4.
56 H. B. Walters, *Ch. Bells of Salop.* (Oswestry, 1915), 93, 402; Heref. Dioc. Regy., reg 1926–38, p. 169.
57 S.R.O. 4323/Rg/1–3; MRg/1–2; regs. at ch.; cf. H.W.R.O.(H.), bp.'s transcripts 1660, 1662–1814, etc.
58 *Kelly's Dir. Salop.* (1937), 119.
59 S.R.O. 2519/1.
60 *Educ. of Poor Digest*, H.C. 224, p. 753 (1819), ix (2); *Educ. Enq. Abstract*, ii, H.C. 62, p. 775 (1835), xlii (refs. supplied by Dr. R. Hume).
61 P.R.O., ED 7/102, ff. 331–2; *Kelly's Dir. Salop.* (1885), 863.
62 S.R.O. 1564/140–1.
63 Cf. P.R.O., ED 7/102, ff. 331–2.
64 *Kelly's Dir. Salop.* (1885), 863; (1900), 52; (1913), 115.
65 Inf. from Miss Nellie Sandells of M. Wenlock, last headmistress of the Eaton sch.
66 *S.C.C. Mins. (Educ.)* 1935–6, 76.
67 Ch. Stretton C.E. sch. log bk. 11 Mar. 1936 (at the sch.).
68 *S.C.C. Mins. (Educ.)* 1947–8, 74, 150.
69 S.P.L., MS 6865, p. 107; *Char. Don. 1786–8*, ii, H.C. 511–II, pp. 1024–5 (1816), xvi (2).
70 *24th Rep. Com. Char.* H.C. 231, p. 409 (1831), xi.
71 *Review of Local Chars.* (S.C.C. 1975), 56.
72 O.S. *Area Bk.* (1884), but deducting Longville, etc. (below, Longville, etc., intro.). This article was written in 1988–9. Mrs. M. Cockin and Mrs. M. B. Pogson, successive archivists of Rushbury & Dist. Record Trust (hereafter R. & D.R.T.) are thanked for help and access to records.
73 S. Bagshaw, *Dir. Salop.* (1851), 545–7; S.R.O. 3573/T/1–3; below, Eaton-under-Heywood; Longville, etc.
74 Above, Cardington, intro.
75 See below, church, for possible Saxon fabric.
76 Figs. 6, 8; S.R.O. 3573/T/1–3.
77 S.R.O. 566/11; 840/2/3/32; 1037/16/12.
78 Larden Ditches: below; below, Shipton.
79 SA 2180.
80 *V.C.H. Salop.* ii. 226 note c.

of Eaton-under-Heywood and Munslow parishes, to Rushbury C.P.[81] This article deals with the parish as it was in the 1830s and with the whole of Gretton township.

The settlements at Gretton and Stone Acton stand on high land flanking the hills of Cardington parish. Rushbury, Wall under Heywood, and East Wall all lie near the top of Ape Dale, which drains south-west across the parish; Rushbury forms an 'island' of higher ground in the Dale, and all the settlements north-west of Wenlock Edge except East Wall stand on prominences. East Wall is in the valley of Lakehouse brook. The Dale's south-eastern edge is formed by the limestone scarp of Wenlock Edge, which rises steeply to *c.* 270 m. at the top of Roman Bank and to the north-east marks the boundary between Rushbury parish and the detachment of Eaton-under-Heywood. The dip slope of Wenlock Edge falls into the shallow Hope Dale containing Wilderhope and Stanway. On the far side of Hope Dale the ground rises to a further ridge, of Aymestry limestone, mostly wooded towards the top and up to the parish boundary; it forms the north-western edge of Corve Dale. Lutwyche is at the head of the valley known in the 18th century as Knaves Dale, also contained by Wenlock Edge and the parallel Aymestry limestone ridge but descending north-east into Easthope.[82] High ground also dominates the north-western part of Rushbury parish, Stone Acton lying towards the eastern end of the group of hills including Cardington, Willstone, and Hope Bowdler hills. There the geological picture is complex, but prominent are Uriconian Andesites as well as igneous Quartz-porphyry at Stone Acton hamlet.[83]

The parish's main watercourse, running down Ape Dale, was known in the later Middle Ages as Strebrook[84] or Stradbrook[85] but in the 20th century as Lakehouse brook above Rushbury, Eaton brook lower down.[86] Heath brook and Coley brook, so known by 1833, drain south into it after the deflection of their courses around opposite ends of the prominence on which Rushbury village stands;[87] the former was perhaps known as Hordersleys brook in 1594.[88] Streams flow down Hope Dale past Wilderhope and the Stanways, uniting as Stanway brook[89] to flow south into Corve Dale. Another, probably the 14th-century Long brook,[90] rises south of Lutwyche Hall and flows north-east into Easthope parish.

Two of the parish place names include the *tun* element: Gretton, the gravelly settlement, and Stone Acton, the oak settlement called stony.[91] No early fortification is known in Rushbury township, and its name may mean the rush manor. Wall under Heywood and East Wall may derive from OE. *waella* (spring). Stanway is stone way and Wilderhope probably Wilthryth's valley. Lutwyche, the most problematical name, may refer to a nearby salt spring in Church Preen.[92]

Most of the roads may be assumed to be medieval, and a few are documented. The principal route was the 'great road' from Church Stretton to Bridgnorth, which ran through Wall under Heywood and crossed Hope Dale between Wilderhope and Lutwyche.[93] In the later 18th century, when Lutwyche was inclosed, it was straightened there; called Pilgrim Lane *c.* 1833, it ceased to be a public road in the 20th century.[94] The green way from Lutwyche to Larden, recorded in 1245,[95] was presumably the first part of the Larden–Plaish road mentioned in 1338.[96] The road from Stone Acton to Cardington was recorded in 1317.[97] The road south-east from Rushbury village over Wenlock Edge was known in 1580 as Rowman Lane.[98] There is no reason to think it Roman, nor need the road past Stanway or the packhorse bridge over Eaton brook on the way from Rushbury to Eaton be so considered.[99]

In 1765, as part of the Much Wenlock turnpike improvements, the road from Much Wenlock to Church Stretton via Wall under Heywood and the road south from Wall under Heywood via Rushbury to Blackwood limeworks were turnpiked.[1] As part of the latter work the bridge across Eaton brook was rebuilt in 1766.[2] A tollgate stood just north of the bridge.[3] Both roads were disturnpiked in 1875.[4] The road from Marshbrook via Ticklerton to Wall Bank was turnpiked under an Act of 1822[5] and disturnpiked in 1878.[6] New roads were laid out in 1806 when Gretton common and Wall's Bank were inclosed.[7]

The Wenlock Railway Co.'s line from Buildwas to Craven Arms, opened in 1867, ran across the parish beneath the scarp of Wenlock Edge. Rushbury station, south of the village, was open 1867–1951.[8]

Local prehistoric activity is attested by various Neolithic and later finds,[9] occupation sites,[10]

81 By the *Salop (No. 2) Order 1966* (Stat. Instr. 1966, no. 1529): *V.C.H. Salop.* ii. 235–6; S.R.O., DA 19/701/6, maps 35, 39.
82 Below, Easthope, intro.
83 For geol. see Geol. Surv. Map 1", drift, sheet 166 (1967 edn.).
84 Eyton iv. 99; below, Eaton-under-Heywood, intro.
85 S.P.L., MS. 2, f. 142; C. Saxton, *Map of Salop.* (1577).
86 O.S. Maps 6", Salop. LVI. SE. (1948 edn.); 1/50,000, sheet 137 (1985 edn.).
87 O.S. Map 1", sheet LXI. SW. (1833 edn.).
88 S.R.O. 840, box 42, lease 25 May 1594.
89 Named in 1665: S.P.L., Deeds 9718, s.a.
90 Staffs. R.O., D. 938/673.
91 *P.N. Salop.* (E.P.N.S.), i. 1–2, 139.
92 Ibid. 186–7, 254–5, 278, 298–9; inf. from Dr. M. Gelling. Cf. *Eng. P.N. Elements* (E.P.N.S.), ii. 266.
93 S.R.O. 4572/3/29.
94 O.S. Maps 1", sheet LXI. SW. (1833 edn.); 6", Salop. LVI. NW. (1928 edn.); 1/50,000, sheet 137 (1985 edn.); below, econ hist.
95 Eyton, iv. 114.
96 S.R.O. 1037/3/31.
97 S.R.O. 840, box 42, deed 20 Feb. 1317.
98 S.P.L., MS. 2, f. 142.
99 *V.C.H. Salop.* i. 273; S.P.L., Chitty File 403/8–17; A. Blackwall, *Historic Bridges of Salop.* (Shrews. 1985), 10.
1 5 Geo. III, c. 86.
2 S.R.O., dep. plan 150; S.R.O. 2118/254.
3 O.S. Map 1", sheet LXI. SW. (1833 edn.); S.R.O. 3573/T/1–2, field 531.
4 Ann. Turnpike Acts Continuance Act, 1873, 36 & 37 Vic. c. 90.
5 3 Geo. IV, c. 49.
6 Ann. Turnpike Acts Continuance Act, 1877, 40 & 41 Vic. c. 64.
7 S.R.O., incl. award B 18; below, econ. hist.
8 *Railway Mag.* xci. 440–4; *T.S.A.S.* lxiv. 102 (cf. 98, *s.v.* Longville); below, M. Wenlock, communications.
9 SA 635, 2748.
10 SA 555, 2174–5, 2180.

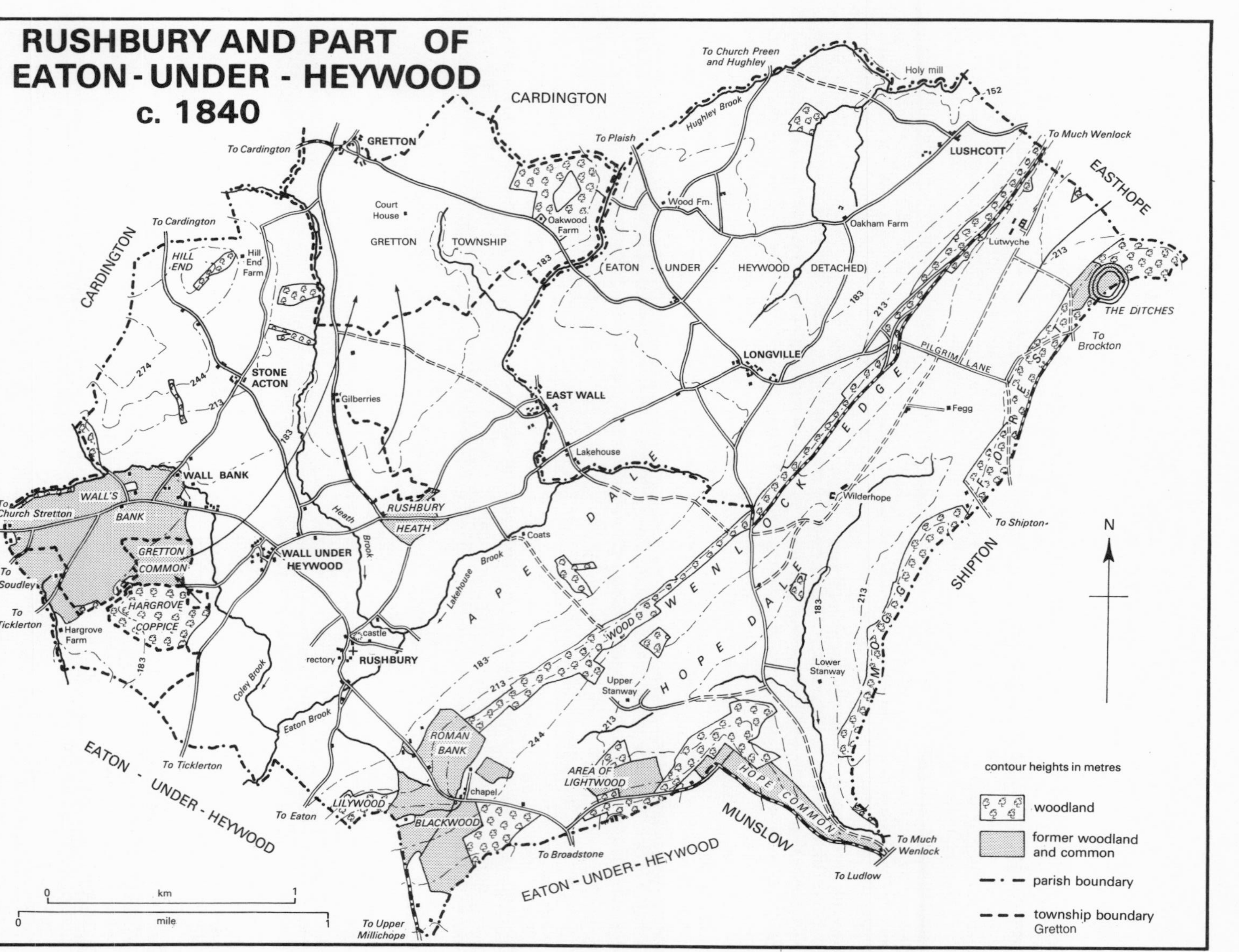
RUSHBURY AND PART OF
EATON - UNDER - HEYWOOD
c. 1840
CARDINGTON
EASTHOPE
SHIPTON
MUNSLOW
EATON - UNDER - HEYWOOD
EATON - UNDER - HEYWOOD
CARDINGTON
THE DITCHES
To Brockton
To Much Wenlock
To Shipton-
To Much Wenlock
To Ludlow
To Broadstone
To Upper Millichope
To Eaton
To Ticklerton
To Ticklerton
To Soudley
To Church Stretton
To Cardington
To Cardington
To Plaish
To Church Preen and Hughley
Hughley Brook
Holy mill
LUSHCOTT
Lutwyche
PILGRIM LANE
Fegg
Oakham Farm
Wilderhope
Lower Stanway
Upper Stanway
(EATON - UNDER - HEYWOOD DETACHED)
LONGVILLE
Wood Fm.
Oakwood Farm
EAST WALL
Lakehouse
Coats
GRETTON TOWNSHIP
GRETTON
Court House
Gilberries
RUSHBURY HEATH
Heath Brook
Lakehouse Brook
RUSHBURY
castle
rectory
WALL UNDER HEYWOOD
Eaton Brook
Coley Brook
STONE ACTON
Hill End Farm
HILL END
WALL BANK
WALL'S BANK
GRETTON COMMON
HARGROVE COPPICE
Hargrove Farm
WENLOCK EDGE
WENLOCK WOOD
HOPE DALE
APEDALE
FORESTS
MOGG
ROMAN BANK
chapel
BLACKWOOD
LILYWOOD
AREA OF LIGHTWOOD
HOPE COMMON
N
contour heights in metres
woodland
former woodland and common
parish boundary
township boundary
Gretton
km
mile

Fig. 8

and perhaps a barrow.[11] The possible barrow lay near the most impressive monument in the parish, an Iron Age hill fort overlooking Hope Dale called the Ditches or Larden Ditches.[12]

Identification of Rushbury as the Antonine Itinerary's *Branogenium* may be discounted,[13] but evidence of Roman occupation has been found near the church.[14] A low motte, presumably Norman, stands at the north end of Rushbury village.[15]

The two larger Domesday manors and their recorded populations, Rushbury 10 and Stanway 8, evidently subsumed more than one settlement. Gretton's recorded population was 5, Lutwyche's 4.[16] Twenty-three paid to the 1327 subsidy from Rushbury parish, including four from Gretton township.[17] Thirty-five men from Rushbury were mustered in 1542 and six from Stone Acton.[18] In 1608, apart from the chief house, there were probably four houses in Coats manor, which was between Rushbury and East Wall.[19] They were apparently included *c.* 1644 in 12 properties returned under the heading Rushbury; the same list gives 12 for Gretton, *c.* 9 for Wall under Heywood, 9 for Stone Acton, 9 for East Wall, and 5 for Stanway.[20] In 1672 hearth tax was paid on 11 houses in Rushbury, 16 in Gretton, 11 in Wall under Heywood, 8 in Stone Acton, 3 in East Wall, and 6 in Stanway and Wilderhope.[21] In 1676 there were 177 adults in the parish.[22]

The parish population rose from 356 in 1801 to 507 in 1831. It remained at about that level until the civil parish was enlarged in 1883; thereafter the C.P.'s population was *c.* 550. Although in 1951 it fell to 466, it rose again to 589 by 1961.[23] After the C.P. was reduced in area in 1967[24] its population averaged *c.* 470.[25]

By the late 17th century cottages were beginning to encroach on the commons. The Benthalls (later Hargrove farm) was established in the western part of Hargrove by 1590.[26] A cottage had been built in Roman wood before 1602,[27] while *c.* 1650 there were seven cottages in or near Musegreave.[28] During the 17th, 18th, and earlier 19th centuries numerous cottages were built on Gretton common, Wall's Bank, Rushbury heath, Roman Bank, and Blackwood.[29]

Both cottages and farmhouses were timber framed in the 16th and 17th centuries, with rubble stone chimneys. Among larger examples of timber framed houses are the Coats[30] and Hall Farm, Wall under Heywood, both 15th-century. Hall Farm is a small **H** plan house of two storeys, with a cruck framed hall and box framed cross wings; originally timber framed on stone, the house was largely cased in brick in the mid 18th century. Seventeenth-century wall paintings, comprising geometric designs and inscriptions, were recorded during building works of the 1970s.[31] Rushbury Manor is late 16th- or early 17th-century,[32] and Church Farm, Rushbury,[33] and the **L** plan Malt House Farm, Wall under Heywood,[34] are early 17th-century. The last mentioned, unusually, is partly cased in stone. Of the two greater houses built in the late 16th century, Lutwyche Hall is of brick, Wilderhope Manor of coursed stone.[35] Before it became common (in the railway age) brick was also used in the Wilderhope Manor stables, perhaps 17th-century, at Wall under Heywood to refront Hall Farm and for Lutwyche House (the former Lutwyche Arms public house) in the mid 18th century, for Stanway Manor Farm in the late 18th or early 19th century, and for the new Manor Farm north-east of Rushbury in the early 19th century.[36] Stone, however, was also used. The early 18th-century Upper Farm, Gretton, is of stone,[37] and at Wall under Heywood Stone House, *c.* 1800, is of coursed and squared stone[38] and Wall House, about the same date,[39] is stuccoed stone. Of the later brick buildings the most notable is Stanway Manor, built in 1863 for William Horton, a retired colliery owner and architect, of Darlaston (Staffs.).[40]

Rushbury village, in 1840 a small settlement away from major roads, did not grow in the next century and a half. The dozen or so dwellings around the castle mound and the church display a variety of timber framing, stone, and brick, and the village was made a conservation area in 1986.[41]

After 1945 Wall under Heywood, on a more important road than Rushbury, slowly grew from a hamlet into a small village, albeit one without amenities beyond a garage (a former traction engine depot),[42] sub-post office, and public house. A wooden parish hall at Wall

11 C. H. Hartshorne, *Salopia Antiqua* (1841), 84.
12 Below, Shipton, intro.
13 Camden, *Brit.* (1772), i. 472; A. L. F. Rivet and C. Smith, *Place-Names of Roman Brit.* (1979), 275.
14 SA 634, 637; S.P.L., Chitty File 44/19; 278/1, 4; Hartshorne, *Salopia Antiqua*, 149.
15 SA 1254. Wrongly called tumulus on early O.S. maps, e.g. 1/2,500, Salop. LVI. 16 (1903 edn.).
16 *V.C.H. Salop.* i. 319–20, 328; below, manors.
17 *T.S.A.S.* 2nd ser. iv. 317–18.
18 *L. & P. Hen. VIII*, xvii, p. 508.
19 S.R.O. 1146/40; below, manors.
20 S.P.L., MS. 6741, pp. 106–7. What constitutes a property in the list (of a levy for Prince Rupert: cf. *V.C.H. Salop.* iii. 359) is unclear.
21 *Hearth Tax 1672* (Salop. Arch. Soc. 1949), 184–6.
22 *Compton Census*, ed. Whiteman, 259.
23 *V.C.H. Salop.* ii. 226; above, this section.
24 Above, this section.
25 *Census*, 1981, Small Area Statistics: Salop.; S.C.C. Property and Planning Services Dept. inf. rep. C91/103.
26 Below, manors (Gretton).
27 S.R.O. 5460/4/7/2.
28 S.R.O. 840, box 120, 'complaint concerning Musegreave'.
29 Ibid. box 112, surv. bk. of Gretton, etc., f. [5]; S.R.O., incl. award B 18; 3573/T/1–3.
30 Below, manors (Coats).
31 Dept. of Environment, *List of Bldgs.: R.D. of Ludlow* (1974), 229; rep. and photos. by Mrs. Moran.
32 Below, manors (Rushbury).
33 Ibid. (Church Yd. fm.).
34 SA 11358. It is hard to relate what survives to the ho. shown in S.R.O. 1242, box 14, map of Randal Cooke's est. 1771.
35 Below, manors (Wilderhope, Lutwyche).
36 SA 11345, 11353, 11355, 11357; below, manors (Stanway).
37 *List of Bldgs.: Shrews. and Atcham (pars. of All Stretton [etc.])* (1986), 25.
38 SA 11356.
39 Though a 16th-cent. date was claimed in 1956: R. & D.R.T., sale partics.
40 Ibid. record sheet and photo.
41 S.R.O. 3573/T/1; inf. from S.C.C. Property and Planning Services Dept.
42 Local inf. Cf. below, econ. hist.

under Heywood had opened *c.* 1930.[43] Ten council houses were built there *c.* 1950[44] and later a number of private houses.

Rushbury wake was held on the Sunday after the feast of St. Peter and St. Paul; it may latterly have been held at Wall under Heywood, where there was a wake until *c.* 1920.[45] Alesellers were licensed in the 17th and 18th centuries at Rushbury and Wall under Heywood.[46] There was only one alehouse in the parish in 1793,[47] but soon after that two public houses were opened at Wall under Heywood: the New Inn (so known in the 1830s and 1840s) had become the Lutwyche Arms by 1851 and closed in the 1920s; the Plough remained open.[48] Stoolball was played in the early 17th century[49] and there is said once to have been a cockpit at Upper Stanway.[50]

About 1892 the former almshouses in Rushbury were converted to a reading and recreation room. It was used by local clubs and contained a library[51] but had closed by 1956.[52]

Rushbury and Eaton-under-Heywood had an Association for the Prosecution of Felons in 1827, subscriptions being based on the poor rate.[53]

The novelist Stella Benson (1892–1933) was born at Lutwyche Hall.[54]

MANORS AND OTHER ESTATES. Alwine (Aelwin), a free man, held *RUSHBURY* in 1066. In 1086 Roger of Montgomery, earl of Shrewsbury, held Rushbury in chief and Roger de Lacy held it of him.[55] Earl Roger's son Robert of Bellême forfeited the lordship in 1102,[56] and the Lacys' estate became a tenancy in chief that descended to their coheirs[57] the Verduns, overlords until at least 1335,[58] and the Mortimers. By 1348, however, Roger de Mortimer (restored as earl of March 1354)[59] held the whole of Rushbury,[60] and the overlordship remained with the earldom of March at least until 1425, when the last Mortimer earl died leaving Richard, duke of York, as his heir.[61] In 1455 the manor was said to be held of the heir of Edward Russell[62] and in 1465 and 1467 of Edmund Russell,[63] possibly under a trust created by an earlier duke of York.[64]

In 1086 Otes of Bernières (fl. 1121) held 5 hides in Rushbury under Roger de Lacy.[65] In 1200 Otes's great-grandson Herbert of Rushbury was lord. He died without issue 1209 × 1221[66] and by 1242 the manor, held as 1 knight's fee, was divided between his sister Parnel, wife of Warner of Willey (d. by 1231),[67] and Stephen of Bitterley (*alias* de Scotot or Esketot), grandson of his other sister.[68] In the royal inquiry of 1255 the jurors returned verdicts on Wall under Heywood and West Wall distinct from that on Rushbury. Nevertheless West Wall seems to have been identical with Wall under Heywood and was then part of Rushbury manor.[69] In 1255 Stephen of Bitterley held half of the manor and Parnel's grandson Andrew of Willey the other half, though part of Andrew's inheritance was held in dower by his mother Burga and the rest, by reason of his minority, was in the hands of Margery de Lacy, who had inherited a moiety of the overlordship and carried it to her husband John de Verdun.[70]

Parnel of Willey's moiety descended with Willey: in 1302 Richard of Harley and his wife Burga of Willey held it, and by 1318 Burga held it in her widowhood. The two moieties, each ½ knight's fee, were probably reunited *c.* 1340 to be held as 1 knight's fee by the Burnells' heirs.[71]

Stephen of Bitterley was lord of the other moiety until 1274 or later, and in 1283 Roger of Bitterley sold it to Hugh Burnell (d. 1286),[72] whose son Philip died in 1294. During part of the minority of Philip's son Edward custody of his moiety was given to Guncelin of Badlesmere (d. 1301).[73] Edward Burnell had livery of his lands in 1307[74] and his moiety then, and the whole manor from *c.* 1340, descended with Acton Burnell until 1485.[75]

On the attainder of Francis, Viscount Lovel, in 1485 the manor was forfeited to the Crown.[76]

43 Inf. from R. & D.R.T.

44 Local inf.

45 S.P.L., MS. 6741, p. 219; S.R.O. 262/3, 5 July 1897, 2 July 1900, 1 July 1901; *T.C.S.V.F.C.* x. 172; P. J. Madeley, 'A geog. descr. of area in par. of Rushbury' (Shenstone Coll., Bromsgrove, dissertation, 1967), 59–60; E. Stokes, 'Local hist. of pars. of Hope Bowdler and Eaton under Heywood' (Wolverhampton Teachers' Coll. dissertation, 1966), 119. Mr. Madeley and Mrs. Stokes are thanked for loan of their work.

46 S.R.O., q. sess. rec. parcel 254, badgers', drovers', and alesellers' licensing bk.; parcels 255–6, regs. of alesellers' recognizances 1753–81.

47 S.P.L., MS. 6865, p. 165.

48 S.R.O. 1210/5–15; 1242, box 13, Lutwyche Arms deeds; box 14, deeds 30–1 Dec. 1824 (innkeeper mentioned); 1709/65/1–10; 3573/T/1–2, fields 455, 561; *P.O.* and *Kelly's Dir. Salop.* (1856–1941); Co. of Salop, *Return of Licensed Hos. 1901* (copy in S.P.L., accession 6117), 94; above.

49 *Salop.* (R.E.E.D.), i. 121–2.

50 H. E. Forrest, *Old Hos. of Wenlock* (Shrews. 1914), 47.

51 S.R.O. 3573/7/17; /9/2–3; *Kelly's Dir. Salop.* (1900–41).

52 Below, educ.

53 Rushbury & Eaton Assoc. for Prosecution of Felons, *Articles, &c.* (Ironbridge, 1827; copy in S.R.O. 1093, box 158).

54 R. Ellis Roberts, *Portrait of Stella Benson* (1939); *D.N.B.* 1931–40.

55 *V.C.H. Salop.* i. 328.

56 Ibid. iii. 9.

57 Eyton, v. 240.

58 *Bk. of Fees*, ii. 964, 972; *Roll of Salop. Eyre 1256* (Selden Soc. xcvi), p. 53; *Cal. Inq. p.m.* v, p. 392; vi, pp. 39–40; vii, p. 495; *Feud. Aids*, iv. 244.

59 *Complete Peerage*, viii. 443–4; G. A. Holmes, *Estates of Higher Nobility in 14th-Cent. Eng.* (1957), 14–16; *D.N.B.*

60 *Cal. Inq. p.m.* viii, p. 496; *Feud. Aids*, iv. 244.

61 *Cal. Inq. p.m.* xiv, p. 350; xviii, pp. 449–50; P.R.O., C 138/54, no. 116; C 139/19, no. 21; *Complete Peerage*, viii. 453.

62 *Cal. Inq. p.m.* (Rec. Com.), iv. 265.

63 P.R.O., C 140/13, no. 27; C 140/19, no. 20.

64 Edw. of York (d. 1415) enfeoffed John Russell (d. 1437, heirs unknown), still a trustee in the 1430s: *Hist. Parl., Commons*, 1386–1421, iv. 247–8.

65 *V.C.H. Salop.* i. 328; viii. 94; Eyton, vi. 83.

66 Eyton, iv. 95–6; vi. 83.

67 Eyton, iv. 96; vi. 83; below, Willey, manor.

68 *Bk. of Fees*, ii. 962, 964; Eyton, iv. 368; vi. 83.

69 Eyton, iv. 100, follows *Rot. Hund.* in noting W. Wall separately.

70 *Rot. Hund.* (Rec. Com.), ii. 70–1.

71 *Roll of Salop. Eyre 1256*, p. 53; *Cal. Chart. R.* 1300–26, 29, 398; *Cal. Inq. p.m.* vii, p. 495; *Feud. Aids*, iv. 229, 244.

72 Eyton, iv. 97, 369–70; vi. 83; ix. 45; *Rot. Hund.* ii. 70.

73 Eyton, iv. 97; *Cal. Inq. Misc.* i, pp. 469–70, 513; *Cal. Inq. p.m.* iii, p. 122; iv, p. 38.

74 *Complete Peerage*, ii. 434.

75 *Cal. Inq. p.m.* (Rec. Com.), iv. 265; *Cal. Inq. p.m.* v, p. 392; vi, p. 39; vii, p. 495; viii, p. 496; xiv, p. 350; xvii, p. 449; *Feud. Aids*, iv. 229, 244, 250, 267; *Cal. Close*, 1346–9, 111; 1419–22, 154; *Cat. Anct. D.* ii, C 2398; P.R.O., C 138/54, no. 116; C 139/19, no. 21; C 140/13, no. 27; C 140/19, no. 20; C 148/45; *T.S.A.S.* xlvii. 50–3; *V.C.H. Salop.* viii. 7; above, this section.

76 *Complete Peerage*, viii. 225.

In 1488 Henry VII granted it in tail male to his uncle and councillor John, Viscount Welles (d.s.p. 1499),[77] but by 1497 it seems to have belonged to Henry, duke of York,[87] who as Henry VIII in 1514 granted Rushbury in tail male to Thomas Howard, newly created duke of Norfolk (d. 1524).[79] In 1533 Norfolk's son and heir Thomas[80] exchanged Rushbury and other manors for estates in Surrey and Sussex with Sir John Dudley,[81] later Lord Lisle and earl of Warwick.[82] In 1549 Warwick exchanged Rushbury with Nicholas Heath, bishop of Worcester, in right of his see,[83] and the freehold and inheritance of the manorial rights then descended with those of Holdgate until 1861.[84]

In 1548 Warwick had leased Rushbury and other properties to Bishop Heath's brother William for 200 years. Heath assigned his lease in 1552 to Henry Cressett (d. 1563), who left his interest to his nephew Richard Cressett (d. 1601) of Upton Cressett. Richard in turn left the property to Edward, grandson of Thomas Cressett of the Coates (in Holdgate), and thereafter, until 1861, the lease descended with Cound manor. In 1861 the lessee, the Revd. Henry Thursby-Pelham, bought the freehold from the Ecclesiastical Commissioners.[85]

Thursby-Pelham sold the manor, probably to the Staffordshire ironmaster W. H. Sparrow (d. 1867), whose son Arthur, of Church Preen, owned it in 1868.[86] On Arthur's death in 1898 the manor passed to his youngest son A. B. H. Sparrow (from 1899 Hanbury-Sparrow) who died in 1936 leaving it to his son Lt.-Col. A. A. H. Hanbury-Sparrow (fl. 1952).[87] By 1949 C. E. Edwards owned the major portion of the Sparrows' former Rushbury estate, which he was then, and in 1951, offering for sale.[88]

Rushbury castle, represented by remains of the motte and its surrounding ditch,[89] was presumably the manor house in the early Middle Ages. The adjacent Rushbury Manor is a late 16th- or early 17th-century timber framed house of two storeys and an attic, with three front and two rear gables. The building and its yards were occupied with Church Yard farm in the mid 19th century; apparently divided into three about then, it was restored as one house *c.* 1966.[90]

After the reunion of the moieties of Rushbury manor *c.* 1340 some interest in Wall under Heywood was apparently retained by the Harleys' heirs, for in 1540 land there was held of Richard Lacon by the Gowers of Stone Acton.[91] In 1613 *WALL UNDER HEYWOOD* was one of several manors or reputed manors mortgaged by Sir Francis Lacon, and in 1616 property there was among that which, with his son Rowland, he sold to Isaac Jones and Richard Newell. Jones's brother Edward sold what was probably all his property in Wall under Heywood in 1636. It belonged to the Baldwins of All Stretton 1636–1722 and in 1770 was bought by Elizabeth Cressett, lady of Rushbury.[92]

In 1495–6 Wenlock priory kitchen received 8*s.* from the tithes of Wall under Heywood,[93] but nothing more is known of the property.

The duke of Norfolk may have retained land in Rushbury after 1533 for in 1574 (after his grandson's forfeiture) the Crown granted a 21-year lease of lands in Rushbury and Chatwall (in Cardington), lately the executed duke's, to Henry Myddelmore, a courtier.[94] The later history of the property has not been traced.

By 1587 the Lees of Langley had land in Rushbury.[95] The property descended with Acton Burnell manor[96] until 1824 when Sir Edward Joseph Smythe sold *RUSHBURY FARM* (later Manor farm) to Barnard Dickinson (d. 1852), manager of the Coalbrookdale Co.'s works.[97] By 1868, with *CHURCH YARD FARM* (evidently acquired from the Thursby-Pelhams with the manor), it was part of Arthur Sparrow's 438-a. estate in Rushbury.[98] The estate belonged to the Sparrows until 1948 and then changed hands more than once before Richard Minton bought it in 1953.[99] The 17th-century Church (formerly Church Yard) Farm, north-east of the church,[1] is a **T** plan building of two storeys, timber framed with stone gable ends.[2]

Francis Leigh (d. 1710), of Puttenham (Surr.), owned property in Rushbury by 1683, and it passed to his daughter and son-in-law Frances and Jasper Jones.[3]

77 Ibid. xii (2), 448–50; *Cal. Pat.* 1485–94, 236; *Sel. Cases in Council of Hen. VII* (Selden Soc. lxxv), pp. xxix, cxii.
78 S.R.O. 3365/165.
79 Formerly earl of Surrey: *L. & P. Hen. VIII*, i (2), p. 1170; *Complete Peerage*, xii (1), 513.
80 *V.C.H. Salop.* viii. 7.
81 P.R.O., CP 40/1079, Carte rott. 1–2; *V.C.H. Surr.* iii. 464–5. Conveyance was completed in 1541–2 after Norfolk had acquired the Crown's reversion: *L. &. P. Hen. VIII*, xvi, p. 240; Staffs. R.O., D. 593/B/2/8/2; P.R.O., CP 25/2/35/234/32 Hen. VIII Hil. no. 8.
82 *Complete Peerage*, ix. 722–4; xii (2), 397.
83 *Cal. Pat.* 1548–9, 255, 298; *V.C.H. Salop.* iv. 130.
84 P.R.O., C 54/3405, m. 27; S.P.L., Deeds 6116, 10195; S.R.O. 2334/1/2, receiver's credit acct. 15 Apr. 1815; below, Holdgate, manors.
85 S.P.L., Deeds 6116, 10195; Bodl. MS. Blakeway 11, f. 113v.; *V.C.H. Salop.* viii. 63–4; S.R.O. 563/2; 933, box 16, abstr. of title to mans. of Holdgate, etc.; 2334/1/2, receiver's credit acct. 15 Apr. 1815; 5460/3/14, scheds.; /5/3/1; /6/1; q. sess. rec. parcel 261, reg. of gamekeepers 1799–1807, f. 106; *P.O. Dir. Salop.* (1856), 107; below, Holdgate, manors (Brookhampton).
86 S.R.O. 536/2; Burke, *Land. Gent.* (1952), 2366–7; *V.C.H. Salop.* iv. 211; viii. 126.
87 *Kelly's Dir. Salop.* (1885–1941); S.R.O. 4044/91, pp. 41–2; Burke, *Land. Gent.* (1952), 2366–7.
88 S.R.O. 508/10; 4654/7.
89 SA 1254.
90 Rep. by Mrs. M. Moran; S.R.O. 536/1–2; 3573/T/1–2; Madeley, 'Geog. descr. Rushbury', 43.
91 P.R.O., C 142/67, no. 142; *V.C.H. Salop.* viii. 87–8.
92 S.R.O. 563/6/1–2; 840, box 41, deed 15 Nov. 1613; 5460/2/2/1, 3; below, this section (Gretton).
93 Eyton, iv. 100.
94 *Cal. Pat.* 1572–5, p. 239; *Complete Peerage*, ix. 623–4.
95 Cf. below, Longville, etc., manors (East Wall).
96 *V.C.H. Salop.* viii. 8; P.R.O., CP 25/2/590/1653 Mich. no. 6; CP 43/412, rot. 12; CP 43/422, rot. 226; S.R.O., q. sess. rec. parcel 281, reg. of papists' deeds 1717–88, pp. 99, 208, 217; S.R.O. 3651, box 87, sched. of deeds.
97 S.R.O. 3573/T/1–2; 3651, box 87, sale papers, etc., 1818, art. of agreement 27 Mar. 1824; 4835/50; *Shrews. Chron.* 17 Sept. 1819, p. 142; A. Raistrick, *Dynasty of Iron Founders: the Darbys and Coalbrookdale* (1953), 3, 227–8, 253, 256.
98 S.R.O. 536/2; 3573/T/1–2.
99 Inf. from R. & D.R.T.
1 Ibid.; S.R.O. 3573/T/1–2.
2 *List of Bldgs.: R. D. of Ludlow*, 228; S.A. 11350.
3 S.R.O. 1007/1. Cf. *V.C.H. Surr.* iii. 54.

The Leightons of Plaish had property in Wall under Heywood and East Wall in the earlier 17th century.[4]

Rushbury manor included land in *EAST WALL* that was subinfeudated in the mid 12th century to Basile (or Sibyl), possibly a relative of Otes of Bernières, the Domesday lord of Rushbury. Basile (d. before 1165) was succeeded by her daughter Eve, who married first Robert of Brimpton, *alias* of Longford (d. by 1185), and secondly Walter de Witefeld (fl. 1200). The estate passed to Eve's son Adam of Brimpton (d. *c.* 1235), who was succeeded by another Adam.[5] The Brimptons' mesne lordship may have lapsed in the next century, for by 1436 Sir John Radcliffe (d. 1441) was lord, presumably in right of his wife Catherine (d. 1452), lady of Rushbury manor.[6]

By 1255 East Wall had been further subinfeudated to the Sprenchoses of Longnor,[7] and the following Sprenchoses held it: Roger, who held 1 hide there in 1255;[8] Roger, fl. *c.* 1316,[9] and Sir John, fl. 1348–1350.[10] The family apparently retained some interest in East Wall in 1483 when John and Maud Sprenchose sold property there to John de Betenhull, clerk.[11]

Lawrence Ludlow held courts for East Wall in 1505 and 1507,[12] and thenceforward the manor descended with the Moorhouse (in Shipton), being sold in 1721 with a share of the Moorhouse by kinsmen of the Ludlows to Samuel Edwards (d. 1738) of West Coppice, described as lord of East Wall in 1733.[13] About 1745 Edwards's trustees sold East Wall manor and 227 a. there to William Beresford.[14] In 1748 Beresford sold it to Godfrey Kneller (d. 1781), of Donhead Hall (Wilts.).[15] By 1775 Charles Maverley (d. by 1795), of Gray's Inn, was lord.[16]

In 1808 Sarah Wildman, of Turnham Green (Mdx.), sold the manor and 242 a. to Thomas Gibbons of Eudon Burnell,[17] who in 1840 had 248 a. in the Rushbury portion of East Wall.[18] John Gibbons farmed at East Wall in 1856.[19] Abraham Haworth, a cotton merchant who owned 731 a. in all at East Wall, had the farm in 1910.[20] Sold with the rest of Haworth's estate in 1925, the farm changed hands several times before being bought in 1947 by the Taylors, owners in 1990.[21]

Manor Farm, presumably the house at East Wall taxed on four hearths in 1672,[22] has a 17th-century core. Refurbished and cased in brick in the mid 18th century, it was modernized again in the mid 19th. Later in the 19th century it was rebuilt in slightly flamboyant gothic as a 1½ storeyed building.

Sir Thomas Lacon (d. 1536) had an estate in Rushbury including property at East Wall which passed to his son Richard (d. 1543).[23] Richard's son Rowland (d. 1608) greatly reduced the family's estate in the parish by the sale in 1581 of Lily wood, south of Rushbury, to Richard Leighton of Coats.[24] In 1616 Rowland's son Sir Francis Lacon sold property, including East Wall 'manor', to Isaac Jones and Richard Newell; the claim to manorial status, like those the Lacons advanced in respect of their properties in Wall under Heywood, Wilderhope,[25] and elsewhere,[26] seems to have been baseless.

From 1616 the Lacons' East Wall property probably descended with Gretton in the Jones family. Like Gretton, a property (38 a.) at East Wall was offered for sale by Sir Thomas John Tyrwhitt Jones (d. 1839) in 1824.[27] It may have failed to sell, for his widow Eliza (d. 1865) had 54 a. at East Wall in 1840.[28] It was worked from a cottage south-west of East Wall, which had been demolished by 1901.[29]

In 1568 Nicholas Crosthwaite, lord of Easthope, sold a messuage and lands in East Wall to John Adys of Frampton on Severn (Glos.), who in 1578 sold it to Edward Lutwyche of Lutwyche. In 1614, when Lutwyche died, the property was held partly of East Wall manor and partly of Rushbury manor.[30] The Lutwyche family evidently continued to own property in East Wall until 1785 when East Wall farm (77 a.) was offered for sale.[31] It was probably withdrawn from sale and then descended with Wilderhope.[32] In 1907 R. B. Benson of Lutwyche sold a farm at East Wall to Rowland Tench,[33] who had apparently sold it to Abraham Haworth

4 P.R.O., CP 25/2/591/1655 Trin. [no. 15].
5 Eyton, iv. 95, 102; vi. 83.
6 S.R.O. 840, box 1, Gretton ct. r. 1436–7; *V.C.H. Salop.* viii. 7; above, this section.
7 Eyton, iv. 102–3; *V.C.H. Salop.* viii. 109.
8 *Rot. Hund.* ii. 70.
9 S.R.O. 840, box 41, deeds of 1315, 1317; Eyton, iv. 103.
10 S.P.L., Deeds 10764; Barnard MSS., Raby Castle, box 1, bdle. 29, no. 8.
11 Barnard MSS., Raby Castle, box 1, bdle 1, no. 53 (dorse).
12 P.R.O., C 116/205.
13 *S.P.R. Heref.* xix (3), p. iv; below, Shipton, manors (Moorhouse); Staffs. R.O., D. (W.) 1788, parcel 43, bdle. 10, deed 14 Nov. 1554; parcel 47, bdle. 3, will of Maurice Ludlow; S.R.O., q. sess. rec. box 160, reg. of gamekeepers 1711–42, 20 Oct. 1733; P.R.O., CP 25/2/654/2 & 3 Phil. & Mary Hil. [no. 21]; CP 25/2/477/8 Chas. I Hil. [no. 23]; CP 25/2/1651 Hil. [no. 5]; CP 25/2/867/3 Wm. & Mary Mich. [no. 19]; CP 25/2/960/11 Anne Mich. [no. 4]; CP 25/2/1054/7 Geo. I Hil. [no. 10].
14 S.R.O. 1359, box 35, deeds 20 Feb. 1743/4, 7–8 Jan. 1744/5; 2089/1/3/38–40; 4572/6/2/56.
15 S.R.O. 1359, box 35, deed 6 Feb. 1747/8; *V.C.H. Wilts.* xiii. 146.
16 S.R.O., q. sess. rec. box 260, reg. of gamekeepers 1742–79, 7 Sept. 1775; *Gent. Mag.* lxv (1), 261.
17 S.R.O. 515/6, pp. 314–15; 1359, box 35, conveyance 24–5 Mar. 1808; cf. *Gent. Mag.* lxv (2), 1060, 1111; *V.C.H. Mdx.* vii. 78; *Hist. Parl., Commons*, 1790–1820, ii. 578.
18 S.R.O. 3573/T/1–2.
19 *P.O. Dir. Salop.* (1856), 108.
20 S.R.O. 4044/91, pp. 48–9; below, Longville, etc., manors (E. Wall); inf. from R. & D.R.T.
21 S.R.O. 5518, pp. 10–12; inf. from R. & D.R.T.
22 *Hearth Tax 1672* (Salop. Arch. Soc. 1949), 185.
23 P.R.O., C 142/68, no. 7; *V.C.H. Salop.* viii. 88.
24 S.R.O. 840, box 41, deed 31 July 1581; *V.C.H. Salop.* viii. 88.
25 S.R.O. 563/6/1–2; P.R.O., CP 25/2/343/14 Jas. I Trin. no. 13; *V.C.H. Salop.* viii. 88; above and below, this section (Wall, Wilderhope).
26 Below, Broseley, manors.
27 Below, Gretton; S.R.O. 840, box 116, draft sale partic. 1824; *V.C.H. Salop.* viii. 316.
28 S.R.O. 3573/T/1–2.
29 Ibid.; O.S. Map 1/2,500, Salop. LVI. 12 (1903 edn.).
30 *S.P.R. Heref.* xix (3), p. iv; P.R.O., C 142/381, no. 160; S.P.L., Deeds 1416; below, this section (Lutwyche).
31 S.R.O. 438/13; 4835/2, p. 18; B.R.L., MS. 577365.
32 S.R.O. 3573/T/1–2; below, this section (Wilderhope).
33 *Shrews. Chron.* 19 July 1907, p. 7.

by 1910.[34] The farm was disposed of with the rest of Haworth's estate in 1925.[35] Brook House Farm, as it was then called, is a small 1½ storeyed timber framed house of the 17th century, later extended.

COATS may early have been part of Rushbury manor.[36] Walter de Witefeld held a freehold there and at Wall in 1200; it included 20 a. of pasture and 40 a. of wood, once his mother-in-law Basile's marriage portion, the status of which was disputed with Herbert, lord of Rushbury. A jury found that Walter held that land in demesne and not of Herbert.[37]

By 1255 Coats, like East Wall, was held in fee by the Sprenchose family. They had subinfeudated Coats to tenants who took their name from it. In 1255 John of Gatacre held Coats as ½ hide as guardian of the heir of John of Coats. That heir, John of Coats (fl. 1263), was apparently succeeded by William of Coats (fl. 1272–92).[38] He or a namesake occurred in 1318.[39] Richard Smallman (fl. 1379) was lord in 1374.[40]

Coats was later held by a branch of the Leightons of Church Stretton.[41] Edward Leighton was perhaps succeeded by a son John (fl. 1487–97),[42] he by his son Ralph (coroner in 1533), and he, by 1557,[43] by his son Richard, perhaps undersheriff 1587–8.[44] Richard (d. 1605) left his second son Nicholas as his heir. Dealings of the eldest son Richard (b. 1562, d.v.p.) led to litigation over the estate between Nicholas and his younger brother William, but Nicholas established his title and in 1610 sold Coats and two mills in Rushbury to Humphrey Lee of Langley.[45]

By 1678 Sir Francis Edwardes (d. 1690), of Meole Brace, owned Coats[46] and his son and namesake was lord in 1721.[47] By 1734 Coats (325 a. in 1785) was part of the Lutwyche estate[48] and it then appears to have descended with Wilderhope.[49] R. B. Benson of Lutwyche sold Coats Hall farm (323 a.) to Abraham Haworth *c.* 1910[50] and it changed hands several times in the 20th century.[51]

The chief house originally stood within a rectangular moat. The box framed hall of *c.* 1486, originally *c.* 30 × 24 ft., was later truncated and a floor was inserted in it; it retains an arch-braced central truss and a spere truss. The screens passage is entered through a 16th-century timber framed porch. A parlour wing incorporates a kitchen, originally detached. In the 17th century that wing was much altered and the hall divided. The whole is now partly cased in brick. The outbuildings include a fine late 16th-century barn.[52]

The early manorial connexions of *WILDERHOPE* are uncertain.[53] The tenancy in chief, like that of Rushbury, was evidently divided between Walter de Lacy's granddaughters and coheirs Margery de Verdun and Maud de Geneville, but the shares of their Wilderhope lordship were not reunited (as those of their Rushbury lordship were) in the Mortimers' hands.[54]

Margery's grandson Tibbald de Verdun (d. 1316) had ½ knight's fee in Wilderhope,[55] at least part of which had passed by 1335 to one of his daughters and coheirs Isabel (d. 1349), wife of Henry, Lord Ferrers (d. 1343).[56] Their son William, Lord Ferrers, had all the ½ knight's fee at his death in 1371.[57] The same estate passed to his son Henry, Lord Ferrers of Groby (d. 1388) and to Henry's son William, Lord Ferrers of Groby.[58]

Maud de Geneville's granddaughter Joan, widow of Roger de Mortimer, earl of March (d. 1330), held lands at Wilderhope in chief at her death in 1356.[59] The descent of the shares of the overlordship of Wilderhope after the 14th century has not been traced, but in 1639 Wilderhope was said to be held in socage of the heirs of Richard Harnage.[60]

Before 1225 the terre tenancy of Wilderhope manor had belonged to Parnel, sister and heir of Herbert of Rushbury, and her husband Warner of Willey.[61] Their son Andrew of Willey (d. 1265) succeeded to Wilderhope[62] and Andrew's daughter and heir Burga of Harley held it in 1283.[63] Burga had married Richard of Harley, and Wilderhope manor descended thereafter with Harley until 1583,[64] when Rowland Lacon sold Wilderhope to Thomas Smalman,[65] a law-

34 S.R.O. 4044/91, pp. 48–9.
35 S.R.O. 5518, pp. 8–9.
36 Eyton, iv. 96, 103.
37 Ibid. 95; *Abbrev. Plac.* (Rec. Com.), 27; *Cur. Reg. R.* i. 351, 360–1.
38 Eyton, iv. 103; above, this section (E. Wall).
39 S.P.L., MS. 4080, p. 2187.
40 S.R.O. 3195/1, ff. 107, 116.
41 For pedigree see *Visit. Salop. 1623*, ii (Harl. Soc. xxix), 323.
42 SA 15506; S.R.O. 3365/165.
43 S.R.O. 1146/38.
44 *V.C.H. Salop.* iii. 76.
45 *Visit. Salop. 1623*, ii. 323; B. Botfield, *Stemmata Botevilliana* (1858), 186; N.L.W., Pitchford Hall 950; S.R.O. 1146/39–40; 3573/Rg/1, bapt. of younger Ric. 13 Dec. 1562; 5001/4/6/1–2; S.P.L., Deeds 2585; P.R.O., C 2/Jas. I/L 13/13; C 142/300, no. 167.
46 N.L.W., Pitchford Hall 831; *T.S.A.S.* 4th ser. xii. 219.
47 *T.S.A.S.* 4th ser. xii. 219; S.R.O., q. sess. rec. box 260, reg. of gamekeepers 1711–42, 13 Dec. 1721.
48 S.R.O., q. sess. rec. box 260, reg. of gamekeepers 1711–42, 25 Oct. 1734.
49 Ibid. 25 Apr. 1735; 1742–79, 7 Sept. 1775; S.R.O. 3573/T/1–2; 4835/2, p. 13; P.R.O., CP 25/2/1396/50 Geo. III Trin. no. 7; below, this section (Wilderhope).
50 Cf. *Shrews. Chron.* 19 July 1907, p. 7; S.R.O. 4044/91, p. 57.
51 Inf. from R. & D.R.T.; S.R.O. 5518, pp. 14–15.
52 S.R.O. 3573/T/1; 3763/78/4/12; SA 553, 15506; M. R. Bismanis, 'Minor domestic archit. of Middle Ages in cos. of Heref. and Salop.' (Nott. Univ. Ph.D. thesis, 1975), i. 139–42; ii. 12, 25; *Vernacular Archit.* xxvii. 104–5.
53 Eyton, iv. 96, 100, is perhaps too definite in stating that it was originally a member of Rushbury and in asserting that its status as a joint township with Stanway is merely modern.
54 Above, this section (Rushbury).
55 *Cal. Inq. p.m.* vi, p. 39. For Verdun pedigree see Eyton, v. 272–9; I. J. Sanders, *Eng. Baronies* (1963), 95–6.
56 *Cal. Inq. p.m.* vii, p. 498. For Ferrers pedigree see *Complete Peerage*, v. 344–54.
57 *Cal. Inq. p.m.* xiii, p. 69.
58 Ibid. xvi, p. 215; xvii, p. 149; *Cal. Close*, 1392–6, 303.
59 *Cal. Inq. p.m.* x, p. 255.
60 *T.S.A.S.* 3rd ser. i. 327.
61 S.R.O. 840, box 41, undated deed, Warner and Parnel to Wm. of Harley (d. 1225: *V.C.H. Salop.* viii. 87) and Engelard the chaplain; above, this section (Rushbury); below, Willey, manor.
62 Eyton, iv. 101.
63 S.R.O. 840, box 41, charter 17 Dec. 1283.
64 *Cal. Inq. p.m.* vi, p. 39; vii, pp. 495, 498; xii, p. 69; xvi, p. 215; xvii, p. 149; *Cal. Chart. R.* 1300–26, 398; *Cal. Close*, 1392–6, 303; S.R.O. 566/11; 1224/3/152–3; P.R.O., C 142/68, no. 7; CP 25/1/288/49, no. 707.
65 *T.S.A.S.* 3rd ser. iii. 17.

yer[66] whose family probably originated in the Rushbury area. In 1583 Smalman also bought a small farm in Wilderhope from Richard Parramore, a London merchant.[67] The estate then descended from father to son in the Smalmans, from Thomas (d. 1590) successively to Stephen (d. 1635),[68] Francis (d. 1639), Thomas (d. 1693) who compounded for the sequestrated estate in 1649, Henry (d. by 1706), and Thomas.[69]

Thomas Smalman sold Wilderhope to Thomas Lutwyche in 1734[70] and Wilderhope descended with Lutwyche[71] until 1785, when it was the subject of a Chancery suit by William Lutwyche, illegitimate son of William Lutwyche (d. 1773) and beneficiary under the wills of two of his father's three sisters.[72] Three estates seem to have been created in the Lutwyche family's landed property and shares in them passed to various members of the family.[73] With the sale of Lutwyche in 1785[74] the estate centred on Wilderhope. A share went to Mrs. Sarah Winford, the elder William Lutwyche's youngest sister and possibly his heir at law;[75] she sold it to Joseph Harris of Bewdley (Worcs.).[76] Other shares went to the younger William Lutwyche and to his sisters Mrs. Eleanor Mayhew (d. 1832) and Mrs. Clementina Handasyd (d. 1838), both latterly of Walcot (Wilts.). Presumably after their brother's death without issue in 1823 they added the surname Lutwyche and set up trusts[77] under which 1,328 a.[78] eventually came to Capt. W. W. T. Bayntun, son of Sir Henry William Bayntun (d. 1840) and Mrs. Mayhew Lutwyche's daughter Sophia (d. 1830).[79] Sir H. W. Bayntun had also acquired Sarah Winford's share in the estate by devise of Joseph Harris in 1833. Capt. Bayntun (d. unm. 1842) was succeeded by his sister Mrs. C. E. M. Boodé. In 1851 some of Mrs. Boodé's land passed to M. G. Benson of Lutwyche, perhaps by exchange. Mrs. Boodé, widowed in 1870, married, probably in 1872, the Baron de Villefranche and died in 1888[80] when Wilderhope passed to her daughter Mrs. C. E. L. Hippisley of Ston Easton (Som.), the owner in 1903.[81]

By 1907 Wilderhope belonged to R. B. Benson of Lutwyche, who sold it that year to T. C. Williams.[82] In 1916 Mary Ann Williams, presumably his widow, sold the estate to William Connell.[83] Wilderhope Manor was bought from Connell's widow Emma Lizzie for the National Trust in 1936 by the Cadbury Trust, which in 1971 also bought the adjacent 216-a. farm from T. C. P. Connell as an endowment for the Manor and thereby reunited the estate.[84]

Francis Smalman built Wilderhope Manor between 1584 (when his brother Thomas granted him a 40-year lease of land bought in 1583 from Richard Parramore) or 1591 (when Thomas's will required all his Wilderhope lands to be leased to Francis) and perhaps 1593 when Francis's wife died.[85]

The house, of six bays and 2½ storeys, faces south-east (assumed south in the following description) across a shallow valley.[86] It is of limestone rubble with quoins, mullions, and pediments of Hoar Edge grit. The upper parts of the chimneys and the shafts are of brick, the former diapered. The roof is of Harnage stone slates. It was taxed on seven hearths in 1672.[87] The hall, presumably with great chamber over, has a screens passage at its west end entered through a projecting porch bay. The hall has a lateral north fireplace and a south-facing oriel at its west end. Like the porch, the oriel rises the full height of the house and is gabled. The south front is generously provided with mullioned and transomed windows. On the north is a projecting semicircular staircase turret, and the great chamber did not therefore have to function also as a first-floor passage room. A secondary newel stair rises in the angle between porch, screens, and

66 Ibid. 2, claiming, prob. incorrectly, that he was a member of the Council in the Marches of Wales: cf. P. Williams, *Council in Marches of Wales* (1958), app. IV (no entry).

67 Eyton, iv. 87, 101; Forrest, *Old Hos. of Wenlock*, 45–6; *T.S.A.S.* 2nd ser. viii, p. xii; above, this section (Coats); P.R.O., C 3/146, no. 101.

68 W.B.R., B3/1/3, p. 447; *T.S.A.S.* 3rd ser. ii. 18.

69 *T.S.A.S.* 3rd ser. ii. 326–7; iii. 8, 13, 18.

70 Ibid. ii. 326–7; iii. 18; P.R.O., C 142/610, no. 97; *Cal. Cttee. for Compounding*, iii. 1646; *Hearth Tax 1672*, 186.

71 S.R.O., q sess. rec. box 260, reg. of gamekeepers 1711–42, 25 Oct. 1734, 25 Apr. 1735; 1742–79, 7 Sept. 1775; S.R.O. 4835/2, pp. 8–9.

72 Lutwyche and others *v.* Winford and others: S.R.O. 1150/201–2; 4835/2.

73 New Ho. fm. (Shipton) deeds, abstr. of title (1909) of trustees of Mr. and Mrs. John Hippisley's marr. settlement. Thanks are due to Mr. and Mrs. B. D. Williams, New Ho., for a sight of these deeds.

74 Below, this section (Lutwyche).

75 Unless his daus. were legitimate: cf. below, n. 77; S.P.L., MS. 2079, p. 403; S.R.O. 589/1, omitting Thos. (d. 1734); *Hist. Parl., Commons*, 1715–54, ii. 61, 231.

76 S.P.L., MS. 4078, pp. 994–5, containing useful details despite being full of genealogical errors (corrected ibid. MS. 2079, p. 403); Loton Hall MSS., Sir B. Leighton's diary 27 Oct. 1865.

77 New Ho. fm. deeds, abstr. of title to Hippisley marr. settlement; S.P.L., MS. 4078, pp. 994–5, according to which the sis. of Wm. Lutwyche (d. 1823) were legitimate, their father having marr. Cath. Lane before their births; P.R.O., CP 43/877, rot. 374; CP 43/960, rot. 49; Weston (Som.) par. reg., bur. 26 Jan. 1832, 10 Dec. 1838, and M.I. in ch.

78 *Ret. of Owners of Land* [C. 1097–I], Salop. p. 18, H.C. (1874), lxxii (2). Refs. (ibid.; S. Bagshaw, *Dir. Salop.* (1851), 545–6; *P.O. Dir. Salop.* (1879), 390; below, n. 80) to 'Mrs. Lutwyche' as a principal landowner in the par. are to the two Mrs. Lutwyches' trustees. Their sis.-in-law, the last Mrs. Lutwyche, d. 1845: Weston (Som.) par. reg., bur. 1 Mar. 1845, and M.I. in ch.

79 *Gent. Mag.* N.S. ii (2), 884; Burke, *Commoners* (1833–8), iv. 330–1; P.R.O., CP 25/2/1396/50 Geo. III Trin. no. 7; S.R.O., q. sess. rec. box 302, reg. of coms. in militia 1834–72; *D.N.B.* s.v. Bayntun, Sir H. W.

80 New Ho. fm. deeds, abstr. of title to Hippisley marr. settlement; Loton Hall MSS., Sir B. Leighton's diary 27 Oct. 1865; S.P.L., MS. 4078, pp. 994–5; S.R.O. 809, parcel 3, Lutwyche est. rental 1843–53; box 10, Lushcott, etc., ests., copy valn. and rep. *re* proposed exchange betw. M. G. Benson and Mrs. Lutwyche 1849.

81 S.R.O. 809, box 9, letter to R. B. Benson, 3 Apr. 1891; *T.S.A.S.* 3rd ser. iii. 19; Burke, *Land. Gent.* (1914), 947.

82 *Wilderhope Man.* (Nat. Trust, n.d.), 5; below, this section (Lutwyche).

83 Inf. from Nat. Trust.

84 Ibid.; *Wilderhope Man.* 5; S.P.L., Caradoc press cuttings, xx. 147–9.

85 *Wilderhope Man.* 2; *T.S.A.S.* 2nd ser. viii, p. xii; 3rd ser. iii. 16.

86 Pl. 12. Brief accts. appear in G. Jackson-Stops, *Wilderhope Man.* (Nat. Trust, 1984); *T.S.A.S.* 2nd ser. viii, pp. xi–xiii; 3rd ser. iii. 15–17; early illustrns. in Bodl. MS. Top. Salop. c. 2, ff. 535–7; Northants. R.O., Hartshorne colln. vol. xxv, pp. 85–7.

87 *Hearth Tax 1672*, 186.

service bay. The parlour range at the east end of the house has an east chimney stack and a projecting north garderobe chute. The service range at the west end of the house extends back north of the hall, and its large west chimney stack suggests that originally its ground floor was mainly taken up with kitchen rather than pantries.

The parlour and hall are among several rooms retaining their original moulded plaster ceilings; devices include Francis and Ellen Smalman's initials and formerly included the family's arms and motto.[88] Some original fireplaces survive. Perhaps in the 17th century the parlour and great chamber were subdivided; otherwise alterations have been few. After 1734 the house probably declined, and it was ruinous and uninhabited by 1936 when renovation began, to make it into a youth hostel.

North-east of the Manor is a smaller brick building of two storeys with projecting gabled end bays, probably built in the 17th century, perhaps as stables. South-west of the Manor is Wilderhope Farm, rebuilt in 1936.[89]

FEGG, a house and 182 a., was owned with Wilderhope in 1785[90] and until 1851 when M. G. Benson acquired it.[91] In the late 1930s G. R. Benson sold it to Mrs. William Connell, whose family owned it in 1990.[92] Fegg Farm is a small 17th-century timber framed building with a brick range of *c.* 1800.

If, as has been suggested, *STONE ACTON* was part of the Domesday manor of Stanway,[93] the connexion may have been recent in 1086. To the west and north the estates in Cardington and Gretton presumed to have belonged to Warin the bald (d. *c.* 1085) almost surrounded Stone Acton:[94] Warin may therefore have owned that too, adding it to his manor of Stanway, on the opposite side of Rushbury, to compensate for Stanway's loss of most of Broadstone which Warin had given to Shrewsbury abbey.[95]

In the earlier 13th century Philip of Broseley held Stone Acton. His immediate overlord was Madoc of Sutton, lord of Stanway *c.* 1240 when Philip gave Stone Acton (½ hide) to the Templars of Lydley.[96] Following the Templars' suppression in 1308[97] Stone Acton passed to the Hospitallers of Dinmore (Herefs.) and from them, in 1540, to the Crown.[98] In 1554 Stone Acton rents formerly the Hospitallers' were granted in fee to Sir Edmund Peckham, Thomas Holmes, and Gilbert Langton.[99]

In 1570 George, son of Roger Smythe of Morville, sold the reputed manor of Stone Acton to Robert Acton of Aldenham.[1] The next lord was Robert's son Walter.[2] Edward Lutwyche (d. 1614) bought the manor from William Tipper and Robert Dawe in 1601.[3] His son Edward (d. 1639) left a 40-year interest in the property to his daughters Elizabeth and Sarah, with remainder to his younger son John.[4] In 1668 John, of Stone Acton, sold the manor to his nephew Edward Lutwyche (kt. 1684, d. 1709).[5] The manor then descended with Lutwyche at least until 1785, when it was among the parts of the Lutwyche estate offered for sale. The Lutwyches' estate in Stone Acton then comprised Stone Acton farm (273 a.), to which was attached a sheep walk of 185 a., probably on Cardington Hill.[6]

Richard Jones, gentleman, lived at Stone Acton in 1800; whether as owner or lessee is unknown,[7] but in 1802 William Jones was lord of the manor.[8] By will of 1868 William Jones, presumably his son or grandson, left his property in Stone Acton, including the manor, to John Farmer of Cound,[9] whose family had it until 1909. The farm then changed hands several times before being bought in 1952 by W. S. Turner, owner in 1990.[10]

The hall of Stone Acton, sold with the manor in 1668,[11] was probably the house of three hearths occupied in 1672 by John Lutwyche.[12] Stone Acton Farm is a mid 19th-century building of brick with stone details and some gothic elements.

Before they bought Stone Acton manor the Lutwyches had begun to buy land there. In 1579 Edward Lutwyche bought three messuages there and at Wall under Heywood from John Hallywell,[13] one of those properties having been bought by Hallywell or his father (also John) from Joan and Richard Lee in 1546.[14] Joan was William Gower's granddaughter and heir.[15]

The Actons evidently retained some interest in Stone Acton after 1601 for in 1741 property there was bought by William Lutwyche from Sir Richard Acton of Aldenham.[16] It probably included the Horse Pool House tenement, which had belonged to George Smythe of Morville in 1568[17] and to the Actons by 1691,[18] and the farm

88 *N. & Q.* 9th ser. ix. 386.
89 Inf. on notice bd. at ho.
90 S.R.O. 4835/2, p. 8.
91 S.R.O. 809, parcel 3, Lutwyche est. rental 1843–53; box 10, Lushcott, etc., ests., copy valn. and rep. *re* proposed exchange 1849; 3573/T/1–2; New Ho. fm. deeds, abstr. of title to Hippisley marr. settlement; cf. below, Easthope, manor.
92 Local inf.
93 Eyton, iv. 91–3; *V.C.H. Salop.* ii. 85; *Rot. Hund.* ii. 72; *Feud. Aids*, iv. 145.
94 Above, Cardington, manors (Cardington); below, this section (Gretton); fig. 8. Reynold of Bailleul's Domesday holdings represent Warin's est.: *V.C.H. Salop.* iii. 9–10.
95 Below, Munslow, manors (Broadstone).
96 Eyton, iv. 91–2; *Rot. Hund.* ii. 72.
97 *V.C.H. Salop.* ii. 86.
98 *Feud. Aids*, iv. 245, 250; P.R.O., C 142/67, no. 142; SC 6/Hen. VIII/7262, m. 17d.; S.R.O. 3365/165.
99 *Cal. Pat.* 1553–4, 184–5; S.P.L., Deeds 1421.
1 S.R.O. 5001/4/1/3; *Visit. Salop. 1623*, i (Harl. Soc. xxviii), 10; ii. 439.
2 P.R.O., C 60/426, m. 10.
3 P.R.O., C 142/381, no. 160; S.R.O. 1093/2/525/2. An Acton claim or interest nevertheless persisted until 1741: S.R.O. 1093/2/526.
4 Glam. R.O., CL/Deeds I, Salop. 1638/9, 2 Feb.; below, this section (Lutwyche).
5 S.R.O. 5001/4/1/5; below, this section (Lutwyche).
6 S.R.O., q. sess. rec. box 260, reg. of gamekeepers 1711–42, 25 Oct. 1734, 25 Apr. 1735; 1742–79, 7 Sept. 1775; S.R.O. 4835/2, pp. 14–15; B.R.L., MS. 577365.
7 S.P.L., Deeds 9989.
8 S.R.O., q. sess. rec. parcel 261, reg. of gamekeepers 1799–1807, f. 70.
9 S.R.O. 1929/34.
10 Inf. from R. & D.R.T.
11 S.P.L., Deeds 1423; S.R.O. 5001/4/1/5.
12 *Hearth Tax 1672*, 184.
13 S.P.L., Deeds 1419–20, 1682.
14 Ibid. 1417–18.
15 P.R.O., C 1/1146, no. 36.
16 S.R.O. 5001/4/1/6.
17 S.R.O. 1146/42.
18 S.P.L., Deeds 1424.

later known as *HILL END*, partly in Cardington parish. The property was presumably sold in Chancery *c.* 1785.[19] Hill End was owned by Daniel Lowe in 1840,[20] Thomas Corfield in 1880,[21] and R. H. Danily in 1910.[22] In 1691 Horse Pool House was described as a mansion.[23] Probably 17th-century, Hill End Farm is a two bayed timber framed house cased in stone.

Aelfric (Aluric), a free man, held *STANWAY* in 1066. In 1086 the sheriff Reynold of Bailleul held it of Earl Roger, the tenant in chief.[24] Soon after 1102, when the earl's son forfeited his English lands, the lordship presumably passed with the rest of Reynold's estates to Alan son of Flaald,[25] whose descendants the FitzAlans, later earls of Arundel, were overlords as late as 1524.[26] By 1567 Rowland Hayward (kt. 1570)[27] was overlord.[28]

In 1086 Stanway was one of the manors of Otes of Bernières,[29] who died some time after 1121.[30] Otes's great-grandson Herbert of Rushbury (fl. 1200–9)[31] made a grant, confirmed in 1227, of 'all the land of the two Stanways with all their appurtenances on Wenlock Edge' to Henry of Audley.[32] Before 1240 Audley exchanged Stanway with Madoc of Sutton for a share of Weston under Redcastle;[33] in 1255 Madoc was John FitzAlan's tenant in the two Stanways.[34] In 1348 Giles Carles held Stanway as ½ knight's fee,[35] as did Sir John Winsbury in 1428 and 1431.[36] Elizabeth Winsbury, perhaps Sir John's widow,[37] claimed it *c.* 1460.[38] By a settlement of 1481 the manor of Over and Nether Stanway was held for life by Sir John Winsbury's daughter Margaret (d. *c.* 1499),[39] widow of Fulk Sprenchose, with remainder to her daughter Margery, wife of Richard Lee of Langley[40] (d. 1498)[41] and secondly of William Leighton.[42]

Margaret Sprenchose's manor may have been divided. The 'townships' of Over and Nether Stanway were later said to have been held (of the earl of Arundel) by Sir Peter Newton (d. 1524) whose heir was his son Arthur.[43] By 1529 Over and Nether Stanway had passed to Sir John Smith,[44] and his son Thomas seems to have sold them, as the 'manor' of Over Stanway and Nether Stanway, to Adam Lutley in 1560.[45] William Powlett, who had married Anne, daughter and heir of Sir John Smith's son Edmund, may have retained some interest in the manor until 1579 or later.[46]

Meanwhile, however, part of the manor of Over and Nether Stanway was said to belong by 1543 to Edward More of Larden; he then settled it on his son Thomas (d. 1567), who held of Rowland Hayward. Thomas's heir was his son Jasper.[47] Jasper's title was disputed in 1569 by William Leighton of Plaish, who claimed a quarter of the manor of Stanway,[48] presumably by descent from Margery Leighton, one of Fulk Sprenchose's coheirs. Margery's coparcenery, however, was not in Stanway manor (her mother's inheritance) but in premises in Over and Nether Stanway that descended with Plaish manor (her father's).[49] Leighton relinquished his claim in 1581[50] and Jasper More then sold his own part of Stanway manor to Adam Lutley (d. 1590).[51]

The whole manor, sometimes called Over Stanway (because Nether Stanway's chief house descended separately),[52] thereafter descended in the Lutleys from father to son, the following being owners:[53] Adam's son John (d. 1645),[54] Adam (d. *c.* 1678),[55] Bartholomew (d. 1716),[56] Philip (d. 1731),[57] and Jenkes (d. unmarried 1746).[58] Three of Jenkes's nephews, John, Richard, and Thomas Barneby, sold the manor in 1797 to William Wainwright (d. 1800).[59] Richard Wainwright owned Upper Stanway in 1840 but later sold it,[60] and William Horton may have been the owner by 1863.[61] It belonged *c.* 1910 to T. C. Williams.[62] The manor was offered for sale in 1933[63] but has not been traced further.

Upper Stanway is an 18th-century brick building, originally of three storeys but later two. A detached timber framed block was demolished in the 20th century.[64] In 1863 William Horton built Stanway Manor on the property as a gentleman's residence.[65] From the early 1890s it was occupied by the railway engineer and 'autocratic ruler' of Crewe, F. W. Webb (d. 1906).[66]

Robert of Beaumais (d. by 1265) held 2

19 S.R.O. 836/23; 5001/4/1/6.
20 S.R.O. 3573/T/1–2.
21 S.R.O. 5001/4/1/6, endorsement.
22 S.R.O. 4044/91, p. 52.
23 S.P.L., Deeds 1424.
24 *V.C.H. Salop.* i. 319.
25 Ibid. iii. 9–10.
26 Eyton, iv. 89–93; *Rot. Hund.* ii. 70; *Cal. Inq. p.m.* i, p. 280; *Cal. Inq. p.m.* (Rec. Com.), iii. 223; P.R.O., C 142/44, no. 147.
27 Shaw, *Kts. of Eng.* ii. 75.
28 P.R.O., C 142/152, no. 163. Hayward bought a large group of mans. from Arundel in 1559–60, but Stanway was not one: P.R.O., CP 25/2/200/2 Eliz. I East. [no. 13]; *Cal. Pat.* 1558–60, 368; S.R.O. 567/2C/2–3.
29 *V.C.H. Salop.* i. 319.
30 Ibid. viii. 94; Eyton, vi. 83.
31 Above, this section (Rushbury).
32 Eyton, iv. 91; *Cal. Chart. R.* 1226–57, 36–7.
33 *Cal. Inq. p.m.* ii, pp. 68, 121–2.
34 *Rot. Hund.* ii. 70.
35 *Feud. Aids*, iv. 245.
36 Ibid. 250, 268.
37 If so, she was not his first wife: *V.C.H. Staffs.* v. 119.
38 P.R.O., C 1/28, no. 42.
39 *V.C.H. Salop.* viii. 45.
40 S.P.L., Deeds 10763.
41 *Cal. Inq. p.m. Hen. VII*, ii, p. 132. Date incorrect in *V.C.H. Salop.* viii. 143.
42 P.R.O., CP 25/1/195/24, no. 12; *Visit. Salop. 1623*, ii. 432.
43 P.R.O., C 142/44, no. 147.
44 H.W.R.O.(H.), LC, R 27/11024. For pedigree see Burke, *Land. Gent.* (1925), 291.
45 P.R.O., CP 25/2/200/2 & 3 Eliz. I Mich. [no. 3].
46 P.R.O., CP 40/1368, rot. 629.
47 P.R.O., C 142/152, no. 163; *S.P.R. Heref.* i (1), 9.
48 S.R.O. 1037/21/198.
49 P.R.O., CP 25/1/195/24, no. 12. Cf. above, Cardington, manors.
50 H.W.R.O.(H.), LC, R 27/11026.
51 N.L.W., Dobell 1; P.R.O., C 142/228, no. 56.
52 Below, this section (Nether Stanway).
53 For pedigree see *T.S.A.S.* 4th ser. vi. 247–67.
54 S.R.O. 783, box 77, deed 10 Nov. 1604.
55 *T.S.A.S.* 4th ser. vi. 258.
56 S.R.O. 783, box 77, deed 1 Oct. 1662.
57 S.R.O., q. sess. rec. box 260, reg. of gamekeepers 1711–42, 28 Nov. 1727.
58 Ibid. 4 Dec. 1731, 27 Nov. 1733.
59 P.R.O., CP 43/855, rot. 266; M.I. in Rushbury ch.
60 S.R.O. 3573/T/1–2; *Bye-Gones*, N.S. xii. 20.
61 *P.O. Dir. Salop.* (1863), 739; above, this article, intro.
62 S.R.O. 4044/91, p. 56.
63 S.R.O. 3573/10/g/2; *Shrews. Chron.* 28 Apr. 1933, p. 8.
64 Rep. by Mrs. Moran.
65 Above, this article, intro.
66 *Kelly's Dir. Salop.* (1895), 182; *D.N.B.*

carucates at Stanway in fee, presumably as tenant of Madoc of Sutton or his successors. The estate had passed by 1270 to Robert's son Hugh, who was said in 1271 to hold the manor of *NETHER STANWAY*. He conveyed it before 1292 to John of Beaumais, lord of Donington, after whose death (1305 × 1315) John's younger son John quitclaimed his rights in Stanway to the elder son Hugh.[67] The further descent of Hugh's Stanway estate has not been traced.

The Lees evidently retained or acquired a freehold in Nether Stanway after Richard Lee's death in 1498, for in 1586 Richard Lee of Langley settled the chief house at Nether Stanway on his sister Jane More for life.[68] Thomas Smalman of Wilderhope (d. 1590) bought it,[69] and it descended with Wilderhope until 1734 when Wilderhope was sold to Thomas Lutwyche; Lutwyche's son William bought Nether Stanway *c.* 1739.[70] Among the Lutwyches' property offered for sale in 1785 was Stanway farm, 206 a. and woods,[71] but it was probably withdrawn, for Sarah Winford (*née* Lutwyche) later sold her share of it to Joseph Harris.[72] By 1840 Lower Stanway was part of Sir H. W. Bayntun's Rushbury estate.[73] In 1909 the 293-a. property was owned by the Websters, formerly tenant farmers there.[74] It later passed by marriage to Thomas Marsden, whose family had it until 1973 when the farm was sold to the Radcliffes, owners in 1990.[75] Lower Stanway is a large 19th-century brick house.

In the 13th century Walter de Kenigford and his wife Margaret had an estate in Nether Stanway. It passed from Margaret to their daughter Alice on her marriage to John Aberd (or Abel). By 1272 John and Alice were divorced but John unlawfully retained 1½ virgate,[76] perhaps including the virgate for which John's daughters sued Herbert Aberd (or Herbert of Stanway) in 1292 and the half virgate of which they had allegedly disseised him.[77] It is possible that Alice Aberd married secondly a Henry son of John; in 1261 he and his wife Alice sold a half virgate in Nether Stanway, in her right, to Robert of Beaumais.[78]

In 1066 Alric and Ottar (Otro), free thegns, held *GRETTON* as two separate estates.[79] In 1086 Earl Roger held the two manors of the king, and that lordship was forfeited in 1102.[80] The sheriff Reynold of Bailleul and one Robert, as mesne lords, held one each of the manors under Earl Roger in 1086; both had the same tenant.[81] Reynold's overlordship descended to the FitzAlans. Nothing is known of Robert but his name, and his interest may have lapsed or been forfeited to the Crown, possibly to be granted in the earlier 12th century to Richard of Beaumais.[82]

The two manors that Otes of Bernières held of the two mesne lords in 1086 evidently became one, and it descended until 1616 with Kenley.[83] In 1613 Sir Francis Lacon mortgaged it to Edward Jones and Richard Newell who probably foreclosed in 1616, the manor passing to Jones's brother Isaac. It probably soon passed to the family of Isaac's brother Edward, and thereafter it descended with Wigmore (in Westbury), at least until 1824, when both were offered for sale.[84] Still in the 1830s, however, Gretton belonged to Sir T. J. Tyrwhitt Jones (d. 1839), whose widow Eliza (d. 1865) later owned it.[85] From 1875 or earlier until 1935 or later Gretton descended with Plaish.[86]

The court of Gretton, mentioned in 1529,[87] presumably stood within the moat that is part of the extensive earthworks south-east of Gretton village.[88] The farmhouse was largely demolished in the mid 19th century,[89] and only a pair of mid or late 16th-century cottages remained, half derelict, in 1986.[90]

William Leighton (d. 1607) of Plaish owned two farms in Gretton in 1602. They passed to his son Henry, of Habberley, who sold them in 1614.[91]

In 1318–19 William, lord of Coats, sold land in *THE GILBERRIES* to Burga of Harley, lady of Gretton, and her son Philip.[92] It descended with Gretton manor until 1887 or later, but by 1910 belonged to William Robinson. In 1824 the farm comprised 59 a.[93] By 1565 there was a house at the Gilberries occupied by Thomas Ridley, gentleman;[94] it was of three bays in 1621 and there was a 2½ bayed barn.[95]

67 Eyton, ii. 178–9, 242–4; iv. 92–3.
68 S.R.O. 5001/4/4/1; *Visit. Salop.* ii. 319, 365.
69 *T.S.A.S.* 3rd ser. iii. 2, 17.
70 P.R.O., C 142/610, no. 97; CP 25/2/591/1656 Trin. no. 7; *T.S.A.S.* 3rd ser. iii. 18–19; above, this section (Wilderhope).
71 S.R.O. 4835/2.
72 S.P.L., MS. 4078, p. 994; above, this section (Wilderhope); below, this section (Lutwyche).
73 S.R.O. 3573/T/1–2.
74 *P.O. Dir. Salop.* (1856, 1871); S.R.O. 4044/91, p. 56; *Kelly's Dir. Salop.* (1885–1909).
75 Inf. from R. & D.R.T.
76 Eyton, iv. 93.
77 *Sel. Bills in Eyre* (Selden Soc. xxx), pp. 12–13.
78 Eyton, ii. 242; iv. 92.
79 *V.C.H. Salop.* i. 319.
80 Ibid.; ibid. iii. 9.
81 Ibid. i. 319; Eyton, iv. 105.
82 Eyton, iv. 105, 107–8.
83 Ibid. 105–8; *Cur. Reg. R.* vii. 207; *T.S.A.S.* 3rd ser. vi. 167–8; *Rot. Hund.* ii. 70; *Cal. Chart. R.* 1300–26, 29, 398; *Cal. Inq. p.m.* xv, pp. 295–6; *Cal. Close*, 1441–7, 435–6; S.R.O. 1224/2/535; P.R.O., C 142/58, no. 60; C 142/68, no. 7; S.R.O. 840, box 40, deeds 4 Dec. 1565, 21 June 1613; 3320/52–3; Barnard MSS., Raby Castle, box 1, bdle. 29, nos. 11–14, 18–22; cf. *V.C.H. Salop.* viii. 87–8, 94–5 (not noting Sir Ric. Lacon's son Ric., lord of Willey and Gretton (and presumably of Harley and Kenley) in 1446, afterwards dying s.p. to be succ. in or before 1454 by his bro. Wm.: S.R.O. 1224/2/535–6; *Cal. Close*, 1441–7, 435–6; *Visit. Salop. 1623*, ii. 306).
84 S.R.O. 563/6/1–2; 840, box 41, deeds of 1613–14, 1616; boxes 112 and 116, draft sale partics., valn., etc., 1824–5; box 1, Gretton ct. r.; 4835/132; q. sess. rec. box 260, reg. of gamekeepers 1711–42, 2 Oct. 1727; *V.C.H. Salop.* viii. 316; *Visit. Salop. 1623*, i. 282.
85 W.S.L. 350/5/40, Cardington p. 3; S.R.O. 3573/T/3; S. Bagshaw, *Dir. Salop.* (1851), 547; Burke, *Peerage* (1938), 292; Blakeway, *Sheriffs*, 194, 240; *T.S.A.S.* 4th ser. v. 71.
86 S.R.O. 1242, box 12, arbitration award *re* Gretton fm.; 3931/1/24, 28; 4044/91, pp. 52–3; above, Cardington, manors (Plaish).
87 S.R.O. 840, box 40, deed 10 Aug. 1529.
88 *Garden Archaeology*, ed. A. E. Brown (1991), 11.
89 S.R.O. 3573/T/3; O.S. Map 6", Salop. LVI. SE. (1883 edn.).
90 *List of Bldgs.: (All Stretton [etc.])*, 26.
91 S.R.O. 189/20; 1104, box 26, deeds 10 Sept. 1602, 24 Oct. 1614; *V.C.H. Salop.* viii. 240; *T.S.A.S.* viii. 197.
92 Eyton, iv. 99; cf. above, this section (Gretton); *V.C.H. Salop.* viii. 95.
93 S.R.O. 840, box 40, deeds 20 May 1603, 21 June 1613, 25 Sept. 1630, 25 Nov. 1738; box 116, draft sale partics. 14 Aug. 1824 (lot 4); 2334/1/2; 3573/T/3; 4044/91, no. 360.
94 S.R.O. 840, box 40, deed 4 Dec. 1565.
95 Ibid. box 113, surv. of Gretton, etc., 1621.

BENTHALLS, mentioned in 1590,[96] occupied most of Gretton's other large detachment and descended with Gretton until 1824 or later.[97] George and Joseph Chune owned it by 1844[98] when it may already, as later, have been known as Hargrove farm.[99] William Hutton of Birmingham owned it in 1910.[1] In 1621 there was a house of three bays with 62 a.[2] Hargrove Farm, the present house, is 19th-century.

Godwine held *LUTWYCHE* in 1066. In 1086 Earl Roger held it in chief, but his son forfeited the lordship in 1102. In 1086 the sheriff Reynold of Bailleul held Lutwyche of the earl and Richard held it of Reynold. Richard also held Brockton (in Shipton and Stanton Long) under Reynold,[3] and probably in the 12th century Richard or one of his successors subinfeudated Lutwyche, for as late as 1639 the lords of Brockton were mesne lords of Lutwyche.[4]

Lutwyche was held by a family which took its name from the place. William of Lutwyche was lord in 1203. Herbert was probably the next lord and was succeeded by his son William (fl. 1240–*c.* 1265). Thomas may have been next lord.[5] The manor was held by men called William 1302–30[6] and in 1366.[7] Hugh may have been lord before another William (fl. 1404–18), after whom Thomas, Richard, Richard, and Richard were successive lords.[8] By 1586 the last named had been succeeded by his son Edward (d. 1614),[9] a Chancery cursitor pardoned of treason in 1605. His son Edward (d. 1639) left a 40-year estate to his daughters Elizabeth and Sarah with remainder to his grandson and heir Edward Lutwyche[10] (kt. 1684), justice of Common Pleas 1685 and chief justice of Chester 1686 (d. 1709).[11] The next lord was Sir Edward's son Thomas. In 1734 Thomas was succeeded by his son William[12] (sheriff 1750) who died, probably unmarried and certainly indebted, in 1773, leaving illegitimate issue by Catherine Lane who had predeceased him.[13]

William's estate was divided between his three sisters. Some part, perhaps most or even all, of the shares of two of them, Elizabeth (d. unmarried 1776) and Anne, Mrs. Fazakerley (d. 1776), passed to William's illegitimate son William Lane (from 1776 Lutwyche).[14] He engaged in a long (*c.* 1778–1785) Chancery suit over his father's will with his father's third sister Sarah Winford (d. 1793), owner of a third of the estate. As a consequence the Lutwyches' estate was partly dispersed by sale in 1785.[15] Lutwyche was sold in 1785, passing to Bartlet Goodrich, owner in 1792,[16] who in turn sold it in 1794 to Thomas Langton (d. 1805) of Easthope.[17] Langton's trustees sold Lutwyche in 1807 to the trustees of Moses Benson (d. 1806), a Liverpool West India merchant.[18] Lutwyche then passed from father to son in the Benson family, successively from Moses' son Capt. Ralph (d. 1845) to Moses George (d. 1871), Ralph Augustus (d. 1886), and Ralph Beaumont (d. 1911).[19]

In 1910 the Bensons' Lutwyche estate comprised *c.* 1,306 a., mainly in Lutwyche and Lushcott.[20] In 1938 *c.* 1,277 a. were put up for sale,[21] and in 1947 R. B. Benson's son Maj. G. R. Benson (d. 1961) sold his interest in what remained of the Lutwyche estate to Accumulated Investments Ltd. of Leicester.[22] The manorial rights were perhaps not conveyed with the estate and so might have passed to G. R. Benson's son Capt. Ralph Benson (b. 1919).[23]

The lord's house was mentioned in the 14th century.[24] Lutwyche Hall is of two storeys with attics. It has main elevations of red brick with black diapering where the original work (allegedly of 1587) survives; the back elevation is of stone.[25] The plan was similar to Shipton Hall's: a short central hall range with symmetrical gabled cross wings and tower-like features in the re-entrants. The eastern tower was above a porch which gave access to a screens passage behind which there was a stair turret. In 1672 the Hall was taxed on 14 hearths.[26] In the early

96 Ibid. box 63, deed 20 Mar. 1609/10; cf. box 40, deed 21 Aug. 1523 (field name).

97 S.R.O. 840, box 112, survs. of Thos. Tyrwhitt Jones's est. 1786 and 1799, valn. of Gretton est. for sale; box 113, surv. of Gretton, etc., 1621.

98 S.R.O. 3573/T/3.

99 O.S. Map 6", Salop. LVI. SE. (1928 edn.).

1 S.R.O. 4044/91, pp. 51–2.

2 S.R.O. 840, box 113, surv. of Gretton, etc., 1621.

3 *V.C.H. Salop.* i. 320; iii. 9.

4 Eyton, iv. 114; *Rot. Hund.* ii. 71; *S.P.R. Heref.* xix (4), pp. ii–iii; C 104/26, deed 25 Mar. 1381; P.R.O., C 116/207; C 142/585, no. 102.

5 Eyton, iv. 114–16; *Rot. Hund.* ii. 71; S.P.L., Deeds 168, 416–18, 421; Staffs. R.O., D. 938/671.

6 S.R.O. 1037/3/23; 3195/1, ff. 50, 77.

7 Barnard MSS., Raby Castle, box 1, bdle. 18, nos. 4a–b.

8 *Visit. Salop. 1623*, ii. 345–6; P.R.O., C 116/207.

9 N.L.W., Pitchford Hall 1534; *Visit. Salop. 1623*, ii. 346; P.R.O., C 142/381, no. 160.

10 Glam. R.O., CL/Deeds I, Salop. 8 Mar. 1604/5; 2 Feb. 1638/9; P.R.O., C 142/585, no. 102.

11 *D.N.B.*; G. Ormerod, *Hist. Co. Palatine of Chester* (1882), i. 66, 222; F. Leach, *Co. Seats of Salop.* (1891), 395.

12 S.R.O., q. sess. rec. box 260, reg. of gamekeepers 1711–42, 25 Oct. 1734, 25 Apr. 1735; *D.N.B.*; *Hist. Parl., Commons*, 1715–54, ii. 231.

13 Pedigree, etc., details from S.R.O. 1150/199–202; S.P.L., MS. 2790, p. 403; S.P.L., MS. 4078, pp. 994–5; J. B. Blakeway, *Sheriffs of Salop.* (Shrews. 1831), 189–90; cf. above, this section (Wilderhope).

14 S.R.O. 589/1; 1150/200; q. sess. rec. box 260, reg. of gamekeepers 1742–79, 7 Sept. 1775; Bodl. MS. Blakeway 6, p. 156; W. P. W. Phillimore and E. A. Fry, *Index to Changes of Name 1760–1901* (1905), 209; S.P.L., MS. 6865, p. 163, calling Wm. 'Col.' Lutwyche (1793). The suggestion that he was an 'eminent physician' (ibid. MS. 2790, p. 403) probably confuses him with his fr.-in-law: Blakeway, *Sheriffs*, 190.

15 S.P.L., MS. 4078, pp. 994–5; 6865, p. 163; S.R.O. 589/1; 1150/199–207; 4835/2; *Hist. Parl., Commons*, 1715–54, ii. 231.

16 S.P.L., MS. 6741, p. 177; 6865, pp. 164–5; S.R.O. 809, box 14, map of Lutwyche fm. 1792.

17 *S.P.R. Heref.* xix (4), pp. iii, 69; W.S.L. 350/5/40, Easthope p. 8; S.P.L., MS. 6865, p. 78.

18 S.R.O. 809, box 10, 'Purchases of freeholds made out of est. of M. Benson' (loose sheet in 'Est. Acct. of M. Benson decd.'); W.S.L. 350/5/40, Easthope p. 8; *V.C.H. Salop.* iv. 211; Forrest, *Old Hos. of Wenlock*, 41–2.

19 Forrest, op. cit. 42; Burke, *Land. Gent.* (18th edn.), ii (1969), 40–2.

20 S.R.O. 4044/91, pp. 54–6.

21 S.R.O. 809, box 14, sale partic. 21 Mar. 1938.

22 Ibid. note from Herb. Smith & Co. 11 Nov. 1947; inf. from Mr. Riou Benson.

23 Cf. below, M. Wenlock, manors (Presthope).

24 Glam. R.O., CL/Manorial, recital of Lutwyche deeds, no. 5.

25 Pl. 14. Mr. Eric Mercer is thanked for discussing the bldg. Date stone 'EL 1587' is later than that date.

26 *Hearth Tax 1672*, 178.

or mid 18th century a brick block of two storeys, containing at its west end a high quality staircase, was added behind the hall. At the same time the principal rooms of the old house were remodelled. The hall lost its screens passage and was decorated with rococo plasterwork, the north-east room was panelled to full height, and the southern rooms in both wings were refitted.[27] Later in the century, before 1792,[28] a long two storeyed service wing was added against the north-east corner of the house. In 1851 the 18th-century back block (now gone) was extended and the front was remodelled in a Jacobean style to a design by S. Pountney Smith.[29] He added two storeyed bay windows to the wings and filled the space between the re-entrant towers with a three storeyed porch with first-floor oriel. Between 1878 and 1886 the front was further raised and remodelled to a design by Mrs. R. A. Benson's brother F. P. Cockerell.[30]

Lutwyche Hall, separated from the estate in or after 1952,[31] housed schools during the Second World War and until 1966.[32] In increasing disrepair the Hall then passed through a succession of owners before being bought *c.* 1981 by Research and Preservation (Historical) Ltd., of Douglas (I.O.M.),[33] and restored under the direction of Dr. Roger Pearson, of Washington, D.C.[34] In 1989 a fire gutted the east wing and destroyed seven years' restoration work.[35]

North-east of the house there is an earlier 18th-century stable block of red brick with a central carriage arch beneath a large pediment. A stone temple stood south-west of the house.[36]

In 1493 an estate in Lutwyche was bought, with Easthope, by Henry and Nicholas Warley. Nicholas (d. 1524) was succeeded by his son Bartholomew (d. 1554), whose property, held of Brockton manor, was described as a moiety of a capital messuage called Lutwyche. His heir was his sister Frances, wife of Nicholas Crosthwaite. In 1566 Nicholas Crosthwaite and Ralph Warley sold Lutwyche farm, probably *c.* 200 a. in Lutwyche and Easthope, to Edward Lutwyche. Thereafter the property presumably descended with Lutwyche.[37]

ECONOMIC HISTORY. Of the four Domesday manors wholly or mainly in the medieval parish, Rushbury had the most arable land. In 1086 it had two ploughteams in demesne worked by 4 *servi*, while 1 *villanus*, 2 bordars, and 3 radmen worked five more. The Stanway demesne also had two teams worked by 4 *servi*, while 3 *villani* and 1 bordar worked two more. At Lutwyche 2 oxmen worked a demesne team, and 1 *villanus* and 1 bordar had a half team. Gretton apparently had no demesne land, but 5 *villani* had 2 teams. Lutwyche was worth 8*s.* in 1066 and 1086, but the other three manors saw a considerable fall in value and were waste when received by their Norman lords. There was room for three more teams at Stanway, and two more each at Rushbury and Gretton.[38]

Expansion of farming throughout the parish in the 12th century is probably indicated by the existence of old assarts at Rushbury, Coats, and Gretton in the mid 13th century.[39] In Lutwyche assarting was probably still in progress in the early 13th century,[40] and in 1250 Parnel of Kenley was fined for an assart into the forest at Wilderhope.[41] By 1341 there had been a drastic fall in agricultural production; among the causes were said to be storm damage to crops, sheep murrain, and the poverty and departure of tenants.[42]

Lutwyche had the best recorded open-field system in the parish,[43] probably occupying much of the lower land in the centre of the manor. Some lay towards Easthope,[44] and the field towards Wilderhope was mentioned in the 13th century[45] and Stowefield, evidently north of Fegg and so in the same part of the manor, in the 14th.[46] Wilderhope too probably had open fields,[47] and at Stanway the Beaumais family had 2 carucates in demesne *c.* 1270.[48]

On the north-west side of Wenlock Edge the medieval open fields are poorly documented. At Rushbury, where the lord had 3 carucates in demesne in 1283,[49] open fields were mentioned in the 16th century, perhaps near the end of their existence.[50] Piecemeal inclosure was then in progress at East Wall and at Stone Acton[51] where Nether field was mentioned in 1541.[52] In 1517 Thomas Lacon was accused of inclosing 20 a. in Gretton,[53] much of which township north of the Cardington–Longville road was open-field land. Gretton's Upper field probably lay north-west of the Gretton–Plaish road (and so in Cardington

27 Pl. 15. For drawing and descr. of Hall *c.* 1730 see Birm. Univ. Libr., Mytton Papers, v. 1097–1100.

28 Shown on S.R.O. 809, box 14, map of Lutwyche fm. 1792. See also S.R.O. 4835/2, p. 2, for descr. of Hall 1785.

29 Leach, *Co. Seats Salop.* 395–6; Forrest, *Old Hos. of Wenlock*, 41–2; *Eddowes's Shrews. Jnl.* 7 Nov. 1883, p. 5; *T.S.A.S.* 2nd ser. viii, pp. xiii–xiv; dates on bldg.; J. Lees-Milne, *Midway on the Waves* (1985), 28–9.

30 S.R.O. 809, box 14, archit. plans; 1119/6, s.v. Lutwyche; Burke, *Land. Gent.* (1937), 139; Leach, op. cit. 396.

31 S.R.O. 809, box 2, sale partic. 1952; inf. from Dr. Rog. Pearson.

32 Below, educ.

33 *Shrews. Chron.* 2 June 1972, p. 16; inf. from Dr. Pearson.

34 Publisher of the cultural and anthropological jnl. *Mankind Quarterly*: *Who's Who in America 1995*, ii. 2863; M. Kohn, *The Race Gallery: The Return of Racial Science* (1995), 51 sqq.; inf. from Dr. Pearson.

35 B.B.C. 1, 'Midlands Today' televised 4 Apr. 1989.

36 O.S. Map 1/2,500, Salop. LVII. 5 (1903 edn.); ruins seen 1991.

37 *S.P.R. Heref.* xix (4), pp. ii–iii; S.P.L., Deeds 1349; P.R.O., C 104/27, deed of 1493; C 116/207; below, Easthope, manor.

38 *V.C.H. Salop.* i. 319–20, 328.

39 *Cal. Pat.* 1258–66, 207; P.R.O., C 47/88/1/15; E 32/147, m. 8; N.L.W., Pitchford Hall 108.

40 S.P.L., Deeds 421; Eyton, iv. 114–15; Glam. R.O., CL/Manorial, recitation of Lutwyche deeds 1589.

41 Eyton, iv. 98.

42 *Inq. Non.* (Rec. Com.), 104.

43 e.g. S.P.L., Deeds 417–20; Glam. R.O., CL/Manorial, recital of Lutwyche deeds 1589; Eyton, iv. 114–16.

44 Staffs. R.O., D. 938/672–5.

45 Eyton, iv. 114; S.P.L., Deeds 421.

46 B.L. Add. Roll 67032.

47 Eyton, iv. 102.

48 Ibid. ii. 244.

49 Ibid. iv. 97.

50 S.R.O. 840, box 41, agreement (n.d.) *re* closing of meadow intercommoned by Gretton and Rushbury.

51 B.L. Lansd. MS. 1, ff. 191, 193.

52 P.R.O., C 116/214, Stone Acton ct. r. 1541.

53 B.L. Lansd. MS. 1, f. 193.

parish),[54] and the Lower field south-east of it.[55] A third field, 'next Cardington', cannot be more precisely located. Gretton's Eastern field and Shirefield, mentioned in 1621,[56] may represent fields known earlier by other names. What remained of the open fields must have been inclosed during the 17th and 18th centuries. Parts of Gretton's Lower field remained common in 1716[57] but were no longer so *c.* 1770.[58] The most systematic inclosure, that of Lutwyche, was probably the last: a date shortly before 1792 seems likely.[59]

The parish, especially its higher parts, was well wooded throughout the Middle Ages. Rushbury manor's Domesday woodland was enough to fatten 40 swine and there was a falcon's eyrie. Woods belonging in the 13th century to Gretton, Lutwyche, and Stanway, however, went unrecorded in 1086.[60]

The parish was in the Long forest and its larger woods were surveyed in 1235. Mullesgreve and Oakwood, both south of Gretton, and Stanway wood, were all said to have been stripped of timber and underwood *c.* 1225. In 1286 Rushbury was among forest parishes from which the Crown granted timber for Acton Burnell castle. The parish was disafforested in 1301, and in 1302 and 1318 the Harleys, lords of Gretton, Wilderhope, and a moiety of Rushbury, were granted free warren in their demesnes there evidently in amplification of a grant of 1283.[61]

About 1250 one pig in ten was due to the lord of Lutwyche for pannage, probably a payment typical of the area.[62] About 1300 the basic stint for ½-virgate holdings in Rushbury was perhaps seven pigs.[63] Very large tracts of common adjoined many of the townships in the Middle Ages. Gretton, for example, intercommoned a large tract of land to the east and north centred on Oakwood, curving 4 miles round from Plaish to Lushcott, Longville, East Wall, and Mullesgreve[64] and so extending into Cardington and Eaton-under-Heywood parishes. Hay wood, west of Rushbury village, lay mainly in Eaton-under-Heywood but part of it extended into the parish; in 1235 the lord of Rushbury's share was well kept, with oaks and underwood.[65] Rushbury, East Wall, Wall under Heywood, and Gretton all claimed common there, but later part of Hay wood became a detached part of Gretton township.[66] Soon after 1500 *c.* 100 a. called Hargreaves was inclosed by a tenant of Thomas Lacon, lord of Gretton. Commoners resisted and continued to put cattle into Hargreaves. Nevertheless, although the tenant said that his inclosure was only for seven years to allow the spring to regrow, it was never common again. Mainly a coppice wood in the 18th and 19th centuries, Hargrove wood survived in the 1980s.[67] The rest of Hay wood in Rushbury parish was known in the 19th century as Gretton common and Wall's Bank, after the principal commoning manors.[68] By then it was largely open common, probably owing to over-grazing by cattle, sheep, and horses.[69] Gretton common and Wall's Bank, in all *c.* 150 a., were inclosed in 1806.[70] The names of fields west of Rushbury village called Wall's moor in the 19th century suggest another former common.[71]

Mullesgreve and Oakwood, perhaps once contiguous, were connected in 1610 by a track ('out rake'). It was probably mainly Gretton that commoned them, although part of Mullesgreve, known as the High or Rough wood, belonged to East Wall. About 1610, prompted by other local woodland inclosures, Gretton's commoners petitioned Sir Francis Lacon to allow the woods' inclosure. He agreed, and commoners received a dole in each wood. Not all were immediately inclosed. About 1659 Francis Ruckley greatly increased his share of Mullesgreve by exchange, although his inclosures were soon broken by associates of George Wilcox, possibly the Gretton manorial bailiff.[72] Mullesgreve was perhaps already open waste when inclosed, but Oakwood, albeit shrunken, remained wooded in the 1980s.[73]

The Gilberries probably originated as detached woodland belonging to Gretton, though perhaps cleared and inclosed by the end of the Middle Ages.[74] Immediately south, and seemingly once part of it, was Rushbury heath, almost 10 a. of which survived in 1840, though much encroached upon. Into it ran roads from Gretton, Wall under Heywood, East Wall, and Rushbury, all of which may once have had right of common there, as had the rector in 1580.[75] It had been inclosed by 1882.[76]

In Stone Acton the lord's wood and the

54 S.R.O. 840, box 40, deed 9 June 1716.
55 Ibid. box 41, agreement 21 Feb. 1658/9.
56 Ibid. box 113, surv. of Gretton, etc., 1621.
57 Ibid. box 40, deed 9 June 1716.
58 Ibid. box 112, surv. bk. of Gretton, etc. [*c.* 1770].
59 S.R.O. 809, bdle. 14, map of Lutwyche fm. The unusually grid-like fields shown on B.L. Maps, O.S.D. 207, suggest recent inclosure.
60 *V.C.H. Salop.* i. 319–20, 328; below, this section.
61 *V.C.H. Salop.* i. 485; Eyton, iv. 91; vi. 337–8; *Cal. Pat.* 1281–92, 228; *Cartulary of Shrews. Abbey*, ed. U. Rees (1975), ii, p. 250; S.R.O. 840, box 41, charter of 1283; *Cal. Chart. R.* 1300–26, 29, 398.
62 Glam. R.O., CL/Manorial, recital of Lutwyche deeds, no. 2; V.C.H. Salop. iv. 62.
63 Loton Hall MSS., vol. called '23 Deeds from 31 Edward I to 6 Henry VIII', p. 5 (deed of *c.* 1300).
64 S.R.O. 840, box 120, complaint concerning Musegreave [c. 1666].
65 Eyton, vi. 338.
66 S.R.O. 840, box 1, Gretton ct. r. 1438, 1465; box 12, Gretton and E. Wall map [late 18th-cent.]; 4835/2, p. 20; P.R.O., C 1/808, no. 47; *Cal. Inq. p.m.* v, p. 392.
67 S.R.O. 840, box 112, surv. bk. of Gretton, f. [5] ('Mr. Lees coppice'); S.R.O., incl. award B 18; P.R.O., C 1/808, no. 47.
68 S.R.O., incl. award B 18. In 1786–8 Gretton's commons there comprised Haywood common (61½ a.): S.R.O. 840, box 112, surv. of Thos. Tyrwhitt Jones's est. f. 66.
69 S.R.O. 840, box 1, presentments 25 Oct. 1804; box 120, examn. of witnesses as to rt. of common on Haywood common, 1803–4.
70 S.R.O., incl. award B 18; S.R.O. 840, box 120, incl. papers.
71 S.R.O. 3573/T/1–2, fields 488, 490–2.
72 S.R.O. 840, box 41, agreements 21 Feb., 21 Mar. 1658/9; memo. 19 Jan. 1660/1; lawsuit papers [*c.* 1661]; box 120, complaint concerning Musegreave; 1264/3.
73 S.R.O. 840, box 113, surv. of Gretton, etc., 1621 ('Mousegreave waste land').
74 Above, this article, intro.; manors (Gretton); S.R.O. 840, box 1, Gretton ct. r. 1441; box 112, surv. bk. of Gretton, etc. [*c.* 1770], f. 4.
75 S.P.L., Deeds 6117; ibid. MS. 2, f. 142; S.R.O. 3573/T/1–2, fields 155, 158, 573.
76 O.S. Map 6", Salop. LVI. SE. (1891 edn.).

common wood (perhaps one and the same) still stood in the mid 16th century; goats were kept there and there was a cockshoot.[77] That woodland was probably cleared in the following century. In the 17th century Stone Acton had waste called the Moor and the Warren, presumably on the hills north and west of the hamlet:[78] in 1750 'Stone Acton hills' were common.[79] In 1775 Manor farm at Stone Acton had a sheep walk of 184 a. on the adjoining hills.[80]

In the Middle Ages, Edge wood ran the whole length of Wenlock Edge, and most townships within a mile of the scarp foot, and some more distant ones, had common in it. By the late Middle Ages each township had a distinct length of woodland, and often those stretches themselves were subdivided. South of Rushbury village lay Blackwood, Lilywood, Short wood, and Roman wood.[81] People from Gretton were depasturing and cutting wood in Blackwood in 1465,[82] and Wilderhope, Fegg, and Stanway were said to have common there in 1785.[83] Rushbury men had common in Roman wood, later Roman bank, in the 17th century and later. Roman bank, 37½ a. of open waste in 1840 but inclosed by 1882, adjoined a stretch of Edge wood known in the 19th century as Crab wood.[84] North-east was Coats wood, and beyond again what was probably once East Wall's share.[85]

Stanway, Wilderhope, and Lutwyche each had woods on the south-east side of Hope Dale. Stanway's wood, mentioned in the 13th century,[86] probably lay in Hope Dale and perhaps included Hope common, although in the early 13th century the two Stanways included appurtenances on Wenlock Edge.[87] Lightwood, one of the Stanways' woods in the early 17th century, lay south of Upper Stanway, adjoining Blackwood.[88] Lower Stanway lay towards the south-western corner of a large block of woodland known since the 16th century as Mogg forest.[89] By 1530 recognized bounds divided Mogg forest between the intercommoning vills,[90] Stanway, Wilderhope, and Lutwyche. The woods were partly waste and partly coppiced in the 1580s, Edward Lutwyche having inclosed his coppice woods within living memory.[91] In the 19th and 20th centuries the slopes of Wenlock Edge and Hope Dale remained as commercial woodland, in the later 20th century under a mixture of conifers (European and Japanese larch, Norway and Sitka spruce, Grandis and Douglas firs) and deciduous trees (oak, ash, poplar, and cherry).[92]

In the 16th century the usual lease in Gretton was probably for 60 years or two or three lives,[93] lengthening in the 17th century[94] to 99-year chattel leases for three lives.[95] Chattel (99-year) leases were granted in Rushbury manor in the 17th century.[96] Mid 18th-century chattel (99-year) leases of Gretton farms for three lives still exacted hen rents and heriots.[97] By the 1770s leases in Gretton were getting shorter, and by 1793 most farms in the parish were probably racked.[98] Farms in Gretton were generally of *c.* 45 a. in 1621,[99] *c.* 80 a. in the 1760s;[1] by 1824 all had been thrown into two farms, of 335 a. and 222 a.[2]

In 1793 the neighbourhood was said to be wet and dirty, with much waste land still uninclosed.[3] Cattle rearing was popular and there was some feeding land. Wheat and oats were the main crops grown, with a little barley and turnips.[4] Labourers received 8*d.* a day with meat and drink, and their condition had evidently worsened in living memory. More than 80 per cent of the parish's population barely subsisted on a diet of bread and potatoes. Few kept pigs; none saved: old labourers who had savings used them to eke out their wages. Some may still have had the hemp plots enjoyed by previous generations.[5]

Cropping patterns were little changed by 1839.[6] Between the mid 19th century and 1938 the proportion of grassland rose, falling back to the mid 19th-century level by 1965. Sheep had long been the main livestock, 5,800 head in 1965. Only after 1938 did cereal growing begin on any appreciable scale. Much of the increase was in barley to feed increasing numbers of dairy cattle.[7] Notable among the farm buildings is the model farm with railway built *c.* 1891 at Upper Stanway for F. W. Webb.[8]

In the late 19th and earlier 20th century the Woolridges of East Wall were steam threshing contractors.[9]

In 1086 the only mill recorded was at Rushbury.[10] There were two water mills, perhaps

77 P.R.O., C 60/426, m. 10; C 116/214; SC 2/197/113–16, 148.
78 S.R.O. 3573/T/1–2, field 336 (Moor leasow); S.R.O. 5001/4/1/5.
79 Bodl. MS. Gough Salop. 4, f. 96.
80 S.R.O. 4835/2, p. 15.
81 S.R.O. 840, box 41, deed 31 July 1581; 1037/3/110; N.L.W., Dobell 1, deed 26 June 1542; below, this section.
82 S.R.O. 840, box 1, Gretton ct. r. 1438, 1465.
83 S.R.O. 4835/2, pp. 8–10.
84 Ibid. p. 14; 3573/T/1–2, fields 687, 705; 5460/4/7/2; O.S. Maps 1", index to tithe survey, sheet LXI. SW. [*c.* 1851]; 6", Salop. LVI. SE. (1891 edn.).
85 Cf. S.R.O. 3573/T/1–2, showing two E. Wall fms. with lands on the Edge; O.S. Map 6", Salop. LVI. SE. (1903 edn.), showing Eastwall Coppice.
86 Above, this section.
87 *Cal. Chart. R.* 1226–57, 36–7.
88 S.R.O. 1037/12/42; P.R.O., C 3/318, no. 20.
89 Below, Shipton, econ. hist.
90 S.R.O. 840, box 42, memo. *re* agreement of 25 Apr. 1528.
91 S.R.O. 566/11; 1037/16/12.
92 S.R.O. 3573/T/1–2; inf. on woodland in 1986 'Domesday' surv. of area (copy with R. & D.R.T.).
93 S.R.O. 840, box 40, deeds 8 Apr. 1529, 19 Oct. 1584, 20 Dec. 1593.
94 Ibid. 70-yr. lease (21 June 1613).
95 Ibid. deeds 1 Mar. 1650/1, 9 June 1716; box 42, deed July 1670; bdle. 104, rental 25 Mar. 1693.
96 S.R.O. 5460/4/7/2–4.
97 S.R.O. 840, box 112, surv. bk. of Gretton, etc. [*c.* 1770], ff. 17–19.
98 S.R.O. 840, box 109, rental 1782–3, ref. to 21-yr. lease 1779; S.P.L., MS. 6865, p. 162.
99 S.R.O. 840, box 113, surv. of Gretton, etc., 1621.
1 Ibid. box 112, surv. bk. of Gretton, etc. [*c.* 1770].
2 S.R.O. 4835/132, pp. 4–5.
3 Para. based on S.P.L., MS. 6865, pp. 161–5.
4 e.g. 10 a. on a Gretton fm.: S.R.O. 840, box 112, valn. of Bolding fm. [etc.] 1796, s.v. Ric. Sheppard's tenement.
5 S.R.O. 1242, box 14, map of Randal Cooke's est. 1771, field name; cf. S.R.O. 5460/4/7/4; /5/3/1.
6 P.R.O., IR 18/8261.
7 Para. based on Table IV and Salop. Agric. Returns, 1905; and see Madeley, 'Geog. descr. Rushbury', 63–81.
8 *Building News*, 18 Dec. 1891.
9 *Kelly's Dir. Salop.* (1891–1941).
10 *V.C.H. Salop.* i. 328.

TABLE IV

RUSHBURY: LAND USE, LIVESTOCK, AND CROPS

		1867	*1891*	*1938*	*1965*
Percentage of	grassland	70	78	89	70
	arable	30	22	11	30
Percentage of	cattle	20	24	23	25
	sheep	70	70	74	63
	pigs	10	6	3	12
Percentage of	wheat	50	31	39	31
	barley	28	32	8	54
	oats	22	37	53	12
	mixed corn & rye	0	0	0	3
Percentage of agricultural land growing roots and vegetables		7	7	3	4

Sources: P.R.O., MAF 68/143, no. 15; /1340, no. 6; /3880, Salop. no. 225; /4945, no. 225.

under one roof, in 1717 but only one in 1737 and 1741;[11] it stood south of the village but had gone by 1841.[12]

There were two water mills at Coats, also perhaps under one roof, in 1608;[13] they probably stood west of Coats.[14]

There was probably a water mill at Gretton from 1236 or earlier. In the 19th century it stood on Heath brook south of the village, and it ceased work in 1948.[15] Another mill, of unknown date, stood south-east of Court House.[16]

Gilberry pool, part of East Wall manor, was said *c.* 1730 to be *c.* 4 a. and to have held fish worth £100 when last drained.[17] It disappeared probably in the early 19th century.[18]

In 1271 Hugh of Beaumais, lord of Nether Stanway, was granted a Thursday market and a fair on the eve and feast of St. Denis (8–9 Oct.).[19] In 1283 the lord of Rushbury was similarly granted a Thursday market and a three-day fair on the eve, feast, and morrow of St. Margaret the Virgin (19–21 July).[20] There is no evidence that either market or fair was ever held.

A tanner lived at Roman Bank in 1602.[21] An early 18th-century tannery was perhaps nearby, in the Lilywood area.[22]

Bricks were made perhaps by 1607,[23] and there was a brickworks east of Hargrove Farm in the late 19th century.[24] Lime kilns were noted from 1703.[25] In 1785 'a particular sort of stone' found in Stone Acton was said to be useful in porcelain manufacture, though it is not certain that any was got in the township.[26] At Hill End there was prospecting for coal in 1914.[27] Road stone got there 1939–45 proved unsatisfactory.[28]

John Moore, an early 19th-century licensee of the New Inn, Wall under Heywood, made clocks.[29]

LOCAL GOVERNMENT. Rushbury and 'Wall' presented at the court leet of Castle Holdgate barony in 1537[30] but they did suit to Munslow hundred by 1781.[31]

Records of Gretton court survive from 1419, 1421, 1436–7, 1441, 1465, 1538, and 1559, and from the later 18th century to 1817. In 1441 a great court was held but the business, as usual, was local and primarily agricultural. A case of lairwite (fornication) was presented in 1436. The record of a single 'view of frankpledge', i.e. great or leet court, that survives for 1538 is insufficient to assess its character.[32]

Court records survive from other manors in the parish: Wilderhope (1441),[33] East Wall (1502, 1505, 1507),[34] Stone Acton (1540s and 1550s),[35] Lutwyche (1588–9),[36] and Rushbury (1509 and early 19th century).[37] The courts' principal concerns were the transfer of copyholds and regulation of woods and other commons.

In the 1740s Rushbury contributed to the joint workhouse at Cleobury Mortimer.[38] By *c.* 1784 Thomas Parker was farming the poor; his salary, unrelated to the number of poor or their needs, rose from £50 to £80 by 1793. He kept a workhouse, and some carding and spinning was done. More children were apprenticed in 1793 than before.[39] In 1802–3 only out-relief was given, at a cost of £242; 23 adults and 9 children received permanent relief, and 10 people occa-

11 S.R.O., q. sess. rec. parcel 281, reg. of papists' deeds 1717–88, pp. 99, 208, 217.
12 S.R.O. 3573/T/1–2, field 533.
13 S.R.O. 1146/40.
14 S.R.O. 3573/T/1–2, fields 578, 647.
15 *T.S.A.S.* 4th ser. vi. 171; S.R.O. 3756/147, p. 13; Madeley, 'Geog. descr. Rushbury', 58; P.R.O., IR 29/29/137; IR 30/29/137, fields 7–10.
16 P.R.O., IR 29/29/137; IR 30/29/137, fields 23–4, 49; R.C.H.M.E., draft field rep. on Gretton Ct. Ho. (1986).
17 S.R.O. 4572/6/2/56.
18 S.R.O. 515/6, p. 314 (Fish pool); S.R.O. 3573/T/1–2, field 102 (Pool field), probably marking the site.
19 *Cal. Chart. R.* 1257–1300, 166.
20 Ibid. 266.
21 S.R.O. 5460/4/7/2.
22 Ibid. /5/3/1; S.R.O., q. sess. rec. parcel 281, reg. of papists' deeds 1717–88, pp. 99, 208, 217.
23 S.R.O. 840, box 113, rental of Gretton, etc., 1607, s.v. John Dawes. For other brick-kiln sites see S.R.O. 3573/T/1–2, fields 620–2, 1017.
24 O.S. Map 6", Salop. LVI. SE. (1891 edn.).
25 S.R.O. 2334/1/2, p. 4; 3573/T/1–2, fields 924, 978, 980; 4835/50; 5460/5/3/1.
26 S.R.O. 4835/2, p. 15. Cf. above, Cardington, econ. hist., for getting of soapstone and quartz.
27 Inf. from Miss Nancy Smout.
28 Madeley, 'Geog. descr. Rushbury', 54.
29 Inf. from Mr. J. Madeley, owner of one; cf. S.R.O., q. sess. rec. parcel 259, reg. of alesellers' recognizances 1822–8.
30 S.P.L., MS. 2, f. 146; cf. below, Holdgate, local govt.
31 S.R.O. 272/1.
32 S.R.O. 840, boxes 1 and 40, ct. r., suit r.
33 S.R.O. 840, box 1, ct. r. 1441.
34 P.R.O., C 116/205.
35 P.R.O., C 116/214; SC 2/197/113–16, 148.
36 Glam. R.O., CL/Deeds I Salop. 1588/9, 14 Jan.
37 P.R.O., C 116/225; S.P.L., Deeds 6117; S.R.O. 2334/1/2, acct. 29 Sept. 1815.
38 S.R.O. 2519/8–13.
39 S.P.L., MS. 6865, p. 166.

sional relief.[40] Ten years later expenditure and the number of recipients were *c.* 10 per cent higher.[41] In the 1830s there were 4 cottages for the poor at Wall Bank.[42]

Rushbury was in Church Stretton poor-law union 1836–1930,[43] highway district 1863–95,[44] rural sanitary district 1872–94, and rural district 1894–1934, and in Ludlow R.D. 1934–74 and South Shropshire district from 1974.[45]

CHURCH. The church contains apparently Saxon fabric[46] and before the Conquest it may have served an area larger than the later, medieval, parish.[47]

The living was a rectory *c.* 1260[48] and has remained so. The patronage belonged to the lord of Rushbury manor,[49] being leased with the manor 1548–1792.[50] A grant of the advowson to Buildwas abbey, proposed in 1406 as the prelude to appropriation,[51] was evidently frustrated. In 1425 a turn was exercised by William Burley, a feoffee for settling the estates of the late lord of the manor, Lord Burnell (d. 1420).[52] Others exercised turns in 1673 and 1684.[53] In 1792 the patronage reverted to the bishop of Worcester as owner of the freehold of the manor,[54] and after the manor had passed to the Ecclesiastical Commissioners the advowson remained with the bishop of Worcester until transferred to the bishop of Birmingham on the creation of that see in 1904.[55] From 1967 Rushbury was held in plurality with the united living of Hope Bowdler with Eaton-under-Heywood, the incumbent to reside temporarily at Rushbury; the patron of Rushbury had the third turn.[56] In 1971 the incumbent became priest in charge of Cardington and the three benefices were held in plurality from 1980, the patrons presenting jointly.[57]

The rectory was worth £14 in 1291, a portion of which, 13*s.* 4*d.*, was due to St. Guthlac's priory, Hereford;[58] the portion represented the share of the rectorial tithes which the Lacys, overlords of Rushbury, had given to the priory *c.* 1100.[59] It was no longer paid in 1535 when the rectory's net annual value was £19 15*s.* 4*d.*[60]

On the eve of tithe commutation moduses were paid in lieu of hay and various small tithes; smoke and garden penny were due, as was an Easter offering of 6*d.* from each house. In the whole parish except Gretton township those payments, along with all the tithes, were commuted to £346 a year in 1842.[61] Gretton's tithes were commuted in 1846: the rector of Rushbury received £40 a year in respect of half of the corn and grain tithes in the whole of the main part of Gretton township (Judge Thomas D'Arcy and his wife Elizabeth received £20 10*s.* in respect of those in the other half) and in respect of all the corn and grain tithes in the whole of the Gilberries and Wall under Heywood detachments of the township and all other tithes in the Rushbury part of the whole township.[62] The living was then worth *c.* £449.[63] The rectory was well endowed with glebe, *c.* 54 a. with rights of common in 1580,[64] 50 a. in 1841,[65] and 70 a. in 1856 and later.[66] About 1920 *c.* 55 a. were sold.[67]

In 1589 the rectory included farm buildings and a pigeon house.[68] The house, just south-west of the church, was described in 1793 as very handsome.[69] Soon after he became rector in 1818 M. Y. Starkie spent much on the house and grounds, but the archdeacon thought he had destroyed the house's 'respectability' by whitewashing good brickwork.[70] In 1852 the house, parts of which may be *c.* 1700, was remodelled and extended in the Elizabethan style to designs by W. J. Donthorn.[71] It presents a symmetrical façade with a projecting central entrance bay and flanking canted bays rising through two storeys. The farm buildings were also remodelled. In 1968 the parsonage was sold with 4 a. Later a dairy wing was demolished.[72]

In the 13th and 14th centuries two rectors, one a pluralist and both probably kinsmen of lords of the manor, were licensed to be absent

40 *Poor Law Abstract*, H.C. 98, pp. 418–19 (1803–4), xiii.
41 *Poor Law Abstract*, H.C. 82, pp. 372–3 (1818), xix.
42 Below, charities.
43 V. J. Walsh, 'Admin. of Poor Laws in Salop. 1820–55' (Pennsylvania Univ. Ph.D. thesis, 1970), 150; *Kelly's Dir. Salop.* (1929), 201.
44 *Lond. Gaz.* 27 Mar. 1863, p. 1770; S.R.O., S.C.C. Local Govt., etc., Cttee. min. bk. 1894–1903, p. 29.
45 *Rural Dist. Councillors Electn. Order, 1894* (Local Govt. Bd. order no. 31847); *V.C.H. Salop.* ii. 215; iii. 178, and sources cited ibid. 169 n. 29.
46 H. M. and J. Taylor, *A.-S. Archit.* ii (1965), 526; M. D. Watson, *Guide to St. Peter's Ch., Rushbury* [Rushbury, 1986], 4–5.
47 Above, this article, intro.
48 Eyton, iv. 101.
49 *Reg. Cantilupe* (C.S.), 212; *Reg. Swinfield* (C.S.), 543; *Reg. Trillek* (C.S.), 389; *Reg. Gilbert* (C.S.), 122; *Reg. Trefnant* (C.S.), 180; *Reg. Mascall* (C.S.), 171; *Reg. Spofford* (C.S.), 356--7; *Reg. Boulers* (C.S.), 22; *Reg. Stanbury* (C.S.), 177, 181; above, manors.
50 *Dioc. of Heref. Institutions (1539–1900)*, ed. A. T. Bannister (Heref. 1923), 7, 9, 25, 28, 51, 53–4, 69, 74, 96; above, manors.
51 *V.C.H. Salop.* ii. 57.
52 *Reg. Spofford*, 352; *T.S.A.S.* lvi. 265; *V.C.H. Salop.* iii. 63, 236; viii. 7.
53 Bannister, *Heref. Institutions*, 39, 47.
54 S.P.L., MS. 6865, p. 169; *State of Bpric. of Worc. 1782–1808* (Worcs. Hist. Soc. N.S. vi), 27–8; H.W.R.O.(H.), HD 9, 'Notitia', f. 55.
55 Heref. Dioc. Regy., reg. 1902–19, p. 425; 1938–53, pp. 193, 434.
56 Ibid. reg. 1953–68, pp. 527, 563; 1969– (in use), p. 50.
57 Ibid. reg. 1969– (in use), pp. 354–5; *Heref. Dioc. Yr. Bk.* (1989), 40; above, Cardington, church.
58 *Tax. Eccl.* (Rec. Com.), 167.
59 Eyton, iv. 104. Cf. ibid. v. 11; *Acta Stephani Langton* (Cant. & York Soc.), i. 147; Dugdale, *Mon.* i. 547.
60 *Valor Eccl.* (Rec. Com.), iii. 209.
61 S.R.O. 3573/T/2–3. Cf. S.R.O. 840, box 112, surv. bk. of Gretton, etc. [*c.* 1770], for moduses, etc., paid.
62 S.R.O. 3573/T/3.
63 S. Bagshaw, *Dir. Salop.* (1851), 545.
64 S.P.L., MS. 2, f. 42.
65 S.R.O. 3573/T/2.
66 *P.O. Dir. Salop.* (1856), 107; S.R.O. 3573/2/3; 4044/91, p. 41.
67 S.R.O. 3573/2/6.
68 H.W.R.O.(H.), HD2/14/52.
69 S.P.L., MS. 6865, p. 169.
70 Ibid. p. 171.
71 Heref. Dioc. Regy., reg. 1847–56, pp. 370, 374, 430–2, 438; H.W.R.O.(H.), Heref. dioc. rec. AA 58, plans, etc., of 1853; H. Colvin, *Biog. Dict. Brit. Architects, 1600–1840* (1978), 270–1.
72 Inf. from dioc. registrar; *Shrews. Chron.* 20 Mar. 1987, p. 21.

for study.[73] Many medieval rectors' names suggest that they were Shropshire men.[74] John Redhode (1461–*c.* 1465) may have studied at Oxford.[75] Adam Littleton, instituted in 1578,[76] and most of his successors were university men.[77] At times in the earlier 17th century the rectory seems to have been held in plurality with Easthope.[78] In the later 17th and earlier 18th century the Cressetts sometimes presented kinsmen or family connexions, some of whom held other family livings in plurality.[79] Edward Cressett, rector in the 1720s (when he succeeded to his brother's estates), was bishop of Llandaff 1749–55. Some rectors employed curates, one of whom, Henry Tilley, succeeded to the rectory in 1690.[80]

Before the Reformation a light in the church was endowed from property in Hope Bowdler.[81] In 1716 there were two Sunday services, one with a sermon, and communion six times a year.[82] In the mid 18th century offerings at the sacrament (called charity money from *c.* 1745) were given to the poor.[83]

The longest-serving rector was William Pemberton, 1761–1813.[84] He resided but occasionally employed a curate. By 1793 he was 'decayed' in mind and irregular in doing his duty, but he enjoyed lucid periods and was later described as pious, the owner of a 1,000-volume library, and one who delighted in showing his church to visitors.[85]

Pemberton's successors to 1851 were pluralists and employed curates. The rector 1814–*c.* 1818 probably lived in Hereford.[86] M. Y. Starkie, 1818–51, was also perpetual curate of Over Darwen (Lancs.) 1815–51.[87] Although in 1820 he had recently refurbished the parsonage and presumably resided, by 1851 he lived in Church Stretton.[88] He tried to improve services and their frequency: in 1836 the singers were paid (an experiment lasting only a year), and by 1849 communion was celebrated about eight times a year;[89] the congregation was then 150 in summer but could fall to 25 in winter because of bad weather and poor roads.[90] F. H. Hotham, rector 1851–87, restored both rectory and church in the 1850s.[91]

The church of *ST. PETER*, so known by *c.* 1740,[92] is of rubble with freestone dressings. It comprises an undivided chancel and nave, south porch, south vestry, and west tower. The oldest fabric, herring-bone work, possibly Saxon, occurs in the lowest courses of the western ends of the north and south nave walls. Inserted through that fabric in the north wall is a tall narrow doorway, probably 12th-century, with a plain tympanum. About 1200 a new chancel, as long as the nave, was added and a tower of almost the same width; a south doorway was inserted. The chancel is defined by an external chamfer and a sill-level string course which appears both internally and externally. It was entered by a central south door, later blocked, and was lit by a triple lancet east window. There were probably once four lancets to both north and south.

Evidence remains of alterations between the 13th century and the 19th. In the chancel the string course is broken internally twice on both the north and south walls; the western break may have been for a chancel screen, the eastern for a wooden screen or partition defining a small sacristy or processional path.[93] Alternatively they may mark the ends of facing pews. A 'Lady chancel' mentioned in 1676[94] may have been a part of the nave once occupied by a guild altar. In 1789 a two-light window, probably late medieval, lit the west end of the south side of the chancel.[95] It probably replaced a lancet. The tower was crenellated, perhaps in the 15th century; pinnacles at the four corners were eroded by 1789.[96] Also 15th-century was the south porch, later much restored. Nave and chancel roofs are late medieval but were embellished in 17th-century style during the 19th century.

In 1793 the church contained some 'modern' windows, all considered by the archdeacon 'unsuitable in form and some whimsical':[97] two such, east and west of the south door, were tall, round-headed, and of two lights.[98] Seats in 1793[99] comprised 29 'irregular' pews in the nave, and two in the chancel.[1] Under the belfry a table on a raised platform and surrounded by benches served as a sort of gallery.

The church was restored in 1855–6,[2] the cost being met by subscriptions, a rate, and a grant from the Hereford Diocesan Church Building

73 *Reg. Cantilupe*, 212; *Reg. Swinfield*, 543; *Reg. Orleton* (C.S.), 296; *Reg. Trillek*, 389; *Cal. Pat.* 1292–1301, 122; S.R.O. 840, box 41, deed 6 May 1338.

74 Sources in preceding note; Eyton, iv. 104; *Cat. Anct. D.* ii, B 3256; *Reg. Mascall*, 44, 171, 182, 185; *Reg. Spofford*, 352, 356–7; *Reg. Boulers*, 22; *Reg. Stanbury*, 177, 181; S.P.L., Deeds 3055.

75 *Reg. Stanbury*, 177, 181; A. B. Emden, *Biog. Reg. Univ. Oxf. to 1500*, iii. 1560.

76 Bannister, *Heref. Institutions*, 25; *Alum. Oxon. 1500–1714*, iii. 919.

77 Records of institutions, subscriptions, etc. (in bps.' regs., etc.).

78 *Alum. Oxon. 1500–1714*, iv. 1684; Bannister, op. cit. 28; S.R.O. 2563/78; P.R.O., E 339/1/5; *T.S.A.S.* 4th ser. ii. 58; mem. slab to Thos. Adney (d. 1672) in ch. porch.

79 Bannister, *Heref. Institutions*, 39, 54, 74; *T.S.A.S.* 3rd ser. v. 375; 4th ser. ii. 65; vi. 219–20; *V.C.H. Salop.* viii. 70–1; Blakeway, *Sheriffs*, 155; *Alum. Oxon. 1500–1714*, i. 348.

80 *T.S.A.S.* 4th ser. ii. 74, 77, 89, 92–3; *V.C.H. Salop.* viii. 70; S.R.O. 3573/Rg/2, curates' signatures.

81 P.R.O., E 302/1/5, no. 43.

82 H.W.R.O.(H.), HD 5/14/1/18.

83 S.R.O. 3573/Ac/1, sacrament money acct.

84 Bannister, *Heref. Institutions*, 96; *T.S.A.S.* 4th ser. ix. 98.

85 S.P.L., MS. 6741, p. 181; 6865, pp. 169–70.

86 Bannister, op. cit. 138, 141–2, 144; *Alum. Oxon. 1715–1886*, iii. 1112; S.P.L., MS. 6741, p. 183.

87 Bannister, op. cit. 142, 167; *Alum. Cantab. 1752–1900*, vi. 16; *Rep. Com. Eccl. Revenues* [67], pp. 448–9, H.C. (1835), xxii.

88 Above, this section; P.R.O., HO 129/354, no. 24.

89 S.R.O. 3573/6/1, vestry min. 30 Mar. 1836; ibid. chwdns.' accts. 1835–6, 1849–50.

90 P.R.O., HO 129/354, no. 24.

91 Bannister, *Heref. Institutions*, 167, 200; above and below, this section.

92 B.L. Add. MS. 30316, f. 30.

93 Suggested by the late Mr. D. C. George.

94 H.W.R.O.(H.), Heref. dioc. rec., AL 19/19, f. 38.

95 Watson, *St. Peter's Ch.* 7.

96 S.P.L., MS. 372, vol. i, f. 91.

97 S.P.L., MS. 6865, p. 171.

98 S.P.L., MS. 372, vol. i, f. 91; J. H. Smith colln., no. 167; Bodl. MS. Top. Salop. c. 2, f. 434.

99 S.P.L., MS. 6865, p. 171.

1 Slightly different no. noted 1851: P.R.O., HO 129/354, no. 24.

2 Acct. based on *Eddowes's Jnl.* 12 Nov. 1856; S.R.O. 3573/5/10; S.P.L., Watton press cuttings, iv. 560–1.

Society. The rector's plans were executed by William Hill of Smethcott, also responsible for carving and installing all the new woodwork. The main work comprised building a south vestry (accessible through the unblocked priest's door) and a new south porch, replacing all windows later than *c.* 1200 with ones in 13th-century style, reopening the north doorway, rebuilding the top stage of the tower, adding seven large buttresses, and lowering the ground around the church. Internally the roof was restored, new benches (incorporating 17th- and 18th-century panelling, some carved with pew owners' names or initials)[3] installed, and new altar rails, pulpit, reading desk, oak chancel arch, and reredos introduced. The church was retiled, with Minton tiles in the chancel. New stained glass in the east window was by Horwood Bros. of Mells (Som.). In 1890 glass by John Hardman & Co. was put in two windows.[4]

Later changes were minor. A screen was introduced into the tower arch in 1912, and in 1932 the chancel was refloored in marble and the pulpit, altar rails, and choir stalls were slightly altered.[5]

The tub font is Norman, its elaborate cover 19th-century. The 17th-century chest was bought in 1950. Painted heraldic shields attached to the chancel roof were made in 1985, being copies of ones there in 1840 but lost by 1955.[6]

The plate includes a chalice of 1619 with contemporary cover, a paten of 1717, flagon of 1810, and chalice and paten of 1869.[7] There were three bells in 1549. A new bell frame was installed in 1621, and in the 18th century five bells by the Rudhalls were hung. A new frame was installed in 1978–9 and a sixth bell added in 1980.[8]

The registers begin in 1538, but there are several gaps in the 16th and 17th centuries.[9]

NONCONFORMITY. At Wilderhope a possible hiding place and motifs in the plastered ceilings suggest that at least one of the Smalman family may have been a Catholic recusant in the late 16th century.[10] No dissent was noted in 1716,[11] but in 1724 Jeremiah Jordan's house at the Gilberries was licensed for Baptists. The religious verses of his wife Judith were published posthumously.[12]

In 1836 Wesleyans built a chapel on the east side of Roman Bank common.[13] In the 1840s there were 20 or more members of the society, but numbers fell in the 1850s and in the 1860s there were only about seven.[14] The small stone chapel, seating 100,[15] closed in 1928.[16]

Primitive Methodists met at East Wall in the 1830s and were served by a chapel built at Lakehouse (in Eaton-under-Heywood) in 1857–8.[17]

EDUCATION. There was a schoolmaster in Rushbury in 1756.[18]

By will proved 1820 Dr. Benjamin Wainwright, son of Richard Wainwright of Upper Stanway, left capital to build a parochial school and teacher's house and endowed a master, a sewing mistress, and a Sunday school master. The master was to teach nine poor children from Rushbury parish and three from Eaton-under-Heywood parish, and the Sunday school master was to teach children from Rushbury and adjoining parishes. In 1821 there was a teacher's house and schoolroom on a piece of rented glebe; a sewing mistress was paid £5 a year, a Sunday school teacher £5, and the master had £20 for teaching day and Sunday schools;[19] he also took private pupils.[20] In 1869–70 the school had 76 pupils, 12[21] of whom were taught free. Its endowment then yielded £15 8*s.* 9*d.* and the school was also supported by £5 a year from Betton's charity, voluntary contributions, and fees that varied according to parents' means. The rector met deficits.[22] The school trustees' funds were increased by legacies of William Jones (d. 1870) and F. H. Hotham (d. 1887), rector.[23]

In 1873 the school was enlarged to accommodate 113, later reduced to 92. The building was again improved in 1889[24] and 1911 but had no separate infant room before 1930.[25] In the 1890s and perhaps later F. W. Webb, of Upper Stanway, gave annual treats; the rector gave prizes and provided clothes and boots for poor pupils.[26] In 1908 and 1912–13 teachers organized train excursions to places as far away as Liverpool and Llandudno.[27] Even for a rural school attendance was exceptionally irregular until the 1920s, averaging 55 in 1885, 75 in 1905, and 93 in 1913;[28] overcrowding caused children under five to be excluded in 1913.[29] In 1915 almost all pupils over 12 had left for work.[30]

The county council rented the school (designated C.E. by 1904) from the Wainwright Trust (which continued to make annual grants to it) and

3 *Salop. N. & Q.* vi. 105.
4 Watson, *St. Peter's Ch.* 12.
5 S.R.O. 3573/5/3, faculties.
6 Watson, op. cit. 12–14.
7 D. L. Arkwright and B. W. Bourne, *Ch. Plate Archd. Ludlow* (Shrews. 1961), 52–3.
8 Watson, op. cit. 14; inf. from the Revd. M. Bromfield.
9 S.R.O. 3573/Rg/1–4; /MRg/1–3; regs. at ch. H.W.R.O.(H.) has transcripts from 1660.
10 M. Hodgetts, 'Topog. index of hiding places', *Recusant Hist.* xvi. 185; *T.S.A.S.* 3rd ser. iii. 16–17 and plates betw.
11 H.W.R.O. (H.), HD 5/14/1/18.
12 S.R.O., q. sess. order bk. 1709–26, f. 177v.; J. Jordan, *Religious Breathings* (Shrews. 1809; copy in S.P.L., class C 94).
13 S.R.O. 2612/11; 3573/T/1–2; R. & D.R.T., record sheet and photo.; K. Edgington, 'Memories of Wesl. Meth. Chap.' (MS. in possession of R. & D.R.T.).
14 S.R.O. 2612/11–12.
15 *Methodist Church Bldgs.: Statistical Returns 1940* (Manchester, *c.* 1947), 271.
16 Madeley, 'Geog. descr. Rushbury', 58.
17 Below, Longville, etc., nonconf.
18 S.R.O. 783, box 79, acct. bk. 1756, 14 May. This section was written *c.* 1983 and later revised.
19 S.R.O. 3573/7/7; P.R.O., ED 7/103, ff. 19–20; S. Bagshaw, *Dir. Salop.* (1851), 546; *9th Rep. Com. Char.* H.C. 258, p. 410 (1823), ix.
20 R. Hume, 'Changing Patterns of Educ. Devt. in Salop. 1660–1833' (Keele Univ. Ph.D. (Educ.) thesis, 1982), 156.
21 Cf. S. Bagshaw, *Dir. Salop.* (1851), 545.
22 P.R.O., ED 7/103, ff. 19-20.
23 S.R.O. 3573/7/6; /7/13.
24 *Kelly's Dir. Salop.* (1891), 400.
25 Rushbury C.E. Sch. log bk. (at the sch.), reps. 1911, 1930.
26 Ibid. *passim*, esp. 7 Feb. 1912.
27 Ibid. 26 June 1908, 22 July 1912, 2 July 1913.
28 *Kelly's Dir. Salop.* (1885), 928; (1895), 182; (1905), 194; (1913), 202.
29 Log bk. 26 Nov. 1906, 5 Aug. 1910, 1 Mar. 1912, 19 Sept. 1913; rep. 1911.
30 Ibid. 30 Aug. 1915.

by 1956 also the parish reading room.[31] Pupils from the closed Eaton-under-Heywood C.E. school were admitted in 1927; the roll was 60 in 1925 but 96 in 1929.[32] Gardening was taught from 1918 and seniors attended Church Stretton domestic science and woodwork centres from 1936.[33] The school became controlled in 1947,[34] and seniors went to Church Stretton Modern school in 1948.[35] The roll was 53 in 1950, 57 in 1973, and 29 in 1981.[36] A demountable classroom, with 30 places, was erected in 1968, and 16 pupils from the closed Cardington C.E. (Aided) Primary school were admitted in 1982.[37] Closure, scheduled for 1983,[38] was averted and the roll was 46 in 1989.[39]

County council evening classes in horticulture, stock management, ambulance work, and hygiene, between 1892 and 1902, and in dressmaking in 1912–13, were well attended.[40]

Lutwyche Hall housed a convent boarding school (evacuated from Brighton) during the Second World War and Wenlock Edge Boys' Boarding school 1948–66, with *c.* 120 boys (including day boys) in 1959.[41]

CHARITIES FOR THE POOR. In 1601 Edward Lutwyche gave a 40*s.* rent charge for weekly bread and annual Good Friday cash doles to six parishioners nominated for life.[42]

Thomas Smalman (d. 1693) left 40*s.* to the poor of the parish,[43] and several small sums of money were employed *c.* 1710, along with *c.* £60 left by a Mr. Leighton and others, to buy land.[44] That was presumably the parish land noted in 1743, which then produced £2 2*s.* a year.[45] In 1830 the *c.* 8 a. of poor's land at Wall Bank was mostly let, the rent providing coals, but paupers occupied two pairs of cottages there rent-free.[46] After the formation of the poor-law union in 1836 the cottages were not so used.[47] About 1920 the land was sold and the proceeds invested.[48]

Anne Tipton (d. 1788) left a rent charge of £1 10*s.* for weekly bread doles.[49]

About 1800 Martha Baker left the interest on £20 for bread doles; soon after her death the capital was used to repair a house (used as a poorhouse) on the poor's land and by 1830 £1 a year from the poor rate was spent on the bread doles.[50] Payment seems to have ceased by 1900.[51]

By will proved 1820 Dr. Wainwright, besides his bequest for a school,[52] left money to build and endow almshouses for two widows on the same plot as the school. In the 19th century the widows each received £2 and coals.[53] The two-roomed almshouses were last occupied *c.* 1875.[54] Under a Scheme of 1893[55] the rector rented them as a parish reading room for 5*s.* a year.[56] By 1942 the eleemosynary part of Wainwright's charity yielded £9 9*s.* 8*d.* including the reading room rent; it was given partly to two widows and partly in money gifts to 18 other recipients.[57]

By the 1890s the annual income of the surviving charities, Lutwyche's, Tipton's, and Wainwright's, and probably of the poor's land, amounted to £34 and was spent on bread, coals, and clothing.[58] In 1975 those four charities were united as the Rushbury charity,[59] with an annual income of £54.[60]

The parish shared in Capt. S. H. Christy's charity for widows.[61]

CHURCH STRETTON

THE extensive parish of Church Stretton contained 10,286 a. (4,163 ha.) *c.* 1831[62] and, save for excrescences at the southern end and the north-western corner, approximated to a compact rectangle over 8 km. from north to south and nearly 5 km. from east to west.[63] The historic

31 *S.C.C. Mins. (Educ.)* 1903–4, 122; 1956–7, 175; 1974–5, 332–3; inf. from headmaster; above, this article, intro.; below, charities.
32 Log bk. 31 Mar. 1925, 8 Feb. 1927, 3 Sept. 1929.
33 Ibid. 27 Mar. 1918, 23 Jan., 25 Mar. 1936.
34 *S.C.C. Mins. (Educ.)* 1947–8, 75.
35 Log bk. 23 Mar., 29 July 1948.
36 Ibid. rep. 1950; S.C.C. Educ. Cttee. *Sch. List* (1973), 8; *Educ. Dir.* (1981), 7.
37 Inf. from S.C.C. Educ. Dept.; log bk. 4 Jan. 1982.
38 *Shropshire Star*, 12 Sept. 1980, p. 4.
39 *Educ. Dir.* (1989), 10.
40 Organizing sec.'s reps. to Intermediate Educ. Cttee. in *S.C.C. Mins.* 1893–1902; reps. on work of Higher Educ. Cttee. in *S.C.C. Mins. (Educ.)* 1912–13.
41 Inf. from Mrs. N. Dale, Rushbury; *Wellington Jnl.* 30 Nov. 1959; personal knowledge.
42 S.R.O. 1661/2, deed poll; S.P.L., MS. 6741, p. 209; MS. 6865, p. 166; P.R.O., C 93/2/31; C 93/3/16A; *24th Rep. Com. Char.* H.C. 231, pp. 411–12 (1831), xi.
43 S.P.L., Deeds 15369; *T.S.A.S.* 3rd ser. iii. 11; *S.P.R. Heref.* iii (5), 22.
44 H.W.R.O.(H.), HD 5/14/1/18.
45 S.R.O. 3573/Ac/1, s.a. 1743.
46 *24th Rep. Com. Char.* 411.
47 S.R.O. 3573/7/4, Jas. Jones to [R. G.] Anning, 20 Nov. 1919; cf. *V.C.H. Salop.* iii. 169.
48 S.R.O. 4693/150, acct. for 1920–1.
49 S.P.L., MS. 6741, p. 209; 6865, p. 166; Watson, *St. Peter's Ch.* 15; *24th Rep. Com. Char.* 412.
50 *24th Rep. Com. Char.* 412; above, local govt.
51 *Kelly's Dir. Salop.* (1895), 181; (1900), 188.
52 Above, educ.
53 S.R.O. 3573/7/7; *24th Rep. Com. Char.* 410; *Salopian Shreds & Patches*, v. 31.
54 S.R.O. 3573/7/17.
55 Ibid. /7/18, Scheme.
56 Ibid. /7/17; above, this article, intro.
57 S.R.O. 4693/150, accts. s.a.
58 Cf. *Kelly's Dir. Salop.* (1895), 181; (1900), 188.
59 Char. Com. Scheme 10 Apr. 1975 (lent by Mrs. J. Ward, correspondent).
60 *Review of Local Chars.* (S.C.C. 1975), 59.
61 Ibid.; above, Cardington, charities.
62 O.S. *Area Bk.* (1884), giving acreage within bounds unchanged since the 1830s: cf. tithe award, calculating the area 40 a. (16 ha.) less. Ch. Stretton tithe apportionment and maps were printed, and for this article copies in S.R.O. 437/3 (apportionment) and 445/13/1–6 (maps) were used. Hereafter refs. (even to pieces of land not strictly fields) are simplified as 'tithe field(s)' followed by the no(s). (for particular features), 'tithe award' (for more general inf. about fam. estates, etc., taken from apportionment and maps), and 'tithe map(s)'.
63 The axes of the parish are in fact more nearly NE.–SW. and SE.–NW., but for simplicity's sake are occasionally treated as N.–S. and E.–W. The rest of the para. and, except where otherwise stated, the next three paras. are based on tithe award; *V.C.H. Salop.* i, map facing p. 23; D. Bilbey, *Ch. Stretton: A Salop. Town and its People* (1985), pl. 150–1; fig. 9 in this vol. Mr. R. D. Bilbey is thanked for much help during the research and writing of this art.

centres of settlement are strung out in a line nearer the eastern than the western edge of the parish. The central and largest settlement, where the church was built, is the small market town of Church Stretton, some 19 km. south-south-west of Shrewsbury and 20 km. north-north-west of Ludlow. South of Church Stretton lie the villages of Little Stretton and Minton and, near the boundary with Wistanstow parish and Old Churchmoor, the hamlet of Hamperley; Marshbrook hamlet lies partly in Wistanstow. To the north are All Stretton and the hamlets of Botvyle and Womerton.

The 19th-century parish included four townships, each centred on one of the main settlements. Minton, the southernmost, was a separate manor[64] extending into Wistanstow parish. The three townships of Church Stretton, All Stretton, and Little Stretton formed the manor of Stretton-en-le-Dale, although All Stretton township then included Botvyle,[65] part of Lydley and Cardington manor[66] which extended into Church Stretton parish to include Caer Caradoc hill.[67] All Stretton township then also included presumably most of the land that had formed the Domesday manor of Womerton. Nevertheless the northernmost parts of the parish (the north-western excrescence and land north and north-east of Womerton) formed detached parts of Church Stretton township,[68] perhaps as a result of the inclosure of 1790.

All the settlements lie near, but not on, the Roman road from *Deva* (Chester) via *Viroconium Cornoviorum* (Wroxeter) to *Isca* (Caerleon, Mon.).[69] The road, itself known as Botte (Bot) Street[70] or (by *c.* 1580) Watling Street, gave a name to the three Strettons,[71] All Stretton apparently taking its particular name from one Alfred, the nature of whose connexion with the settlement is not known.[72] Minton is named from its proximity to the Long Mynd, Womerton perhaps from an early English owner of that estate.[73]

In the 1830s the parish boundary followed major or minor natural features or roads or field boundaries,[74] save in the north-east against Leebotwood parish where, in 1340, it was defined by a trench.[75] South of the trench the boundary with Cardington coincided with a short stretch of the Roman road[76] and then crossed fields towards Caer Caradoc hill. Along the top of the Long Mynd the north-western boundary followed the Port Way, which also marked part of the boundary of the north-western excrescence that was otherwise largely defined by enclosures on Wilderley Hill.[77] Much of the northern boundary (with Smethcott and Woolstaston parishes) followed Betchcott and Broad brooks.[78] On the east and south-east the boundary with Hope Bowdler and Acton Scott was marked by minor streams near the Cwms and ran along the eastern slopes of Helmeth and Ragleth hills but across the summit of Hazler Hill lying between them. On the south-east and south roads and streams marked the boundary with Acton Scott and Wistanstow parishes, but around Hamperley, at the southern extremity of the parish, the boundary followed field boundaries and minor streams as far west as Minton Batch, which it ascended to the Port Way on the Long Mynd.[79]

In 1899 the civil parish was split into three[80] whose combined areas coincided with that of the ancient parish until 1986. In 1986 the most distant part of the long strip of All Stretton C.P.'s territory that ran up beyond the north end of the Long Mynd, to the area around New Leasowes, was transferred to Ratlinghope C.P.,[81] the rest of the strip to Church Pulverbatch and Smethcott C.P.s, whose new boundary there was formed by part of the Picklescott–Stitt road via Thresholds.[82]

The parish is hilly and most land lies over 220 m. The highest point (490 m.) is on the Long Mynd, near the north-western boundary of the parish and the springs of the streams that drain down Ashes Hollow;[83] the lowest land (161 m.) lies around Marshbrook.[84] The settled part of the parish consists of the dale referred to in the manorial name Stretton-en-le-Dale and confined by the steep sides of the Long Mynd on the north-west and by Ragleth, Hazler, Helmeth, and Caer Caradoc hills on the south-east. The dale is narrowest at Little Stretton. Church Stretton town stands on the dale's watershed. Water flowing through the rectory grounds, it was said *c.* 1838, could be turned either north or south:[85] that was Town brook, now culverted. The streams draining the dale north and south are fed from the west by substantial tributaries springing from the heads of the narrow valleys (batches) cut into the eastern flank of the Long Mynd; no such streams rise on the eastern side of the dale.[86] The northward stream, Ash (Nash) brook,[87] which later takes its name from the places through which it flows,[88] rises in Carding Mill valley and receives tributaries from the

64 Below, manors.

65 Tithe award.

66 For descent see above, Cardington, manors.

67 Cf. S.R.O. 3908/Pa/1; 1011, box 172, papers *re* boundary fences; incl. award C 4/36, map II.

68 Tithe award; Bilbey, *Ch. Stretton*, pl. 150.

69 *V.C.H. Salop.* i. 270–1 and map facing p. 205; O.S. Map, *Roman Brit.* (1978), S. sheet.

70 B. Botfield, *Stemmata Botevilliana* (1858), 21.

71 S.R.O. 1709, box 203, glebe terrier; *P.N.Salop* (E.P.N.S.), i. 286–7.

72 Eyton, xii. 27.

73 *P.N. Salop.* i. 209, 217, 320–1.

74 Early 17th-cent. descr.: *T.S.A.S.* xlix. 250.

75 *V.C.H. Salop.* viii. 98; SA 246.

76 At O.S. Nat. Grid SO 4755 9700: *V.C.H. Salop.* i. 270; O.S. Map 1/25,000, SO 49 (1956 edn.).

77 For the inclosure of Wilderley Hill (1790) see below, fig 9.

78 *V.C.H. Salop.* viii. 146, 170.

79 O.S. Maps 1/25,000, SO 48 (1957 edn.), SO 49 (1956 edn.).

80 Below, local govt.

81 Above, Hope Bowdler, intro.; *Salop. (Dist. Boundaries) Order 1985* (Stat. Instr. 1985, no. 1891).

82 *Shrews. and Atcham (Parishes) Order 1985* (Stat. Instr. 1985, no. 2056).

83 O.S. Nat. Grid SO 4169 9420: O.S. Map 1/25,000, SO 49/59 (1981 edn.).

84 O.S. Nat. Grid SO 4423 8989 (spot height a few m. outside the par.): O.S. Map 1/25,000, SO 48/58 (1983 edn.).

85 W.S.L. 350/5/40, Ch. Stretton p. 47.

86 O.S. Maps, 1/25,000, SO 48 (1957 edn.), SO 49 (1956 edn.).

87 Giving its name to Nashbrook field: cf. below, econ. hist. (agric.).

88 *Route of Shrews. & Heref. Rly.* (Leominster, 1860), 51.

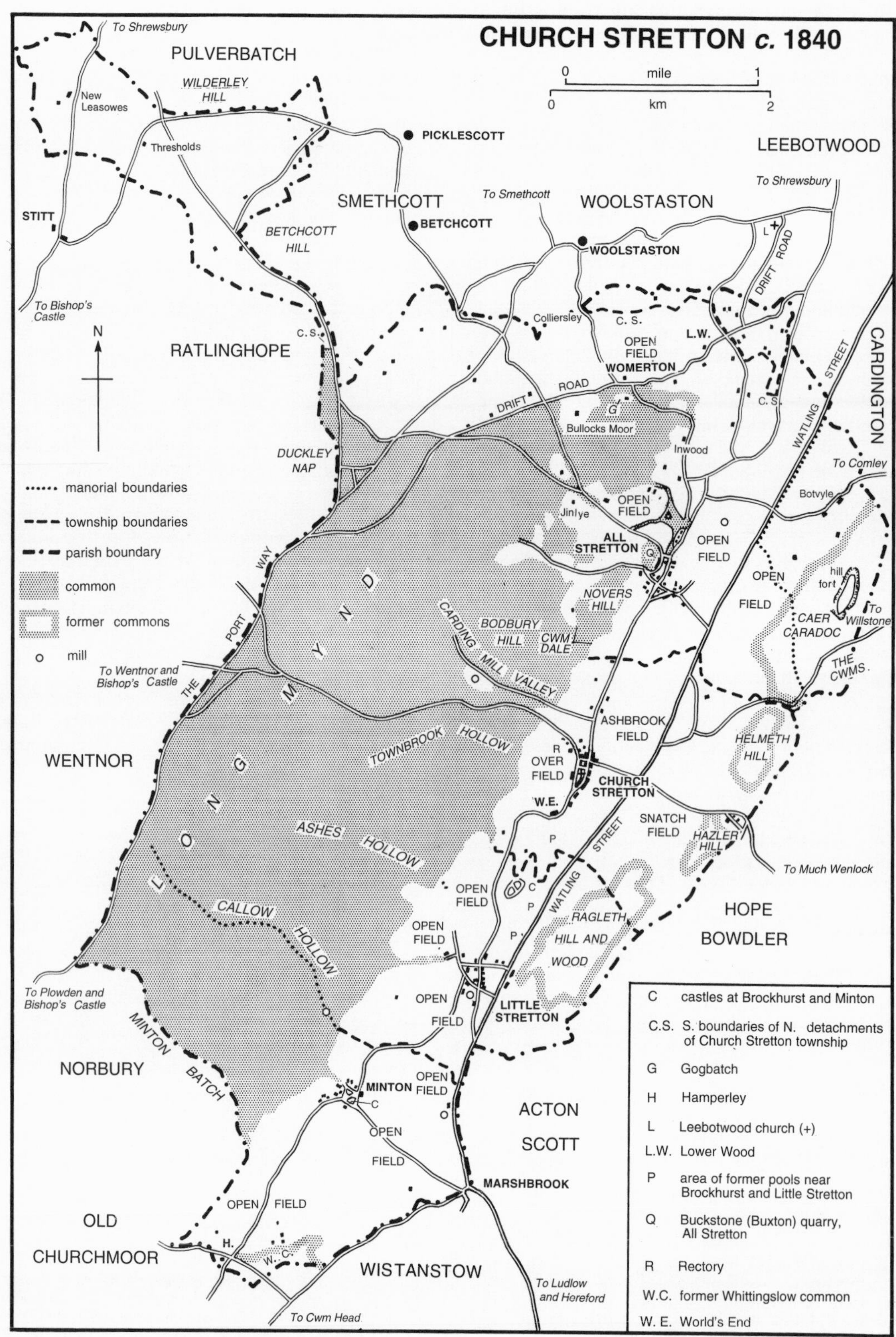

Fig. 9

Hazler hill and commons west of Bullocks Moor and around Betchcott hill were inclosed in 1790, Caer Caradoc and Whittingslow common in 1822 (Acts of 1788, 1814, and 1816).

Batch and Gogbatch; it feeds the Cound brook system, joining the Severn near Lower Cound. The southward stream flowing round the west of Brockhurst and through Little Stretton is fed from Ashes and Callow hollows and Minton Batch; variously known as Quinny[89] or Marsh[90] brook it flows into the Onny near the Grove, Wistanstow.

The parish's geology is almost entirely Pre-Cambrian.[91] The principal feature is the Church Stretton Fault running along the east side of the dale. East of the fault, broadly speaking, the hills are formed of what, apart from some small areas of schists near the Wrekin,[92] are Shropshire's oldest rocks, the Uriconian volcanics: mainly Ragleth Tuffs, though Caer Caradoc's geology is complicated by Caer Caradoc Andesites and Cwms Rhyolites with intrusive igneous Dolerite. West of the fault the younger Longmyndian sedimentary rocks form the Long Mynd, their strata dipping almost vertically[93] to the north-west, throwing up the Stretton Series of fine-grained siltstones and a thin band of Cardingmill Grit and, further west and beyond the parish boundary, the newer coarse-grained Wentnor Series;[94] the higher parts of the Long Mynd are covered with head[95] and, between All Stretton and Colliers Lye, areas of boulder clay.[96] In the centre of the dale Longmyndian rocks are exposed on both sides of the fault[97] so that Stretton Shales form the lowest slopes not only of the Long Mynd but also of Ragleth and Helmeth hills and the south-western slope of Caer Caradoc hill; on the western slopes of the eastern hills, though not on the Long Mynd, Helmeth Grit, oldest of the Longmyndian rocks, appears from beneath the Stretton Shales. Small areas at the south end of Ragleth hill (around Wiresytch coppice) and at the eastern end of Minton township (around Queensbatch mill and Marshbrook) are Ordovician: Caradoc shales, flags, and sandstone. The floor of the dale consists of glacial deposits of boulder clay[98] overlying Silurian shales and limestone; some of those shales, of the Llandovery and Wenlock Series, are exposed in the southern part of the dale, particularly around Minton. There are alluvial deposits along the courses of the streams and, here and there, islands of sand and gravel. Coal Measures have been encountered near Botvyle.

Palaeontological data from the late 7th millennium B.C., *c.* 2,500 years before subsistence agriculture began to appear in Britain, have been interpreted as evidence of a pastoral people's felling and burning of trees in the centre of Stretton dale, near the north–south watershed; similar evidence from further south, in the ill drained land near Little Stretton, is somewhat later and more tenuous.[99] Mesolithic stone mace-heads have been found on the north-western slopes of Ragleth hill[1] and worked flints of uncertain date near the Port Way or its suggested north-west branch; some are possibly Neolithic[2] and an axe from Carding Mill valley is certainly so.[3]

The higher land in the parish, principally the Long Mynd, affords much evidence of prehistoric activity, though difficult to interpret within the limits of a single parish. From the Bronze Age, however, some four millennia after the first suggestion of local human activity, 20 round barrows are known[4] and possibly a ring ditch or additional round barrow[5] and other earthworks,[6] together with 'swords', flints, and stone hammers or axe hammers.[7]

On top of Caer Caradoc hill in the mid or later 1st millennium B.C. Iron Age people constructed an oval enclosure (2.6 ha.) defended by two ditches. The main rampart was a stone wall following the crest of the slopes, and the main entrance, at the south-east, had guard chambers and an inturned rampart on the north;[8] there are building platforms within the fort.[9] Bodbury Ring promontory fort, above Carding Mill valley, may be Iron Age,[10] though some earthworks and lynchets could be 7th- or 8th-century Mercian (cross-ridge) dykes[11] and other enclosures or evidence of field systems may be medieval or later.[12]

The name Battle Field[13] and Caratacus legends[14] and his supposed cave below Caer Caradoc hill fort[15] are inadequate evidence for local scenes of violent resistance to early Roman

89 J. Rocque, *Map of Salop.* (1752), mistakenly follows earlier maps in making the 'Quanny' (or 'Quenny') drain the whole dale southwards, ignoring the Ch. Stretton watershed: cf. J. Speed, *Shropshyre Descr.* (1611); J. Blaeu, *Com. Salop.* (1645).

90 O.S. Map 1/25,000, SO 48/58 (1983 edn.).

91 Para. based on Geol. Surv. Maps, *Ch. Stretton* (SO 49) (O.S. for Inst. Geol. Sciences, 1968), *Craven Arms* (SO 48) (O.S. for Inst. Geol. Sciences 1969). Cf. *V.C.H. Salop.* i. 5–10; iv. 11–12; below, econ. hist. (manufactures and trade).

92 P. Toghill, *Geol. in Salop.* (Shrews. 1990), 10, 17–18.

93 Ibid. 10–11, 29 sqq.

94 D. C. Greig and others, *Geol. of Country around Ch. Stretton, Craven Arms, Wenlock Edge and Brown Clee* (Mem. Geol. Surv. 1968), 6.

95 Ibid. 284, 298–9.

96 Ibid. 280.

97 Ibid. 282; cf. ibid. 284 sqq.

99 P. J. Osborne, 'Insect faunas of Late Devensian and Flandrian age from Ch. Stretton', *Philosophical Trans. of Royal Soc.* Ser. B, cclxiii. 327–67 (ref. owed to Miss C. M. Sheard); *V.C.H. Salop.* iv. 20–2.

1 SA 1909, 1911.

2 SA 196, 594, 1900, 1904, 1912–13, 2664. The provenance of one, a (lost) stone scraper, was simply Ch. Stretton. Cf. S.P.L., Chitty colln. 807/LVI.SW; *V.C.H. Salop.* i. 202.

3 SA 3562.

4 SA 190, 193–5, 218, 236, 284, 1236–9, 1243–4, 1246–8, 1252, 1562, 4341; *V.C.H. Salop.* i. 411.

5 SA 3908.

6 SA 199, 1253; *V.C.H. Salop.* i. 407–8, 410.

7 SA 240, 243, 1893, 3564; *V.C.H. Salop.* i. 202.

8 SA 226; *Ch. Stretton: Some Results of Local Scientific Research*, ed. C. W. Campbell-Hyslop and E. S. Cobbold (3 vols. 1900–4), iii. 25–33; *V.C.H. Salop.* i. 361–2; A. H. A. Hogg, *Hill-Forts of Brit.* (1975), 153–4, pl. 15; J. Forde-Johnston, *Hillforts of the Iron Age in Eng. and Wales* (1976), 40, 43 n. 3, 54, 129, 141–2, 153, 225–6, 229, pls. 12–13.

9 T. Rowley, *Landscape of the Welsh Marches* (1986), 32.

10 SA 1245; Campbell-Hyslop and Cobbold, op. cit. iii. 10- -14; *V.C.H. Salop.* i. 354–5; Forde-Johnston, *Hillforts*, 67, fig. 29.

11 SA 251; cf. Sir C. Fox, *Offa's Dyke* (1955), 165 n. and map; *V.C.H. Salop.* i. 409–10.

12 SA 231, 241–2, 244, 1895, 1899, 4046; *V.C.H. Salop.* i. 360.

13 SA 1905; W.S.L. 350/5/40, Ch. Stretton p. 24. The name occurs in S.R.O. 567, box 10, deed of 1623.

14 *Hillforts: Later Prehistoric Earthwks. in Brit. and Irel.* ed. D. W. Harding (1976), 290.

15 SA 248; *V.C.H. Salop.* i. 362.

rule, though Caratacus's last stand in battle (A.D. 50) probably occurred somewhere in what became the Shropshire sector of the Anglo-Welsh borderland.[16] The Romans' most obvious local legacy is their road along the east side of the dale, away from the valley bottom.[17] A couple of coins found at opposite ends of the parish,[18] a brooch found near Battle Field,[19] and a supposed Roman milestone[20] suggest traces of Roman travel through the area, for all the finds were made near the Roman road or a suggested north-west branch of the Port Way.[21] Evidence of Roman settlement is more elusive,[22] and native British settlement can only be presumed.

By the mid 12th century there was a royal castle on Brockhurst hill, defended by steep slopes and streams and marshes on the west and south; its keepers were paid out of the manorial revenues. It was possibly destroyed in the earlier 13th century and not rebuilt in consequence of Hubert de Burgh's construction of the new castle at Montgomery. In the 1890s there were still some remains of stonework lying about the earthworks, possibly part of the massive stone wall that had once defended the inner bailey.[23]

In the Middle Ages such importance as Church Stretton had derived from its location on the main Shrewsbury–Hereford road and its status as a royal manor rather than from the size of the settlement. An attempt to establish a market there probably failed, though a fair seems to have survived and there were probably decent inns there by the 14th century. A market was established in the early 17th century, but Stretton long remained Shropshire's smallest market town. Notwithstanding its small size, and perhaps from its situation on an important road and the lack of a dominant local landowner, the early 19th-century town seems to have enjoyed a livelier social life than (for instance) the rather more populous Much Wenlock.[24] After the railway's arrival in 1852 the town began to develop as a health resort and even to nurture aspirations, never realized, to become a spa. It nevertheless grew, especially in the Edwardian period when many fine villas were built. In the 20th century its population overtook Much Wenlock's, but Stretton's growth was owed largely to its popularity as a retirement town, and to an extent it remained, as in some respects it had always been, peculiar among Shropshire towns.

There is a healing well beside the lane from Minton to Hamperley.[25]

Notable people connected with Stretton, apart from lords of manors[26] and rectors,[27] include four landowners in the parish: Sir Thomas Leighton (1443–1519), courtier and founder of the family (for whom a baronetcy was created in 1692) seated at Wattlesborough and later (from *c.* 1711) at Loton;[28] Sir John Thynne (d. 1580), builder of Longleat;[29] Bonham Norton (1565–1635), the London stationer who laid out much of the money needed to print the Authorized Version of the Bible (1611);[30] and the antiquary and bibliographer Beriah Botfield (1807–63), member of the family of which the Thynnes were a branch.[31] The Revd. A. H. Johnson (1845–1927), one of the most influential tutors in the newly established school of Modern History at Oxford,[32] was a director of Church Stretton Developments Ltd. and indeed owned the greatest share of that concern's capital, an interest which passed to his son Sir Robert (1874–1938), deputy master and comptroller of the Royal Mint.[33] Dr. Roger Mainwaring (1590–1653), bishop of St. David's from 1635 to *c.* 1641,[34] the animal and genre painter Philip Eustace Stretton (b. 1863, fl. 1919),[35] and the gardener and plantsman John Treasure (1911–93)[36] were all natives. Stretton, *né* Smith, was the son and grandson of artists, and his father John Halphed Smith (1830–96) lived in All Stretton *c.* 1862–1883.[37] Stretton's aunt, Sarah Smith (1832–1911), the writer 'Hesba Stretton', had a cottage at All Stretton, where she spent holidays.[38] Lt.-Col. C. W. Campbell Hyslop (1860–1915), owner of Stretton House asylum, did distinguished service for the reserve forces[39] while his brother Dr. T. B. Hyslop (1863–1933) achieved pre-eminence in the family trade as

16 Suggested sites include ones near Bucknell and Clunbury, in the Newtown (Mont.) area, and at Llanymynech hill fort (cf. SA 1117): *T.S.A.S.* 3rd ser. viii, pp. vii–xii; liii. 37–52; G. Webster, *Rome against Caratacus* (1981), 28–30, 120; G. D. B. Jones, 'Searching for Caradog', *Trivium*, xxx. 57–64.

17 SA 108; *V.C.H. Salop.* i. 270–1 and map facing p. 205; I. D. Margary, *Roman Roads in Brit.* ii (1957), 51–2; below, communications.

18 On Wilderley Hill and nr. the Wayside inn, Marshbrook: SA 220, 4093.

19 SA 3567.

20 From nr. Marshbrook and now lost: SA 256.

21 Towards Cothercott hill: cf. below, communications.

22 A suggested quarry (SA 238), on Watling St. nr. Botvyle, and a possible Roman wooden drain from near Battle Field (SA 3566).

23 SA 1250; *V.C.H. Salop.* i. 353, 393; iii. 38; below, manors.

24 Cf. *Bye-Gones*, 1 Feb. 1911, 15–22 (reminiscences of the 19th cent.); below, M. Wenlock, social and cultural activities.

25 SA 1897.

26 Below, manors.

27 Below, church.

28 E. G. Salisbury, *Border Counties Worthies*, i (Oswestry, 1878), 138; Botfield, *Stemmata Botevilliana*, 165–70, 184; J. B. Blakeway, *Sheriffs of Salop.* (Shrews. 1831), 80–1; *V.C.H. Salop.* viii. 198.

29 *D.N.B.*; Botfield, op. cit. 30–3, 59.

30 *D.N.B.*; *Dict. of Printers and Booksellers 1557–1640*, ed. R. B. McKerrow (1910), 32, 201–3; below, manors (the Hall).

31 *D.N.B.*; Botfield, op. cit. 25–6, 58 (where a misprint falsifies the paternity of John Botvyle fl. 1439) sqq., 84–7, 99–100; below, manors (Botvyle).

32 Ford's lecturer 1908, fellow of All Souls: *Who Was Who 1916–28*, 558; *The Times*, 1 Feb. 1927, p. 17*a*; R. Soffer, 'Hist. at Oxf. 1850–1914', *Hist. Jnl.* xxx. 95, 98–9. He is mentioned in the article on his wife in *D.N.B. Missing Persons*. Dr. J. F. A. Mason is thanked for the last two refs.

33 P.R.O., BT 31/32100/116650; *Who Was Who 1929–40*, 717.

34 *D.N.B.*; *Alum. Oxon.* 1500–1714, iii. 960. He lost all his preferment when imprisoned by the Long Parliament.

35 C. Wood, *Dict. of Victorian Painters* (1978), 457; S.R.O. 6296/6/1, p. 5.

36 *The Independent*, 23 Dec. 1993, p. 14; *The Times*, 30 Dec. 1993, p. 17*a*.

37 S.R.O. 6296/6/1, pp. 1, 3, 5; *P.O. Dir. Salop.* (1863), 671, 804; (1879), 300. For his grandfather John Homes Smith see G. A. Godden, *Coalport and Coalbrookdale Porcelains* (1970), 96, 125; *Eng. County Histories: A Guide*, ed. C. R. J. Currie and C. P. Lewis (1994), 344.

38 Below, econ. hist. (resort); cf. *V.C.H. Salop.* xi. 198.

39 *Who Was Who 1897–1915*, 267; *The Times*, 8 (p. 10*f*), 22 (p. 7*a*) Apr. 1915; *Shrews. Chron.* 9 (pp. 4–5), 16 (p. 3) Apr. 1915; below, econ. hist. (manufactures and trade [asylums]).

'head of Bedlam' 1898–1910.[40] The Revd. D. H. S. Cranage (1866–1957), having moved to Cambridge in 1902, acquired a house in Madeira Walk (1906) whence to complete work on *An Architectural Account of the Churches of Shropshire*.[41] The Revd. C. S. Horne (1865–1914), politician and eminent Congregational divine, built the White House, Sandford Avenue, as a retirement home; he did not live to enjoy it,[42] but it was the home, in youth, of his son Kenneth (1907–69), broadcaster and businessman.[43]

COMMUNICATIONS. The main long distance communications through the parish have always been aligned with its north–south topography centring on the dale.[44] The earliest such route was the Port Way, possibly in use from Neolithic and Bronze Age times and traceable north from Plowden. In Stretton it is a ridgeway along the top of the Long Mynd, after which it keeps to the high ground across Betchcott hill and heads towards Cothercott hill, possibly then linking with routes to Pontesbury and thence to Bayston Hill. Recognized as a highway in the Middle Ages,[45] the Port Way may have been the way that Bishop Swinfield travelled from Stretton to Pontesbury in 1290.[46] Another route he might have taken is the road from All Stretton via Jinlye through Betchcott and Picklescott villages (where, in the 15th century, that road too was known as a portway),[47] but his employment of a guide suggests that he went over the hills rather than through the villages: to lose the way in bad weather on the wild wastes of the Long Mynd is to risk death.[48] At Bullocks Moor the road from All Stretton to Betchcott village crossed a drift road from the Port Way towards Leebotwood and a little further north, near Greenway Hill (as Woolstaston people called it in the 18th century), it crossed the main way down from the Long Mynd to Woolstaston village.[49]

Perhaps for centuries drovers taking cattle from central Wales to Shrewsbury via Bishop's Castle used the Port Way from Plowden to the north end of the Long Mynd. The Port Way's name indicates a road to a town, or here, more probably, the road to the local market towns, and in the early 19th century it was also used by farm wagons, perhaps to avoid toll gates; the steep ascent was probably no more laborious than the lower country roads. The drovers, when they descended the Long Mynd, probably avoided the roads connecting the main settlements: after passing Duckley Nap the 18th-century 'driving road' seems to have turned right out of the direct way to Woolstaston and then passed by Bullocks Moor, Womerton, and Lower Wood, turning north past the Malt House to run past the east end of Leebotwood church.[50] From where the drift road turned north a lane continued north-east to the Shrewsbury–Stretton road near the confluence of Broad brook with the main stream; known as Bog Lane in 1866, it was then inconvenient and little used.[51] Other north-bound traffic descending the Long Mynd probably used the road that left Stretton parish near Greenway Hill to run through Woolstaston and Smethcott villages towards Dorrington, a road that was known, in part at least, as the Portway in the 17th century.[52]

South-bound travellers from villages north of the parish did not have to use the Shrewsbury–Ludlow road north of Gorsty Bank to enter the parish, even if going to Church Stretton: in the 17th century Stankleys Lane (so called in 1777), entering the parish near Colliersley, was the high road from Woolstaston (and so in all probability from Smethcott) to Church Stretton,[53] evidently via Womerton and All Stretton. To travel from Woolstaston to Stretton by joining the Shrewsbury–Stretton turnpike at Leebotwood was in any case impossible before the 'new road' was made through Woolstaston parish in 1776–7; and long afterwards that road, not well maintained, was hardly ever used by wheeled traffic.[54] The Cartway was a route into Stretton parish from Leebotwood that avoided the Shrewsbury–Stretton turnpike north of Gorsty Bank: it turned south a few yards west of Leebotwood church to run parallel to the drift road across the south-east corner of Woolstaston parish and so to Lower Wood and the Strettons.[55]

40 *Who Was Who 1929–40*, 689; *The Times*, 15 Feb. 1933, p. 17*a*; inf. from Bethlehem Royal Hosp. Archives, Beckenham.

41 Published in parts 1894–1912. See Cranage, *Not Only a Dean* (1952), 75–7, 106, 115–16, 132, 146, 214–15; *V.C.H. Salop*. xi. 198; S.R.O. 2079/LVI. 5, no. 398; 4044/39, p. 44 no. 398.

42 *D.N.B. Missing Persons*; cf. *V.C.H. Salop*. iii. 348.

43 *D.N.B. Missing Persons*; N. Hackforth, *Solo for Horne: biog. of Kenneth Horne* (1976), 7–33.

44 See plate 3. For this section generally see Rocque, *Map of Salop*. (1752); R. Baugh, *Map of Salop*. (1808); B.L. Maps, O.S.D. 200, 207; C. & J. Greenwood, *Map of Salop*. (1827); tithe maps; O.S. Maps 1", Salop. LXI. SW (1833 edn.); 1/25,000, SO 49/59 (1981 edn.), and adjoining sheets where necessary.

45 Bilbey, *Ch. Stretton*, pl. 151; L. F. Chitty, 'Bronze Age Trade-Ways of Salop.' *Observation*, ii. 11; *T.S.A.S*. liii. 31; S.P.L., Chitty colln. 803/12; SA 157; Campbell-Hyslop and Cobbold, *Ch. Stretton*, iii. 36, 50–1.

46 Rest of para. based on *Household Roll of Ric. de Swinfield* (Camd. Soc. [1st ser.] lix), 79; ibid. (Camd. Soc. [1st ser.] lxii), pp. cxc–cxci; W.S.L. 350/5/40, Ch. Stretton pp. 96–7.

47 *V.C.H. Salop*. viii. 148. 'Port' way may thus be a generic term that includes roads linking in to the main Port Way. Dr. M. Gelling is thanked for advice on the Port Way's name.

48 E. D. Carr, *A Night in the Snow* (1865); *V.C.H. Salop*. viii. 177; *Shrews. Chron*. 3 Jan. 1902, p. 8.

49 For the last two roads see the next para.

50 R. J. Colyer, *Welsh Cattle Drovers* (1976), 102, 136; Campbell-Hyslop and Cobbold, *Ch. Stretton*, iii. 50–1; W.S.L. 350/5/40, Ch. Stretton p. 98, whose 'driving road' seems to follow the footpath from Malt Ho. to Leebotwood ch. shown on O.S. Map 6", Salop. XLIX. SW. (1903 edn.).

51 S.R.O. 1168/2/1, p. 95.

52 *V.C.H. Salop*. viii. 148, 171; W.S.L. 350/5/40, Ch. Stretton pp. 96–7. This may be the N. continuation of the main Port Way rather than a branch (cf. above, n. 47).

53 *V.C.H. Salop*. viii. 171 (corr. below, Corrigenda).

54 Ibid.; S.R.O. 567/5/3/1/14, 27 May 1776; /1/15, 18 Apr. 1777; 2282/2/3, pp. 11–12. The road was called new in 1766–7, though later local tradition maintained that Cath. Pope (d. 1754) used it with a coach and six.

55 S.R.O. 3628/1, map 14; W.S.L. 350/5/40, Ch. Stretton p. 98. It cannot be identified securely with the 13th-cent. *alta via* referred to in *V.C.H. Salop*. viii. 171; the word there interpreted as *cimeterium* seems to read *cunetam*, of doubtful meaning and providing no identifiable point to fix the boundary being defined. Cf. *Cart. Haughmond*, p. 144.

As has been seen, the road from Woolstaston up the north end of the Long Mynd, joining the Port Way near Duckley Nap, was part of a road to Bishop's Castle in the 17th century.[56] About 2 km. south of Duckley Nap the Port Way crossed the main route west across the Long Mynd: known as Burway Road at its eastern end, it was a carriage road, 'much improved' in the mid 19th century, leading from Church Stretton to Ratlinghope and earlier perhaps as far as Welshpool (Mont.).[57] Its crossing with the Port Way offered southbound travellers alternative routes to Bishop's Castle: continuing south along the Port Way to Plowden on the road from Wistanstow to Bishop's Castle or turning west to Ratlinghope, whence it was a short way to the road from Shrewsbury to Bishop's Castle. Further north the latter road crosses the remote corner of Church Stretton parish near New Leasowes, but it ceased to be the main route from Shrewsbury to Bishop's Castle *c.* 1838 after a new one had been made through Minsterley and the Hope valley[58] further west.

Another road from Church Stretton to the top of the Long Mynd (whence roads or tracks lead to villages between it and the Stiperstones) ascends from Carding Mill valley and is called Mott's Road after Dr. Charles Mott, the Church Stretton doctor in whose honour it was improved by public subscription in 1850.[59]

The way to the top of the Mynd from Little Stretton up Ashes Hollow is really a scramble for the 'youthful and agile', but farther south, going round Callow and Round hills, there was evidently a way from Little Stretton to Bishop's Castle (via the Port Way or Wentnor) in the late 17th century.[60]

Watling Street, the Roman road from Chester to Caerleon, was skilfully made along the eastern side of the dale.[61] In Stretton it had no influence on post-Roman settlement (which was all on the western side) before the end of the 19th century.

The Shrewsbury–Ludlow road entered the parish from Leebotwood near the present Brook House and ran through the three Strettons, joining Watling Street south of Little Stretton. In the later 17th century it was part of the Chester–Bristol road, and as late as 1841 Church Stretton High Street was known as Bristol Road. North of All Stretton lanes from the road to Watling Street enabled through travellers to use the Roman road as a bypass in the late 17th century.[62] The Stretton–Ludlow road was a turnpike 1756–1873, with a toll gate (and a stop gate into Watling Street) in Little Stretton.[63] The Stretton–Shrewsbury road was a turnpike 1756–1877, and improvements may have included minor modifications of route.[64] After much local opposition a new bypass was opened in 1941; leaving the Shrewsbury–Stretton road near Gorsty Bank, *c.* 700 m. to the south it joined Watling Street, following that route for 2 km. and then running parallel to, and west of, Watling Street, which it rejoined after another 1.5 km. A roundabout planned for the new road at Crossways was never made.[65]

Minton is reached by lanes leaving the Shrewsbury–Ludlow road at Little Stretton and Marshbrook. From Minton a lane south-west to Hamperley was presumably also a route to Hawkhurst hay and to lanes leading towards Old Churchmoor and Cwm Head. Ways up to the Long Mynd around Minton hill lead to the Port Way.

The principal road east out of the dale ran from Church Stretton along the line of the present Hazler Road, through the gap between Hazler and Helmeth hills to Hope Bowdler, and then across Ape Dale and over Wenlock Edge to Much Wenlock; by 1675 a branch out of it, presumably at Longville in the Dale, ran to Bridgnorth.[66] The Stretton–Wenlock road was a turnpike 1765–1875. In 1855 the Hazler Road route was superseded by the straighter line of what became Sandford Avenue, laid out a little further north.[67] A road past Botvyle runs via Comley to Cardington, and another between Helmeth and Caer Caradoc hills, via the Cwms, was perhaps an old road to Cardington from the town, where it seems to align with the front of Spring Cottage, which may thus preserve an old building line where the Bristol road widened out north of the market place.[68]

The railway from Shrewsbury arrived at Church Stretton in 1852 when a station was opened north of the bridge made to carry the road to Hope Bowdler (the later Sandford Avenue) over the line. The line opened to Hereford in 1853.[69] The station was replaced in 1914 by a larger one south of the road bridge to cater for holidaymakers and visitors;[70] it was an unstaffed halt from 1967. All Stretton and Little Stretton halts were opened probably in the 1930s to compete with buses; both were open until 1958, though All Stretton halt had been closed 1943–6 as a wartime economy.

GROWTH OF SETTLEMENT. The recorded population in 1086 was 35 in Stretton

56 *V.C.H. Salop.* viii. 171.

57 Ogilby, *Britannia* (1675), pl. 57; Windsor, *Handbk.* 27.

58 *V.C.H. Salop.* viii. 301; cf. Loton Hall MSS., Sir Baldwin Leighton's diary 25 May 1842.

59 *Stretton Focus*, Mar. 1982, p. 10; Windsor, *Handbk.* 27–8.

60 Windsor, *Handbk.* 27; Ogilby, *Britannia* (1675), pl. 57.

61 Margary, *Roman Roads*, ii. 51–2.

62 Ogilby, *Britannia* (1675), pl. 57; *Stretton Focus*, Oct. 1983, p. 9.

63 29 Geo. II, c. 59; S.R.O. 356, box 312, Ludlow 2nd turnpike trust min. bk. 1756–70, p. 4; Ann. Turnpike Acts Continuance Act, 1872, 35 & 36 Vic. c. 85.

64 29 Geo. II, c. 61; *T.S.A.S.* lix. 55; Ann. Turnpike Acts Continuance Act, 1874, 37 & 38 Vic. c. 95; Campbell-Hyslop and Cobbold, *Ch. Stretton*, ii. 197 n.

65 *Shrews. Chron.* 9 Jan. (p. 3), 28 Aug. (p. 10) 1931; 7 Feb. (p. 11), 31 July (p. 5) 1936; S.R.O. 340/1; 1738, boxes 14–15, co. surveyor's files on by-pass; *S.C.C. Mins.* 1936–7, 308–9; 1938–9, 328; 1941–2, 98–9; Bilbey, *Ch. Stretton*, pl. 109–10.

66 Ogilby, *Britannia* (1675), pl. 57; below, Shipton, intro.

67 Above, Hope Bowdler, intro.; *Stretton Focus*, Aug. 1986, p. 9.

68 See Mr. Bilbey's suggestion: *Ch. Stretton*, pl. 125; cf. *Ch. Stretton Illustrated*, ed. E. S. Cobbold (1908), 18.

69 Para. based on R. K. Morriss, *Rlys. of Salop.* (1991), 14–15; *T.S.A.S.* lxiv. 89–90, 97.

70 Below, econ. hist. (the resort).

manor and 2 in Womerton; Lydley, where 2 were recorded, may have included Botvyle, but Domesday Book recorded no population figure for Minton.[71] The 1327 subsidy was paid by 38: 11 in Church Stretton, 11 in All Stretton, 10 in Minton, and 6 in Little Stretton.[72] Population at Botvyle was perhaps recorded under Lydley (5 taxpayers),[73] and the Minton figure may have included part of Wistanstow,[74] as it evidently did in 1524–5 when 4 paid to the subsidy in Minton and Whittingslow. That year 11 paid in Church Stretton and 7 in All Stretton. There were then perhaps two taxpayers in Botvyle, probably bringing the parish total to just under two dozen, perhaps representing a population of 100–200.[75]

In 1667 poll tax was assessed on 489 men, women, and children in the Strettons and Minton.[76] In 1672 hearth tax was paid for 98 houses there[77] and in 1676 there were 434 adults in the parish, perhaps representing a population approaching 500.[78] By 1792 there were 168 houses: 87 in Church Stretton, 42 in All Stretton, 26 in Little Stretton, 11 and some cottages in Minton, and 2 at Botvyle. The population was growing rapidly by the 1790s, and by 1801 there were 924 inhabitants (199 families) in the parish.[79]

The population increased erratically from 1801 to 1871, with rapid spurts 1811–21 and in the 1830s. It was 1,756 by 1871 but declined slightly in the 1870s and by 1901 had still not recovered to the 1871 level.[80]

The greatest increase of population was in the Edwardian period and was concentrated in Church Stretton town, always the largest settlement: the total population of the three new civil parishes grew from 1,749 in 1901 to 2,435 in 1911 and to 2,650 by 1921. It was probably in the Edwardian period that the population of Church Stretton town passed that of Much Wenlock town, having been about half its size in the mid 19th century. For forty years after 1921 decennial increases were small, and the population of the three C.P.s was only 2,977 in 1961. Growth then quickened, bringing their population to 3,514 by 1971, 3,945 by 1981, and 4,184 by 1991.[81]

In 1593 a fire destroyed part of Church Stretton town probably leaving other parts unscathed. The inhabitants were licensed to collect for the town's rebuilding. In the event the necessary rebuilding may have owed less to charitable collections than to Bonham Norton's investment in town properties.[82] On Sir Henry Townshend's warrant Norton received building timber from the lord of the manor's demesne woods of Hawkhurst and Womerton not only for his fine new market house but also for a school and a court house, and it seems clear that Norton (who also built himself a house) was granted a market to assist him with the improvement of the town by the building or rebuilding of inns and lodging houses.[83]

The rebuilding seems not to have destroyed Church Stretton's simple original plan, which remained apparent *c.* 1840.[84] It lined both sides of Bristol Road, renamed High Street in the 19th century. Most of the town was south of the Bristol road's crossing of the road down from the Long Mynd towards Hope Bowdler, then apparently part of a route from Welshpool to Much Wenlock and Bridgnorth; that road became known as Brook Street (later Burway Road) west of the crossing, and Lake Lane (later Station Road, later again Sandford Avenue) east of it. South of the crossing, probably immediately south in early times,[85] the Bristol road widened into a market place. West of the crossing Church Street (formerly Back Lane) runs south from Burway Road to join High Street at the south end of the town. In the centre of the town Churchway (formerly Cub Lane) links High Street and the Square to Church Street, which has more consequence than most back lanes as it is the way to the church, built *c.* 1200, and was also the way to the Hall in the 17th and 18th centuries;[86] at that point the churchyard occupies most of the land between Church Street and High Street, and it is possible that the buildings east of it are encroachments on a market place once considerably larger. Encroachment may have begun early: the town's oldest known building apart from the church, the Buck's Head built as a hall and cross wing, occupies the southern end of this suggested encroachment; the hall has gone, but the cross wing, with crown-post roof and dragon ties, was built 1287–1321.[87]

The railway's arrival in 1852 stimulated the town's aspirations (apparent by the early 1860s) to develop into a resort, but growth was long delayed. Its population was probably rather more than 500 in the 1840s[88] and little more 40 years later.[89] Some building and embellishments were undertaken in the 1880s. In 1884–5 Station

71 *V.C.H. Salop.* i. 317, 326, 342, 344.

72 *T.S.A.S.* 2nd ser. iv. 303, 322.

73 Ibid. 316.

74 Into which par. that man. extended: above, this article, intro.

75 P.R.O., E 179/166/127, m. 2r.–d.; E 179/166/205, m. 1, where the name of the place recorded betw. All Stretton and Cardington is torn away, but the taxpayers include [John] of the Inne (Thynne) who lived at Botvyle (below, manors). Cf. *T.S.A.S.* lxiv. 36–8.

76 Staffs. R.O., D.(W.) 1788, P. 46, B. 8, assessment of Ch. Stretton Mar. 1666/7.

77 *Hearth Tax 1672* (Salop. Arch. Soc.), 179–81.

78 *Compton Census*, ed. Whiteman, 259. The poll tax figs. suggest a multiplier for the hearth tax data rather higher than that favoured ibid. p. lxvii.

79 S.P.L., MS. 6865, pp. 185–6.

80 *V.C.H. Salop.* ii. 228.

81 Ibid. 228–9; *Census* 1971, *Co. Rep. Salop.* i. 2, 4; *Census*, 1981, Small Area Statistics: Salop.; S.C.C. Property and Planning Services Dept. inf. rep. C91/103. For the town pop. in 1876 see below, n. 89.

82 Bilbey, *Ch. Stretton*, intro.; P.R.O., C 2/Jas. I/B 30/56; S.R.O. 3365/2621, Wm. Leighton and Hen. Townshend (Council in Marches of Wales) to bailiffs of Shrews. 21 Oct. 1593.

83 Longleat MSS., unbound, 3804, note taken from ct. r. 3 Jan. 1616; S.R.O. 2956/1.

84 Para. based on tithe map; cf. above, communications; Bilbey, *Ch. Stretton*, pls. 38, 44.

85 Above, communications.

86 Below, manors (the Hall); church (bldg.).

87 *Vernacular Archit.* xxvi. 69, 71.

88 Fig. suggested after rough deduction of out-of-town pop. (in P.R.O., HO 107/913/22, ff. 11–30v.; HO 107/1984, ff. 170–92), though the town is hard to define. Cf. above, communications; below, econ. hist. (resort).

89 The 1876 drainage dist. pop. was 425: below, public services.

Road and the new road (1855) which continued east to the Hope Bowdler boundary were planted as an avenue of limes on the initiative of Holland Sandford, rector of Eaton-under-Heywood and donor of the first trees. Sandford hoped thereby to improve the landscape and climate of the dale and to provide visitors with the amenity of a sheltered walk similar to that he had known as a Shrewsbury schoolboy. The road was later called after him.[90] At the same time the lord of the manor built five 'beautiful villas' in Church Street and planted a 'charming little enclosure of shrubs and trees at the top of the town' to add to the town's attractions.[91]

Nevertheless land was not made available for new building before 1892: the rebuilding of Bank House at the northern end of the town that year was later seen as marking the beginning of the town's growth.[92] In 1893 some four or five new houses appeared, and more followed in succeeding years.[93] Notable houses built before 1900 included Brockhurst, designed by A. E. Lloyd Oswell (perhaps for Mrs. Proffit),[94] beyond the south end of the town; it was a large three-storeyed house with small timber-decorated gables. More notable aesthetically was Woodcote (1896–8), secluded from the south end of the town and designed for Maj. C. W. Campbell Hyslop by Parker & Unwin.[95]

Parker & Unwin also designed the pair of cottages built in 1900–1 for Campbell Hyslop at the bottom of Cunnery Road, opposite the entrance to Woodcote. They were prototypes of Parker & Unwin's influential designs for cottages at New Earswick.[96] About 1900 the lord of the manor laid out over 200 building plots on *c.* 27 a. bounded by Shrewsbury Road, Sandford Avenue, the railway line, and Ash brook.[97]

Meanwhile, in 1896, a syndicate had bought up a considerable area, probably *c.* 300 a., for development, which they conveyed to the new Church Stretton Land Co. Ltd. in 1897. Two years later Church Stretton Building Co. Ltd. was formed, with a registered office at the same London address as the Land Co.'s. Those companies, with several 'allied organizations', invested capital running into six figures to develop the town as a superior residential district and to attract a good class of visitor.[98]

New roads, carefully planned to respect the scenic beauty, were laid out on the slopes of the hills. By 1901 Cunnery Road ran uphill from the south-west end of the town, and Madeira Walk, Trevor Hill, Stanyeld Road, and Links Road had been laid out on the slopes north-west of the town near the entrance to Carding Mill valley; Crossways had been laid out in the centre of the dale, and Clive Avenue, the beginnings of Hazler Crescent, and Kenyon Road on the dale's eastern slopes. There were then few houses in any of them, except the newly opened Hydropathic Establishment and Tiger Hall at the top of Cunnery Road and the terraced Cunnery Cottages near the bottom, two or three houses in Carding Mill valley, one (Staniel Villa) in Madeira Walk, the golf course clubhouse at the top of Links Road, and four houses at the lower (north) end of Clive Avenue. For the first time in its long history Watling Street had begun to be settled.[99]

Within ten years the urban district's rateable value doubled[1] as large villas were built on the sides of the dale and many new houses and shops in the centre. By 1905 the focus of intended development in the centre of the dale was Crossways, four shopping streets laid out by the Land Co. south of Sandford Avenue between the railway line and Watling Street. It included Tower Buildings, an impressive row of shops, with living quarters over, built *c.* 1905 to A. B. and W. S. Deakin's design in an elaborate 'black and white' style reminiscent of Victorian Chester. Vernon House, on the next corner, was a more commonplace corner shop.[2] In the same period *c.* 60 small houses, semi-detached or in short terraces, were built at the southern end of Crossways, in the part of Watling Street adjoining Crossways, and further south along Watling Street. Hazler Crescent's detached houses and the grander villas of Sandford Avenue and Watling Street east and north of their crossing point added over 30 more. Along the dale's eastern and western slopes fewer houses were built: only 3 were added in Clive Avenue in the east, and on the western side 2 in Cunnery Road, 5 in Madeira Walk, and 9 in Trevor Hill and Stanyeld Road. Almost all were detached villas in ample grounds, similar to those in the eastern stretch of Sandford Avenue.

Church Stretton's early 20th-century villas exemplify the rich variety of Edwardian architecture: Miss Brace's Overdale (*c.* 1903),[3] Clive Avenue; Emil Quäck's Mynd Court (*c.* 1905), Longhills;[4] Denehurst; the neo-timber-framed

90 Windsor, *Handbk.* 51–8, 106–13; S.P.L., Deeds 2747–8; Bilbey, *Ch. Stretton*, pls. 95–6; idem, *Sandford Ave.* (Stretton Soc. 1984; copy in S.P.L., class R 64.8 v.f.); *The Strettons*, pl. 3.

91 S.R.O. 809, box 14, plans and elevations of hos. in Church St.; Bilbey, *Ch. Stretton*, pl. 97; S.P.L., MS. 2748, p. [5].

92 Cf. below, manors (Bank Ho.).

93 Cobbold, *Ch. Stretton Illustr.* (1908), 21; O.S. Maps 1/2,500, Salop. LVI. 5, 9 (1883, 1903 edns.).

94 *Shrews. Chron.* 14 Nov. 1930, p. 7 (Oswell's obit.); *Kelly's Dir. Salop.* (1900), 60. For the Proffits see *Bye-Gones*, 1 Feb. 1911, p. 22; Bilbey, *Ch. Stretton*, pls. 76, 81.

95 B. Parker and R. Unwin, *The Art of Building a Home* (1901), pls. 47–52; Bilbey, *Ch. Stretton*, pls. 105–6;

96 M. Miller, *Raymond Unwin: Garden Cities and Town Planning* (1992), 29, 31; Bilbey, *Ch. Stretton*, pl. 108; S.R.O. 2079/LVI. 9; 4044/39, p. 29 nos. 261–2. Dr. M. Miller is thanked for inf. about Parker & Unwin's work in Ch. Stretton.

97 S.R.O. 809, box 14, allotted sale plan of R. B. Benson's bldg. est.

98 *Shrews. Chron.* 17 June 1898, p. 6; 13 Mar. 1903, pp. 5, 6; P.R.O., BT 31/7597/54215; BT 31/16320/64651.

99 Cobbold, *Ch. Stretton Illustr.* 14; O.S. Map 1/2,500, Salop. LVI. 5, 9 (1901 edn.); below, econ. hist. (the resort).

1 From £7,716 (1900) to £11,311 (1905) and £14,007 (1911): S.R.O., DA 7/516/1; /531/1. For rest of para. cf. O.S. Maps 1/2,500, Salop. LVI. 5, 9 (1903 edns.); S.R.O. 2079/LVI. 5, 9.

2 S.R.O., DA 7/111/1, pp. 234, 242, 274; S.R.O. 2079/LVI. 9, nos. 415–17, 446, 450; 4044/39, pp. 46 nos. 416–17, 49 no. 446, 50 no. 450; Bilbey, *Ch. Stretton*, pls. 109–10; *The Strettons*, pl. 23.

3 S.R.O., DA 7/531/1, 1904 rate p. 19 no 223; *Shropshire Star*, 23 May 1992, p. 13; Bilbey, op. cit. pl. 113.

4 S.R.O., DA 7/111/1, p. 367.

Arden;[5] and the Rowans,[6] Burway Road, may be cited. Towards the end of the grandest phase of Church Stretton's development were Scotsman's Field (1908), Burway Road, designed by Ernest Newton for Mrs. H. B. Quick,[7] and the White House (1913), Sandford Avenue, designed for the Revd. C. S. Horne by P. R. Morley Horder.[8]

The first half of the Edwardian decade saw a burst of building activity probably unparalleled since that presumed to have followed the 1593 fire. Nevertheless the lord's plan to develop the north-eastern end of the town was not realized; nor, after the great sale of the Land Co.'s building plots in 1905 (which may have brought the company's disposals up to *c.* 100 a.),[9] did the next twenty or so years see much more development on the company's remaining property.[10] The rate of submission of building plans to the U.D.C.'s Buildings Committee halved between 1905 and 1910.[11] Even where development had been quickest many houses stood among vacant plots. Some of the new roads were never completed, some never begun.[12] The developers were too optimistic. In 1908 the Land Co. renamed itself Church Stretton Ltd. and set about raising almost £29,000 by a new share issue. In its prospectus the company outlined plans to make the town a spa by buying the Longmynd Hotel, enlarging it to accommodate 120–130 visitors, and piping water from a saline spring near Wentnor to a new Pump Room to be built in the 9-a. grounds of Woodcote, which the company had contracted to buy. It still owned *c.* 200 a. of building land in and around the town, but growth was slowing, and in 1909 the company's assets were put in receivership for the debenture holders. In 1911 they were acquired by the new Church Stretton Developments Ltd., which continued in business, presumably with more realistic expectations, until its voluntary liquidation in 1935–6.[13]

By the mid 1920s little had been added since the Edwardian period except the 20 council houses at Cross Bank in Little Stretton township.[14] The Crossways shopping streets had not developed as hoped and were awkwardly related to the town: too cut-off from the old centre to benefit from High Street trade and not well positioned for the railway station until a new one opened in 1914 with its up platform at the west end of Crossways. (The main buildings were on the down platform, approached from the old town centre.) In 1941 Crossways was bisected by the new bypass, and the increase of traffic after the war eventually led to the demolition (1965) of the area's only grand feature, Tower Buildings.[15]

The largest elements in the town's growth in the 1930s and 1940s were the 30 council houses built in Essex Road *c.* 1930[16] and later the substantial detached houses along Hazler Road and at around the east end of Sandford Avenue. Property in the town between Beaumont and Essex roads, including part of the south side of Lutwyche Road and part of the north side of Sandford Avenue, was developed. There was also infilling in Carding Mill Valley Road, Madeira Walk, Shrewsbury Road, and the south ends of Watling Street South and Clive Avenue.

In the half century after the end of the Second World War the town's 'rounding-off' between Shrewsbury Road and the railway line involved some north and south extension of the built-up area, northward growth being limited to retain open country between the town and All Stretton village east of Shrewsbury Road.[17] Council housing was mainly in the central and northern parts of the growing town, private housing at the south end and on the east side of the dale. Growth was particularly marked in the 1960s, when the housing estates east of the bypass were built, even up the slopes of Hazler and Helmeth hills. Development on the east side of the dale, however, was limited after the 1960s.

Initially the main new developments, to meet an urgent housing shortage,[18] were near the town centre: in 1947 10 council houses were completed in Lutwyche Road and Essex Road,[19] and soon afterwards 14 prefabs were built at the south end of Easthope Road.[20] Over the next six or seven years 72 more council houses were built in Lutwyche Road and Central Avenue[21] in semi-detached pairs and short terraces.[22] Also in the early 1950s the council housing in Essex Road was continued north.[23] There was housing along the east side of Shrewsbury Road, south of Carding Mill Valley Road, by 1963–4 when 22 council houses and bungalows in Brooksbury were built between it and the houses in Lutwyche Road.[24] In the late 1970s and early 1980s Essex Road was extended further north (including old people's flatlets in Windsor Place, opened 1978) while Churchill Road was extended east

5 Bilbey, op. cit. pl. 111.

6 Ibid. pl. 112.

7 Ibid. pl. 107; A. Stuart Gray, *Edwardian Archit.: A Biog. Dict.* (1985), 273; S.C.C. deed Gen. 147. Mrs. Quick was widow of the Revd. R. H. Quick, the educational writer (*D.N.B.*).

8 Above, this article, intro. and sources there cited.

9 Bilbey, *Ch. Stretton*, pl. 104; *Stretton Focus*, Feb. 1986, pp. 10–11; P.R.O., BT 31/7597/54215.

10 For what remained *c.* 1910 (much then in Hoare & Co.'s hands for the mortgagees: see below) and where it lay cf. S.R.O. 2079/LVI. 5, 9; 4044/39 (developed land), 40 [after Wistanstow par.] nos. 1192–1373 (undeveloped land). For later development cf. O.S. Map 6", Salop. LVI. NW., SW. (1928 edn.).

11 Almost 3 per month 1904–6, less than 1 per month by 1909–10: S.R.O., DA 7/111/1–3 (Bldgs. Cttee. mins.).

12 Cobbold, *Ch. Stretton Illustr.* 18; Bilbey, *Ch. Stretton*, pls. 103–4, 114, 116, 145.

13 P.R.O., BT 31/7597/54215; BT 31/32100/116650; S.R.O. 1642, box 27, plan of property of Stretton Land Co. Ltd. [1908].

14 Below, this section; cf. S.R.O. 2079/LVI. 5, 9; O.S. Map 6", Salop. LVI. NW., SW. (1928 edn.).

15 Bilbey, *Ch. Stretton*, pls. 109–10.

16 S.R.O., DA 7/722; DA 7/701/1–2. The main source for changes up to *c.* 1980 described in this and the next four paras. are the O.S. 6" and 1/10,000 Maps following Salop. LVI. NW., SW. (1928 edn.).

17 Para. based on *Stretton Focus*, May 1972, p. 9.

18 *Shrews. Chron.* 7 May 1948, p. 3.

19 S.R.O., DA 7/602/1.

20 Site prepared 1947:

21 S.R.O., DA 7/725/7, esp. U.D.C. clk.'s letters to Min. of Housing and Local Govt. 4 and 18 Feb. 1954.

22 S.R.O., DA 7/725/6, plans, elevations, etc.

23 S.R.O., DA 7/111/14, p. 148.

24 S.R.O., DA 7/725/8. Plate 4 in this vol. shows the town *c.* 1962, just before Brooksbury was built.

to meet it and so complete the housing encirclement of Brooksbury recreation ground and Russells Meadow playing fields.[25] West and north of the town private houses were built on the south side of Burway Road and on the west side of Shrewsbury Road around the Yeld; building further north was seen as ribbon development threatening to link Church Stretton to All Stretton.

On the eastern side of the dale infilling of Clive Avenue, especially at the south end, and of the south side of Sandford Avenue were small by comparison with the building, in the 1960s, of a large private estate at Battlefield, north of Sandford Avenue. In the same period more private housing was built in Poplar Drive up the northern slope of Ragleth hill.[26] The extension of Poplar Drive, with Chelmick Drive and the upper part of Ragleth Road, higher up the side of the dale than any comparable area of small houses and bungalows[27] occasioned some disquiet,[28] and a civic society, the Stretton Society, was formed in 1974–5.[29] One critic alleged that it was against development,[30] but another (albeit slightly lower) hillside development, Hazler Orchard off Hazler Road, went ahead.[31]

At the south end of the town Woodcote Edge's houses were built in the grounds of Woodcote in the mid 1960s.[32] On the opposite side of Ludlow Road Stretton House (which had been flatted like some other older and larger houses)[33] was demolished in 1976[34] and the Stretton Farm private estate of bungalows was built over its grounds.[35]

The town was designated a conservation area in 1986.[36] Though 'half-timber' (both original and revived) had been designated its 'hallmark' thirty years before, the small town centre contains a wide range of building styles: 17th-century brickwork encasing the old part of the Buck's Head; the elegant town house that replaced 'Berry's messuage' in High Street; and Victorian buildings—the Hotel, H. Salt's ironmongery, and Ashlett House—impressive by their greater size and varied styles.[37]

In the 1980s and 1990s there was infilling between the railway and the bypass (the short terraces and semis of Swain's Meadow private estate) and in the town centre, with developments like Rectory Gardens, King's Court (off Easthope Road), and the housing on the north side of the town-centre part of Sandford Avenue.[38] The post-war prefabs had given way to a car park *c.* 1966,[39] and the largest change to the town-centre plan was made when, after long delayed planning permission, a superstore was opened next to the car park in 1994:[40] the central part of High Street was thus opened up to Easthope Road and Central Avenue.

All Stretton was perhaps a straggling settlement that grew together from two groups of houses on the Shrewsbury–Ludlow road. At the south end of the village a lane down Batch valley ran into the village nearly opposite the end of Farm Lane, reaching the village from Watling Street. The other, perhaps larger, group was 250 m. north, where the way from Picklescott and Betchcott joins the main road. East of the main road *c.* 1840 All Stretton Hall and its grounds filled most of the space between the two ends. To the west a few cottages strung along the Row connected the two ends;[41] high above the village, its approaches narrow and steep, the Row was not a normal back lane. The furlongs north-west of the village must have been reached via Castle Hill, and access to the village's largest areas of open field[42] was by Farm Lane and two minor lanes north and south out of it just beyond Old Hall Farm at the south end of the village.

Old Hall Farm is the most complete of the village's larger and older timber-framed buildings. Its low western cross wing (1564) has a northern jetty. Abutting it on the east is a taller lobby-entry block of 1630 with rooms either side of a large stack. The attic storey was fitted for domestic living.[43] The farmhouse known since the 1920s as the Manor House, at the northern end of the village, is early 17th-century with a main east-extending range and a northern parlour wing at the west end. The building is notable for the quality of its exposed timber framing and the panelled ceilings of the principal rooms. The eastern room was rebuilt in brick in the early 19th century. In the late 19th century the house was a lodging house, but in the 1920s it was remodelled and 17th-century panelling and a 19th-century staircase, the latter said to come from Preen Manor, were introduced.[44] Maj. T. E. Price-Stretche lived there from *c.* 1926 to the early 1940s;[45] he regarded himself as the village squire, perhaps in rivalry with Dr. McClintock of the Grove.[46] The timber-framed cottage Marylis bears the date 1603, and the box-framed Yew Tree inn is probably 17th-century but was altered and extended in 1720.[47] Other cottages in local stone or brick are probably later.

Essex Lodge is ostensibly early 19th-century, but its kitchen preserves 17th-century timber

25 Cf. O.S. Map 1/25,000, SO 49/59 (1981 edn.); *Stretton Focus*, Feb. 1992, p. 16.
26 S.R.O., DA 7/100/25, p. 65.
27 O.S. Map 1/25,000, SO 49/59 (1981 edn.).
28 *Stretton Focus*, May 1972, p. 9.
29 Ibid. May 1975, p. 3.
30 Ibid. Sept. 1974, p. 7.
31 Ibid. May 1975, p. 5.
32 See e.g. advt. in *Shrews. Chron.* 8 April 1966, p. 13.
33 Below, econ. hist. (manufactures and trade [asylums]).
34 *Stretton Focus*, Jan. 1989, p. 13.
35 Bilbey, *Ch. Stretton*, pl. 146.
36 Inf. from S.C.C.
37 Pevsner, *Salop.* 101–2; Bilbey, *Ch. Stretton*, *passim.*
38 Personal observation.
39 S.R.O., DA 7/100/25, pp. 23, 58, 65.
40 N. Watson, *A Family Business: Morris & Co. 1869–1994* (1995), 150–1, 159–60.
41 Para. based on Bilbey, *Ch. Stretton*, pl. 159.
42 Below, econ. hist. (agric.).
43 Dendrochronological dates from Mr. D. H. Miles, additional inf. from Mrs. Moran. Mrs. I. E. Jones is thanked for much help during the investigation of her house and otherwise.
44 Thanks are due to Mrs. A. R. Lofthouse for allowing a visit and to Mr. Eric Mercer for additional comment.
45 S.R.O., electoral regs.; cf. *T.S.A.S.* xlvi. 74.
46 See the exchange betw. them in *Ch. Stretton Adv.* 24 May 1935, p. 1. Price-Stretche's attendance at worship in St. Mic.'s ch. was still remembered as impressive in the 1990s.
47 SA 10765; Whately, *Old Hos. in All Stretton*, i. 4; ii. 6–7; Bilbey, *Ch. Stretton*, pl. 166.

framing.[48] Stretton Hall, perhaps late 18th-century, belonged to the Wildings who, by 1838, were letting it as a farmhouse.[49] The Grove, by 1838 second only to Stretton Hall in the size and extent of its pleasure grounds, was of early 19th-century appearance; then a boarding school and later (1851–1969) a private asylum, it is said to have taken the place of a cottage.[50] A cottage occupied by a smith in 1767, later the Lion inn, was enlarged in Victorian times by the Leebotwood coalmaster James Smith to become Caradoc Lodge.[51] Other cottages were once larger houses: White Heart Cottage, built in the 1750s and possibly an inn in the 1850s, may have had its roof lowered in 1910 and its stable was demolished in 1940.[52]

The west end of Farm Lane began to be built up in the mid 19th century. James Smith's two cottages, later made into one called Cloverley, were built or extended then.[53] Further east down Farm Lane, beyond White Heart Cottage, Minton Cottage probably represents the old copyhold messuage called Vernolds and Hayles;[54] it stood apart from the village until, from the early 20th century, detached houses were built on the opposite side of what became Heighways Lane.[55] By 1925 almost all that side of Heighways Lane had been built, and 4 council houses were built in Farm Lane, on the other side of Minton Cottage. By 1970 15 detached and semi-detached houses and bungalows had been built in Farm and Heighways lanes[56] to fill up a substantial south-eastern extension of the village.

Other extensions to the village in the later 20th century were mainly at the southern end: in the triangle formed by Shrewsbury Road, Star Lane, and Farm Lane; along Batch valley; and in the Grove's grounds, where bungalows were built in 1972.[57] Over many years development of the west side of Shrewsbury Road had linked the village to Church Stretton, though the houses, standing high above the road and looking over farm land, do not look like ribbon development.

Womerton Farm and the two farmhouses at Botvyle presumably represent shrunken hamlets, though three modern bungalows have been added at Botvyle. Nevertheless settlement north of All Stretton, from Botvyle to the homesteads at New Leasowes and Jinlye, is, and long has been, very scattered, a pattern distinguishing the north end of the parish, and to a lesser extent its south end, from the centre, where settlement was nucleated until recent times.[58] Besides small farmhouses the area included cottages associated with piecemeal inclosures from the waste. Some cottages were probably fairly ramshackle and either improved or destroyed as inclosure proceeded more systematically in the late 18th century:[59] in the early 19th century a 'wretched' dwelling near Womerton wood was thrown down even as the corpse of its last resident, one Bowdler, was taken out for burial.[60] In the earlier 19th century Dudgeley House was an admired *cottage ornée*.[61] Many older houses have been modernized, and there has been some 20th-century development between Castle Hill and Inwood. The few substantial 20th-century houses include Acrebatch at Lower Wood and Maidenhill Wood.

Little Stretton village is a rough quadrilateral formed by two lanes forking out of one descending from Ashes Hollow: the northern lane runs due east and the southern one south and then south-east,[62] both (as Ashes Road and Brook Lane) to form crossroads (250 m. apart) with Ludlow Road and continue (as Elms Lane and Crown Lane) to Watling Street.

At the northern crossroads stands the Ragleth (earlier Sun) inn, the former Pigg's or Lloyd's copyhold messuage rebuilt in the early 19th century.[63] On Ludlow Road between the northern and the southern crossroads several timber-framed buildings date from the late Middle Ages to the 17th century. South of the church (1903)[64] is the late medieval farmhouse known as the Manor House;[65] an adjacent 17th-century farm building, restored in the 20th century, is now Courtyard Cottage.[66] Further south is Bircher Cottage, a cruck-framed house of two bays, made **L** shaped by a southern box-framed cross wing. An upper floor was put into the main room, probably in the 17th century, and there is a large stack with a bread oven against the north gable. East and west additions were made in the 20th century.[67] Next door is the Malt House, a 16th-century **T** shaped box-framed former farmhouse, with 17th-century alterations. The hall has an inserted floor and raised roof, and at the north end there is a flattened-ogee headed internal door into the cross wing, which is built over a cobbled cellar. The cross-wing framing includes a cambered tie beam and arch braces and its gable contains an ulenlok. The hall range has square framing three panels high. On the main, west, front the 19th-century leaded casements, with pointed Gothick heads in wooden mullioned frames beneath

48 Whately, op. cit. ii. 1.
49 Ibid. 5–6; tithe award.
50 Bilbey, *Ch. Stretton*, pls. 159–60; Whately, op. cit. i. 4; *Stretton Focus*, Jan. (p. 2) and Feb. (p. 3) 1969; below, econ. hist. (manufactures and trade [asylums]); educ.
51 Whately, op. cit. i. 7.
52 Ibid. 1.
53 Ibid. ii. 5; O.S. Map 6", Salop. LVI. NW. (1883 edn.).
54 Mr. Ivar Romo is thanked for making his research on the 18th- and 19th-cent. manor ct. bks. available.
55 Inf. from Mr. Romo.
56 Cf. S.R.O., electoral regs.; O.S. 6" maps.
57 *Stretton Focus*, Feb. 1992, p. 16. This para. and the next based on personal observation.
58 Tithe maps; O.S. Map 6", Salop. XLIX. SW., LVI. NW. (1903 edn.); O.S. Map 1/10,000, SO 49 NW., NE. (1980 edn).
59 W.S.L. 350/5/40, Ch. Stretton pp. 96–8.
60 Ibid. p. 26. He was presumably a relative of the Bowdlers who had owned land in the area since Eliz. I's time: ibid. pp. 25–6.
61 Ibid. p. 29.
62 Bilbey, *Ch. Stretton*, pl. 156.
63 SA 10801; cf. S.R.O. 1643/118–19. Many of the bldgs. descr. here, incl. the four farmhos., were bought by the Gibbons in the 18th–20th cents.: below, manors (Lt. Stretton Manor Ho.).
64 Below, church.
65 Below, manors (Manor Ho.).
66 SA 10794.
67 Thanks are due to Mr. and Mrs. A. M. Jenkinson for allowing a visit. Cf. SA 10795.

bracketed hoods, have wooden drip moulds; the doorway is pedimented.[68] The Tan House[69] has been remodelled. In the 17th century it comprised two adjacent timber-framed structures, the northern one perhaps a cross wing. The walls of the southern range were later partly rebuilt in rubble and the northern range was reduced in size. Mrs. A. B. Wood, *née* Maw, owned the house 1875–1909,[70] and it was probably early in her time[71] that the timber framing was restored and matching additions were made to the north and west; the interior was fitted out with a collection of 17th- and 18th-century woodwork, much of it elaborately carved; and a stone fireplace with flanking terms of *c.* 1600, said to have been brought from Devon by Mrs. Wood's father, was put into the central room.

Old Hall Farm in Ashes Road is a 16th-century or earlier timber-framed farmhouse, roughly **E** shaped; the gable in the centre of the main, east, front has exposed vertical timber framing, the later north and south gables are of random stone. To the north is an 18th-century rubble stone barn.[72] The nearby Brook Farm is a late 18th-century farmhouse of coursed stone; the windows have wooden mullions and transoms, those on the ground floor with stone lintels and raised centre key blocks. Two cottages on the opposite side of the road are early 17th-century.[73]

The village has some early 19th century buildings[74] but grew little before the mid 20th century.[75] Half a dozen small scattered houses were built north of the Sun (later Ragleth) inn in the later 19th and earlier 20th century, but it was only the addition of *c.* 20 more, mainly in the 1950s and 1960s, that formed a continuous northern extension of the village along Ludlow Road.[76] By 1949 the village had begun to extend south with six semi-detached houses in the angle between Ludlow Road and the railway, built by the owner of the adjacent saw mill for his workers; some became council houses after the closure of the mill, whose site was redeveloped as private bungalows (Crown Close) in the earlier 1960s. There was later some infilling in the centre of the village, which was designated a conservation area in 1986.[77]

North of the village, just within Little Stretton township, Church Stretton U.D.C. built 20 houses at Cross Bank 1920–2;[78] in the mid 1960s private bungalows were built opposite them, between the brook and Brockhurst wood.[79]

Minton village is 'very singularly situated' on a spur of land which slopes down to the south and east, between Callow Hollow and Minton Batch. It has changed very little since the early 19th century. It may have shrunk slightly since *c.* 1838 when it was said to be 'overspread with many ancient timber and plaster farmhouses and smaller dwellings'.[80] Longmynd House near the northern corner of the village, has a main cruck-framed range of two bays and a short jettied cross wing to the west.[81]

The village centres on a green where three ways meet, one down from the Port Way over Minton and Packetstone hills, two others approaching Minton from Little Stretton to the north-east and Hamperley to the south-west. East of the green stands Manor House Farm, said *c.* 1838 to be the manor house; the timber-framed east end was then said to be the oldest part, dating from the 1630s; a new kitchen and brewhouse were built in 1723, and later still the house was extended in brick when a parlour and chamber were built at the west end. Between the manor house and the village green was the chapel yard,[82] which, with the manor house and its curtilage, and the property to the north, may indicate the shape of the former bailey[83] of a castle whose motte survives to the south-east.[84] The biggest house, Minton House, a little south-west of the village, has a stone Georgian front dated 1757, but a massive stone stack suggests an earlier house.[85]

Settlement in the southern part of Minton township is sparse and scattered. About 1900 Hamperley, in the south-west corner, was a farmstead at the meeting of four lanes. Marshbrook, in the south-east corner of the parish, had an inn and railway station in the parish but otherwise straggled into Wistanstow parish. Between Hamperley and Marshbrook there were a few isolated cottages and houses, including Minton Oaks and New House Farm. Little changed after 1900,[86] though within a few years White Birches, a gentleman's house in the Elizabethan style, was built above the lane from Marshbrook to Cwm Head.[87] In the mid 20th century, when E. W. Minton Beddoes lived

68 Inf. from Mrs. M. Moran; SA 10796; Bilbey, *Ch. Stretton*, pl. 158.

69 Cf. below, econ. hist. (manufactures and trade) for the Bridgmans' tannery.

70 Deeds in possession of Sqn. Ldr. and Mrs. G. K. Larney, who are thanked for their help.

71 Pevsner, *Salop.* 102, attributes the ho.'s restoration and enrichment to her son, the sculptor F. D. Wood (1871–1926), but he seems to have lived only briefly (1889–90) in Salop. (*D.N.B.* 1922–30), perhaps not in Lt. Stretton. SA 10798 dates the restoration *c.* 1910, but a memo. (probably 1919; in Sqn. Ldr. and Mrs. Larney's possession) implies that the fireplace was inserted in the 1870s.

72 SA 10804–5.

73 SA 10802–3.

74 See e.g. SA 10759 (Ragleth Ho.) and 10797.

75 Cf. Bilbey, *Ch. Stretton*, pl. 156; O.S. Map 6", Salop. LVI. SW. (1903 edn.).

76 Cf. O.S. Maps 6", Salop. LVI. SW. (1889–1953 edns.), with ho. names on 1/2,500, SO 4491–4591 (1974 edn.) and SO 4492–4592 (1975 edn.) and their appearances in S.R.O., electoral regs.

77 O.S. Map 6", Salop. LVI. SW. (1953 edn.); inf. from Mrs. J. G. Tyldesley; inf. from S.C.C.

78 S.R.O., DA 7/111/6, pp. 198, 382, etc.

79 Cf. O.S. Map 6", Salop. LVI. SW. (1953 edn.), with ho. names on 1/2,500, SO 4492–4592 (1975 edn.) and their appearance in S.R.O., electoral regs.

80 W.S.L. 350/5/40, Ch. Stretton p. 41; Bilbey, *Ch. Stretton*, pl. 152; O.S. Map 1/10,000, SO 49 SW. (1980 edn.).

81 Cf. Bilbey, op. cit. pl. 154; inf. from Mrs. M. Moran. The Misses Downes are thanked for allowing a visit.

82 O.S. Map 1/10,000, SO 49 SW. (1980 edn.); W.S.L. 350/5/40, Ch. Stretton p. 41.

83 Bilbey, *Ch. Stretton*, pl. 152.

84 Ibid. pls. 152–3; W.S.L. 350/5/40, Ch. Stretton p. 35; D. J. Cathcart King, *Castellarium Anglicanum* (1983), ii. 426.

85 Bilbey, *Ch. Stretton*, pl. 155; W.S.L. 350/5/40, Ch. Stretton p. 42; tithe field 1896.

86 Cf. O.S. Maps 6", LV. SE. (1903 edn.), LXIII. NE. (1903 edn.), LXIV. NW. (1903 edn.); 1/10,000, SO 48 NW. (1981 edn.).

87 O.S. Map, 6", Salop. LXIII. NE. (1903 edn.); S.R.O., electoral reg. S. divn. 1910, p. 229; S.P.L., SC3/24, cover and p. 3.

there, it was called Minton House, Minton House in the village being renamed the Well House;[88] the houses resumed their former names, Minton House *c.* 1955 and White Birches *c.* 1965.[89]

SOCIAL AND CULTURAL ACTIVITIES. In 1392–3 alesellers in the manor were required to display their 'signs' outside their houses when they were selling ale.[90] Bonham Norton was expected to set up inns and lodging houses as an encouragement to the town's trade after the 1593 fire,[91] and two alesellers were licensed in 1613.[92] In the mid 18th century there were about a dozen licensed premises in the parish, probably three quarters of them in the town, where the Buck's Head, the Red Lion, the Plough, and the Raven all seem to have existed by the end of the 17th century,[93] as did the Swan (later the Swan and Malt Shovel) by 1757 and the Fox from *c.* 1770.[94] The Talbot and the Crown, at the south and north ends of the town respectively, were probably also in existence by then.[95] By the earlier 1750s there were two alesellers in Little Stretton and one (perhaps the Lion)[96] in All Stretton; there seems to have been one at Minton, perhaps intermittently, in the 1760s.

The number of licensees in the parish fell from 12 in 1786 to eight by 1789 and seven by the 1820s; All Stretton and Minton may have lost their taverns and Little Stretton may have lost one too.[97] The number of inns and alehouses in Church Stretton town also fell, the Swan and the Fox probably closing in or before the early 19th century.[98] In the 1820s there were apparently only six public houses in the town. The Talbot was then the best inn, with a good coaching trade; the excise office was there and two of the licensees served as the town's postmaster.[99]

By 1851 the Talbot's best days were over; the post office was elsewhere, and the opening of the railway in 1852 probably fixed the superiority of the Crown, the inn nearest to the railway station. The Talbot closed *c.* 1853.[1]

Meanwhile, with the end of licensing in 1828,[2] inns, taverns, and beer sellers had increased. By 1835 Little Stretton had two taverns again, the Sun and the Crown,[3] and a beer seller.[4] All Stretton had the White Horse, the New Inn, and the Yew Tree,[5] and in the 1860s the White Heart may have been a short-lived enterprise at the south-east corner of the village, well placed to catch railway navvies' custom.[6] The New Inn at Marshbrook, on the south side of the Bishop's Castle road, was open by 1838, but the opening of the railway in 1853 caused it to be renamed the Station inn, and about the same time, or early in the 1860s when the track was doubled, it was rebuilt on the opposite side of the road.[7] By 1835 there was a new beer seller in Church Stretton, perhaps at the King's Arms or the Queen's Head, probably both in existence by 1841, and by 1851 the town also had the Britannia and, at World's End just south of the town, the Grapes.[8] The Britannia closed *c.* 1895,[9] so by *c.* 1900 the number of licensed premises in the parish was at the mid 18th-century level again, with 1 at Marshbrook, 3 at Little Stretton, 2 at All Stretton (where the New Inn had closed in the late 1880s),[10] 7 in the town,[11] and 1 at World's End.

The opening of the Hotel in 1865 marked the town's developing role as a resort,[12] which in due course attracted a better trade to the High Street inns: the Buck's Head and the Raven, and the King's Arms further south, all provided good accommodation and stabling *c.* 1900. Before the First World War the smaller pubs in the town—the Lion, the Queen's Head, and the World's End (the former Grapes)—closed, and the Raven became an hotel.[13] The town's only pubs were then the Plough (whose licence was transferred to the Sandford House Hotel, Watling Street South, in 1947), the King's Arms (which seems to have closed for a time in the 1960s),[14] and the Buck's Head. By *c.* 1990 the Buck's Head, the reopened King's Arms, and the Hotel (which resumed the old Crown's public-house role after a fire in 1968)[15] were the town's only public houses, though two hotels, the Denehurst

88 S.P.L., SC3/23, frontispiece and p. 4; *Kelly's Dir. Salop.* (1941), 69.

89 S.R.O. 657/2, p. 177; 725/4, p. 175; 1490/1, p. 187; 1627/2, pp. 181–2.

90 S.R.O. 125/1.

91 S.R.O. 2956/1.

92 S.R.O., q. sess. rec. parcel 254, badgers', drovers', and alesellers' licensing bk.

93 This and the next four paras. based on ibid. parcels 255–9, regs. of alesellers' recognizances 1753–1828 (naming premises, as distinct from licensees, only from 1822); Co. of Salop, *Reg. of Public Hos. 1901* (copy in S.P.L., accession 6117), 89–93, 96, some of whose first-licence dates must be regarded with caution; J.P.s' licensing regs. 1928–54, 1955–92 (in possession of magistrates' clk.).

94 *Stretton Focus*, June 1986, p. 11.

95 Below; the Hotel's late 17th-cent. licence (*Reg. of Public Hos. 1901*, 89) presumably represents the Crown's.

96 Whately, *Hos. in All Stretton*, i. 7.

97 Though the Sun and the Crown are said to have been first licensed in the 18th cent.: *Reg. of Public Hos. 1901*, 92.

98 *Stretton Focus*, June 1986, p. 11.

99 Ibid. Nov. 1981, p. 8; Oct. 1983, p. 9; Tibnam & Co. *Salop. Dir.* (1828), 34; Pigot, *Nat. Com. Dir.* (1835), 352–3; (1842), 11.

1 *Stretton Focus*, Nov. 1981, p. 8; May 1982, pp. 8–9; Oct. 1986, p. 10; S. Bagshaw, *Dir. Salop.* (1851), 529; Bilbey, *Ch. Stretton*, pl. 91; above, communications.

2 Cf. *V.C.H. Salop.* iii. 136.

3 Pigot, *Nat. Com. Dir.* (1835), 353; Slater, *Nat. Com. Dir.* (1850), 14; cf. tithe fields 1624, 1726 (wrongly printed '1626' on map); P.R.O., HO 107/1984, ff. 223v., 224v.

4 Mentioned in Pigot, *Nat. Com. Dir.* (1835), 353, and Slater, *Nat. Com. Dir.* (1850), 15, but not in P.R.O., HO 107/913/22, ff. 6–10, or HO 107/1984, ff. 221v.–227v. Perh. he kept the later Green Dragon, reputedly first licensed in 1818: *Reg. of Public Hos. 1901*, 92.

5 Pigot, *Nat. Com. Dir.* (1835), 353; tithe fields 769, 875; Whately, *Hos. in All Stretton*, i. 6; ii. 1, 6–7.

6 Slater, *Nat. Com. Dir.* (1850), 14–15; Whately, op. cit. i. 1; P.R.O., HO 107/1984, ff. 209–10, 212, 214v.

7 Tithe field 1968; P.R.O., HO 107/1984, f. 228; Slater, *Nat. Com. Dir.* (1850), 14; S.R.O., dep. plan 336, plan 4 no. 359; *T.S.A.S.* lxiv. 99; O.S. Map 1/2,500, Salop. LXIV. 1 (1884 edn.).

8 Pigot, *Nat. Com. Dir.* (1835), 353; (1842), 11; tithe fields 1145, 1178, 1184, 1213, 1221, 1304, 1321, 1389; P.R.O., HO 107/913/22, ff. 14–31v. (naming 8 publicans); HO 107/1984, ff. 170–177v. (naming 10 inns incl. 1 at World's End).

9 *Stretton Focus*, Nov. 1981, p. 8; June 1982, p. 8; May 1984, p. 10; Bilbey, *Ch. Stretton*, pl. 64.

10 *Kelly's Dir. Salop.* (1885, 1891).

11 Counting the Hotel, which had absorbed the Crown.

12 Below, econ. hist. (the resort).

13 *Kelly's Dir. Salop.* (1913), 67–8.

14 *Stretton Focus*, Sept. 1982, p. 10; G.P.O. *Telephone Dir.* (1960), sect. 72, p. 2090 (last mention of King's Arms).

15 Bilbey, *Ch. Stretton*, pl. 22. The Hotel was known as Strettondale Hotel 1945–50.

(Shrewsbury Road) and Sandford House (closed *c.* 1990),[16] served areas north and east of the town centre.

Outside the town, by *c.* 1990, there were the Wayside Inn (the Station Inn, renamed *c.* 1972)[17] at Marshbrook; the Green Dragon and Ragleth (formerly Sun) inns at Little Stretton, where the Crown had closed *c.* 1907;[18] and at All Stretton the Yew Tree[19] and Stretton Hall hotel, with a pub licence from 1976.

Stretton's church ale was abolished in 1595.[20] In the later 18th century Little Stretton still had its wake on the Sunday after 21 August ('Old St. Lawrence's Day' after 1752). All Stretton wake was celebrated on the first Sunday after Trinity and Minton wake on the Sunday after 15 October. 'Caradoc Wakes', recollected as formerly held on Trinity Sunday on Caer Caradoc,[21] was evidently a distinct occasion from the annual meeting of the 18th-century Caractusian Society there.[22] By the mid 19th century, however, it was not a wake but the May fair,[23] the annual 'Mop and Statute' hiring fair, that was the main event in the parish's social life. The September horse fair was also observed as a local holiday as late as the end of the century.[24] The May pleasure fair was still a considerable attraction in the early 20th century, and in 1926, besides various sideshows, the amusements had for some years included Mr. Marshall Hill's scenic railway from Bristol; that year, however, the fair was poorly attended by previous years' standards,[25] and it later lapsed. It was revived in 1984 by the efforts of the local fire brigade.[26]

A new town hall was built by public subscription in 1838–9 on the site of the old market house. Designed in a 17th-century style by Edward Haycock, the hall was intended for town and public use and as a polling place[27] for the county's Southern parliamentary division.[28] The hall accommodated a subscription library by the mid 19th century,[29] and the U.D.C. met there 1899–1920.[30] Other buildings for public resort and assembly were later erected in the town: a parish hall *c.* 1913 (rebuilt in 1989–90)[31] and the Silvester Horne Institute, built in 1915–16 in memory of the Revd. C. S. Horne and designed by P. R. Morley Horder.[32] By 1963 the town hall had become unsafe and was then demolished.[33]

By the mid 19th century, besides the library in the town hall, there was a news room in the Crown. A Working Men's Club and Reading Room was established in 1880, and by 1909 W. H. Smith's had a circulating library.[34] The Silvester Horne Institute, conveyed to the U.D.C. in 1946, was used for many educational and social purposes[35] and from 1920 included a reading room and library. The county library opened a book centre there in 1929; stocked with 600 books, it was run by the Institute's own librarian and was open longer hours than most centres in the county. Book issues were high and opening hours were extended *c.* 1950; by 1956 the branch had paid staff[36] and in 1968 it was moved into the former primary school in Church Street.[37]

G. R. Windsor published two issues of a weekly *Church Stretton Times and Visitors' List* in September 1881; it was intended to come out during the town's 'season' but failed to appear again.[38] The weekly *Church Stretton Advertiser and Visitors' List* was started in 1898 by W. F. and G. J. Marks, who had taken over the *Ludlow Advertiser*. It proclaimed from the first that it would support 'every movement by which the development of the district will be advanced' without serving any political party,[39] though W. F. Marks (sole owner after his brother's departure)[40] was a radical.[41] The Conservative *Ludlow and Church Stretton Chronicle* was published in Ludlow 1910–12.[42] Owing to rising production costs the *Church Stretton Advertiser*, with three other papers in the same group,[43] was incorporated in the *Ludlow Advertiser* in 1938.[44] H. D. Woods published the *Stretton Gazette* for about a year *c.* 1964 from a High Street office.[45] *The Stretton Focus*, a monthly 'interchurch and local newspaper', was published from February 1967, though its title appeared on its masthead only in June 1969 and the explanatory gloss only in November 1980.[46] The *Stretton Times*, a local edition of a quarterly magazine called the *Castle Times*, was published in Bishop's Castle and first appeared in 1983.[47]

A branch of the Shropshire Provident Society

16 Not in telephone dir. after 1988, licence not renewed Feb. 1992.

17 P.O. *Telephone Dir.* (1971), sect. 303, p. 225; (1972), sect. 303, p. 267.

18 *Kelly's Dir. Salop.* (1905–9); Bilbey, *Ch. Stretton*, pl. 171f; O.S. Map 1/2,500, Salop. LVI. 13 (1903 and 1927 edns.); G.P.O. *Telephone Dir.* (1960), sect. 72, p. 2065; (1964), sect. 72, p. 2069 (not in intervening issues).

19 Whately, *Hos. in All Stretton*, ii. 6.

20 Below, church; educ.

21 *Salop. Folk-Lore*, ed. C. S. Burne (1883), 436; *T.C.S.V.F.C.* x. 172.

22 Above, Cardington, intro. The Caractusians met later in the summer, usually Aug.

23 Cf. below, econ. hist. (mkts. and fairs).

24 Windsor, *Handbk.* 58, 68–75; S.R.O. 4505/4, pp. 14, 23, 171, 185; /5, p. 112.

25 *Ch. Stretton Adv.* 20 May 1926, p. 2.

26 *Shropshire Mag.* June 1984, 26.

27 S.R.O. 1642, box 27, mkt. hall papers; Pevsner, *Salop.* 102; Loton Hall MSS., Sir B. Leighton's diary 14 Sept. 1859; below, econ. hist. (mkts. and fairs).

28 *V.C.H. Salop.* iii. 314–15.

29 R. C. Elliott, 'Development of Public Libraries in Salop.' (Loughborough Univ. M.A. thesis, 1970; copy in co. libr.), 9, 118.

30 Below, local govt.

31 Below, church; *Stretton Focus*, July 1989, p. 1; Mar. 1990, p. 1.

32 *Kelly's Dir. Salop.* (1922), 63; inf. from Mr. T. S. Acton; for Horne see above, this article, intro.

33 Bilbey, *Ch. Stretton*, pl. 72.

34 Elliott, 'Librs.' 9, 23, 118.

35 *Kelly's Dir. Salop.* (1929), 65; S.R.O., DA 7/100/6, pp. 418, 425; DA 7/119/7, pp. 254 sqq.

36 Elliott, 'Librs.' 9, 22, 55, 60, 94–6, 99, 118, 126.

37 Ibid. 100, 102–3; inf. from co. libr.

38 *Shropshire Mag.* Feb. 1980, pp. 32–3.

39 *Ch. Stretton Adv.* 7 July 1898, p. 4.

40 To take over the *Ripon Observer*: ibid. 31 Mar. 1927, p. 3.

41 A firm believer in Hen. George's single tax, he stood unsuccessfully for Labour at Ludlow in the 1922 co.-council electn.: *Ch. Stretton Adv.* 31 Mar. 1927, p. 3 (obit.); *Shrews. Chron.* 3 (p. 8) and 17 (p. 2) Mar. 1922.

42 Set in S.P.L.

43 *Bp.'s Cas. Adv.* (1900–38), *Cleobury Mortimer Jnl.* (1933–8), and *Tenbury Wells News* (1935–8).

44 *Ch. Stretton Adv.* 4 Nov. 1938, p. 1.

45 *Stretton Focus*, Nov. 1985, pp. 11–12.

46 Set in S.P.L.

47 Set in S.P.L.

existed by 1883 and until 1948.[48] There was an independent Odd Fellows' lodge at the King's Arms by 1850 and a Manchester Unity lodge by 1885. By 1895 there was a court of Foresters at the Red Lion; all three were named after Caratacus (Caradoc). The Odd Fellows' lodges may have amalgamated soon after 1905. The Foresters ceased about the end of the First World War, the Odd Fellows about the beginning of the Second World War.[49] Freemasons' lodges were formed in 1926 (at the Longmynd hotel) and 1946. In 1973 the lodges moved from the Denehurst hotel to a newly purchased building (the old Queen's Head) in High Street, officially opened as a masonic hall in 1975.[50]

Walter Burrie, the schoolmaster, was prosecuted in the church courts in 1589 for producing plays and interludes on Sunday.[51] In 1777 travelling comedians staged a Molière double bill, 'The Miser & Lyar', at 'Stretton Theatre', staying a month or more.[52] Strolling players and mountebanks performed in the grounds of Park House or the old barn there in the 19th century,[53] but no permanent theatre in the town is mentioned before the early 20th century. The Barn Theatre opened *c.* 1905 at the southern end of the town in an outbuilding of Stretton House asylum; played by a theatre group called the Barn Owls and managed by the asylum's resident proprietor Dr. Horatio Barnett. Later the theatre passed to Church Stretton Entertainments Ltd., formed in 1910 with mainly local shareholders but liquidated in 1914. The theatre closed *c.* 1920.[54] By 1922 touring companies occasionally performed in the Silvester Horne Institute.[55]

The first movies in Stretton were shown in the Barn Theatre,[56] but early in 1919 and during 1921–2 they were shown in the Silvester Horne Institute, whose management committee was concerned to prevent the building of a cinema and so retain influence over the choice of films shown in the town. The parish hall was used for cinema shows from 1922.[57] By the later 1930s, however, there was evidently a demand for showings six days a week, which could not be satisfied by rented premises,[58] and Craven Cinemas Ltd. opened the Regal, Sandford Avenue, in 1937; by the beginning of 1962 the cinema was used by a bingo club two days a week, and it evidently closed later that year.[59]

Part of the 1st Shropshire Artillery Volunteer Corps, formed in 1860 (and known after consolidation in 1880 as the 1st Shropshire & Staffordshire Artillery Volunteers),[60] trained at Church Stretton: a position battery stationed there (or partly there) by 1868 was under the command of Lt. (Capt. 1894, later Maj.) W. Campbell Hyslop in the 1880s and 1890 and of Maj. Horatio Barnett later; there were 63 men in 1891.[61] A gun platform was established on the Long Mynd *c.* 1865, and by 1883 there was a carbine range between Stretton House and Brockhurst.[62] In 1885 the drill hall in the Lion Yard contained a 32-pounder, but guns were later kept in the grounds of Stretton House.[63] As a result of the Territorial reorganization of 1908 the gunners stationed at Church Stretton formed half of the Welsh Border Mounted Brigade Ammunition Column, Shropshire Royal Horse Artillery, not re-formed after the First World War.[64]

Church Stretton was in the recruiting area of Ludlow Platoon, A (Shrewsbury) Company, 4th Battalion, King's Shropshire Light Infantry (T.A.) 1920–39. Ludlow Platoon was expanded during the Second World War to become the new D Company with a Church Stretton platoon; the platoon was suspended in 1947 but re-formed in A Company in 1963. The Territorials were again reorganized in 1967[65] and the drill hut near the railway station was demolished about then.[66]

About 1840 William Pinches of Ticklerton and the Revd. R. J. Buddicom introduced a few pair of red grouse (from Yorkshire) to the Long Mynd. Though it was the bird's southernmost habitat in 19th-century England, the high, treeless, heather-and-bilberry moorland suited well,[67] and the sport which the common afforded (apparently unaffected by the volunteer gunners' summer practices)[68] became one of the manorial property's most desirable features.[69] Mrs. Coleman let Pinches have it but on his death in 1849

48 *Eddowes's Shrews. Jnl.* 24 Jan. 1883, p. 8 (obit. of Dr. Ric. Wilding); S.R.O. 436/6733, pp. 13–14; /6750, f. 2.
49 *Kelly's Dir. Salop.* (1885–1941); S.R.O. 1672/4.
50 H. Temperton, *Hist. of Craft Freemasonry in Salop. 1732–1982* [1982], 62–3, 73–4, 83, 108, 115; *Stretton Focus*, Apr. 1982, p. 9.
51 *Salop.* (R.E.E.D.), i. 22.
52 Cf. S.R.O. 567/5/3/1/15, 25 Apr. 1777; *S.P.R. Heref.* viii (2), pp. x, 165 (25 May 1777).
53 *Bye-Gones*, 1 Feb. 1911, 15.
54 *Kelly's Dir. Salop.* (1905), 60, 62, 434; (1917), 57, 59, 431; S.R.O., DA 7/531/1, 1905 rate p. 5 no. 48a (assembly rm., previously wkshop. and yd.); S.R.O. 2079/LVI. 9, no. 124; 4044/39, p. 16 no. 124; P.R.O., BT 31/13099/107747.
55 S.R.O., DA 7/119/5, pp. 163–5, 171–2, 214.
56 Bilbey, *Ch. Stretton*, pl. 132.
57 S.R.O., DA 7/119/5, pp. 30–1, 57–8, 68–9, 115, 122–3, 125, 154–7.
58 S.R.O., DA 7/119/7, pp. 108–13, 115.
59 *Shrews. Chron.* 10 Dec. 1937, p. 1; 5 Jan. (p. 12), 25 May (p. 16: last advertised programme) 1962; *The Strettons*, pls. 25–7; J. Critchley, *A Bag of Boiled Sweets: An Autobiog.* (1994), 8.
60 N. E. H. Litchfield and R. Westlake, *Volunteer Artillery 1859–1908* (Nottingham, 1982), 3–4, 150–2.
61 *Stretton Focus*, May 1982, p. 9; *Kelly's Dir. Salop.* (1885), 945; (1891), 244; (1895), 8; (1900), 8, 61; W. Mate & Sons Ltd. *Shropshire: Historical, Descriptive, Biographical* (1906), pt. 2, p. 138.
62 At O.S. Nat. Grid 4314 9395 and 4494 9302 (target): Windsor, *Handbk.* 28; O.S. Map 1/2,500, Salop. LV. 8, LVI. 9 (1883 edn.).
63 Windsor, op. cit. 44; *Shropshire Mag.* July 1980, 34.
64 Cf. *V.C.H. Salop.* iii. 224; Litchfield and Westlake, *Vol. Artillery*, 151; W. Richards, *H.M. Territorial Army*, iv [1911], 18–19; G. A. Parfitt, 'Short Hist. of Salop. Royal Horse Artillery 1860 to 1966' (TS. n.d.), 2.
65 Under the Reserve Forces Act, 1966, c. 30. Para. based on inf. from the late G. A. Parfitt (hon. curator, Salop. Regtl. Mus., Shrews.) and Mr. N. G. Phillips, who are thanked for their help.
66 *Shropshire Mag.* July 1980, 36 (wrongly connecting the hut's disappearance with the end of the Salop. Royal Horse Artillery, which survived only as an honour title for 240 Medium Battery at Shrews. and Wellington).
67 *V.C.H. Salop.* i. 160, 178; ii. 190; J. T. R. Sharrock, *Atlas of Breeding Birds in Brit. and Irel.* (1976), 132–3; below, Eaton-under-Heywood, manors (Ticklerton).
68 *Shrews. Chron.* 21 June 1935, p. 8.
69 R. J. More, *Hints to Strangers who may visit the R. Agric. Soc.'s Show at Shrews. in 1884* (Shrews. 1884), 5 (copy in S.P.L.); *V.C.H. Warws.* ii. 391.

his brother-in-law Buddicom lost it after Moses Benson, of Lutwyche, 'treacherously applied over his head to Mrs. Coleman'.[70] Benson's grandson R. B. Benson, who also leased the shooting,[71] bought the manor in 1888, and A. S. Browne, who bought the manor from Maj. G. R. Benson in 1925, was another tenant of the shooting before his purchase.[72] Such continuous interest produced good sport: a day's bag of 96 brace by four or five guns was remembered in 1935.[73] Browne improved the shooting to the satisfaction of his successor R. D. Cohen.[74] William Humphrey, lord 1937–63 and previously agent to his predecessor M. V. Wenner, was the breeder of a unique strain of English 'Llewellin' setters.[75]

Wenner and Humphrey both enjoyed shooting over their setters, but their attempts to confine a potentially careless public to rights of way over the common had little success. Public access led to damage: a match dropped by a labourer more used to town than country life destroyed 1,000 a. of heather in 1922, and in the spring of 1935 alone there were three fires.[76] In 1935 Humphrey admitted that 'hikers' behaved well on the hill,[77] but there were other classes of visitor who perhaps did not;[78] and the beginning of flights by the Midland Gliding Club in 1934 was said to have attracted too many spectators, they (and their dogs) probably doing more harm to the grouse than the gliders did.[79] During the Second World War Humphrey could not exercise his sporting rights; afterwards, however, he resumed his 'days at grouse' with a mounted party, flying falcons at birds found by his setters.[80] In 1965–6 the manor and common were acquired by the National Trust, which was faced with potentially difficult management problems in reconciling agricultural and recreational interests.[81] By then, however, recreational interests were primarily those of visitors to the area[82] rather than sportsmen, though bags of 113 brace for the 1975 season and 32 brace in 1990 were recorded; the latter was the highest seasonal bag for a decade and indicated the need for conservation.[83]

By the 1880s lawn tennis,[84] quoits, bowls, football, and cricket were favourite amusements for visitors and local people. Tennis was presumably played on private courts, quoits perhaps on public-house premises. Bowls, football, and cricket were club activities, and in the 1880s and 1890s the bowling club was at the Hotel, the football club at the Red Lion and later the King's Arms, the cricket club at the Raven and later the Buck's Head.[85] Clubs and teams for those sports, especially bowls, football, and later golf, remained a feature of local life. There was a cricket club between the wars,[86] but some other sports failed to support long-lived clubs. A rifle club, evidently formed during the First World War, seems not to have long outlasted it.[87] There was a lawn tennis club *c.* 1926[88] and a hockey club in the later 1920s.[89] Even soccer clubs needed occasional reanimation,[90] but *c.* 1990 three teams regularly played on Brooksbury recreation ground (given by Richard Robinson in 1924) and Russells Meadow playing field (opened 1928): two, one of them an All Stretton team, played in the Shrewsbury Sunday League but Church Stretton Town played in the county league and also in the Shrewsbury and West Shropshire Alliance League.[91] There were grass and hard tennis courts, a bowling green, and children's amusements in Broad Meadow park between the railway line and the by-pass; given by the Bensons, its gates were made by a Belgian refugee living in the town *c.* 1915.[92] Beyond it, *c.* 1990, was an 18-hole miniature golf course.

In 1898 Church Stretton Golf Club was formed, and an 18-hole course, designed by James Braid and one of the highest in England, was laid out between Bodbury Hill and Cwmdale on part of the Long Mynd common leased to Church Stretton Land Co. Ltd. by the lord of the manor. The Shropshire amateur championship was played there in 1913,[93] and golf, tennis, and cricket competitions added to the attractions of Church Stretton's visitor season.[94]

The Church Stretton and South Shropshire arts festival began in 1967.[95] By 1990 it extended over 2 weeks during late July and early August and included choral, musical, and poetry recitals, concerts, professional acting, opera, and dance, and an exhibition, illustrated lecture, craft fair, and film show. Most events that year took place in schools in the town but two were performed in nearby villages.[96]

70 '[Buddicom] Family Sketches' (MS. vol. in possession of Lady Brown, Ticklerton Cottage), p. 116.

71 S.R.O. 809, box 10, draft lease 1875; Windsor, *Handbk.* 29. For the Bensons see above, Rushbury, manors (Lutwyche).

72 S.R.O. 1904/89; cf. below, manors.

73 *Shrews. Chron.* 21 June 1935, p. 8.

74 *Ch. Stretton Adv.* 21 Oct. 1926, p. 2.

75 *The Field*, Dec. 1963, p. 1201 (obit.); will pr. 29 Jan. 1964.

76 *Shrews. Chron.* 17 (p. 4), 24 (p. 8), and 31 (p. 8) May, 14 (p. 5), 21 (p. 8), and 28 (p. 11) June, 5 July (p. 7) 1935; S.R.O. 1904/89.

77 *Ch. Stretton Adv.* 15 Mar. 1935, p. 8.

78 Below, econ. hist. (resort).

79 The club's soaring site was on the W. side of the Long Mynd, nr. Asterton (in Norbury): *Ch. Stretton Adv.* 15 (pp. 1, 8) and 22 (p. 3) Mar., 2 Aug. (p. 8) 1935.

80 S.R.O. DA 7/111/14, p. 146; *The Field*, Dec. 1963, p. 1201.

81 *V.C.H. Salop.* iv. 256; below, manors; econ. hist. (agric.).

82 Below, econ. hist. (the resort).

83 *Atlas of Breeding Birds of Salop.* ed. P. Deans *et al.* (Salop. Ornithological Soc. 1992), 53–4.

84 Then in its infancy as an organized sport: *Tennis, Lawn Tennis, Rackets, Fives* (Badminton Libr. 1890), 127 sqq.

85 Windsor, *Handbk.* 14; *Kelly's Dir. Salop.* (1885–1905).

86 *Kelly's Dir. Salop.* (1926), 67, 390; (1941), 67, 381.

87 Ibid. (1917), 59, 352; (1922), 65, 354.

88 Ibid. (1926), 67, 389.

89 Ibid.; (1929), 68, 385.

90 See e.g. *Stretton Focus*, Dec. 1970, p. 7.

91 Salop. F.A. *Official Handbk. 1989–90*, 138–9, 141; dates, etc., of recreation ground and playing field from par. council via Mr. A. J. Crowe.

92 S.R.O., DA 7/100/2, pp. 279–80, 284, 288; *Shrews. Chron.* 5 Mar. 1915, p. 7.

93 *Shropshire Mag.* Jan. 1951, 17–19; Oct. 1986, 40–1; S.R.O. map. For Braid see *D.N.B.* 1941–50.

94 Below, econ. hist. (the resort).

95 *Stretton Focus*, July (p. 4), Sept. (p. 4) 1967.

96 Programme 1990.

MANORS AND OTHER ESTATES. In 1066 the manor of *STRETTON*, later known as *STRETTON-EN-LE-DALE*, was held by Edwin, earl of Mercia (d. 1071). Roger of Montgomery, created earl of Shrewsbury *c.* 1068, held it in chief in 1086, and it was forfeited to the Crown by the rebellion of his son Earl Robert in 1102.[97] The manor remained in the Crown until 1229. For much of the reigns of Henry II and his sons its revenues were assigned to successive keepers of Stretton castle. Between 1192 and 1194, however, they were enjoyed by William and James, sons of a former keeper, Simon, but not themselves keepers of the castle.[98]

In 1229 Henry III granted the manor in fee to Hubert de Burgh, earl of Kent, who had formerly farmed it.[99] He forfeited it in 1232.[1] In 1238 Henry III granted the manor *in tenenciam* to Henry de Hastings and his wife Ada, a sister and coheir of John, earl of Chester (d. 1237), in lieu of her purparty of the earldom of Chester,[2] but in 1245 it was resumed by the Crown.[3] In 1267 Henry III granted the manor, with other estates, to Hamon le Strange of Wrockwardine, an old friend and companion in arms of the king and of his son Edward; the grant was to Hamon and his heirs until the king should provide them with other land worth £100 a year.[4] About 1270, before leaving on the ninth crusade, Hamon assigned Stretton to his sister Hawise, wife of Gruffudd ap Gwenwynwyn, lord of southern Powys.[5] Early in 1273, when Hamon's death overseas became known, Stretton was resumed by the Crown as an unlicensed alienation, though from 1275 Hawise was allowed all the manor's revenues for life. Hawise died in 1310 and Edmund FitzAlan, earl of Arundel, then entered into possession, having been granted the reversion of the manor for life in 1309.[6]

Arundel's estates were forfeited to the Crown on his execution in 1326, and in 1327 Stretton was granted for life to Roger de Mortimer of Wigmore, created earl of March in 1328. In 1330 March was granted the manor in fee simple but later that year, on his fall from power, the manor reverted to the Crown,[7] and in 1336 Edward III granted it in fee to Richard FitzAlan, earl of Arundel (d. 1376).[8] In 1397, after the impeachment, forfeiture, and execution of his son Earl Richard, the king granted the manor to the steward of his household Thomas Percy, earl of Worcester. Worcester surrendered it to the Crown in 1399 in exchange for an Exchequer annuity granted by Henry IV. Thomas FitzAlan, restored in 1400 to the earldom of Arundel and to his father's estates,[9] died seised of the manor in 1415 when it passed to his cousin Sir John d'Arundel. Sir John, probably never recognized as earl of Arundel, died in 1421[10] and his son John inherited the manor. He was certainly recognized as earl in 1433, was created duke of Touraine in France in 1434, and died in 1435.[11] Thereafter the manor descended with the earldom of Arundel until its presumed settlement on Arundel's elder daughter and coheir Jane on her marriage to Sir John Lumley, Lord Lumley. The Lumleys had an interest in the manor by 1562, when it was probably mortgaged,[12] and courts were held in Lumley's name 1566–7. In 1576 the childless Lumleys sold it to a former lord mayor of London, Sir Rowland Hayward, probably a mortgagee since 1566.[13] Hayward settled it in marriage on his daughter and son-in-law Joan and John (kt. 1603) Thynne.[14]

Sir John Thynne died in 1604,[15] his widow Joan in 1612.[16] After Joan's death the manor descended with the manors of Caus and Minsterley[17] until 1714 when, upon the 1st Lord Weymouth's death, Stretton manor passed to his widowed daughter-in-law, Mrs. Grace Thynne, for life. On her death in 1725[18] the manor again descended with Caus and Minsterley in the Thynne family[19] until 1803 when Lord Bath sold it to Thomas Coleman of Leominster (Herefs.).[20]

In 1808 Coleman settled the manor on the marriage of his son T. B. Coleman, rector 1807–18, with Anne Gregory Stackhouse. Mrs. Coleman was lady of the manor during her widowhood, 1818–62, and was succeeded by her grandson E. B. Coleman (from 1878 Proctor) of

97 *V.C.H. Salop.* i. 317; iii. 7, 9–10.

98 Eyton, xii. 18–21.

99 Ibid. 21–2; *Cal. Chart. R.* 1226–57, 103; *Close R.* 1227–31, 492.

1 Eyton, xi. 138–9; xii. 21–2; *Bk. of Fees*, i. 541; *V.C.H. Salop.* iii. 14; Sir M. Powicke, *13th Cent.* (1962), 44–51.

2 *Cal. Pat.* 1232–47, 224; *Close R.* 1237–42, 60; *Cal. Lib.* 1240–5, 124; Eyton, xii. 22; R. Stewart-Brown, 'End of Norman Earldom of Chester', *E.H.R.* xxxv. 39.

3 Eyton, xii. 22.

4 *Cal. Pat.* 1266–72, 39; *Cal. Inq. Misc.* i, p. 295; H. le Strange, *Le Strange Rec.* (1916), 140–1, 144; Eyton, xii. 24.

5 Le Strange, op. cit. 145, 224.

6 Ibid. 148, 163–5; Eyton, xii. 25–7; *Cal. Pat.* 1272–81, 30, 131; *Cal. Fine R.* 1272–1307, 4, 64; 1327–37, 190; *Cal. Inq. Misc.* ii, pp. 13, 18; *Feud. Aids*, iv. 229.

7 Eyton, xii. 27; G. A. Holmes, *Estates of Higher Nobility in 14th-Cent. Eng.* (1957), 13; *Cal. Pat.* 1327–30, 192; 1330–4, 5, 143; *Cal. Fine R.* 1327–37, 190; *V.C.H. Salop.* iii. 20.

8 Eyton, xii. 27; *Cal. Chart. R.* 1327–41, 353. Cf. *Cal. Pat.* 1343–5, 488; 1345–8, 328–9; 1350–4, 524; 1354–8, 131; *Cal. Close* 1346–9, 244.

9 P.R.O., C 145/263, no. 12; *Cal. Inq. Misc.* vi, p. 114; *Complete Peerage*, i. 244–6; *Cal. Pat.* 1396–9, 213, 248, 250.

10 *Cal. Fine R.* 1413–22, 165–6; *Complete Peerage*, i. 247.

11 *Complete Peerage*, i. 248.

12 Longleat MSS., unbound, 4071 note on endpaper.

13 P.R.O., CP 25/1/293/71, no. 330; CP 25/2/200/18 & 19 Eliz. I Mich. [no. 24]; CP 25/2/259/5 Eliz. I East. [no. 16]; CP 40/1158, rot. 616d.; CP 40/1351, rot. 1296; Arundel Jointure Act, 1545, 37 Hen. VIII, c. 32 (Private, not printed); *L. & P. Hen. VIII*, xx (2), p. 414; *Cal. Pat.* 1461–7, 443; 1553–4, 315; 1560--3, 582, 615; 1575–6, p. 98; *T.S.A.S.* 3rd ser. iv. 115–28; *Complete Peerage*, i. 253; Longleat MSS., unbound, 4071 note on endpaper. For Hayward cf. *V.C.H. Salop.* iv. 130–2.

14 *Two Elizabethan Women* (Wilts. Rec. Soc. xxxviii), p. xix; P.R.O., C 142/241, no. 125; W. A. Shaw, *Kts. of Eng.* (1906), ii. 105.

15 *Two Elizabethan Women*, p. xxiv.

16 Ibid. p. xxv.

17 P.R.O., C 142/535, no. 47; CP 25/2/616/1652 Trin. [no. 34]; CP 43/147, rot. 85; CP 43/281, rot. 216; CP 43/283, rot. 68; CP 43/284, rot. 140; CP 43/362, rot. 86; CP 43/409, rot. 269; *V.C.H. Salop.* viii. 311.

18 Burke, *Peerage* (1949), 145; W.S.L. 350/5/40, Ch. Stretton p. 6; P.R.O., CP 43/449, rot. 180; S.R.O., q. sess. rec. box 260, reg. of gamekeepers 1711–42, 14 July 1721.

19 P.R.O., CP 25/2/1477/29 Geo. III Hil. no. 12; CP 43/593, rot. 144; CP 43/712, rot. 167; S.R.O., q. sess. rec. box 260, reg. of gamekeepers 1742–79, 21 July 1756, 15 July 1760, 17 July 1771, 4 Aug. 1778; parcel 261, reg. of gamekeepers 1799– 1807, f. 14; *V.C.H. Salop.* viii. 311.

20 W.S.L. 350/5/40, Ch. Stretton p. 6.

Aberhafesp (Mont.).[21] In 1888 Proctor sold the manor with 433 a. to R. B. Benson of Lutwyche.[22] Benson died in 1911 and the manor passed to his son Maj. G. R. Benson, who sold it in 1925 to A. S. Browne of Hanwood House.[23] Rex D. Cohen of Condover, a Liverpool businessman, bought it in 1926. He died in 1928 and in 1934 his representatives sold it to Max V. Wenner of Betchcott.[24] Wenner died in 1937 leaving it to his friend and agent William Humphrey, of Stiperstones and later of Walcot.[25] Humphrey died in 1963[26] and in 1964 his executors sold the manor and his land on the Long Mynd to Ingleby Holdings Ltd. of Birmingham. The company, which had acquired the estate in trust for the National Trust conveyed it to the Trust in 1965 and the Trust has remained owner of the manor.[27]

West of the Port Way the land bought from Humphrey's executors in 1964 consisted of some 1,205 a. of open common, parts of Ratlinghope and Medlicott manors;[28] east of the Port Way the land comprised almost all the uninclosed common of Stretton-en-le-Dale, evidently some 3,260 a. In 1965, soon after its acquisition of the manor, the Trust extended its property southwards by buying Minton Hill, the 755 a. of common belonging to Minton manor.[29] Later, between 1972 and 1986, it rounded off its Long Mynd estate by buying a small property in Carding Mill valley with 250 a. of surrounding common,[30] several small parcels of land formerly belonging to water authorities,[31] and the 25-a. Batch Land, All Stretton.[32]

Before 1066 *WOMERTON* was held as four manors by four free thegns Auti, Einulfr (Einulf), Argrimr (Aregrim), and Arnketil (Archetel). In 1086, as part of Condover hundred, it was held of the earl of Shrewsbury by Robert fitz Corbet. The earl's tenure in chief lapsed after 1102.[33] Robert died after 1121.[34] Womerton seems not to have been retained by the descendants of either of Robert's daughters and coheirs[35] but was eventually absorbed into the royal manor of Stretton and thus transferred to Munslow hundred.[36]

Leofric, earl of Mercia (d. 1057), held *MINTON* and Whittingslow as 4 hides; by 1086 they lay within Earl Roger's 'farm' at Stretton.[37] Earl Roger's son, Earl Robert, forfeited his English estates by rebellion in 1102,[38] and perhaps from Henry I's reign Minton came to be held of the Crown in serjeanty.

One Fulk may have received an estate in Minton as a king's serjeant during Henry I's reign,[39] but the first certainly recorded serjeant there was Walter of Minton, fl. 1199–1211; he held 1½ carucate in Minton as forester or keeper of the Long forest. His successor, probably his son, Richard of Minton occurred in the 1220s and early 1230s[40] and alienated some of his estate.[41] Peter of Minton, whose relationship to Richard is uncertain, held the serjeanty in the late 1240s and 1250s and was said to be keeper of the Long forest, of its hays of Bushmoor and Hawkhurst, of the forest of Stretton, and of Heywood on Wenlock Edge. He died *c.* 1261. His son John of Minton died in 1263 leaving, besides a widow Isabel who claimed dower, three sisters as coheirs: Alice, the wife of Saer Mauveysin of Berwick; Agnes, the wife of Richard de Grymenhull; and Margery, who married William le Fleming of Whitcot.[42] John's inheritance was divided between his sisters in 1266: the widowed Margery held property in Minton as late as 1292 and made provision for her daughters there, and Agnes's widower Richard de Grymenhull held her part of the Minton estate by the curtesy until he died (leaving three married daughters) in 1308. Alice and Saer Mauveysin, however, seem to have received more of her father's estate than her sisters, and Saer (d. 1283) and his son Peter (d. 1298) did the serjeant's duties, did homage for the estate, and were regarded as tenants of the vill.[43] Peter Mauveysin's son John died in 1324[44] and John's son John (II) in 1326. John's son John (III) was lord of Minton in 1347–8,[45] but the male line of the Mauveysins was probably extinct by 1397 or thereabouts.[46] The Mauveysins' successors held the manor divided into fractions which (at least as recorded in their respective deeds) did not add up to unity.

Hugh Stapleton owned half of Minton in 1478 and sold it in 1484 to Sir Robert Corbet of Moreton Corbet, owner in 1509–10. It evidently descended with Moreton until Robert Corbet's death in 1583, when his share of Minton passed

[21] Ibid.; *S.P.R. Heref.* viii (2), p. vi; Burke, *Land. Gent.* (1914), 3, 1488; Loton Hall MSS., Sir B. Leighton's diary 28 June 1857; inf. from Mr. T. S. Acton; *Lond. Gaz.* 8 Nov. 1878, p. 5937.

[22] S.R.O. 809, box 10, sched. of property purchased from Proctor 1888; box 14, plans.

[23] Burke, *Land. Gent.* (1914), 137; *Kelly's Dir. Salop.* (1913), 64; S.R.O. 2408/106A, ff. 442 sqq.; /109, Soames & Thompson to C. E. Wace 21 Jan. 1925; cf. *Kelly's Dir. Salop.* (1926), 111; file on 'Salop. Manorial Records' in archivist's office.

[24] *Ch. Stretton Adv.* 12 June (p. 3), 21 Oct. (p. 2) 1926; S.R.O. 1709, box 202, compensation agreement forms referring to conveyance of 13 June 1934; 2408/106A, f. 455; *Kelly's Dir. Salop.* (1934), 66, 84; (1937), 65, 260; *Shrews. Chron.* 9 and 16 Mar. 1928; *V.C.H. Salop.* viii. 39–40.

[25] *Shrews. Chron.* 8 and 15 Jan. 1937; M. V. Wenner's will pr. 26 May 1937; *Ch. Stretton Adv.* 8 July 1938, p. 1; *Kelly's Dir. Salop.* (1941), 65, 117; *Reg. Electors: Ludlow*, Mar. 1951, p. 328; Mar. 1952, p. 348.

[26] MS. note (1978) by A. H. Horrocks in Longmynd Hills Cttee. *Rules and Regulations under the Commons Act, 1908* (Ch. Stretton, 1928; copy in S.R.O. DA 7/134/11/3).

[27] Nat. Trust deeds, conveyances of 22 Sept. 1964, 11 May 1965; cf. *S.C.C. Mins.* 1964–5, 33–4, 274.

[28] Nat. Trust deeds, deed of 22 Sept. 1964; S.R.O. 552/8/902.

[29] Nat. Trust deeds, deeds of 22 Sept. 1964, 23 Sept. 1965. For the Long Mynd commons see below, econ. hist. (agric.).

[30] From Harold Holmes: Nat. Trust deeds.

[31] Incl. 3 reservoirs taken out of the common: ibid.

[32] Ibid.

[33] *V.C.H. Salop.* i. 326; iii. 10.

[34] Eyton, vii. 9–10; *Cartulary of Shrews. Abbey*, ed. U. Rees (1975), i, p. 36.

[35] i.e. the Boterells and FitzHerberts: *V.C.H. Salop.* i. 297; Eyton, vi. 158; vii. 40, 148, 159; xi. 192. The FitzHerberts received a poorer share of Rob.'s est. and were not in Hen. II's favour: ibid. vii. 151–2, 156.

[36] Eyton, vi. 158; *V.C.H. Salop.* viii. 1.

[37] *V.C.H. Salop.* i. 344.

[38] Ibid. iii. 10.

[39] Eyton, xii. 4, 12.

[40] Ibid. 5.

[41] Ibid. 6; *Rot. Hund.* (Rec. Com.), ii. 84.

[42] Eyton, vi. 341; xii. 6–8.

[43] Ibid. xii. 9–12.

[44] *Cal. Inq. p.m.* vi, p. 289.

[45] Ibid. p. 457; W.S.L. 350/5/40, Ch. Stretton p. 39.

[46] Eyton, vii. 396; S. Shaw, *Hist. Staffs.* i (1798), 167 n. 8, 168 and n. 7.

to his daughter Elizabeth, who married Sir Henry Wallop, of Farleigh Wallop (Hants). Their son Robert, the regicide, sold it to Richard Minton of Minton in 1655.[47]

In 1442–3 Ralph Lingen died owning a third of Minton,[48] which then descended, in the Lingens of Sutton St. Nicholas (Herefs.), with Yockleton and Stoney Stretton (in Westbury) until they were sold in 1641; Minton and Yockleton may have been in the hands of the Crown or trustees after the death (1610) of Jane Shelley (*née* Lingen), who left many charitable legacies and was the widow of a recusant involved in Throckmorton's plot (1583).[49] In 1660 Sir Henry Lingen and his wife Alice sold their share of Minton to two brothers Richard and Thomas Minton, of Minton; in 1668 Richard conveyed his interest, perhaps including his interest in the Wallop share, to Thomas (d. 1674).

Thomas Kynaston, of Shotton, owned another third of Minton in 1509–10. He died without issue, probably leaving the Minton estate to his first cousin George Kynaston, of Oteley, owner in the 1520s and 1541–2. George died in 1543 and the property descended in the Kynastons of Oteley from father to son, the following being owners: Francis (d. 1581), Sir Edward (d. 1641), Sir Francis (d. 1652), Edward (d. 1656), and Sir Francis who died childless in 1661. The estate then passed successively to Sir Francis's brother Edward and to Edward's son Charles. Charles Kynaston and his wife Alice sold the property to Thomas Minton in 1704.[50]

Thus in 1704 Thomas Minton, son of the Thomas who had died in 1674, became owner of the whole manor. He died in 1726 and the manor passed successively to his son Thomas (d. 1737) and to the younger Thomas's son Thomas. The last named died in 1765 leaving a widow Sarah (d. 1789), who had a life interest in his estate, and three young daughters, Anne, Priscilla who married Thomas Beddoes of Cheney Longville in 1773, and Mary who married Delabere Pritchett of Brimfield (Herefs.) in 1777. Anne died a minor, unmarried, in 1766. On Mary Pritchett's death (by 1784) without surviving issue her interest in the estate passed to her husband; he died in 1806 and the whole estate thus came eventually to Priscilla (d. 1819) and Thomas (d. 1822) Beddoes and descended to their son Thomas Beddoes (d. 1837)[51] and then to his widow Jane.[52] By 1851 their son Dr. W. M. Beddoes was lord. He died in 1870 leaving his estate to his widow Laura Seraphina as his 'executrix for life' and trustee; she died in 1890.[53] The estate descended to the Beddoeses' eldest son W. F. Beddoes, a barrister, on whose death without issue in 1928 it passed to his nephew E. W. Minton Beddoes.[54] When the latter died in 1952 his executors immediately offered Minton House (formerly White Birches) for sale with *c.* 208 a., and later that year *c.* 1,360 a. of settled estate was offered for sale, though without mention of any manorial rights.[55] E. W. Minton Beddoes's son and heir S. W. Minton Beddoes, who sold Minton hill common to the National Trust in 1965,[56] remained lord of the manor in 1969.

BOTVYLE may have been the mainly demesne portion of an estate in Lydley manor, 2 tenanted virgates of which, called 'Botley', were given to the Templars in the later 1150s and included in their parish of Cardington.[57] Botvyle, though mainly in Stretton parish,[58] remained wholly in Lydley and Cardington manor, and Thomas Botvyle held a copyhold estate there by 1439, as did his descendants until the 18th century and again in the 19th.[59]

Richard Botvyle (d. 1732) of Ludlow, formerly of Botvyle, left all his estate to his cousin Richard Botvyle, a Shrewsbury saddler. Nevertheless Botvyle descended to his nephew and heir Benjamin Botvyle, a minor, and in 1742 Benjamin, then a London vintner, sold Botvyle to the son and namesake of his uncle's legatee. Like his father the younger Richard Botvyle was a Shrewsbury saddler and, as tenant of 'Berry's messuage', a Stretton copyholder too.[60] After the younger Richard's death Botvyle, mortgaged since 1724 or earlier, was held by his widow Martha.[61] In 1760 she passed it to her son Thomas, a Shrewsbury saddler, and he immediately sold it to Moses Luther. It later passed to Luther's son-in-law, the Revd. Richard Wilding (d. 1820).[62] By 1838 the Wilding estate in Stretton parish amounted to 762 a., almost all around Botvyle.[63] In 1856 the Wildings sold it, encumbered, to Beriah Botfield of Norton Hall (Northants.), a descendant of Thomas Botvyle (fl. 1439). The same year Botfield also bought the Botvyle property of Thomas Duppa Duppa, of Cheney Longville, in 1838 the owner of 72 a.

47 S.R.O. 665, box 42, deeds of 1478–84; P.R.O., C 141/2, no. 17; CP 25/2/616/1653 Mich. [no. 8]; W.S.L. 350/5/40, Ch. Stretton p. 39. For Rob. Wallop see *D.N.B.*

48 Para. based on W.S.L. 350/5/40, Ch. Stretton p. 40, corr. by Burke, *Land. Gent.* (1914), 282; *V.C.H. Salop.* viii. 312 (corr. below, Corrigenda); *Cal. Pat.* 1554–5, 88; P.R.O., C 142/402, no. 151; C 142/535, no. 132; CP 25/2/712/13 Chas. II Trin. [no. 14]; N.L.W., Chirk Castle, Group F no. 1415; H.W.R.O.(H.), Heref. dioc. rec., Thos. Minton's will pr. 5 June 1694.

49 Cf. *V.C.H. Suss.* vi (1), 13; P.R.O., C 66/1876, no. 4.

50 W.S.L. 350/5/40, Ch. Stretton pp. 39–40; P.R.O., C 1/423, no. 23; CP 25/2/200/8 & 9 Eliz. I Mich. [no. 16]; CP 25/2/201/26 Eliz. I East. [no. 27]; CP 25/2/477/10 Chas. I Hil. [no. 17]; *Visit. Salop. 1623*, ii. 294, 298; Burke, *Land. Gent.* (1914), 1260.

51 W.S.L. 350/5/40, Ch. Stretton pp. 40–1; P.R.O., CP 25/2/1055/10 Geo. I Trin. [no. 2]; *S.P.R. Heref.* viii (2), 90, 94, 117–18, 132, 135, 139, 149–50, 183; S.R.O., q. sess. rec. box 260, reg. of gamekeepers 1742–79, 19 July 1769, 26 Dec. 1770; 1799–1807, ff. 8, 18; S.R.O. 1150/815.

52 Tithe award; Burke, *Land. Gent.* (18th edn.), ii (1969), 39 (on which rest of para. based, though there are some incorrect dates).

53 S. Bagshaw, *Dir. Salop.* (1851), 530; *Alum. Oxon. 1715–1886*, i. 86; S.R.O. 1206/27, pp. 237–41; *P.O. Dir. Salop.* (1879), 299.

54 *Kelly's Dir. Salop.* (1885), 825; (1929), 66; (1941), 65; *Shrews. Chron.* 30 Nov. 1928, p. 3 (obit.).

55 S.P.L., SC3/23–4.

56 Above, this section.

57 Above, Cardington, intro., manors, church.

58 S.P.L., MS. 6741, p. 3.

59 Botfield, *Stemmata Botevilliana*, 71–5, 91–2.

60 Ibid. 75–6, 91–2; *S.P.R. Heref.* xiv. 798; S.R.O. 3288/2/1, pp. 122–3, 125–6, 161–2.

61 S.R.O. 567/1/360; 3288/2/1, pp. 101 sqq., 123–4.

62 S.R.O. 3288/2/1, pp. 223–4; Botfield, *Stemmata Botevilliana*, 76, 92. For Wilding cf. *S.P.R. Heref.* viii (2), 118; S.R.O. 248/15, ff. 73v.–74; *Alum. Cantab. 1752–1900*, vi. 468.

63 Tithe award.

there,[64] where the Duppas had been copyholders since 1709.[65]

Botfield died in 1863, and his relict Mrs. Alfred Seymour (d. 1911) held the estate (*c.* 650 a.) for life. Botfield's disposition of his whole estate, no less than his acquisitions of parts of it, was dictated by genealogical sentiment, and under his will it passed in 1911 to Lord Alexander Thynne. He was killed in action in 1918,[66] and his estate passed to his sister Lady Beatrice Thynne. She sold some of the Botvyle property in 1920, but at her death in 1941 what remained passed to her nephew Henry Frederick Thynne, Viscount Weymouth. He, having succeeded as 6th marquess of Bath in 1946, sold the rest next year 'solely' to pay death duties.[67]

The house that descended from Moses Luther to the Wildings and in 1792 was reputed the Thynnes' old seat (though mistakenly, as it had descended in the younger, Botvyle, line) is Upper Botvyle Farmhouse or Botvyle Farm. It has a cement-rendered Georgian north-west front with a central door in panelled pilastered frame beneath a fanlight and bracketed hood. That suggests an early 19th-century house, but the front was rebuilt after a fire, and timber framing is exposed at the rear; a timber-framed cross wing was demolished, probably *c.* 1980. Lower Botvyle, or Botvyle Farmhouse, on the Duppa estate in the early 19th century, is said to have a possibly early 17th-century core; greatly altered in modern times, it was for a time called the Old Manor.[68]

Long before the final definition of Stretton-en-le-Dale's manorial customs in 1670,[69] indeed before the end of the Middle Ages, Stretton customary tenants seem to have cast off the character of a peasantry in preparation for that of a parish gentry. Their progress, running ahead of the conversion of villeinage to copyhold,[70] doubtless sprang from the relative prosperity and independence which they enjoyed without a resident lord.[71] The Heynes and Higgins (or Hughes) families (both eventually armigerous), for example, were settled in the manor by the 14th century,[72] and in the 15th century the Higginses provided two rectors of the parish church[73] while in the early 16th century Thomas Heynes married a daughter of Humphrey Gatacre of Gatacre.[74] The Thynnes were an offshoot of the Botvyles. In 1439 Thomas Botvyle, the reputed restorer of the family fortunes, settled the family's ancient copyhold estate on his younger son John, separating it from their freehold property there and elsewhere in the parish: that evidently went to the elder son William, who bought other land. William's grandson John Botvyle, perhaps from residence in the family house or inn in Church Stretton, was called Thynne (o'th'Inn). The 1439 division of property did not deprive the elder line of all land at Botvyle, for in 1497 Thomas Thynne and William Botvyle, descendants of the elder and younger lines respectively, both held land there, as did John Thynne in 1524. Thomas Thynne's younger brother William held land in Church Stretton in 1497, and the Thynnes remained Stretton copyholders, though they were of much greater consequence elsewhere after the first Thynne's great-grandson, Sir John (d. 1580), had built Longleat. Sir John's son (d. 1604) and namesake became lord of Stretton-en-le-Dale in his wife's right in 1576, and his descendants retained the manor until 1803.[75]

Landed families established elsewhere became Stretton copyholders. The Leightons, lords of Leighton, obtained land in the manor, and began to live there, in the later 14th century when John Leighton married Walter Cambray's daughter and heir Maud; about that time the Leightons also gained forfeited lands of the Botvyles. John Leighton's successors as head of the family continued to live in Stretton until Sir Edward moved to Wattlesborough, leasing his 'great house' in Stretton to his younger brother Devereux *c.* 1592.[76] Meanwhile other Leightons had acquired Stretton lands, and among the copyholds which Bonham Norton bought in the early 17th century[77] were those of Sir Edward's kinsmen William Leighton (probably of Plaish)[78] and Nicholas Leighton (probably of Coats).[79]

The existence of a brisk land market and the occasional growth of some copyhold estates at the expense of others are themes latent in the court records from the time (1721) of their regular survival[80] and assumable for earlier periods as the processes which brought some parish families into prominence. Those same processes also continued to make Stretton land available to gentry landowners from outside the manor: in 1742, for instance, the heirs of Thomas Duppa of Rye Felton (in Bromfield) sold Bright's messuage to William Davies, gent-

64 Botfield, op. cit. pp. 77–87, 99–100, 156, ccli*; *V.C.H. Salop.* iv. 209, 211; tithe award.

65 S.R.O. 3288/2/1, pp. 60 sqq.

66 *D.N.B.* s.v. Botfield, Beriah; S.R.O. 4044/39, pp. 60–1, 63, 67–72, 74–5, 82; *V.C.H. Salop.* iv. 211; Burke, *Peerage* (1967), 189, 1483.

67 Longleat MSS., Norton Hall papers, Ch. Stretton est. xv.1, 3, 7, 9–10. Also at Longleat there are bound maps (one dated 1903) of the Ch. Stretton est.

68 Dept. of Environment, *List of Bldgs. of Special Arch. or Hist. Interest: R.D. of Ludlow* (1974), 28; Bilbey, *Ch. Stretton*, pls. 167–9; S.P.L., MS. 6865, p. 186; tithe award; S.P.L., SC20/35.

69 Below, econ. hist. (agric.).

70 A. H. Johnson, *Disappearance of the Small Landowner* (1909), 28–5, 38, 61–74; cf. *V.C.H. Salop.* iv. 110–11, 137–8.

71 Above, this section (Stretton-en-le-Dale); below, econ. hist. (agric.).

72 S.R.O. 125/1.

73 Below, church.

74 Botfield, *Stemmata Botevilliana*, 138. But his fr.-in-law cannot (as there stated) have been a courtier of Hen. VI.

75 Botfield, op. cit. 23–6, 27 sqq., 52, 58 (where a misprint wrongly transfers Wm. and John's paternity from Thos. to Wal., fl. 1388), 63–4; W.S.L. 350/5/40, Ch. Stretton p. 19–22, 29–30; S.R.O. 3365/165; P.R.O., E 179/166/205, m. 1; above, this article, intro.; above, this section.

76 Botfield, op. cit. 163 sqq., 165, 170–1, 184.

77 Longleat MSS., unbound, 3804, list of Stretton tenants 9 Sept. 1613; 3814, ct. 9 Jan. 1603; 4072, f. 165r.–v.

78 His rank 'esquire' (Longleat MSS., unbound, 4072, f. 165r.–v.) suits Wm. (d. 1607) of Plaish or his son and heir (kt. 1603) better than other contemporary namesakes.

79 Called 'gent.' (ibid.): cf. Botfield, *Stemmata Botevilliana*, 186; above, Rushbury, manors (Coats). Nic.'s gt.-grandfather had been steward of Stretton-en-le-Dale in 1490.

80 Below, local govt.

leman, of Charlton (in Wrockwardine),[81] and in 1750 the Sandfords of the Isle sold the Little Stretton Hall copyhold (including Bright's messuage also known as the Lower living) to John Baker of Uppington, gentleman.[82] Among outsiders who seized opportunities to invest in Stretton land on a significant scale two men, Bonham Norton in the early 17th century and the Revd. R. N. Pemberton in the earlier 19th century, are particularly noteworthy for seeming to fulfil, even if briefly, some of the functions of a principal resident landowner in the lord of the manor's absence.

The London stationer Bonham Norton (d. 1635)[83] bought up 9 or 10 copyholds in the manor and probably the former demesne wood at Bushmoor (in Wistanstow) too; many of his estates were acquired from prominent manorial families. Perhaps most of his purchases were made soon after the town fire of 1593, for in 1603 he was licensed to let his customary lands for 500 years and by 1613 he evidently owned much land in the manor.[84] In 1616 he was described as 'lord [*sic*] of the larger part of the lands and possessions' in the town and was then granted a market. Tacitly or otherwise, therefore, the lord of the manor seems to have waived his own claim to market rights (doubtless long neglected),[85] perhaps in acknowledgment of Norton's role as the town's leading landowner and rebuilder; and it was from the lord's demesne woods that Norton received building timber.[86] Probably well supplied with ready money, Norton may have aimed to profit from the fire's effects on local property values and from building work. He was also intent on establishing a seat there, in the county from which his family sprang and where he was sheriff in 1611: for, besides his market house, a school, and a court house,[87] his other known building work was *THE HALL* on the west side of the back lane, just north of the end of Cub Lane.[88] Westwards his private grounds evidently ran uphill to include, on the edge of the Long Mynd common, a warren including Over field, one of the town's open fields 'above Mr. Norton's house'.[89] Park House, opposite the Hall, may thus have originated as a parker's or warrener's lodge, but later the Hall stables seem to have been there.[90] Norton's son Arthur married the heiress of George Norton of Abbot's Leigh (Som.), where their descendants lived,[91] and the Hall, the town's principal house,[92] was probably let. Sold when the Norton estate was broken up in 1714, the Hall, a 'large timbered mansion', was taken down by the rector, T. B. Coleman, probably not long before his death in 1818.[93]

R. N. Pemberton, rector 1818–48 and patron, accumulated a considerable private estate in the parish, much of it adjoining the glebe so that his two estates, fenced as one, surrounded the Rectory with large private grounds to the west of the town but secluded from it; his grounds probably occupied much of the same land as Bonham Norton's two centuries before. In accordance with Pemberton's will a kinsman succeeded to his benefice and also to his private estate; but he died within a year, and, although succeeding rectors lived in gentlemanly style in the best house in the parish,[94] their inheritance was less splendid than Pemberton had planned for one who, though not lord of the manor, would in all other ways have been a very well-to-do 'squarson'.

Stretton copyhold estates, though heritable, have not left notable or easily identifiable houses: standing in the principal settlements, they were liable to tenurial, as well as physical, separation from their lands and also to rebuilding. Houses of the Higginses and Brookes and the Gibbon family's estate are cases in point.

The copyhold 'house on the Bank called Higgins House' was in All Stretton, where Higginses had been settled by the 14th century. In 1658 it belonged to John and Elizabeth Kyte, probably as heirs to a branch of the Higginses since their son was called Higgins Kyte;[95] it probably stood just a little south of the Grove.[96] There was another *BANK HOUSE* in Church Stretton: that was the 'pretty house' north of the church, *c.* 1540 residence of the attorney Francis Brooke, fifth son of John Brooke of Blacklands (in Bobbington). Francis had settled in the town and become deputy steward of the manor; he prospered and in 1563 bought from the earl of Arundel a farm, Ragleth wood, and the demesne mill on Nash brook, an estate that was held in chief by knight service; the farmstead was evidently in Church Stretton town, probably near the north end, as that was where the town fire of 1593 began. Brooke died in 1582.[97] In 1603 his grandson Edward Brooke the younger married Elizabeth, daughter of Richard Higgins of All Stretton, evidently a freeholder, most of whose land the couple evidently obtained.[98] Another Edward Brooke owned the Bank House in 1681,[99] and it descended to Thomas Brooke (d. 1742). Thomas's daughter and heir Elizabeth (d. 1785) married a Shrewsbury solicitor Edward Lloyd (d. 1790), and in 1835 his kinswomen, the

81 S.R.O. 248/11, p. 223; /13, f. 10. The Davieses were later of Brook fm.: tithe award.
82 S.R.O. 248/13, f. 12v.; 465/599.
83 Above, this article, intro.
84 Longleat MSS., unbound, 3804, list of Stretton tenants 9 Sept. 1613; 3814; 4072, ff. 132v.–133, 165 r.–v. For Bushmoor see below, econ. hist. (agric.), for the fire above, growth of settlement.
85 P.R.O., C 66/2059, no. 6; below, econ. hist. (mkts. and fairs).
86 Above, growth of settlement.
87 McKerrow, *Dict. of Printers and Booksellers 1557–1640*, 202; J. B. Blakeway, *Sheriffs of Salop*. (Shrews. 1831), 102; below, econ. hist. (mkts. and fairs); local govt.; educ.
88 W.S.L. 350/5/40, Ch. Stretton p. 9.
89 Longleat MSS., unbound, 4072, f. 120; below, econ. hist. (agric.).
90 Windsor, *Handbk*. 89; Bilbey, *Ch. Stretton*, pl. 80.
91 J. Collinson, *Hist. and Antiquities of Som.* (1791), iii. 153–4.
92 Ogilby, *Britannia* (1675), pl. 57.
93 W.S.L. 350/5/40, Ch. Stretton p. 9.
94 Below, church.
95 P.R.O., C 1/815, no. 37; C 1/1010, nos. 69–70; C 3/457, no. 127; S.R.O. 125/1; *Visit. Salop. 1623*, i. 240.
96 Inf. from Mr. Romo.
97 Leland, *Itin.* ed. Toulmin Smith, ii. 80; Blakeway, *Sheriffs*, 188; *V.C.H. Staffs*. xx. 68; P.R.O., C 2/Jas. I/B 30/56; C 142/201, no. 137; C 142/379, no. 15; REQ 2/260, no. 8; below, econ. hist. (mills).
98 P.R.O., C 2/Jas. I/B 20/4; C 2/Jas. I/H 35/45; *Visit. Salop. 1623*, i. 80.
99 N.L.W., Glansevern 9361; *T.S.A.S.* l. 183.

Misses Lloyd, sold the estate, or part of it, to the rector, R. N. Pemberton. In the 18th century the Brookes built a brick mansion, evidently near the old Bank House, which still stood in 1861. Both had gone by 1892 (when the building of the present Bank House began), the old house some years before.[1]

A Little Stretton estate comprised three ancient copyhold messuages (eventually two houses only): Bonham Norton's, John Thynne's of Deverill, and the Medlicotts (earlier Vernolds and Hayles),[2] or parts of their lands. It was acquired by the Jones family, whose estate was sold out of Chancery in 1724. The purchaser John Brewster, of Burton Court (in Eardisland, Herefs.), sold it in 1761 to Thomas More the younger (d. 1767), of Millichope, whose representatives sold it to Thomas Gibbon (d. 1789), of the Marsh (in Wistanstow), in 1781.[3] In 1796 Gibbon's son and namesake owned 97 a. extending along most of the northern boundary of Little Stretton township as far east as the lowest slopes of Ragleth hill; the chief house, presumably representing one or more of the old copyhold messuages, stood apart from the lands, in Little Stretton village, and was later known as the *MANOR HOUSE*.[4] The younger Thomas Gibbon's estate passed to his brother Edward, after whose death in 1855 it remained in the Gibbons' hands for a century or more.

In the 19th century the head of the Gibbon family was often an absentee, residing near Liverpool, but other members lived in the Manor House,[5] and the estate was enlarged to from time to time. Still 97 a. in 1838,[6] it was *c.* 332 a. by *c.* 1910.[7] To Manor House farm Edward Gibbon (d. 1897) added the small Malt House farm (formerly Thynne's messuage) bought from the Robinsons in 1872. His executors continued to buy land: notably, in 1902 and 1904, most of Old Hall farm (including, besides the Hall, the ancient Medlicott's and one of the Bright's messuages, both enfranchised in 1881) and in 1920 the 150-a. Brook farm (including the other Bright's messuage and Harrington's).[8] Those acquisitions were made during the time of Edward Gibbon's daughter-in-law, Mrs. A. E. Gibbon, who lived in the Manor House from 1896 until her death in 1932. In 1942 her sons sold *c.* 58 a. of the land bought in 1902 (which had enlarged Malt House farm), and the estate was presumably broken up *c.* 1958 when her younger son, E. L. L. Gibbon, left the Manor House.[9] At its greatest extent the Gibbons' Little Stretton estate included several ancient copyhold messuages: besides those mentioned above, Humphrey Child's[10] and Lloyd's or Pigge's.[11] The Gibbons were descended from Thomas Bridgman, a Little Stretton tanner[12] and owner of part of Lloyd's or Pigge's copyhold,[13] the chief messuage of which was added to the Gibbon estate in 1901.[14] There was more than one branch of Little Stretton Bridgmans, and in the earlier 18th century a John Bridgman had been tenant, under the copyhold owner, of the Hall farm,[15] most of which the Gibbons bought in 1902 and 1904.[16]

The Manor House has a cruck hall with inserted floor and cross wings at the north and south ends. The main front, to the west, is of five bays, with brick covering some of the framing; the two cross wings have restored jettied tiebeams and brackets; the central entrance has an 18th-century pilastered doorcase with moulded pediment. The north wing is 17th-century with later additions, some of the visible timbers covering earlier framing. A stone chimney projecting from the restored north wall has a tall brick stack. Inside there is a Jacobean staircase.[17]

ECONOMIC HISTORY. AGRICULTURE. By 1086 the 8-hide manor of Stretton had 3 ploughteams on the demesne, and 12 other teams belonged to 27 other men: 18 *villani*, 8 bordars, and a priest. There was room to employ 6 more teams. The teams were presumably distributed between the Strettons and perhaps Minton and even Whittingslow too, for no such information is recorded for those two manors, together rated as 4 hides; in 1086 both lay in Earl Roger's farm at Stretton and may earlier (by 1066) have been two of Stretton's four berewicks, the others likely to have been All and Little Stretton.[18] At Womerton (2½ hides) 2 *villani* had ½ ploughteam, but most of that manor was waste and there was land enough for 5 teams.[19] Botvyle was probably in the Domesday manor of Lydley.[20]

Church Stretton seems to have had three open fields: the largest was probably Ashbrook or Nashbrook field north-east of the town and east of the road to All Stretton;[21] Snatch field lay beneath Hazler hill;[22] and Overfield or the Upper field, probably the smallest, was above the town

1 W.S.L. 350/5/40, Ch. Stretton pp. 18–19; *T.S.A.S.* l. 183; drawing of ho. stuck to a screen in Loton Hall (Sir Michael Leighton is thanked for drawing attention to it); *The Strettons*, pl. 18; Cobbold, *Ch. Stretton Illustr.* (1908), 21.

2 For the eponyms of these messuages see e.g. S.R.O. 3933/1–4, etc.

3 S.R.O. 1643/1–2; 3933/82–140; cf. below, Munslow, manors (Millichope).

4 Cf. S.R.O. 3933/140, 282; O.S. Map 1/2,500, Salop. LVI. 13 (1883 edn.).

5 For the fam. see Burke, *Land. Gent.* (1952), 971–2, omitting the younger Thos. (fl. 1796–9), presumably d. s.p.

6 Tithe award.

7 S.R.O. 2079/LV. 12, 16, LVI. 9; 4044/40, pp. 1 nos. 708, 713, 716, 2 nos. 717, 719, 721–2, 4 no. 738, 6 nos. 757–9, 8 nos. 769–70, 773–7, 10 no. 792.

8 S.R.O. 1371/1–22; 1643/42, 70; 3933/42–56, 290–1.

9 *Shrews. Chron.* 26 Feb. 1932, p. 8; 27 Apr. 1962, p. 6; S.R.O. 888/1, p. 169; 949/1, p. 16 ; 1643/143 (abstr. of 1942 deed endorsed).

10 S.R.O. 1643/105.

11 Ibid. /118.

12 *S.P.R. Heref.* viii (2), 112; S.R.O. 3933/264.

13 S.R.O. 1643/53.

14 Ibid. /118–30.

15 S.R.O. 248/13, f. 12v.

16 Above, this para.

17 SA 10793.

18 *V.C.H. Salop.* i. 317, 344. Eyton's suggestion (xii. 28) that Botyvle was a berewick seems less likely.

19 *V.C.H. Salop.* i. 326.

20 Above, Cardington, manors (Lydley).

21 Cf. H.W.R.O.(H.), HD 2/14/17–18; tithe award *passim*, esp. fields 1037–8.

22 Cf. H.W.R.O.(H.), HD 2/14/17–18; tithe fields 1405, 1417, 1474.

to the west.[23] Open fields in Womerton probably lay north and east of the settlement, with Womerton wood and Lower wood beyond.[24] All Stretton had two or three open fields. North of the village lay what, in the mid 17th century, was called the field towards the Long Mynd;[25] north-east of the village, and as far east as the lowest slopes of Caer Caradoc field names indicate other areas of former open field.[26] Nearby, in Botvyle, field names and perhaps shapes suggest the existence of small open fields to the south.[27] Little Stretton's Ashletts or Ashley field and Raven field lay north and north-west of that village, separated by the stream draining down Ashes Hollow. West and south of the village were other open fields, perhaps fragmented by 1597 when several names are recorded: Callow field, perhaps containing Oxen field and Accurse (Skerrs?) field, to the west beneath Callow hill; Knappall (Napper) field south of the village; and farther south Hawarton field probably extending from the south end of Ragleth to the lane to Minton, and so crossed by the road to Marshbrook.[28] Minton's open fields seem to have lain south-east of the village (between the lanes to Marshbrook and Whittingslow), east of it, and farther away to the south-west either side of the lane to Hamperley and near that hamlet.[29]

The open fields were probably disappearing in the early 17th century when, for example, Church Stretton's Overfield or Upper field was absorbed into Bonham Norton's new rabbit warren.[30]

By far the greatest parts of the territories of the manors of Stretton (which absorbed Womerton after 1086) and Minton were occupied by the vast Long Mynd forest or common to the west.[31] Callow brook formed the boundary between the two manors and eventually separated their Long Mynd commons too.[32] Botvyle, along with other settlements in Lydley and Cardington manor, enjoyed common rights on Caer Caradoc hill, which was wooded perhaps as late as Charles I's reign.[33]

There were 5 'hays' in Stretton's woodland in 1086.[34] 'Stretton forest' and the Long Mynd were in the Long forest, whose keeper or forester, probably from Henry I's time, was the lord of Minton.[35] Stretton forest presumably comprised the demesne woods (perhaps identifiable with the Domesday hays) of the large royal manor of Stretton-en-le-Dale: on the east side of the dale Ragleth hill and presumably at least the western sides of Hazler and Helmeth hills;[36] in the north Womerton wood; and on the west the Long Mynd itself, where the wood of 'Netebech' (mentioned in 1235) probably lay, perhaps extending from Church Stretton to All Stretton and centred on the Batch north of Novers hill. When the Long forest was surveyed in 1235 the oak and underwood of the Long Mynd and Ragleth were well kept. In the northern part of 'Netebech', however, much oak had been felled for dread, it was alleged, of Welshmen, perhaps raiders lurking thereabouts: such perhaps had been the 57 whom Richard of Minton had killed in the dale two years before, receiving 57*s.* bounty for their heads; the Batch is overlooked by defensive enclosures at its head and on Novers hill. In Womerton wood much timber had formerly been felled for work on Shrewsbury and Stretton castles and for Roger Sprenchose's house at Longnor, but more recently the wood had been well kept.[37] Other gifts of timber suggest that the manor was well supplied: in 1245 the king gave three oaks from Stretton wood for an anchoress's house.[38] In the mid 13th century the lord of Minton, keeper of the forest, and the poor people of Stretton (as their only livelihood) kept goats on the manor's hills and in its woods, though generally goats were excluded when common woods were not plentiful.[39]

In the mid 13th century Stretton men with tenancies dating from King John's early years could take housebote and haybote under the oversight of the king's bailiff and had common for all their beasts at all seasons. Evidently free tenants could pannage their swine in the woods, giving the lord only the third best pig of the first seven and at no charge if they had fewer than seven. Copyholders had to give every tenth pig and 1*d.* for each pig over. Holders of more recent tenancies were at the king's will, as were tenants in avowry, who had no right to housebote and haybote save at the king's will.[40]

In the 13th century pressure on the king's forest and demesnes increased from the encroachments of landowners and others. The manor was amerced by the forest justices in 1209 for having openly made an assart. Haughmond abbey made a 2-a. purpresture *c.* 1235, and in 1250 the justice of the forest fined William of Church Stretton 10 marks for improving parts of the forest waste. Richard of Minton and Stephen of Hope had taken 50 a. of forest by 1255, and William English and the prior of Ratlinghope had made purprestures of ½ a. and 2 a. respectively. During the forest eyre of 1262 (when the regard was defined as that of the Long forest, Stretton dale, and the Long Mynd) continued waste of the king's wood of Stretton was alleged against the men of Stretton. Later the Templars were said to have taken 150 a. of land

23 Around the present Tiger Hall. Cf. H.W.R.O.(H.), HD 2/14/17; Longleat MSS., unbound, 4072, f. 120 (mentioning, besides Overfield, Ashbrook and 'Knatts' (Snatch?) fields).

24 Tithe fields 353–4, 470.

25 Longleat MSS., unbound, 4072, f. 120; tithe fields 664–6.

26 Tithe fields 713, 794, 891, 932. The 'acres' (tithe fields 795a, 796) look like strips, the Houghs north of them (fields 784–7, 789), with other adjacent fields (790–2), like consolidated and inclosed strips. Cf. H. D. G. Foxall, *Salop. Field-Names* (1980), 15.

27 Tithe fields 696 (Ridges), 709 (Houghs).

28 Field names of 1597 (*T.S.A.S.* li. 48–51) are recognizable, though changed, in some of those recorded in 1840 (tithe award).

29 S.R.O., incl. award C 3/43.

30 Longleat MSS., unbound, 4072, f. 120.

31 Fig. 9.

32 W.S.L. 350/5/40, Ch. Stretton p. 47.

33 Above, Cardington, econ. hist.

34 *V.C.H. Salop.* i. 317.

35 Above, manors (Minton).

36 Fig. 9.

37 Eyton, vi. 339; F. C. Suppe, *Military Institutions on the Welsh Marches: Salop. 1066–1300* (1994), 21, 109–11, 146; SA 244, 4046; *V.C.H. Salop.* i. 407.

38 *Close R.* 1242–7, 368.

39 *V.C.H. Salop.* iv. 61–2.

40 *Cal. Inq. Misc.* i, p. 43; *Close R.* 1247–51, 514.

and 40 a. of wood in Stretton-en-le-Dale, part of which the king recovered in 1292. Peter Corbet of Caus was prosecuted for taking 40 a. of wood and 40 a. of pasture in Stretton, and his defence, that the premises were in Wentnor,[41] suggests encroachment on even the highest parts of the Long Mynd, near the boundary between the manors.

Minton and the demesnes of Stretton-en-le-Dale were not disafforested in 1301, although parts of the Long Mynd in other manors apparently were.[42] In 1309 Ragleth, a surviving wood of the Long forest in Stretton, was valued at 6*s.* 8*d.* a year: there was no high timber and the underwood could not be valued because Ragleth was a game covert. Womerton wood then consisted of tall oaks but no underwood; it was common pasture, and pannage yielded 6*s.* 8*d.* a year. The common pasture of the Stretton hills extended *c.* 10 leagues in circumference but was not valued because it was open to the whole country.[43] The canons of Haughmond, for example, who had estates around the northern end of the Long Mynd, had enjoyed large horse-pasture rights on it since 1175.[44]

The valuation of 1309 preceded the grant of the reversion of the manor in fee to the earl of Arundel,[45] and from 1310 the woods and demesnes of Stretton were evidently the earl's private chase,[46] which probably included the two hays of Bushmoor and Hawkhurst (in Wistanstow parish), where attachments and wood sales were being made for him in 1417–18; the lord of Stretton seems to have sold Bushmoor by 1613 but he still had the wood of Hawkhurst in the 1630s.[47] The chase evidently included Minton, for as late as 1582 that vill swore in Stretton court that their lordship had no land outside the vill's ring hedge and claimed nothing of the soil of Minton wood and the Long Mynd except common of pasture for their beasts.[48] In 1392–3 there were wood sales (old wood and an oak) from Womerton wood and attachments there, and Richard Hughes (Euges) was fined 3*s.* 4*d.* for entering the wood and cutting down ivies and branches of trees, presumably for litter and browse in the winter. Stray cattle and sheep in Minton were seized for the lord of Stretton, and in 1393 Arundel wrote of his concern for the damage done to 'our forest of Longmynd' by wild and other beasts. Accordingly his steward John Burley proclaimed in the manor court that all the lord's tenants and all others who intercommoned within the forest should mark their animals before Whit Sunday. Every year in Whit week and at All Saints the lord's officers were to ride the forest and seize every unmarked beast for him, the sale prices to be recorded in the manor court roll.[49]

Just as the extensive commons of the Long Mynd were intercommoned by surrounding vills so too some of Stretton-en-le-Dales's tenants, and other Church Stretton parishioners also, had additional rights elsewhere: still in the 1530s All Stretton and Botvyle were allegedly among the many townships entitled to intercommon Hay wood (in Eaton-under-Heywood)[50] and, more generally, the manor of Stretton was then claiming (though unsuccessfully) wide and exclusive common rights extending north into Church Pulverbatch parish around the open fields of Cothercott and Wilderley; in the mid 17th century similar claims were made, with slightly more success, against Betchcott and Picklescott (in Smethcott parish).[51]

Stretton never had a resident lord before 1808,[52] and the manorial demesnes were possibly let from an early date: in the later 1250s the men of Stretton were farming them for £24 a year,[53] and after the manor passed to the earl of Arundel in 1310 it is unlikely that much, if any, of the demesne arable was cultivated directly.[54] The lord had a flock of 233 sheep in 1349 and one of 240 in 1351,[55] and the demesne meadows were probably kept in hand only while such flocks were run: the former lord's goods seized in April 1331 had included hay sold for 6*s.* 8*d.*[56] Thus the demesne flock had probably gone by May 1393 when six lots of demesne meadow were let for a year to eight men for rents totalling £3 19*s.* 10*d.*[57] The lord's meadows were still farmed out in 1418 and 1531–2.[58] In 1418 the lord profited from agistment in 'Poulez' meadow, presumably one of the manor's common meadows,[59] and agistment was an obvious means of developing his income from a manor with such extensive commons. Though tenants were probably never stinted, the manor court could amerce individuals, whether tenants or strangers, who overburdened the commons. In 1596, however, it was stated that the lord could let agistments for sheep on the Long Mynd at his pleasure.[60]

Demesne enterprises were not easily kept profitable. The extensive wet land around Brockhurst[61] was to an extent organized as fishponds; in the 13th century, when the manor was royal demesne, the sheriff had been responsible for fishing and restocking them.[62] The

41 Eyton, vi. 341; xii. 20, 23, 26–7.

42 *T.S.A.S.* lxxi. 26–8; *Cartulary of Shrews. Abbey*, ed. U. Rees (1975), ii, p. 247. Like Hawkhurst and Bushmoor they should be shown as continuing forest (though soon to become a private chase) on the map in *V.C.H. Salop.* iv. 45.

43 Eyton, xii. 26–7; cf. *Cal. Inq. Misc.* ii, pp. 13, 18.

44 *Cartulary of Haughmond Abbey*, ed. U. Rees (1985), p. 149.

45 Above, manors.

46 Above, n. 42.

47 Longleat MSS., unbound, 3804 note from ct. r. 3 Jan. 1616; 4072 notes from ct. r. 1633–6; 4080; below, this section (for the alienation of Bushmoor).

48 Longleat MSS., unbound, 4071 ct. 26 Apr. 1582. Later Callow brook divided the Long Mynd commons of Minton and Stretton-en-le-Dale: above, this section.

49 S.R.O. 125/1. For Burley cf. *V.C.H. Salop.* iii. 62–3, 235–6.

50 P.R.O., C 1/808, no. 47.

51 *V.C.H. Salop.* viii. 130–1, 148.

52 Above, manors.

53 Eyton, xii. 24.

54 *V.C.H. Salop.* iv. 103–4.

55 S.R.O. 552/1/1164; 1093, box 1, view of acct. 28 Sept. 1349.

56 P.R.O., E 142/68.

57 S.R.O. 125/1, m. 4.

58 Longleat MSS., unbound, 3804 notes from acct. r. 1531–2, 4080.

59 For refs. to common meadows cf. e.g. ibid. 4077 (resettlement of Medlicott fam. property excepting common meadows, etc.), 4080.

60 Ibid. 4071 customs; cf. 4072, f. 133.

61 For 'pools' and 'marshes', surrounded by meadows, see tithe fields 1399–1401, 1465–7, 1506–7, 1513, 1525, 1532, 1544, 1562–5, 1575–7, 1579–80, 1639–40.

62 *Close R.* 1237–42, 104; *V.C.H. Salop.* iv. 65.

waters also harboured swans: the earl of March's goods seized in the manor in 1331 included 5 swans,[63] and the earl of Arundel had 11 there in 1349 and 17 in 1351.[64] By the early 15th century, however, the ponds were shrinking, for in 1418–19 the tenants, provisioned with bread and ale by the reeve, assembled to search for fish in the parts that were drying out and moved them to parts still under water.[65] Parts of the ponds, or former ponds, were evidently let out at that time,[66] probably as meadow.[67] Two cockshoots of the lord's yielded nothing in 1418,[68] but 'fishing' still brought him £1 13*s.* 4*d.* in 1531–2.[69] The sale of some of the demesne pool land and marshy meadows near Brockhurst to Francis Brooke in 1563,[70] however, suggests that the pools had dried out by then. The lord let pastures in the demesne woods (e.g. Womerton and Ragleth) in the later Middle Ages, but income from the demesne woods could fall temporarily, as in 1418 when the lord received no pannage dues from Womerton because the mast had failed in 1417.[71] The lord's alienation (by 1613) of his demesne wood of Bushmoor,[72] however, meant a permanent loss of income. Bonham Norton seems to have acquired Bushmoor, probably soon after 1613, so it was probably still a useful source of timber then.[73]

At the 1255 inquest into regalian rights and foresters' doings Church Stretton was represented by its reeve,[74] whose office (mentioned in the 1230s) later evidence shows to have been served annually[75] by one of the principal tenants. The reeve, by the early 17th century known as the bailiff-reeve, was then accountable to the lord for manorial copyhold rents that were fixed and customary, set out in a rental supplied to him by the steward of the manor court and totalling £20 6*s.* 3½*d.* year after year,[76] about the same as the sums recorded in 14th-, 15th-, and 16th-century valors and rentals.[77] Each of 52 ancient tenements also owed 2*d.* a year 'green',[78] representing the old forest vert. By the early 17th century the bailiff-reeve's office seems to have fossilized somewhat, like the rents for which he was responsible but which an under-bailiff collected.[79] Unlike his medieval predecessors[80] the bailiff-reeve could pass no arrears to his successor, and the lord could repossess his tenement for failure to account.[81] This primitive administration suggests some circumscribing of the lord's position within the manor just as, from the later 1630s, reliance on a distinct, probably newer, official suggests a seignurial reaction: the 'bailiff of the liberties of the manor', more directly the lord's appointee,[82] served during pleasure[83] and was called the 'deputed bailiff' in 1566.[84] The bailiff of the liberties was responsible for such casual income as felons' goods,[85] heriots, and waifs and strays, but by the later 1630s he was additionally called 'bailiff of the improved rents of Sir Thomas Thynne'.[86]

In 1634 a manorial jury inquired into many matters including particulars and bounds of the lord's demesnes, the number of mills, and the proliferation of cottages. The commons and wastes and the nature of copyhold titles, however, formed the burden of the jurors' inquiry.[87] Whether Stretton copyholds were heritable or transferred at the lord's will had been in contention since the 16th century and from the 1630s the lord was at odds with a generation of copyholders.[88] In 1625–6 Heynes's tenement was rented to the lord's brother, John Thynne, for an improved rent of £14 (in place of the old copyhold rent of *c.* 5*s.*) for which, from 1633–4, the bailiff of the liberties was answerable.[89] By the early 1660s Elizabeth Hearne and other copyholders were at law with the lord, Sir Henry Frederick Thynne, and his bailiff Thomas Harris, and eventually the lord lost: Stretton copyholds were adjudged heritable in 1670 when a body of manorial custom was confirmed in Chancery;[90] disputes between lord and tenants over heriots, however, were then still unsettled.[91]

Alienations of demesne in the 1560s and 1570s by the last FitzAlan earl of Arundel[92] and the copyholders' victory in 1670 meant that thereafter the lord could not hope materially to increase his income by improving his rental. He was left with copyhold incidents (heriots and fare fees, for example), pannage and wood sales, sale of agistments on the common, and such casual income as was afforded by felons' goods, waifs

63 P.R.O., E 142/68.

64 S.R.O. 552/1/1164; 1093, box 1, view of acct. 28 Sept. 1349.

65 S.P.L., Deeds 7530.

66 The *gurgitus* then farmed out (Longleat MSS., unbound, 4080) probably indicates weir meadowland, increasing as the pools dried out.

67 Above, notes 61, 66.

68 Longleat MSS., unbound, 4080.

69 Ibid. 3804.

70 Ibid. 3625 purchase among the leases and sales noted on the last 4 folios; cf. ibid. 3813 (poss. incomplete 17th-cent. rental), giving details of the Brooke est.

71 Longleat MSS., unbound, 4080.

72 By 1613 Edw. and Ric. Lewes, gents., evidently held Bushmoor as free tenants in tail: ibid. 3625, notes of leases and sales on last 4 folios; 3804, list of Stretton tenants 9 Sept. 1613.

73 Ibid. 4072, f. 132v.

74 *Rot. Hund.* ii. 83.

75 Cf. S.P.L., Deeds 7528–30; Longleat MSS., unbound, 4080; below, local govt.

76 S.P.L., Deeds 6573, bailiff-reeves' accts. 1623–36 (that for 1628–9 printed in *T.S.A.S.* l. 180–2); Longleat MSS., unbound, 4071.

77 Ranging from £23 6*s.* 8*d.* (1350–1) to £20 12*s.* (1403–4) and £20 18*s.* 6*d.* (1590): S.R.O. 552/1/1164–5, 1201; Longleat MSS., unbound, 3805.

78 See e.g. *T.S.A.S.* l. 180.

79 Receiving 2*s.* 6*d.*, the bailiff-reeve's fee being 5*s.*: S.P.L., Deeds 6573, bailiff-reeve's acct. 1622–3.

80 e.g. Longleat MSS., unbound, 4080 (1417–18).

81 Ibid. 4071 customs.

82 S.P.L., Deeds 6573, accts. of bailiff of libs. 1625–6, 1630–6.

83 See e.g. ibid. 6166.

84 *T.S.A.S.* 3rd ser. iv. 121.

85 Evidently relying on estreats sent to the Exchequer for the green wax: cf. S.P.L., Deeds 6573, bailiff-reeve's acct. 1625–6. *T.S.A.S.* 3rd ser. iv. 116, misinterprets the ld.'s right to felons' goods (*temp.* Eliz. I) as the power to hang felons.

86 S.P.L., Deeds 6573; Longleat MSS., unbound, 3804 acct. 1636–8.

87 Longleat MSS., unbound, 4072, ff. 132–3.

88 *V.C.H. Salop.* iv. 137–8.

89 S.P.L., Deeds 6573, bailiff-reeves' accts. 1625–36, John Kyte's (1625–6) specifying the old rent. Thynne gave up the tenancy *c.* 1635.

90 Longleat MSS., unbound, 3803, 6169; *V.C.H. Salop.* iv. 138; Botfield, *Stemmata Botevilliana*, pp. lxxi–lxxvii.

91 Longleat MSS., unbound, 3804 ld.'s letter to Harris 10 June 1671.

92 e.g. in 1563 to Fra. Brooke (above, manors (Bank Ho.); above, this section), Mic. Oakes (P.R.O., C 142/633, no. 43), and others (Longleat MSS., unbound, 3625, notes of leases and sales on last 4 folios).

and strays, and perquisites of court. Even the market was not the lord's. After 1670 distinctions between the manor's copyholders and its ten or so free tenants were probably few, largely those associated with legal technicalities of inheritance and conveyancing. The enhanced security and capital value of copyhold estates produced a lively land market, and there were 87 landowners in the parish by 1792, 49 of them resident; in Church Stretton it was chiefly the smaller owners who resided.[93] Copyhold enfranchisement proceeded throughout the 19th century,[94] and the number of landowners increased greatly between *c.* 1840 and 1910, by the latter date including large numbers of householders living on their own property.[95] Except for the Long Mynd common, the land owned by the 19th- and 20th-century lords of the manor was not historic demesne but property acquired independently of the lordship.[96]

In 1280–1 a flock of 120 sheep belonging to Haughmond abbey was driven to the Long Mynd,[97] and sheep were always important in the local economy. Reference to the lord's flock in 1349 and 1351,[98] however, is not matched by much evidence concerning tenants' flocks. Sheep were occasionally recorded as strays.[99] The lord's right to sell sheep agistments, recorded in 1596,[1] indicates the Long Mynd's plentiful summer grazing, and tenants presumably took no less advantage of it than strangers did.

In the later 17th and early 18th century sheep and flock sizes were apparently increasing.[2] In the 1660s there were some very small flocks whose owners were probably not principally occupied in agriculture.[3] Although some leaving modest possessions[4] had sizeable flocks,[5] some apparently substantial farmers seem to have had no sheep: in March 1668 the goods of Randolph Jones, a Little Stretton yeoman, were valued at £243, but his livestock contributed little of the total value and included 4 cattle and *c.* 10 horses but no sheep. By the 1690s small flocks and substantial farmers without sheep seem to have been rarer. In the 1660s, moreover, men whose sheep were worth more than their cattle had few cattle, while a generation later men in the same situation seem to have had larger numbers of cattle but very many more sheep: flocks of 100 or more, and some of several hundred, were run.[6] Moses Eaton (d. 1702), a Church Stretton yeoman whose grandson and namesake (d. 1776) was to be described as 'gentleman' in 1757,[7] left a flock of 700 worth £140 and 51 cattle worth £98; he also had 13 horses and colts (£80), 18 swine (£6 10*s.*), and geese and poultry (£1).

Farming was mixed, if with a pastoral emphasis. Most substantial farmers kept livestock and grew corn and other grains: barley, oats, and peas were often specified, rye much more rarely. Hemp and flax were grown, and linen yarn and cloth, as well as wool, was stored, probably for domestic use. Pigs were widely kept but usually in small numbers that suggest domestic consumption, though William Tomkins (d. 1667), who had cattle but no sheep, may have kept pigs as part of a dairy enterprise, for he also left 100 cheeses. Some larger herds (e.g. 10, 12, and 18) were being kept by *c.* 1700, mainly by more substantial farmers;[8] they could perhaps afford to bring their stock to the attention of buyers attending the important swine fairs of north Shropshire.[9]

In the 1790s Edward Harries regarded the Long Mynd as among the principal 'extensive commons' of south-west Shropshire that were 'so elevated and so well calculated for sheep pastures, that perhaps they cannot be better applied'.[10] The Mynd gave its name to an indigenous breed, horned and black faced, nimble, hardy, and *c.* 10 lb. a quarter fatted; fleeces could yield ½ lb. of coarse wool and 2 lb. of finer wool.[11] Late 18th-century improved farming claimed good results from crossing Longmynds and Southdowns, but the Longmynd became extinct in 1926.[12] In 1838 the commons were said to feed large numbers of sheep each summer, and 7,825 had been sheared. In winter, however, the dale could not support so many, and they had to be sold or 'tacked out'.[13]

Cattle may have been turned out on the common, as the names 'Netebech' and Bullocks Moor may suggest, and one farmer was alleged in 1760 to have turned out large numbers of sheep, horses, and cattle in the course of a dispute with a neighbour.[14] For centuries, however, sheep shared the Long Mynd principally with horses, and after the 1540 Act[15] the lord's

93 S.P.L., MS. 6865, pp. 185–6.

94 S.R.O. 248/17–23; 3613/3; *20th Rep. Copyhold Com.* [4221], p. 30, H.C. (1862), xix; *21st Rep.* [6471], p. 28, H.C. (1863), xxviii.

95 Tithe award; S.R.O. 4044/39–40.

96 e.g. for the Benson est. *c.* 1840: tithe award.

97 *V.C.H. Salop.* iv. 59.

98 Above, this section.

99 e.g. S.R.O. 125/1, m. 3.

1 Above, this section.

2 This para. and the next based on H.W.R.O.(H.), Heref. dioc. rec., invs. of Thos. Reynolds, 1663; Ric. Howells, 1665; Ric. Jarrett, 1665; Wm. Cornes, 1666; Thos. Kyte, 1667; Wal. Brooke, 1668; Wm. Tomkins, 1667; Randolph Jones, 1668; Eleanor Cornes, 1668; Wm. Crippin, 1668; Ric. Crippin, 1668; Wm. Wilkes, 1668; John Kyte, 1669; John Woodhouse, 1669; Wm. Urwicke, 1670; Wm. Wood, 1670; Ric. Wilding, 1670; Thos. Powell, 1670; Ric. Bowdler, 1670; Thos. Botfield, 1671; Wm. Berry, 1689; John Poston, 1690; Edw. Kite, 1691; John Harrington, 1693; Thos. Minton, 1694; Evan Lloyd, 1697; John Oakes, 1699; Griffith Gough, 1699; John Kyte, 1700; Ben. Kite, 1700; Wm. Painter, 1701; Wm. Woodhouse, 1701; John Harrington, 1702; Ric. Poston, 1702; Moses Eaton, 1702; John Cross, 1702; Eliz. Paddy, 1702; Thos. Burges, 1703; and Ric. Minton, 1706.

3 Thos. Reynolds (4 sheep), Eleanor Cornes (10), Thos. Powell (15), corvisor, and Thos. Kyte (17), shoemaker.

4 Paucity of inventoried goods does not always indicate poverty: Eliz. Paddy's were worth £8 0*s.* 1*d.* in 1703, but she was the former Eliz. Hearne, gentleman's relict and Chancery plaintiff against the ld. Cf. above, this section; *S.P.R. Heref.* viii (2), pp. vii, 3–4, 11, 80.

5 Wm. Crippin and John Woodhouse (60 each).

6 e.g. Wm. Berry, John Poston, Evan Lloyd, Wm. Woodhouse, and John Harrington, yeoman and miller.

7 *S.P.R. Heref.* viii (2), pp. ix, 35, 61, 88, 111; S.R.O. 4323/Rg/1, bur. 8 July 1702, 5 Sept. 1776.

8 e.g. Griffith Gough, Moses Eaton, and John Cross.

9 *V.C.H. Salop.* iv. 162, 167.

10 J. Plymley, *Gen. View of Agric. of Salop.* (1803), 222. For Harries cf. *V.C.H. Salop.* iv. 226; viii. 274, 277–8.

11 Plymley, op. cit. 260.

12 *V.C.H. Salop.* iv. 197–8.

13 P.R.O., IR 18/8015.

14 S.R.O. 3614/9/4. The nos. of animals are incredibly high for one farmer.

15 32 Hen. VIII, c. 13: *V.C.H. Salop.* iv. 160.

officers took substandard horses and colts off the common.[16] By the later 17th century most husbandmen's livestock included horses, often one or two mares and colts, sometimes just an old nag. A few more substantial men[17] left horses numerous or valuable enough to suggest that they were breeding and rearing them. Moses Eaton had 13 horses and colts worth £80. His nearest rival was Griffith Gough (d. 1698)[18] who had 2 horses and 4 colts worth £15 10*s*. altogether, but the colts were probably on his Frodesley farm, for, like Eaton who had property in Hope Bowdler,[19] Gough's farming interests were not confined to one parish.

The importance of cattle, sheep, and horses at Stretton fairs[20] reflected a predominantly pastoral local economy. Fields tended to be small; so did farms, which averaged *c.* £40 a year in 1792. The most usual course of husbandry then was wheat, barley, oats, and fallow; some turnips were grown.[21] Arable farming became more profitable during the Napoleonic wars and was extended to parts of the Long Mynd that were then inclosed, sometimes temporarily.[22] The high grain prices of wartime,[23] however, did not last, and the common remained open, *c.* 1840 occupying *c.* 5,000 a. or virtually half of the parish. Less than a quarter of the rest of the parish was arable (1,227 a.), almost two thirds meadow or pasture (3,455 a.).[24] The arable lands, often on steep hillsides, were hard to cultivate: those facing north-west were very poor, ripening crops to perfection only in exceptional seasons. Over a shale rock the parish had two soil types. One, the 'sharp soil', was suited to barley and turnips, and the course there was turnips, barley, clover, and wheat; the other soil, cold poor clay, yielded only three white-straw crops in five years, the course being fallow, wheat, oats, clover, and wheat. In both courses the clover was half mown, half grazed. The only improvement detected was meadow irrigation; perhaps conversion of the old manorial fish pools to meadow in previous centuries had helped to establish the practice. Hauling manure up the steep hillsides and carrying produce home were difficult, and there were no signs of high farming or the necessary manuring.[25] Nevertheless in the mid 19th century the area of arable cultivation expanded slightly.[26]

From the mid 19th century arable enterprise declined sharply, and as it did so oats became the most important crop. In the 1960s barley replaced oats, though arable acreages were by then very small, having shrunk from 944 a. in 1867 to 893 a. in 1905 (when 3,411 a. were under permanent grass) and 382 a. by 1965. The number of pigs declined in relative importance, varying little from an average of just under 300. Cattle remained fairly constantly *c.* 9 per cent of livestock, a proportion which masks an increase in numbers from 425 in 1867 to 974 in 1938 and

TABLE V

CHURCH STRETTON: LAND USE, LIVESTOCK, AND CROPS

		1867	*1891*	*1938*	*1965*
Percentage of	grassland	73	84	96	93
	arable	27	16	4	7
Percentage of	cattle	8	10	9	9
	sheep	87	80	86	90
	horses	0	6	2	0
	pigs	5	4	3	1
Percentage of	wheat	35	24	14	12
	barley	31	33	0	63
	oats	32	41	80	12
	mixed corn & rye	2	1	6	1
Percentage of agricultural land growing roots and vegetables		8	5	1	2

Sources: P.R.O., MAF 68/143, no. 20; /1340, no. 6; /3880, Salop. nos. 217--18, 220; /4945, nos. 217--218, 220. The 1938 return has been brougth into conformity with the others by excluding the area of the Long Mynd registered common (cf. *V.C.H. Salop.* iv. 256) from the 'rough grazings'.

1,708 by 1957, with a slight drop by 1965 to 1,632. What kept the increasing numbers of cattle a steady percentage of livestock was the very great increase in sheep stocking levels in the 20th century: by 1938 there were 9,500 in place of the 19th-century average of just under 7,600, but there were 10,106 by 1945, 13,396 by 1957, and 16,410 by 1965.[27]

The great increase of sheep was made possible by the Long Mynd's unstinted[28] supply of common grazing, whose preservation was the responsibility of a committee appointed under an agreement concluded in 1869 between the lord of the manor and a commoners' association formed in 1868. Sheep and ponies were the objects of concern:[29] cattle and pigs were then animals of enclosed lands, but for centuries horses had shared the Long Mynd with sheep, and in the late 19th and early 20th century they did so in considerable numbers. A Long Mynd hill pony improvement association was formed in 1890, under the presidency of John Hill of Felhampton. Its work included the elimination of substandard stallions, and it held an annual show with prizes and Board of Agriculture pre-

16 S.P.L., Deeds 6573 accts. of bailiff of liberties 1630--6.
17 e.g. Randolph Jones, Ric. Wilding.
18 *S.P.R. Heref.* viii (2), 79.
19 H.W.R.O.(H.), Heref. dioc. rec., Eaton's will pr. 8 Sept. 1702.
20 Below, this section.
21 S.P.L., MS. 6865, p. 186.
22 Plymley, *Agric. of Salop.* 222. Ridge and furrow on Ch. Stretton golf course may be of this period.
23 *V.C.H. Salop.* iv. 168, 171–2.
24 Tithe award.
25 P.R.O., IR 18/8015.
26 Sources used for Table V.
27 Table V and sources there cited; Agric. Returns 1905; P.R.O., MAF 68/4139, nos. 217–18, 220; MAF 68/4583, nos. 217–18, 220.
28 *Shrews. Chron.* 21 June 1935, p. 8.
29 S.R.O. 1709, box 203, mins., agreement, etc.

miums.[30] The association necessarily worked closely with the Longmynd Hills Committee, formed after the 1908 Commons Act was adopted in 1913, to keep up the standard of rams and stallions on the common, which it drove regularly.[31] By the mid 1930s, however, interest in pony improvement was falling off, and after the Second World War the Long Mynd became in effect a sheep common.[32]

By 1990 there were thought to be *c.* 18,000 sheep on the Long Mynd as a whole, and in 1994 its owner, the National Trust, estimated that an average of 5½ ewes per hectare were grazing the Long Mynd as a whole 'most of the year'. Such stocking levels, a result of subsidy payments to hill farmers, were 5½ times the level that the common could sustain: combined with bracken spraying and taking feed out to sheep, overstocking was destroying the historic vegetation that had resulted from centuries of manorial management. In 1994, with the National Trust's concurrence, the Ministry of Agriculture and the commoners agreed to halve stocking levels over the next few years.[33]

About a twentieth of the parish (564 a.) was wooded *c.* 1840.[34] The largest surviving woods, then as a century and a half later, clothed the hillsides in the central part of the parish: from the Rectory grounds to Brockhurst, and, across the dale, Helmeth hill and the western slopes of Hazler and Ragleth hills. Elsewhere some of the more isolated woods, coppices, and plantations, especially in the north, disappeared as the wooded area shrank, a notable example being most of the 46 a. of plantations south-west of High Park House, which had gone by 1882.[35] Woods and plantations occupied 473 a. in 1905. There were more losses in the north in the 20th century, but the central part of the dale lost little woodland in the 20th century, though Helmeth (previously coppiced) seems to have been cleared during the First World War[36] and Hazler coppice had gone by 1925,[37] though the woodland later recovered.

MILLS. The mill in Stretton manor in 1086 and 1309[38] may have been 'Brooks mill', the later Carding Mill. In 1563 the lord sold to Francis Brooke a mill on Nash brook, which was said in 1885 to have been a demesne mill for upwards of four centuries; soon after buying it the Brookes rebuilt it.[39] Called Stretton's Mill in the 1680s and 1690s, it then worked in conjunction with a forge.[40] It was an old thatched building called Brooks mill *c.* 1812 and was then demolished; the new building, intended for a corn mill, was adapted to become the Carding Mill.[41]

Thomas Hawkes (d. 1704), of Botvyle, owned Church Stretton property on which, it was said in 1733, two fulling mills had once stood; the property, near Brook House, was still known as the walk mills in 1817.[42]

Richard Higgins owned a mill in All Stretton in 1599.[43] Neither its site, nor that of Borton's or Burton's mill, All Stretton, mentioned in 1663 and occupied by the prosperous yeoman farmer John Harrington (d. *c.* 1702),[44] is definitely known. One or both may have been the mill between All Stretton and Botvyle[45] eventually known as Dudgeley mill. Nevertheless there was possibly a mill near the village.[46]

In 1808 the only mill in All Stretton seems to have been that known by 1785 as Dagers mill, formerly William Lutwyche's.[47] About 1812 it was carding wool, a business then transferred to the rebuilt Brooks mill, Church Stretton. John Williams worked Dagers mill *c.* 1840 on the Wilding estate.[48] The mill became known as Dudgeley mill, and the Hince family, also farmers, worked it throughout the later 19th century and for a few years thereafter; in 1871 George Hiles was probably running the mill for Charles Hince of Dudgeley House.[49] By 1909 it was occupied by the Williamses[50] who bought it from Lady Beatrice Thynne[51] in 1920 and owned it until the mid 1960s. Bread flour was ground until 1917, thereafter barley and other meals and animal feed. New machinery was installed in 1941 and the mill was grinding *c.* 300 tons a year during the Second World War but only 150–200 tons by 1964, when, for 'a few years' past, it had been driving a dynamo. When sold in 1968 the mill property included *c.* 20 a. of pasture and pools, buildings for a small farm, and common

30 *Kelly's Dir. Salop.* (1895), 57; *Ch. Stretton Adv.* 25 Sept. 1913, p. 5; 26 Mar. (p. 5), 16 Apr. (p. 4) 1914; 10 Sept. 1925, p. 3; 29 Apr. 1926; 16 Feb. 1928, p. 3 (obit.).

31 *Ch. Stretton Adv.* 23 Jan. (p. 5), 28 Aug. (p. 5) 1913; 17 Jan. 1918, pp. 2–3; 29 Jan. 1925; 30 Dec. 1926, p. 2; 4 Feb. 1938, p. 3; *Shrews. Chron.* 28 June 1935, p. 11; S.R.O. 2563/66, rules, etc., 1928; DA 7/134/11.

32 See e.g. *Ch. Stretton Adv.* 10 May 1935, p. 1; Bilbey, *Ch. Stretton*, pl. 128.

33 J. S. Ellett III, 'Sheep Stocking Densities and Vegetation Change on the Long Mynd Common' (Univ. Coll., London, M.Sc. thesis, 1984); *Shrews. Chron.* 21 Sept. 1990, p. 9; Nat. Trust, *Mercia* newsletter, summer 1995, p. [3].

34 Para. based on tithe award; Agric. Returns 1905; O.S. Maps 6", Salop. XLVIII. SE., XLIX. SW., LV. SE., NE., LVI. SW., NW., LXIII. NE. (1903 edns.); 1/25,000, SO 49/59 (1981 edn.).

35 Cf. tithe field 233; O.S. Maps 1/2,500, Salop. XLVIII. 16 (1883 edn.), XLIX. 13 (1883 edn.), LV. 4 (1884 edn.).

36 Bilbey, *Ch. Stretton*, pl. 131.

37 O.S. Map 1/2,500, Salop. LVI. SW. (1928 edn.).

38 *V.C.H. Salop.* i. 317; Eyton, xii. 27.

39 P.R.O., C 142/201, no. 137; C 142/379, no. 15; REQ 2/260, no. 8; Longleat MSS., unbound, 3625, notes of leases and sales on last 4 folios; Windsor, *Handbk.* 79.

40 N.L.W., Glansevern 9361; Glam. R.O., Cardiff, CL/Deeds II, no. 6005.

41 Windsor, *Handbk.* 79; below, this section (manufactures and trade).

42 S.R.O. 248/11, 19 Oct. 1733; /17, pp. 208, 295; 809, box 14, map *c.*1817; *S.P.R. Heref.* viii (2), pp. vii, 81. Refs. provided by Mr. Romo.

43 Longleat MSS., unbound, 4142.

44 *S.P.R. Heref.* viii (2), 2; H.W.R.O.(H.), Heref. dioc. rec., prob. inv. of John Harrington 14 July 1702.

45 O.S. Nat. Grid SO 4665 9597.

46 Tithe fields 780, 803 (Mill yd.).

47 R. Baugh, *Map of Salop.* (1808); S.R.O. 4835/2. For the Lutwyches' est. see below, this section (mkts. and fairs).

48 Tithe fields 685–7; for the wool carding see below, this section (manufactures and trade).

49 *P.O. Dir. Salop.* (1863), 671; *Kelly's Dir. Salop.* (1905), 63; P.R.O., RG 10/2734, ff. 38v., 39v.

50 Rest of para. based on S.R.O. 4044/39, p. 68 nos. 553–4; *Kelly's Dir. Salop.* (1909), 67; (1941), 69; *Stretton Gaz.* Aug. 1964 (cutting in possession of Mrs. Carole Llewellyn, Dudgeley Mill, who is thanked for much help); *Shropshire Star*, 10 Feb. 1968, p. 13.

51 Cf. above, manors (Botvyle).

rights on the Long Mynd and the Cwms. It ceased working *c.* 1970.

In 1327 Lawrence the miller paid tax in Little Stretton.[52] Little Stretton mill yielded the lord 6*s.* 8*d.* in 1531–2[53] and was probably the mill of 'Lytyleston' which had not yielded the 6*s.* 8*d.* due in 1528–9 because it was untenanted and in need of rebuilding.[54] It is probably the one that stood in the village, on Ashes brook just above the Ludlow road; in 1838 it belonged to John Bridgman who had the adjacent tanyard.[55] Nevertheless a second mill site is known, that of Oakley or Hockley mill on the right bank of Callow brook, just above a waterfall on the Long Mynd common;[56] it is not known when it worked.

In 1392 Roger Salter held a mill in Minton manor.[57] It was probably the later Quembatch or Quenbatch mill, two corn mills under one roof near the Acton Scott boundary in 1597.[58] In 1723 Richard Leighton, of Leighton, leased it for 21 years, with land, to Robert Powell, a Whittingslow yeoman; then described as three corn or grist mills under one roof, it stood on Caudwell brook,[59] presumably an alternative name for Quinny brook.[60] In 1803 Robert Pemberton leased it for 19 years to Jasper Jones of Ryton after they had combined to build a new mill designed by the Shrewsbury ironfounder William Hazledine.[61] By 1840 James Hiles occupied it, with *c.* 10 a., under Pemberton's son, the rector.[62] From the mid 19th century until 1941 or later, known eventually as Queensbatch mill, it was worked by the Edwardses, tenants of W. F. Beddoes *c.* 1910.[63] The mill ceased working *c.* 1949.[64]

MARKET AND FAIRS. In 1214 the Crown advertised a Wednesday market and a one-day August fair in Stretton, and in 1252 a Tuesday market and a four-day fair 2–5 May.[65] In 1337 the earl of Arundel obtained a Thursday market and a three-day fair 13–15 September for his manor of Stretton,[66] but in the event no market seems to have been established, or else it fell into disuse.[67] The May and September fairs, however, evidently continued: in 1591 the lord leased their tolls for lives, and the lease was still in effect in 1626–7.[68]

In 1616, despite opposition from the borough of Bishop's Castle, Bonham Norton, owner of a considerable estate in and around the town,[69] was granted a Thursday market in Church Stretton and a court of pie powder.[70] The market became notable for corn and provisions.[71] A market house was built,[72] and the Nortons owned the market until Sir George Norton began to sell off his Shropshire estates.[73] In 1715 Edward and Sarah Appleyard bought it, and in 1721 it passed from them to Thomas Lutwyche of Lutwyche (in Rushbury). William Cheney Hart, of Hope Bowdler, bought it from the Lutwyche estate in 1787, and after his death (1819) it was evidently sold out of Chancery, probably to one Robinson *c.* 1830.[74]

The market was described as 'small' in 1803,[75] and in 1836 market and market house were bought from the Bensons of Lutwyche by trustees for the county's Southern parliamentary division; their purpose was to abolish the market tolls and to build a town hall (convenient also as a polling place for the division) on the site of the market house. The new building, designed in a 17th-century style by Edward Haycock, was put up in 1838–9.[76] About 1890 foodstuffs (including butcher's meat, fish, and poultry), haberdashery, clothing, and earthenware were sold from boards and trestles beneath the town hall and open-air standings around it; stallage produced about £30 a year but the town hall trustees charged no tolls.[77] The town hall became unsafe and was demolished in 1963, but an open-air market continued in the Square.[78]

The lord of the manor's May and September fairs were held on 14 May and 25 September from 1752–3,[79] and by 1803 two other fairs had been added 'by custom', on the third Thursday in March and the last Thursday in November. By 1888 fairs on the second Thursday in January and on 3 July had been added.[80] Thirty ewes were bought at Stretton for Willey farm in September 1748,[81] and in 1803 the September fair was said to be a 'very established mart' for sheep, as was the May fair for cows and calves.[82] The September fair remained important for store-sheep sales in the early 20th century,[83] and colts too were sold then. Stretton horse fairs

52 *T.S.A.S.* 2nd ser. iv. 303.
53 Longleat MSS., unbound, 3804, notes from Stretton acct. r. 1531–2.
54 S.R.O. 567, box 30, enrolled accts. of earl of Arundel's Salop. ministers 1528–9. 'Lytyleston' may be a mistake for Lt. Stretton in the fair copying of the Stretton acct.
55 Tithe field 1724; below, this section (manufactures and trade).
56 Name deduced from tithe fields 1770, 1770a, 1772, 1774; cf. O.S. Map 1/2,500, Salop. LV. 16 (1883 edn.).
57 S.R.O. 125/1, m. 1.
58 P.R.O., C 142/278, no. 194; *T.S.A.S.* li. 47.
59 S.R.O. 5724/1.
60 J. Rocque, *Map of Salop.* (1752).
61 S.R.O. 837/94.
62 Tithe fields 1848, 1918, 1922.
63 S. Bagshaw, *Dir. Salop.* (1851), 530; *Kelly's Dir. Salop.* (1885), 826; (1941), 69; S.R.O. 2079/ ; 4044/39, p. no.
64 S.R.O. 3756/147, no. 56.
65 Eyton, xii. 20; *Close R.* 1251–3, 321; S.R.O. 2833/2–3; *V.C.H. Salop.* iv. 68 (corr. below, Corrigenda), 70.
66 S.R.O. 2833/1; *Cal. Chart. R.* 1327–41, p. 421.
67 Above, manors (the Hall).
68 S.P.L., Deeds 6573, bailiff-reeve's acct. 1626–7.
69 Above, manors (the Hall).
70 P.R.O., C 66/2059, no. 6; S.R.O. 2956/1; *Cal. S.P. Dom.* 1603–10, 570; Hist. MSS. Com. 13, *10th Rep. IV, Bp.'s Castle*, 401, 406.
71 *V.C.H. Salop.* iv. 164.
72 See pl. 39 in this vol. Cf. Northants. R.O., Hartshorne albums, xxii, p. 39; xxv, p. 7; T. F. Dukes, *Antiquities of Salop.* (1844), 233.
73 W.S.L. 350/5/40, Ch. Stretton pp. 12, 17; above, manors (the Hall).
74 S.R.O. 1642, box 27, mkt. hall papers; W.S.L. 350/5/40, Ch. Stretton pp. 17, 53; P.R.O., CP 25/2/1053/2 Geo. I Trin. [no. 16]; CP 25/2/1054/7 Geo. I East. [no. 2].
75 Plymley, *Agric. of Salop.* 335.
76 S.R.O. 1642, box 27, mkt. hall papers and deed of 1836; Pevsner, *Salop.* 102. Cf. *V.C.H. Salop.* iii. 314–15.
77 *Rep. R. Com. Mkt. Rights*, xiii (2) [C. 6268–VIa], pp. 424–6, 428, 430, H.C. (1890–1), xl.
78 Bilbey, *Ch. Stretton*, pls. 39, 67, 72.
79 Under 24 Geo. II, c. 23: Plymley, *Agric. of Salop.* 338.
80 Ibid.; *Rep. R. Com. Mkt. Rights*, i [C.5550], pp. 197–8, H.C. (1888), liii.
81 Plymley, op. cit. 338; S.R.O. 1224, box 171, acct. of stock of Willey fm. 11 Nov. 1748, f. 3.
82 Plymley, op. cit. 338.
83 *V.C.H. Salop.* iv. 247.

remained important in the early 20th century, but in the mid 20th century the livestock fairs dwindled away, though sheep sales were long held in the Lion field, Church Stretton, and a field in Little Stretton.[84]

MANUFACTURES AND TRADE. In 1626 the lord of Stretton's bailiff was paid £5 'to search for coals within this lordship',[85] and the name Colliersley (on the Woolstaston boundary)[86] may suggest a location for his efforts. Field names[87] and an abandoned shaft (date unknown) north of Botvyle suggest the site of explorations in Lydley and Cardington manor where the Upper Coal Measures' Coed-yr-Allt beds have been found at *c.* 21 m.[88] in Coalpit piece.[89] At the south end of the parish, in Minton manor, there were 'old trial shafts' in White Birches wood, which may have been sunk for coal in ignorance of local geology.[90]

Stone, brick clay, and gravel were extracted and there are references to stone cutters in the early 18th century[91] and masons in the 19th.[92]

In 1901 the Ordnance Survey plotted twenty-odd quarries in the parish, not all that there were. Most were small and probably then disused. The quarry near the way out of Minton village to the Long Mynd common is one of those whose purpose is no longer obvious. About a third of the quarries were near the main settlements, and some of them evidently provided rubble for nearby buildings, such as the diorite dug for the old Tiger Hall, Church Stretton, or the stone for All Stretton church (opened 1902). A string of quarries runs south from Dudgeley House (north of All Stretton) to the entrance to Carding Mill valley (in Church Stretton) and coincides with the outcrop of Buxton Rock that bore the name of the quarry in All Stretton. Half of the quarries near the main settlements were near Church Stretton.[93] There was, however, no large source of stone suitable for modern building, and the railway station (opened 1852) was built of Soudley sandstone.[94]

Some of the remoter quarries were evidently sources of limestone to be burnt for agricultural lime: such presumably was Botvyle quarry in the Aymestry limestone, and there seem to have been similar smaller workings three fields to the south.[95] Other quarries away from the settlements yielded road stone, for example the diggings into the Helmeth Grits at the eastern end of Hazler Road and the south-western end of Ragleth hill. Road metal was presumably also got, probably for local use only, from a dozen or so gravel pits, mainly around Ragleth and Hazler hills and in the north-eastern corner of the parish; probably other pits survived as ponds.[96]

In the 1890s road metal was got from a quarry west of the brickworks at Brockhurst. A little farther south one of the largest gravel pits in the parish apparently obliterated an early brickworks,[97] and at some time one of the old coalpit fields north of Botvyle is said to have been worked as a brickyard.[98] Claypits presumably yielded marl or brick clay,[99] but brickmaking was probably intermittent, fluctuating with a demand that was purely local: the three main brickyards were very close to the railway line but not connected to it. Near Dagers mill a field called Brick yard in 1838 was again part of a 4½-a. brickyard, occupied by Church Stretton Brick & Tile Co., *c.* 1910.[1] Bricks were being made at Minton in 1856 and near Little Stretton by 1879 and still in 1885;[2] those enterprises (latterly Marshbrook Brick Works) probably worked the same site, a large claypit in a field east of Minton known in 1838 as Quarry leasow.[3] The Church Stretton Terra Cotta Works established by 1891 was presumably that near Brockhurst,[4] but it had probably closed by 1900.

Malting was established in Stretton by 1587 when a malthouse was built near Lake Lane's corner with the Shrewsbury road.[5] In 1621, when Shrewsbury corporation may have been trying to control the grain market, that town's great brewer William Rowley sent his malt mill to Stretton 'upon wains'.[6] Malting continued, though, as a small-scale subsidiary occupation, probably under-recorded: William Corfield (d. 1751) and his son Richard (fl. 1762) were maltsters.[7] In the mid and later 19th century some

84 Ibid. pl. facing p. 252; *Kelly's Dir. Salop.* (1900), 8, 58–9; Bilbey, *Ch. Stretton*, intro.; *Stretton Focus*, July 1986, p. 9.

85 S.P.L., Deeds 6573, bailiff-reeve's acct. 1625–6.

86 Around O.S. Nat. Grid SO 452 974: tithe fields 188, 263, 345–7. Name first recorded 1743: *V.C.H. Salop.* viii. 172.

87 Coalpit piece and meadow, Gin leasow: tithe fields 546–8.

88 Evidently before the 1838 record of field names.

89 Geol Surv. Map 1/25,000, *Ch. Stretton* (O.S. for Inst. Geol. Sciences, 1968); Greig, *Geol. of Country around Ch. Stretton*, 257–8. Cf. S.R.O. 3651, bdle. 20, map of Lydley and Cardington man.

90 O.S. Map 1/2,500, Salop. LXIII. 4 (1903 edn.); Geol. Surv. Map 1/25,000, *Craven Arms* (O.S. for Inst. Geol. Sciences, 1969); cf. Greig, op. cit. 145 (fig. 13), 150, 173.

91 *S.P.R. Heref.* viii (2), p. ix.

92 Scattered refs. in directories and census enumerators' bks.; cf. Bilbey, *Ch. Stretton*, intro.

93 O.S. Maps 1/2,500, Salop. XLVIII. 7, 11–12, 15–16; XLIX. 13–14; LV. 4, 7–8, 11–12, 15–16; LVI. 1–2, 5–6, 9–10, 13; LXIII. 4; LXIV. 1 (1902–3 edns.); Geol. Surv. Map 1/25,000, *Ch. Stretton* (1968); tithe field 754 (Buckstone); Campbell-Hyslop and Cobbold, *Ch. Stretton*, i. 80–1, 110, 112; iii. 97. In his geol. survey Cobbold mentions quarries not on the O.S. maps.

94 Bilbey, *Ch. Stretton*, pl. 118; cf. above, Hope Bowdler, econ. hist.

95 Campbell-Hyslop and Cobbold, op. cit. 43–4; tithe fields 698, 705 (Limekiln leasows).

96 Campbell-Hyslop and Cobbold, op. cit. i. 20, 82–3; O.S. Maps as cited above.

97 Campbell-Hyslop and Cobbold, op. cit. i. 111–12; tithe field 1541 (Brick-kiln leasow).

98 Campbell-Hyslop and Cobbold, op. cit. i. 44.

99 O.S. Maps as cited above.

1 Tithe field 690; S.R.O. 2079/LVI. 2, no. 518; 4044/39, p. 63 no. 518.

2 *P.O. Dir. Salop.* (1856), 170; (1879), 475; *Kelly's Dir. Salop.* (1885), 1031.

3 Tithe field 1813; O.S. Map 1/2,500, Salop. LV. 10 (1883 edn.).

4 *Kelly's Dir. Salop.* (1891), 517 (only mention); O.S. Map 1/2,500, Salop. LVI. 9 (1903 edn.); Campbell-Hyslop and Cobbold, *Ch. Stretton*, i. 111–12.

5 Bilbey, *Ch. Stretton*, intro. and pl. 91.

6 S.R.O., q. sess. rec., parcel 254, badgers', drovers', and ale-sellers' licensing bk. Epiph. 18 Jas. I. For Rowley cf. *V.C.H. Salop.* iv. 167; *Travels by Sir W. Brereton* (Chetham Soc. i), 186.

7 S.R.O. 248/13, ff. 18v.–19; Corfield, *The Corfields* 59, 62; *S.P.R. Heref.* viii (2), 145. Ric. is presumably one of two namesakes d. 1770 and 1787: cf. ibid. 155, 180.

farmers and publicans were maltsters, and in the 1850s John Lewis combined malting with plumbing, painting, and glazing. In the early and mid 19th century there were often half a dozen or more maltsters in the town and as many more in the rest of the parish. Soon after 1851 Robert McCartney, a travelling tea dealer in Stretton, became a hop merchant and maltster. By 1900 there was still a farmer-maltster in Little Stretton, but Robert McCartney & Sons (also hop and seed merchants),[8] who built the large malthouse, warehouse, and shop in Station Road *c.* 1904,[9] ran Stretton's only big 20th-century malting business until it closed *c.* 1940.[10]

There were fulling mills in Stretton in the late 17th century,[11] and in the early 18th century local textile trades included weaving and tailoring; the leather trades comprised tanning, shoemaking, and gloving; and there were blacksmiths, carpenters, and coopers.[12]

Weaving was locally established by 1570 when Thomas Hayles, a Little Stretton weaver, bought land in Cardington.[13] In 1631 William Pinches of All Stretton left his looms to his cousin William Corfield,[14] and weaving still continued in the early 19th century,[15] when the town's 'poor' were said to be 'chiefly employed in making a coarse linen cloth for packing hops and wool'.[16] By then the rebuilding of Brooks corn mill (*c.* 1812)[17] allowed the transfer of wool carding from Dagers mill in All Stretton to the new building, which became known as the Carding Mill.[18] The first tenant Ashworth Pilkington ('Pilkington & Co.') soon left, so that the owner, G. W. Marsh, rector of Hope Bowdler, had to work the mill for a time on his own account. The mill stimulated domestic spinning within the pull of the town's market and may explain the existence of a busy wool fair in the early 19th century. George Corfield bought the mill *c.* 1824, enlarged it, and took on more hands, but his business failed at his death in 1836. His successor, Evans, made coarse flannels for two or three years but then died, leaving a widow who soon became insolvent. Edward Wilding, wool manufacturer, was probably the employer of 12 hands in 1841. About 1850 Duppa, Banks & Co. took a lease of the mill and engaged hands for flannel and cloth manufacture: 19 (9 of them from the Welsh flannel centre of Newtown) were employed in 1851, but never so many thereafter. The firm gave up, and in 1854 the tenancy was acquired by James Williams, Corfield's former manager. Williams died in 1866 and until *c.* 1900 his son Richard continued to manufacture tweed cloth, blankets, rugs, and woollen yarn in a small way, offering farmers an exchange of cloth for wool. In the mid 1920s Harry Page, in Churchway, began to work a hand loom to revive the former renown of Church Stretton homespun, though producing a lighter cloth than the old Carding Mill tweed. He was still at work in 1937.[19]

The leather trades were represented by such occupations as currier, skinner, saddler, and harness maker in the 1840s; there was a dealer in skins in All Stretton in 1841.[20] In 1851 the Beddoes family, farmers and fellmongers, had a skinner's yard near the town crossroads, but by 1861 they had moved their business out of the town.[21] In 1838 John Bridgman owned a tanyard in Little Stretton adjoining his mill building on Ashes brook; William Simpson was running the yard by 1851 and did so until the 1870s.[22]

As manufactures dwindled the range of shops and services expanded to serve the needs of a town increasingly intent on attracting visitors and new residents. Between 1841 and 1895[23] trades such as brickmaker, cooper, ropemaker, sawyer, and tanner ceased, and only one wheelwright remained (at Little Stretton). Blacksmiths, saddlers, shoemakers, and tailors survived from the old crafts by adapting to the town's new role alongside new businesses and shops serving middle-class needs, from hairdressing to laundry, livery and jobmastering, and a wider range of retailing, including dealing in wines and provisions. To the medical profession, represented in Stretton since the earlier 18th century,[24] were added bankers and solicitors. The town's 20th-century growth, though intermittent, also favoured the building trade.[25]

Three quarters of the 20th century were to pass before plans to bring industry to the town again bore fruit. In 1976–7 the railway station yard became an industrial estate[26] and the land between the railway line and the Shrewsbury–Ludlow road was brought into use. R. A. Swain, haulage contractor by the early 1960s, had premises there, but the business outgrew them, and in the mid 1980s Swains of Stretton Ltd., international hauliers, moved to Stafford Park, Telford.[27] Light industry was encouraged and in the 1990s the industrial area was expanded south with speculative factories being erected on the Mynd industrial estate by English Partnerships.

8 S. Bagshaw, *Dir. Salop.* (1851), 529; Trinder, *Ind. Arch. Salop.* 47; Windsor, *Handbk.* 88; *P.O. Dir. Salop.* (1856–79); *Kelly's Dir. Salop.* 1885–1900.

9 Cf. O.S. Map 1/2,500, Salop. LVI. 9 (1903 edn.); S.R.O. 2079/LVI. 9; S.R.O., DA 7/531/1, 1903 rate p. 9 no. 89, 1904 rate p. 21 no. 247; Bilbey, *Ch. Stretton*, pl. 115.

10 *Kelly's Dir. Salop.* (1937), 68 (last mention).

11 Above, this section (mills).

12 *S.P.R. Heref.* viii (2), p. ix.

13 S.R.O. 567, box 10, deed 4 Jan. 1570.

14 J. H. Pinches, *Fam. of Pinches* (1981), 15, 45.

15 A. Dakers, *Fordritishope* (1986), 21.

16 G. A. Cooke, *Topog. and Statistical Descr. of Salop.* (2nd edn. n.d.), 175.

17 Above, this section (mills).

18 Rest of para. based on S. Bagshaw, *Dir. Salop.* (1851), 529; Windsor, *Handbk.* 74–5, 79–82; *Salop. N. & Q.* 3rd ser. iv. 71–2; J. J. Corfield, *The Corfields* (Rosanna, 1993), 61–2; P.R.O., HO 107/913/22, ff. 19r.–v., 24; HO 107/1984, ff. 176v.–177; Trinder, *Ind. Arch. Salop.* 136–7.

19 *Kelly's Dir. Salop.* (1926), 68; (1937), 68.

20 For All Stretton trades see P.R.O., HO 107/913/22, ff. 37v. sqq.

21 *Stretton Focus*, Aug. 1982, p. 12; May 1983, p. 10; cf. *Kelly's Dir. Salop.* (1885), 826.

22 Tithe field 1697; S. Bagshaw, *Dir. Salop.* (1851), 530; *P.O. Dir. Salop.* (1870), 37 (last mention).

23 Rest of para. based on P.R.O., HO 107/913/22, ff. 14 sqq.; HO 107/1984, ff. 173 sqq.; *Kelly's Dir. Salop.* (1895–1941).

24 W.S.L. 350/5/40, Ch. Stretton p. 53; *T.S.A.S.* 4th ser. vii. 215.

25 Cf. *Stretton Focus*, Sept. 1974, p. 7.

26 Ibid. Feb. 1992, p. 16.

27 G.P.O. *Telephone Dir.* (Aug. 1963), p. 2162; cf. Brit. Telecom, *Phone Bk.* (sectn. 303), July 1983 (p. 468), Dec. 1986 (p. 705); local inf.

The old Stretton Laundry site, further south on the main road, also attracted light industry. There was little industry in the villages, though after the Second World War Wetcowood Ltd. established a saw mill south of Little Stretton village; after the mill closed the site ceased to be industrial: a chicken hatchery was established there for a time, but the area was developed as housing in the earlier 1960s.[28]

The purity of Long Mynd spring water was proclaimed as Stretton aspired to become a health resort and residential area, and springs were first exploited in 1881 when Church Stretton Aerated Water Co. opened in part of the Carding Mill, which had been advertised in 1870 as suitable for a hydropathic establishment or brewery. Two years later Stretton Hills Mineral Water Co. opened a factory at Cwm Dale in Shrewsbury Road. The Carding Mill firm had ceased by 1906. The Shrewsbury Road factory, however, continued: nicknamed the 'Pop Works', it was later taken over by Jewsbury & Brown. Schweppes owned the factory in the 1950s but used it merely as a distribution centre. It was later bought by Wells Drinks, of Tenbury Wells, who bottle the water, renowned for its purity and low mineral content, for sale throughout the country.[29] Proposals (eventually fruitless) to develop a spa in the town *c.* 1908 had depended on the piping of water from a spring at Wentnor on the western side of the Long Mynd.[30]

By 1841 a dozen people of independent means were living in the town,[31] forerunners both of those who, in the later 19th century, sought recreation and health in Stretton[32] and also of those who, at a later period, went to live there in retirement. From the mid 19th century private middle-class lunatic asylums catered for a particular type of the former; in the later 20th century the establishment of homes for old people and others provided retreats which paralleled the independent retirement of many householders on the new, predominantly bungalow, estates built mainly around the town.[33] Both developments contributed to the growth of the town and its peculiar economy.

Dr. S. G. Bakewell, a Staffordshire man, established two lunatic asylums in the parish in the 1850s. In 1851 the Grove, All Stretton, was licensed for the reception of 10 female patients[34] and later for 12 (1855) and 14 (1856); after Bakewell's death in 1865 his widow Harriet ran the asylum, whose licensed number was increased to 25 in 1868 and 45 in 1871.[35] Her niece married Dr. J. R. McLintock (also medical officer of Stretton House asylum until his death in 1883), and their family (eventually spelling their name McClintock) owned and ran the Grove for a hundred years until it closed and was demolished in 1969.[36] Bakewell's other asylum, established in 1854, was the Retreat, or Stretton House asylum, for men; built where the Talbot inn had stood, at the south end of the town, it was first licensed for 16 patients, later for 18 (1856).[37] On Bakewell's death William Hyslop bought it, and in 1868 it was licensed for 28 patients. Hyslop enlarged and reconstructed it and added new 'gothic' buildings (designed by Thomas Tisdale) in 1869, thus allowing the reception of 40. Patients were classified socially as well as clinically: in addition to cricket, gardening, billiards, and music the richer patients could ride or enjoy 'carriage exercise'. The grounds, like those of the Bakewells' earlier establishments in Staffordshire, had always been spacious, and the asylum was supplied from its garden and model farm and in the mid 1930s continued to provide 'the comforts of a first-class home'.[38] It closed, evidently in 1948 when it was divided into flats.[39]

Stretton's reputation as a health resort in a quiet corner of England and its Edwardian inheritance of large houses attracted convalescent and other homes and, particularly during the world wars, hospitals. In the First World War Church Stretton had housed Belgian refugees,[40] and Essex House had been a V.A.D. hospital.[41] In the 1930s, and perhaps for longer, the Odd Fellows Friendly Society had Holmwood as a convalescent home.[42] On the outbreak of the Second World War St. Dunstan's, the charity for rehabilitating men and women blinded on war service, was evacuated to the town from the south coast and remained until 1946. Hotels and other premises were requisitioned, a hospital was established in Tiger Hall, and workshop huts were built in the town and in the grounds of the Longmynd Hotel and Brockhurst. Staff and V.A.D. houses too were needed, and the town 'had a marvellous talent for producing houses and sites'.[43] Later the county council used Holmwood as an old people's home[44] and (in 1977) built May Fair House, with 50 places for old people.[45] In the 1980s, when the view prevailed that private and voluntary homes could offer more choice,[46] seven registered homes in the Strettons afforded 97 places, 9 of them (in Arden House, an Edwardian villa) for mentally ill people; in

[28] Inf. from Mrs. J. G. Tyldesley; above, growth of settlement.

[29] *V.C.H. Salop.* i. 421; *Shropshire Star*, 31 Oct. 1978; Nat. Trust, *Carding Mill Valley* (1981); Bilbey, *Ch. Stretton*, pls. 89–90; *S. Salop. Jnl.* 1 Aug. 1986, p. 7; *Stretton Focus*, Aug. 1983, p. 11; Sept. 1983, p. 9; Aug. 1991, p. 14.

[30] Above, growth of settlement.

[31] P.R.O., HO 107/913/22, ff. 16v.–30v.

[32] Below, this section (the resort).

[33] Above, growth of settlement.

[34] *Orders of Q. Sess.* iv, pp. xx, 87; cf. W. Ll. Parry-Jones, *The Trade in Lunacy* (1972), 49, 77, 93–4, 101, 107; P.R.O., RG 9/1844, f. 9v.; *Stretton Focus*, Jan. 1985, p. 9.

[35] *Orders of Q. Sess.* iv. 104, 112, 181, 195.

[36] Whately, *Old Hos. in All Stretton*, i. 4; *Eddowes's Jnl.* 14 Apr. 1869 [p. 5]; *Shrews. Jnl.* 28 Mar. 1883, p. 7; below.

[37] *Orders of Q. Sess.* iv, pp. xx, 107, 113; *Stretton Focus*, Nov. 1981, p. 8.

[38] *Eddowes's Jnl.* 14 Apr. 1869, [p. 5]; 7 Sept. 1870, p. 8; *Orders of Q. Sess.* iv. 181; Whately, op. cit. i. 4; S.R.O. 3209/175.

[39] S.R.O., DA 7/516/24, pp. 2, 67–8.

[40] Bilbey, *Ch. Stretton*, pl. 132.

[41] *Red Cross and Voluntary Aid in Salop. 1915–17* (Shrews. 1918), 88–9, 91.

[42] *Kelly's Dir. Salop.* (1929), 68; (1941), 67.

[43] Bilbey, *Ch. Stretton*, pls. 135–9; Ld. Fraser of Lonsdale, *My Story of St. Dunstan's* (1961), esp. cap. 14; *St. Dunstan's: a story of accomplishment* [*c.* 1975], 12–16 (copy in S.P.L.).

[44] Inf. from S.C.C.

[45] *S.C.C. Mins.* 1976–7, 74, 145, 216.

[46] D. C. Cox, *Salop. County Council: A Centenary Hist.* (Shrews. 1989), 67.

Shropshire only Shrewsbury had more.[47] Private residential homes continued to increase (*c.* 1990 Sandford House hotel became a residential nursing home),[48] and the county council converted Holmwood to a children's home *c.* 1987 and closed May Fair House in the 1990s.[49]

THE RESORT. The railway's arrival in 1852[50] gave Shropshire's smallest market town[51] the opportunity to develop into the county's principal resort by advertising the beauty of its scenery. By 1860 the railway company was alerting passengers to the attractions of a country already accessible by half a dozen well conceived excursions from the town and said to be 'far superior' to that which had given Malvern 'deserved celebrity'.[52]

The Hotel superseded the Crown in 1865,[53] but change came slowly. G. R. Windsor's arrival in the town gave something of an impetus. In 1879 Windsor, by then postmaster,[54] was probably behind a curious advertisement which proclaimed that Stretton's climatic 'salubrity' and atmospheric 'purity' were demonstrated by the annual returns of its lunatic asylums (showing high percentages of recoveries) and by the churchyard gravestones recording the inhabitants' 'patriarchal' ages. Nevertheless the claim that Stretton was 'becoming more and more the resort of the denizens of . . . the large English Towns' seems to have been wishful thinking: the advertisement admitted that there were few places to stay apart from the modern Hotel and 'wayside-like Inns', that capital and enterprise were much wanted to supply the deficit of 'suitable up-putting', and that the town's destiny as 'a popular Summer Retreat' still lay in the future.[55]

In 1881 Windsor, who was also printer, stationer, and bookseller, launched a newspaper and *Visitors' List* intended for the Stretton 'season',[56] but it did not appear again. In 1885 he published *Laura Heathjohn*,[57] a 'sensational local descriptive novel'.[58] It was not the first such that had appeared, for the area had an enduring appeal to artistic and literary people in the later 19th and earlier 20th century. From *c.* 1862 to 1883 the artist John Halphed Smith (1830–96) lived in All Stretton,[59] where his wife had inherited property including a cottage then or later called Cloverley; it was occupied by her sister Sarah Smith, the writer 'Hesba Stretton', who spent holidays there until late in life; All Stretton apparently provides the background of her stories *Fern's Hollow* (1864) and *The Children of Cloverley* (1865).[60] In 1869 Henry Kingsley's novel *Stretton* appeared,[61] the work of a writer with a talent for landscape description.[62] Rosa Mackenzie Kettle's 1882 novel *The Carding-Mill Valley* was subtitled *A Romance of the Shropshire Highlands*,[63] using a phrase that was later to be hard worked in publicity for the area.[64] The Kailyard writer 'Ian Maclaren'[65] is said to have written his most popular book, *Beside the Bonnie Brier Bush* (1894), while staying at the Tan House, Little Stretton;[66] and Little Stretton was the scene of a story ('At the Green Dragon') in Beatrice Harraden's *In Varying Moods* (1894).[67] Mary Webb spent her honeymoon in Little Stretton in 1912, and much of the atmosphere of her first novel, *The Golden Arrow* (1916), was contributed by the landscape of the Long Mynd, disguised, inappropriately, as 'Wilderhope'.[68]

In 1885, the year that his novel appeared, G. R. Windsor brought out *A Handbook to the Capabilities, Attractions, Beauties, and Scenery of Church Stretton.*[69] Not the first local guide,[70] it was certainly the most literary, but between the verses and local stories the *Handbook* makes it clear that few houses had yet been built specially for letting. Most accommodation apart from that in the inns and the Hotel was provided by householders letting their best rooms during the season; farmhouses let rooms outside the town and in All Stretton and Little Stretton villages. Such lodgings varied greatly in size and could amount to apartments for families or large parties. Visitors' facilities were becoming available: David Hyslop's posting establishment with horses and conveyances of all sorts for hire; Mrs. James's temperance refreshment rooms, where cyclists were 'specially attended to'; and in Carding Mill valley, 'the most Romantic Valley of the Long Mynd', tea gardens and refreshment rooms.[71]

Boarding houses apparently began to trade in the 1890s, though Mrs. H. Salt's Ashlett House in High Street appears to have been the only purpose-built one;[72] others, like the Central

47 'Homes for Disabled or Old Persons' registered under the Registered Homes Act, 1984, c. 23 (list provided by S.C.C. Social Services Dept. 1986). Registered-homes places were then increasing rapidly throughout the county: *S.C.C. Mins.* 1985–6, 39, 450.

48 Personal observation.

49 *S.C.C. Mins.* 1985–6, 390–2, 446; inf. from S.C.C.

50 Morriss, *Rlys. of Salop.* 14–15.

51 S. A. Lewis, 'Hist. and Geog. Study of the small towns of Salop. 1600–1830' (Leic. Univ. Ph.D. thesis, 1990), 240–2.

52 *Route of Shrews. & Heref. Rly.* 45–51.

53 Above, social and cultural activities.

54 *Shrews. Chron.* 5 July 1912, p. 7 (obit.).

55 *P.O. Dir. Salop.* (1879), 299, county advts. p. 82.

56 Above, social and cultural activities.

57 Copy in S.P.L.

58 Windsor, *Handbk.* title page and pp. 104–6.

59 Above, this article, intro.

60 S.R.O. 2079/LVI. 2, 5; 4044/39, pp. 71 no. 577, 75 no. 609, 77 nos. 622–7; 6296/1/1, p. 1; /1/3, pp. 3–4; Whately, *Old Hos. in All Stretton*, i. 5, 7; ii. 5; S.R.O. 6296/2/4 (art. from *The Sunday at Home* (1911), 121–2); *Salop. N. & Q.* 3rd ser. ii. 104; above, this article, intro.

61 Copy of 2nd edn. (1896) in S.P.L. For Kingsley see F. Boase, *Modern Eng. Biog.* ii (1897), 236.

62 *Oxf. Companion to Eng. Literature*, ed. M. Drabble (1985), 536.

63 Copy in S.P.L. For Kettle see Boase, op. cit. v (1912), 818.

64 Below, this section.

65 The Revd. John Watson (1850–1907): *D.N.B.* 1901–11.

66 *Ch. Stretton Official Guide to the Holiday and Health Centre of the Salop. Highlands* (Shrews. [1950]), 3 (copy in S.P.L.).

67 Ibid.; for Harraden (1864–1936) cf. *D.N.B.* 1931–40.

68 G. M. Coles, *The Flower of Light: biog. of Mary Webb* (1978), 113, 127–9, 332–3. The OE. *hop* means a valley, not a hill: cf. below, Rushbury, intro.

69 Subtitled *with a description of objects of interest; pleasant walks; its hills, dells, valleys, and waterfalls* (copy in S.P.L.).

70 Cf. Jas. Phillips, *Illustr. Guide to Ch. Stretton* (Shrews. 1869; copy in S.P.L.).

71 Windsor, *Handbk.* 1, 13–15, advts.

72 To judge from its appearance: depicted in *Ch. Stretton Adv.* 9 Aug. 1900, p. 1.

Boarding House and Family Hotel on the opposite side of High Street, were adapted buildings.[73] Not for about a decade did directories begin to list boarding houses: there were six in 1905 and nine (out of thirteen in the county) in 1909. By 1909 apartments were being let by 45 householders (mainly in the town), the same number as in Shrewsbury,[74] a town twelve times more populous than the three Strettons.[75] Numbers listed remained at that level until the First World War but apparently declined then.[76]

From 1898 numbers of seasonal visitors can be estimated from the visitors' lists in the new *Advertiser*.[77] At the August bank holiday that year probably *c.* 120 people arrived: 34 (including the Hon. Charles Lawrance and Sir John Ramsden) at the Hotel, 10 each at the Buck's Head and Ashlett House, 6 at the Priory, and 5 at the Central Hotel and Boarding House.[78] Stretton's season was naturally mainly a summer one, with the emphasis on outdoor pursuits. Ashlett House, however, offered special terms for the winter months,[79] and there were 29 visitors in Stretton at the end of December 1898, some of whom had stayed longish periods.[80] Such figures for summer and winter visitors may not be wide of the mark for the years before the First World War. Titled people began to figure in the lists before 1900 and good numbers of visitors seem to have been attracted from the west midlands, Merseyside, and the north: in 1900 there were *c.* 175 visitors at the beginning of August and *c.* 10 a fortnight before Christmas;[81] in 1908 the 23 after Christmas included Sir Charles and Lady Ottley and Lady Banks, and the large numbers recorded that August (*c.* 128 in the middle of the month) included the dean of Windsor and the Misses Eliot, who spent the whole month at the Longmynd Hotel. Stretton seems to have been favoured by the senior clergy: Canon Holmes was at the Longmynd at the same time as Dean Eliot, and in June Bishop Gibson of Gloucester and his wife had been there.[82]

During its Edwardian heyday Church Stretton prospered. By 1903 it had been puffed 'in a Monte Carlo journal', and in 1905 it was advertised in the society weekly *Truth* as 'the Highlands of England', recommended as a winter resort by the medical profession. In 1908 Church Stretton Ltd. was planning to make a spa. The firm's plans were too ambitious to be realized,[83] but the town grasped the need to plan attractions and to advertise itself. On 8–10 July 1913, to publicize 'the Highlands of England' and attract visitors,[84] an ambitious historical pageant was staged in the natural amphitheatre formed by the slope between Cunnery Road and the Rectory wood: long remembered locally, it dramatized episodes of local history from the capture of Caratacus to the visit of James II.[85] Church Stretton Advancement Association, formed as an 'advertising committee' in 1903, published a guide in which the 'Highlands' phrase was well used.[86] The local press warned the Association to attend to signposting,[87] and by December 1914 £53 (subscribed) had been spent on newspaper and railway advertising and on putting up signposts; results, it was claimed, would have been better but for the war,[88] which brought the Association to an end.[89]

From the 1890s 'day excursionists' formed an important part of Stretton's custom. At the 1898 August bank holiday nearly 700 arrived by rail; the return fare from Shrewsbury was 1*s.*[90] On 4 August 1913 excursions from the Shrewsbury and Wellington districts and also from Birkenhead and Liverpool brought in *c.* 800 whose day on the hills and in the vales brought no casualties.[91] Early next year the new station, with a better platform and passenger accommodation, was completed in time for the Whit holiday,[92] but days in June and August, bringing in *c.* 500, were perhaps not quite up to expectation.[93]

After the war Carding Mill valley, long felt to be romantic and by then free of industry (a 'chalet' refreshment pavilion was built next to the mill in 1920),[94] increasingly became the principal attraction for day trippers: in 1918, despite food controls, the influx of Whitsun visitors was 'quite on a par with old times' and on the Monday the valley was well patronized. People then came in by brake,[95] but by 1926 it was cars, buses, and charabancs that brought them to the valley. A 'tremendous rush' of visitors that August, when the valley was the centre of attraction, packed the town streets with cars, though many also came by charabanc.[96] Next Easter the charabancs were less in evidence, but there were more smaller cars than before: 'hundreds', their occupants intent on picnicking in the valley. By August bank holiday 1927 the valley was 'simply one mass' of cars 'of all descriptions', the hills scattered with trippers 'dressed in various colours'; children paddled and bathed while 'their elders were content to lounge on the banks'.[97] In 1937 one motorist who regularly visited the valley wrote to protest that

73 Descr. in *Stretton Focus*, Feb. 1982, p. 10.

74 *Kelly's Dir. Salop.* (1905), 62–3; (1909), 65–7, 343–4, 348.

75 *V.C.H. Salop.* ii. 227–8.

76 *Kelly's Dir. Salop.* (1913–29).

77 Cf. above, social and cultural activities.

78 *Ch. Stretton Adv.* 4 Aug. 1898, p. 5.

79 Ibid. advt.

80 Ibid. 29 Dec. 1898, p. 5, and earlier issues.

81 Ibid. 9 Aug. (p. 5), 13 Dec. (p. 5) 1900.

82 Ibid. 2 Jan. (p. 1), 11 June (p. 1), 6 (p. 1), 13 (p. 1), 20 (p. 1), and 27 (p. 1) Aug. 1908.

83 Above, growth of settlement; *Shrews. Chron.* 13 Mar. 1903, p. 5; *Truth*, 21 and 28 Dec. 1905 (ref. provided by Dr. J. F. A. Mason).

84 *Ch. Stretton Adv.* 12 (p.4) and 19 (p. 4) June 1913.

85 Descr. ibid. 10 July 1913, p. 5; *Shrews. Chron.* 11 July 1913, pp. 4, 9; cf. S.R.O. 1666/1, p. 46.

86 Edited by E. S. Cobbold: *Ch. Stretton Illustrated* (3rd edn. 1908–9; copy in S.P.L.); (4th edn. 1912; copy in possession of Mrs. I. E. Jones, All Stretton). Cf. Ellesmere's characterization as the Salop. Lake Dist.: *Kelly's Dir. Salop.* (1895).

87 *Ch. Stretton Adv.* 3 July 1913, p. 4.

88 Ibid. 31 Dec. 1914, p. 4.

89 S.R.O., DA 7/137/2/1.

90 *Ch. Stretton Adv.* 4 Aug. 1898, p. 4.

91 Ibid. 7 Aug. 1913, p. 4.

92 Ibid. 30 Apr., 21 May (p. 5) 1914.

93 Ibid. 4 June (p. 4), 6 Aug. (p. 4) 1914.

94 Above, this section (manufactures and trade); *Carding Mill Valley* (Nat. Trust, 1981).

95 *Ch. Stretton Adv.* 23 May 1918, p. 2.

96 Ibid. 27 May (p. 2), 5 Aug. (p. 2) 1926.

97 Ibid. 28 Apr. (p. 2), 4 Aug. (p. 2) 1927; Bilbey, *Ch. Stretton*, pl. 143.

for weeks past it had been spoilt by 'hordes of holiday makers from certain parts of the Midlands who with their motor coaches and barrels of beer gave the valley the appearance of a fair ground'. He suggested supervision or a nominal charge.[98] By Easter 1938 the scene 'had to be seen to be believed': thousands in the valley and climbing the hills, both sides of the valley road parked up from the valley entrance as far as the swimming pool, and the town full of parked cars too.[99] By then the spectacle provided by the gliding club and visits by the aviator Amy Johnson were added to natural attractions, and in July the U.D.C. was planning to charge for car parking in the valley; the lord of the manor was asked to withdraw his request for a share of profits as the council wished only to recoup the cost of cleaning up the valley after the trippers had gone.[1] One of those who disliked Carding Mill valley's 'commercialization' in the late 1930s was the children's writer Malcolm Saville, who centred his Shropshire stories mainly on the remoter country farther south, around Marshbrook, Minton, and Hamperley. Concentration of the trippers in the valley was nevertheless some consolation for those who sought unfrequented countryside.[2]

Thus in the 1920s and 1930s the town, the Long Mynd, and Carding Mill valley acquired a role that lasted the rest of the 20th century as cars brought bank holiday and summer weekend crowds.[3] Day or weekend trippers did not, however, monopolize Stretton. The Advancement Association, revived 1922–9, resumed its advertising work,[4] and the hotel and other residential trade continued, though boarding and apartment houses were perhaps gradually transmuted into private hotels and guest houses. In 1925 a public meeting was told that 'It was better to get people to come to Stretton for months at a time than just for a day. Everyone in Stretton wanted that class of visitor, especially hotels, boarding houses, and apartment houses'. One of the meeting's intentions was to improve the golf links, 'one of the greatest assets of the place'[5] for that kind of visitor. At a meeting of the U.D.C. a month later it was claimed that 'to expect visitors to come to a place where there were no attractions' was a short-sighted policy and that not everyone played golf.[6] In fact the town did its best to provide 'attractions' for a wide range of visitors, both resident and day visitors, always aware that it was competing with other English 'health resorts'.[7] It hoped to keep pace with them even if it did not expect to overtake them.[8] At Easter and other times there were golf competitions.[9] The new park and recreation grounds[10] provided for bowls and tennis (eventually open tournaments were played) on grass and hard courts,[11] and from time to time there was cricket to watch.[12] Carding Mill valley and the town were often enlivened in the summer by local musical societies[13] and brass bands;[14] the occasional entertainment of the bandsmen by the hotels[15] was an acknowledgment of their value to the resort. The May fair had a wide range of attractions,[16] and at Whit 1927 there was another pageant.[17] As in other resorts the clergy held open-air services at busy times like August bank holiday.[18] The resort continued to be popular with the clergy (Bishop Carr of Hereford and his wife were at the Longmynd Hotel in April 1938),[19] and the hotels catered for a middle class clientele.

White Christmases gave much scope for tobogganning and skating, and in milder winters golf and events like the five-mile paper chase of Christmas 1925 afforded 'immense sport'. Hotels and boarding houses entertained their winter guests indoors: whist, billiards, concerts and dancing (occasionally with a Shrewsbury orchestra), and perhaps fancy dress balls. At Christmas 1925 the Longmynd Hotel employed a 'novelty entertainer' from Manchester.[20] Visitors to that hotel in January 1938 came mainly from Cheshire, Derbyshire, Lancashire, and Staffordshire,[21] and it was perhaps not only in winter that Stretton's role was primarily that of a regional resort for north and midland England and perhaps parts of Wales.[22]

After the war Stretton hotels resumed business and in 1949 were patronized by some of those (including the actress Jennifer Jones) involved in David O. Selznick's film *Gone to Earth* (1950).[23] The fire at the Hotel in 1968 caused one of the town's two best hotels to become simply a public house, but its loss was compensated by others elsewhere in the parish. In the 1990s, besides the main hotels and inns in the Strettons, there were at least 15 other guest houses, farmhouses, or family homes advertising accommodation, in two cases self-catering.[24] Self-catering lodges and apartments were provided in the Longmynd Hotel grounds[25] too, and there were caravan and camping sites.[26] Day visitors, as always, tended to congregate in Card-

98 *Ch. Stretton Adv.* 4 June 1937, p. 1.

99 Ibid. 22 Apr. 1938, p. 5.

1 Ibid. 14 Apr. (p. 1), 8 (p. 1) and 29 (p. 7) July 1938. For Amy Johnson cf. *D.N.B.* 1941–50. The gliding club was not in the par.

2 M. O'Hanlon, *The Complete Lone Pine: The 'Lone Pine' Bks. of Malcolm Saville Explored* (Worc. 1996), 9, 11–12, 18, 26–7, 148, 152, 155–60; cf. *Who Was Who 1981–90*, 669.

3 Personal observation 1970s–90s.

4 S.R.O., DA 7/137/1–7 (esp. /137/1/1).

5 *Ch. Stretton Adv.* 5 Feb. 1925, p. 2.

6 Ibid. 5 Mar. 1925, p. 2.

7 Ibid. 9 Apr. 1925, p. 2; 8 July 1938, p. 1.

8 Ibid. 5 Mar. (p. 2), 9 Apr. (p. 2) 1925.

9 Ibid. 9 Apr. 1925, p. 2 (mentioning the Stretton Laundry cup); 5 Aug. 1926, p. 2; 14 and 28 (p. 2) Apr. 1927.

10 Above, social and cultural activities.

11 See e.g. *Ch. Stretton Adv.* 8 Apr. (p. 2), 27 May (p. 2) 1926; 4 Aug. 1927, p. 2; 29 July 1938, p. 7.

12 Ibid. 4 Aug. 1927, p. 2.

13 Ibid. 7 May 1925, p. 2; 13 Jan. 1926, p. 2.

14 Ibid. 8 Apr. (p. 2), 5 Aug. (p. 2) 1926.

15 Ibid. 4 Aug. 1927, p. 2.

16 Above, social and cultural activities.

17 *Ch. Stretton Adv.* 26 May 1927, p. 2.

18 Ibid. 5 Aug. 1926, p. 2.

19 Ibid. 1 Apr. 1938, p. 8.

20 Ibid. 1 Jan. 1925; 29 Dec. 1927, p. 2.

21 Ibid. 14 Jan. 1938, p. 8.

22 Cf. the visitors' lists for the Hotel and the Longmynd Hotel ibid. 1 Apr. 1938, p. 8.

23 D. Thomson, *Showman: The Life of David O. Selznick* (1993), 540–8, 550–1, 554, 562, 757–8; below, M. Wenlock, intro., and sources there cited.

24 *S. Salop.: Where to Stay 1991* (S. Salop. Tourism Assoc.).

25 Brochure.

26 e.g. in Ashes Hollow.

ing Mill valley, where the National Trust had acquired the refreshment chalet.[27] They came mostly at weekends and bank holidays, enjoying special attractions like the vintage cars and old steam vehicles paraded in August 1961.[28]

LOCAL GOVERNMENT. After 1102 Stretton was a manor of royal demesne and was separately represented by its reeve and six men at the eyre and similar inquiries.[29] Though said *c.* 1830 to owe 3*s.* 4*d.* a year to the lord of Munslow hundred, with suit and service,[30] the manor was in fact exempt from the hundred and enjoyed a court leet. That is clear from court records for 1392–3,[31] 1566–7,[32] 1634–5,[33] 1697,[34] 1721–1893,[35] 1895, 1902, and 1906;[36] in 1832 more 16th- and 17th-century rolls, and perhaps medieval ones, were apparently extant,[37] though those for 1630–95 were then said to be 'wanting'.[38]

Minton and Whittingslow were evidently subject to the jurisdiction of Stretton manor by 1086, but Minton's lord had wide powers as keeper of the Long forest and in the early 13th century he and the reeve of Stretton were important representatives of the Crown in the area. In 1233 the two men, attended by the men of the district, were formally appointed to ward and defend Stretton dale, particularly from the Welsh against whom they had already been active.[39] Minton had a court baron: a session of 1608 dealt with copyhold matters.[40]

Stretton's leet jurisdiction[41] extended over the whole parish, except for Botvyle (in Lydley and Cardington manor),[42] and over an adjoining part of Wistanstow parish: presentments were made by All Stretton, Church Stretton, Little Stretton, Minton, Whittingslow, and Womerton (or Woodhouse), the last named having been absorbed by Stretton manor some time after 1086;[43] constables were apparently appointed for those places until 1876, though appointments for Minton and Whittingslow had ceased earlier. The great or leet court was evidently held in April or May and October until 1840; thereafter it seems to have become annual, in May or June or October or November. After 1870 it was held less regularly, and the session of November 1880 was probably the last.

In 1554 the lord was granted return of writs, an administrative privilege excluding the sheriff and other Crown officials.[44]

In 1393 the 'small' court, or court baron, met every three weeks during the summer but less often in the winter. By 1567 winter meetings, though still irregular, were more frequent. In the earlier 18th century the small court met on the same days as the court leet and also at intervals between them. It was usually called the court baron and customary court and was increasingly preoccupied with the descent and conveyancing of copyhold estates. A 'purchased' court baron of 1736 and 'special' sessions of 1863 and 1872[45] were presumably held at the instance of people with urgent business. Until 1871 there seem to have been meetings of the small court every year, though they were becoming less frequent. After 1871 sessions were increasingly rare and what were probably the court's last three meetings took place in 1895, 1902, and 1906.[46] Thereafter the steward dealt with copyhold business out of court.[47]

The court house which Bonham Norton undertook to build may well have been his market house,[48] but by the 19th century the manor courts normally met in the Buck's Head, then also called the Manor House. The inn yard, on the east side of High Street, remained the manorial pound at the end of the 19th century.[49]

In the late 18th and early 19th century young paupers were apprenticed[50] and in 1816 the vestry assigned liability to take one or more such apprentices between 100 persons.[51] That system, if adopted, seems to have been discontinued by the early 1830s.[52] In the early 19th century pauperism evidently increased towards the end of the Napoleonic wars, and expenditure on the poor increased greatly during the years 1817–20, reaching a peak of £527 in 1818. Otherwise the burden on the parish seems to have varied little from a post-war average of £370 a year. Maintenance allowances for bastard children (some 25 a year) averaged £62 a year net 1828–32. In the earlier 1830s labourers were seldom unemployed[53] and the parish poor-house in High

27 Above, manors.

28 *Shropshire Mag.* Sept. 1961, pp. 11, 37.

29 *V.C.H. Salop.* iii. 48–9, and sources there cited; *Rot. Hund.* (Rec. Com.), ii. 83–4; cf. the Crown pleas presenting dists. in D. Crook, *Rec. of Gen. Eyre* (P.R.O. Handbks. xx, 1982), 234–5.

30 W.S.L. 350/5/40, Ch. Stretton p. 6; cf. *V.C.H. Salop.* iii. 47 and n. 3.

31 S.R.O. 125/1.

32 S.P.L., Deeds 2630; cf. *T.S.A.S.* 3rd ser. iv. 115–28.

33 S.R.O. 1709, box 202, verdict 1634, ct. r. 1635.

34 S.R.O. 1011, box 166, jury presentment.

35 S.R.O. 248/11–23; 1242, box IV, estreat 1880; 1709, box 202, suit r. 1735–9, 1745–50, 1824–32, ct. r. 1865–70, 1873, 1876–7, 1880, 1884, 1892, presentments 1863–71, estreats 1865, 1867–73, receipt bks. for fines 1866–7, forms for holding cts., etc.; 3616/3.

36 S.R.O. 1709, box 202, ct. r. A proposed ct. Nov. 1898 apparently attracted no business.

37 At Acton Scott: W.S.L. 350/5/40, Ch. Stretton pp. 73–8; cf. Campbell-Hyslop and Cobbold, *Ch. Stretton*, ii. 170.

38 W.S.L. 350/5/40, Ch. Stretton p. 78.

39 F. C. Suppe, *Military Institutions on the Welsh Marches: Salop. A.D. 1066–1300* (1994), 109–10; above, econ. hist. (agric.).

40 S.R.O. 1011, box 166, ct. r.

41 Summarized in the *quo warr.* procs. agst. the ld. begun 1622: S.R.O. 1709, box 203, exemplificn. of rec. for ascertaining privs. of man. of Stretton 1629. Para. based on sources in notes 31–6, above.

42 W.S.L. 350/5/40, Ch. Stretton p. 30; *Salop. N. & Q.* 8 May 1925.

43 Above, manors (Womerton).

44 S.R.O. 1709, box 203, exemplificn. of rec. for ascertaining privs. of man. of Stretton 1629; cf. *V.C.H. Salop.* iii. 46–7.

45 S.R.O. 248/11, p. 148; 3616/3, pp. 13–16, 188–200. Para. based on sources cited above, notes 31–6.

46 S.R.O. 2408/109, requisitions on title 1924, question 4.

47 Cf. S.R.O. 1709, box 202, steward's fees out of, and at, ct. 1864.

48 Above, growth of settlement; econ. hist. (mkts. and fairs).

49 Bilbey, *Ch. Stretton*, intro.; local inf.

50 S.R.O. 1642, box 28.

51 Ibid. box 29, 'rule or plan' 27 Sept. 1816 (incomplete).

52 *Rep. Poor Law Com.* H.C. 44, p. 662A (1834), xxviii; ibid. p. 388C (1834), xxxii.

53 Ibid. p. 388A (1834), xxx; ibid. p. 388E (1834), xxxiv; *Poor Rate Returns*, H.C. 556, suppl. app. p. 142 (1822), v; H.C. 334, p. 177 (1825), iv; H.C. 83, p. 165 (1830–1), xi; H.C. 444, p. 160 (1835), xlvii.

Street (in existence 1733)[54] seems to have been little used. Applications for sick and accident relief were judged individually.[55] There was an assistant overseer but no select vestry; the vestry itself fixed the rate on the parish officers' advice[56] and examined the annual accounts.[57] Poor cottagers paid no rates.[58]

The whole area of the ancient parish was in Church Stretton poor-law union 1836–1930.[59] At first the union used the parish poor-house but in 1838 a new union workhouse to accommodate 120, designed by T. D. Duppa of Cheney Longville, was built north of Ashbrook by S. Pountney Smith.[60] Soon afterwards the parish sold the old poor-house, divided into two dwellings.[61] In the 1930s the county council used part of the former union workhouse as a children's home; before it closed in 1939 the institution had also housed mental defectives.[62]

The whole area of the ancient parish was in Church Stretton highway district 1863–94,[63] Church Stretton rural sanitary district 1872–94, and Church Stretton rural district 1894–9. In 1899 most of Church Stretton ward,[64] one of three formed in the parish in 1894,[65] became an urban district; Little Stretton and All Stretton wards, each slightly enlarged, became civil parishes.[66] In 1934 the U.D. was enlarged to include the villages of All Stretton and Little Stretton; at the same time Church Stretton R.D. was abolished and the reduced C.P.s of Little Stretton and All Stretton were transferred to Ludlow R.D. and Atcham R.D. respectively.[67] In 1967, on the abolition of Church Stretton U.D., Church Stretton C.P. absorbed Little Stretton C.P. and was included in Ludlow R.D.[68] From 1974 Church Stretton C.P. was in South Shropshire district, All Stretton C.P. in the borough of Shrewsbury and Atcham.[69]

U.D.C. meetings were at first in the town hall.[70] When a new depot was completed in Beaumont Road offices were provided there in 1912 to replace rented ones in High Street.[71] From *c.* 1920 U.D.C. meetings were held at the council offices.[72] The U.D.C.'s first clerk (1899–1932) was Samuel M. Morris (kt. 1920).[73] A. E. D. de S. Zrinyi, rate collector 1899–1915,[74] was also bailiff of the manor court;[75] he was succeeded as rate collector by his son.[76]

PUBLIC SERVICES. In 1856 promoters of the Church Stretton Water Co. secured the goodwill of the rector, H. O. Wilson, and of C. O. Childe-Pemberton for a scheme to bring water to the town from a reservoir on Town brook above the rectory.[77] By 1870 the water supplied was good,[78] comparable to 'the best upland waters', and distributed by gravity from the Long Mynd to the whole town.[79] Little Stretton and All Stretton were less efficiently supplied by other companies, formed in 1865 and 1870 respectively: in 1894 the All Stretton company's supply was little more than nominal. Some improvements in reservoir storage were made,[80] but in 1899 Church Stretton Waterworks Co. was incorporated to build waterworks and improve the parish's supply. A reservoir was built in New Pool Hollow and mains ran down Carding Mill valley to the town and to All Stretton and Little Stretton.[81] The undertaking was acquired by the U.D.C. in 1912.[82] The town and both villages were still so supplied in 1946, water being taken from Town brook and a stream at All Stretton; in 1953 the All Stretton company's undertaking, including a small service reservoir, was acquired by the U.D.C., which remained the authorized supplier for the whole of the ancient parish area until 1964; by 1946, however, mains had not reached Minton village or the scattered population of All Stretton C.P.[83]

H. O. Wilson was active in promoting sewerage schemes for the town in 1865–6 and 1874.[84] In 1876 the town, some 35 a. with a population of 425, became a special drainage district[85] and a disposal scheme was carried out *c.* 1878–80; by

54 *Stretton Focus*, Jan. 1982, p. 10; tithe field 1312.
55 *Rep. Poor Law Com.* p. 388B (1834), xxxi.
56 Ibid. 388C.
57 Ibid. 388E.
58 Ibid. 388B.
59 V. J. Walsh, 'Admin. of Poor Laws in Salop. 1820–55' (Pennsylvania Univ. Ph.D. thesis, 1970), 148–50; *Kelly's Dir. Salop.* (1929), 4, 66; cf. *V.C.H. Salop.* iii. 170.
60 S.R.O. 19/2/1, 13 Oct., 29 Dec. 1837, 16 Feb., 2 Mar., 20 Apr., 7 and 21 Dec. 1838; tithe field 1044; Bilbey, *Ch. Stretton*, pl. 83.
61 S.R.O. 3908/Ch/1, notes of vestry mtgs. 2 and 19 Mar. 1840.
62 *S.C.C. Mins.* 1933–4, 493; 1936–7, 403–4; 1938–9, 414, 569; 1939–40, 284.
63 *Lond. Gaz.* 27 Mar. 1863, p. 1767.
64 Except Carding Mill valley (put in All Stretton C.P.) and Ragleth and Hazler hills (put in Lt. Stretton C.P.).
65 *S.C.C. Mins.* 1894–5, rep. of subcttee. to form par. councils, 10.
66 Ibid. 1898–9, 155; ibid. 11 Mar. 1899, 3; S.R.O., S.C.C. Local Govt., etc., Cttee. min. bk. 1894–1903, pp. 184, 186, 190, 203; S.R.O. 3977/PC/1, pp. 36, 46, 49, 59–60, 65, 71, 77–8; *V.C.H. Salop.* ii. 217, 228.
67 *V.C.H. Salop.* ii. 228; *Census, 1931: Herefs. and Salop. (Pt. II)* (H.M.S.O. 1936), 6, 8–9, 11; cf. *V.C.H. Salop.* iii. 179.
68 *V.C.H. Salop.* ii. 236; cf. ibid. xi. 376, correcting ibid. ii. 235.
69 Sources cited ibid. iii. 169 n. 29.
70 S.R.O., DA 7/100/1–3.
71 Ibid. /2, pp. 181–2, 184, 196, 306–8, 314, 318–19, 327, 372, 393, 437, 445; DA 7/124/1, pp. 5–6.
72 Ibid. DA 7/100/4; *Kelly's Dir. Salop.* (1922), 63.
73 S.R.O., DA 7/100/1, pp. 27–8; /5, pp. 19, 29; *Shrews. Chron.* 26 Mar. 1937, p. 7.
74 A former hussar officer exiled from Austria-Hungary. See S.R.O., DA 7/100/1, p. 24; /3, pp. 174, 179; *Shrews. Chron.* 9 Apr. (p. 8), 29 Oct. (p. 7) 1897; 10 June 1898, p. 8; 5 Mar. 1915, p. 7; P.R.O., HO 144/45/86747; HO 334/9, no. 3006; RG 10/2734, f. 19v.; RG 11/2623, f. 11 (no. 61).
75 See e.g. *Shrews. Chron.* 28 June 1935, p. 11 (recollection of Zrinyi's manorial and council offices).
76 A. E. J. D. Zrinyi was rate collector until his d. in 1930: S.R.O., DA 7/100/4, p. 317; *Shrews. Chron.* 11 Apr. 1930, p. 2.
77 S.R.O. 1642, box 27, drainage papers, C. Hicks to Timotheus Burd 19 Aug. 1856.
78 *P.O. Dir. Salop.* (1870), 35.
79 Windsor, *Handbk.* 31–2; *S.C.C. Mins.* 1897–8, 624.
80 P.R.O., BT 31/1070/1940C; *S.C.C. Mins.* 1894–5, Sanitary and Roads and Bridges Cttee. 7 July 1894, 21; *S.C.C. Mins.* 1895–6, 88; 1896–7, 296. The All Stretton co.'s no. (5122) indicates formation in 1870.
81 Under Ch. Stretton Water Act, 1899, 62 & 63 Vic. c. 92 (Local): copy, with plans and sections, in S.R.O. 1242 maps.
82 Under Ch. Stretton U.D. Water Act, 1912, 2 & 3 Geo. V, c. 15 (Local): A. H. S. Waters, *Rep. on Water Supplies* (S.C.C. 1946), 19.
83 Ibid. 19–20, 31, 76; S.R.O., DA 7/100/9, p. 330; /100/12, p. 297; /100/23, pp. 112–13, 126–7, 132; *V.C.H. Salop.* iii. 208.
84 S.R.O. 1642, box 27, drainage papers.
85 *P.O. Dir. Salop.* (1879), 298; *6th Ann. Rep. Local Govt. Bd.* [C. 1865], p. 389, H.C. (1877), xxxvii.

February 1880 a hundred cottages and buildings in the district were connected to the main sewers and few houses were not.[86] A new sewerage scheme was carried out 1904–6.[87] A long deliberated[88] U.D.C. scheme to sewer All Stretton and Little Stretton was effected in the mid 1960s.[89]

A nursing charity for the sick poor established in 1880 gave rise in 1900 to the Church Stretton Nursing Association.[90] A child welfare centre, started by the association in 1921, was recognized by the county council in 1924.[91] The association ended in 1948 when the council became responsible for district nursing.[92]

In the 1880s a bier, probably belonging to the parish, was kept in the old lock-up at the almshouses.[93] In 1942, when the church's additional burial ground[94] was almost full,[95] the U.D.C. opened a cemetery near Brockhurst.[96]

A gas works was built at World's End *c.* 1860.[97] By 1867 parish gas-lighting inspectors[98] had arranged for the town to be lit,[99] and in or shortly before 1885 mains were laid to All Stretton.[1] The works was owned privately or by limited companies until nationalization in 1949.[2] From *c.* 1904 electricity was supplied from a works at Crossways; generating there ceased in the mid 1930s, a few years after the liquidation of the local company.[3]

John Broome of the Talbot inn was postmaster in 1828[4] and was succeeded as innkeeper and postmaster by the Haverkams.[5] G. R. Windsor, bookseller, stationer, and local writer, was postmaster from the 1870s to 1892 and kept the post office in Shrewsbury Road, opposite the Hotel; he was succeeded by the retired schoolmaster Samuel Darlington.[6] A new post office was later built in Sandford Avenue.[7]

On the formation of the county constabulary in 1840[8] the superintendent in charge of 'E' division and a constable were stationed at Church Stretton.[9] A police station, comprising lock-up and superintendent's house, was built north of the town in Shrewsbury Road in 1846–7;[10] the new lock-up replaced one built on the almshouse property twenty years before.[11]

A volunteer fire brigade was established in 1881, the engine being kept at David Hyslop's posting stables in Brook Street.[12] The brigade was taken over and re-formed by the U.D.C. in 1901,[13] and the council depot built in Beaumont Road in 1911 included accommodation for the engine.[14] In 1964 the county council opened a new fire station in Essex Road.[15]

CHURCH. There was evidently a church at Stretton in 1086,[16] and the nave of the present building is 12th-century.[17]

Save for two short periods (1229–32 and 1327–30, in neither of which are any vacancies known to have occurred) the rectory was in the Crown's patronage until 1336, though on two occasions the Crown's presentee was evidently not instituted.[18] Henry III granted the advowson in fee, with the manor, to Hubert de Burgh, earl of Kent, in 1229 and resumed it in 1232.[19] Edmund FitzAlan, earl of Arundel, who had a life interest in the manor from 1310, presented in 1316[20] and 1321.[21] In 1327, after Arundel's execution and forfeiture, the Crown presented[22] and then granted the advowson for life, with the manor, to Roger de Mortimer, created earl of March in 1328.[23] In 1330 March was granted the advowson in fee and licensed to alienate it to the chaplains of his chantry in Leintwardine church,[24] but later that year he forfeited his estates to the Crown.[25]

In 1336 Edward III granted the advowson in fee to Richard FitzAlan, earl of Arundel,[26] and it then descended with the manor until *c.* 1800.[27]

86 S.R.O. 1168/1/114, pp. 6 sqq., 9 sqq., 14–16, 19, 28, 33, 40–2, 46–7, 49, 52.

87 S.R.O., DA 7/100/1, pp. 379–80, 449–51; DA 7/152/1.

88 S.R.O., DA 7/100/9–22.

89 Ibid. /100/19, pp. 34, 40, 146; /23, p. 25; /25, pp. 69, 92, 103–4, and treasurer's rep. (p. 3) betw. pp. 87 and 88; DA 7/742/6.

90 S.R.O., DA 7/137/1, *Ch. Stretton Nursing Assoc. Ann. Rep. 1947–8*; below, chars.

91 S.R.O., DA 7/136/3, 26 Feb., 11 Apr., 3 May 1921, 5 Feb. 1924; /5, p. 88; rep. in S.R.O., S.C.C. Public Health and Housing Cttee. min. bk. 1923–6.

92 S.R.O., DA 7/136/5, pp. 70–2, 79, 96–7; *V.C.H. Salop.* iii. 209.

93 Windsor, *Handbk.* 92.

94 Below, church.

95 S.R.O., DA 7/111/12, pp. 990, 1008; /13, p. 17.

96 Ibid. /12, pp. 569–70, 711; /13, pp. 15–17; DA 7/724, order of service at consecration.

97 P.R.O., BT 31/327/1155; RG 9/1844, f. 9v.

98 Appointed under 3 & 4 Wm. IV, c. 90, s. 17.

99 As a lighting dist.: cf. ibid. s. 73; S.R.O. 1168/1/192, 7 Mar. 1867; Windsor, *Handbk.* 62; Bilbey, *Ch. Stretton*, pl. 144.

1 Windsor, op. cit. 49; S.R.O. 2079/LVI.9, no. 94; 4044/39, p. 13 no. 94.

2 P.R.O., BT 31/327/1155; BT 31/34604/60106.

3 P.R.O., BT 31/17230/80857; S.R.O. 2079/LVI.9, no. 371; 4044/39, p. 41 no. 371; Bilbey, *Ch. Stretton*, pls. 100, 104; *Stretton Focus*, Nov. 1984, p. 8.

4 Tibnam & Co. *Salop. Dir.* (1828), 34.

5 Pigot, *Nat. Com. Dir.* (1842), 10.

6 Windsor, *Handbk.* 5–6; Bilbey, *Ch. Stretton*, pl. 127; *Shrews. Chron.* 17 June 1892, p. 8; 23 Nov. 1894, p. 6 (obit.).

7 Land bought by postmaster gen. 20 Sept. 1939: S.C.C. deeds ED. 152.

8 *V.C.H. Salop.* iii. 157.

9 S.R.O., q. sess. Const. Cttee. rep. bk. 1839–53, p. 77; Bodl. MS. Top. Salop. c. 1, f. 482; D. J. Elliott, *Policing Salop. 1836–1967* (1984), 20.

10 S. Bagshaw, *Dir. Salop.* (1851), 526; S.R.O., q. sess. Const. Cttee. rep. bk. 1839–53, pp. 285–6; 289–90, 297, 301, 315.

11 *Orders of Q. Sess.* iii. 259; S.R.O., q. sess. Auditing Cttee. and Finance Cttee. rep. bk. 1837–43, p. 146; Const. Cttee. rep. bk. 1839–53, pp. 266–7, 276–7; Windsor, *Handbk.* 92.

12 Windsor, op. cit. 14, 49–50; Bilbey, *Ch. Stretton*, pl. 126.

13 S.R.O., DA 7/100/1, pp. 85–6, 91, 97, 177, 186–7, 198–9; /111/1, pp. 3, 15, 21–2, 26–7, 33.

14 Cf. *Wellington Jnl.* 24 Sept. 1910; above, local govt.

15 *S.C.C. Mins.* 1962–3, 419; 1964–5, 182.

16 *V.C.H. Salop.* i. 317.

17 Below, this section (building).

18 *Pat. R.* 1216–25, 353; 1225–32, 170; *Cal. Pat.* 1232–47, 190, 473; 1247–58, 167, 206; 1258–66, 508; 1266–72, 319; 1307–13, 186; 1313–17, 397; 1321–4, 30; 1327–30, 133; 1330–4, 39, 339, 518; 1334–8, 4; *Cal. Inq. Misc.* ii, p. 2.

19 *Cal. Chart. R.* 1226–57, 103; above, manors.

20 Frustrating the Crown presentee Thos. of Charlton: cf. *Reg. Swinfield* (C.S.), 543; *Cal. Pat.* 1313–17, 397; Emden, *Biog. Reg. Oxf. to 1500*, i. 392 (confusing the ch. with Stretton Sugwas, Herefs.); above, manors.

21 Cf. *Reg. Orleton* (C.S.), 387; *Cal. Pat.* 1321–4, 30.

22 *Cal. Pat.* 1327–30, 133.

23 Ibid. 192.

24 Ibid. 484, 494.

25 Above, manors. Cf. *Cal. Pat.* 1334–8, 4.

26 *Cal. Chart. R.* 1327–41, 353.

27 *Reg. Trillek* (C.S.), 390; *Reg. L. Charlton* (C.S.), 63; *Reg. Gilbert* (C.S.), 122; *Reg. Trefnant* (C.S.), 177, 180; *Reg. Lacy* (C.S.), 113; *Reg. Spofford* (C.S.), 362; *Cal. Pat.* 1396–9, 213; *Dioc. of Heref. Institutions (1539–1900)*, ed. A. T. Bannister (Heref. 1923), 6, 36, 38, 71, 87, 133; *T.S.A.S.* 3rd ser. v. 361; 4th ser. viii. 47; cf. above, manors.

The earls conveyed turns to others in the earlier 16th century, the Crown apparently presented by lapse *c.* 1576, and Sir Rowland Hayward may have granted a turn soon after that.[28] About 1800 Thomas Thynne, marquess of Bath, sold the advowson to Thomas Coleman, of Leominster (Herefs.),[29] who presented his son T. B. Coleman in 1807 and later conveyed the advowson to him. T. B. Coleman's representatives presented in 1818 and evidently sold the advowson before 1834 to Coleman's successor as rector, R. N. Pemberton, whose trustees presented in 1849. That year the patronage was exercised again, by Pemberton's devisee C. O. Childe-Pemberton of Millichope, who remained patron until his death in 1883.[30] In 1886 the advowson was conveyed in trust,[31] evidently to the Church Patronage Trust,[32] patron in 1990.[33]

In 1255 and 1292 the rectory was said to be worth £26 13*s.* 4*d.* a year,[34] though in 1291 the annual value was given as £15.[35] The living was valued at £16 a year in 1535: £14 13*s.* 4*d.* from tithes, £1 6*s.* 8*d.* from glebe.[36] In the later 16th century the rector possessed an extensive glebe, over 55 a. including closes around the parsonage and acres, lands, and butts in Nashbrook field; then, and in 1699, he also owned all the tithes of the parish and took housebote, firebote, and hedgebote in the lord's wood and common. By 1699 the glebe was said to amount to over 76 a.,[37] and in 1839 it amounted to some 67 a. The tithes were commuted to £505 in 1839,[38] and in 1885 the living was said to be worth £580 a year gross, when the 66 a. of glebe was worth £145.[39] By 1911 the tithe rent charges were worth only £353 7*s.* 6*d.*[40] and the net value of the benefice little more.[41] The rectory house and its grounds are discussed below.

In the 1220s the living was held by two prominent royal officials. Ralph de Neville, rector 1214–22 and later bishop of Chichester, was keeper of the great seal from 1218 and chancellor 1226–44.[42] Walter of Brackley, rector 1222–7, was joint keeper of the Wardrobe 1222–32.[43] Three mid 13th-century rectors were foreigners,[44] perhaps appointed by Savoyard influence;[45] the first, Guillaume *de Pinu* presented in 1237, was archdeacon of Vézelay (Yonne).[46] Such rectors were absentees and from 1227 they had 25 marks a year from the living while a vicar had been beneficed with the rest.[47] Even the vicarage, however, seems occasionally to have been conferred on men unlikely to have resided: in 1253 the vicar, chaplain to the royal chancellor, was induced by promised compensation of £20 a year to resign in favour of a nephew of the prior of le Mas.[48] The vicarage's existence, however, extenuated the nomination of rectors unqualified for cure of souls. In 1277 the rector was only sixteen years old and not yet a subdeacon; he was a pupil of one Philip Walsh who obtained the rectory later that year, fraudulently it was said in 1283 when he himself was neither priest nor resident. The bishop then claimed that a vicar could not be appointed and in 1285 he abolished the vicarage. Walsh, protected by royal service, remained rector until 1292[49] or later.

In the 14th century incumbencies, with perhaps two exceptions,[50] were apparently short and frequently ended by an exchange of livings. William of Hartshill, not yet a subdeacon, was presented by the Crown in 1327 and was an absentee.[51] In 1331 he exchanged with a namesake,[52] presumably a relative. The second William of Hartshill, a royal clerk, twice considered an exchange[53] before effecting one with another royal clerk, John de Watenhull, in 1335.[54] Watenhull was still rector in 1347.[55] John Sprott, rector in 1349–50 and until his death in 1358, presented by the earl of Arundel, was a feoffee of the earl's estates.[56] Dr. Nicholas de Chaddesden, rector 1358–61 and only in minor orders when presented, later enjoyed a distinguished legal career.[57] Of Chaddesden's seven recorded 14th-century successors, four exchanged the rectory for other livings.[58] The rector in 1366 was a pluralist.[59]

Only ten rectors' names are known for the 15th and 16th centuries[60] and incumbencies, especially perhaps those of local men, may have been longer than in the 14th century. Dr. William Corfe, rector 1405–17, was provost of Oriel College, Oxford, 1415–17 and, as one of the

28 *Reg. Mayew* (C.S.), 282 n. 8; H.W.R.O.(H.), Heref. dioc. rec. AL 19/14, ff. 57, 59r.–v.; P.R.O., C 2/Jas. I/T 12/17.

29 S.R.O. 802, box 51, arts. of agreement 12 Oct. 1799.

30 Bannister, *Heref. Institutions*, 133, 142, 164–5, 192; S.R.O. 1011, box 241, draft settlement (11 Aug. 1849) of est. devised by the Revd. R. N. Pemberton; 2563/123.

31 Heref. Dioc. Regy., reg. 1883–1901, p. 119.

32 Ibid. reg. 1969– (in use), p. 114.

33 *Heref. Dioc. Yr. Bk. 1991*, 39.

34 Eyton, xii. 29.

35 *Tax. Eccl.* (Rec. Com.), 167.

36 *Valor Eccl.* (Rec. Com.), iii. 208.

37 H.W.R.O.(H.), HD 2/14/17–18.

38 Tithe award.

39 *Kelly's Dir. Salop.* (1885), 824; *Return of Glebe Land, 1887*, H.C. 307, p. 61 (1887), lxiv.

40 S.R.O. 4044/39, pp. 54 no. 486, 85 no. 178; /40, p. 16 no. 838.

41 *Kelly's Dir. Salop.* (1909), 63 (£400 net yearly value with resid.); (1913), 64 (£350).

42 *D.N.B.*; Eyton, xii. 29; T. F. Tout, *Chapters in Admin. Hist.* i (1937), 185, 284; vi (1933), 4.

43 Retired as bp. of Ossory 1233–43: Tout, op. cit. i. 190–200; vi. 25.

44 *Cal. Pat.* 1232–47, 190, 473; 1258–66, 508.

45 Sir M. Powicke, *13th Cent.* (1962), 74.

46 *Cal. Pat.* 1232–47, 190.

47 *Pat. R.* 1225–32, 170; *Cal. Pat.* 1247–58, 167.

48 *Cal. Pat.* 1247–58, 206. L. H. Cottineau, *Répertoire topo-bibliographique des abbayes et prieurés* (Mâcon, 1939–70), ii. 1782–3, lists 11 hos. so called.

49 *Reg. Cantilupe* (C.S.), 119–21, 302; *Reg. Swinfield*, 3–6, 89–90; Eyton, xii. 31; *Cal. Chanc. Wts.* i. 14 (misnaming the rector John).

50 Sprott and Watenhull: below, this para. It is not known who was rector 1366–86.

51 *Cal. Pat.* 1327–30, 133; *Reg. T. Charlton* (C.S.), 85, 89; cf. ibid. 29–30, 44.

52 *Cal. Pat.* 1330–4, 39.

53 Ibid. 339; 1334–8, 4; cf. Eyton, x. 283.

54 *Reg. T. Charlton*, 79, 83; *Cal. Pat.* 1330–4, 518; cf. Eyton, x. 71; *V.C.H. Suss.* ii. 112.

55 *Reg. Trillek*, 405. Cf. *Cal. Pat.* 1334–8, 181.

56 *Cal. Inq. Misc.* iii, p. 377; *Reg. Trillek*, 390.

57 *Reg. Trillek*, 390, 397; *Alum. Oxon. to 1500*, i. 380.

58 Eyton, xii. 33; *Reg. L. Charlton*, 63, 71; *Reg. Gilbert*, 121–2; *Reg. Trefnant*, 188–9; *Cal. Pat.* 1396–9, 258.

59 *Reg. S. Langham* (C. & Y.S.), 40.

60 In addn. to those mentioned below, John Fox, pres. 1439 (*Reg. Spofford*, 362), and John Marett, pres. 1549 occ. 1553 (Bannister, *Heref. Institutions*, 6; *S.P.R. Heref.* viii (2), p. v).

English delegation at the council of Constance from 1414, participated in Hus's trial.[61] Thomas Oswestry was rector 1417–39[62] and William Higgins, probably one of the All Stretton family,[63] was rector 1465–1514.[64] Dr. Edward Higgins, rector 1514–15,[65] was one of only four or five known graduate rectors[66] during the period. Of the other graduates Richard Norys, 1454–9,[67] and Master David (or William) Holywell, 1459–65,[68] had short incumbencies but George Dycher,[69] was rector 1515–48.[70] William Harris, presented *c.* 1576 and still rector in 1609, had married the widowed mother of a Church Stretton yeoman.[71] In 1595 he secured the suppression of the church ale, until then celebrated after evening prayer on Easter Day at the rector's expense: he agreed to pay 20*s.* a year for a school and schoolmaster, the ale to be revived if he defaulted.[72]

In the Middle Ages there was a service of the Blessed Virgin Mary in the south transept. It was apparently endowed with lands at Hodghurst from the mid 13th century and in 1512 the wardens acquired small properties in All Stretton and at Dudgeley. Sir Thomas Leighton (d. 1519) left 8 marks a year for masses to be said before Our Lady.[73] At Womerton there was a chapel dedicated to St. Peter. The manorial officers were putting it to secular uses by the early 1560s, and by 1622 it was said to be 'wholly defaced', most of its stones carried off;[74] its last remains were carted off in the early 19th century to build a garden wall at Womerton Farm.[75] At the opposite end of the parish Minton chapel, for which a dedication to St. Thecla has been suggested,[76] stood next to the village green; in 1562 the inhabitants wished to restore it for worship and keep the chalice and bell,[77] but it too disappeared. Thus from the 17th century to the 20th the parish church alone served the whole of the very extensive parish.

Anthony Hawkes, presented in 1621, conformed as a presbyterian and was still rector in 1647. He was an Oxford graduate,[78] and all but one[79] of his 19 known[80] successors until 1974 were university men,[81] 12 of Oxford,[82] 6 of Cambridge.[83]

John Mainwaring, rector 1749–1807, was fellow of St. John's College, Cambridge, 1748–88 and Lady Margaret professor of divinity 1788–1807.[84] He published several Cambridge sermons but is best remembered as Handel's first biographer.[85] His successors, T. B. Coleman 1807–18, who was also lord of the manor, R. N. Pemberton 1818–48, H. O. Wilson 1849–79, and Charles Noel-Hill 1879–1904, lived in gentlemanly style, and Coleman and Pemberton were patrons of the living. Under Pemberton's will his kinsman C. A. Salusbury was presented in 1849, but he died within the year. For half a century, from the 1820s to the 1870s, successive rectors employed Preston Nunn as their curate.[86] Wilson and Noel-Hill were exceptionally energetic incumbents.

Twentieth-century incumbencies were shorter, averaging little over eight years. Dr. H. T. Dixon, 1923–37, and R. W. Morley, 1948–64, served longest.[87] Dixon was archdeacon of Ludlow 1932–9, and H. E. Whately succeeded him both as rector (1937–47) and archdeacon (1939–47).[88]

In 1819 the vestry decided to remove the 'old gallery' (possibly in the chancel) and re-site the organ; during the 1820s the psalm singers were probably dispensed with; and in 1832 the organist was replaced by a barrel organ presented by the rector.[89] In 1839, when 440 of the 1,500 or so parishioners lived over two miles from the church, there were 500 sittings, 120 of them free; 200 more free places were then needed to accommodate all the poor. In 1851 attendance was said to average 300 at morning service, 120 in the afternoon; there was then an evening service at the workhouse in a chapel or room holding 65, where attendance averaged 53.[90] More sittings were provided by extensions to the church in 1867–8[91] and two new chapels of ease in 1902–3. St. Michael and All Angels, All Stretton, was opened in 1902; built in stone to a design by A.

61 Emden, *Biog. Reg. Oxf. to 1500*, i. 487; *T.S.A.S.* vi. 319.
62 *Reg. Lacy*, 113; *Reg. Spofford*, 362.
63 Above, manors (Bank Ho.).
64 *Reg. Stanbury*, (C.S.), 181; *Reg. Mayew*, 282.
65 *Reg. Mayew*, 282–3.
66 *Biog. Reg. Oxf. to 1500*, ii. 932.
67 Ibid. 1376.
68 *Reg. Stanbury*, 181, 193.
69 *Biog. Reg. Oxf. 1501–40*, 180.
70 *Reg. Mayew*, 283; *T.S.A.S.* vi. 120.
71 P.R.O., C 2/Jas. I/T 12/17.
72 W.S.L. 350/5/40, Ch. Stretton p. 52.
73 Ibid. pp. 25, 50; Loton Hall MSS., Sir Thos. Leighton's will. Edw. Leighton had been bur. in St. Mary's chap. in the ch. *c.* 65 yrs. before: *T.S.A.S.* vi. 320–1.
74 P.R.O., E 302/1/5, no. 41; S.P.L., Deeds 6573.
75 S.R.O. 2282/2/3, p. 22.
76 *Salop. Folk-Lore*, ed. C. S. Burne (1883), 436 and n. 1. If all the evidence there adduced is later than the 1752 calendar reform (as some is), the argument for St. Thecla is weakened.
77 W.S.L. 350/5/40, Ch. Stretton pp. 41–2; P.R.O., E 178/3075; E 302/1/5, no. 34.
78 *T.S.A.S.* 3rd ser. v. 361; vii. 269; viii. 47; H.W.R.O.(H.), Heref. dioc. rec., visit. bk. 17; *Alum. Oxon. 1500--1714*, ii. 675.
79 Rob. Catterall 1912–14: *Crockford* (1910), 251.
80 The yrs. 1647–67 yield no names.
81 See below, this section, and next two notes.
82 For Peter Dormer d. 1667, Geo. Roberts 1668, Hen. Maurice 1668–71, Hen. Clayton 1671–1725, and Alex. Roberts 1904–11, see *Alum. Oxon. 1500–1714*, i. 287, 415; iii. 991, 1261; *1715–1886*, iii. 1204.
83 For Rowland Tench 1725–48, S. C. Woods 1914–22, W. H. Wilson 1964–71, and F. P. B. Ashe 1972–4, see *Alum. Cantab. to 1751*, iv. 214; *1752–1900*, vi. 574; *Crockford* (1971–2), 1050; (1973–4), 29.
84 Bannister, *Heref. Institutions*, 87; *S.P.R. Heref.* viii (2), 208; *Alum. Cantab. to 1751*, iii. 127; *Admissions to Coll. of St. John the Evangelist Camb.* iii, ed. R. F. Scott (1903), 105, 526–7; J. Cradock, *Literary and Misc. Memoirs* (1828), i. 189–92; iv. 228–34.
85 B.M. *Gen. Cat. of Printed Bks. to 1955* (photolithographic edn. 1959–66), cl, cols. 698–9; P. H. Lang, *Geo. Frideric Handel* (1967), 16, 85–6, 598–9, 682, 713.
86 For Mainwaring's successors see above and below, this section; refs. in other sections. For Nunn see *Stretton Focus*, May 1982, p. 9; Jan. 1989, p. 9.
87 Heref. Dioc. Regy., regs. 1902–19 sqq.
88 *Shrews. Chron.* 4 Aug. 1939, p. 4; 12 Dec. 1947, p. 3.
89 S.R.O. 3908/Ch/1 *passim*, esp. 24 June 1819, 25 July 1822, 26 June 1832. The rector was intent on beautifying the chancel in 1819 (below, this section). Mr. G. C. Ashman is thanked for comment and for lending his notes on this source.
90 S.R.O. 3908/AV/1–2; P.R.O., HO 129/354, no. 6; *V.C.H. Salop.* ii. 228.
91 Below, this section.

E. Lloyd Oswell, it held 230. In 1903 the timber-framed All Saints', Little Stretton, was built on Mrs. A. E. Gibbon's property and at her expense to hold *c.* 150;[92] it was conveyed to the church in 1958.[93]

The opening of the new chapels of ease came as the culmination of Noel-Hill's energetic 25 years' incumbency and the funds for All Stretton chapel were raised largely by his exertions.[94] Besides his invigoration of local benefit clubs and charities[95] Noel-Hill had promptly organized mission services in outlying parts of the parish and district visiting. He had immediately introduced a daily service, more frequent celebrations of communion, and a surpliced choir of boys, while the church and its services were embellished with flowers and pictures, the latter arousing fears of Roman 'imagery'.[96] In 1883 a new organ was installed in a new chamber off the chancel,[97] and it was probably *c.* 1886 that 16th- and 17th-century Flemish glass was put in chancel windows.[98] Noel-Hill founded a ringing society in 1880,[99] and in 1890 two of the six bells of 1711 were recast, two trebles added, and the whole peal rehung.[1] Probably about the same time a chalice—in a medieval style, perhaps by Bodley—and paten were acquired and added to earlier gifts of plate by Mrs. Coleman (1818) and R. N. Pemberton (1823).[2] A chancel screen was fitted in 1898.[3]

In the 20th century the ownership of the patronage[4] produced a consistently Evangelical emphasis. In the parish church Sunday communicants averaged 34 in 1904 and 67 by 1967, an increase proportionately greater than that of the population,[5] not counting communicants in the chapels of ease. Easter communicants numbered 251 in 1905 and 276 in 1967, but Christmas communicants rose from 146 in 1904 to 346 by 1967, apparently owing to the increasing popularity of the midnight service introduced in 1946.[6] There was normally a curate,[7] and from 1973 there was a lay worker.[8]

John Mainwaring's parsonage, and residence in the Cambridge vacation,[9] was perhaps the 'decent house' recorded in the 16th and 17th centuries[10] and sketched in 1767. If so a single range, with a lower building to the east and what were probably two stacks on the south or garden side,[11] comprised two parlours, two butteries, five chambers, a kitchen, a boulting house, a malt chamber, a stable, and an ox house all under one roof; there were also a barn and a sheepcot, each of five bays.[12] How much of it survived the late 18th century is uncertain,[13] though thicker walls in the north-west part[14] may be stone or brick-clad timber.

Great changes to the house and its grounds were made by Mainwaring and his successors.[15] In the 1770s Mainwaring, a friend of 'Capability' Brown, was improving part of the glebe around his house:[16] to the west part of Townbrook hollow was laid out with walks and provided with an artificial pool and small cascade overlooked by a gothick summer-house;[17] then or later an ice-house was made near the pool.[18] In the late 18th century a west end or wing of the rectory probably comprised drawing room and (to the north) dining room; there was perhaps an entrance hall in the centre of the south front. It was evidently T. B. Coleman, rector 1807–18,[19] who undertook the remodelling that shifted the main entrance to the west in order to locate the principal rooms on the south so as to command a fine prospect: the town did not intrude on the distant view of Ragleth hill and on the west there was a nearer view of the intricately folded, well planted flanks of the Long Mynd interrupted by a grassy field sloping up out of sight. Across the view,[20] *c.* 130 m. south of the house, a new drive was made (probably by T. B. Coleman, after his demolition of Stretton Hall)[21] to run west from a lodge in Back Lane; after turning north it swung round to the west front where a neo-classical, apparently recessed entrance, flanked by Doric columns seemingly *in antis*, was contrived between the projecting stacks of the late 18th-century drawing and dining rooms. The dining room was reduced to make a vestibule and a staircase was built between the west and south wings.[22] Coleman's successor R. N. Pemberton, 1818–48,[23]

92 Par. rec., papers on St. Mic.'s, All Stretton 1901–3; Pevsner, *Salop.* 101; Bilbey, *Ch. Stretton*, pl. 157; *Kelly's Dir. Salop.* (1905), 60, 62; above, manors (Lt. Stretton Manor Ho.).

93 Heref. Dioc. Regy., reg. 1953–68, pp. 255–6.

94 *Shrews. Chron.* 8 Jan. 1904, p. 3; 27 Nov. 1911, p. 7; cf. W. Mate & Sons Ltd. *Shropshire: Historical, Descriptive, Biographical* (1906), pt. 2, p. 102.

95 Below, chars.

96 S.R.O. 2495 uncat., vol. of Ch. Stretton newscuttings.

97 Below, this section.

98 Par. rec., invoice for glass 1886.

99 S.R.O. 2495 uncat., vol. of Ch. Stretton newscuttings.

1 For the bells see H. B. Walters, *Ch. Bells Salop.* (Oswestry, 1915), 88–90.

2 D. L. Arkwright and B. W. Bourne, *Ch. Plate Archd. Ludlow* (Shrews. 1961), 19.

3 Below, this section.

4 Above, this section.

5 Trinitytide statistics in S.R.O. 3908/Rg 16, 26; cf. *V.C.H. Salop.* ii. 228.

6 S.R.O. 3908/Rg 23, p. 54; ibid. /Rg. 23–6.

7 Heref. Dioc. Regy., regs. 1902–19 sqq.

8 Ibid. 1969– (in use), p. 157; local inf.

9 D. Stroud, *Capability Brown* (1975), 171 (ref. owed to Mr. J. B. Lawson).

10 H.W.R.O.(H.), HD 2/14/17–18.

11 S.R.O. 3357 uncat., map of Ch. Stretton glebe 1767. The features here interpreted as stacks were just possibly gables. Mr. Eric Mercer is thanked for comment on the ho.

12 H.W.R.O.(H.), HD 2/14/17–18.

13 S.R.O. 3357 uncat., plan of lands to be exchanged 1811, marks the ho. but without details to relate to the 1767 sketch.

14 For this and what follows thanks are due to Mr. and Mrs. R. D. Bilbey and Mr. and Mrs. J. H. Meynall for allowing insp. of their homes.

15 W.S.L. 350/5/40, Ch. Stretton p. 17; cf. Dept. of Environment, *List of Bldgs. of Special Archit. or Hist. Interest: R.D. of Ludlow* (1974), 31.

16 Cradock, *Memoirs*, i. 82–3; iv. 147; Stroud, *Brown*, 171–2, locating Mainwaring's improvements on the slopes of Caer Caradoc (where his wife's fam., the Wildings, had an est.), but descriptions and other evidence suggest the glebe on the Long Mynd's slopes. Cf. *S.P.R. Heref.* viii (2), 120; S.R.O. 567/5/3/1/19, 19 Aug. 1781.

17 S.R.O. 3357 uncat., map of Ch. Stretton glebe 1767.

18 O.S. Map 1/2,500, Salop. LVI.5 (1883 edn.); Bilbey, *Ch. Stretton*, pl. 55.

19 Bannister, *Heref. Institutions*, 133, 143; cf. next note.

20 And so across the lands bought in 1801 and 1804 by Thos. Coleman (S.R.O. 248/17, pp. 44, 57–64, 101–2), the new patron (above, this section), evidently with these changes to the ho. in mind.

21 Above, manors (the Hall).

22 S.R.O. 299/3; Bilbey, *Ch. Stretton*, pl. 53–4.

23 Bannister, *Heref. Institutions*, 142, 164.

raised the height of the large central room on the south, probably in the earlier 1830s;[24] a passage and a service wing east and north of the staircase block were perhaps built or rebuilt by him.

The 19th-century rectors lived in gentlemanly style. Coleman was lord of the manor and patron as well as parson. His successor Pemberton bought the patronage and much land in the parish; some of his purchases adjoining the 29 a. of glebe around the parsonage had been let to him, before being sold to him in 1833, by Coleman's widow. By 1834 a high brick boundary wall secluded Pemberton's rectory, glebe, and private estate from the town. His property comprised virtually all the land between the town and the Mynd and a wide tract of hill and dale as far as the township boundary; near World's End a lodge marked the beginning of a carriage drive through Pemberton's new plantations.[25] Pemberton inherited the Millichope estate in 1832[26] and built Millichope Park (in Munslow) where he lived from 1841.[27] In accordance with Pemberton's will his second cousin's son, C. A. Salusbury, was presented to the living in 1849. Thereby he became entitled to Pemberton's private estate in Church Stretton and Acton Scott parishes during his incumbency; but he died the same year, and his successor H. O. Wilson, 1849–79,[28] spent over £1,000 on furniture, glass, china, linen, books,[29] and cellar stock[30] which had belonged to Pemberton and Salusbury.[31] In 1853 an exchange of land with C. O. Childe-Pemberton of Millichope increased the glebe south of the parsonage by more than 9½ a. which Wilson's two predecessors had owned privately.[32] Eventually Wilson also bought property of his own in the parish[33] as did his successor Charles Noel-Hill, 1879–1904, a grandson of the 4th Lord Berwick.[34] In 1885 Noel-Hill bought 14 a. adjoining the glebe north of the parsonage from Charles Baldwyn Childe of Kinlet; parts of that were added to the glebe before 1906 and *c.* 2 a. more in that year.[35] When he died in 1911 Noel-Hill owned seven houses and twelve cottages in the town with other small properties.[36]

Dr. H. T. Dixon and his successors lived in Mynd Court, Longhills Road, built *c.* 1905 on former glebe,[37] and Dixon let the Old Rectory to tenants until its sale *c.* 1935. Mynd Court was replaced as the rectory in 1981 when Norfolk Lodge, Carding Mill Valley Road, was bought.[38]

The cruciform church of *ST. LAWRENCE*, so called by *c.* 1740,[39] is built partly of uncoursed rubble and partly of ashlar. It consists of chancel, embattled and pinnacled central tower, transepts with west aisles, and a nave with south vestry in place of a former porch. The nave is 12th-century and has nearly opposing north and south doorways of the period. Seen from outside, the blocked north doorway, recessed in a thicker part of the wall, has a semicircular arch and original abaci on the west; reset above the doorway are fragments of 12th-century carved stone and a sheela-na-gig. The south doorway, now connecting nave and vestry, is of one order with attached shafts. About 1200 the church became cruciform with the building of transepts, tower, and a new chancel. Chancel and north transept have doorways contemporary with their build: towards the west end of the chancel a priest's doorway pierces the south wall, and until 1882[40] another doorway pierced the north wall and perhaps gave access to the tower stair; the blocked doorway in the north transept ceased to be external when the west aisle was added in 1868. There were two almost opposing lancets in the north transept but the western one was reset in the aisle added in 1868. The south transept has an original south doorway and a lancet in the east wall; another lancet, reset in the aisle added in 1867, ceased to be external when the vestry was extended in 1882. In the nave the double lancet in the south wall may be 13th-century. In the chancel a new east window was inserted probably in the 14th century, and the north and south windows of the transepts, though possibly repaired in the early 17th century, may also be 14th-century insertions. The nave and chancel roofs are of coupled rafters, the former with straight braces to the collars, the latter with curved braces; the north-transept coupled rafters have alternating curved and straight braces.

A low side window and a window above it, at the south-west corner of the chancel, are probably 15th-century.[41] The sill of the upper window, recut from a tomb cross, contains a piscina presumed to have served an altar in a rood loft at the west end of the chancel; window and piscina are the only evidence of the existence of a loft. The low side window may have lit a priest's desk. The font also is 15th-century,[42] and the ashlar upper storey of the tower and the

24 Pemberton crest in ceiling; cf. 1st-floor fenestration 1834 in S.R.O. 299/3.

25 Above, this section; above, manors; tithe award; S.R.O. 299/3; 1045/525; W.S.L. 350/5/40, Ch. Stretton p. 35.

26 From his uncle Thos. Pemberton: cf. J. B. Blakeway, *Sheriffs of Salop.* (Shrews. 1831), 192; Burke, *Land. Gent.* (1914), 368 n.; cf. *V.C.H. Salop.* iv. 204.

27 Pevsner, *Salop.* 200; Heref. Dioc. Regy., reg. 1822–42, pp. 575, 649; reg. 1847–56, p. 147; *S.P.R. Heref.* viii (2), p. v.

28 S.R.O. 1011, box 241, draft settlement (11 Aug. 1849) of est. devised by the Revd. R. N. Pemberton, Pemberton pedigree; *S.P.R. Heref.* viii (2), pp. v–vi.

29 Pemberton left over 900 vols. at the rectory: S.R.O. 1011, box 241, bdle. of executorship papers, inv. of bks.

30 Comprising 55 doz. of sherry, port, and madeira.

31 S.R.O. 1011, box 241, statement of effects to be taken by Wilson.

32 S.R.O. 3908/Gl/1–3.

33 *S.P.R. Heref.* viii (2), p. vi; Burke, *Peerage* (1949), 185.

34 S.C.C deeds Gen. 147.

35 Ibid.

36 S.R.O. 4044/39, pp. 11 no. 77, 14 nos. 105–9, 18 no. 148, 24–8 nos. 209–13, 229–34, 237, 245–6; /40 [after Wistanstow] no. 1192.

37 Cf. par. rec., corresp. *re* purchase of Mynd Ct. 1922; S.R.O., DA 7/531/1, p. 26; *Kelly's Dir. Salop.* (1909), 65; O.S. Map 1/2,500, Salop. LVI.5 (1938 edn.).

38 Heref. Dioc. Regy., reg. 1919–26, p. 238; 1926–38, p. 461; 1969– (in use), p. 396; Bilbey, *Ch. Stretton*, pl. 58; cf. *Ludlow Parl. Divn. Spring Reg. 1923*, 237–48; *Autumn Reg. 1923*, 235–47.

39 B.L. Add. MS. 30316, ff. 29v.–30. This para. and the next two are based on Cranage, ii. 80–3; Pevsner, *Salop.* 100–1; S.R.O. 3908/Ch/12.

40 When an organ chamber was built: below, this section.

41 For these two windows cf. Cranage, x. 1059–60, 1075–7, 1079, 1083–6.

42 Bodl. MS. Top. Salop. c. 2, f. 457.

south-transept roof, arch-braced with the wind braces arranged in quatrefoils, perhaps date from *c.* 1500.[43]

In the early 17th century Bonham Norton's widow Jane (*née* Owen) rebuilt the west wall of the church, and at her death in 1640 she endowed the repair of the west end.[44] Probably about the same time the two-light south window in the chancel replaced a smaller window and other repairs to doors and windows were made.

About 1830 the church's 'beautiful appearance' inside was attributed to R. N. Pemberton's activity and taste. Perhaps in 1819 he had provided a new east window, with glass by David Evans of Shrewsbury, and fitted up the chancel with Jacobean and earlier woodwork collected from various places.[45] Repairs to the end of the south transept involved considerable rebuilding in 1827.[46] On Pemberton's proposal in 1831 a new west entrance was provided and a vestry room was built on the site of the old wooden south porch; a west gallery was built with pews in the front rows. The north transept was roofed with Broseley tiles in 1833.[47] The tower was repaired in 1839,[48] and in 1841 the nave was roofed with Broseley tiles and crests.[49]

The church was restored in 1867–8. S. Pountney Smith's original scheme[50] was considerably modified[51] to achieve, in the end, the removal of the west gallery and the addition of a west aisle to each transept; encaustic tiles were laid, new seats replaced the old pews in nave and transepts, and new choir seats replaced the rector's pews at the west end of the chancel. The font was moved across the nave from the north doorway to the south.[52] In 1880 a pulpit of mixed native and foreign marbles on a Caen stone base, designed by Smith in an Early English style, was installed at the corner of the chancel and north transept in memory of H. O. Wilson;[53] it replaced a three-decker Jacobean pulpit at the corner of the chancel and south transept, parts of which, in 1885, were arranged around the font,[54] probably then moved down the nave to the south-west corner. The top of the tower was rebuilt with a new, pyramidal, roof and new pinnacles in 1880–1.[55] The vestry was extended probably in 1882,[56] when a new organ chamber was built north of the chancel.[57] It was probably in Noel-Hill's time that the inside walls were scraped.[58]

A carved oak chancel screen by S. Bodley was fitted in 1898.[59] Much restoration work was carried out in the 1930s.[60] In 1977 the sanctuary was enlarged and the altar-rail entrance widened. In 1984 the chancel screen was removed and the north transept aisle, enclosed with glass fitted to parts of the screen, became an Emmaus chapel for worship and private prayer.[61]

In the chancel the north window and the low side window contain Flemish roundels and panels of the late 16th and 17th centuries;[62] the high window includes fragments said to have come from St. Mary's, Shrewsbury.[63] Several windows have Victorian glass[64] but the glass in the north and south windows of the transepts is 20th-century, the latter replacing glass given by Edward Gibbon of Little Stretton *c.* 1873.[65] The south-transept lancet depicts 'Jessica' in memory of the writer 'Hesba Stretton' (Sarah Smith, d. 1911).[66] The south window of the south-transept aisle contains glass commemorating Edward (d. 1455) and Elizabeth Leighton, of Stretton, and Lord Leighton of Stretton (1830–96), P.R.A. 1878–96.[67]

In 1553 the church had five bells and a sanctus bell and a silver chalice. Except for a paten of 1798 the other plate was 19th-century or later.[68]

The registers begin in 1662 and are complete thereafter.[69]

The churchyard occupied *c.* ¾ a. in 1839.[70] In the early 19th century its wall was divided into some 76 'hayments' whose repair, with the repair of the gates and stile, was apportioned to the

43 Pountney Smith considered the tower's upper storeys 16th-cent. Perp.: S.R.O. 3908/Ch/12. Mr. Eric Mercer is thanked for comment.

44 *T.S.A.S.* 3rd ser. i. 356. Cf. Owen of Condover arms in W. window: A. H. Horrocks, *Story of St. Laurence Par. Ch., Ch. Stretton* (Cheltenham, 1982), [6].

45 St. Deiniol's Libr., Hawarden, Sir Steph. Glynne's ch. notes, xcvi, f. 2; cf. Cranage, ii. 80; x. 978; *V.C.H. Salop.* viii. 236.

46 S.R.O. 3908/Ch/1, note of vestry mtg. 11 Jan. 1827; ibid. disbursements 1827.

47 Ibid. notes of vestry mtgs. 17 Mar. 1831, 13 June 1833; St. Deiniol's Libr., Glynne's ch. notes, xcvi, ff. 1–2.

48 S.R.O. 3908/Ch/1, note of vestry mtg. 22 July 1839.

49 Ibid. 17 June 1841.

50 Ibid. /Ch/12 (16 July 1867).

51 By enlarging the S. transept aisle (cf. ibid. /13–15) and adding a N. transept aisle (ibid. /17). A new choir (where the later organ chamber was built) and sacristy proposed by Smith (ibid. /16, n.d.) were not built.

52 Ibid. /Ch/1, notes of vestry mtgs. 11 Jan., 12 Apr. 1867, 27 Apr. 1868, and printed accts. 1867–8; ibid. /Ch/4, 12– 17; Horrocks, *St. Laurence Par. Ch.* [1].

53 S.R.O. 2495 uncat., Ch. Stretton cuttings bk. 23 Aug. [1880]; 3908/Ch/5–8.

54 Bodl. MS. Top. Salop. c. 2, f. 458; St. Deiniol's Libr., Glynne's ch. notes, xcvi, f. 2; Cranage, ii. 82.

55 S.R.O. 2495 uncat., Ch. Stretton cuttings bk., loose cutting prob. Jan. 1881; 3908/Ch/2, note of vestry mtg. 23 Sept. 1880.

56 In which case a 1913 faculty (Heref. Dioc. Regy., reg. 1902–19, p. 550) presumably refers to the demolition of the internal wall shown on Pountney Smith's plan of Dec. 1881 (S.R.O. 3908/Ch/18).

57 S.R.O. 2495 uncat., Ch. Stretton cuttings bk., loose cutting July or Aug. 1881; 3908/Ch/2, offertory acct. 1883–4; Cranage, ii. 80.

58 Mr. D. C. George's suggestion. In 1867 the vestry had instructed Pountney Smith to clean and colour the walls and fit oak to the bottom of the nave walls: S.R.O. 3908/Ch/1, note of mtg. 12 Apr. 1867.

59 Heref. Dioc. Regy., reg. 1883–1901, pp. 616–17; par. rec., plan, accts. etc. 1898; Horrocks, *St. Laurence Par. Ch.* [7].

60 Par. rec., vouchers, corresp., etc., 1932–3, 1936–8; SA 10770.

61 Heref. Dioc. Regy., reg. 1969– (in use), pp. 255–6, 456.

62 Pevsner, *Salop.* 101; Horrocks, op. cit. [5]; W. Cole, 'Glass-Paintings after Heemskerck in Eng.' *Antiquaries Jnl.* lx. 251, 258, 261–2.

63 *Par. Ch. of St. Laurence, Ch. Stretton* [1985].

64 Horrocks, op. cit. [5–6].

65 Heref. Dioc. Regy., reg. 1926–38, pp. 241, 426; 1953–68, p. 63; S.R.O. 3908/Ch/1, note on accts. for 1872–3; cf. E. Cassey & Co. *Dir. Salop.* (1871), 113, 115.

66 Best known for *Jessica's First Prayer* (1866): *D.N.B.* 1901–11; plaque of 1914 in ch.; above, intro.

67 *D.N.B.*; *Complete Peerage*, vii. 572; R. Jenkyns, *The Victorians and Ancient Greece* (1980), 300, 305–8, 310–13, 319–20, 323.

68 *T.S.A.S.* 2nd ser. xii. 306; Arkwright and Bourne, *Ch. Plate*, 19.

69 S.R.O. 3908/Rg/1–15; *S.P.R. Heref.* viii (2); modern regs. in ch. Transcripts for 1638 and 1660 survive in H.W.R.O.(H.), Heref. dioc. rec.

70 Tithe field 1216.

landowners.[71] The churchyard was slightly reduced on the west for road widening in 1934.[72] An additional burial ground, *c.* 1 a. at the south end of the town, was consecrated in 1869.[73]

ROMAN CATHOLICISM. There was one papist in the parish in 1676 and 1686[74] but none in 1767.[75] A mission opened in 1907–8, when the Catholic population was 20, was served for some years from neighbouring Catholic parishes. At first mass was celebrated in a house in Watling Street, later in Manchester House, Churchway. The first resident priest arrived in 1923, and St. Milburga's church opened in 1929 with seating for 70. Designed by F. H. Shayler of Shrewsbury, church and presbytery were built at the corner of Sandford Avenue and Watling Street North on land given by Mrs. Sarah Dutton of Shrewsbury.[76] The Church Stretton priest served Acton Burnell until 1939–40 when sisters of Our Lady of Sion established a convent in the Hall there and a resident priest was appointed.[77] By *c.* 1990 the Catholic population was 185, and Craven Arms and Plowden were then served from Church Stretton.[78]

In 1946 Brockhurst[79] was opened as St. Mary's scholasticate by missionaries of the Company of Mary (Montfort Fathers). The scholasticate professors served regular mass centres at Clun, Knighton (Radnors.), Mawley (in Cleobury Mortimer), Middleton Priors, Shipton, and Much Wenlock but left *c.* 1968.[80]

PROTESTANT NONCONFORMITY. Henry Maurice, rector 1668–71, favoured the nonconformists and resigned the living. He preached at Church Stretton as a nonconformist before receiving his licence, soon establishing himself in Much Wenlock and becoming an itinerant preacher in Breconshire.[81] At Stretton he left a small dissenting congregation. Thomas Sankey and his wife and Thomas Gallier's wife Elizabeth had been presented as 'anabaptists' in 1662,[82] and in 1669 Joan, widow of Jerome Zankey, and Elizabeth Gallier were reputed 'schismatics'.[83] Joan Zankey's house in All Stretton was licensed for Congregational worship in 1672[84] and that year three men and the wife of one of them were presented for frequenting conventicles.[85] There were two dissenters in 1676[86] and next year John Gallier, anabaptist, was apparently converted and baptized into the church.[87] A meeting house was licensed in 1725 and the Baker family were anabaptists in the early 1730s[88] but there were no dissenters in the parish by 1767.[89] Meeting houses were registered in 1808 and 1833.[90]

Primitive Methodists of the Bishop's Castle circuit (founded 1832) were at work in Church Stretton in the 1830s. From 1837 or earlier there were meetings in the town. It was not fertile ground, but the northern and southern parts of the parish were, and meetings just beyond the parish boundary were probably accessible to the remoter parishioners. It was the success of the area's scattered rural meetings that enabled a Church Stretton branch (with 121 members) to organize itself within the circuit from 1844 and the branch became a circuit (with 154 members) in 1872.[91] Church Stretton was in Shrewsbury Methodist circuit 1952–64, Craven Arms and Church Stretton circuit 1964–72, and Shropshire South circuit from 1972.[92]

In the northern part of the parish there were Primitive Methodist meetings at All Stretton by 1837, Bullocks Moor by 1838,[93] and Lower Wood by 1842.[94] Pennsylvania, on plan from 1854, became the strongest of the area's meetings.[95] In 1866 the All Stretton meeting was using a private house[96] and may have ceased soon after. Lower Wood throve less than other meetings in the parish in the 1860s and came off plan in 1872;[97] soon afterwards, however, the Pennsylvania meeting began to plan the building of a chapel at Lower Wood, which opened in 1876.[98] It closed *c.* 1950.[99]

In the southern part of the parish there were Primitive Methodist meetings at Minton and Little Stretton by 1839.[1] By 1851, when there was a Hamperley meeting just over the boundary

71 S.R.O. 3908/Chy/1.
72 Par. rec., faculties of 1934 and corresp.
73 S.R.O. 3908/Ch/1, notes of vestry mtgs. 1867–8, accts. 1868–78; /2, accts. 1878–83; /Chy/2–4; Heref. Dioc. Regy., reg. 1857–69, pp. 626, 657–9; O.S. Map 1/2,500, Salop. LVI.9 (1903 edn.); par. rec., interment bk.
74 *Compton Census*, ed. Whiteman, 259; M. D. G. Wanklyn, 'Recusants in Dioc. of Heref. 1660–1688', *Worcs. Recusant*, liv. 26, 28–9, 33.
75 H.W.R.O.(H.), Heref. dioc. rec., return of papists 1767.
76 *Dioc. of Shrews. Centenary Record 1851–1951* (1951), 29; Bilbey, *Ch. Stretton*, pl. 35; S.R.O. 2079/LVI.9, no. 1280; 4044/40, no. 1280; *Kelly's Dir. Salop.* (1929), 373; O.N.S. (Birkdale), Worship Reg. no. 55995.
77 *Dioc. of Shrews. Centenary Rec.* 26–7, 29; cf. *V.C.H. Salop.* viii. 8, 12–13.
78 *Shrews. Dioc. Yr. Bk. 1991*, 29.
79 Former prep. sch.: below, educ.
80 *Dioc. of Shrews. Centenary Rec.* 29, 33–4, 37; cf. *Shrews. Dioc. Yr. Bk. 1968*, 112 (last mention); *Shropshire Mag.* June 1968, 44.
81 Below, M. Wenlock, prot. nonconf.; *Calamy Revised*, ed. A. G. Matthews, 346; *Dict. Welsh Biog.* 622–3.
82 H.W.R.O.(H.), HD 7/18, 1662.
83 Ibid. 1669. For Jerome Zankey see *T.S.A.S.* l. 171–8; R. Gough, *Myddle* (Shrews. 1875), 142.
84 *Cal. S.P. Dom.* 1672, 401; Hen. Maurice's diary (MS. in possession of the late Dr. Basil Cottle, Bristol Univ., who kindly supplied a transcript), 26 June, 2 July, 27 Sept. 1672.
85 H.W.R.O.(H.), HD 7/67, 1672.
86 *Compton Census*, ed. Whiteman, 259.
87 *S.P.R. Heref.* viii (2), 21.
88 Ibid. 69; *Orders of Q. Sess.* ii. 54.
89 H.W.R.O.(H.), Heref. dioc. rec., return of papists, 1767.
90 *Orders of Q. Sess.* iii. 145; Heref. Dioc. Regy., reg. 1822–42, p. 213.
91 *V.C.H. Salop.* ii. 15; S.R.O. 2138/54, 82; 3219/1, 4 Dec. 1871 (no. 27), 3 June (no. 19) and 2 Sept. (no. 26) 1872; *Prim. Meth. Min.* (1872), 13.
92 W. E. Morris, *Hist. of Methodism in Shrews. & Dist.* (Shrews. 1960), 27; *Meth. Conf. Min.* (1952), 92; (1964), 170; S.R.O. 3938/6/7–44; 4286/2/10; /5/10–37. The last named was briefly called Ludlow and Craven Arms circuit.
93 S.R.O. 2138/48, [pp. 2, 6, 11, 23, 27].
94 Ibid. /49 *passim* esp. 5 Sept. 1847 (protracted mtg. at Lr. Wood), 53–4, 57–8, 61, 63.
95 Ibid. /62, 64; 3219/1.
96 S.R.O. 3219/1, June 1866.
97 Ibid. esp. 4 Mar. 1872 (no. 10).
98 Ibid. 7 Dec. 1874 (no. 11), 8 Mar. (no. 10), 6 Sept. (no. 18), and Dec. (no. 5) 1875.
99 S.R.O. 3212/4/50; cf. ibid. /6/1–7.
1 S.R.O. 2138/48, [pp. 17, 19, 23, 25, 27].

in Wistanstow parish,[2] the Minton meeting may have ceased, but the Little Stretton meeting prospered in the 1860s: in 1863–4 there were camp and protracted meetings there and plans were formed to build a chapel.[3] Opened in 1868, it stood at the northern end of the village.[4] There was a resident minister by 1885 and until 1906; his manse was a small cottage nearby.[5] The chapel had closed by the mid 1950s.[6]

A 'preaching house' in Church Stretton was in use in 1837 but seems to have been given up on grounds of expense next year. There were camp meetings and open-air preachings, and travelling preachers evidently stayed in the town, but it was a difficult place, mission territory, taken off plan in 1840.[7] Carding Mill came on plan in 1855 but was off next year.[8] A regular meeting in the town in the 1860s had no premises of its own: the town hall was used at Christmas 1863. A year later hopes of building a chapel were entertained, but in 1865 it was agreed to try to get the Congregationalists' room should they give it up.[9] Not until 1906, however, was a Methodist chapel opened in the town: of Ruabon brick and to a design by W. Scott Deakin of Shrewsbury, it was built at the corner of Crossways and Watling Street in a rapidly developing area.[10] A manse nearby was taken in 1906 and the Little Stretton cottage was given up; *c.* 1922 a manse was built on land adjoining the church, partly with materials from the recently demolished Preen Manor.[11] A Sunday school was built between church and manse in 1956.[12]

By 1850 there were Wesleyan meetings on the Ludlow circuit at All Stretton (6 members) and Minton (4). There may have been a failed attempt to establish one at Little Stretton next year, but in 1858 a meeting started there and over the next ten years membership doubled from 7 to 14. The Minton meeting, though it had doubled its membership by 1860, ceased in 1860 and the All Stretton meeting ceased in 1862.[13] At Little Stretton, however, a chapel was opened in the 1870s and there was a resident minister.[14] The chapel closed soon after 1922.[15]

Congregational worship in Church Stretton began in the summer of 1858 on the initiative of ministers and laymen from Shrewsbury, Dorrington, and Ludlow. The first services were open-air, under the town hall. Later a room that had been a carpenter's workshop was taken; despite its shortcomings (approach by a narrow stepladder and inconveniently low) the cause prospered. A Sunday school was established and services began at an out-station at All Stretton. In 1860 a church of seven members was formed under the auspices of the Castle Gates Congregational church in Shrewsbury. In 1865–6 a chapel was built in High Street on a site for which Thomas Barnes, M.P., had advanced the money.[16] Designed in a gothic style by Joseph Bratton of Birkenhead, the chapel was renovated in 1886 and 1900 and refurbished in 1937.[17] It prospered in the 1870s and from the beginning there was a resident minister[18] save for the years 1882–99;[19] in the early 20th century the manse was in Watling Street[20] but later elsewhere in the town.[21] In 1957 a hall was added south of the church.[22] The church had 72 members in 1985.[23]

In All Stretton a cottage in the Row was used for Congregational worship until 1895, and then larger premises in the Old Room, farther along the lane, until 1907.[24] A mission church seating 120 was built at the northern end of the Row in 1907.[25] It closed in 1984 when United Reformed Church members in the village began to use St. Michael's.[26]

EDUCATION. There were two principal schools in the parish: an endowed or charity[27] church school that existed by the end of the 16th century and became a primary school in 1948, and a modern school which opened that year and later became comprehensive. There were also, however, private schools from the late 18th century and a workhouse school in the 19th century.

Private schools were held by Mr. J. Meredith, master of an 'academy', from 1791 to 1801, by a Mrs. Johnson in 1797, and by Miss Perkins and Miss Rogers in 1806.[28] In 1819, besides the endowed school and a Sunday school, there were five small schools containing *c.* 46 young children. By 1835 there were two infant schools

2 P.R.O., HO 129/354, no. 4A.
3 S.R.O. 3219/1, Nov.–Dec. 1866, Mar. Sept. 1867, Mar. 1868.
4 Ibid. Mar. 1868; ibid. /104–5; O.N.S. (Birkdale), Worship Reg. no. 19351 (cancelled 1964 on revision of list); O.S. Map 1/2,500, Salop. LVI.13 (1883 edn.).
5 *Kelly's Dir. Salop.* (1885–1905); Morris, *Methodism in Shrews.* 56; below, this section.
6 S.R.O. 3212/4/13–14; 3219/71.
7 S.R.O. 2138/48, [pp. 3–4, 6, 8, 10–12, 14, 17, 25, and pp. 1–2 and 8 from end].
8 Ibid. /63–4.
9 S.R.O. 3219/1, Aug. 1863, Dec. 1864, Dec. 1865.
10 S.R.O. 3212/1/1–93; 3219/2, s.a. 1905 sqq.; Bilbey, *Ch. Stretton*, pl. 34; O.N.S. (Birkdale), Worship Reg. no. 41946.
11 S.R.O. 3219/2, 5 Dec. 1905 (no. 15), 6 Mar. 1906 (no. 14); S.R.O., DA 7/516/1, p. 25 (no. 305); *Kelly's Dir. Salop.* (1905), 62–3; Morris, *Methodism in Shrews.* 56; *V.C.H. Salop.* viii. 125.
12 Morris, op. cit. 57; S.R.O. 3212/4/1–294.
13 S.R.O. 2612/12, s.a.
14 E. Cassey & Co. *Dir. Salop.* (1874), 113 (no mention); *P.O. Dir. Salop.* (1879), 299–300.
15 *Kelly's Dir. Salop.* (1922), 64 (last mention).
16 *Utd. Ref. Ch. Yr. Bk. 1985–6*, 59; S.R.O. 3219/1, Dec. 1865.
17 Bilbey, *Ch. Stretton*, pl. 33; S.R.O. 4950/2/1, 3 Apr. 1900; O.N.S. (Birkdale), Worship Reg. no. 17370; inscr. on bldg.
18 S.R.O. 4950/2/1–7; *P.O. Dir. Salop.* (1870), 36; (1879), 299; E. Cassey & Co. *Dir. Salop.* (1871), 114; (1874), 114; *Kelly's Dir. Salop.* (1900–41).
19 When the ch. was served from Dorrington: S.R.O. 4950/2/1, hist. acct. and min. 27 June 1899; cf. *V.C.H. Salop.* viii. 56.
20 *Kelly's Dir. Salop.* (1900–41); S.R.O. 2079/LVI.9, no. 393; 4044/39, p. 432 no. 393.
21 Local inf.
22 Bilbey, *Ch. Stretton*, pl. 33.
23 *Utd. Ref. Ch. Yr. Bk. 1985–6*, 59.
24 Bilbey, op. cit. pls. 164–5.
25 Ibid.; *Kelly's Dir. Salop.* (1909), 63; O.S. Map 6", Salop. LVI.NW. (1928 edn.).
26 O.N.S. (Birkdale), Worship Reg. no. 76889.
27 The term used *c.* 1790: *24th Rep. Com. Char.* H.C. 231, p. 406 (1831), xi. This section was written 1982–3 and later revised.
28 R. Hume, 'Changing Patterns of Educ. Development in Salop. 1660–1833' (Keele Univ. Ph.D. (Educ.) thesis, 1982), 238, 312–13, 381.

attended by 13 boys and 21 girls, whose parents paid fees. There were also two fee-paying schools for older children. One, kept by the Misses Corfield in Ragleth House, High Street, until the 1850s, had 30 girls. The other had 32 boys; it was a commercial boarding school kept by William Craig in Grove House, All Stretton, from 1830 or earlier to 1842 or later.[29] In 1856 there were three private schools: a boarding school in the town (the Park) and another at All Stretton and a day school at Little Stretton. The two last were short-lived but Park House was a school until *c.* 1870.[30] Ashbrook Villa, north of the town, was a school *c.* 1885–1900. In the years before 1914 five private schools were started in or near the town: at Brockhurst, Burway House (the old church school), and Clivedon by 1905, Ashlett House, High Street, by 1909, and Mount View, Hazler Lane, by 1913. Only the first two survived the First World War, lasting into the early 1940s, when Brockhurst preparatory school was moved to Staffordshire. The Mount, Sandford Avenue, was a private school *c.* 1929–41.[31]

Church Stretton poor-law union school was held at the workhouse built in 1838.[32] It had 21 pupils in 1849 and was fairly efficient except in industrial training; the mistress was paid only £4 a year.[33] In 1893, the school's last year, the mistress received £23 17*s.* 4*d.*[34] From 1894 workhouse children attended the church school.[35]

There was a schoolmaster in 1589. Sir Rowland Hayward (d. 1593) left £1 13*s.* 4*d.* a year towards his maintenance, and the rector added 20*s.* a year in 1595 when the parish agreed to abolish the church ale.[36] Robert Taylor taught school in 1676,[37] Edmund Cheese in 1693. Although Bonham Norton had been expected to build a school, Cheese apparently taught school in the church.[38] In 1716 the master, duly licensed, was teaching the catechism and taking his pupils to church.[39] In 1720 Thomas Bridgman left the master 40*s.* a year to teach four poor children to read. Eventually a school was built by subscription on roadside waste opposite the Hall lawn. A new school and house were built there in 1779. By then some encroachments on the commons and wastes were evidently appropriated to the school. Under the 1788 Inclosure Act *c.* 27 a. in Womerton wood were confirmed to the school and a body of endowment trustees was formed.[40]

In 1790 Edward Lloyd of Bank House left a stock of £50 to apprentice two pupils; the apprenticeship fund, still managed by the school trustees in 1926, was well used. Lloyd also left £50 to increase the salary of the master, who was then teaching reading, writing, and arithmetic to 15 poor scholars, aged 7–11 and elected by the trustees, who paid him £1 a year for each.[41] In 1831 the school received £42 12*s.* 4*d.*, almost wholly from endowment; a Sunday school, in existence by 1790, then received £9 14*s.*, £7 13*s.* of it from legacies of Lloyd and John Mainwaring (d. 1807), rector. The master had £40 a year and his house. In the day school there were 60 free pupils, labourers' children, and 11 whose fees varied from 2*s.* to 7*s.* a quarter; coal, books, and slates were provided from the endowment. Fifteen children attended the Sunday school only. The school was conducted on the National system and girls learned sewing.[42] In 1851 there were 120 pupils.[43]

The school building[44] was sold when a new National school and teacher's house were built, with the aid of voluntary contributions and grants, on a site in Back Lane given by C. O. Childe-Pemberton; it opened, with 144 places, in 1861.[45] Income for 1864–5 exceeded expenditure by *c.* £20, and over 60 per cent of it came from endowment (£46 9*s.* 6*d.*) and voluntary contributions (£8); fees varied according to parents' means. The master (certificated) and his wife had a joint salary of £65. In 1867 there were 65 boys and 65 girls in school, tradesmen's and farm labourers' children; one boy learned mensuration or book keeping.[46] The school, under inspection from 1869, had one or two pupil teachers in training between 1870 and 1907. By 1870 there was a Standard VI, and grammar and geography were taught. Usually efficient, the school earned government grant by 1870,[47] drawing grant from 1892.[48] Conditions, however, were difficult[49] and staffing not always adequate.[50] Alterations in 1894 increased places to 220, much of the cost being raised by sale of endowment stock and an appeal for a voluntary rate as the alternative to a school board. Further alterations in 1912 produced 235 places, later reduced to 191.[51] Attendance was often well below the number on roll, but the badly venti-

29 Ibid. 170, 316, 370; *Digest Educ. Poor*, H.C. 224, p. 762 (1819), ix (2); *Educ. Enq. Abstract*, H.C. 62, p. 785 (1835), xlii; Bilbey *Ch. Stretton*, pls. 65–6, 160; W.S.L. 350/5/40, Ch. Stretton p. 31; S.R.O. 1150/953; Pigot, *Nat. Com. Dir.* (1835), 353; (1842), 12.

30 *P.O. Dir. Salop.* (1856), 33; (1870), 37; *Eddowes's Jnl.* 7 Jan. 1857, p. 4; Bilbey *Ch. Stretton*, pl. 80.

31 *Kelly's Dir. Salop.* (1885–1941); Bilbey, op. cit. pl. 81; S.R.O. 1334/2, pp. 64, 94; Critchley, *Bag of Boiled Sweets*, 7–19.

32 S. Bagshaw, *Dir. Salop.* (1851), 527.

33 *Mins. of Cttee. of Council on Educ., Schs. of Parochial Unions, 1848–50* [1256], p. 169, H.C. (1850), xliii.

34 *S.C.C. Mins.* Finance and G.P. Cttee. rep. 25 Feb. 1893, 13.

35 S.R.O. 4505/5, pp. 43, 351.

36 W.S.L. 350/5/40, Ch. Stretton pp. 6, 52; above, social and cultural activities; church.

37 Hume, 'Changing Patterns of Educ. Dev.' 311.

38 Above, growth of settlement (for Norton); H.W.R.O.(H.), Heref. dioc. rec. AL 19/20, f. 165.

39 H.W.R.O.(H.), Heref. dioc. rec., reply to visit. articles 1716 (ref. supplied by Dr. R. Hume).

40 *24th Rep. Com. Char.* 402–3, 405; *S.P.R. Heref.* viii (2), 87; tithe fields 298–300, 336–8, 365, 1131; 4505/1.

41 *24th Rep. Com. Char.* 406; S.R.O. 4505/1, 21 Jan., 20 Feb. 1791, 26 Feb. 1926; S.R.O. 1642, box 29, apprenticeship papers.

42 *24th Rep. Com. Char.* 403, 406–7.

43 S. Bagshaw, *Dir. Salop.* (1851), 527.

44 See Bilbey, *Ch. Stretton*, pls. 77–8, 82.

45 Ibid. pl. 79; S.R.O. 3105/4; P.R.O., ED 7/102/169; *P.O. Dir. Salop.* (1870), 36. The rector and his fam. subscribed *c.* £320.

46 P.R.O., ED 7/102/169; *Schs. Inquiry Com.* [3966–XIV], pp. 536–7, H.C. (1867–8), xxviii (12).

47 S.R.O. 4505/5, reps. 1891–1906; ibid. p. 190; ibid. /4, reps. to 1890.

48 Ibid. /5, e.g. p. 14; /1, accts. 1892–3.

49 Ibid. /5, pp. 23–5, 38–9, 201–2, 210–11, 228–30, 238.

50 Ibid. pp. 183, 201, 210–11, 228–9, 238–9; /4, reps. 1878–80.

51 Ibid. /5, pp. 23–4, 201–2, 442–3, and endpapers; /1, 12 Nov. 1892 sqq., 7 June 1909 sqq.; *Kelly's Dir. Salop.* (1895), 58; (1913), 66.

lated building was often overcrowded.[52] A night school was held from 1869 or earlier to 1880.[53] Gardening was taught from 1902 and domestic science in the Silvester Horne Institute from 1918; domestic science and woodwork centres in the parish hall opened in 1936.[54] An infant class was held in the same hall from 1932.[55] The roll was *c.* 184 in 1926 and *c.* 243 in 1934. The school took Liverpool and other evacuees from 1939, and until 1941 it used rooms at the Methodist and Congregational chapels.[56]

The school became a junior and infant school in 1948 when seniors transferred to the new modern school.[57] It became controlled in 1954 and was then renovated.[58] It was overcrowded in the 1950s:[59] one class used an upper room in the parish hall 1953–60,[60] another used a room in the Silvester Horne Institute 1956–60.[61] From 1961 juniors were taught in huts in Essex Road, vacated by the modern school, infants at the old school.[62] A new open-plan building, with 250 places, opened next to the modern school in Shrewsbury Road in 1968, and two demountable classrooms were added next year.[63] The numbers on roll rose in the 1950s and 1960s to peak at 357 in 1968; they remained over 300 throughout the 1970s but fell thereafter.[64]

Church Stretton Modern school, with 200 places, opened in 1948[65] in huts at the corner of Sandford Avenue and Essex Road, formerly a St. Dunstan's workshop and instruction centre.[66] New buildings on the workhouse site in Shrewsbury Road opened in 1960;[67] the 240 places increased to 600[68] after enlargements in 1965 and in the 1970s.[69] In 1977, as Church Stretton school, it became compehensive for pupils aged 11–16; older pupils could go to schools in Ludlow or Shrewsbury or to Shrewsbury Technical College.[70] The roll was 173 in 1948, 248 in 1960, and 310 in 1970, rising thereafter to a peak of 629 in 1983; in 1986 it was 569.[71]

County-council classes in cookery, horticulture, chemistry, botany, and insect pests were held in 1891–2, in hygiene 1893–1900, in horticulture in 1901–2, and in music and drawing in 1905–6. There was a continuation school in 1894–5 and 1899–1903. Attendance was usually poor.[72] Evening classes for boys and girls were held 1932–4, and an evening institute at the modern school from 1948.[73]

CHARITIES FOR THE POOR. In 1677 the parish stock was said to have been almost all lost through the 'incuriousness' of past churchwardens.[74] Soon thereafter, however, it began to grow again as gifts and legacies were made for bread and cash doles, principally at Easter and about Christmas time.[75]

In 1684 a meadow in Little Stretton pools was settled in trust for poor parishioners and in 1704 Thomas Hawkes of Botvyle[76] left £30 to buy land to endow weekly bread doles for the neediest churchgoers or parishioners disabled from getting to church. In 1708 Hawkes's legacy was used to buy a house in the town as an endowment or dwelling for the poor; house and Pools meadow were then vested in trustees and it was perhaps on those trustees[77] that, in 1735, Edward Phillips the elder settled Street meadow (*c.* 2¾ a.) for the poor. Appointment of trustees being neglected, the trust seems to have devolved on the rector and churchwardens by the early 19th century. Meanwhile bread and cash doles at Easter and about Christmas time had been endowed with capital amounting by 1830 to £268 10*s.*:[78] William Minton of Minton[79] had left £6 in 1701, Randolph Jones £10 in 1710, Thomas Bridgman 30*s.* in 1720, Edward Phillips the younger £30 in 1781,[80] Edward Lloyd of Bank House[81] £21 in 1790, John Bridgman £100 in 1804, and John Mainwaring, rector, £100 in 1807. About 1830 those sums produced £13 17*s.* a year and Stretton Pools meadow, Hawkes's charity, and Street meadow produced another £13 10*s.*; except for a 6*s.* rent charge representing Minton's legacy, the income was then carried to a fund augmented with sacrament money from the church and other voluntary contributions. The whole income was spent on Sunday bread doles and in gifts of bread and cash at Easter and about Christmas time.

About 1830 the poor rate contributed £3 1*s.* of the parish charities, representing interest on Hawkes's, Jones's, and Lloyd's charities: the house bought with Hawkes's legacy had been taken over as the parish poor-house and the

52 P.R.O., ED 7/102/169; S.R.O. 4505/5 *passim*; /4, 29 May 1875; *Kelly's Dir Salop.* (1900), 60; (1913), 66.
53 S.R.O. 4505/4 *passim.*
54 Ibid. /5, pp. 133, 282, 473; /3, pp. 28, 30–1.
55 Ibid. /5, pp. 443, 445–6.
56 Ibid. pp. 375, 456, 490, 499 sqq.
57 Ibid. /3, pp. 97–8.
58 Ibid. pp. 150, 159–60, 163–4, 175–6.
59 Ibid. *passim.*
60 Ibid. pp. 149–50, 152–4, 156.
61 Ibid. pp. 182–3; *S.C.C. Mins. (Educ.)* 1956–7, 102; 1960–1, 18.
62 *S.C.C. Mins. (Educ.)* 1960–1, 160; S.R.O. 4505/3, pp. 195 sqq.
63 Inf. from Mr. L. Cunnick, headmaster.
64 S.C.C. Educ. Cttee. *Sch. List*, continued as *Educ. Dir.*
65 Inf. from S.C.C. Educ. Dept.
66 *S.C.C. Mins. (Educ.)* 1945–6, 174–5; Bilbey, *Ch. Stretton*, pl. 138. Seniors came from ch. schs. at Ch. Stretton, Acton Scott, Cardington, Hope Bowdler, Longnor, Rushbury, and Smethcott.
67 S.R.O. 3346/2/19, 25 Nov. 1960, 26 May 1961.
68 Inf. from S.C.C. Educ. Dept.
69 S.R.O. 3346/2/19, 4 June, 12 Nov. (H.M.I.'s rep.) 1965; *S.C.C. Mins. (Educ.)* 1970–1, 62–4; 1971–2, 208; 1972–3, 77; 1976–7, 48, 94, 312.
70 *S.C.C. Mins. (Educ.)* 1975–6, 168–70; inf. from S.C.C. Educ. Dept.
71 S.R.O. 3346/2/19, 28 May 1948, 12 Feb. 1960 (H.M. Inspector's reps.); *Sch. List* (1970), 1; *Educ. Dir.* (1983), 2; (1986), 2.
72 Organizing sec.'s ann. reps. to Intermediate Educ. Cttee. in *S.C.C. Mins.* 1892–1901; S.C.C. *Higher Educ. Dept. Rep.* 1903–7 (copies in S.R.O.).
73 *S.C.C. Mins. (Educ.)* 1932–3, 63; 1933–4, 54; 1948–9, 77; *et al.*
74 H.W.R.O.(H.), Heref. dioc. rec., visitations box 20.
75 See next two paras., based on *24th Rep. Com. Char.* H.C. 231, pp. 403–8 (1831), xi; S.C.C. chars. index.
76 Cf. *S.P.R. Heref.* viii (2), 81.
77 Thos. Brooke was a trustee in 1708 and 1735.
78 Excl. £10 left in 1794 spent as capital: below, this section.
79 Cf. above, manors (Minton).
80 Cf. *S.P.R. Heref.* viii (2), 172, 178 (burials of two Edw. Phillipses, 1782 and 1785).
81 Cf. above, manors (Bank Ho.).

other two legacies had evidently been spent on it. Under the 1788 Inclosure Act two small inclosures were allotted in respect of Stretton Pools meadow and Street meadow; £10 which Thomas Harrison left in 1794 for Christmas gifts to the poor was spent on the allotments but they were too small to be worth keeping. They were therefore conveyed to John Robinson, a mercer of the town, and in return he built two almshouses next to the parish workhouse in 1829; at the same time two more were built, partly at Robinson's expense and partly with contributions from others.[82] The rector and churchwardens nominated the almshouse residents, who paid 4*s*. a year rent to a repair fund.[83] The almshouses, perhaps never very eligible accommodation, were sold in 1921.[84]

In 1841 Elizabeth Metcalf left money for the use of the poor. Her legacy and all those previously mentioned were united in 1907 as the Church Stretton consolidated charities; property and investments then produced £48 13*s*. 8*d*. a year.[85] About 1975 annual income was *c*. £100.[86]

The Church Stretton Nursing Charity and Nunn's Hospital Fund was established in 1880 by gift of Harriet Esther Nunn to provide a nurse, in cases of severe illness, for such of the sick poor as could not otherwise obtain one. About 1975 annual income was £34. In 1978 the Fund was united with the Shropshire Sanatorium Care Committee Fund, then governed under schemes of 1955 and 1967 for the benefit of poor residents of Church Stretton parish or the surrounding district suffering, or lately suffering, from tuberculosis; *c*. 1975 annual income had been some £9. By 1982 the annual income (*c*. £100) of the amalgamated charity, known since 1978 as the Church Stretton Nunn Trust and Sickness Charity, was used to alleviate sickness or disability or to assist convalescence.[87]

The Arthur George Woolley Trusts were established in 1957 to relieve poverty in the parishes of Church Stretton and All Stretton and the neighbourhood; *c*. 1975 annual income was £149.[88]

ABDON

THE SPARSELY populated rural parish of Abdon, comprising 1,263 a.[89] (511 ha.) until 1884, is 13 km. north-east of Ludlow on the western flank of Brown Clee. Much of its boundary, especially on the south and west, followed streams, but on the east it followed the upper limits of Abdon common, which were not finally fixed until the 17th or early 18th century.[90] In 1884 the civil parish absorbed Earnstrey Park, a detached township of Diddlebury parish, and a small detachment of Tugford parish around New House.[91] About 0.1 ha. of Ditton Priors C.P. was added in 1967[92] and the whole of Tugford C.P. in 1987.[93] This article deals with the area of the pre-1884 parish and the adjoining detachment of Tugford.

The eastern third of the parish, Abdon common, falls steeply from 505 m. on the east, below the prehistoric rampart of Abdon Burf, to *c*. 325 m. above Abdon village. The land then falls more gradually to 180 m. at the parish's western tip. Most of the parish drains south and west towards Tugford (or Norncott)[94] brook, which forms the parish boundary on those sides. The parish's north-western part drains north and west towards tributaries of the brook, at or beyond the parish boundary.

The lower, western, two thirds of the parish are on the Ditton Series of the Lower Old Red Sandstone, with no significant drift except for an area of head near Marsh Farm. The steeper eastern third, Abdon common, is on the Clee Group of the Lower Old Red Sandstone. The Upper and Lower Abdon limestones run in two narrow parallel bands along the foot of the common.[95]

Abdon village was loosely grouped around the head of a valley below Brown Clee, between *c*. 240 m. and *c*. 300 m. Extensive earthworks east of the churchyard[96] include at least one house platform occupied until the 14th century,[97] and early buildings may have stood northwards as far as Marsh Farm.[98] The village evidently shrank in the 14th century because of economic adversity.[99] Nevertheless the township could muster 10 able men in 1539[1] and had at least 11 houses in 1642.[2] Expansion of mineral working in and near the parish[3] was accompanied by squatter settlement along the lower edge of Abdon common;[4] thus by 1662, of 20 houses in the township that paid hearth tax, 14 had only

82 Cf. tithe fields 1311–13; S.R.O. 2079/LVI.9, nos. 101, 154; 4044/39, pp. 13 no. 101, 19 no. 154; *S.P.R. Heref.* viii (2), p. vii.
83 Cf. S.R.O. 3908/AH/1–3.
84 Windsor, *Handbk.* 92; S.R.O., DA 7/111/6, p. 183; /119/5, pp. 113–16, 125–30.
85 S.R.O. 3601/Admin/2, Char. Com. scheme 27 Aug. 1907.
86 *Review of Local Chars.* (S.C.C. 1975), 42, 54.
87 Ibid. 54; Windsor, *Handbk.* 103–4; S.R.O. 3908/Rg 8, p. 26; S.R.O., DA 7/137/1, acct. bk. (1880) and copy trust deed; S.C.C. chars. index; *Stretton Focus*, Mar. 1982, p. 11.
88 *Review of Local Chars.* 42, 54.
89 P.R.O., IR 30/29/1; O.S. Maps 1/2,500, Salop. LXV. 6–7, 10–11, 14–15 (1884 edn.); O.S. *Area Bk.* (1884). This article was written in 1991.
90 Fig. 10; below, econ. hist.
91 *14th Ann. Rep. Local Govt. Bd.* [C. 4515], pp. xlvii–xlviii, 200, H.C. (1884–5), xxxii.
92 *Salop (No. 2) Order 1966* (Stat. Instr. 1966, no. 1529); S.R.O., DA 19/701/6, map 43.
93 *S. Salop. (Pars.) Order 1987* (Stat. Instr. 1987, no. 496).
94 So called 1605: H.W.R.O.(H.), HO 2/14/2.
95 Geol. Surv. Maps 1/50,000, solid, sheet 166 (1974 edn.); 1", drift, sheet 166 (1967 edn.).
96 *Salop. News Letter*, xxix. 4–5; T. Rowley, *Salop. Landscape* (1972), 117; SA 184; R.C.H.M.E., draft field rep. (1987).
97 *Salop. News Letter*, xxxi. 1–2; *Med. Arch.* xi. 310–12.
98 Irregularities in pasture S. of Marsh Fm.
99 Below, econ. hist.
1 P.R.O., E 36/48, f. 19v.
2 Bodl. MS. Gough Salop. 11, ff. 51–4.
3 *T.S.A.S.* lviii. 66.
4 Below, econ. hist.; S.R.O., incl. award B 33; P.R.O., IR 30/29/1.

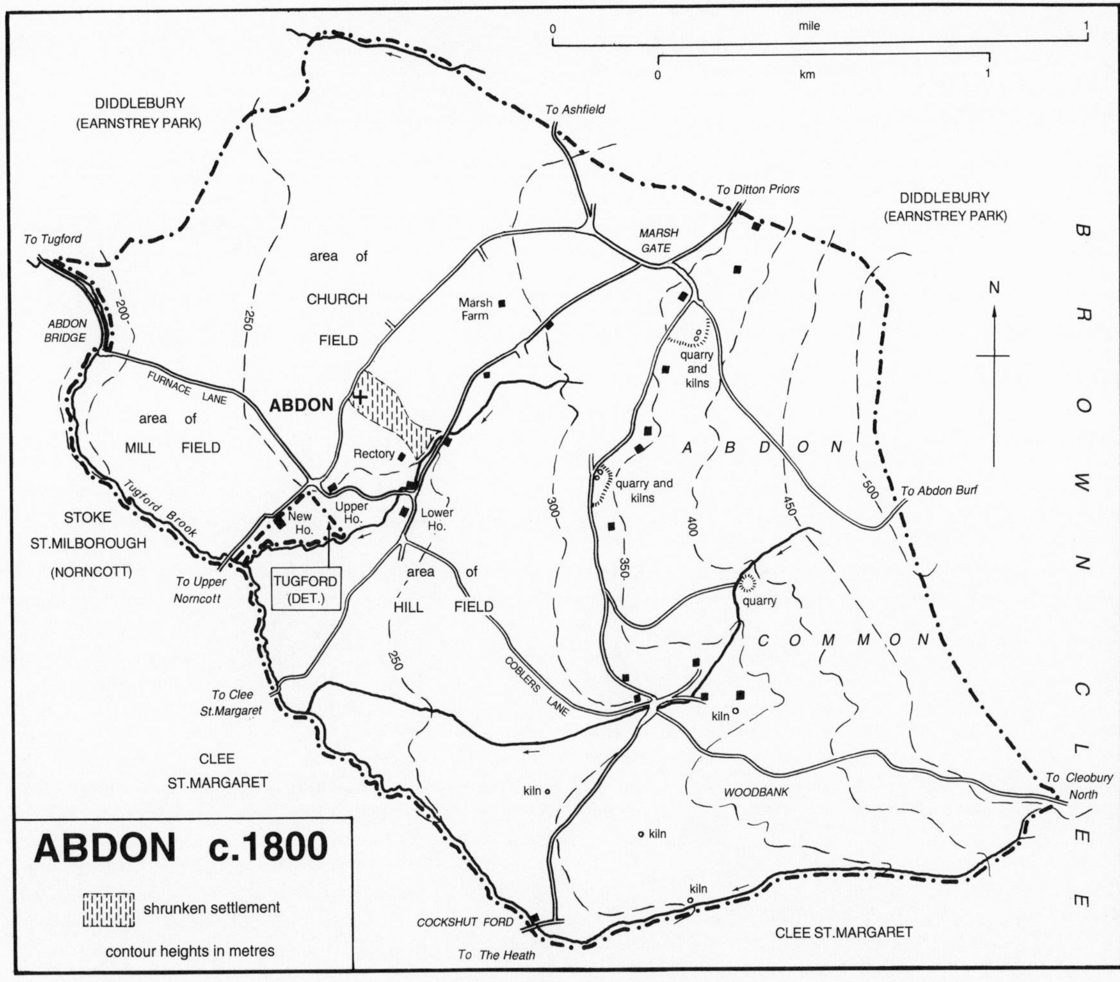

Fig. 10

one hearth,[5] and by 1684 there were said to be *c.* 30 squatters.[6] Houses were abandoned in the later 18th century.[7] Some were probably in Abdon village and became redundant through farm amalgamations;[8] at least one house platform among the earthworks east of the church seems to have fallen vacant at that time.[9] Others were probably miners' cottages at the edge of Abdon common[10] and were abandoned when local demand for ironstone ceased.[11] Nevertheless the parish had 30 houses in 1793, an unusually high number for the district, and many were occupied by miners.[12] After the common was inclosed in 1813[13] a scattering of houses arose on the plots sold at Woodbank,[14] and the parish's population grew from 137 to 170 between 1811 and 1831.[15] Changes in the character and extent of mineral extraction on Brown Clee[16] may have been the main causes of marked population loss in the 1860s and, in the enlarged civil parish, in the 1890s and mid 20th century.[17] The civil parish had 70 inhabitants in 1971[18] and 85 in 1981.[19] Population decline after the mid 19th century, however, did not result in the loss of many houses.[20] In 1991 the former squatter cottages, which enjoyed long views over Corve Dale and had been much modernized and extended in recent years, were mostly occupied by commuters to the west midlands.[21] The old farmhouses and cottages are all of local stone, some with brick additions of the 18th century or later.

Two minor thoroughfares served Abdon village.[22] One of them, south-west from Ditton Priors,[23] descended through the village to Clee St. Margaret and Stoke St. Milborough. The other, west from Cleobury North (and thus from Bridgnorth),[24] descended between Abdon Burf and Clee Burf and crossed Abdon common to the village, via the sunken Coblers Lane; thence Furnace Lane ran west by Abdon bridge to Tugford.[25]

5 P.R.O., E 179/255/35, m. 48.
6 *T.S.A.S.* lviii. 66.
7 S.P.L., MS. 6865, p. 4.
8 Below, econ. hist.
9 *Salop. News Letter*, xxix. 4; Deserted Medieval Village Research Group, *17th Ann. Rep.* (1969), 27.
10 Several vacant plots in 1848: P.R.O., IR 30/29/1.
11 Below, econ. hist.
12 S.P.L., MS. 6865, p. 4.
13 S.R.O., incl. award B 33.
14 P.R.O., IR 30/29/1.
15 *V.C.H. Salop.* ii. 219.
16 Below, econ. hist.
17 *V.C.H. Salop.* ii. 219; cf. below, Stoke St. Milborough, intro.
18 *Census*, 1971, *Co. Rep. Salop.* i. 5.
19 *Census*, 1981, Small Area Statistics: Salop.
20 P.R.O., IR 30/29/1; O.S. Map 1/10,000, SO 58 NE. (1978 edn.).
21 Local inf.
22 Descr. of roads based on O.S. Map 1", sheet LXI. SW. (1833 edn.); P.R.O., IR 30/29/1.
23 By 1712: S.R.O. 1037/21/6.
24 By 1813: S.R.O., incl. award B 33.
25 Named 1692: *S.P.R. Heref.* xix (1), p. vi; Bodl., Craven dep. 16, f. 21. The furnace was at Lr. Norncott: below, the Heath, econ. hist.

Marsh gate, on the road from Ditton Priors to Clee St. Margaret, where it touched the lower edge of Abdon common, gave access to the common for the 'strakers' (commoners) of Holdgate[26] and Brookhampton; they came through Earnstrey park[27] and probably joined a road to Marsh gate from Ashfield. A southward lane from Marsh gate followed the western edge of Abdon village, passing the church, and led to Upper Norncott, the Heath, and Bouldon.[28] Another lane from Marsh gate followed the edge of the common southwards, thus serving the squatter cottages and limekilns and leading via Cockshutford[29] across Tugford brook to the Heath.[30] Strakers from Tugford crossed the ford from the south side to reach the common at Woodbank.[31] A sunken track from Marsh gate to the top of Brown Clee[32] linked the squatter cottages and limekilns to the coal pits across the parish boundary.[33]

In 1991 metalled roads ran from Abdon village to Tugford, Ditton Priors, and Clee St. Margaret, and from Marsh gate to Ashfield and Cockshutford.

In the Whitsun morris dancing at Clee St. Margaret in 1619 the 'carpet' from the communion table at Abdon was used as a flag.[34] The parish seems to have had no public house in the 19th or 20th centuries. The county library opened a part-time 'book centre' at Abdon *c.* 1927.[35] The closed school[36] became a village hall in 1991.[37]

MANOR AND OTHER ESTATES. Wulfwine (Ulwin) held *ABDON* in 1066. Roger of Montgomery, earl of Shrewsbury, held it in chief in 1086, and Reynold of Bailleul, the sheriff, held it of him.[38] At Earl Robert's forfeiture in 1102 the chief lordship seems to have passed to Reynold's successors in the shrieval estates;[39] William FitzAlan (d. 1160)[40] held it;[41] so did Richard FitzAlan, earl of Arundel and Surrey (d. 1397),[42] and Beatrice, countess of Arundel and Surrey (d. 1439).[43]

In 1086 Azo held Abdon of Reynold.[44] He is assumed to have been Azor Bigot,[45] who gave a fardel (¼ virgate) of land in Abdon to Shrewsbury abbey between 1121 and 1135.[46] The land probably passed at that time to Tugford manor. Robert, a knight, perhaps Azor's son,[47] gave Abdon to Shrewsbury abbey in the later 1150s with William FitzAlan's consent.[48] The gift, although confirmed by the king in 1332 and 1346,[49] seems to have been void by 1255, when John le Strange held Abdon,[50] and it is assumed that Azor's Abdon estate had passed before 1166 to John's grandfather, John le Strange.[51] The younger John's grandson John le Strange, later Lord Strange of Knockin, held it *c.* 1284[52] and in 1292.[53] John, Lord Strange, grandson of the last named, held it in 1315.[54]

The estate had been subinfeudated by the mid 13th century. In 1226 Geoffrey of Ledwich held land in Abdon.[55] He was perhaps the man who died in or before 1253[56] and whose son and namesake[57] held Abdon in 1255[58] and was perhaps the lord of that name in 1294.[59] Geoffrey of Ledwich's unnamed heir held it in 1363.[60]

Roger of Ledwich held Abdon under Geoffrey of Ledwich *c.* 1284,[61] but Roger's estate later passed to Robert Burnell (d. 1292), bishop of Bath and Wells.[62] It then followed the descent of Acton Burnell until Sir John Dudley sold Acton Burnell in 1542,[63] except that Sir Edward Burnell's widow Aline held it in dower 1315–63.[64] In 1548 Dudley, then earl of Warwick, leased the manor for 200 years to William Heath. Heath assigned the lease in 1559 to Henry Cressett of Upton.[65] The freehold, which had presumably escheated to the Crown in 1553 on the attainder of Dudley, then duke of Northumberland, was acquired by Cressett (d. 1563) who left the manor to his nephew John Cressett of Upton (d. *c.* 1566). John's brother Richard had succeeded by 1572[66] and sold it in 1598 to Humphrey Briggs (d. 1626).[67] It then passed from father to son,[68] through Moreton (cr. bt. 1641; d. by 1647), Sir Humphrey (d. 1691),[69] Sir Humphrey (d. 1700),[70] and Sir Humphrey (d. 1734),[71] and then to Sir Hugh, brother of the last named.[72]

On Sir Hugh Briggs's death in 1767 his estates passed to Richard Cavendish (formerly Chan-

26 By 1632: S.R.O. 1359, box 20, Holdgate terrier.
27 By 1810: S.R.O., incl. award B 21, brief of [1810], ff. 1v., 5.
28 Below, the Heath, intro.
29 Named 1675: *S.P.R. Heref.* xix (1), 24.
30 By 1813: S.R.O., incl. award B 33.
31 Ibid. B 21, brief of [1810], f. 11v.
32 By 1712: S.R.O. 1037/21/6.
33 By 1813: S.R.O., incl. award B 33.
34 *Salop.* (R.E.E.D.), i. 40–50.
35 R. C. Elliott, 'Development of Public Libraries in Salop.' (Loughborough Univ. M.A. thesis, 1970; copy in co. libr.), 125.
36 Below, educ.
37 Local inf.
38 *V.C.H. Salop.* i. 319.
39 Cf. ibid. iii. 10–12, 34–5.
40 Eyton, vii. 237.
41 *Cartulary of Shrews. Abbey*, ed. U. Rees (1975), ii, p. 286.
42 *Cal. Inq. Misc.* vi, p. 111; *Complete Peerage*, i. 244.
43 *Cal. Inq. p.m.* (Rec. Com.), iv. 199; *Complete Peerage*, i. 426.
44 *V.C.H. Salop.* i. 319.
45 Eyton, iv. 127.
46 *Cart. Shrews.* ii, pp. 258, 262.
47 Eyton, iv. 128–9.
48 *Cart. Shrews.* ii, p. 286.
49 *Cal. Chart. R.* 1327–41, 288; 1341–1417, 50.
50 *Rot. Hund.* (Rec. Com.), ii. 71.
51 Eyton, iv. 128; cf. *V.C.H. Salop.* viii. 18, 109. For le Strange pedigree see H. le Strange, *Le Strange Records* (1916), 58, 98, 153, 323; *Complete Peerage*, xii (1), 347–56.
52 *Feud. Aids*, iv. 223.
53 *Cal. Inq. p.m.* iii, p. 51.
54 Ibid. v, p. 392.
55 P.R.O., JUST 1/1172, m. 3d.
56 *Ex. e Rot. Fin.* (Rec. Com.), ii. 172.
57 Eyton, iv. 373.
58 *Rot. Hund.* ii. 71.
59 *Cal. Inq. p.m.* iii, p. 443; *Cal. Inq. Misc.* i, p. 470.
60 *Cal. Inq. p.m.* xi, p. 373.
61 *Feud. Aids*, iv. 223.
62 *Cal. Inq. p.m.* iii, p. 51.
63 Ibid. pp. 51, 443–4; v, p. 392; *Cal. Inq. Misc.* vi, p. 111; *Cal. Close*, 1419–22, 154–5; S.P.L., MS. 2, f. 4v.; *Cal. Inq. p.m.* (Rec. Com.), iv. 265, 325; *Cal. Pat.* 1485–94, 64; *L. & P. Hen. VIII*, i (2), p. 1170; vi, p. 89; xvi, p. 240; P.R.O., CP 40/1079, Carte rot. 1; cf. *V.C.H. Salop.* viii. 7; above, Rushbury, manors.
64 *Feud. Aids*, iv. 229; *Cal. Inq. p.m.* xi, pp. 372–3.
65 B.L. Add. MS. 31932, f. 283.
66 Bodl. MS. Blakeway 11, ff. 113v.–114; *T.S.A.S.* 4th ser. vi. 217.
67 S.R.O., incl. award B 21, abstr. of title, m. 1; P.R.O., C 142/424, no. 86.
68 Burke, *Ext. & Dormant Baronetcies* (1841), 82–3; G.E.C. *Baronetage*, ii. 134–5.
69 P.R.O., C 142/424, no. 86; CP 25/2/477/13 Chas. I Trin. no. 17; CP 25/2/478/23 Chas. I East. no. 2; S.R.O. 1335/Rg/1, f. 49v.
70 *T.S.A.S.* i. 448.
71 S.R.O. 1238/3; 1335/Rg/1, f. 166.
72 S.R.O. 1238/3; q. sess. rec. box 260, reg. of gamekeepers 1711–42, 13 July 1736.

dler) and Wadham Brooke as coparceners.[73] When Cavendish died in 1769 his moiety passed to Brooke (d. 1770), from whom the whole passed to the Revd. John Brooke.[74] On John's death in 1786 Cavendish's former moiety was shared by the Revd. Richard Huntley (d. 1794), who left his share to his son and namesake, and Gen. John Fitzwilliam (d. 1789),[75] who left his share to Richard, Viscount Fitzwilliam; John Brooke left the other moiety to George Brooke Brigges Townshend, who changed his name to George Brooke in 1797.[76]

In 1800 Huntley, Fitzwilliam, and Brooke partitioned Sir Hugh's former estates: Abdon manor was allotted to Fitzwilliam,[77] who died in 1816,[78] leaving it to George Augustus Herbert, earl of Pembroke and Montgomery (d. 1827), with remainder to the earl's son Sidney Herbert,[79] cr. Baron Herbert of Lea 1861. Herbert died in 1861[80] and under Fitzwilliam's will[81] Abdon passed to Herbert's son George Robert Charles, the 2nd baron, who succeeded as earl of Pembroke and Montgomery in 1862. He sold the manor in 1873 to William Bradley (d. 1905), tenant of Lower House farm,[82] who was succeeded by his widow Helen (d. 1933),[83] followed by T. W. Bradley (d. 1959), whose cousin T. J. Bradley owned the manorial estate in 1991.[84]

By the mid 17th century the chief house was perhaps Lower House; it had by far the largest farm,[85] which may have been that called the Farm in 1754.[86] Edward Millichope, tenant in 1642,[87] rebuilt or altered it in 1647.[88] It may then have consisted of a single stone range. It was enlarged in stone on the south side *c.* 1800 to create a double-pile house, which was roofed and extensively remodelled to resemble a new building. It was renamed the Manor House after 1873.

Before 1291 Geoffrey of Ledwich enfeoffed Richard (perhaps fl. 1256),[89] son of Philip of Sutton, with a house and land in Abdon. Later Adam of Sutton held a house and land in Abdon, which his kinsman and successor Richard Sutton conveyed *c.* 1410 to his son Geoffrey.[90] John Sutton acquired more Abdon property *c.* 1434.[91] William Sutton (fl. 1561) sold Abdon property in 1566 to John Harryes, who conveyed a house and land there in 1573 to Francis Cressett of Stanton Lacy; Cressett sold it immediately to William Barker.[92]

The Abdon estate of William Burley (d. 1458)[93] seems to have descended with Broncroft (in Diddlebury) until the mid 16th century or later.[94] John de Vere, earl of Oxford, sold his moiety of the Abdon estate in 1552 to John Stringfellow,[95] who sold it to Thomas Barker in 1553.[96] In 1620 William Barker sold two houses and land in Abdon, perhaps consisting of what had been bought from Cressett and Stringfellow, to Moreton Briggs,[97] who became lord of the manor.[98]

Richard Tasker sold an estate to the lord *c.* 1734, called *ABDON'S MARSH* (47 a.).[99] Marsh Farm, presumably its house, may date from the 16th century or earlier. Built of stone, it consists of a hall range and cross wing, each having two units, 1½ storey, and an axial stack.

A farm at Abdon that belonged in 1608 to Thomas Sheppard of Baucott[1] (in Tugford) seems to have been *NEW HOUSE*,[2] in a detachment of Tugford parish[3] and therefore perhaps the Abdon land acquired by Shrewsbury abbey, lord of Tugford, in the 12th century.[4] By 1640 it belonged to John Page of Oxenbold,[5] whose family still had it in 1729. By 1744 it belonged to a relative,[6] Caleb Stedman of Elsich, and in 1813 to Sarah Stedman.[7] Thomas Bradley of Lower House, Abdon, owned it by 1841.[8] It thus joined the Abdon manorial estate when William Bradley bought that in 1873, and remained with it in 1991.[9] The house, a two storeyed range of three units with an axial stack against a cross passage, is probably 17th-century. It is built of rubble, neatly dressed and coursed, with dressed copings on the end gables. Internal brick stacks have been added at each gable end.

William Fewtrell (d. 1625) of Wrickton (in Stottesdon) owned lands between Abdon and Cockshutford called Bromley. He was succeeded by a grandnephew William Jenkes, whose daughter married Anthony Kynnersley.[10] Anthony Kynnersley of Leighton (d. 1760)[11] left *COCKSHUTFORD FARM* to his sons R. L.

73 Para. based on S.R.O. 1238/14; Brigges Estates Act, 1800, 39 & 40 Geo. III, c. 114 (Local and Personal).
74 S.R.O., q. sess. rec. box 260, reg. of gamekeepers 1742–79, 4 Dec. 1770.
75 *Ann. Register*, xxxi, Chronicle, 244.
76 Burke, *Land. Gent.* (1952), 271.
77 S.R.O. 1238/6; 39 & 40 Geo. III, c. 114 (Local and Personal).
78 *Complete Peerage*, v. 529.
79 Fitzwilliam Estates Act, 1833, 3 & 4 Wm. IV, c. 26 (Private). For pedigree of Herbert earls of Pembroke see *Complete Peerage*, x. 405–30; Burke, *Peerage* (1967), 1961–3.
80 *Complete Peerage*, vi. 445; *D.N.B.*
81 3 & 4 Wm. IV, c. 26 (Private).
82 S.R.O. 1037/21/37; *P.O. Dir. Salop.* (1879), 269; grave stone at Abdon.
83 *Kelly's Dir. Salop.* (1909), 19; grave stone at Abdon.
84 *Kelly's Dir. Salop.* (1934), 21; grave stone at Abdon; inf. from Mr. Bradley.
85 Bodl. MS. Gough Salop. 11, f. 54.
86 *S.P.R. Heref.* xix (1), 60.
87 Bodl. MS. Gough Salop. 11, f. 54.
88 Date stone in garden.
89 *Roll of Salop. Eyre 1256* (Selden Soc. xcvi), p. 337.
90 S.P.L., MS. 2, f. 127.
91 Ibid. f. 131.
92 B.L. Add. MS. 31932, ff. 283–4.
93 *T.S.A.S.* lvi. 272.
94 *Cal. Inq. p.m. Hen. VII*, ii, pp. 210–11, 427, 577–8; iii, pp. 127–8; cf. *T.S.A.S.* 4th ser. vi. 231–6, 244–52.
95 S.R.O. 20/23/13.
96 P.R.O., CP 40/1156, rot. 13.
97 B.L. Add. MS. 31932, f. 287.
98 Above, this section.
99 S.R.O. 5735/G/1/1.
1 S.R.O. 4260/1/2.
2 John Sond, Sheppard's tenant (S.R.O. 4260/1/2), was presumably predecessor of Eliz. Sande, whose fm. was in Abdon and Tugford pars. 'or one of them' in 1640 (S.R.O. 171, box 2, deed). Edw. Sandes, an Abdon pewholder in 1655, lived in Tugford par.: *S.P.R. Heref.* xix (1), 15.
3 P.R.O., IR 29/29/324; IR 30/29/324, field 250.
4 Above, this section.
5 S.R.O. 171, box 2, deed of 1640.
6 Deeds in possession of Mr. T. J. Bradley; S.P.L., Deeds 630.
7 S.R.O., incl. award B 33.
8 P.R.O., IR 29/29/1; IR 30/29/1, field 198; IR 30/29/324, field 250.
9 Above, this section; inf. from Mr. Bradley.
10 *S.P.R. Heref.* xix (1), p. v.; Shrews. Sch. Libr., James Deed 75. Located from P.R.O., IR 29/29/1; IR 30/29/1, field 193.
11 *S.P.R. Heref.* xiv (1), 67.

Kynnersley and Capt. Anthony Kynnersley (d. 1804);[12] Anthony was sole owner after his brother's death in 1781.[13] His son Thomas (d. 1843) left the farm to a niece (d. 1865), whose husband Robert Gardner (formerly Panting) sold it (26 a.) to Viscount Boyne in 1867.[14] The farm was later renamed Brook House. The house is a two storeyed stone range of three units, with a lobby entry against an axial stack; it is probably 17th-century. An internal stack has been added at the west gable end.

ECONOMIC HISTORY. The parish has always been mainly agricultural. In 1086 there were two ploughteams but capacity for three more; the manor's value had fallen from 20*s.* to 12*s.* since 1066.[15] The arable seems to have been enlarged in the 12th and 13th centuries,[16] and a marl pit was mentioned in 1256.[17] In the 13th century the township had autumn grazing over the hay meadow of Corfham manor in return for rent and mowing services.[18] By 1340, however, Abdon's tenants were said to be so poor that most of the arable lay uncultivated.[19] About 1600 the open fields included Mill field west of the village, Church field north-west, and Hill field south-east.[20]

In the Middle Ages Abdon was among the townships that intercommoned over the great uninclosed part of Brown Clee, which belonged to the lord of Clee chase and was regulated by his swainmote. He also allowed grazing on the uninclosed hill by inhabitants of outlying townships within the chase, who were called strakers.[21] By *c.* 1620 the lower parts of the uninclosed hill had been divided among the townships that adjoined it, as their exclusive commons.[22] In the earlier 17th century the swainmote lapsed and by 1712 the whole of the uninclosed hill had been apportioned, probably in the later 17th century, among the adjoining townships as their own commons.[23] Strakers from Holdgate, Brookhampton, and Tugford nevertheless continued to exercise grazing rights on Abdon common or 'liberty' until the later 18th century.[24] It occupied the eastern third of the parish, and its upper limit was marked by the massive dry stone 'Burf wall',[25] of which there were some remains in 1991. A manorial rabbit warren on the common at Coneybury[26] was in use in 1708 but had disappeared by 1810.[27]

By the 1640s the open fields had been almost wholly inclosed; only parts of Hill and Little fields remained. The manorial estate then had five large farms, of which Lower House[28] (perhaps the former demesne)[29] was valued twice as highly as any other, and five much smaller farms. No cottagers, smallholders, or squatters were mentioned.[30] In the later 17th and earlier 18th century sheep and cereals were more important than cattle, but there was some dairying on a domestic scale.[31]

By the mid 18th century the lord of Abdon was seeking to amalgamate farms. In 1734, on leasing two farms (47 a. and 52 a.) and a smallholding to a single tenant, Sir Humphrey Briggs reserved the right to demolish buildings;[32] by 1800 the combined holding was a single farm (122 a.) with only the farmhouse on it. The manorial estate then had five farms between 64 a. and 170 a., another of 28 a., and 10 resident smallholders or cottagers,[33] at least some of whom were squatters on the common.[34] In 1793 oats were considered the main cereal.[35] There was more wheat than oats in 1801, but in some years the parish could not grow enough grain to supply the inhabitants.[36] Abdon common was inclosed in 1813. A portion was allotted to each freeholder of Holdgate and Brookhampton, and to Lord Craven (for his Tugford estate), in lieu of straker rights, as well as to each of the Abdon freeholders; 96 a. at Woodbank were sold to defray expenses.[37] By 1850, after inclosure of the common and evidently some further amalgamations, the parish had three large farms: Upper House (278 a.) and nearby Lower House (230 a.) with houses in the hamlet, and Marsh farm (140 a.) Three other farms had 30–40 a. each and occupied old inclosures at the edge of Abdon common. There were also *c.* 15 resident smallholders, similarly located, with up to 16 a. each; eight of them were principally farmers, the others also had a trade.[38] Much of the parish's arable was put down to grass in the late 19th and early 20th century but was ploughed up again later, especially for barley.[39] In 1941 there remained seven farmers, a smallholder, and five cowkeepers.[40] At Upper House George Bradley was a noted breeder of Hereford cattle and Shropshire sheep,[41] and in the late 20th century beef cattle and sheep remained the parish's chief enterprises.[42]

There seems to have been no mill by the mid 17th century. The names Mill field and Mill

12 S.R.O. 3320/30G/1; *S.P.R. Lich.* xiv (1), 107.
13 S.R.O. 802, box 38, surv. of 1782, pp. [6–7]; 3320/30G/2.
14 S.R.O. 802, box 38, deed of 1867.
15 *V.C.H. Salop.* i. 319.
16 Eyton, iv. 129; P.R.O., E 32/144, m. 2.
17 *Roll of Salop. Eyre 1256* (Selden Soc. xcvi), p. 222; cf. *V.C.H. Salop.* iv. 51–2.
18 *Close R.* 1256–9, 488.
19 *Inq. Non.* (Rec. Com.), 186.
20 H.W.R.O.(H.), HD 2/14/1, 2; Bodl. MS. Gough Salop. 11, ff. 51, 52v., 53. Located from P.R.O., IR 29/29/1; IR 30/29/1, fields 23–4, 29, 49, 194.
21 *T.S.A.S.* lviii. 48–67.
22 Ibid. 2nd ser. viii. 195–8.
23 S.R.O. 1037/21/6, 8.
24 Below, Holdgate, econ. hist.; S.R.O., incl. award B 21, brief of [1810], ff. 10, 11v.
25 So called in 1810: S.R.O., incl. award B 21, brief of [1810], f. 5v.
26 O.S. Nat. Grid SO 585 852.
27 S.R.O., incl. award B 21, brief of [1810], ff. 7v.–8v.
28 Identified as Edw. Millichope's fm. of 1642 from a date stone 'EM 1647' in garden.
29 Above, manors.
30 Bodl. MS. Gough Salop. 11, ff. 51–4 (surv. of 1642).
31 H.W.R.O.(H.), Heref. dioc. rec., invs. of Sam. Weaver, 1664; Mary Millechap, 1667; Jane Barker, 1668; Joan Millichap, 1671; Thos. Page, 1685; John Ball, 1699; Wm. Blakeway, 1720; Geo. Rushbury, 1725; Wm. Tasker, 1733; Fra. Glaze, 1742; John Preece, 1743; Ric. Rushbury, 1749 (transcripts supplied by Dr. B. S. Trinder).
32 S.R.O. 5735/G/1/1.
33 Ibid. /G/1/6.
34 Above, this article, intro.; below, this section.
35 S.P.L., MS. 6865, p. 5.
36 P.R.O., HO 67/12/1.
37 Under Abdon and Stoke St. Milborough Incl. Act, 49 Geo. III, c. 109 (Local and Personal): S.R.O., incl. award B 33.
38 P.R.O., HO 107/1982, ff. 519v.–523v.; IR 29/29/1.
39 Table VI; Salop. Agric. Returns, 1905.
40 *Kelly's Dir. Salop.* (1941), 19 (excluding those outside the ancient par.).
41 Ibid. (1905), 17.
42 Local inf.

TABLE VI

ABDON: LAND USE, LIVESTOCK, AND CROPS

		1867	*1891*	*1938*	*1965*
Percentage of	grassland	78	84	95	78
	arable	22	16	5	22
Percentage of	cattle	14	16	13	14
	sheep	81	79	86	85
	pigs	5	5	1	1
Percentage of	wheat	42	36	32	18
	barley	40	27	12	63
	oats	18	37	56	19
	mixed corn & rye	0	0	0	0
Percentage of agricultural land growing roots and vegetables		1	2	1	4

Sources: P.R.O., MAF 68/143, no. 20; /1340, no. 6; /3880, Salop. no. 95; /4945, no. 95.

furlong, mentioned in 1642,[43] probably refer to a nearby mill at Lower Norncott.[44]

Limestone quarrying and lime burning were probably established by the late 17th century; early 18th-century farm leases allowed lime making for use on the premises.[45] Quarrying followed the two narrow bands of limestone.[46] In 1810 'Abdon limeworks'[47] were above Marsh gate, with 'new' kilns apparently nearby.[48] The kilns were associated with three quarries along the lower margin of Abdon common.[49] By 1807 the works were let to a single undertaker, who sublet parts.[50] They were fuelled with Brown Clee coal.[51] Before the mid 19th century a scattering of kilns also stood farther south towards Cockshutford.[52] In 1841, however, working was probably intermittent, for there were no resident quarrymen or limeburners.[53] Production seems to have ceased with the closure of the nearby collieries.[54] The last man to burn lime regularly was Levi Cooper, a farmer and coal owner in 1851,[55] whose main occupation was lime burning in the period 1856–70.[56] Some kilns remained in 1883[57] but all were disused by 1902.[58] Roofing slates were got on Abdon common in the early 18th century.[59] A sandstone quarry on the common,[60] reached by an old sunken track, was disused by 1883.[61]

There were coal and ironstone mines east and south of the parish boundary, on the higher parts of Brown Clee.[62] Commercial extraction seems to have begun in the 17th century.[63] A miner was mentioned in 1715.[64] Demand for local ironstone fell in the later 18th century with the decline of nearby furnaces,[65] but in 1793 nearly half of the 31 households at Abdon were of miners, most of whom probably had agricultural smallholdings too; they kept pigs, worked only part time at mining, and at harvest helped on the farms.[66] In 1851 Abdon had four resident coal-pit owners, evidently self-employed, of whom at least three also had smallholdings,[67] a coal haulier, and four coal miners, probably wage earners.[68] Coal mining on Brown Clee declined in the later 19th century,[69] and only one coal miner remained at Abdon in 1881.[70] From 1907 to 1936 jobs were available on Abdon Burf in roadstone extraction,[71] but agriculture became otherwise the only nearby employment.

LOCAL GOVERNMENT. In 1571–2 Abdon presented at Richard Cressett's court leet of Holdgate,[72] but in the 1770s was doing suit to Munslow hundred.[73] A court baron, mentioned in 1734,[74] met biennially in the later 18th century.[75] Abdon was also subject in the 16th century to the swainmote of Clee chase.[76] The 'old pound and drift place' mentioned in 1580[77] may have been used in connexion with it. After the swainmote lapsed, its jurisdiction over parts of the former chase was claimed to subsist in the court leet of Earnstrey Park (in Diddlebury),[78] and when Sir Humphrey Briggs sold Earnstrey Park

43 Bodl. MS. Gough Salop. 11, ff. 51v.–52.
44 Below, the Heath, econ. hist.
45 S.R.O. 1141, box 175, deed of 1718; 5735/G/1/1.
46 Above, this article, intro.
47 O.S. Map 1", sheet LXI. SW. (1833 edn.).
48 S.R.O. 1037/21/23.
49 O.S. Maps 1/2,500, Salop. LXV. 10, 11 (1884 edn.).
50 S.R.O., incl. award B 21, Rob. Brigges to Jos. Loxdale 4 Sept. 1807.
51 G. L. A. Price, 'Coal mining in the Clee Hills', *Birm. Enterprise Club Trans.* ii. 15 (copy in S.P.L.).
52 P.R.O., IR 29/29/1; IR 30/29/1, fields 225, 245, 248; O.S. Maps 1/2,500, Salop. LXV. 14, 15 (1884 edn.).
53 P.R.O., HO 107/912/1, ff. 2–4v.
54 *Salop. Mining Club Jnl.* (1975), 21.
55 P.R.O., HO 107/1982, f. 521.
56 *P.O. Dir. Salop.* (1856), 7; (1863), 644; (1870), 7.
57 O.S. Maps 1/2,500, Salop. LXV. 10, 11, 14, 15 (1884 edn.).
58 Ibid. (1903 edn.).
59 S.R.O. 5735/G/1/1. Such tiles were used on the ch.: below, church.
60 D. C. Greig and others, *Geol. of Country around Ch. Stretton, Craven Arms, Wenlock Edge and Brown Clee* (Mem. Geol. Surv. 1968), 245.
61 O.S. Map 1/2,500, Salop. LXV. 11 (1884 edn.).
62 S.R.O. 1037/21/6; J. Rocque, *Map of Salop.* (1752); R. Baugh, *Map of Salop.* (1808); O.S. Maps 1", sheet LXI. SW. (1833 edn.); 1/2,500, Salop. LXV. 11, 15 (1884 edn.); Geol. Surv. Map 1/50,000, solid, sheet 166 (1974 edn.).
63 Downton Hall muniments, deed of 1650 (Sir Humph. Briggs to Edw. Baldwin); *T.S.A.S.* lviii. 66–7.
64 *S.P.R. Heref.* xix (1), 46.
65 *T.S.A.S.* lviii. 67; T. Rowley, *Salop. Landscape* (1972), 219–20; below, Bouldon, econ. hist.; Stoke St. Milborough, econ. hist.
66 S.P.L., MS. 6865, p. 4.
67 P.R.O., IR 29/29/1.
68 P.R.O., HO 107/1982, ff. 519v.–523v.
69 *Birm. Enterprise Club Trans.* ii. 15.
70 P.R.O., RG 11/2617, f. 7.
71 *Salop. Mining Club Jnl.* (1975), 22; W. Smith and K. Beddoes, *Cleobury Mortimer and Ditton Priors Lt. Rly.* (1980), 83.
72 S.P.L., MS. 2, f. 146v.
73 S.R.O. 272/1.
74 S.R.O. 5735/G/1/1.
75 Ibid. /G/1/6; S.R.O., incl. award B 21, abstract of ct. r.
76 S.R.O., incl. award B 21, ct. r.; S.R.O. 1037/21/1.
77 B.L. Add. MS. 31932, f. 285.
78 *T.S.A.S.* lviii. 66.

in 1709 he is said to have 'removed' his chase jurisdiction, perhaps reduced in extent, to Abdon; by 1744, however, it was not exercised there.[79]

The parish was in Ludlow poor-law union 1836–1930,[80] Ludlow highway district 1863–95,[81] Ludlow rural sanitary district 1872--94, and Ludlow rural district 1894–1974, and in South Shropshire district from 1974.[82] The civil parish had a joint council with the Heath C.P. in 1992.[83]

CHURCH. About 1138 Aelfric (Eluericus) 'the dean' gave Abdon chapel to Shrewsbury abbey in recompense for having wronged the monks.[84] By 1148 the chapel had long been paying the abbey a pension of 2*s*.,[85] which was still owed in 1419.[86] The living was a rectory by 1346.[87] In 1407 it was said to owe another pension, 3*s*. 4*d*., to Tugford church,[88] to which it may therefore at one time have been joined or subordinate.[89] In 1240 Geoffrey of Ledwich quitclaimed the adowson to the abbey,[90] which held it until 1407[91] or later; the bishop collated by lapse in 1462 and 1530.[92] In 1551 Jerome Dudley, the lord of the manor's brother,[93] presented, and in 1556 Henry Cressett, perhaps already lord, with William Heath. Edward Cressett presented in 1577,[94] but from 1580 the advowson was regularly exercised by the lord[95] until 1873 when Lord Pembroke sold the manor but kept the advowson. The earls of Pembroke remained patrons after 1873 and alternate patrons from 1928, when Abdon and Clee St. Margaret became a united benefice,[96] until 1962[97] when the earl conveyed his advowson to the bishop of Hereford. From 1957 the united living was held in plurality with Stoke St. Milborough and Cold Weston benefices.[98] The patronage was suspended 1973–83 and the cure served by the incumbent of Diddlebury with Bouldon and Munslow as curate (or priest) in charge.[99] In 1983 Abdon rectory was separated from Clee St. Margaret and was thereafter held in plurality with the united benefice of Diddlebury with Munslow, Holdgate, and Tugford.[1]

The living was valued at less than £4 in 1291,[2] at £5 3*s*. 4*d*. in 1407,[3] at £2 19*s*. 6*d*. in 1535,[4] and at £32 *c*. 1708.[5] In 1768, to meet a benefaction in augmentation of the living, Queen Anne's Bounty gave £200,[6] with which glebe at Clee Stanton was bought in 1785.[7] In 1793 there were 22 a. of glebe in the parish and 25 a. in Clee Stanton, yielding £29 altogether, and all the tithes in Abdon were let to the occupiers for £30.[8] The tithes were commuted to £128 in 1848.[9] The glebe at Clee Stanton was sold in 1863,[10] leaving 28 a. in Abdon.[11] Earnstrey Park township (in Diddlebury) had been added to the ecclesiastical parish of Abdon in 1858,[12] from which time the dean and chapter of Hereford paid the rector £20 a year for his duty there;[13] in 1885 £33 of annual tithe rent charges in the township, thitherto the vicar of Diddlebury's property, were annexed to Abdon rectory.[14] The rectory house was reckoned 'equal to the living' in 1793 and was rebuilt or much improved by Lord Pembroke *c*. 1825.[15] The incumbents did not live there after 1920,[16] and 21 a. of glebe were sold in 1922.[17]

The rectors seem to have been normally resident until 1780.[18] Edward Baldwyn, 1780–1817, always employed curates; he was a schoolmaster in Bradford (Yorks. W.R.) in 1793 and afterwards lived in London.[19] His immediate successors,[20] though non-resident, served the cure in person.[21] The rectors from *c*. 1825 to *c*. 1920 lived in the parish.[22] From 1920 they lived in the nearby parishes of which they were also incumbents.[23]

The small church of *ST. MARGARET*, so dedicated by 1793,[24] consists of chancel and nave with south porch and west bellcot. The walls are of coursed rubble with ashlar quoins and were rendered externally until after 1854. In 1854 the roofs were of stone slates,[25] later replaced by clay

79 S.R.O. 1037/21/9–10, 27.

80 V. J. Walsh, 'Admin. of Poor Laws in Salop. 1820–55' (Pennsylvania Univ. Ph.D. thesis, 1970), 150; *Kelly's Dir. Salop*. (1929), 21.

81 *Lond. Gaz*. 27 Mar. 1863, p. 1771; S.R.O., S.C.C. Local Govt., etc., cttee. min. bk. 1894–1903, p. 29.

82 *Rural Dist. Councillors Electn. Order, 1894* (Local Govt. Bd. order no. 31847); *V.C.H. Salop*. ii. 215; iii. 179, and sources cited ibid. 169 n. 29.

83 Local inf.

84 *Cart. Shrews*. ii, p. 303. Aelfric's deanery is unidentified: *V.C.H. Salop*. ii. 3.

85 *Cart. Shrews*. ii, p. 304.

86 *Reg. Lacy* (C.S.), 77.

87 *Reg. Trillek* (C.S.), 405.

88 *Reg. Mascall* (C.S.), 171 n.

89 There seems no evid. for the suggestion (Eyton, iv. 131; *Minsters and Par. Churches*, ed. J. Blair (1988), 74) that Abdon chap. was once a dependency of Morville ch.

90 *T.S.A.S*. 4th ser. vi. 177.

91 *Reg. Swinfield* (C.S.), 537; *Reg. Courtenay* (C.S.), 12; *Reg. Mascall*, 169, 171.

92 *Reg. Stanbury* (C.S.), 178; *Reg. Bothe* (C.S.), 343.

93 Burke, *Ext. Peerage* (1840), 182.

94 *Dioc. of Heref. Institutions (1539–1900)*, ed. A. T. Bannister (Heref. 1923), 7, 11, 24.

95 Ibid. 26, 141, 145–6, 148–9, 166; H.W.R.O.(H.), HD 2/14/1; Bodl. MS. Gough Salop 11, f. 55; *T.S.A.S*. 4th ser. ii. 80, 97–8, 101–2; vi. 317.

96 Heref. Dioc. Regy., reg. 1926–38, p. 99.

97 Bannister, *Heref. Institutions*, 189, 205; *Kelly's Dir. Salop*. (1992), 19; (1934), 21; (1941), 19.

98 Heref. Dioc. Regy., reg. 1953–68, pp. 190, 419.

99 *Crockford* (1975–6), 490; (1989–90), 441.

1 Heref. Dioc. Regy., reg. 1969– (in use), pp. 457–9. For the subsequent patronage arrangements see below, Holdgate, church.

2 *Tax. Eccl*. (Rec. Com.), 167, 176.

3 *Reg. Mascall*, 37.

4 *Valor Eccl*. (Rec. Com.), iii. 209.

5 J. Ecton, *Liber Valorum et Decimarum* (1711), 147.

6 C. Hodgson, *Q. Anne's Bounty* (2nd edn.), p. cclxxxix.

7 Downton Hall muniments, deed.

8 S.P.L., MS. 6865, p. 7; P.R.O., IR 29/29/84, fields 3, 11, 14, 16–17, 24.

9 P.R.O., IR 29/29/1.

10 Downton Hall muniments, deed.

11 S.R.O. 1037/21/37, p. 13.

12 Heref. Dioc. Regy., reg. 1857–69, pp. 52–6.

13 S.R.O. 1037/21/37, p. 13.

14 Heref. Dioc. Regy., reg. 1883–1901, p. 61.

15 S.P.L., MS. 6865, pp. 7, 9.

16 *Kelly's Dir. Salop*. (1917), 14; (1922), 19.

17 *S.P.R. Heref*. xix (1), p. vi.

18 *T.S.A.S*. 4th ser. xi. 186; *S.P.R. Heref*. xix (1), 12, 37, 54, 70.

19 *S.P.R. Heref*. xix (1), pp. ix, 70–1, 75–7, 81–2, 87--9; Heref. Dioc. Regy., reg. 1772–1802, f. 126; 1791–1821, ff. 35v., 131; S.P.L., MS. 6865, pp. 7, 9.

20 Bannister, *Heref. Institutions*, 141, 145.

21 S.P.L., MS. 6865, pp. 9, 102; S.R.O. 1661/2.

22 S.P.L., MS. 6865, p. 9; P.R.O., HO 107/912/1, f. 2; S. Bagshaw, *Dir. Salop*. (1851), 517; *P.O. Dir. Salop*. (1856–79); *Kelly's Dir. Salop*. (1885–1917).

23 *Crockford* (1924 and later edns.).

24 S.P.L., MS. 6865, p. 7. St. Mary Magdalen was noted as patron in 1741 (B.L. Add. MS. 30316, f. 29v.), perhaps in error.

25 S.P.L., MS. 372, vol. ii, f. 38; St. Deiniol's Libr., Hawarden, Sir Steph. Glynne's ch. notes, xcvii, f. 45.

tiles. In 1731 the church was 'very ruinous' and needed complete rebuilding.[26] A brief for £1,120 was issued *c.* 1737,[27] and it appears from the surviving fabric that a thorough rebuilding took place, the old materials being re-used.[28]

The plain font may date from *c.* 1200. The chancel has a two-light south window of the earlier 14th century and remains of a piscina. The south door, and perhaps its timber framed porch, may also be 14th-century. The chancel roof timbers may be of the later 15th. There was a timber framed west bell turret by 1731.[29] An open timber truss serves as a chancel screen;[30] it is apparently integral with the nave roof, which probably dates from the 1730s. The east window of the chancel and south window of the nave were plain and square-headed in 1790,[31] so perhaps were replacements of the 1730s; the north nave window[32] was similar.[33] By the late 18th century the pulpit was in the north-east angle of the nave. Men sat on the north side of the nave, women on the south.[34] There seems to have been a west gallery by 1790[35] and it was greatly enlarged in 1831. The communion rail stood then on three sides of the table. The chancel had two pews on the south,[36] one of them perhaps that erected for Edward Sandes's farm in 1655.[37]

W. S. Dear, rector 1829–50,[38] inserted a new east window in the Decorated style.[39] A thorough restoration was completed in 1860.[40] The nave was extended west, with a stone bellcot in place of the turret. The nave south window was replaced by a new one, the north one by three new ones.[41] It may have been then that the gallery was taken down and the pews replaced by benches. Wainscot from the pews was re-used as a nave dado. The pulpit, reading desk, and communion rail may all be *c.* 1860 too. All the communion plate dates from 1846.[42] Two new bells were substituted in 1860 for the three recorded in 1740.[43]

The registers begin in the 1560s and entries survive for 1583–5, but they are complete (save for a gap 1641–9) only from 1614.[44]

NONCONFORMITY. None known.

EDUCATION. The rector had a school in 1662,[45] and there was a day school in 1831.[46] Abdon C.E. school opened in 1850 as a parochial school, in a new building provided by the lord of the manor and managed by the rector, who by 1870 made up any annual deficit. It consisted of two rooms and a teacher's house under one roof. There were *c.* 20 pupils in 1870. Boys and girls were taught together in the larger room in the morning; in the afternoon the master's wife taught the girls sewing in the other.[47] The school closed in 1946 and the children went to Burwarton C.E. school.[48]

CHARITIES FOR THE POOR. Robert Ellis of Earnstrey Park,[49] by will dated in or before 1652, gave a 10*s.* rent charge in Llanwyddelan parish (Mont.); still received in 1820, it afterwards lapsed.[50]

By 1787 there was a poor's stock of £12 10*s.*[51] The annual income, 12*s.* in the early 20th century, was distributed in cash to widows until 1927 or later,[52] but the charity ceased before 1975.[53]

EASTHOPE

EASTHOPE parish is a single township of 331 ha. (817 a.)[54] 7 km. south-west of Much Wenlock. It is bounded westwards by Plaish[55] brook, also called Rey brook[56] and Hughley brook;[57] a tributary forms part of the southern boundary. Elsewhere the boundaries mostly follow unbroken lines, probably fixed in the 13th century by division among townships of formerly shared woods and pastures: the boundary between Easthope and Patton (in Stanton Long) crosses Natal common and by 1332 Easthope wood was separated from Hughley manor by a ditch, and Easthope from Presthope (in Much Wenlock) by a hedge.[58]

Wenlock Edge bisects the parish. Beneath its escarpment, facing north-west, the land slopes down to Plaish brook. The rest of the parish, named in relation to Westhope and Middlehope, occupies a broad-headed valley (OE. *hop*),[59] called Knaves Dale in the 18th century,[60] which

26 S.R.O., q. sess. order bk. 1726–41, f. 69v.
27 W. A. Bewes, *Ch. Briefs* (1896), 318.
28 e.g. tracery of chancel S. window, remains of piscina: below, this section.
29 S.R.O., q. sess. order bk. 1726–41, f. 69v.
30 Cf. above, Acton Scott, church.
31 S.P.L., MS. 372, vol. ii, f. 38.
32 S.R.O. 4644/MRg/2, front pastedown (plan).
33 St. Deiniol's Libr., Glynne's ch. notes, xcvii, f. 45.
34 *S.P.R. Heref.* xix (1), 15.
35 Small skylight shown on S.P.L., MS. 372, vol. ii, f. 38.
36 S.R.O. 4644/MRg/2, front pastedown and tipped-in sheet.
37 *S.P.R. Heref.* xix (1), 15.
38 Bannister, *Heref. Institutions*, 149, 166.
39 St. Deiniol's Libr., Glynne's ch. notes, xcvii, f. 45; *S.P.R. Heref.* xix (1), p. v.
40 S.R.O. 4644/Ser/3, 22 Feb. 1860.
41 Cranage, ii. 61.
42 D. L. Arkwright and B. W. Bourne, *Ch. Plate Archd. Ludlow* (Shrews. 1961), 1.
43 H. B. Walters, *Ch. Bells of Salop.* (Oswestry, 1915), 83.
44 S.R.O. 4644/Rg/1–3; /MRg/1–2; regs. at ch.; *S.P.R. Heref.* xix (1), esp. pp. vi–vii.
45 H.W.R.O.(H.), HD 7, chwdns.' presentment of 1662.
46 R. Hume, 'Changing Patterns of Educ. Devt. in Salop. 1660–1833' (Keele Univ. Ph.D. (Educ.) thesis, 1982), 316.
47 P.R.O., ED 7/102, ff. 14–15.
48 *S.C.C. Mins.* 1947–8, 166.
49 S.P.L., MS. 6865, p. 97.
50 *3rd Rep. Com. Char.* H.C. 5, p. 265 (1820), iv. Not mentioned in *Review of Local Chars.* (S.C.C. 1975).
51 *Char. Don. 1786–8*, ii, H.C. 511–II, pp. 1022–3 (1816), xvi (2).
52 S.R.O. 4644/MRg/2, front endpaper; 4693/1; *Kelly's Dir. Salop.* (1941), 19.
53 *Review of Local Chars.* 52.
54 O.S. *Area Bk.* (1883). This article was written 1990–1.
55 So called 1332: S.R.O. 1224/2/11.
56 By 1538: P.R.O., C 116/213, m. 1.
57 By *c.* 1735: S.R.O. 4572/6/2/56.
58 Fig. 11; S.R.O. 1224/2/11.
59 *P.N. Salop.* (E.P.N.S.), i. 114, 156.
60 Bodl. MS. Gough Salop. 4, f. 96.

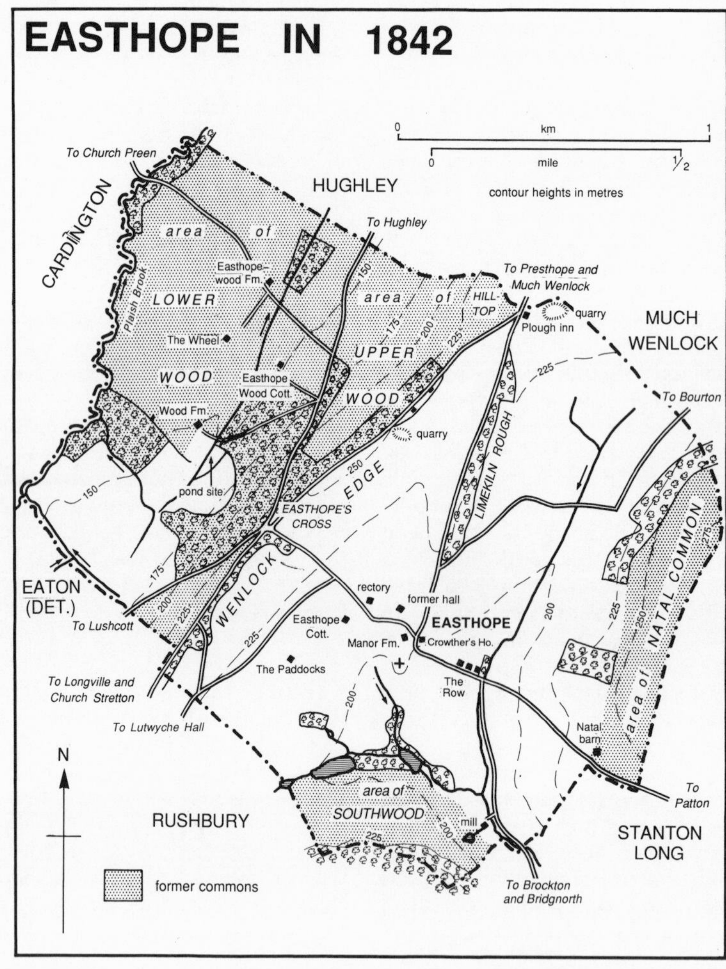

Fig. 11

lies between the dip slope of the Edge and a parallel ridge to the south-east. Two streams, the north-eastern called Natal brook in 1509,[61] drain the valley and meet, as Brockton brook, to cut the south-eastern ridge at the parish boundary before descending to the Corve.

The rock below and at the base of Wenlock Edge is Wenlock Shale.[62] The soils there are poorly drained.[63] The top of the Edge is formed by a band of Wenlock Limestone. On the dip slope the rock is mainly Lower Ludlow Shale, with a narrow outcrop of Wenlock Limestone extending from the village northwards to Hilltop. The higher part of Natal common consists of Aymestry Group limestone. Boulder clay overlies most of that and the shale.

Apart from a neolithic stone axe found just south of the village,[64] direct evidence of prehistoric or Romano-British activity is lacking. In 1086 the recorded population consisted of four demesne *servi*, a *villanus*, and five bordars.[65] By 1306 there were 16 tenants,[66] and a similar number was recorded in 1383 and 1493.[67] There were five taxpayers in 1525.[68] Nine households paid hearth tax in 1672[69] and there were *c.* 50 adults in 1676.[70] By 1801, however, the total population was only 85. It was 109 in 1811, and until the 1960s remained about 100.[71] By 1991, however, it had fallen to 74.[72]

By the 16th century, and still in the 20th, the principal houses, some stone and others timber framed,[73] stood close to the north side of the church, just below the head of the valley. They fronted a north-westward lane from Patton to Easthope's Cross (a junction on Wenlock Edge). The mill was lower down the valley. In addition there was dispersed settlement between the Upper and Lower woods, beside a stream that ran at the foot of the Edge: Wood Farm probably existed by the late 16th century,[74] the timber framed Easthope Wood Cottage (later Hollybank Villa) was evidently built before 1700,[75]

61 P.R.O., C 116/213, m. 5.
62 Para. based on Inst. Geol. Sciences Map 1/25,000, SO 59, *Wenlock Edge* (1969 edn.).
63 Soil Surv. Map 1", sheet 166 (1972 edn.).
64 SA 3593.
65 *V.C.H. Salop.* i. 319–20.
66 P.R.O., C 133/121, no. 23.
67 P.R.O., C 116/213, mm. 9, 15.
68 P.R.O., E 179/166/127, m. 4.
69 *Hearth Tax 1672* (Salop. Arch. Soc. 1949), 178.
70 *Compton Census*, ed. Whiteman, 259.
71 *V.C.H. Salop.* ii. 222.
72 S.C.C. Property and Planning Services Dept. inf. rep. C91/103.
73 Below, manor.
74 Its associated pond was probably that mentioned 1576: below, econ. hist.
75 SA 15490.

and a house at what was later called the Wheel was standing in 1732. By then a cottage also stood on the edge of Natal common.[76] Two roadside cottages stood by 1833 on the road along the Edge, next to a quarry and limekiln.[77] The Plough inn (later Hilltop Farm) and Easthopewood Farm were built in isolated positions between 1732 and 1833.[78] By the early 19th century Easthope had begun to take on the character of an estate village dependent on Lutwyche Hall (in Rushbury),[79] and the few changes were mostly in the nature of estate improvements. In the village three pairs of cottages, the Row, were built *c.* 1794,[80] Ivy Cottage and Sniper's House in the mid 19th century,[81] and Allenby and Birdwood cottages *c.* 1920.[82] Towards Lutwyche Hall a pair of cottages was built at the Paddocks *c.* 1800,[83] a gate lodge by 1851,[84] and the Pheasantry bungalow *c.* 1920.[85] There has been little new building since then.

The road from Much Wenlock to Church Stretton ran along the Edge.[86] From Easthope's Cross a lane descended south-west to Lushcott (in Eaton-under-Heywood) and another, called 'Colway' or 'Calloweie',[87] north-east to Hughley; from the latter a lane leading north-westwards, perhaps the 'Preen way' mentioned in 1576, went through Easthope wood.[88] A south-eastward lane from the Edge road at Easthope's Cross reached Patton by way of Natal common;[89] Easthope village used it to reach Easthope wood.[90] That lane was joined at the village by others from Brockton and Bourton, the latter called Easthope's way in 1332,[91] and by a lane from the Edge road at Hilltop. The route from Easthope's Cross to Brockton was part of the road from Church Stretton via Longville to Bridgnorth by the mid 18th century.[92] The Edge road was turnpiked from Much Wenlock to Church Stretton in 1765.[93] It was disturnpiked in 1867[94] and was a main road by 1889.[95] From Easthope's Cross the road via Easthope and Brockton was turnpiked to Weston in 1839[96] and disturnpiked in 1872.[97] With the branches from Easthope's Cross to Lushcott and from Hilltop to Easthope, they were the parish's principal roads in 1990.

The railway from Much Wenlock to Craven Arms, beside and below the road along the Edge, opened in 1867,[98] with a halt for Easthope opened in 1936. That closed in 1951 and the line in 1963.[99]

There was a sub post office from the 1850s[1] to the 1950s[2] or later, and a resident police constable from the 1860s[3] to *c.* 1920.[4]

The Plough inn stood on the turnpike road at Hilltop by 1841.[5] The sign moved to Presthope *c.* 1862. It returned to Hilltop in the early 20th century, but to a house outside Easthope parish.[6] The Lutwyche Club was built in the early 1920s,[7] and St. Philip's Sunday school was sometimes used as a parish room by 1929.[8] The county library started a voluntary book centre at Easthope in that year.[9] There was a cricket club in 1926,[10] and a youth hostel at Manor Farm until *c.* 1936.[11] The club house and the parish room closed before 1952.[12]

MANOR AND OTHER ESTATES. One of the estates 'by the river Corve' given to St. Mildburg by her half-brothers Merchelm and Mildfrith before 704 may have been *EASTHOPE*, for in 901 Aethelraed, ealdorman of Mercia, and his wife Aethelflaed received three *manentes* there from the church of Wenlock.[13] The manor belonged in 1066 to two free men, Earnwig (Ernu) and Wulfric (Uluric). In 1086 it was held of Roger of Montgomery, earl of Shrewsbury and tenant in chief, by the sheriff Reynold of Bailleul;[14] after Earl Robert's forfeiture in 1102 it was evidently held in chief by Reynold's successors in the shrieval estates[15] and thus had come to William FitzAlan by 1166.[16] The FitzAlans remained overlords until the later 16th century[17] and in 1581 Easthope was said to be held of Sir Rowland Hayward's manor of Acton Round,[18] which Hayward had bought from Henry FitzAlan, earl of Arundel.[19] Before 1615, however, Easthope was said to be held of Thomas Howard, earl of Suffolk.[20]

76 S.R.O. 809, parcel 14, Easthope map.
77 O.S. Maps 1", sheet LXI. SW. (1833 edn.); 1/2,500, Salop. LVII. 2 (1883 edn.); P.R.O., IR 29/29/116; IR 30/29/116, fields 73–7.
78 O.S. Map 1", sheet LXI. SW. (1833 edn.); S.R.O. 809, parcel 14, Easthope map.
79 Cf. below, manor.
80 S.P.L., MS. 6865, p. 78.
81 P.R.O., IR 30/29/116 (not shown); O.S. Map 1/2,500, Salop. LVII. 2 (1883 edn.).
82 S.R.O., DA 18/640 (1168/3/304).
83 O.S. Map 1", sheet LXI. SW. (1833 edn.).
84 P.R.O., IR 30/29/116 (not shown); HO 107/1984, f. 97.
85 S.R.O., DA 18/640 (1168/3/318, 321).
86 Para. based on S.R.O. 809, parcel 14, map of 1732.
87 S.R.O. 2922/1/2/11.
88 S.P.L., Deeds 1174.
89 Below, Stanton Long, intro.
90 H.W.R.O.(H.), HD 2/14/24.
91 S.R.O. 1224/2/11.
92 Below, Shipton, intro.
93 5 Geo. III, c. 86.
94 Ann. Turnpike Acts Continuance Act, 1867, 30 & 31 Vic. c. 121.
95 *S.C.C. Mins.* Main Roads and Bridges Cttee. rep. 27 Apr. 1889.
96 2 Vic. c. 30 (Local and Personal); S.R.O., dep. plan 249.
97 Ann. Turnpike Acts Continuance Act, 1871, 34 & 35 Vic. c. 115.
98 Below, M. Wenlock, communications.
99 *T.S.A.S.* lxiv. 94, 98.

1 *P.O. Dir. Salop.* (1856), 46.
2 O.S. Map 1/25,000, SO 59 (1956 edn.).
3 *P.O. Dir. Salop.* (1863), 684; S.R.O. 3900/Ve/2, 19 Feb. 1868.
4 *Kelly's Dir. Salop.* (1917), 83; (1922), 89.
5 P.R.O., HO 107/912, no. 20, f. 4; IR 29/29/116; IR 30/29/116, field 171.
6 Below, M. Wenlock, social and cultural activities.
7 S.R.O., DA 18/640 (1168/3/304); O.S. Map 1/2,500, Salop. LVII. 2 (1926 edn.).
8 Heref. Dioc. Regy., reg. 1926–38, p. 121; cf. below, educ.
9 R. C. Elliott, 'Development of Public Libraries in Salop.' (Loughborough Univ. M.A. thesis, 1970; copy in co. libr.), 126.
10 *Kelly's Dir. Salop.* (1926), 93; no mention in later edns.
11 S.P.L., Caradoc press cuttings, xx. 147–9.
12 S.R.O. 809, box 2, sale partic.
13 Birch, *Cart. Sax.* ii, p. 230 (no. 587); H. P. R. Finberg, *Early Charters of W. Midlands* (1972), p. 148.
14 *V.C.H. Salop.* i. 319.
15 Cf. ibid. iii. 10–12.
16 *Red Bk. Exch.* (Rolls Ser.), i. 273.
17 *Bk. of Fees*, ii. 963; *Cal. Inq. p.m.* iv, p. 236; *Feud. Aids*, iv. 244, 267; P.R.O., C 142/117, no. 12; E 150/846, no. 7.
18 P.R.O., C 142/216, no. 16.
19 *T.S.A.S.* li. 136.
20 Ibid. 4th ser. iii. 3. Cf. below, Shipton, manors (Brockton).

The terre tenant in 1086 was Fulcher.[21] Easthope was held in 1166 by Roger of Easthope (fl. 1154).[22] Thomas of Easthope was lord in 1242[23] and his son[24] John of Easthope by 1255.[25] That or another John (d. c. 1306)[26] was succeeded by Thomas of Easthope (d. 1348 × 1349),[27] perhaps a grandson.[28] Thomas's son John was lord in 1357[29] and died c. 1383,[30] leaving his relict Edith,[31] who held the manor in 1405 and 1414,[32] though their son John Easthope was named as lord in 1396 and 1412.[33] He may have been the John Easthope who was lord in 1431 and 1440.[34] Another John Easthope had the manor in 1483;[35] his relict quitclaimed it to their son Edward in 1489.[36] Henry and Nicholas Warley acquired it in 1493 from Thomas Janyns and William Adams.[37] In 1497 Henry conveyed his interest to Nicholas[38] (d. 1524), from whom it descended to his son Bartholomew[39] (d. 1554), whose sister and heir Frances was the wife of Nicholas Crosthwaite.[40] Crosthwaite sold the manor in 1566 to Thomas Ludlow.[41] It then descended with the Moorhouse (in Shipton)[42] until 1745, when Samuel Edwards's trustees sold it to William Lutwyche,[43] after which it descended with Lutwyche (in Rushbury)[44] except for 125 a., which descended with Wilderhope (in Rushbury) to Mrs. C. E. M. Boodé,[45] who conveyed them to M. G. Benson of Lutwyche in 1851, perhaps by exchange.[46]

About 1557[47] the Crosthwaites had sold off most of the manorial estate to the tenants.[48] The chief house and demesne lands were bought in 1557 by the tenant, William Ball (d. 1605).[49] By c. 1610 they had passed to Thomas Ball[50] (d. 1641), who left them to his widow Eleanor (d. 1647) with remainder to their son William[51] (d. 1665). William left the estate to his widow Mary (d. 1691) with remainder to his brother-in-law Thomas Mason (d. 1705).[52] Mason's son Charles[53] sold it in 1702 to Samuel Edwards,[54] who acquired the manor in 1721,[55] with which Ball's farm[56] was thus reunited. The chief house of the manor, mentioned in 1306[57] and owned since the 16th century by the Ball family, may therefore have been the farmhouse that a Mr. Corfield held of the manorial estate in 1732; at that time the only other large holding on the manorial estate was attached to Manor Farm,[58] the former freehold of the Fewtrells.[59] Corfield's house[60] included part of a timber framed hall of c. 1431 with a box framed cross wing of c. 1454. It may have been the 'Hall house, now used by farmers' mentioned in 1793.[61] About 1800 it was converted to a malthouse and cased in brick, probably to serve the new Easthope Cottage,[62] to which it remained a farm building in 1990.

Edward Fewtrell bought his farm from the Crosthwaites,[63] and in 1588 Roger Fewtrell sold 'Dyke's house' to his brother John (fl. 1593).[64] John's son Edward (fl. 1640) was the owner c. 1610.[65] John Fewtrell (fl. 1661, d. 1690)[66] owned two farms and a cottage in Easthope, one of which was *MANOR FARM*.[67] In 1712 his grandchildren Samuel Fewtrell and Mary Harris[68] conveyed the farms and cottage to William Russell of Enchmarsh.[69] By 1732 the farms had been reunited with the manor.[70] Manor Farm has an east–west timber framed range that included a late medieval open hall. A two storeyed box framed cross wing was built at the east end, perhaps c. 1600; it has a contemporary plaster ceiling by craftsmen whose work has been found in several other Shropshire houses.[71] It may have been then that an upper floor and central stack were inserted in the medieval hall.[72]

In 1566 Edward Lutwyche bought land at Easthope from Nicholas Crosthwaite and Ralph

21 *V.C.H. Salop.* i. 319.
22 *Red Bk. Exch.* (Rolls Ser.), i. 273; S.R.O. 1/17/2 (witnessed by Rog., earl of Heref).
23 *Bk. of Fees*, ii. 963.
24 P.R.O., C 104/27, undated deed (Ric. son of Bernard to Agnes dau. of Rob.).
25 *Rot. Hund.* (Rec. Com.), ii. 70.
26 *Cal. Inq. p.m.* iv, pp. 236–7.
27 P.R.O., CP 25/1/194/9, no. 48; *Feud. Aids*, iv. 244; *Reg. Trillek* (C.S.), 381.
28 *Cal. Inq. p.m.* iv, p. 237, naming Thos.'s father as Thos. of Easthope. John of Easthope, ld. in 1260, had a son Thos.: P.R.O., C 104/23, pt. 2, fine.
29 P.R.O., C 104/25, deed.
30 *Reg. Gilbert* (C.S.), 24–5.
31 Ibid. 119, 125; P.R.O., C 116/213, m. 9.
32 *Reg. Mascall* (C.S.), 168; P.R.O., C 104/25, deed.
33 S.R.O. 1037/3/72; P.R.O., C 104/25, deed.
34 *Feud. Aids*, iv. 267; P.R.O., C 104/27, deed.
35 P.R.O., C 104/23, pt. 2, deed.
36 P.R.O., C 104/25, deed.
37 P.R.O., C 104/27, deed.
38 P.R.O., C 104/25, deed.
39 P.R.O., E 150/846, no. 7.
40 P.R.O., C 142/117, no. 12.
41 P.R.O., C 104/23, pt. 1, deed.
42 Ibid. pt. 2, memo. [of early 17th cent.]; P.R.O., C 142/216, no. 16; S.R.O. 1037/21/180–1; 2922/1/2/11. Cf. below, Shipton, manors.
43 Inscr. on S.R.O. 809, parcel 14, Easthope map of 1732.
44 S.R.O., q. sess. rec. box 260, reg. of gamekeepers 1742–79, 7 Sept. 1775; 809, box 1, deeds 26–7 Dec. 1806; 4835/2; S.P.L., MS. 6865, p. 78; S. Bagshaw, *Dir. Salop.* (1851), 535; *P.O. Dir. Salop.* (1879), 316; *Kelly's Dir. Salop.* (1891), 311; (1913), 91. Cf. above, Rushbury, manors (Lutwyche).
45 P.R.O., IR 29/29/116. Cf. above, Rushbury, manors (Wilderhope).
46 New Ho. fm. (Shipton) deeds, abstr. of title (1909) of trustees of Mr. and Mrs. John Hippisley's marr. settlement (thanks are due to Mr. and Mrs. B. D. Williams, New Ho., for sight of this abstr.); S.R.O. 809, parcel 3, Lutwyche est. rental 1843–53; box 10, Lushcott, etc., ests., copy valn. and rep. *re* proposed exchange betw. M. G. Benson and Mrs. Lutwyche 1849.
47 S.P.L., Deeds 1174.
48 H.W.R.O.(H.), HD 2/14/24.
49 P.R.O., C 104/26, deed of 1554; C 104/27, deed of 1557; H.W.R.O.(H.), Heref. dioc. rec., bp.'s transcripts, Easthope, 20 Dec. 1605.
50 Bodl. MS. Blakeway 8, f. 364.
51 S.R.O. 5001/4/5/3; *S.P.R. Heref.* xix (4), 6, 9.
52 S.P.L., Deeds 1352; *S.P.R. Heref.* xix (4), 19, 29; *Hearth Tax 1672* (Salop. Arch. Soc. 1949), 178; S.R.O. 4649/Rg/1, bur. 13 Nov. 1705.
53 Cf. *V.C.H. Salop.* iii. 298–302.
54 S.R.o. 4573/2.
55 S.R.O. 1037/21/181.
56 S.R.O. 2089/9/2/11.
57 P.R.O., C 133/121, no. 23.
58 S.R.O. 809, parcel 14, Easthope map of 1732.
59 Below, this section.
60 O.S. Nat. Grid SO 5661 9530; SA 17196 (incl. surv. and drawings); *Vernacular Archit.* xxv. 31, 33–4.
61 S.P.L., MS. 6865, p. 78.
62 Below, this section.
63 H.W.R.O.(H.), HD 2/14/24.
64 S.R.O. 1146/18; 5001/4/5/1; S.P.L., Deeds 1351.
65 Bodl. MS. Blakeway 8, f. 364; S.R.O. 2922/1/2/11.
66 P.R.O., E 179/168/214, m. 21d.; *S.P.R. Heref.* xix (4), 29.
67 S.R.O. 5001/4/5/4; W.S.L. 350/5/40, Easthope p. 1.
68 Cf. *S.P.R. Heref.* xix (4), 7, 11, 24, 27, 29.
69 S.R.O. 5001/4/5/5.
70 S.R.O. 809, parcel 14, Easthope map of 1732.
71 H. E. Forrest, *Old Hos. of Wenlock* (Shrews. 1914), 40–1; Pevsner, *Salop.* 72, 207, 307, 319; *T.S.A.S.* 3rd ser. iii. 15–16.
72 Mrs. M. Moran is thanked for advice on this bldg.

Warley[73] to add to that acquired from the Crosthwaites by his father Richard.[74] It probably followed the descent of Lutwyche (in Rushbury) and was thus reunited to the Easthope manorial estate in 1745.[75]

John Harriots (d. 1572) of Chorley bought a house and land from the Crosthwaites,[76] to which his son Robert succeeded.[77] Robert settled it in 1601 on his son John[78] (d. 1650) and the farm later belonged to John's great-grandson Robert Harriots[79] (d. 1699). His representatives sold it to the Lutwyche estate in 1721.[80] The Harriots family probably owned a house on the site, which the Lutwyches owned in 1732, of the later Easthope Cottage.[81] Easthope Cottage was built *c.* 1800 in polite style, presumably by Thomas Langton (d. 1805),[82] the first lord of the manor to live at Easthope[83] since the Middle Ages.

Edward Crowther, also a purchaser from the Crosthwaites,[84] was succeeded before 1593 by his son Edward (fl. 1620).[85] George Crowther was in possession of that estate in 1641,[86] and Simon Crowther (d. 1676) in 1658.[87] It descended from father to son through George (d. 1705),[88] Edward (d. 1729),[89] John (d. 1776), John (d. 1801), and William, who sold it to Moses Benson's trustees in 1810,[90] thus reuniting it to the manorial estate. Crowther's House (later Cottage) had a late medieval north–south cruck framed open hall of two bays with a contemporary cruck framed 1½ storeyed solar cross wing on the north. The hall was later divided into two floors and two units, with a central stack dated 1658.[91] The southern unit was later demolished, apparently in the 19th century.[92]

In 1938 Maj. G. R. Benson sold the western part of the Easthope manorial estate in separate lots,[93] and Accumulated Investments Ltd. sold the rest to the tenants in 1952.[94]

ECONOMIC HISTORY. Wenlock Edge marked the western limit of Easthope's open fields in the Middle Ages. Easthope common wood, comprising Upper wood and Lower wood, lay on and below the Edge, Natal common, used for pasture by 1424, on the ridge between Easthope and Patton, and Southwood common, still a wood in 1469,[95] on the slopes of Mogg Forest bordering Brockton and Lutwyche.[96] In the 15th century several of the tenants pastured small herds of swine in the woods.[97] Easthope also had grazing rights next to Easthope wood in Hughley's Over field after harvest, while Hughley had rights in the wood.[98]

The manor was worth 15*s.* in 1066; it was found waste *c.* 1070, but by 1086 had risen in value to 20*s.* There was one ploughteam in demesne and one between a single *villanus* and five bordars, with capacity for two more teams.[99] Asserting was reported in the early 13th century,[1] and by the late 14th the land cleared below the Edge was divided into four small and equal leaseholds.[2] The demesne included 80 a. arable in the early 14th century and small amounts of meadow and woodland. Outside the demesne were 2 freeholders, 9 villeins, and 5 other tenants. The freeholders and villeins occupied a ½ virgate each, except for one villein with a nook (¼ virgate). All owed cash rents except for one freeholder who rendered 1 lb. of cumin. The manor yielded £3 8*s.* 7*d.* a year *c.* 1306.[3] Later devastated by murrain, Easthope had no sheep in 1340.[4] By 1383 the number of tenants was similar to that of eighty years earlier, but holdings were more varied in size and rents higher; there was a mixture of copyholds and leaseholds; and the demesne remained in hand. By 1483 the demesne was at farm. Outside it were 1 freeholder, 2 leaseholders, and 11 tenants at will; rents ranging from 2*s.* to 26*s.* 8*d.* indicate a wide diversity of holdings. A three-course rotation seems to have been practised in the open fields: the winter and Lent fields were mentioned in March 1498.[5]

In the open fields consolidation of holdings by exchange, followed by inclosure, was in progress in the late 16th century after the manorial estate was broken up,[6] and there was no open-field land by 1732.[7] In 1736 the parish was mainly arable but with a 'good deal' of pasture.[8] About 1558 part of each common had been divided among the purchasers of the manorial estate,[9] and by 1593 more of Natal common had been partitioned between the commoners.[10] Pieces of Easthope wood were inclosed for coppicing in the 16th and 17th centuries[11] and it was fenced off from Hughley *c.* 1628.[12] Assarting in the wood was associated with dispersed settle-

73 S.P.L., Deeds 1349.
74 H.W.R.O.(H.), HD 2/14/24.
75 Above, this section.
76 H.W.R.O.(H.), HD 2/14/24. For Harriots pedigree see S.P.L., MS. 4646, p. 109.
77 S.P.L., Deeds 9721.
78 B.R.L., Homer colln. no. 48.
79 S.P.L., Deeds 1488.
80 P.R.O., CP 25/2/1054/7 Geo. I East. no. 2.
81 S.R.O. 809, parcel 14, Easthope map.
82 *S.P.R. Heref.* xix (4), 69.
83 S.P.L., MS. 6865, p. 80.
84 H.W.R.O.(H.), HD 2/14/24.
85 S.P.L., Deeds 1351; H.W.R.O.(H.), Heref. dioc. rec., bp.'s transcripts, Easthope, 31 Mar. 1620.
86 S.R.O. 2922/1/2/10.
87 Forrest, *Old Hos. of Wenlock*, 41; *S.P.R. Heref.* xix (4), 25.
88 In occupation 1672: *Hearth Tax 1672*, 178. For burials 1705–1801 see *S.P.R. Heref.* xix (4), 32, 41, 60, 67.
89 For descent from Edw. see S.R.O. 809, box 1, deed of 1810.
90 Ibid. deed.
91 Forrest, *Old Hos. of Wenlock*, 41. Mrs. Moran is thanked for advice on this bldg.
92 It seems to be shown in 1839 in S.R.O., dep. plan 249 (field 356).
93 S.R.O. 809, box 14, sale partic.
94 Ibid. box 2, sale partic.; *Shrews. Chron.* 15 Feb. 1952, p. 3.
95 P.R.O., C 116/213, mm. 10, 12.
96 H.W.R.O.(H.), HD 2/14/22; S.R.O. 809, parcel 14, map of 1732.
97 P.R.O., C 116/213, mm. 5, 10.
98 S.R.O. 2922/1/2/1–3, 10–11.
99 *V.C.H. Salop.* i. 319–20.
1 P.R.O., E 32/144, m. 1.
2 P.R.O., C 116/213, m. 9.
3 P.R.O., C 133/121, no. 23.
4 *Inq. Non.* (Rec. Com.), 186.
5 P.R.O., C 116/213, mm. 9, 14–15.
6 H.W.R.O.(H.), HD 2/14/22. Cf. above, manor.
7 S.R.O. 809, parcel 14, map.
8 Birm. Univ. Libr., Mytton Papers, ii. 422.
9 S.P.L., Deeds 1174; H.W.R.O.(H.), HD 2/14/24.
10 S.P.L., Deeds 1351.
11 S.R.O. 2922/1/2/1–3, 10–11.
12 Ibid. /1/2/11.

ment there.[13] Nevertheless considerable areas of the commons were open in the 1730s.[14] Fifty years later all that remained open was part of Southwood, though tenants' cattle could 'by mere indulgence' graze in the Lower wood.[15]

In the late 18th century the farms needed much 'new modelling'[16] and in 1794, when the lord of the manor was proposing great improvements, the main farms were using a rotation of fallow, wheat, barley, oats, and clover ley.[17] Henry Wadlow, who occupied more than half of the parish 1809–*c.* 1834, was a successful racehorse breeder and trainer but left his land exhausted, and in 1844 the parish was thought ill cultivated. There were then equal amounts of arable and grass, the latter mostly east of the Edge. The soil was better there and a four- or five-course 'turnip and barley shift' suited it. Below the Edge a rotation of fallow, wheat, and oats suited the thin undrained soil;[18] underdraining was carried out there later in the century.[19]

In 1845 there were four main farms: Easthope Cottage and Manor farms east of the Edge, and Wood and Easthopewood farms below it.[20] Their composition later changed markedly.[21] Easthope Cottage (which had had 339 a. in 1845) had no farm land from the 1870s to the 1920s,[22] and by 1882 some of its former land had been taken into the grounds of Lutwyche Hall.[23] In the later 19th century grass reached four times the acreage of arable, and kept that proportion in the 20th. Dairying grew at the expense of beef cattle and sheep.[24] The parish's woods varied little in extent after the early 19th century.[25] In the early 20th much of Easthope wood, between the Edge road and the railway, was felled and planted with conifers.[26] A commercial sawmill was set up *c.* 1920 at the Lutwyche estate yard in Easthope village; it made fencing and gates[27] and was linked by a tramway to Mogg Forest (in Rushbury),[28] but it closed before 1929.[29] Flat coppice and Natal plantation were later cleared.[30] More of Easthope wood was cleared for conifers *c.* 1960, but in the 1980s the National Trust began to replace them with hardwoods.[31]

Easthope mill, mentioned in 1306,[32] used both steam and water power by 1891.[33] It served several nearby parishes until closure *c.* 1930.[34]

TABLE VII

EASTHOPE: LAND USE, LIVESTOCK, AND CROPS

		1867	*1891*	*1938*	*1965*
Percentage of	grassland	60	83	85	81
	arable	40	17	15	19
Percentage of	cattle	12	25	29	27
	sheep	78	65	68	58
	pigs	10	10	3	15
Percentage of	wheat	47	39	50	27
	barley	37	15	22	38
	oats	16	46	27	26
	mixed corn & rye	0	0	1	9
Percentage of agricultural land growing roots and vegetables		14	6	4	1

Sources: P.R.O., MAF 68/143, no. 15; /1340, no. 5; /3880, Salop. no. 223; /4945, no. 223.

Edward Lutwyche created a fishpond next to Robert Harriots's land *c.* 1591.[35] It was probably that above Easthope mill mapped in 1732,[36] which had two smaller ponds linked to it; all were fish pools in 1845.[37] Another pond, perhaps the fishpond called Easthope's pool in 1559,[38] lay near Lower wood before 1576[39] and was presumably that controlled by a sluice on the stream at Wood Farm, mapped in 1732.[40]

Thomas le Tyler was a tenant in 1413, and clay was being dug for tiles in 1497.[41] Wenlock limestone was quarried by the 1730s[42] and occasionally until the early 20th century.[43] Some of the stone went for iron smelting in the late 18th century,[44] but the workings did not expand as at Presthope nearby.[45] Associated kilns[46] had closed by the 1880s.[47] In 1806

[13] Above, this article, intro.
[14] S.R.O. 809, parcel 14, map of 1732; 4572/6/2/56.
[15] S.R.O. 4835/2.
[16] Ibid.
[17] S.P.L., MS. 6865, p. 78.
[18] E. C. Wadlow, 'A Hist. of the Horse Racing and Training Interests of the Shropshire Wadlows' (TS. 1973 in S.P.L., C 38.7 v.f.), 2–9; S.R.O. 809, box 2, rep. to tithe comrs. 1844.
[19] S.R.O. 5093/1.
[20] P.R.O., IR 29/29/116; 30/29/116.
[21] S.R.O. 809, parcel 3, rental 1843–53; parcel 6, rentals 1853–66; box 13, rentals 1866–98; box 14, sale partic. of 1938; box 2, sale partic. of 1952.
[22] *P.O. Dir. Salop.* (1879), 316; P.R.O., RG 11/2624, f. 27; *Kelly's Dir. Salop.* (1885–1926).
[23] O.S. Map 6", Salop. LVII. NW. (1890 edn.).
[24] Table VII.
[25] B.L. Maps, O.S.D. 207; P.R.O., IR 29/29/116; IR 30/29/116; O.S. Maps 6", LVII. SW. (1890, 1903, and 1928 edns.); 1/25,000, SO 49/59 (1981 edn.).
[26] O.S. Map 6", Salop. LVII. NW. (1903 and 1928 edns.)
[27] *Kelly's Dir. Salop.* (1922), 89.
[28] O.S. Map 6", Salop. LVII. NW. (1928 edn.).
[29] *Kelly's Dir. Salop.* (1929), 93.
[30] O.S. Maps 1/25,000, SO 59 (1956 edn.); 49/59 (1981 edn.).
[31] *Shrews. Chron.* 7 Sept. 1984, p. 9.
[32] P.R.O., C 133/121, no. 23.
[33] *Kelly's Dir. Salop.* (1891), 311.
[34] SA 15777; *Shropshire Mag.* Sept. 1974, 27.
[35] S.P.L., Deeds 1173.
[36] At O.S. Nat. Grid SO 564 948: S.R.O. 809, parcel 14, Easthope map.
[37] P.R.O., IR 29/29/116; IR 30/29/116, field 108.
[38] P.R.O., C 104/24, pt. 2, deed.
[39] S.P.L., Deeds 1174.
[40] At O.S. Nat. Grid SO 559 957: S.R.O. 809, parcel 14, Easthope map.
[41] P.R.O., C 116/213, mm. 8, 10.
[42] S.R.O. 4572/6/2/56.
[43] O.S. Map 1/2,500, Salop. LVII. 2 (1902 and 1926 edns.); J. Glyn Williams, *The Wenlock Limestone Ind.: an Hist. Note* (M. Wenlock, 1990; copy in S.P.L.), 42.
[44] S.R.O. 4835/2.
[45] Below, M. Wenlock, econ. hist.
[46] S.R.O. 809, box 2, rep. to tithe comrs.
[47] O.S. Map 1/2,500, Salop. LVII. 2 (1883 edn.).

there was a colliery at a smallholding[48] below the Edge,[49] later called the Wheel.[50] The associated house was standing by 1732,[51] and next to it in 1845 was Pit meadow.[52]

LOCAL GOVERNMENT. Manor court rolls or drafts survive for many dates between 1383 and 1538.[53] Courts seem to have ceased when the manorial estate was dispersed *c.* 1558,[54] and by 1565 Rowland Hayward treated Easthope's inhabitants as subject to his manor of Acton Round,[55] which he had bought from the earl of Arundel, Easthope's overlord.[56] In 1732 a pinfold, probably that mentioned in 1503,[57] stood opposite the junction of the lanes from Natal common and Brockton.[58]

The parish was in Church Stretton poor-law union 1836–1930,[59] Church Stretton highway district 1863–95,[60] Church Stretton rural sanitary district 1872–94, and Church Stretton rural district 1894–1934. In 1934 it passed to Bridgnorth rural district and in 1974 to Bridgnorth district.[61] In 1970 a joint parish council was formed for Easthope, Shipton, and Stanton Long C.P.s.[62]

CHURCH. Parts of the church may be 12th-century,[63] and the living, mentioned *c.* 1240,[64] is a rectory. In 1927 it was united to that of Stanton Long.[65] By 1260 the advowson descended with the manor[66] and it usually did so,[67] save during the years 1559–66 when Ralph Warley (1559–63) and Thomas Ludlow (from 1563) were patrons.[68] From 1927 it was a turn of the united benefice, and in consequence of the break-up of the manorial estate (from 1938) the turn descended with Larden Hall (in Shipton) from 1948.[69]

The rectory was worth under £4 gross in 1291[70] and £3 6*s.* 8*d.* in 1535.[71] By 1243 most of Easthope's grain tithes belonged to the rector of Cound,[72] whose Easthope 'portion' was valued at 3*s.* in 1291[73] and commuted by 1535 to a pension of 3*s.* 4*d.*,[74] still payable in 1793.[75] The glebe was *c.* 32 a. in 1607[76] and 36½ a. in 1845.[77] The living was worth £30 *c.* 1708[78] but by 1785 had £25 from glebe and £37 from tithes.[79] Queen Anne's Bounty gave £200 in 1792,[80] to make the rector's gross income £133 by 1835.[81] In 1845 the tithes were commuted to £97 10*s.* 6*d.*[82] In 1887 the glebe (46 a.), which had been increased with land in Clun parish, was worth £44 a year.[83]

The parsonage, mentioned in 1589,[84] was in good repair in 1716[85] but by 1793 seemed 'little better than a cottage'.[86] Deemed unfit in 1835[87] but 'neat' in 1851,[88] it was much enlarged *c.* 1859.[89] It was the benefice house for Stanton Long with Easthope from *c.* 1927[90] until the last incumbent left in 1975.[91]

Several pre-Reformation rectors bore local surnames,[92] and from the 16th century, or earlier, until *c.* 1772 the incumbents seem to have done the duty in person,[93] whether they lived in the parish or not. Thomas Adney, 1639–*c.* 1651,[94] signed the Presbyterian 'testimony' of 1648.[95] Curates were employed from *c.* 1772,[96] when the incumbent was also rector of Hughley.[97] Easthope parsonage was let by 1785,[98] and by 1793 no rector had resided for many years.[99] The incumbent 1780–1820[1] was

48 S.R.O. 809, box 1, deeds 26–7 Dec. 1806 (9a. 1r. 6p.).
49 P.R.O., IR 29/29/116; IR 30/29/116, fields 30–7, 54–5. Identified by area (9a. 2r. 2p.).
50 O.S. Map 1/2,500, Salop. LVII. 1 (1883 edn.).
51 S.R.O. 809, parcel 14, Easthope map.
52 P.R.O., IR 29/29/116; IR 30/29/116, fields 36–7.
53 P.R.O., C 116/213.
54 Above, manor.
55 S.R.O. 1093, box 1, acct. r. of 1564–5; S.P.L., Deeds 9721.
56 Above, manor.
57 P.R.O., C 116/213, m. 14d.
58 At O.S. Nat. Grid SO 568 951: S.R.O. 809, parcel 14, Easthope map.
59 V. J. Walsh, 'Admin. of Poor Laws in Salop. 1920–55' (Pennsylvania Univ. Ph.D. thesis, 1970), 150; *Kelly's Dir. Salop.* (1929), 93.
60 *Lond. Gaz.* 27 Mar. 1863, p. 1769; S.R.O., S.C.C. Local Govt., etc., Cttee. min. bk. 1894–1903, p. 29.
61 *Rural Dist. Councillors Electn. Order, 1894* (Local Govt. Bd. order no. 31847); *V.C.H. Salop.* ii. 213, 217; iii. 179, and sources cited ibid. 169 n. 29.
62 *Easthope, Shipton and Stanton Long Combined Par. Council Order 1970* (copy in S.R.O. 4873/1/205).
63 Below, this section.
64 Eyton, iv. 114.
65 Below, Stanton Long, church (where the later history of the benefice is treated).
66 P.R.O., C 104/23, pt. 2, deed.
67 *Reg. Swinfield* (C.S.), 540, 543; *Reg. Trillek*, 381; *Reg. L. Charlton* (C.S.), 67; *Reg. Gilbert*, 125; *Dioc. of Heref. Institutions (1539–1900)*, ed. A. T. Bannister (Heref. 1923), 15, 30, 39, 61, 76, 109, 112, 143, 167, 215; P.R.O., C 104/23, pt. 2, deed of 1483; C 104/25, deed of 1497; C 142/117, no. 12; CP 25/1/194/9, no. 48; CP 25/1/195/24, no. 8; H.W.R.O.(H.), HD 2/14/22; S.P.L., Deeds 1353; MS. 6865, p. 80; *Kelly's Dir. Salop.* (1913), 91. Cf. above, manor.
68 P.R.O., C 104/23, pt. 1, deed; C 104/24, pt. 2, deeds.
69 Above, manor; below, Stanton Long, church.
70 *Tax. Eccl.* (Rec. Com.), 167.
71 *Valor Eccl.* (Rec. Com.), iii. 209.
72 *Cal. Pat.* 1266–72, 721; *Inq. Non.* (Rec. Com.), 186; cf. below, Lib. and Boro. of Wenlock (early est.).
73 *Tax. Eccl.* 167.
74 *Valor Eccl.* iii. 209.
75 S.P.L., MS. 6865, p. 80.
76 H.W.R.O.(H.), HD 2/14/23.
77 P.R.O., IR 29/29/116.
78 J. Ecton, *Liber Valorum et Decimarum* (1711), 147.
79 S.R.O. 4835/2.
80 C. Hodgson, *Q. Anne's Bounty* (2nd edn.), p. ccxc.
81 *Rep. Com. Eccl. Rev.* [67], p. 437, H.C. (1835), xxii.
82 P.R.O., IR 29/29/116.
83 *Return of Glebe Land, 1887*, H.C. 307, p. 59 (1887), lxiv.
84 H.W.R.O.(H.), HD 2/14/22.
85 Ibid. HD 5/14/1/11.
86 S.P.L., MS. 6865, p. 80.
87 *Rep. Com. Eccl. Rev.* p. 437.
88 S. Bagshaw, *Dir. Salop.* (1851), 535.
89 H.W.R.O.(H.), Heref. dioc. rec. AA 58 (1860), drawings, specification, etc. (ref. supplied by Mr. C. J. Pickford); Heref. Dioc. Regy., reg. 1857–69, p. 133.
90 *Kelly's Dir. Salop.* (1926), 279; (1929), 93.
91 Heref. Dioc. Regy., reg. 1969– (in use), p. 206; S.R.O. 3523/1, p. 169; 3658/2, p. 162; 3926/1, p. 166.
92 *Reg. Swinfield*, 546; *Reg. Trillek*, 381; *Reg. Gilbert*, 24–5, 119, 125; *Reg. Mascall* (C.S.), 168.
93 *S.P.R. Heref.* xix (4), *passim*; *T.S.A.S.* 4th ser. xi. 185; H.W.R.O.(H.), HD 7, chwdns.' presentments 2 May 1663, 7 Nov. 1694; HD 5/14/1/11.
94 *T.S.A.S.* 4th ser. ii. 58, 298; P.R.O., E 339/1/5.
95 *Calamy Revised*, ed. A. G. Matthews, 556.
96 *S.P.R. Heref.* xix (4), 74 sqq.; S.R.O. 3900/Rg/3, *passim.*
97 Bannister, *Heref. Institutions*, 76, 84, 108–9.
98 S.R.O. 4835/2.
99 S.P.L., MS. 6865, p. 80.
1 Bannister, *Heref. Institutions*, 112, 143.

buried at Church Stretton;[2] he was assistant curate there until 1808[3] and then perpetual curate of Leebotwood.[4] His curates for Easthope[5] also lived outside the parish;[6] from *c.* 1780 to *c.* 1800 the church was served weekly from Cressage,[7] over 10 km. away. Edward Homfray, 1820–5,[8] kept the living warm for R. L. Benson,[9] the patron's son,[10] who served as his curate[11] and succeeded him.[12] Benson was non-resident from 1829.[13] His curate,[14] and successor in 1831,[15] was perpetual curate of Church Preen.[16] By 1839 he did not live at Easthope, but had no curate until 1840[17] and died *c.* 1843.[18] The curate lived in the rectory from *c.* 1840[19] and the rectors returned to live there before 1851.[20]

The small parish church of *ST. PETER*, so dedicated by 1741[21] but called St. John the Baptist in 1557,[22] consisted of undivided chancel and nave with south porch and west bell turret, all rendered externally.[23] A narrow splayed light in the nave north wall may have been 12th-century. Until 1928 the font was circular and tub shaped.[24] Otherwise there were no datable features earlier than the 14th-century east and south windows of the chancel. Square-headed windows in the nave were evidently much later. The roofs were of trussed rafter construction. Edward Ball of London, a native of the parish, gave the pulpit and nave pews in 1623. In 1662 the rector gave a decorative iron bracket for a preaching glass. The communion rails, on three sides of the table,[25] were made in the early 18th century, as were two sanctuary chairs, one dated 1713. William Lutwyche had a west gallery built *c.* 1742.[26] In 1860 the church was re-roofed and an open timber truss, serving as a chancel screen, was put up.[27] Stained glass was placed in the chancel south window *c.* 1872, and glass by C. E. Kempe in the east window in 1887.[28] In the 19th century the communion rails were altered to span the chancel. In 1928 fire nearly destroyed the church; parts of the walls remained[29] and the communion rail, sanctuary chairs, and preaching-glass bracket were saved. The church was rebuilt to its former appearance, with a north vestry added, and dedicated in 1929. The interior, however, was altered; the font was reconstructed[30] in plain octagonal form, the gallery was omitted, benches replaced the pews, a carved stone and alabaster pulpit was provided, and a light gothic chancel screen of wood was inserted in 1931.[31] In 1933[32] glass by W. E. Tower was put in the chancel windows.

In 1961 the plate consisted of a chalice of 1640 or 1642, an unmarked cover paten, and a paten of 1698.[33] One bell was given by Richard Lutwyche in 1584; another was made by Richard Oldfield in 1638; the third (replacing a medieval bell)[34] was by Thomas Rudhall, 1764.[35] In 1920 they were recast and two new ones added; a sixth was added in 1921.[36] The peal was destroyed in the fire and replaced by eight new bells.[37] The registers begin in 1624 and are complete.[38]

NONCONFORMITY. Easthope was in the Hopton Bank Primitive Methodist circuit from 1831 but the society, with only four members, ceased next year. Preaching was briefly revived in 1835.[39]

EDUCATION. A private school mentioned in 1663[40] had closed by 1719.[41] From 1844 children attended Brockton National school.[42] St. Philip's Sunday school was built in 1867 at Mrs. Charlotte Benson's expense; the school was apparently still held there in 1941[43] but it became a private house *c.* 1951.[44]

CHARITIES FOR THE POOR. None known.

2 S.R.O. 3908/Rg/7, 8 June 1820.
3 *S.P.R. Heref.* viii (2), 118.
4 *T.S.A.S.* 4th ser. vii. 166; S.R.O. 3992/BRg/1.
5 *S.P.R. Heref.* xix (4), 68–9, 74–5; S.R.O. 3900/Rg/3; Heref. Dioc. Regy., reg. 1791–1821, f. 129v.
6 S.P.L., MS. 6865, p. 80; *S.P.R. Lich.* v (6), 72; S.R.O. 4791/1/8, p. 114; *S.P.R. Heref.* xix (3), 124, 175.
7 *S.P.R. Heref.* xix (4), 74–5; *S.P.R. Lich.* ii (3), pp. iii, 60; S.P.L., MS. 6865, p. 80.
8 Bannister, *Heref. Institutions*, 143; S.R.O. 3900/Rg/3.
9 S.P.L., MS. 6865, p. 81.
10 *S.P.R. Heref.* xix (4), p. vi.
11 Heref. Dioc. Regy., reg. 1822–42, pp. 28, 40.
12 Bannister, *Heref. Institutions*, 146.
13 S.P.L., MS. 6865, p. 81.
14 Ibid.; *S.P.R. Heref.* xix (4), 76–7.
15 Bannister, *Heref. Institutions*, 151.
16 Ibid. 148, 160.
17 Heref. Dioc. Regy., reg. 1822–42, pp. 395, 458, 631.
18 Bannister, *Heref. Institutions*, 159.
19 Heref. Dioc. Regy., reg. 1822–42, pp. 458, 667; Brookes fam. letter bk. (MS. in private hands; Mr. W. M. Motley arranged access), p. 17.
20 S. Bagshaw, *Dir. Salop.* (1851), 536.
21 B.L. Add. MS. 30316, f. 29v.
22 *T.S.A.S.* vi. 126.
23 Descr. based on S.P.L., MS. 372, vol. i, f. 34; W.S.L., 350/5/40, Easthope p. 6; St. Deiniol's Libr., Hawarden, Sir Steph. Glynne's ch. notes, xc, f. 22; Cranage, ii. 93; x. 1089.
24 St. Deiniol's Libr., Glynne's ch. notes, xc, f. 22.
25 B.L. Add. MS. 21237, f. 115.
26 H.W.R.O.(H.), Heref. dioc. rec. AL 19/22, f. 95.
27 S.P.L., photo.; *P.O. Dir. Salop.* (1863), 46. Cf. above, Abdon, church.
28 *Ch. Cal. Dioc. Heref.* (1872), 118; (1888), 138–9.
29 *Shrews. Chron.* 22 June 1928, p. 12 (with photo. of ruin).
30 Ibid. 29 Mar. 1929, p. 7.
31 Inscr. plate on screen.
32 Heref. Dioc. Regy., reg. 1926–38, p. 358; S.R.O. 3901/SRg/2, 5 Feb. 1933.
33 D. L. Arkwright and B. W. Bourne, *Ch. Plate Archd. Ludlow* (Shrews. 1961), 28.
34 Notice in ch.
35 H. B. Walters, *Ch. Bells of Salop.* (Oswestry, 1915), 90–1.
36 Birm. Univ. Libr., Mytton Papers, ii. 422b.
37 *Shrews. Chron.* 29 Mar. 1929, p. 7.
38 S.R.O. 3900/Rg/1–10; regs. at ch.; *S.P.R. Heref.* xix (4), esp. p. iv.
39 S.R.O. 2941/2/2, 20 June 1831, 29 Dec. 1834; /2/3.
40 H.W.R.O.(H.), HD 7, chwdns.' presentment 2 May 1663 (ref. provided by Dr. R. Hume).
41 Ibid. HD 5/15, Easthope (ref. from Dr. Hume).
42 P.R.O., ED 7/103, ff. 67–8. Cf. below, Stanton Long, educ.
43 *P.O. Dir. Salop.* (1870), 52; *Kelly's Dir. Salop.* (1941), 92.
44 Reg. of electors, Ludlow const. (1952), 265.

HOLDGATE

THE QUIET parish of Holdgate, also called Castle Holdgate,[45] lies in Corve Dale 12 km. south-west of Much Wenlock and remote from main thoroughfares. It had *c.* 1,973 a. until 1883 and consisted mainly of Holdgate and Brookhampton townships. It seems to have been formed in the late 11th century by diversion of the tithes from the lord of Holdgate's demesnes, perhaps from a church at Patton (and in Bouldon's case from Diddlebury church), to his new castle church;[46] the dispersed character of the demesne lands may explain why the parish had several small detachments and two large ones, the Coates and Bouldon. In 1883 seven detachments (38 a.) were absorbed by Stanton Long civil parish; in 1884 the Coates and three remaining detachments (264 a. altogether) passed to Stanton Long, and Bouldon (*c.* 417 a.) to Diddlebury,[47] leaving 1,254 a. (507 ha.).[48] In 1967 almost all of Holdgate C.P. was absorbed by Tugford C.P., the rest (*c.* 1 ha.) going to Munslow C.P.[49] This article deals with the area of the pre-1883 parish except for Bouldon, which has a separate article.

Holdgate and Brookhampton lay on the eastern side of Corve Dale. Their territory was roughly square, bounded on the west by Trow brook and on the east by the rising edge of the Clee plateau. The virtually unbroken line of the eastern boundary and its northward continuation in the boundary of Stanton Long parish suggest that it was fixed along the contours of the plateau when Holdgate, Brookhampton, and Stanton Long were still within an undivided pre-Conquest estate called 'Stantune'.[50] Holdgate and Brookhampton lie wholly on the Ledbury Group of the Downton Series of the Lower Old Red Sandstone, except where the land rises beyond 190 m. east of New Buildings; there the Ditton Series overlies the Downton and is separated from it by a narrow layer of '*Psammosteus*' Limestone.[51] The soils are mostly red-brown loams, with alluvial soils along the watercourses.[52] The land slopes down north-westwards from 235 m. at the Clee plateau to 135 m. at Trow brook, except for an intervening sandstone ridge that rises to 169 m. Streams from the Clee plateau converge south of Brookhampton and then flow to Trow brook through a gap in the ridge.

No evidence of settlement in the prehistoric and Roman periods is known. In 1086 Holdgate manor had a recorded population of 13.[53] There was evidently much growth in Holdgate manor before 1315, when it had 12 freeholders, 21 customary tenants, and 12 cottagers.[54] In 1676 the whole parish had *c.* 80 adults.[55] In 1793 there were 202 inhabitants in 42 families.[56] Between 1811 and 1821 the population rose from 197 to 238. It never again reached that level. The population of Holdgate and Brookhampton declined markedly in the 1820s, as did that of Brookhampton in the 1860s. The population of the civil parish continued to fall 1891–1951. The total remained at 47 during the 1950s,[57] after which no separate figures are available. It seems that most of the people have lived since the Middle Ages in the three villages or hamlets of Holdgate, Brookhampton, and Bouldon.

Helgot's castle, from which the village and parish were named, and the church[58] were built at the highest part of the central ridge and overlooked Corve Dale. A raised wedge-shaped area (*c.* 1.5 ha.) tapers from the castle north-eastwards along the ridge and is bisected lengthwise by an abandoned roadway, which is aligned on the castle motte and continues the former line of the Stanton Long road, which was represented in 1990 by a low linear bank that climbs from the stream at Brookhampton. The raised area is unexplained and undated;[59] it may be the abandoned site of the 13th-century market[60] or of an unrecorded attempt at town plantation. The modern road from Stanton Long skirts its southern boundary. Shrinkage of settlement at Holdgate after the 13th century may be indicated, too, by some of the earthworks on the ridge's south-eastern flank. The later medieval village was probably confined to the narrow ridge top south of the castle, as in 1989.

There was presumably new building below and beyond the ridge top before the late 17th century, for in Holdgate township 18 houses paid to the hearth tax in 1672, eight of which had more than one hearth.[61] By 1842 the township had only 10 houses in all, half of which ranked as farms. The village then lay along the ridge top for *c.* 500 m. from the Hall to Lower Farm. Two cottages stood farther south-west along the ridge, at Gallitree bank. Another cottage, Blue Hall, and one farm, Castlemoor, lay isolated in the fields.[62] Castlemoor, a timber framed house with early 19th-century brick and stone additions,[63] dated from the clearance of woodland in the 16th or 17th century.[64] The village had probably contracted during amalgamations of farms in the 18th century;[65] some of the earthworks on the south-eastern side of the

45 *P.N. Salop.* (E.P.N.S), i. 155. This article was written in 1989.
46 Below, church.
47 Divided Parishes and Poor Law Amendment Act, 1882, 45 & 46 Vic. c. 58; *14th Ann. Rep. Local Govt. Bd.* [C. 4515], pp. xlvii–xlviii, 200, H.C. (1884–5), xxxii; *Census*, 1891, ii. 652. Areas calculated from P.R.O., IR 29/29/161; O.S. Maps 1/2,500, Salop. LVII. 14–15; LXV. 3, 9, 13 (1903 edn.).
48 O.S. *Area Bk.* (1884).
49 *V.C.H. Salop.* ii. 235–6 (corr. ibid. xi. 376); S.R.O., DA 19/701/6, map 40.
50 Fig. 12; below, manors.
51 Geol. Surv. Map 1/50,000, solid, sheet 166 (1974 edn.).
52 Soil Surv. Map 1", sheet 166 (1972 edn.).
53 *V.C.H. Salop.* i. 337.
54 P.R.O., C 134/48, no. 9.
55 *Compton Census*, ed. Whiteman, 246, 248, 259 n.
56 S.P.L., MS. 6865, pp. 95–6.
57 *V.C.H. Salop.* ii. 223.
58 Below, manors; church.
59 R.C.H.M.E., draft field rep. (1986), which suggests that it may have been a post-medieval garden or orchard.
60 Below, econ. hist.
61 *Hearth Tax 1672* (Salop. Arch. Soc. 1949), 177.
62 P.R.O., IR 29/29/161; IR 30/29/161.
63 SA 17446.
64 Below, econ. hist.
65 Ibid.

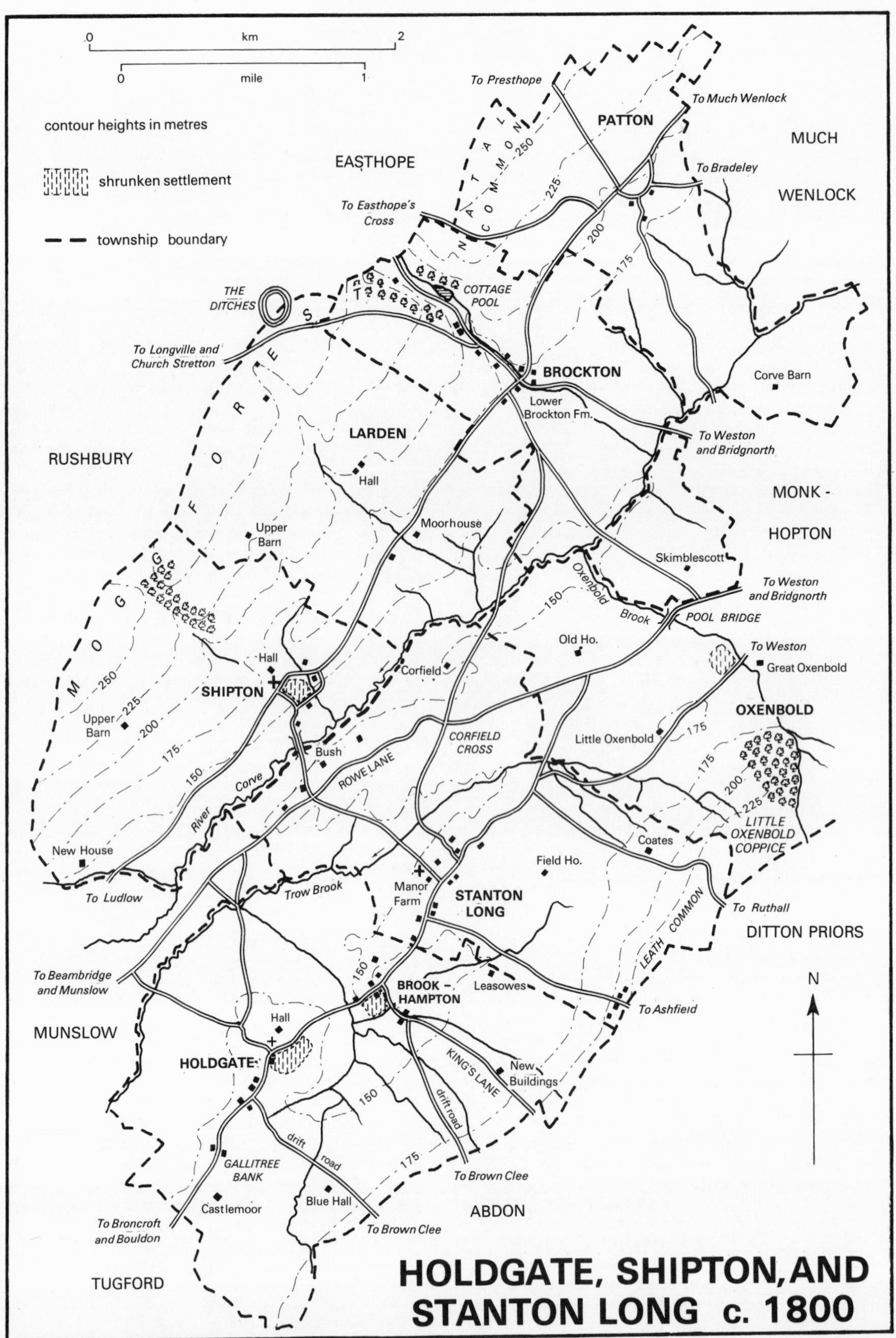

Fig. 12

For parish boundaries in the area covered by this map see above, fig. 3. The boundary between Shipton and Stanton Long parishes ran east–west through Brockton village.

ridge seem to represent houses abandoned then.[66] Amalgamations in the later 19th century[67] left Holdgate township with only the rectory, three farms, and four cottages by 1907,[68] and there has been almost no change since.

In 1672 Brookhampton had 10 houses liable to the hearth tax, six with more than one hearth.[69] In 1842 there were seven farms and eight cottages. The houses lay mostly on a 500-m. length of the lane from Stanton Long to Holdgate, on the central ridge where it descended south to the brook. The Leasowes and New Buildings stood among fields to the east, the smithy and two cottages *c.* 300 m. along King's Lane.[70] Earthworks south of the junction of King's Lane and the Stanton Long lane represented several former buildings, perhaps houses abandoned in the 18th century or much earlier.[71] Brookhampton township's population fell from 86 to 47 in the 1860s,[72] and in 1907 there were only five farms or smallholdings and four cottages.[73] There has been no contraction since.

The lane from Bridgnorth through Stanton Long[74] followed the ridge south-west through Brookhampton and Holdgate villages to Broncroft; thence by the 13th century it led, perhaps via Bouldon, past Corfham (in Diddlebury) to Ludlow.[75] It offered an alternative Bridgnorth–Ludlow route to those via Burwarton and Ditton Priors. In 1989 it was the only road out of Holdgate and Brookhampton for wheeled traffic, but other lanes formerly ran from it across the parish boundary in several directions. Next to the smithy in King's Lane a drift road branched south-east towards the Brown Clee;[76] beyond the parish boundary it was joined by another drift road running south-east from Holdgate village.[77]

The Coates, which lies *c.* 500 m. north-east of Brookhampton and beyond Stanton Long village, forms an irregular east–west rectangle. Its eastern boundary is part of the northern continuation of Stanton Long's parish boundary and so probably coincides with part of the boundary of pre-Conquest 'Stantune'. Its northern boundary continues westwards as that of Stanton Long township, to which the Coates then probably belonged;[78] it shared in that township's open fields.[79] Its geology is the same as Holdgate's but without limestone.[80] No evidence of settlement other than at the main house[81] is known.

A wake on Trinity Sunday was still observed *c.* 1840.[82] An aleseller lived near Holdgate church in 1719.[83] In 1841[84] and 1851[85] Mary Howells kept a public house at Brookhampton, opposite the later Brook Farm;[86] it had gone by 1881.[87] The county library opened a book centre at Holdgate *c.* 1927,[88] but no public room remained after the school closed in 1948.[89]

MANORS AND OTHER ESTATES. Called 'Stantune' in 1086,[90] *HOLDGATE* had presumably been part of the greater 'Stantune' that was restored to the church of Wenlock in 901 by Aethelraed and Aethelflaed. In their time 'Stantune' seems also to have included Stanton Long.[91] By 1066 the 'Stantune' that became Holdgate had again ceased to belong to the church of Wenlock and consisted of five estates held freely by Ketil (Chetel), Genust, Alweard (Aelward), Dunning, and Aelfgifu (Elueua). By 1086 Helgot held them of Roger of Montgomery, earl of Shrewsbury (the tenant in chief) as two estates.[92] He was called Helgot of 'Reisolent',[93] perhaps from Résenlieu (Orne) in or near Roger's *vicomté* of the Hiémois, and was the eponymous lord who gave his name to his chief manor and to the barony centred on it. Honor and manor descended together.[94] Helgot's son Herbert of Clee,[95] nephew of Geoffrey of Clee ('de Clive'), bishop of Hereford,[96] succeeded before 1116[97] and was living in 1121. The family is presumed to have held the manor in chief after Earl Robert's forfeiture in 1102. Herbert's son Herbert[98] of Castle Holdgate ('de castello Holgot')[99] was chief lord in 1166[1] and died in 1189 or 1190.[2] His widow died childless in 1192 or 1193.[3] By 1194 Ralph of Arden held the manor,[4] apparently in right of his wife Agnes, daughter and heir of Robert de la Mare (perhaps a nephew of Herbert of Castle Holdgate)[5] and widow of Robert Mauduit of Warminster (Wilts.).[6] Between 1197 and 1199 Ralph was succeeded as lord by Agnes's son Thomas Mauduit.[7] In 1244, after Thomas's

66 Medieval Village Research Group, *Ann. Rep.* xxxi. 9–11; R.C.H.M.E., draft field rep. (1986).
67 Below, econ. hist.
68 S.P.L., Deeds 4099.
69 *Hearth Tax 1672*, 177.
70 P.R.O., IR 29/29/161; IR 30/29/161.
71 SA 1274.
72 *V.C.H. Salop.* ii. 223.
73 S.P.L., Deeds 4099.
74 S.R.O. 356, box 327, Brookhampton surv. of 1657. Para. based on ibid. parcel 416, map of 1785; R. Baugh, *Map of Salop.* (1808); B.L. Maps, O.S.D. 206–7; O.S. Map 1", sheet LXI. SW. (1833 edn.); P.R.O., IR 30/29/161.
75 *Rot. Hund.* (Rec. Com.), ii. 101; S.R.O. 1359, box 20, terrier of 1632.
76 S.R.O., incl. award B 21, brief [of 1810], f. lv.
77 S.R.O. 1359, box 20, terrier of 1632; below, econ. hist.
78 i.e. before the Coates passed to Holdgate par.: below, church.
79 Below, Stanton Long, econ. hist.
80 Geol. Surv. Map 1/50,000, solid, sheet 166 (1974 edn.); Soil Surv. Map 1", sheet 166 (1972 edn.).
81 Below, manors.
82 W.S.L. 350/5/40, Castle Holdgate p. 11.
83 H.W.R.O.(H.), HD 5/15, Holdgate.
84 P.R.O., HO 107/912/22, f. 8v.
85 P.R.O., HO 107/1982, f. 536v.
86 P.R.O., IR 29/29/161; IR 30/29/161, field 143.
87 P.R.O., RG 11/2617, ff. 17–18.
88 R. C. Elliott, 'Development of Public Libraries in Salop.' (Loughborough Univ. M.A. thesis, 1970; copy in co. libr.), 125.
89 Below, educ.
90 *V.C.H. Salop.* i. 337.
91 Below, Stanton Long, manors.
92 *V.C.H. Salop.* i. 337.
93 P.R.O., SP 16/124, f. 165 (17th-cent. transcript of an undated medieval doc.).
94 *P.N. Salop.* (E.P.N.S.), i. 155–6; I. J. Sanders, *Eng. Baronies* (1960), 28–9.
95 Eyton, iv. 53, 75.
96 P.R.O., SP 16/124, f. 165.
97 *Reg. Regum Anglo-Norm.* ii, no. 1051.
98 *Cartulary of Shrews. Abbey*, ed. U. Rees (1975), i, pp. 2, 36.
99 *Cartulary of Haughmond Abbey*, ed. U. Rees (1985), p. 212.
1 *Red Bk. Exch.* (Rolls Ser.), i. 275.
2 *Pipe R.* 1190 (P.R.S. N.S. i), 126.
3 Ibid. 1193 (P.R.S. N.S. iii), 90; Eyton, iii. 82; iv. 57; vi. 190–1.
4 *Pipe R.* 1194 (P.R.S. N.S. v), 143.
5 Eyton, iv. 57–8.
6 *Cart. Haughmond*, pp. 224–5.
7 *Pipe R.* 1197 (P.R.S. N.S. viii), 158; 1199 (ibid. x), 78; Eyton, iv. 59.

death, Holdgate passed to his son William[8] who alienated it in 1256 to Richard, earl of Cornwall and king of the Romans (d. 1272).[9] Richard's son Earl Edmund succeeded as lord,[10] although the Templars of Lydley had held the manor of the earl of Cornwall in fee farm since 1263.[11] The Templars' tenure lasted until some time between 1276[12] and *c.* 1284.[13] Between *c.* 1284 and 1292 Earl Edmund's feudal tenant of Holdgate, Robert Burnell, bishop of Bath and Wells, acquired the chief lordship,[14] which thereafter followed the descent of Acton Burnell until 1542 when Sir John Dudley exchanged Acton Burnell.[15] As earl of Warwick he gave Holdgate in 1549 to the see of Worcester in an exchange.[16] In 1648 Parliament sold it to Thomas Groome and Henry Fewtrell[17] but it had been returned to the bishop by 1661.[18] It remained with the see until Bishop Pepys died in 1860, when it passed to the Ecclesiastical Commissioners.[19] They sold the freehold *c.* 1861 to their lessee, the Revd. Henry Thursby-Pelham[20] (d. 1878). He was succeeded by his grandson J. A. H. Thursby-Pelham[21] (d. 1947), whose daughter Mrs. M. A. N. Chapman was lady of the manor in 1965.[22] Its descent thereafter has not been traced.

In 1548 the earl of Warwick leased Holdgate manor for 200 years to William Heath,[23] the bishop of Worcester's brother,[24] who assigned it in 1551 to Henry Cressett,[25] second son of Richard Cressett of Upton.[26] Henry died in 1563, leaving the lease to his nephew Richard Cressett of Upton; Henry's widow Mary was still in possession in 1566, but Richard held the lease by 1572. At his death in 1601 it passed to Henry's cousin Francis Cressett of the Coates,[27] who assigned it in 1603 to Henry Townshend of Cound (kt. 1604),[28] father-in-law of his son Edward. In 1611 Townshend assigned the lease to Edward,[29] who bought Cound manor in 1623;[30] the lease, periodically renewed, seems to have passed with Cound thereafter.[31] At John Cressett Pelham's death[32] in 1838 moieties of his leasehold and freehold estates passed to his sister Mrs. Frances Thursby and brother-in-law Thomas Papillon.[33] In 1842 Papillon assigned his Shropshire moieties to Frances[34] (d. 1852), and her son the Revd. Henry Thursby-Pelham bought the Holdgate manorial freehold *c.* 1861.[35]

J. A. H. Thursby-Pelham, who had, in addition to the manor, acquired or succeeded to other estates in Holdgate, offered all his Holdgate estate for sale, except the manor, in 1907,[36] though some farms were not sold until later.[37] Holdgate Hall farm (484 a. in 1907)[38] remained with J. A. H. Thursby-Pelham in 1913[39] but seems to have been sold by 1917 to John Allen (d. 1939).[40] In 1941 A. G. Allen sold it to P. G. Holder (d. 1945),[41] whose sister Maude Mary (d. 1953),[42] was probably the Miss Holder said to be the owner in 1946.[43] P. G. Holder's daughter Mrs. D. M. Gamble[44] sold the house and farm in 1954 to J. L. Hartley.[45] The Hartleys retained the property in 1989.

Holdgate had a castle in 1086,[46] represented by the surviving motte, which stands 9 m. high. The motte is sited between two apparently contemporary and symmetrical triangular enclosures, that on the north-east seemingly a bailey, that on the south-west the churchyard. Inside the northern edge of the supposed bailey a free-standing tower house with massive round corner turrets seems to have been built in the late 13th or early 14th century. One turret remains on the west and the base of that next to it on the north (still standing in 1737),[47] with the lower part of the wall between them. In 1292 the site consisted of an old castle, worth nothing, a chief house, a garden, and a dovehouse.[48] The chief house may thus have been the tower house. In 1383 the old castle was almost wholly in ruins, but the chief house remained then and in 1420.[49] Its gardens and curtilages were mentioned in 1315.[50] A castle yard was mentioned in 1544.[51] Two parks mentioned in 1428[52] were perhaps the great and little parks (together 16 a.) that in 1842 lay immediately east of the castle site, on the other side of the lane.[53] Parts of the castle

8 *Ex. e Rot. Fin.* (Rec. Com.), i. 418.
9 P.R.O., E 36/57, ff. 26v.–27; *D.N.B.*
10 *Feud. Aids*, iv. 224.
11 P.R.O., E 36/57, f. 45 and v.
12 Eyton, iv. 68.
13 *Feud. Aids*, iv. 224.
14 Ibid. 224, 268; *Cal. Inq. p.m.* iii, p. 50.
15 *Cal. Inq. p.m.* iii, p. 121; v, p. 393; viii, p. 495; xv, pp. 288–9; *Cal. Pat.* 1313–17, 554; 1485–94, 64; *Cal. Close*, 1346–9, 111; 1419–22, 154; *Reg. Gilbert* (C.S.), 118; *Cal. Inq. p.m.* (Rec. Com.), iv. 265; P.R.O., C 140/13, no. 27; CP 40/1079, Carte rot. 1; *L. & P. Hen. VIII*, i (2), p. 1170; vi, p. 89; xvi, p. 240; cf. *V.C.H. Salop.* viii. 7; above, Rushbury, manors (Rushbury).
16 *Cal. Pat.* 1548–9, 255, 298.
17 P.R.O., C 54/3405, mm. 27–8.
18 S.R.O. 1359, box 20, Thos. Martin to Ric. Holman 26 June 1661 (copy).
19 Under the Eccl. Com. Act, 1860, 23 & 24 Vic. c. 124.
20 S.R.O. 933, box 16, abstr. of title of 1861.
21 *Salopian Shreds & Patches*, iii. 126; Burke, *Land. Gent.* (1937), 1782.
22 Burke, *Land. Gent.* (18th edn.), i (1965), 558.
23 S.R.O. 563/2.
24 H.W.R.O.(W.), ref. 009:1 BA 2636/197, no. 325122, p. 163.
25 S.P.L., Deeds 6116.
26 For pedigree to 1792 see *T.S.A.S.* 4th ser. vi. 215–22.
27 Bodl. MS. Blakeway 11, ff. 113v.–14; S.P.L., MS. 14, p. 33.
28 S.R.O. 563/2; S.P.L., MS. 2, f. 149; *T.S.A.S.* 2nd ser. vii. 19.
29 W.B.R., M4/2.
30 *V.C.H. Salop.* viii. 63.
31 S.P.L., Deeds 722, 6116; S.R.O. 5460/3/16, 22; S.R.O., q. sess. rec. box 260, reg. of gamekeepers 1711–42, 19 Aug. 1727; 1742–79, 19 Oct. 1749; parcel 261, reg. of gamekeepers 1799–1807, f. 106; Bodl. MS. Blakeway 11, f. 114v. Cf. *V.C.H. Salop.* viii. 63–4.
32 For pedigree see Burke, *Land. Gent.* (1937), 1782–3.
33 S.P.L., Deeds 6118; S.R.O. 933, box 16, sched. of 1842.
34 S.R.O. 4152/1/49; S.P.L., MS. 2493.
35 Above, this section.
36 S.P.L., Deeds 4099.
37 *Shrews. Chron.* 19 July 1907, p. 7. Cf. below, this section (Lower fm.; Brook fm.).
38 S.P.L., Deeds 4099, lot 14.
39 S.R.O. 4011/46, no. 44.
40 *Kelly's Dir. Salop.* (1917), 104; grave stone at Holdgate.
41 *Birm. Post*, 10 Dec. 1941; grave stone at Holdgate.
42 Grave stone at Holdgate. Holder's daus. had other names: *Shrews. Chron.* 4 Sept. 1925, p. 12.
43 *Woolhope Trans.* xxxii (1), p. xxxvii.
44 *Shrews. Chron.* 22 June 1934, p. [16].
45 S.P.L., SC12/49; *Salop. N.F.U. Jnl.* cxxv. 8.
46 *V.C.H. Salop.* i. 337. Following descr. based on R.C.H.M.E., draft field rep. (1986).
47 Birm. Univ. Libr., Mytton Papers, iv. 747.
48 Eyton, iv. 69
49 P.R.O., C 136/24, no. 19; C 138/54, no. 116.
50 P.R.O., C 134/48, no. 9.
51 *Salop. N. & Q.* i. 47.
52 Loton Hall MSS., transcript (in blue bks.) from bound vol. of 'Seven Rolls of Steward's Accts. 1375–1457'.
53 P.R.O., IR 29/29/161; IR 30/29/161, fields 301a, 302.

(perhaps the tower house) remained standing until the Civil Wars, when Royalists pulled them down.[54] The motte may have been adapted as a garden mount. In 1737 a small tower, not necessarily medieval, was said formerly to have stood on it,[55] and indications of a rectangular stone building remain there. It was said *c.* 1840, however, that the motte had been lowered by 6 ft. in modern times.[56] A vaulted chamber in its base may have been an icehouse. The stone-built Hall Farm, presumably the building described in 1648 as a 'fair' house with dovehouse, barns, and outhouses for cattle,[57] seems to have been built on the broken walls of the tower house; it incorporated the western and northern turrets and the wall between them. The house was later extended south, and in 1763 the northern end was rebuilt,[58] its corner turret having been recently demolished.[59]

The Revd. Henry Thursby-Pelham, who bought the manor *c.* 1861, had inherited a freehold estate in Holdgate that his family held in the 16th century. Henry Cressett (d. 1563), lessee of Holdgate manor,[60] had freehold property there, which he left to his nephew Richard Cressett (d. 1601).[61] The property seems to have descended thereafter with the leasehold of the manor, for Henry Cressett Pelham (d. 1803) had the freehold of 79 a. in Holdgate parish.[62] About 1825 John Cressett Pelham gave 67 a. of that to the living of Clee St. Margaret,[63] but he had bought another 44 a. in 1806 from Charles Hanbury-Tracy,[64] and his sister and heir Frances Thursby thus owned 56 a. freehold in the parish in 1842.[65]

In 1568 Francis Cressett of the Coates (d. 1606)[66] had a freehold in Holdgate.[67] It descended with the Coates until Edward Cressett's death in 1672[68] when it passed to his son Thomas (d. 1679),[69] who was succeeded by his daughter Elizabeth. In 1698 she married John Minton,[70] who later sold the Holdgate freehold to Richard Phillips of Brockton (in Sutton Maddock).[71] Capt. Richard Phillips owned it in 1787[72] when it comprised 118 a. with two houses,[73] and G. M. Phillips in 1863.[74] By 1874 it had been added to the Holdgate manorial estate,[75] and by 1907 had been reorganized as a farm of 162 a.[76] Between then and 1913 it passed from J. A. H. Thursby-Pelham to Arthur Morgan of Tugford.[77] It was known by 1874 as *LOWER FARM*,[78] and also by 1978 as *HOLDGATE FARM*.[79] The 17th-century house is timber framed on a rubble base and was originally of one storey and thatched; a framed upper storey and tiled roof were added.[80]

BROOKHAMPTON, styled a manor in 1256 and later,[81] was part of Holdgate manor and descended with it.[82]

The Russell family was living at Brookhampton by 1308. William Russell, son and heir of Richard Russell of Brookhampton, had a freehold there in 1460.[83] It belonged by 1475 to Walter Russell (fl. 1487) of Ludlow, a baker,[84] and by 1504 to his son Richard Russell (or Baker), who sold it in 1508 to Richard More of Thonglands.[85] More gave it in 1523 to his son Robert,[86] at whose death in 1545 it passed to his son Edward, a minor, who obtained livery in 1555. When Edward died in 1558 it passed to his brother Thomas,[87] who sold it in 1565 to Ralph Jurden of Sutton[88] (in Diddlebury). Ralph died in 1587[89] and Thomas Jurden was probably in possession in 1604.[90] By 1659 the property belonged to John Churchman, and it then descended with his Stanton Long property and in 1806 was sold (44 a.) by Charles Hanbury-Tracy to John Cressett Pelham.[91] It then descended with Cressett Pelham's other freehold and leasehold property in Holdgate parish.[92] The house, occupied in 1805,[93] had gone by 1842 when the land was farmed by the undertenant of Holdgate Hall farm.[94]

In 1444 William Walle the elder and William Walle the younger had property in Brookhampton. Thomas Walle sold it in 1513 to Thomas Skrymsher.[95] It descended thereafter with Malt House farm, Stanton Long,[96] until 1863 when Edward VI's charity, Ludlow, conveyed it (67 a.) to the Revd. Henry Thursby-Pelham in exchange for Lower House farm, Stanton Long.[97] It then descended with Holdgate manor until sold to F. W. Blake of Ludlow in 1907.[98] By 1910 it was called *BROOK FARM*.[99] It

54 S.P.L., Deeds 6116; *T.S.A.S.* 4th ser. vi. 223.
55 Birm. Univ. Libr., Mytton Papers, iv. 747.
56 W.S.L. 350/5/40, Castle Holdgate p. 7.
57 S.P.L., Deeds 6116.
58 Date stone.
59 W.S.L. 350/5/40, Castle Holdgate p. 7.
60 Above, this section.
61 S.P.L., MS. 2, f. 149v.; MS. 14, p. 33.
62 S.P.L., Deeds 724.
63 Below, this section.
64 S.R.O. 2334/2, f. 2; 4835/28, lot 7.
65 P.R.O., IR 29/29/161.
66 S.P.L., MS. 14, p. 33.
67 S.R.O. 563/1.
68 Glam. R.O., CL/Deeds II, no. 8131; below, this section (the Coates).
69 S.R.O., incl. award B 21, brief of [1810], f. lv.; *S.P.R. Heref.* iv (2), 16.
70 Glam. R.O., CL/Deeds I, Salop. 2 Jan. 1684/5; *S.P.R. Lich.* v (6), 41.
71 S.R.O., incl. award B 21, brief of [1810], f. lv.
72 S.R.O. 1359, box 20, land tax assessment.
73 S.R.O. 515/1, pp. 125–7 and index at front of vol.
74 H.W.R.O.(W.), ref. 823.1 BA 2500(i), G. M. Phillips to A. C. Hooper 17 Mar. 1863.
75 S.R.O. 4367/Gl/15.
76 S.P.L., Deeds 4099, lot 15.
77 Ibid.; S.R.O. 4011/46, no. 59.
78 S.R.O., reg. of electors, Southern divn. (1874), 115; *Kelly's Dir. Salop.* (1922), 111; local inf.
79 O.S. Map 1/10,000, SO 58 NE. (1978 edn.).
80 SA 11392.
81 P.R.O., E 36/57, f. 27; *Cat. Anct. D.* ii, C 2398; S.R.O., q. sess. rec. box 260, reg. of gamekeepers 1711–42, 2 Oct. 1722.
82 P.R.O., C 138/54, no. 116; S.P.L., Deeds 6116; sources cited above, this section (Holdgate).
83 Glos. R.O., D2153 D/2, 9; S.P.L., MS. 2, f. 126v.
84 Glos. R.O., D2153 D/11–12.
85 Ibid. A/16; D/13.
86 S.P.L., MS. 2342, no. 12937.
87 S.R.O. 3320/24/4, 6.
88 Glos. R.O., D2153 A/17; D/15.
89 *S.P.R. Heref.* xv (1), 8.
90 Glos. R.O., D2153 D/14.
91 Ibid. J/3, 6; As/6–7, 9–10; S.R.O. 2334/2, f. 2; 4835/28, lot 7. Cf. below, Stanton Long, manors (Lower Ho.).
92 Above, this section.
93 S.R.O. 4835/28, lot 7.
94 P.R.O., IR 29/29/161; IR 30/29/161.
95 S.R.O. 356/MT/1092–4.
96 S.P.L., MS. 2, f. 149; *Cal. Pat.* 1550–3, 345–6; S.R.O. 356, box 363, lease of 1567; parcel 416, map of 1785; Ludlow (Charity Estates) Act, 1846, 9 & 10 Vic. c. 18 (Private). Cf. below, Stanton Long, manors (Malt Ho.).
97 S.R.O. 5353/6.
98 S.P.L., Deeds 4099, lot 11; *Shrews. Chron.* 19 July 1907, p. 7.
99 S.R.O., reg. of electors, Southern or Ludlow divn. (1910), 497; O.S. Map 1/10,000, SO 58 NE. (1978 edn.).

belonged by 1913 to William Haynes.[1] Between 1863 and 1907 the farmhouse became a cottage, called King's Croft in 1990, and the house of an adjacent smallholding became the farmhouse.[2]

In 1842 the incumbent of Clee St. Margaret had 108 a. of glebe in Holdgate parish,[3] 67 a. of it given by John Cressett Pelham *c.* 1825 and the rest bought soon afterwards with a grant from Queen Anne's Bounty.[4] The farmhouse site[5] was added to the Holdgate rectorial glebe in 1864 as a site for the new rectory house.[6] J. A. H. Thursby-Pelham acquired the rest in 1882 from the vicar of Clee St. Margaret by exchange[7] and added it to his manorial estate.

The Wele (or Weole) family was living by the late 14th century at *THE COATES*, also called Coates under Leath[8] or White Coats,[9] and was headed in 1422[10] and *c.* 1440 by William Wele,[11] probably Edmund Wele's son and heir of that name.[12] In 1488 another William Wele, with Alice his wife, was said to hold the estate of the earl of Shrewsbury in fee.[13] It was called a manor by 1501.[14] On William's death the estate was shared by his mistress Alice Roberts (later Langworth) and their son John Wele (or Roberts). John was in sole possession from her death *c.* 1538[15] until 1557 or later.[16] He or his son John Wele[17] sold the Coates in 1560 to Thomas Cressett of Stanton Lacy (d. 1566),[18] who was succeeded by his son Francis (d. 1606).[19] By 1615 Francis's son Francis was in possession.[20] He died in 1640 or 1641,[21] and by 1648 the Coates was owned by his son Edward (d. 1672).[22] Thereafter the reputed manor was held by a trustee, Thomas Wolley, until he relinquished it in 1699 to Edward's granddaughter and heir Elizabeth Cressett, wife of John Minton.[23] By 1724 it had passed to the Mintons' son Edward (d. 1781),[24] who left it to a nephew Edward Minton (fl. 1787)[25] for life, with remainder to the latter's nephew Capt. William Slack. Slack, who lived in France, was unable to get possession until 1815. He sold the reputed manor to Edward Howells in 1825. By will proved 1830 Howells left the Coates farm to his daughter Sarah, wife of Thomas France, and after her death to their son E. H. France, who sold it in 1867 to G. F. Hamilton-Russell, Viscount Boyne[26] (d. 1872), whose son G. R. Hamilton-Russell, the 8th viscount (d. 1907), left it to his second son F. G. Hamilton-Russell,[27] who sold it in 1919 to T. Howard of Medley Park (in Culmington).[28] A. E. Gough owned it in 1945.[29] It was bought before 1974[30] by H. S. Killick, whose widow owned it in 1990. The stone house, of two storeys and three bays, dates from the 18th century, probably from 1777.[31] Moulded joists of *c.* 1600 were re-used within. The house was uninhabited after the Second World War until the Killicks restored it, introducing on the ground floor panelling from Eaton Hall (Ches.), demolished 1961–5,[32] and adding a stone wing at the rear.[33]

ECONOMIC HISTORY. In 1086 there were two estates. The larger had 3 hides and 5½ ploughlands; having been 'waste' when Helgot took possession, it was then worth 25*s.* The smaller estate, perhaps at Brookhampton, had 2 hides and 2½ ploughlands; its value had fallen from 8*s.* to 3*s.*[34]

In 1292 the Holdgate demesne included 3 carucates of arable and 5 a. of wood. The manor was valued at £19 11*s.* 8½*d.* a year.[35] By 1315 its value was £14 10*s.* 5½*d.* The demesne arable had been reduced to 2 carucates while the cash rents of freeholders, customary tenants, and cottagers had increased, from £7 6*s.* 8½*d.* in 1292 to £10 13*s.* 5½*d*:[36] it may be that declining income from the demesne had induced the lord to let off part of it and accept cash rents in lieu of labour services. By 1428 the whole demesne was let to tenants, and the manor's gross income that year, excluding arrears, was £26 16*s.* 2¼*d.*[37] In 1515 Robert Legge took a 49-year lease of the demesne.[38]

In the 16th century the arable at Brookhampton lay in Broadmoor field north-east of the village, Park field to the south-east, and Brook (or Nether) field to the west;[39] part of Broadmoor field was in Stanton Long parish.[40] In the early

1 S.R.O. 4011/46, no. 43.
2 P.R.O., IR 29/29/161; IR 30/29/161, fields 200, 203; S.P.L., Deeds 4099 (nos. 56, 60).
3 P.R.O., IR 29/29/161.
4 S.P.L., MS. 6862, f. 48; C. Hodgson, *Q. Anne's Bounty* (2nd edn.), p. ccxc.
5 P.R.O., IR 29/29/161; IR 30/29/161, field 63.
6 Heref. Dioc. Regy., reg. 1857–69, p. 423; below, church.
7 S.P.L., Deeds 4099 (ref. to Order of Exchange by Incl. Comrs. 11 May 1882); S.R.O. 4367/Gl/14–15, 48.
8 Heref. D. & C. mun., chapter act bk. 1512–66 (folio), f. 216v.
9 J. Rocque, *Map of Salop.* (1752).
10 S.P.L., MS. 2342, no. 12878.
11 Heref. D. & C. mun., chapter act bk. 1512–66 (folio), f. 216v.
12 P.R.O., C 1/1088/22.
13 S.R.O. 1037/12/40.
14 Heref. D. & C. mun., chapter act bk. 1512–66 (folio), f. 216v.
15 S.R.O. 1037/25/1.
16 Glam. R.O., CL/Deeds I, Salop. 14 Jan. 1556/7.
17 Ibid. /Deeds II, no. 7577.
18 Ibid. /Deeds I, Salop. 24 and 30 July 1560; *S.P.R. Heref.* iv (1), 5. For Cressett pedigree see *T.S.A.S.* 4th ser. vi. 217–18, 221.
19 S.R.O. 563/1; S.P.L., MS. 14, p. 33.
20 Glam. R.O., CL/Deeds II, no. 8131.
21 Ibid. no. 10028; S.P.L., MS. 2, f. 150.
22 Glam. R.O., CL/Deeds II, no. 8124; S.R.O. 4131/Rg/1, bur. 4 June.
23 S.R.O. 171, box 2, deed.
24 S.R.O. 3532/1/3/2; 4131/Rg/3, bur. 25 Feb.
25 S.R.O. 1359, box 20, Holdgate land tax assessment.
26 W.S.L. 350/5/40, Castle Holdgate p. 10; S.R.O. 757, box 50, will (extract), replies to requisitions on title, 1867, and deed of 1867; 1037/21/98; Sarah's husb. identified from P.R.O., IR 29/29/161; IR 30/29/161.
27 S.R.O. 5236/A/49, abstr. of title. For dates of death of 7th and 8th viscounts see *Complete Peerage*, ii. 268–9.
28 S.R.O. 4190/2, lot 109; *Shrews. Chron.* 26 Sept. 1919.
29 S.R.O., DA 17/516/13, f. 132.
30 S.R.O., reg. of electors, Ludlow const. (1974), 172.
31 Date stone lying in outbuilding.
32 J. Martin Robinson, *Archit. of N. Eng.* (1986), 24.
33 Inf. from Mrs. H. Killick.
34 *V.C.H. Salop.* i. 337.
35 Eyton, iv. 69.
36 P.R.O., C 134/48, no. 9.
37 Loton Hall MSS., transcript (in blue bks.) from bound vol. of 'Seven Rolls of Steward's Accounts 1375–1457'.
38 S.P.L., MS. 2, f. 151.
39 Glos. R.O., D2153 D/14; S.R.O. 356, box 327, surv. *c.* 1575, pp. 171, 173, 176. Cf. field names in P.R.O., IR 29/29/161; IR 30/29/161.
40 H.W.R.O.(H.), HD 2/14/40. Cf. field names in P.R.O., IR 29/29/297; IR 30/29/297.

17th century Holdgate had a separate set of open fields: Perell field south-west of the village, Park field to the south-east, and Church field to the north-west.[41] Inclosure of open-field arable was very gradual in Holdgate and Brookhampton; in 1842 a considerable acreage of uninclosed strips remained in nine fields, presumably fragments of the former six. At the Coates, which had land in Stanton Long's open fields,[42] everything was inclosed before 1842.[43]

Medieval clearances of woodland were indicated at Brookhampton in 1549 by the name 'Stocking' in Brook and Broadmoor fields;[44] the name referred to 35 a. at Brookhampton in 1842, around New Buildings on the rising ground below the Clee plateau.[45] Blackmoor, a 10-a. pasture at Holdgate in 1648,[46] may also have represented a former wood, waste, or marsh, as perhaps did Gamesmoor and Shot moor, west of Brookhampton, together 13 a. in 1842.[47] In 1546 there was a neglected demesne wood, Castlemoor, near Holdgate's southern boundary; it was probably the common wood called the Moor in 1383,[48] whose underwood and pasture were worth nothing to the lord in 1420.[49] In 1546 Henry Cressett and the rector received a 21-year lease of three quarters of the herbage of Castlemoor on condition that they cleared the undergrowth, leaving only the saplings of oak, ash, and fruit trees.[50] By 1648, however, there was said to be no wood in Holdgate or Brookhampton other than in hedges and in 3 a. of coppice felled every 20 years. Castlemoor was presumably by then the 'farm at the wood now laid to the demesnes', 60 a. of pasture and 10 a. of meadow.[51]

The coppice mentioned in 1648 was probably in that 'land or wood ground' called the Edge, which in 1654 occupied the escarpment at the parish's boundary with Ditton Priors[52] and was represented in 1842 by 22 a. of pasture called the Coppice.[53] Only 16 a. in Holdgate parish were then woodland, and that of no annual value.[54]

There seem to have been no common wastes at Holdgate or Brookhampton by the 17th century, but the inhabitants were said in 1617 to have, as strakers, right of common on the waste of Brown Clee, *c.* 4 km. south-east.[55] Allegedly that right was allowed by the lord of Clee chase in return for their not harming stray deer among their crops.[56] Cattle were normally driven through Earnstrey park (in Diddlebury) and Abdon Marsh to the 'driving out' above Ditton's wood and there turned out to graze.[57] In the later 18th century sheep, normally wintered on farms in Holdgate and Brookhampton, were driven to Brown Clee in spring. The drift road from Brookhampton ran south-south-east from King's Lane and converged with that from Holdgate in Earnstrey park; it ran thence to Marsh gate (in Abdon), above which the sheep were turned out on Abdon common or 'liberty'; some were driven to the adjacent Earnstrey Liberty. Those movements had virtually ceased[58] by 1813, when Abdon common was inclosed; the freeholders of Holdgate and Brookhampton were then awarded portions of it totalling 152 a.[59]

In 1648 the eight principal farms in Holdgate and Brookhampton on the manorial estate, apart from the 300-a. demesne at Holdgate, varied in size between 24 a. and 100 a., the average being 60 a.; the Holdgate farms, other than the demesnes, were much smaller than the Brookhampton ones. Except for the 'farm at the wood' the Holdgate farms, including the demesne, had as much arable as pasture. At Brookhampton, however, the farmers had considerably more arable than pasture.[60]

At Brookhampton a three-year rotation of oats, wheat, and fallow based on the three open fields was maintained in the late 16th century.[61] In the 17th century farmers seem to have grown a variety of grains. In May 1626 Edward Cressett sowed 140 a. of arable with wheat (20 a.), mixed corn (30 a.), rye (20 a.), barley (20 a.), and oats (50 a.).[62] Early 18th-century inventories mention corn in the ground in December and January,[63] and peas, vetches, and other pulses.[64] Clover was used at the Coates by 1693.[65] At Brookhampton there was a former hopyard and a kiln in 1657.[66] In the late 17th and early 18th century the farmers seem to have kept many more cattle than sheep. One of the largest, Francis Hudson, had 50 cattle in January 1701 and only 18 sheep.[67] By the later 18th century, however, it was almost exclusively sheep that the farmers of Holdgate and Brookhampton grazed on Brown Clee. Flocks of up to 100 were then known.[68]

By 1793 the larger farms in Holdgate and Brookhampton had absorbed some of the cottage holdings, and the cottages were sublet to labourers, but none of the farms was considered large.[69]

41 Glam. R.O., CL/Deeds II, no. 8031; S.R.O. 1359, box 20, terrier of 1632. For locations see P.R.O., IR 29/29/161; IR 30/9/161, fields 62, 74–88, 90–122, 356, 358–61.
42 Below, Stanton Long, econ. hist.
43 P.R.O., IR 29/29/161; IR 30/29/161.
44 Glos. R.O., D2153 D/14.
45 P.R.O., IR 29/29/161; IR 30/29/161, fields 238, 241, 246–8, 274–5.
46 S.P.L., Deeds 6116.
47 P.R.O., IR 29/29/161; IR 30/29/161, fields 170, 183–4, 187.
48 P.R.O., C 136/24, no. 19.
49 P.R.O., C 138/54, no. 116.
50 P.R.O., E 326/11742.
51 S.P.L., Deeds 6116.
52 S.R.O. 5460/4/4/1; /5/3/1.
53 P.R.O., IR 29/29/161; IR 30/29/161, fields 232–3, 239–40.
54 P.R.O., IR 18/8115.
55 *T.S.A.S.* 2nd ser. viii. 196–7, dated by S.R.O. 334/1.
56 S.R.O., incl. award B 21, brief of [1810], f. 4v.
57 *T.S.A.S.* 2nd ser. viii. 197.
58 S.R.O., incl. award B 21, brief of [1810]. The drift rds. appear as public footpaths on O.S. Map 1/25,000, SO 48/58 (1983 edn.).
59 Abdon and Stoke St. Milborough Incl. Act, 1809, 49 Geo. III, c. 109 (Local and Personal); S.R.O., incl. award B 33.
60 S.P.L., Deeds 6116.
61 S.R.O. 356, box 327, surv. *c.* 1575, pp. 171, 173, 176.
62 S.R.O. 5460/7/4/1.
63 H.W.R.O.(H.), Heref. dioc. rec., invs. of Fra. Hudson, 1701; Edw. Onslowe, 1711; Thos. Pritchard, 1717.
64 Ibid. invs. of Edw. Fewtrell, 1667; Edw. Onslowe, 1711.
65 S.R.O. 173, box 2, deed of 1693.
66 S.R.O. 356, box 327, Brookhampton surv. of 1657.
67 H.W.R.O.(H.), Heref. dioc. rec., invs. of Edw. Fewtrell, 1667; Fra. Hudson, 1701; Edw. Onslowe, 1711; Edm. Jones, 1716; Thos. Pritchard, 1717; Jas. Page, 1723.
68 S.R.O., incl. award B 21, brief of [1810].
69 S.P.L., MS. 6865, p. 95.

TABLE VIII

HOLDGATE: LAND USE, LIVESTOCK, AND CROPS

		1867	1891[a]	1938[a]	1965[a]
Percentage of	grassland	70	80	91	71
	arable	30	20	9	29
Percentage of	cattle	18	29	21	20
	sheep	74	66	76	78
	pigs	8	5	3	2
Percentage of	wheat	49	29	44	63
	barley	35	35	18	21
	oats	16	36	38	14
	mixed corn & rye	0	0	0	2
Percentage of agricultural land growing roots and vegetables		6	7	1	2

[a] Excluding Bouldon and the Coates.

Sources: P.R.O., MAF 68/143, no. 15; /1340, no. 6; /3880, Salop. no. 108; /4945, no. 108.

In 1842 the farms were intermixed,[70] but the manorial estate absorbed the intermingled freeholds from the 1860s onwards,[71] and before 1907 Holdgate and Brookhampton were reorganized in six compact farms: one of 48 a., four between 101 a. and 225 a., and Holdgate Hall, 484 a. In the process the surviving parts of the open fields were inclosed.[72]

On farms over 25 a. grass and arable were held in roughly equal amounts in 1842.[73] The grassland was 'very poor'. About 150 a. of arable near Holdgate village were of 'turnip' soil, well farmed in five courses: wheat, turnips, barley, and clover (grazed) for two years. The remaining arable (*c.* 580 a.) was of a 'weak' soil on a water-retentive subsoil, and there had been no draining; the courses there were fallow and vetches (eaten by cart horses), wheat, oats, clover (half mown, half grazed by cart horses), and clover (grazed by sheep and young cattle).[74] From the mid 19th century to the early 20th the main farms moved increasingly towards livestock. By the 1960s they had seen some movement towards cereals again,[75] mainly winter wheat: at Holdgate it was the only grain that could yield more than 2 tons an acre.[76] In 1965, however, there was still more than twice as much grass as arable.[77]

In 1222 Thomas Mauduit was granted a weekly market at Holdgate until the king should come of age;[78] no renewal at the end of that term is known. In 1253 William Mauduit obtained a Thursday market;[79] it was active in 1285[80] but may have lapsed by 1291 when Robert Burnell, bishop of Bath and Wells, was granted a Tuesday market and an annual fair on the eve, feast, and morrow of Trinity.[81] No later evidence of markets or fairs has been found, and it therefore seems that those of the 13th century failed to become established.[82] By 1515 the inhabitants went to market outside the parish.[83]

There was a water mill in Holdgate manor by the earlier 13th century; in 1248 or 1249 William Mauduit granted it in fee to Haughmond abbey. The manor's customary tenants were required to haul its millstones and to do suit when the mill was able to work. After 1264[84] the abbey seems to have given up the mill; in 1292 it was held of Bishop Burnell by Roger de Bradeleye.[85] It was mentioned in 1346 but not in 1383[86] or later. The mill seems to have stood at Brookhampton; the 'Mill weir acre' was in Brook field in 1549.[87]

A cooper lived at Brookhampton in 1385,[88] and two tailors were mentioned in Holdgate manor in 1576.[89] In 1841 Holdgate and Brookhampton each had a shoemaker. Brookhampton also had a stonemason and a blacksmith.[90]

LOCAL GOVERNMENT. By 1255 the barony of Holdgate had its own court, some of whose suitors were exempt from suit of their hundreds. The exemption did not then apply to all the estates of the barony, but within the liberty William Mauduit claimed the right to have a gallows, to hear pleas of bloodshed, of hue and cry, and breaches of the assize of ale, and pleas under writ of right.[91] The gallows presumably stood on Gallitree bank[92] next to the road *c.* 1 km. south-west of the castle.[93] Richard of Cornwall annexed more of the barony's members to the liberty between 1256 and 1272, and the Templars, who held the barony of him, extended the court's jurisdiction to pleas *de vetito namio*.[94] By 1422 at least 15 separate places did suit.[95] The court met twice a year in the late 13th century[96] and was still meeting in the 1590s, when May and November sessions were recorded. By then it was combined with the court baron of Holdgate manor, which elected two constables.[97] In 1793 Henry Cressett Pelham had a court leet

70 P.R.O., IR 29/29/161; IR 30/29/161.
71 Above, manors.
72 S.P.L., Deed 4099.
73 P.R.O., IR 29/29/161.
74 P.R.O., IR 18/8115.
75 Table VIII.
76 *Salop. N.F.U. Jnl.* cxxv. 8.
77 Table VIII.
78 P.R.O., C 60/18, m. 10.
79 *Cal. Pat.* 1247–58, 252.
80 *V.C.H. Salop.* iv. 68.
81 *Cal. Chart. R.* 1257–1300, 389.
82 For the possible mkt. site see above, this article, intro.
83 *Salop. N. & Q.* i. 33.
84 *Cart. Haughmond*, pp. 122–3.
85 Eyton, iv. 69.
86 P.R.O., C 135/82, no. 1; C 136/24, no. 19.
87 Glos. R.O., D2153 D/14.
88 S.R.O. 1037/3/63.
89 *Salop. N. & Q.* i. 21.
90 P.R.O., HO 107/912/22, ff. 5 and v., 6v.–8v.
91 *Rot. Hund.* ii. 71–2. Only Holdgate and Clee St. Margaret were then expressly stated to do suit.
92 P.R.O., IR 29/29/161; IR 30/29/161, field 8.
93 At O.S. Nat. Grid SO 557 889.
94 *Rot. Hund.* ii. 91, 100; cf. *V.C.H. Salop.* iii. 48.
95 S.P.L., MS. 2, f. 146.
96 *Cart. Haughmond*, p. 226.
97 *Salop. N. & Q.* i. 13, 19, 21, 33, 47, 53; S.P.L., MS. 2, ff. 127v., 146 and v., 149.

and court baron;[98] an annual manor court was being held 1813–15;[99] a court leet met in the 1840s; and in 1863 the Revd. Henry Thursby-Pelham held a 'view of frankpledge, court leet, and court baron', which elected constables for Brookhampton and Bouldon. It met at Jeremiah Cocks's house, Holdgate Hall.[1]

In the mid 16th century Holdgate was subject to the earl of Shrewsbury's swainmote of Clee chase,[2] which in 1561 amerced a Holdgate farmer for overcharging the common with cattle.[3]

Average annual expenditure on the poor 1782–5 was £44. In 1802–3, however, £153 was spent, and only eight out of 37 recipients of permanent or occasional relief were old or disabled.[4] Expenditure fluctuated over the next thirty years, peaking at £200 in 1831.[5]

The parish was in Ludlow poor-law union 1836–1930,[6] Ludlow highway district 1863–95,[7] Ludlow rural sanitary district 1872–94, and Ludlow rural district from 1894.[8]

CHURCH. Holdgate had a church and a priest in 1086,[9] and Helgot was posthumously credited with having founded a church there. A church, probably a new building, was consecrated by Geoffrey of Clee, bishop of Hereford 1115–19, uncle of Helgot's son Herbert. It was then called the castle church ('ecclesia de castello')[10] and seems to have been part of the castle; the churchyard, roughly triangular, was one of two enclosures adjoining the motte.[11]

Before 1121 Herbert son of Helgot gave the church to Shrewsbury abbey[12] subject to the life interest of Warin, the clerk who held it in the 1120s.[13]

Before 1189 the rectory was divided into portions for a priest, a deacon, and a subdeacon,[14] described as canons in 1205.[15] It is difficult not to connect the portionary constitution of the church with the unusual character of the generous endowment conferred on it by Helgot or his son Herbert,[16] and, if the portions existed in the 1120s, Warin may have held them all, rather as the Beaumais family engrossed prebends in St. Alkmund's, Shrewsbury.[17] The priest and his portion were later often referred to as the rector and the rectory. The canons may have been the baron's household clerks, like Earl Roger's, who had earlier been beneficed at Quatford and in his castle chapel at Shrewsbury.[18] In 1210 Shrewsbury abbey granted the advowson of the deaconry to Thomas Mauduit,[19] lord of the honor and manor, and in 1283 conveyed those of the rectory and subdeaconry to the bishop of Hereford.[20] The subdeaconry lapsed after its advowson was last exercised by Bishop Godwin[21] (1617–33). From 1831 to 1861 the rectory was united with that of Tugford, also in the bishop's gift,[22] and in 1888 it was united with the deaconry.[23]

The advowson of the deaconry followed the lordship of the manor from 1210 until 1860,[24] but it did not, apparently, pass to Sir Nicholas Burnell until Dame Aline Burnell's death[25] in 1363.[26] Joan, widow of John, Lord Lovel, and wife of Sir William Stanley, had the advowson in 1466.[27] The bishop of Hereford collated to the deaconry in 1603, 1632 (twice),[28] and 1704.[29] The advowson was leased with the manor by 1551 and until Elizabeth Cressett's death in 1792,[30] when the bishop of Worcester resumed possession;[31] the bishop retained the advowson when the manor passed to the Ecclesiastical Commissioners in 1860.

On the union of the rectory and deaconry the bishop of Worcester had every fourth turn and the bishop of Hereford the other three.[32] In 1926 Bouldon was transferred to a new benefice, Diddlebury with Bouldon, and the rest of Holdgate benefice was united to that of Tugford as Holdgate with Tugford, the bishop of Worcester to have the second turn, the bishop of Hereford the first, third, and all subsequent turns.[33] The patronage was suspended from 1958 to 1983 when the benefice was united to that of

98 S.P.L., MS. 6865, p. 95.

99 S.R.O. 2334/2.

1 S.P.L., Deeds 6120–1, 10194; cf. Cocks's grave stone (1872) at Holdgate.

2 S.R.O., incl. award B 21, ct. r. of 1554, 1561–4 (copies); S.R.O. 1037/21/1.

3 S.R.O., incl. award B 21, ct. r. 28 Apr. 1561 (copy).

4 *Poor Law Abstract*, H.C. 175, pp. 418–19 (1803–4), xiii.

5 Ibid. H.C. 82, pp. 370–1 (1818), xix; *Poor Rate Returns*, H.C. 556, suppl. app. p. 142 (1822), v; H.C. 334, p. 177 (1825), iv; H.C. 219, p. 165 (1830–1), xi; H.C. 444, p. 160 (1835), xlvii.

6 V. J. Walsh, 'Admin. of Poor Laws in Salop. 1820–55' (Pennsylvania Univ. Ph.D. thesis, 1970), 150; *Kelly's Dir. Salop.* (1929), 116.

7 *Lond. Gaz.* 27 Mar. 1863, p. 1772; S.R.O., S.C.C. Local Govt., etc., Cttee. min. bk. 1894–1903, p. 29.

8 *V.C.H. Salop.* ii. 215 (corr. ibid. xi. 376); *Rural Dist. Councillors Electn. Order, 1894* (Local Govt. Bd. order no. 31847). For the govt. of detached areas after their transfer to Stanton Long and Diddlebury C.P.s 1883–4 see below, Bouldon, local govt.; Stanton Long, local govt. For the govt. of the C.P.s which absorbed Holdgate C.P. see above, Abdon, local govt.; below, Munslow, local govt.; Tugford, local govt.

9 *V.C.H. Salop.* i. 337.

10 P.R.O., SP 16/124, f. 165; *Cart. Shrews.* i, p. 2.

11 Above, manors (Holdgate).

12 *Cart. Shrews.* i, p. 33.

13 Ibid. ii, p. 307.

14 P.R.O., SP 16/124, f. 165.

15 *Cur. Reg. R.* iv. 45.

16 Below, this section.

17 Cf. *V.C.H. Salop.* ii. 71.

18 *T.S.A.S.* lvi. 252–3; *V.C.H. Salop.* ii. 123–4.

19 *T.S.A.S.* 2nd ser. x. 327–8.

20 *Charters and Rec. of Heref. Cath.* ed. W. W. Capes (1908), 172, dated by Heref. D. & C. mun. 2131 (ref. supplied by Mrs. M. T. Roberts).

21 P.R.O., SP 16/124, f. 165v.

22 Heref. Dioc. Regy., reg. 1822–42, pp. 165–9; 1857–69, pp. 188–90.

23 Bannister, *Heref. Institutions*, 151.

24 *Reg. Swinfield* (C.S.), 525; *Cal. Close*, 1313–18, 488; *Reg. Gilbert* (C.S.), 119; *Reg. Spofford* (C.S.), 350, 359; *L. & P. Hen. VIII*, vi, p. 89; xvi, p. 240; *Cal. Pat.* 1548–9, 298; Bannister, op. cit. 141, 144, 151. Cf. above, manors (Holdgate).

25 *Reg. Trillek* (C.S.), 392; *Cal. Inq. p.m.* xv, pp. 288–9.

26 *Complete Peerage*, ii. 434.

27 *Reg. Stanbury* (C.S.), 183 and n.

28 *T.S.A.S.* 3rd ser. viii. 42, 53.

29 Bannister, *Heref. Institutions*, 59.

30 Ibid. 86, 119; S.P.L., MS. 2, f. 137v.; Birm. Univ. Libr., Mytton Papers, iv. 753.

31 *State of Bishopric of Worc.* (Worcs. Hist. Soc. N.S. vi), 28.

32 *Lond. Gaz.* 24 May 1881, pp. 2677–8; Heref. Dioc. Regy., reg. 1883–1901, p. 194.

33 Heref. Dioc. Regy., reg. 1919–26, pp. 440–1; 1926–38, p. 7.

Diddlebury with Bouldon and Munslow to form Diddlebury with Munslow, Holdgate, and Tugford. The new benefice was to be held in plurality with Abdon, and from 1988 patronage was shared between the bishop and the dean and chapter of Hereford.[34]

Helgot or his son Herbert[35] endowed the church with the tithes of his demesne and part of the tithes of his knights' demesnes in various parts of the barony. Thus tithes became due to it from Holdgate township (presumably with Brookhampton) and from parts of the townships of Bouldon, Oxenbold (probably including 'Parva Bentley'),[36] and Stanton Long (probably including the Coates), and fractions of certain tithes from Belswardine (in Leighton), Charlcotte (in Neenton), Clee St. Margaret, Corfield (in Stanton Long), Felton Butler (in Great Ness), Meadowley (in Morville), Oxenbold (in Monkhopton and Stanton Long), Great Poston (in Diddlebury), Stanton Long, Great Sutton (in Diddlebury), and Uffington.[37] It thus appears that those lands of Helgot (or of Herbert) that were not subinfeudated formed Holdgate parish, while the estates of his feudal tenants remained outside. Of the new parish's components Holdgate and part of Stanton Long (as members of pre-Conquest 'Stantune') and Oxenbold had probably been originally in Much Wenlock parish, but by Helgot's day they were perhaps attached to a church at Patton; Bouldon was probably formerly in Diddlebury.[38] By the 1630s no tithes were received from Meadowley, Charlcotte, Uffington, or 'Parva Bentley',[39] but in the 1840s tithes or moduses were still payable from certain farms in Clee St. Margaret, Corfield, Felton Butler, Oxenbold, Great Poston, Stanton Long, and Great Sutton.[40] In 1291 a pension of 10*s.* was payable from the church of Bold[41] (in Aston Botterell); in 1478 a pension may have been payable to Holdgate from Uffington chapel;[42] and in 1535 another of 5*s.* was payable by the vicar of Leighton.[43] Helgot was said to have exacted perpetual annual sums from all his lands, including Belswardine (in Leighton), Bold, and Uffington, to provide a paschal candle at Holdgate.[44]

Herbert was said to have given the church 1 hide of land in Holdgate and his wife to have given 1 carucate. When the rectory was divided the priest was assigned a house near the church and glebe comprising 70 a. of arable, 2 crofts (containing 2 a. of pasture), and 3 a. of meadow; and two thirds of all tithes in the parish and one third of all tithes due from other parishes.[45] His annual income was put at £6 in 1291, when he was owed 3*s.* 6*d.* from the pension from Bold;[46] the rector of Aston Botterell still owed 4*s.* a year in 1535 to the priest or rector of Holdgate,[47] who from the later 16th century also had the income of the subdeaconry.[48] In the 14th and early 15th century the rectors were usually Hereford cathedral or diocesan office-holders and large pluralists outside Shropshire;[49] Roger of Ottery, rector 1364–*c.* 1387, claimed that the benefice required no resident incumbent.[50]

From 1529 the rectors may have been required to reside. Walter Blunt, a graduate pluralist,[51] resigned the rectory *c.* 1528 in return for a pension of £5 6*s.* 8*d.*[52] His successor Edward Strete, 1529–*c.* 1549,[53] is not known as a pluralist; Maurice Monyngton, 1549–54, was married in the parish;[54] and Edward Fewtrell, *c.* 1554–*c.* 1601,[55] certainly resided.[56] The priest's buildings were in disrepair in 1533,[57] and by 1614 they had been replaced by a 'goodly' glebe house in a detached part of the parish at Stanton Long.[58] The four priests from *c.* 1601 to *c.* 1640 were pluralists[59] and none is likely to have resided, but Dr. Patrick Panter, rector 1640–70, and his three successors to 1729[60] did reside.[61] In 1705 the rector acquired most of the deacon's tithes.[62]

The rectors 1729–1860, except perhaps Daniel Price (1772–5),[63] were pluralists in Shropshire[64] and none seems to have resided.[65] They employed curates throughout.[66] Not used as a parsonage after 1729,[67] the rectory house at

34 Ibid. 1953–68, p. 249; 1969– (in use), pp. 395, 458–9, 568; *Crockford* (1977–9), 408, 504; (1987–8), 392; *Heref. Dioc. Yr. Bk.* (1989), 44–5; inf. from the rector.

35 *Cart. Shrews.* i, p. 33.

36 'Bentley' was a parcel of land in Oxenbold man. in the 15th cent. (S.P.L., MS. 2342, nos. 12870, 12873) and there was a 'Bentley' field at Stanton Long (P.R.O., SP 16/124, f. 165v.).

37 P.R.O., SP 16/124, f. 165.

38 Below, Stanton Long, church; Bouldon, intro.

39 P.R.O., SP 16/124, f. 165v.

40 S.R.O. 1565/5; 4367/Ti/2; P.R.O., IR 29/29/126; IR 29/29/255; IR 29/29/297.

41 *Tax. Eccl.* 166.

42 *Cart. Haughmond*, p. 226.

43 *Valor Eccl.* (Rec. Com.), iii. 184.

44 P.R.O., SP 16/124, f. 165.

45 *Cart. Shrews.* i, p. 41; ii, p. 258.

46 *Tax. Eccl.* 166–7.

47 *Valor Eccl.* iii. 209, 211.

48 Below.

49 For names see *Reg. Trillek*, 378, 387; *Reg. L. Charlton* (C.S.), 67; *Reg. Gilbert*, 121; *Reg. Spofford*, 351–2, 356. For careers see Le Neve, *Fasti, 1300–1541, Heref.* 4, 7, 10, 28–9, 32, 35–6, 41, 51; A. B. Emden, *Biog. Reg. Univ. Oxf. to 1500*, ii. 921, 1068–9, 1409; iii. 1906–7; idem, *Biog. Reg. Univ. Camb.* 215.

50 A. H. Thompson, *Eng. Clergy and their Organization in Later Middle Ages* (1947), 246–7. The deacon made a similar claim: *Reg. Langham* (Cant. & York Soc.), 39–40.

51 Emden, *Biog. Reg. Oxf. to 1500*, i. 203–4.

52 *Reg. Bothe* (C.S.), 342.

53 Ibid.; S.P.L., MS. 2, f. 137.

54 Bannister, *Heref. Institutions*, 7; Heref. D. & C. mun., chapter act bk. 1512–66 (folio), ff. 129, 130v.

55 S.P.L., MS. 2, f. 146c; P.R.O., C 3/399/150; *T.S.A.S.* 3rd ser. viii. 42.

56 *T.S.A.S.* 4th ser. xi. 186; xlvi. 45.

57 *Reg. Bothe*, 264.

58 Bodl. MS. Top. Salop. c. 6, ff. 18, 64.

59 The names and succession are given in S.R.O. 4131/Rg/1, s.a. 1668–70. For careers see *T.S.A.S.* 3rd ser. viii. 42, 44–6, 54; *Alum. Oxon. 1500–1714*, i. 92, 213, 612; S.R.O. 4131/Rg/1, s.a. 1668–70; *D.N.B.*; Bannister, *Heref. Institutions*, 27.

60 *T.S.A.S.* 4th ser. ii. 58; Bannister, op. cit. 38, 46, 58.

61 All bur. in par.: S.R.O. 4131/Rg/1, 30 Sept. 1670; 4 Nov. 1683; /Rg/2, 5 Jan. 1703/4; 6 Dec. 1729.

62 Below, this section.

63 Bannister, *Heref. Institutions*, 104, 106.

64 For names and succession see Bannister, op. cit. 74, 104, 106, 130, 175; *Alum. Oxon. 1715–1886*, i. 297. For careers see *T.S.A.S.* 4th ser. v. 193, 207; vi. 328–9; *S.P.R. Lich.* v (7), 34; xi (2), 321, 343; Bannister, op. cit. 116, 139, 144–6, 175; S.P.L., MS. 6865, p. 102.

65 Birm. Univ. Libr., Mytton Papers, iv. 747; S.P.L., MS. 6865, pp. 98–9, 102; S. Bagshaw, *Dir. Salop.* (1851), 553).

66 S.R.O. 3901/Rg/1, 5 Jan. 1733/4; Birm. Univ. Libr., Mytton Papers, iv. 747; S.R.O. 4131/Rg/2, 3, 5; Heref. Dioc. Regy., reg. 1772–1802, ff. 78, 93; S.P.L., MS. 6865, p. 102.

67 Death of last resident rector: S.R.O. 4131/Rg/2, bur. 6 Dec. 1729.

Stanton Long was considered in 1793 to be insufficient; though in average repair for a farmhouse, it had only three small rooms downstairs and four, even smaller, in the roof space.[68] In 1813 the rector received 8¾ a. glebe in Abdon parish at the inclosure of Abdon common.[69] His tithes in Holdgate parish were commuted to £222 in 1842[70] and those from other parishes to £25 11*s.* 3*d.* 1842–7.[71] In 1793 there were weekly prayers morning and evening, and a morning sermon. Holy communion was celebrated at Easter, Whitsun, Michaelmas, and Christmas, with *c.* 60 communicants.[72] In 1851 Sunday congregations averaged 30–40 adults, with *c.* 35 Sunday school children.[73]

The rectors 1861–1958[74] lived in the parish,[75] except that R. E. Haymes lived in Herefordshire near the end of his life.[76] A large brick rectory house with gothic details, by J. P. Seddon,[77] was built near the church in 1865;[78] the house at Stanton Long became Glebe Farm.[79] There were 83 a. of glebe in 1887[80] and 113 a., including Glebe farm and the Leasowes, were sold *c.* 1920.[81]

Incumbents of other parishes served the cure intermittently 1958–83 as priests or curates in charge.[82] From 1983 the incumbent of the united benefice lived at Munslow. The rectory house at Holdgate was sold *c.* 1959, and became Holdgate House.[83] In 1963 the bishop bought land for a new parsonage[84] but none was built.

The deacon was in the 12th century assigned 40 a. of arable, 5 crofts (containing 2½ a. of pasture), 1 a. of meadow, and a third of the tithes due from Holdgate and the other parishes.[85] In 1291 his annual income was reckoned to be £4 6*s.* 8*d.*, with 3*s.* 3*d.* from Bold.[86] Few deacons are known to have been graduates or pluralists in the later Middle Ages.[87] In 1551 the deacon leased his tithes for 80 years to Robert Cressett of Upton, who was succeeded soon afterwards by Henry Cressett,[88] patron of the deaconry. The deacons instituted in 1554 and 1556 were rectors of Abdon[89] and probably lived there.[90] No deacon seems to have been instituted after 1556[91] until 1603. From 1555 successive patrons sublet the tithes to the rectors, reserving only the deaconry tithes from the Holdgate demesne and Felton Butler, which the patron (as lessee) assigned to the deacon when the deaconry was revived[92] in 1603.[93] By 1631, when the 80-year lease expired, the deacon's house near the church had long been occupied by tenants[94] and the deacons had performed no duties for many years.[95] No deacon was instituted after 1632 until 1704.[96] The revenues were said to have been assigned in that period to the rector, the Cressetts being allowed a third turn of the rectory patronage in lieu of their patronage of the deaconry.[97]

Under an agreement of 1705 the deacon was to receive the rector's tithes (as well as his own) from Felton Butler but to relinquish all his other tithes to the rector; the rector, in return, was to do the deacon's duty.[98] That arrangement subsisted in the mid 19th century.[99] The deacon's duties were said in the 18th century to be those of a deacon in the Church of England[1] and of reading the second lesson[2] and so to be in 'constant attendance',[3] but after 1705, since he performed no duties, he was probably always non-resident.[4] The deacon's house was occupied by an aleseller in 1719 and 'ready to drop down'.[5] In 1782 the deacon's glebe consisted of 20 a. called the Leasowes,[6] *c.* 1 mile from the church,[7] which yielded £12 rent in 1793;[8] the tithes from Felton Butler, let to Lord Powis, were producing another £50 in 1782[9] and in 1847 were commuted to £54 6*s.*[10]

Before 1189 the subdeacon was assigned ½ a. of arable and two crofts (containing 1 a. of pasture) with a third of tithes arising outside the parish.[11] In 1291 his income was said, implausibly, to be the same as the deacon's.[12] In 1366 its true annual value was put at 30*s.*[13] The subdeaconry revenues hardly sufficed to maintain a

68 S.P.L., MS. 6865, pp. 98–100.
69 S.R.O., incl. award B 33.
70 P.R.O., IR 29/29/161.
71 P.R.O., IR 29/29/255; IR 29/29/297; S.R.O. 1565/5; 4367/Ti/2.
72 S.P.L., MS. 6865, pp. 100–1.
73 P.R.O., HO 129/352, no. 56.
74 Bannister, *Heref. Institutions*, 175, 191; Heref. Dioc. Regy., reg. 1902–19, p. 357; 1926–38, p. 7; 1938–53, pp. 450–1; 1953–68, p. 249.
75 *P.O. Dir. Salop.* (1870), 64; (1879), 331; *Kelly's Dir. Salop.* (1905), 108; (1913), 114; (1922), 111; (1929), 116; S.R.O., reg. of electors, Ludlow divn. (civilian) (1948), p. 347; Ludlow const. (1951), 441; S.R.O. 888/1, 445.
76 *Kelly's Dir. Salop.* (1909), 111; *Crockford* (1932), 688.
77 H.W.R.O.(H.), Heref. dioc. rec. AA 58, plans, specifications, etc., of 1865 (ref. supplied by Mr. C. J. Pickford).
78 *Rep. of Heref. Dioc. Ch. Bldg. Soc., Archd. of Salop 1869* (Ludlow, 1870; copy in S.P.L.), 18; Heref. Dioc. Regy., reg. 1857–69, pp. 386, 423, 449; P.R.O., IR 29/29/161, altered appt.
79 S.R.O. 3901/Rg/4, 31 Oct. 1915.
80 *Return of Glebe Land, 1887*, H.C. 307, p. 59 (1887), lxiv.
81 Par. rec., statement 21 Mar. 1921.
82 *Heref. Dioc. Yr. Bk.* (1964–5), 40; (1965–6), 40; *Crockford* (1977–9), 408, 504; (1987–8), 392.
83 S.R.O. 1038/1, p. 447; O.S. Map 1/10,000, SO 58 NE. (1978 edn.).
84 Heref. Dioc. Regy., reg. 1953–68, p. 437.
85 P.R.O., SP 16/124, f. 165.
86 *Tax. Eccl.* 166–7.
87 *Reg. Trillek*, 392; *Reg. L. Charlton*, 71; *Reg. Spofford*, 350, 359; *Reg. Beauchamp* (C.S.), 15; *Reg. Bothe*, 331; Emden, *Biog. Reg. Oxf. to 1500*, ii. 713; *Reg. Langham*, 39–40.
88 P.R.O., C 3/399/150.
89 Bannister, *Heref. Institutions*, 7, 9, 11.
90 *T.S.A.S.* 4th ser. xi. 186.
91 Bannister, op. cit. 11.
92 P.R.O., C 3/399/150; S.P.L., MS. 2, ff. 145 and v., 146c.
93 *T.S.A.S.* 3rd ser. viii. 42. There was no deacon 1601: Bodl. MS. Top. Salop. c. 6, f. 10.
94 P.R.O., SP 16/124, f. 165v.; S.P.L., MS. 2, f. 145v.
95 Bodl. MS. Top. Salop. c. 6, f. 29v.
96 *T.S.A.S.* 3rd ser. viii. 53; Bannister, *Heref. Institutions*, 59.
97 Birm. Univ. Libr., Mytton Papers, iv. 753.
98 S.P.L., MS. 2, f. 142.
99 S.R.O. 1565/5; 4367/Ti/2; P.R.O., IR 29/29/126 (referring incorrectly to the 'subdeacon'); IR 29/29/161; IR 29/29/255; IR 29/29/297.
1 Birm. Univ. Libr., Mytton Papers, iv. 753.
2 S.P.L., MS. 6865, p. 100.
3 S.P.L., MS. 2, f. 142.
4 e.g. Bannister, *Heref. Institutions*, 59, 86, 119, 131, 134, 141, 144, 148, 151–2, 154; S.P.L., MS. 2, f. 142; MS. 6865, p. 100; *T.S.A.S.* 4th ser. vii. 103; *State of Bishopric of Worc.* 28, 41, 136–7, 216; *Alum. Oxon. 1715–1886*, iii. 1111.
5 H.W.R.O.(H.), HD 5/15, Holdgate.
6 *State of Bishopric of Worc.* 28.
7 B.L. Maps, O.S.D. 207.
8 S.P.L., MS. 6865, p. 96 (there incorrectly called the 'subdeacon's land').
9 *State of Bishopric of Worc.* 28.
10 P.R.O., IR 29/29/126.
11 P.R.O., SP 16/124, f. 165.
12 *Tax. Eccl.* 166–7.
13 *Reg. Langham*, 103.

non-pluralist, and some subdeacons are known to have enjoyed or proceeded to higher preferment.[14] In 1551 the subdeacon leased his revenues to Henry Cressett, lessee of the manor, for 80 years, and from 1555 to 1631 the successive lessees sublet them to the rectors, reserving only the subdeaconry tithes from Felton Butler.[15] From the later 16th century the revenues of the subdeaconry were held by the rectors.[16] The last subdeacon performed no duties[17] and had no income from the benefice in the 1630s.[18]

The small church of the *HOLY TRINITY*, so dedicated by 1737[19] and possibly by 1291,[20] consists of chancel, nave with south porch, and west tower.[21] It is built of coursed sandstone rubble with tiled roofs. None of the fabric can be securely dated as early as the consecration of *c.* 1117, but the exceptionally ornate south doorway and font are 12th-century. The door had wrought ironwork that was apparently of that period.[22] The chalice shaped font, its bowl covered with bold abstract and animal carving, may be *c.* 1140, resembling those at Eardisley and Castle Frome (Herefs.) and Chaddesley Corbett (Worcs.).[23] The nave has a small splayed west window, pierced through a 12th-century central buttress, which was external until the tower was added. The chancel, slightly lower and narrower than the nave, is assumed to be mainly 12th-century but retains no feature datable to that period, except perhaps for a sheela-na-gig in its south wall outside.

The chancel's east end is clearly of the 13th century; the two east lancets are integral with the walling and there seem to be breaks near the east ends of the north and south walls; what seem to be the lower courses of an earlier north wall are visible inside. There is another lancet in the chancel's north wall. That wall also has a plain aumbry. The lower part of the tower seems to date from the 13th century; its battered plinth has a prominent round moulding. The tower was said in 1862 to be entered from the nave through a narrow pointed archway; if so, it was blocked by 1894 to form a window,[24] south of which is a plain doorway of unknown date. A low arched recess in the south wall of the nave, presumably covering a grave, is believed to be 14th-century; a grave slab, incised with a floriated cross, which forms the interior sill of the south-east chancel window, seems to be earlier. New windows were inserted at various dates in the late 13th or earlier 14th century: one on the north side of the chancel and two on the south, and a pair on each side of the nave. The chancel's south-west window was a low-side window, with shutters at the bottom and two lights above. The head of the chancel piscina is the re-used head of a cusped lancet.

The porch was probably 14th-century; its bargeboards were apparently of that date. The nave door seems to have been replaced in the 14th or 15th century, with some of the earlier ironwork rearranged on it.[25] The embattled upper stage of the tower was added in the later 14th or 15th century. The nave benches seem late medieval, and wooden stalls for the portioners may have been provided in the chancel: 'ancient elbow chairs, richly carved' for the rector and deacon stood within the communion rail[26] in 1794; one of them had a late medieval misericord showing two wyverns fighting and two as supporters.[27] The stalls disintegrated and had been removed by *c.* 1840[28] but the misericord survives; it is by the same hand as the four in Enville church (Staffs.).[29] The late medieval nave roof, lower pitched than its predecessor, had king posts.[30] Two plain chests were noted in 1912, one medieval, the other 16th- or 17th-century, but both were missing by 1983.[31]

The upper stage of the tower appears to have been rebuilt in the 17th century. In 1915 there were three bells, of 1657 (by John Martin), 1666, and 1754 (by Abel Rudhall).[32] In the 17th century a communion rail was made round three sides of the table. A 17th-century chair inscribed 'IH' stands in the chancel. In the nave carved doors were added to some of the benches, and a low box pew was made east of them on each side. A richly carved double seat, made in the 16th or earlier 17th century, stood against the north wall of the nave in 1737. It was probably the Cressett (of the Coates) seat, banished from the chancel *c.* 1623,[33] or a replacement of it. Above the seat a wooden aedicule, described *c.* 1840 as at the 'north end of the Coates pew', frames a carving of the Cressett arms.[34] There seems never to have been a west gallery.[35] Singers or musicians probably used the rear bench on the north side of the nave, as at Langley chapel;[36] a desk

14 *Reg. Trillek*, 376, 407; *Reg. Mascall* (C.S.), 168, 181; *Reg. Boulers* (C.S.), 22; *Reg. Myllyng* (C.S.), 194; *Reg. Mayew* (C.S.), 281; *Reg. Bothe*, 333, 335; Le Neve, *Fasti, 1300–1541*: *Heref.* 9, 15–16, 25, 33, 39–40; *Welsh Diocs.* 32; Emden, *Biog. Reg. Oxf.*: *to 1500*, iii. 1941; *1500–40*, 601; *Reg. Langham*, 103.

15 P.R.O., C 3/399/150; S.P.L., MS. 2, ff. 145 and v., 146c.

16 Birm. Univ. Libr., Mytton Papers, iv. 752–3.

17 Bodl. MS. Top. Salop. c. 6, f. 29v.

18 P.R.O., SP 16/124, f. 165v.

19 Birm. Univ. Libr., Mytton Papers, iv. 749.

20 When a Trinitytide fair was granted: above, econ. hist.

21 Archit. hist. based on Birm. Univ. Libr., Mytton Papers, ii. 884v.; S.P.L., MS. 372, vol. i, f. 100; MS. 3065, no. 88; St. Deiniol's Libr., Hawarden, Sir Steph. Glynne's ch. notes, xc, ff. 9–10; Cranage, ii. 98–101; x. 992–3, 1028, 1056, 1063, 1077, 1091; Pevsner, *Salop.* 151–2. The Revd. I. E. Gibbs contributed valuable observations.

22 Inf. from Dr. J. Geddes; Eyton, iv, facing p. 70, probably from S.P.L., MS. 203, f. 32. A mid 19th-cent. drawing also shows a plain round-headed N. doorway at the W. end: Northants. R.O., Hartshorne colln. vol. xx, p. 24.

23 F. Bond, *Fonts and Font Covers* (1908), 51–5; *Eng. Romanesque Art 1066–1200*, ed. G. Zarnecki, J. Holt, and T. Holland (1984), p. 178.

24 St. Deiniol's Libr., Glynne's ch. notes, xc, f. 10; Cranage, ii. 99.

25 Inf. from Dr. Geddes.

26 W.S.L. 350/5/40, Castle Holdgate p. 11.

27 B.L. Add. MS. 21237, f. 55; G. L. Remnant, *Cat. of Misericords in Gt. Brit.* (1969), 133.

28 W.S.L. 350/5/40, Castle Holdgate p. 11.

29 Inf. from Mr. P. Klein; cf. *V.C.H. Staffs.* xx, pl. facing p. 113.

30 Cranage, ii. 99.

31 Inf. from Mr. Gibbs.

32 H. B. Walters, *Ch. Bells of Salop.* (Oswestry, 1915), 92.

33 Bodl. MS. Top. Salop. c. 6, ff. 22v.–24v.

34 W.S.L. 350/5/40, Castle Holdgate p. 11. For similar seats see Cranage, iv. 299; Pevsner, *Salop.* 107, 121.

35 No S. window to light a gallery in 1730s (Birm. Univ. Libr., Mytton Papers, ii. 884v.) or 1789 (S.P.L., MS. 372, vol. i, f. 100).

36 Cranage, vi. 496.

inscribed 'MC 1707' is fixed to the back of the next bench ahead. The royal arms on wood, dated 1753,[37] hang on the north wall of the nave. By 1793 the pulpit and communion table were described as new, and the church was ceiled over. There were then three pews in the chancel.[38]

The west end of the nave, unoccupied in 1793,[39] was later partitioned off as a schoolroom. The church was restored and repewed 1854–5 under the supervision of a Mr. Davies.[40] The ancient nave pews seem merely to have been refurbished. It was probably during the later 19th century that the communion rail was altered to span the chancel. The church was restored 1894–5 by St. Aubyn & Wadling: a chancel arch was inserted, windows renewed, the ceilings taken down, new roofs and porch built, and the western partition (latterly enclosing a vestry) removed.[41] It was probably then that the Cressett seat was moved to the south side of the nave.[42]

Twentieth-century additions included stained glass in the chancel's north lancet (*c.* 1930)[43] and east lancets,[44] and a carved wooden altar (*c.* 1922).[45]

The plate in 1793 was pewter except for a small cup.[46] In 1961 it consisted of a plated chalice and two plated patens.[47]

The registers[48] begin in 1660,[49] except for a single entry of 1651.

The churchyard contains the remains of a medieval cross; above the base only the top of the shaft and part of the cross remain, upside down and with a sundial of 1657 fixed on the broken end of the shaft.

NONCONFORMITY. Edward Cressett of the Coates was returned fit to be of the fifth Shropshire classis in 1647[50] and there were four recusant families in 1673, but no nonconformists were reported in 1676 or 1767.[51]

At Brookhampton a room in William Peck's farmhouse was licensed for Methodists in 1804.[52] Wesleyans continued to meet at Brookhampton until 1817.[53] By 1828 there was regular Primitive Methodist preaching at Brookhampton, then in the Hopton Bank circuit. The society had eight members in 1831.[54] In 1850 and 1851 Brookhampton was the head of a mission within the Ludlow circuit; it covered seven other places and comprised *c.* 70 members.[55] In 1853 worship was twice every Sunday.[56] The class had 15 members in 1863.[57] By 1898 Brookhampton's Primitive Methodists belonged to the society at Stanton Long,[58] where a chapel had been built in 1880.[59] The Haynes family had been prominent ever since the 1830s.[60]

EDUCATION. Probably from the early 19th century school was held in the west end of the church nave.[61] A church school, established as a dame school, opened in 1866. In 1876 Holdgate and Stanton Long National school, designed by F. R. Kempson, was built in red brick beside the church on land leased from the Revd. Henry Thursby-Pelham.[62] In 1876 fees were charged but 8 of the 40 pupils went free. The clergy sometimes taught the older pupils. Attendance averaged 31 in 1876.[63]

No teacher stayed long, and the school was understaffed by 1905; a young monitress taught the infants 1912–15.[64] There was never more than one schoolroom. Gardening was introduced before 1919.[65] In 1920–1, when attendance averaged only 21, the county council wished to close the school,[66] but the managers opposed it[67] and soon afterwards the neglected building was repaired.[68] In 1948 the school, with a roll of only 13, closed because it was impossible to obtain a permanent headmistress.[69] The building became a farm store. Pupils went to Diddlebury C.E. school, but from 1958 Holdgate children attended Brockton C.E. (Controlled) Primary school.[70]

CHARITIES FOR THE POOR. Robert Ellis of Earnstrey Park,[71] by will dated in or before 1652, gave a 10*s.* rent charge in Llanwyddelan parish (Mont.). The charity disappeared after 1820.[72] Several small capital sums, amounting to £14 10*s.* in 1671, yielded nothing by 1787 and the biggest, £5 given by Henry Fewtrell in 1661, had been lost.[73]

37 Date deciphered from named chwdns.' yr. of office: B.L. Add. MS. 21237, f. 56.
38 S.P.L., MS. 6865, p. 101.
39 Ibid.
40 S.R.O. 4131/Ch/1, s.a.; *P.O. Dir. Salop.* (1856), 59.
41 *Ch. Cal. Dioc. Heref.* (1896), 142–3; Cranage, ii. 98–9; x. 992; par. rec., acct. 24 Aug. 1899.
42 Cf. Cranage, ii. 98–9.
43 Heref. Dioc. Regy., reg. 1926–38, p. 249.
44 Inscr. on glass.
45 Heref. Dioc. Regy., reg. 1919–26, p. 186.
46 S.P.L., MS. 6865, p. 101.
47 D. L. Arkwright and B. W. Bourne, *Ch. Plate Archd. Ludlow* (Shrews. 1961), 33.
48 S.R.O. 4131/Rg/1; regs. in ch.
49 As do the bp.'s transcripts in H.W.R.O.(H.).
50 *T.S.A.S.* 3rd ser. vii. 268.
51 *Compton Census*, ed. Whiteman, 259; *Worcs. Recusant*, xxv. 34; liii. 28.
52 Heref. Dioc. Regy., reg. 1791–1821, f. 40v.
53 S.R.O. 5630/1/1.
54 S.R.O. 2941/2/1, 17 July 1828; /2/3, Dec. 1831.
55 S.R.O. 2612/22, 16 Dec. 1850–16 June 1851, 15 Sept. 1851.
56 S.R.O. 2138/61.
57 S.R.O. 3544/4/17.
58 Wm. Haynes of Brookhampton (*Kelly's Dir. Salop.* (1900), 105) was its steward: S.R.O. 2612/43.
59 Below, Stanton Long, nonconf.
60 S.R.O. 2138/61; 2612/17, pp. 89, 93; 2941/2/3.
61 Cranage, ii. 99.
62 P.R.O., ED 7/102, ff. 329–30; S.R.O. 1564/137.
63 P.R.O., ED 7/102, ff. 329–30; cf. managers' min. bk. *passim*, for causes of irregular attendance.
64 P.R.O., ED 7/102, ff. 329–30; *Kelly's Dir. Salop.* (1885), 862, and later edns.; managers' min. bk. *passim.*
65 Managers' min. bk. p. 165.
66 *S.C.C. Mins. (Educ.)* 1921–2, 10, 85.
67 Managers' min. bk. pp. 197–200.
68 Ibid. (at front) 1 Sept. 1922.
69 *S.C.C. Mins. (Educ.)* 1945–6, 75.
70 Inf. from Mr. R. J. Hartley, Holdgate Hall.
71 S.P.L., MS. 6865, p. 97.
72 *3rd Rep. Com. Char.* H.C. 5, p. 265 (1820), iv; cf. *Review of Local Chars.* (S.C.C. 1975).
73 *Char. Don. 1786–8*, ii, H.C. 511–II, pp. 1024–5 (1816), xvi (2).

BOULDON

UNTIL 1884 Bouldon, *c.* 11 km. north of Ludlow, was a detached township of Holdgate parish and had *c.* 417 a. (*c.* 169 ha.).[74] Until the late 11th century[75] it had probably been part of Diddlebury parish; ½ virgate was in that parish until the 15th century,[76] and 1⅔ a. of Bouldon village was in Diddlebury parish before 1884.[77] In that year the rest of Bouldon was transferred to Diddlebury civil parish.[78]

Bouldon township lies about *c.* 4.5 km. south of Holdgate village in a fold of the Clee plateau whence Pye (or Clee) brook drains west towards the river Corve. The township is roughly triangular, its apex to the south-east, with a narrow southward extension. The northern boundary followed a stream that descends to Pye brook at Peaton. The eastern and the higher part of the western boundary may have been drawn when the margins were still intercommoned, for there are some long unbroken lengths. On the Clee plateau the land rises to 235 m. in the east, and on Pye brook in the west falls to 130 m.[79] The higher parts of the township lie on the Ditton Series of the Lower Old Red Sandstone and the lower on the Ledbury Group of the Downton Series; where the series meet are two narrow layers of '*Psammosteus*' Limestones.[80] The soils are mostly red-brown silt loams, with alluvial soils on the west.[81]

There was a recorded population of 4 in 1086.[82] Bouldon village, strung out along Pye brook, seems to have changed little in extent since the 17th century; no outlying houses are known. Eight houses paid hearth tax in 1672, four having more than one hearth.[83] From the 1820s to the 1880s the population varied little from a median of 59.[84] In 1842 the houses extended *c.* 500 m. through the valley from Bank Farm in the east to the later Tally-Ho public house.[85] The houses and cottages are almost all 16th- or 17th-century plain structures of coursed stone rubble or of some mixture of stone, timber framing, and brick, with tiled roofs.[86] Farm buildings of similar period and materials survive at Bank Farm,[87] Bouldon Farm,[88] and Bouldon House.[89]

Several routes radiated from the village.[90] That on which most of the houses stood followed Pye brook west through Peaton and thence ran to Ludlow. It was turnpiked from Bouldon westwards in 1794,[91] disturnpiked in 1873,[92] and ceased to be a main road in 1879.[93] From the village lanes ran via Broncroft and Tugford to Holdgate, via the Heath to Bridgnorth[94] and to Cockshutford, and to Clee St. Margaret (via Peckledy) and Cold Weston. The lane to Clee and Cold Weston was no longer open to public wheeled traffic in 1989.

The Tally-Ho was licensed in 1844.[95]

MANOR. In 1066 Siward (Seward) and Almund (Elmund) held *BOULDON* as two manors. Helgot held it of Earl Roger by 1086,[96] and the chief lordship seems to have descended thereafter with that of Holdgate.[97]

By 1135 Bouldon had been subinfeudated. The tenant in 1166 was William of Bouldon,[98] and in 1199 Robert of Bouldon;[99] Robert was probably the tenant of that name recorded in 1205.[1] The tenant bore the same name *c.* 1242[2] and in 1255.[3] Hugh of Bouldon (perhaps fl. 1327)[4] was tenant by 1285[5] and in 1294,[6] and Giles Carles by 1348.

John Talbot, Lord Furnivalle, later earl of Shrewsbury (d. 1453), held Bouldon by 1428 and in 1431.[7] The manor later descended, through Sir Humphrey Talbot (d. 1493),[8] to John Grey, Viscount Lisle (d. 1504),[9] and thereafter followed the descent of Aston (in Munslow) until 1963,[10] except that Sir John

74 Area calculated from P.R.O., IR 29/29/161; O.S. Maps 1/2,500, Salop. LXV. 9, 13 (1903 edn.). This article was written in 1989.
75 Above, Holdgate, church.
76 Heref. D. & C. mun., chapter act bk. 1512–66 (folio), f. 217v.
77 P.R.O., IR 29/29/161; IR 30/29/161.
78 *Census*, 1891, ii. 652.
79 Fig. 13.
80 Geol. Surv. Map 1/50,000, solid, sheet 166 (1974 edn.).
81 Soil Surv. Map 1", sheet 166 (1972 edn.).
82 *V.C.H. Salop.* i. 338.
83 *Hearth Tax 1672*, (Salop. Arch. Soc. 1949), 178.
84 *V.C.H. Salop.* ii. 223. No later figs. available.
85 P.R.O., IR 30/29/161.
86 SA 10875–6, 16569, 16571–2, 16602–4.
87 SA 16568.
88 SA 10877–8; inf. from Mrs. M. Moran.
89 SA 16570.
90 Para. based on R. Baugh, *Map of Salop.* (1808); B.L. Maps, O.S.D. 206; O.S. Map 1", sheet LXI. SW. (1833 edn.); P.R.O., IR 30/29/161.
91 34 Geo. III, c. 123.
92 Ann. Turnpike Acts Continuance Act, 1872, 35 & 36 Vic. c. 85.
93 Local Govt. Bd.'s (Highways) Prov. Orders Conf. (Dorset, &c.) Act, 1879, 42 & 43 Vic. c. 85 (Local).
94 Below, the Heath, intro.
95 Co. of Salop, *Return of Licensed Hos. 1896* (copy in S.R.O., q. sess. rec. box 148), p. 84.
96 *V.C.H. Salop.* i. 338.
97 *Red Bk. Exch.* (Rolls Ser.), i. 276; *Abbrev. Plac.* (Rec. Com.), 48; *Rot. Hund.* (Rec. Com.), ii. 71, 100; *Feud. Aids*, iv. 224; *Cal. Inq. p.m.* iii. 124; below, local govt. Cf. above, Holdgate, manors.
98 *Red Bk. Exch.* i. 275–6.
99 *T.S.A.S.* 2nd ser. x. 314.
1 *Abbrev. Plac.* 48.
2 *Bk. of Fees*, ii. 965, 973.
3 *Rot. Hund.* ii. 71.
4 *T.S.A.S.* 2nd ser. iv. 297.
5 *Feud. Aids*, iv. 224.
6 *Cal. Inq. p.m.* iii, p. 124.
7 *Feud. Aids*, iv. 245, 251, 268.
8 *Cal. Inq. p.m. Hen. VII*, i, pp. 428–9.
9 P.R.O., SP 1/4, f. 15; *Complete Peerage*, viii. 61.
10 P.R.O., C 142/293, no. 70; C 142/448, no. 110; CP 40/1137, Carte rot. 8; IR 29/29/161; SP 1/4, f. 15; S.P.L., MS. 2, f. 135v.; S.P.L., Deeds 2537; S.R.O., q. sess. rec. parcel 281, reg. of papists' deeds 1717–88, pp. 16–17, 203, 249; parcel 261, reg. of gamekeepers 1799–1807, f. 148; S.R.O. 4440/2; *P.O. Dir. Salop.* (1879), 331; *Kelly's Dir. Salop.* (1909), 86; (1913), 88; (1941), 89. Cf. below, Munslow, manors.

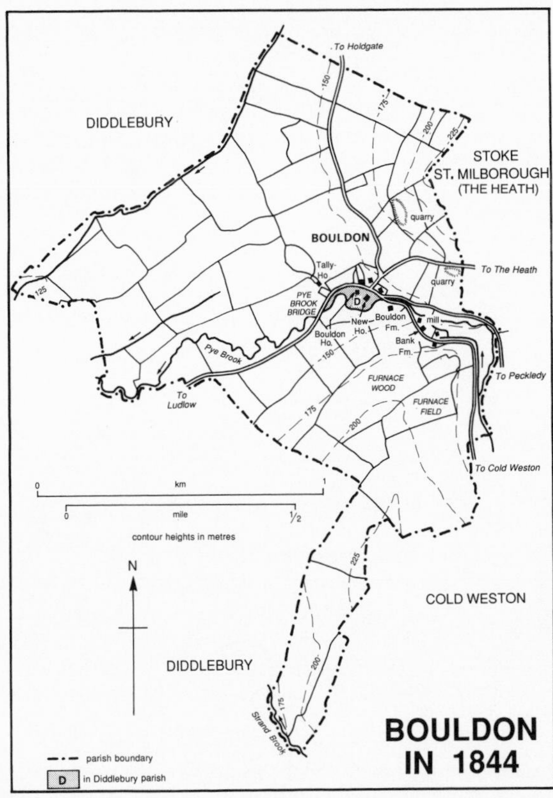

Fig. 13

Smith's widow Agnes (d. 1562) did not hold Bouldon.[11] G. M. G. Hamilton-Russell, Viscount Boyne, bought the manorial estate from the Church Commissioners in 1964[12] but retained only a part in 1992.[13]

The chief house in 1670[14] was called the Farm House in 1733,[15] and later Bouldon Farm.[16] Mainly of coursed rubble, with some timber framing, it contains a 16th-century hall of one bay, formerly open with a louvre in the roof and with a contemporary or near-contemporary cross wing at the east end, which had a smoke bay at the southern end. In the 17th century a 2½ storeyed cross wing was added to the west end, and the hall was probably converted to two storeys.[17]

A freehold belonging to Thomas Hawlyn in 1486[18] passed before 1530 to Richard Brecknock.[19] The farm, with 21 a. of arable, was called *HAWLYN'S HOUSE* in 1532.[20] Randle Brecknock sold it in 1578 to Maurice Ludlow (d. 1595),[21] who left it to his nephew William Baldwyn (d. *c.* 1614).[22] It descended from father to son[23] to Charles[24] (d. 1675), Sir Samuel[25] (d. 1683), Charles[26] (d. 1706), and Acton (d. 1727), from whom it passed to his brother Charles[27] (d. 1751). It was added to the manorial estate before 1842.[28]

ECONOMIC HISTORY. In 1086 Bouldon, with 2 hides and 3 ploughlands, and 2 ploughteams on the demesne, was worth 15*s.*, having earlier been found 'waste'; the demesne's four oxmen were the only recorded inhabitants.[29] The estate was valued at £4 6*s.* a year in 1295[30] and at £3 in 1431.[31] There was some woodland in the late 13th century.[32]

In the early 16th century the open fields were Cross, Flotmere, and Rye fields.[33] Some recent inclosure of arable, resulting in the loss of two farms, was reported in 1517.[34] Corn and barley were harvested on Charles Baldwyn's land in August 1618.[35] By 1733 only fragments of open-field land remained, as Crow pit and Withy pit fields, and Upper and Lower Rye fields. The manorial estate then comprised only two farms and the furnace. Bouldon farm (224 a.) had absorbed most of the other holdings, and their houses were occupied by the farmer's 'undertenants',[36] probably labourers.

By 1842, after the manorial estate had acquired that of the Baldwyns, Bouldon farm (288 a.) included Bouldon House and New House, both of which had substantial old farm buildings in 1989.[37] Each of the two farms of 1842 had twice as much grass as arable. The whole township was inclosed and only 3 a. were woodland.[38] By 1942 Bouldon farm had been reduced to 186 a. and Bank farm to two holdings of 41 a. and 33 a. But for recent wartime ploughing, their proportion of grass to arable would have been far greater than in 1842.[39]

A water mill on the manorial estate, mentioned in 1611,[40] was described as a muncorn mill in

11 P.R.O., C 142/132, no. 16.
12 Inf. from Ch. Com.
13 Inf. from the agent, Vct. Boyne Ests.
14 *T.S.A.S.* 4th ser. xi. 109.
15 S.P.L., Deeds 2538; S.R.O., q. sess. rec. parcel 281, reg. of papists' deeds 1717–88, p. 15; P.R.O., C 103/164, pt. 1, surv. of 1733, f. 38.
16 Cf. P.R.O., C 103/164, pt. 1, surv. ff. 38–43; IR 29/29/161.
17 Descr. based on inf. from Mrs. M. Moran.
18 Staffs. R.O., D.(W.) 1788, parcel 38, bdle. 11, deed.
19 Ibid. parcel 35, bdle. 11, deed.
20 Ibid. parcel 43, bdle. 8, deed.
21 Ibid. parcel 36, bdle. 10, deed; below, Shipton, manors (Moorhouse).
22 Staffs. R.O., D.(W.) 1788, will; *T.S.A.S.* 4th ser. ii. 149; P.R.O., C 142/346, no. 184.
23 For Baldwyn pedigree see *T.S.A.S.* 4th ser. ii. 133–85, 299–385, *passim.*
24 P.R.O., C 142/346, no. 184; Staffs. R.O., D.(W.) 1788, vol. 13.
25 Staffs. R.O., D.(W.) 1788, parcel 36, bdle. 4, deed 1675.
26 *T.S.A.S.* 4th ser. ii. 339, 344.
27 S.R.O., q. sess. rec. parcel 281, reg. of papists' deeds 1717–88, pp. 17, 203.
28 P.R.O., IR 29/29/161.
29 *V.C.H. Salop.* i. 338.
30 Eyton, v. 61.
31 *Feud. Aids*, iv. 268. Cf. P.R.O., C 140/488, no. 27.
32 *Select Bills in Eyre, A.D. 1292–1333* (Selden Soc. xxx), p. 31.
33 Staffs. R.O., D.(W.) 1788, parcel 43, bdle. 8, deed of 1532.
34 P.R.O., C 104/26, comrs.' return.
35 Staffs. R.O., D.(W.) 1788, vol. 13, f. 7.
36 P.R.O., C 103/164, pt. 1, surv. of 1733, ff. 38–43; S.P.L., MS. 6865, p. 96.
37 SA 16570–1, 16603.
38 P.R.O., IR 29/29/161; IR 30/29/161.
39 S.R.O. 4440/2, sched.
40 P.R.O. C 66/1921, m. 6.

1733.[41] It was presumably the mill that, by the late 18th century, stood at the east end of the village on a leat from Pye brook.[42] It was rebuilt in stone in the later 18th century[43] and ceased working in 1934.[44] Another water mill, on the Brecknock estate, was mentioned in 1570[45] and was presumably that called 'Mr. Legas's mill' in 1712[46] to distinguish it from the manorial mill held by the Crumpe family.[47] It had gone by 1842; the site was probably west of the village, near Old Mill meadow, where Pye and Strand brooks met at the boundary with Peaton township.[48]

An iron furnace at Bouldon was said to have been established by one of the Smiths, lords of the manor;[49] it was on the manorial estate by 1670.[50] In 1647 Sir William Blount had it,[51] presumably as tenant. William Hall was the lord's lessee from 1696 until 1702 or later, and Thomas Read from 1718. By 1721 Sir Edward Blount (d. 1758) was tenant, by 1761 Sir Edward Blount (d. 1765),[52] and by 1793 Sir Walter Blount.[53]

In 1643 Francis Walker, 'clerk of the furnace' until 1661 or later, a kinsman of Richard Cressett of Upton[54] (d. 1677) and lessee of the Bringewood ironworks (Herefs.),[55] was paid for making 63 tons of ordnance for the king, delivered from Bouldon to Bridgnorth and Shrewsbury. In 1644 he made a similar quantity, including a gun for the defence of Ludlow.[56] Presumably he worked the furnace under licence from the Blounts. It was supplied with cordwood from Ditton Priors and elsewhere, with ironstone from Brown Clee, and with Bouldon limestone.[57]

By the early 18th century the furnace produced mainly pig iron. Annual output was estimated at 400 tons in 1717.[58] Pig was supplied to forges as far away as Pool Quay (in Guilsfield, Mont.), Ffridd Mathrafal, Park Mathrafal (both in Llangynyw, Mont.),[59] and probably to the Blounts' forges at Cleobury Mortimer.[60] The furnace was alleged in 1737 and 1795 to produce the finest pig iron in England. In 1795 the lord offered it to let as a going concern,[61] and cordwood was being supplied in 1798,[62] but no later reference is known. The works was presumably on Pye brook and probably on a leat upstream of the village;[63] masonry and a large slag heap have been recorded next to the mill.[64]

The ironworks is believed to have become the paper mill,[65] near to Furnace field and Furnace wood in 1842.[66] Peter Medlicott was making paper at Bouldon by 1803, when his partnership with Henry Proctor, Thomas Green, and Thomas Lawley was dissolved, and still in 1816. By 1832 the paper mill was run by Simon Cox,[67] who still held it in 1842 as part of the later Bank farm; it was attached to the farmhouse on a leat from Pye brook.[68] By 1841 the paper makers were William Cox and William Baker.[69] Production had ceased by 1851.[70]

Of several quarries,[71] one in the earlier 19th century was north of the former furnace,[72] which it had probably supplied with limestone.[73] In 1774 Bouldon supplied stone for building Downton Castle (Herefs.)[74] and in the early 19th century was one of the best local sources of sandstone flags.[75] John Smallman of Bouldon Rock was a builder in 1811.[76] Bouldon was still producing 'considerable quantities' of building stone *c.* 1850.[77] Three masons lived there in 1841[78] but none in 1851.[79]

Richard Amies, who operated the furnace in the 1720s,[80] was also a timber dealer.[81] In 1841 there were a shoemaker, a sawyer, a blacksmith, and a wheelwright.[82]

LOCAL GOVERNMENT. By 1422 Bouldon was subject to the court of Holdgate barony.[83] In 1863 Holdgate manor court still appointed the Bouldon constable.[84]

As part of Diddlebury C.P. from 1884 Bouldon remained in the same poor-law union and highway, rural sanitary, and rural districts as

41 P.R.O., C 103/164, pt. 1, surv. f. 40.
42 P.R.O., IR 29/29/161; IR 30/29/161, field 430.
43 *Trans. Newcomen Soc.* xxxvi. 163.
44 *Shropshire Mag.* Feb. 1966, 29.
45 Staffs. R.O., D.(W.) 1788, parcel 36, bdle. 4, deed.
46 Bodl. MS. Top. Salop. c. 6, f. 66 (presumably ref. to Sebastian Legas, fl. 1698–1717: S.R.O., q. sess. rec. parcel 281, reg. of papists' deeds 1717–88, p. 16). John Legas held pt. of the Baldwyn (formerly Brecknock) est. in 1733: P.R.O., C 103/164, pt. 1, surv. f. 43.
47 P.R.O., C 66/1921, m. 6; S.R.O., q. sess. rec. parcel 281, reg. of papists' deeds 1717–88, p. 15; P.R.O., C 103/164, pt. 1, surv. f. 40.
48 P.R.O., IR 29/29/161; IR 30/29/161, fields 420–1.
49 Birm. Univ. Libr., Mytton Papers, iv. 753.
50 *T.S.A.S.* 4th ser. xi. 109.
51 R. T. Rowley, 'Hist. of S. Salop. Landscape' (Oxf. Univ. B.Litt. thesis, 1967), 170 n. For pedigree see G.E.C. *Baronetage*, ii. 202–3.
52 S.R.O., q. sess. rec. parcel 281, reg. of papists' deeds 1717–88, pp. 16, 202, 249; ibid. ff. 184–5.
53 S.P.L., MS. 6865, p. 96.
54 S.R.O. 1359, box 20, Thos. Martin to Ric. Holman 26 June 1661 (copy).
55 K. W. G. Goodman, 'Hammerman's Hill: Land, People, and Inds. of Titterstone Clee Area 16th to 18th Cents.' (Keele Univ. Ph.D. thesis, 1978), 106.
56 *Cal. S.P. Dom.* 1641–3, 488; 1644, 108; *V.C.H. Salop.* i. 473.
57 *Salopian Jnl.* 5 Aug. 1795; Birm. Univ. Libr., Mytton Papers, iv. 753.
58 *Trans. Newcomen Soc.* ix. 22.
59 S.R.O. 5403/7/7/4b.
60 Goodman, 'Hammerman's Hill', 107.
61 *Salopian Jnl.* 5 Aug. 1795; Birm. Univ. Libr., Mytton Papers, iv. 753.
62 *Shropshire Mag.* Feb. 1966, 29.
63 'Mill Race' on O.S. Map 1/2,500, Salop. LXV. 13 (1884 edn.).
64 S.R.O. 5403/7/7/2a; *Shropshire Mag.* Feb. 1966, 29.
65 Rowley, 'S. Salop. Landscape', 178–9.
66 P.R.O., IR 29/29/161; IR 30/29/161, fields 449, 452.
67 *T.S.A.S.* liii. 147, 149, 157.
68 P.R.O., IR 29/29/161; IR 30/29/161, field 443.
69 P.R.O., HO 107/912/22, ff. 5v., 6.
70 P.R.O., HO 107/1982, ff. 541–542v.
71 O.S. Map 1/2,500, Salop. LXV. 13 (1884 edn.).
72 O.S. Map 1", sheet LXI. SW. (1833 edn.); P.R.O., IR 29/29/161; IR 30/29/161, field 437.
73 *Salopian Jnl.* 5 Aug. 1795.
74 H.W.R.O.(H.), T 74/414, acct.
75 S.R.O. 4367/Ch/1, s.a. 1818–19; R. I. Murchison, *The Silurian System* (1839), i. 179.
76 W.B.R., Q2/1/3.
77 S. Bagshaw, *Dir. Salop.* (1851), 538.
78 P.R.O., HO 107/912/22, ff. 5v., 6v.
79 P.R.O., HO 107/1982, ff. 541–542v.
80 S.R.O., q. sess. rec. parcel 281, reg. of papists' deeds 1717–88, f. 185 and p. 202.
81 S.R.O. 5460/2/3/15–16.
82 P.R.O., HO 107/912/22, ff. 5v.–6v.
83 S.P.L., MS. 2, f. 146. Cf. above, Holdgate, local govt.
84 S.P.L., Deeds 10194.

Holdgate C.P.[85] and after 1967 in the same rural district and district as Tugford C.P. (1967–87) and Abdon C.P. thereafter.[86]

CHAPEL OF EASE. Bouldon was said in 1737 formerly to have had a chapel,[87] which was believed *c.* 1840 to have been at Bouldon Farm where burials had been found *c.* 1800 under the house and in the garden.[88] The inhabitants attended neighbouring churches[89] until an iron chapel of *ALL SAINTS*, by Croggon & Co., opened in 1873.[90] It was built at the rector of Holdgate's expense[91] on land provided by E. C. Wright.[92] In 1900 there was one service weekly.[93] The chapel was served from Holdgate until 1926 when Bouldon was transferred to the new ecclesiastical parish of Diddlebury with Bouldon,[94] and it remained in use in 1989.

NONCONFORMITY. The Smiths and the Wrights, lords of Bouldon, were Roman Catholics,[95] as were the Blounts, tenants of the furnace.[96] There were three Roman Catholic households in 1604, including those of Lewis Brecknock and Adam Crumpe,[97] and the Crumpe and Latchard families were papists in the late 17th century.[98] Later James and Isabella Blount were papists; they moved to Cleobury forge *c.* 1766,[99] and no papist was reported in 1767.[1]

The Hopton Bank Primitive Methodist circuit had preaching at Bouldon from 1828,[2] when John Jones's house was licensed;[3] the society had 21 members in 1831.[4] Bouldon was served by the Brookhampton mission of 1850–1[5] and the class had 20 members in 1863.[6] Primitive Methodists were still represented at Bouldon in 1909.[7]

EDUCATION. No evidence.

CHARITIES FOR THE POOR. Bouldon shared in Holdgate's charities.[8]

MUNSLOW

MUNSLOW parish lies along the north-west side of Corve Dale.[9] Aston Munslow, one of its two surviving villages, is on the principal road down the dale, *c.* 16 km. south-west of Much Wenlock and *c.* 10 north-east of Craven Arms. Munslow, the other village, is just over 1 km. north-east of Aston Munslow, and other smaller or shrunken settlements are strung out further to the north-east.

Until 1883 the parish's six townships comprised 3,545 a.[10] (1,435 ha.) and included two detachments, one to the north at Topley (101 a., 41 ha.), a part of Lower Millichope township surrounded by Eaton-under-Heywood parish, and the other to the south at Little Poston, a small township (343 a., 139 ha.) almost completely surrounded by Diddlebury parish.[11]

The two southern townships in the main part of the parish, Aston and Munslow, represented the Domesday manor of Aston[12] and probably a parish as originally formed out of Diddlebury parish: Aston's name records its geographical relation to Diddlebury whose parish surrounds Aston and Munslow townships on three sides[13] and may have done so completely.

Of the parish's three northern townships Lower Millichope was formed by the parochial division of the Domesday manor of Millichope *c.* 1115 when Wenlock priory's parochial rights over Upper Millichope were confirmed but Lower Millichope was assigned to Munslow parish.[14] It was presumably after the two estates were separated manorially, by subinfeudation, that *c.* 101 a. of woodland on Topley hill was allocated to Lower Millichope as common[15] and so eventually to Munslow parish. Millichope's parochial connexions before *c.* 1115 are uncertain.[16] Thonglands was a separate parish until its union with Munslow in 1442 and probably included Little Poston as a detached township.[17] In 1066 Broadstone was part of Stanway manor which was in the medieval parish of Rushbury; within the next twenty years, however, Broadstone became part of Shrewsbury abbey's

85 *Kelly's Dir. Salop.* (1885), 780; (1929), 4; S.R.O., q. sess. order bk. 1861–9, p. 127; *V.C.H. Salop.* ii. 215.
86 *V.C.H. Salop.* ii. 215; iii. 168, 179, and sources cited ibid. 169 n. 29.
87 Birm. Univ. Libr., Mytton Papers, iv. 753.
88 W.S.L. 350/5/40, Castle Holdgate p. 8. Ho. identified from P.R.O., IR 29/29/161; IR 30/29/161, field 428.
89 H.W.R.O.(H.), Heref. dioc. rec., bp.'s transcripts, Tugford; P.R.O., HO 129/352, no. 56.
90 *Ch. Cal. Dioc. Heref.* (1874), 100, 122.
91 *Kelly's Dir. Salop.* (1900), 104.
92 Heref. Dioc. Regy., reg. 1869–83, p. 186.
93 *Kelly's Dir. Salop.* (1900), 104.
94 Ibid. (1922), 111; (1926), 116; Heref. Dioc. Regy., reg. 1919–26, pp. 440–1.
95 S.R.O., q. sess. rec. parcel 281, reg. of papists' deeds 1717–88, pp. 17, 203, 249.
96 S.R.O., q. sess. rec. parcel 281, reg. of papists' deeds 1717–88, ff. 185, 261; above, econ. hist.
97 *Miscellanea*, ii (Cath. Rec. Soc. ii), 295. Cf. P.R.O., C 66/1921, m. 6.
98 *Worcs. Recusant*, liii. 28; *T.S.A.S.* 3rd ser. iii, p. *vi*; 4th ser. xi. 108 n.; S.R.O. 567, box 47, assoc. oath return.
99 *S.P.R. Rom. Cath.* 87–8.
1 *Worcs. Recusant*, xxv. 34.
2 S.R.O. 2941/2/1, 15 Nov. 1828.
3 Heref. Dioc. Regy., reg. 1822–42, p. 91.
4 S.R.O. 2941/2/3, Dec. 1831.
5 S.R.O. 2612/22, 16 Dec. 1850–16 June 1851, 15 Sept. 1851.
6 S.R.O. 3544/4/17.
7 S.R.O. 2612/17, p. 96.
8 Above, Holdgate, charities.
9 This article was written 1990–1.
10 Area given in *Census* (1891), plus Little Poston (below, Lesser Poston, intro.) and Topley (P.R.O., IR 30/29/229; O.S. Map 1/2,500, Salop. LXIV. 4 (1903 edn.)).
11 Figs. 14 and 29.
12 Below, manors.
13 Fig 3; below, churches.
14 Below, manors; below, Eaton-under-Heywood, manors.
15 Below, econ. hist.
16 Below, Eaton-under-Heywood, church.
17 Below, churches; below, Lesser Poston, intro.

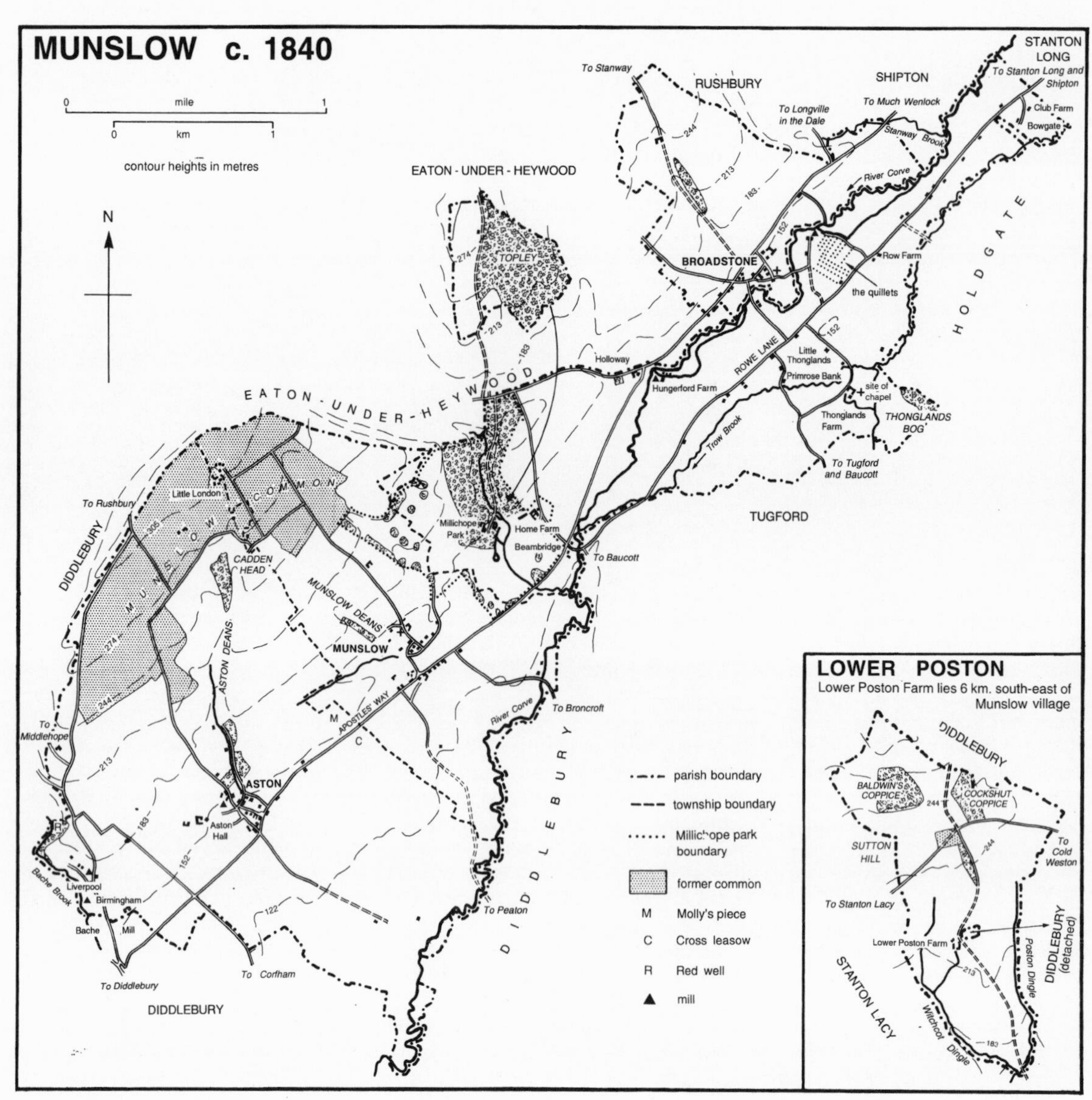

Fig. 14

possessions and was separated from Stanway.[18] Broadstone formed part of Munslow parish by 1589, but when and how it became part of the parish are unknown.[19]

West of Aston and Munslow townships the parish boundary runs mainly along the limestone ridge separating Hope Dale from Corve Dale, to the east along the river Corve. Further north the Corve marks the western parish boundary above and below Broadstone; the eastern boundary follows Trow brook except around Thonglands, where, however, a tributary of Trow brook marks part of it. Otherwise around Thonglands, Broadstone, and Topley and across the southern end of the parish the boundary follows artificial features, save for short stretches coinciding with minor streams.[20]

The main 19th-century changes to the civil parish were the transfers of detachments at Topley (1883) and Little Poston (1884) to Eaton-under-Heywood and Hopton Cangeford C.P.s respectively.[21] The area of Munslow C.P. was thus reduced to 3,101 a.[22] (1,255 ha.). In

18 Above, Rushbury, manors; below, manors.
19 Below, churches.
20 e.g. on Bache and Stanway brooks: cf. O.S. Maps 1/25,000, SO 48 (1957 edn.), 58–9 (1956 edn.); fig. 14.
21 *V.C.H. Salop*. ii. 225 n.
22 *Census* (1891).

1967 Munslow C.P. was enlarged by 450 ha. in Upper Millichope, Hungerford, and Topley taken from Eaton-under-Heywood C.P. and by *c.* 1 ha. from Holdgate C.P. At the same time the part of Bache Mill in Munslow was transferred to Diddlebury C.P. and another small area to Tugford C.P.[23] This article deals with the whole of the parish as it was in the earlier 19th century, apart from Lesser Poston, treated separately.[24]

The four townships west of the Corve have similar physical characteristics: they slope up from alluvial soils along the right bank of the river (*c.* 120 m.) to higher ground (up to *c.* 325 m. north of Little London) occupied historically by woods and commons. The settlements stand at *c.* 150 m., by springs and streams at the foot of shallow valleys (deans) cut through the Aymestry Group limestone and Upper Ludlow Shales that form the higher ground and supply the local building and road stone. South of Aston Munslow village and north-east of Thonglands Farm the geology is different, the drift consisting of red marls, cornstones, and sandstones of the Ledbury Group, while west and south of Thonglands Manor is Downton Castle Sandstone.[25]

Streams draining south and east into the Corve include Bache brook, so called in 1660,[26] Dean brook,[27] on which Munslow stands, Millichope brook,[28] and Stanway brook.[29] Trow brook flows south-west into the Corve near Thonglands, whose name may allude to the confluence.[30]

By 1653 and until the 19th century the road from Much Wenlock to Craven Arms and Ludlow, south-west of Munslow village and probably as far as the parish boundary, was known as the Apostles' Way.[31] It was turnpiked in 1756 and disturnpiked in 1867.[32] There were tollgates at Munslow and 1.3 km. north-east at Beambridge.[33] In the 18th century minor routes led south-east out of the road.[34] From Munslow Churley way[35] ran, perhaps past Marston,[36] to Corfham and Peaton, and a second route, via Brook House (presumably the Brook Hall of 1589),[37] ran to Baucott and Broncroft. Minor ways also led from Broadstone to Thonglands and Tugford, and from Beambridge to Baucott. North and west from the Wenlock–Ludlow road led the ways from Diddlebury to Middlehope via Bache Mill; from Beambridge and from Hungerford to Upper Millichope and Rushbury (the former a new road of *c.* 1835);[38] and from a point 1 km. north-east of Broadstone to Longville in the Dale, probably the Bromedge Way of 1662.[39] A supposed Roman road, believed to run from Greensforge (Staffs.) to central Wales[40] and known locally as Rowe Lane, originally ran from Shipton parish along the slight ridge between the Corve and Trow brook to Beambridge; it was the Bridgnorth–Munslow road *c.* 1575 and was probably known in the 17th century as Marsh, or Bowgate (or Bodgate or Bog gate), Lane;[41] its modern name derives from Cuckolds' Row, the usual name for the squatter settlement along it in the 18th and 19th centuries.[42] From Rowe Lane tracks ran south to Tugford and to Holdgate, the latter crossing Trow brook by Agnes bridge, so called in the 16th century.[43]

Finds of Neolithic and Bronze Age material, crop marks,[44] and perhaps the mound from which Munslow was named[45] supply evidence of prehistoric activity. A barrow may have been destroyed at Thonglands in 1827, and Gills hill (the Gill hill in 1685) in Aston village was conjectured in the early 19th century to be a British burial mound.[46]

In 1086 Aston manor had a recorded population of 22.[47] In 1327 subsidy was paid by 7 in Munslow (presumably including Aston), 6 in Broadstone, and 13 in Millichope (which, besides Lower Millichope, may have included Upper Millichope and Thonglands).[48] About 1490 Shrewsbury abbey had 10 tenants in Broadstone.[49] There was at least one house outside the parish's main settlements in the Middle Ages, at Red well on the western parish boundary, mentioned in 1267[50] and 1652–3.[51]

In 1676 the parish's adult population was 404;[52] 82 houses then paid the parish rate, 9 more than in 1663. Settlement in Broadstone (*c.* 8 ratepaying houses in 1676) and Lower Millichope (3) seems to have continued small in scale. Aston (27 ratepaying houses), Munslow (20), and Thonglands (*c.* 24) townships provided most of the increase; although the Thonglands figure probably included part of Hungerford (a settlement mainly in Eaton-under-Heywood parish), there had been some recent cottage building in Thonglands. Larger houses were

23 *Salop (No. 2) Order 1966* (Stat. Instr. 1966, no. 1529); S.R.O., DA 19/701/6, maps 40–2.
24 Below.
25 Inst. Geol. Sciences Map 1", drift, sheet 166 (1967 edn.).
26 Glam. R.O., CL/Deeds II, no. 7590.
27 S.R.O. 1705/29.
28 W.S.L. 350/5/40, Munslow p. 1.
29 S.P.L., Deeds 9718, s.a. 1665.
30 i.e. the element *tang* (forceps) or possibly *tweonga* (something pinched): inf. from Dr. M. Gelling.
31 W.S.L. 350/5/40, Munslow pp. 7–8; Glam. R.O., CL/Deeds I/Salop., 1652/3, Jan. 15; CL/Deeds II, no. 7591.
32 Below, Stanton Long, intro.
33 O.S. Map 1", sheet LXI. SW. (1833 edn.); S.P.L., SC5/48; tollho. photo.
34 J. Rocque, *Map of Salop.* (1752); R. Baugh, *Map of Salop.* (1808); B.L. Maps, O.S.D. 206–7; S.R.O. 1705/26.
35 So called in 16th cent.: H.W.R.O.(H.), HD 2/14/50–1; cf. S.R.O. 1705/25–6, field 774.
36 SA 991.
37 S.R.O. 1705/29.
38 Below, manors (Lr. Millichope).
39 S.R.O. 1037/21/187.
40 *T.S.A.S.* lvi. 233–43.
41 *S.P.R. Heref.* xv (2), 90; S.P.L., Deeds 6373; S.R.O. 356, box 327, surv. of 1657; below, Stanton Long, intro.
42 Below, this section.
43 S.R.O. 356, box 327, 16th-cent. surv.
44 SA 631, 2161, 2163, 2176, 3207, 3210.
45 *P.N. Salop.* (E.P.N.S.), i. 215–16.
46 W.S.L. 350/5/40, Munslow pp. 10, 16; S.R.O. 3614/3/32. Neither location is identifiable.
47 *V.C.H. Salop.* i. 322.
48 *T.S.A.S.* 2nd ser. iv. 298, 331, 338.
49 S.P.L., Holy Cross par. rec., Shrews. abbey rental, dated from H. Owen and J. B. Blakeway, *Hist. Shrews.* (1825), ii. 532.
50 Eyton, v. 142.
51 Glam. R.O., CL/Deeds I, Salop., 1652/3, Jan. 15.
52 *Compton Census*, ed. Whiteman, 259. The fig. presumably includes Little Poston; others in this para. do not.

concentrated in Aston and Munslow, particularly the latter.[53] By then there were squatters in Aston wood, later a hamlet known as Bache Mill, parts of which were called Liverpool and Birmingham;[54] at Broadstone; in Millichope wood; and on Munslow common, a settlement known by the 1840s as Little London.[55] Building of the cottages later known as Cuckolds' Row had begun by the mid 17th century,[56] and there were *c.* 20 in the 1840s.[57]

The population, 610 in 1801, rose to a peak of 767 in 1851 and fell to 475 in 1901 as cottages were demolished and multiple occupation declined.[58] Broadstone village shrank considerably in the century after 1770, a change to which the late inclosure of open-field land may have contributed. Half a dozen houses with their outbuildings were demolished, and the network of lanes serving them fell into disuse. One or two new cottages were built and, beyond the old village to the north-east, Broadstone Farm (*c.* 1800) with modern buildings.[59] Cottages were also abandoned along Cuckolds' Row, at least six being demolished between 1843 and 1891.[60]

The population and number of dwellings continued to fall until the mid 20th century.[61] Thereafter the attractions of rural residence for those who could afford a car halted the population decline and led to the renovation of dilapidated buildings and the construction of new houses (especially in Aston Munslow) for newcomers. Other and less welcome changes were the closure of shops and businesses and the loss of bus services.[62]

Aston Munslow and Munslow villages, roughly equal in size by *c.* 1990,[63] and what is left of Broadstone village exhibit similar characteristics, though Munslow may have developed as a settlement later than the others.[64] All stand away from the main road, with buildings widely spread and served by networks of lanes, tracks, and footpaths. In Munslow lanes loop round a spur of ground called Castle Hill in 1834 and the Rock in the later 20th century.[65] Part of it was common called the village green, inclosed and sold in 1847.[66]

A cottage at Hungerford has a cruck truss.[67] Where other buildings in the parish[68] retain 17th-century and earlier elements much of the work is box framed, as at Thonglands Farm, the Crown inn and the Chains in Munslow village and the White House, Lower Farm, the Swan inn, Tudor Cottage, Arbour Cottages (dated 1632), and numbers 8–9 in Aston Munslow. Aston Hall, probably the parish's most important house in the 16th and 17th centuries, is stone. So, externally, is the Old School House in Munslow, a fine **L** shaped house with stone mullioned and transomed windows, built in 1658 apparently for John Baldwin (d. 1680) and his wife Abigail; Baldwin's will mentions the wainscot chamber over the buttery.[69] In the 18th and 19th centuries stone, readily got in the parish, became almost ubiquitous, both for superior houses, such as the new rectory (before 1793) and Miller House (probably *c.* 1799) in Munslow and Hungerford Farm (*c.* 1800), and for farm buildings and squatters' cottages.

Before the mid 19th century brick was rarely used, though it can be seen in a 17th-century range at Munslow Farm, in the mid 18th-century Crown inn, Munslow, and in Little Thonglands, a small, polite 18th-century building. Thereafter brick became commoner, being used to extend and raise cottages.

Stone, however, was consistently employed in the 1830s in a wholesale rebuilding programme in the Greek style on the Millichope Park estate. Most of the buildings have raised pilasters to their principal elevations, as on the north lodge to the park. The most ambitious scheme was Home Farm, remodelled *c.* 1836[70] around the sides of a courtyard on whose fourth side is a free-standing kennels block surmounted by a cupola. Nearby at Beambridge a polite building of four bays and two storeys with a low hipped roof was constructed; at least part of it probably served as the Millichope Park laundry, the whole being called the Old Laundry in the 20th century. A row of cottages (1838), with a projecting and pedimented central bay, stands to the north-east. Also at Beambridge is a gothick smithy once surmounted by a crenellated parapet;[71] it is unlike the other buildings in style and may be of a slightly different date.

Alesellers at Aston Munslow, Munslow, and Thonglands were licensed in the 17th century.[72] In the 18th and early 19th century the main, and long the only, public houses were the Crown at Munslow and the Swan at Aston Munslow, both licensed in 1790[73] and open two centuries later. The Crown may once have been the 'court house' of Munslow hundred,[74] while the Swan was also known as the

53 S.R.O. 1705/43, s.a. 1663, 1676–7; *Hearth Tax 1672* (Salop. Arch. Soc. 1949), 39, 173–5. For Hungerford, below, manors; Eaton-under-Heywood, manors; for Thonglands, below, this section.

54 S.R.O. 1705/26.

55 *S.P.R. Heref.* xv (2), 69, 75, 77, 80, 82–3, 85, 87, 91–2, 94; *Orders of Q. Sess.* i. 6, 9, 72; S.R.O. 3614/3/16; S.P.L., Deeds 9712, ct. r. 28 Oct. 1702.

56 Glos. R.O., D2153/J/8; S.R.O. 4131/Rg/2, 24 June 1705.

57 S.R.O. 1705/25–6.

58 *V.C.H. Salop.* ii. 225, 232.

59 R.C.H.M.E. draft field rep. (1986); S.P.L., MS. 2481, map XI; S.R.O. 1705/25–6; O.S. Map 1/2,500, Salop. LXV. 1 (1884 edn.).

60 S.R.O. 1705/25–6; O.S. Maps 6", Salop. LVII. SW.; LXV. NW. (1891 edn.).

61 *V.C.H. Salop.* ii. 225.

62 Local inf.; *The Observer*, 20 Mar. 1994, news p. 3.

63 Cf. O.S. Maps 1/2,500, SO 5086–5186, 5287–5387 (1973 edn.); S.R.O. 2893/1, pp. 431–4; elect. reg. S. Salop. Dist. (1991), AX3.

64 Above, Munslow Hundred (*part*); below, churches.

65 S.P.L., MS. 201, f. 55; inf. from Revd. I. E. Gibbs. There is no evidence of a castle.

66 W.S.L. 350/5/40, Munslow p. 6; S.R.O., incl. award C 6/54.

67 No. 21: inf. from Mrs. M. Moran.

68 For what follows cf. Dept. of Environment, *List of Bldgs.: R. D. of Ludlow* (1974), 209–16.

69 Date stone; *T.S.A.S.* 4th ser. ii. 175–7.

70 *Country Life*, 10 Feb. 1977, 313.

71 N.B.R., photo.

72 S.R.O., q. sess. rec., parcel 254, badgers', drovers', and alesellers' licensing bk.

73 Ibid. parcels 255–9, regs. of alesellers' recognizances 1753–1828; Co. of Salop, *Return of Licensed Hos. 1896* (copy in S.R.O., q. sess. rec., box 148), pp. 80, 82, 86.

74 W.S.L. 350/5/40, Munslow p. 7.

Hundred House,[75] probably from meetings of the Lower Munslow divisional magistrates there.[76] Two other public houses had long lives: the Seven Stars north-east of Broadstone, open by 1851 and still in 1941, and the Butcher's Arms at Primrose Bank in Thonglands, open by 1851 and until *c.* 1920.[77]

In the early 19th century[78] it was apparently still within recollection that banners, including the 'great banner' of the Crucifixion and of St. Michael (patron of the church), were borne in annual procession from Munslow village along the Apostles' Way[79] to the Aston boundary: there the banner of the Cross was fixed to the fence of Cross leasow,[80] a well beside the road (in Molly's piece) was dressed, and refreshments were enjoyed. Beyond Aston, on the western edge of the parish, was another holy well, a healing well called Red (or Red Wall) well from the local soil colour; still in the mid 18th century the cured hung up their crutches nearby.

A Sunday bear-baiting was presented in 1606.[81] Munslow common was hunted over in the 1820s,[82] and wakes may have been held there.[83] There were 70–100 members of friendly societies living in the parish in the early 19th century,[84] and in the 1840s and later Munslow had a cricket club.[85] In 1847, at the inclosure of Munslow common, 4 a. near Little London were allotted as a recreation ground;[86] it was sold in 1968 and deregistered as common in 1973.[87] When a youth club was formed in the late 1940s the Millichope estate made a converted cowshed available; in due course it became the parish hall, known as Beambridge club room.[88]

Four Parliamentarian troopers were buried at Munslow in 1645 after Royalists had forced the Parliamentarians' abandonment of Broncroft castle.[89]

Besides members of the Lyttelton (or Littleton) family,[90] notable people connected with the parish were Richard Baldwin (1616–89), a Paracelsian physician whose nephew Richard Baldwin (licensed 1674) and grandson Edward Baldwin (licensed 1702) also practised medicine locally,[91] and Samuel Pountney Smith (1812–83), architect, who was a native.[92]

MANORS AND OTHER ESTATES. In 1066 Almund (Elmund) held *ASTON*. An extensive manor of 8½ hides, it was held in chief at Domesday by Roger of Montgomery, cr. earl of Shrewsbury in 1068, from whom the sheriff Reynold of Bailleul then held it.[93] The earl's tenancy in chief ended in 1102,[94] and by 1115 the sheriff's interest had ceased too.[95]

Aston, which included Munslow,[96] was held in chief by Richard Banastre in 1115. Richard's son and heir Thurstan Banastre (fl. *c.* 1150) was succeeded as tenant in chief by his daughter Maud, wife of William de Hastings (d. by 1182). She had the lordship until her death *c.* 1222 when it passed to their son William (d. *c.* 1225). William's son Sir Henry[97] held Aston and Munslow in chief as ¼ knight's fee by 1243.[98] From him (d. 1250) the tenancy in chief appears to have descended from father to son through Sir Henry, at first a minor[99] (d. *c.* 1269), Sir John[1] (Lord Hastings 1290, d. 1313), John, Lord Hastings[2] (d. 1325), Lawrence, Lord Hastings (cr. earl of Pembroke 1339, d. 1348), and John, earl of Pembroke[3] (d. 1375), to John, earl of Pembroke, who died childless in 1389. It seems likely that the tenancy in chief was afterwards disputed. Under a settlement of 1372 it should have passed to William Beauchamp, Lord Bergavenny, a kinsman of the last John, earl of Pembroke;[4] Beauchamp had the advowson of Munslow church by 1396.[5] Nevertheless Reynold, Lord Grey of Ruthin, Pembroke's heir general,[6] was named as tenant in chief of Aston in 1401.[7] It seems that by then a compromise had been reached, involving separation of the tenancies in chief of Aston and Munslow.[8]

The tenancies in chief may have been the more easily separated *c.* 1400 because Aston and Munslow had been separately subinfeudated since the mid 13th century or earlier. In the 1160s, Aston and Munslow may have been held together in fee, under Maud de Hastings, by

75 S. Bagshaw, *Dir. Salop.* (1851), 541; *S.P.R. Heref.* xv (2), p. iv, probably implying too early a date for the name.

76 e.g. in 1825 (S.R.O., q. sess. rec. parcel 259, reg. of alesellers' recognizances 1822–8, s.a.) and perh. the mid 19th cent. (sources in previous note).

77 S. Bagshaw, *Dir. Salop.* (1851), 541–2; *P.O. Dir. Salop.* (1856–79); *Kelly's Dir. Salop.* (1885–1941); O.S. Map 6" LXV. NW. (1903 edn.) for locations.

78 W.S.L. 350/5/40, Munslow pp. 7–8, confounds the ann. procession with an acct. of Red well, which topog. evidence shows to be distinct.

79 Above, this section.

80 S.R.O. 1705/25–6, fields 7, 753–4; cf. fig. 14.

81 *Salop.* (R.E.E.D.), i. 116–17.

82 *V.C.H. Salop.* ii. 173.

83 S.R.O. 1705/25–6, 'wake' names in fields 51, 57.

84 *Poor Law Abstract*, H.C. 82, pp. 372–3 (1818), xix.

85 *V.C.H. Salop.* ii. 195; *Kelly's Dir. Salop.* (1885), 901; *The Observer*, 20 Mar. 1994, news p. 3.

86 S.R.O. 3043/1. Cf *V.C.H. Salop.* iv. 176–7.

87 Inf. from S.C.C. Chief Exec.'s Dept.

88 Inf. from Dr. S. M. Williams, Baucott; S.C.C. Ch. Exec.'s dept., chars. index.

89 *S.P.R. Heref.* xv (2), 86; W. J. Farrow, *Gt. Civil War in Salop. (1642–9)* (1926), 88.

90 Sir Thos. Lyttelton (d. 1481), the jurist (*D.N.B.*), who held the man. *jure uxoris*; Ld. Keeper Littleton (d. 1645), a native; and his grandson Speaker Littleton (d. 1710), ld. of the man.: below, manors (Munslow).

91 *T.S.A.S.* l. 95–104; cf. ibid. 4th ser. ii. 170–1. Ric.'s grandson, rather than Ric.'s son (the Revd. Edw., d. 1709), is taken to be the licenciate of 1702.

92 *Shrews. Jnl.* 7 Nov. 1883, p. 5 (obit.).

93 *V.C.H. Salop.* i. 322.

94 Ibid. iii. 9–10.

95 Eyton, v. 130, giving a different explanation from that offered above, Munslow Hundred (*part*).

96 Names used together and interchangeably in sources of 13th–15th cents.

97 Eyton, v. 130–3, 135, 137–40. For Hastings pedigree, etc., see *Complete Peerage*, vi. 345–51.

98 *Bk. of Fees*, ii. 964.

99 *Rot. Hund.* (Rec. Com.), ii. 71; cf. *Complete Peerage*, vi. 345; Eyton, iii. 108.

1 *Feud. Aids*, iv. 223.

2 Claimed advowson of Munslow: *Reg. Orleton* (C.S.), 322.

3 *Cal. Inq. p.m.* xiv, p. 154.

4 *Cal. Close*, 1374–7, 286–8; *Complete Peerage*, i. 24 notes b–c.

5 *Reg. Trefnant* (C.S.), 181.

6 *Complete Peerage*, vi. 155.

7 *Cal. Inq. p.m.* xviii, p. 192.

8 Below, this section (Munslow).

Robert son of Waukelin, who forfeited his lands for his part in the rebellion of 1173, but whose widow Amice retained an interest in Munslow as late as 1199.[9]

The tenant in chief of Aston in 1428 was Sir John Talbot, Lord Furnivalle,[10] cr. earl of Shrewsbury in 1442. He died in 1453[11] and under a settlement of 1452 his tenancy in chief descended successively to his sons Sir Lewis (d. by 1458) and Humphrey (later Sir Humphrey).[12] It seems afterwards to have merged in the terre tenancy, which Humphrey acquired in 1463.[13]

Aston was subinfeudated by the mid 13th century, when Adam Hertwell's son John was terre tenant. By 1255 Aston had passed to John's heir, a minor in the custody (during his overlord's minority) of Geoffrey of Lusignan.[14] By 1284 Adam Hertwell was in possession.[15] John Hertwell was lord in 1348[16] and Richard Hertwell in 1375 when he was leasing the manor to John FitzWarin,[17] allegedly descended from the FitzWarins of Whittington by an illegitimate line.[18] FitzWarin acquired the freehold before his death in 1401 and his son William succeeded.[19] In 1463 Edward FitzWarin quitclaimed it to the overlord Humphrey Talbot.[20]

From Sir Humphrey (d. 1493)[21] Aston descended successively to his grand-nephew John Grey, Viscount Lisle (d. 1504),[22] and to Lisle's daughter and heir Elizabeth, Lady Lisle and countess of Devon[23] (d. 1519). In 1529 it was held by Sir Arthur Plantagenet, Viscount Lisle, second husband of the countess of Devon's aunt and heir Elizabeth. In 1529 Lady Lisle's son (by her first husband) Sir John Dudley sold his reversionary interest in the manor to Sir John Alleyn, who sold it next year to John Smith,[24] a baron of the Exchequer from 1539.[25] Smith (kt. by 1541)[26] presumably came into possession on Viscount Lisle's death in 1542.

Smith's widow Agnes (d. 1562)[27] had Aston,[28] and from her it descended with Wootton Wawen (Warws.) until 1758,[29] except that Aston passed directly to Sir Francis Smith in 1605,[30] and that Charles Carington (or Smith), Viscount Carrington (d. 1706), was evidently succeeded by his cousin's son[31] Francis Smith (d. 1721),[32] who was succeeded by his son[33] Francis Smith (or Carington),[34] to whom Wootton passed in 1748.

Aston is presumed to have descended from William Smith (d. 1758)[35] to his grand-nephew John Wright, in possession by 1787,[36] perhaps through John's mother, Mrs. Constantia Holford.[37] John died in 1792 and was succeeded by his son John[38] (d. 1826); the latter's grandson and heir J. F. Wright (d. 1868) was in possession by 1843[39] and was followed by his nephew E. C. Wright.[40] In 1911 Wright sold Aston Hall and 100 a. to P. G. Holder, who sold that property next year to J. I. Benson. In 1978 Maj. D. Benson sold the Hall and 13 a. to R. N. Broad. Broad sold it in 1985 to Cdr. J. L. Skinner, who sold it in 1988 to Mr. and Mrs. P. A. G. Cressall.[41]

Aston Hall[42] is a stone **H** plan building, but a two storeyed porch gives the front (south-eastern) elevation a symmetrical **E** shaped appearance. Timber framing in the north-east wing—large jowled posts and parts of the roof—and a break-back at the south-west corner indicate the incorporation of a timber-framed building to the west when the Hall was built, perhaps *c.* 1665; a skewed stack may be later. The plan, a widespread use of panelling and bolection moulding, and the quality of the principal staircase all suggest the intention to create a substantial and superior gentleman's house. So too do the three gardens, walled in brick (with some diaper work) and partly terraced, and the household's stables at one end of a threshing barn, both perhaps contemporary with the remodelling of the house.

After the sale of Aston Hall in 1911 E. C. Wright retained 661 a. at Aston and *c.* 1914 he sold that property too to P. G. Holder.[43] In 1942 Holder sold it to the Ecclesiastical Commissioners,[44] and in 1963 the Church Commissioners sold Lower Aston Farm, 244 a. of a small estate that John Smith had owned in 1843.[45] The farmhouse is a late 16th-century **L** shaped timber framed building of two storeys; the south-east wing has an overhanging gabled end.

There were Stedmans at Aston by the 15th

9 Eyton, v. 140–1.
10 *Feud. Aids*, iv. 250, 268.
11 *Complete Peerage*, xi. 702.
12 P.R.O., C 139/179, no. 58 (25); *Cal. Inq. p.m. Hen. VII*, i, pp. 428–9; *Index of P.C.C. Wills, 1383–1558*, ii (Index Libr. xi), 517.
13 Below, this section.
14 *Rot. Hund.* ii. 71; Eyton, v. 49, 141.
15 *Feud. Aids*, iv. 223.
16 Ibid. 245.
17 *Cal. Inq. p.m.* xiv, p. 154.
18 S.P.L., MS. 2788, p. 406.
19 *Cal. Inq. p.m.* xviii, p. 192; *Cal. Close*, 1399–1402, 457.
20 *Cal. Close*, 1461–8, 177.
21 *Cal. Inq. p.m. Hen. VII*, i, p. 428.
22 For Lisle peerages see *Complete Peerage*, viii. 55–68.
23 P.R.O., SP 1/4, f. 15.
24 P.R.O., CP 40/1137, Carte rot. 8.
25 *L. & P. Hen. VIII*, xiv (2), p. 30.
26 W. A. Copinger, *Hist. and Rec. of Smith-Carington Fam.* (1907), 123.
27 *V.C.H. Warws.* iii. 198.
28 P.R.O., C 142/132, no. 16.
29 P.R.O., C 142/448, no. 110; CP 25/2/713/26 & 27 Chas. II Hil. [no. 13]. Cf. *V.C.H. Warws.* iii. 197–9.
30 P.R.O., C 142/293, no. 70; C 142/448, no. 110.
31 *Complete Peerage*, iii. 66–7; Burke, *Land. Gent.* (1925), 291, where Fra. is identifiable as Cath. Southcote's husb. (*S.P.R. Heref.* xv (2), 176).
32 S.R.O., q sess. rec. parcel 281, reg. of papists' deeds 1717–88, p. 17; *S.P.R. Heref.* xv (2), 177.
33 Burke, *Land. Gent.* (1925), 291.
34 P.R.O., C 103/164, pt. 2, rent r. of 1745–6.
35 *V.C.H. Warws.* iii. 199.
36 P.R.O., CP 43/817, rot. 50.
37 Cf. *V.C.H. Warws.* iii. 199. She is called Cath. there but Constantia in Burke, *Land. Gent.* (1894), ii. 2275; cf. ibid. 2275–6, Wright pedigree.
38 S.R.O. 515/4, p. 288.
39 S.R.O. 1705/25–6.
40 S.R.O., electoral reg. S. Divn. (1874), p. 116. Cf. *V.C.H. Essex*, iv. 66.
41 Deeds in possession of Mr. and Mrs. Cressall.
42 Descr. based on rep. by Mrs. M. Moran; H. E. Forrest, *Old Hos. of Wenlock* (Shrews. 1914), 65, and pl. facing p. 1.
43 S.R.O. 4011/46, nos. 206, 331–2; *S.P.R. Heref.* xv (2), p. iv.
44 S.R.O. 4440/2.
45 Inf. from Ch. Com.; S.R.O. 1705/25–6.

century.[46] In the 17th century one line lived in a house at the Bank, not now identifiable. Perhaps the main line lived, by the 16th century, at a house known by 1648 as the White House.[47] John Stedman (d. 1804) left the White House to his nephew Thomas Smith, who had *c.* 415 a. in 1808.[48] Smith's descendants lived there until 1945 when A. H. Davies bought it;[49] he sold it to Walter Purser in 1947.

The oldest part of the White House[50] would seem to be a three bayed range of mixed cruck and box frame construction. A dovecot too may be medieval.[51] In the late 16th century a cellared, box framed west wing was added, perhaps in place of a pre-14th-century range. The 17th century saw a first floor and chimney inserted in the medieval range and perhaps its casing in stone. In the late 18th century the house was modernized, refronted, and extended to the west. Walter Purser's daughter Jessie Constance, who formed a museum of country life there and opened it to the public from 1965 to *c.* 1986, gave the house to the Landmark Trust in 1990.[52]

Land owned by the Ludlow Palmers' guild passed in 1552 to Ludlow corporation which had 13 a. at Aston in 1562[53] and 10 a. in 1843.[54] Vested in the trustees of Edward VI's charity, Ludlow, in 1846, the land was sold after 1876.[55]

The tenancy in chief of *MUNSLOW* may have been separated from that of Aston *c.* 1400, for William Beauchamp, Lord Bergavenny, is said to have sold what was probably the tenancy in chief to John Burley, Reynold, Lord Grey of Ruthin's brother-in-law.[56] Burley also acquired the terre tenancy of the manor, and the tenancy in chief presumably merged with it.

Munslow had been subinfeudated by 1255, when the terre tenants, evidently coparceners, were John de Chandurs, Nicholas Seymour, and Ermyntrude, a daughter of John Hertwell, son of John Hertwell, the late terre tenant of Aston. They held Munslow of a mesne lord, William de Venables, whose tenure was evidently resumed by the chief lord before 1285. Ermyntrude's daughter Agnes conveyed her share to Seymour and his wife Alice. Seymour predeceased Alice, who was in sole possession of their Munslow estate by 1285. She conveyed it to Robert de Beke and his wife Maud, Ermyntrude's sister;[57] Robert and Maud presumably possessed John de Chandurs's share, for by 1316 Robert was sole lord of Munslow.[58] Maud predeceased him *c.* 1324[59] and by 1348 his son Nicholas de Beke (kt. 1348, d. 1369) was lord.[60] Sir Nicholas's heir was his daughter Elizabeth, who married and predeceased Sir Robert Swynnerton (d. 1386).[61] After Swynnerton's death Munslow seems to have passed to their daughter and heir Maud Peshall.[62] Maud's second husband (from *c.* 1388) was William Ipstones (d. 1399),[63] whose father Sir John (d. 1393) had Munslow manor, apparently as Maud's feoffee.[64] After William's death Maud may have had only a third of Munslow; in 1404 she and her third husband John Savage conveyed a third of the advowson to John Burley,[65] tenant in chief of the manor. The other two thirds of the manor may have passed in 1399 to William's daughters and coheirs Christine and Alice[66] and were apparently later acquired by Burley.

By 1428 John Burley's son William (d. 1458) was in sole possession.[67] Munslow passed to William's daughters, Sir Thomas Trussell's wife Elizabeth and Sir Thomas Lyttelton's wife Joan. The Trussells' share descended with Acton Trussell (Staffs.) until 1552 when John de Vere, earl of Oxford,[68] sold his moiety of Munslow manor to John Stringfellow.[69] In 1553 Stringfellow sold it to John Littleton,[70] rector.

Lady Lyttelton died a widow in 1504 and her moiety then passed to her son Sir William Lyttelton of Frankley[71] (d. 1507) and then to his son John[72] (d. 1532), who left it to his son John.[73] The last named had the moiety in 1556,[74] but it was soon acquired by his cousin John Littleton (d. 1560), former rector and the owner of the other moiety, who left the whole manor to his son Thomas (d. 1622).[75]

From Thomas it descended, presumably through his son Sir Adam (d. 1647) and Sir Adam's son Sir Thomas Littleton or Poyntz (d. 1681), to Sir Thomas Littleton, speaker of the Commons (1698–1700), son of the last named,[76] who sold Munslow in 1706 to his cousin Sir Littleton Powys (d. 1732),[77] who was succeeded

46 What follows is based on W.S.L. 350/5/40, Munslow p. 24; *T.S.A.S.* lviii. 140–52; S.R.O. 3614/3/5–7, 10, 27, 36a–c, 38.

47 S.R.O. 3614/3/13a–b.

48 S.R.O. 515/7, pp. 25–7.

49 Inf. from the Landmark Trust.

50 Descr. based on *T.S.A.S.* lviii. 140–52.

51 P. Stamper, *The Farmer Feeds Us All* (Shrews. 1989), 18.

52 Corresp. 1963–9 betw. Miss J. C. Purser and A. T. Gaydon, in possession of editor *V.C.H. Salop.*; inf. from the Landmark Trust.

53 S.R.O. 356, box 327, surv. of 1562; *V.C.H. Salop.* ii. 138–9; *Cal. Pat.* 1550–3, 345–6.

54 S.R.O. 1705/25–6.

55 Ludlow (Charity Estates) Act, 1846, 9 & 10 Vic. c. 18 (Private); inf. from Mr. D. J. Lloyd.

56 *T.S.A.S.* 4th ser. xi. 5; Owen and Blakeway, *Hist. Shrews.* ii. 139; S.P.L., MSS. 2788, p. 375; 2789, p. 214.

57 *Rot. Hund.* ii. 71, where Nic. de 'Stubbings' probably represents Nic. de Sancto Mauro; *Pedigrees from the Plea Rolls*, ed. G. Wrottesley (1905), 509–10; *Feud. Aids*, iv. 223.

58 *Feud. Aids*, iv. 229.

59 Wrottesley, *Pedigrees from Plea Rolls*, 509–10.

60 *Feud. Aids*, iv. 245; *S.H.C.* 1917–18, 105–6.

61 *S.H.C.* 1917–18, 106, 125.

62 *Cal. Inq. p.m.* xvi, p. 170.

63 *S.H.C.* 1917–18, 145; *V.C.H. Staffs.* iv. 65.

64 *Cal. Inq. p.m.* xvii, pp. 157; *Cal. Fine R.* 1391–9, 115. Cf. *S.H.C.* xiii. 114–15.

65 P.R.O., CP 25/1/195/20, no. 8.

66 Cf. *S.H.C.* xiii. 114–15.

67 *Feud. Aids*, iv. 250.

68 *T.S.A.S.* 4th ser. vi. 231–4; lvi. 263–4, 271–2; *Cal. Inq. p.m. Hen. VII*, iii, pp. 127–8, 148–9; cf. *V.C.H. Staffs.* v. 13; *Complete Peerage*, x. 247 sqq.

69 S.R.O. 20/23/13.

70 P.R.O., CP 40/1156, Carte rot. 5.

71 *Cal. Inq. p.m. Hen. VII*, ii, p. 577. For pedigree to 1590 see Burke, *Peerage* (1967), 553.

72 P.R.O., C 142/21, no. 78; C 142/78, no. 140.

73 P.R.O., C 142/54, no. 137.

74 P.R.O., CP 25/2/77/655/3 & 4 Ph. & M. Mich. no. 37.

75 *T.S.A.S.* 4th ser. iii. 303, 316.

76 G.E.C. *Baronetage*, ii. 204.

77 *S.P.R. Heref.* iv (2), 78.

by his grand-nephew Thomas Powys (d. 1767). In 1772 Thomas Powys's son Thomas[78] sold the lordship of the manor, without the manorial estate, to Robert, Lord Clive, whose descendant and heir Edward Herbert, earl of Powis, sold it in 1842 to the Revd. R. N. Pemberton of Millichope Park.[79] Munslow manor then descended with the Millichope Park estate.[80]

The Littletons' house was Munslow Farm,[81] an L shaped building with a brick wing of the 1660s or 1670s and an 18th-century stone wing. The upper parlour of the older portion of the house has some panelling and a series of 17th-century painted cloth hangings, perhaps Flemish.[82]

The only real estate which Lord Clive bought with the manor of Munslow was the 'manor' house. By 1793 it had been divided into two dwellings[83] and its later history has not been found. The rest of the former Littleton estate had passed by 1793 to one Walker, a serjeant-at-law,[84] who had 300 a. in the parish in 1801.[85] In 1833 his son Charles conveyed that estate by way of exchange to the Revd. R. N. Pemberton, who bought the lordship of the manor in 1842.[86]

Sir Edward Littleton, brother of the lord of Munslow, is said to have bought from John Lutley, before 1581, a considerable estate in Munslow owned by the Lutleys since the 13th century.[87] Sir Edward's son Sir Edward, cr. Lord Lyttelton in 1641 soon after his appointment as lord keeper, died in 1645[88] leaving a daughter Anne his sole heir. She married her second cousin Sir Thomas Littleton or Poyntz, lord of the manor.[89] In the 1830s it was recounted that the Lutleys' 'manor house' had stood on an 'eminence'. Partly burnt down in the 16th century, its ruins were removed *c.* 1799 when a new stone house (later known as the Miller House) was built for William Wainwright to John Smalman's design.[90]

In 1428 William Baudewyn (fl. 1433) was listed with William Burley and Lord Furnivalle as a principal landowner; he was a Munslow freeholder, as were his descendants until the 18th century or later.[91] One of them, Richard Baldwin (fl. 1523), was ancestor of Earl Baldwin of Bewdley, prime minister 1923–4, 1924–9, and 1935–7.[92] A chief house that belonged to John Baldwin (d. 1605) passed to his son William (fl. 1620) and was possibly the 'Farm of Munslow' that Roger Baldwin, John's uncle, had bought from John Stringfellow (purchaser of a moiety of the manor) in 1553; for the house in which William Baldwin's son John lived in 1658 was called Munslow Old Farm House by 1838. It then belonged to the Revd. R. N. Pemberton and was later called the Old School House.[93]

In 1607 William Baldwyn of Elsich (d. *c.* 1614) sold a house, later called the Chains, to Thomas Varnolds, in whose family it remained until the early 19th century.[94]

LOWER MILLICHOPE was separated parochially from Upper Millichope *c.* 1115[95] and manorially, perhaps earlier, by subinfeudation. The prior of Wenlock was overlord, so described until 1420 or later.[96]

Peter de Lacy held the manor under the prior in 1255.[97] Peter's heir was apparently William de Schippeye's wife Amice. In 1293 the couple exchanged the manor with Philip Burnell (d. 1294).[98] During the minority of Burnell's son Edward the manor was among those given in custody to Guncelin of Badlesmere (d. 1301).[99] From 1307 until 1542 Lower Millichope descended with Acton Burnell.[1]

About 1544 Sir John Dudley, Viscount Lisle, sold his Lower Millichope estate, although no mention was made of the manorial rights, to Richard Adams, who in turn sold it in 1544 to Robert More of Thonglands,[2] already a Lower Millichope landowner.[3] More (d. 1545)[4] was probably succeeded by Edward More (d. 1558), whose heir was his brother Thomas.[5] Thomas or a namesake was succeeded in 1620 by his son Charles (d. 1646).[6] The claimed manor of Nether Millichope was an estate which, in 1685, Charles's son Thomas (d. 1689)[7] settled on his son Henry (d. 1689)[8] and daughter-in-law Mary.[9] Henry's son Thomas was lord in

78 *D.N.B.*; Burke, *Peerage* (1967), 1512.
79 S.R.O. 3651, parcel 17C, sched. of deeds, pp. 40–1; *V.C.H. Salop.* iv. 205–6; S.P.L., MS. 4645, p. 35.
80 *S.P.R. Heref.* xv (2), p. iii; W.S.L. 350/5/40, Munslow pp. 6–7; S.R.O. 3651, box 17D, bur. certif. (copy); *P.O. Dir. Salop.* (1856–79); *Kelly's Dir. Salop.* (1885–1941); below, this section.
81 W.S.L. 350/5/40, Munslow p. 6; S.R.O. 1011, parcel 248, Millichope est. rentals Lady Day 1836 to Mich. 1840; P.R.O., IR 29/29/229; IR 30/29/229, field 723.
82 W.S.L. 350/5/40, Munslow p. 6. Mrs. Moran is thanked for her remarks on the ho.
83 S.P.L., MS. 6865, p. 148.
84 Ibid. pp. 148–9; W.S.L. 350/5/40, Munslow p. 6.
85 S.R.O. 515/4, p. 288.
86 W.S.L. 350/5/40, Munslow pp. 6–7; above, this section.
87 *Visit. Salop. 1623*, ii (Harl. Soc. xxix), 343–5; *T.S.A.S.* 4th ser. vi. 242–3; W.S.L. 350/5/40, Munslow pp. 1–3. See also S.P.L., MS. 2794, p. 91 n. 1.
88 *D.N.B.*
89 *T.S.A.S.* 3rd ser. ii. 328; 4th ser. iii. 313, 325, 332.
90 W.S.L. 350/5/40, Munslow pp. 1–2; P.R.O., IR 29/29/229; IR 30/29/229, field 286.
91 *Feud. Aids*, iv. 250; *T.S.A.S.* 4th ser. ii. 141, 168–85.
92 Burke, *Peerage* (1967), 154.
93 P.R.O., CP 40/1156, Carte rot. ld.; C 2/Jas. I/B 3/46; IR 29/29/229; IR 30/29/229, field 272; *T.S.A.S.* 4th ser. ii. 170, 173–5; S.R.O. 1011, parcel 248, Millichope est. rentals Lady Day 1838 to Lady Day 1843; above, this article, intro.; this section.
94 Staffs. R.O., D.(W.) 1788, parcel 38, bdle. 12, deed of 1607; W.S.L. 350/5/4, Munslow p. 7; P.R.O., IR 29/29/229; IR 30/29/229, field 720; above, this article, intro.
95 Below, Eaton-under-Heywood, manors.
96 *Rot. Hund.* ii. 85; *Cal. Inq. p.m.* iii, pp. 122, 443; viii, p. 496; x, pp. 499–500; xiv, p. 258; xviii, p. 201; P.R.O., C 138/54, no. 116.
97 *Rot. Hund.* ii. 85.
98 P.R.O., C 133/68, no. 10; CP 25/1/193/6, no. 71.
99 *Cal. Inq. p.m.* iii, p. 443.
1 *V.C.H. Salop.* viii. 7; W.S.L. 350/5/40, Munslow p. 10; *Cal. Close*, 1346–9, 111; 1419–22, 154–5; *Cal. Pat.* 1485–94, 64; *L. & P. Hen. VIII*, i, pp. 1170–1; xvi, p. 240; P.R.O., C 138/54, no. 116; C 148/45; cf. above, Rushbury, manors.
2 S.R.O. 3320/24/1–2.
3 S.P.L., Deeds 12937.
4 S.R.O. 3320/24/4.
5 S.R.O. 3320/24/5; P.R.O., C 142/115, no. 59.
6 S.R.O. 3320/24/12; P.R.O., C 142/388, no. 53; S.P.L., Deeds 15687.
7 *S.P.R. Heref.* xv (2), 49, 132.
8 Ibid. 133.
9 S.R.O. 4055/6/4–5.

1752. On his death without surviving sons in 1767[10] Lower Millichope passed to Thomas More's daughter Catherine (d. 1792), who left it to her cousin Robert Pemberton (d. 1794). Robert's son Thomas[11] (d. 1832) was succeeded by his nephew the Revd. R. N. Pemberton (d. 1848), who left most of his estates to his cousin C. O. Childe (from 1849 Childe-Pemberton). Childe-Pemberton died in 1883, and his son C. B. Childe-Pemberton (Childe from 1884),[12] who had been offering the Millichope Park estate for sale since 1886,[13] sold it in 1896 to Capt. H. J. Beckwith (d. 1927), heir of a Durham landowning family, whose father had been rector of Eaton Constantine 1832–88.[14] Beckwith's daughter Kathleen Frances Malebisse (d. 1932) married L. E. Bury, and their great-grandson L. C. N. Bury owned Lower Millichope in 1990.

The old hall at Millichope, perhaps of the later 16th century, was timber framed and of two storeys with attics on a high basement.[15] The east front was symmetrical, with a full-height central porch and projections of similar size at each end of the elevation. The south front was cased in brick in the 18th century. The old hall was demolished *c.* 1843.[16]

Meanwhile a new house had been built 1835–40 on a higher site just to the south-west.[17] House, stables, and terraces cost over £30,000, which a contemporary considered a high figure in view of the lack of accommodation and 'many faults'[18] which he detected in this splendidly original house, one of the finest of the Greek Revival.[19] The approach through a deep cutting and tunnel postponed the visitor's prospect of the grounds until the Hall itself had been entered. Designed by Edward Haycock of Shrewsbury, the house is of Grinshill ashlar,[20] with a large central Ionic hexastyle portico to the east. Ostensibly only two storeys high it sits on a terrace within which were the main and service entrances. The principal entrance was below the portico and between short Tuscan columns *in antis*. From the basement a wide flight of stairs rose into the central two storeyed hall which was galleried in Ionic style. The ceiling is raised above the first-floor gallery by a glazed 'attic storey' lighting the hall. The service rooms were originally in the basement, but a north service wing was added in the later 19th century.

The house was remodelled in the 1970s.[21] The basement entries were closed and a new entry formed in the north front of the principal floor. The stairs from the basement and one branch of the stairs to the gallery were removed, new gallery railings put in, and the central portion of the service wing demolished.

Millichope Hall's surroundings were embellished in the mid 18th century, probably in the 1760s by Thomas More (d. 1767) as a memorial to his sons Leighton (d. 1744), John (d. 1762), and Thomas (d. 1767).[22] An Ionic rotunda, completed in 1770 to George Steuart's design,[23] faces the Hall across a shallow valley; it contains a memorial to Leighton and John More, a putto on a pedestal, which may once have been elsewhere in the grounds.[24] In the valley three ponds had been made by 1817.[25] A fine obelisk (10 m. high) south-west of the Hall and a deer park extending mainly west and north of the Hall may also date from the 1760s.[26] A rustic summer house called the Moustry and a sheepcot with stone corner towers, both north-west of the Hall, may also be of that period.[27]

In the early 1830s, before building the new Hall, the Revd. R. N. Pemberton made substantial changes to its surroundings.[28] Home Farm was rebuilt as were other buildings on the estate,[29] and extensive walled kitchen gardens were laid out. Beyond, additional walks may have been made around the rotunda and the ponds and associated streams altered. The park was enlarged but no longer stocked with deer.[30] Access to Church Stretton, where Pemberton was rector (absentee from 1840),[31] was improved by the creation of a new private drive to the Hall (with a lodge at its north end), and a new public road from Beambridge via Home Farm and Rushbury.[32]

Between 1843 and 1884[33] there were further changes. A large new pool, with boathouse, was created in front of the Hall, partly by quarrying which formed a picturesque cliff beneath the rotunda. Waterfalls were built across the stream that fed the pool. The walks around the rotunda

10 S.R.O., q. sess. rec. box 260, reg. of gamekeepers 1742–79, 17 Jan. 1752; S.P.L., MS. 4645, p. 439; *S.P.R. Heref.* xv (2), 224. Rest of para. based on *T.S.A.S.* 4th ser. ix. 99–105; Loton Hall MSS., Sir B. Leighton's diary 18 Dec. 1848, 27 Jan. 1862; W.S.L. 350/5/40, Munslow p. 10; *Lond. Gaz.* 13 July 1849, p. 2225; *Shrews. Chron.* 10 Jan. 1930; Burke, *Land. Gent.* (1952), 142–3; inf. from Mrs. L. C. N. Bury.

11 For him see *V.C.H. Salop.* iii. 117, 360.

12 Burke, *Land. Gent.* (1952), 430.

13 Copy of sale cat. at Millichope Pk.; cf. *V.C.H. Salop.* iv. 212 n. 89.

14 *Alum. Cantab. 1752–1900*, i. 211.

15 Pl. 20. For illus. of the old ho. see Northants. R.O., Hartshorne colln., vol. xxv, pp. 61–2; Bodl. MS. Top. Salop. c. 2, ff. 374–5, 377; S.P.L., MS. 201, ff. 48, 53.

16 *T.S.A.S.* 3rd ser. vii. 135; Loton Hall MSS., Sir B. Leighton's diary 18 Dec. 1848.

17 Pl. 20; W.S.L. 350/5/40, Munslow p. 10; *Country Life*, 10 and 17 Feb. (pp. 310–13, 370–3), 17 Mar. (pp. 654, 656), 21 Apr. (p. 1014) 1977. For illus. see also Bodl. MS. Top. Salop. c. 2, ff. 376–8; N.B.R., photos.

18 Loton Hall MSS., Sir B. Leighton's diary 2 Oct. 1857. The 'stables' were perh. Home Fm.: below.

19 Pevsner, *Salop.* 41, 200.

20 Its carriage cost £1,500: Leighton's diary 2 Oct. 1857.

21 *Country Life*, 10 Feb. 1977, 310–13; 17 Feb. 1977, 370–-3.

22 *S.P.R. Heref.* xv (2), 224; J. B. Blakeway, *Sheriffs of Salop.* (Shrews. 1831), 208. Blakeway's story that John (d. 1762) left money for work is not substantiated by his will: P.R.O., PROB 11/889, ff. 30–1.

23 Blakeway, *Sheriffs*, 208.

24 Rotunda and putto each has its own inscr. and distinct stone. Blakeway, op. cit. 208, notes, 'little memorials . . . scattered up and down' Millichope grounds.

25 B.L. Maps, O.S.D. 206.

26 Park not on J. Rocque, *Map of Salop.* (1752), but on Baugh, *Map of Salop.* (1808). See also W.S.L. 350/5/40, Munslow p. 15.

27 S.R.O. 1705/25–6; O.S. Map 1/2,500, Salop. LXIV. 8 (1884 edn.); Millichope Pk., 1886 sale cat.

28 W.S.L. 350/5/40, Munslow p. 15; cf. B.L. Maps, O.S.D. 206; S.R.O. 1705/26.

29 Above, this article, intro.

30 S.P.L., MS. 226, f. 37v.; O.S. Map 1", sheet LXI. SW. (1833 edn.); S.R.O. 1705/25–6.

31 Above, Ch. Stretton, church.

32 W.S.L. 350/5/40, Munslow p. 15; W.B.R., Q1/12/93. Cf. B.L. Maps, O.S.D. 206; S.R.O. 1705/26.

33 Cf. S.R.O. 1705/26; O.S. Map 1/2,500, Salop. LXIV. 8 (1884 edn.).

were changed and a new stable block (demolished in the 1970s)[34] was made north of the new pool. A new south drive and lodge were built *c.* 1907.[35] Later changes were minor.

What was described as a third of Lower Millichope's great *TITHES* was offered for sale in 1788.[36] The tithes arose from *c.* 50 a. at the western edge of Millichope park, around the Eaton-under-Heywood parish boundary intrusion.[37] They had evidently been enjoyed by Wenlock priory with its appropriated rectory of Eaton, and they descended as an impropriation from John Pakington, who bought them from the Crown in 1544,[38] to the Littletons and then to the Actons,[39] subsequently to William Churchman of Thonglands and so, in 1722, to Arthur Weaver of Bridgnorth.[40] The purchaser *c.* 1788 was presumably Richard Powell, rector. In 1843 the tithes belonged to Powell's son Richard, also rector, and were commuted to £10 10*s.*[41]

In 1086 *THONGLANDS* was an unnamed hide in Tugford manor held by Reynold the sheriff.[42] It remained part of the fee of the earls of Arundel, Reynold's successors, until 1439–40 or later.[43] In 1504, 1509 and 1532 Thonglands was said to be held of the earl of Shrewsbury.[44]

The Domesday tenant was Rayner of Thonglands, who by *c.* 1114 had been succeeded by his son William.[45] Robert was lord in 1165, perhaps William *c.* 1240,[46] Richard in 1242–3,[47] Roger in 1256, and Sir Roger de Bradeleye by 1280, in 1313, and probably in 1317; he held it as ½ knight's fee.[48] Roger de la Mare had Thonglands in 1322,[49] Henry de Bradeley in 1328–9 and probably in 1326.[50]

By 1330 Thonglands had apparently passed to John of Hadlow (d. 1346)[51] and thereafter, increasingly often called a manor, it descended with Acton Burnell until the death of Hugh, Lord Burnell, in 1420.[52] In 1425 one of Burnell's feoffees, William Burley, acquired it[53] and it then descended with Munslow until the mid 17th century,[54] probably being sold by the Littletons in 1654 to George Ludlow[55] of the Moorhouse (in Shipton). The Moorhouse and Thonglands then descended together, and Thonglands was part of the estate of Samuel Edwards (d. 1738) of West Coppice (in Buildwas).[56] In 1745 Edwards's trustees sold the manor and property there to Thomas More (d. 1767) of Millichope, from whom they passed to his son-in-law Dudley Ackland, owner in 1776.[57] The manorial estate has not been noticed thereafter.

Walter de Beysin (d. 1344) owned an estate in Thonglands, which descended with his share of Broseley manor until the division of the Harewells' estate in 1534. Rents from Thonglands then passed to John Smith's wife Agnes and Thomas Aston's wife Bridget, who were sisters.[58] Nicholas Purslow bought the Smiths' interest in 1559[59] and died in 1563;[60] it passed to his brother John (d. 1594) but has not been traced further.[61]

Edward Lacon, a son of Sir Richard Lacon of Willey, lived at Thonglands in the mid 16th century.[62] His elder son Robert died childless, and a Thonglands property passed to Robert's brother William. William's son Edward (d. 1637) was next owner. Thonglands farm, as it was later known, then passed from father to son, to Edward's son Richard, Francis (d. 1686), Edward (d. 1709), Francis (d. 1735),[63] Thomas (d. 1809),[64] Frederick, and the Revd. Frederick (in possession 1851).[65] By 1896 the farm had been acquired by the Millichope Park estate,[66] with which it remained.[67]

Thonglands Farm, by the 19th century the township's principal residence, stands within a partly filled moat, the remaining portion of which is semicircular. The **T** plan building comprises a late 16th-century hall range, originally timber framed, to which an elaborate parlour range, also timber framed, was added in the early 17th century. About 1700 the hall range was cased in stone, and soon afterwards brick additions were made to both ends of the building. West of the house and also within the moat are the ruined church and a ruinous circular stone dovecot formerly with 250 nesting holes.[68]

The Ludlow Palmers' guild acquired land in

34 Inf. from Mrs. Bury.
35 Date stone on lodge.
36 S.P.L., MS. 6865, p. 150.
37 S.R.O. 1705/25–6; fig. 14. For what follows cf. Eaton-under-Heywood, manors (rectory).
38 *L. & P. Hen. VIII*, xix, p. 633.
39 *Cal. Pat.* 1563–6, p. 128.
40 S.R.O. 4023/1.
41 S.R.O. 1705/25–6. For the Powells see below, churches.
42 *V.C.H. Salop.* i. 319; Eyton, iv. 80, 85.
43 Eyton, iv. 85–6; *Cal. Inq. p.m.* i, p. 280; viii, p. 496; xv, p. 289; *Cal. Inq. p.m.* (Rec. Com.), iv. 199; *Feud. Aids*, iv. 223, 244, 267.
44 P.R.O., C 142/54, no. 137; *Cal. Inq. p.m. Hen. VII*, ii, pp. 577–8; iii, pp. 331–2.
45 Eyton, iv. 85; *Cartulary of Shrews. Abbey*, ed. U. Rees (1975), ii, pp. 2, 4, 37.
46 Eyton, iv. 85.
47 *Bk. of Fees*, ii. 963.
48 Eyton, iv. 86, 88; *Feud. Aids*, iv. 223; *Reg. Orleton* (C.S.), 5.
49 *Cal. Pat.* 1321–4, 52.
50 P.R.O., CP 25/1/194/11 [no. 10]; *Reg. Orleton*, 389.
51 *Cal. Inq. p.m.* viii, p. 496.
52 *Cal. Close*, 1346–9, 111; 1419–22, 154–5; *Cal. Inq. p.m.* xv, p. 289; *Cal. Inq. p.m.* (Rec. Com.), iv. 56; *Cat. Anct. D.* ii, C 2398; *Feud. Aids*, iv. 249; cf. *V.C.H. Salop.* viii. 7.
53 *Cal. Close*, 1422–9, 207; cf. *T.S.A.S.* lvi. 265–6, 269.
54 *Feud. Aids*, iv. 267; S.R.O. 20/23/13; P.R.O., C 142/54, no. 137; CP 25/1/195/22, no. 9; CP 40/1156, Carte rot. 5; *Cal. Inq. p.m. Hen. VII*, ii, pp. 577–8; iii, pp. 127–8, 331–2; above, this section.
55 P.R.O., CP 25/2/591/1654 East. no. 18.
56 S.R.O. 4572/6/2/56; P.R.O., CP 25/2/867/3 Wm. & Mary Mich. no. 19; below, Shipton, manors.
57 S.R.O. 1224, box 101, abstr. of title of Dudley Ackland, 1790; above, this section (Lr. Millichope).
58 P.R.O., CP 25/1/194/13, no. 33; *Cal. Inq. p.m.* xviii, pp. 199–202; *Cal. Inq. p.m.* (Rec. Com.), iv. 35, 41; *Cal. Inq. p.m. Hen. VII*, iii, pp. 141–2; *Cal. Fine R.* 1413–22, 263–5; Dugdale, *Warws.* (1730), ii. 810; T. F. Dukes, *Antiquities of Salop.* (1844), 264; above, this section (Aston); below, Broseley, manor.
59 *Cal. Pat.* 1558–60, 10.
60 S.P.L., MS. 2792, p. 411.
61 *T.S.A.S.* 4th ser. iii. 113; *S.P.R. Heref.* i (7), 5.
62 For pedigrees see S.P.L., MS. 4360, pp. 275–6; 4645, p. 413.
63 S.P.L., Deeds 276; MS. 4645, p. 413.
64 S.R.O. 4131/Rg/4.
65 S. Bagshaw, *Dir. Salop.* (1851), 542; W.S.L. 350/5/40, Munslow p. 10.
66 *S.P.R. Heref.* xv (2), p. v.
67 S.R.O. 4044/46, no. 119; local inf. Cf. above, this section.
68 Below, churches; A. O. Cooke, *Bk. of Dovecotes* (1920), 77.

Thonglands in the later Middle Ages, and *c.* 11 a. there passed with the rest of its property to Ludlow corporation in 1552.[69] The corporation still had 8 a. in Thonglands in 1843.[70] Vested in the trustees of Edward VI's charity, Ludlow, in 1846, the land was sold after 1876.[71]

Wenlock priory had 2 a. in Thonglands at the Dissolution.[72]

William Churchman (d. 1602) owned two farms at *HUNGERFORD*, Muxhill and Holloway (or the 'hall of Hungerford').[73] Muxhill had probably been the home of Richard More of Thonglands (fl. 1497–1529),[74] and in 1575 Thomas More sold it to Thomas Tedstill[75] who sold it to Edward Lacon in 1581.[76] Churchman bought it from Lacon in 1596.[77] Holloway had been inherited by Roger Churchman from his brother Thomas. William Churchman was Roger's son; the property was part of the settlement when he married in 1593.[78] Those two properties then descended in the Churchman family[79] until 1685 when Arthur Weaver (d. 1710) bought Muxhill.[80] It passed to his son Arthur,[81] who bought Holloway from the Churchmans' representatives in 1722.[82] The properties descended thereafter with Lower House, Stanton Long, until 1806, when Lower House was sold.[83] In 1809 Charles Hanbury-Tracy sold Muxhill and Holloway to Richard Pee of the Bold (in Willey).[84] J. F. Wright, lord of Aston, owned them later,[85] but by 1843 they were part of the Millichope Park estate.[86]

Muxhill Farm probably adjoined Holloway. The house had been demolished by 1805, though its buildings still served a 68-a. farm.[87] The house site[88] is probably occupied by Hungerford Farm of *c.* 1800, an elegant stone house of three storeys. It has raised stone quoins, a slightly projecting central section, and a Venetian window to the second storey. Holloway Farm of *c.* 1600, which had 37 a. in 1805,[89] is a timber framed building of two storeys cased in stone, perhaps in the 18th century. West of it is a large improved farmyard of the early 19th century.

In 1066 *BROADSTONE* was part of Stanway. Most of Broadstone was given by the sheriff Warin the bald (d. *c.* 1085) to Shrewsbury abbey. Otes of Bernières, lord of Stanway, gave the abbey 1 fardel or 1 virgate there 1121 × 1136.[90] The abbey's Broadstone property was surrendered with the rest of its estates in 1540.[91] It then descended with Tugford until 1843 or later.[92] Since 1913 or earlier Broadstone and Mill farms (*c.* 511 a. in all) have belonged to the Millichope Park estate.[93]

ECONOMIC HISTORY. Aston, a manor of 8½ hides, had two ploughteams and six *servi* on the demesne in 1086; five other teams belonged to the tenants: 5 *villani*, 8 bordars, a priest, a Frenchman, and a radman. Nine more teams might have been employed.[94] In 1340 it was said that 5 carucates in the parish lay untilled, sheep had been killed by murrain, and corn lost in storms.[95]

Each of the five townships had its own fields and access to woods, commons, and meadows. Aston's open-field land seems to have been mainly in three fields in the 16th century, worked in a three-course rotation:[96] Mynde field, under corn in 1575, was west of Aston village; Clay field, under oats, lay to the south-east; and the Nether (or Lower)[97] field, then fallow, was perhaps north of the village. Some open-field land in 1575 also lay in the Over field, north of Mynde field and probably a late intake from the common. In 1664 Aston's farm land was reckoned at 11¼ yardlands, in 1694 at 12¼.[98]

Munslow's open-field land lay in four fields in the later 16th century: Over (or Calden) field north-west of Munslow village, Clay field to the north-east, Bricknall field to the east, and Churley field to the south.[99] The township's farm land was reckoned at 6¾ yardlands in 1669, 10¾ in 1694.[1]

Broadstone's open-field land was in three fields in the 16th and 17th centuries: the Brook field, probably east of the village and adjoining the Corve; Hill field, presumably north and west of Broadstone; and the Deane field, separated from Hill field by a ring hedge, also north of the village.[2] The township's farm land was reckoned at 5⅓ yardlands in 1669, and just over 4½ in 1694.[3]

At Thonglands in the early 14th century strips lay in fields including Necroft (near Thonglands mill) and Westcroft.[4] In 1502 the three open fields were the field by Hungerford, Over field (south of the later Upper mill), and the Muxhill

69 S.R.O. 356, box 327, surv. of 1562; 356/MT/87, 1094, 1190–3, 1362; *Cal. Pat.* 1550–3, 345–6; *V.C.H. Salop.* ii. 138–9.
70 S.R.O. 1705/25–6. Cf. S.R.O. 356, box 416 (3).
71 9 & 10 Vic. c. 18 (Private); inf. from Mr. Lloyd.
72 N.L.W., Chirk Castle, F 13350.
73 P.R.O., C 142/273, no. 83; S.P.L., Deeds 6395. For another estate in Hungerford see below, Eaton-under-Heywood, manors.
74 S.P.L., Deeds 12937; N.L.W., Dobell 1; Glos. R.O., D2153/D/13; S.R.O. 3365/165.
75 S.R.O. 4055/6/1; Glos. R.O., D2153/A/24–5.
76 Glos. R.O., D2153/F/1.
77 S.P.L., Deeds 6395.
78 Glos. R.O., D2153/D/17.
79 Ibid. A/28; D/17, 19; E/7; F/2–3, 6, 8; P.R.O., C 142/273, no. 83; S.R.O. 837/49; 1037/21/189.
80 S.R.O. 837/49; *Mont. Coll.* xxii. 86.
81 Glos. R.O., D2153/J/6.
82 S.R.O. 837/49.
83 *Mont. Coll.* xxii. 90; Glos. R.O., D2153/H/20; J/6; cf. below, Stanton Long, manors.
84 S.R.O. 837/49.
85 W.S.L. 350/5/40, Muslow p. 10; above, this section (Aston).
86 S.R.O. 1705/25–6.
87 S.R.O. 4835/28, p. 4.
88 Cf. (for field names) S.R.O. 837/49; 1705/25–6.
89 S.R.O. 4835/28, p. 4.
90 Eyton, iv. 89–90; *V.C.H. Salop.* i. 319; ii. 30; iii. 9; above, Rushbury, manors; *Cart. Shrews.* i, pp. 15–16, 43, 258, 262.
91 S.P.L., Holy Cross par. rec., Shrews. abbey rental [*c.* 1490]; *V.C.H. Salop.* ii. 36.
92 Below, Tugford, manors; S.R.O. 1705/25–6; 4260/1/6; S.P.L., Deeds 8403.
93 S.R.O. 4011/46, nos. 68, 117; local inf.
94 *V.C.H. Salop.* i. 322.
95 *Inq. Non.* (Rec. Com.), 186.
96 S.R.O., 356, box 327, surv. of *c.* 1575, pp. 115–17. Fields located from 1705/25–6.
97 S.R.O. 3614/3/13a.
98 S.R.O. 1705/43, s.a.
99 Ibid. /29; H.W.R.O.(H.), HD2/14/50–1.
1 S.R.O. 1705/43, s.a.
2 S.R.O. 1037/21/187; Bodl., Craven dep. 3; S.P.L., Deeds 7467.
3 S.R.O. 1705/43, s.a.
4 Eyton, iv. 86–7.

field or Mide field (perhaps east of Over field).[5] About 1575 a three-course rotation was followed: Over field was fallow, Mill field (probably the earlier Mide field) grew oats, and Croft or West Croft field (earlier the field towards Hungerford) corn.[6] Thonglands' farm land, apparently 7½ virgates in the mid 14th century,[7] was reckoned at 8¼ yardlands in 1669 and just over 9 in 1694.[8] In and after the later 17th century only the Upper or Further field was mentioned;[9] it was called Thonglands field in 1785.[10]

Open-field land at Lower Millichope in 1316 lay in the Muned field and the field between 'Bynnesden' and 'Bullesden'. What may have been a separate field (probably that later reckoned as Hungerford's)[11] extended to the Wenlock–Ludlow road near Hungerford.[12] Millichope's farm land was reckoned at 4 yardlands in 1669 and 1694.[13]

The high ground forming the north-western parts of Munslow and Aston townships was used by them as a large open common, *c.* 2 km. east–west by 1 km. north–south in the 18th century.[14] Roads ran up to the common from both villages, and access may also have been gained via the deans (shallow valleys). When the common was cleared of woodland is unknown; none of the Domesday manors[15] is said to have had woodland. Most of the parish was disafforested from the Long Forest in 1301.[16] In the 17th century an area called Cadden head, apparently common pasture, lay between Aston's dean and the common.[17] Whether then or later there was any demarcation of Aston's common from Munslow's is uncertain.[18] In 1793 the whole common was reckoned at 300 a.[19] By *c.* 1817 two thirds, mainly in Aston, had been inclosed;[20] the remaining 94 a., in Munslow township, were allotted in 1847.[21]

Aston anciently had woodland between Bache brook and Mynde field, perhaps the wood of Sir Roger of Ridware recorded in 1262 as wasted of old.[22] By the 17th century it was home to several squatters and parts at least were inclosed.[23] Only fragments survived into the 19th century.[24]

The manor best supplied with woodland was Lower Millichope. Until the 19th-century expansion of Millichope park, much of the northern part of the township was wooded.[25] The manor also included a wooded hill known in the 16th century as Millichope Knoll[26] and in the 19th as Topley,[27] part of which was presumably allotted to Lower Millichope after subinfeudation separated it from Upper Millichope.[28] Outsiders were licensed to common in Millichope in 1462,[29] and in 1669 a cottager living in Millichope wood had the right to pasture 20 sheep in the common wood.[30] Charcoal was burnt in the manor's woods in the mid 17th century.[31]

The north-western extremity of Broadstone township, between Eaton-under-Heywood and Rushbury parishes, was called the Yeld and was common in 1665.[32]

Thonglands apparently had no wood but had a moor, called Wolful in the early 14th century[33] and presumably the same as the later Thonglands bog, east of Thonglands Farm.[34] There was probably also a large amount of pasture, much of it wet, along Rowe (or Marsh) Lane north-east of Row Farm.[35]

In general the parish was well supplied with meadow, mainly along the Corve and Trow brook; some of it was floated in the 18th and 19th centuries.[36]

Inclosure of the parish's open-field land was mostly piecemeal. Lower Millichope's may not have outlasted the Middle Ages,[37] while Aston's and Munslow's seems to have been inclosed mainly in the 17th century.[38] Broadstone's fields were inclosed by Lord Craven *c.* 1800,[39] and Broadstone Farm was probably built then. At Thonglands two large areas of open strips survived in 1843[40] and a few 'quillets' (strips) south of Broadstone mill until the early 20th century.[41]

Thomas Brooke (d. 1668), of Broadstone, was probably typical of the parish's more prosperous mid 17th-century farmers: he had 4 oxen and grew corn, barley, oats, and peas, worth in all £28 14*s.* His livestock included 9 cows (£14 10*s.*), 3 horses (£3 10*s.*), 6 pigs (£2), 65 sheep (£10), and bees (£1).[42] In the 19th and 20th centuries cattle and sheep rearing remained important in the parish's mixed farming regime. Some outlying barns and folds were built as part

5 S.R.O. 356/MT/1192.
6 S.R.O. 356, box 327, surv. of *c.* 1575, pp. 168–70.
7 *Inq. Non.* 186; Eyton, iv. 88.
8 S.R.O. 1705/43, s.a.
9 S.R.O. 1037/21/189.
10 S.R.O. 356/416/2.
11 Below, Eaton-under-Heywood, econ. hist.
12 S.R.O. 3195/1, p. 66.
13 S.R.O. 1705/43, s.a.
14 Sources cited below, this section; S.R.O. 1705/25–6, field names. See fig. 14.
15 *V.C.H. Salop.* i. 313, 322, 337.
16 *Cart. Shrews.* ii, p. 250. Cf. *V.C.H. Salop.* iv. 45.
17 H.W.R.O.(H.), HD2/14/50.
18 S.R.O. 3614/3/45 (1–2), hints at divn. by 1702.
19 S.P.L., MS. 6865, p. 149.
20 B.L. Maps, O.S.D. 206.
21 Under Bp.'s Cas. and Munslow Incl. Act, 1838, 1 & 2 Vic. c. 13 (Private): S.R.O., incl. award C 6/54.
22 Eyton, v. 142.
23 Glam. R.O., CL/Deeds I, Salop., 1652/3, Jan. 15; CL/Deeds II, no. 7590; *S.P.R. Heref.* xv (2), 80, 82–3; S.R.O. 356, box 327, surv. of 1562; 3614/3/67.
24 S.R.O. 1705/25–6.
25 Rocque, *Map of Salop.*
26 S.R.O. 3320/24/9.
27 S.R.O. 1705/25–6.
28 Above, this article, intro.; manors.
29 Birm. Univ. Libr., Mytton Papers, i. 198.
30 S.R.O. 3320/25/1.
31 *S.P.R. Heref.* xv (2), 90.
32 S.P.L., Deeds 9718 s.a.
33 Eyton, iv. 86.
34 S.R.O. 1705/25–6, fields 632–3. O.S. Map 1", sheet LXI. SW. (1833 edn.), marks Thonglands bog along Trow brook, W. of Thonglands Fm.
35 S.R.O. 4055/6/1; cf. field boundaries on S.R.O. 1705/26.
36 S.R.O. 356, box 327, surv. of 1562; 3614/3/43; 4835/28, p. 4.
37 No later mention noted.
38 'Ridges' last noted at Aston in 1717 (Glam. R.O., CL/Deeds II, no. 4987) and at Munslow in 1589 (S.R.O. 1705/29).
39 Extant in 1770 (S.P.L., MS. 2481, map XI), incl. by 1843 (S.R.O. 1705/25–6). Cf. *V.C.H. Salop.* iv. 136, 144–5.
40 S.R.O. 1705/25–6.
41 Ibid. /148; O.S. Map 6", Salop. LXV. NW. (1903 edn.); cf. H. D. G. Foxall, *Salop. Field-Names* (Salop. Arch. Soc. 1980), 8.
42 H.W.R.O.(H.), Heref. dioc. rec., inv. 4 Feb. 1667/8.

TABLE IX

MUNSLOW: LAND USE, LIVESTOCK, AND CROPS

	1867[a]	1891	1938	1965
Percentage of grassland	71	60	84	69
arable	29	40	16	31
Percentage of cattle	17	21	15	17
sheep	75	74	81	79
pigs	8	5	4	4
Percentage of wheat	47	37	8	25
barley	38	35	10	57
oats	15	28	82	18
mixed corn & rye	0	0	0	0
Percentage of agricultural land growing roots and vegetables	11	7	6	3

[a] Presumably including Lower Poston.

Sources: P.R.O., MAF 68/143, no. 20; /1340, no. 6; /3880, Salop. no. 113; /4945, no. 113.

of the agricultural improvements of the late 18th and early 19th century; in the late 20th century they were becoming derelict.[43]

There was a water mill at Aston in 1086,[44] and William the miller held land in Aston in 1341.[45] Aston's mill was called Bache mill by 1651.[46] It closed *c.* 1920.[47]

A mill associated with a tannery at Hungerford by the early 19th century was used to crush bark as well as grind corn. It closed in the 1890s.[48] Broadstone, or Upper, mill was built in 1794 by William Hazledine for Richard Grant. It last worked in the 1930s.[49] Hungerford's mill, or Broadstone's, or both, may earlier have belonged to Thonglands, which had two mills in 1272[50] and at least one until the mid 18th century.[51]

A windmill near Bache mill in the early 19th century was disused by the 1880s.[52]

There was weaving and glove making in the parish in the 17th and 18th centuries[53] and a tannery on the Corve at Hungerford between the mid 18th and mid 19th centuries.[54] Numerous small quarries supplied Corvedale siltstones, Upper Ludlow Shales, and Aymestry limestone for building and road stone.[55]

LOCAL GOVERNMENT. In 1462 William Harewell's tenants in Thonglands and Hungerford (noted under the general heading of Millichope) appeared at a Broseley court of recognition and did fealty to him.[56] Courts were said to be held for Munslow manor in the 1730s,[57] but no records survive. Broadstone was a member of Tugford manor, and Broadstone presentments survive from the mid 16th century and 1808.[58]

Each township had a constable in 1793.[59]

In the late 17th and early 18th centuries the parish poor were relieved with cash, clothing, fuel, and medicine. Flax and hemp were occasionally bought to provide them with work.[60] By 1803 the poor were contracted for. Out-relief was given to 70 adults and 8 children, and there were 8 adults in a workhouse. Annual expenditure rose from *c.* £150 in the 1770s to a peak of £627 in 1812–13 and stood at £293 in 1834.[61]

The parish was in Ludlow union 1836–1930,[62] Ludlow highway district 1863–95,[63] Ludlow rural sanitary district 1872–94, Ludlow rural district 1894–1974, and South Shropshire district from 1974.[64]

CHURCHES. There was a priest, and so perhaps a church, at Aston in 1086. Within the next few years the sheriff may have shifted the hundred meeting place from Corfham to Munslow, a change perhaps stimulating the development of a new settlement at Munslow and the move of the church there.[65] There was a rector of Munslow by *c.* 1115.[66] The church is 12th-century. Thonglands was a separate parish with its own church until 1442. A chapel at Broadstone is probably medieval but no evidence of its parochial affiliation before 1589 has been found.[67]

43 e.g. N. of Aston, of Munslow, and of Broadstone; cf. Table IX.
44 *V.C.H. Salop.* i. 322.
45 Glam. R.O., CL/Deeds I, Salop., 1341, July 26.
46 S.R.O. 3614/3/16.
47 *Kelly's Dir. Salop.* (1917), 152; (1922), 159.
48 Forrest, *Old Hos. of Wenlock*, 64; *Kelly's Dir. Salop.* (1891), 371; (1900), 154.
49 *Trans. Newcomen Soc.* xxxvi. 159–63.
50 Eyton, iv. 86.
51 Ibid.; S.R.O. 356, box 327, surv. of 1657; 566/51; 1037/21/189; 3651, parcel 17C, sched. of deeds, pp. 22–3; P.R.O., C 104/22, pt. 2, deed 29 Sept. 1731.
52 O.S. Maps 1", sheet LXI. SW. (1833 edn.); 6", Salop. LXIV. SE. (1891 edn.); S.R.O. 1705/25–6, field 111.
53 *S.P.R. Heref.* xv (2), 72, 146, 150.
54 Ibid. 212, 223; Forrest, *Old Hos. of Wenlock*, 64; S.R.O. 837/102; 3320/17; S.P.L., Deeds 8605, 10856, 12976.
55 S.P.L., Deeds 9718, ct. r. of 1671; S.R.O., incl. award C 6/54; O.S. Maps 1/2,500, Salop. LXIV. 4, 7–8, 11; LXV. 1 (1884 edn.); Inst. Geol. Sciences Map 1", drift, sheet 166 (1967 edn.); D. C. Greig and others, *Geol. of Country around Ch. Stretton, Craven Arms, Wenlock Edge and Brown Clee* (Mem. Geol. Surv. 1968), 194–6.
56 Birm. Univ. Libr., Mytton Papers, i. 198.
57 Ibid. iv. 907.
58 S.P.L., Deeds 7146, 9721; S.R.O. 1011, box 167, Tugford ct. r.; cf. below, Tugford, local govt.
59 S.R.O., MS. 6865, p. 149.
60 S.R.O. 1705/43, s.a. (e.g.) 1692–3, 1701, 1708; *S.P.R. Heref.* xv (2), 153.
61 *Poor Law Abstract*, H.C. 98, pp. 418–19 (1803–4), xiii; H.C. 82, pp. 372–3 (1818), xix; *Poor Rate Returns*, H.C. 556, suppl. app. p. 142 (1822), v; H.C. 444, p. 160 (1835), xlvii.
62 V. J. Walsh, 'Admin. of Poor Laws in Salop. 1820–55' (Pennsylvania Univ. Ph.D. thesis, 1970), 148–50; *Kelly's Dir. Salop.* (1929), 164.
63 S.R.O., q. sess. order bk. 1861–9, p. 127; S.C.C. Local Govt., etc., Cttee. min. bk. 1894–1903, p. 29.
64 *V.C.H. Salop.* ii. 215; iii. 178, and sources cited 169 n. 29.
65 Ibid. i. 322; Eyton, v. 129; above, Munslow Hundred (*part*).
66 Eyton, v. 130–1, 144.
67 Below, this section.

The advowson of Munslow rectory appears to have descended with the chief lordship of Munslow until 1772.[68] In 1324 Lord Hastings's right of patronage was challenged, unsuccessfully, by Robert de Beke, terre tenant of Munslow,[69] and the advowson, like the tenancy in chief, seems to have been disputed after the death of John, earl of Pembroke, in 1389; William Beauchamp, Lord Bergavenny, presented to the living in 1396[70] and the patronage was still in dispute in 1407.[71] In 1772 Thomas Powys sold it to Thomas Powell of Bridgnorth, whose family owned it for the next two centuries.[72] In 1967 Munslow was united to the benefice of Diddlebury with Bouldon, and the Revd. Edward Powell became alternate patron with the dean and chapter of Hereford. In 1980 Powell's son the Revd. R. M. W. Powell conveyed his patronage to the bishop of Lichfield, and when, in 1983, a new benefice of Diddlebury with Munslow, Holdgate, and Tugford was created the bishop of Lichfield had one turn of its advowson in every four. In 1988 the bishop of Lichfield conveyed his turn to the bishop of Hereford who then had three turns in every four.[73]

The rectory was worth £11 6*s.* 8*d.* a year in 1291.[74] There was then a separately endowed vicarage too: not known to have existed save in the late 13th and early 14th century,[75] the vicarage was worth less than £4 a year in 1291.[76] The rectory was worth £21 15*s.* 2*d.* net in 1535,[77] *c.* £200 in 1771, *c.* £300 in 1793,[78] £500 in 1826,[79] and £665 net in 1835.[80]

On the eve of commutation tithes were paid mainly in kind, although customary payments of 1*d.* for a milch cow and a garden and 4*d.* for a colt were due, and also two moduses (totalling 21*s.*) from *c.* 36 a. at the north-eastern extremity of Thonglands (and the parish) near the Stanton Long boundary. In 1843 the rector *ex officio* owned all the tithes except a third of those in Little Poston, appropriated to Hereford cathedral, and an impropriated third of the corn and grain tithes from 50 a. at the western edge of Millichope park. His tithes were commuted to £514 10*s.* with an additional £20 due from the glebe whenever it, or parts of it, were not in his hands.[81]

The living was worth £747 in 1851: £525 tithe rent charge, £215 from the glebe, and £7 in surplice fees.[82] In 1885 its gross value was £740.[83] In 1793 there had been 80 a. of glebe,[84] much of it owned before 1600;[85] in 1843 there were *c.* 116 a.[86] Glebe farm, Munslow, comprised 137 a. in 1888,[87] and 125 a. in 1941.[88] The Church Commissioners sold the farmhouse in 1968 but retained the land.[89]

There was a five bayed parsonage with attached farm buildings *c.* 1600.[90] By 1793 Richard Powell, rector 1776–1806,[91] had built a substantial three storeyed stone parsonage[92] west of the church, with a coach house north-east of the church. A new parsonage was built in Park Lane by 1967, when the old one was sold.[93]

In the later 12th century the son of a former rector claimed to have been wrongfully excluded from the living.[94] Ellis, one of two known medieval vicars, was murdered *c.* 1298.[95] William of Rowton (or of Ludlow), rector from 1324, was cited in 1333 for non-payment of procurations and later excommunicated and sought for arrest.[96] Walter Lawrence, rector 1418–22, resigned after having been castrated.[97] John Littleton, rector from 1528 and a graduate,[98] was deprived for marriage in 1554, as was his curate.[99]

An obit was endowed with land in Thonglands yielding 12*d.*[1] John Lloyd, rector 1506–28, endowed St. Mary's service with land in Hungerford.[2] A stipendiary priest received *c.* 40*s.* a year.[3]

George Littleton, rector 1630–75, was a grandson of John, rector 1528–54;[4] he celebrated communion four times a year.[5] In 1761 Thomas Powys put in a namesake, doubtless a kinsman.[6] In 1776, four years after he bought the advowson from Powys, Thomas Powell presented his son Richard.[7] That began a remarkable hold on the living by successive fathers and sons (all after 1776 presenting themselves) for almost 200 years until Edward Powell's resignation in

68 Eyton, v. 144; *Cal. Pat.* 1247–58, 125; *Cal. Close,* 1251–3, 206; *Cal. Inq. p.m.* xiv, p. 154; P.R.O., CP 25/1/195/20, no. 8; CP 25/2/77/654/3 & 4 Phil. & Mary Mich. no. 37; CP 25/2/959/5 Anne East. [no. 11]; CP 40/1156, m. 5; H.W.R.O.(H.), HD 2/14/51; *T.S.A.S.* 3rd ser. v. 362, 375; viii. 52; 4th ser. ii. 66, 81, 104–5; vi. 306; *Reg. Courtenay* (C.S.), 11; *Reg. Mascall* (C.S.), 175, 182; *Reg. Lacy* (C.S.), 119; *Reg. Spofford* (C.S.), 247, 350–1, 359; *Reg. Myllyng* (C.S.), 187; *Reg. Mayew* (C.S.), 274; *Reg. Bothe* (C.S.), 342. Cf. above, manors.

69 Wrottesley, *Pedigrees from Plea Rolls*, 509–10; Eyton, v. 144; *Reg. Orleton* (C.S.), 299–301, 304, 322.

70 *Reg. Trefnant* (C.S.), 181. Cf. above, manors.

71 *Reg. Mascall*, 38–9, 47, 50.

72 S.P.L., MS. 6865, p. 151; below, this section.

73 *T.S.A.S.* 4th ser. vi. 313; vii. 170; *Dioc. of Heref. Institutions (1539–1900)*, ed. A. T. Bannister (Heref. 1923), 162, 205; Heref. Dioc. Regy., reg. 1969– (in use), pp. 131, 382, 458, 568; *Heref. Dioc. Yr. Bk.* (1967–8), 34; (1989), 44; inf. from Ch. Com.

74 *Tax. Eccl.* (Rec. Com.), 167.

75 *Cal. Chanc. Wts.* i. 88; *S.P.R. Heref.* xv (2), p. vi.

76 *Tax. Eccl.* 167.

77 *Valor Eccl.* (Rec. Com.), iii. 209.

78 S.P.L., MS. 6865, p. 151.

79 H.W.R.O.(H.), HD 9, 'Notitia', f. 47.

80 *Rep. Com. Eccl. Rev.* [67], pp. 446–7, H.C. (1835), xxii.

81 S.R.O. 1705/25; above, manors (Lr. Millichope, tithes); below, Lesser Poston, intro.

82 P.R.O., HO 129/352, no. 58.

83 *Kelly's Dir. Salop.* (1885), 900.

84 S.P.L., MS. 6865, p. 151.

85 H.W.R.O.(H.), HD 2/14/50–1.

86 S.R.O. 1705/25.

87 S.R.O. 1705/30.

88 *Kelly's Dir. Salop.* (1941), 166.

89 Inf. from Ch. Com. and Mrs. E. Hughes.

90 H.W.R.O.(H.), HD 2/14/50; S.R.O. 1705/29.

91 Bannister, *Heref. Institutions*, 107, 133.

92 S.P.L., MS. 6865, p. 151.

93 Inf. from Ch. Com. and the Revd. I. E. Gibbs.

94 B.L. Egerton MS. 2819, ff. 39, 94v.; Royal MS. 15 B. iv, f. 111v.

95 *Cal. Chanc. Wts.* i. 88; Eyton, v. 144.

96 Eyton, v. 144; *Reg. Orleton*, 388; *Reg. T. Charlton* (C.S.), 24, 30.

97 *Reg. Spofford*, 9, 350; *Reg. Lacy*, 119.

98 *Reg. Bothe*, 342; S.P.L., MS. 5589.

99 Heref. D. & C. mun., chapter act bk. 1512–66 (folio), ff. 129, 130v.

1 *Cal. Pat.* 1548–9, 395; *T.S.A.S.* 3rd ser. x. 373.

2 *Cal. Pat.* 1572–5, p. 324; *Reg. Mayew*, 274; *Reg. Bothe*, 342; *S.P.R. Heref.* xv (2), p. vi.

3 *S.P.R. Heref.* xv (2), p. vi, citing no source.

4 *T.S.A.S.* 3rd ser. v. 362, 375; viii. 52; 4th ser. vi. 250–2.

5 S.R.O. 1705/43, s.a. e.g. 1669.

6 Bannister, *Heref. Institutions*, 95.

7 Ibid. 107; *S.P.R. Heref.* xv (2), p. vii; above, this section.

1965.[8] In 1793 Richard Powell, who had recently rebuilt the parsonage, held two Sunday services and celebrated communion monthly for 20 or more parishioners. Occasional services on saints' days drew up to 60 to church.[9] On Census Sunday 1851 *c.* 65 adults were at the morning service and *c.* 55 at that in the afternoon, in each case with *c.* 45 children; the adult figures were said to be slightly below average.[10]

The church of *ST. MICHAEL*, so dedicated by *c.* 1740,[11] consists of chancel with south chapel (now the vestry), nave with north aisle, west tower, and south porch. The medieval fabric is rubble stone including much soft siltstone with dressed openings; rebuilding in 1869–70 employed ashlar, including red sandstone, to give an irregular chequerboard effect.

The nave is 12th-century. The tower, entered by a broad arch, was added late in the same century. The chancel may be 13th-century; there is a piscina in the south wall. In the 14th century a north aisle was built, the arcade of three arches being built within the existing nave whose north wall was then removed. Also 14th-century are three windows in the south nave wall, the east window and south door in the chancel, perhaps the south chapel, the top storey of the tower, and the cruck framed south porch with its elaborate wooden tracery.

Fifteenth- and 16th-century work includes the middle window in the north aisle, the font, and painted glass, some of it given by John Lloyd, rector 1506–28 and depicted in one window.[12] In the 15th or early 16th century a large rood loft was inserted, approached by a staircase in the south wall of the nave. It was probably removed before the 17th century.[13] A number of bench ends carved with simple geometric patterns may also date from the later 15th or early 16th century. In the 16th century both nave and chancel roofs were renewed and a window inserted at the west end of the north wall of the aisle. Box pews were introduced in the 17th century, and a parapet added to the tower in the 18th.

By the late 18th century the church was in decay, especially the south (or Aston) chapel.[14] The 'Millichope chancel' may then have occupied the east end of the north aisle.[15] Substantial repairs were made in 1815.[16] In 1839 the vestry asked Mrs. Wright of Aston to give up the south chapel so that it could be fitted up as a vestry room,[17] and in 1841 the church was repewed with aid from the Incorporated Church Building Society and the Hereford Diocesan Church Building Society.[18] The change produced 148 more seats, 133 of them free, to give a total of 370 sittings.[19] Pulpit and reading desk were moved from the middle of the south wall to the south-east corner of the nave.[20]

S. Pountney Smith's restoration of the church in 1869–70 was also grant-aided.[21] Roofs and floors were renewed, a west gallery and high pews removed, the internal walls scraped and pointed, and new furnishings and glass introduced.[22] A wooden screen[23] was replaced by a stone chancel arch and a new eastern arch was made into the aisle.[24] In 1954 a crucifix was placed above the pulpit, in 1968 an aumbry was put in the north aisle, and in 1980 a Lady chapel was made in that aisle.[25]

The plate is of 1674 and later.[26] Four bells hang in a 17th-century frame.[27] Fittings include a late medieval chest[28] and some good 16th-century and later monuments.[29]

The registers begin in 1538 and are largely complete.[30]

The 'cross',[31] a re-used lych-gate[32] in the churchyard over the tomb of the Revd. F. W. Read (d. 1774), a former rector, remained until the 1890s or later.[33] Additional burial ground south of the church was consecrated in 1873 and 1930.[34]

There was a parish church by 1280 at *THONGLANDS*, which had its own rector[35] and burial rights until 1425 or later.[36] Little Poston probably formed a detached part of Thonglands parish.[37] The advowson seems to have descended with the reputed manor.[38] In 1425 William Burley acquired both and so, in 1442, was able to unite Thonglands rectory to Munslow, also in his patronage.[39] Thonglands rectory was worth £4 in 1291.[40]

8 *S.P.R. Heref.* xv (2), pp. vi–vii; Bannister, op. cit. 107, 133, 162, 205; *Guide to St. Mic.'s Ch., Munslow* (priv. print. *c.* 1985).

9 S.P.L., MS. 6865, pp. 151–3.

10 P.R.O., HO 129/352, no. 58.

11 B.L. Add. MS. 30316, f. 31.

12 For glass see S.P.L., MS. 6820, f. 72; S.R.O. 1865/1, pp. 147–50; Birm. Univ. Libr., Mytton Papers, iv. 920–3.

13 A wooden chancel screen survived to *c.* 1870: below.

14 S.P.L., MS. 6865, pp. 152–3. See also W.S.L. 350/5/40, Munslow p. 26; St. Deiniol's Libr., Glynne's ch. notes, xcvi, f. 7.

15 Mentioned in W.S.L. 350/5/40, Munslow pp. 25–6, and distinct from the 'rectory chancel' (ibid. p. 31); it is otherwise difficult to suggest a location.

16 S.R.O. 1705/54; S.P.L., MS. 6865, p. 153.

17 S.R.O. 2788/41, mtg. 17 July 1839.

18 S.R.O. 1705/58, 60–1, 65–7; Heref. Dioc. Regy., reg. 1822–42, pp. 592–3; H.W.R.O.(H.), HD 8, box 45, pew plans, etc.

19 S.R.O. 2580/67, s.v. Munslow.

20 H.W.R.O.(H.), HD 8, box 45, pew plans, etc.

21 S.R.O. 1705/70–81, 92; *Shrews. Jnl.* 7 Nov. 1883, p. 5.

22 S.R.O. 1705/75; *Ch. Cal. Dioc. Heref.* (1871), 157; (1872), 119.

23 S.R.O. 1865/1, p. 147.

24 S.R.O. 1705/75; Cranage, ii. 143.

25 Heref. Dioc. Regy., reg. 1953–68, pp. 87, 301; 1969– (in use), pp. 373, 552.

26 D. L. Arkwright and B. W. Bourne, *Ch. Plate Archd. Ludlow* (Shrews. 1961), 47.

27 H. B. Walters, *Ch. Bells of Salop.* (Oswestry, 1915), 96–7.

28 Cranage, ii. 143; S.P.L., MS. 6767, no. 59.

29 *T.S.A.S.* l. 95–104; Birm. Univ. Libr., Mytton Papers, iv. 908–18; S.R.O. 1865/1, pp. 151–7; Pevsner, *Salop.* 214.

30 S.R.O. 1705/1–12; 2788/1–4; regs. at ch.; cf. *S.P.R. Heref.* xv (2).

31 W.S.L. 350/5/40, Munslow pp. 26–7.

32 Perh. that repaired in 1688: S.R.O. 1705/43, s.a.

33 *S.P.R. Heref.* xv (2), p. vii; W.S.L. 350/5/40, Munslow pp. 26–7; S.P.L., MS. 372, vol. ii, f. 59; S. Bagshaw, *Dir. Salop.* (1851), 541; S.P.L., photos.; N.B.R., photos.; Cranage, ii. 146.

34 Heref. Dioc. Regy., reg. 1869–83, p. 202; 1919–26, p. 330; 1926–38, p. 243.

35 *S.P.R. Heref.* xv (2), pp. v, 7; S.R.O. 1037/3/83, 92; S.P.L., Deeds 12873.

36 *T.S.A.S.* 4th ser. ii, p. xxi; S.P.L., MS. 1119/6, drawing of coffin lid.

37 Below, Lesser Poston, intro.

38 *Reg. Cantilupe* (C.S.), 203; *Reg. Orleton*, 5, 389; *Cal. Inq. p.m.* xv, p. 289; *Cal. Inq. p.m.* (Rec. Com.), iv. 56; *Cal. Close*, 1419–22, 154–5; above, manors (Thonglands).

39 *Cal. Close*, 1422–9, 207; *Reg. Spofford*, 247–8; above, manors (Thonglands).

40 *Inq. Non.* 186.

The small church, built within the manor-house moat, may have been in occasional use when George I's arms were hung in it, but by the 1830s it was ruinous and by 1883 had gone.[41]

BROADSTONE chapel was mentioned in 1589, but the plain round-headed south doorway suggests a medieval origin. In 1589, as later, it was reckoned a chapel of ease to Munslow. It was endowed with a house and curtilage, 1 yardland of arable, and 1 a. of wood at Stanway,[42] but no record of a chaplain is known. In 1716 the only services there were Christmas and Easter communions.[43] In 1793 glebe (49 a. *c.* 1830)[44] and tithe income were worth £63.[45] Broadstone remained little used in the early 19th century,[46] but services were more regular after the chapel's refurbishment in 1842–4.[47] On Census Sunday 1851 all 70 free seats were occupied for the monthly service.[48] There was a monthly service in 1990.[49]

In 1793 the single-cell, three bayed stone chapel, entered by a round-headed south door, was lit by several small unglazed windows. The nave, earth-floored, had no seats except a stone wall bench. In the south-east corner was a carved 'tub or pulpit'. The chancel, floored with pebbles, had a communion table,[50] probably the 17th-century one there in 1990. The chapel was restored in 1842–4, with grants from the Hereford Diocesan Church Building Society and the Incorporated Church Building Society.[51]

Plate in 1793 comprised a pewter tankard and plate of 1708.[52] There was no plate in 1961.[53]

NONCONFORMITY. In the later 17th and early 18th century several Aston families were papists, including the Smiths, lords of that manor.[54] The Augustinian canonesses' chapel at Millichope Hall was used by local Catholics 1943–5 and perhaps until 1947 during the subsequent occupancy of the Hall by some Benedictines from Prinknash (Glos.).[55]

Methodists met in Aston in 1804,[56] and they or other dissenters had a house in the parish licensed for worship in 1827.[57] Aston Munslow Wesleyan chapel was built in stone in 1862[58] and remained in use in 1990. Other Methodist chapels were a Primitive one at Primrose Bank (1861, closed by 1963)[59] and a Wesleyan one at Bache Mill (1879, closed by 1964).[60]

EDUCATION. Roger Stedman, rector, kept school in 1573.[61] In the 18th century the only teaching in the parish seems to have been at dame schools.[62] In 1819 and 1835 there was said to be no school,[63] but a school in Munslow Old Farm House closed *c.* 1842.[64]

A National school, supported by voluntary contributions, school pence, and a small endowment, opened in the former Munslow Old Farm House *c.* 1849. The building, rented from the owner of Millichope Park, provided a master's house containing a first-floor schoolroom and second-floor classroom;[65] it was extended in 1872.[66] In 1870[67] there was an adult evening school from which nine were struck off. Attendance then averaged *c.* 65 at the day school but rose to over 80 at times in the 1880s and 1890s, although numbers often fell off owing to bad weather or the demands of farm work; in 1895 76 pupils had to walk between 1 and 2½ miles and only 11 lived in Munslow village. There were 98 on roll in 1902, but by 1922 attendance averaged 55. The school closed in 1982, the 29 pupils going to the new Corvedale school, Diddlebury.[68]

A Roman Catholic school run by Augustinian canonesses was evacuated from Westgate-on-Sea (Kent) to Millichope Hall in 1943 and remained until 1945.[69] The Hall was used by the county council 1948–62 for Millichope school, a boys' secondary boarding (or 'camp') school. The pupils, normally *c.* 60, came from all-age schools with limited opportunities for senior boys' education. In 1962 the school moved to Apley Park.[70]

CHARITIES FOR THE POOR. There was a poor's stock when Charles More (d. 1646)[71] of Millichope left 40*s.* to increase it.[72] Nothing more is known of the legacy.

By 1716 the parish had an almshouse given by a 'Mr. Hanson', a former minister,[73] perhaps William

41 W.S.L. 350/5/40, Munslow p. 10; O.S. Map 6", Salop. LXV. NW. (1891 edn.).

42 S.R.O. 1705/29.

43 H.W.R.O.(H.), HD 5/14/1/19.

44 W.S.L. 350/5/40, Munslow p. 9.

45 S.P.L., MS. 6865, pp. 53, 151.

46 W.S.L. 350/5/40, Munslow p. 9; S. Bagshaw, *Dir. Salop.* (1851), 542.

47 Cranage, ii. 69; below, this section.

48 P.R.O., HO 129/352, no. 57.

49 Inf. from Mr. Gibbs.

50 S.P.L., MS. 6865, p. 52.

51 S.R.O. 2788/41, s.a.

52 S.P.L., MS. 6865, p. 52.

53 D. L. Arkwright and B. W. Bourne, *Ch. Plate Archd. Ludlow* (Shrews. 1961), 12.

54 B.L. Add. MS. 30211; H.L.R.O., Main Papers, 3 Dec. 1680 (papist returns); *S.P.R. Heref.* xv (2), pp. iv–vi, 154, 161, 170, 195, 210; *Worcs. Recusant*, liii. 28, 34–5; liv. 31; S.P.L., MS. 6865, p. 152; *Compton Census*, ed. Whiteman, 259.

55 E. M. Abbott, *Hist. Dioc. Shrews. 1850–1986* [1987], 78; below, educ.

56 Heref. Dioc. Regy., reg. 1791–1821, f. 40v.

57 Ibid. reg. 1822–42, p. 82.

58 O.N.S. (Birkdale), Worship Reg. no. 15497; date stone; inf. from Mr. Gibbs.

59 O.N.S. (Birkdale), Worship Reg. no. 12821.

60 Ibid. no. 25186; date stone.

61 S.R.O. 3320/21/2.

62 H.W.R.O.(H.), HD 5/14/1/19; S.P.L., MS. 6865, p. 150.

63 *Digest Educ. Poor*, H.C. 224, p. 756 (1819), ix (2); *Educ. Enq. Abstract*, ii, H.C. 62, p. 779 (1835), xlii.

64 S.R.O. 1011, parcel 248, Millichope estate rentals 1842–3.

65 S. Bagshaw, *Dir. Salop.* (1851), 541; S.C.C. *Salop. Char. for Elem. Educ.* (1906), 61–2; P.R.O., ED 7/102, ff. 446–7; S.R.O. 1705/25–6, field 271; above, this article, intro.

66 *Shropshire Mag.* Jan. 1975, 16.

67 Rest of para. based on S.R.O. 4322/1/1.

68 R. J. Phillips, *Ch. and State: Heref. Dioc. Schs.* (Heref. Dioc. Council of Educ. [1987]), table 2 (copy in S.R.O. 5101); S.C.C. Educ. Cttee. *Educ. Dir.* (1981), p. 6.

69 Abbott, *Hist. Dioc. Shrews.* 78.

70 *S.C.C. Mins. (Educ.)* 1946–7, 208, 213, 229–30; 1947–8, 127, 171; 1948–9, 10, 22, 91–2; 1961–2, 133; S.R.O. 2782/16; *Shropshire Mag.* Dec. 1950, 23–5.

71 *S.P.R. Heref.* xv (2), 87.

72 S.P.L., Deeds 15687.

73 H.W.R.O.(H.), HD 5/14/1/19.

Honsome, rector (d. *c.* 1471).[74] It may still have existed in 1827, but had apparently gone by 1883.[75]

In 1786 land given at an unknown date produced 10*s.* a year and land devised by Samuel Amies (d. 1750) £2; disbursements from both had ceased long before.[76]

John (d. 1762) and Catherine (d. 1792) More left £100 and £200 respectively. Their charities produced £13 2*s.* 6*d.* in 1823, £8 in 1975.[77]

By will proved in 1849 the Revd. R. N. Pemberton left money which produced £5 in 1975.[78]

LESSER POSTON

AT THE time of its transfer to Hopton Cangeford civil parish in 1884 Little Poston (343 a., 139 ha.) had long been a detached township of Munslow parish, the main part of which lay *c.* 6 km. north-west.[79] Earlier, until 1442, it had probably formed a detached township of Thonglands parish and earlier still, it is presumed, was part of Diddlebury parish.

In the late Saxon period Little Poston and Great Poston adjoining it to the north-east had presumably formed a single estate in Diddlebury parish; thus perhaps it was to Diddlebury church that a Domesday tenant of the manor had to render a bundle of box on Palm Sunday.[80] A 1¼-a. close near Little Poston Farm remained in Diddlebury parish until the 19th century.[81] The dean and chapter of Hereford cathedral, to whom Diddlebury rectory was appropriated in 1237, owned a third of Little Poston's tithes.[82] The other two thirds were evidently granted away before 1237, probably to the rector of Thonglands, for the lord of Little Poston seems also to have been lord of Thonglands manor and patron of that church. It was thus almost certainly the absorption of Thonglands by Munslow parish in 1442[83] that made Little Poston a detached part of Munslow parish. Little Poston, with Great Poston, was transferred to Hopton Cangeford ecclesiastical parish in 1858.[84]

The name Poston may have reference to a thorn tree used as a boundary marker of the combined estate.[85] Little Poston's own boundary was marked in the south by the streams running down Poston and Witchcot dingles. A small tributary of Pye brook marked part of the township's northern boundary, but elsewhere the boundary followed field edges.[86]

Little (now Lesser) Poston lies towards the western edge of the Clee Hills plateau. The land slopes up from *c.* 170 m. at the confluence of Witchcot and Poston dingles, to 254 m. on Sutton hill, south of Baldwin's coppice; to the north-west it dips towards the Pye brook valley. Lesser Poston Farm stands at *c.* 220 m.[87] The soil is a silty loam, overlying the red marls of the Old Red Sandstone.[88]

Crossing the highest land in the township is the road north-east from Ludlow bound for villages around the western side of the Clees including Cold Weston, Clee St. Margaret, and Stoke St. Milborough. Footpaths lead north-west and north from Little Poston to Sutton, Diddlebury, and Peaton, and south to Hopton Cangeford.[89]

There is nothing to suggest that before the 19th century Little Poston ever comprised more than one or two farms, and the township was not taxed separately in the Middle Ages. In the later 17th century there were two farmhouses there[90] but by the early 19th century only one,[91] Little Poston Farm;[92] that was last inhabited *c.* 1950.[93] By 1843 there were cottages at Red Furlong in the north-eastern part of the township and at Sutton Hill in the north-west.[94] Eight houses, Cedarwood Cottages, were built *c.* 1953 in the north, next to the Ludlow road.[95]

MANOR. Ketil (Chetel) held *LITTLE POSTON* in 1066. By 1086 Earl Roger had given it to his chapel of St. Michael in Shrewsbury castle.[96] In 1102 the Crown resumed the castle, which was usually in the sheriff's custody thereafter. By 1255 John FitzAlan (II), heir of the men who had enjoyed a virtually hereditary shrievalty in the 12th century, was overlord of Little Poston.[97] Little Poston was said to be held of Hugh, Lord Burnell, in 1418–19[98] and of the duchy of York 1501–1606.[99]

74 *Reg. Stanbury* (C.S.), 187.

75 C. & J. Greenwood, *Map of Salop.* (1827); O.S. Map 6", Salop. LXIV. NE. (1890 edn.).

76 *Char. Don. 1786–8*, ii, H.C. 511–II, pp. 1024–5 (1816), xvi (2); *S.P.R. Heref.* xv (2), 212.

77 *9th Rep. Com. Char.* H.C. 258, pp. 409–10 (1823) ix; *Review of Local Chars.* (S.C.C. 1975), 58.

78 *Salop. Char. for Elem. Educ.* 61–2; *Rev. Local Chars.* 58; above, manors (Lr. Millichope).

79 Cf. *V.C.H. Salop.* ii. 223 n., 225 n.; S.R.O. 1705/25–6; above, Munslow, intro.; fig. 14. Township area calculated from P.R.O., IR 30/29/229; O.S. Maps 1/2,500, Salop. LXXI. 4; LXXII. 1, 5 (1884 edn.); O.S. *Area Bk.* Hopton Cangeford (1885). The farm was successively 'Little', 'Lower' (from *c.* 1890), and 'Lesser' Poston (from *c.* 1930): *Kelly's Dir. Salop.* (1885–1941); O.S. maps; S.R.O., regs. of electors.

80 *V.C.H. Salop.* i. 313, 338.

81 P.R.O., IR 29/29/255; IR 30/29/255, field 61. S.R.O. 783, box 183, sale partic., wrongly assumes that still to be the case in 1913 (cf. O.S. Map 1/2,500, Salop. LXXII. 5 (1884 edn.)).

82 Below, manor (tithes).

83 Above, Munslow, manors (Thonglands); churches; below, manor.

84 Heref. Dioc. Regy., reg. 1857–69, pp. 61–5.

85 *P.N. Salop.* (E.P.N.S.), i. 239–40.

86 O.S. Maps 1/2,500, Salop. LXXI. 4; LXXII. 1, 5 (1884 edn.).

87 O.S. Map 1/25,000, SO 48/58 (1983 edn.).

88 Inst. Geol. Sciences Map 1", drift, sheet 166 (1967 edn.); *Field Studies*, ii (1), map of 'Soil Associations of Salop.'; *V.C.H. Salop.* iv. 6–7.

89 O.S. Map 1/25,000, SO 48/58 (1983 edn.).

90 e.g. S.R.O. 1705/43, s.a. 1663, 1670, 1676.

91 B.L. Maps, O.S.D. 206.

92 Below, manor.

93 S.R.O., reg. of electors, Ludlow const. (1950), p. 473; (1951), p. 473.

94 S.R.O. 783, box 183, sale partic.; 1705/25–6.

95 S.R.O., reg. of electors, Ludlow const. (1954), p. 473; (1955), p. 483.

96 *V.C.H. Salop.* i. 313; Eyton, v. 206.

97 *V.C.H. Salop.* iii. 10, 12–13, 31; *Rot. Hund.* (Rec. Com.), ii. 70.

98 P.R.O., C 138/32, no. 31; C 138/39, no. 46.

99 *Cal. Inq. p.m. Hen. VII*, ii, p. 268; iii, pp. 141–2; P.R.O., C 142/35, no. 103; C 142/293, no. 70.

Richard of Thonglands was terre tenant in 1255[1] as were his successors as lords of Thonglands, Sir Roger de Bradeleye in 1284 and Roger de la Mare in 1316.[2] Before 1344 the principal holding in Little Poston, occasionally described as a manor, passed to the Beysin family.[3] It descended with their share of Broseley until the division of the Harewell estate in 1534 when Little Poston fell to Agnes, wife of John Smith.[4] From her (d. 1562) the estate, usually described as two farms, seems to have descended with Wootton Wawen (Warws.)[5] until 1673 when Francis Smith, Viscount Carrington, sold Little Poston to Richard Coling. Coling sold it in 1693 to Thomas and Elizabeth Lee[6] whose descendants sold it in 1802 to Valentine Vickers of Cranmere (in Worfield).[7] Vickers died in 1814;[8] his son, the Ven. William Vickers, owned all Little Poston in 1843[9] but evidently sold it shortly before his death in 1851[10] to Richard Mason, owner *c.* 1850 of the 739-a. Poston estate, including all of Little Poston.[11] Mason or a namesake was evidently owner in 1913,[12] but in that year Lower, formerly Little, Poston farm (*c.* 263 a.) was bought, probably from trustees, by James Mason, John K. Mason, and Zachariah Mason, coal merchants of Dudley. James was mentioned as owner until the late 1920s when the estate evidently passed to P. G. Holder of Corfton Hall.[13]

In 1942 Holder sold Lesser, formerly Little, Poston farm (205 a.), as part of his Corfton estate, to the Ecclesiastical Commissioners.[14] The Church Commissioners sold it to Lord Boyne in 1964,[15] and he sold it later.[16] The owner in 1991 was T. R. Gough.

Lesser Poston Farm, a long stone building of two storeys and an attic, semi-derelict in 1991, includes elements of a substantial late medieval timber framed building.[17] Those include a stud partition at the north end of the principal first-floor room and, in the roof, intermediate trusses, probably not *in situ*; one of them is elaborately stopped. About 1600, or perhaps a little later, the house was altered to give it a principal ground-floor room (26 × 19 ft.) served by a chimney stack placed centrally in the rear wall; much of the room's elaborately carved compartmented ceiling remains *in situ*. The room above was the same size. What comprised the rest of the house, probably that occupied with 3 yardlands by Thomas Baldwin (fl. 1661, d. 1708), gentleman, and his son Edward (d. 1730),[18] is unknown. The house was substantially altered in the 18th and 19th centuries when it was progressively clad in stone. The south, or parlour, end was rebuilt, the hall was foreshortened at the north to form a new kitchen, and the timber ceiling was cut down to fit the new, smaller, hall place.

A third of the *TITHES* of Little Poston belonged to the dean and chapter of Hereford cathedral, presumably from 1237, when Diddlebury rectory was appropriated to them.[19] In 1844 the tithes were commuted to £6.[20] The cathedral's appropriated tithe of Barn close, that part of the township in Diddlebury parish, had been discharged of appropriated and vicarial tithe at commutation in 1843.[21]

ECONOMIC HISTORY. In 1086 there was 1 virgate of land sufficient for ½ ploughteam.[22] Furlongs in the north-eastern part of the township[23] and ridge and furrow around Lesser Poston Farm[24] may indicate medieval open-field land. In the later 17th century the township's farm land was reckoned at 3 yardlands.[25] Flax or hemp may have been grown there.[26]

A large wood, probably called Brockhurst, seems to have occupied the township's southern end;[27] it was cleared before the 19th century.[28] In the northern part of the township Baldwin's and Cockshut coppices, both so called in the early 19th century, survived.[29] A small common on Sutton hill, mentioned in 1802, was inclosed after 1843.[30]

There was a quarry north of Baldwin's coppice and another near Lower, formerly Little, Poston Farm. A shaft north of the farm buildings may represent old copper workings.[31]

LOCAL GOVERNMENT. In 1462 Little Poston did suit to a Broseley court of recognition at which William Harewell's tenants appeared.[32]

As part of Munslow parish Little Poston was in Ludlow poor-law union from 1836, Ludlow highway district from 1863, and Ludlow rural sanitary district from 1872, and after its transfer

1 *Rot. Hund.* ii. 70.

2 *Feud. Aids*, iv. 223; *Kts. of Edw. I*, iii (Harl. Soc. lxxxii), 113; above, Munslow, manors.

3 P.R.O., CP 25/1/194/13, no. 33.

4 *Cal. Fine R.* 1413–22, 263–5; *Cal. Inq. p.m.* xviii, pp. 199–202; *Cal. Inq. p.m.* (Rec. Com.), iv. 35, 41; *Cal. Inq. p.m. Hen. VII*, ii, p. 268; iii, pp. 141–2, 297; below, Broseley, manor; Dugdale, *Warws.* (1730), ii. 810; T. F. Dukes, *Antiquities of Salop.* (1844), 263–4.

5 P.R.O., C 142/132, no. 16; C 142/293, no. 70. Cf. *V.C.H. Warws.* iii. 197–9.

6 S.R.O. 1005/1; 2496/13, 15–17.

7 S.R.O. 837/104; 1005/2–4; 2496/18–22; S.P.L., Deeds 10520–1, 11231.

8 S.R.O. 4208/103, no. X2.

9 S.R.O. 1374/6, s.a. 1789; 1705/25–6.

10 *Gent. Mag.* N.S. xxxv (1), 679.

11 S.R.O. 2521/1.

12 *Kelly's Dir. Salop.* (1891), 331; (1909), 113.

13 Ibid. (1926), 118; (1929), 118; S.R.O. 783, box 183, sale partic. and corresp.; 4011/44, no. 294.

14 S.R.O. 4440/2.

15 Inf. from Ch. Com.

16 Inf. from the agent, Vct. Boyne Ests.

17 Mr. E. Mercer and Mrs. M. Moran are thanked for their comments and help with survey work.

18 *T.S.A.S.* 4th ser. ii. 159–60; *S.P.R. Heref.* xv (2), pp. 141, 165; Glam. R.O., CL/Deeds I, Salop. 13 Feb. 1688/9; S.R.O. 1705/43 (lewns).

19 *Charters and Rec. of Heref. Cath.* ed. W. W. Capes (1908), pp. xiii, 74–5; Heref. D. & C. mun. 4836 (xlviii) (1725).

20 S.R.O. 1705/25–6.

21 P.R.O., IR 29/29/255; IR 29/30/255, field 61.

22 *V.C.H. Salop.* i. 313.

23 S.R.O. 1705/25–6, fields 821–2.

24 SA 4367.

25 S.R.O. 1705/43, s.a. 1669, 1694.

26 Ibid. /25–6, field 866 (Hoddy field); cf. H. D. G. Foxall, *Salop. Field-Names* (Salop. Arch. Soc. 1980), 31.

27 S.R.O. 1705/25–6, fields 858–60.

28 B.L. Maps, O.S.D. 206.

29 Ibid.; O.S. Map 1/25,000, SO 48/58 (1983 edn.).

30 S.R.O. 837/104; 1705/25–6, tithe-free area; fig. 14.

31 O.S. Maps 6", Salop. LXXI. NE. (1903 edn.); LXXII. NW. (1891 edn.); SA 6993 (suggesting purpose of shaft from proximity of Hayton's Bent copper mine).

32 Birm. Univ. Libr., Mytton Papers, i. 198.

to Hopton Cangeford civil parish in 1884 remained with that C.P. in the same poor-law union, highway district, rural (sanitary) district, and district as Munslow.[33]

STANTON LONG

SITUATED in Corve Dale, about 10 km. south-west of Much Wenlock, the agricultural parish of Stanton Long consisted *c.* 1831 of Patton township and parts of Brockton, Stanton Long, and Oxenbold townships.[34] The parish forms two compact blocks joined by a narrow isthmus, the southern block formerly containing several detached parts of Holdgate parish. The irregular shape probably resulted from the 12th-century separation of estates (perhaps all once served from a church at Patton) into the parishes of two newly founded manorial churches at Stanton Long and Holdgate. The southern part of the parish is bounded by the river Corve on the north-west, Oxenbold brook on the north-east, and the edge of the Clee plateau on the south-east; the northern part by the Corve on the south-east and Brockton brook on the south-west; elsewhere the boundary mostly follows artificial features. The parish had *c.* 2,423 a. from 1844, when its boundary with Shipton was defined,[35] until 1883 when some detachments of Holdgate civil parish in Stanton township were absorbed. In 1884 the Coates and three other Holdgate detachments in Stanton were added,[36] bringing the civil parish to 2,725 a. (1,103 ha.).[37] This article treats the parish as defined before 1883.

In Oxenbold and Stanton townships, in the southern part of the parish, the land rises from the Corve to the lower slopes of the Clee plateau. Trow brook runs down a shallow valley to cross the boundary on the south-west. In Brockton and Patton townships in the north the land rises more steeply from the Corve to the ridge behind Wenlock Edge on the north-west; at Brockton a deep valley cuts the ridge and runs down to the Corve.

The underlying strata dip from north-west to south-east. Most of Stanton and Oxenbold townships, and the eastern parts of Brockton and Patton townships, are on the Ledbury Group of the Downton Series of the Lower Old Red Sandstone; the highest parts of Stanton and Oxenbold are on the Ditton Series. Narrow bands of '*Psammosteus*' Limestone lie near the junction of the series east of Little Oxenbold. Most of Patton and Brockton are on the Upper Ludlow Shales and, on the higher side, the Aymestry Group limestone, the highest parts of which are overlain by boulder clay. The soils are mainly red-brown loams; at Patton a freely drained silt loam is usual.[38]

A neolithic flint scraper was found at Brockton,[39] but the only clear evidence of pre-Roman activity is at Patton, on rising ground west of the main road, where indications of a Bronze Age round barrow[40] and several ditched enclosures of Iron Age or Romano-British date[41] have been observed.

St. Mildburg Way, so called in 1332,[42] ran from Much Wenlock through Bourton, Patton, and Brockton to Shipton and beyond.[43] It was turnpiked in 1756[44] and used thereafter as the road from Much Wenlock to Ludlow.[45] It was disturnpiked in 1867[46] and became a main road in 1879.[47] Branches ran from Patton to Easthope (the Greenway),[48] Presthope, Bradeley (in Much Wenlock), and Weston (in Monkhopton) but none of them was metalled in 1990.

A supposed Roman road, believed to run from Greensforge (Staffs.) to central Wales, crossed Oxenbold and Stanton townships on high ground.[49] It was the Bridgnorth–Munslow road *c.* 1575.[50] It was turnpiked in 1839 from Morville to Corfield Cross, in Stanton township, and thence by a new stretch to Shipton, to meet the turnpike from Much Wenlock to Ludlow. A branch from Weston via Brockton to Easthope's Cross was turnpiked at the same time.[51] The supposed Roman road south of Corfield Cross was then abandoned as far as the road from Stanton Long to Shipton, beyond which it remained in use as Rowe Lane.[52] The Morville–Shipton road and its branch from Weston were disturnpiked in 1872[53] and became main roads in 1878.[54]

A lane from the supposed Roman road at Weston ran via Great and Little Oxenbold along high ground to Stanton Long, Holdgate, and beyond. It was the Bridgnorth–Stanton road in the 17th century.[55] South of Stanton Long it

33 Cf. V. J. Walsh, 'Admin. of Poor Laws in Salop. 1820–55' (Pennsylvania Univ. Ph.D. thesis, 1970), 148–50; S.R.O., q. sess. order bk. 1861–9, p. 127; *Kelly's Dir. Salop.* (1929), 118; *V.C.H. Salop.* ii. 215; sources cited ibid. iii. 169 n. 29; above, Munslow, local govt.

34 Fig. 12. This article was written 1989–90.

35 S.R.O. 1681/76/21–2.

36 Above, Holdgate, intro.

37 O.S. *Area Bk.* (1884).

38 Inst. Geol. Sciences Map 1/25,000, SO 59 *Wenlock Edge* (1969 edn.); Soil Surv. Map 1", sheet 166 (1972 edn.).

39 SA 2823.

40 O.S. Nat. Grid SO 578 947: SA 2188.

41 R. Whimster, *The Emerging Past* (R.C.H.M.E. 1989), 56–7.

42 S.R.O. 1224/2/11. Cf. below, M. Wenlock, communications.

43 Descr. of rds. based on J. Rocque, *Map of Salop.* (1752); S.R.O. 356, parcel 416, map of 1785; R. Baugh, *Map of Salop.* (1808); B.L. Maps, O.S.D. 207; C. & J. Greenwood, *Map of Salop.* (1827); P.R.O., IR 29/29/248, 297.

44 29 Geo. II, c. 60.

45 N.L.W., Wynnstay, box 56/6.

46 Ann. Turnpike Acts Continuance Act, 1867, 30 & 31 Vic. c. 59.

47 Under the Highways and Locomotives (Amendment) Act, 1878, 41 & 42 Vic. c. 77: S.R.O. 560/744.

48 P.R.O., IR 29/29/248; IR 30/29/248, fields 3, 10, 11, 17, 47.

49 *T.S.A.S.* lvi. 233–43.

50 S.R.O. 356, box 327, surv. *c.* 1575, p. 161.

51 2 Vic. c. 30 (Local and Personal); S.R.O., dep. plan 249.

52 *T.S.A.S.* lvi. 233, 238–9.

53 Ann. Turnpike Acts Continuance Act, 1871, 34 & 35 Vic. c. 115.

54 Highways and Locomotives (Amendment) Act, 1878, 41 & 42 Vic. c. 77.

55 S.R.O. 356, box 327, Brookhampton surv. of 1657.

remained open to wheeled traffic in 1990, though in 1633 it was 'bad to go on foot and a dangerous way to ride'.[56] From Stanton Long a footway, mentioned in the 13th century,[57] branched to Brockton and crossed the supposed Roman road at Corfield Cross.[58] Another road linked Stanton Long to Shipton, and left the parish by Shipton's bridge, so called in 1591;[59] the road remained in use in 1990. Other lanes ran from Stanton Long to Ashfield and to Ruthall (both in Ditton Priors) via the Leath and the Coates respectively. That to Ruthall survived in 1990 only in part and as a footpath.

In 1676 the parish had 110 adult inhabitants.[60] From a total population of 184 in 1793[61] there was marked growth, especially in the 1800s and 1830s, to a total of 327 in 1841;[62] the number of houses rose from 35 in 1793[63] to 54 in 1845.[64] By 1851, however, there were only 224 inhabitants. Further decline after 1931 brought the number down to 148 by 1961,[65] at which level it remained in 1981.[66] By 1991 it had climbed to 170.[67]

The only nucleated settlements seem to have been Brockton,[68] Patton, and Stanton Long. In 1086 Patton had six recorded inhabitants, twice as many as Stanton. It had a priest, unlike Stanton,[69] and had been *caput* of a hundred.[70] By the mid 14th century Patton's economic difficulties[71] had probably reduced the size of the settlement; only a freeman and two neifs were paying cash rents in 1363.[72] Earthworks suggest the sites of houses abandoned at that period.[73] Nevertheless there were five tenants (not necessarily resident) in 1447,[74] and in the 1540s Patton had four farms[75] and in 1542 mustered seven men, nearly as many as Stanton.[76] By 1716 there were three farmhouses.[77] The Farm (probably the former chief house), the Upper House, and the Middle House stood close to each other south-east of the Wenlock–Ludlow road near a stream draining to the Corve; they were the only dwellings in 1746.[78] They were replaced when Patton House was built *c.* 1800[79] and Patton Grange *c.* 1830, both north-west of the road,[80] but they were not demolished. In 1845 the Farm remained a house, later converted to a pair of cottages and ruinous by 1987; it was built of local sandstone, with a timber framed western gable. The Middle House was represented in 1845 by 'old buildings' (cattle sheds by 1987),[81] near which Patton Grange Cottages were later built;[82] the Upper House had been converted by 1845 to four cottages,[83] which were demolished in the early 20th century.[84] Farther south two cottages next to an isolated brick kiln in 1845[85] were gone by 1901.[86]

As its affix indicates,[87] Stanton Long is strung out, along the road to Holdgate above Trow brook. Only three inhabitants were recorded in 1086,[88] but by 1315 the manor had 13 freeholders and four customary tenants[89] as well as farm servants, of which the demesne had eight or more in 1308.[90] It may be that dense occupation of the higher ground *c.* 1200 caused the church to be built farther down the slope.[91] The withdrawal of 11 tenants from their holdings by 1340[92] presumably caused the settlement to shrink; the township mustered eight men in 1542, only one more than Patton.[93] The village was known locally as Dirty Stanton in the 17th and 18th centuries.[94] Nine houses owed hearth tax in 1672, of which five had more than one hearth.[95] In 1845 the village had four farmhouses, the vicarage, and 10 cottages (one a smithy, another a wheelwright's shop).[96] By 1990 the pattern had changed little. Most of the old houses were timber framed.

Stanton township had several early outlying houses, especially near the supposed Roman road. Corfield ('Corve hill'), occupied by the 13th century,[97] stands on a knoll above the river Corve. The Bush, apparently mentioned in 1589,[98] likewise overlooks the Corve; as part of Stanton's demesne lands,[99] its farm may have been 'Harley's tenement' in the 16th and 17th centuries.[1] Nearby cottages, New York (later

56 *T.S.A.S.* lviii. 60.
57 S.R.O. 3195/1, f. 23.
58 Cf. S.R.O. 356, parcel 416, map of 1785; 1141, box 20, deed.
59 S.P.L., Deeds 6333.
60 *Compton Census*, ed. Whiteman, 259 n.
61 S.P.L., MS. 6865, p. 178.
62 *V.C.H. Salop.* ii. 227.
63 S.P.L., MS. 6865, p. 178.
64 P.R.O., IR 29/29/248, 297. Glebe Fm. (standing in a detachment of Holdgate par.) is also counted here.
65 *V.C.H. Salop.* ii. 227.
66 *Census*, 1981, Small Area Statistics: Salop.
67 S.C.C. Property and Planning Services Dept. inf. rep C91/103.
68 Brockton's settlement hist. is mainly treated below, Shipton, intro.
69 *V.C.H. Salop.* i. 328.
70 By 1086 Patton hund. was said to 'belong' to the royal man. of Corfham (in Diddlebury): ibid. 316; iii. 6.
71 Below, econ. hist.
72 P.R.O., C 143/349, no. 4.
73 SA 948 (at O.S. Nat. Grid SO 585 947, 585 948); R.C.H.M.E., draft field rep. (1987).
74 P.R.O., C 116/213, m. 11.
75 *L. & P. Hen. VIII*, xx (1), pp. 222–3.
76 Ibid. xvii, p. 508.
77 S.R.O. 566/59, dated by *Orders of Q. Sess.* ii. 25.
78 S.R.O. 168/2, ff. 96 (no. 220), 97 (no. 216), 99 (no. 217). Locations inferred from those of nos. 215 (Dove's yard), 219 (Barn yard), mapped in 1845: P.R.O., IR 29/29/248; IR 30/29/248, fields 59, 72.
79 Baugh, *Map of Salop.*
80 O.S. Map 1", sheet LXI. SW. (1833 edn.); cf. B.L. Maps, O.S.D. 207; Greenwood, *Map of Salop.* (1827).
81 P.R.O., IR 29/29/248; IR 30/29/248, fields 47, 70; R.C.H.M.E., draft field rep. (1987).
82 O.S. Map 1/2,500, Salop. LVII. 7 (1902 edn.).
83 At O.S. Nat. Grid SO 585 948: P.R.O., IR 29/29/248; IR 30/29/248, field 54.
84 O.S. Map 1/2,500, Salop. LVII. 6 (1902 and 1926 edns.).
85 At O.S. Nat. Grid SO 588 943: P.R.O., IR 29/29/248; IR 30/29/248, field 75.
86 O.S. Map 1/2,500, Salop. LVII. 7 (1902 edn.).
87 *P.N. Salop.* (E.P.N.S), i. 277.
88 *V.C.H. Salop.* i. 328.
89 P.R.O., C 134/48, no. 9.
90 P.R.O., E 358/18, m. 4.
91 T. Rowley, *Salop. Landscape* (1972), 76–7. For date see below, church.
92 *Inq. Non.* (Rec. Com.), 186.
93 *L. & P. Hen. VIII*, xvii, p. 508.
94 *P.N. Salop.* (E.P.N.S), i. 277; Staffs. R.O., D.(W.) 1788, parcel 45, bdle. 11, canvass bk. of 1766.
95 *Hearth Tax 1672* (Salop. Arch. Soc. 1949), 179.
96 P.R.O., IR 29/29/297; IR 30/29/297.
97 Eyton, iv. 24, 37.
98 H.W.R.O.(H.), HD 2/14/39.
99 S.R.O. 757, box 50, deed of 1754.
1 H.W.R.O.(H.), HD 2/14/39; S.P.L., Deed 7145; S.R.O. 1037/21/105A, deed 30 July 1661.

York Cottage) and Stonehouse, occupied a single smallholding in the early 19th century.[2] East of Stanton village the isolated Field House, mentioned in 1584,[3] remained in 1990 as a rubble cottage with modern extensions. Cottages had begun to encroach on the Leath common by the mid 18th century;[4] there were five by 1845,[5] of which some remained in 1990.

In Oxenbold township the houses called Little Oxenbold and Oxenbold Leasows stood on isolated sites *c.* 1700. Little Oxenbold may have had open fields in the Middle Ages[6] and therefore may once have been a nucleated settlement.

The Feathers, Brockton, was probably the alehouse mentioned in 1793.[7] The Brockton Queen Dowager Benefit Society met there by 1855.[8] Harvest homes were held at Patton in the mid 19th century, and in 1869 an annual harvest thanksgiving was started, with a church service, a dinner for men and tea for women and children, and sports.[9] A parochial and school lending library began in 1868.[10]

MANORS AND OTHER ESTATES. The lands by the river Corve that Merchelm and Mildfrith gave to their half-sister St. Mildburg before 704[11] may have included 'Stantune', first named in 901 when Aethelraed, ealdorman of Mercia, and his wife Aethelflaed restored 10 *cassatae* in 'Stantune' to the church of Wenlock, which had granted the land into 'royal lordship' ('*in dominium regalem*').[12] The estate is presumed to have included the later manor of *STANTON LONG*. By 1066, however, the church of Wenlock no longer owned Stanton Long; it then belonged to Alwine (Elwin) a free man,[13] who may have been the son of Eadwig *cild*, a considerable landholder in Herefordshire.[14]

By 1086 Earl Roger held Stanton Long in chief. His overlordship presumably escheated to the Crown on Earl Robert's forfeiture in 1102. Roger de Lacy had a mesne lordship in 1086.[15] After his banishment in 1096 it is presumed to have passed by 1100 to his brother Hugh, and after Hugh's death, before 1121, to have escheated to the Crown.[16]

The terre tenant in 1086 was Herbert,[17] probably Herbert of Fourches.[18] His manorial estate of 3 hides[19] was later divided, apparently in the 12th century.

Part of Stanton Long may have been among the Shropshire lands that Roger of More, said to be an ancestor of the Mores of Linley,[20] held of the king in serjeanty in 1199,[21] for *c.* 1250 another Roger of More held an estate in Stanton by the serjeanty of acting as a constable of infantry whenever the king invaded Wales.[22] Before the end of the 12th century a predecessor had subinfeudated his Stanton Long property and Simon of Stanton (fl. *c.* 1174–*c.* 1180)[23] may have been the terre tenant of that part of Stanton; his son Thomas of Stanton (or of Long Stanton), fl. 1250,[24] certainly was by *c.* 1215. Between *c.* 1215 and 1251 Thomas alienated much of his land by subinfeudations or sales, but in 1247 he still held 1 carucate in Stanton Long.[25] By *c.* 1251 the serjeant Roger of More was liable to pay the Crown (in addition to the serjeanty that he owed) 5*s.* a year, which he collected from the various tenants in fee, as composition for his ancestor's alienation of the serjeanty's Stanton Long estate.[26] Thomas's grandson Thomas of Stanton had succeeded to the family property by 1255 when he sold a moor in Stanton to the Templars of Lydley and soon afterwards conveyed the rest of his estate to them.[27] The Templars held courts for Stanton Long by 1273[28] and before long were paying the king the serjeanty rent of 5*s.*[29]

Another part of Stanton Long had passed after 1086, perhaps in the period 1154–65,[30] to the baron of Castle Holdgate, who held it in chief in 1255.[31] In the late 12th century one of the barony's undertenants may have been Robert Walsh (fl. 1171 × 1176);[32] about 1225 a Robert Walsh gave 4 virgates in Stanton Long to the Templars of Lydley, who held them of Castle Holdgate barony in 1255.[33]

From 1263 to 1276 or later the Templars held Castle Holdgate manor and barony of the earls of Cornwall and thus owned a mesne lordship, as well as two demesne estates, in Stanton Long. Between *c.* 1284 and 1292 the chief lordship of Holdgate passed to the Burnells, who had succeeded to the Templars' mesne lordship,[34] and after Lydley preceptory was dissolved in 1308[35] the Stanton Long demesne estate that the Templars had acquired from Robert Walsh escheated to Edward Burnell. After Burnell's death in 1315[36] his widow Aline held it in dower and it was called a manor in 1316,[37] but nothing further is known of its descent. The Templars' other demesne estate, that which they had received

2 S.R.O. 3901/Rg/4, 25 May 1816, 30 July 1826; P.R.O., IR 29/29/297; IR 30/29/297, fields 226, 255.
3 S.R.O. 3901/Rg/1, 15 Feb. 1583/4. Cf. ibid. 5 Nov. 1607.
4 Ibid. /Rg/3, 4 Dec. 1746, 22 July 1753.
5 P.R.O., IR 29/29/297; IR 30/29/297.
6 Below, manors (Oxenbold); econ. hist.
7 S.P.L., MS. 6865, p. 180; Co. of Salop, *Return of Licensed Hos. 1896* (copy in S.R.O., q. sess. rec. box 148), 9.
8 Registrar of Friendly Socs. *List of Friendly Socs. in Co. of Salop, 1793–1855* (H.M.S.O. 1857; copy in S.R.O. 119/27), 5.
9 *Shrews. Chron.* 24 Sept. 1869, p. 7.
10 S.R.O. 3901/Rg/4, front endpaper.
11 H.P.R. Finberg, *Early Charters of W. Midlands* (1972), p. 203.
12 Birch, *Cart. Sax.* ii, p. 230 (no. 587).
13 *V.C.H. Salop.* i. 328.
14 W. E. Wightman, *Lacy Fam. in Eng. and Normandy, 1066–1194* (1966), 157–8.
15 *V.C.H. Salop.* i. 328; iii. 10.
16 Eyton, iv. 32; v. 237, 239–41; Wightman, op. cit. 170–1, 173–5.
17 *V.C.H. Salop.* i. 328.
18 Wightman, op. cit. 154 n.
19 *V.C.H. Salop.* i. 328.
20 Eyton, xi. 209–10.
21 *Pipe R.* 1199 (P.R.S. N.S. x), 78.
22 *Bk. of Fees*, ii. 1183, 1284; *Rot. Hund.* (Rec. Com.), ii. 72.
23 Eyton, ii. 66 n.; iv. 112.
24 S.R.O. 1224, box 342, Prior Gosnell's reg. f. 4; *Bk. of Fees*, ii. 1183.
25 *Rot. Hund.* ii. 72.
26 Eyton, iv. 35.
27 *Rot. Hund.* ii. 72, 101.
28 *Cartulary of Haughmond Abbey*, ed. U. Rees (1985), p. 143.
29 P.R.O., E 358/18, m. 4.
30 Eyton, v. 65.
31 *Rot. Hund.* ii. 72.
32 S.R.O. 1224, box 342, Prior Gosnell's reg. f. 7 v., dated by Peter de Leia's priorate of Wenlock (*V.C.H. Salop.* ii. 46).
33 *Rot. Hund.* ii. 72.
34 Above, Holdgate, manor.
35 *V.C.H. Salop.* ii. 86.
36 *Cal. Inq. p.m.* v, p. 392.
37 *Cal. Close*, 1313–18, 263–4; *Cal. Pat.* 1313–17, 554–5.

from Thomas of Stanton, passed to the Hospitaller preceptory of Dinmore (Herefs.),[38] with which it remained until confiscated by the Crown in 1540.[39]

In 1547 the Crown granted the former Hospitaller estate, then called Stanton Long manor, to John Dudley, earl of Warwick.[40] In 1549 Dudley conveyed it, except for the chief house and demesne lands, to the see of Worcester, together with Holdgate manor.[41] The Stanton Long manorial rights thereafter descended with those of Holdgate.[42]

In 1554, after the attainder of Dudley, by then duke of Northumberland, the Crown sold the chief house and demesne lands of Stanton Long to Rowland Hayward (kt. 1570).[43] That estate was termed a manor before his death in 1593,[44] but it had no separate court and by 1560 was subject to Hayward's manor of Tugford.[45] Hayward's widow Catherine still held the Stanton Long estate in 1617,[46] but it was probably sold by their son Sir John, who died without issue in 1636.[47] By 1661 it had been severed from Tugford manor and was owned as a reputed manor by John Browne of Sowbach, who settled it on his son William. William's widow Anne settled it in 1702 on their son Richard. By 1732 Richard's son William was in possession. William Browne left the reputed manor to Thomas Tomkys the elder of Neachells (Staffs.),[48] who sold it in 1754 to Henry Mytton of Shipton (d. 1757).[49] Mytton's son Thomas (d. 1787)[50] left it to his widow Mary,[51] who sold off the estate in parts.[52]

The chief house, called the Manor House by 1873,[53] and its farm land were bought by 1793 by a Mr. Adney,[54] and in 1823 by Edward Howells.[55] In 1825 Howells bought the Coates (in Holdgate),[56] with which the Stanton Long estate thereafter descended[57] until F. G. Hamilton-Russell sold it as Manor farm in 1919 to the tenant George Bebbington.[58] Bebbington was succeeded in 1947 by W. A. Davies,[59] the owner in 1965.[60] The house has a 16th-century north–south range of 1½ storey, which may originally have consisted of an open hall and parlour. A south cross wing of 2½ storeys was built in the 17th century, probably replacing the original service end; it had a basement kitchen. The wing is stone except for the gable end towards the street, which is brick.[61]

About 1679 William Browne, owner of the demesne lands, bought the Stanton Long property of George Ludlow[62] of the Moorhouse (in Shipton), whose father had owned it in 1625.[63]

Another undertenant of the barons of Castle Holdgate was probably[64] Robert de Girros (d. 1190 × 1191); he had property in Stanton,[65] which may have come, by further subinfeudation, to another branch of that family and thus to Roger de Girros of Stanton (fl. 1225–31). If so, Roger was probably succeeded at Stanton by his son and namesake.[66] Henry Girros (fl. 1308–22) held property at Stanton Long[67] and Robert Girros (fl. 1358) at Corfield.[68] By 1366 Sibyl Girros, wife of John Jenkyns, held property at Stanton Long and Corfield,[69] presumably by inheritance from Robert. At Sibyl's death her property descended, in whole or in part, to Margaret, wife of Thomas Russell. In 1432 their son Roger quitclaimed a moiety of her estate in Stanton Long and Corfield to his brother John.[70] In 1590 John Russell and his brother William, presumably descendants, sold what was evidently the same property to Richard Churchman, the vicar,[71] who bought more in 1591 from Richard Reynoldes.[72] On Churchman's death in 1621[73] his son Joseph sold the premises, later represented by *LOWER HOUSE* farm, to Osias his brother,[74] whose son John[75] sold them in 1659 to Arthur Weaver (d. 1710).[76] Weaver left the estate to his son Arthur (d. 1764),[77] who left it to his niece Susannah Weaver.[78] She later married Henry Leigh Tracy[79] and at her death in 1783 left it to their daughter Henrietta Susanna.[80] On her marriage in 1798 to Charles Hanbury, who took the additional surname of Tracy,[81] Henrietta settled

38 L. B. Larking, *Kts. Hospitallers in Eng.* (Camd. Soc. [1st ser.] lxv), 199.

39 W. Rees, *Hist. of Order of St. John of Jerusalem in Wales and on Welsh Border* (1947), 85.

40 *Cal. Pat.* 1547–8, 252–4.

41 Ibid. 1548–9, 255, 298.

42 Above, Holdgate, manor.

43 *Cal. Pat.* 1553–4, 479; W. A. Shaw, *Kts. of Eng.* (1906), ii. 75.

44 P.R.O., C 142/241, no. 125.

45 S.P.L., Deeds 7146, ct. r.

46 P.R.O., C 142/363, no. 194.

47 *T.S.A.S.* 4th ser. v. 53. Cf. *V.C.H. Salop.* viii. 8, 63; xi. 80–1, 113–14, 188.

48 S.R.O. 1037/21/105A.

49 S.R.O. 757, box 50, deed; S.P.L., Deeds 676.

50 *S.P.R. Heref.* i (1), 53.

51 S.R.O. 1037/21/105A.

52 Ibid. /21/105; S.R.O. 757, box 50, deed of 1789; S.P.L., MS. 6865, p. 179.

53 S.R.O. 3901/BRg/1, 17 Oct. 1873.

54 S.P.L., MS. 6865, pp. 179, 181.

55 S.R.O. 757, box 50, replies to requisitions on title of 1867.

56 Above, Holdgate, manor.

57 S.R.O. 757, box 50, extract of E. Howells's will, deed of 1867; P.R.O., IR 29/29/297; *P.O. Dir. Salop.* (1879), 417; *Kelly's Dir. Salop.* (1909), 258.

58 S.R.O. 2030/6/41; 4190/2; *Shrews. Chron.* 19 and 26 Sept. 1919.

59 S.R.O., DA 17/516/17, f. 132.

60 Ibid. /516/37, f. 232.

61 SA 12041; inf. from Mrs. M. Moran.

62 S.R.O. 1224, box 248, deed of 1696.

63 P.R.O., C 116/210.

64 It is certain that the baron of Holdgate had feudal tenants in Stanton Long but not certain that the Walsh or Girros fams. held of the barony. The Girros fam., however, were the most widely enfeoffed in the barony lands: Eyton, iv. 37.

65 *Pipe R.* 1190 (P.R.S. N.S. i), 124; 1191 & 92 (P.R.S. N.S. ii), 78; 1194 (P.R.S. N.S. v), 6; 1195 (P.R.S. N.S. vi), 42; cf. Eyton, iv. 37.

66 Eyton, iv. 22, 37; v. 95.

67 Glos. R.O., D2153/D/2–5.

68 P.R.O., C 143/325, no. 12.

69 Glos. R.O., D2153/D/7.

70 Ibid. /D/8.

71 Ibid. /D/16; *Dioc. of Heref. Institutions (1539–1900)*, ed. A. T. Bannister (Heref. 1923), 21.

72 S.P.L., Deeds 6333.

73 S.R.O. 3901/Rg/1, bur. Aug. 1621.

74 S.P.L., Deeds 6383; S.R.O. 840, box 63, deed of 20 Mar. 1609/10.

75 *Alum. Cantab. to 1751*, i. 337.

76 Glos. R.O., D2153/Am/1; /J/3, 8.

77 *Mont. Colln.* xxii. 87; Morville par. reg., bur. 2 Nov. (transcript in S.P.L.).

78 *Mont. Colln.* xxii. 90.

79 *Complete Peerage*, xii (2), 5.

80 Glos. R.O., D2153/H/20.

81 Burke, *Peerage* (1967), 2412.

the estate on him.[82] In 1806 he sold it to John Cressett Pelham.[83] Its descent then followed that of Holdgate manor[84] until 1863 when the Revd. Henry Thursby-Pelham conveyed it (66 a.) to Edward VI's charity, Ludlow,[85] the owner in 1913.[86] In 1921 it belonged to T. W. Howard[87] and by 1934 was called Lower House.[88] The timber framed house of 1½ storey was built in the 17th century. It had two units, separated by a lobby entry and stack. Another bay was added at the north end.[89]

About 1215 Thomas of Stanton, son of Simon of Stanton, sold 3 bovates in Stanton Long to Geoffrey Griffin. Geoffrey granted them to Haughmond abbey *c.* 1235 for the support of infirm canons, in exchange for land in Besford (in Shawbury).[90] In 1539 the estate passed to the Crown,[91] which sold it in 1560 to Thomas Reve and Nicholas Pynde.[92]

In 1513 Thomas Walle sold his Stanton Long property to Thomas Skrymsher, one of the executors of Thomas Cookes of Ludlow; the executors had by 1516 bought lands in Stanton Long, later represented by *MALT HOUSE FARM*, for the Ludlow Palmers' guild.[93] The guild was dissolved in 1551,[94] and in 1552 the Crown granted its property to Ludlow corporation,[95] which owned an 80-a. farm in Stanton Long in 1785.[96] In 1846 the farm was vested in the trustees of Edward VI's charity, Ludlow,[97] which still owned it, as Malt House farm (63 a.), in 1913.[98] By 1921 it belonged to Richard Jones.[99] The house is cruck-built, with an added 16th- or early 17th-century box framed cross wing.[1]

In 1245 Roger, son of William of Corfield, and Roger's son Robert granted lands in *CORFIELD* to Wenlock priory.[2] In 1358 William of Kinnersley and John de Chay, holding of Robert Girros, conveyed further property in Corfield to the priory.[3] The priory's Corfield estate became part of its manor of Oxenbold[4] (called Shipton after 1522)[5] and passed to Sir Thomas Palmer in 1548 with Shipton manor,[6] to which it belonged thereafter.[7] Mrs. Mary Mytton sold Corfield (83 a.) to a Mr. Whitehurst *c.* 1791,[8] and it later passed through the Deighton,[9] Jones,[10] Lewis,[11] and Allsop[12] families.

PATTON may have been among the lands 'by the Corve' given to St. Mildburg by her half-brothers before 704, for in 901 five *manentes* there belonged to the church of Wenlock: that year the church gave them to Aethelraed, ealdorman of Mercia, and his wife Aethelflaed, in part exchange for land in 'Stantune'.[13] Alwine (Alwin), a free man, held Patton in 1066.[14] He was presumably the man who owned Stanton Long.[15]

In 1086 Earl Roger held Patton in chief. The chief lordship presumably passed on Earl Robert's forfeiture in 1102 to Hugh de Lacy, whose brother Roger had the mesne lordship of Patton in 1086;[16] if so, Hugh's estate at Patton is presumed, like that at Stanton Long, to have escheated before 1121.[17] The Fourches family, to whom Herbert, Roger de Lacy's tenant at Patton in 1086,[18] probably belonged,[19] may then have become tenants in chief.

By 1166 Patton had been divided into moieties. The Crown had apparently restored the chief lordship of one of them to the Lacy honor. The subsequent descent of that tenure in chief has not been traced. The Fourches family seems to have held a mesne lordship of the moiety from the Lacy honor[20] and that mesne lordship had evidently descended by 1363 to Sir Nicholas Burnell,[21] beyond whom it has not been traced. Under the Fourches family, Walter of Hopton held a further mesne lordship of the moiety (½ hide) in 1255 and 1284,[22] not further traced. The terre tenancy of this moiety was united with the terre tenancy of the other by the mid 13th century.[23]

The chief lordship of the other moiety of Patton seems to have remained with the Fourches family in 1255[24] and that too had evidently descended by 1363 to Sir Nicholas Burnell,[25] beyond whom it has not been traced. In the mid 12th century William of Middlehope seems to have held the moiety under the Fourches family, and he sold ½ hide at Patton to Joce of Dinham. Between 1143 and 1154 Joce gave it to Wenlock priory,[26] which held a moiety of Patton by *c.* 1170 and (as ½ hide) in 1255.[27]

Stephen of Patton, fl. 1226–30, lord of Patton, may have been terre tenant of both moieties, as

82 Glos. R.O., D2153/J/6.
83 S.R.O. 4835/28, lot 8. Cf. ibid. lot 7; S.R.O. 2334/2, ff. 1 (no. 13), 2 (no. 24).
84 P.R.O., IR 29/29/297; above, Holdgate, manor.
85 S.R.O. 5353/6.
86 S.R.O. 4011/46, no. 267.
87 S.R.O. 2030/6/41.
88 S.R.O., DA 17/518/2, f. 133.
89 Inf. from Mrs. M. Moran.
90 *Cart. Haughmond*, p. 151.
91 *V.C.H. Salop.* ii. 68.
92 *Cal. Pat.* 1558–60, 302.
93 S.R.O. 356/MT/1094, 1362.
94 *V.C.H. Salop.* ii. 139.
95 *Cal. Pat.* 1550–3, 345–6.
96 S.R.O. 356, parcel 416, map.
97 Ludlow (Charity Estates) Act, 1846, 9 & 10 Vic. c. 18 (Private).
98 S.R.O. 4011/46, no. 273; S.R.O., reg. of electors, Southern or Ludlow divn. (1913), 519.
99 S.R.O. 2030/6/41.
1 *T.S.A.S.* lxiii. 16.
2 Barnard MSS., Raby Castle, box 1, bdle. 16, nos. 3a–b, 5a–b.
3 P.R.O., C 143/325, no. 12; *Cal. Pat.* 1358–61, 41.
4 P.R.O., SC 6/Hen. VIII/3021, m. 7.
5 Below, Monkhopton, manors.
6 *Cal. Pat.* 1548–9, 14.
7 S.R.O. 566/8; 1037/15/28; P.R.O., C 142/374, no. 91; below, Shipton, manors.
8 S.R.O. 5555; S.P.L., MS. 6865, pp. 179, 181.
9 P.R.O., IR 29/29/297; S. Bagshaw, *Dir. Salop.* (1851), 550.
10 S.R.O. 1356/9, Stanton Long; 4011/46, no. 238.
11 S.R.O., DA 17/518/2, f. 134.
12 Ibid. /516/37, f. 233.
13 Birch, *Cart. Sax.* ii, p. 230 (no. 587); Finberg, *Early Charters of W. Midlands*, p. 148.
14 *V.C.H. Salop.* i. 328.
15 Wightman, *Lacy Fam.* 157–8.
16 *V.C.H. Salop.* i. 328; iii. 10.
17 Eyton, iv. 32; v. 237, 239–41; Wightman, op. cit. 170–1, 173–5. Cf. above, this section (Stanton Long).
18 *V.C.H. Salop.* i. 328.
19 Wightman, op. cit. 154 n.
20 *Red Bk. Exch.* (Rolls Ser.), i. 282. Cf. Eyton, iv. 46.
21 P.R.O., C 143/349, no. 4. Cf. Eyton, v. 47.
22 *Rot. Hund.* ii. 70; *Feud. Aids*, iv. 223. Cf. Eyton, iv. 46.
23 Below, this section.
24 *Rot. Hund.* ii. 70. Cf. Eyton, iv. 43.
25 P.R.O., C 143/349, no. 4. Cf. Eyton, v. 47.
26 Barnard MSS., Raby Castle, box 1, bdle. 17, no. 2. Cf. Eyton, v. 52.
27 S.P.L., Deeds 398; *Rot. Hund.* ii. 70, 85.

was Hugh of Patton, lord in 1255 and 1256.[28] The demesne lordship belonged to Sibyl of Patton (fl. 1327) in 1316,[29] to another Hugh of Patton in 1329 and 1348,[30] and to Philip of Patton (fl. 1352) by 1360.[31] Philip's trustees conveyed Patton manor to Wenlock priory in 1364.[32] Patton was later part of the priory's manor of Oxenbold[33] (called Shipton after 1522).[34] In 1545 the Crown sold Patton to Thomas Ireland,[35] acting for Thomas Bromley,[36] with whose manor of Oxenbold it descended until the early 20th century[37] when Lord Barnard sold the farms separately.[38] In 1934 Patton House belonged to T. J. Wadlow and Patton Grange to the Misses A. J. and G. Wadlow.[39]

The later manor of *OXENBOLD* was sold to Thomas Bromley in 1544.[40] Part of it lay within Stanton Long parish and may have included, besides part of Great Oxenbold, the farm called Nether Old Oxenbold, held of Wenlock priory *c.* 1522,[41] and that let by the priory in 1533 as Old Oxenbold.[42] A farm called Little Oxenbold was mentioned in 1697,[43] and another was called Oxenbold Leasows (or Leasow House) in the earlier 18th century[44] and Old House in the early 19th.[45] Old House was held by the tenant of Skimblescott (in Shipton) in 1846, when it served as a cottage,[46] and in 1913 by the tenant of Little Oxenbold.[47] Lord Barnard sold the farms *c.* 1919.[48] By 1922 the Poplars had been built to replace Old House, which was demolished, and its farm was again in separate tenure from that of Little Oxenbold.[49] James Carter sold the Poplars in 1945 to T. F. M. Corrie, who sold it to Albert Curry as part of the Larden Hall estate in 1947. Curry sold it separately to E. G. Brown in 1952,[50] to whose family both it and Little Oxenbold belonged in 1990; the early buildings at Little Oxenbold were demolished in the mid 20th century.[51]

BROCKTON[52] was probably wholly in Stanton Long parish (as successor to Patton) until 1271 or later, thereafter only partly so.[53] In 1895 R. J. More sold Upper (or Upper House) farm, Brockton, at 204 a. the largest of his farms in the parish, to the Revd. J. Hodgson.[54] By 1913 it belonged to the Philpott family,[55] owners in 1939.[56] H. Lewis owned it in 1965.[57] In 1987 J. Hayward sold the house alone, then called Brockton House.[58]

In the late 12th century *CORVE*, later called Corve Park[59] or Corve Barn,[60] was held, apparently in chief, by Robert son of Nicholas,[61] probably lord of Brockton.[62] By 1255 the tenancy in chief had passed to Wenlock priory.[63] Corve was later reckoned part of the priory's manor of Oxenbold[64] (called Shipton after 1522). After the priory's surrender in 1540 the overlordship of Corve was probably sold to Thomas Bromley, for in 1555 Richard Newport, Bromley's successor as chief lord of Oxenbold,[65] held Corve of the king and queen as of their manor of Stanton Lacy.[66] Corve was still said to be held of that manor in 1623.[67]

An apparent mesne lordship of Corve, with entitlement to a chief rent of 7*s.* (part of a 15*s.* rent that Robert son of Nicholas had in the 12th century),[68] belonged in 1255 to Robert de Emsteleg.[69] In 1555 Thomas Ludlow quitclaimed the 7*s.* rent to Sir Thomas Bromley.[70]

Ralph son of Edward became terre tenant of Corve in the late 12th century by feoffment from Robert son of Nicholas.[71] In 1255 John of Corve was terre tenant.[72] By 1350 Thomas, son of William of Corve, had succeeded Hugh of Corve in an estate there.[73] In 1410 Roger of Corve's son and heir Philip quitclaimed his estate to Thomas of Corve, whose widow married Thomas Hustyng (d. 1446).[74] Ralph Poyner, son-in-law of William Hustyng,[75] had William's estate by 1522,[76] and in 1545 sold it to Thomas Bromley,[77] with whose Oxenbold manor the estate descended until the early 20th century.[78] Corve belonged in 1934 to John

28 Eyton, iv. 43–4, 116; *Roll of Salop. Eyre 1256* (Selden Soc. xcvi), pp. 301, 320.
29 *Feud. Aids*, iv. 229; *T.S.A.S.* 2nd ser. iv. 330.
30 Barnard MSS., Raby Castle, box 1, bdle. 18, nos. 2, 5a- -b.
31 S.R.O. 1037/3/50, 53.
32 Staffs. R.O., D. 938/767; P.R.O., C 143/349, no. 4; Barnard MSS., Raby Castle, box 1, bdle. 17, no. 17.
33 P.R.O., SC 6/Hen. VIII/3021, m. 7.
34 Below, Monkhopton, manors.
35 *L. & P. Hen. VIII*, xx (1), pp. 222–3.
36 Barnard MSS., Raby Castle, abstr. of writings, pt. 1, f. 50.
37 P.R.O., IR 29/29/248; SC 2/197/118; S.R.O. 168/2, ff. 96, 97, 99; 4011/46, nos. 286, 288; S.P.L., Deeds 1361, f. 6. Cf. below, Monkhopton, manors.
38 S.P.L., SC1/13.
39 S.R.O., DA 17/518/2, f. 135.
40 For descent see below, Monkhopton, manors.
41 N.L.W., Wynnstay, RA 2.
42 S.R.O. 1/74.
43 S.R.O. 3901/Rg/1, 27 Sept. 1697. Cf. Birm. Univ. Libr., Mytton Papers, v. 1207.
44 S.R.O. 168/2, f. 94.
45 S.R.O. 3901/Rg/4, 26 June 1825; O.S. Map 1", sheet LXI. SW. (1833 edn.).
46 P.R.O., IR 29/29/288, 297; IR 30/29/288, 297.
47 S.R.O. 4011/46, no. 226.
48 Below, Monkhopton, manors (Oxenbold).
49 O.S. Map 1/2,500, Salop. LVII. 10 (1902 and 1927 edns.); *Kelly's Dir. Salop.* (1922), 260; local inf.
50 S.R.O. 5321/A73; below, Shipton, manors (Nether Larden).
51 Local inf.
52 For descent see below, Shipton, manors.
53 Below, church.
54 S.R.O. 1242, box 15, sale partic. (lot 4); *Shrews. Chron.* 25 July 1895.
55 S.R.O. 4011/46, no. 233.
56 S.R.O. 1356/9, Stanton Long.
57 S.R.O., DA 17/516/37, f. 234.
58 S.P.L., SC13/45.
59 S.R.O. 171, box 2, deed of 1636.
60 S.R.O. 4011/46, no. 289.
61 S.P.L., Deeds 377, dated by Eyton, i. 140.
62 Below, Shipton, manors.
63 *Rot. Hund.* ii. 85.
64 P.R.O., SC 6/Hen. VIII/3021, m. 6d.
65 Below, Monkhopton, manors.
66 Barnard MSS., Raby Castle, box 2, bdle. 1, no. 5.
67 P.R.O., C 142/402, no. 146.
68 S.P.L., Deeds 377.
69 *Rot. Hund.* ii. 85.
70 Barnard MSS., Raby Castle, abstr. of writings, pt. 1, f. 53.
71 S.P.L., Deeds 377.
72 *Rot. Hund.* ii. 85.
73 P.R.O., C 104/26, deed of 1350.
74 Barnard MSS., Raby Castle, box 1, bdle. 18, nos. 12–14; *Cal. Pat.* 1452–61, 514.
75 Barnard MSS., Raby Castle, abstr. of writings, pt. 1, f. 53.
76 S.R.O. 1224, box 342, Prior Gosnell's reg. f. 39.
77 Barnard MSS., Raby Castle, abstr. of writings, pt. 1, f. 53.
78 S.R.O. 168/2, f. 98; 566/34–5, 48; 4011/46, no. 289; S.P.L., Deeds 1361, f. 7; P.R.O., IR 29/29/248. Cf. below, Monkhopton, manors.

Childe,[79] and in 1965 to E. G. Brown of the Poplars.[80]

Stanton Long *RECTORY* was appropriated to the dean and chapter of Hereford cathedral in 1295.[81] In 1315 the rectorial glebe included two barns, one of 11 bays.[82] By 1725 it consisted only of a meadow, Canons' close.[83] The rectorial tithes were commuted to £198 4*s.* 10*d.* in 1845.[84] About 1881 the rent charges passed to the Ecclesiastical Commissioners.[85] In 1938 they acquired Canons' close (3½ a.),[86] which the Church Commissioners sold in 1963.[87]

ECONOMIC HISTORY.[88] No woodland was recorded in 1086.[89] Patton manor later included part of Cawley wood, which stood between Stanton parish and Monk Hall.[90] Cawley wood was being assarted from Corve in the early 13th century[91] and in 1545 was represented in Patton by only a 2-a. wood, Cawley grove.[92] Brockton had woods in 1301.[93] Ancient woodland also stood on the escarpment south-east of Little Oxenbold,[94] where some of it was in Oxenbold's new park, formed *c.* 1250;[95] Little Oxenbold Coppice (36 a.) remained wooded in the 1970s.[96] The old park of Oxenbold had lain farther west; land in Corfield lay between it and the river Corve in the 1250s.[97] On the escarpment south-east of Stanton Long, the Leath common remained open until the early 18th century,[98] and until the late 18th century farmers in Stanton township drove their animals annually to Earnstrey liberty on the slopes of Brown Clee.[99] Natal (or Natle) common, mentioned *c.* 1300,[1] covered the hill where Patton township met those of Brockton, Easthope, and Presthope[2] and remained partly open in 1746.[3]

Patton, Stanton Long, Brockton, and probably Little Oxenbold had each its own open fields. Two fields at Patton were mentioned in 1301.[4] In the 16th and 17th centuries Stanton had Rea field west of the village, Fulsich (or Leath) field east, and Coates field north.[5] Part of Rea field lay within the Coates (in Holdgate) and within Oxenbold township. In Stanton Long parish in 1494 Oxenbold township also had Tycley (or Ticknel) field, Pew field, Steward's field, and the field 'beneath the park', and Bentley field was mentioned in the 16th century;[6] those presumably were centred on Little Oxenbold.

Common meadows included Fulsich, north-east of Stanton Long village, in 1589.[7] Fulsich remained at least partly open in 1707, when others were already inclosed.[8]

Inclosure of the open fields was very gradual. In 1517 William Blakeway at Patton and the abbot of Haughmond at Stanton Long had recently inclosed arable for pasture.[9] Between 1589 and 1607 tenants of the Stanton Long demesne and Lower House inclosed some arable for pasture after consolidating it by exchange.[10] Parts of Rea field were 'lately inclosed' in 1648.[11] Nevertheless considerable open-field land remained on Manor farm in 1661,[12] Malt House farm in 1701,[13] and the glebe in 1707.[14] By 1747 the open fields of Patton and Oxenbold townships were wholly inclosed.[15] Malt House farm was all inclosed by 1785,[16] and virtually the whole parish was by 1793 except for little-used 'slips' of common at the edges.[17]

In Stanton township, with many freeholders in 1315[18] and ever since,[19] consolidation and amalgamation of farms has been difficult to arrange; in the 1840s the holdings were still intermingled and fairly small.[20] At Patton, by contrast, the four farms of 1545[21] were reduced to three by the early 18th century,[22] and to two large compact farms by 1845. In Oxenbold township, too, the farms were large and compact in 1845.[23]

In 1086 Patton had 1 hide but was worth twice as much as Stanton Long with 3, and had twice the recorded population. Both had increased in value since 1066.[24] In 1308 the former Templar estate at Stanton Long had much of its income in cash rents; on the demesne, cash was paid for

79 S.R.O., DA 17/518/2, f. 135.
80 Ibid. /516/37, f. 233.
81 Below, church.
82 Heref. D. & C. mun. 1836; cf. *Charters and Rec. of Heref. Cath.* ed. W. W. Capes (1908), p. 234.
83 Heref. D. & C. mun. 4836 (xlvi).
84 P.R.O., IR 29/29/248, 297.
85 Heref. D. & C. mun. 4836 (xliv).
86 Order in Council 21 Dec. 1937 (copy in Heref. D. & C. mun. 6154).
87 Inf. from Church Com.
88 Brockton's econ. hist. is mainly treated below, Shipton, econ. hist.
89 *V.C.H. Salop.* i. 320, 328.
90 Below, Monkhopton, econ. hist.
91 Eyton, iv. 44. Located from P.R.O., IR 29/29/248; IR 30/29/248, fields 105–8.
92 *L. & P. Hen. VIII*, xx (1), p. 223.
93 *Cartulary of Shrews. Abbey*, ed. U. Rees (1975), ii, p. 250.
94 P.R.O., IR 29/29/297; IR 30/29/297, fields 148, 151, 153–6.
95 Heref. D. & C. mun., chapter act bk. 1512–66 (folio), f. 186; cf. P.R.O., IR 29/29/297; IR 30/29/297, field 143. Cf., for Oxenbold new pk., below, Monkhopton, econ. hist.
96 O.S. Maps 1/2,500, Salop. LVII. 15 (1903 edn.); 1/25,000, SO 49/59 (1981 edn.).
97 Eyton, iv. 24.
98 S.R.O. 1141, box 20, deed of 1701; H.W.R.O.(H.), HD 2/14/41; R. T. Rowley, 'Hist. of S. Salop. Landscape' (Oxf. Univ. B.Litt. thesis, 1967), 136.
99 S.R.O., incl. award B 21, brief of [1810], f. 6.

1 S.R.O. 3195/1, f. 31.
2 S.R.O. 809, parcel 14, map of 1732; P.R.O., IR 29/29/248, 297; IR 30/29/248, fields 4–6, 9; IR 30/29/297, fields 48, 50.
3 S.R.O. 168/2, f. 102.
4 *Cart. Shrews.* ii, p. 250.
5 S.R.O. 356, box 327, surv. *c.* 1575, pp. 159–67; Bodl. MS. Top. Salop. c. 6, ff. 18–20v.; H.W.R.O.(H.), HD 2/14/40–1. Cf. field names in P.R.O., IR 29/29/297; IR 30/29/297.
6 Heref. D. & C. mun., chapter act bk. 1512–66 (folio), ff. 186, 216v.–217. Cf. field names in P.R.O., IR 29/29/297; IR 30/29/297.
7 H.W.R.O.(H.), HD 2/14/39.
8 Ibid. /14/41.
9 B.L. Lansd. MS. 1, ff. 191, 193. Patton's chief ho. was held by the Blakeway fam. in 1545: *L. & P. Hen. VIII*, xx (1), p. 223.
10 H.W.R.O.(H.), HD 2/14/39–40.
11 S.P.L., Deeds 6516.
12 S.R.O. 1037/21/105A.
13 S.R.O. 1141, box 20, deed.
14 H.W.R.O.(H.), HD 2/14/41.
15 S.R.O. 168/2, ff. 93–4, 96–9, 102.
16 S.R.O. 356, parcel 416, map.
17 S.P.L., MS. 6865, p. 180.
18 P.R.O., C 134/48, no. 9.
19 Above, manors.
20 P.R.O., IR 29/29/297; IR 30/29/297.
21 *L. & P. Hen. VIII*, xx (1), pp. 222–3.
22 S.R.O. 566/59, dated by *Orders of Q. Sess.* ii. 25.
23 P.R.O., IR 29/29/248, 297; IR 30/29/248, 297.
24 *V.C.H. Salop.* i. 328.

mowing, reaping, and threshing work, and wages were paid to a carter, four ploughmen, a maid, and other servants. The demesne had 2 ploughs and 12 oxen, 2 wagons and 2 workhorses. Wheat and oats were the only crops, and in January 1308 there were no dairy cattle or sheep.[25]

By 1315 the Stanton demesne had no buildings[26] and its land was uncultivated.[27] There was a marked recovery before 1338,[28] but in 1340 the parish's cereal crop had recently been destroyed by storms, and its sheep attacked by disease; 11 tenants had abandoned their holdings.[29] When Wenlock priory acquired the demesne lordship of Patton in 1364[30] the chief house was worth nothing and the demesne arable was decayed (*debilis*). In the next six years the value per acre of the demesne arable fell by half and of the meadow by a third. Meanwhile, however, the priory had reduced the acreage of demesne arable by a third and of meadow by half, and had increased the income from assize rents. Those measures raised Patton's value from 17*s.* 2*d.* in 1363[31] to 47*s.* 8*d.* in 1370.[32] At Stanton Long the Hospitallers let the demesne on a long lease in 1506.[33]

At Stanton a three-year rotation of wheat, oats, and fallow based on the three open fields was maintained in the late 16th century.[34] In the 17th and 18th centuries arable farming was usually combined with dairying, and cheese was commonly made. Only the larger farms normally had sheep. Besides the usual cereals, some farmers grew hemp and flax.[35] In the Great pool at Corfield carp and perch were reared in quantity for the table *c.* 1770.[36]

At the close of the 18th century wheat and oats, in equal proportions, were the parish's principal cereals, with barley too at Patton,[37] where soils were different.[38] By 1844 the landlord stipulated a three-course rotation at Patton, but at Corve Park the rotation was fallow, wheat, clover (fed as hay to cart-horses), and oats.[39] By the late 19th century and more so in the early 20th, grass greatly exceeded arable. Cattle increased in the late 19th century but sheep were still important in the mid 20th. Arable then occupied a greater proportion of land than before, especially for barley, but remained subordinate.[40]

Wenlock priory had a mill at Stanton Long in 1291.[41] No later record is known, but the 'mill bridge' was mentioned in 1420[42] and the 'mill fleam' and Mill Bridge leasow in 1701.[43] The mill had probably been on Trow brook north of the village.[44] Another early mill, probably associated with the nearby shrunken settlement at Great Oxenbold (in Monkhopton),[45] evidently stood on Oxenbold brook, which formed the parish boundary through Oxenbold township; on the Stanton Long side Mill meadow and Mill leasow lay immediately downstream of a field called the Pools,[46] which is bounded west by an earth dam or causeway that carries the Ludlow–Bridgnorth road over Pool bridge. It was perhaps the 'mill of the park', which stood near there in 1339.[47]

TABLE X

STANTON LONG: LAND USE, LIVESTOCK, AND CROPS

		1867	*1891*	*1938*	*1965*
Percentage of	grassland	72	73	86	70
	arable	28	27	14	30
Percentage of	cattle	16	26	22	23
	sheep	74	67	75	69
	pigs	10	7	3	8
Percentage of	wheat	53	40	55	42
	barley	47	22	8	45
	oats	0	38	33	11
	mixed corn & rye	0	0	4	2
Percentage of agricultural land growing roots and vegetables		7	7	3	4

Sources: P.R.O., MAF 68/143, no. 15; /1340, no. 5; /3880, Salop. no. 212; /4945, no. 212.

LOCAL GOVERNMENT. By 1422 Stanton Long and Corfield presented at the court leet of Castle Holdgate barony; Corfield also did so in 1551 and Stanton in 1577.[48]

In the 16th century Stanton Long manor court had jurisdiction over most of Stanton township. A court roll survives for 1541 and transcripts of four from the period 1561–77.[49] After 1554[50] the Stanton demesne lands were

25 P.R.O., E 358/18, m. 4 and d.
26 P.R.O., C 134/48, no. 9.
27 Heref. D. & C. mun. 1836.
28 Larking, *Kts. Hospitallers*, 199.
29 *Inq. Non.* 186.
30 Above, manors.
31 P.R.O., C 143/349, no. 4; B.L. Add. MS. 6165, p. 99.
32 B.L. Add. MS. 6164, p. 410.
33 P.R.O., SC 6/Hen. VIII/7263, mm. 18d.–19.
34 S.R.O. 356, box 327, surv. *c.* 1575, pp. 159, 164–5.
35 H.W.R.O.(H.), Heref. dioc. rec., probate invs. of Fra. Wier, 1665; Mary Cocks, 1678; Hugh Floyd [*c.* 1680]; Wm. Watkins, 1686; John Blakeway, 1690; Ric. Hotchkis, 1693; Eleanor Baxter, 1702; John Rogers, 1717; Thos. Farnalls, 1722; Anne Easthope, 1726; Wm. Philpott, 1727; Adam Griffithes, 1729.
36 S.R.O. 3385/5/3.
37 S.P.L., MS. 6865, p. 180; P.R.O., HO 67/12/220.
38 Soil Surv. Map 1", sheet 166 (1972 edn.).
39 P.R.O., IR 18/8230.
40 Table X.
41 *Tax. Eccl.* (Rec. Com.), 164.
42 N.L.W., Pitchford Hall 197.
43 S.R.O. 1141, box 20, deed.
44 S.R.O. 356, parcel 416, map of 1785; P.R.O., IR 29/29/297; IR 30/29/297.
45 Below, Monkhopton, intro.
46 S.R.O. 168/2, f. 94; P.R.O., IR 29/29/297; 30/29/297, fields 121, 123, 136.
47 P.R.O., C 104/27, deed 21 Dec. 1339.
48 S.P.L., MS. 2, f. 146 and v.; *Salop. N. & Q.* i. 19; cf. above, Holdgate, local govt.
49 P.R.O., C 116/214; S.P.L., MS. 2, f. 149v.
50 Above, manors.

subject to Tugford manor court[51] but ceased to be so before 1808.[52]

The prior of Wenlock had a court baron for Patton in 1421, of which a roll survives.[53] By 1522, however, Patton presented at the prior's court baron of Oxenbold manor (later called Shipton). In that year Patton was released from its suit there and agreed to present instead at the prior's court baron of Bourton.[54] By 1610, however, Patton owed suit again to Shipton court baron,[55] and Patton supplied one of Shipton manor's constables in 1650 and 1793.[56] But Patton presented at the new Oxenbold court leet and court baron in 1566[57] and owed suit there in 1821.[58]

Corve, a manor in 1255,[59] was presumably subject before the Dissolution to Oxenbold (later called Shipton) court baron.[60] Corve owed suit to Shipton between 1561 and 1650[61] and Matthew Churchman of Corve[62] was elected a constable by Shipton manor court in 1655.[63] Nevertheless Corve presented at the new Oxenbold court leet and court baron in 1566[64] and owed suit there in 1636.[65]

Brockton, partly in the parish, was a separate manor in 1066 and remained so.[66]

The parish was in Bridgnorth poor-law union 1836–1930,[67] Bridgnorth highway district 1863–95,[68] Bridgnorth rural sanitary district 1872–94, Bridgnorth rural district 1894–1974, and Bridgnorth district from 1974.[69] From 1970 it had a joint council with Easthope and Shipton civil parishes.[70]

CHURCH. 'Stantune' (which included the later townships of Stanton and Holdgate), Brockton, Oxenbold, and Patton probably formed part of the large parish dependent on the minster church of Wenlock in St. Mildburg's time.[71] Nevertheless the church lost lordship over 'Stantune' and Patton during the 10th and 11th centuries,[72] and it may have been 10th- or 11th-century lay owners of those estates (or parts of them) who founded the benefices indicated by the existence of a priest at Patton and a priest and a church at Holdgate in 1086.[73] No priest or church at Patton was recorded thereafter, but by *c.* 1200 there was a church at Stanton Long,[74] where none had been recorded in 1086. It was to the Stanton Long undertenant that the patronage of the new church belonged in the earlier 13th century.

In or before 1245 Thomas of Long Stanton gave the advowson to Wenlock priory.[75] By 1270 the priory had also acquired some of the tithes,[76] and in 1271, when the priory conveyed the advowson to the dean and chapter of Hereford, it reserved such tithes as it had been receiving and any it that it might in future receive from newly cultivated lands.[77] The part of Brockton that was afterwards in Shipton parish may thus have been united to the parish of Holy Trinity, Much Wenlock. In or before 1272 the cathedral had acquired from the priory a house and 4 bovates of land in Stanton Long,[78] and in 1272 the bishop appropriated the rectory to the dean and chapter at the next vacancy.[79] That took effect in 1295, when the bishop ordained a vicarage in the dean and chapter's gift.[80]

Thereafter the dean and chapter exercised the advowson of the vicarage[81] until the benefice was united in 1927 with that of Easthope to form the rectory of Stanton Long with Easthope,[82] to which the dean and chapter had the right to present alternately with Maj. G. R. Benson;[83] Benson conveyed his right to Albert Curry of Larden Hall in 1948. After the rector's resignation in 1975 the patronage was suspended and the vicar of Much Wenlock with Bourton was appointed priest-in-charge. In 1981 the rectory was merged in the united benefice of Wenlock, of which the dean and chapter and Curry were among the joint patrons.[84]

In 1291 Stanton Long rectory was worth £13 6*s.* 8*d.*[85] The vicarage was worth £6 13*s.* net in 1535.[86] About 1535 the dean and chapter, which recognized the living to be 'over slender', was augmenting it annually[87] and in 1607 was still doing so by £2 3*s.* 4*d.*[88] The vicarage was valued at £40 *c.* 1708.[89] In 1726 Samuel Baldwyn, until recently farmer of the rectory,[90] gave £200, which was matched by £200 from Queen Anne's Bounty;[91] the capital was used in 1785 to buy

51 S.P.L., Deeds 7141, 7146, 7182–3, 7396, 7446, 7467, 7526A, 7527; MS. 2, f. 148.
52 S.R.O. 802, box 167, ct. r. of 1808.
53 S.R.O. 1224/2/7.
54 S.R.O. 566/2; cf. below, Monkhopton, local govt.; M. Wenlock, local govt.
55 S.R.O. 637/3.
56 S.R.O. 566/47; S.P.L., MS. 6865, p. 178.
57 P.R.O., SC 2/197/118.
58 S.R.O. 284/35.
59 *Rot. Hund.* ii. 85.
60 Above, manors (Corve).
61 S.R.O. 566/30, 34–5, 48, 54.
62 Ibid. /43.
63 Ibid. /49.
64 P.R.O., SC 2/197/118.
65 S.R.O. 171, box 2, deed.
66 Below, Shipton, manors; local govt.
67 V. J. Walsh, 'Admin. of Poor Laws in Salop. 1820–55' (Pennsylvania Univ. Ph.D. thesis, 1970), 150; *Kelly's Dir. Salop.* (1929), 273.
68 *Lond. Gaz.* 27 Mar. 1863, pp. 1767, 1769; S.R.O., S.C.C. Local Govt., etc., Cttee. min. bk. 1894–1903, p. 29.
69 *Rural Dist. Councillors Electn. Order, 1894* (Local Govt. Bd. order no. 31847); *V.C.H. Salop.* ii. 213; iii. 179.
70 *Easthope, Shipton and Stanton Long Combined Par. Council Order 1970* (copy in S.R.O. 4873/1/205).
71 Below, Lib. and Boro. of Wenlock (early est.).
72 Ibid.; above, manors; below, Monkhopton, manors (Oxenbold); Shipton, manors (Brockton).
73 *V.C.H. Salop.* i. 328, 337.
74 Below, this section [archit.].
75 S.R.O. 1224, box 342, Prior Gosnell's reg. f. 4.
76 Birm. Univ. Libr., Mytton Papers, v. 1209.
77 Capes, *Charters and Rec. Heref. Cath.* p. 126.
78 *Cal. Close*, 1296–1302, 453 (mentioning Prior Aymo, d. or res. 1272: *V.C.H. Salop.* ii. 46).
79 Capes, op. cit. pp. 127–8.
80 Heref. D. & C. mun. 1061; *Reg. Swinfield* (C.S.), 314–15; above, manors (rectory).
81 *Reg. Swinfield*, 535–6; *Reg. Trillek* (C.S.), 380, 390; *Reg. Myllyng* (C.S.), 185, 188; Bannister, *Heref. Institutions*, 21, 32, 36, 44, 49, 66, 73, 77, 112, 124, 139, 145, 179, 190, 205, 214; *T.S.A.S.* 3rd ser. v. 362–3; *Kelly's Dir. Salop.* (1900), 246; (1909), 258.
82 Heref. Dioc. Regy., reg. 1926–38, p. 76.
83 *Kelly's Dir. Salop.* (1929), 273.
84 Heref. Dioc. Regy., reg. 1938–53, p. 384; reg. 1969–(in use), pp. 206, 397–9; *Crockford* (1977–9), 3.
85 *Tax. Eccl.* 167.
86 *Valor Eccl.* (Rec. Com.), iii. 210.
87 Heref. D. & C. mun. 4575.
88 H.W.R.O.(H.), HD 2/14/40.
89 J. Ecton, *Liber Valorum et Decimarum* (1711), 147.
90 Heref. D. & C. mun. 4836 (viii).
91 C. Hodgson, *Q. Anne's Bounty* (2nd edn.), pp. cxlii, ccxc.

land in Clee Stanton,[92] and by 1793 the vicarage was worth *c.* £81, of which the glebe yielded *c.* £40, tithes £25, and the Clee Stanton land £16.[93]

The vicar's glebe was reckoned to be 40 a. in 1589.[94] In 1845 it included 67 a. in Stanton township.[95] The Clee Stanton land (32 a.) was sold in 1868.[96] The remaining glebe was slightly reduced by exchanges *c.* 1875 and in 1878[97] and was worth £72 a year in 1887.[98] In 1707 the vicarage house had four bays and the barn three, with a stable and a wainhouse built into it. There were two cowhouses with haylofts over them, and other buildings for feeding swine and geese and for coal.[99] In 1733 the incumbent rebuilt the vicarage house at his own expense.[1] It was extended *c.* 1846 and in 1867, and in 1869 stables and a dairy were built.[2] It was sold in 1930,[3] after the incumbent moved to Easthope,[4] and was afterwards named Stanton Long House.[5]

In 1707 the vicar was entitled to the small tithes and half of the hay tithes, except from Brockton's 'franchise land' (the part of the township that was in Wenlock borough), and to all the 'tithe tilling' of Corve farm. From a number of holdings the vicar received moduses called 'custom money'.[6] In 1793 he was leasing his tithes.[7] In 1815 the new vicar refused to accept the customary moduses from 266 a. in Brockton, which then yielded a mere £3 18*s.*, but neither he nor his successor was able to obtain tithes in kind from those farms.[8] By 1733 there had also been disputes over farms that lay partly in Shipton parish;[9] such difficulties recurred until the Tithe Commissioners defined the boundary between Shipton and Stanton Long in 1844.[10] In 1845 the vicar was adjudged to be owed no moduses but all the small and half of the hay tithes, except from the rectorial glebe, and all the tithes from the vicarial glebe and Corve farm. His tithes were then commuted to £135 6*s.* 11*d.*[11]

The surnames of some pre-Reformation incumbents[12] suggest that they were local men. Until 1780 the post-Reformation vicars usually lived in the parish and remained until death;[13] there were thus some long incumbencies.[14] The only known non-resident was John Tudor, 1729–33, who lived at Ross-on-Wye (Herefs.).[15] He employed a curate at Stanton Long;[16] no other seems to have been needed before the last years of Charles Hicks (d. 1780).[17] Of the four vicars 1780–1866[18] the first three lived at Hereford[19] and the fourth was master of Eardisland endowed school (Herefs.).[20] The parish was served by assistant curates, most of whom lived at the vicarage.[21] From 1866 until the union with Easthope in 1927 the vicars resided.[22] In 1793 people in the northern part of the parish seldom came to church because of the distance,[23] but from 1867[24] to 1909[25] services were held for them in Brockton school.

The small parish church of *ST. MICHAEL*, so dedicated by 1835,[26] is built of rubble with tiled roofs and consists of chancel with north vestry and nave with south porch and timber framed west bell turret. The chancel and wide nave appear to date from *c.* 1200; the south doorway of the nave, with its original door and decorative ironwork, is of that date, and plain lancets remain in the west wall and in the north wall of the chancel. The south wall of the chancel seems to have been rebuilt by the later 13th century; it is thinner than the north wall and has a two-light window. The north wall of the nave, too, was evidently rebuilt before 1300; its plinth is discontinuous with that of the west wall, and a blocked lancet remained in 1862. Two vertical masonry breaks inside the south wall indicate alterations there as well. The church acquired several new features in the later 13th and earlier 14th century. On the south side of the chancel are a tomb recess, a priest's door, and a single-light low-side window. In the nave a two-light south window was inserted, and east of it a piscina marks the site of an altar, lit by a cusped lancet. Nave and chancel received new timber roofs in the later Middle Ages; the wind braces form quatrefoils, and in the chancel the collar beams have carved bosses. The porch was of

92 Heref. D. & C. mun., chapter act bk. 1860–71 (quarto), p. 300.
93 S.P.L., MS. 6865, pp. 182–3.
94 H.W.R.O.(H.), HD 2/14/39.
95 P.R.O., IR 29/29/297; IR 30/29/297.
96 Heref. D. & C. mun., chapter act bk. 1860–71 (quarto), pp. 300, 318, 339.
97 P.R.O., IR 18/8284; S.R.O. 757, box 50, deed.
98 *Return of Glebe Land, 1887*, H.C. 307, p. 61 (1887), lxiv.
99 H.W.R.O.(H.), HD 2/14/41.
1 S.R.O. 3901/Rg/1.
2 Ibid. /BRg/1, front endpaper; /Rg/4, front endpaper; Heref. D. & C. mun., chapter act bk. 1844–60 (quarto), pp. 44, 65–6; H.W.R.O.(H.), HD 8, box 49, plans, specification, etc. (ref. supplied by Mr. C. J. Pickford).
3 Heref. D. & C. mun., chapter act bk. 1916–48 (quarto), pp. 245, 253.
4 *Kelly's Dir. Salop.* (1926), 279; (1929), 273.
5 S.R.O., DA 17/518/2, f. 133.
6 H.W.R.O.(H.), HD 2/14/41.
7 S.P.L., MS. 6865, p. 182.
8 S.R.O. 1681/76/8–15.
9 S.R.O. 3901/Rg/1, memo. 5 Nov. 1733.
10 S.R.O. 1681/76/21–2
11 P.R.O., IR 29/29/248, 297.
12 *Reg. Trillek*, 380 (Tugford), 390 (More); S.P.L., Deeds 6986 (Holgot).
13 *T.S.A.S.* 4th ser. xi. 186; xlvi. 43; S.R.O. 3901/Rg/1, 14 Dec. 1571, [—] Aug. 1621, 22 May 1639, 8 May 1668, 12 Nov. 1670, 13 Mar. 1716/17; B.L. Add. MS. 21237, f. 57; H.W.R.O.(H.), Heref. dioc. rec., invs. of Hugh Floyd [*c.* 1680]; Wm. Watkins, 1686; John Rogers, 1717; John Rogers, 1728; HD 5/14/1/22; HD 7, presentment of 1663.
14 Heref. D. & C. mun., chapter act bk. 1512–66 (folio), f. 30; S.R.O. 3901/Rg/1, 14 Dec. 1571, [—] Aug. 1621, 13 Mar. 1716/17; /Rg/3, 29 Jan. 1780; Bannister, *Heref. Institutions*, 21, 49, 77.
15 Bannister, op. cit. 73; S.R.O. 3901/Rg/1, 25 Aug. 1733 (and preceding memo.).
16 S.R.O. 3901/Rg/1, 13 June 1729, 5 Jan. 1733/4.
17 Ibid. /Rg/3, signatures s.a. 1777–9 and bur. 29 Jan. 1780.
18 Bannister, *Heref. Institutions*, 112, 124, 139, 145, 179.
19 S.P.L., MS. 6865, pp. 182, 184.
20 *Crockford* (1865), 507; Heref. Dioc. Regy., reg. 1857–69, p. 478.
21 S.P.L., MS. 6865, pp. 182–3; S.R.O. 3901/Rg/3, flyleaf and signatures; /Rg/4, signatures, and lic. 14 Dec. 1860 (loosely inserted); Heref. Dioc. Regy., reg. 1772–1802, f. 231; 1791– 1821, f. 129 and pp. 154, 196; 1822–42, pp. 8, 115; *P.O. Dir. Salop.* (1856), 127.
22 *P.O. Dir. Salop.* (1870 and later edns.); *Kelly's Dir. Salop.* (1885 and later edns.).
23 S.P.L., MS. 6865, p. 182.
24 S.R.O. 3901/Rg/4, front endpaper.
25 Ibid. /SRg/1, 14 Feb. 1909.
26 Lewis, *Topog. Dict. Eng.* (1835), iv, s.v. Stanton Long.

similar date.[27] Barrelled plaster ceilings were made over nave and chancel in the 16th or 17th century. The bell turret was present by 1736.[28]

The church was restored in 1842. There was a further restoration 1869–70 by S. Pountney Smith. A chancel arch was then inserted, the ceilings were removed, new north windows were provided in the nave, and the porch walls were rebuilt in stone. The east wall and east window were rebuilt in 1869, with stained glass by Done & Davies of Shrewsbury. The vestry was added in 1871.[29] In 1879 stained glass by John Davies of Shrewsbury was placed in the larger south chancel window,[30] and the chancel's north lancet received its glass in 1893.

A lamp in the church was endowed with land, which the Crown confiscated *c.* 1547,[31] and in 1547 an 'image' of St. Blase, patron saint of wool combers, was removed to Much Wenlock and burnt in the market place.[32] In the 17th century a communion rail was placed round three sides of the table.[33] The plate consisted in 1961 of a silver cup and paten of 1571, a silver paten of 1700, and a flagon of 1725.[34] Until 1893, when they were recast, one of the three bells was probably by Richard le Belyetere of Worcester (fl. 1464), another was pre-Reformation or Marian, and the third was dated 1676.[35] The seating[36] and the plain font's octagonal stem[37] may date from the 1842 restoration. A harmonium was acquired in 1861.[38] The stone reredos and flanking blind arcades were designed by F. R. Kempson, carved by Robert Clarke of Hereford, and erected in 1888.[39] Also of the 19th century are the wooden pulpit, reading desk, brass lectern, and wooden communion rail, and the floor tiles of chancel and porch; the nave tiles are of 1954.[40] A clock was placed in the bell turret in 1927.[41]

The registers begin in 1546[42] but the earliest is damaged so that few entries remain before 1568, and the register of marriages 1754–1813 was missing by 1903.[43]

NONCONFORMITY. Five papists were reported in 1767.[44] Primitive Methodists, apparently of the former Brookhampton society,[45] built a plain brick chapel, Bethel, on the north side of Stanton Long village in 1880.[46] It had seats for 75 in 1940[47] but had closed by 1955.[48]

EDUCATION. With the aid of government and other grants[49] a long needed[50] National school opened at Brockton in 1845. Designed by S. Pountney Smith, it adjoined a teacher's house and had ground- and first-floor schoolrooms, the lower floored in brick. Boys and girls were taught separately in 1854 but together by 1871. During those years attendance averaged 38–9, and the school received £5 a year from 'Betton's charity'[51] and was supported by voluntary contributions; school pence varied with parents' occupations. Besides those from Stanton,[52] some pupils came from Church Preen in 1846 and from Easthope, Shipton,[53] and Weston (in Monkhopton); some children from the southern end of the parish presumably began to attend Holdgate and Stanton Long National school when it opened at Holdgate in 1876.[54] Attendance at Brockton averaged 70 in 1885, 81 in 1900, and 70 in 1913; the 120 places were reduced to 113 by 1910.[55] By 1907 the school was earning what were usually good reports.[56]

Gardening was introduced in 1925, and from 1936 11-year-old boys and 12-year-old girls attended Much Wenlock woodwork and domestic-science centres.[57] The roll was 60 in 1920, 57 in 1930, and 60 (including 25 evacuees) in 1941. In 1939 the school had admitted pupils from Middlemore Emigration Homes, evacuated from Birmingham to Wilderhope Manor, and two years later Wallasey evacuees with their teacher.[58]

Brockton school became controlled in 1948 and was much renovated.[59] In 1949 13-year-old pupils went to Much Wenlock C.E. school and in 1953, when 11-year-olds went to the new Much Wenlock Modern school, the roll fell to

27 St. Deiniol's Libr., Hawarden, Sir Steph. Glynne's ch. notes, xc, ff. 9v.–11; S.P.L., MS. 372, vol. i, f. 101; Cranage, ii. 152–4; Pevsner, *Salop.* 291–2.

28 Birm. Univ. Libr., Mytton Papers, v. 1207.

29 *Ch. Cal. Dioc. Heref.* (1870), 139; (1872), 99, 120; Cranage, ii. 153.

30 *Salopian Shreds & Patches*, iii. 184.

31 The land changed hands four times 1573–1601 and Fra. Cressett bought it *c.* 1621: P.R.O., C 66/1111, m. 4; E 178/1879, m. [2]; N.L.W., Chirk Castle F, nos. 766, 788, 791–2, 13349; Staffs. R.O., D.(W.) 1788, vol. 13, s.a. 1617–21.

32 *T.S.A.S.* vi. 120; cf. *V.C.H. Salop.* i. 431.

33 B.L. Add. MS. 21237, f. 57.

34 D. L. Arkwright and B. W. Bourne, *Ch. Plate Archd. Ludlow* (Shrews. 1961), 56–7.

35 H. B. Walters, *Ch. Bells of Salop.* (Oswestry, 1915), 99–100, 408, 461.

36 *P.O. Dir. Salop.* (1856), 127.

37 New in 1862: St. Deiniol's Libr., Glynne's ch. notes, xc, f. 10.

38 S.R.O. 3901/BRg/1, front endpaper.

39 *Ch. Cal. Dioc. Heref.* (1889), 139–40; (1894), 144.

40 S.R.O. 3901/Rg/4, front endpaper.

41 Ibid. /SRg/2, 9 Oct. 1927.

42 Ibid. /Rg/1, 3–4; BRg/1; MRg/1–2; regs. from 1970s at ch.

43 E. C. Peele and R. S. Clease, *Salop. Par. Doc.* (Shrews. [1903]), 318–19. Bp.'s transcripts for that period are in H.W.R.O.(H.).

44 *Worcs. Recusant*, xxvi. 22.

45 Above, Holdgate, nonconf.

46 Date stone.

47 *Methodist Church Bldgs.: Statistical Returns 1940* (Manchester [*c.* 1947]), 271.

48 O.N.S. (Birkdale), Worship Reg. no. 25621.

49 Para. based on *Eddowes's Jnl.* 28 Aug. 1844, p. [3]; Heref. D. & C. mun., chapter act bk. 1844–60 (quarto), pp. 9, 60; S.R.O. 1564/36–8; *Mins. of Educ. Cttee. of Council 1849–50* [1215], p. 233, H.C. (1850), xliii; P.R.O., ED 7/103, ff. 65–8. This section written *c.* 1982 and later revised.

50 *Digest Educ. Poor*, H.C. 224, p. 761 (1819), ix (2); *Educ. Enq. Abstract*, H.C. 62, p. 784 (1835), xlii.

51 Not recorded in S.C.C. *Salop. Char. for Elem. Educ.* (1906).

52 E. Cassey & Co. *Dir. Salop.* (1871), 348; *Kelly's Dir. Salop.* (1885), 968, and later edns.; Brockton C.E. sch. admissions bk. (at the sch.).

53 *V.C.H. Salop.* viii. 128; cf. *Kelly's Dir. Salop.* (1900), 83, 199.

54 Above, Holdgate, educ.

55 *Kelly's Dir. Salop.* (1885), 963; (1900), 247; (1913), 265; Brockton C.E. sch. log bk. (at the sch.), 4 Apr. 1910.

56 Log bk. *passim.*

57 Ibid. 19 June 1925, 10 and 12 Nov. 1936.

58 Ibid. 5 Jan. 1920, 2 May 1930, 22 Sept., 7 Oct., and 20 Nov. 1939, 24 Mar., 7 and 21 Apr., and 6 Oct. 1941.

59 *S.C.C. Mins. (Educ.)* 1947–8, 73; log bk. reps. 1950, 1953.

1860 and there was only one teacher 1953–8.[61] Thereafter several Much Wenlock children attended.[62] By 1962 the roll was 47 and in 1966 a demountable classroom was added.[63] As had long been planned, pupils from the closed Bourton C.E. (Aided) Primary school were admitted in 1967,[64] and in 1971 the building was replaced by an open-plan school with 90 places,[65] the old school serving as a field study centre 1973–*c.* 1986.[66] The school had 71 pupils in 1980[67] and by 1986–7, with over 80 pupils and an additional teacher, was in danger of being overcrowded.[68] By 1990 the roll was 77.[69]

County-council classes in poultry keeping and ambulance work held at Stanton Long and in dressmaking and horticulture at Brockton were usually well supported 1898–1902.[70]

CHARITIES FOR THE POOR. In 1712 Mrs. Anne Browne gave £5, the interest to provide bread doles; the charity lapsed before 1820. There was a poor's stock of £12 in 1758, allegedly the remains of an earlier single benefaction of £40.[71] The annual income was 12*s.* in 1787[72] but the capital was lost after 1820.[73] Tasker's Charity, mentioned in 1869,[74] yielded £1 a year for bread in 1975.[75]

TUGFORD

A QUIET rural parish on the eastern side of Corve Dale, *c.* 13 km. north-east of Ludlow, Tugford is shaped like a ragged ellipse.[76] A detachment (*c.* 7 a.) in Abdon village[77] was transferred to Abdon civil parish in 1884,[78] leaving Tugford C.P. with 1,346 a.[79] (545 ha.), the area treated in this article. In 1967 the parish absorbed most of Holdgate C.P. and a small part of Munslow C.P.[80] In 1987 it was absorbed by Abdon C.P.[81]

By the mid 17th century the parish was bounded north and east by fences, ditches, and other artificial features, probably made through former woods and wastes. South and west, however, the boundary followed streams.[82] East of Tugford village the land rises steeply at the edge of the Clee plateau; westwards it descends gently to the Corve and is drained by its tributaries. The parish lies mostly on the Ledbury Group of the Downton Series of the Lower Old Red Sandstone. At the edge of the Clee plateau is an overlying stratum of the Ditton Series, including bands of '*Psammosteus*' Limestone.[83] A drift of head covers most of the parish, and alluvium borders Trow brook and the Corve.[84] The soils are mostly sandy or silt loams, freely drained except in the area of Balaam's heath,[85] where dhu stone boulders also have impeded the plough, and in boggy areas near the streams.[86]

Tugford and Baucott had chapels in the early 12th century,[87] presumably for existing settlements. In the 13th century Great Tugford was distinct from Little Tugford.[88] Little Tugford was probably Nether (or Lower) Tugford, apparently at or near Hall yards[89] midway between Great Tugford and Baucott.[90] It was still represented at the manor court in the later 16th century,[91] but by 1631 the last house was only a memory.[92]

Great (or Church or Over) Tugford[93] lay at the lower end of a steep-sided valley cut through the western escarpment of the Clee plateau by Tugford brook, a tributary of the Corve. The houses, church, and mill stood together on converging lanes that led south to a crossing of the brook, presumably the ford from which the village was named.[94] There were six taxpayers in 1327[95] and in 1631 six farmhouses; other houses were the rectory, the miller's house, and two cottages.[96] The village's appearance did not change markedly thereafter, though farm amalgamations *c.* 1800 reduced two of the farmhouses to cottages and did away with another.[97] Only a pair of cottages was added in the later 19th century[98] and a bungalow in the 20th.

Baucott lay on the western side of the parish. Its clay subsoil was well suited to the construction of cattle ponds,[99] several of which remained

60 Log bk. 29 July 1949; rep. 1953.
61 Log bk.
62 Personal knowledge.
63 Log bk. 10 Jan. 1962, 19 Dec. 1966.
64 Ibid. 5 Sept. 1967; cf. S.C.C. *Development Plan of Primary and Secondary Educ.* (1947; copy in S.R.O.), 56; *S.C.C. Mins. (Educ.)* 1969–70, 44.
65 Log bk. 7 Sept., 5 Nov. 1971.
66 Ibid. 30 Mar., 2 July 1973; *S.C.C. Mins. (Educ.)* 1986–7, 345, 366.
67 S.C.C. Educ. Cttee. *Educ. Dir.* (1980), 5.
68 *S.C.C. Mins.* 1986–7, 451; S.R.O., M 1037, S.C.C. Educ. Cttee. mins. 1987–8, p. 501.
69 *Educ. Dir.* (1990), 9.
70 Organizing sec.'s ann. reps. to Intermediate Educ. Cttee. in *S.C.C. Mins.* 1898–1901.
71 *3rd Rep. Com. Char.* H.C. 5, p. 265 (1820), iv.
72 *Char. Don. 1786–8*, ii, H.C. 511–II, pp. 1024–5 (1816), xvi (2).
73 *3rd Rep. Com. Char.* p. 265.
74 S.R.O. 3901/Rg/4, front endpaper.
75 *Review of Local Chars.* (S.C.C. 1975), 26.
76 Fig. 15. This article was written in 1990.
77 P.R.O., IR 30/29/324, fields 250–5.
78 *14th Ann. Rep. Local Govt. Bd.* [C. 4515], pp. xlvii–xlviii, 200, H.C. (1884–5), xxxii. The detached area is treated with Abdon, above.
79 O.S. *Area Bk.* (1884).
80 *V.C.H. Salop.* ii. 235–6 (corr. ibid. xi. 376); S.R.O., DA 19/701/6, map 40.
81 *S. Salop. (Pars.) Order 1987* (Stat. Instr. 1987, no. 496).
82 S.P.L., Deeds 9718, 14 Apr. 1665.
83 Geol. Surv. Map 1/50,000, solid, sheet 166 (1974 edn.).
84 Ibid. 1", drift, sheet 166 (1967 edn.).
85 Soil Surv. Map 1", sheet 166 (1972 edn.).
86 Local inf.
87 Below, church.
88 Eyton, iv. 81; *Cartulary of Shrews. Abbey*, ed. U. Rees (1975), i, p. 97.
89 Bodl., Craven dep. 16, f. 33.
90 P.R.O., IR 29/29/324; IR 30/29/324, fields 112–14.
91 S.P.L., Deeds 7146.
92 Bodl., Craven dep. 40, p. 83.
93 *P.N. Salop.* (E.P.N.S.), i. 294; S.P.L., Deeds 7146.
94 *P.N. Salop.* i. 294.
95 *T.S.A.S.* 2nd ser. iv. 298.
96 Bodl., Craven dep. 40, pp. 73–80.
97 S.P.L., MS. 2481, ff. 37–50 and map IX; P.R.O., IR 29/29/324; IR 30/29/324; below, econ. hist.
98 O.S. Map 1/2,500, Salop. LXV. 9 (1884 edn.).
99 Local inf.

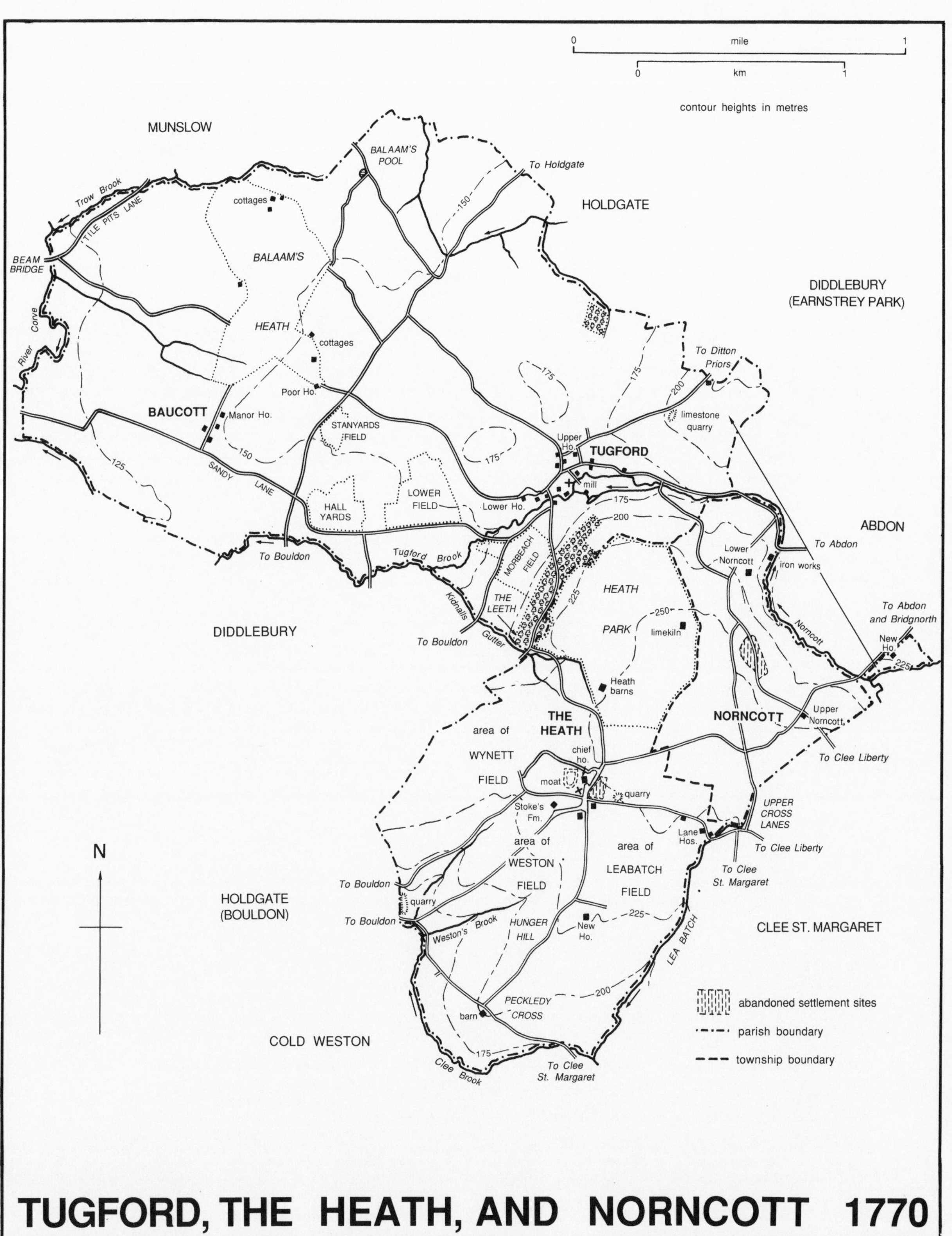
0 mile 1
0 km 1
contour heights in metres
MUNSLOW
BALAAM'S POOL
To Holdgate
HOLDGATE
DIDDLEBURY (EARNSTREY PARK)
Trow Brook
TILE PITS LANE
cottages
BEAM BRIDGE
BALAAM'S
HEATH
cottages
River Corve
Poor Ho.
BAUCOTT
Manor Ho.
STANYARDS FIELD
SANDY LANE
HALL YARDS
LOWER FIELD
Lower Ho.
Upper Ho.
TUGFORD
mill
To Ditton Priors
limestone quarry
To Bouldon
Tugford Brook
MORBEACH FIELD
THE LEETH
Kidnalls Gutter
HEATH PARK
limekiln
Lower Norncott
iron works
ABDON
To Abdon
To Abdon and Bridgnorth
New Ho.
Norncott
DIDDLEBURY
To Bouldon
Heath barns
THE HEATH
NORNCOTT
Upper Norncott
To Clee Liberty
area of WYNETT FIELD
chief ho.
moat
quarry
Stoke's Fm.
UPPER CROSS LANES
Lane Hos.
To Clee Liberty
area of WESTON FIELD
area of LEABATCH FIELD
To Clee St. Margaret
N
To Bouldon
quarry
HOLDGATE (BOULDON)
To Bouldon
Weston's Brook
HUNGER HILL
New Ho.
LEA BATCH
CLEE ST. MARGARET
PECKLEDY CROSS
barn
abandoned settlement sites
parish boundary
township boundary
COLD WESTON
Clee Brook
To Clee St. Margaret
TUGFORD, THE HEATH, AND NORNCOTT 1770

Fig. 15

in 1990. It had three taxpayers in 1327[1] and four farmhouses in 1631,[2] grouped along a lane;[3] two of them were abandoned in the earlier 19th century after farm amalgamations.[4] A pair of cottages in Sandy Lane was the only later addition at Baucott.[5]

In the mid 17th century most of the parish's farmhouses had three, sometimes two, ground-floor rooms, with chambers over. The houses of the largest farms on the manorial estate had four downstairs rooms: hall, parlour, buttery, and kitchen. One small farm had lofts rather than chambers,[6] and some of the houses seem to have had earlier open halls.[7] All were probably timber framed. Some were later cased in stone or extended but none was rebuilt, and most of the houses remaining in 1990 were timber framed.

In 1676 the parish had 103 adult inhabitants.[8] The population was 165 in 1801, but it was 197 ten years later and remained at that level until the 1830s, since when it has tended to fall; it was 86 in 1961.[9] There were at least two cottages on Balaam's heath in 1680,[10] *c.* 10 on or near it in 1770,[11] and 18 in 1851,[12] but only four in 1989.[13]

A supposed Roman road, believed to run from Greensforge (Staffs.) to central Wales, entered the parish by a ford on Trow brook and crossed its north-western extremity as what was called Tile Pits Lane,[14] and left by Beam bridge on the Corve.[15] It was said to be the Bridgnorth–Munslow road *c.* 1575.[16] From Tugford village early roads led to Bridgnorth via Ditton Priors, to Ludlow via Bouldon, and to nearby Abdon, Holdgate, the Heath, and Clee St. Margaret (via Lower Norncott). Part of the last-named route was probably the route of the commoners or 'strakers' from Tugford to Clee common or 'liberty'. West of the parish the road from Much Wenlock to Ludlow was accessible over Beam bridge or via Broadstone 2 km. north-east. In 1990 there were no classified roads and the parish was little frequented.[17]

In the early 18th century wakes were held on the Sunday after St. Catherine's day.[18] No public house is known to have existed, but there was a village hall from the 1920s to the 1950s.[19] Mary Sargeon, a 'wise woman', died at Balaam's Heath in 1832, aged 101.[20]

MANORS AND OTHER ESTATES. In 1066 *TUGFORD* manor belonged to Alwine (Elwin).[21] Warin the bald (d. *c.* 1085)[22] gave it to the church of St. Peter, Shrewsbury,[23] and it belonged to Shrewsbury abbey until 1540, when the abbey surrendered to the Crown.[24] Rowland Hayward (kt. 1570)[25] bought it from the Crown in 1554.[26] He died in 1593 leaving the manor to trustees,[27] who held it in 1598;[28] his son George (kt. 1604)[29] was in possession by 1609.[30] At George's death in 1615 it passed to his brother John (kt. 1619),[31] who sold it in 1623 to William Craven,[32] created Baron Craven in 1627.[33] Parliament confiscated Craven's estates in 1651[34] and sold Tugford in 1653 to Richard Sheppard of Baucott, Lewis Edwards, and Ralph Accom;[35] Accom conveyed his interest to Sheppard and Edwards the same year, and Sheppard still owned a portion in 1655.[36] Craven (cr. earl of Craven 1665)[37] regained the manor at the Restoration in 1660.[38] The earl died unmarried in 1697 and the earldom of Craven then became extinct but the manor and the barony passed to his cousin William Craven (d. 1711), whose eventual successor, William Craven, Baron Craven, was created earl of Craven in 1801. The manor descended with the barony (and from 1801 the earldom) of Craven[39] until 1853, when the Revd. R. N. Pemberton's trustees bought it and conveyed it to C. O. Childe-Pemberton of Millichope (in Munslow),[40] and it remained with the Millichope estate in 1990.[41]

William Burley (d. 1458) of Broncroft (in

1 *T.S.A.S.* 2nd ser. iv. 298.
2 Bodl., Craven dep. 40, pp. 81–3 (excludes Manor Ho. Fm.).
3 S.P.L., MS. 2481, ff. 44–6, 49, and map IX.
4 W.S.L. 350/5/40, Tugford p. 3; P.R.O., IR 29/29/324; IR 30/29/324; below, econ. hist.
5 O.S. Map 1/2,500, Salop. LXV. 5 (1884 edn.).
6 Bodl., Craven dep. 16, ff. 12–36.
7 e.g. no. 5 Tugford (SA 15138); Manor Ho. Fm., Baucott (inf. from Mrs. M. Moran).
8 *Compton Census*, ed. Whiteman, pp. lxvii, 259 n.
9 *V.C.H. Salop.* ii. 228. No later figs. are available for the par. area.
10 S.P.L., Deeds 7142.
11 S.P.L., MS. 2481, ff. 45, 47, and map IX.
12 S.R.O. 3392/27.
13 S.R.O., reg. of electors, S. Shropshire dist. (1990), section AX.
14 Recorded 1652: Bodl., Craven dep. 16, f. 30. Located from P.R.O., IR 29/29/324; IR 30/29/324, fields 226–8.
15 *T.S.A.S.* lvi. 239.
16 S.R.O. 356, box 327, surv. c. 1575, p. 161.
17 Bodl., Craven dep. 16, ff. 12–30; S.P.L., MS. 2481, map IX; P.R.O., IR 30/29/324; O.S. Map 1", sheet LXI. SW. (1833 edn.); above, Bouldon, intro.; below, Ditton Priors, intro.; Shipton, intro.; the Heath, intro.
18 Birm. Univ. Libr., Mytton Papers, vii. 1493.
19 Local inf.
20 *Salopian Jnl.* 25 Jan 1832, p. 2 (ref. supplied by Mr. D. J. Lloyd); cf. E. G. Salisbury, *Border Cos. Worthies*, 1st ser. (1879), 222.
21 *V.C.H. Salop.* i. 319.
22 *T.S.A.S.* lvi. 246.
23 *Cart. Shrews.* i, pp. 33, 41, 256. Cf. *V.C.H. Salop.* i. 319.
24 *V.C.H. Salop.* ii. 36.
25 W. A. Shaw, *Kts. of Eng.* (1906), ii. 75.
26 Cal. Pat. 1553–4, 478–9.
27 P.R.O., C 142/241, no. 125; *T.S.A.S.* li. 130, 132.
28 S.P.L., Deeds 7527.
29 Shaw, *Kts.* ii. 135.
30 S.P.L., Deeds 13116.
31 P.R.O., C 142/363, no. 194; S.P.L., Deeds 8430; Shaw, *Kts.* ii. 174.
32 Bodl., Craven dep. 69, deed 10 Oct. 1623; 70, deeds 16 Oct., 28 Nov. 1623.
33 *Complete Peerage*, iii. 500.
34 *Cal. Cttee. for Compounding*, ii. 1617.
35 S.R.O. 4260/1/6.
36 S.R.O. 171, box 2, deed 5 May 1655.
37 *Complete Peerage*, iii. 501.
38 *D.N.B.*; S.P.L., Deeds 9718.
39 S.P.L., Deeds 7976, 7989, 8014, 8043a, 8046, 8063. Cf. *Complete Peerage*, iii. 500–5.
40 S.R.O. 3651, parcel 17c, sched. of deeds, pp. 158–9.
41 *P.O. Dir. Salop.* (1879), 423; *Kelly's Dir. Salop.* (1885 and later edns.); local inf. Cf. above, Munslow, manors.

Diddlebury)[42] held freehold estates in Baucott and Tugford of Shrewsbury abbey. One farm followed the descent of Broncroft[43] until after 1770, when B. R. Barneby owned 46 a. in the parish.[44] By 1810 the farm had been broken up; Benjamin Blockley then owned the house, known as *POOR HOUSE* c. 1900, and 8 a.[45]

From William Burley the reputed manor of *BAUCOTT* followed the descent of Brockton[46] until the 1550s. By 1555 Nicholas Gravenor had bought one moiety, which his son Edward sold to the lord of Tugford in 1588.[47] John de Vere, earl of Oxford, sold the other moiety in 1552 to John Stringfellow in fee farm.[48] Stringfellow sold it in 1553 to John Sheppard (d. *c.* 1568).[49] By 1608 it belonged to Thomas Sheppard (d. 1638)[50] and by 1655 to his son Isaac (d. 1667),[51] who was succeeded by his son Richard (d. 1682).[52] By 1685[53] it belonged to Richard's daughter Mary (d. 1705) and her husband Henry More (d. 1689) of Millichope. It passed to their son Thomas and descended thereafter with Millichope.[54] Baucott was joined to Tugford's manorial estate when the Revd. R. N. Pemberton's trustees bought that in 1853,[55] making C. O. Childe-Pemberton virtually the parish's sole landowner by 1856.[56]

The chief house of Baucott, probably mid 16th-century and known by 1990 as Manor House Farm, has a box framed north–south range parallel with the road; it may have included an open hall. In 1652 Isaac Sheppard[57] added a two storeyed stone wing in the middle of the range, towards the road; the timber framed range was cased in stone about the same time.[58]

ECONOMIC HISTORY. Tugford and Baucott each had its own set of open fields by the late Middle Ages.[59] Field names indicate former woodland on the high ground north and east of Tugford,[60] and Leeth common (15 a. in 1652)[61] lay on the escarpment south of the village.[62] Many 'moor' and 'marsh' names occur on the low lying north and west sides of the parish,[63] and Balaam's heath was a large common north of Baucott.[64] Some farms in Tugford also had, as strakers, common of pasture on Brown Clee.[65] By the 16th century, and until the 18th, cattle were more important than sheep to many, perhaps most, farmers,[66] and a butcher lived at Nether Tugford in 1560.[67]

In 1341 it was said that the land was untilled, and that six tenants had resorted to begging;[68] the statement may indicate economic collapse. By *c.* 1490 Shrewsbury abbey had 12 tenants at Tugford and 3 at Baucott.[69] In 1540 the farmers held by copy or at will.[70] Between the late 16th and mid 17th century all received leases, usually for three lives.[71] In 1631 Tugford had six farms between 55 a. and 138 a., and one of 22 a.; Baucott had three, between 64 a. and 139 a.[72]

By 1600 there had been much piecemeal inclosure of arable, pasture, and meadows.[73] Nevertheless in the 1650s Tugford had over 150 a. of open-field arable in Street, Willsmore, Morbeach, Buffe (i.e. Above) town, and Neath town fields. Baucott had some open arable in Gey field,[74] but its Little and Brunslow fields[75] had been inclosed for some time.[76] Grazing on Balaam's heath was unstinted in 1652, but only named leaseholders were allowed on Leeth common, with no more than four beasts each.[77] By 1770 the only remaining open arable was 36 a. at Tugford in Stanyard, Morbeach, and Lower fields.[78] Balaam's heath was much reduced on its east side between the mid 17th century[79] and the late 18th, and Leeth common, open in 1680,[80] was inclosed for coppicing before 1770. Little other woodland remained.[81]

Between the late 18th and early 19th century the agricultural landscape was rapidly modernized. Tugford's common of pasture on Brown

42 *T.S.A.S.* lvi. 272.
43 *Cal. Inq. p.m. Hen. VII*, ii, pp. 210–11, 577–8; iii, pp. 127–8, 331–2; P.R.O., C 142/228, no. 56; CP 25/2/77/653, no. 6; CP 25/2/200/4 Eliz. East. no. 2; S.P.L., Deeds 7145; *T.S.A.S.* 4th ser. vi. 257–9, 263–4.
44 S.P.L., MS. 2481, f. 49 and map IX.
45 S.R.O., incl. award B 37; O.S. Map 1/2,500, Salop. LXV. 5 (1903 edn.).
46 *Cal. Inq. p.m. Hen. VII*, ii, pp. 210–11, 577–8; iii, pp. 127, 331–2. Cf. below, Shipton, manors (Brockton).
47 Bodl., Craven dep. 66, deed of 1588.
48 S.R.O. 20/23/13.
49 P.R.O., CP 40/1156, m. 3; S.R.O. 4260/1/1.
50 S.R.O. 4260/1/2; H.W.R.O.(H.), Heref. dioc. rec., bp.'s transcripts, Tugford.
51 S.R.O. 4260/1/4, 10; H.W.R.O.(H.), Heref. dioc. rec., bp.'s transcripts, Tugford.
52 S.P.L., Deeds 9718, 25 Oct. 1667; S.R.O. 4260/1/12; H.W.R.O.(H.), Heref. dioc. rec., bp.'s transcripts, Tugford. Cf. W.S.L. 350/5/40, Tugford p. 3.
53 S.R.O. 4260/1/15.
54 W.S.L. 350/5/40, Tugford p. 3. Cf. above, Munslow, manors (Lr. Millichope).
55 Above, this section.
56 *P.O. Dir. Salop.* (1856), 133.
57 Date stone 'IERS': inf. from Mrs. Moran. Isaac's wife was Eliz. and their s. was Ric.: S.R.O. 4260/1/10.
58 Descr. based on inf. from Mrs. Moran.
59 Below, this section.
60 P.R.O., IR 29/29/324; IR 30/29/324, fields 15, 21, 26–7, 30–1, 37.
61 Bodl., Craven dep. 16, f. 45.
62 S.P.L., Deeds 9718, 14 Apr. 1665.
63 *Rot. Hund.* (Rec. Com.), ii. 101; Heref. D. & C. mun., chapter act bk. 1512–66 (folio), f. 217v.; P.R.O., IR 29/29/324; IR 30/29/324, fields 2, 4–5, 7, 10, 234, 236, 248–9.
64 S.P.L., MS. 2481, f. 48 and map IX.
65 *T.S.A.S.* 2nd ser. viii. 196–7; Bodl., Craven dep. 40, pp. 76–9; S.R.O., incl. award B 21, brief of [1810], ff. 10–11v.
66 H.W.R.O.(H.), Heref. dioc. rec., invs. of Rob. Dyke, 1571; Fra. Bishop, 1664; Thos. Turner, 1665; Edw. Reinolds, 1688; John Grennows, 1693; Thos. Clinton, 1698; Adam Bishop, 1698; Thos. Clinton [1699: ibid. bp.'s transcripts, box 475]; John Sheppard, 1701; Fra. Childs, 1706; Fra. Bishop, 1719; Edw. Dayas, 1726; Edw. Dayas, 1728; John Smout, 1733. Transcripts supplied by Dr. B. S. Trinder.
67 S.P.L., Deeds 7146.
68 *Inq. Non.* (Rec. Com.), 186.
69 S.P.L., Holy Cross par. rec., Shrews. abbey rental, dated from H. Owen and J. B. Blakeway, *Hist. Shrews.* (1825), ii. 532.
70 P.R.O., SC 6/Hen. VIII/3010, m. 65.
71 S.P.L., Deeds 8403; S.R.O. 4260/1/6.
72 Bodl., Craven dep. 40, pp. 73–83.
73 H.W.R.O.(H.), HD 2/14/55, 57.
74 Bodl., Craven dep. 16, ff. 12–36.
75 S.P.L., Deeds 7146.
76 Bodl., Craven dep. 40, pp. 81–3.
77 Ibid. 16, f. 45.
78 S.P.L., MS. 2481, ff. 37, 40–1, 43–5, 48–50, and map IX.
79 When it included Balaam's pool (ibid. map IX): S.P.L., Deeds 9718, 14 Apr. 1665.
80 S.P.L., Deeds 7142.
81 S.P.L., MS. 2481, map IX.

Table XI

Tugford: Land use, livestock, and crops

	1867	*1891*	*1938*	*1965*
Percentage of grassland	73	76	91	60
arable	27	24	9	40
Percentage of cattle	17	18	15	16
sheep	79	79	84	84
pigs	4	3	1	0
Percentage of wheat	49	37	47	40
barley	0	37	19	49
oats	40	26	34	11
mixed corn & rye	11	0	0	0
Percentage of agricultural land growing roots and vegetables	9	8	2	4

Sources: P.R.O., MAF 68/143, no. 21; /1340, no. 7; /3880, Salop. no. 119; /4945, no. 119.

Clee was extinguished by inclosure in 1813,[82] and in 1815 Balaam's heath (91 a.) was inclosed by agreement.[83] Farms were enlarged by amalgamation, the last open-field arable was inclosed, and dispersed parcels were exchanged and consolidated.[84] Much draining was carried out. In 1839 there were roughly equal amounts of arable and grass. The better arable, about a third, was on the higher ground, 'very fair turnip and barley land'; a rotation of wheat, barley, turnips, and clover (two years) suited it. The rest, stiffer and colder, required a rotation of wheat, oats (or beans), and dead fallow but produced fair crops. The grassland was 'indifferent' or 'very bad'.[85] Some isolated barns were built at or near Balaam's Heath in the earlier 19th century. From the mid 19th to the early 20th century arable was increasingly converted to pasture, but the balance was later redressed, especially for growing barley. Sheep overtook cattle as the main livestock before the late 19th century.[86] Nevertheless the Shirley family of Baucott were celebrated breeders of Hereford cattle in the later 19th and early 20th.[87]

A mill, mentioned in 1086,[88] stood by 1770 near the church on a leat from Tugford brook[89] and closed *c.* 1900.[90] The derelict waterworks, buildings of *c.* 1800, and machinery remained in 1990.

Field names indicate pre-19th-century charcoal and lime burning east of Tugford, quarrying north-west, and tile making next to Trow brook.[91] Weavers were mentioned in the 17th and 18th centuries,[92] and a tow dresser in 1752,[93] but no such occupations were mentioned in 1841.[94] Two small quarries remained in use along Sandy Lane in the late 19th century.[95]

LOCAL GOVERNMENT. Tugford presented at the court leet of Castle Holdgate barony in 1537.[96]

By the mid 16th century the manor of Tugford had a biannual court baron with view of frankpledge. At that time separate presentments were made by Nether Tugford, Over Tugford, and Baucott, and separate constables were elected for each. The court then also exercised baron and leet jurisdiction outside the parish: in Broadstone (in Munslow), Burley (in Culmington), the Heath (in Stoke St. Milborough), Stanton Long, and Cold Weston. By the later 17th century it elected one constable for Tugford township, apparently the whole parish, and in 1662 two highway surveyors for the 'manor'. The courts, annual by 1660, were held regularly until 1808 or later. They were by then concerned with regulating the remaining wastes and electing constables for Tugford, Broadstone, Burley, and Cold Weston townships. Court rolls survive for most years 1556–98 and 1660–1808.[97]

In the 16th and early 17th century Tugford was subject to the swainmote of Clee chase.[98]

The parish was in Ludlow poor-law union 1836–1930,[99] Ludlow highway district 1863–95,[1] Ludlow rural sanitary district 1872–94, and Ludlow rural district 1894–1974, and in South Shropshire district from 1974.[2]

CHURCH. About 1138 the bishop of Hereford ordered Tugford and Baucott chapels to be counted as one ('pro una capella computari')[3] and no later reference to Baucott chapel is known. The abbot of Shrewsbury conveyed

82 Abdon and Stoke St. Milborough Incl. Act, 49 Geo. III, c. 109 (Local and Personal); S.R.O., incl. award B 33.

83 S.R.O., incl. award B 37.

84 S.P.L., MS. 2481, ff. 37–50 and map IX; P.R.O., IR 29/29/324; IR 30/29/324.

85 P.R.O., IR 18/8316.

86 Table XI.

87 J. Macdonald and J. Sinclair, *Hist. of Heref. Cattle* (1909), 226–7, 488.

88 *V.C.H. Salop.* i. 319.

89 S.P.L., MS. 2481, f. 47 (field 240) and map IX.

90 *Kelly's Dir. Salop.* (1900), 256; O.S. Map 1/2,500, Salop. LXV. 9 (1903 edn.).

91 P.R.O., IR 29/29/324; IR 30/29/324, fields 8–9, 40–1, 43, 45–6, 228.

92 H.W.R.O.(H.), Heref. dioc. rec., inv. of Thos. Turner, 1665; S.R.O. 4132/Rg/1, 24 Aug. 1766.

93 H.W.R.O.(H.), Heref. dioc. rec., bp.'s transcripts, Tugford, 4 June 1752.

94 S.R.O. 3392/27.

95 O.S. Maps 1/2,500, Salop. LXV. 5, 9 (1884 edn.).

96 S.P.L., MS. 2, f. 146; cf. above, Holdgate, local govt.

97 S.P.L., Deeds 7141–3, 7146, 7182–3, 7396, 7446, 7467, 7526–7, 7976–8039, 8043–77, 9713–21; S.R.O. 1011, box 167, ct. r. of 1808. There is a copy ct. r. of 1553 in P.R.O., SC 2/197/148, m. 1.

98 S.R.O., incl. award B 21, ct. r. 1553–4, 1561; S.R.O. 1037/21/1; *T.S.A.S.* 2nd ser. viii. 198.

99 V. J. Walsh, 'Admin. of Poor Laws in Salop. 1820–55' (Pennsylvania Univ. Ph.D. thesis, 1970), 150; *Kelly's Dir. Salop.* (1929), 284.

1 *Lond. Gaz.* 27 Mar. 1863, p. 1772; S.R.O., S.C.C. Local Govt., etc., Cttee. min. bk. 1894–1903, p. 29.

2 *Rural Dist. Councillors Electn. Order, 1894* (Local Govt. Bd. order no. 31847); *V.C.H. Salop.* ii. 215; iii. 179, and sources cited ibid. 169 n. 29.

3 *Cart. Shrews.* i. 30–1; ii, pp. 302–3. There seems no evid. for the tentative suggestion (Eyton, iv. 82–3) that the chaps. were once in Morville par.

the advowson of Tugford to the bishop of Hereford in 1283,[4] and the living was a rectory in 1291.[5] In 1554 Rowland Hayward bought the advowson from the Crown[6] but probably in error,[7] for the patronage continued to be exercised by the bishop.[8] The living was united to that of Holdgate in 1831, separated from it in 1861, and joined to it again in 1926.[9]

The rectory was taxed in 1291 on a net annual value of £5 6*s*. 8*d*., of which £2 was said in 1341 to come from altar dues and £1 6*s*. 8*d*. from glebe.[10] By 1148[11] and until 1419[12] or later Shrewsbury abbey received a pension of 2*s*. from Tugford. In 1535 the rector's net income was only £4 6*s*. 2*d*.[13] It was estimated at £100 in 1793, of which *c*. £85 came from letting the tithes.[14] In 1839 the glebe (19 a.),[15] though improved by exchange and consolidation in 1825,[16] yielded only *c*. £1 rent.[17] The tithes were commuted to £182 10*s*. in 1842.[18] The small rectory house, perhaps dating from the 16th century, was a single range built of stone rubble,[19] which the rector enlarged with a parallel range *c*. 1822.[20] The house was sold with the glebe in 1930.[21]

Before the Reformation one rector,[22] Stephen of Thanet, was or had been a household clerk of Bishop Swinfield;[23] another was a canon of Hereford;[24] another had leave of absence in 1319.[25] The rectors normally resided in the 16th and early 17th century.[26] In 1617 the pluralist rector of Holdgate,[27] a prebendary of Hereford,[28] acquired the living; his successor at Tugford held the deaconry of Holdgate[29] and in 1639 an assistant curate was employed.[30] Hugh Pugh, rector 1665–1723,[31] resided[32] but by 1743 and until 1860 his successors were, or became, pluralists;[33] they employed curates at Tugford from *c*. 1731 until 1811[34] and are assumed or known[35] to have been absentees until then. Only from 1758 to 1766 did the rector reside and have no curate.[36] There were two services every Sunday in 1716[37] and 1793.[38]

The rectors usually resided 1811–1926,[39] with a curate only 1831–61 during the union with Holdgate;[40] in 1839 the rector was 'chiefly occupied in hunting'.[41] Under Richard Woodhouse, rector 1861–1918,[42] the church band was discontinued[43] and in 1869 choir stalls were provided.[44] R. H. Jeffrey, rector 1918–26, was also vicar of Shipton and, until 1920, sequestrator of Acton Round. He published *Village Sermons on Some Strange Texts* in 1921.[45]

The small parish church of *ST. CATHERINE*, so dedicated by 1733,[46] and probably by the 16th century,[47] consists of chancel and nave without structural division, and south porch and west tower.[48] The walls are of coursed rubble and the roofs tiled. The nave seems to be early 12th-century; there is a narrow splayed north window. A blocked north doorway and, within, small sheela-na-gigs either side of the south doorway, may also be of that period. The chancel seems to have been wholly rebuilt, perhaps about 1200; a north lancet remains from that period. The chancel, which is longer than the nave, has an external string course all round it; the floriated tympanum, perhaps 11th-century, of the former priest's

4 *Charters and Records of Heref. Cath.* ed. W. W. Capes (C.S.), 172; dated from Heref. D. & C. mun. 2131 (ref. supplied by Mrs. M. T. Roberts).

5 *Reg. Swinfield* (C.S.), 276.

6 *Cal. Pat.* 1553–4, 478–9.

7 For a similar case see below, Deuxhill, church.

8 *Dioc. of Heref. Institutions (1539–1900)*, ed. A. T. Bannister (Heref. 1923), 23. The patron in 1560 is unnamed (ibid. 13), but many benefices were being filled by Bp. Scory that yr. (ibid. 13–14) and, if the rector was the Ric. Dyke who d. 1604 (*Alum. Oxon. 1500–1714*, i. 438), then he was a Herefs. man, and so perhaps the likelier to have been the bp.'s appointee.

9 Above, Holdgate, church (where the later hist. of the advowson is treated).

10 *Tax. Eccl.* (Rec. Com.), 167; *Inq. Non.* 186.

11 *Cart. Shrews.* ii, p. 304.

12 *Reg. Lacy* (C.S.), 77.

13 *Valor Eccl.* (Rec. Com.), iii. 209.

14 S.P.L., MS. 6865, p. 196.

15 P.R.O., IR 29/29/324.

16 S.P.L., MS. 6865, p. 198; Heref. Dioc. Regy., reg. 1822–42, pp. 56–8.

17 P.R.O., IR 18/8316.

18 P.R.O., IR 29/29/324.

19 S.P.L., SC11/2, SC31/91.

20 S.P.L., MS. 6865, p. 198.

21 H.W.R.O.(W.), ref. 823.1, BA 2500 (ix), dioc. registrar to bp.'s sec. 20 Jan. 1927; par. rec., statement of stock held by Eccl. Comrs. 30 July 1930.

22 For rectors' names to 1926 see *Reg. Swinfield*, 276, 358, 533–4; *Reg. Trillek* (C.S.), 374, 381, 405; *Reg. Mascall* (C.S.), 183; *Reg. Spofford* (C.S.), 275, 362; *Reg. Myllyng* (C.S.), 195–6; *Reg. Mayew* (C.S.), 236, 275; *Reg. Foxe* (C.S.), 381; Eyton, iv. 84; *Cal. Pat.* 1388–92, 97; Heref. D. & C. mun., chapter act bk. 1512–66 (folio), f. 129; Bannister, *Heref. Institutions*, 13, 23–4, 70, 145, 175; Heref. Cath. Libr., M.R. 6.A.iv, f. 8v.; *T.S.A.S.* 3rd ser. v. 361, 376; 4th ser. ii. 90, 100, 111; vi. 312, 326; vii. 171; Bodl. MS. Gough Salop. 11, f. 71; P.R.O., E 339/1/5; *Crockford* (1932), 688.

23 *Household Roll of Bp. Swinfield* (Camd. Soc. [1st ser.], lix), 116, 119, 158, 209.

24 *Reg. Trillek*, 43–4.

25 *Reg. Orleton* (C.S.), 390; Eyton, iv. 84.

26 e.g. Heref. D. & C. mun., chapter act bk. 1512–66 (folio), f. 129; *T.S.A.S.* 4th ser. xi. 185; xlvi. 45; S.P.L., MS. 14, p. 29.

27 *T.S.A.S.* 3rd ser. viii. 4, 45.

28 Bannister, *Heref. Institutions*, 27.

29 *T.S.A.S.* 3rd ser. viii. 46, 53.

30 H.W.R.O.(H.), Heref. dioc. rec., bp.'s transcripts, Tugford.

31 T.S.A.S. 3rd ser. v. 376; S.P.L., MS. 14, p. 29.

32 S.R.O. 4132/Ch/1; S.P.L., MS. 14, p. 29.

33 Jos. Careless (Bannister, *Heref. Institutions*, 83); Jas. Pratchet (S.P.R. Lich. xi (2), 178, 321, 343–4), Thos. Williams (Bannister, op. cit. 105–6, 127), Ric. Walond (ibid. 115, 130; *Alum. Oxon. 1715–1886*, iv. 1491; *Alum. Cantab. 1752–1900*, vi. 331), John Morgan (Bannister, op. cit. 142, 145), Jos. Corbett (ibid. 145–6; *Alum. Oxon. 1715–1886*, i. 297).

34 H.W.R.O.(H.), Heref. dioc. rec., bp.'s transcripts, Tugford; S.R.O. 4132/Rg/1–3, 5; Heref. Dioc. Regy., reg. 1772–1802, ff. 69, 107, 177.

35 Pratchet from 1766 (*S.P.R. Lich.* xi (2), 178, 321); Williams in 1793 (S.P.L., MS. 6865, p. 196).

36 S.R.O. 4132/Rg/3; S.P.L., MS. 6865, p. 196.

37 H.W.R.O.(H.), HD 5/14/1/23.

38 S.P.L., MS. 6865, p. 197.

39 Ibid. p. 102; S.R.O. 4132/Rg/2, 4; S. Bagshaw, *Dir. Salop.* (1851), 553; *P.O. Dir. Salop.* (1870), 153; *Kelly's Dir. Salop.* (1917), 262; (1926), 290; (1929), 284. For absences see Heref. Dioc. Regy., reg. 1847–56, pp. 362, 369, 373.

40 Heref. Dioc. Regy., reg. 1822–42, p. 171; 1847–56, pp. 362, 373.

41 P.R.O., IR 18/8316.

42 Bannister, *Heref. Institutions*, 175; M.I. in Tugford ch.

43 H. T. Timmins, *Nooks and Corners of Salop.* (1899), 120.

44 *Ch. Cal. Dioc. Heref.* (1870), 139.

45 *Crockford* (1932), 688.

46 Birm. Univ. Libr., Mytton Papers, vii. 1493.

47 St. Cath. was represented in medieval chancel glass: ibid. 1494.

48 Descr. based on Cranage, ii. 164–6; xii. 1012; Pevsner, *Salop.* 305.

doorway was cut down from round to pointed shape and re-used. Two external tomb recesses, north and south, are slightly later, for that on the north interrupts the string course. The south doorway of the nave, and perhaps the font, are roughly contemporary with the chancel.

The tower was added in the 13th century; the lower stage has lancets, a west doorway, and an arch to the nave. In the earlier 14th century large windows were inserted in the chancel, and its east wall was rebuilt; other windows were provided on the south side of the nave. Much medieval glass, perhaps of that period, remained in 1733. The main panels of the east window depicted the Crucifixion, the Resurrection, and Christ in Glory.[49] In the late 13th or early 14th century the chancel received a conjoined pair of external tomb recesses on the north. West of the priest's doorway is a rectangular low-side window of unknown date. A wooden screen evidently divided nave and chancel in the 15th century; tracery from such a screen is re-used in the west gallery; and in the nave, next to the junction with the chancel, a blocked rectangular opening in the south wall may have lit stairs to a rood loft. A plain beam spanning the chancel farther east may once have been part of the screen. A few fragments of medieval stained glass survive in the east window tracery.

The upper stages of the tower were rebuilt in 1720.[50] The porch was standing by 1721.[51] The gallery was built before 1790;[52] its dormer was removed after 1949.[53] The communion rail is dated 1716. A 'great pew' was mentioned in 1733.[54] In 1793 the chancel had two pews, the nave two pews and twenty benches;[55] and plain early benches remain, the rest being 19th-century copies. In the 19th century a separate wooden lectern, reading desk, pulpit, and (in 1869)[56] choir stalls were also provided. The barrelled plaster ceiling and the west gallery with its four-sided music stand have been allowed to remain.

A bier is dated 1617. The five bells are dated 1636–95.[57] A chancel chair is perhaps early 18th-century. Royal arms repainted 1732–3[58] had gone by 1990. So had a silver chalice and tankard recorded in 1793;[59] by 1961 the only plate was 19th-century.[60] In the early 19th century the registers dated from 1594[61] but by 1870 only from 1754;[62] transcripts survive for 1638–9 and from 1661 onwards.[63]

NONCONFORMITY. Members of the Turner family were Baptists in the 1670s[64] and John Edwards and his wife were recusants in 1684[65] but no dissenters were reported in 1716.[66] A Balaam's Heath society of Primitive Methodists with 13 members was on the Hopton Bank circuit by 1832[67] and the Much Wenlock circuit in 1847.[68]

EDUCATION. A schoolmistress was mentioned in 1719[69] but there was no school in 1835.[70] By 1885 the children attended Munslow school.[71]

CHARITIES FOR THE POOR. A poor's stock managed in 1695[72] had gone by 1787.[73] Robert Ellis of Earnstrey Park,[74] by will dated in or before 1652, gave a 10*s*. rent charge in Llanwyddelan parish (Mont.); still received in 1820, it afterwards lapsed.[75] Thomas Clinton, by will dated 1815, gave £100 stock for 10 widows,[76] which yielded £3 a year in 1975.[77]

49 Birm. Univ. Libr., Mytton Papers, vii. 1494 (drawings).
50 S.R.O. 4132/Ch/1; date stone.
51 S.R.O. 4132/Ch/1.
52 S.P.L., MS. 372, vol. ii, f. 35.
53 S.P.L., photo. by S. A. Jeavons.
54 S.R.O. 4132/Ch/1.
55 S.P.L., MS. 6865, p. 197.
56 *Ch. Cal. Dioc. Heref.* (1870), 139.
57 H. B. Walters, *Ch. Bells of Salop.* (Oswestry, 1915), 100–1, 469.
58 S.R.O. 4132/Ch/1; cf. ibid. s.a. 1702–3.
59 S.P.L., MS. 6865, p. 197.
60 D. L. Arkwright and B. W. Bourne, *Ch. Plate Archd. Ludlow* (Shrews. 1961), 59.
61 S.P.L., MS. 14, p. 29.
62 *P.O. Dir. Salop.* (1870), 153; S.R.O. 4132/Rg/1–5; regs. at ch.
63 H.W.R.O.(H.), Heref. dioc. rec., bp.'s transcripts, Tugford.
64 H.W.R.O.(H.), HD 7, chwdns.' presentment of 1669; H.W.R.O.(H.), Heref. dioc. rec., bp.'s transcripts, Tugford, 18 Feb. 1675/6; *Compton Census*, ed. Whiteman, 259 n.
65 *Worcs. Recusant*, liv. 30.
66 H.W.R.O.(H.), HD 5/14/1/23.
67 S.R.O. 2941/2/3.
68 S.R.O. 1861/4.
69 R. Hume, 'Changing Patterns of Educ. Devt. in Salop. 1660–1833' (Keele Univ. Ph.D. (Educ.) thesis, 1982), 190.
70 *Educ. Enq. Abstract*, ii, HC 62, p. 785 (1835), xlii.
71 *Kelly's Dir. Salop.* (1885), 971.
72 S.R.O. 4132/Ch/1.
73 No mention in *Char. Don. 1786–8*, ii, H.C. 511–II, pp. 1024–5 (1816), xvi (2).
74 S.P.L., MS. 6865, p. 97.
75 *3rd Rep. Com. Char.* H.C. 5, p. 265 (1820), iv. Not mentioned in *Review of Local Chars.* (S.C.C. 1975).
76 *3rd Rep. Com. Char.* pp. 265–6.
77 *Review of Local Chars.* 60.

THE LIBERTY AND BOROUGH OF WENLOCK

AT THE beginnning of 1966 fourteen Shropshire towns enjoyed municipal self-government: five larger and older ones under municipal borough councils, nine newer and smaller ones under urban district councils.[1] A sixth municipal borough, that of Wenlock, was unique, not only for the singular extent of its territory (which contained four small towns set in 92 sq. km. of countryside)[2] but also because its legal identity and constitution arose from the fact that it was a rump of Wenlock priory's 'monkish domains'[3] which, since before the Norman Conquest, had been administered under successive forms of fiscal, seignorial, and municipal privilege. The borough's uniqueness derived from unforeseen, probably unintended, effects of an early 12th-century declaration that all the lands of the Cluniac priory of Wenlock constituted one parish. They never did, but the declaration, its original purpose obscure, survived as an oracle, obfuscating the changing character and extent of Holy Trinity parish, Much Wenlock, and working on the ambiguities of royal charters to influence the exercise of secular franchises: thus the priory, and eventually its borough, were enabled to extend their liberties over almost the whole of the priory estate.

The early estate: parishes and fiscal privilege

Most of the estates received by the priory at its foundation *c.* 1080 had already belonged for four centuries to the church of Wenlock, founded as a double monastery and later to become a minster of secular priests.[4] Well before the Conquest they shared a common fiscal privilege. All lay in south Shropshire, scattered around a large central estate at Much Wenlock and at no great distance from it. Despite some changes, moreover, the church of Wenlock's estate was one of those[5] notable for long maintained territorial integrity. The earliest documents, embedded in the *Testament* of St. Mildburg (transcribed into the life of the saint attributed to Goscelin), have been taken to suggest that the monastery was originally much more widely endowed, with estates in Wales and what were to become Herefordshire and Worcestershire.[6] Probably, however, the monastery's early endowment never formed more than part (albeit much the greatest part) of the extensive lands given to Mildburg, a daughter of King Merewalh of the West Hecani.[7]

1 *V.C.H. Salop.* iii. 179.

2 Broseley, Ironbridge, Madeley, M. Wenlock: *Census*, 1961.

3 316 *H.L. Deb.* 5th ser. 1181–2.

4 Below, M. Wenlock, churches.

5 Cf. those of Barking, Ely, Evesham, Peterborough, etc.: *Med. Art, Archit. and Arch. at Heref.* (Brit. Arch. Assoc. Conf. Trans. xv), 5.

6 H. P. R. Finberg, *Lucerna* (1964), 74–5; idem, *Early Charters of W. Midlands* (1972), pp. 208, 215, equates Mildburg's *Testament* with 'the Wenlock title-deeds', but the 'titles' were hers. *V.C.H. Salop.* ii. 39, mentions only Lingen or Upper Lye (Herefs.), Wyre Piddle (Worcs.), and the est. in Wales; for suggestions about those places see below, this section. For Goscelin cf. *D.N.B.*; Finberg, *Early Charters*, pp. 199–201.

7 Apparently predecessors (7th–8th cents.) of the Magonsaete (9th–11th cents.): *Woolhope Trans.* xlii. 33, 36–45; *Origins of A.-S. Kingdoms*, ed. S. Bassett (1989), 181–2; but cf. P. Sims-Williams, *Religion and Literature in W. Eng. 600–800* (1990), 40–3.

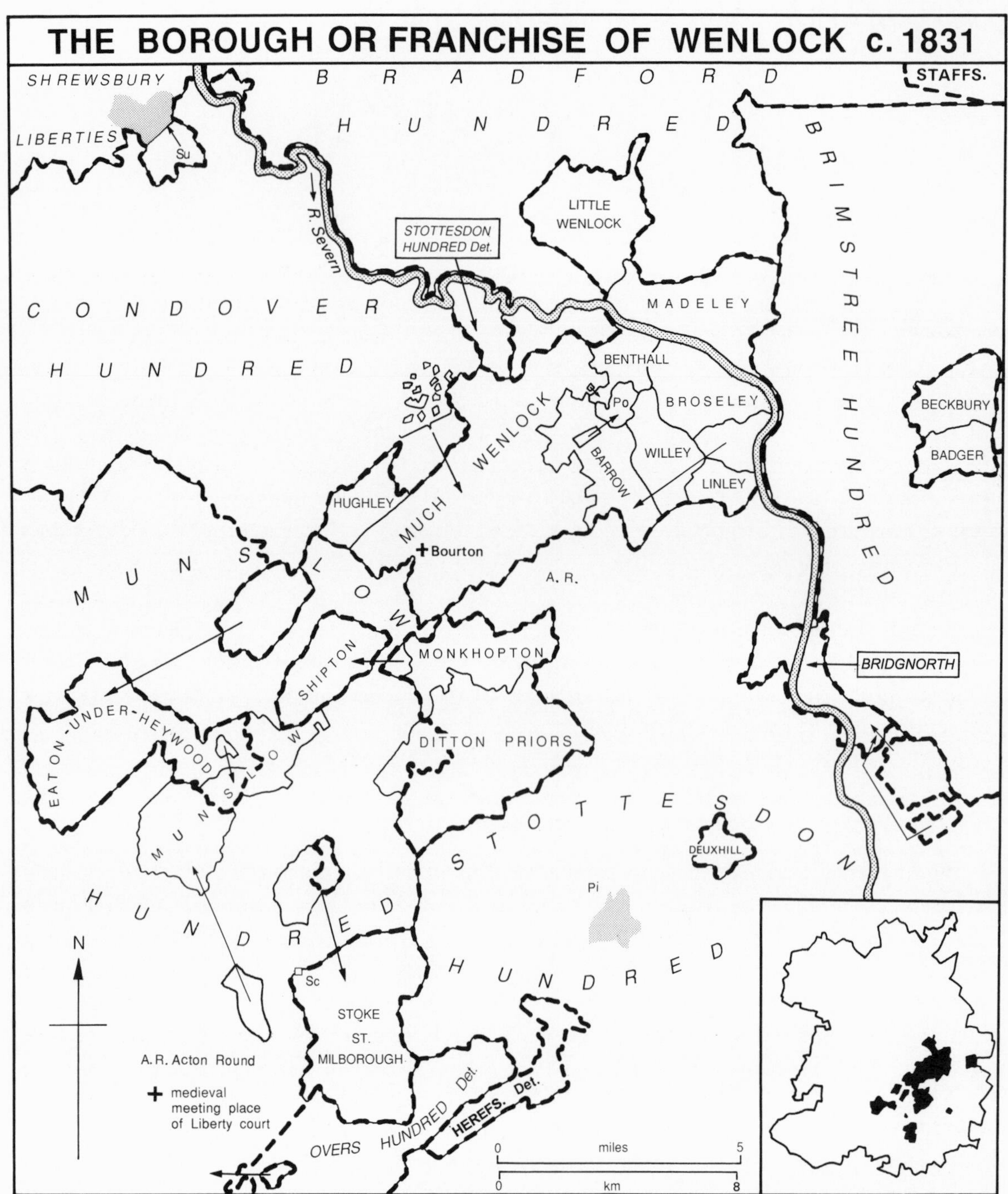

Fig. 16
The boundary of the parliamentary borough was not affected when the area of the municipal borough was reduced under the Municipal Corporations Act, 1835, and the parliamentary boundary was recorded in the 1880s on the first edition of the 1/2,500 Ordnance Survey plans, which are thus the best available evidence for the precise boundary of the borough *c.* 1831 and so of the old liberty. Abbreviations: Pi, Pickthorn; Po, Posenhall; Sc, the Scirmidge; Su, Sutton.

Before 690 Aethelheah, abbot of Iken (Suff.), gave Mildburg 144 hides (*manentes*) which his monastery[8] had bought from her father (probably dead by *c.* 685). Of those hides 47 were within the later Herefordshire, at 'Magana', 'Lydas', and 'another place by the river Monnow'.[9] The gift implies a monastic foundation at 'Wininicas', under Iken's tutelage and perhaps in existence since *c.* 680,[10] but there is nothing to suggest that Mildburg was obliged to use, or did use, all her lands to endow one monastery,[11] for all that Aethelheah gave her was to be absolutely at her disposal, by gift or legacy, to promote monastic life,[12] and Mildburg's *Testament*,[13] though occasionally read aloud in the Cluniac priory,[14] was no *historia fundationis*.[15] It is thus not known to what purposes Mildburg's 'Herefordshire' or Welsh lands were devoted. Rulers enjoyed much proprietorial freedom with church lands,[16] and Mildburg would doubtless have been expected to foster her family's dynastic interests, centred on the Lugg valley, heartland of the kingdom.[17] 'Magana' (Maund, later in Bodenham parish) possibly formed part of the large minster parish of Leominster, where monastic life flourished in Saxon times[18] and which was the ecclesiastical centre of Merewalh's kingdom. 'Lydas', a large estate near Hereford, seems to have passed to the minster at Hereford, founded by Mildburg's half-brother Mildfrith and destined, as the cathedral church of a diocese created *c.* 690 for his subjects, to surpass Leominster.[19] An estate by the Monnow, implausible as an endowment for a monastery at the opposite end of the kingdom, may have furthered other, unrecorded, initiatives by Mildburg or her family, as may the estate in Wales[20] that she is said to have owned.

Ninety-seven of the 144 hides which the young[21] virgin, already consecrated to religion, received from Abbot Aethelheah were in exchange for 60 at 'Homtun' (possibly near Leominster and later part of the Leominster monastic estate)[22] and were 'in the place called Wininicas'; that is usually assumed to include the site of Mildburg's monastery at Much Wenlock and was thus the first instalment and core of those estates which she did use to endow the monastery there.[23] 'Skilled in monastic life' she ruled it as abbess until her death some time after 727, increasing its estates with gifts from her kinsmen and others and purchases from neighbouring landowners.[24] Before 704 her half-brothers Merchelm and Mildfrith gave her 63 hides around Clee Hill (where the Cluniac priory owned Stoke St. Milborough, Clee Downton and the Moor, Clee Stanton, the Heath, and Norncott),[25] by the river Corve

8 The summarizing phrase about 'the land of this minster' amounting to 144 hides probably paraphrases words of Aethelheah referring to a total surrendered by Iken ('this minster') rather than one received by 'Wininicas'; the paragraphing of Finberg's translation of B.L. Add. MS. 34633, f. 210v., shows that better than the paragraphing of his transcript: *Early Charters*, pp. 202, 205.

9 Ibid. 138, 147, 202, 204–5, 217–18, 239–40.

10 Ibid. 202, 205, 220.

11 Her *Testament* simply lists all her acquisitions of lands. The last word in the phrase *ignoracione agrorum ecclesie* (ibid. 201, 204) may not specify the monastery at 'Wininicas'.

12 Ibid. 202, 205.

13 Not a devising document: ibid. 200–1.

14 Ibid. 213.

15 Above, notes 6, 11.

16 F. M. Stenton, *A.-S. Eng.* (1971), 149–50, 155–6. D. M. Hadley, 'Conquest, Colonization and the Church: Eccl. Organization in the Danelaw', *Hist. Research*, lxix. 109–28, exemplifies pre-Viking royal depredation of church property, not only in the Danelaw (e.g. pp. 110–12).

17 Bassett, *A.-S. Kingdoms*, 177.

18 *Minsters and Par. Chs.* ed. J. Blair (1988), 83, 85; cf. *Med. Art at Heref.* 6–11. Bodenham, adjoining Leominster's *parochia*, is said never to have formed pt. of it (Blair, op. cit. 86, 88, 92), though the early *parochia* is admitted to have been more extensive (ibid. 83). For Leominster priory's 13th-cent. interests in Bodenham see ibid. 93 n. 26.

19 Finberg, *Early Charters*, pp. 220–3; idem, *Lucerna*, 75; *Woolhope Trans.* xlii. 16–52; *Med. Art at Heref.* 4–6; *V.C.H. Herefs.* i. 323–4.

20 On the opposite side of the Black Mts. from the Monnow, at Llanfilo (Brec.) whose ch. is dedicated to her: Finberg, *Early Charters*, p. 210. Evesham abbey's ch. at Offenham (Worcs.) was dedicated to her, perh. in the early 12th cent. when her cult was publicized: *V.C.H. Worcs.* ii. 421, 423; *T.S.A.S.* lvii. 136–7.

21 Finberg, *Early Charters*, pp. 217–18, 220.

22 Ibid. p. 208 n. 2.

23 Finberg, *Lucerna*, 73–4; below, M. Wenlock, manors.

24 Finberg, *Early Charters*, pp. 201–6, 220.

25 Cf. below, Stoke St. Milborough, manors; the Heath, manors.

(probably the later estates of Bourton, Easthope, Larden, Patton, Shipton, Skimblescott, and 'Stantune'),[26] in 'Kenbecleag' (possibly Beckbury, and, if so, lost by 1066),[27] and in Chelmarsh (probably Deuxhill and Eardington).[28] King Ceolred of Mercia (709–16) gave her 4 hides at 'Peandan Wrye',[29] perhaps an estate that had belonged to their grandfather King Penda.[30] In Ceolred's reign a nun gave her 8 hides at 'Lingen', probably 'Lege' lying below Wenlock Edge and including the place later called Hughley, where the priory retained ½ hide in 1086.[31] Late in life Mildburg spent much on buying Madeley.[32]

Though it remained largely intact, the landed endowment of St. Mildburg's abbey was subject to occasional royal interference. 'Stantune' was surrendered to royal lordship late in the 9th century,[33] but in 901 it was restored to the minster, with Caughley added, in exchange for Easthope and Patton;[34] Patton subsequently became the *caput* of a hundred.[35] By 1066 'Stantune' had been lost again,[36] but the minster then owned, in addition to Mildburg's early endowment, a large estate at Ticklerton[37] in Ape Dale and smaller manors at Pickthorn near Stottesdon, Sutton in Shrewsbury hundred,[38] and Little Wenlock[39] north-west of Madeley. Penda's 'Wrye' was perhaps among those estates.[40] Little Wenlock (3 hides in 1086) presumably had a different name before it was acquired by the church of Wenlock,[41] and Ticklerton (10 hides in 1086), perhaps another renamed settlement,[42] lies on the north-west side of central Ape Dale, where streams deflected by the lumpy topography[43] may suggest a possible 'Wrye'.[44]

Roger of Montgomery, earl of Shrewsbury from 1068,[45] was almost the last secular ruler to tamper with the minster estate, but his changes, like those of *c.* 900[46] and the 10th or 11th century,[47] were in the end fairly minor. He took Stoke St. Milborough to give to his chaplains,[48] but by 1086 he had taken Eardington to endow a new college at Quatford for them,[49] and the Cluniac monks whom he had brought to Much Wenlock *c.* 1080 soon regained Stoke; the earl compensated them for distant Eardington with the baron of Castle Holdgate's manor of Millichope[50] adjoining their Ticklerton (later Eaton-under-Heywood) estate. Nevertheless the priory's estate was still clearly that which St. Mildburg had assembled, centred on the great, though probably diminished, minster parish of Holy Trinity and mostly concentrated in Patton hundred. An oddity of Patton hundred in 1086 was its detached member of Beckbury: lending support to the identification of Beckbury with 'Kenbecleag', the link gives a first hint of the new priory's early ambition to

26 Cf. above, Easthope, manor; Holdgate, manors; Stanton Long, manors; below, Shipton, manors. 'Stantune' comprised the later Holdgate and Stanton Long.

27 Cf. below, Beckbury, manor.

28 Cf. below, Deuxhill, manor.

29 Earning little gratitude: Finberg, op. cit. pp. 203, 205–6, 211; B. Yorke, *Kings and Kingdoms of Early A.-S. Eng.* (1990), 112; Sims-Williams, *Religion and Literature*, 243, 246–7, 267, 269–72.

30 For the relationships see Yorke, op. cit. 104. The name Penda is rare: *P.N. Worcs.* (E.P.N.S.), pp. xxii, 223.

31 Below, Hughley, manor.

32 *V.C.H. Salop.* xi. 35.

33 To benefit the minster estate as a whole: below, this section.

34 Finberg, *Early Charters*, p. 148.

35 And then perh. acquired a church: cf. above, Munslow Hundred (*part*); below, this section.

36 Above, Stanton Long, manors.

37 Cf. below, Eaton-under-Heywood, manors.

38 *V.C.H. Salop.* i. 312–13.

39 Cf. ibid. xi. 80.

40 Finberg, *Early Charters*, p. 89, suggests Wyre Piddle nr. Pinvin ('Penda's fen'), but that was in the Hwiccan kingdom and in the 690s probably part of an est. given to Bp. Oftfor to re-establish monastic life at Fladbury. Metathesis cannot be presumed in 'Wyre'. See *P.N. Worcs.* pp. xiii, 155, 223; *Trans. Worcs. Arch. Soc.* 3rd ser. ii. 26; D. Hooke, *A.-S. Landscape: Kingdom of the Hwicce* (1985), 134, 136.

41 S. Bassett, 'Medieval Eccl. Organisation in Vicinity of Wroxeter', *Jnl. Brit. Arch. Assoc.* cxlv. 17.

42 *P.N. Salop.* (E.P.N.S.), i, pp. xv, 292, for remarks on the 'worthign' element.

43 Above, Intro.; Rushbury, intro.; below, Eaton-under-Heywood, intro.

44 As in the area called 'Wryme', perh. from the deflection of Checkley brook where it marks the Ches.–Staffs. boundary (O.S. Nat. Grid 750460–744456): *P.N. Ches.* (E.P.N.S.), iii. 56–8; O.S. Map 1/25,000, SJ 64/74 (1987 edn.).

45 C. P. Lewis, 'Early Earls of Norman Eng.' *Ang.-Norman Studies*, xiii. 219–20.

46 Above, this section.

47 When 'Stantune' was lost: preceding para.

48 For them see *T.S.A.S.* lvi. 252–4 (superseding Finberg's speculation in *Early Charters*, p. 198 n. 4).

49 *V.C.H. Salop.* i. 312, 318; ii. 39, 123–4.

50 Ibid. ii. 39–40.

draw the church of Wenlock's ancient estates into one hundred, an aim realized almost completely more than a century after 1086.[51] Before that, however, the priory succeeded in regaining for Holy Trinity parish some of its semi-detached members by means that were to contribute to the success of its wider hundredal policy.

The church of Wenlock's estates were always too scattered to form one parish. For its larger estates away from Much Wenlock the Saxon minster presumably provided churches[52] over which, as landowner, it exercised proprietary rights. Smaller distant estates are likely to have been served from independently established churches nearby,[53] as probably were Deuxhill and Eardington (possibly in a parish of Chelmarsh),[54] Pickthorn (in Stottesdon),[55] and Sutton[56] (perhaps associated with Meole Brace church).[57] Even Hughley, adjoining Holy Trinity parish but in Condover hundred in 1086, probably depended on a church to the north, perhaps Cound.[58]

The religious influence of the Wenlock community, however, would have been exercised most directly throughout the large parish centring on it and probably once stretching from 'Stantune' and Shipton in Corve Dale to Benthall, Broseley, and Linley in the Severn Gorge.[59] In time the community probably built local chapels, the surviving evidence of which is the Saxon fabric in Barrow church.[60] The church of Wenlock's own lands presumably dominated the parish, reinforcing the community's religious influence there by its power as a landowner. Within the area suggested for the parish, however, Caughley did not belong to the minster until 901, and the minster is not known to have had a temporal estate in (for example) Broseley, Willey,[61] Brockton,[62] or Linley[63] before 1086 or ever any in Acton Round.[64] So the parish evidently included lay estates,[65] and from the 10th century, certainly by the time of Edgar's law on tithe payment,[66] lay landowners were weakening the cohesion of minster parishes by founding local churches.[67] Although Barrow is the only known pre-Conquest chapel in Holy Trinity parish, there may have been another at Shipton. The priest at Patton in 1086 may have served a church founded after the minster's estate there became royal property (901) and a hundred *caput*,[68] and, whenever founded, a church at Patton, by separating Shipton and Larden from Holy Trinity parish, could have led to the foundation of a chapel at Shipton to safeguard the minster's parochial rights there.

51 Ibid. i. 341; above, this section; below, this article (Lib.: Bourton hund.).

52 Archit. remains at Stoke St. Milborough suggest a pre-12th-cent. ch.: below, Stoke St. Milborough, church.

53 Beckbury e.g. adjoined the large minster par. of Shifnal (Eyton, ii. 331).

54 Below, Deuxhill, church.

55 Where it remains.

56 Notwithstanding S. Bassett, 'A.-S. Shrews. and its Churches', *Midland Hist.* xvi. 5. Nothing is known of Sutton ch.'s 'parochial affiliation' before *c.* 1110 (date of the *Dictum* of St. Mildburg: below, this section) and thereafter the ch. is indistinguishable in status from other priory chs. outside H. Trin. par. as defined in 1332 (below, this section).

57 Implausibly suggested as a minster (ibid. 5, 15–16; *Jnl. Brit. Arch. Assoc.* cxlv. 3 (fig. 1), 12–14), pretermitting possible connexions betw. it and Sutton.

58 *Jnl. Brit. Arch. Assoc.* cxlv. 6–8, 13–17. All Condover hund. manors seem originally to have been in Lichfield dioc.

59 Eyton, iii. 264–70, suggesting that the medieval par. comprised the early 19th-cent. pars. of Acton Round, Barrow, Benthall, Broseley, Hughley, Linley, Monkhopton, Shipton, M. Wenlock (incl. Bourton), and Willey. Cf. below, M. Wenlock, churches. But the pre-10th-cent. par. must have excluded the pts. of Harley later in M. Wenlock par., Hughley, and Wigwig while including Easthope, Patton, 'Stantune', and any intervening places not minster property.

60 Below, Barrow, church; cf. M. Deanesly, *Pre-Conquest Church in Eng.* (1963), 197–8.

61 Below, Broseley, manor; Willey, manor. They were in Alnodestreu hund. in 1086 (*V.C.H. Salop.* i. 335, 338) and so perh. not owned by the minster when the hunds. were formed or reorganized in the 10th or early 11th cent. (ibid. iii. 6).

62 Below, Shipton, manors (Brockton).

63 First recorded in the 1130s as held of the priory in socage: below, Linley, manor.

64 Eyton, iv. 121 sqq. Acton Round will be treated with other Stottesdon hund. pars. in a future vol. of this *Hist.*

65 Above, n. 59.

66 *Eng. Hist. Doc. c. 500–1042*, ed. D. Whitelock (1955), pp. 47, 395–6; *Dom. Bk. Studies*, ed. A. Williams and R. W. H. Erskine (1987), 65.

67 Deanesly, *Pre-Conquest Ch.* 191, 207–8, 309–11, 347.

68 Above, Munslow Hundred (*part*); Stanton Long, church; *V.C.H. Salop.* iii. 6.

By *c.* 1110 Shipton chapel's own independence was being asserted,[69] a claim that may suggest its foundation long before. Dismissal of the claim led Richard of Beaumais, bishop of London and probably already a benefactor to Wenlock priory,[70] to declare the land of St. Mildburg all 'one parish' subject to the mother church of Wenlock. Beaumais pronounced his sentence, the so-called *Dictum* of St. Mildburg, as justiciar of Shropshire,[71] not in the ecclesiastical role of judge-delegate presumed for him when Bishop Vere confirmed the *Dictum* eighty-odd years later.[72] The *Dictum*'s claim that the parochial unity of St. Mildburg's lands was ancient need not be taken literally or as a guide to Saxon parochial arrangements. The English clergy who attested the *Dictum* were interpreting the past in terms appropriate to the age of reform in which they lived, when ownership of churches was being redefined: lay proprietorship was seen as mere patronage while churches were conceived as owned by their rectors and monastic ownership of rectories was encouraged.[73] Accordingly to declare that Wenlock's estates were one parish subject to one church was in effect to give the monks of Wenlock, owners of Holy Trinity church,[74] a monopoly of rectorial rights throughout their estates and on other men's estates within their parishes, the newly defined arrangements being sanctioned as immemorial.[75]

The *Dictum*'s significance was probably enhanced by further developments which it helped to warrant. They may be considered first in relation to four manors east of Much Wenlock: Badger, Beckbury, Broseley, and Willey. Although only Broseley and Willey[76] were probably ancient members (perhaps *membra disjecta* by the early 12th century) of Holy Trinity parish, the four form a distinctive group among the estates that the priory owned or which were to come within its liberty. All were in lay hands in 1086 and Domesday Book states no ostensible connexion between them and the priory;[77] all four were also distinguished by a two-stage system of church patronage. Domesday Book's one hint of a temporal link with Wenlock priory is the record of Beckbury as a detached member of Patton hundred: making identification of Beckbury with Wenlock's early estate of 'Kenbecleag' more plausible, it also suggests that the priory was trying to establish or revive seignorial links with Beckbury.[78] By what tactics its 'strong and progressive' strategy[79] was pursued must be guessed. The *Dictum*'s declaration that the priory lands were one parish implied the corollary that places linked to the priory ecclesiastically were among its lands or estates, posing a dilemma to the manorial lords. Thus the priory may have followed up the temporal claims which it was making on Beckbury *c.* 1086 by the advancement, after *c.* 1110, of parochial claims (perhaps including Badger),[80] success reinforcing the earlier temporal claims. So, by analogy with Beckbury and Badger, the recovery of Broseley and Willey for Holy Trinity parish with the *Dictum*'s aid may have prompted the priory's forging of temporal links with them too.

The two-stage church patronage (contrasting with more conventional advowsons

69 Eyton, iii. 232–3; below, Shipton, church.

70 *T.S.A.S.* lxx. 194.

71 Eyton, iii. 232–4; *V.C.H. Salop.* iii. 10.

72 *Heref. 1079–1234*, ed. J. Barrow (Eng. Episcopal Acta, vii), pp. 167–8.

73 Stenton, *A.-S. Eng.* 668–9; G. Tellenbach, *Church, State and Christian Soc. at time of Investiture Contest*, transl. R. F. Bennett (1959), 117–25; D. Knowles, *Monastic Order in Eng.* (1966), 595–600.

74 Formally appropriated *c.* 1190: below, n. 10; M. Wenlock, churches.

75 Cf. M. T. Clanchy, 'Remembering the Past and the Good Old Law', *History*, lv. 171.

76 Notwithstanding Eyton, ii. 76. Cf. ibid. 33, 60; above, notes 53, 59.

77 *V.C.H. Salop.* i. 333, 335, 338, 341. For the rest of this para. cf. below, manor and church sections for the four manors.

78 *V.C.H. Salop.* i. 341; above, this section; below, this section.

79 Eyton, iii. 232, calling it 'influence' rather than policy.

80 If Badger and Beckbury were once a single estate (below, Beckbury, intro.), Badger ch. may have depended on Beckbury's.

of churches on other priory manors that were subinfeudated)[81] is so similar in all four manors[82] as to suggest that the arrangements originated in similar circumstances and at the same time. It is not only the *Dictum* which suggests that that time was the early 12th century. For what may not have been the first time[83] Prior Humbald (1155 × 1175) granted the lord of Badger the right to nominate an incumbent for the prior to present to the bishop.[84] Although comparable arrangements for Beckbury, Willey, and Broseley are not recorded unambiguously until 1303,[85] 1324,[86] and 1359[87] respectively,[88] it seems reasonable to deduce the priory's seignorial links with Beckbury (striven for *c.* 1086, achieved by 1120),[89] Badger (inferable from 1198, confirmed in the 1220s),[90] and Broseley and Willey (inferable from 1198)[91] from the early 12th century and the ecclesiastical links that had probably preceded them. Broseley had formed part of a ring of manors belonging to the baron of Castle Holdgate and the sheriff (later to the FitzAlans) hemming the priory's central estate,[92] and about the time that the *Dictum* was issued Henry I altered the feudal tenure of Broseley, enfeoffing the Lorrainer Warin of Metz in the baron's place,[93] at the same time conferring on the Breton royal protégé Alan fitz Flaald (brought to Shropshire by 1114) the chief lordship of Willey over Turold of Verley's heirs or successors.[94] About 1115 Warin of Metz and Warner, the new terre tenant of Willey, attested Richard of Beaumais's declaration supplementing the *Dictum*.[95] Their attestations suggest that they were already in some sense the prior's men[96] and that the *Dictum* had quickly reasserted the rights of the priory's parish of Holy Trinity over their estates, fixing the pensions that the incumbents of Broseley and Willey, as those of Badger and Beckbury,[97] are later known to have owed and which were probably secured by the two-stage patronage.[98]

The four manors seem to have been the only ones over whose feudal tenants the priory intruded itself as lord (as distinct from becoming overlord by the enfeoffment of tenants on the priory demesne), probably soon after the *Dictum* was issued. In Badger and Beckbury the lay overlords continued to be recorded, and the terre tenants evidently held their estates of two overlords concurrently; the service which they owed to the priory included rents (secular analogues of the church pensions) and, from 1198, afforcement of the liberty court.[99] Broseley and Willey too were held of the priory for suit of court from 1198, though after the displacement of their lay overlords—Broseley's early and Willey's after 1256—the prior seems to have felt free to exact further services from those two nearby manors: ceremonial attendance at his table by the lord of Broseley and the carrying of his frock in Parliament by the lord of Willey.[1] The assertion of ecclesiastical and seignorial rights over the four manors, probably from the early 12th century, had

81 e.g. Hughley (with Bourton the only priory estate mentioned in Domesday Bk. as tenanted), to whose lord the prior granted a normal advowson in the 1170s: below, Hughley, church.

82 Many of the similarities betw. Badger and Beckbury (Eyton, iv. 138) extend to Broseley and Willey.

83 The grant was to a lord who had bought Badger, so may have renewed an earlier arrangement.

84 Bodl. MS. ch. Shrops. 106; below, Badger, church.

85 Eyton, iv. 138.

86 Eyton, ii. 60.

87 Ibid. 36; *Cal. Pat.* 1358–61, 264.

88 Full and regular inf. about patronage is in bps.' regs., Heref.'s first being Cantilupe's 1275–82: D. M. Smith, *Guide to Bps.' Regs. of Eng. and Wales* (1981), pp. ix, 95.

89 Above, this section; below, Beckbury, manor.

90 Dugdale, *Monasticon*, v. 76 no. vi; below, Badger, manor.

91 From the suit of ct. they made from 1198: *Rot. Hund.* ii. 84–5.

92 See e.g. tabulated Dom. Bk. inf. on tenures in Eyton, i. 18; ii. 258; iii. 220; v. 2; vi. 2, 4; vii. 198; xi. 294.

93 Below, Broseley, manor.

94 Who became mesne lords: below Willey, manor. For Alan see *V.C.H. Salop.* iii. 10.

95 Eyton, iii. 233–4.

96 It is not known when (before the 13th cent.) Broseley's lord was overlord of estates carved out of priory demesnes at Arlescott and Bradeley (below, Barrow, manors; M. Wenlock, manors) or why he held Shushions (Staffs.) of the priory (*V.C.H. Staffs.* iv. 97).

97 Below, Badger, church; Beckbury, church; Broseley, churches; Willey, church

98 Cf. Eyton, vii. 111.

99 Below, Badger, manor; Beckbury, manor.

1 Below, Broseley, manor; Willey, manor; cf., for their suit at Bourton hund. small ct., below, this article (Lib.: Bourton hund.).

made them parts of the priory's lands and so, in the *Dictum*'s terms, also parts of the 'one parish' which all those lands formed.

The *Dictum* also helped to reassert the rights of Holy Trinity church over the FitzAlan demesne manor of Acton Round[2] in the earlier 12th century when, showing the family's constant solicitude for its demesnes, the lord reserved a third of the manor's tithes for Cound church on another of his demesne manors.[3] Besides the restoration of Holy Trinity parish to something like its original extent, however, other conveniently adjoining manors were absorbed, the long-possessed Hughley and the newly acquired Wigwig probably in the earlier or mid 12th century.[4] Significantly, however, it proved impossible to absorb Church Preen. Preen parish adjoined Hughley and most of it fell within Church Preen manor, which had probably been given to Wenlock priory in the late 11th or early 12th century. Nevertheless the baron of Castle Holdgate, overlord of Church Preen and of the parish's other manor, Holt Preen, seems to have succeeded in maintaining the existence of the cell at Church Preen as his *Eigenkloster* and thereby preserving the separateness of Preen parish in his own patronage.[5]

The *Dictum* did not unite all the priory's churches and estates in one parish. In 1332 the bounds of Holy Trinity parish[6] excluded the priory's parishes of Badger, Beckbury, Clun, Preen,[7] and Sutton and its estates of Deuxhill, Ditton Priors (containing Middleton Priors), Eaton-under-Heywood, Madeley, Stoke St. Milborough, and Little Wenlock; those places, some including adjacent subinfeudated estates,[8] functioned as independent parishes in the Middle Ages and later.[9] Rather, it seems, the *Dictum*'s authority assisted the monks first (as has been seen) to reintegrate Holy Trinity parish, then freely to reorganize benefices on their estates in ways that best suited their house's interests as occasion arose—essentially by justifying the monks' continued exercise of a landowner's old proprietorial freedom with churches.[10] Thus *c.* 1115, with Bishop Beaumais's renewed sanction and in an evident compromise of claims, the priory conceded the tithes and burial rights of its estate at Lower Millichope to the rector of Munslow,[11] keeping those of its estate at Upper Millichope for its own neighbouring church of Eaton-under-Heywood.[12] Simultaneously the priory's small manor of Deuxhill was separated from Glazeley parish,[13] though its prospects as an independent benefice were not good; later, after the priory had acquired Ditton (*c.* 1175) and the appropriation of its church (in the mid 1220s), the monks chose to forgo the tithes of its chapel of Middleton and to unite Middleton to Deuxhill and so make a viable living, if not a convenient parish, of two places 8 km. apart.[14]

Though never united parochially, the minster estate had a long-established unity in secular affairs, for its freedom from secular dues was secured by the surrender of 'Stantune' to royal lordship, apparently in the late 9th century.[15] That unity of

[2] The *Dictum* was adduced to reassert Wenlock's rights in Acton Round again in 1284: below, this article (Lib.: Bourton hund.).

[3] He also gave Criddon and Easthope tithes to Cound (*Cal. Pat.* 1266–72, 721): early (Eyton, i. 183; iv. 126) and coeval gifts evidently made when the FitzAlans held Acton Round, Cound, Criddon, and Easthope in demesne. The two last were subinfeudated by 1166: ibid. i. 191; above, Easthope, manor. *V.C.H. Salop.* viii. 70, wrongly dates the grant early 13th-cent.

[4] Below, Hughley, church; M. Wenlock, churches.

[5] *T.S.A.S.* lxx. 194–6.

[6] S.R.O. 1224/2/11.

[7] *T.S.A.S.* lxx. 194, 196, 199 n. 68.

[8] i.e. Clee Stanton, Hatton, the Heath, Upper Millichope, Norncott, Sidnall, and Wolverton: below, Ditton Priors, manors; Eaton-under-Heywood, manors; the Heath, manors; Stoke St. Milborough, manors.

[9] See par. hists. below; *V.C.H. Salop.* xi. 21–92.

[10] But H. Trin. (1186 x 1198: below, M. Wenlock, churches) and other chs. were formally appropriated to the priory in order to define rectorial and vicarial rights.

[11] Possibly a new benefice then: above, Munslow Hundred (*part*); Munslow, churches.

[12] Possibly also new: below, Eaton-under-Heywood, church.

[13] Eyton, i. 217, 220; iii. 233.

[14] Below, Deuxhill, church; Ditton Priors, churches.

[15] Finberg, *Early Charters*, p. 148.

fiscal privilege was probably confirmed over a century later in Cnut's reign when 4 of Much Wenlock's 20 hides were acquitted of liability to pay geld.[16] In 1086 many of Wenlock priory's other estates enjoyed similar concessions, perhaps also since Cnut's time:[17] 13 of its hides were then exempt from geld, all in Patton hundred where the priory held 63¾ of the hundred's original 101 hides.[18] The priory's 4½ (formerly 9½) hides scattered in four other hundreds were not exempt.[19] Fiscal privilege was thus confined to the priory's estates in Patton hundred, and the priory's privileged and dominant position there, though falling short of making Patton a private hundred,[20] perhaps suggests a twofold motive for Beckbury's inclusion in it by 1086:[21] first as a reinforcement of priory claims on the manor that were probably at best only shadowy ones from a remote past,[22] and secondly to strengthen the priory's position within the hundred. Modification of hundreds[23] and even shires[24] for the convenience of great landowners was not unusual in the early Middle Ages.

Patton hundred, however, where the priory enjoyed such privileged pre-eminence, was to disappear. It merged, perhaps gradually, with Culvestan hundred after the choice of a new *caput* at Munslow *c.* 1100 or shortly before, the resulting hundred taking the new *caput*'s name.[25] Munslow hundred naturally included the priory's manors from the former Patton and Culvestan[26] hundreds, but it also came to include Broseley and Willey, whose transfer from Alnodestreu hundred or its successor Brimstree[27] before 1198[28] was presumably eased partly by their nearness to Much Wenlock but mainly by their reintegration with Holy Trinity parish probably soon after *c.* 1110.[29] The ecclesiastical and seignorial links forged with Badger and Beckbury,[30] however, while they evidently made them a detached part of Hereford diocese,[31] did not serve to make them a detachment of Munslow hundred, and Beckbury was restored to what was apparently its original hundred of Alnodestreu (or to Brimstree).[32] Within the new and far larger hundred of Munslow, moreover, the priory's landowning position was much less dominant, the extent of its privileges less outstanding. New initiatives were needed to secure the liberty of a private hundred into which Beckbury and Badger, along with the rest of the priory estates, could be drawn—as, after 1198, almost all were.

The Liberty: Bourton hundred and other leets

In 1138 King Stephen freed the priory and its tenants from suit to shire and hundred: though the priory was to be represented there by its steward, its tenants need not attend unless specially summoned in a Crown plea or complaining of lack of justice in the prior's own court.[33] In fact the privilege seems not to have given

16 *V.C.H. Salop.* i. 312.

17 Ibid. 282, 312.

18 Not counting Ditton's 12 hides (not known to have been in Patton hund.) and Beckbury's 1 (seemingly in Patton hund. only temporarily): ibid. 282–3, 285 (giving Patton hund. as 114 hides), 317; next para. (for Beckbury).

19 *V.C.H. Salop.* i. 312–13. Eardington's 5 hides (almost certainly in Alnodestreu hund.: Eyton, i. 103) were lost 1068×1086: *V.C.H. Salop.* i. 318.

20 See R. Allen Brown, *Origins of Eng. Feudalism* (1973), 52 sqq., for an outstanding example, the 3 hunds. of Oswaldslow lib. (Worcs.).

21 Above, this section.

22 For 'Kenbecleag' see below, Beckbury, manor.

23 See e.g. *V.C.H. Salop.* viii. 1–2; xi. 93, 95.

24 Ibid. i. 286–7; iii. 33–42; viii. 179–80.

25 Above, Munslow Hundred (*part*).

26 In Culvestan there was only Clee Stanton: cf. *V.C.H. Salop.* i. 313; *Rot. Hund.* ii. 85.

27 *V.C.H. Salop.* iii. 43, may suggest too early a date for Alnodestreu hund.'s disappearance. Parts of what is now SE. Salop. may still have been in Staffs. and Warws. in 1130, so Brimstree and Stottesdon hunds. may have been formed 1130×1198: Eyton, i. 23–4; iii. 174–5; *T.S.A.S.* lvii. 157–60; *Rot. Hund.* ii. 84–5.

28 Cf. above, n. 61; *Rot. Hund.* ii. 84–5.

29 Above, this section.

30 Below, Badger, church; Beckbury, church.

31 That detachment is unlikely to have been ancient, and there is no evidence that it was. An 11th-cent. record of Heref. dioc.'s E. boundary (*T.S.A.S.* lvii. 158) does not go that far N.

32 In 1086 Alnodestreu hund. surrounded Beckbury save where it adjoined Staffs., and until 1198 the man. did suit to Brimstree hund.: *Salop. acc. to Dom. Bk.* (map, 1990) in *Salop. Domesday: Folios and Maps*, ed. R. W. H. Erskine (1988); *Rot. Hund.* ii. 85.

33 *T.S.A.S.* lxvi. 56–8.

rise to the priory's exercise of hundredal jurisdiction over its estates. That jurisdiction was exercised only from 1198, when Richard I freed all the priory's men, lands, and tithes and whatever was theirs from all exactions of royal foresters and sheriffs, from shire and hundred courts, and from other customs. The priory was also to hold a court: the usual formula of sac and soc, toll and team, and infangthief[34] indicated a court leet co-ordinate with the sheriff's tourn in the hundreds.[35] Later privileges granted to the lord and inhabitants of the liberty were economic in character: quittance of murage, toll, pontage, etc., throughout the realm in 1265 and free warren on their estates in 1291.[36] By 1292 outfangthief was apparently an unchallenged constituent of the prior's jurisdiction over the liberty, which was thus slightly more privileged than most Shropshire leets.[37]

The 1198 charter, confirmed by Henry III in 1227 and Edward I in 1290,[38] conferred hundredal jurisdiction[39] not merely over the priory's temporalities but also over its spiritualities, principally tithes,[40] which, since *c.* 1110, the priory could claim as *de jure* one rectorial estate notwithstanding the existence *de facto* of several parochial benefices. The 1255 inquiry into regalian rights in hundreds and shires[41] reveals the priory's liberty as comprising its demesne manors of Much Wenlock,[42] Bourton, Deuxhill, Ditton Priors, Eaton-under-Heywood,[43] Madeley, Great Oxenbold, Shipton, Stoke St. Milborough,[44] Little Wenlock, and Weston (with Hopton and Monk Hall) and the subinfeudated estates of Badger, Beckbury, Benthall, Broseley (including Arlescott and Bradeley), Caughley, Corve, Hatton, Hughley, Over and Nether Larden, Linley, Upper and Lower Millichope, Norncott, part of Patton, Pickthorn, Posenhall, Presthope, Skimblescott, Clee Stanton, Willey, and Wolverton. The demesne manor of Sutton and the subinfeudated manor of the Heath were also included in the jurors' verdict. Sutton, however, unlike all the other demesne manors, was never within the priory liberty.[45] No particulars of suits owed to the priory liberty or diverted from shire or hundred are given for Sutton, but that is true of all the demesne manors save Much Wenlock itself and the very recently acquired Great Oxenbold. Sutton's inclusion in the Wenlock verdict moreover suggests that the priory produced evidence about all its lordships, whether it exercised jurisdiction over them or not, and that the jurors consequently found a verdict encompassing all of them. Such a supposition is strengthened by the terms in which the Heath is mentioned in the Wenlock verdict of 1255. Diversions of suits from shire or hundred to the liberty are particularized for all the subinfeudated estates except the Heath, an exception indicating that the Heath was probably not in the liberty then, as it certainly was not later; that is to be expected of an estate which the baron of Castle Holdgate held of the priory in 1255 and which soon afterwards became a demesne manor of the FitzAlans.[46] In the mid 13th century, and in fact long after the close of the Middle Ages, Patton[47] and Brockton were only partly in the liberty:

34 *Cal. Chart. R.* 1257–1300, 357–8; Eyton, iii. 237–8; *Rot. Hund.* ii. 84–6.

35 *V.C.H. Salop.* iii. 33, 47; *Pipe R.* 1199 (P.R.S. N.S. x), 73.

36 *Cal. Chart. R.* 1257–1300, 358, 406; Eyton, iii. 243–4.

37 *V.C.H. Salop.* ii. 40; iii. 50.

38 *Rot. Litt. Claus.* (Rec. Com.), ii. 173; *Cal. Chart. R.* 1226–57, 17; 1257–1300, 357–8.

39 *V.C.H. Salop.* ii. 40.

40 *Cal. Chart. R.* 1257–1300, 357 ('omnes terras suas, et homines suos et decimas et omnes res suas').

41 For this para. see *Rot. Hund.* ii. 84–5 (and for Patton ibid. 70).

42 Incl. Atterley and Walton, Barrow, Callaughton, Wigwig, and Wyke and Bradley. Some members of demesne manors (as given ibid.) were partly or wholly subinfeudated. For details of the manors mentioned in this para. see the appropriate sections of par. hists. in this vol.; *V.C.H. Salop.* xi. 35, 80.

43 Incl. Harton, Longville, Lushcott, and Ticklerton.

44 Incl. Bockleton, Clee Downton, Kinson, and Newton.

45 Below, this section.

46 Below, this section, for the Castle Holdgate manors and FitzAlan demesnes.

47 When last recorded in the boro. (in the 18th cent.) it was still only partly so: below, this article (parl. boro.).

the prior had become mesne lord of the liberty part of Patton by *c.* 1170[48] and acquired the tithes of the liberty part of Brockton in the mid 13th century,[49] the century in which, by and large, liberties were formed and fixed.[50] The priory's acquisition of the whole terre tenancy of Patton in 1364 was too late to alter the liberty boundary so as to include the whole of Patton.

Some priory estates were excluded from its liberty as its limits were fixed in the 13th century when neighbouring lords' defences of liberties overlapping the priory's constrained the priory's freedom of action. The excluded estates[51] were Holy Trinity parish's chapelry of Acton Round (where the priory had asserted rectorial rights but had no temporal estate), Clun rectory, Church Preen manor, Preen rectory,[52] the Heath, and Sutton.[53] All but the last were connected with the FitzAlan and Castle Holdgate baronies.

Generations of FitzAlans safeguarded the integrity of their demesne manors, duly securing their exemption from hundred courts but showing no such concern for their subinfeudated estates.[54] Thus Willey, their subinfeudated manor whose tithes had all passed to Holy Trinity, was later included in Munslow hundred and, from 1198, the priory liberty there.[55] Similarly the priory had established a feudal tie with the FitzAlans' subinfeudated manor of Beckbury by 1120 and made it part of the priory liberty from 1198.[56] By contrast the FitzAlans' demesne manor of Acton Round, part of whose tithes had been denied to Holy Trinity,[57] was kept out of the priory liberty:[58] the FitzAlans withdrew it from Munslow hundred court before 1255[59] to create their own court leet.[60] Other examples show the FitzAlans' disregard of subinfeudated manors and tenacity of their demesnes. In the mid 13th century the priory acquired some of the tithes of the FitzAlans' subinfeudated manor of Brockton and, in accordance with the 1198 charter, that part of Brockton passed into the priory liberty.[61] By contrast the Heath, probably not in the priory liberty in 1255 (when the baron of Castle Holdgate held it under the priory), was certainly denied to the prior's jurisdiction after John FitzAlan became terre tenant.[62] At Acton Round it was probably the FitzAlans who intruded a chaplain in the early 1280s[63] in violation of the priory's right to present,[64] and for fifty years they did not recognize the appropriation of Clun church *c.* 1220 to the priory;[65] thus Clun tithes, when considered as outside the priory liberty, should be seen not merely as the most distant priory estate and a late acquired spirituality but also (like Acton Round's tithes, belonging of old to nearby Wenlock) as an accessory to FitzAlan demesnes.[66]

48 Above, Stanton Long, manors (Patton). *Roll of Salop. Eyre 1256* (Selden Soc. xcvi), pp. 240, 301, 316, 320, shows Patton in the lib. and its ld. as a Munslow hund. juror but is an unreliable guide to the lib.'s extent (cf. ibid. pp. 239–42, 304, 316–17).

49 Above, Stanton Long, church; below, this section.

50 *V.C.H. Salop.* iii. 46 sqq.

51 Besides very small ones: Eyton, *passim*.

52 Ch. Preen man. and Preen rectory endowed the cell known as Preen priory, but the cell, and ultimately its property, belonged to Wenlock priory: *T.S.A.S.* lxx. 193–6.

53 Fig. 16.

54 *V.C.H. Salop.* xi. 98–100. But in the marcher lordships at the heart of their Clun and Oswestry baronies franchisal and feudal jurisdictions were consolidated: ibid. iii. 33–6.

55 Above, this article (early est.).

56 Below, Beckbury, manor; *Rot. Hund.* ii. 85. The FitzAlan overlordship is recorded from the 13th cent.

57 Above, this article (early est.).

58 The parson of Acton Round's attendance at the prior's ct. at Bourton in 1227 (Dugdale, *Mon.* v. 74 notes (no. 5)) may indicate a priory attempt to exact suit.

59 *Rot. Hund.* ii. 71.

60 A ct. leet was still being summoned in 1826: S.R.O. 775/152–66.

61 Above, Stanton Long, church.

62 *Rot. Hund.* ii. 85; Eyton, iv. 16 sqq.; below, the Heath, manors.

63 The intruded chaplain Hugh of Pedwardine (*Reg. Swinfield* (C.S.), 62–3; cf. above, this article) was perh. a connexion of Sir Wal. of Pedwardine who was of service to the FitzAlans (*V.C.H. Salop.* xi. 97; Eyton, xi. 257).

64 *T.S.A.S.* 4th ser. i. 347–8

65 Possible technical defects in the priory's title were soon made good when the FitzAlans were willing: ibid. 342–7.

66 Where most firmly consolidated: above, n. 54.

Despite early 12th-century changes[67] and losses then and later,[68] Castle Holdgate barony comprised half a dozen manors in Corve Dale and the neighbouring dales, centring on Holdgate (the only demesne manor) and with outliers further afield. The canons of Holdgate castle church owned tithes in all parts of the barony,[69] their property reinforcing the honor's cohesion and helping to counteract difficulties of exacting suit to its court from scattered feudal tenants.[70] So from the mid 13th century successive owners of the barony—the Mauduits, the king of the Romans, and the Templars—were diverting to Holdgate the suits which their manors owed at hundred courts.[71] The two manors in Preen parish, whose tithes were appropriated to the monks, made no suits to Condover hundred from *c.* 1245. It is not stated who then withdrew their suits,[72] but Preen was not merely a priory cell but also a small *Eigenkloster* of the baron,[73] to whose Holdgate court Preen suits were rendered,[74] and Preen was never in the priory liberty. Jurisdiction over the Heath, a manor which the baron held of the priory, may have been in contention in 1255 and the priory never acquired the jurisdiction.[75] Where the baron had lordship he tried to keep jurisdiction, and so he, like the FitzAlans, set limits to the expansion of the priory's liberty. Nevertheless after the priory acquired Great Oxenbold from the baron's feudal tenant in 1244 and drew the manor into its liberty the baron surrendered both overlordship and jurisdiction in 1256.[76]

Sutton, the priory estate neither in its liberty nor connected with the FitzAlan and Castle Holdgate estates, fell under the borough of Shrewsbury's jurisdiction,[77] as well defended as any liberty in the county,[78] baronial or monastic.

Thus were the liberty's territorial limits fixed, somewhat short of the whole priory estate, during the 13th century. In 1274 there were many complaints of exactions and illegalities perpetrated in the liberty by sheriffs and undersheriffs, escheators and subescheators, and bailiffs, under-bailiffs, and beadles of Munslow hundred;[79] the administrative privilege of return of writs would have excluded such officers,[80] but they were not definitively excluded until the incorporation of the priory's borough in 1468.[81] Nevertheless within the liberty the priory's courts were free to develop hundredal or leet jurisdiction; and, since the principal court was held at Bourton, that was known by the 1220s as Bourton hundred,[82] though occasionally as Wenlock hundred.[83]

All Bourton hundred's 'ancient court rolls' were lost when its lord, the younger Sir John Weld, was taken prisoner at the fall of Shrewsbury to Parliamentarian forces in 1645.[84] Nevertheless it is clear in general how the courts operated. By 1231 Bourton hundred small court met fortnightly.[85] Its twice yearly great court had the marks of a court leet in the 13th century, gallows and jurisdiction over the assize of bread and of ale,[86] and it doubtless met at the usual times—after Easter

67 The baron's losses of Broseley, Harley, and Millichope (below, p.266 n.11) and of feudal status in Gt. Sutton (Eyton, v. 64 sqq.) were perh. compensated by grants to Helgot's sons in Dowles, Quatt, and Stanton Long (ibid. iii. 174–5, 177, 185–7; iv. 160; above, Stanton Long, manors) and the acquisition of a mesne lordship at the Heath (Eyton, iv. 13 sqq., dating it early but giving no evidence before the early 13th cent.).

68 Adley, Bucknell, Burwarton, Norton-in-Hales: Eyton, iii. 31–2; ix. 366–7; xi. 312–13, 318. For Gt. Oxenbold see below, this para.

69 Above, Holdgate, church.

70 *V.C.H. Salop.* iii. 34.

71 *Rot. Hund.* ii. 62, 70–1, 82, 105, 108; cf. Eyton, iv. 67.

72 *Rot. Hund.* ii. 62, misleadingly paraphrased in Eyton, vi. 221.

73 Above, this article (early est.) and source there cited.

74 Eyton, vi. 222; *Rot. Hund.* ii. 91.

75 Above, this section.

76 Eyton, iv. 22–4; below, Monkhopton, manors.

77 *V.C.H. Salop.* i. 313; ii. 211; iii. 8, 40.

78 *V.C.H. Salop.* iii. 46–7.

79 *Rot. Hund.* ii. 110–12

80 Ibid. 110; *V.C.H. Salop.* iii. 46–7.

81 Below, this article (boro. 1468–1836).

82 Dugdale, *Mon.* v. 74 notes (no. 5); *V.C.H. Salop.* iii. 49–50, 52.

83 *Abbrev. Plac.* (Rec. Com.), 254.

84 S.R.O. 1224, box 158, Remembrances concerning the Hund. of Bourton 27 Oct. 1651; H. Owen and J. B. Blakeway, *Hist. Shrews.* (1825), i. 453, 455.

85 *Curia Regis R.* xiv. 245.

86 *Rot. Hund.* ii. 110; *Plac. de Quo Warr.* (Rec. Com.), 684; cf. *V.C.H. Salop.* iii. 47.

and after Michaelmas, as recorded in 1369. Its pleas and perquisites were then worth 20*s.*,[87] £4 in 1390.[88] The small court met every three weeks by the 1360s; its pleas and perquisites were worth 6*s.* 8*d.* a year. The lords of Broseley, Linley, and Willey and two tenants in Much Wenlock[89] then owed three-weekly suit to the small court. Other socage tenants owed suit to the hundred and rendered money dues there that were said to amount to £8 in 1369 and to £6 13*s.* 4*d.* in 1379.[90]

Particular suits owed by individual tenants apart, it seems likely that Bourton hundred's jurisdiction extended over the whole liberty except the priory's town and township of Much Wenlock, a demesne manor which, probably by 1272, had its own court leet.[91] The Much Wenlock burgesses[92] were thus privileged within the liberty, and in Much Wenlock, between the spring and autumn great courts, there were frequent and regular small courts, often every three weeks. That was also the early 14th-century pattern in Madeley new town, in another of the priory's demesne manors; a separate court for the manor's unfree tenants was absorbed by the new town little court, possibly in 1380 but certainly by 1411, and eventually only the great court survived, though that seems not to have excluded the jurisdiction of Bourton hundred's leet twice a year. In the priory's other demesne manors within the liberty[93] great courts were rendered superfluous by that of Bourton hundred, and small courts were held much less frequently than in Much Wenlock: evidently three or four times a year in Eaton-under-Heywood in the 13th and 14th centuries and once or twice a year in the earlier 15th century. Similar patterns appear in the other demesne manors. After the priory acquired a third of Broseley manor in 1363 it held a separate small court there, probably once or twice a year as in 1406–8;[94] later Broseley's 'Priory land' was evidently absorbed into Marsh manor.[95] The priory acquired Patton manor in 1364 and held the court baron as late as 1421, though how often is unknown; by 1522 it was absorbed into Oxenbold manor.[96] Such changes suggest some late medieval reorganization of the demesne manors' small courts, of which there are other hints: from some time between 1450 and 1477 the Marsh court may have been organized separately from the others,[97] perhaps with a view to the delegation of some leet business to it, and Oxenbold court was dealing with breaches of the assize of bread and of ale in the late Middle Ages.[98] Callaughton, perhaps previously subject to Much Wenlock court, acquired its own court baron before 1540.[99] The priory's holding of a court in the subinfeudated manor of Wolverton in 1334 may have had some special cause, perhaps a minority.[1]

The development of Bourton hundred and some other separate, or embryo, leets within Wenlock priory's liberty, withdrawn from Munslow hundred's jurisdiction, did not alter the hundred-based divisions of the county for government purposes. Places in the liberty of Wenlock were taxed in Munslow hundred in 1327 and 1497[2] and mustered with Munslow hundred in 1542.[3] Nevertheless the creation (in 1468)

87 B.L. Add. MS. 6165, p. 100.

88 S.R.O. 1224, box 342, Prior Gosnell's reg. f. 35v.

89 John Bastard and Nic. Carewell.

90 B.L. Add. MS. 6164, p. 385; 6165, p. 100.

91 For this para. see the surviving ct. r. of 'the whole land of St. Milburga': S.R.O. 566/1 (1333–4); 1224/2/1–5 (1344–5, 1379–80); 1190/1, unlisted ct. r. 1403–4; 1224/2/6–9 (1411–12, 1420–1, 1431–2, 1449–50); below, M. Wenlock, local govt.; *V.C.H. Salop.* xi. 56.

92 i.e. tenants of burgages. Cf. below, n. 59.

93 Bourton, Ditton Priors, Eaton-under-Heywood, Stoke St. Milborough, and Lt. Wenlock. Ch. Preen and Sutton were in other liberties: above, this section. Marsh and Oxenbold cts. may have had leet business devolved to them: below, this section.

94 Below, Broseley, local govt.

95 S.R.O. 1224/3/81, listing, apparently correctly, members of Marsh in the last prior's time but, with palpable untruth, asserting that none was 'any manor of itself'.

96 Above, Stanton Long, local govt.

97 Cf. S.R.O. 1224/2/9, 16 sqq.

98 Below, Monkhopton, local govt.

99 Below, M. Wenlock, local govt.

1 S.R.O. 566/1; below, Eaton-under-Heywood, manors (Wolverton).

2 *T.S.A.S.* 2nd ser. iv. 287–338; S.R.O. 3365/165.

3 *T.S.A.S.* 3rd ser. viii. 251–2, misdated (cf. *L. & P. Hen. VIII*, xvii, p. 508).

of a quarter sessions borough effectively conterminous with the liberty began to change the administrative map of Shropshire,[4] and in 1524 tax was collected in the liberty separately from Munslow hundred.[5] From the 16th century Wenlock borough, or 'Franchise' as it was generally known,[6] was a normal division of the county.[7]

The prior of Wenlock was lord of Bourton hundred (let in 1528 and 1540) until the surrender to the Crown in 1540.[8] On 12 December 1573 Henry Welby, of Goxhill (Lincs.), and George Blythe of London bought the hundred from the Crown to hold of the manor of East Greenwich in socage for 20*s*. a year.[9] Next day they sold it to David Deley, a London goldsmith.[10] In 1595, shortly before his death, Deley mortgaged it to another Londoner Thomas Myddleton, who acquired it next year from Deley's son and heir Jerome, a London schoolmaster.[11] Myddleton sold it in 1601 to William Baldwyn (d. 1614) of Elsich, who was evidently tenant of the hundred[12] and to whom, in 1595, the Crown had leased Munslow hundred for 21 years.[13] Baldwyn's son Charles owned Bourton hundred when he came of age in 1619[14] and as a minor had presumably inherited the lease of Munslow hundred too; indeed the lease may have been renewed or extended for he bought Munslow hundred *c*. 1630.[15] In 1639 Baldwyn sold Bourton hundred to the younger John Weld (kt. 1642), of Willey,[16] and after Weld succeeded his father in 1666[17] Bourton hundred and Marsh leet both descended with Willey in the Weld and (from 1748) Forester families. George Forester (d. 1811) devised it with the rest of his estates to his cousin Cecil (cr. Lord Forester 1821),[18] but by 1811 the hundred jurisdiction had presumably ceased to exist for practical purposes, though the Marsh court leet maintained a formal existence as late as the 1870s.[19]

The area over which Bourton hundred's jurisdiction was exercised had probably begun to shrink by the time the priory's borough received its first charter in 1468.[20] It did not include Much Wenlock itself,[21] and in the late Middle Ages some of the leet functions appropriate to Bourton hundred (such as the assize of bread and of ale) seem to have been devolved by the priory to the Marsh and Oxenbold manor courts, each of whose jurisdictions came to include several townships.[22] Between its acquisition of the priory in 1540 and its sale of Bourton hundred in 1573 the Crown sold former priory manors to men whose grants included general words which, by entitling them to a court leet, actually or potentially[23] reduced Bourton hundred and the Marsh and Oxenbold leets. Richard Lawley acquired the right to a court leet with the manor of Bourton itself in 1543,[24] and Bourton manor was lost to Bourton hundred.[25] The purchasers of Ditton Priors and Eaton-under-Heywood manors each

4 Below, this article (boro. 1468–1836); *V.C.H. Salop*. iii. 40 (corr. below, Corrigenda), 43–4.

5 P.R.O., E 179/166/200.

6 See e.g. R. Baugh, *Map of Salop*. (1808); C. and J. Greenwood, *Map of Salop*. (1827).

7 See e.g. *V.C.H. Salop*. ii. 211 (corr. below, Corrigenda). Some inaccuracies or omissions in the *Census* (e.g. the fact that pt. of Munslow par. was in Wenlock boro. in 1831) are not corrected there.

8 P.R.O., LR 2/184, f. 95; SC 6/Hen. VIII/3021, m. 6; N.L.W., Chirk Castle, Group F nos. 13347–8; *V.C.H. Salop*. ii. 45; iii. 49–50, 52; above, this section.

9 *Cal. Pat*. 1572–5, pp. 220–1.

10 N.L.W., Chirk Castle, Group F nos. 788, 1996.

11 Ibid. nos. 766, 791. For Myddleton see *D.N.B.*

12 N.L.W., Chirk Castle, Group F nos. 792, 11424; Staffs. R.O., D.(W.) 1788, P. 43, B. 8, deed 4 July 1601; *T.S.A.S*. 4th ser. ii. 149; P.R.O., C 142/346, no. 184.

13 S.P.L., MS. 2790, p. 77.

14 Staffs. R.O., D.(W.) 1788, vol. 13 (Baldwyn's acct. bk. *c*. 1617–25). Cf. *T.S.A.S*. 4th ser. ii. 149 (some errors of date); *S.P.R. Heref*. xiii. 117; S.P.L., MS. 2790, pp. 77, 94.

15 *V.C.H. Salop*. iii. 45 n. 65.

16 Staffs. R.O., D.(W.) 1788, P. 33, B. 10, deed 29 Oct. 1639.

17 Below, Willey, manor.

18 S.R.O. 1224/2/510–11; box 272, Geo. Forester's will 3 Nov. 1805, pr. 18 Feb. 1812; below, Willey, manor.

19 J. Randall, *Broseley and Its Surroundings* (Madeley, 1879), 33–4.

20 Below, this article (boro. 1468–1836).

21 Above, this section.

22 Above, Stanton Long, local govt.; below, Barrow, local govt.; Shipton, local govt.; Monkhopton, local govt.

23 Below, this para. for Eaton-under-Heywood and Lt. Wenlock.

24 P.R.O., C 66/725, m. 26.

25 But there is no evidence of a Bourton leet: below, M. Wenlock, local govt.

acquired the right to a court leet in 1544, and one was being held in Ditton in 1570, though there is no evidence that one was ever held in Eaton.[26] The new lords of manors that had formed part of the large priory manor of Shipton (earlier called Oxenbold) acquired courts leet: the lord of Oxenbold was granted one in 1544 as were the purchasers of Hopton and Monk Hall next year,[27] and by 1553 the lord of Shipton had leet jurisdiction in Shipton, Larden, and Skimblescott, though only claims to suit from Corve and Patton (in Oxenbold leet).[28] The purchaser of Patton and Weston bought the right to a court leet in 1545.[29] Also in 1545 the Crown sold Little Wenlock with the right to hold a court leet,[30] though it was probably almost ninety years before the right was exercised there.[31] Under the priory Much Wenlock manor had been administered separately from Bourton hundred, and it remained Crown property longer than the hundred; when it was finally sold in 1600 its court leet was conveyed with it.[32]

Fifty years after the Crown's sale of Bourton hundred in 1573 the process of reducing its territory received new impetus. In the mid 16th century a leet jurisdiction had been claimed for the Marsh manor over all the places that had belonged to that manor in the Middle Ages, but there had been much uncertainty about which those places were. In fact they were Barrow, Atterley, and Walton, Benthall, Posenhall, part of Harley, Wigwig, and Wyke and Bradley, but the only places to make presentments at the Marsh court in 1622–3 were Posenhall and Wyke and Bradley, with parts of Barrow (i.e. Shirlett) and Willey (the Smithies). The Marsh, however, had just been bought by the pertinacious John Weld[33] who wished 'to be free of Wenlock' (by which he evidently meant Bourton hundred) and who intended to reinvigorate his manorial courts of the Marsh and Willey, especially with regard to their jurisdiction over commons and the rights to drive them and make inclosures.[34] In 1634 he restored the extent of the Marsh's jurisdiction almost completely by buying out Bourton hundred's rights over Barrow, Atterley, and Walton, part of Harley, Willey, and Wyke and Bradley and annexing them to his court leet of the Marsh,[35] which also had jurisdiction over Broseley's 'Priory land'.[36] In 1637 he completed the restoration by securing Bourton hundred's jurisdiction over Benthall for the Marsh leet; simultaneously he divided the commons with the lord of Benthall.[37] Later, when the Welds also owned Bourton hundred (which had jurisdiction over Broseley's 'socage land'), they demarcated the Broseley commons (1648) and thwarted the lord of Broseley's attempt to usurp a court leet and take felons' goods and waifs and strays (1677).[38] In 1634 the lord of Bourton hundred sold his rights over Little Wenlock to its lord, who was either ignorant of the terms of the grant to his predecessor in 1545 or believed that purchase that was the uncontentious way to acquire a court leet of his own.[39]

Conflicts of jurisdiction between Bourton hundred and the priory's other leets on the one hand and the new borough on the other were presumably easily avoided as long as the borough and other jurisdictions[40] were all the priory's. After 1540

26 P.R.O., C 66/743, mm. 41–2; C 66/747, m. 4; below, Ditton Priors, local govt.; Eaton-under-Heywood, local govt.

27 Below, Monkhopton, local govt. Cf. P.R.O., C 66/739, m. 26; C 66/770, m. 26.

28 Below, Shipton, local govt.

29 P.R.O., C 66/750, m. 42.

30 P.R.O., C 66/771, m. 10.

31 Next para.

32 Above, this section; P.R.O., C 66/1531, m. 4.

33 S.R.O. 1224/3/81; below, Barrow, manors and local govt.

34 S.R.O. 1224, box 163, Mr. Weld's memo. bk. 1619/20, ff. 2–4.

35 Below, Barrow, local govt. Caughley was probably included with Barrow.

36 And, by 1680, socage lands owned by the Welds since the 1620s: below, Broseley, local govt.

37 S.P.L., Deeds 18120; below, Benthall local govt.

38 S.R.O. 1224/2/510, 22 Apr. 1674, 10 July 1677.

39 Staffs. R.O., D.(W.) 1788, P. 33, B. 10, deed 29 Oct. 1639 (citing deed of 14 Nov. 1634); *V.C.H. Salop.* xi. 87–8.

40 Esp. the Marsh, Oxenbold, and M. Wenlock manor cts.

there was greater potential for conflict, for a borough incorporated by royal charter normally exercised leet jurisdiction through its own great court, whereas in the borough of Wenlock that jurisdiction belonged to private lords. The borough may have been strengthened, relatively to the lords, by the morcellation of Bourton hundred and Shipton (formerly Oxenbold) leet as new courts leet were created and by the passing of the Marsh (its jurisdiction temporarily enfeebled) and Much Wenlock leets to different lords.[41]

In the earlier 17th century, however, the acquisition of Bourton hundred and the reinvigoration of Marsh leet gave the Welds an impressive extent of 'leet' territory stretching south-west from Madeley to Presthope and west from Linley to Hughley, interrupted only by Much Wenlock township under Much Wenlock manorial leet. Farther afield (yet within the borough) Bourton hundred gave them jurisdiction over Badger, Beckbury, Brockton, Clee Downton, Clee Stanton, and the Moor, Deuxhill, Hughley, Hungerford and Millichope, and Stoke St. Milborough. Such jurisdictions, administered together though in distinct courts,[42] made the Welds natural leaders of any resistance to borough encroachments on manorial leets.[43] In 1651, evidently hoping for the support of 'Mr. Jenkes, my Lord Newport, Mr. Forester, Mr. Penruddock, Sir Francis Lawley, & others that have bought part of the manors within the Hundred[44] from the Crown with waifs & strays & felons' goods, etc.', it seems that Sir John Weld was sufficiently agitated to contemplate *quo warranto* proceedings against the borough. He considered representing himself as merely the fee-farmer of the hundred so that the corporation, evidently considering litigation, would have to sue the state. The main causes of concern seem to have been the rights to felons' goods, deodands, and other 'royalties' including rights to waifs and strays that were valued the more because of their connexion with the management of commons. The Welds were considering whether the lords might forbid their tenants to present matters to the borough sessions of the peace that belonged rather to Bourton hundred and the other leets. How matters were settled is unknown, but the rights then at issue seem to have been those that the lord of Bourton hundred continued to exercise almost as long as his court retained any vigour at all.

Bourton hundred court had met at Bourton in the Middle Ages and as late as 1536. After the earlier 16th century, however, it presumably ceased to do so. By the later 17th and early 18th centuries the court's spring meeting was at Broseley, the autumn one usually at Brockton, though occasionally at Linleygreen in the later 1670s and early 1680s; Broseley and Brockton were clearly chosen to accommodate suitors from as far apart as Beckbury and Madeley in the north and Clee Stanton in the south. Bourton hundred court usually met the day after the Marsh court leet (invariably held at Hangstree Gate at that period). By 1723, perhaps from 1711, Bourton hundred court always met in Broseley, and in some years there was only one meeting.[45]

In the early 18th century a carefully guarded part of Bourton hundred's jurisdiction was the right to round up strays. Sheep were taken at Clee Downton in 1701, and in 1704 George Weld appointed a Beckbury man 'to take all strays

41 Cf. two preceding paras.; below, Barrow, manors (the Marsh); M. Wenlock, manors.

42 S.R.O. 1224/2/47–344, 346–508, 515–27.

43 Rest of para. based on ibid. box 158, Remembrances concerning Hund. of Bourton 27 Oct. 1651. Herb. Jenkes was lord of Eaton-under-Heywood, Ld. Newport lord of Oxenbold, Fra. Forester lord of Lt. Wenlock, Geo. Penruddock lord of M. Wenlock, and Sir Fra. Lawley lord of Bourton, Callaughton, and Hopton and Monk Hall: below, manors sections of par. hists.; *V.C.H. Salop.* xi. 80; cf. above, this section, for their predecessors' acquisitions of leets.

44 Sc. Liberty or Franchise.

45 Para. based on sources in n. 42, above; cf. S.R.O. 1224/2/46; below, Barrow, local govt.

in Beckbury or Badger or elsewhere within his manor [*sic*]' and John Mason, a Shirlett man, to deputize for the hundred bailiff in the same work elsewhere in Bourton hundred.[46] In Madeley, despite the emergence of a great court, the lord of Bourton hundred retained the right to take strays.[47] The interlocking townships of Bourton and Munslow hundreds[48] made vigilance necessary: a week after his appointment Mason reported that the bailiff of Munslow hundred 'doth employ idle persons to convey strays away' and all had gone from Millichope common.[49]

Useful as it had been to its 17th-century lords in the management of commons and the accompanying 'royalties',[50] by the 18th century Bourton hundred court was becoming a relic,[51] commanding little respect. In 1725 William Roper was fined 2*s.* 6*d.* for refusing to join in a presentment, defying the steward and abusing his fellow jurors, and saying 'he did not value the court of a farthing'.[52] Other men were involved in similar incidents 1726–8.[53] The latest surviving court records (estreat rolls) end in 1769, but for twenty-five years before that only Hungerford and Millichope (until 1754), Linley (until 1763), and townships in Stoke St. Milborough parish (still in 1769) had figured in them with any regularity.[54]

The borough 1468–1836

In 1468, a few weeks after the first successful royal appointment of a prior of Wenlock[55] and at the instance of Lord Wenlock, chief butler of England,[56] Edward IV, recalling the 'laudable and acceptable services' of his 'liege men and residents of the town of Wenlock' in his gaining of the crown,[57] granted them a charter conferring on the town the status of a 'free borough incorporate forever'.[58] A bailiff, burgesses, and commonalty were to have a liberty extending over 'the parish of Holy Trinity'. Among the franchises granted to the new burgesses[59] were some that had already been long enjoyed by the prior and the inhabitants of his hundredal liberty: such were Much Wenlock's Monday market and June fair, the exemption from various dues throughout the realm, and freedom from serving with jurors from outside the liberty. The exclusion of the sheriff and other Crown ministers from the borough was new, but pre-eminent among new privileges were the rights to elect a member of Parliament[60] and to have its own gaol and sessions of the peace. The bailiff and recorder were to be the king's justices of gaol delivery and of the peace to the exclusion of others, and a borough coroner was to exclude the county coroners and the sheriff. The corporation was granted all fines, amercements, and forfeitures of residents, whether levied in the borough or in the Westminster courts, and, within the borough and liberty, burgesses' deodands, the chattels of outlaws and felons, and (for a year and a day) their forfeited lands or tenements. The corporation was also to have cognizance of all pleas of land and debt to be held before the bailiff. The bailiff's Tuesday court was to determine all

46 S.R.O. 1224/2/511, [ff. 22v., 24v.].
47 *V.C.H. Salop.* xi. 56.
48 Figs. 3, 16.
49 S.R.O. 1224/2/511, f. [25].
50 Whether or not such matters belonged strictly to leet jurisdiction: *Leet Jurisdiction in Eng.* (Southampton Rec. Soc. 1908), 207, noting abundance of presentments about the common lands in the Southampton leet.
51 Cf. ibid. 354–5.
52 S.R.O. 1224/2/397.
53 Ibid. /2/400, 402, 404.
54 Ibid. /2/414–32.
55 The late Mr. V. H. Deacon suggested the significance of the timing. Earlier Crown attempts to appoint the prior had involved the same men as at Monkton Farleigh: cf. *V.C.H. Salop.* ii. 44, 46–7; *V.C.H. Wilts.* iii. 265, 268.
56 *D.N.B.*; *Wenlock, 1468–1968*, ed. L. C. Lloyd (M. Wenlock, 1968), 9–12.
57 As in his 1461 charter to Ludlow: *V.C.H. Salop.* iii. 244.
58 W.B.R., B1/1; transcript and transl. in S.R.O. 81/490–1; *Translation of the Charters of the Corpn. of Wenlock* (Shrews. 1820), 1–19 (copy in S.P.L., accession 5213); cf. *Cal. Chart. R.* 1427–1516, 229–32.
59 Eyton (iii. 253 sqq.), encountering M. Wenlock examples of burgage tenure (cf. below, p. 405), wrongly supposed the earlier existence of a corporate boro.
60 Below, this article (parl. boro. 1468–1885).

pleas of trespass within the liberty and to have jurisdiction over contracts even if they exceeded 40*s*.

The borough initially had two odd characteristics, fairly soon reduced to one. The corporation officers, though acting for the Crown, were not accountable to it because the town was not 'immediately' under the Crown but held by the prior of Wenlock, whose seignorial rights were recognized. The prior was 'chief burgess' and played a part, early defined, in the annual election of the borough bailiff: on 2 October the prior nominated the first of two men (the second being the retiring bailiff's nominee) who joined themselves to the six men to co-opt five burgesses and so form thirteen to elect the new bailiff. In 1540 the prior's seignorial interest in the borough passed to the Crown and his role in forming the jury to elect the bailiff was filled by the lord of Much Wenlock manor until 1704.[61]

The charter's other oddity arose from the vagueness with which it defined the borough liberty as 'the parish of Holy Trinity'. That the intention was to make Much Wenlock town a borough seems clear both from the charter's references to the town and from its tacit transfer to the new borough of the priory's markets and fairs in Much Wenlock, while the priory's markets and fairs in its other demesne manors were never borough property. The charter's manipulation of the market and fair rights did not perhaps matter as long as the borough and the manor of Much Wenlock both belonged to the same lord. That ceased to be the case in 1600, and in the earlier 1670s the lady of Much Wenlock manor attempted a *quo warranto* challenge to the borough's market and fair rights in Much Wenlock, though unsuccessfully.[62] Nevertheless the phrase defining the liberty as 'the parish of Holy Trinity', had it been construed in accordance with the ecclesiastical realities of 1468, ought to have indicated the parish defined in 1332, and that was a much greater area than the town or even the manor. In fact, however, the borough was to occupy an area greater still. The *Dictum* of *c.* 1110 had stated that all the priory's lands were one parish, and the significance of that sentence had been enhanced by the 1198 charter, which had given the priory hundredal jurisdiction over all its tithes as well as its lands: thus the priory's liberty, as settled in the 13th century, had in a significant sense become identifiable with Holy Trinity parish. For two generations after 1468 the new borough, like Bourton hundred and other leets in the liberty, was the priory's, and, with more justification from historical precedent than from logic or the tenor of the 1468 charter, the priory evidently took the borough to include the whole priory liberty—all those estates over which it exercised hundredal or leet jurisdiction. The chancellor's power to amend legal defects in the charter was apparently not used, and the borough's uniquely extensive territory was not further defined until the municipality was reduced by statute in 1835–6.[63]

The borough obtained a new charter in 1631.[64] It too was ambivalent about the extent of the borough liberty. It was not to prejudice the Much Wenlock manorial leet ('Sir Roger Bertie's liberties') but expressed no protection for other courts leet functioning elsewhere in the borough, in particular Bourton hundred's and the Marsh leet.[65] The implication was that the borough liberty extended no farther than the parish of Holy Trinity, which was then smaller than it had been in 1468, although still larger

[61] W.B.R., B3/1/1, p. 84; B3/1/2, p. 153.

[62] Ibid. /1/2, pp. 36, 49; above, this section.

[63] Below, this article (boro. 1836–89). Political challenges to the boundary were occasionally considered: below, this article (parl. boro. 1468–1885).

[64] For this and the next para see W.B.R., B1/2; transcript in S.P.L., Deeds 12685, transl. in *Transl. of Charters of Wenlock*, 21–46. Cf. P.R.O., C 66/2565, no. 5; *Cal. S.P. Dom.* 1631–3, 153.

[65] Above, this article (Lib.: Bourton hund.).

than the area under the jurisdiction of Much Wenlock court leet.[66] Nevertheless the charter's final clause, that it was to be interpreted for the borough's 'greatest good and benefit', perhaps justified the borough's continuing jurisdiction over the whole of the former priory liberty. Another clause confirmed all ancient jurisdictions lawfully used.

In other ways the 1631 charter confirmed that of 1468, amplifying the corporation's powers of government and peace-keeping by giving them fuller legal definition. Power to make ordinances was vested in the bailiff, a majority of his peers, and the burgesses and commonalty. The bailiff's peers were all those who had previously served his office, and it was from them that a deputy bailiff was to be appointed during the bailiff's incapacity or absence. In legislative practice, however, the need for a majority among the bailiff's peers came to be ignored. There were other changes too. In 1704 the lord of the manor's right to nominate a juror for the election of the bailiff, as of the other annual officers (coroner and treasurer) chosen with him, were transferred by borough ordinance to the bailiff and his peers. The fourth annual officer, the serjeant at mace who was also gaoler, high constable, and server of process out of the court of record, was appointed by the bailiff.[67] The 1631 charter appointed new borough magistrates: the recorder Sir John Bridgeman,[68] Richard Jones, esquire, bailiff 1630–1,[69] and the bailiff for the time being and his immediate predecessor; Jones was to be succeeded as magistrate by one chosen annually from the bailiff's peers at the first common hall after Michaelmas. Sessions were to be kept for all matters 'except such as concern title', and the town clerk was to be clerk of the peace.

In the mid 17th century disputes about commons and the associated 'royalties' strained relations between the corporation and the lords of leet jurisdictions (formerly the priory's) within the borough,[70] as did uncertainties about market and fair rights in Much Wenlock town. There were other potential conflicts too. In normal boroughs a range of administrative responsibilities and jurisdiction over nuisances and trespasses was divided between the borough great (i.e. leet) court and its sessions of the peace,[71] but in Wenlock leet jurisdiction was in private hands. Court leet and Wenlock borough records hint that in the 17th and 18th centuries the different interests achieved some sort of *modus vivendi*, though they do not reveal its continuous operation. A petty constable absent from the court of Bourton hundred or the Marsh leet at which he was appointed had to swear his oath of office before a borough magistrate within an appointed time.[72] Borough magistrates were exercising control over alehouse keepers by the mid 17th century[73] while later in the century (but perhaps rarely after the 1680s) Bourton hundred and the Marsh leet (for example) were evidently fining alesellers and victuallers for breaking the assize of bread and of ale.[74] In 1719 all unlicensed alesellers were ordered to be brought before the next borough sessions,[75] and by then the borough magistrates' oversight of parish government was probably a matter of course, highway surveyors and churchwardens and overseers routinely attending their special sessions.[76]

66 M. Wenlock leet was wholly within H. Trin. par., other pts. of which were subject to Bourton hund. (in the S.) and the Marsh leet (in the N.): above, this article (Lib.: Bourton hund.).

67 *1st Rep. Com. Mun. Corp.* H.C. 116, App. III, pp. 2076–7 (1835), xxv; cf. above, this section; below, this article (parl. boro. 1836–85); *V.C.H. Salop.* iii. 293.

68 Vice-pres. of Council in Marches of Wales: cf. *T.S.A.S.* 3rd ser. ii. 327; *V.C.H. Salop.* iii. 248.

69 W.B.R., B3/1/1, pp. 638–9.

70 Above, this article (Lib.: Bourton hund.).

71 As e.g. in Southampton: *Leet Jurisdiction in Eng.* 198, 222–30.

72 S.R.O. 1224/2/510, 7 Apr. 1669.

73 W.B.R., Q1/11/1 (datable by Elias Birch, fl. 1630s: *Alum. Oxon. 1500–1714*, i. 125).

74 See e.g. S.R.O. 1224/2/510, 7 Apr. 1669; /2/511.

75 W.B.R., Q1/11/12.

76 W.B.R., Q/1/12/1–85; /13/1–195. Cf. *T.S.A.S.* lvi. 314–27.

The corporation governed the borough in accordance with its charters until 1836. Its income came from rates[77] and the profits of its markets and fairs.[78] A gift (*c.* 1675) of £200 from Sir Thomas Littleton, M.P. for the borough 1640–6 and 1661–79, was used in 1720 to buy a charter for two more fairs.[79] The corporation's only property[80] was the guildhall, built on the edge of Holy Trinity churchyard *c.* 1540; by 1577 a borough gaol adjoined it.[81] In other ways, perhaps because of its widely scattered territory, the borough relied periodically on county facilities. From *c.* 1630 a county house of correction at Bridgnorth was used, but in 1707 the mastership of a house in Much Wenlock was added to the serjeant at mace's duties;[82] a local house may still have been used in 1771.[83] Prisoners for debt were the serjeant's responsibility by the 17th century, and in 1648 seven were accommodated in two upper rooms over the guildhall.[84]

Capital sentences were passed at quarter sessions, and in 1542 the execution ground was 'on the Edge Top'.[85] One of the serjeant's duties in 1687 was 'so often as occasion shall require [to] procure, find, and maintain a topman or executioner to execute all felons condemned to die'.[86] In the earlier 18th century executions were carried out in the town, but by the 1830s it was long since capital felonies had been tried there.[87]

By the later 1750s, when repairs to the borough gaol were very frequent and gaol breaks not unknown, prisoners charged with the more serious crimes were sent to the county gaol in Shrewsbury.[88] In 1786 a prisoner was being held in Wenlock gaol against the next quarter sessions,[89] but probably soon thereafter[90] committals were invariably to Shrewsbury, as in the 1830s. Regular petty sessions were then fortnightly but also as occasioned by the need to avoid confining lesser offenders. In 1835 the magistrates were castigated for negligence, perhaps largely owing to the recent signing of a blank committal warrant procured by a constable who wanted his travel expenses paid for a day at Shrewsbury races.[91]

In the later 17th and the 18th centuries, when parish highway surveyors and overseers of the poor were summoned to the magistrates' special sessions, they had to appear at 'the serjeant's house' or 'town hall';[92] those were doubtless other names for the guildhall, which was probably also the venue for quarter sessions.[93] By 1803, however, it was said that 'the regular courts' (evidently petty sessions, including the special alehouse licensing sessions)[94] were kept at the Raven inn belonging to George Forester,[95] and that was where the bailiff's feast (and from 1836 the mayor's) was often held.[96] The creation of the Broseley court of requests in 1782,[97] with simpler and cheaper procedure, greatly reduced the borough court of record's business, which had apparently also suffered because successive bailiffs had allowed it to become the preserve of a few local attorneys, 'agents of influential

77 Levied on allotments as used throughout the county: see e.g. W.B.R., B3/1/1, pp. 625–7; Mumford, *Wenlock in Middle Ages*, 138, 181; P.R.O., E 179/168/219; B.U.L., Mytton papers, vii. 1523; *V.C.H. Salop*. iii. 85–6.

78 *1st Rep. Com. Mun. Corp*. App. III, 2078.

79 W.B.R., B3/1/2, pp. 51–2; *V.C.H. Salop*. iii. 250, 291–2; below, M. Wenlock, econ. hist. (mkts. and fairs).

80 *1st Rep. Com. Mun. Corp*. App. III, 2073–80.

81 Below, M. Wenlock, growth of settlement.

82 *V.C.H. Salop*. iii. 105, 127; W.B.R., B3/1/2, 29 Sept. 1707; *Orders of Q. Sess*. i. 235.

83 S.P.L., Deeds 19294, 12 and 20 Nov. 1764, 1 July 1771.

84 Ibid. Deeds 1566; P.R.O., C 104/23, pt. 1, sched. of items surrendered by outgoing to incoming bailiff 31 Oct. 1648; *T.S.A.S*. xi. 39.

85 *T.S.A.S*. vi. 100.

86 S.P.L., Deeds 1566.

87 *1st Rep. Com. Mun. Corp*. App. III, 2077.

88 S.P.L., Deeds 19294.

89 W.B.R., P4/5/3, 15 Jan. 1786.

90 Under the Salop Gaol Act, 1786, 26 Geo. III, c. 24: *1st Rep. Com. Mun. Corp*. App. III, 2078.

91 Ibid. 2077, 2079–80.

92 Examples in sources cited in n. 76, above.

93 S.R.O. 1681/193/1.

94 W.B.R., Q1/11/2–4.

95 S.R.O. 1224/7/20.

96 S.R.O. 1681/47, p. 25; Brookes fam. letter bk. (MS. in private hands; access kindly arranged by Mr. W. M. Motley) Nov. 1842.

97 Below, Broseley, local govt.

parties connected with the borough'. By the 1830s the court met only fortnightly, and cases then, as in busier times, rarely came to trial.[98]

The parliamentary borough 1468–1885

Wenlock's charter empowered it to elect one M.P., but by 1491 writs to elect two were being issued.[99] From 1544 to 1629 the representation was mostly dominated by the Lawleys, kinsmen seated at Spoonhill and Wenlock Abbey, and to a lesser extent by the Lacons of Willey. Unrepresented 1646–59, the borough returned a Lawley in 1659, but thereafter the Welds, of Willey from 1618, and the Foresters of Watling Street, later of Dothill, families whose landed interests coalesced in 1748,[1] dominated the borough's representation until 1885, though rarely free of the threat of opposition before 1826. Interests based on the Lawleys' property and the Much Wenlock manorial estate[2] would have profited politically from a restriction of the parliamentary boundary to Much Wenlock itself; legal challenges were periodically meditated or threatened[3] but never pushed to a conclusion. The Foresters easily met the cost of defending their interests and of creating[4] and treating large numbers of burgesses in the 18th and early 19th century. After 1826, however, they were concerned to hold only one seat; the other was occupied by men (Peelite from the 1850s, then Liberal) connected with the manorial estate and the Lawleys' interest. After 1832, despite the electorate's increasingly industrial character and its sudden great growth[5] in 1868 to 3,445 (including many rural labourers),[6] there were few contests, mainly no doubt because of the balance of power and influence between the Conservative Weld-Foresters (who always topped the poll when there was one) and the Liberals.

The parliamentary borough survived the 1832 Reform Act intact and weathered later political criticism.[7] Its survival meant the persistence of ancient boundaries until 1885. They puzzled canvassers for the radical candidate in November 1832: it was hard for them to discover which south Shropshire villages were in the parliamentary borough and which were not, and the locals misled them.[8] Eventually all the eccentric detail of the parliamentary boundary had to be worked out for the Ordnance Survey's 25-in. plans, and in 1881 the town clerk attempted to help and advise, adducing the evidence of old poll books and electoral registers and even sending a translation of the *Dictum* of *c.* 1110.[9] With such aid and other local information the Survey thus recorded[10] the closest approximation there is to the boundary of the priory's medieval liberty and the borough of 1468–1836.[11] The main discrepancy between the

98 *1st Rep. Com. Mun. Corp.* App. III, 2077–8; L. C. Lloyd, 'Rec. of a Boro. Ct. in 17th Cent.' *Archives*, vii. 13–14.

99 Para. based on *V.C.H. Salop.* iii. 246–8, 250–3, 291–7, 339–43. Since that acct. appeared *Hist. Parl., Commons*, 1509–58, ed. S. T. Bindoff (1982), 1558–1603, ed. P. W. Hasler (1981), 1660–90, ed. B. D. Henning (1983), and 1790–1820, ed. R. G. Thorne (1986), have appeared covering periods after 1468.

1 Below, Willey, manor; *V.C.H. Salop.* iv. 204–5; xi. 80, 216, 220. The Foresters' main property in the boro. before 1748 was Lt. Wenlock, bought 1623. John Forester, M.P. 1529–36, may have been a courtier (*T.S.A.S.* 3rd ser. ii. 151–2) rather than a man with influence in the boro.; he sat with the historian Edw. Hall.

2 Also originally Lawley property: below, Monkhopton, manors; M. Wenlock, manors (M. Wenlock, Bourton, Spoonhill).

3 e.g. in 1710, 1722, 1780, 1820, and 1822.

4 Cf. W.B.R., B3/1/9.

5 The pre-1832 electorate fluctuated, but cf. 790 burgesses in 1710, and 691 and 961 electors in 1832 and 1866.

6 In consequence of the 1868 Reform Act. Cf. *V.C.H. Salop.* iv. 231 n. 3; J. Davis and D. Tanner, 'Boro. Franchise after 1867', *Hist. Research*, lxix. 306–27.

7 *1st Rep. Com. Mun. Corp.* App. III, 2078–9.

8 B.L. Add. MS. 44161, ff. 90v.–91; cf. *V.C.H. Salop.* iii. 340–1.

9 W.B.R., B3/5/51–3.

10 O.S. Maps 1/2,500, Salop. XXXVI. 14; XLII. 4, 8, 12; XLIII. 1–2, 6–7, 9–16; XLIV. 14–15; L. 3–4, 7–8, 10–11, 13–16; LI. 1, 3–4, 7–8, 11, 13–15; LII. 1–3, 5–7, 9–11; LVI. 8, 10–16; LVII. 1–15; LVIII. 5, 9, 13; LXIV. 1–4, 6–8; LXV. 1, 3–4, 7–8, 10–11, 14–15; LXVI. 7–8, 11; LXXII. 1–3, 5–7, 9–11, 13–15 (1882–5 edns.).

11 See fig. 16 and caption.

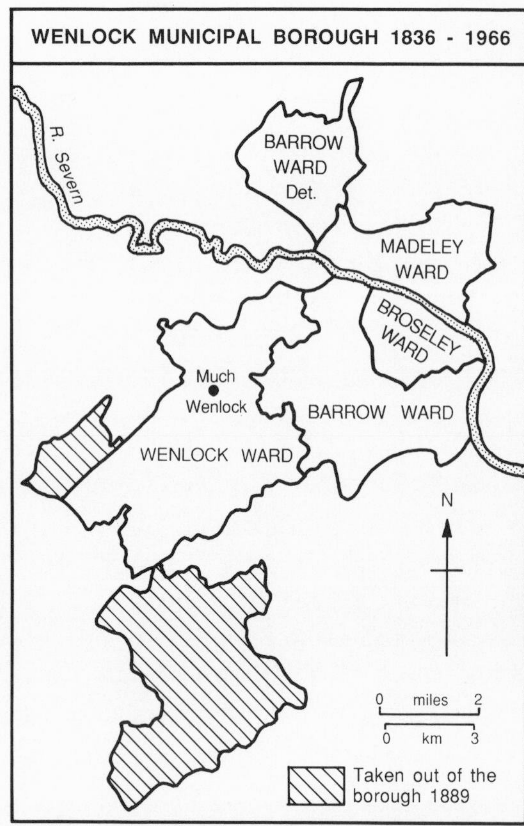

Fig. 17
The borough lost its detached parts (shown on fig. 16) in 1836. The wards shown are those created in 1889.

Ordnance Survey plans and the borough incorporated in 1468 was the omission of small areas like Pickthorn and parts of Oxenbold or Patton, lost to the borough apparently in the late 17th or early 18th century.[12]

The borough 1836–89

The most obvious impact of the 1835 Municipal Corporations Act on the borough was the loss of its detached parts,[13] rather more than a third of its territory. In 1836 the county magistrates assigned Badger, Beckbury, Eaton-under-Heywood, and most of Shipton[14] and Stoke St. Milborough[15] parishes to neighbouring petty sessional divisions of the county.[16] They clearly had little idea of where Deuxhill was: having assigned it to Bridgnorth division, they soon had to reassign it to Chelmarsh division.[17] The resulting municipal borough, still very extensive, was divided into three wards. Madeley ward consisted of Madeley and Little Wenlock parishes, Broseley ward included Barrow, Benthall, Broseley, Linley, and Willey parishes and Posenhall extra-parochial place, and Wenlock ward comprised the rest: Hughley, Monkhopton, and Much Wenlock parishes, most of Ditton Priors parish, and Skimblescott.[18] Each ward elected six councillors to the borough council of 24, whose number was completed by six aldermen; in place of the bailiff of the old corporation a mayor was to preside.[19] The last bailiff completed his term of office after becoming mayor on 1 January 1836.[20]

Besides territory Wenlock lost its quarter sessions and coroner,[21] though it was granted a commission of the peace in 1836.[22] The borough was therefore assessed to the county rate[23] and became a county coroner's district.[24] The skill with which the landed interests had combined to manipulate the old borough institutions in the 1820s[25] may have persisted: for half a century after 1835 there was little political excitement in borough affairs,[26] and the changes introduced by the 1835 Act were, from the beginning, endured with 'more moderation, and less of party feeling'

[12] Pickthorn was in the boro. in 1674 (S.R.O. 5709, Wenlock q. sess. order book 1661–90, p. 90), parts of Oxenbold and Patton in 1715–16: S.R.O. 566/59.

[13] Under the Municipal Corporations Act, 1835, 5 & 6 Wm. IV, c. 76, s. 7. Cf. fig. 17.

[14] All but Skimblescott, the only pt. of Shipton par. not detached from the main body of the boro.

[15] The Heath had never been in the lib or boro.: above, this article (Lib.: Bourton hund.).

[16] Under 9 Geo. IV, c. 43: S.R.O., q. sess. order bk. 1833–9, ff. 129v., 168v.

[17] Cf. ibid. ff. 184v., 203.

[18] *Lond. Gaz.* 8 Dec. 1835, p. 2406.

[19] 5 & 6 Wm. IV, c. 76, s. 25 and sched. A (2).

[20] H. E. Forrest, *Old Hos. of Wenlock and Wenlock Edge* (Shrews. [1914]), 122.

[21] 5 & 6 Wm. IV, c. 76, ss. 1, 64, 101.

[22] Ibid. s. 98; S.R.O. 1922/7–8, 10.

[23] S.R.O. 119/115; assessments in S.R.O., q. sess. order bks. 1833–43; *V.C.H. Salop.* iii. 152.

[24] *Orders of Q. Sess.* iii. 310, 312.

[25] *1st Rep. Com. Mun. Corp.* App. III, 2078–9.

[26] *V.C.H. Salop.* iii. 340.

than in some other reformed Shropshire boroughs.[27] In 1840 Wenlock was prompt to join the new county constabulary.[28]

By 1841, however, earlier moves to petition for the restoration of a court of quarter sessions were being revived. Some (including at least one resident magistrate and perhaps the town clerk) disapproved, but a petition succeeded,[29] and in November 1842 Much Wenlock was reported 'rather bustling' on account of the court's revival under the new recorder, Uvedale Corbett: at his first sessions, after a trial of over five hours, he sentenced Thomas Halford, shoemaker and Chartist lecturer, to three months' imprisonment for incitement to steal during that summer's disturbances over wage reductions.[30] With its quarter sessions (which it retained until 1949)[31] the borough regained its coroner.[32] Although it ceased to pay the county rate from 1842, the borough continued its partnerships with the county, paying to the county police rate,[33] paying to use the county gaol[34] (keeping its own merely as a lock-up),[35] and in 1844 forming a partnership with the county to found the pauper lunatic asylum.[36]

Nevertheless the borough and its still extensive and eccentric territory remained in many ways an obstacle to the rationalization and unification of local government so notably advanced by the Public Health Act of 1872.[37] Most of the borough was then within Madeley poor-law union, formed 1836.[38] The union's twelve parishes, however, included three (one of them populous) outside the borough boundary,[39] while outlying parts of the borough had been included in Atcham and Bridgnorth unions since their formation in 1836.[40] The borough was accordingly excluded from the Public Health Act's provisions,[41] as it was retrospectively from those of the 1870 Education Act concerning school board elections.[42] Later three urban parishes within the borough and the Madeley union became urban sanitary and highway districts under local boards of health:[43] Much Wenlock in 1873,[44] Broseley in 1876,[45] and Madeley in 1880.[46] The Atcham, Bridgnorth, and Madeley rural sanitary authorities continued to be responsible for the remaining parts of the borough.[47] The borough's existence also frustrated the introduction of new highway authorities. The county magistrates, on adopting the 1862 Highways Act, had tried to form rural highway districts that coincided with the poor-law unions,[48] but they had no authority within the quarter sessions borough of Wenlock, where nine rural parishes accordingly continued as highway authorities.[49]

The borough, so anomalous as to require regular exclusion from important pieces of general legislation, was clearly ready for a second dose of reform, and the 1888 Local Government Act provided the means of administering it.[50]

27 C. Hulbert, *Hist. and Descr. of Salop.* ii (1837), 359.

28 S.R.O. 4774/11, 13; *Orders of Q. Sess.* iv, p. xii; *V.C.H. Salop.* iii. 157.

29 W.B.R., boro. council min. bk. 1836–65, 9 Feb., 9 and 30 May 1836; boro. council min. bk. 1810–74, 9 and 23 Nov., 20 Dec. 1841, 3 Aug. 1842; S.R.O. 2924/82, W. Anstice to J. J. Peele 24 Sept. 1841.

30 Brookes fam. letter bk. 18 Nov. 1842; S.R.O. 1681/193/1, 15 Nov. 1842; *Salopian Jnl.* 23 Nov. 1842. Cf. B. Trinder, *Ind. Rev. Salop.* 235–8.

31 *V.C.H. Salop.* iii. 227.

32 Under 5 & 6 Wm. IV, c. 76, ss. 62, 103: W.B.R., boro. council min. bk. 1810–74, 3 Aug. 1842.

33 *V.C.H. Salop.* iii. 152.

34 *Orders of Q. Sess.* iv. 22.

35 *1st Rep. Com. Mun. Corp.* App. III, 2078.

36 S.R.O. 819/21–4; *V.C.H. Salop.* iii. 160.

37 *V.C.H. Salop.* iii. 177.

38 *P.O. Dir. Salop.* (1879), 261, 433.

39 Buildwas, Dawley, and Stirchley.

40 V. J. Walsh, 'Admin. of Poor Laws in Salop. 1820–55' (Pennsylvania Univ. Ph.D. thesis, 1970), 148–50, 167.

41 And from the subsequent consolidating Act: Public Health Acts, 1872, 35 & 36 Vic. c. 79, s. 4, and 1875, 38 & 39 Vic. c. 55, s. 6.

42 37 & 38 Vic. c. 39.

43 Under the Local Govt. Act, 1858, 21 & 22 Vic. c. 98. Cf. *Pratt and Mackenzie's Law of Highways*, ed. H. Parrish and P. Freeman (1952), 135–6.

44 Below, M. Wenlock, local govt.

45 Below, Broseley, local govt.

46 *V.C.H. Salop.* xi. 57.

47 Local Govt. Bd.'s Prov. Order Conf. (No. 4) Act, 1889, 52 & 53 Vic. c. 22 (Local).

48 *V.C.H. Salop.* iii. 178.

49 Under the Highways Act, 1835, 5 & 6 Wm. IV, c. 50: below, local govt. sections for Barrow, Benthall, Ditton Priors, Hughley, Linley, Monkhopton, Posenhall, and Willey; *V.C.H. Salop.* xi. 88 (for Lt. Wenlock). But Gt. Oxenbold and Skimblescott went into Bridgnorth highway dist.: S.R.O. 560/78–81, 339 (1–3).

50 Local Govt. Act, 1888, 51 & 52 Vic. c. 41, s. 52.

The borough 1889–1966

In 1889 the borough was further reduced, to half of its ancient (pre-1836) area, by the loss of Hughley and Monkhopton civil parishes and the part of Ditton Priors C.P. that was in the borough. The remaining borough territory was divided into four wards: Barrow, Broseley, Madeley, and Wenlock.[51] Madeley ward was to elect 9 borough councillors, Broseley and Wenlock wards 6 each, and Barrow ward 3, and the 24 councillors, with 8 aldermen, were to form the new council. The borough was reformed by a special Act,[52] providing it with a unique, truly federal, constitution. Although the borough became an area for the administration of sanitary affairs, as had been the case with normal boroughs since 1872, the borough council was not the sanitary authority. Instead four district committees were created, each to be the autonomous authority of a sanitary district conterminous with a borough ward. Thus the borough's Broseley, Madeley, and Wenlock district committees took over the responsibilities of the Broseley, Madeley, and Wenlock local boards, then abolished; its Barrow district committee took over the responsibilities within the borough of the Madeley rural sanitary authority and those of the six former highways parishes remaining within the borough, all in Barrow ward.[53] Each district committee consisted of the aldermen assigned to it by the borough council and the councillors elected for the ward.

The borough became a 'Part III' local education authority in 1903.[54] There were no elementary board schools for it to take over,[55] but it formed a school attendance committee[56] and, in 1905, a higher education committee.[57] In 1912 it relinquished its education powers to the county council,[58] a move in the tradition of Wenlock's mid 19th-century co-operation with the county and consonant with general trends in the earlier 20th century as education devolved on county authorities,[59] housing on minor authorities. In the 20th century the borough's district committees thus became housing authorities, that of the most populous district an important one within Shropshire. When the Addison housing programme began in 1919[60] the populous industrial parishes of Broseley and Madeley had accumulated housing problems and their district committees needed to plan for the elimination of slums and insanitary houses as well as to provide for post-war needs. Between the 1920s and 1966 the Madeley district committee built over 1,400 dwellings,[61] more than twice the combined total of the other three district committees: over the same period the Broseley committee built some 420,[62] the Wenlock committee some 230;[63] the Barrow committee built very few.[64]

Such statistics point to social and economic contrasts between the borough's different parts that had been noted as early as the 1830s.[65] By the mid 20th century the wards had developed correspondingly distinct political identities to which the council officers serving those committees had regularly to adapt.[66] The 6th Lord

51 Fig. 17. The area in 1835 had been 184 sq. km.: *V.C.H. Salop*. iii. 339.

52 For this para. see 52 & 53 Vic. c. 22 (Local).

53 Those (except Ditton Priors, Hughley, and Monkhopton) listed in n. 49, above.

54 Under the Education Act, 1902, 2 Edw. VII, c. 42, s. 1.

55 *V.C.H. Salop*. iii. 175, and source first cited ibid. n. 17.

56 S.R.O., DA 6/119/1.

57 W.B.R., P10/1/81.

58 Under 2 Edw. VII, c. 42, s. 20(*b*): W.B.R., B3/5/46.

59 *V.C.H. Salop*. iii. 177 (corr. ibid. xi. 377), 199.

60 K. and J. Morgan, *Portrait of a Progressive: Political Career of Chris., Vct. Addison* (1980), 74–5, 81–2, 96 sqq.

61 *V.C.H. Salop*. xi. 30–1.

62 Below, Broseley, growth of settlement.

63 Below, M. Wenlock, growth of settlement.

64 Eight hos. built at Benthall in 1953 (below, Benthall, intro.) seem to be all. Cf. below, intro. sections for Barrow, Linley, Posenhall, and Willey; and (for Lt. Wenlock) *V.C.H. Salop*. xi. 78, 80.

65 *R. Com. Mun. Corp. Boundaries (Eng. and Wales) Pt. III*, H.C. 238 (1837), xxviii (copy in W.B.R., B3/5/48).

66 Inf. from Mr. J. L. McFall, boro. public health insp. 1956–66.

Forester (twice mayor)[67] was a member of the small Barrow committee from 1899 until his death in 1932, when his son the 7th baron (also twice mayor) succeeded to his father's seat and went on to chair the committee 1945–66, latterly as an alderman;[68] business went through smoothly. By contrast in Broseley ward, and perhaps even more in Madeley, councillors were sharply divided by party politics, and those wards contributed most to the Labour party's strength in the borough.[69]

In 1947 the deadlocked Madeley district committee (6 Labour, 6 independents) was unable to elect a chairman and the ensuing dispute revealed that the town clerk and district committee members had for years misconceived the committees as district councils.[70] In 1949 a council subcommittee, recommending administrative changes within the borough, was unable to agree whether repeal of the 1889 constitution should be sought; the process was likely to prove expensive, and later that year the borough decided against seeking a change, though the reformers predicted that the Boundary Commission would return to sweep away what had 'amazed' them the year before. Meanwhile different rates for different parts of the borough, multiplication of work for the council's officers, and the alleged existence of 42 borough banking accounts were said to amount to 'parochialism run mad',[71] a claim that a recent contest between Broseley and Madeley for a meagre Ministry of Health housing allocation went far to justify.[72]

In such circumstances interest revived in a rearrangement of local authorities in the east Shropshire coalfield area. Dawley's inclusion in Wenlock borough had been proposed more than once in the 19th century,[73] and in the 1930s the county council had explored the possibility of amalgamating Dawley and Oakengates.[74] In 1948, under the stimulus of the Boundary Commission's work, there was much local support in principle for schemes to amalgamate local authorities in the Wrekin area, where Wellington rural district was half urban and Wenlock borough half rural. The press too pushed such schemes.[75] By 1956, when the Conservative government was beginning to prepare for local-government reform,[76] there was talk of a 'borough of the Wrekin' to include territory ceded by Wenlock, whose unique system of semi-autonomous wards was considered 'not satisfactory'.[77] In 1963 the government designated Dawley urban district, Madeley ward, and small parts of Barrow and Broseley wards as Dawley new town.[78] The move 'took the ground from under our feet' confessed Lord Forester, a county as well as a Wenlock alderman and chairman of the county Planning Committee 1962–6; he claimed that Wenlock's 'somewhat peculiar system of local government since 1468' had 'worked very well'.[79] The designation nevertheless fitted in with the county council's scheme (being prepared in accordance with the Conservatives' 1958 Act) for reorganizing the Shropshire minor authorities. After 1964 the scheme survived the Labour government's new ideas on local-government reform: a deal struck over the new

67 In 1920–2: W.B.R., M 5/68, p. 10 (obit.).

68 W.B.R., Barrow dist. cttee. min. bks. Mayor 1936–7 and 1961–2, he (like his father) was also a co. council member: cf. Burke, *Peerage* (1967), 973–4; *V.C.H. Salop.* iii. 182 n. 20; *Shrews. Chron.* 27 Jan. 1967, p. 1; 7 Jan. 1977, p. 2 (obit.).

69 Local inf.

70 *Wellington Jnl.* 13 Dec. 1947 (in W.B.R., vol. of news cuttings 1937–49, p. 108); S.R.O., DA 6/112/7; *V.C.H. Salop.* xi. 58.

71 *Wellington Jnl.* 10 Dec. 1949 (in W.B.R., vol. of news cuttings 1937–49, back endpaper); S.R.O. 1721/31.

72 *Shrews. Chron.* 23 July 1948 (in W.B.R., vol.of news cuttings 1937–49, p. 113).

73 *R. Com. Mun. Corp. Boundaries Pt. III*; S.R.O., q. sess. rec. box 30, cuttings bk. 1872–7, corresp. 1877.

74 *S.C.C. Mins.* 1930–1, 457; 1932–3, 133–5; 1933–4, 50–3.

75 *Shrews. Chron.* 19 Dec. 1947, p. 3; 7 (p. 3) and 28 (p. 3) May, 4 June (p. 3) 1948; 26 Jan. 1951, p. 6.

76 *The Times*, 1 Aug. 1956, p. 8*g*; cf. 3 May (p. 5*e*), 11 July (p. 6*f*) 1957.

77 *Shrews. Chron.* 6 Jan. 1956, pp. 1, 9.

78 *V.C.H. Salop.* iii. 220; xi. 2, 4, 88; below, Benthall, intro.; Broseley, intro.

79 *Shrews. Chron.* 8 Nov. 1963, pp. 1, 8–9, 18; *S.C.C. Mins.* 1962–3, 34; 1966–7, 47; above, n. 68.

town's expansion saved it,[80] and it came into effect in 1966, bringing the borough to an end. Madeley ward, the Severn Gorge parts of Benthall and Broseley civil parishes, and part of Little Wenlock C.P. were transferred to Dawley U.D. Bridgnorth rural district received the rest of the borough except for the rest of Little Wenlock C.P., which went to Wellington R.D.[81]

On the evening of 28 March 1966, three days before its dissolution, Wenlock corporation met for the last time. Business over, it passed from the guildhall into Holy Trinity for a thanksgiving service.[82] No scene for the final act could have been fitter than the church whose parish, equivocally defined, had spelled the extension of such privileges and so odd a system of local government over so wide an area for so many centuries.

Bailiffs, mayors, seals, arms, and insignia

A list of bailiffs 1468–1835 and mayors from 1836 is on a board in the Guildhall court room.[83]

A late 15th-century circular corporation seal, 50 mm. in diameter, displays figures under three gothic canopies, the Holy Trinity in the centre, on the left St. Mildburg holding a crozier and book, and on the right St. Michael; in the base are three escutcheons, the right-hand one Lord Wenlock's, and either side the main design are words and devices relating to a rebus or motto of his. A surrounding legend, black letter, has been read as: SIGILLUM COM*M*UNE BURGI DE WENLOK. The seal in use in the 19th century—presumably until *c.* 1884 when a new one 'on the embossing principle' was acquired—was said to be 'a shallow modern copy of the old one, with various errors of detail'.[84] A rebus formed by the letters W, E, and N and a fetterlock was on a 'seal of office for common processes', elliptical 25 × 23 mm., drawn in the mid 18th century.[85]

The corporation had no official arms, but used the fetterlock, in blue and gold, as a badge. An escutcheon, charged with three inescutcheons from the corporation seal, otherwise did duty as unofficial arms.[86]

The borough insignia comprise a mid 17th-century sword, evidently given in 1757; two silver gilt maces, one (the serjeant's mace) 17th-century, the other (the great mace) given by George Forester and hallmarked 1811–12; and a set of six staves, two with more ornamental gilt heads than the others.[87] There was no plate.[88] By the 1890s the mayor was scarlet robed and the town clerk had a black gown,[89] and in 1899 Lord Forester and members of the corporation presented the borough with a mayoral chain and pendant badge (containing a reproduction of the corporation seal), gothic in design.[90]

80 *V.C.H. Salop.* iii. 168–9 (corr. below, Corrigenda); H. Wilson, *The Labour Govt. 1964–70* (1971), 204; R. Crossman, *Diaries of a Cabinet Minister*, i (1975), 331, 367, 386, 439–41, 452–3, 485, 491.

81 *V.C.H. Salop.* ii. 236–7 (corr. ibid. xi. 376).

82 W.B.R., B3/1/11, pp. 585–7; B3/5/123.

83 Cf. lists (differing slightly) in Forrest, *Old Hos. of Wenlock*, 115–23 (1468–1913); Mumford, *Wenlock in Middle Ages*, 179–81 (1468–1602).

84 Ll. Jewitt, *Corporation Plate and Insignia of Office of the Cities and Towns of Eng. and Wales*, ed. W. H. St. John Hope (1895), i, pp. xciv, xcviii; ii. 292, 587; T. F. Dukes, *Antiquities of Salop.* (1844), 66; *T.S.A.S.* 2nd ser. viii. 18; W.B.R., boro. council min. bk. 1865–90, p. 246. Cf. wax impression in B.U.L., Mytton Papers, vii. 1534; cf. *Jnl. Brit. Arch. Assoc.* vii. 162.

85 B.U.L., Mytton Papers, vii. 1534; *T.S.A.S.* 2nd ser. viii. 19.

86 *T.S.A.S.* 2nd ser. viii. 19.

87 Jewitt, *Corp. Plate and Insignia*, i, pp. lxx, cxxvi, cxxxi, cxxxv; ii. 291–2; *Cat. of Loan Exhibn. of Salop. Antiquities 1898* (*T.S.A.S.* 2nd ser. x, Special Exhibn. Part), 162–3.

88 Just two pieces of china: Jewitt, op. cit. ii. 293.

89 Ibid.; cf. pl. 40 in this vol. Cf. W.B.R., boro. council min. bk. 1865–90, p. 246.

90 By Hen. Wells, jeweller, of Shrews.: *Shrews. Chron.* 10 Nov. 1899, p. 5 (full descr.); illustr. on cover of W. F. Mumford, *M. Wenlock: a Short Hist.* (M. Wenlock Mus. Cttee. 1971; copy in S.P.L., class M 64 v.f.).

BADGER

BADGER is a small rural parish on the Shropshire–Staffordshire boundary. In the Middle Ages (perhaps from the 12th century) and until 1905 it formed, with the adjoining parish of Beckbury, a detached part of Hereford diocese.[1]

Parish and manor, roughly rectangular, are conterminous.[2] On the west and south-west Badger is bounded by the meandering river Worfe,[3] also known in the 19th century as Cosford brook;[4] on the east and south it is bounded by a tributary called the Batch, Heath[5] or Snowdon brook, or the Mert.[6] Badger's northern boundary, with Beckbury, follows field edges and ditches and required clarification in 1229.[7] The boundary did not alter after the early 19th century and the 374-ha. (924-a.) parish[8] extends *c.* 2.5 km. from west to east and *c.* 2 km. from north to south. From over 90 m. in the north-west, high ground perhaps referred to in the name Badger (which probably means 'Baecg's ridge tip'),[9] the land falls steeply west to the river and more gradually to the south and east.[10]

The western half of Badger lies mainly on Upper Mottled Sandstone, the eastern on boulder clay and sand and gravel. A small area of peat lies in the extreme north-east.[11]

From Badger village minor roads run north to Beckbury, south to Ackleton, east to Pattingham (Staffs.), and south-west to Stableford. Stableford bridge was rebuilt in 1834–5 to Francis Halley's design.[12] In 1757 a road also ran west from Badger and over a bridge to join the Wellington–Worcester road;[13] by 1808 the road was no more.[14]

There were 4 bordars in 1086.[15] In 1642 the Protestation was taken by 25 men in the parish.[16] In the 1670s the parish had an adult population of *c.* 45 in seven houses; only the manor house was taxed on more than one hearth.[17] In 1801 the parish had 88 inhabitants. By 1811 the population had risen to 123, and slow increase brought it to 178 in 1861. Numbers then gradually fell, to 88 in 1951, though rising again to 114 by 1981.[18]

The medieval village was probably small and surrounded by open fields; there were large woods to the west and north and an extensive tract of heath along the eastern side of the parish.[19] The settlement pattern changed little between the 18th and 20th centuries and had probably been much the same in the Middle Ages.[20] Manor house, church, and rectory stood together in the southern half of the parish, with the village's few other houses a little farther south along the Stableford–Pattingham road. Some of the older ones are timber framed with brick nogging. There were few outlying houses. Badger Heath Farm, centre of the Heath copyhold estate enfranchised in 1662, stands in the south-east corner of the parish.[21] Badger Farm, a large improved set of buildings north of the village, was built *c.* 1810.[22] In the late 1970s a small sewage works opened on the north bank of the Upper Pool in Badger Dingle; effluent was pumped for further treatment in the Ackleton works in Worfield parish.[23] The village was made a conservation area in 1981.[24]

In 1835 there was a parish lending library provided by the lady of the manor. It was probably due to the lord of the manor's influence that there was no public house in the parish in the 19th and 20th centuries.[25]

In the later 18th and in the 19th century Badger Dingle, south of the village, was a much admired picturesque attraction.[26] The steep-sided dell or batch, 1 km. long, cut through the Red Sandstone by Snowdon brook, was improved *c.* 1780 by I. H. Browne, lord of the manor, to a design by William Emes (d. 1803), probably in conjunction with his pupil, partner, and successor John Webb (d. 1828).[27] Two miles of walks were laid out on the north side of the renamed 'Dingle', with a connecting walk to Badger Hall near its east end; the latter walk ran under the public road to Pattingham. A 'chase' looped north-east from the west end of the Dingle to complete the circuit. Forming the west end of the Upper pool, a dam, probably with the cascades found later, was built across the brook.

1 *V.C.H. Salop.* ii. 1; above, Lib. and Boro. of Wenlock (early est.). This article was written in 1985.

2 Bodl. MS. Blakeway 10, f. 145; S.R.O. 4001/Misc/1, box 311, ct. r. of 1774.

3 So called by 11th cent.: *P.N. Salop.* (E.P.N.S.), i. 326–7.

4 R. Baugh, *Map of Salop.* (1808); S. Bagshaw, *Dir. Salop.* (1851), 456.

5 S.R.O. 513, box 2, bdle. 1, deed 4 Nov. 1662; 4001/Misc/1, box 311, ct. r. of 1774.

6 D. H. Robinson, *The Wandering Worfe* (Albrighton, 1980), 82; *V.C.H. Staffs.* xx. 161.

7 Fig. 18; *Cal. Close*, 1227–31, 242–3.

8 O.S. *Area Bk.* (1883).

9 *P.N. Salop.* (E.P.N.S.), i. 30; M. Gelling, *Place-Names in Landscape* (1984), 176, 259.

10 O.S. Maps 1/25,000, SJ 70 (1951 edn.), SO 79 (1956 edn.).

11 Geol. Surv. Map 1", drift, sheet 153 (1901 edn.).

12 S.R.O. 4480/H/2; SA 13786.

13 J. Rocque, *Map of Salop.* (1757); *V.C.H. Salop.* xi. 201.

14 Baugh, *Map of Salop.*

15 *V.C.H. Salop.* i. 333. Badger does not appear in records of the 1327 subsidy.

16 Ho. of Lords papers 1641–2, Protestations Oxon. and Salop. f. 180.

17 *Hearth Tax 1672* (Salop. Arch. Soc. 1949), 36; *T.S.A.S.* 2nd ser. i. 91; W.B.R., B3/6/77(1).

18 *V.C.H. Salop.* ii. 220; *Census*, 1971, *Co. Rep. Salop.* ii. 6; *Census*, 1981, Small Area Statistics: Salop.

19 Below, econ. hist.

20 Rocque, *Map of Salop.*; Baugh, *Map of Salop.*; C. & J. Greenwood, *Map of Salop.* (1827); S.R.O. 4792; fig. 18.

21 Below, manor.

22 Cf. Baugh, *Map of Salop.*; B.L. Maps, O.S.D. 213.

23 Robinson, *Wandering Worfe*, 19, 85.

24 Inf. from S.C.C. Planning Dept.

25 *Educ. Enq. Abstract*, H.C. 62, p. 769 (1835), xlii.

26 Fig. 19. Descr. of Dingle based on Bodl. MS. Blakeway 10, f. 145; W.S.L. 350/3/40, Badger pp. 58–9; S.P.L., J. H. Smith colln. no. 236; N.B.R., copies of watercolours; SA 13788; Robinson, *Wandering Worfe*, 83; S.R.O. 4792; P.R.O., IR 29/29/26; IR 30/29/26; S.C.C. Planning Dept., Sites and Monuments, Badger Dingle file; C. Howard, 'Badger Est. and its Pleasure Grounds' (Wolverhampton Polytechnic B.A. dissertation, 1985; copy in S.P.L.). Dr. K. M. Goodway is thanked for help on Emes.

27 H. Colvin, *Biog. Dict. Brit. Architects, 1600–1840* (1978), 874; I. C. Laurie, 'Landscape Gardeners at Eaton Pk.', *Garden Hist.* xii. 50–7.

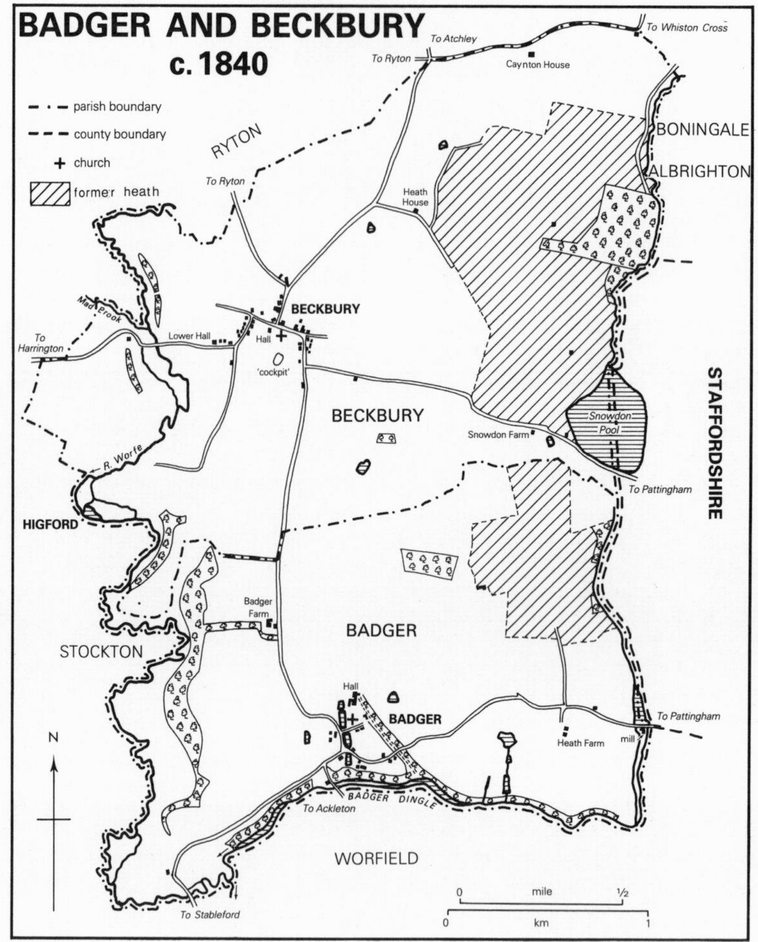
BADGER AND BECKBURY
c. 1840
parish boundary
county boundary
church
former heath
To Atchley
To Whiston Cross
To Ryton
Caynton House
BONINGALE
ALBRIGHTON
RYTON
To Ryton
Heath House
BECKBURY
Lower Hall
Hall
'cockpit'
To Harrington
BECKBURY
Snowdon Farm
Snowdon Pool
STAFFORDSHIRE
To Pattingham
R. Worfe
HIGFORD
Badger Farm
BADGER
STOCKTON
Hall
BADGER
To Pattingham
Heath Farm
mill
N
BADGER DINGLE
To Ackleton
WORFIELD
To Stableford
mile
km

Fig. 18

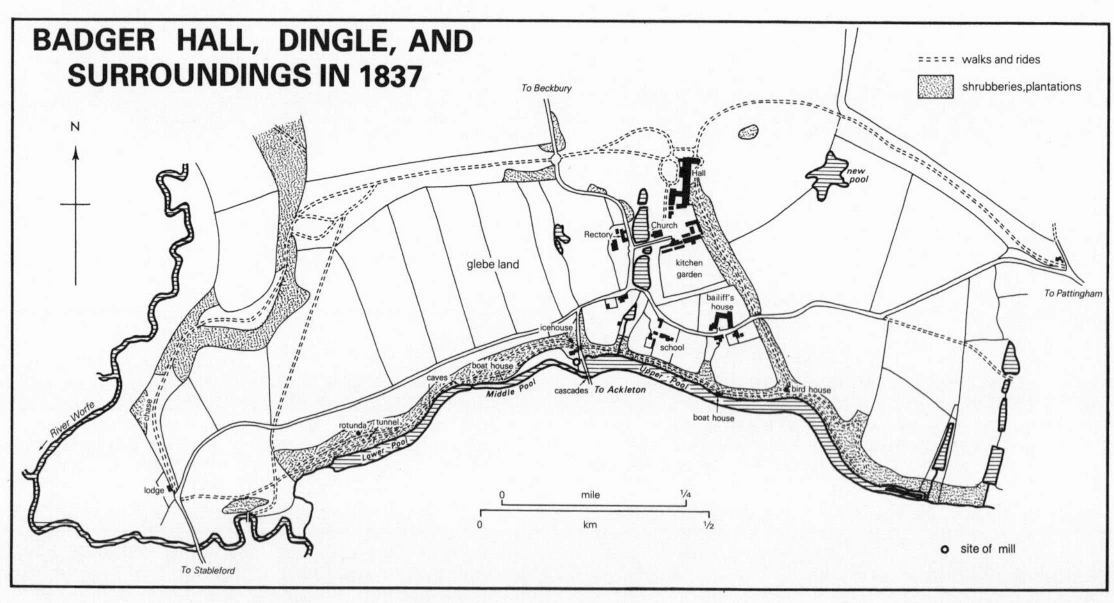
BADGER HALL, DINGLE, AND SURROUNDINGS IN 1837
walks and rides
shrubberies, plantations
To Beckbury
N
Hall
new pool
Rectory
Church
glebe land
kitchen garden
To Pattingham
bailiff's house
icehouse
school
boat house
caves
Middle Pool
cascades
To Ackleton
Upper Pool
bird house
boat house
River Worfe
rotunda
tunnel
Lower Pool
lodge
mile
km
site of mill
To Stableford

Fig. 19

Alpine plants, American rhododendrons, azaleas, and camelias were planted in the Dingle, and tulip trees and magnolias in the shrubbery along the hall walk. A summer house or banqueting room with a basement kitchen, possibly designed by James Wyatt,[28] was built where walk and Dingle met. In the early 19th century it was known as the Doric Temple, later as the bird house.[29] A boathouse *c.* 150 m. to the west was probably also an original feature. A rock-cut icehouse mid way along the Dingle may have been incorporated in the design. A rotunda was built near the west end of the Dingle.

In 1828 the dam burst after a storm, and *c.* 40 men from the Brownes' coalfield manor of Malinslee (in Dawley) spent nine weeks reconstructing the Dingle. In the mid 19th century other alterations were made: the original boathouse was replaced or supplemented by ones on the Middle and Upper pools; a pond was made north of Upper pool to provide a waterfall down the Dingle's side; and various walls, caves, and gateways were made in the side of the Dingle. Badger mill on the north side of the main dam, built probably in the 1830s, was perhaps designed as a scenic addition to the Dingle; a rock cut path, with a bridge over the main Dingle path, led down to it from the road to the north. Initially the Dingle was private, but by 1851 it was open to the public and visited by workers' outings from the Wolverhampton and Birmingham areas.[30] The Dingle was well maintained until the later 1930s but by the 1970s was overgrown, its buildings in disrepair.[31]

MANOR AND OTHER ESTATES. In 1066 Bruning (Bruniht) held *BADGER*. In 1086 Roger of Montgomery, earl of Shrewsbury, held it in chief and Osbern fitz Richard, baron of Richard's Castle, held it of him.[32] Earl Roger's son Earl Robert forfeited his lordship in 1102[33] and the baron of Richard's Castle was evidently tenant in chief thereafter until the early 15th century or later.[34]

By the mid 1170s Guy le Strange (d. *c.* 1179), of Alveley, held Badger immediately under Osbern fitz Hugh, baron of Richard's Castle, probably for 4*s*. a year.[35] After the death of Guy's son Ralph in 1195, that lordship was divided among Ralph's sisters and coheirs Margaret Noel, Gillian of Wappenbury, and Maud of Sutton.[36] It was acquired in the later 13th century by the terre tenant; the barony of Richard's Castle belonged then to the Mortimers and later to their coheirs the Talbots and the Cornwalls.[37] A baron of Richard's Castle may have interposed another lord between himself and the Stranges or their coheirs,[38] for possibly in 1211–12, and certainly by 1274, Badger and Romsley (in Alveley) were held as 1 knight's fee under the baron by the Poer family (who had held Romsley of the baron probably since 1165 or earlier) and in 1307 by Leo of Romsley who had evidently succeeded to their mesne lordship.[39] Ives of Romsley had the mesne lordship in 1348[40] but its later descent has not been traced.

By Richard I's reign the terre tenant of Badger held his manor of the prior of Wenlock for 20*s*. a year and evidently suit of court, an arrangement confirmed in the mid 1220s by Prior Humbert.[41]

Robert was terre tenant in 1086[42] as was William of Badger in the mid 12th century.[43] William sold the manor to Philip son of Stephen, later known as Philip of Badger (d. *c.* 1196).[44] Son then followed father, the following, usually called 'of Badger', being lords: Philip's son Roger (d. 1220 × 1225),[45] Thomas (d. by 1246), Philip (d. *c.* 1258),[46] Philip (d. *c.* 1291),[47] Thomas (d. by 1316), and Philip (d. 1345).[48] The estate belonged to Philip's son and heir William in 1347[49] but not in 1349 at William's death without issue.[50] By 1361 it belonged to John of Badger,[51] Philip's brother,[52] and John's widow Alice had it from *c.* 1366[53] until her death in 1404. Under a settlement of 1361 Badger was then shared by William's coheirs Catherine Sevile, Elizabeth Maundevile, Elizabeth Fraunceys, Catherine Mercher, and Margaret Overton.[54] Catherine Sevile's husband Thomas may have had a share in 1413, when he nominated the rector,[55] but in 1430 the rector was nominated by Roger Elmbridge.[56] Roger is said to have been the husband of Alice's granddaughter Elizabeth Coleson, and the Elmbridges' daughter Alice is said to have married Richard Petit.[57] In 1435 Roger quitclaimed his interest in Badger to Richard,[58] who nominated the rector in 1435, had a moiety of

28 Wyatt did much work at Badger Hall and worked elsewhere with Emes (below, manor; inf. from Dr. Goodway) but Wyatt's design for a dovecot at Badger (*Cat. of Drawings Colln. of R.I.B.A.: Wyatt Fam.* (1974), p. 37 and fig. 27) resembles neither of the Dingle's 'temples'.

29 Gracilla Boddington's diary (in possession of Mrs. S. Whitley, Kingsley Green, Surr.) 25 July 1830, 25 Mar. 1840.

30 S.R.O. 4792; S. Bagshaw, *Dir. Salop.* (1851), 456; 'Viator', *Guide to View from Brimstree Hill* (Shifnal, 1858), 38–9 (copy in S.P.L.).

31 *Shropshire Mag.* Feb. 1955, 25, 27, 29; Sept. 1962, 18, 20; *Shropshire Star*, 7 May 1985, p. 17.

32 *V.C.H. Salop.* i. 333.

33 Ibid. iii. 9–10.

34 Eyton, ii. 62–3, 66, 74–5; *Cal. Inq. p.m.* v, p. 24; viii, p. 418; xiv, p. 228; xvi, p. 299; xviii, p. 327.

35 Eyton, ii. 63; S.R.O. 513, box 1, no. 4 (printed in Eyton, ii. 66–7 n. 5); H. le Strange, *Le Strange Rec.* (1916), 40.

36 Eyton, ii. 74–5; iii. 131–43; le Strange, op. cit. 42.

37 Eyton, ii. 74–5; I. J. Sanders, *Eng. Baronies 1086–1327* (1960), 75.

38 As Eyton (ii. 75 n. 35) considered possible. Cf. Sir F. Pollock and F. W. Maitland, *Hist. Eng. Law* (1898), i. 346–8.

39 Eyton, ii. 75 n. 35; iii. 197–8, 202–3; *Cal. Inq. p.m.* ii, p. 489; v, p. 24; *Cal. Close*, 1307–13, 178.

40 *Cal. Inq. p.m.* xii, p. 428.

41 Eyton, ii. 69, 71, 73–5; iv. 135.

42 *V.C.H. Salop.* i. 333.

43 Eyton, ii. 62–3.

44 Ibid. 63, 67–8.

45 Ibid. 68–71.

46 Ibid. 71–4; *Cal. Close*, 1227–31, 242–3; S.R.O. 513, box 1, no. 9.

47 Eyton, ii. 74–6; *Cal. Inq. p.m.* ii, p. 489.

48 Eyton, ii. 75–6; *Cal. Pat.* 1321–4, 17, 53; *Cal. Inq. p.m.* viii, p. 418.

49 *Cal. Inq. p.m.* viii, p. 418; *Cal. Pat.* 1345–8, 284.

50 *Cal. Inq. p.m.* ix, p. 293.

51 S.R.O. 513, box 1, nos. 12–13.

52 Bodl. MS. ch. Shrops. 121.

53 Bodl. MS. Rolls Shrops. 7.

54 *Cal. Inq. p.m.* xviii, pp. 326–7; *Cal. Close*, 1402–5, 341–2.

55 *Reg. Mascall* (C.S.), 186.

56 *S.P.R. Heref.* xvi (3), p. v.

57 S.P.L., MS. 4645, p. 186; cf. W.S.L. 350/3/40, Badger pp. 3–4, which makes Eliz. dau. of Alice by a second marriage.

58 Bodl. MS. ch. Shrops. 129.

the manor in 1437, and was living in 1447.[59] Roger Elmbridge's brother John quitclaimed his interest in Badger to Richard in 1440.[60] Richard's son Robert (fl. 1465–6) was succeeded by his brother John (d. 1501), whose son Thomas died seised of the manor in 1504.[61] Thomas was succeeded by 1495 by his brother Henry (fl. 1507–8) and he by his daughter Dorothy who married first her stepbrother John Kynnersley (d. 1514–15), of Loxley (Staffs.), and secondly Thomas Nowell of Pelsall (Staffs.).[62] In 1560 Dorothy, then a widow, and her son James Nowell conveyed the manor to her son Thomas Kynnersley[63] (fl. 1577), from whom it passed from father to son, the following being lords:[64] Anthony (d. 1621), Francis (d. 1633), a magistrate,[65] Thomas (d. 1680), sheriff of Staffordshire 1646–7[66] and of Shropshire 1654, Thomas (d. 1689), and John, sheriff 1721. John (d.s.p. 1750) was succeeded by his brother Clement (d. unmarried 1758) of Uttoxeter (Staffs.). In 1774 Clement Kynnersley of Loxley, grandson of John and Clement's nephew, sold the manor, with the Badger estate also including lands in Beckbury and Ackleton, to Isaac Hawkins Browne of Foston (Derb.).[67]

Browne, sheriff in 1783 and M.P. for Bridgnorth 1784–1812, was an essayist and editor of the poems of his father and namesake (d. 1760). He died childless in 1818[68] leaving a life interest in Badger to his wife Elizabeth (d. 1839), with remainder to his cousin's son R. H. Cheney (d. 1866) who was succeeded by his brother Edward. On Edward's death in 1884 the estate passed to his nephew Col. Alfred Capel Cure of Blake Hall, Ongar (Essex).[69] Capel Cure died in 1896 and was followed by his nephew Francis Capel Cure (d. 1933). In 1937 the estate passed from Francis's widow to his nephew G. N. Capel Cure of Blake Hall. By 1953 Capel Cure had disposed of Badger Hall and estate to John Swire & Sons.[70] Sir Adrian Swire was lord of the manor in 1985.[71]

About 1719 John Kynnersley demolished the timber framed moated house just west of the church, although part of the moat remained, probably as a garden canal, until *c.* 1780. Kynnersley built a new house just to the north;[72] it was occupied by the ironmaster William Ferriday (d. 1801) from *c.* 1761 to 1775[73] and in his day was approached along an avenue of elms.[74] In 1761 the Hall had six ground floor rooms: at the front the hall was flanked by a drawing room and common parlour, to the rear were a best parlour, smoking room, and kitchen.[75] Service buildings, perhaps of 1698, stood to the south[76] and were retained when, in 1779–83, James Wyatt extended and remodelled the Hall for I. H. Browne. A large new block of eight bays and three storeys was built on the north end of the old Hall. It was principally of brick (made on site) with stone quoins. New rooms included a museum, library, and conservatory, and fine plasterwork by Joseph Rose of London included a frieze depicting classical gods and heroes and Shakespearean characters.[77] In 1783 Browne commissioned chiaroscuro paintings from Robert Smirke (d. 1845) for the library and dining room.[78] The Hall was further enlarged in the later 19th century. At the north entrance rooms were added on two storeys, a carriage entrance and conservatory were added to the east side of them, and additional service rooms were built on the south side of the house. A chapel was added in 1886.[79] Swire & Sons demolished most of Badger Hall *c.* 1953 but the service range of *c.* 1700 was refurbished as a private house in the early 1980s.[80]

In 1781 and 1785 William Emes, the designer of Badger Dingle, submitted estimates for landscaping around the Hall.[81] It included levelling the ground and making ha-has, planting a shrubbery east of the Hall and around the stables and clumps of trees elsewhere, altering the approach roads, and making walks, including one (called the 'pleasure ground' in 1837)[82] to the Dingle. Perhaps also at that time the pools[83] west and south-west of the church were enlarged; they drained into the Dingle. In the early 19th century extensive parkland around the Hall was

59 Ibid. 128; *S.P.R. Heref.* xvi (3), p. v; *Visit. Salop. 1623*, ii (Harl. Soc. xxix), 300; *Cal. Pat.* 1446–52, 76.

60 Bodl. MS. ch. Shrops. 131.

61 Ibid. 133; *Visit. Salop. 1623*, ii. 300 (misdating Thos.'s death); *Cal. Inq. p.m. Hen. VII*, ii, pp. 378, 542.

62 *Visit. Salop. 1623*, ii. 300; *S.P.R. Heref.* xvi (3), p. iv.

63 Bodl. MS. ch. Shrops. 137; P.R.O., CP 25/2/200/3 Eliz. I East. [no.12].

64 Descent based on *Visit. Salop. 1623*, ii. 301; *S.P.R. Heref.* xvi (3), pp. iv, ix, 3; J. B. Blakeway, *Sheriffs of Salop.* (Shrews. 1831), 128–9, 172; S.R.O. 513, box 1, no. 15; box 7, abstr. of title to Mr. Browne's est.; P.R.O., C 142/728, no. 9; S.P.L., MS. 4078, pp. 886–9; W.S.L., S. MS. 47/42.

65 P.R.O., STAC 8/192/2–3.

66 *S.H.C.* 1912, 287.

67 *S.P.R. Heref.* xvi (3), p. iv; S.R.O. 513, box 7, abstr. of title to Mr. Browne's est.; W.S.L. 350/3/40, Badger p. 12; S. Shaw, *Hist. Staffs.* i (1798), 79.

68 *D.N.B.*; B.M. *Gen. Cat. of Printed Bks. to 1955* (photolithographic edn. 1959–66), xxvii, cols. 1251–2; M.I. in St. John's Coll., Camb., chapel.

69 *Miscellanea Genealogica et Heraldica*, N.S. iii. 43; W. Hughes, *Sheriffs of Salop. 1831–86* (Shrews. 1886), 43–4; M.I. in Badger ch.

70 *S.P.R. Heref.* xvi (3), p. iv; M.I.s in Badger ch.; *Kelly's Dir. Salop.* (1900–41); S.R.O., archivist's office file 'Badger', corresp.; Howard, 'Badger Est.' 34; S.R.O. 5071 (sale of ho. contents 1945); Burke, *Land. Gent.* (18th edn.), i. 179.

71 Inf. from Sir Adrian.

72 SA 14773; Dept. of Environment, *List of Bldgs.: Bridgnorth (pars. of Albrighton [etc.]*, 16; M.U.L., Botfield Papers, Badger memo. bk. 1779–89, Mr. Emes's estimate 24–5 Sept. 1781; W.S.L. 350/3/40, Badger p. 12.

73 *S.P.R. Heref.* xvi (3), p. xii; S.R.O. 1681/183/15; 2280/BRg/1, f. 53; Trinder, *Ind. Rev. Salop.* 24, 26, 88, 228–9; *V.C.H. Salop.* xi. 120.

74 S.R.O. 4001/Misc/1, box 378, deed 12 July 1771.

75 Bodl. MS. Gough Salop. 11, f. 11v.

76 *S.P.R. Heref.* xvi (3), p. iv.

77 S.R.O. 1232/1; 4187/4; Colvin, *Biog. Dict. Brit. Architects*, 940, 947; N.B.R., photos.; S.P.L., photos.; pls. 18–19; 'Viator', *View from Brimstree Hill*, 37; *Cat. of Drawings Colln. of R.I.B.A.: Wyatt Fam.* pp. 36–7; M.U.L., Botfield Papers, Badger memo. bk. 1779–89, lists of prices, estimates, details, etc., of plasterwork, etc., 1781–2, and Wm. Emes's estimates 24–5 Sept. 1781, 28 Nov. 1785 (for brick kiln).

78 Essex R.O., A 8403, box B misc., corresp. from Smirke to Browne; *D.N.B.*

79 *Salop.: short hist., with genealogies and current biogs.* ed. J. Grant [1911], 252; Howard, 'Badger Est.' 34.

80 S.R.O., archivist's office file 'Badger', corresp.; inf. from Miss C. Ryan, S.C.C. Planning Dept. conservation officer.

81 M.U.L., Botfield Papers, Badger memo. bk. 1779–89, Emes's estimates 24–5 Sept. 1781, 28 Nov. 1785.

82 S.R.O. 4792.

83 Lawn, Church, and Town pools: O.S. Map 1/2,500, Salop. LII. 6 (1902 edn.).

crossed by numerous walks and rides.[84] George Cooke, head gardener, made changes to the grounds *c.* 1850.[85]

An icehouse, used until the 1930s, stood 0.5 km. south-west of the Hall, in the Dingle. Ice was got from a specially dug pool east of the Hall.[86]

In 1662 the Badger Heath farm copyhold estate, in the south-western part of the parish, was enfranchised. It was then owned by Francis Taylor of Wootton (in Quatt) and occupied by Richard Taylor. After enfranchisement £2 a year, twice yearly suit of court, and a £5 relief on the death of each freehold tenant were due to the lord of the manor in lieu of chief rents, heriots, and all other services.[87] Francis Taylor died in 1689 and *THE HEATH* passed to his brother Richard (d. 1697), who left the estate to his wife Margaret (d. 1698) for life and then to their son William. William (d. 1713) was succeeded by his son Richard, and Richard (d. 1741) by his son Richard. In 1748 the Heath comprised 180 a.[88] The younger Richard died in 1757 and the estate passed to his nephew William Taylor[89] who sold it to Joseph Green in 1796. The Heath then consisted of 184 a. in Badger and 16 a. in Ackleton.[90] The Greens probably owned the Heath until the 1870s, when it was sold to A. S. Trevor.[91] By 1910 the Heath estate had been sold to the lord of the manor.[92] Badger Heath Farm is a 2½ storeyed **T** plan stone house of *c.* 1600, much extended in the 18th, 19th, and 20th centuries.

Wenlock priory received a pension of 3*s.* 4*d.* from the rector of Badger from the 12th century[93] and a 'free' or assize rent of £1 perhaps representing the annual rent for Badger due from the lord of the manor *c.* 1258. In 1544 the Crown sold pension and rent to Robert Brooke, the purchaser of Madeley manor (the former priory's nearest demesne manor, where they had been payable).[94] They descended with Madeley (after 1763 with the Slaughter share) until 1782 or later.[95]

ECONOMIC HISTORY. In 1086 there was enough land for two ploughteams; one belonged to the demesne, the other to four bordars.[96] The presence of bordars and the existence of enough woodland for 30 swine suggest an estate still under development. In 1291 the manor consisted of a house and 4½ virgates, also defined as 1 carucate, 8 a. of wood, and 4 a. of meadow.[97] As on other manors subject to Wenlock priory's lordship terciary was exacted: in 1502 the priory was entitled to 3 qr. of wheat and 3 of oats on a lessee's death.[98]

In the 17th and 18th centuries the medieval landscape of Badger was transformed. Until then open fields had probably lain east, west, and north of the Hall.[99] By 1662, when three leet or open fields were mentioned, Batch and Middle fields and Uppsfield, inclosure had begun.[1] In that year waste amounting to 176 a., probably of heath[2] along the east side of the parish, was divided. By 1689 the part of Badger heath belonging to the manor was kept free of gorse and furze.[3] An eighth of the heath was allotted to the newly enfranchised Heath estate, whose owner was allowed to make ditches from Snowdon pool and streams to bring water to his land on Sundays.[4] The Heath estate, 50 per cent arable, 36 per cent pasture, 8 per cent meadow, and 3 per cent woodland in 1748, had then only 3 per cent heath.[5] In the 1730s it had been stated that there were no commons in the parish,[6] and the division of 1662 may have put an end to them. Two woods survived in 1752: Badger wood along the west side of the parish and Beckbury wood straddling the northern boundary; both had gone by 1808.[7]

In 1594 copyholders had held in yardlands or half-yardlands since time immemorial.[8] In 1615 a demesne ploughteam consisted of 6 oxen.[9] Some hemp was grown in the later 17th century.[10] In the late 18th century the welfare of labouring families was promoted by the generosity of I. H. Browne, who gave allowances for coal and to the sick and aged.[11]

In 1801 94 a. of wheat, 92 a. of barley, 8 a. of oats, and 124 a. of turnips were grown in the parish.[12] In 1837 66 per cent of the land was arable, 26 per cent pasture and 8 per cent under woods and plantations.[13] In the late 19th and early 20th century the proportion of grassland gradually increased, with sheep the commonest livestock. Wheat and barley were grown in

84 S.R.O. 4792; above, this article, intro.; Greenwood, *Map of Salop.*

85 S. Bagshaw, *Dir. Salop.* (1851), 457; 'Viator', *View from Brimstree Hill*, 36–7.

86 Robinson, *Wandering Worfe*, 83–5; above, this article, intro.

87 Bodl. MS. Blakeway 10, f. 146a; S.R.O. 513, box 2, bdle. 1, abstr. of title of Wm. Taylor; 4001/Misc/1, box 378, deed 4 Nov. 1662.

88 S.R.O. 513, box 4, bdle. 3, abstr. of title pt. 2; *S.P.R. Heref.* xvi (3), 7, 9, 15; S.R.O. 4237/Rg/1, 17 May 1689.

89 S.R.O. 513, box 4, bdle. 4, abstr. of title pt. 3; *S.P.R. Heref.* xvi (3), 16.

90 S.R.O. 513, box 2, bdle. 5, deed 20 Apr. 1796; box 3, bdle. 2, deed 2 June 1795.

91 *P.O. Dir. Salop.* (1856), 13; (1879), 276; E. Cassey & Co. *Dir. Salop.* (1871), 59; *S.P.R. Heref.* xvi (3), p. v.

92 S.R.O. 4044/5.

93 Below, church.

94 Eyton, ii. 74; S.R.O. 245/1–2; N.L.W., Wynnstay, RA 2; cf. *V.C.H. Salop.* xi. 35; *Rot. Hund.* (Rec. Com.), ii. 85.

95 *V.C.H. Salop.* xi. 35–6; S.R.O. 2280/14/1; P.R.O., CP 25/2/1394 pt. 2/22 Geo. III East. [no. 8]; *Cal. Pat.* 1575–8, p. 272.

96 *V.C.H. Salop.* i. 333. Eyton, ii. 61, erroneously gives 3 bordars.

97 Eyton, ii. 75–6.

98 *V.C.H. Salop.* ii. 43; xi. 43, 81.

99 P.R.O., IR 29/29/26; IR 30/29/26, fields 39, 95–6; below, this section.

1 S.R.O. 513, box 2, bdle. 1, abstr. of title of Wm. Taylor. For Batchfield cf. P.R.O., IR 29/29/26; IR 30/29/26, field 13.

2 Fig. 18, for probable extent of heath.

3 S.R.O. 513, box 7, agreement 7 Oct. 1689.

4 Ibid. box 2, bdle. 1, abstr. of title, deed of enfranchisement of 1662; 4001/Misc/1, box 378, deed 4 Nov. 1662. See also Bodl. MS. ch. Shrops. 139.

5 S.R.O. 513, box 4, bdle. 3, abstr. of title, pt. 2.

6 Birm. Univ. Libr., Mytton Papers, i. 114.

7 Cf. Rocque, *Map of Salop.*; Baugh, *Map of Salop.*; P.R.O., IR 29/29/26; IR 30/29/26, fields 37, 48, 50, 53–5, 63, 65, 71.

8 P.R.O., C 78/86, no. 6.

9 P.R.O., STAC 8/193/5.

10 S.R.O. 513, box 2, bdle. 1, abstr. of title, deed of enfranchisement of 1662 (field names); cf. P.R.O., IR 29/29/26; IR 30/29/26, field 4.

11 *V.C.H. Salop.* iv. 221.

12 P.R.O., HO 67/12/15.

13 P.R.O., IR 29/29/26.

Table XII

Badger: Land use, livestock, and crops

	1867	*1891*	*1938*	*1965*
Percentage of grassland	48	58	60	42
arable	52	42	40	58
Percentage of cattle	3	7	24	25
sheep	88	87	72	62
pigs	9	6	4	13
Percentage of wheat	54	40	32	14
barley	45	41	34	75
oats	0	19	34	0
mixed corn & rye	1	0	0	11
Percentage of agricultural land growing roots and vegetables	20	16	14	29

Sources: P.R.O., MAF 68/143, no. 9; /1340, no. 12; /3880, Salop. no. 176; /4945, no. 176.

roughly equal, but declining, proportions as more oats were grown. Turnips and later sugar beet were usually grown on some scale.[14]

There was a water mill at Badger by the early 13th century. A rent of 10*s*. issuing from it was granted to Wenlock priory kitchen by Roger of Badger (d. by *c*. 1225)[15] and was bought from the Crown in 1828 by Mrs. I. H. Browne.[16] Badger water mill or mills were mentioned in the mid 17th and mid 18th centuries.[17] The principal or sole mill stood in Badger Dingle by the Ackleton road. That was apparently pulled down before 1811 for when Badger Heath mill, east of Heath Farm, was rebuilt in 1811, it was said to be the only mill in the parish; it was demolished 1948–50. The mill pool was used to wash sheep and had a great local reputation as a source of eels.[18] Another mill built in Badger Dingle, probably in the 1830s, was perhaps intended as a picturesque feature.[19]

In 1834 stone was got from the church quarry to rebuild Stableford bridge.[20] The same quarry was perhaps also the source of roadstone used locally.[21] Gravel was dug in the parish.[22]

LOCAL GOVERNMENT. Rolls for Badger manor court survive for various years between 1350 and 1532. They include presentments from Ackleton (in Worfield).[23] A court baron held in October 1774 for I. H. Browne, the new lord, was probably the first for many years.[24]

In 1642 one man was perhaps both churchwarden and parish constable.[25] In the 1660s and later three parish offices, those of churchwarden, overseer of the poor and highway surveyor, and constable, were served in rotation by the occupants of certain houses. A separate highway surveyor was probably appointed from 1692.[26] In the 1680s Badger had a pound and stocks.[27]

In 1740 £5 12*s*. was expended on the poor in cash, corn, rent, and burial expenses. Between 1812 and 1815 over £80 a year was paid as out relief, but expenditure then fell rapidly and between 1818 and 1836 the largest annual expenditure was £32 6*s*., in 1822–3. In 1830–1, as an exceptional measure, the poor were paid for picking and breaking stones.[28]

Badger was in Shifnal poor-law union 1836–1930,[29] Bridgnorth highway district 1863–95,[30] Shifnal rural sanitary district 1872–94, Shifnal rural district 1894–1974, and Bridgnorth district from 1974.[31]

CHURCH. There was a priest, and so presumably a church, at Badger by *c*. 1174, and the living was called a rectory in 1246.[32] In the Middle Ages the lord of the manor had the right to nominate a new incumbent to the prior of Wenlock (or to the Crown during its seizure of the alien priory in the 14th century) and the prior presented him to the bishop.[33] Prior Humbald granted the right of nomination to the lord 1155 × 1175, and the parson (*persona*) or clerk was to pay the priory 3*s*. 4*d*. a year.[34] At the Dissolution that pension was paid at Madeley, where dues from Beckbury and Badger were collected by *c*. 1523. The lord of Madeley bought it in 1544 and it was paid to his successors until the late 18th century or later.[35] After the Dissolution each new rector was usually nominated by the lord of the manor and presented by the Crown (as successor to the priory's rights). In 1941 the lord

14 Table XII.
15 Eyton, ii. 69, 71.
16 S.R.O. 513, box 6, corresp., etc., *re* fee-farm rent, certif. of common of woods and forests.
17 Ibid. box 2, bdle. 1, abstr. of title of Wm. Taylor, f. 6; box 7, abstr. of title of Mr. Browne, f. 2.
18 Robinson, *Wandering Worfe*, 82–3, misdating a source of *c*. 1830 as 1877; Bodl. MS. Blakeway 10, f. 145; M.U.L., Botfield Papers, Badger memo. bk. 1779–89, estimate by Geo. Beswick to clean pools 22 Oct. 1781; SA 15035.
19 Above, this article, intro.
20 Ibid.; S.R.O. 4480/H/2.
21 S.R.O. 4480/CW/1, s.a. 1692.
22 S.P.L., SC1/76.
23 S.R.O. 513, box 1, ct. r.; Staffs. R.O., D.(W.) 1733, bdle. 19; Bodl. MS. Rolls Shrops. 7.
24 Bodl. MS. Blakeway 10, f. 145; S.R.O. 4001/Misc/1, box 311, ct. r. 1774. It was evidently a ct. of survey, at which the death (1757) of Ric. Taylor of the Heath was presented.
25 Ho. of Lords papers 1641–2, Protestations Oxon. and Salop. f. 180.
26 S.R.O. 4480/CW/1; Bodl. MS. ch. Shrops. 139.
27 S.R.O. 4480/CW/1, s.a. 1684, 1686.
28 Ibid. at end, overseers' accts. 1740; /P/1.
29 V. J. Walsh, 'Admin. of Poor Laws in Salop. 1820–55' (Pennsylvania Univ. Ph.D. thesis, 1970), 147–50; *Kelly's Dir. Salop*. (1929), 30.
30 *Lond. Gaz*. 27 Mar. 1863, p. 1767; S.R.O., S.C.C. Local Govt., etc., Cttee. min. bk. 1894–1903, p. 29.
31 *V.C.H. Salop*. ii. 217; iii, sources cited 169 n. 29, 177–9.
32 Eyton, ii. 72, 78; S.R.O. 513/9.
33 Eyton, ii. 77; *Cal. Pat*. 1345–8, 284; *Reg. Trillek* (C.S.), 257, 301–2, 375; *Year Bk*. 19 Edw. III (Rolls Ser.), 469.
34 Eyton, ii. 77; Bodl. MS. ch. Shrops. 106.
35 Above, manor [pension and assize rent].

chancellor was patron on the nomination of G. N. Capel Cure, but by 1964 the lord chancellor alone was mentioned.[36] From 1956 the living was held in plurality with those of Beckbury (where a new house was built) and Ryton.[37]

The church was worth less than £4 a year in 1291, £3 6*s*. 8*d*. in 1379, and £4 11*s*. 2*d*. in 1535.[38] In the late 16th century the glebe comprised 8 a. of arable, a little grazing, and common for *c*. 40 sheep. Besides the tithes the rector had 8*s*. from a house occupied by Humphrey Blakeman.[39] In 1615 the rector had 19 a. of glebe and rent from ½ yardland; Blakeman's cottage was uninhabited and decayed.[40] How hay and corn tithes were then paid is unknown but most other tithes, and Easter offerings, were rendered in cash. Poultry tithes were paid in eggs.[41] About 1708 the living was worth £39.[42] In 1774 I. H. Browne rented the tithes for £80.[43] The rector exchanged part of his ancient glebe with Clement Kynnersley for other land in 1771.[44] About 1805 the living was said to be worth £400.[45] In 1837, when the tithes were commuted to £254 10*s*., there were 25 a. of glebe in a block west of the church.[46] The living was worth £292 10*s*. in 1851, £254 in 1879, and £175 in 1900.[47]

About 1700 the parsonage was a house of three bays with 2½-bayed barn.[48] The absentee rectors of the 18th century left the house in disrepair and it was substantially renovated and enlarged in 1795 when William Smith became rector.[49] In 1838 a new house, designed by Francis Halley, was built on the site of the old one, south-west of the church.[50] It was sold with 7 a. in 1944.[51]

If Roger, clerk of Badger (fl. *c*. 1174 and *c*. 1211), was the incumbent, he is the first known.[52] Philip of Badger, presented in 1291, was the lord of the manor's son, and John of Beckbury, 1344–9, was a son of the lord of Beckbury.[53] Roger Hondeslowe, rector for 40 years from 1368, was latterly also rector of Hope Bowdler.[54]

In 1614 the king presented Richard Froysall to the living without the lord of the manor's nomination. Francis Kynnersley vigorously opposed Froysall, attempting to prevent his entering the church. Ordering the parishioners not to attend services, Kynnersley deprived Froysall of his tithes and dues and planted trees on his glebe; he threatened to cut off the rector's head and throw it in Badger pool; and finally he had Froysall gaoled in Shrewsbury. Froysall's supporters seized a team of Kynnersley's oxen to try to make him restore Froysall's rights.[55]

John London, 1622–41, is the first known graduate rector. Like most of his 17th- and 18th-century successors he was a pluralist, being rector of Wheathill from 1624.[56] Benjamin Taylor, rector 1677–1704 and vicar of Madeley 1672–1704, was a son of Richard Taylor of the Heath;[57] he employed a curate.[58] Communion was normally celebrated four times a year in the late 17th century and five in the 18th century. Thomas Green, rector of Badger and of Beckbury 1705–24, lived in Beckbury in 1716. He then conducted two Sunday services in Badger, one with a sermon.[59] R. C. Hartshorne, rector 1724–52 and rector of Broseley from 1727, was succeeded by his son Thomas, rector 1753–79.[60] Between 1780 and 1795 the living was one of several held by Dr. James Chelsum (d. 1801), author of sermons, of a work on mezzotint engraving, and of criticism of Gibbon's *Decline and Fall*.[61]

By arrangement with the patron Chelsum resigned to make way for William Smith, probably the first resident for over a century.[62] I. H. Browne (d. 1818) left Smith the right to nominate the next rector; in 1820 Smith sold the turn to Browne's widow Elizabeth (d. 1839) for £1,200.[63] When Smith died in 1837, three years after the church's rebuilding, he was said never to have been more than two Sundays absent from Badger.[64] T. F. Boddington, rector 1838–71, lived at Shifnal in 1851. On Census Sunday 1851 morning service was attended by 70 adults, evening service by 75; 48 children were at both. Many Worfield parishioners attended Badger church in the 1840s and 1850s.[65]

36 *Dioc. of Heref. Institutions (1539–1900)*, ed. A. T. Bannister (Heref. 1923), 22, 33, 41, 45, 59, 70, 89, 112, 124, 155, 185, 194, 212; *S.P.R. Heref.* xvi (3), p. v; below, this section; *Kelly's Dir. Salop.* (1941), 29; *Lich. Dioc. Dir.* (1964), 101; (1985), 34.

37 Below, Beckbury, church.

38 Eyton, ii. 77–8.

39 S.R.O. 513, box 6, bdle. *re* living, terrier *temp.* Eliz. I.

40 Ibid. terrier 1615.

41 Ibid. acct. of tithes payable.

42 J. Ecton, *Liber Valorum et Decimarum* (1711), 147.

43 M.U.L., Botfield Papers, Badger memo. bk. 1779–89.

44 S.R.O. 4001/Misc/1, box 378, deed.

45 Bodl. MS. Blakeway 10, f. 147.

46 P.R.O., IR 29/29/26; IR 30/29/26.

47 P.R.O., HO 129/357, no. 1A; *P.O. Dir. Salop.* (1879), 276; *Kelly's Dir. Salop.* (1900), 26.

48 S.R.O. 513, box 6, bdle. *re* living, terriers *temp.* Eliz. I and 1615.

49 Ibid. corresp. 5 Sept. 1793, 18 Apr. 1795, 25 Feb. and 13 Apr. 1796; 4791/1/6, p. 160; below, this section. Thos. Telford's design for a new ho. was rejected as submitted too late and too expensive (S.R.O. 513, box 6, corresp. 13 Apr. 1796). For later inv. of ho. see S.R.O. 4480/Rec/3.

50 S.R.O. 4480/Rec/5; 4792; Heref. Dioc. Regy., reg. 1822–42, pp. 375, 415; Gracilla Boddington's diary 20 Feb. 1838.

51 Inf. from Lich. dioc. registrar.

52 Eyton, ii. 67 n. 5, 70 n. 18, 78.

53 Ibid. 78–9; *Reg. Swinfield* (C.S.), 528; *Reg. Trillek*, 257, 301–2, 375; *Cal. Pat.* 1345–8, 284.

54 *Reg. Mascall* (C.S.), 174, 189; *Reg. L. Charlton* (C.S.), 69.

55 P.R.O., STAC 8/147/22; STAC 8/193/5.

56 *S.P.R. Heref.* xvi (3), p. vi; Bannister, *Heref. Institutions*, 20, 22 (Thos. Gwilliam); below, Beckbury, church.

57 *S.P.R. Heref.* xvi (3), p. vi; *V.C.H. Salop.* xi. 61 n. 51; above, manor.

58 H.W.R.O.(H.), HD 7, petition for appointment of Mic. Shelden 1678; ibid. presentment of 1694.

59 *S.P.R. Heref.* xvi (3), pp. vi, ix; H.W.R.O.(H.), HD 5/14/1/5.

60 *S.P.R. Heref.* xvi (3), p. vi; Bannister, *Heref. Institutions*, 70, 72, 89, 112.

61 *S.P.R. Heref.* xvi (3), p. vi; *D.N.B.*; B.M. *Gen. Cat. of Printed Bks. to 1955*, xxxvii, col. 1013.

62 S.R.O. 513, box 6, Wm. Smith to [I. H. Browne] 5 Sept. 1793, 18 Apr. 1795; Bannister, *Heref. Institutions*, 124; W.S.L. 350/3/40, Badger pp. 53–4.

63 Above, manor; S.R.O. 513, box 6, deed 5 July 1820.

64 *Gent. Mag.* N.S. ix (1), 215.

65 P.R.O., HO 129/357, no. 1A; Bannister, *Heref. Institutions*, 155, 185; S. Bagshaw, *Dir. Salop.* (1851), 456.

The church of *ST. GILES*, so known by *c.* 1740,[66] was rebuilt in 1833–4. The old church comprised chancel, nave, and west tower; the body of the church measured 51 by 21 ft.[67] Men and women may have sat separately in 1662.[68] In 1713 John Kynnersley refurbished the interior; he railed round the communion table, improved the seating, and gave fittings including a communion set.[69] Nave and chancel were of Old Red Sandstone,[70] and the chancel seems to have been slightly longer than the nave. Windows, at least on the north and west, were late- or post-medieval. By 1805 heavy buttresses supported the south wall. The entrance then, as perhaps long before, was in the west wall of the tower. A west gallery, used by I. H. Browne's tenants and servants, was enlarged in 1809.[71]

In 1833–4 the dilapidated nave and chancel and the upper part of the tower were rebuilt at the expense of Mr. Green of the Heath (£100) and Mrs. I. H. Browne (£1,100). Designed by Francis Halley of Shifnal, the church consisted of a broad undivided nave and chancel in an early gothic style, with a thin pinnacled and crenellated west tower.[72] In 1851 there were 40 free and 118 rented adult seats and 60 for children.[73] Heating was installed in 1847.[74] A small north chapel for use by the Badger Hall family and a south porch, designed by F. Francis of London, were added in 1886–7. At the same time the gallery was removed and the nave repewed.[75] Preserved from the old church is a 15th-century wooden screen which separated nave and chancel in 1823[76] but screened the north chapel in 1985. Also kept were three 17th-century bells.[77] There are several notable monuments, including one by Chantrey.[78]

A tall headless cross, probably 14th- or 15th-century, was moved to the churchyard from 'the road' before 1789.[79] The churchyard was extended in 1853 and 1904.[80]

The registers begin in 1713 and are complete.[81]

NONCONFORMITY. None known.

EDUCATION. In 1819 there were two schools in the parish.[82] One had 8–12 pupils, the other, supported by Mrs. I. H. Browne, had 22. The latter was probably the private school, with teacher's house, in existence in 1837.[83] It had *c.* 50 pupils in 1851 but was limited to 30 by 1905 and to 25 by 1913. Owned and supported by the lord of the manor until 1933,[84] it was called a church school in 1876. That year three quarters of the school's income came from voluntary contributions, the rest from school pence, though the patron paid some expenses; attendance averaged 25.[85] By 1885 pupils above infant age left for Beckbury National school or Burnhill Green school.[86]

Attendance averaged 15 in 1900 and 20 in 1913.[87] Emma Grainger, mistress since 1891, and Francis Capel Cure, the school's patron, both died in 1933,[88] and the school closed. The roll was then *c.* 20. Girls were taught needlework, but the school was not under inspection and fees were still paid, 1*d.* a week for Badger children, 2*d.* for others; only slates were used for writing and arithmetic. After it closed pupils went to Beckbury or Worfield C.E. schools.[89]

CHARITIES FOR THE POOR. R. C. Hartshorne (d. 1752), rector, gave £5 in his lifetime and £5 by will. His son Thomas, also rector, gave £10 in 1779, shortly before he died. In 1783 the £20 was given to I. H. Browne, who charged one of his houses in Badger with £1 a year, which in 1820 was distributed annually.[90]

Bequests by William Smith (d. 1837), rector, Harriet Margaret Pigot (d. 1852), sister of R. H. Cheney, lord of the manor, and T. F. Boddington (d. 1871), rector, yielded £3 6*s.* a year in 1885.[91]

In 1975 the Badger charities yielded £4 a year.[92]

66 B.L. Add. MS. 30316, f. 29v.
67 Ibid. 21013, f. 65.
68 Bodl. MS. ch. Shrops. 139.
69 S.R.O. 4480/CW/1, s.a.; S. A. Jeavons, *Ch. Plate Archd. Salop.* (Shrews. 1964), p. 53.
70 S.P.L., MS. 372, vol. i, f. 123.
71 S.P.L., MS. 3065, no. 17; Bodl. MS. Blakeway 10, f. 147 (watermarked 1805); S.R.O. 4480/CW/1, 3 Oct. 1809.
72 S.R.O. 4480/CW/1, 15 Sept. 1833; /ChF/1, 4, 7; Cranage, iii. 173–4; Pevsner, *Salop.* 67–8; S.P.L., J. H. Smith colln. no. 13; *List of Bldgs.* 15; Heref. Dioc. Regy., reg. 1822–42, pp. 233–6.
73 P.R.O., HO 129/357, no. 1A.
74 S.R.O. 4480/CW/1, s.a. 1847, 1848.
75 Cranage, iii. 173; Heref. Dioc. Regy., reg. 1883–1901, pp. 111–12; *Ch. Cal. Dioc. Heref.* (1887), 138.
76 Cranage, iii. 183; B.L. Add. MS. 21013, f. 65.
77 H. B. Walters, *Ch. Bells of Salop.* (Oswestry, 1915), 20–1.
78 Cranage, iii. 173–4; Pevsner, *Salop.* 67–8.
79 Cranage, iii. 174; SA 13787; S.P.L., MS. 372, vol. i, f. 123; *List of Bldgs.* 16; Birm. Univ. Libr., Mytton Papers, i. 114.
80 S.R.O. 4480/Chyd/1; Heref. Dioc. Regy., reg. 1902–19, p. 95.
81 S.R.O. 4480/Rg/1, incl. transcribed entries 1662–81 from an earlier (lost) reg.; /MRg/1–3; regs. at ch.; *S.P.R. Heref.* xvi (3); cf. H.W.R.O.(H.), bp.'s transcripts 1602, 1622, 1638, 1640, 1660, 1662–1833, etc.
82 *Digest Educ. Poor*, H.C. 224, p. 746 (1819), ix (2). This section was written in 1982.
83 P.R.O., ED 7/103, ff. 367–8; S.R.O. 4792; *Educ. Enq. Abstract*, H.C. 62, p. 769 (1835), xlii.
84 S. Bagshaw, *Dir. Salop.* (1851), 457; *Kelly's Dir. Salop.* (1905), 26; (1913), 29; (1926), 29; inf. from Mrs. Doreen Ford, Beckbury.
85 P.R.O., ED 7/103, ff. 367–8.
86 *Kelly's Dir. Salop.* (1885), 797. For Burnhill Green sch. see *V.C.H. Staffs.* xx. 172.
87 *Kelly's Dir. Salop.* (1900), 26; (1913), 29.
88 M.I. in ch.; Burke, *Land. Gent.* (18th edn.), i. 179.
89 Inf. from Mrs. Ford.
90 S.R.O. 2991/Rg/4, 11 Oct. 1752; *S.P.R. Heref.* xvi (3), pp. xii, 19; *3rd Rep. Com. Char.* H.C. 5, pp. 299–300 (1820), iv.
91 *S.P.R. Heref.* xvi (3), pp. vi, 24; Burke, *Land. Gent.* i (1846), 211; Burke, *Peerage* (1967), 1987; *Kelly's Dir. Salop.* (1885), 797.
92 *Review of Local Chars.* (S.C.C. 1975), 20.

BARROW

THE HEAVILY wooded rural parish of Barrow, as it was in the mid 20th century, centred on the small hamlet of Barrow just over 3 km. east of Much Wenlock and 2.5 km. south-west of Broseley. In the Middle Ages Shirlett forest's demesne woods occupied the southern part of that area, and between the 16th and 18th centuries its commons, wastes, and minerals attracted numerous smallholders and miners. In the 19th century population declined and J. G. W. Weld-Forester, Lord Forester (d. 1874), became virtually the sole landowner; much of the area south of Barrow hamlet was private woodland in the 1980s.

By the late 11th century there was a chapel, evidently a dependency of the church of Wenlock. By the late 13th century, and probably long before, the area served from Barrow chapel was within the parish of Holy Trinity, Much Wenlock, and its parochial independence was gained only in the early 17th century, probably the period when Caughley became dependent on it.[93] In the earlier 19th century the main part of Barrow parish comprised 911 ha. (2,250 a.)[94] and extended *c.* 6 km. from north to south and a maximum of *c.* 2.5 km. from east to west. The Caughley detachment contributed 332 ha. (821 a.) to the total parish area of 1,243 ha. (3,071 a.). In 1883 a detached part (21 ha., 51 a.) of Posenhall civil parish was added to Barrow C.P., and in 1934 Caughley was transferred to Linley C.P. In 1966 Linley, Posenhall, and Willey C.P.s were abolished and added to Barrow C.P., as was almost the whole of Benthall C.P.[95] This article deals with the main part of the earlier 19th-century parish, a separate account of Caughley following.

On the east Barrow was partly bounded by Linley brook, probably the Atherwell brook mentioned in 1620,[96] and on the south by a tributary of Linley brook;[97] it had no other natural boundaries. On the south-west the parish boundary followed boundaries of the medieval forest of Shirlett.[98] The angular notched boundary in the north and north-west suggests widespread inclosure at the time of its delineation.

Barrow hamlet stands on a slight rise in the Broseley–Wenlock road. Most of the land is over 180 m. and rises to *c.* 230 m. near White Mines in the south-west and Arlescott in the north-west.[99] Barrow hamlet and part of Shirlett lie on productive Upper Middle Coal Measures, the rest of the south on Downtonian Ledbury and Temeside shale beds. South-west and north-east of the Marsh are Upper Ludlow shales, north of which (though largely outside the parish) Aymestry limestone occurs.[1] A chalybeate spring rises at the north end of Shirlett Common;[2] no evidence of its use has been found.

In 1625,[3] as later, the parish's principal thoroughfare was the Wenlock–Broseley road on which Barrow hamlet and the Marsh stood. A road south-east from Barrow led via Hangstree Gate to Willey; it formed part of the Wenlock–Bridgnorth road turnpiked in 1756.[4] Another road from Wenlock to Broseley ran north-east from Marsh green via Posenhall, where it was joined by a road from Hangstree Gate; that was part of the Wenlock–Broseley road turnpiked in 1756. North-west of the last mentioned road ran one from Posenhall to Arlescott which continued towards Much Wenlock, joining the Barrow–Wenlock road 750 m. west of the Marsh.[5] South-east of the Marsh roads and tracks bounded and crossed Marsh green whence a road ran south forking at White Mines, south-west to Rowmers corner and south-east towards Haughton (via the later Maypole Bank)[6] and Bridgnorth. In the south-east roads ran from Upper Smithies north to Willey via Harper's mill and south-west to the road to Haughton. From Barrow hamlet a road ran south-west to a group of houses, perhaps the hamlet of Prestenden.[7] The road north from Hangstree Gate was presumably closed when that settlement was cleared, *c.* 1818.[8] There was little later change in the road pattern, although several smaller roads had become tracks or footpaths by the 1980s.

The Saxon chapel was built at what was probably the northern edge of an extensive tract of woodland, the later Shirlett forest.[9] The name Barrow ('grove') sometimes occurs on the outskirts of a heavily wooded area.[10] The medieval landscape was apparently similar to that of the 17th century, when there was a clear division between the wooded southern half of the parish and the agricultural northern part, separated by the hamlet of Barrow and its open fields.[11] Arlescott was mentioned in the early 13th century,[12] the Marsh in 1291;[13] both were probably hamlets.[14] On the eastern edge of the parish the hamlet of 'Hanesty', whose name perhaps refers to a high, climbing track, probably existed by

93 Above, Lib. and Boro. of Wenlock (early est.); below, church; below, Caughley, intro. This article was written in 1984.

94 O.S. *Area Bk.* (1883).

95 Below, Caughley, intro.; Posenhall, intro.; *V.C.H. Salop.* ii. 229 note u, 235–7.

96 Below, Willey, intro.

97 O.S. Map 6", SO 69 NE. (1954 edn.).

98 Mapped in 1625: S.R.O. 1224/1/15; below, econ. hist. (agric.).

99 O.S. Maps 1/25,000, SJ 60 (1958 edn.), SO 69 (1956 edn.).

1 Geol. Surv. Map 1", drift, sheet 152 (1906 edn.).

2 O.S. Map 6", Salop. LI. SW. (1883 edn.).

3 S.R.O. 1224/1/15; fig. 20.

4 Trinder, *Ind. Rev. Salop.* 88; 29 Geo. II, c. 60.

5 Below, Broseley, communications; S.R.O. 1224/1/51; O.S. Map 6", SJ 60 SE. (1954 edn.).

6 O.S. Map 6", SO 69 NE. (1954 edn.).

7 S.R.O. 1093, parcel 161, Barrow map of 1721; 1224/1/15; below, this section.

8 S.R.O. 3375/77 (road not shown); below, this section.

9 Below, church; econ. hist. (agric.).

10 *P.N. Salop.* (E.P.N.S.), i. 30; M. Gelling, *Place-Names in Landscape* (1984), 189–90.

11 Below, econ. hist. (agric.).

12 Below, manors.

13 *Tax. Eccl.* (Rec. Com.), 164.

14 For Arlescott see S.P.L., MS. 292, ff. 77–81; R.C.H.M.E., draft field rep. (1986). For the Marsh see Clwyd–Powys Arch. Trust colour slides 92/C/949–52.

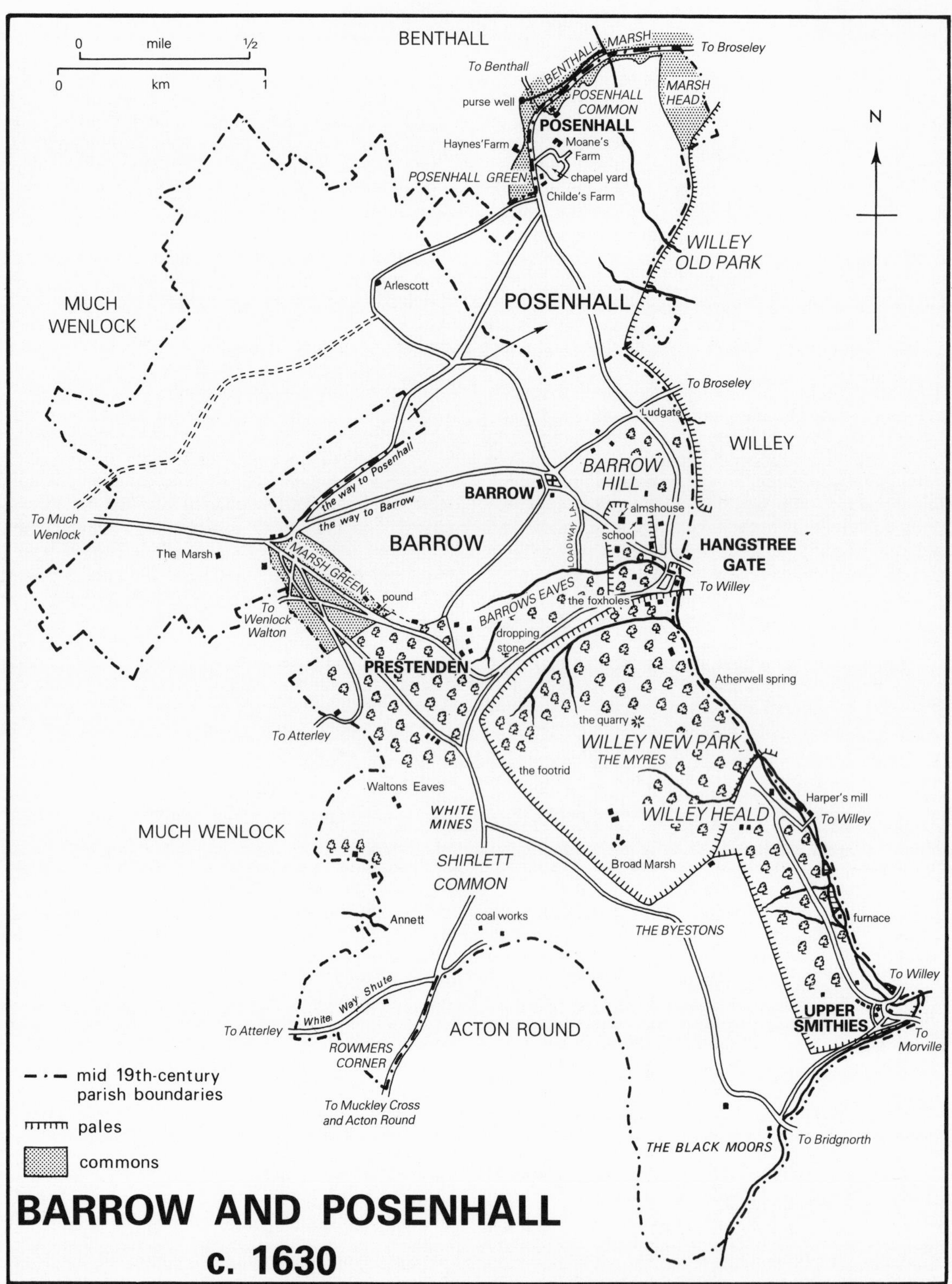

BARROW AND POSENHALL c. 1630
0 mile ½
0 km 1
N
BENTHALL
To Broseley
To Benthall
BENTHALL MARSH
MARSH HEAD
purse well
POSENHALL COMMON
POSENHALL
Moane's Farm
Haynes'Farm
POSENHALL GREEN
chapel yard
Childe's Farm
WILLEY OLD PARK
Arlescott
POSENHALL
MUCH WENLOCK
To Broseley
Ludgate
WILLEY
BARROW HILL
the way to Posenhall
the way to Barrow
BARROW
almshouse
school
HANGSTREE GATE
To Much Wenlock
The Marsh
BARROW
LOADWAY LA.
MARSH GREEN
To Willey
BARROWS EAVES
the foxholes
pound
To Wenlock Walton
dropping stone
PRESTENDEN
Atherwell spring
the quarry
WILLEY NEW PARK
To Atterley
THE MYRES
the footrid
Harper's mill
Waltons Eaves
WILLEY HEALD
To Willey
WHITE MINES
MUCH WENLOCK
SHIRLETT COMMON
Broad Marsh
furnace
Annett
coal works
THE BYESTONS
To Willey
White Way Shute
To Atterley
ACTON ROUND
UPPER SMITHIES
To Morville
ROWMERS CORNER
To Muckley Cross and Acton Round
To Bridgnorth
THE BLACK MOORS
mid 19th-century parish boundaries
pales
commons

Fig. 20

1262; from the 17th century it was usually called Hangstree Gate.[15]

There was mining and ironworking in Shirlett in the Middle Ages. Economic activity, increasing in the early 17th century (as in Broseley), led to an agreement to divide Shirlett in 1625.[16] Although, by 1625, the parish was populous, Barrow hamlet, perhaps never large, then consisted only of Barrow Farm and two or three other houses.[17] There were several loose clusters of houses in the northern part of the parish. To the east of Barrow hamlet was Barrow Hill where, in 1618, John Slaney, lord of Marsh, had built almshouses and a school[18] among *c.* 10 squatters' cottages. The more nucleated settlement of Hangstree Gate, where a cottage was mentioned in 1540, stood immediately to their east.[19] East of the Marsh lay Marsh green, around whose edge were several cottages and Marsh manorial pound. South-east of Marsh green was a hamlet of *c.* 5 houses, already suggested as the hamlet of Prestenden noted in that area between the 12th and 17th centuries: in the 14th and 16th centuries Prestenden was near 'Gonninghford' or 'Guynyfordes yate', presumably the 'Winneford yate' owned in 1797 by Samuel Yate of the Marsh.[20] In the southern half of the parish there were cottages at Waltons Eaves, the coal works, the Black Moors, and Upper Smithies. The last named settlement, about a dozen houses, at least some inhabited by furnacemen, was partly in Willey parish.[21] In all there were perhaps 50–60 squatters' and miners' cottages *c.* 1620 in the part of Shirlett that was in Barrow.[22]

In 1327 Barrow was taxed with Benthall and Posenhall, and 17 paid.[23] Nine Barrow men were mustered in 1542, 2 fewer than the combined Benthall and Posenhall roll.[24] Barrow's population probably reached its peak in the 17th and 18th centuries. In 1642 the Protestation was taken by 67 adult men in the parish.[25] About 24 householders, excluding those in Caughley, paid hearth tax in 1672,[26] and there were 123 adult parishioners in 1676.[27] In 1729 there were 65 cottages 'about the furnace and Shirlett', and 11 at Barrow Hill and Hangstree Gate; some of those would have been in Willey parish.[28] In 1784 it was said that 82 cottages had been erected in Shirlett since 1625.[29] In 1721 three or four farms flanked the road around Barrow church; just north of the church were Barrow green and pound.[30]

The population of 1801–21, at *c.* 470, was perhaps already slightly below its peak. In the 1820s it fell to 351;[31] coal had begun to run out around Broseley, and Caughley porcelain works had closed.[32] Population then stabilized until it fell again, in the 1880s and 1890s, to 242.[33] In the 1920s and 1930s it recovered towards late 19th-century levels.[34]

About 1818, to improve the prospect from the new Willey Hall, Barrow Hill was cleared, part of the area being taken into the new park, and the school and almshouses were moved nearer to the church.[35] At the same time Hangstree Gate was cleared away.[36] Thereafter only gradual shrinkage altered the settlement pattern. By 1838 the hamlet of Barrow had dwindled to a farmhouse (Barrow House) and, to the east, the new almshouses, school, and school house.[37] Marsh green had been inclosed in the preceding 20 years.[38] By 1941 gas and electricity were available and water supplied by the Wenlock Corporation.[39] Nevertheless in the 1980s much of what settlement existed was scattered and isolated: in the southern woodland cottages were accessible only by minor roads and tracks.

There is no evidence of organized social life in Barrow outside the alehouse, perhaps because of the nearness of towns at Much Wenlock and, from the 17th century, Broseley. Between the later 15th and the 19th centuries the number of alesellers fluctuated between one and eight, averaging half a dozen.[40] Drink played a part in bannering in the earlier 18th century.[41] A friendly society was founded in 1797.[42]

Perhaps by 1803[43] a chimney-like obelisk had been built in Shirlett, reputedly by George Forester (d. 1811), squire of Willey, either to mark the spot where a dog fell to its death or as the plinth of a pole from which a flag flew when Forester was at home.[44]

The King Edward VII Memorial Sanatorium was opened in Shirlett in 1910 by the Association for the Prevention of Consumption. Initially for

15 Below, this section; Willey, intro.; *Cal. Chart. R.* 1327–41, 488; P.R.O., C 143/2, no. 16. Dr. M. Gelling is thanked for comment on the name.
16 Below, econ. hist. (agric.; ind.).
17 Descr. of 1625 based on S.R.O. 1224/1/15.
18 Below, educ.; charities.
19 P.R.O., SC 6/Hen. VIII/3021, m. 8; below, Willey, intro.
20 Eyton, iii. 293–5; *Docs. illustr. rule of Wal. de Wenlok* (Camd. 4th ser. ii), pp. 52, 84, 147, 187; *Cal. Pat.* 1327–30, 473; N.L.W., Wynnstay, RA 2; Nott. Univ. Libr. MSS. Dept., Mi. D. 3756; S.R.O. 840, box 30, deeds of 1412, 1417; 1224/3/8, f. 2v.; box 342, Prior Gosnell's reg. f. 39; 1987/3/13–14; 5460/7/8; S.P.L., Deeds 1542; SA 3579.
21 Below, Willey, intro.
22 S.R.O. 1224/1/15; /2/71, 79.
23 *T.S.A.S.* 2nd ser. iv. 333.
24 *L. & P. Hen. VIII*, xvii, p. 508.
25 Ho. of Lords papers 1641–2, Protestations Oxon. and Salop. f. 181. Ric. Knott, signatory, probably lived in Willey.
26 *Hearth Tax 1672* (Salop. Arch. Soc. 1949), 34, 42–4.
27 *T.S.A.S.* 2nd ser. i. 91.
28 S.R.O. 1224, box 81, tithe acct. Jos. Barney.
29 S.R.O. 163/47. Some are shown on S.R.O. 3628/1, map IV.
30 S.R.O. 1093, bdle. 161, Barrow map of 1721.
31 *V.C.H. Salop.* ii. 220.
32 Below, Broseley, intro.; econ. hist. (ind.); Caughley, econ. hist. (ind.).
33 *V.C.H. Salop.* ii. 220; Barrow Sch. log bk. (at sch. 1982), 29 Apr. 1887, 19 Mar. 1897.
34 *V.C.H. Salop.* ii. 220, 229. No figs. after 1951.
35 Below, church; educ.; charities; Willey, intro.; manor.
36 Below, Willey, intro.; econ. hist. (agric.).
37 Above and below, this section; P.R.O., IR 30/29/28.
38 Cf. B.L. Maps, O.S.D. 207; P.R.O., IR 30/29/28.
39 A.H.S. Waters, *Rep. on Water Supply* (S.C.C. 1946), 16.
40 W. F. Mumford, *Wenlock in the Middle Ages* (Shrews. 1977), 74; S.R.O. 1224/2/368; 3385/1/5 (mention of the Raven); W.B.R., Q1/11/2.
41 S.R.O. 2992/ChW/1, s.a. 1708–9, 1727, 1745.
42 S.R.O., q. sess. rec. parcel 285, index to club articles.
43 S.R.O. 515/5, pp. 84–5 (Monument Bank 1803).
44 At O.S. Nat. Grid SO 666 976: B.L. Maps, O.S.D. 207; B. Jones, *Follies and Grottoes* (1974), 381; 'Viator', *Guide to View from Brimstree Hill* (Shifnal, 1858), 7 (copy in S.P.L.); 'The little known Shirlett Monument' (MS. [*c.* 1964?] in S.P.L., class MY 72.1 v.f.).

36 patients it was extended in 1913 to provide 60 places. It was improved in 1923[45] and closed *c.* 1961.[46]

MANORS AND OTHER ESTATES. *BARROW*, probably part of the Domesday manor of Much Wenlock, remained part of Wenlock priory's demesnes, probably by 1291 a member of Marsh manor, until they were surrendered to the Crown in 1540.[47]

In 1544 the manorial rights of *BARROW*, *ATTERLEY*, and *WALTON*, which thenceforward descended as one manor, were sold by the Crown to the attorney general William Whorwood.[48] On Whorwood's death in 1546 his estates, subject to his widow's dower, passed to his daughters Anne, wife of Ambrose Dudley (cr. earl of Warwick 1561), and Margaret, a minor, later the wife of Thomas Throckmorton.[49] Anne died without surviving issue in 1552, and on Warwick's death in 1590 her property passed to her cousin's son Thomas Whorwood (kt. 1604, d. 1616) of Compton (Staffs.), who had already acquired Margaret Throckmorton's interest.[50]

In 1613 Sir Thomas Whorwood sold the manor to Walter Acton[51] of Aldenham. Acton (d. 1641) was succeeded by his son Edward (cr. bt. 1644, d. 1659), and the manor subsequently descended with the baronetcy.[52] In an exchange of 1814 Sir Ferdinand Acton conveyed much of his Barrow land, with the manorial rights over that part, to Cecil Weld-Forester,[53] whose son J. G. W. Weld-Forester, Lord Forester, seems to have acquired the rest of the manorial rights *c.* 1855.[54] Barrow remained part of the Willey estate in 1984.[55]

In 1602 Thomas Whorwood sold *BARROW FARM* to its tenant Thomas Ruckley.[56] In 1622 Ruckley sold it to his brother and sister-in-law Edward and Anne Ruckley. Edward Ruckley (d. 1638)[57] was succeeded by his son William (fl. 1672) whose daughter and heir Judith married Francis Tarver. In 1743 the Tarvers' son William sold the 130-a. farm to the Revd. R. C. Hartshorne (d. 1752).[58] Hartshorne entailed it on members of the Garrett family of Weston-under-Lizard (Staffs.). In 1765 the farm belonged to Elizabeth Garrett who then married Jonathan Key (d. 1805). Elizabeth and her son John Key sold the farm to George Forester's trustees in 1812, and it remained part of the Willey estate in 1984.[59]

Barrow Farm or House, south-west of the church, is a big brick building incorporating early 17th-century fabric.[60]

ARLESCOTT, perhaps part of Much Wenlock manor in 1086, was said in 1484 to be held of the prior of Wenlock.[61] A mesne lordship was said in 1377 to belong to Fulk FitzWarin,[62] perhaps as heir to Warin of Metz or his male descendants, lords of Broseley until the 13th century.[63]

In the 13th century Arlescott was held by the Beysins, lords of Broseley. Philip of Broseley (d. *c.* 1240) held Arlescott in 1230.[64] He was apparently succeeded in Arlescott, as in Broseley, first by his brother Roger (d. 1243) then by their three sisters. About 1244 Mabel, widow of Adam de Beysin (d. 1238), granted her interest there to her younger son Warin (fl. 1244 × 1262). He in turn granted half of his land in Arlescott to his daughter Margaret. Robert of Arlescott, perhaps her brother, may also have had an interest.[65] In 1255 Robert de Beysin (d. 1267), son of Adam de Beysin, Mabel's eldest son and lord of Broseley, was lord of Arlescott. Alice, one of Mabel's sisters, granted all her interest in Arlescott to her daughter Amice between 1244 and 1249.[66]

By 1313 Arlescott belonged to Richard Burnell and it seems to have descended with his manor of Oaks (in Pontesbury),[67] coming by 1478 into the possession of Hugh Stapleton (d. 1484). Stapleton's heirs were Sir Richard Corbet of Moreton Corbet, Robert Coyney (or Coyne), and Richard Lee, the last two presumably by virtue of their descent from the coheirs of Sir Edward Burnell (d. 1377).[68] Corbet died in 1492 and the coparceners of Arlescott *c.* 1497 were Coyney and Fulk Lee, Richard's son.[69] Lee conveyed his portion to Coyney *c.* 1505[70] and by 1509 Arlescott belonged to Richard Forster of Evelith (in Shifnal). Forster's son Thomas (d. by 1560), M.P. for Wenlock, owned Arlescott, as did Thomas's grandson Richard Forster (d. 1605). In 1610, when Richard's son and heir Walter died, Arlescott comprised a house and 252 a. Walter Forster left an infant son and heir

45 *V.C.H. Salop.* iii. 211; *Kelly's Dir. Salop.* (1913), 29; (1929), 31; S.R.O. 1147/1.

46 S.R.O., DA 6/119/1, pp. 360, 364.

47 Eyton, iii. 223–4, 279, 281–2; *V.C.H. Salop.* ii. 42; *Rot. Hund.* (Rec. Com.), ii. 85; *Bracton's Note Bk.* ed. Maitland, iii, pp. 239–40; below, M. Wenlock, econ. hist. (agric.); local govt.

48 S.R.O. 1224/3/135, f. 2; *L. & P. Hen. VIII*, xix (1), p. 638.

49 P.R.O., C 142/104, no. 89; *Cal. Pat.* 1578–80, p. 241; *V.C.H. Staffs.* xx. 130.

50 S. Shaw, *Hist. Staffs.* ii (1801), 129; *Hist. Parl., Commons*, 1558–1603, iii. 614–15; *Complete Peerage*, xii (2), 402, 404; *V.C.H. Staffs.* xx. 130, 133.

51 J. Randall, *Broseley and Its Surroundings* (Madeley, 1879), 299; P.R.O., CP 25/2/343/11 Jas. I Trin. [no. 22]. Cf. S.R.O. 775/151.

52 S.R.O. 775/77–137; q. sess. rec. box 260, reg. of gamekeepers 1742–79, 9 Oct. 1771; parcel 261, reg. of gamekeepers 1799–1807, ff. 11, 61, 82; Burke, *Peerage* (1938), 77–8; P.R.O., C 142/611, no. 120 (1).

53 S.R.O., incl. award B 38.

54 S. Bagshaw, *Dir. Salop.* (1851), 588; *P.O. Dir. Salop.* (1856), 86.

55 Inf. from Ld. Forester.

56 For what follows see S.R.O. 1224, box 67, abstr. of title.

57 P.R.O., C 142/561, no. 33.

58 S.R.O. 2991/Rg/4, Oct. 1752.

59 Inf. from Ld. Forester.

60 SA 11471.

61 Eyton, iii. 223; P.R.O., C 141/2, no. 19.

62 *Cal. Inq. p.m.* xiv, p. 304; cf. xvii, p. 23

63 Below, Broseley, manor.

64 Ibid.; Eyton, ii. 10, 15.

65 Eyton, ii. 12–13, 18, 36–7; iii. 272.

66 Ibid. ii. 12–13, 19, 22; below, Broseley, manor.

67 *Cal. Chart. and Rolls in Bodl.* ed. W. H. Turner and H. O. Coxe (1878), p. 385; *Cal. Inq. p.m.* xiv, p. 304; xv, p. 3; *V.C.H. Salop.* viii. 266.

68 P.R.O., C 141/2, no. 19; S.R.O. 665, box 42, deeds 10 July 1478, 25 Jan. 1484; *V.C.H. Salop.* viii. 143; Burke, *Land. Gent.* i (1846), 272. Cf. above, Ch. Stretton, manors (Minton).

69 *Cal. Inq. p.m. Hen. VII*, i, p. 476; S.R.O. 3365/165.

70 S.P.L., MS. 2, f. 12v.

George.[71] In 1681 Charles Forster of Vernhams Dean (Hants) sold Arlescott to the tenant, his kinsman Samuel Bowdler, and in 1691 Bowdler settled it on his daughter and heir, Joyce, on her marriage to Thomas Sprott (d. 1710). The Sprotts' son Henry succeeded to Arlescott and in 1721 came into possession of the Marsh house and demesnes, with which Arlescott thereafter descended.[72]

Arlescott Farm, taxed on seven hearths in 1672,[73] is probably late 16th- or early 17th-century. It stands on the east side of a small brick walled courtyard which in part may be late 16th-century. The courtyard is bounded on the west by an 18th-century stable and granary.

After Wenlock priory's surrender in 1540 its manor of *MARSH* remained with the Crown until 1554[74] when it was granted for life to Stephen Hadnall, a courtier.[75] Hadnall bought the reversion in fee in 1558,[76] died in 1580, and was survived by his wife Margaret who later married Serjeant Richard Lewkenor (kt. 1600).[77] In 1600 Hadnall's daughter and son-in-law Ann and Hampden Powlett sold Marsh to John Slaney, a London merchant tailor.[78] In 1620 Slaney sold Marsh to John Weld[79] (kt. 1642, d. 1666). In 1658–9 Weld evidently settled a joint life interest in the manor on his daughters Dorothy Weld (d. 1674) and Mary Saltonstall (d. probably in 1674), widow. Thereafter it descended with Willey.[80]

In 1540 the manor house of Marsh, with the demesne lands, was separated from the manor and sold to Thomas Lokier, a Bristol merchant.[81] Lokier (d. 1546) was succeeded by his son Thomas, on whose death in 1603 the house with 300 a.[82] passed to Thomas's son Francis (d. 1636).[83] Francis was succeeded by his son Thomas (d. 1676),[84] followed by Thomas's daughter Ann (d. 1721), relict of Henry Sprott of Ashmore Brook (Staffs.). At Ann's death the house and demesnes passed to her grandson, the Revd. Henry Sprott (d. 1744). He was succeeded by his brother Dr. Samuel Sprott (d. 1760), who left the estate to a nephew Thomas Yate (d. 1772). Yate was succeeded by a cousin Mrs. Elizabeth Toldervey (d. 1797) and she by Yate's son Samuel. Samuel, having taken the additional surname of Sprott, died in 1802, leaving the estate to a cousin's son William Moseley,[85] who sold it in 1816 to Cecil Weld-Forester[86] (cr. Baron Forester 1821).[87] It remained in the Willey estate in 1984.

The Marsh is an early 19th-century red brick house. Apparently incorporating rubble walls of an earlier building, it stands on the south side of a walled court which is in part 18th-century. In 1672 the Marsh had thirteen hearths.[88] A stone building, used as a barn and forming the west side of the court, is probably late 16th-century. It has three low storeys, and the east elevation has, besides several windows, three identical doorways which may imply that it was once a lodging. To the north of the buildings earthworks and ponds are probably the relics of a small 17th- or 18th-century garden.

PRESTENDEN, a member of Marsh manor *c.* 1523,[89] was among the lands of Wenlock priory held in the early 16th century by Arthur Plantagenet, Viscount Lisle (d. 1542) and may thus have passed to Sir John Smith;[90] in 1550 another John Smith, perhaps a son or grandson of that name, was lord of Prestenden.[91] In 1636 Francis Lokier of the Marsh died seised of Prestenden, and his son Thomas was given seisin in 1637, when Prestenden was said to be held of Walter Acton's manor of Barrow.[92] No later mention of Prestenden is known.

In 1446 Richard Lacon, lord of Willey, had a pasture called Prestenden.[93]

The *TITHES* belonged to Wenlock priory[94] and were surrendered to the Crown in 1540.[95]

In 1554 the Crown granted the great tithes of Arlescott and of Barrow to Stephen Hadnall (d. 1580) for life, and in 1581 sold them to two speculators.[96] Not long before 1631 John Clarke sold them (without the tithes of Barrow farm) to John Weld, lord of the manor of Marsh,[97] with which they seem to have descended thereafter.[98]

The great tithes of the Marsh demesnes descended from 1540 with that estate[99] but passed before 1773 to the lord of Marsh manor. Those of Barrow farm were sold in 1622 by Edward and Anne Littleton to Thomas Ruckley and descended with that estate until 1743 or later. They too belonged to the lord of Marsh by 1773.[1]

In an exchange of 1814 Cecil Weld-Forester

71 P.R.O., C 3/448, no. 25; C 142/337, no. 101; C 142/353, no. 71; W.B.R., M4/1; S.P.L., MS. 2790, p. 282; *Hist. Parl., Commons*, 1509–58, ii. 163–4 (wrongly identifying Thos. Forster as one of the Foresters of Watling St.); Turner and Coxe, *Chart. and Rolls in Bodl.* pp. 385–6.

72 S.R.O. 1224, box 74, abstr. of title of Wm. Moseley and deed of 1816; 1224/3/127–8; S.P.L., MS. 2790, p. 282; *V.C.H. Staffs.* xiv. 208; inf. from Ld. Forester; below, this section.

73 *Hearth Tax 1672*, 34.

74 *Cal. Pat.* 1554–5, 21; S.R.O. 1224/3/12, 14, 16.

75 *V.C.H. Salop.* ii. 45; S.R.O. 1224/3/19, 97.

76 S.R.O. 1224/3/13/1–2; /3/15; *Cal. Pat.* 1557–8, 378–9.

77 W. A. Shaw, *Kts. of Eng.* (1906), ii. 98; S.R.O. 1224/3/63–4; P.R.O., C 142/224, no. 32. Marsh ct., however, was held in Steph. Hadnall's name until 1589 or later: S.R.O. 1224/2/38–44.

78 S.R.O. 1224/3/71–3, 78, 84, 102, 126; *Cal. Pat.* 1578–80, p. 312.

79 S.R.O. 1224/3/98–100, 113, 131; box 163, John Weld's bk. 1631, f. 7.

80 S.R.O. 1224/2/47–344; 1224, parcel 385, Weld-Forester pedigree roll; 3568/Rg/1; inf. from Ld. Forester; cf. below, Willey, manor.

81 *L. & P. Hen. VIII*, xv, p. 468; S.R.O. 1224/3/9/1.

82 P.R.O., C 142/75, no. 73; C 142/281, no. 34.

83 S.P.L., Deeds 1542.

84 Ibid. 1501, 1509, 1542; *T.S.A.S.* xi. 46.

85 S.R.O. 1224, box 74, abstr. of title of Wm. Moseley; *V.C.H. Staffs.* xiv. 208; S.P.L., MS. 4081, pp. 2212–15.

86 S.R.O. 1224, box 74, deed.

87 *Complete Peerage*, v. 553.

88 *Hearth Tax 1672*, 34.

89 N.L.W., Wynnstay, RA 2.

90 S.R.O. 1224, box 342, Prior Gosnell's reg. f. 39; P.R.O., CP 25/2/35/233, no. 5; cf. above, Munslow, manors (Aston).

91 P.R.O., LR 2/184, f. 59; S.R.O. 757, box 69, deed of 1544; Burke, *Land. Gent.* (1925), 274.

92 S.P.L., Deeds 1542.

93 S.R.O. 1224/2/536.

94 Ibid. /3/8, ff. 4v.–5.

95 S.P.L., Deeds 8892, f. 1.

96 *Cal. Pat.* 1580–2, p. 5; above, this section (Marsh).

97 S.R.O. 1224, box 163, John Weld's bk. 1631, f. 8.

98 Shirlett Incl. Act, 1773, 13 Geo. III, c. 105 (Priv. Act).

99 *L. & P. Hen. VIII*, xv, p. 468; P.R.O., C 142/281, no. 34.

1 Shirlett Incl. Act, 1773; S.R.O. 1224, box 67, abstr. of title of 1812.

conveyed the impropriate tithes of 162 a. to Sir Ferdinand Acton.[2]

Lord Forester's impropriate tithes were commuted to £283 2*s.* in 1839. The only other impropriator was Sir John Dalberg-Acton, whose tithes were then merged and extinguished.[3]

ECONOMIC HISTORY. AGRICULTURE. In the Middle Ages the southern half of Barrow was wooded, the core of the royal forest of Shirlett, while the northern half was farm land. Between them lay Barrow's open fields and, north of them, the large freeholds of Arlescott and the Marsh.

Until 1301 Shirlett forest extended *c.* 20 km. from Buildwas in the north to Aston Botterell in the south, and *c.* 9 km. west from the Severn. That year the forest charter reduced it to two hays, one of which, Shirlett,[4] occupied the southern half of Barrow and the northern ends of Acton Round and Morville.[5] Over a century before, in 1190, the prior of Wenlock had paid 20 marks to remove his demesne wood in Shirlett from the royal forest.[6] Presumably that was the later Prior's wood covering most of the south-western part of what eventually became Barrow parish.[7] In the 13th century the priory was assarting there;[8] in the 14th century it had a woodward whose duties included allotting housebote and hedgebote.[9] In 1379–80 18 people paid pannage for 178 pigs; peat was cut and probably bees yielded honey. Browsing of goats was restricted, if not banned altogether.[10] The Crown exploited its woodland in the normal way, selling underwood[11] and, in the 13th century at least, granting oaks to local people and local religious houses.[12] In 1557 the woodward general authorized the sale of 100 old trees from Shirlett to the poor for fuel.[13]

At the Dissolution Wenlock priory's part of Shirlett covered *c.* 910 a. and was said to contain only oaks and to be without deer, although pigs were pannaged by commoners. Some income also came from the sale of dead oaks.[14] Priory tenants still received wood from the woodward.[15] Bounding Prior's wood were the other divisions of Shirlett: Willey Heald or Hill (*c.* 340 a.), a ½-km.-wide strip down the east side of Barrow; King's Hay (*c.* 698 a.) in the northern part of Morville; and Earl's wood (*c.* 411 a.) in the northern part of Acton Round.[16] With the break-up of the priory estate ancient common rights were frequently the subject of litigation. In 1554 the Crown ordered a recently inclosed wood on Barrow hill to be thrown open.[17] Stephen Hadnall, who bought Marsh manor from the Crown later that year, sought to clarify the bounds of Shirlett in 1562 and 1568, and throughout the 1570s and 1580s he was involved in a series of disputes over Shirlett, particularly Prior's wood, and the extent of his manorial jurisdiction there.[18] Hadnall's successors as lords of Marsh, Hampden Powlett and John Slaney, were similarly embroiled in the late 1590s, early 1600s, and 1609–11.[19] Common rights nevertheless survived. In the late 16th and early 17th century the inhabitants of Barrow, Atterley, Walton, and Willey were entitled to wood from Shirlett and could pannage ringed swine there; food offerings were due to the lord of Marsh at certain times of year in return for wood, and cash in respect of each pig killed or sold.[20] In 1618 tenants of the manor owed the carting of 140 loads of wood from Shirlett to Willey Hall.[21] Possibly there were then few standards, for in 1619 John Weld, the new lord of Willey, intended to sow acorns.[22] Certainly there was some clearance about then, and 50 a. were inclosed as small plots for tillage.[23]

In 1625 Shirlett, 2,300 a. of waste and commons, was divided between the surrounding manors.[24] In Barrow John Weld, lord of Willey and Marsh, received 410 a., i.e. almost all of Willey Heald and part of Prior's wood; the Willey commoners (including those of the Bold and Dean) obtained 300 a., i.e. the rest of Willey Heald and a large central area of Prior's wood; Francis Lokier of the Marsh received 102 a., the northern tip of Prior's wood. The Barrow commoners received 100 a. at the northern ends of Prior's wood and Willey Heald, the Atterley and Walton commoners 100 a. for each vill on the western edge of Barrow (Prior's wood). The commons at the south end of Barrow were divided between the commoners of Astley Abbots[25] and those of Haughton Croft and Kingsley in Morville parish.[26] Walter Acton (*inter alia* as lord of Barrow, Atterley, and Walton)[27] received an allotment of 350 a. in King's Hay where Aldenham Park was later made. Nevertheless only land allotted to the manorial lords (Weld and Acton) and to Francis Lokier and freeholders in Barrow, in all *c.* 1,112 a., could be inclosed; the rest were to remain open. Lokier and the Barrow freeholders apparently soon inclosed

2 S.R.O., incl. award B 38.
3 P.R.O., IR 29/29/28.
4 Eyton, iii. 297–8; *Cartulary of Shrews. Abbey*, ed. U. Rees (1975), ii, pp. 245–51.
5 Below, this section.
6 Eyton, iii. 296; *Cal. Chart. R.* 1226–57, 17; *Itin. of Ric. I* (P.R.S. N.S. xiii), pl. facing p. 174.
7 S.R.O. 1224/1/15.
8 *V.C.H. Salop.* ii. 41; P.R.O., C 143/2, no. 16.
9 Mumford, *Wenlock in Middle Ages*, 154.
10 Ibid. 72, 170, 172; S.R.O. 1224/2/1–9.
11 *Cal. Pat.* 1247–58, 115.
12 *V.C.H. Salop.* i. 490; ii. 56, 89, 98; iv. 47.
13 Ibid. i. 492.
14 S.R.O. 1224/3/8, ff. 6, 8. For sale of oaks in 1556–7 see *V.C.H. Salop.* i. 492.
15 S.R.O. 1224/3/24.
16 Ibid. /1/15.
17 P.R.O., SC 2/197/148, m. 9.
18 S.R.O. 1224/3/22–54.
19 Ibid. /3/66–9, 74–7, 79–81, 83, 86–95.
20 S.R.O. 1175/1. For ringing see S.R.O. 1224/2/367.
21 M. D. G. Wanklyn, 'John Weld of Willey 1585–1665', *W. Midlands Studies*, iii. 89.
22 S.R.O. 1224, box 163, Mr. Weld's memo. bk. 1619/20, f. 19.
23 S.P.L., MS. 8892.
24 What follows based on S.R.O. 1093/2/453–4; 1224/1/15; box 147, award; box 163, articles of 1625; 1952/11; S.P.L., MS. 8891. Cf. fig. 21.
25 Their Shirlett commons, extending also over the N. tip of Morville par. (King's Hay), amounted to *c.* 200 a. being then distinct from their 307 a. of commons in Astley Abbots: S.R.O. 1224/1/16–17.
26 And ancient members of Astley Abbots man. (cf. Eyton, i. 43, 50–4). Their commons (250 a.) extended W. from Barrow into Acton Round par. (Earl's wood) and S. and E. into Morville par. (King's Hay).
27 Above, manors.

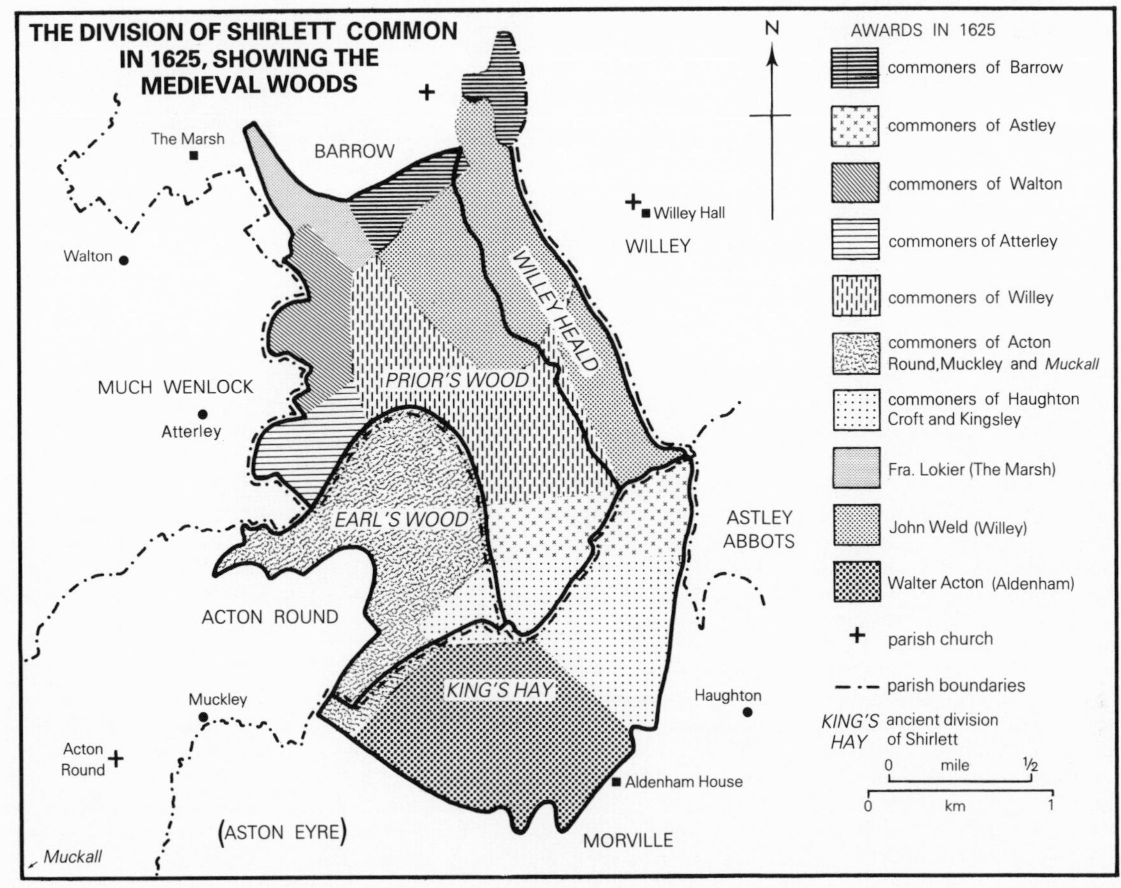

Fig. 21

their allotments, as did Weld who largely incorporated his in his new park at Willey. All Weld's portions were bounded with a pale.[28] Abuses continued: in 1631 the inhabitants of Barrow still put cattle on others' commons.[29] In 1775 the remaining Shirlett commons in Barrow and Morville parishes, perhaps some 662 a.,[30] were inclosed by Act,[31] most of the new inclosures there going to Sir Richard Acton (201 a.), George Forester (155 a.), and Thomas Whitmore (90 a.) in respect of common rights belonging to their properties in Walton and Atterley, Willey, Haughton Croft and Kinsley, and Astley Abbots.

Barrow's open-field land was mentioned in 1262 and 1321–2.[32] In 1340 it was said that corn was deficient after an unfavourable season, that there were no sheep, and that several peasants were too poor to till their lands.[33] In the 16th and early 17th century Shirlett and Cross fields were mentioned;[34] Shirlett field lay west of Barrow church,[35] and other open-field land lay north, east, and perhaps south-west of the church. Final inclosure probably occurred in the 17th century.[36]

The Marsh demesne was cultivated separately in the Middle Ages and later. In 1369 and 1379 it was estimated as 2 carucates (*c.* 240 a.) and was cropped in a three-course rotation.[37] In 1468 Wenlock priory leased the Marsh to William Clerk, Wenlock's first known M.P.; the lease was renewed in 1475.[38] Arlescott too had its own land: 2 carucates in 1229.[39] Lynchets lie north-east of Arlescott Farm.[40] In the later 17th century Arlescott was a rich farm, with cattle worth £150, horses (£60), sheep (£29), and corn (£26) in 1677.[41]

By 1608 leases for three lives were being granted in Barrow. The lord exacted terciary and heriot. One condition of a lease of 1769 required

28 S.R.O. 1224/1/14 (the Plankes), 15; box 163, articles of 1625 (marginalia); cf. below, Willey, econ. hist. (agric.).
29 S.R.O. 1224/2/64.
30 i.e. the 854 a. inclosed minus the 192 a. inclosed from Nordley wood, Colemoor green, and Dunnelley's common in Astley Abbots.
31 Shirlett Incl. Act, 1773; S.R.O. 1224, box 147, award.
32 Mumford, *Wenlock in Middle Ages*, 172; P.R.O., C 143/2, no. 16.
33 *Inq. Non.* (Rec. Com.), 187.
34 S.R.O. 1093/2/459; 1224/2/19; box 67, abstract of title.
35 S.R.O. 1093, parcel 161, Barrow map of 1721.
36 Field names: S.R.O. 1093/2/459; parcel 161, Barrow map of 1721; /2/49; box 67, abstr. of title.
37 B.L. Add. MSS. 6164, p. 382; 6165, p. 97. Mumford, *Wenlock in Middle Ages*, 60, wrongly gives the fig. as three.
38 S.R.O. 1224, box 342, Prior Gosnell's reg. f. 16v.; *V.C.H. Salop.* iii. 247.
39 *Cal. Close*, 1227–31, 251.
40 SA 661.
41 S.P.L., Deeds 1549.

the tenant to be ready to keep a hound or spaniel for Sir Richard Acton.[42] In 1785 leases for three lives were introduced for all Shirlett cottagers on the Forester estate. The uniformity did not last long and in the early 19th century, as before 1785, various short-term leases were created.[43]

In the 1720s most land (348 a.) around Barrow hamlet, apart from Barrow farm, was owned by Sir Whitmore Acton and was divided into four scattered farms, two of *c.* 110 a., and two of *c.* 60 a. Acton also owned six smallholdings on *c.* 13 a.[44] In 1814 much of Sir Ferdinand Acton's land in Barrow passed to Cecil Weld-Forester by exchange,[45] and by 1828, following the acquisition of the Marsh and Arlescott farms (in all 736 a.) from William Moseley and of Barrow farm (112 a.) from the Keys, J. G. W. Weld-Forester, Lord Forester, was virtually the sole landowner in Barrow.[46] The former Acton land had been taken into Barrow farm, then 440 a.; the Marsh extended to 412 a., Arlescott to 312 a., and two Shirlett farms to 141 a. and 54 a. There were three smallholdings of 14–24 a. and *c.* 25 of under 10 a.; most of the last were west of Shirlett where commons had been inclosed by Act of 1773.[47]

By 1910 Arlescott, Barrow, and the Marsh farms had been reduced to 264 a., 346 a., and 290 a. respectively. Smallholding land had increased correspondingly: there were 5 holdings of 20– 30 a., 12 of 10–20 a., and 20 under 10 a.[48] Later the number of smallholdings fell, and by 1965 only six agricultural holdings had fewer than 30 a.[49]

In 1801 twice as much wheat as barley and oats was grown.[50] In 1838 48 per cent of Barrow was arable, 32 per cent meadow and pasture, and 20 per cent woodland.[51] By 1867 three times as much grassland as arable was recorded, and only after the Second World War did the amount of arable again approach its early 19th-century level. Between the mid 19th and mid 20th centuries barley replaced wheat as the main cereal. The proportion of cattle among livestock remained fairly constant, while pigs became more numerous than sheep or cattle.

INDUSTRY. A smithy in Shirlett was occupied by John Myston and Thomas Venymer *c.* 1532; they paid £13 rent to Wenlock priory, and the priory also received £5 13*s.* from the quarrying of stone, presumably ironstone.[52] In 1532 the priory let a smithy in Shirlett, near the house of Thomas Ellestone, in Marsh manor, to the Caughley ironmaster Thomas Munslow. The furnace was to be supplied with ironstone from Shirlett and wood from Willey and Caughley.[53]

TABLE XIII

BARROW: LAND USE, LIVESTOCK, AND CROPS

		1867	*1891*	*1938*	*1965*
Percentage of	grassland	73	76	80	58
	arable	27	24	20	42
Percentage of	cattle	17	24	19	19
	sheep	68	64	71	34
	pigs	15	12	10	47
Percentage of	wheat	57	43	62	30
	barley	26	35	1	59
	oats	17	22	37	11
	mixed corn & rye	0	0	0	0
Percentage of agricultural land growing roots and vegetables		7	7	8	6

Sources: P.R.O., MAF 68/143, no. 15; /1340, no. 5; /3880, Salop. no. 257; /4945, no. 257.

The works, called a forge, was leased by the Crown to Reginald and Thomas Ridley in 1541 and in 1554 Stephen Hadnall was granted the reversion. At the same time the Crown granted Hadnall a second Shirlett forge, occupied by Alexander Wood;[54] that was perhaps the 'new smithy' noted in 1552.[55] In the 1550s ironstone was mined at Barrow hill and Willey Heald.[56]

Mineral rights passed with Marsh manor to John Weld in 1620.[57] Weld intended to sell ironstone and to let a coalpit, both probably in Shirlett. The Shirlett agreement of 1625 gave the manorial lords sole rights to dig for coal, ironstone, and 'slate', though obliging them to repair damaged roads and fill worked-out pits.[58] The main coal-producing area, worked by William Porter, then lay on the south-western boundary of Barrow and extended into Acton Round. An area called White Mines lay 0.5 km. north, with a 'footrid' nearby.[59]

By 1630 Weld, as lord of Marsh, had increased the ironstone yield and installed a sough to drain the coal delph.[60] His annual income from the Marsh then included £50 a year from coal and *c.* £40 from ironstone.[61] Weld was aware that

42 S.R.O. 775/151, 238.
43 S.R.O. 1224, boxes 141–2, deeds *passim*.
44 Above, manors; S.R.O. 836/23, f. 26; 1093, parcel 161, Barrow map of 1721.
45 Above, manors; below, M. Wenlock, manors; S.R.O. 1224/1/50; box 162, bdle. *re* exchange.
46 S.R.O. 515/5, pp. 80–1; /10, pp. 37–40; 1224/7/44, f. 6; above, manors.
47 S.R.O. 1224/7/44, ff. 4–6; 1681/177/14, Geo. Price's evid. f. 1; above, this article, intro.; above, this section.
48 S.R.O. 4044/89, f. 1v.
49 P.R.O., MAF 68/4945, no. 257.
50 P.R.O., HO 67/12/17.
51 P.R.O., IR 29/29/28. The total (3,013 a.) suggests that the surv. incl. Caughley. Rest of para. based on Table XIII.
52 N.L.W., Wynnstay, RA 2.
53 S.R.O. 1224/3/6. See also Dugdale, *Mon.* v. 81; *V.C.H. Salop.* ii. 44; S.R.O. 1224/3/8, f. 6; P.R.O., E 303/14/Salop. no. 263; below, Caughley, econ. hist. (ind.).
54 S.R.O. 1224/3/12, 97.
55 *T.S.A.S.* vi. 108.
56 *Cal. Pat.* 1557–8, 379; S.R.O. 3898/Rg/1, 28 May 1559, 18 Sept. 1561.
57 Above, manors (Marsh), and sources there cited.
58 S.R.O. 1224, box 163, Mr. Weld's memo. bk. 1619/20, f. 19; above, this section (agric.).
59 *V.C.H. Salop.* i. 459; S.R.O. 1224/1/15. See fig. 20.
60 S.R.O. 1224, box 163, J. Weld's bk. 1631, f. 6.
61 Ibid. f. 6 and figs. at end.

unexploited reserves of coal and ironstone, the latter saleable to Sir Richard Newport,[62] lay under Barrow hill, Atterley, and Francis Lokier's Marsh demesne.[63] Cottagers were digging coal at Barrow green by 1639, and small pits proliferated in Shirlett in the 1670s.[64] As in other coalfield parishes,[65] smallholders combined mining or coal carrying with agriculture. Anthony Jenks (d. 1663), of Barrow, left personalty worth £27 3*s.* 6*d.*, including 4 horses, 2 pigs, 6 lambs, 3 hens, hay, fodder, and clover, coal-working tools (including three picks), coal sacks, and four pack saddles.[66]

Limited coal and ironstone mining probably continued in the 18th and 19th centuries. In 1702 George Weld obtained the right to make a sough draining on to Edward Acton's land at Aldenham from a prospective coal and ironstone mine in Shirlett.[67] A month later Weld leased mining rights in Shirlett to William Daughton of Willey, Joseph Read of Atterley, and Nicholas Harrison of Broseley on condition that they supplied reasonably priced ironstone to Willey furnace.[68] In 1711 the tenant of Willey furnace was allowed to mine ironstone in Willey new park.[69] Agreements of 1757 and 1759 between George Forester and the New Willey Co. allowed the company to dig coal and ironstone in Barrow.[70] Furnacemen and colliers were among the parish's cottagers in 1785,[71] and some coal was still got in Barrow *c.* 1800.[72]

There was a quarry south of Maypole Bank in the late 19th century.[73]

LOCAL GOVERNMENT. Marsh manor court existed by 1291.[74] In the Middle Ages its jurisdiction evidently coincided with the area of Wenlock priory's Marsh grange,[75] which originally consisted of Atterley, Walton, and Barrow and was enlarged between 1379 and 1390 to include Bradley grange (Wyke, Bradley, Posenhall, Benthall, Wigwig, and part of Harley) and at some time between 1379 and 1540 to include the Broseley 'Priory land' and probably Caughley. The demesne part of Presthope was apparently in Marsh manor by 1540.[76] Records survive for 1334, 1344–5, 1379–80, 1403, 1411–12, 1420–1, 1431, 1449, 1477, 1482, and 1530. Several Marsh court rolls survive from most decades after 1540 and large numbers from the years 1620–1840.[77]

It seems likely that the one court had originally both 'baron' jurisdiction (withdrawn from Much Wenlock manor after 1255)[78] and some limited 'leet' jurisdiction, which did not involve more than hearing breaches of the assize of ale (e.g. in 1403)[79] and electing constables for the member townships (e.g. for Barrow in 1477).[80] Most business concerned agricultural matters such as encroachment and making waste, and many presentments were made of vert and pannaging offences in Shirlett.[81] The court often met at Wyke (in Much Wenlock) in the later 16th and early 17th century,[82] and surviving records of the 1580s call the manor Wyke.[83]

In 1554 Marsh manor was deemed to have leet jurisdiction over every place that had been in the manor at any time before the Dissolution; in 1568, however, there was some uncertainty as to Marsh's former constituents.[84]

The court's interests and ambitions widened in the early 17th century: regular presentments began to be made of breaches of the assize of ale.[85] In 1619 John Weld intended to 'keep a leet' for Shirlett[86] and in 1620 started to call Marsh court a 'court leet and court baron'.[87] In 1622–3 only Posenhall, Shirlett, the Smithies (in Willey), and Wyke and Bradley presented,[88] but from 1634, evidently under an agreement that year between Weld and Charles Baldwyn, lord of Bourton hundred,[89] Barrow (probably including Caughley),[90] Atterley and Walton, Broseley (probably the 'Priory land' only),[91] Wigwig and Harley, and Willey also began to make regular presentments to Marsh court leet.[92] In effect Weld bought Baldwyn's claim to those places as parts of Bourton hundred. Presthope and properties in Benthall and Broseley had also been discussed,[93] but Presthope stayed under the jurisdiction of Bourton hundred[94] despite Weld's attempts until 1640 (unsuccessfully except in 1635) to exact the suit of its inhabitants,[95] and relations between Marsh and Benthall manors, whereby Benthall was held in socage of Marsh manor for 4*s.* 6*d.* a year and suit to Marsh leet, were agreed in 1637.[96]

The court's main concerns were the assize of

62 Presumably for his Leighton furnace, blown in *c.* 1632: inf. from Mr. J. B. Lawson.
63 S.R.O. 1224, box 163, John Weld's bk. 1631, f. 6v.
64 S.R.O. 1224/2/83, 116.
65 *Yeomen and Colliers in Telford*, ed. B. Trinder and J. Cox (1980), pp. 70–2; *V.C.H. Salop.* xi. 328.
66 H.W.R.O.(H.), Heref. dioc. rec., inv. of Ant. Jenks, 1663.
67 S.R.O. 1093/2/456.
68 S.R.O. 1224, box 141, deed 4 July 1702.
69 Ibid. box 140, deed 16 Oct. 1711.
70 Ibid. box 143, deeds 13 June 1757, 24 Sept. 1759; below, Willey, econ. hist. (coal and ironstone).
71 S.R.O. 1224, boxes 141–2, leases of 1785.
72 J. Plymley, *Gen. View of Agric. of Salop.* (1803), 52; S.R.O. 1681/177/14, Geo. Price's evid. f. 1.
73 O.S. Map 6", Salop. LI. SW. (1883 edn.).
74 *Tax. Eccl.* (Rec. Com.), 164.
75 S.R.O. 1190/1, unlisted ct. r. 1403–4; 1224/2/1, 6, 16.
76 Below, Broseley, local govt.; M. Wenlock, manors (Presthope); econ. hist. (agric.).
77 S.R.O. 566/1; 840, box 1, Marsh ct. r. 1641–71; 1190/1, unlisted ct. r. 1403–4; 1224/2/1–344; P.R.O., SC 2/197/117; SC 2/197/148, mm. 7, 9; Mumford, *Wenlock in Middle Ages*, 62.
78 Below, M. Wenlock, local govt.
79 S.R.O. 1190/1, unlisted ct. r. 1403–4
80 S.R.O. 1224/2/6.
81 e.g. ibid. /2/19–43.
82 Ibid. /2/21–3, 25, 27, 30–1, 34, 36, 44.
83 Ibid. /2/38, 531–3.
84 Ibid. /3/12, 24.
85 Ibid. /2/50.
86 S.R.O. 1224, box 163, Mr. Weld's memo. bk. 1619/20, f. 19.
87 S.R.O. 1224/2/48, 50 sqq.
88 Ibid. /2/52, 54.
89 Cf. ibid. /2/65–6 (Marsh ct. r. 8 Oct. 1634); /3/101.
90 S.R.O. 1224, box 75, interrogatories in Weld *v.* Dawes 2 Oct. 1652, no. 2; S.R.O. 840, box 1, Marsh ct. r. of 1641, ff. 2, 4.
91 Below, Broseley, local govt.
92 S.R.O. 1224/2/65–9.
93 Ibid. /2/65–6.
94 Ibid. /2/376, 390–2, 396–8, 400–1, 404, 406, 411–12, 419–22, 427.
95 Ibid. /2/65–88.
96 S.P.L., Deeds 18120; cf. below, Benthall, local govt.

ale, pannaging, taking in lodgers, and the appointment of constables; it also dealt with the reservation of minor game and bees to the lord, with failures to keep up shooting butts, bows and arrows, and with minor breaches of the peace. In 1624 Phoebe Coulton was presented as a scold and for cursing a man and his cattle.[97] The court met in Broseley in the 1640s and earlier 1650s, but Hangstree Gate was the usual meeting place from 1655 or 1656.[98] By the early 18th century two Coalbrookdale farms also did suit to the court. Presentments by then were few, apart from cottage encroachments on the waste.[99] A separate constable was elected for Caughley from 1792.[1] The court last met at Hangstree Gate in 1811, shortly before the settlement was cleared away; thereafter it met in Broseley again.[2] After 1816 the court met once a year; previously, since at least the 1590s, it had met twice yearly.[3] Records cease in 1840,[4] though the court still met at the Lion in Broseley *c.* 1879. It appointed 31 constables but neither they nor the court retained any function.[5]

In 1619 John Weld planned to erect a pound for Shirlett,[6] and there was a pound at Marsh Green *c.* 1625.[7] There was a pound for the manor of Barrow, Atterley, and Walton north of the church in 1721.[8]

A separate court baron for Barrow, Atterley, and Walton probably began to be held following their acquisition by William Whorwood in 1544,[9] although the three places presented at Marsh leet from 1634.[10] In 1602 the court baron was being held twice yearly.[11] In the late 17th century presentments were mainly agricultural. In the late 18th century the few presentments at the twice yearly court were for encroachment. Presentment ceased in the early 19th century although suit continued to be exacted until 1836 or later.[12] Sir Ferdinand Acton retained the right to hold a court baron for Barrow after the 1814 exchange of lands with Cecil Weld-Forester.[13]

Two churchwardens were apparently appointed (from 1629) by rotation, and there was a highway surveyor in 1635. By the 1650s two surveyors and two overseers of the poor were appointed annually.[14] Barrow vestry remained a highway authority until 1889.[15]

In the years 1812–15 *c.* 45 people usually received permanent out-relief and another 30 or so occasional relief. Expenditure on the poor after 1816, when it was £320 10*s*., was almost always over £400 and sometimes over £500.[16] In 1822 the Barrow overseers occupied part of Caughley Place (formerly Thomas Turner's house), presumably as a poor house.[17]

Barrow was in Madeley poor-law union 1836–1930[18] and in Madeley rural sanitary district from 1872[19] until 1889, when it was included in the Barrow ward and sanitary division of the borough of Wenlock,[20] under a largely autonomous district committee.[21] After the dissolution of Wenlock M.B. in 1966 Barrow C.P.[22] was in Bridgnorth rural district until 1974[23] and Bridgnorth district thereafter.[24]

Barrow was within the jurisdiction of the Broseley court of requests from 1782[25] until its abolition under the County Courts Act, 1846.[26]

CHURCH. Barrow was part of the large parish of Holy Trinity, Much Wenlock. Probably by the mid 11th century the minster at Much Wenlock had built a chapel at Barrow.[27] By 1277 Wenlock priory was presenting a rector of Barrow chapel[28] who presumably received the tithes of Barrow. In 1283 the priory reasserted Wenlock's ancient parochial rights and the rector was reduced to the status of chaplain, owing dues to the vicar of Much Wenlock, who was declared to have cure of souls in Barrow.[29] In 1321 the prior appointed a chaplain to serve Barrow and evidently Posenhall, either personally or through another, demising to him all the chapel's lands and the altarages and offerings.[30] That arrangement may have been encouraged by the Crown in 1349–50, exercising the alien priory's patronage of Barrow chapel. By 1540 the priory seems to have conceived of Marsh manor as also a parish, centred on Barrow church.[31] Nevertheless Barrow chapel reverted to being, or remained, a dependency of Holy Trinity, Much Wenlock, until the early 17th century.[32] It had a graveyard in 1568 and burial rights by 1611.[33] At that time Barrow was still occasionally said to be in 'Marsh' parish.[34]

Patronage of the chaplaincy remained with Wenlock priory until it surrendered in 1540,

97 S.R.O. 1224/2/347, 349–51.
98 Cf. ibid. /2/87 sqq.
99 Ibid. /2/151; *V.C.H. Salop.* xi. 37.
1 Cf. S.R.O. 1224/2/270–1.
2 Below, Willey, intro.; above, this article, intro.; econ. hist. (agric.); S.R.O. 1224/2/310–11.
3 Cf. S.R.O. 1224/2/319–21; /3/135, f. 5.
4 Ibid. /2/344.
5 Randall, *Broseley*, 34.
6 S.R.O. 1224, box 163, Mr. Weld's memo. bk. 1619/20, f. 19.
7 S.R.O. 1224/1/25.
8 S.R.O. 1093, bdle. 161, Barrow map of 1721.
9 S.R.O. 1175/1, Anne Heely's answers; above, manors (Barrow, Atterley, and Walton).
10 Above, this section.
11 S.R.O. 1093/2/459.
12 S.R.O. 775/85–6, 110, 112, 121–50.
13 S.R.O. 1224/1/50; box 162, bdle. *re* exchange 1812–14; above, manors (Barrow, Atterley, and Walton).
14 S.R.O. 2992/ChW/1, s.a.
15 Local Govt. Bd.'s Prov. Order Conf. (No. 4) Act, 1889, 52 & 53 Vic. c. 22 (Local).
16 *Poor Law Abstract*, H.C. 82, pp. 376–7 (1818), xix; *Poor Law Returns*, H.C. 556, suppl. app. p. 143 (1822), v; H.C. 334, p. 179 (1825), iv; H.C. 219, p. 167 (1830–1), xi; H.C. 444, p. 162 (1835), xlvii.
17 S.R.O. 1224/7/41.
18 V. J. Walsh, 'Admin. of Poor Laws in Salop. 1820–55' (Pennsylvania Univ. Ph.D. thesis, 1970), 148–50; *Kelly's Dir. Salop.* (1929), 31.
19 *V.C.H. Salop.* ii. 216.
20 Ibid. 204 (corr. below, Corrigenda), 215 (corr. ibid. xi. 376).
21 W.B.R., Barrow dist. cttee. min. bks. 1889–1966.
22 Enlarged: above, this article, intro.
23 *V.C.H. Salop.* ii. 236.
24 Sources cited ibid. iii. 169 n. 29.
25 Broseley, etc., Small Debts Act, 1782, 22 Geo. III, c. 37.
26 9 & 10 Vic., c. 95.
27 Below, this section; M. Wenlock, churches.
28 Eyton, iii. 280.
29 *Reg. Swinfield* (C.S.), 62.
30 Eyton, iii. 281; Mumford, *Wenlock in Middle Ages*, 171–2.
31 *Cal. Pat.* 1348–50, 372, 468; P.R.O., SC 6/Hen. VIII/3021, mm. 8, 9d.
32 *Cal. Pat.* 1575–8, p. 282; S.R.O. 1037/19/21.
33 *Cal. Pat.* 1566–9, p. 163; P.R.O., E 178/1879; S.R.O. 2992/1/1.
34 e.g. *Cal. Pat.* 1575–8, p. 282.

although Wenlock's alien status allowed the Crown to present.[35] After 1540 officiating ministers were apparently appointed by the vicar of Much Wenlock.[36] In the mid 17th century the inhabitants of Posenhall attended Barrow church and made payments to the minister there, and by then Barrow was frequently under the care of the rector of Willey; the two livings were formally united in 1822.[37] In 1835 Barrow was described as a perpetual curacy annexed to the rectory of Willey.[38] The united benefice of Linley with Willey and Barrow was created in 1976.[39]

In 1601 the minister received an income from small tithes and Easter offerings,[40] and between 1611, or earlier, and 1616 he received burial fees by consent of Much Wenlock vestry.[41] A commission of inquiry into Shropshire livings and parishes, probably that appointed in 1649,[42] found that the church had little value and no glebe or tithes. The minister's income comprised Easter offerings and money given by some parishioners in lieu of small tithes; it came to some £7 or £8 a year and was augmented by parishioners' money gifts. Proposals to combine Barrow with other livings came to nothing. Between 1671 and 1734 communicants (other than the principal ratepayers and the poor) paid the churchwardens church pence of 2*d.* towards church expenses; between 7*s.* and £1 a year was usually raised,[43] payments which presumably explain the statement in 1668 that the minister was paid 'by custom'.[44] The importance of church pence declined after 1709, when they produced 7*s.* 6*d.* while the nine ratepayers contributed £4 5*s.* 4*d.* In 1716 the living was said to be worth £5.[45] It was augmented five times between 1745 and 1810 by Queen Anne's Bounty.[46] In 1783 a 43-a. farm in Clee Stanton was bought, and the living was worth *c.* £28 a year *c.* 1790.[47] In 1839 the minister's income from customary payments (including 18*s.* from Caughley and 8*s.* from Swinney) was commuted to a rent charge of £3 15*s.* 2*d.* on certain lands,[48] and in 1851 his total income in respect of Barrow parish was £56.[49] The Clee Stanton farm was sold in 1855.[50]

There may have been a chaplain's house in 1321, when the chaplain was required to build a new barn in the rectory close at Barrow and to maintain other 'buildings' there.[51] In 1716, 1819, and probably at other times the minister lived in the school house at Barrow school, where he was the master.[52] In 1740, on his arrival as incumbent, John Fayle bought a house in Barrow.[53] The 'old clergyman's house' on the bank between Barrow and Willey was demolished in 1816, apparently because it was visible from the new Willey Hall.[54]

The first known incumbent, John de Wicumbe, was not in holy orders and his living was sequestrated.[55] James de Tyceford, deprived in 1284, was perhaps related to the prior of Wenlock.[56] Richard, who had died or resigned by 1321, appears to have officiated at Barrow as an appointee of the prior.[57] In 1321 Hamon Corn became incumbent by an agreement made in the prior's court. He, or another priest, and a clerk were to serve the chapel, Hamon receiving all lands and tenements belonging to it there and in Posenhall, with altarages and offerings; he was to maintain all the glebe buildings in Barrow and Posenhall, receiving housebote and hedgebote from the prior's woodward and firebote when resident, and was to pay the prior a rent of twelve capons a year.[58]

In or before the 1520s a boy fell into St. Mildburg's well in Much Wenlock. Among the actions taken to revive him was a barefoot pilgrimage by his father and monks from Wenlock to Barrow.[59] In 1547 an image of the Blessed Virgin from Barrow was burnt in Much Wenlock market place.[60] Thomas Acton *alias* Doughtie (d. 1551), a former monk of Wenlock, conducted a wedding at Barrow in 1549 perhaps as the regular minister.[61] Randal Massey (d. 1592), schooled in Much Wenlock in his youth, was curate at Barrow in 1563.[62]

In the 1630s communion was celebrated four times a year.[63] Richard Knott, curate in 1642, signed the Shropshire presbyterian ministers' *Testimony* (1648) but conformed in 1662.[64] In 1649 he preached once a Sunday at Barrow and Willey.[65] From the 1680s the rector of Willey served Barrow.[66] In the 1670s communion began to be celebrated five times a year, increasing to six times (though not invariably) in the late 1690s. Large amounts of wine were bought, 8 qt. for Easter 1692. At Christmas 1695 the borough bailiff and a magistrate received communion at Barrow separately from the parishioners.[67] In 1716 there was a morning service every Sunday and an afternoon service every other Sunday, with communion six times a year.[68]

In 1756 the parishioners proceeded against

35 Ibid. 1348–50, 372, 468; Eyton, iii. 280–1; Mumford, *Wenlock in Middle Ages*, 171–2; S.R.O. 1037/19/1.
36 L. F. Peltor, *Pars. of Willey and Barrow* (Glouc. 1966; copy in S.P.L.).
37 Ibid.; below, Posenhall, chapel of ease; Willey, church.
38 Lewis, *Topog. Dict. Eng.* (1835).
39 Heref. Dioc. Regy, reg. 1969– (in use), pp. 228–9.
40 S.R.O. 1175/1, Anne Heely's answers.
41 S.R.O. 2992/1/1.
42 For that see *T.S.A.S.* 3rd ser. vii. 279.
43 S.R.O. 1224, box 163, 'Inf. of parishioners of Barrow to commissioners [etc.]'; 2992/ChW/1.
44 H.W.R.O.(H.), HD 7, 1668/402.
45 Ibid. HD 5/14/1/6; S.R.O. 2992/ChW/1.
46 C. Hodgson, *Q. Anne's Bounty* (2nd edn.), pp. clxxiv, cclxxix.
47 S.R.O. 2992/Ben/1; Downton Hall muniments, abstr. of title to Stocking fm.
48 P.R.O., IR 29/29/28.
49 P.R.O., HO 129/358, no. 39.
50 Downton Hall muniments, deed 19 Nov. 1855.
51 Mumford, *Wenlock in Middle Ages*, 171.
52 H.W.R.O.(H.), HD 5/14/1/6; below, educ.
53 S.R.O. 2992/1/2, verso of front endpaper.
54 S.R.O. 2992, TS. on par. chars.
55 Eyton, iii. 280.
56 Ibid.; *V.C.H. Salop.* ii. 46.
57 Eyton, iii. 281.
58 Ibid.; Mumford, *Wenlock in Middle Ages*, 171–2.
59 Mumford, op. cit. 148.
60 *T.S.A.S.* vi. 120.
61 Ibid. 107, 121; lx. 99; Mumford, op. cit. 178.
62 *T.S.A.S.* lx. 105.
63 S.R.O. 2992/ChW/1.
64 *Calamy Revised*, ed. A. G. Matthews, 556; Ho. of Lords papers 1641–2, Protestations Oxon. and Salop. f. 181; R. F. Skinner, *Nonconf. in Salop.* (Shrews. 1964), 102.
65 S.R.O. 1224, box 163, 'Inf. of parishioners of Barrow to commissioners [etc.]'.
66 Below, Willey, church.
67 S.R.O. 2992/ChW/1, s.a.
68 H.W.R.O.(H.), HD 5/14/1/6.

John Fayle, minister 1740–71 and rector of Beckbury from 1754, for neglecting to read prayers; proceedings were later dropped,[69] but Fayle began to employ curates.[70] In 1778–9 a psalm teacher was employed.[71] In 1851 55 adults and 95 children attended the fortnightly service.[72]

The church of *ST. GILES*, so dedicated by *c.* 1740,[73] comprises chancel, nave, north chapel, south porch, and west tower. The chancel, 5.74 by 3.88 m. internally, may date from the early or mid 11th century. It is built of good quality dressed and coursed stone and originally had a steeply pitched gable roof. Externally the walls rest upon a triple plinth visible on the north, south, and east sides. A defaced pilaster strip with a possible naturalistic capital runs up the lower part of the centre of the north wall. Perhaps also original are a double-splayed window high in the east part of the north wall, and the chancel arch with through-stone jambs, originally flat-faced imposts, and a square-sectioned hood moulding on the west face. The visible former gable suggests that the original nave was probably of wood. If so, it was rebuilt in rubble, perhaps in the mid or late 11th century. Internally the nave measures 15.38 m. by 6.45 m., and was entered by a tall west door (later the tower arch) surmounted by a tympanum decorated with diaper-type work and by a similar south door, also with tympanum. The south door was set between windows piercing the centre and west end of the side wall, an arrangement probably mirrored in the north wall. There may also originally have been a third, easternmost, window on each side.[74] In the earlier 12th century a rubble west tower of at least three low stages was built. It had a west door and lancet windows. About the same time a single-splayed window was inserted in the south wall of the chancel. That was soon half cut away by the insertion of a priest's door. It was perhaps also at that time that a north door, opposite the south one, was added to the nave.

The only major addition to the church in the Middle Ages was a north chapel.[75] In the 15th century the west window in the south wall was renewed. In the 1520s work was undertaken on the *cancellum*,[76] probably the chancel;[77] the east wall of the latter was certainly rebuilt in or after the late Middle Ages.[78]

By 1618 the church had a south porch and the tower a pyramidal roof.[79] Perhaps about then tall rectangular windows were inserted in the north wall of the chancel and the south wall of the nave. The north chapel was rebuilt in brick in 1688 by Samuel Bowdler of Arlescott. The south porch was rebuilt in brick with stone details and with an iron gate in 1705.[80] About the same time an upper stage in brick was added to the tower. Much was spent *c.* 1778 inserting a ceiling.[81] About 1800 there was talk of adding two pews to one which Edward Ruckley had built in the chancel *c.* 1634; the patron George Forester threatened to pull down the chancel were that to happen.[82]

The east wall of the chancel was rebuilt in 1844. During G. E. Street's restoration in 1852 medieval wall paintings, including a life-sized mounted knight, were briefly revealed as the plaster was stripped.[83] At the same time the decoration on the south door's tympanum was cut off, the chancel arch imposts were chamfered, a two-light window replaced the rectangular one in the south nave wall, squints were made into the chancel, and oak benches were installed.[84] In Ewan Christian's more sympathetic restoration of 1894–5 the east wall of the chancel was again rebuilt and the porch restored. It was probably then that the north chapel was rebuilt in stone. Before 1937 the west tympanum was pierced for electric cable.[85]

The churchyard, which contains several cast iron memorials, was closed in 1882 and a new burial ground opened nearby on land given by Lord Forester.[86] The burial ground was extended in 1935.[87]

One of the two bells is dated 1661.[88] The plate includes a chalice of 1625 and a paten of 1700.[89] Parts of the register survive for 1611–15 and 1633–7 and from 1727 it is complete.[90]

NONCONFORMITY. Mrs. Mary Twyne was a recusant in 1680,[91] and in 1716 a Roman Catholic gentlewoman and her two maids lived in the parish.[92] In 1811 a house was licensed for Particular Baptists.[93]

EDUCATION. In 1618[94] John Slaney, lord of Marsh,[95] built a school on Barrow hill, which he

69 S.R.O. 2992/ChW/1, s.a.; S.R.O. 2992/2, verso of front endpaper and s.a. 1740; below, Beckbury, church.

70 S.R.O. 2992/ChW/1, s.a. 1758, 1764, 1767.

71 Ibid. s.a.

72 P.R.O., HO 129/358, no. 39.

73 B.L. Add. MS. 30316, f. 29v. Following acct. based on Cranage, iii. 175–83; H. M. and J. Taylor, *A.-S. Archit.* (1965), i. 49–51; E. D. C. Jackson and E. Fletcher, 'Barrow: Surviving Saxon Oratory in Salop.' *Jnl. Brit. Arch. Assoc.* 3rd ser. xxix. 52–60; H. M. Taylor, 'St. Giles' Ch., Barrow', *Arch. Jnl.* cxxvii. 211–21. Interpretation of chancel follows Taylor in *Arch. Jnl.*

74 The spacing suggests this possibility.

75 For evid. of date see Cranage, iii. 182.

76 S.R.O. 1224, box 342, Prior Gosnell's reg. f. 22v.

77 Brit. Acad. *Dict. of Medieval Lat. from Brit. Sources*, i (2), 255, which does not offer the translation 'screen', used in *T.S.A.S.* 4th ser. ix. 156.

78 S.P.L., MS. 372, vol. i, f. 113.

79 S.R.O. 1224/1/9, 14–15.

80 S.R.O. 2992/ChW/1, s.a. 1704–5.

81 Ibid. /Ch/1.

82 Randall, *Broseley*, 299–301; H.W.R.O.(H.), Heref. dioc. rec. AL 19/18, f. 140v.

83 *P.O. Dir. Salop.* (1856), 13; *Salop. N. & Q.* iii. 70; *Ch. Cal. Dioc. Heref.* (1871), 154.

84 For appearance of ch. *c.* 1856 see Eyton, iii, pl. facing p. 279.

85 S.R.O. 2992/Chyd/1–7; *Ch. Cal. Dioc. Heref.* (1895), 142.

86 E. A. Gee, 'Hist. and arch. acct. of Wenlock priory and its dependent churches' (Birm. Univ. M.A. thesis, 1937), 231 (plate).

87 Heref. Dioc. Regy., reg. 1926–38, p. 460.

88 H. B. Walters, *Ch. Bells of Salop.* (Oswestry, 1915), 64.

89 D. L. Arkwright and B. W. Bourne, *Ch. Plate Archd. Ludlow* (Shrews. 1961), 6.

90 S.R.O. 2992/1/1–14.

91 *Worcs. Recusant*, liii. 32.

92 H.W.R.O.(H.), HD 5/14/1/6.

93 *Orders of Q. Sess.* iii. 172; S.R.O., q. sess. file 10/219.

94 S.R.O. 1224/1/9. This section was written in 1983 and later revised.

95 Above, manors (Marsh).

1. Wenlock Edge from near Presthope (centre), looking north-east in December 1965. The Lilleshall Co.'s limestone quarry lies (bottom centre) next to the Much Wenlock–Craven Arms railway. Much Wenlock is in the distance (top centre). The farms and cottages at Presthope were later demolished.

2. Much Wenlock *c.* 1973, looking north-east. The three main streets meet just south of the parish church. In the background are the priory ruins incorporating the house known as Wenlock Abbey.

3. THE STRETTON GAP in 1947, looking south-west from the neighbourhood of Frodesley (bottom left). The Strettons lie in the distance, flanked (right) by the Long Mynd and (left) by Caer Caradoc and (beyond) the Ragleth. Nearer the camera (left) is the Lawley and (behind and parallel) Hoar Edge, beyond which is Wenlock Edge. Watling Street enters at bottom left and runs towards Leintwardine (*Bravonium*).

4. CHURCH STRETTON *c.* 1962, looking north-east. The old centre of the town, High Street (formerly Bristol Road) and Church Lane (Back Lane), is bottom left.

1. WENLOCK EDGE from near Presthope (centre), looking north-east in December 1965. The Lilleshall Co.'s limestone quarry lies (bottom centre) next to the Much Wenlock–Craven Arms railway. Much Wenlock is in the distance (top centre). The farms and cottages at Presthope were later demolished.

2. MUCH WENLOCK *c.* 1973, looking north-east. The three main streets meet just south of the parish church. In the background are the priory ruins incorporating the house known as Wenlock Abbey.

3. THE STRETTON GAP in 1947, looking south-west from the neighbourhood of Frodesley (bottom left). The Strettons lie in the distance, flanked (right) by the Long Mynd and (left) by Caer Caradoc and (beyond) the Ragleth. Nearer the camera (left) is the Lawley and (behind and parallel) Hoar Edge, beyond which is Wenlock Edge. Watling Street enters at bottom left and runs towards Leintwardine (*Bravonium*).

4. CHURCH STRETTON *c.* 1962, looking north-east. The old centre of the town, High Street (formerly Bristol Road) and Church Lane (Back Lane), is bottom left.

ACTON SCOTT HALL from the south-west.
The main entrance, originally central, was moved to one side in the early 19th century.

38. MUCH WENLOCK: the guildhall (right), market hall (dated 1878), and Holy Trinity church *c.* 1887, looking north. The spire was taken down in 1930.

39. CHURCH STRETTON market house in 1832

40. MUCH WENLOCK: mayoral group outside the market hall, Sunday 15 November 1896. The new mayor, Thomas Cooke, was a rich grocer and philanthropist, who left his entire estate to charity. The mace bearer, Sgt. Albert Darbyshire, is accompanied by officers of the Shropshire Constabulary stationed at Much Wenlock.

41. MUCH WENLOCK: the council chamber at the guildhall, 1904. The furniture and panelling had been introduced in the mid 19th century.

38. MUCH WENLOCK: the guildhall (right), market hall (dated 1878), and Holy Trinity church *c.* 1887, looking north. The spire was taken down in 1930.

39. CHURCH STRETTON market house in 1832

40. Much Wenlock: mayoral group outside the market hall, Sunday 15 November 1896. The new mayor, Thomas Cooke, was a rich grocer and philanthropist, who left his entire estate to charity. The mace bearer, Sgt. Albert Darbyshire, is accompanied by officers of the Shropshire Constabulary stationed at Much Wenlock.

41. Much Wenlock: the council chamber at the guildhall, 1904. The furniture and panelling had been introduced in the mid 19th century.

maintained during his life and endowed by will proved in 1632: he left the school a £30 rent charge (bought from John Weld) on Willey manor and left lands in Astley Abbots and at the Hem (in Linley) to Slaney's nephew John Slaney (d. *c.* 1654),[96] charged in perpetuity with a rent to maintain the school. The master, preferably to be a 'preaching minister', was to have £10 a year and the school house; a great part of 6 a. nearby and free coals were also assigned to the school. The master might take private pupils, but to earn his full salary he was to teach, free of charge, 20 poor boys to read and write, fitting them for apprenticeship. The stone schoolroom had a brick floor.[97]

In 1671 the master was a clergyman[98] and in 1716 and 1819 minister of Barrow; in 1819 he received the £10 but an usher taught the boys. The owners of the Hem continued to maintain the school until, in 1816, John Stephens gave it and adjoining land to Cecil Weld-Forester in exchange for a site near the church where Weld-Forester built a new school *c.* 1819. Pupils from Barrow and Willey, chosen by the master under Weld-Forester's 'sanction', usually left before they were 11.[99] Weld-Forester thus probably became the school's trustee, and his heirs, the Lords Forester, were its patrons and later rebuilt it again.[1]

By 1837 the school was mixed on the National system.[2] Its endowment continued, but pupils also paid fees until 1891 and the patron met any annual deficit. With a new classroom built in 1877 the school had 65 places.[3] By 1887 it was overcrowded[4] and in 1891 was rebuilt on the same site, two rooms providing 58 places.[5] Closely associated with the church, the school was known as Barrow-cum-Willey C.E. school.[6] Exceptionally irregular attendance helped to mar pupils' progress.[7]

During the Second World War the school admitted evacuees from London, Liverpool, and Chingford.[8] Boys aged 13 attended woodwork centres at Broseley 1936–40 and Much Wenlock 1947–9, girls aged 13 attended Much Wenlock cookery centre 1946–9.[9] Thirteen-year-olds transferred to Much Wenlock C.E. school in 1949, 11-year-olds to Much Wenlock Modern school opened in 1952.[10]

The school became aided in 1957[11] and was improved in 1958.[12] The roll was 32 in 1967 but 63 in 1973, an increase due entirely to extra-parochial admissions: by 1972 half of the pupils came from Broseley and its neighbourhood.[13] The roll was falling in the earlier 1980s.[14]

CHARITIES FOR THE POOR. In 1618 John Slaney built almshouses along with the school on Barrow hill. He maintained them during his life and endowed them by will proved in 1632. They formed a row of two-storeyed houses with three chimneys and three side entrances, each probably admitting to a lower and an upper apartment. They housed six local almspeople who received money, clothing, and coal. Cecil Weld-Forester demolished them *c.* 1818 and built a single-storeyed row of six near the church. In 1819 allowances remained the same those in the founder's will. Lord Forester (d. 1874) and his widow (d. 1894)[15] each left £500 to provide income for the almspeople. The charity's income was £510 in 1975.[16]

In 1788 £9 of poor's money was applied to church repairs. In return the parish was to pay 10*s.* yearly for ever to the poor. It was still paid in 1899.[17]

J. M. Howells, by will proved 1868, left £50, the interest to be spent on bread. Distribution began in 1878 and continued in 1905.[18]

CAUGHLEY

CAUGHLEY, part of the medieval parish of Holy Trinity, Much Wenlock, lay 2 km. east of Barrow and contained 821 a. (332 ha.) in 1883.[19] Caughley's demesne was in Barrow parish by 1649,[20] and by 1838 the perpetual curate of Barrow was owed customary payments from Caughley (18*s.*) and Swinney (8*s.*).[21] In 1934 the Caughley detachment of Barrow civil parish was transferred to Linley C.P., itself absorbed by Barrow C.P. in 1966.[22] The township[23] was roughly triangular, bounded on the east by the Severn and on the south-west largely by Dean brook.[24] To the north Caughley's irregular boundary followed no natural feature or field

96 *Index of P.C.C. Wills*, vii (Index Libr. liv), 475.
97 P.R.O., PROB 11/161, ff. 326–7, 329; *3rd Rep. Com. Char.* H.C. 5, pp. 300–2 (1820), iv; S.R.O. 1224/1/14.
98 H.W.R.O.(H.), HD 7, chwdns.' presentment 20 Sept. 1671 (ref. owed to Dr. R. Hume).
99 Ibid. HD 5/14/1/6 (ref. owed to Dr. Hume); *3rd Rep. Com. Char.* 300–3; *Educ. of Poor Digest*, H.C. 254, pp. 745–6 (1819), ix (2); cf. below, Linley, manor (the Hem).
1 P.R.O., ED 7/103, ff. 139–40; log bk. (at Barrow C.E. (Aided) Primary sch.), 21 Sept. 1891.
2 C. Hulbert, *Hist. and Descr. of Salop.* ii (1837), 341–2.
3 J. McFall, 'Educ. in Madeley Union of Salop. in 19th Cent.' (Keele Univ. M.A. (Educ.) thesis, 1973), 36, 98, 153, 282; P.R.O., ED 7/103, ff. 139–40.
4 Log bk. (at Barrow C.E. (Aided) Primary sch.) rep. 1887.
5 Ibid.; ibid. 21 Sept. 1891; *Kelly's Dir. Salop.* (1900), 26.
6 Log bk. 4 Nov. 1907.
7 Cf. ibid. 17 Sept. 1886, 27 Sept. 1901; *Kelly's Dir. Salop.* (1885), 797; (1900), 26; log bk. *passim*.
8 Log. bk. 20 June, 4 Nov. 1940, 6 Jan. 1941, 13 July, 9 Oct. 1944.
9 Ibid. 6 Mar. 1940, 13 Nov. 1946, 13 May 1947, 5 Sept. 1949; inf. from Mr. W. F. R. Miles, woodwk. master 1936–40.
10 Log bk. 5 Sept. 1949, 7 Jan. 1952.
11 *S.C.C. Mins. (Educ.)* 1957–8, 28.
12 Log bk. 8 Jan. 1959.
13 *S.C.C. Mins. (Educ.)* 1972–3, 83–4, 386–7.
14 S.C.C. Educ. Cttee. *Educ. Dir.* (1980–4).
15 Burke, *Peerage* (1949), 1036.
16 P.R.O., PROB 11/161, ff. 326–7, 329; S.R.O. 1224/1/9, 14–15; 2992/Cy/1, ff. 1–4; *3rd Rep. Com. Char.* 300–2; *Review of Local Chars.* (S.C.C. 1975), 20; above, educ.
17 S.R.O. 2992/Cy/1, ff. 5–6.
18 Ibid.; S.R.O. 1206/23, pp. 298, 301.
19 S.R.O. 1224/2/11; O.S. *Area Bk.* Barrow (1883). This article was written in 1984.
20 S.R.O. 1224, box 163, 'Inf. of parishioners of Barrow to commissioners [etc.]' (for date see *T.S.A.S.* 3rd ser. vii. 279).
21 P.R.O., IR 29/29/28.
22 *V.C.H. Salop.* ii. 229 note u.
23 So called in the late 19th cent.: E. Cassey & Co. *Dir. Salop.* (1871), 59; *Kelly's Dir. Salop.* (1891), 261.
24 S.R.O. 1224, box 75, Caughley map of 1609.

edges and may have marked the former northern boundary of Caughley wood. The township at its longest extended *c.* 2 km. from north-west to south-east and from north-east to south-west. The land, highest (*c.* 150 m.) in the west, falls south-eastwards to *c.* 40 m. where Caughley's southern boundary reaches the Severn.[25] The geology is mixed: in the east are the Upper Coal Measures, containing siltstones, mudstones, and some *Spirorbis* limestone, all of the Coalport Formation, and marls of the Hadley Formation; to the west the Lower Coal Measures outcrop and are partly overlain by boulder clay. A broad band of terrace gravels stretches along the Severn.[26]

Caughley, perhaps 'daw wood',[27] existed by 901 when the minster at Much Wenlock acquired property there[28] but was unmentioned in Domesday Book.[29] Swinney was mentioned as a residence in 1199[30] but may then have been long established[31] like Caughley, mentioned in 1221.[32] In the late 13th century Little Caughley was mentioned along with Caughley and Swinney.[33] Inett, whose name suggests an origin as an assart farm, was probably also established by the 13th century.[34]

It seems that the only nucleated settlement was the hamlet of Darley straddling the south-west boundary of the township: its field was mentioned in 1341.[35] Largely bounded by woodland in 1618, Darley then apparently comprised three houses in Caughley township and two in Willey.[36] By 1609 there were several cottages east of Darley in former common woodland, inclosed *c.* 1590. Cottages at Little Caughley in 1609[37] were perhaps on the site of the 13th-century hamlet, and by 1693 a woodland clearing had expanded outwards from some of them[38] to cover *c.* 21 a. by the late 18th century.[39] In 1714 the Browne estate had 13 houses or cottages, including Caughley Hall and Inett.[40] By 1780 there were 6 dwellings at Darley, irregularly scattered around a few acres of common, and others at Little Caughley.[41]

In the late 18th century, as later, the main farms were Caughley, Swinney, and Inett, those at Caughley and Swinney adjoining the halls, while coal mines flanked a newly built porcelain factory whose saggar works stood east of Darley. A few buildings, one or two of them perhaps alehouses or warehouses, stood along the river bank.[42] The clearing by the river at the end of the road from the Dean (in Willey) was known by 1752 as Roving, and the Rovings public house was open there in the early 19th century.[43]

There were some changes between 1780 and 1795: the saggar works closed, Inett Farm was rebuilt south of its previous position,[44] and Caughley Place was built north-east of the porcelain factory for its managing partner Thomas Turner. Reputedly designed by one of Turner's French employees,[45] Caughley Place was in the mid 18th-century French style with a projecting bow[46] and a tall central feature surmounted by a mansard gable. It was perhaps demolished with the factory *c.* 1821.[47] Swinney and Caughley halls were both demolished after those estates were sold to George Forester and his trustees in 1790 and 1822.[48]

Between the earlier 19th and the later 20th century there was little change. The riverside area lost importance after the railway arrived in 1862, and between 1882 and 1901 the cleared area around Little Caughley reverted to woodland.[49] In 1931 the township's population was 48.[50] By the early 1980s settlement comprised Caughley, Swinney, and Inett farmhouses together with a few isolated cottages; Darley was no longer recognizable as a hamlet.

In 1609 a north–south road from Rowton and Swinbatch in Broseley crossed Caughley township via Caughley Hall. It was crossed near the Hall by another running west from Swinney and forking at Inett: north-west towards Broseley and south-west towards the Dean and thence to Bridgnorth.[51] By 1790 there had been changes: the road to Broseley from Inett then left the Dean road a little farther west than it previously had. The road from Swinney then also had a branch south-east from near Caughley Hall to the Rovings by the Severn, while the road south from Caughley Hall had apparently lost importance.[52] In the 19th century the western part of the road to the Dean was straightened.[53]

Tarbatch dingle railway, built in the early 18th century from Broseley, terminated at Willey wharf on the Severn east of Swinney. By 1882 the western end of the line in Broseley was at Upper Riddings Farm, whence a branch ran south-east to Turnersyard colliery in the township. That line closed between 1901 and 1925.[54] In the later 18th century other lines linked coal

25 O.S. Maps 6", Salop. LI. NE., SE. (1903 edn.).
26 Inst. Geol. Sciences Map 1/25,000, *Telford* (1978).
27 Ekwall, *Eng. Place-Names* (1960), 91.
28 Below, manors.
29 Cf. Eyton, ii. 69; below, econ. hist. (agric.).
30 Eyton, ii. 38.
31 Below, econ. hist. (agric.). Cf. C. Taylor, *Village and Farmstead* (1983), 192.
32 Eyton, ii. 43.
33 Ibid. iii. 297.
34 Below, manors.
35 S.R.O. 1224/3/143.
36 Ibid. /1/9; below, fig. 46.
37 S.R.O. 1224, box 75, Caughley map of 1609; below, econ. hist. (agric.).
38 S.R.O. 1224/7/2, at end; above, this section.
39 S.R.O. 1224/1/47.
40 Ibid. box 76, deed 26 Apr. 1714.
41 Ibid. /1/47; above, this section.
42 S.R.O. 1224/1/47. For alehos. see also S.R.O. 2992/1/2, pp. 102, 104 (Thos. Guest).
43 J. Rocque, *Map of Salop.* (1752); S.R.O. 515/5, pp. 78–9; 1224/7/41.
44 S.R.O. 1224/1/48. For Inett see below, manors.
45 J. Randall, *Broseley and Its Surroundings* (Madeley, 1879), 302; C. Roberts, 'Salopian China', *The Connoisseur*, liv. 192.
46 Descr. based on photo. of model of Caughley Place: *Connoisseur*, liv. 192.
47 Below, econ. hist. (ind.). Not on C. & J. Greenwood, *Map of Salop.* (1830), or O.S. Map 1", sheet LXI. NE. (1833 edn.).
48 Below, manors.
49 Below, this section; O.S. Map 6", Salop. LI. SE. (1888 and 1903 edns.).
50 *V.C.H. Salop.* ii. 229 note u.
51 S.R.O. 1224, box 75, Caughley map of 1609.
52 S.R.O. 604, box 4, plan of Riddings and Swinney est. 1790; 1224/1/48. Cf. R. Baugh, *Map of Salop.* (1808); B.L. Maps, O.S.D. 213.
53 Cf. S.R.O. 1224/1/48; O.S. Map 6", Salop. LI. NE. (1887 edn.).
54 Below, Broseley, communications; Trinder, *Ind. Rev. Salop.* 73; *Jnl. Wilkinson Soc.* xiii. 4–11.

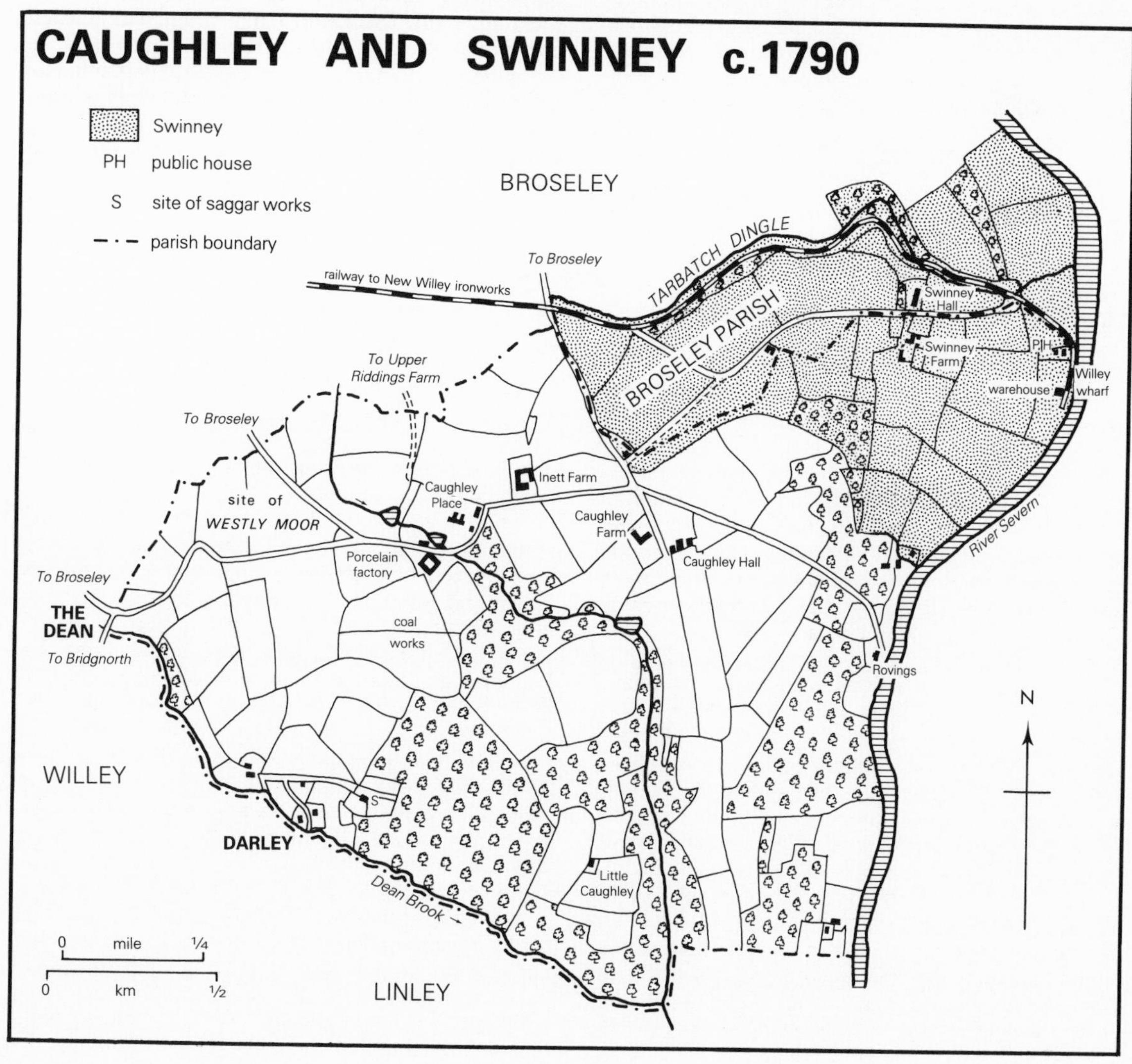

Fig. 22

pits in the centre of the township with the Severn.[55] In 1822 there were 80 tons of jenny rails and sleepers at Caughley colliery that were 'nearly new'.[56]

For much of the 18th and 19th centuries Willey wharf was an important outlet for Broseley's industrial products, particularly those of the New Willey Co. from which it presumably took its name.[57] A public house and warehouse served the wharf in the late 18th century. There was perhaps also a wharf at the Rovings 1 km. south. Along the Severn bank ran the Coalbrookdale–Bewdley tow path, made *c.* 1800.[58] The wharves' importance probably declined rapidly after 1862 when the Severn Valley line of the West Midland Railway (later G.W.R.) opened along the river bank.

MANORS AND OTHER ESTATES. Aethelraed, ealdorman of Mercia, and his wife Aethelflaed gave three *manentes* at *CAUGHLEY* to the church of Wenlock in 901.[59] In the 13th century Wenlock priory (the Cluniac refoundation of the Saxon minster) was overlord of estates there which it acquired in demesne during that century and held until it surrendered to the Crown in 1540.[60]

In 1255 Ralph of Caughley (fl. 1274)[61] held a carucate in Caughley of the prior of Wenlock for 40*s.* a year and suit to the prior's court.[62] In 1296 Philip of Caughley and Margery of Presthope held what was evidently that estate—a house, 4 virgates, and 10 a. of wood—for 40*s.* a year and suit to Bourton hundred.[63] In 1299 they were licensed to grant their property to Wenlock priory.[64]

55 S.R.O. 515/2, pp. 185–6. It is not clear whether S.R.O. 1224/1/47, a map of 1780, depicts rds. or rlys.

56 *Wolverhampton Chron.* 24 July 1822.

57 For this para. see below, Broseley, communications; O.S. Maps 6", Salop. LI. NE. (1887 edn.), SE. (1888 edn.); S.R.O. 1224/1/47–8.

58 Under 39 Geo. III, c. 8 (Local and Personal): C. Hadfield, *Canals of W. Midlands* (1969), 124.

59 H. P. R. Finberg, *Early Charters of W. Midlands* (1972), p. 148.

60 Below, this section; Eyton, ii. 43–5; iii. 223-4; *V.C.H. Salop.* ii. 38.

61 Eyton, ii. 45.

62 *Rot. Hund.* (Rec. Com.), ii. 85.

63 Eyton, ii. 44.

64 *Cal. Pat.* 1292–1301, 401.

In 1290 Nicholas Brisebon of Montgomery held 1 carucate, described as the manor of Caughley, of the prior of Wenlock and was licensed to grant it to the priory.[65] It must have been that carucate, worth 12*s.* a year, which the priory owned in 1291. Besides that carucate the priory was said in 1291 to have 20*s.* annual rent from Caughley property:[66] that figure (evidently mis-stated) must have included the rent due from the Caughleys' carucate.

Another estate in Caughley was held in 1221 by Walter the smith and his wife Agnes.[67] It may have been the house and virgate, held of Wenlock priory, that Walter the goldsmith conveyed to the priory in 1342.[68]

Wenlock priory's Caughley demesne consisted in 1369 of a house and 2 carucates.[69] In 1540, shortly after the priory's surrender, Thomas Lokier, a Bristol merchant, bought the chief house and demesne lands of Caughley manor from the Crown. Lokier sold the estate to the tenant John Munslow in 1541.[70] In 1564 Munslow conveyed the manor to William Bentley of Bridgnorth, who sold it in 1567 to John Dudley. Dudley sold it in 1569 to Richard Onslow (d. 1571), the solicitor general.[71] In 1584 Onslow's son and heir Edward sold the manor to Thomas Owen, a London lawyer, who sold it in 1586 to John Dawes (d. 1595) of Shrewsbury.[72] The manor remained with his relict Margaret, who married Thomas Jewkes. In 1632 she settled the chief house and certain lands on her grandson John Dawes, to whom the rest of her Caughley estate passed at her death in 1634.[73] Dawes (d. 1680)[74] left the manor to his grandson Ralph Browne (d. 1707),[75] who left it to his son Edward (d. 1740),[76] husband of Laconia (*née* Berkeley), supposed original of Sylvia in Farquhar's *The Recruiting Officer* (1706).[77] After Edward Browne's death the manor may have passed first to his eldest son Ralph (d. 1763), but Ralph's brother Edward had it at his death in 1751[78] and left it to his widow Jane (d. 1779);[79] she left it to their grandnephew R. B. Wylde (d. 1810) who added the name Browne on inheriting. Wylde Browne's son T. W. Wylde Browne, of Glazeley, succeeded; his trustees sold the manor to George Forester's trustees in 1823,[80] and thereafter it was part of the Willey estate.[81]

In 1609 Caughley Hall stood on the site of the later Caughley Farm. It had a central range with cross wings and was of two storeys with attics covered by a slated or tiled roof.[82] There was probably a nearby dovehouse in or before the late 17th century.[83] In 1672 the Hall was taxed on 13 hearths.[84] Ralph Browne built a new Hall in the early 1680s[85] a little east of the old. It was rebuilt or greatly enlarged *c.* 1790 as a plain building of seven bays and three storeys, with a central entrance facing south. An adjoining coach house and stables, with pedimented front and gothick windows, faced west. All were demolished in 1833.[86] Caughley Farm is an early 19th-century brick building slightly in the Tudor style and incorporating probably older stonework.

The Sandfords owned property in Caughley from the 13th to the 16th century. About 1221 Ralph of Sandford unjustly disseised Walter the smith and his wife Agnes of their free tenement in Caughley, and Wenlock priory's tenant Ralph of Caughley also owed Ralph of Sandford's son Richard (d. 1249) 8*s.* rent for land in Caughley.[87] Richard Sandford of Sandford had land at Caughley in 1497[88] and his son Hugh (d. 1530) held it of the prior of Wenlock. The estate then included the houses and land called *INETT*. It passed to Hugh Sandford's son Richard (d. *c.* 1532) and then to Richard's son George who, in 1552, sold it to Richard Moreton (fl. 1578) of Haughton (in Shifnal).[89]

In 1623 Humphrey Briggs, husband of Moreton's granddaughter Anne, sold Inett and the rest of his Caughley estate to Francis Billingsley, Francis Adams, and John Huxley,[90] presumably interested in the minerals.[91] By 1651 the Dawes family had bought the property and added it to the manorial estate.[92] Inett Farm, 'lately erected' in 1683,[93] was demolished *c.* 1790 and a plain brick house of three bays and three storeys was built just to the south.[94]

Several possible medieval holders of the freehold or reputed manor[95] of *SWINNEY* are

65 Ibid. 1281–92, 369; P.R.O., C 143/12, no. 21.
66 *Tax. Eccl.* (Rec. Com.), 164.
67 *Rolls of Justices in Eyre, 1221–2* (Selden Soc. lix), pp. 443–4.
68 P.R.O., C 143/263, no. 6; *Cal. Pat.* 1340–3, 529.
69 B.L. Add. MS. 6165, p. 100.
70 *L. & P. Hen. VIII*, xv, p. 468; xvi, pp. 278–9; S.R.O. 1224, box 75, deed 17 Feb. 1541.
71 S.R.O. 1224, box 75, deeds 9 July 1564, 31 Oct. 1567, 15 Jan. 1568/9; *Hist. Parl., Commons*, 1558–1603, iii. 153–5.
72 S.R.O. 1224, box 75, deeds 4 Nov. 1584, 26 Nov. 1586; *T.S.A.S.* xi. 12.
73 S.R.O. 840, box 1, Marsh ct. r. of 1641; 1224, box 75, deeds 9 Jan. 1595/6, 27 Sept. 1620, 20 Apr. 1632; *T.S.A.S.* xi. 28.
74 S.P.L., MS. 2793, p. 106.
75 S.R.O. 1224, box 75, deeds 1 May 1677, 28 May 1683; 2993/Rg/2, bur. 26 Aug. 1707.
76 S.R.O. 1224, box 76, Ralph Browne's will 2 Jan. 1704/5; 2993/Rg/3, bur. 31 May 1740.
77 G. Farquhar, *The Recruiting Officer*, ed. J. Ross (1991), pp. xvi–xvii; *N. & Q.* ccxxvi. 216–17.
78 S.R.O. 1224, box 77, deed 5 Apr. 1732, Jane Browne's will 25 Dec. 1773; 2993/Rg/3, bur. 15 Mar. 1750/1, 13 May 1763.
79 S.R.O. 1224, box 77, Edw. Browne's will 27 Aug. 1749; 2992/1/2, bur. 15 May 1779; S.P.L., MS. 2793, p. 99.
80 S.R.O. 1224, box 77, Jane Browne's will 25 Dec. 1773; box 78, abstr. of title, deeds 24–5 Mar. 1823; S.P.L., MSS. 2792, p. 462; 2793, p. 99.
81 For descent see *V.C.H. Salop.* xi. 80; below, Willey, manor.
82 S.R.O. 1224, box 75, Caughley map of 1609.
83 Ibid. /7/2, at end (Doveho. orchard).
84 *Hearth Tax 1672* (Salop. Arch. Soc. 1949), 34.
85 S.R.O. 1224, box 75, deed 28 May 1683.
86 Ibid. bdle. 384, elevations of Caughley Hall; H. E. Forrest, *Old Hos. of Wenlock* (Shrews. 1914), 93–4; Greenwood, *Map of Salop.*; *Salopian Jnl.* 27 Feb. 1833.
87 Eyton, ii. 43.
88 S.R.O. 3365/165.
89 *Visit. Salop. 1623*, ii (Harl. Soc. xxix), 431; Eyton ix. 236–7; S.R.O. 2/92, 94, 96, 99; 1224, box 75, deed 15 Jan. 1568/9; S.P.L., MS. 2793, p. 281.
90 S.R.O. 5735/U/1/9; *Visit. Salop. 1623*, i (Harl. Soc. xxviii), 69; ii. 368.
91 Below, Broseley, econ. hist. (coal and ironstone) for Huxleys and Adamses.
92 S.R.O. 1224, box 75, bill in Weld *v.* Dawes, John Dawes's objections 14 Apr. 1651.
93 Ibid. deed 28 May 1683.
94 Ibid. /1/47–8.
95 Ibid. box 75, Caughley map of 1609.

known.[96] By 1446 four virgates at Swinney belonged to Richard Lacon, lord of Willey.[97] The estate presumably descended with Willey until 1618 when Sir Francis Lacon conveyed it to Sir Francis Newport, who sold it immediately to Sir Edward Bromley[98] (d. 1626), a baron of the Exchequer.[99] Bromley's purchase included other premises in Broseley, probably *HIGH* or *UPPER RIDDINGS* and part of *THE WOODHOUSE*.[1] He bought other parts of the Woodhouse (which were part of the Broseley 'socage land' in 1421) from William Whitmore, probably in 1621.[2] The estate, which by 1641 evidently also included *LOWER RIDDINGS* in Broseley (part of the 'Priory land'),[3] remained with Sir Edward's widow Margaret in 1656 but by 1657 had passed to John Bromley[4] (d. 1674) of Worcester, his heir. John's successor was his grandnephew William Bromley (d. 1707) of Holt (Worcs.). William was succeeded by his cousin William Bromley (d. 1769) of Abberley (Worcs.), who left the whole estate to his son Robert. Robert Bromley sold Swinney and Upper Riddings to George Forester in 1790, having sold Lower Riddings in 1788 to John Guest. Guest sold Lower Riddings in 1789 to Daniel Onions, from whom Forester bought it in 1790.[5]

In 1687 Swinney Hall was on the Caughley side of the parish boundary, Swinney Farm on the Broseley side.[6] By 1790 the names seem to have been reversed.[7] The Swinney Hall then in Broseley parish, perhaps the earlier Farm, was probably demolished soon after George Forester bought the estate in 1790.[8] Swinney Farm, perhaps the earlier Hall, comprises two ranges: one, timber framed and with a large stone end stack, is perhaps 17th-century, the other, of brick with plat bands, is *c.* 1700. Upper Riddings stands inside Broseley's southern boundary and is 18th-century and later. Lower Riddings, a 1½ storeyed building just south-east, is 17th-century and later.

Wenlock priory, as appropriator of Holy Trinity, Much Wenlock,[9] owned the *TITHES*. From 1540 the tithes of Caughley's demesnes, later called the manor, descended with that estate[10] and in 1809 the demesnes were described as tithe free.[11] The rest of the impropriate tithes, including Swinney's, descended after 1540 with those of Barrow.[12]

ECONOMIC HISTORY. AGRICULTURE. It seems likely that the three Caughley *manentes* of 901 were represented by the 13th-century estates at Caughley (2 carucates) and Swinney (4 virgates).[13] In 1290, when land in Caughley was granted to the priory, it was agreed that the villeins' status should remain unchanged.[14] In 1321 Wenlock priory had a bailiff for Caughley.[15]

Despite the disafforestation of Caughley and Little Caughley from Shirlett forest in the 13th century,[16] much of Caughley remained wooded. Over 90 pigs were pannaged in Caughley wood in 1380,[17] and in 1532 the right to take wood from Caughley between Michaelmas and Lady Day was included in a lease of Shirlett smithy to Thomas Munslow, later, if not then, lessee of Caughley manor.[18] About 1590, soon after his purchase of Caughley, John Dawes inclosed much of Caughley wood, *c.* 100 a. between Darley and Little Caughley. That large area of common woodland adjoined Rudge wood in Willey and they had been intercommoned at the time of the Dissolution. Dawes also inclosed a second common, Westly moor, to the north-west. John Weld disputed those inclosures after he had bought Marsh manor in 1620, claiming, in part successfully, rights of lordship over the inclosed areas.[19] John Slaney, Weld's predecessor as lord of Marsh, had apparently also inclosed a part of Caughley wood. As late as 1722 rival claims of the lords of Caughley and Marsh led to litigation.[20] By *c.* 1650 the Dawes family had also considerably extended the Caughley estate by purchase,[21] and in 1693 the lordship of Caughley totalled 647 a. including 52 a. of Caughley wood.[22]

No large areas of open field land are known, although the field of Darley was noted in 1341,[23] and there were 'furlongs' south-east of Caughley Hall in 1609 and at Little Caughley in 1780.[24] The main concentration of arable land in 1795 was in the north-west. When George Forester's trustees bought Caughley manor in 1823 the 701-a. estate included 215 a. in hand and the 216-a. Hall farm, while in 1832 Inett farm covered 248 a.[25] In the late 19th and early 20th century there was a pheasantry at Caughley Farm.[26]

Swinney extended to at least 4 virgates in 1446,[27] and to *c.* 248 a. in the 1790s.[28] In 1794

96 Eyton, ii. 38–9.
97 S.R.O. 1224/2/536; cf. below, Willey, manor.
98 Barnard MSS., Raby Castle, box 1, bdle. 29, nos. 45, 55, 59.
99 *Hist. Parl., Commons*, 1558–1603, i. 489. For Bromley pedigree: S.P.L., MS. 2790, pp. 242, 244.
1 S.R.O. 1224/1/32; /2/546; /3/22, 24.
2 S.R.O. 1190/1, unlisted acct. r. 1417–27; 1224/1/32; /3/244–6 (docketing); cf. below, Broseley, manor.
3 S.R.O. 840, box 1, Marsh ct. r. of 1641; 1224/3/238, 545; P.R.O., STAC 8/242/12, f. 5; below, Broseley, manor.
4 S.R.O. 840, box 1, Marsh ct. r. of 1641, 1656, 1657.
5 S.R.O. 1224/3/528, 543, 545, 552–3, 560–1, 564–5, 569–70.
6 Ibid. /3/545.
7 S.R.O. 604, plan of Riddings and Swinney est. 1790.
8 Not on R. Baugh, *Map of Salop.* (1808), and certainly demolished by 1840: S.R.O. 1313/149.
9 Below, M. Wenlock, manors (rectory).
10 *L. & P. Hen. VIII*, xv, p. 468; S.R.O. 1224, box 75, deed 26 Nov. 1586; box 163, 'Inf. of parishioners of Barrow to commissioners [etc.]'.
11 S.R.O. 515/7, p. 243.
12 *Cal. Pat.* 1580–2, p. 5; S.R.O. 1224, box 163, John Weld's bk. 1631, ff. 8, 13; cf. above, Barrow, manors (tithes).
13 Above, this article, intro.; manors.
14 Eyton, ii. 43.
15 W. F. Mumford, *Wenlock in the Middle Ages* (Shrews. 1977), 64.
16 Eyton, iii. 297; *Cartulary of Shrews. Abbey*, ed. U. Rees (1975), ii, p. 251.
17 S.R.O. 1224/2/3.
18 Ibid. /3/6; above, manors.
19 See S.R.O. 1224, boxes 75–6, Caughley map of 1609, and memoranda, depositions, etc., *re* dispute.
20 Ibid. box 75, interrogatories in Weld *v.* Dawes 2 Oct. 1652, no. 18; box 76, Hardwick *v.* Browne, bill.
21 Above, manors.
22 S.R.O. 1224/7/2, at end.
23 Ibid. /3/143.
24 Ibid. /1/47; box 75, Caughley map of 1609.
25 Ibid. /1/48; /7/41, 47.
26 O.S. Maps 6", Salop. LI. NE. (1887 edn.); 1/2,500, Salop. LI. 7 (1902 and 1927 edns.).
27 Above, manors.
28 Area calculated from S.R.O. 604, box 4, plan of Riddings and Swinney est. 1790.

the farm was said to be undergoing 'much improvement'.[29] In 1910 Swinney farm comprised 89 a., much of its land having apparently been transferred to Inett farm, then 353 a.[30]

INDUSTRY. Coal, ironstone, and limestone were probably all mined in Caughley in the 16th century and used in the ironworks there. John Dawes and John Weld, lords of Caughley and Marsh, defined their mining rights in Caughley *c.* 1650.[31] How much mining was then actually going on, however, is unknown. Larger scale coal mining perhaps began in the north in the earlier 18th century after the opening of pits at Rowton and Gitchfield in Broseley.[32] Some of the coal was carried west by crickers (packhorse drivers).[33] By 1752 there were pits around Swinney.[34] Exploitation in the later 18th and early 19th century was haphazard and centred on 200 a. north-east and south-west of the porcelain factory and bounded by faults. Coal was carried to the Severn. The clod or furnace coal was of variable quality but local ironworks used it if other supplies were short. A little ironstone was probably got with the coal.[35] Between 1823 and 1825 Robert Evans & Son took a lease of the Caughley coalworks. In 1825 both the Caughley and the Swinney coalworks were taken over by John Onions and Thomas Rose, still lessees in 1834.[36] Small scale digging continued around the site of the porcelain factory and north of Inett Farm, and in 1910 Broseley Tileries Co. Ltd. held the lease. Extraction continued until 1927 or later.[37] There was some opencast mining around Turnersyard colliery by the National Coal Board after the Second World War. From 1955 Coalmoor Refractories (Horsehay) Ltd. and its subsidiary Prestage & Broseley Tileries Ltd. got high quality alumina fireclay there; extraction continued in the earlier 1980s.[38]

Walter the smith lived in Caughley in 1221, though he may not have been an iron smith.[39] Thomas Munslow, lessee of Inett from 1524,[40] had an ironworks at Caughley by *c.* 1523.[41] Munslow, a furnace technologist who worked at several ironworks in the county,[42] probably used foreign expertise; a Frenchman, John Morell (d. 1556) of Caughley wood, was the 'founder' and chief workman at Munslow's 'smithy'.[43] In 1541 the works was leased to Reynold and Thomas Ridley of Caughley for 21 years: for £13 6*s.* 8*d.* a year they enjoyed the same rights as Munslow had. The works then comprised an 'ironhouse' and an 'iron mill called an iron smythe place'. The Ridleys' forge was probably still working in 1568 when another ironworks was probably run by the 40-year old John Munslow who had liberty to dig ironstone in Shirlett.[44] He was presumably the tenant, and from 1541 to 1564 the owner, of the Caughley demesnes[45] and a kinsman of Thomas Munslow.[46] But the location of his works, even its parish, is unknown.

About 1590 John Dawes, lord of Caughley,[47] built an iron smithy in Caughley wood to use the coal and ironstone there. It was leased to others and probably short lived.[48]

Benjamin Ball leased a warehouse and land at Willey wharf in 1816,[49] and between 1817 and 1838 he leased the Swinney iron foundry there from the Willey estate.[50] It stood beside the railway from Willey ironworks, on the site of the public house of 1790.[51] Possibly he was the Benjamin Ball who managed the Barnett's Leasow furnaces in Broseley from *c.* 1821.[52]

Inferior limestone was got in the early 19th century and burnt for local agricultural use.[53] It was also used for a cottage limewash known as 'Lord Forester's livery'.[54]

There was probably a pottery at Caughley from *c.* 1750;[55] a 62-year lease of it is said to have been taken in 1754 by Ambrose Gallimore, a native of the Staffordshire Potteries. Traditional coarse and slip coated wares were made. About 1772 Gallimore was joined by Thomas Turner,[56] a former apprentice at the Worcester Porcelain Manufactory. Turner was the creative force, but Gallimore retained an interest in 1787.[57] The two- and three-storeyed Salopian China Manufactory,[58] was built south-west of Inett Farm, and porcelain was produced by 1775. Saggars were made, presumably from local refractory clay,[59] at a works to the south,[60] and coal was got

29 S.R.O. 515/2, pp. 185–6.

30 S.R.O. 4044/89, p. 8.

31 S.R.O. 1224, box 75, deposition *re* Caughley 1651, interrogatories in Weld *v.* Dawes 2 Oct. 1652 (no. 12), and articles for Sir John Weld, John Dawes, Fra. Adams, John Baldwin to peruse.

32 Below, Broseley, econ. hist. (coal and ironstone).

33 S.R.O. 1224, box 147, depositions 7 Oct. 1728, f. 1.

34 Rocque, *Map of Salop.*

35 S.R.O. 1224/1/47; box 77, Mr. Smith's rep. as to Caughley mines, 1822.

36 Ibid. box 174, royalty acct. bk. 1815–34.

37 Greenwood, *Map of Salop.*; O.S. Map 1/2,500, Salop. LI. 7 (1902 and 1927 edns.); S.R.O. 4044/89, p. 9 (no. 78).

38 Inf. from S.C.C. Planning Dept.

39 *Rolls of Justices in Eyre, 1221–2* (Selden Soc. lix), p. 444; above, manors.

40 S.R.O. 1224, box 75, deed 31 Oct. 1567; 5735/U/1/4; cf. above, manors.

41 S.R.O. 1224/3/6; N.L.W., Wynnstay, RA 2.

42 Inf. from Mr. J. B. Lawson, who is thanked for reading and commenting on this section.

43 *T.S.A.S.* vi. 110.

44 *L. & P. Hen. VIII*, xvii, p. 696; S.R.O. 1224/3/9/2; /3/16, 24.

45 Above, manors.

46 John Munslow, like Thos., also had ironwks. elsewhere, e.g. at Caus: Longleat, unbound MSS. 3993.

47 Above, manors.

48 S.R.O. 1224, box 75, deposition *re* Caughley, 1651.

49 Ibid. box 138, deed 1 Sept. 1816.

50 Ibid. /7/44, f. 4; parcel 190, rentals 51 (f. 1), 52 (f. 1); cf. parcel 193, rentals 1838; Tibnam & Co. *Salop. Dir.* (1828), 27; O.S. Map 1", sheet LXI. NE. (1833 edn.).

51 S.R.O. 604, plan of Riddings and Swinney est. 1790; above, this article, intro.

52 Below, Broseley, econ. hist. (iron); Trinder, *Ind. Rev. Salop.* 143.

53 S.R.O. 1224, box 77, Mr. Smith's rep. f. 2; J. Plymley, *Gen. View of Agric. of Salop.* (1803), 66; O.S. Map 1/2,500, Salop. LI. 7 (1902 edn.).

54 Randall, *Broseley*, 131.

55 This and the next two paras. based on G. A. Godden, *Caughley and Worc. Porcelains 1775–1800* (1969); [M. Messenger], *Caughley Porcelains: Bi-centenary Exhibn.* (Shrews. Art Gallery [1972]; copy in S.R.O. 2766/1); Trinder, *Ind. Rev. Salop.* 126–8; *Country Life*, 11 Oct. 1962, 846–7.

56 For the Gallimores and Turners see *Connoisseur*, liv. 187–94.

57 S.R.O. 1224, box 78, abstr. of title, Caughley, f. 8.

58 *The Reliquary*, xv. 161 (this article, fig. 23); C. Mackenzie, *Ho. of Coalport 1750–1950* (1951), 13.

59 Above, this section.

60 S.R.O. 1224/1/47.

Fig. 23
CAUGHLEY: THE SALOPIAN CHINA MANUFACTORY *c.* 1800

from adjacent mines. Soapstone came from Cardington as well as from the Lizard (Cornw.), and china clay was presumably also brought from Devon or Cornwall.[61] Grinding was done in mills at the Smithies (in Willey) and Calcutts (in Broseley). The Salopian China Warehouse opened in London in 1783.[62] The works employed *c.* 100 in 1793. There were three kilns in 1795, but the saggar works had apparently been demolished.[63]

From the beginning production concentrated on transfer printed imitation Chinese porcelain table wares. Turner had learned transfer printing at Worcester, and in 1775 Robert Hancock, then the most celebrated engraver for porcelain, joined Caughley from Worcester. 'Salopian' china enjoyed aristocratic patronage yet undersold Worcester. From *c.* 1780 there was much French influence on style and design, and gilt began to be used on its own for decoration. Those changes reflect the work of the decorating establishment of Humphrey and Robert Chamberlain at Worcester, and increasingly from the 1780s Caughley porcelain was sent away for decoration.

In the 1790s the Chamberlains began to produce their own porcelain, and it was perhaps that, together with the establishment (1795–6)[64] and growth of the Coalport porcelain works, and perhaps Turner's ill health, that led in 1799 to his sale of the Caughley lease, works, and stock.[65] The buyers were the Coalport partners Edward Blakeway and Richard and John Rose, the last named a native of Barrow and former Caughley apprentice. Caughley continued to make porcelain, much for decoration and finishing at Coalport, until 1814 when the two works were bought by John Rose. He closed Caughley, and by 1821[66] most of the factory had been taken down and the materials taken to Coalport for re-use. Two brick cottages, derelict in the early 1980s, may have been made from parts of the works left behind.[67] Among Rose's apprentices at Caughley was probably T. M. Randall, a native of Caughley who later had his own porcelain works in Madeley.[68]

LOCAL GOVERNMENT. Caughley seems to have been subject to the prior of Wenlock's Broseley manor court in 1379.[69] That Broseley estate was later absorbed by the priory's manor of Marsh.[70] There is no evidence of a separate court being held for Caughley, and in 1568 Caughley was stated to be in Marsh manor; in

61 Plymley, *Agric. of Salop.* 69–70.

62 F. A. Barrett, *Caughley and Coalport Porcelains* (Leigh on Sea, 1951), 15.

63 S.R.O. 1224/1/47–8; S.P.L., MS. 6865, p. 33.

64 *V.C.H. Salop.* xi. 53–4.

65 Turner was still selling stock in 1800: *Aris's Birm. Gaz.* 31 Mar. 1800.

66 Randall, *Broseley*, 306.

67 The cottage illustr. in *Shropshire Mag.* Mar. 1954, p. 24, cannot be identified with either.

68 *V.C.H. Salop.* i. 440; xi. 54; E. G. Salisbury, *Border Cos. Worthies*, 2nd ser. (1879), 243.

69 S.R.O. 1224/2/3. The chronological arrangement of the roll requires a date in Jan. 1380 for this entry, but the dating formula, though partly destroyed by rubbing, appears to make that impossible.

70 Above, Barrow, local govt.; below, Broseley, local govt. The rest of Barrow par. was in the man. of Barrow, Atterley, and Walton after the Dissolution.

the earlier 17th century the lord of Marsh claimed suit to his court leet and baron from Caughley and at least part of Swinney.[71]

Roger Halghton of Swinney owed suit at Willey court baron in 1438, and Swinney was said to be in Willey manor in 1573.[72]

Caughley was absorbed by Linley civil parish in 1934 and thus remained in the Barrow ward of Wenlock borough. On the borough's dissolution in 1966 Caughley, like the rest of Linley C.P., was absorbed by Barrow C.P. and so was in Bridgnorth rural district 1966–74 and Bridgnorth district thereafter.[73]

NONCONFORMITY. A papist in Barrow parish in 1676 was perhaps one of the Brownes of Caughley.[74]

CHARITIES FOR THE POOR. Barrow parish charities[75] presumably applied to Caughley.

BECKBURY

THE SMALL rural parish of Beckbury lies on the Shropshire–Staffordshire border *c.* 6 km. south of Shifnal. In the Middle Ages (perhaps from the 12th century)[76] and until 1905 it formed, with the adjoining parish of Badger, a detached part of Hereford diocese,[77] and it is possible that the two parishes were once a single estate.[78]

Beckbury (Becca's burh or house)[79] is bounded on the west partly by the river Worfe and its tributary Mad brook; in the centre of the western side of the parish, however, the boundary turns west to include land on the right bank of the Worfe. On the east the boundary is Snowdon brook, which rises near the north-eastern corner of the parish (called 'the marshes' in the early 19th century)[80] and has had several other names. Beckbury's northern boundary partly follows a tributary of the Worfe flowing from Denton pool (mentioned 1585) and partly the Ryton–Whiston road. Beckbury's southern boundary, with Badger, follows no natural features and required clarification in 1229.[81] The early 19th-century parish and manor were conterminous.[82]

The parish covers 545 ha. (1,346 a.)[83] and extends *c.* 2 km. from north to south and a maximum of 3.5 km. from west to east. Beckbury village lies on the western slope of Wall or Hine Hill,[84] a low north–south ridge of Keuper sandstone occupying the western half of the parish and rising to over 90 m.[85] West of the ridge is Upper Mottled Sandstone and some sand and gravel, and to the east boulder clay and sand and gravel, with peat along Snowdon brook.[86]

From Beckbury village a minor road, mentioned in 1285,[87] runs north to Albrighton and to Shifnal via Ryton, and others run east to Burnhill Green (Staffs.), south to Badger, south-west to Higford, and west via Harrington to the Wellington–Worcester road. The last was turnpiked in 1764 with the Shropshire part of the main road[88] and disturnpiked in 1867.[89]

There was prehistoric or Roman occupation on the (western) boundary with Sutton Maddock.[90] In the early 19th century fields called Golden hill and Urn field, north of Beckbury on the west side of the Shifnal road, were assumed to be named from 'antiquarian curiosities' found there,[91] but no such finds are recorded. Until 1840 there was a mound in Windmill field; it was then believed to be a barrow but was probably made as a windmill mound.[92]

On a hill top south of the church is an amphitheatre *c.* 30 m. in diameter, surrounded by a tall holly hedge and entered through opposing gates; in the centre is a raised circular platform *c.* 4 m. across. In 1839 it was described as a garden to Beckbury Hall. The garden was probably made in the 18th century, with a temple or summer house on the platform. Though it became known as the cockpit, it is unlikely that cocks were matched there.[93]

Around the church by the later Middle Ages there was probably a nucleated settlement, the present village, amid open fields. About 1 km. north-east of the village was the freehold property eventually known as Heath House, on the edge of a broad expanse of heath running down the eastern side of the parish. In the south-east corner of the parish was Snowdon pool, a large fishpond created before 1255.[94] Snowdon was

71 S.R.O. 804, box 1, Marsh ct. r. of 1641; 1224/3/24; ibid. box 75, articles for Sir John Weld, John Dawes, Fra. Adams, John Baldwin to peruse, f. 2.

72 S.R.O. 840, box 1, Willey ct. r. 1438; 1224/2/540; cf. above, manors.

73 Above, fig. 17; Barrow, intro.; local govt.; below, Linley, intro.; local govt.

74 *Compton Census*, ed. Whiteman, 259; *T.S.A.S.* iv. 294–5; 2nd ser. i. 91.

75 Above, Barrow, charities.

76 Above, Lib. and Boro. of Wenlock (early est.). This article was written in 1985.

77 O.S. Map, *Monastic Brit.* (1978), S. sheet; *V.C.H. Salop.* ii. 1.

78 The ld. of Badger owned an est. in Beckbury: below, manor.

79 *P.N. Salop.* (E.P.N.S.), i. 35.

80 W.S.L. 350/3/40, Beckbury p. 1.

81 Above, Badger, intro.; O.S. Map 1/25,000, SJ 70 (1951 edn.); S.R.O. 513, box 7, deed 30 Mar. 1585; *Cal. Close*, 1227–31, 242–3.

82 Bodl. MS. Blakeway 10, f. 143.

83 O.S. *Area Bk.* (1882).

84 Both names recorded *c.* 1735: Birm. Univ. Libr., Mytton Papers, i. 125.

85 O.S. Map 1/25,000, SJ 70 (1951 edn.).

86 Geol. Surv. Map 1", drift, sheet 153 (1907 edn.).

87 *Cal. Pat.* 1281–92, 151.

88 4 Geo. III, c. 81; S.R.O., dep. plan 219; cf. *V.C.H. Salop.* xi. 201.

89 Ann. Turnpike Acts Continuance Act, 1867, 30 & 31 Vic. c. 121

90 SA 2363.

91 W.S.L. 350/3/40, Beckbury p. 14.

92 Precise location unknown: not in P.R.O., IR 29/29/30; IR 30/29/30. For 1840 excavation rep. see par. rec., bur. reg. 1813–1973, note on flyleaf.

93 W.S.L. 350/3/40, Beckbury p. 13; D. H. Robinson, *The Wandering Worfe* (Albrighton, 1980), 79; H. E. Forrest, *Old Hos. of Wenlock* (Shrews. 1914), 111; *Country Life*, 11 July (p. 75), 8 Aug. (p. 267) 1957.

94 Below, econ. hist.

mentioned as a member of Patshull (Staffs.) manor in 1279.[95]

Beckbury's oldest houses are the Hall and the White House, both 16th- or 17th-century though later remodelled. Cheriton Cottage and Church Farm are 17th-century, and there are several 18th-century barns. Between 1752 and the mid 20th century the village altered little in size or plan, though there are some 19th-century buildings: Quarry House (early 19th century), a pair of estate cottages (mid century) in Caynton Road, and the school (1852).[96]

In the 18th century drinking water came from a well on Wall Hill. A second source, Fulwell, lay south-east of the village. By the 1730s some private wells had been sunk,[97] and by the late 19th century the Capel Cures' tenants had piped water, a supply that was extended to the rest of the village *c.* 1910.[98] In 1938 Wenlock Corporation opened a borehole and pumping station at Beckbury.[99]

After the Second World War the village grew considerably, especially northwards, as private and council houses were built, though there was no street lighting in 1952.[1] It was made a conservation area in 1981.[2] Snowdon Farm, at the north end of Snowdon pool in 1752, was rebuilt west of the pool *c.* 1810. The pool itself was drained in the 1850s.[3]

Eleven men from Beckbury and Badger were mustered in 1542.[4] In 1642 the Protestation was taken by all 36 men of the parish.[5] In 1672 hearth tax was paid by 19 householders.[6] In 1676 there were 25 adults in the parish.[7] There were 31 houses in the parish in 1732,[8] and by 1801 the population was 231. It rose to 307 in 1831 and remained at that level until the end of the century. It fell to 262 in 1921 but after the Second World War it rose again and was 372 in 1951 and 367 in 1981.[9]

In the 1630s or thereabouts John Wilde, victualler and alehouse keeper, lived in a house that had been an alehouse for forty years and was recommended as the best man in Beckbury to be licensed.[10] Ale sellers were mentioned occasionally in the late 17th century.[11] The Seven Stars, open by 1846, was presumably one of the two beerhouses noted in 1851. Thereafter, as in 1985, it was the village's only pub.[12] The Oddfellows had a Prince of Wales lodge and owned four cottages in the village by 1910.[13] A recreation and reading room was built in 1889 at Col. Alfred Capel Cure's expense; in 1891 the room's secretary was a blacksmith. About 1930 the room became the village hall.[14] The county library established a voluntary book centre in the village in 1926.[15]

MANOR AND OTHER ESTATES. It is possible that 'Kenbecleag', given to St. Mildburg by her half-brothers 690 × 704, was the later manor of *BECKBURY*.[16] By 1066, however, Azur (Azor), a free man, held Beckbury.[17]

In 1086 Roger of Montgomery, earl of Shrewsbury, held Beckbury in chief,[18] but his son Earl Robert presumably forfeited it with the rest of his English estates in 1102.[19] Roger the huntsman (*venator*) had held Beckbury under Earl Roger in 1086,[20] and the huntsman's estates went to form the barony of Pulverbatch.[21] About 1240 John of Beckbury, lord of the manor of Beckbury, was coparcener in a knight's fee held of the baron of Pulverbatch, but that holding is said to have been in Pulverbatch[22] and no certain post-Domesday connexion between Beckbury and the barony of Pulverbatch is known. Instead Beckbury is recorded as being held of the FitzAlans between the 13th and the 16th centuries. In 1242–3 John of Beckbury, whose predecessor, Hugh of Beckbury, had witnessed a FitzAlan charter *c.* 1196, held ⅛ knight's fee in Beckbury of John FitzAlan (II), baron of Oswestry[23] and John's overlord at Golding.[24] The FitzAlans' overlordship[25] of Beckbury was recorded again in 1348[26] and 1595.[27]

Wenlock priory had established a tenurial hold by 1120, and in 1255 the manor was simply said to be held of the prior for 25*s.* a year, the rent specified as due to the priory in 1120 and paid to the priory until the Dissolution.[28] Thereafter a fee-farm rent was evidently due to the

95 *V.C.H. Staffs.* xx. 162.

96 Dept. of Environment, *List of Bldgs.: Bridgnorth (pars. of Albrighton [etc.])* (1984), 20–7; J. Rocque, *Map of Salop.* (1752); R. Baugh, *Map of Salop.* (1808); B.L. Maps, O.S.D. 213; P.R.O., IR 30/29/30.

97 S.R.O. 2664, box 13, draft ct. r. of 1774; Birm. Univ. Libr., Mytton Papers, i. 125. For Fulwell see P.R.O., IR 29/29/30; IR 30/29/30, fields 157–9.

98 S.R.O. 3630, 5 May 1898, 4 Apr. 1910.

99 A.H.S. Waters, *Rep. on Water Supply* (S.C.C. 1946), 88; Robinson, *Wandering Worfe*, 18, 79.

1 *Manchester Guardian*, 19 Feb. 1952, p. 5.

2 Inf. from S.C.C. Planning Dept.

3 'Viator', *Guide to View from Brimstree Hill* (Shifnal, 1858), 39 (copy in S.P.L.).

4 *L. & P. Hen. VIII*, xvii, p. 508.

5 Ho. of Lords papers 1641–2, Protestations Oxon. and Salop. f. 182 and v.

6 *Hearth Tax 1672* (Salop. Arch. Soc. 1949), 36.

7 *Compton Census*, ed. Whiteman, 259.

8 Birm. Univ. Libr., Mytton Papers, i. 123.

9 *V.C.H. Salop.* ii. 220; *Census*, 1981, Small Area Statistics: Salop.

10 W.B.R., Q1/11/1 (dated by ref. to Elias Birch: *Alum. Oxon. 1500–1714*, i. 125).

11 S.R.O. 1224/2/511.

12 S. Bagshaw, *Dir. Salop.* (1851), 458; Co. of Salop, *Return of Licensed Hos. 1901* (copy in S.P.L., accession 6117), 172; *P.O. Dir. Salop.* (1856–79); *Kelly's Dir. Salop.* (1885–1941).

13 *Shropshire Mag.* Oct. 1955, 11; S.R.O. 3630, 7 Mar., 18 June 1912; 4044/6, p. 5.

14 *Kelly's Dir. Salop.* (1891–1941).

15 R. C. Elliott, 'Development of Public Librs. in Salop.' (Loughborough Univ. M.A. thesis, 1970; copy in co. libr.), 125.

16 H. P. R. Finberg, *Early Charters of W. Midlands* (1972), pp. 147–8. The ch.'s dedication to St. Mildburg (below, church) cannot be used as evidence of early manorial hist.

17 *V.C.H. Salop.* i. 341.

18 Ibid.

19 Ibid. iii. 10.

20 Ibid. i. 341.

21 Ibid. 298; viii. 133.

22 Eyton, iv. 137. But no such est. is mentioned in *V.C.H. Salop.* viii. 133–4.

23 *Bk. of Fees*, ii. 962, 971; cf. Eyton, iv. 136–7.

24 *V.C.H. Salop.* viii. 64.

25 Which Eyton (iv. 137 n. 19) dismisses as an error of the medieval record.

26 *Feud. Aids*, iv. 244.

27 P.R.O., C 142/254, no. 14.

28 Below, this section; *Rot. Hund.* (Rec. Com.), ii. 85.

Crown until Mrs. Elizabeth Browne, lady of the manor, redeemed it, then £1 8*s.* 6*d.* a year, in 1828.[29]

In 1086 an unnamed man-at-arms (*miles*) was paying 20*d.*, perhaps as rent for the manor.[30] A certain Reynold held 1 hide (the Domesday assessment of the manor) in Beckbury and in 1120, after his death, Wenlock priory granted his Beckbury land, his widow, and the wardship of his son to Walter son of Warin for 15 years for 25*s.* a year payable on the feast of St. Mildburg.[31]

Hugh of Beckbury (fl. 1190) was lord of Beckbury *c.* 1220.[32] He died in 1226 or 1227 and his heir John of Beckbury (d. 1248 × 1254) seems to have succeeded him there for John's son Philip (fl. 1292) was in possession by 1255.[33] John of Beckbury, lord in 1316,[34] was perhaps John of Beckbury, son and heir of Philip of Beckbury[35] and lord in 1347[36] and 1351. In 1351 John settled the manor on his daughter Parnel and her husband Thomas de la Lowe.[37] Beckbury descended in that family and passed to the Greys of Whittington (Staffs.). The Greys also held Enville (Staffs.), with which Beckbury apparently descended in the 16th and 17th centuries.[38] In 1674 Henry Grey sold Beckbury to Thomas Kynnersley[39] (d. 1680), lord of Badger, and thereafter the two manors descended together.[40]

The lords of Badger held an estate in Beckbury; like Badger it formed part of the barony of Richard's Castle and a mesne lordship was mentioned *c.* 1200. Later, however, like the manors of Badger and Beckbury it was said to be held of the prior of Wenlock. In the later 12th century Philip of Badger held 1 hide in Beckbury and in 1196, shortly before his death, he surrendered half of it to Ralph de Herleton. The half remaining to him passed to his son Roger of Badger and was said *c.* 1200 to be held of Philip of Greete, tenant of other estates in the barony of Richard's Castle. After Roger's death in the earlier 1220s his younger son Philip held the Beckbury estate under his older brother Thomas of Badger, lord of Badger. Probably in 1227 Philip, about to go on crusade, sold his estate to Thomas[41] and thereafter it evidently descended with the manor of Badger until the early 16th century.[42] John Petit (d. 1501), lord of Badger, had two messuages and two virgates in Beckbury worth £4 a year and held of the prior of Wenlock.[43] They passed to his son Thomas (d. 1504) who was succeeded by his brother Henry. Half a virgate of that land then formed a separate tenement, variously held by Richard the chaplain (probably in the late 15th century), Thomas of Badger (to 1506), Reynold de Penhill (from 1506), Roger Beston (to 1530), and Richard and Elizabeth Ascall (from 1530).[44]

By 1541 the two messuages inherited by Petit in 1504 had perhaps passed to the Haughtons.[45] John Haughton of Beckbury greatly enlarged his estate in the parish in 1585 when he bought the manor house, demesne lands, and rights in the Worfe between Denton pool and Badger wood from his kinsman John Grey, lord of the manor.[46] On Haughton's death in 1595 his estate included the manor house and two other messuages. They were all said (probably erroneously) once to have belonged to John Grey as of his manor of Beckbury.[47] John Haughton was succeeded by his son Roger (fl. 1623), whose son and heir was called Francis.[48] In 1668 William Haughton probably owned the estate.[49] About then it was sold to Richard Astley of Patshull (cr. bt. 1662, d. 1688). Sir Richard's son Sir John (d. 1772) left the estate to F. D. Astley, who sold his estate in Beckbury to Dr. Thomas Wyndham,[50] owner of *BECKBURY HALL* and 353 a. in the parish in 1837.[51] In 1850 Wyndham sold the Hall and 68 a. to Walter Stubbs, owner of Lower Hall, with which it was bought by William Stubbs. In 1896 William Stubbs's executrix Miss E. M. Stubbs sold Beckbury Hall with 14 a. to Lt.-Col. Lionel Tillotson;[52] Tillotson sold it in 1907 to Lt.-Col. A. C. Yate (d. 1929).[53] His son A. C. McC. Yate lived at Beckbury Hall until *c.* 1934[54] and Lt.-Col. H. P. Sykes from *c.* 1936 until his death in 1942.[55] His widow Mrs. W. C. J. Sykes remained there until her death in 1955,[56] and the Hall was bought *c.* 1956 by E. H. Browne (kt. 1964), mining engineer and businessman. Sir Humphrey re-

29 S.R.O. 513, box 6, corresp., etc., *re* fee-fm. rent; Bodl. MS. Blakeway 10, f. 144v.

30 *V.C.H. Salop.* i. 341; *Domesday Bk.: Salop.* ed. F. and C. Thorn (1986), n. 4.26.5.

31 Eyton, iv. 133–4; viii. 159; *V.C.H. Salop.* i. 341.

32 Eyton, iv. 136; *V.C.H. Salop.* viii. 64.

33 Eyton, ii. 134; iv. 136–7; vi. 101; *Rot. Hund.* ii. 56, 85; *Feud. Aids*, iv. 225.

34 *Feud. Aids*, iv. 228.

35 Eyton, viii. 161.

36 S.R.O. 905/3–4.

37 P.R.O., CP 25/1/195/15, no. 3; *V.C.H. Salop.* viii. 64.

38 *V.C.H. Staffs.* xx. 96–7, 135; W.S.L. 350/3/40, Beckbury pp. 4–8; P.R.O., C 2/Jas. I/G 7/42; CP 43/128, mm. 7, 70. The 14th–16th-cent. descent given in *T.S.A.S.* 4th ser. iii. 3, is confused and erroneous but apparently preserves a memory of the truth.

39 S.R.O. 513, box 7, deed 3 Mar. 1673/4.

40 Bodl. MS. Blakeway 10, ff. 143–4; above, Badger, manor; S.R.O., q. sess. rec. box 260, reg. of gamekeepers 1742– 79, 11 Aug. 1777; S.R.O. 513, box 7, abstr. of title to Mr. Browne's est.; 924/587; 1265/218; *P.O. Dir. Salop.* (1856–79); *Kelly's Dir. Salop.* (1885–1941).

41 Eyton, ii. 67, 70–2; cf. above, Badger, manor.

42 *Bk. of Fees*, ii. 962, 971; cf. Eyton, iv. 137.

43 *Cal. Inq. p.m. Hen. VII*, ii, pp. 379, 542; cf. above, Badger, manor.

44 S.R.O. 905/5–7.

45 Rog. Haughton descr. as 'of Beckbury' 1541: *L. & P. Hen. VIII*, xvi, p. 293.

46 S.R.O. 513, box 7, deed 30 Mar. 1585; Bodl. MS. Blakeway 10, f. 143. For the Haughtons see *T.S.A.S.* 4th ser. iii. 1–3; Forrest, *Old Hos. of Wenlock*, 111; *Visit. Salop. 1623*, i (Harl. Soc. xxviii), 230–1.

47 P.R.O., C 142/254, no. 14.

48 Ibid.; Barnard MSS., Raby Castle, box 2, bdle. 3, no. 3; *Visit. Salop. 1623*, i. 231.

49 S.R.O. 513, box 7, deeds 20 Aug. 1668.

50 *T.S.A.S.* 4th ser. iii. 3; viii. 131; S.R.O. 2664, box 13, draft ct. r. of 1774; *V.C.H. Staffs.* xx. 165; S. Shaw, *Hist. Staffs.* ii (1801), 203; *V.C.H. Wilts.* xi. 254.

51 W.S.L. 350/3/40, Beckbury p. 14; P.R.O., IR 29/29/30.

52 S.R.O. 1681/96/5, 33; /97/52; below, this section.

53 Forrest, *Old Hos. of Wenlock*, 111; Burke, *Peerage* (1938), 2641.

54 S.R.O., reg. of electors, Wrekin divn. (1933), p. 667.

55 Ibid. (1936), p. 686; *Shrews. Chron.* 16 Jan. 1942, p. 8.

56 S.R.O., reg. of electors, Wrekin const. (1955), p. 180; Burke, *Peerage* (1967), 2617.

mained the owner in 1985.[57] By 1910 the rest of the former Wyndham estate was part of the manorial estate of Francis Capel Cure.[58]

Beckbury Hall is a 16th- or early 17th-century timber framed house, perhaps originally comprising hall and cross wing. It was bricked up in the early 18th century and extended in the later 19th.[59]

A term of three lives in Beckbury Hall and in an estate in the parish was given by Sir Richard Astley to his daughter Ann on her marriage with Walter Stubbs (d. 1697). It was probably their son Walter (d. 1754) who bought *LOWER HALL*, on the south-west edge of the village. He bought other lands in the parish: six inclosed pieces of heath in 1712, 30 a. in 1726, a house called the Heath in 1727, and the 82-a. Heath House estate in 1734. The estate passed from father to son the following being owners: Walter (d. 1766), Walter (d. 1815), and Walter who, in 1837, owned Lower Hall and 18 a. in the parish. After the last named died in 1865 his trustees sold Lower Hall to his brother William (d. 1879). In 1880 William's mortgagees sold Lower Hall with 26 a. to Alfred Capel Cure.[60] The owner of Lower Hall in 1910 was Mary Ann Cartwright.[61]

Lower Hall is a small timber framed house of the 16th and 17th centuries.

In 1761 Humphrey Pitt of Priorslee owned two farms (179 a.) in Beckbury,[62] probably part of the former Haughton estate and including *HEATH HOUSE*, so known by the early 17th century.[63] That year Pitt settled three quarters of his property on three of his daughters. He died in 1769 and when his coheirs divided the estate in 1782 his daughter Mrs. Maria Edwards received the Beckbury property. Mrs. Edwards (fl. 1787, d.s.p. by 1800) left it to her American brother-in-law W. J. Yonge until his son Henry came of age, when it was to become his.[64] The Yonges built *CAYNTON HOUSE* on the estate in 1803.[65]

It seems that Henry Yonge (d. 1833), an army officer and evidently a spendthrift, sold the estate to Capt. William Horton (d. 1844), who in 1837 owned 293 a. in the parish including Heath House and Caynton. The estate was up for sale in 1850; it was probably then that it was acquired by the family of William Legge, earl of Dartmouth (d. 1853), who in 1848 had bought the adjoining Patshull estate. In 1856 the owner of Caynton House was his brother Col. (later Gen.) A. C. Legge. Legge died in 1890 and in 1941 the estate belonged to the trustees of his daughter-in-law Mrs. L. A. G. Legge (d. 1931).[66] By 1948 Caynton Hall belonged to D. G. Hann who sold it *c.* 1957 to Philip Trevor-Jones.[67]

Caynton House, or Hall, was built by the Yonges in 1803,[68] perhaps on the site of a late 18th-century farmhouse called Dennetts Hays (or Dennetts Heys).[69] Caynton was reputedly styled on an earlier residence of W. J. Yonge's, perhaps Pirbright Lodge (Surr.). Elements of the design are also claimed to have been inspired by mansions in the southern states of North America. The building, of seven bays and two storeys, has a low-pitched slate roof. Office and stable blocks are connected to both sides of the house by arcades. The north (entrance) façade has a projecting centre bow with colonnade. To the rear is a semicircular pillared portico, off which opens a circular hall rising the full height of the house. Caynton was altered in the 1850s by Col. Legge,[70] and again in the 1960s when a second bay to the south was added, the hall extended east to give a balanced effect, and the stables renovated. The house was divided into three *c.* 1977.[71]

Cut into a disused quarry 250 m. west of the house is a small neo-Romanesque grotto with irregular ambulatories opening into inner sanctuaries. It is locally reputed to have been made by Gen. Legge but could be older. In the early 1980s it seemed to be in use for black magic rituals.[72]

Heath House, 1 km. north-east of the village, is a large brick house of 1957. It replaced a three storeyed brick house, perhaps early 19th-century, demolished in the early 1970s.[73]

In the mid 18th century Richard Fowler (d. *c.* 1774) owned a messuage and yardland. He was succeeded briefly by his widow.[74] In the mid 19th century Dr. Richard Fowler was a principal landowner in the parish,[75] and in 1910 a Miss Fowler owned 88 a., including *QUARRY FARM* (56 a.)[76] whose house, later Quarry House, is an early 19th-century brick building.

57 S.R.O., reg. of electors, Wrekin const. (1957), p. 165; S.R.O., DA 25/516/3, Beckbury f. 2; *Who Was Who, 1981–90*, 98.

58 S.R.O. 4044/6.

59 Forrest, *Old Hos. of Wenlock*, 111; *List of Bldgs.* 25.

60 T. E. Sharpe, *A Royal Descent with Other Pedigrees and Memorials* (1875), 21–7; Forrest, op. cit. 111; P.R.O., IR 29/29/30; S.R.O. 498/11; 1681/96/7–8, 21. The Heath Ho. of the Stubbs fam. was distinct from that of Humph. Pitt (below, this section).

61 S.R.O. 4044/6, p. 3.

62 S.R.O. 1238/15, 21; Pitt Estate Act, 1800, 39 & 40 Geo. III, c. 115 (Local and Personal) (copy in S.R.O. 1238/27).

63 Above and below, this section; P.R.O., C 2/Jas. I/H 16/60.

64 S.R.O. 1238/28; Pitt Estate Act, 1800; E. Yonge, *The Yonges of Caynton, Edgmond* (priv. print. 1969), 133, 159–60.

65 Below, this section.

66 P.R.O., IR 29/29/30; IR 30/29/30; S.P.L., SC6/34; W.S.L. 350/3/40, Beckbury p. 14; Robinson, *Wandering Worfe*, 82; 'Viator', *Guide to View from Brimstree Hill*, 39–41; *V.C.H. Staffs.* xx. 165; Burke, *Peerage* (1949), 546; *Kelly's Dir. Salop.* (1900–41); S.R.O. 4044/6; Yonge, op. cit. 162–5; S.R.O. 515/7, p. 24; M.I.s in Beckbury ch.

67 S.R.O., reg. of electors, Wrekin (1948), 321; (1957), 165; (1958), 170; Yonge, op. cit. 162.

68 W.S.L. 350/3/40, Beckbury p. 14. The date 1775–80 (Robinson, op. cit. 82) seems too early as the Yonges acquired the est. only after 1787. Yonge (op. cit. 82, 133, 163) says that Bp. Yonge of Norwich provided financial aid towards the bldg., but he died in 1783.

69 Rocque, *Map of Salop.* showing no ho.; S.R.O. 2664, box 13, draft ct. r. of 1774, first recording existence of Dennetts Heys fm.; cf. P.R.O., IR 29/29/30; IR 30/29/30, fields 81–3, 87–8, 94, 96; S.R.O. 1238/27, pp. 16–17.

70 'Viator', *View from Brimstree Hill*, 39–40; Robinson, op. cit. 82; *List of Bldgs.* 22; I. Nairn and N. Pevsner, *Surr.* ed. B. Cherry (Bldgs. of Eng. 1971), 414; *Surr. Times*, 26 Sept. 1953; Yonge, op. cit. 163.

71 Inf. from Mr. P. Trevor-Jones.

72 *List of Bldgs.* 22; *Bridgnorth Jnl.* 26 June 1970; Robinson, op. cit. 82.

73 Local inf.

74 S.R.O. 2664, box 13, draft ct. r. of 1774.

75 S. Bagshaw, *Dir. Salop.* (1851), 457; *P.O. Dir. Salop.* (1856), 14–15; S.P.L., SC6/34; P.R.O., IR 29/29/30.

76 S.R.O. 4044/6.

In the earlier 19th century Thomas Whitmore (d. 1846) of Apley Park bought *c.* 117 a. in the parish, formerly part of the Haughtons' and Astleys' estate and including *BROOK FARM*. W. O. Foster bought the Whitmore estate in 1867 and his great-grandson Brig. Cuthbert Goulburn was owner in 1985.[77]

Before 1254 St. Leonard's priory (White Ladies), Brewood, was given the rent from two mills in Beckbury. In that year, after a dispute, the new lord of the manor, Philip of Beckbury, undertook to pay 1 mark a year. The canonesses still derived income from Beckbury at the Dissolution.[78]

Thomas Acton (d. 1514), of Longnor, endowed a chantry in Condover church out of lands in Beckbury and elsewhere.[79]

ECONOMIC HISTORY. Beckbury's open fields lay north, east, and south of the village. The three fields, known after the Middle Ages as Marsh, Wood, and Depdale fields, were inclosed by the early 18th century.[80] In 1732 the arable, *c.* 14 yardlands *c.* 1768,[81] was 'mostly rye land'.[82] Beckbury was well supplied with meadows along the Worfe, some of them common.[83] The eastern third of the parish was mainly heath.[84] It was presumably there that the rector had the right *c.* 1600 to pasture 50 sheep and some young beasts.[85] As in Badger, the heath may have been inclosed in the 17th century; it certainly was by 1712.[86] Reinvasion by gorse, however, remained a problem in 1800.[87] West of the Worfe was wet moor.[88] In the late 18th century some flax was grown.[89] Most farm work was done by contract between farmers and labourers. At 1*s.* a day with beer labourers' wages were low; they were supplemented by I. H. Browne, who gave weekly doles of 1*s.* 6*d.* to 2*s.* 6*d.* to those who attended church.[90]

In 1801 the main arable crops were barley, wheat, and turnips.[91] In 1839 over four fifths of the parish was arable,[92] but by 1867 there was more grassland than arable. Thereafter the proportion of arable recovered, and in 1965 the amount of arable was close to early 19th-century levels. The proportion of wheat fell while that of barley rose, with oats being quite widely grown in the parish in the late 19th and early 20th century. From the late 19th century about a quarter of the land was usually given over to root crops. Until after the Second World War sheep were by far the most widely kept livestock, but thereafter their numbers declined as pig-keeping increased.

TABLE XIV

BECKBURY: LAND USE, LIVESTOCK, AND CROPS

		1867	*1891*	*1938*	*1965*
Percentage of	grassland	42	45	59	30
	arable	58	55	41	70
Percentage of	cattle	3	9	21	7
	sheep	85	87	71	0
	pigs	12	4	8	93
Percentage of	wheat	49	19	37	17
	barley	50	58	31	81
	oats	0	23	32	2
	mixed corn & rye	1	0	0	0
Percentage of agricultural land growing roots and vegetables		18	22	20	27

Sources: P.R.O., MAF 68/143, no. 9; /1340, no. 12; /3880, Salop. no. 177; /4945, no. 177.

Three areas of woodland survived until the later 18th or early 19th century:[93] Ellston (or Elslow) wood in the south-west adjoining Badger wood, Beckbury wood west of Snowdon pool on the Badger boundary, and a wood east of Beckbury village.

Snowdon pool, created before 1255 as a fishpond, belonged to the lord of Patshull by the early 15th century. In good repair in the 17th century, the pool was drained in the 1850s and planted with trees.[94] There was perhaps a weir on the Worfe north of Higford (in Stockton).[95]

There was a mill at Beckbury *c.* 1200,[96] perhaps on the Worfe near Mill croft, due west of the village.[97] White Ladies priory had the rent from two mills in Beckbury by 1254.[98] There was probably a windmill before the early 19th century.[99]

In 1732 *fluor metallorum*, probably the smelting flux fluorspar, was got in the parish, presumably from the local sandstone.[1] A family of ropemakers worked in Beckbury in the mid 18th century.[2] In the later 19th century Beck-

77 W.S.L. 350/3/40, Beckbury p. 14; P.R.O., IR 29/29/30; *V.C.H. Salop.* iii. 335; Burke, *Land. Gent.* (1952), 1030, 2707; *P.O. Dir. Salop.* (1856–79); *Kelly's Dir. Salop.* (1885–1941); S.R.O. 4044/6; inf. from the late Brig. C. Goulburn.

78 Eyton, iv. 137; *V.C.H. Salop.* ii. 83.

79 *Cal. Pat.* 1563–6, p. 63; *V.C.H. Salop.* viii. 52, 109.

80 S.R.O. 498/11; 1681/98, f. 7; field names in P.R.O., IR 29/29/30 and IR 30/29/30.

81 S.R.O. 4481/CW/1.

82 Birm. Univ. Libr., Mytton Papers, i. 123.

83 S.R.O. 498/11 (10–12), 12 (1); 905/3; 1681/98, ff. 2, 4.

84 Fig. 18.

85 H.W.R.O.(H.), HD 2/14/10.

86 Above, Badger, econ. hist.; S.R.O. 498/11.

87 Pitt Estate Act, 1800.

88 Birm. Univ. Libr., Mytton Papers, i. 125.

89 S.R.O. 2664, box 13, draft ct. r. of 1774.

90 Trinder, *Ind. Rev. Salop.* 203.

91 P.R.O., HO 67/12/28.

92 P.R.O., IR 29/29/30. Rest of para. based on Table XIV and sources there cited.

93 Rocque, *Map of Salop.*; P.R.O., IR 29/29/30; 30/29/30; S.R.O. 4792, no. 46.

94 *V.C.H. Staffs.* xx. 169; S.R.O. 513, box 2, agreement 4 Mar. 1535/6, agreement *re* Snowdon pool 4 Nov. 1661, ct. order 29 Mar. 1658.

95 P.R.O., IR 29/29/30; IR 30/29/30, field 230.

96 Eyton, ii. 70.

97 P.R.O., IR 29/29/30; IR 30/29/30, field 225.

98 Above, manor.

99 Above, this article, intro.

1 Birm. Univ. Libr., Mytton Papers, i. 123; *O.E.D.*; inf. from S.C.C. Planning Dept.

2 S.R.O. 4481/P/2/4.

bury was a thriving village with half a dozen food shops; usually there were also at least one blacksmith, a wheelwright, a plumber, a builder, a draper, and a shoemaker. In 1941 there were four food shops, a carpenter, and a wheelwright,[3] but in the later 20th century the number of shops and services declined.

LOCAL GOVERNMENT. Beckbury manor court rolls survive from 1415, when it was mainly grazing offences that were presented, and 1774. The record of a court of recognition of *c.* 1400 also survives.[4]

The office of churchwarden (only one usually being appointed by the 1760s) was served by householders in rotation according to ancient custom. In 1768, when one man served as both churchwarden and parish constable, his activities were financed by a levy of 8*s.* per yardland;[5] by the early 19th century, however, properties were rated.[6] In 1711 the parish overseers rented a cottage for use as a poorhouse.[7] Between 1744, from when regular accounts survive, until the early 19th century, there was one overseer, appointed annually. Between the 1740s and early 1770s *c.* £8 was raised each year and disbursed, as later, in cash, clothing, and coal. From 1774 expenditure rose rapidly, to £38 in 1785. It then fell, before rising again in the early 1790s to peak several times in the post-war period: £214 was spent in 1814,[8] £290 10*s.* in 1817, and £232 7*s.* in 1824.[9] Between 1812 and 1815 about a dozen adults usually received permanent out-relief and another 4 or 5 occasional relief.[10]

Beckbury was in Shifnal poor-law union 1836–1930,[11] Bridgnorth highway district 1863–95,[12] Shifnal rural sanitary district 1872–94, Shifnal rural district 1894–1974, and Bridgnorth district from 1974.[13]

CHURCH. The incumbent was described as rector in 1279,[14] though the church was often called a chapel in the earlier 14th century and perhaps later. By 1303 the lord of the manor nominated each new incumbent to the prior of Wenlock (or to the king when the priory was in his hands as an alien house), who presented him to the bishop. An incoming rector had to covenant to pay a pension of 3*s.* to the priory, and after the Dissolution the pension was part of an annual rent paid by the lord to the Crown, which presented to the living. The lord's right of nomination seems to have lapsed after 1695, perhaps in 1724. Payment of the 3*s.* ceased in 1872.[15] The lord chancellor was patron by 1879.[16] The living was held in plurality with those of Badger and Ryton from 1956.[17]

The church, worth less than £4 a year in 1291, was valued at £3 18*s.* in 1379, £4 in 1426, and £5 6*s.* 8*d.* in 1535.[18] About 1600 the glebe comprised 16 a. of arable and common for 50 sheep and some young beasts.[19] About 1708 the living was worth £49.[20] In 1839 the tithes were commuted to £333.[21] In 1851 the rector received £321 from tithe rent charges and £41 from 31 a. of glebe.[22] Glebe of *c.* 26 a. was being let in 1990.[23]

About 1600 the parsonage was of two bays and had a barn and sheepcote.[24] The house, east of the church, was in good repair in the early 18th century[25] but was evidently unfit for the successor of H. R. Smythe (d. 1882) until enlarged and improved in 1891.[26] It was sold in 1955 and a new one was built to the south.[27]

Rectors' names in the later 13th and 14th century suggest that they were local men.[28] Thomas Gwilliam, rector from 1571 until 1607 or later, was also rector of Badger.[29] William James, rector 1661–98, was said in 1672 to be a 'railer and quarreller' who was not ordained, qualified, or instituted.[30] Thomas Green, rector 1698–1724, apparently resided; he conducted two Sunday services, one with sermon, and then, as usually in the 18th and 19th centuries, communion was celebrated five times a year.[31] John Fayle, rector 1754–78, was also rector of Barrow and Willey.[32]

By the mid 18th century and until the later 19th the employment of a curate was usual; the curate 1757–60 and in 1766 was Jonathan Stubbs (d. 1789), a younger son of Walter Stubbs (d. 1754).[33] For most, if not all, of the incumbency of the pluralist William Bates, rector 1824–50, the cure was served by R. P. Thursfield.[34] H. R. Smythe, rector 1850–82,

3 S. Bagshaw, *Dir. Salop.* (1851), 458; *P.O. Dir. Salop.* (1856–79); *Kelly's Dir. Salop.* (1885–1941).

4 S.R.O. 513, box 1, ct. r. 1415; 2664, box 13, draft ct. r. 1774; Staffs. R.O., D.(W.) 1733, bdle. 19, ct. of recognition.

5 H.W.R.O.(H.), HD 5/15, Beckbury; S.R.O. 4481/CW/1.

6 e.g. S.R.O. 4481/CW/1, s.a. 1819.

7 S.R.O. 4481/P/5/2.

8 Ibid. /P/1/1.

9 *Poor Rate Returns*, H.C. 556, suppl. app. p. 143 (1822), v; H.C. 334, p. 179 (1825), iv; H.C. 219, p. 167 (1830–1), xi; H.C. 444, p. 162 (1835), xlvii.

10 *Poor Law Abstract*, H.C. 82, pp. 376–7 (1818), xix.

11 V. J. Walsh, 'Admin. of Poor Laws in Salop. 1820–55' (Pennsylvania Univ. Ph.D. thesis, 1970), 147–50; *Kelly's Dir. Salop.* (1929), 34.

12 S.R.O., q. sess. order bk. 1861–9, p. 127; S.C.C. Local Govt., etc., Cttee. min. bk. 1894–1903, p. 29.

13 *V.C.H. Salop.* ii. 217.

14 *Reg. Cantilupe* (C.S.), 209.

15 Eyton, ii. 77; iv. 138–9; *Cal. Pat.* 1358–61, 27; 1377–81, 407; *Reg. Mascall* (C.S.), 174; *Reg. Stanbury* (C.S.), 174; Bodl. MS. Blakeway 10, f. 144 and v.; *Dioc. of Heref. Institutions (1539–1900)*, ed. A. T. Bannister (Heref. 1923), 20, 59, 71, 90, 110, 129, 146, 165, 195; S.R.O. 4481/Inc/3.

16 *P.O. Dir. Salop.* (1879), 278; *Lich. Dioc. Dir.* (1985), 35.

17 *Crockford* (1957–8), 130; *Lich. Dioc. Dir.* (1985), 35.

18 *Tax. Eccl.* (Rec. Com.), 167, 176; Dugdale, *Mon.* v. 78; *Valor Eccl.* (Rec. Com.), iii. 216. Eyton, iv. 138, incorrectly gives 5 marks in 1379.

19 H.W.R.O.(H.), HD 2/14/10, 11 (noting 10 a. of glebe in 1607).

20 J. Ecton, *Liber Valorum et Decimarum* (1711), 147.

21 P.R.O., IR 29/29/30.

22 P.R.O. HO 129/357, no. 5; S. Bagshaw, *Dir. Salop.* (1851), 457.

23 Inf. from Lich. dioc. registrar.

24 H.W.R.O.(H.), HD 2/14/10.

25 Ibid. HD 5/14/1/7; HD 5/15, Beckbury.

26 *Kelly's Dir. Salop.* (1885), 799; (1891), 263; below, this section (for Smythe).

27 O.S. Map 1/10,000, SJ 70 SE. (1975 edn.); inf. from Lich. dioc. registrar.

28 Eyton, iv. 138.

29 Bannister, *Heref. Institutions*, 20; above, Badger, church.

30 H.W.R.O.(H.), HD 7, chwdns.' presentment of 1672; Birm. Univ. Libr., Mytton Papers, i. 123.

31 Bannister, op. cit. 55, 59, 71; H.W.R.O.(H.), HD 5/14/1/7; HD 5/15, Beckbury; S.R.O. 4481/CW/1.

32 Bannister, op. cit. 81, 90, 110–11.

33 Heref. Dioc Regy., curates' licences in bps.' regs.; S.R.O. 4481/MRg/1–2; Sharpe, *Royal Descent*, 29; *Alum. Oxon.* 1715–1886, iv. 1369; above, manor (Lower Hall).

34 Bannister, op. cit. 146, 165; *Rep. Com. Eccl. Revenues* [67], pp. 428–9, H.C. (1835), xxii; S.R.O. 4481/MRg/2.

lived in Shifnal in 1851 and spent time in Italy in 1852;[35] for much of the 1850s and 1860s he was absent because of illness[36] and employed curates, who lived at the rectory.[37] On Census Sunday 1851 morning service was attended by 40 adults, evening service by 30; 15 children attended both.[38] Girls were paid to sing in church in 1835. By 1866 the church had a harmonium.[39]

The church of *ST. MILBURGA*, so dedicated by *c.* 1740,[40] comprises chancel, nave, north and south aisles, north porch, and west tower. The chancel is probably early 14th-century and has east, north, and south windows of that date.[41] At the west ends of the side walls are also cusped lancets above blocked low side windows, the southern one retaining its external iron bars and recesses for a bolt.

After a brief was issued in 1731[42] a new nave and tower were built. The old nave was probably small with only one (north) entrance.[43] The new nave was of red ashlar sandstone with rusticated quoins and had two semicircular headed windows on each side. The two-stage tower has a pyramidal roof and a Gibbs doorway on the west. Round windows containing 19th-century clock faces pierce its north and west faces. Above the west round window is a semicircular headed window; a shorter one is in the east face of the tower. About 1800 a north gallery for Caynton House was built in the nave; it was entered by an external staircase and a door made from the eastern window in the nave's north wall.[44]

In 1851 the church had 100 seats, half of them free.[45] It was much altered in the later 19th century. In 1855 two three-light windows replaced the gallery entrance and surviving window of 1731 in the north wall.[46] In 1856 a south aisle designed by Edward Banks was added, the chancel repaired, and the pews cut down.[47] Two stained glass windows by Wailes & Strang were introduced in 1877. In 1879–80 a north aisle, transept, and nave clerestory designed by William Martin of Hereford and at least partly financed by the Incorporated Church Building Society were built, the north gallery being removed.[48] In 1884, to a design by T. H. Fleeming of Wolverhampton, the chancel was raised by 4 ft. and a new east window (by Burlison & Grylls), screen, and stalls provided.[49] In 1887–8 the west end was restored; an oak screen, choir vestry, and new tower arch were erected. At the same time the nave was reseated and a north porch added.[50]

Externally on the north wall is an empty tomb recess, heavily restored in concrete. Internally in the south wall is a piscina, and on the north wall an incised alabaster slab to Richard Haughton (d. 1505) and his wife Margaret; it was moved there in 1856 when an altar tomb on the north side of the chancel was destroyed. Other furnishings include a probably medieval chest, a Perpendicular font (restored 1892), and a stone pulpit of 1867. There are three bells: one of 1615 and two of 1658.[51] The plate includes an Elizabethan silver chalice.[52]

The churchyard was extended in 1894 (on the east) and 1969.[53] The registers are complete from 1661.[54]

NONCONFORMITY. There was a dissenter in 1676[55] but none in 1716.[56]

In 1807 Thomas Harrison of Beckbury was a Baptist minister.[57] Wesleyans met at Beckbury from *c.* 1812 until 1834–5. In 1815 the society had four members.[58] In 1840 the house of Richard Adams, an 81-year-old farm labourer,[59] was licensed for dissenting worship.[60] Primitive Methodists built Provident chapel in 1866. By 1963 services were poorly attended and preachers few. The chapel was sold in 1966.[61]

EDUCATION. In 1716 and 1719 the rector kept a school; pupils had to attend Saturday catechism and church services.[62] Samuel Hill (d. 1789) kept a school for boys and girls in a cottage near Lower Hall. In the early 19th century the curate R. P. Thursfield took in pupils to read classics.[63] The Misses Belton kept a school in the 1800s. In 1819 there were two unendowed schools in the parish with 51 pupils in all. A Sunday school had failed through non-attendance, but another, begun in 1825, had 15 boys and 15 girls in 1835, when there was also a day school, begun in 1829, with 34 boys and 21 girls.[64]

Beckbury National school, a two storeyed brick building in the Tudor style,[65] was built in

35 Bannister, op. cit. 165, 195; P.R.O., HO 129/357, no. 5; S.R.O. 4481/T/1–2.

36 Heref. Dioc. Regy., reg. 1847–56, pp. 316, 459, 536; 1857–69, pp. 133, 318–19, 432, 548, 637.

37 P.R.O., RG 9/1852, f. 103v.; RG 10/2746, f. 73.

38 P.R.O., HO 129/357, no. 5.

39 S.R.O. 4481/CW/1, s.a.

40 B.L. Add. MS. 30316, ff. 5, 29v.

41 Descr. based on Cranage, iii. 184–5; x. 1081–2; Pevsner, *Salop.* 71; *List of Bldgs.* 26; S.P.L., MS. 372, vol. i, f. 124; Bodl. MS. Top. Salop. c. 2, f. 108; W.S.L. 350/3/40, Beckbury pp. 15–16.

42 *Orders of Q. Sess.* ii. 77.

43 Birm. Univ. Libr., Mytton Papers, i. 123.

44 W.S.L. 350/3/40, Beckbury p. 15; S.P.L., J. H. Smith colln. no. 18.

45 P.R.O., HO 129/357, no. 5.

46 [J. P. R. Baggaley], *Notes on Par. and Ch. of St. Milburga, Beckbury* (1979), 21–2 (copy in S.P.L.); S.R.O. 4481/ChF/2.

47 S.R.O. 4481/ChF/1; /CW/1, s.a. 1857; *P.O. Dir. Salop.* (1856), 14.

48 *Ch. Cal. Dioc. Heref.* (1878), 111; (1880), 127; S.R.O. 4481/ChF/2.

49 *Kelly's Dir. Salop.* (1885), 799 (cf. N. Pevsner, *Staffs.* (1974), 199, 318, 321, 326); *Ch. Cal. Dioc. Heref.* (1887), 138.

50 *Kelly's Dir. Salop.* (1900), 31.

51 H. B. Walters, *Ch. Bells of Salop.* (Oswestry, 1915), 21.

52 S. A. Jeavons, *Ch. Plate Archd. Salop.* (Shrews. 1964), pp. 32, 100, 108, 124.

53 Heref. Dioc. Regy., reg. 1883–91, pp. 458, 472–3; Baggaley, *Notes on Beckbury*, 26.

54 S.R.O. 4481/Rg/1–3; /MRg/1–2; regs. at ch. Cf. H.W.R.O.(H.), bp.'s transcripts for 1610, 1620, 1622, 1628, 1630, 1660–1833, etc.

55 *Compton Census*, ed. Whiteman, 259.

56 H.W.R.O.(H.), HD 5/14/1/7.

57 S.R.O. 3235/1.

58 Heref. Dioc. Regy., reg. 1791–1821, f. 118; Shrews. Sch. Libr., Broseley circuit bk. 1815–41.

59 P.R.O., HO 107/909, f. 9v.

60 Heref. Dioc. Regy., reg. 1822–42, p. 500. For location of ho. see L.J.R.O., B/A/15, Beckbury (no. 7).

61 *Kelly's Dir. Salop.* (1885), 799; S.R.O. 2533/134, 11 Nov. 1963; *Shropshire Mag.* Oct. 1955, 11.

62 H.W.R.O.(H.), HD 5/14/1/7; HD 5/15, Beckbury (refs. supplied by Dr. R. Hume). This section was written in 1982 and later revised.

63 W.S.L. 350/3/40, Beckbury pp. 13–14.

64 R. Hume, 'Changing Patterns of Educ. Devt. in Salop. 1660–1833' (Keele Univ. Ph.D. (Educ.) thesis, 1982), 170, 315, 366; *Educ. of Poor Digest*, H.C. 224, p. 746 (1819), ix (2); *Educ. Enq. Abstract*, H.C. 62, p. 769 (1835), xlii.

65 *Kelly's Dir. Salop.* (1885), 799; S.R.O. 1564/10.

1852 by the owner of Beckbury Hall on a site that later passed to the diocese.[66] The teacher's house was on the ground floor; a stone staircase at each end led to the schoolroom above. The school received £10 a year from the parish, the rest of its income in voluntary contributions and school pence (2*d.* a week). Attendance averaged 53 in 1854,[67] 50 in 1885, 36 in 1909, and 50 in 1913.[68] The building was much improved in the years 1898–1904, 1928,[69] and 1964.[70] An evening school was held 1925–6 and 1928–31.[71] Twelve Smethwick evacuees were admitted in 1939. In 1949 13-year old pupils, and next year 11-year-olds, left for Shifnal Modern school.[72] Beckbury school, controlled from 1957,[73] admitted 11 pupils from Kemberton and 22 from Ryton C.E. (Controlled) primary schools, both closed in 1964; a demountable unit including two classrooms and a kitchen was erected then and extended in 1976.[74] The roll was 45 in 1954, 81 in 1965, 89 in 1974, and 64 in 1985.[75]

CHARITY FOR THE POOR. H. R. Smythe (d. 1882), rector, left £200. In the late 20th century his charity yielded *c.* £5 a year.[76]

BENTHALL

BENTHALL lies on the right bank of the Severn facing the town of Ironbridge.[77] The former parish is largely rural, but in earlier centuries its extensive reserves of coal, ironstone, limestone, and clay were exploited, at times intensively as economic activity quickened in the neighbouring parishes of Broseley and Madeley. Benthall, however, never rivalled Broseley as an industrial and market centre and was in effect merely an adjunct to it.[78]

By the early 19th century the parish covered *c.* 844 a. (*c.* 342 ha.) and extended a maximum of 2.5 km. north-west to south-east and 3 km. north-east to south-west. Its bounds remained unaltered (except for the loss of a tiny detachment in 1883) until the parish was abolished in 1966.[79] To the east it was mainly bounded by Benthall brook[80] draining north to the Severn. To the north-west the boundary with Buildwas followed for a short distance the Hunger Dale stream, called Mallebroch when the boundary was defined in the later 13th century,[81] and near the Severn ran along the base of Benthall Edge. The notched south-west boundary of the parish followed field edges; a tongue of land protruding south-west from it included part of the hamlet of Posenhall and, having been bought by Lawrence Benthall in 1576 and probably incorporated in his manor of Benthall,[82] probably transferred to Benthall parish from Posenhall chapelry.[83] With the Posenhall land Lawrence acquired land in Wyke, which may explain the origin of a 1½-a. detachment of Benthall parish at Wyke,[84] transferred in 1883 to the surrounding civil parish of Much Wenlock.[85] To the south Benthall's boundary followed the Wenlock–Broseley road before swinging south and then east to follow the northern boundary of Willey's medieval park.[86]

Most of the parish is fairly flat, lying at *c.* 180 m. To the north and north-west, along Benthall Edge, the ground falls sharply towards the Severn and Buildwas to 60 m. and less. It also falls eastwards towards Benthall brook, the main natural route down to the Severn.[87] The early topography is apparently alluded to in some way by Benthall's name, meaning 'bent-grass nook'.[88] Much of the centre of the parish is covered by boulder clay. Workable Lower Coal Measures outcrop everywhere save in the area towards Posenhall. Benthall Edge is formed by an outcrop of Silurian limestone.[89]

About 1250 Philip of Benthall gave Buildwas abbey free right of way across Benthall for the carriage of coal, stone, and timber. Until the 19th century a road ran north and then west from a point east of Benthall Hall to Buildwas, although stone and timber for the abbey had probably been carried to the Severn and so up river rather than overland.[90]

The principal road, at least until the 18th century, was that from Much Wenlock to Broseley; it was a medieval route turnpiked in 1756.[91] In the 1630s, as later, a road forked north-west from it to Benthall Hall and church. There was probably then a second route to Hall and church, north from Posenhall; it was disused by 1808

66 S.R.O. 2699/37, no. 17; *S.C.C. Mins. (Educ.)* 1972–3, 127.

67 P.R.O., ED 7/102, ff. 68–70; S.R.O. 1564/10.

68 *Kelly's Dir. Salop.* (1885), 799; (1909), 31; (1913), 32.

69 Beckbury Nat. sch. log bk. (at Beckbury C.E. (Contr.) Primary Sch.) 25 Nov. 1898, 11 Sept. 1899; *S.C.C. Mins. (Educ.)* 1904–5, 110; 1928–9, 64.

70 Personal knowledge; below, this section.

71 Log bk. 7 Oct. 1928 (night sch. reopened, 12 boys, 2 girls attending); *S.C.C. Mins. (Educ.)* 1925–6, 73; 1929–30, 65; 1930–1, 64.

72 Log bk. 11 Sept. 1939, 28 Oct. 1949, 25 Jan. 1950.

73 *S.C.C. Mins. (Educ.)* 1957–8, 80.

74 Log bk. 1 Sept., 19 June 1964, 19 Aug. 1976.

75 Ibid. rep. 1954, 5 Jan. 1965, 14 Jan. 1974; S.C.C. Educ. Cttee. *Educ. Dir.* (1985), 4.

76 *Kelly's Dir. Salop.* (1900), 29; S.R.O. 4693/18; *Review of Local Chars.* (S.C.C. 1975), 21.

77 This article was written in 1985 and revised in 1995.

78 Below, this section; econ. hist. (ind.).

79 *Census* (1891); S.R.O. 294/2; below, this para.; local govt.

80 Below, Broseley, intro.

81 Below, manor; Dugdale, *Mon.* v. 360; S.R.O., archivist's office file 'Benthall', letter from Sir Paul Benthall 11 May 1972; O.S. Map 1/25,000, SJ 60 (1958 edn.).

82 Below, manor.

83 Below, Posenhall, chapel of ease.

84 S.R.O. 294/2, fields 365–6; 3956.

85 Under 45 & 46 Vic. c. 58: O.S. *Area Bk.* M. Wenlock (1883; with amendment slip).

86 Below; below, Willey, econ. hist. (agric.).

87 O.S. Map 1/25,000, SJ 60 (1958 edn.).

88 *P.N. Salop.* (E.P.N.S.), i. 37.

89 Inst. Geol. Sciences Map 1/25,000, *Telford* (1978 edn.); C. Clark and J. Alfrey, *Benthall and Broseley Wood* (Nuffield Arch. Surv. [of Ironbridge Gorge] 3rd Interim Rep.; Ironbridge, 1987), 38–9, 163–4.

90 Clark and Alfrey, op. cit. 30; Eyton, iii. 276; cf. below, Broseley, communications.

91 Below, Broseley, communications; M. Wenlock, communications.

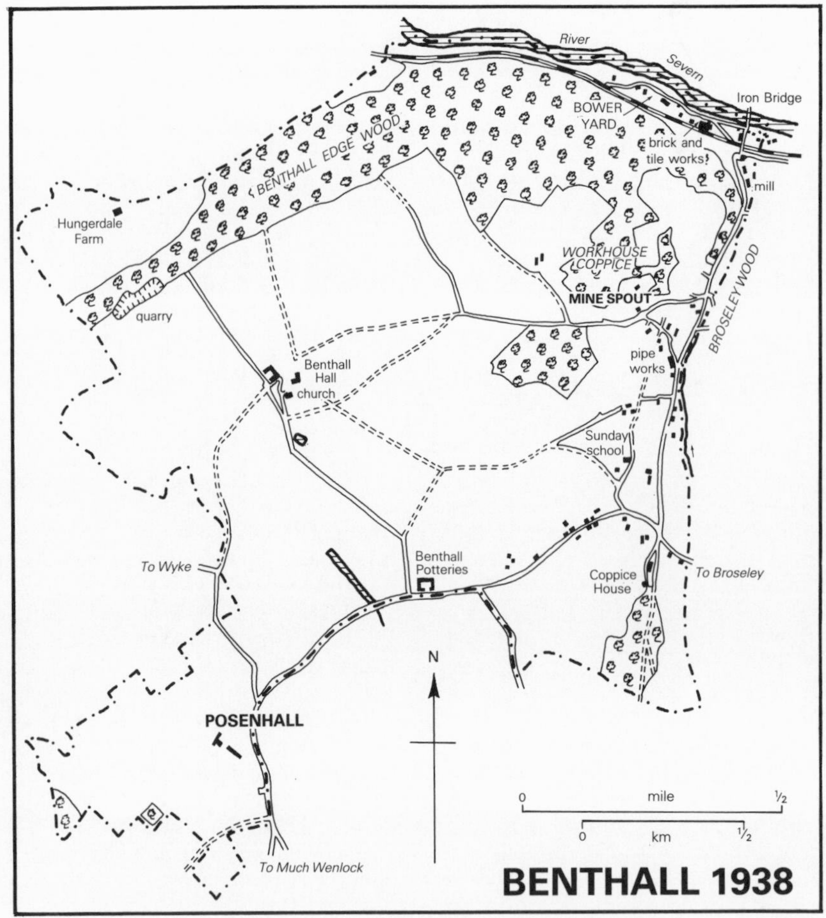

Fig. 24

when that road turned west to Wyke, just north of Posenhall. Perhaps already by 1630 the road that led out of the Wenlock–Broseley road to run north along the left bank of Benthall brook had become especially important.[92] In 1776 the Iron Bridge proprietors decided to improve the road up Benthall Bank to the Broseley–Wenlock turnpike, but it was steep and often obstructed and was replaced in 1828 by a new road looping east of Broseley town.[93]

By the mid 17th century coal from Benthall was shipped down the Severn,[94] and the barges, trows, and watermen working from the Bower Yard wharves were mainstays of the local economy until the 1860s. Eight owners had 13 barges or trows in 1756,[95] while in 1851 there were *c.* 11 families of watermen in the parish.[96] Along the Severn bank ran the Coalbrookdale–Bewdley tow path, made *c.* 1800.[97] River use declined after the railway came in 1862, though lime was still carried by barge in the late 19th century.[98] Benthall ferry was replaced as the main crossing of the Severn by the Iron Bridge, built 1777–80 from the eastern end of Bower Yard to Hodgebower in Madeley Wood; the bridge closed to vehicles in 1934.[99] A small ferry owned by the Maws operated across the Severn at the western end of the parish in the later 19th century.[1]

The Severn Valley line of the West Midland Railway (later G.W.R.), which ran along the base of the Edge, opened in 1862. Ironbridge and Broseley station, near the Iron Bridge, closed in 1963 and the line in 1970.[2]

Seventeen people from Barrow, Benthall, and Posenhall paid to the 1327 subsidy,[3] and 11 men from Benthall and Posenhall were mustered in 1542.[4] The 1642 Protestation was taken by 84 adult male parishioners.[5] In 1672 hearth tax was paid by 29 households; 20 of the houses had just one or two taxed hearths and 7 had three or four.[6] In 1676 there were 241 inhabitants of Benthall,

92 S.R.O. 1224/1/32; S.P.L., Deeds 18120; fig. 24; R. Baugh, *Map of Salop.* (1808).

93 Below, Broseley, communications; Trinder, *Ind. Rev. Salop.* 90; J. Randall, *Broseley and Its Surroundings* (Madeley, 1879), 238, 315–16; Clark and Alfrey, *Benthall and Broseley Wood*, 31–3.

94 Below, econ. hist. (coal and ironstone).

95 *V.C.H. Salop.* i. 426.

96 S.R.O. 2979/3.

97 Under 39 Geo. III, c. 8 (Local and Personal): C. Hadfield, *Canals of W. Midlands* (1969), 124.

98 Clark and Alfrey, *Benthall and Broseley Wood*, 35–6, 56.

99 A. Young, *Tours in Eng. and Wales* (1932), 150; *V.C.H. Salop.* i. 416; xi. 150; Severn Bridge Act, 16 Geo. III, c. 17, s. 18.

1 Clark and Alfrey, op. cit. 36.

2 Below, Broseley, communications; *V.C.H. Salop.* xi. 27; *Railway Mag.* cxi. 375; *T.S.A.S.* lxiv. 96; O.S. Map 6", Salop. XLIII. SW. (1890 edn.).

3 *T.S.A.S.* 2nd ser. iv. 333.

4 *L. & P. Hen. VIII*, xvii, p. 508.

5 Ho. of Lords papers 1641–2, Protestations Oxon. and Salop. f. 184.

6 *Hearth Tax 1672* (Salop. Arch. Soc. 1949), 33. The total may include the pt. of Posenhall hamlet that was apparently added to Benthall man. in or after 1576: below, manor.

perhaps including children.[7] By 1700 the parish's population was over 500,[8] in 1801 *c.* 600.[9] Thereafter it fell to 530 in 1851. It eventually stabilized at *c.* 320 in the 1920s.[10]

A local tradition states that when Benthall Hall was taken by Parliamentarian forces in 1645 the village to the north was razed.[11] It seems more likely that any surviving settlement around the Hall was gradually deserted at that time in favour of the new industrial areas of Bower Yard and Broseley Wood, the latter spilling over from Broseley into Benthall as an area of settlement called the Mines. Both had probably begun to grow in the late 16th century.[12] In 1635 John Weld of Willey asserted that Lawrence Benthall had built, or encouraged 'poor and disorderly people' to build, cottages both in Benthall and in Broseley (presumably Broseley Wood). Benthall denied it, saying that he had built only two cottages, at Benthall Marsh and for miners not disorderly people.[13] Nevertheless settlement along Benthall brook expanded in the 17th century. By contrast with Broseley the parish had few large houses: apart from Benthall Hall the only substantial house was one with six hearths, probably Thomas Hartshorne's and possibly the house in Spout Lane, near Broseley Wood, known as the Bailiff House: dated 1672, it has early 16th-century internal features, is built of well coursed and squared sandstone, and formerly had exposed timber framed gable ends.[14]

Most 17th-century cottages were probably of stone or timber. In the early 18th century, however, brick became ubiquitous and most dwellings were still detached cottages, often of 1½ storey. Sometimes in the later 18th and 19th centuries such buildings were incorporated in semi-detached or terraced houses. The Old Vicarage, a three storeyed brick house with a symmetrical façade of *c.* 1700, is the only 18th-century house of any distinction.[15]

Benthall's population in 1700 was only a quarter the size of Broseley's, and Benthall never rivalled Broseley as an industrial and market centre. The reasons are not far to seek: large-scale coal mining began at least a generation earlier in Broseley (*c.* 1580) than in Benthall (*c.* 1630), and Benthall's winnable coal, ironstone, and good clays proved more limited. Benthall's commons, on which incomers could be settled, were smaller than Broseley's, whose natural advantages were fully exploited by its landowners, particularly James Clifford (d. 1613) and Sir John Weld (d. 1666).[16]

A few substantial brick houses, mainly farmhouses, were built in the first third of the 19th century, notably Hill Top Farm, Barratts Hill Farm, Benthall Hall Farm, Benthall Villa Farm, and Benthall House. Otherwise the quality of housing was poor.[17] In 1801 Bower Yard was a small village and boat yard, described as sunless for over a third of the year.[18] Most settlement remained, as before, along the Wenlock–Ironbridge road, close to the eastern parish boundary. The densest cluster of houses was at Mine Spout where the parish workhouse, the New Inn, lime kilns, and a clay-pipe works also stood.[19] In the later 19th century there was some piecemeal slum clearance, and in the 20th century older cottages continued to be demolished, often to be replaced by fairly insubstantial bungalows. The eight houses of Haybrook Terrace were completed by Wenlock borough's Barrow district committee in 1953. The only privately built estate is the Bentlands, *c.* 30 houses built in the later 1970s.[20]

Houses near the river presumably drew their water thence until the Madeley & Broseley Water Works began a piped supply in the early 20th century.[21] The southern parts of the parish obtained water from two main springs or wells. Purse well, near Posenhall, was in use by the early 17th century[22] and supplied Benthall Hall, presumably by pipe, from 1754.[23] The mine, or main, spout was in use by the 19th century.[24] In the 20th century Purse well was used as the basis of the Broseley (or Posenhall) reservoir whence water was piped to the locality.[25]

Benthall wake was held in October until the early 20th century.[26] Between the 1630s and *c.* 1790 there were usually *c.* 8 alesellers in Benthall. Numbers then steadily declined:[27] in the mid and late 19th century there were two public houses, from 1895 only one, the New Inn near Mine Spout, licensed by 1821[28] and remaining in 1985. Four friendly societies were formed in the parish 1800–10;[29] they had 407 members in 1802–3. One was a Female Society with 94 members.[30] Coursing greyhounds were kept at Benthall Hall in the early 19th century.[31]

7 *Compton Census*, ed. Whiteman, 248, 259.

8 M. D. G. Wanklyn, 'Ind. Devt. in Ironbridge Gorge before Abraham Darby', *W. Midlands Studies*, xv. 4; *T.S.A.S.* xi. 55.

9 Allowing *c.* 20 for Posenhall: *V.C.H. Salop.* ii. 220, 226 note h; below, Posenhall, intro.

10 *V.C.H. Salop.* ii. 220, 229. For navvies living in par. in 1861 see *Victorian Shrews.* ed. B. Trinder (Shrews. 1984), 100–2.

11 *Benthall Hall* (Nat. Trust, 1976), 17; [F. Stackhouse Acton], *Garrisons of Salop., during the Civil War, 1642–8* (Shrews. 1867), 28–9; *V.C.H. Salop.* i. 454.

12 Cf. R.C.H.M.E., draft field rep. (1987); below, Broseley, growth of settlement.

13 S.R.O. 1224, box 66, John Weld's evid. (ff. 10–11), Lawr. Benthall's answer 16 Nov. 1635 (ff. 33, 36).

14 Clark and Alfrey, *Benthall and Broseley Wood*, 98, 212; inf. from the late Mr. D. Worthington.

15 Discussion and inv. of bldgs. in Clark and Alfrey, op. cit. 94–102, 108, 118–32, 206–53.

16 Cf. above and below, this section; below, Broseley, intro.

17 Clark and Alfrey, op. cit. 94–113, 118–32.

18 *T.S.A.S.* lviii. 250.

19 S.R.O. 294/2.

20 Clark and Alfrey, *Benthall and Broseley Wood*, 113–14, 222; W.B.R., Barrow dist. cttee. min. bk. 1946–66, p. 107; inf. from Bridgnorth Dist. Council.

21 *Kelly's Dir. Salop.* (1941), 34; cf. *V.C.H. Salop.* xi. 58; below, Broseley, public services.

22 Below, Posenhall, intro.; fig. 20; perh. the Benthall well of 1730: Birm. Univ. Libr., Mytton Papers, i. 128.

23 S.R.O. 1224, box 66, memo. *re* Weld–Benthall agreement, 1754.

24 At O.S. Nat. Grid SJ 669 028; below, Broseley, public services; Randall, *Broseley*, 315.

25 A. H. S. Waters, *Rep. on Water Supply* (S.C.C. 1946), 17.

26 M. J. Taylor, 'Study of Origins of the Local Name "Pitchyard" given to "The New Inn" Benthall' (TS. in I.G.M.T. Libr., accession 1983.2590).

27 W.B.R., Q1/11/2; S.R.O. 1224/2/359, 361, 368, 375.

28 Co. of Salop. *Return of Licensed Hos. 1901* (copy in S.P.L., accession 6117), 342; *P.O. Dir. Salop.* (1856), 15; (1879), 279; *Kelly's Dir. Salop.* (1885–1941).

29 S.R.O., q. sess. rec. parcel 285, index to club articles.

30 *Poor Law Abstract*, H.C. 98, pp. 422–3 (1803–4), xiii.

31 Randall, *Broseley*, 315.

George Maw (d. 1912) moved to Benthall Hall *c.* 1852, when Maw & Co. began to make tiles in the parish. A writer on subjects including agriculture and geology, Maw was a notable botanist, amassing 3–4,000 distinct species of plants, principally alpines, at the Hall. In 1866 he published *A Monograph of the Genus Crocus*.[32] The actress Ruby Hermione Yolande (Clinton-)Baddeley (1906–86) was born in the parish.[33]

MANOR AND OTHER ESTATES. *BENTHALL* was probably part of the Domesday manor of Much Wenlock,[34] and the prior of Wenlock remained overlord until the priory's surrender in 1540.[35] In the late 16th and early 17th century the manor was said to be held of the Crown in free and common socage, and not in chief.[36]

Anfred of Benthall was probably lord in the early 12th century.[37] He had two sons, Hamon and Robert. Hamon's son Robert enfeoffed Siward the champion (or of Frankton) in his Benthall lands, Siward in turn granting them to Wenlock priory. Following Robert's death *c.* 1204, however, they were restored to his son Robert, a minor. That Robert (d. by *c.* 1249) was succeeded by Philip of Benthall (d. by 1283), apparently his brother,[38] who settled Benthall on his second cousin Roger of Benthall.[39] The manor then passed to John Burnell, who married Roger's daughter Margery.[40] After 1294 John became a monk and was succeeded as lord by his son Philip of Benthall (fl. 1330).[41] Philip's son John probably succeeded him, for John's son and heir, Walter, was lord in 1363 and the manor was later claimed by Walter's son John.[42] After 1383[43] Benthall passed to the Benthalls' kinsman Hugh, Lord Burnell,[44] who also had another estate in Benthall.[45] Thenceforth the manor descended with Acton Burnell until 1562.[46] The Benthalls seem to have retained possession as tenants; the last John's grandson Robert Benthall (fl. 1521) was a freeholder *c.* 1497, as was Robert's son William in 1540.[47]

In 1562 Thomas Crompton, lord of Acton Burnell, sold most of Benthall to William's son Richard (d. 1575),[48] and the estate passed successively to Richard's sons Lawrence (d. 1603) and John (d. 1633)[49] and then to John's son Lawrence (d. 1652) who compounded in 1645.[50] Lawrence's son Philip (d. 1713) succeeded, and his son Richard died unmarried in 1720, the manor passing to his cousin and fiancée Elizabeth Browne. Elizabeth (d. 1738) left the estate to her brother John Browne (d. 1746) who in turn left it to his brother Ralph. Dying childless in 1763 Ralph left Benthall to his wife Anne (d. 1767), who in turn left it to her brother Francis Turner Blithe (d. 1770). Blithe left the manor to his daughter Lucia, widow of Francis Turner. In 1771 she (d. 1781) married the Revd. Edward Harries (d. 1812), of Cruckton and Hanwood, and in 1844 their son Thomas sold Benthall to J. G. W. Weld-Forester, Lord Forester,[51] with whose heir the manor remained in the earlier 1980s.[52]

In 1934 C. G. W. Weld-Forester, Lord Forester, sold Benthall Hall and the adjoining 134-a. farm to James Floyer Dale (d. 1942) and his wife and cousin Mary Clementina, *née* Benthall; the couple changed their surname to Benthall in 1935. In 1958 Mrs. Benthall (d. 1960) and her cousin Sir Edward Benthall transferred the property bought in 1934 to the National Trust.[53] Sir Edward's brother Sir Paul became the Trust's tenant at the Hall in 1962, but by 1985 Sir Paul's son James was tenant.[54]

Benthall Hall was probably built *c.* 1580 by Lawrence Benthall on the site of an earlier house. It is of brick faced with red sandstone and has, on the whole, a conventional plan with central hall, eastern service wing and western parlour wing. An unusual element is introduced, however, by an additional bay between the hall and parlour. The main section of that bay is now occupied by a staircase of *c.* 1620–30, but it is likely that the original stair was in the square turret immediately to the north. The southern entrance to the hall is protected by a two-storeyed porch and there are two-storeyed semi-octagonal bays on the west side of the parlour, on the hall and on the service end. The last may be an addition of the early 17th century when the southern rooms were richly panelled and made into additional parlours or bedrooms. Panelling and a moulded plaster ceiling in the parlour and the overmantel in the hall are prob-

32 P. Benthall, 'Geo. Maw: Versatile Victorian', *Nat. Trust Studies* (1980), 11–20; D. E. Owen, 'Silurian Polyzoa from Benthall Edge', *Bull. of Brit. Mus. (Nat. Hist.), Geol.* x. 96–7; *Wellington Jnl.* 17 Feb. 1912, p. 10; below, econ. hist. (ind.).

33 *Shrews. Chron.* 20 Apr. 1928, p. 12; *Who Was Who, 1981–90*, 31; H. Baddeley, *The Unsinkable Hermione Baddeley* (1984), 18–19; par. reg.

34 Eyton, iii. 223–4.

35 Ibid. 273–7.

36 P.R.O., C 142/179, no. 71; C 142/299, no. 130.

37 Eyton, iii. 273; Benthall pedigree (giving fuller descent than Eyton) in possession of the late Sir Paul Benthall and of Mr. Jas. Benthall, who are thanked for its loan and for comment on fam. pedigree.

38 Eyton, iii. 273–6; *Rolls of Justices in Eyre, 1221–2* (Selden Soc. lix), pp. 615–16; Benthall pedigree.

39 *T.S.A.S.* xi. 63.

40 Ibid.; Eyton, iii. 277.

41 *Cal. Inq. p.m.* iii, pp. 122, 443; Dugdale, *Mon.* v. 360; Eyton, iii. 277; S.R.O., archivist's office file 'Benthall', transcript of deed 2 Sept. 1330.

42 P.R.O., C 260/119, no. 24; *Cal. Inq. p.m.* xi, p. 373.

43 *Cal. inq. p.m.* xv, p. 289.

44 *T.S.A.S.* xlvii. 51; P.R.O., C 148/45.

45 Below, this section.

46 *T.S.A.S.* xlvii. 51; *Cal. Inq. p.m.* (Rec. Com.), iv. 56, 265, 325; *L. & P. Hen. VIII*, xvii, p. 28; *Cal. Pat.* 1547–8, p. 280; P.R.O., C 140/13, no. 27 [ff. 10–11]; C 142/213, no. 149; cf. *V.C.H. Salop.* viii. 7–8.

47 *Visit. Salop. 1623*, i (Harl. Soc. xxviii), 41; P.R.O., SC 6/Hen. VIII/3021, m. 8; S.R.O. 3365/165; Eyton, iii. 278.

48 *Cal. Pat.* 1560–3, 425; P.R.O., C 142/179, no. 71; *Visit. Salop. 1623*, i. 41.

49 P.R.O., C 142/505, no. 103.

50 *T.S.A.S.* 4th ser. ii. 232–3; *Cal. Cttee. for Compounding*, ii. 1040–1; *Cal. Cttee. for Money*, ii. 782–3.

51 *T.S.A.S.* xi. 66; lix. 146; P.R.O., C 78/1835, no. 2; S.P.L., Deeds 11244; MS. 2793, pp. 99–101; *V.C.H. Salop.* iv. 209–10. Randall, *Broseley*, 314–15, wrongly suggests that the vendor was Thos.'s bro. F. B. Harries, whom *T.S.A.S.* xi. 66, confuses with the latter's son Fra.

52 Inf. from Ld. Forester.

53 S.P.L., MSS. 4676–8; Burke, *Land. Gent.* (18th edn.), iii. 62–3; A. R. Wagner, *Eng. Genealogy* (1972), 223–4; inf. from Sir Paul Benthall and Mr. Jas. Benthall.

54 *Who's Who* (1991), 140–1; inf. from Sir Paul Benthall, for whom see *The Times*, 20 Jan. 1992, p. 14 (obit.).

ably contemporary with the new staircase. The service wing was extended north, probably in the 17th century when the status of its south end was raised. Its older fittings are now of the 18th century and perhaps contemporary with alterations, including new fireplaces in both wings, attributed to T. F. Pritchard. New doorcases at the foot of the staircase and a new ceiling there were probably inserted after a fire in 1818.[55]

Robert Burnell (d. 1292), chancellor of England and bishop of Bath and Wells, had an estate at Benthall, perhaps that held by Richard son of John in 1277–8. The bishop's nephew Sir Philip Burnell enlarged the estate and died in 1294 seised of lands held of John Burnell, lord of the manor. On the death of Philip's son Edward, Lord Burnell, in 1315, the estate was said to be held directly of the prior of Wenlock.[56] It was then assigned in dower to Edward's widow Aline,[57] who was said to hold it of the Benthall family and was succeeded in 1363 by his nephew and heir Nicholas, Lord Burnell (d. 1383),[58] who held an assize rent at Benthall of the prior of Wenlock.[59] Under Nicholas's son Hugh, Lord Burnell, the estate was presumably absorbed into the manor.[60]

Possibly because a fishery there was reserved to Wenlock priory in the late 11th or early 12th century, when the rest of Benthall was subinfeudated, *c.* 2 a. at Bower Yard were in Madeley, a demesne manor of the priory until 1540. In 1704 Comberford Brooke, lord of Madeley, sold the land to John Ashwood of Madeley.[61]

About 1560 the Crown seized as alleged chantry land 30 a. of arable in Benthall, which from the 13th to the 16th century had been glebe for Holy Trinity church, Much Wenlock. Within a year or so the land was sold to Edward Stephens and by him to Lawrence Benthall.[62]

In 1576 Stephen Hadnall, lord of Marsh, alienated land in Benthall, Posenhall, and Wyke to Lawrence Benthall.[63] It is likely that the land was incorporated in Benthall manor.

In the later Middle Ages the *TITHES* of Benthall were probably owned by Wenlock priory as appropriator of Holy Trinity church, Much Wenlock. They were among those which the Crown granted in 1554 to Stephen Hadnall (d. 1580) for his life. In 1581 the Crown sold them to two speculators.[64] The lord of the manor was impropriator of all the great tithes in 1844 when they were commuted to £150.[65]

ECONOMIC HISTORY. AGRICULTURE. There was open-field land south, east, and perhaps north-east of Benthall church. In 1517 it was said that Robert Benthall had inclosed 20 a. for pasture. To the north Benthall Edge's steep slopes supported woodland, and to the east, on slopes towards Broseley, were Hazel wood and Astwood, the latter partly in Broseley. Field names suggest woodland clearance. The southern part of the vill probably comprised common pasture.[66]

In the later 16th and early 17th century much common was inclosed. In the 1630s the process brought John Weld of Willey, lord of Marsh, and Lawrence Benthall, lord of Benthall, into conflict; both were enterprising landowners. Benthall denied Weld's claim that large areas of wood and waste in Benthall were commonable and asserted that Benthall Edge (*c.* 60 a.), Hazel wood (*c.* 30 a.), and Marsh field (*c.* 50 a.) had been inclosed time out of mind and were demesne land and that Astwood had been inclosed for *c.* 60 years. He claimed the Marsh Head (adjoining Willey park, in the south-east of the parish) as part of his manor (by implication demesne land) but conceded that Benthall Marsh (*c.* 60 a. north of the Wenlock–Broseley road) was open common and that the tenants of Posenhall (mainly Weld's property) had grazing rights in Benthall. In 1637 arbitrators allotted the Marsh Head to Weld and Benthall Marsh to Lawrence Benthall, and final inclosure presumably soon followed.[67]

In the later 16th and early 17th century cattle were important in a mixed economy, 8 oxen perhaps then being the preferred team. When Richard Benthall died in 1720 his demesne farm had cattle worth £93 (perhaps *c.* 50 beasts in all, including 8 oxen), 6 horses (£15 15*s.*), sheep worth £17, pigs (£10), poultry (10*s.*), and corn, peas, vetches, and hay (£64). Flax and hemp worth £5 and 8 st. of wool (£4) were stored in Benthall Hall.[68]

Arthur Young visited Benthall in 1776 and was told that farms were usually 100–200 a., the arable normally being ploughed by six oxen 3–5 years old, although alternatively four horses might be used. Fairly few sheep were kept. Turnips were being introduced, while hemp was 'almost universally' grown by both farmers and cottagers, who also dressed and spun it before it was passed on to be woven into linen 'in the country'. Cottagers usually also grew potatoes and kept a pig. Young described a farm of 320 a., presumably the Hall demesne, which employed 7 men and 2 dairymaids. Half was grass supporting 8 horses, 6 oxen, 38 cattle, and 80 sheep. The arable was growing 35 a. of wheat, 35 a. of barley, 40 a. of oats, 20 a. of peas, 20 a.

55 *V.C.H. Salop.* v (forthcoming); H. A. Tipping, *Eng. Homes, Period III*, i. 147–53; *Benthall Hall* (Nat. Trust, 1976); Pevsner, *Salop.* 72–3; J. Randall, *Severn Valley* (Madeley, 1882), 307; H.W.R.O.(H.), Heref. dioc. rec., inv. of Ric. Benthall, 1720.

56 Eyton, iii. 276–7; *Complete Peerage*, ii. 434; *Cal. Inq. p.m.* (Rec. Com.), i. 64.

57 *Cal. Close*, 1313–18, 264.

58 Ibid. 1360–4, 471; *Cal. Inq. p.m.* xi, p. 373; *Complete Peerage*, ii. 435; *V.C.H. Salop.* viii. 7.

59 *Cal. Inq. p.m.* xv, pp. 287–9.

60 Above, this section.

61 *V.C.H. Salop.* xi. 36, 42; S.R.O. 1681/132/3.

62 Below, M. Wenlock, churches; H.W.R.O.(H.), HD 2/14/48; *Cal. Pat.* 1560–3, 257.

63 *Cal. Pat.* 1575–8, p. 164.

64 Ibid. 1554–5, 22; 1580–2, p. 5; cf. above, Barrow, manors (tithes).

65 S.R.O. 294/2.

66 S.R.O., archivist's office file 'Benthall', transcript of deed 2 Sept. 1330; S.R.O. 294/2, fields 251–2, 280–7, 309–10, 325, 345–6; 1224, box 66, Weld *v.* Benthall, evid. of John Weld and Lawr. Benthall; 4704/1, p. 1; S.P.L., Deeds 18120; B.L. Lansd. MS. 1, f. 191; below, Broseley, growth of settlement.

67 S.R.O. 1224, box 66, Weld *v.* Benthall, evid. of John Weld and Lawr. Benthall; S.P.L., Deeds 18120; *W. Midlands Studies*, iv. 65; cf. fig. 20; below, Posenhall, econ. hist. (agric.).

68 H.W.R.O.(H.), Heref. dioc. rec., invs. of Naboth Dawley, 1677; Wm. Rutter, 1679; John Rutter, 1708/9; Ric. Benthall, 1720. Young cattle valued at *c.* £1: cf. *Yeomen and Colliers in Telford*, ed. B. Trinder and J. Cox (1980), pp. 74–5.

TABLE XV

BENTHALL: LAND USE, LIVESTOCK, AND CROPS

		1867	*1891*	*1938*	*1965*
Percentage of	grassland	65	74	77	49
	arable	35	26	23	51
Percentage of	cattle	16	40	23	21
	sheep	68	47	63	71
	pigs	16	13	14	8
Percentage of	wheat	49	36	55	43
	barley	51	36	0	55
	oats	0	27	45	2
	mixed corn & rye	0	1	0	0
Percentage of agricultural land growing roots and vegetables		12	9	8	7

Sources: P.R.O., MAF 68/143, no. 15; /1340, no. 5; /3880, Salop. no. 258; /4945, no. 258.

of clover, and 10 a. of turnips, with 10 a. of fallow. Much, if not all, of the wood around Benthall was then in demesne and managed as coppice: cut at 21 years the oak poles were barked before being sold as pit props.[69] In 1837, however, 'thousands of flourishing fir trees' covered Benthall Edge. None remained in 1986, when rough deciduous woods covered much of the slopes down to the Severn.[70]

In 1801 oats comprised 48 per cent of the recorded cereal acreage, wheat 46 per cent, and barley 6 per cent.[71] Until after the Second World War, when the amount of arable increased, it usually occupied only about a third or half as much land as did grass. During that time the proportion of wheat grown was fairly constant, although those of barley and oats fluctuated considerably. The proportions of animals kept remained stable: sheep were the most common, followed by cattle and then pigs. There was much intensive poultry rearing in the 1930s.

In the late 16th and early 17th century Benthall manor had a weir in the Severn.[72] Bower weir, near Bower Yard, was in Madeley manor.[73]

A water mill in the late 16th and early 17th century presumably stood on Benthall brook where there were two ponds in 1618.[74] In the late 18th century a corn mill with an overshot wheel 60 ft. in diameter was built *c.* 200 m. south of the Iron Bridge. Like the bridge, Benthall wheel soon attracted tourists.[75] By the mid 19th century steam power was also employed. Used only occasionally by 1900, the mill was dismantled in 1935 and ruinous in the earlier 1980s.[76]

A windmill north-west of Posenhall in 1808[77] had been demolished by 1845.[78]

INDUSTRY. Coal was probably dug by 1250, and was certainly got in the 14th century when it was exported via the Severn.[79]

Large-scale coal extraction perhaps did not begin as early in Benthall as in Broseley,[80] and it was apparently Lawrence Benthall (born *c.* 1589)[81] who accelerated exploitation of the parish's mineral reserves. By 1634 he had sunk pits for coal and ironstone, perhaps particularly in Benthall Marsh, and had allegedly encouraged the settlement of 'many poor and disorderly people' as workmen. By the terms of his agreement with John Weld in 1637 Benthall was able to mine throughout Benthall Marsh and the Marsh Head and to lay railways.[82] By 1645, when they were seized by Parliament, Benthall's collieries ranked with those of Broseley and Madeley, and it was said that each year 30,000 tons of Benthall coal were shipped down the Severn to Worcester or beyond.[83] Benthall remained one of the Severn's pre-eminent collieries in 1695.[84]

After the mid 17th century, when many of the easily won reserves were probably worked out, Benthall's mines may never again have equalled Broseley's.[85] Pierce & Co., who ran potteries in the parish in the early 19th century, got coal and clay there.[86] In 1851 the inhabitants included 30 miners, three-quarters of them coal miners and the rest ironstone miners,[87] but most probably worked in Broseley pits.[88] There was some mining in the late 19th and the 20th century.[89]

Small amounts of ironstone were also mined in the parish.[90]

69 Young, *Tours in Eng. and Wales*, 145–9.
70 C. Hulbert, *Hist. and Descr. of Salop.* ii (1837), 348; W. E. Wiggins, *Ancient Woodland in Telford Area* (T.D.C. 1986; copy in S.P.L.).
71 P.R.O., HO 67/12/27. Rest of para. based on Table XV.
72 *T.S.A.S.* xi. 425; cf. *V.C.H. Salop.* xi. 42; Bodl. MS. Top. Salop. c. 2, f. 177.
73 *V.C.H. Salop.* xi. 36, 42.
74 P.R.O., C 142/299, no. 130; Bodl. MS. Top. Salop. c. 2, f. 177; S.R.O. 1224/1/32; 3898/Rg/1, 30 Mar. 1598; W.B.R., Q2/2/27.
75 S. Smith, *View from the Iron Bridge* (I.G.M.T. 1979), pp. 58–9, 64, 71–2; S.R.O. 294/2; Clark and Alfrey, *Benthall and Broseley Wood*, 143–52; pl. 33.
76 *P.O. Dir. Salop.* (1856), 15; *Kelly's Dir. Salop.* (1900), 29; (1929), 34 (last mention); *Shropshire Mag.* Dec. 1984, 70; inf. from Mr. F. R. Ball, neph. of John Bennett, owner in 1935.
77 R. Baugh, *Map of Salop.* (1808).
78 S.R.O. 294/2, field 362.
79 Eyton, iii. 276; *V.C.H. Salop.* i. 454; ii. 52; Bodl. MS. Blakeway 2, p. 68.
80 Cf. below, Broseley, econ. hist. (coal and ironstone).
81 P.R.O., C 142/505, no. 103.
82 S.R.O. 1224/1/32; 1224, box 66, John Weld's evid. (f. 10), Lawr. Benthall's answer (ff. 31–3); S.P.L., Deeds 18120.
83 *V.C.H. Salop.* i. 454; A. Raistrick, *Dynasty of Iron Founders: the Darbys and Coalbrookdale* (1953), 25; S.R.O., archivist's office file 'Benthall', transcript of petition [1645?] to Cttee. at Goldsmiths' Hall.
84 J. U. Nef, *Rise of Brit. Coal Ind.* (1932), i. 360.
85 H.W.R.O.(H.), Heref. dioc. rec., invs. of Ric. Benthall, 1720; Wm. Smith, 1752; J. Plymley, *Gen. View of Agric. of Salop.* (1803), 52.
86 S.R.O. 515/9, pp. 56–7.
87 S.R.O. 2979/3.
88 Cf. absence of pits on S.R.O. 294/2.
89 Clark and Alfrey, *Benthall and Broseley Wood*, 41.
90 Ibid. 42–3; S.R.O. 515/9, p. 57.

Benthall ironworks was built in the 1770s on Benthall brook, *c.* 400 m. from the Severn. The Harries family and William Banks and John Onions were operating the works together by 1778 and in formal partnership 1797–1801.[91] The lord of the manor's younger son F. B. Harries remained active in the works until 1814 or later.[92] Initially the blast for the two furnaces was provided by a water wheel, a pumping engine returning the water to pools above the works. Later an atmospheric engine blew the furnaces. The furnaces specialized in pig for casting, sent in the late 1770s to the ironworks in Wolverley (Worcs.), and between *c.* 1797 and 1801 to the Soho foundry in Smethwick (Staffs.). In 1803 there were two furnaces but the engine could blow only one at a time. Production was 30 tons a week, part of which was used in the adjoining foundry and the rest sold. The works, employing *c.* 700, had a water-powered boring mill by 1781 and a forge. By 1784 the works was capable of manufacturing steam engines, although in the early 19th century domestic goods were probably the main manufacture. The furnaces went out of blast in 1821 but the foundry, under Stephen Hill, and the boring mill worked until the 1840s.[93]

There was a 'pitchhouse' in 1712.[94] A range of ovens for the manufacture of coke and tar, similar to those at Calcutts (in Broseley), was built by Lord Dundonald *c.* 1787, next to the ironworks. By 1799 they had been demolished.[95]

In 1731 Thomas Barker, chief agent in North Wales for the London Lead Co., leased land in Benthall, probably on the river bank near the Broseley boundary.[96] A smeltery of Barker's design, with two coal-fired reverberatory furnaces or cupolas, was in use later that year. It used ore from the company's mines in Llandrinio (Mont.) and coal from Little Dawley. The ore supply, however, proved unsatisfactory and in 1736 the works was leased to Matthew Dore & Partners of the Bog mine (in Wentnor), who used it until the mid 1740s.

In the 18th and 19th centuries vast amounts of limestone were got from Benthall Edge for fluxing and burning. In the late 18th century at least some of the limeworks were run as a joint venture with Benthall ironworks.[97] In the late 19th century three groups of kilns survived: one west of Bower Yard, one on the top of Benthall Edge, and one west of Mine Spout.[98] There was some quarrying and lime burning in the 1920s and 1930s.[99]

Local railways served the parish's industries by the 17th century. By 1636 Lawrence Benthall was laying wooden railways to his mines, and in 1637 he gained permission to cross the land of John Weld of Willey.[1] The main line in the parish, down its eastern side, was Benthall rails, apparently in existence by 1686. In the late 18th century the New Willey Co. used it, as an alternative to the Tarbatch Dingle railway, to carry iron to a Severn wharf. At that time, therefore, the line probably ran from Willey furnaces to the neighbourhood of Benthall ferry. The southern part of the line probably fell into disuse when Willey ironworks closed in the early 19th century, but the northern section probably took limestone and Benthall ironworks' products to the river until 1856 or later.[2] Short railways probably served various extractive industries in the parish.[3] In 1801 and later an inclined plane carried limestone from Benthall Edge to kilns at Bower Yard.[4] In 1833 it ran south-east from the top of the Edge before turning north-east, probably to join Benthall rails near Benthall ironworks.[5] At least two other short inclined planes also served the limestone quarries.[6]

In the early 18th century brown lead-glazed ware, yellow slipware, and salt-glazed dipped stoneware were made near Coppice House.[7] Eleanor and John Lyster had a kiln in 1735.[8] William Booth was leasing an 'old pottery' in the parish in 1801.[9] The Pitchyard pottery, on the site later occupied by E. Southorn's clay pipe works, probably also began in the 18th century.[10] The Pitchyard pottery was leased to Jasper Cox in 1800[11] and was run from before 1814 until 1826 by William Lloyd of Pitchyard House, and from 1826 until 1833 or later by Mrs. Lloyd, presumably his widow.[12]

The main pot works in the parish, the Benthall Pottery, was founded in 1772 when John Thursfield (d. 1789) built a new manufactory north of his existing Haybrook Pottery in Posenhall, which he soon afterwards gave up. John's son John later entered the business and was joined by his brother-in-law William Pierce.[13]

91 Para. based on Trinder, *Ind. Rev. Salop.* 39–40, 51, 90, 143, and sources there cited; Randall, *Broseley*, 124; idem, *The Wilkinsons* (Madeley, n.d.), 37 (copy in S.R.O. 245); *John Rennie's Diary of a Journey Through N. Eng. 1784*, ed. R. B. Matkin (E. Kent Marine Trust Hist. Study ii), 24–5; S.R.O. 245/71; 1190/4/250. Cf. S.R.O. 2993/P/1. For site see S.R.O. 294/2, field 67.

92 S.R.O. 4791/1/7, pp. 134, 370. Cf. above, manor; Burke, *Land. Gent.* (1858), 524.

93 Clark and Alfrey, *Benthall and Broseley Wood*, 83; Tibnam & Co. *Salop. Dir.* (1828), 27; Pigot, *Nat. Com. Dir.* (1835), 351; (1842), 9; S.R.O. 294/2, field 67; not in S. Bagshaw, *Dir. Salop.* (1851).

94 W.B.R., Q2/2/27.

95 Trinder, *Ind. Rev. Salop.* 40, 55–7.

96 Para. based on *Salop. News Letter*, xli. 16–19; Trinder, op. cit. 8, 10; Smith, *View from Iron Bridge*, pp. 27, 29.

97 *Shrews. Chron.* 1 Jan. 1802; pl. 27.

98 O.S. Maps 1/2,500, LI. 2 (1882 edn.); 6", Salop. XLIII. SW. (1890 edn.); S.R.O. 3956.

99 Clark and Alfrey, *Benthall and Broseley Wood*, 53–4.

1 S.R.O. 1224, box 66, further answer of Lawr. Benthall 1636 (f. 11); S.P.L., Deeds 18120.

2 O.S. Arch. Div. record card SJ 60 SE. 7; Randall, *Broseley*, 315; Trinder, *Ind. Rev. Salop.* 70–1, 73; I.G.M.T. Libr., watercolour of Benthall rails 1856 (accession 1975.169); below, this section; Broseley, communications; Willey, intro.; econ. hist. (iron).

3 Clark and Alfrey, *Benthall and Broseley Wood*, 33–4.

4 Terminus at O.S. Nat. Grid SJ 671 033; S.R.O. 1888/17.

5 O.S. Map 1", sheet LXI. NE. (1833 edn.).

6 Clark and Alfrey, *Benthall and Broseley Wood*, 49–50.

7 *Jnl. Wilkinson Soc.* vi. 9–20. At *c.* O.S. Nat. Grid SJ 668 020.

8 W.B.R., Q1/3/1, 17 June 1735: ref. supplied by Dr. D. Higgins.

9 S.R.O. 515/4, p. 182.

10 At O.S. Nat. Grid SJ 670 026: J. Randall, *Hist. Madeley* (Madeley, 1880), 184; below, this section.

11 S.R.O. 515/4, p. 283.

12 S.R.O. 2993/P/1.

13 *T.S.A.S.* lv. 160–1; S.R.O. 1224/1/51; below, Posenhall, econ. hist.

Pierce & Co. ran the Benthall Pottery until 1817–18. It was then taken by Samuel Roden & Co., who had the lease until 1823–4 when John Farnall became proprietor. Farnall still ran the works in 1837[14] and perhaps remained in charge until *c.* 1845 when W. T. Jones and Edwin Bathurst, lessees of the Haybrook Pottery, reunited the two concerns.[15] They remained a single business, the works being known collectively as the Benthall Potteries, although in the early 1850s, when there were 31 employees at the Benthall Pottery, Jones and Bathurst may have divided the managerial responsibility with the latter running the Benthall concern.[16] The main products were then Rockingham-style ware and stoneware.[17]

Between *c.* 1862 and *c.* 1907 the Benthall Pottery Co. was run by William Allen and thereafter, until the early 1920s, by his son W. B. Allen.[18] In 1880 the traditional coarse 'red and yellow' ware still sold readily in Wales. Allen, however, was beginning to promote the works as the Salopian Decorative Art Pottery Co. In 1882 its products included copies and 'adaptations' of vessels from the ancient world, pots based on flower heads, and barbotine ware. By 1901 Allen's attempt to 'raise the character' of the products had largely foundered, and, apart from a few Greek- and Hispano-style vessels, the manufacture was mainly coarse wares, lamp bases, and electrical engineering ceramics.[19] In 1929 the company was re-formed as the Benthall & Ironbridge Pottery Co. Ltd., which continued trading until the Second World War.[20]

In 1795 and 1805 John Thursfield also held a pottery formerly run by Joseph Glass (d. 1790), where one kiln produced earthenware.[21] Pierce & Co. had it in 1811,[22] and it was presumably the single-kiln pottery held in 1845 by Jones & Bathurst on the north side of the Wenlock–Broseley road 0.5 km. east of their Benthall Pottery.[23]

By the time that Maw & Co. moved from Benthall in 1883 they were making decorative vases.[24]

In 1922 Woolfson, Rowe & Co. made earthenware in Bridge Road as the Salop Pottery Co. Ltd. The works was operated between *c.* 1929 and 1937 by the Leigh Pottery Co. Ltd. The works had three kilns, and the main product was probably domestic ware such as teapots. Production was restarted by a Stoke-on-Trent firm *c.* 1950, but it soon ceased.[25]

In 1635 Lawrence Benthall was promoting the manufacture of bricks at Benthall Marsh.[26] The Burton family had a brickworks which was perhaps, by *c.* 1800 as in 1845 and later, at Bower Yard. By 1856 white refractory firebricks were the main product, although floor and roofing tiles were also possibly made there in the later 19th century. Burtons built the coalfield's first down-draught chimney in 1874. About 1895 control of the firm passed to the Jones family, and *c.* 1917 to Bennett Bros. Known as Benthall Firebrick Works from *c.* 1900, it closed *c.* 1930.[27] A second brickyard at Bower Yard in 1845 belonged to F. B. Harries.[28] In 1852 George and Arthur Maw, who for some time had used clay from the area in their Worcester factory, opened a tileworks on the site of the former ironworks. In the early years the Maws concentrated on development, and production was not on a commercial scale, but by the early 1860s Maws had a highly regarded design team and were receiving awards and commissions for products which included tile mosaics, friezes, and chimney pieces. Roof tiles were designed by Sir Matthew Digby Wyatt. The Benthall works closed in 1883 when the Maws' new Broseley works opened.[29] Between the late 1930s and *c.* 1955 the Benthall Stoneware Co. made sanitary pipes at the former Raleigh Pipe works, employing 30 or 40 people. Between 1930 and 1982 the Benthall Pipe Co. made agricultural and sanitary pipes at the former Benthall pottery.[30]

Clay tobacco pipes were made in Benthall from the later 17th century or earlier. As in Broseley local clays were used in the 17th century.[31] Apparently prominent in the 17th and 18th centuries were the Bradley and Hartshorne families,[32] and in the 19th the Shaws and Rodens.[33] About 1858 Edwin Southorn took over Noah Roden's business adjoining the New Inn in Bridge Road. An important and innovative factory, the Broseley Pipe Works, was soon established, employing 28 pipemakers in 1861

14 S.R.O. 515/9, pp. 56–7; 2993/P/1; Hulbert, *Hist. Salop.* ii. 342.

15 Below, Posenhall, econ. hist.; S.R.O. 294/2, field 234; 1224, bdle. 193, rental 29 Sept. 1846, s.v. Posenhall.

16 S. Bagshaw, *Dir. Salop.* (1851), 555; S.R.O. 2979/3.

17 E. Cassey & Co. *Dir. Salop.* (1871), 67.

18 A keen naturalist and contributor (on fungi) to *V.C.H. Salop.* i. 84–5, 93–8; cf. *T.S.A.S.* lv. 167; C. A. Sinker and others, *Ecological Flora of Salop. Region* (1985), 33–4.

19 E. Cassey & Co. *Dir. Salop.* (1871), 67; Randall, *Madeley*, 184; idem, *Severn Valley*, advt.; *V.C.H. Salop.* i. 424, 434; *Kelly's Dir. Salop.* (1885–1922); *Staffs. and Salop. at Opening of 20th Cent.* ed. W. T. Pike (1907), 245.

20 *Kelly's Dir. Salop.* (1926–41); S.R.O. 1681/190/6; inf. from Mr. R. S. Edmundson; Clark and Alfrey, *Benthall and Broseley Wood*, 198–201.

21 S.R.O. 4791/1/3, p. 272; /1/5, p. 444 (refs. supplied by Mr. Edmundson); H.W.R.O.(H.), Heref. dioc. rec., inv. of Jos. Glass, 1790.

22 S.R.O. 515/9, pp. 56–7.

23 S.R.O. 294/2, field 168; 3956, no. 168.

24 Below; below, Broseley, econ. hist. (clay inds. [pottery]).

25 *Kelly's Dir. Salop.* (1922–41); Clark and Alfrey, *Benthall and Broseley Wood*, 190; Taylor, 'Local Name "Pitchyard"'; inf. from Mr. Ball.

26 S.R.O. 1224, box 66, John Weld's evid. (f. 10), Lawr. Benthall's answer (ff. 31–2).

27 S.R.O. 294/2, field 57; 2993/P/1; 3956; Randall, *Broseley*, 148, and advt.; Clark and Alfrey, op. cit. 74–5; *V.C.H. Salop.* i. 443; *Wellington Jnl.* 27 June 1874; *P.O. Dir. Salop.* (1856), 15; (1879), 279; *Kelly's Dir. Salop.* (1891–1909) s.v. Benthall, (1913–29) s.v. Ironbridge; O.S. Map 6", Salop. XLIII. SW. (1928 edn.).

28 S.R.O. 294/2, field 273.

29 *V.C.H. Salop.* i. 446; *Eddowes's Jnl.* 26 Mar. 1856, p. 5; 13 Mar. 1867, p. 6; Randall, *Broseley*, 140, 144–7; Ll. Jewitt, *Ceramic Art of Gt. Brit.* (1883), 182–90; J. M. Robinson, *The Wyatts* (1969), 253; Clark and Alfrey, op. cit. 184–5; below, Broseley, econ. hist. (clay inds. [pottery]).

30 *Kelly's Dir. Salop.* (1934–41); local inf.; Clark and Alfrey, op. cit. 66, 75–6.

31 S.R.O. 1224/2/124; below, Broseley, econ. hist. (clay inds. [tobacco pipes]).

32 H.W.R.O.(H.), Heref. dioc. rec., invs. of Thos. Hartshorne, 1743, and Geo. Bradley, 1788; D. R. Atkinson, *Tobacco Pipes of Broseley* (1975), 46, 58–9; SA 3788, 3820; *Post-Medieval Arch.* xix. 177; Clark and Alfrey, op. cit. 139–40.

33 Atkinson, op. cit. 76–9, 82; Clark and Alfrey, op. cit. 140–1; S.R.O. 294/2, field 123; 2979/3; 3956, no. 123; Tibnam & Co. *Salop. Dir.* (1828), 29; *P.O. Dir. Salop.* (1856), 15.

and 40 in 1871. After Southorn's death in 1876 Hopkins & Co. ran the works as the Raleigh Pipe Works, said in 1885 to be one of the largest factories of its kind in England. About 1882 control of the works reverted to the Southorns, who kept up production there until *c.* 1900.[34]

Boats were built and repaired at Bower Yard in the 18th and 19th centuries for the local community of Severn watermen.[35]

There was a short-lived ropewalk *c.* 1821.[36]

LOCAL GOVERNMENT. By 1369 at least part of Benthall was in Wenlock priory's Bradley grange[37] and thus presumably owed suit at the prior's court of Bradley, absorbed in the 1380s into that of Marsh.[38] Benthall presented at the Marsh court in 1477 and still in 1530.[39]

In 1635 a dispute arose between Lawrence Benthall, lord of the manor, and John Weld of Willey, who was then seeking to extend the jurisdiction of his manor of Marsh.[40] Default of suit to Marsh court was alleged against Benthall men in 1636. In 1635 Lawrence Benthall claimed that courts had been held for Benthall manor but agreed that there had not lately been a court baron. He said Benthall's inhabitants had 'constantly' appeared at Bourton hundred court[41] but not elsewhere. Weld disputed that, and in 1637 the parties agreed that in future Benthall manor was to be held of Marsh, freely and in socage, paying 4*s.* 6*d.* a year, with its inhabitants appearing at the Marsh leet and indemnified against proceedings for non-appearance at Bourton hundred court. Benthall continued to appear at Marsh court until 1879[42] or later.

Benthall had a highway surveyor by 1718[43] and the vestry remained a highway authority until 1889.[44]

Out relief was given in 1737–8.[45] In 1775–6 £38 was spent on the poor, and in 1782–5 an average of £65. By 1802–3 expenditure had risen to £154, spent on out relief for 30 adults and 10 children.[46] By 1814 *c.* £300 a year was being spent.[47] Some of the poor then lived in a poorhouse and two cottages, for which cheese, potatoes, and flour were bought; others received out relief. In 1816–17 expenditure doubled to £680; for the only time in the surviving accounts the 17th-century house at Mine Spout (the later Bailiff House), which was used as the poorhouse or workhouse,[48] was referred to as Benthall School of Industry. Also apparently exceptional was the setting to work of the poor as labourers in the district. By *c.* 1820 annual expenditure had returned to *c.* £300. In 1835–6 most expenditure was on weekly pay, although there was still a poorhouse, presumably that at Mine Spout:[49] 'old workhouse cottages' there were so called in 1910.[50]

Benthall was in Madeley poor-law union 1836–1930,[51] and in Madeley rural sanitary district from 1872 until 1889, when it was transferred to the Barrow ward of Wenlock borough.[52] On the borough's dissolution in 1966 Benthall civil parish was abolished, most being absorbed by Barrow C.P., then assigned to Bridgnorth rural district and in Bridgnorth district from 1974. Bower Yard, however, was included in Dawley C.P. and U.D.,[53] abolished in 1974. Thereafter the Bower Yard area formed part of Wrekin district, unparished until 1988 when the Bower Yard area was included in the Gorge C.P.[54]

The 16-ha. area around Bower Yard was included in the designated area of Dawley (from 1968 Telford) new town[55] whose development corporation was dissolved in 1991.[56]

Benthall was within the jurisdiction of the Broseley court of requests from 1782[57] until its abolition under the County Courts Act, 1846.[58]

CHURCH. Benthall had a chapel by 1221, when Robert of Benthall conceded the advowson to the prior of Wenlock. In 1274 Benthall's tithes and 30 a. of glebe were given to the vicar of Holy Trinity, Much Wenlock,[59] and independence of Holy Trinity parish was achieved only slowly. In the early 17th century Benthall was served by a curate appointed by the vicar of Holy Trinity. The curate could baptize and solemnize marriages, but burial rights were acquired only in 1702.[60] With its endowment in the 18th century the curacy was a perpetual curacy, later styled a vicarage, in the gift of the vicar of Holy Trinity until 1930. The united benefice of Broseley with

34 Clark and Alfrey, op. cit. 141–2; Atkinson, op. cit. 82; Randall, *Broseley*, 313; P. and D. N. Brown, 'Broseley—1851 and after', *Soc. for Clay Pipe Research Newsletter*, viii. 32; O.S. Map 1/2,500, Salop. LI. 2 (1902 edn.); S.R.O. 1681/41/14.

35 *T.S.A.S.* lviii. 250; Smith, *View from Iron Bridge*, pp. 62–3; Pigot, *Nat. Com. Dir.* (1835), 350; *P.O. Dir. Salop.* (1856), 15; S.R.O. 2979/3.

36 S.R.O. 2993/P/1, 1 June 1821.

37 B.L. Add. MS. 6165, p. 98.

38 Below, M. Wenlock, local govt.

39 S.R.O. 1224/2/16–18.

40 Para. based on P.R.O., C 3/418, no. 115; S.R.O. 1224, box 66, Weld *v.* Benthall, evid. of Lawr. Benthall and John Weld; S.P.L., Deeds 18120; cf. above, Barrow, local govt.

41 *Rot. Hund.* (Rec. Com.), ii. 84, states that they began to do so in 1198.

42 Randall, *Broseley*, 34.

43 *T.S.A.S.* lvi. 315.

44 Local Govt. Bd.'s Prov. Order Conf. (No. 4) Act, 1889, 52 & 53 Vic. c. 22 (Local).

45 S.R.O. 5709, Benthall overseers' accts.

46 *Poor Law Abstract*, H.C. 98, pp. 422–3 (1803–4), xiii.

47 Para. based on S.R.O. 2993/P/1. Randall's statement (*Broseley*, 49, 315) that the poor were farmed refers, if correct, to years before 1814, when extant accts. begin.

48 Above, this article, intro.; SA 11472; Clark and Alfrey, *Benthall and Broseley Wood*, 212; Randall, op. cit. 315.

49 Randall, op. cit. 315.

50 S.R.O. 4044/89, p. 19 nos. 208–9.

51 V. J. Walsh, 'Admin. of Poor Laws in Salop. 1820–55' (Pennsylvania Univ. Ph.D. thesis, 1970), 148–50; *Kelly's Dir. Salop.* (1929), 34.

52 *V.C.H. Salop.* ii. 215–16 (corr. below, Corrigenda).

53 Ibid. ii. 236, and (for detail) source cited.

54 Sources cited ibid. iii. 169 n. 29; *The Wrekin (Pars.) Order 1988* (Stat. Instr. 1988, no. 156); O.S. Map 1/100,000, *Salop. Admin. Areas* (1988 edn.).

55 Area calculated from *Dawley New Town (Designation) Order, 1963* (Stat. Instr. 1963, no. 64) and map; *Dawley New Town (Designation) Amendment (Telford) Order, 1968* (Stat. Instr. 1968, no. 1912) and map.

56 *Telford Devt. Corpn. (Transfer of Property and Dissolution) Order* (Stat. Instr. 1991, no. 1980).

57 Broseley, etc., Small Debts Act, 1782, 22 Geo. III, c. 37.

58 9 & 10 Vic. c. 95.

59 Eyton, iii. 274, 278–9; *Rolls of Justices in Eyre, 1221–2*, p. 472.

60 S.R.O. 2993/Chyd/1.

Benthall was then formed, with Lord Forester as patron; at the same time Posenhall extra-parochial place was joined to Benthall ecclesiastical parish.[61]

The curate of Benthall had no glebe and no tithes except the small tithes of that part of the parish which had probably formed part of Posenhall chapelry. From the rest of the parish £1 13*s*. 4*d*. was paid prescriptively to the curate in lieu of all small tithes. In 1844 that payment and the small tithes were commuted to £8.[62] Between 1735 and 1816 the living had been augmented six times by Queen Anne's Bounty.[63] By the mid 19th century it had been endowed with the 15-a. Coxfold farm at Barr Beacon (Staffs.) and in 1851 was worth £98.[64] The living's value varied little until *c*. 1920 when it began to rise considerably.[65] In 1923 the glebe was sold.[66]

Before the Reformation there was land endowing the celebration of Our Lady's service in the chapel.[67] Baptisms and marriages in the chapel became more frequent from the 1570s,[68] perhaps as the mining population increased,[69] but in the later 16th and the 17th century it may have been poorly furnished: in 1552 there had been one little bell and a poor chasuble, and the chalice used belonged to William Benthall. Impiety was said to be 'too much used' in 1716; the minister of Much Wenlock then came to conduct a Sunday afternoon service once a month with communion three or more times a year.[70] On Census Sunday 1851 morning service was attended by 70 adults and 30 children, afternoon service by 110 and 30 respectively.[71]

There was an incumbent curate between 1609 and 1622–3[72] and in 1642,[73] but thereafter until the mid 18th century Benthall probably did not have a resident minister, and there seems to have been no benefice house.[74] Some, probably all, of the curates instituted thereafter were absentees until *c*. 1880.[75] They normally employed an assistant curate who, by 1851, usually lived at Benthall House;[76] one such was the antiquary C. H. Hartshorne (1827–8).[77] The perpetual curates lived at Benthall House from *c*. 1880 to 1898,[78] and at Benthall Vicarage (the former Coppice House) from 1902 until the living was united with Broseley.[79] They had no salaried curates except 1899–1902, when the vicar of Much Wenlock was incumbent.[80]

Between 1893 and the 1940s a mission room at Hilltop was used for Sunday evening services, and Sunday school continued to be held there in 1948. In 1948 Mrs. M. C. Benthall gave it to the parish, and it was named the Floyer Hall after her husband.[81]

The medieval chapel was dedicated to *ST. BRICE*, bishop of Tours (d. 444).[82] It was 'burnt down to the ground', probably in 1645, and 'wholly demolished'; afterwards no warden was appointed until the building of a new church was undertaken.[83] A new church of *ST. BARTHOLOMEW*, so known by *c*. 1740,[84] was built in or soon after 1667[85] probably on the medieval chapel's foundations.[86] Consisting of chancel and nave with a west bell turret,[87] it had a hammer-beam roof with carved decoration. There are some medieval floor tiles which, with pews, panelling, and furnishings that are mostly early 17th-century, were perhaps salvaged from the old chapel. In 1673 the lord of the manor owned several seats in the chancel,[88] and it was probably late in the 17th century that the west gallery was added. The font may be of *c*. 1670 and the bell is of 1671. The royal arms, painted on plaster, filled the space over the chancel arch but were half whitewashed over when a nave ceiling was inserted.[89]

In 1884 a vestry was built between nave and chancel on the south side, and the chancel was gothicized.[90] It was perhaps then that high square pews, said in 1878 to block the chancel, were removed. In 1893 a western apse was added, with a porch replacing the old south door. At the same time the external stairs to the gallery

61 *Lond. Gaz*. 28 Feb. 1930, p. 1286.

62 S.R.O. 294/2; below, Posenhall, chapel of ease.

63 C. Hodgson, *Q. Anne's Bounty* (2nd edn.), p. cclxxxix.

64 P.R.O., HO 129/358, no. 28a; S.R.O. 2992/ChW/1, f. 142.

65 E. Cassey & Co. *Dir. Salop*. (1871), 67; *Kelly's Dir. Salop*. (1885–1926); Heref. Dioc. Regy., reg. 1919–26, pp. 19, 242, 344.

66 S.R.O. 2993/ChW/1, f. 176.

67 *Cal. Pat*. 1560–3, 257, 260.

68 S.R.O. 2993/Rg/1, f. 15 and *passim* (entries transcribed from M. Wenlock reg.).

69 Welsh names begin to appear. Cf. above, this article, intro.; econ hist.

70 *T.S.A.S*. 2nd ser. xii. 93, 312; H.W.R.O.(H.), HD 2/14/12; HD 5/14/1/8.

71 P.R.O. HO 129/358, no. 28a.

72 S.R.O. 2993/Rg/1, ff. 19–20; *Short Hist. of Par. Ch. at Benthall* [1948], 2 (copy in S.R.O. 3756/74).

73 Ho. of Lords papers 1641–2, Protestations Oxon. and Salop. f. 179.

74 Eyton, iii. 279; H.W.R.O.(H.), HD 2/14/12; HD 5/14/1/8.

75 H.W.R.O.(H.), Heref. dioc. rec., vol. 'Notitia', f. 6; *Dioc. of Heref. Institutions (1539–1900)*, ed. A. T. Bannister (Heref. 1923), 99, 119, 125, 127, 142, 158–9; *P.O. Dir. Salop*. (1870), 15; (1879), 278.

76 Heref. Dioc. Regy., reg. 1822–42, pp. 84, 115, 201; 1847–56, pp. 220, 255, 684; S. Bagshaw, *Dir. Salop*. (1851), 556; *P.O. Dir. Salop*. (1856), 15.

77 *D.N.B.*; E. Glasgow, *Hartshorne, Charles Henry* (issued with St. John's Coll., Camb., mag. *The Eagle*, Easter 1984).

78 *Kelly's Dir. Salop*. (1885), 800; (1895), 29; Bannister, *Heref. Institutions*, 214.

79 *Kelly's Dir. Salop*. (1905), 30; (1929), 35; SA 11473.

80 Bannister, op. cit. 214; *Kelly's Dir. Salop*. (1900), 29; Heref. Dioc. Regy., reg. 1902–19, pp. 11, 15.

81 *Kelly's Dir. Salop*. (1895–1941); S.R.O. 2993/ChW/1, ff. 153, 177; *Hist. Ch. at Benthall*, 6; S.R.O., archivist's office file 'Benthall', corresp. of Mrs. M. C. Benthall with co. archivist.

82 *T.S.A.S*. vi. 124; D. H. Farmer, *Oxf. Dict. of Saints* (1987), 61.

83 H.W.R.O.(H.), Heref. dioc. rec. AL 19/19, f. 12v.; HD 7, 1668/414; Stackhouse Acton, *Garrisons of Salop*. 28–9.

84 B.L. Add. MS. 30316, f. 29v. Nevertheless the dedication to St. Brice was still current in 1789: S.P.L., MS. 372, vol. i, f. 117.

85 The date is given in a contemporary inscription (B.L. Add. MS. 21237, f. 320) but by July 1668 the work was allegedly unfinished (H.W.R.O.(H.), HD 7, 1668/414); ch. 'lately erected' by Oct. 1673 (H.W.R.O.(H.), Heref. dioc. rec. AL 19/19, f. 12v.).

86 As the proportions suggest.

87 Descr. from Cranage, iii. 186–7; Pevsner, *Salop*. 72; *Hist. Ch. at Benthall*; *Benthall Hall* (Nat. Trust, 1976), 24–5; Bodl. MS. Top. Salop. c. 2, f. 109; B.L. Add. MS. 21237, f. 318.

88 H.W.R.O.(H.), Heref. dioc. rec. AL 19/19, f. 13.

89 S.R.O. 2993/ChW/1, f. 157v. The arms could hardly have been Jas. I's (as suggested for the first time ibid.) if the chapel was completely destroyed before 1667.

90 Para. based on S.R.O. 2993/ChW/1, ff. 136–9, 150, 155; *Ch. Cal. Dioc. Heref*. (1879), 125; Heref. Dioc. Regy., reg. 1883–1901, pp. 438–9.

were removed, the pulpit was moved from the south wall to the east end of the nave, and the lion's head bee bole[91] over the old south door was renewed. The nave ceiling was removed *c.* 1950.[92] In 1974 a painting of the Coronation of the Virgin was hung in the church.[93]

The churchyard was extended in 1868 and 1937, and in 1964 it was levelled and the stones were removed.[94]

The earliest register begins in 1640 and is complete from 1670 except for marriages 1752–5.[95]

NONCONFORMITY. In the later 16th century the Benthalls of Benthall Hall were recusants or sympathizers and the Hall has a priest's hole.[96] Four papists, including Edward Benthall's widow Fortunata, lived in Benthall in 1680,[97] eight in 1716,[98] and one in 1767.[99]

An ostensibly medicinal cold bath, built by Isaac Wyke, a Broseley surgeon, on land near Coppice House which he had leased in 1744, may really have been a baptism pool for the Broseley Baptists whose chapel had recently opened nearby.[1]

William Genner's house near the Iron Bridge was licensed for protestant meetings in 1811.[2]

EDUCATION. Day schools and a Sunday school, supported by subscription and later partly by an endowment of £3 10*s.* a year, had *c.* 45 pupils in 1820 and *c.* 30 in 1835. There was also an infant school begun in 1821; in 1835 it had 12 pupils.[3]

Benthall Parochial Mixed school, with 80 places[4] in a schoolroom and classroom,[5] opened in 1872;[6] there was also a teacher's house.[7] Annual income in 1890 included £2 15*s.* from endowment besides school pence and voluntary contributions; pupils bought their books.[8] Attendance averaged 60 in 1885 and 71 in 1891.[9] The school closed in 1891, mistress and pupils transferring to the new Broseley Wood C.E. Infant school.[10]

CHARITIES FOR THE POOR. Mrs. Anne Browne (d. 1767) left £200, the income (£6) distributed in small doles in 1820 and later. After 1820 Edward Brown left £200, the income to repair a tombstone and to relieve the poor; in 1857 £6 12*s.* 4*d.* was given in small sums for clothing. Samuel Roden (d. 1854) left £100 to maintain a tombstone and to provide cash doles for ten widows; the first distribution (£3 6*s.* 6*d.*) was in 1858. Edward Roden, by will proved 1883, left £100 for annual cash doles to widows, and Elizabeth Morgan, by will proved 1886, left £100 to maintain tombs and provide doles for widows.

By 1975 the parish charities had been combined with those of Broseley civil parish.[11]

BROSELEY

THE NAME Broseley probably means 'woodland clearing of the fort guardian', and much of Broseley remained wooded in the Middle Ages.[12] For 350 years from the late 16th century coal, ironstone, and clay were successively exploited in the riverside parish, and Broseley grew rapidly from an agricultural village with extensive wood–pasture reserves to be, by the 18th century, one of the county's most populous towns, with mazes of hilly lanes winding around jumbles of brick cottages and the occasional larger house. The town's prosperity ended as the coal ran out in the early 19th century, and it then stagnated and the population declined. Recovery of a sort came after the Second World War when the building of over 1,000 new houses brought the population back to its early 19th-century level. Many of the new houses, however, were for commuters, and there was still little employment to be had locally. The parish also includes Jackfield, the port from which coal and ironstone were shipped out of Broseley, and the main site in the 19th and early 20th century of the parish's celebrated brick and tile industries. When Dawley (later Telford) new town was planned in the early 1960s largely aesthetic considerations demanded the inclusion of 63 ha. of Jackfield in the designated area.[13] The rest of the parish, which did not contribute to the spectacular scenery of the Severn Gorge, was excluded from the new town. By 1983 Telford's effects were clear: Ironbridge, on the opposite bank of

91 Alluding to Judg. 14: 5–18.
92 *Hist. Ch. at Benthall*, 5; Pevsner, *Salop.* 72.
93 Heref. Dioc. Regy., reg. 1969– (in use), p. 180.
94 S.R.O. 2993/ChW/1, f. 176; Heref. Dicc. Regy., reg. 1857–69, pp. 610–11, 629; 1919–26, p. 170; 1926–38, p. 530; 1953–68, p. 456.
95 S.R.O. 2993/Rg/1–4; /BRg/1; /MRg/1–2; regs. at ch. Cf. H.W.R.O.(H.), bp.'s transcripts 1630, 1674–5, 1677–1812, etc.
96 Above, this article, manor; *Benthall Hall* (Nat. Trust, 1976), 15–16.
97 *Worcs. Recusant*, liii. 32.
98 H.W.R.O.(H.), HD 5/14/1/8.
99 *Worcs. Recusant*, xxv. 29.
1 S.R.O. 294/2, field 204; 515/2, p. 132; /4, p. 282; 1224, box 40, deed 1 Aug. 1744; below, Broseley, intro.; prot. nonconf.
2 *Orders of Q. Sess.* iii. 172.
3 R. Hume, 'Changing Patterns of Educ. Devt. in Salop. 1660–1833' (Keele Univ. Ph.D. (Educ.) thesis, 1982), 314; *Digest Educ. Poor*, H.C. 224, p. 746 (1819), ix (2); *Educ. Enq. Abstract*, H.C. 62, p. 769 (1835), xlii.
4 *Kelly's Dir. Salop.* (1885), 800.
5 P.R.O., ED 7/103, ff. 147–8.
6 J. McFall, 'Educ. in Madeley Union of Salop. in 19th Cent.' (Keele Univ. M.A. (Educ.) thesis, 1973), 51.
7 Ibid. 144.
8 P.R.O., ED 7/103, ff. 147–8.
9 *Kelly's Dir. Salop.* (1885), 800; (1891), 264.
10 P.R.O., ED 7/103, ff. 147–8.
11 S. Bagshaw, *Dir. Salop.* (1851), 556; S.R.O. 2993/P/1; /Rg/3, p. 151; /BRg/1, p. 67; *3rd Rep. Com. Char.* H.C. 5, p. 303 (1820), iv; S.R.O. 1206/54, pp. 879–85; /60, pp. 537–40; *Review of Local Chars.* (S.C.C. 1975), 21.
12 *P.N. Salop.* (E.P.N.S.), i. 63–4. This article was written in 1983 and revised 1985–6 and later.
13 *Dawley New Town (Designation) Order 1963* (Stat. Inst. 1963, no. 64) and map; *Dawley New Town (Designation) Amendment (Telford) Order 1968* (Stat. Instr. 1968, no. 1912) and map; S.R.O., DA 6/112/13, 12 Sept. 1962.

the Severn, had gained an international reputation as an historic centre and had been physically and economically regenerated, while Broseley town centre remained shabby and depressed.[14]

The parish is roughly triangular, the Severn forming its north-east boundary for 5 km. Extending *c.* 3 km. north–east and *c.* 4 km. east–west the parish is bounded on the west partly by Benthall brook, so called by 1686,[15] which drains to the Severn, and partly by Dean brook, so called by 1609, draining south-east.[16] The southern boundary follows no natural feature and may once have marked the northern edge of woodland in Caughley.[17] Until 1966 the parish covered 1,991 a. (806 ha.),[18] but that year it was reduced to 743 ha. by the transfer of part of Jackfield to Dawley C.P.;[19] that part was included in the new civil parish of the Gorge in 1988.[20]

Broseley lies on the southern edge of the east Shropshire coalfield. Most of the parish lies between 122 and 152 m., rising higher in the west between Hockley Bank and Broseley Wood and around the Dunge. Dingles or baches run down from the higher ground to the Severn, the descent to which is steep and extensively wooded. Jackfield, on the river bank, lies at *c.* 40 m. Extensive outcrops of the Lower Coal Measures occur in the west. To the east the workable coal seams are overlain by the Carboniferous sandstones, marl, and mudstones of the Hadley and Coalport formations. Pockets of sand and gravel occur across the parish, while at the Dunge there is a kilometre-long spread of boulder clay. The slopes down to the Severn are unstable and landslips have occurred, notably in 1881 and 1952.[21]

Natives of Broseley include John Langley (1596–1661) of the Amies, who was private secretary to the earl of Leicester (d. 1626) and later manager of Sir Richard Leveson's Shropshire estates, and whose knowledge of antiquities was commended by Dugdale.[22] John Randall (1810–1910), local historian and artist, was born in Broseley.[23] John Guest, member of a long-established Broseley family of colliers, moved to Dowlais (Glam.) *c.* 1758 to manage the ironworks, becoming a partner in 1782. His family prospered, becoming baronets (1838) and Barons Wimborne (1880).[24] Also originally from Broseley were the Hornblowers, several of whom made notable contributions to engineering in the 18th and early 19th century.[25] Osborne Gordon (1813–83), a leading Oxford figure of the 1840s and 1850s, was a Broseley man.[26] Richard Wyke, who like several members of his family was a Broseley surgeon, published *Belisarius, Buildwas Abbey, Ludlow Castle, and Other Poems* in 1844.[27]

COMMUNICATIONS. The medieval roads probably differed little from those of *c.* 1620.[28] Broseley village then extended along the road from Bridgnorth that entered the parish at its southern extremity. It continued to Much Wenlock via Posenhall and either Benthall or Arlescott; the Wenlock–Broseley road via the latter route was among those turnpiked in 1756.[29] About 1220 the lord of the manor allowed Buildwas abbey to make a road from quarries in Broseley wood to the Severn (perhaps the later Quarry Road).[30]

About 1620[31] a road ran from Benthall village down Benthall brook towards Ladywood; the later Ball's Lane ran north-east from Woodlands towards Jackfield. From the south end of Broseley village roads and tracks radiated west, south, and east. West ran a track across or along the northern part of West field to Broseley Gate on the parish boundary, thence via Willey park to Barrow and Wenlock. South ran the 'horseway' to Bridgnorth, from which Hatch Lane[32] branched south to Willey and Hangstree Gate. In the early 19th century Hatch Lane increased in importance when the road across Willey park was closed.[33] Lampas Lane ran south-east towards Caughley. East ran a second road to Caughley, off which stood the Amies, Lower Riddings, Rowton, and Swinbatch. Near Broseley that road was called Rough Lane, and to the east Riddings Lane. A track ran north of Riddings Lane and later superseded it, probably by 1757 when the new route was known as Amies Lane. In 1687 the owner of Rowton was granted a way to the Severn (possibly the road closed before 1787 by Thomas Stephens), another to the Broseley–Caughley road, and a burial way to Broseley church.[34]

Two bridges across the Severn, opened in 1780, greatly altered the local road pattern. A bridge from Preen's Eddy in Broseley to Sutton Maddock[35] was completed in 1780 under an Act of 1776.[36] It was known as Preen's Eddy or

[14] Below, local govt.; *V.C.H. Salop* xi. 1–19.

[15] S.R.O. 1224/1/34. Possibly Shyer's brook, mentioned 1729: ibid. /2/480–1; /1/32 for position of Thos. Syner's ho.

[16] Ibid. /3/523–4; 1224, box 75, Caughley map of 1609; O.S. Map 6", LI. NW., NE. (1983 edn.); 1/25,000, SO 79 (1956 edn.).

[17] Above, Caughley, intro.

[18] *Census*, 1891.

[19] *Census*, 1971, *Co. Rep. Salop.* i. 10; O.S. Map 1/10,000, SJ 60 SE. (1981 edn.).

[20] *The Wrekin (Parishes) Order 1988* (Stat. Instr. 1988, no. 156); O.S. Map 1/100,000, Salop. Admin. Areas (1988 edn.).

[21] Inst. Geol. Sciences Map 1/25,000, *Telford* (1978 edn.); W.B.R., Broseley dist. cttee. min. bk. 1946–52, pp. 325, 329, 336, 342; *Manchester Guardian*, 10 Apr. 1952; *Bye-Gones*, v. 314; pl. 35.

[22] *T.S.A.S.* 2nd ser. 119–21; *Cal. Cttee. for Compounding*, ii. 1453; E. G. Salisbury, *Border Cos. Worthies*, 2nd ser. (1879), 176; *Par. Regs. of Broseley*, ed. A. F. C. C. Langley (2 vols. 1889–90), i. 47.

[23] L. C. Lloyd, *Boro. of Wenlock Official Guide* (1964), 55; *V.C.H. Salop.* xi. 23.

[24] Burke, *Peerage* (1938), 2601; Trinder, *Ind. Rev. Salop.* (1981), 123; S. Baring Gould, *Bk. of S. Wales* (1905), 113–14.

[25] *D.N.B.* s.v. Hornblower, Jonathan.

[26] *D.N.B.*

[27] Salisbury, *Border Cos. Worthies*, 2nd ser. 305; cf. (for Isaac Wyke) above, Benthall, nonconf.; below, prot. nonconf.

[28] S.R.O. 1224/1/32. Cf. fig. 25.

[29] Below, M. Wenlock, communications; 29 Geo. II, c. 60.

[30] *V.C.H. Salop.* ii. 52, 56; below, econ. hist. (other ind.); J. Randall, *Broseley and Its Surroundings* (Madeley, 1879), 14–15; O.S. Map 1/2,500, Salop. LI. 2. (1902 edn.).

[31] S.R.O. 1224/1/32; O.S. Maps 1/2,500, Salop. XLIII. 14, LI. 2 (1902 edn.).

[32] S.R.O. 1224/1/9.

[33] Below, Willey, intro.

[34] S.R.O. 1224/3/536, 578, 597; Randall, *Broseley*, 70.

[35] Following based on Trinder, *Ind. Rev. Salop.* 88–9; idem, 'Coalport Bridge', *Ind. Arch. Rev.* iii. 153–7; A. Blackwall, *Historic Bridges of Salop.* (Shrews. 1985), 21–2.

[36] 17 Geo. III, c. 12.

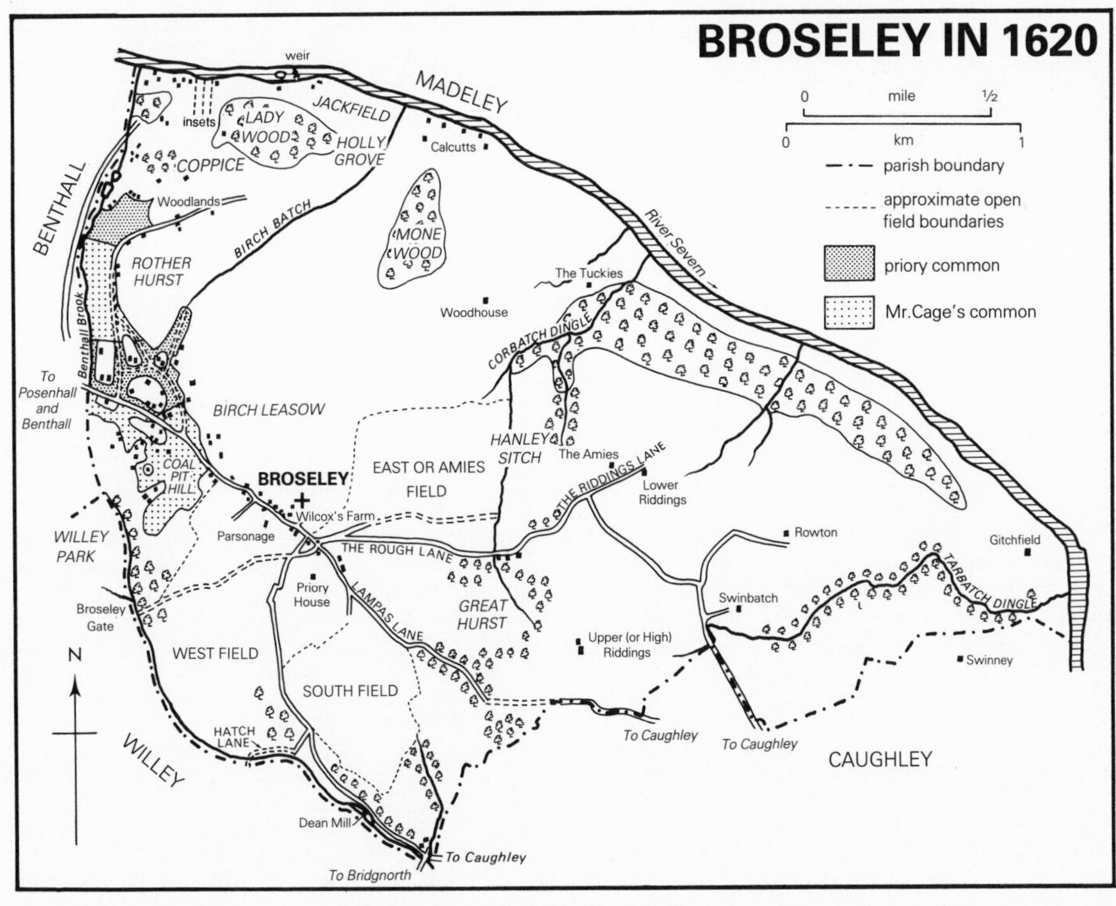

Fig. 25

Wood bridge and, from the growth of Coalport in the 1790s, as Coalport bridge. A two-span wooden bridge, it was designed by William Hayward and built by Robert Palmer, a Madeley timber merchant. It was rebuilt in 1799 as a single-span bridge with cast-iron main ribs. The bridge's proprietors had powers to build connecting roads; that to Bridgnorth opened in 1796[37] and that from Broseley to the Wellington–Worcester road near Brockton (in Sutton Maddock), along the former Amies Lane, was completed in 1797.[38]

The Iron Bridge, from Benthall to Madeley Wood, opened in 1780.[39] At first the road from the bridge to the Wenlock–Broseley turnpike ran through Benthall parish.[40] In 1828 a new route from Ironbridge was built using the parish poor as labourers: from the bridge it ran east for 1 km. before turning south for 1.5 km., past a tollhouse, to the south end of Broseley town. Among those involved in its construction were Benjamin Ball, manager of James Foster's Barnett's Leasow ironworks, and Silvanus Ball, a Broseley ironfounder. A private carriageway, with a lodge at its entrance, extended from the road to Willey Hall.[41]

The Iron Bridge closed to vehicles in 1934. By then two more bridges had opened across the Severn: the ferro-concrete Haynes Memorial (or Free) bridge between the Lloyds and Jackfield in 1909, and the War Memorial footbridge from Coalport to the Tuckies in 1922.[42]

Even after the bridging of the Severn in 1780[43] ferries continued to ply between Broseley and Madeley. After the Coalport china works opened in Madeley in the late 18th century large numbers of workers had daily to cross the river from their homes in Broseley and Jackfield.[44] In 1799 a Jackfield ferry overturned with 41 Coalport workers on board.[45] William Reynolds had a private ferry at the Tuckies.[46] In 1840 three services crossed the river:[47] Adam's ferry, between Ladywood and Ironbridge; a horse ferry, between Jackfield and the Lloyds; and the Werps, or Tuckies,[48] ferry, connecting with Coalport. The horse ferry had ceased operating by 1856;[49] Adam's ferry stopped in 1912, and

37 R. Baugh, *Map of Salop.* (1808); S.P.L., MS. 2479.
38 *V.C.H. Salop.* xi. 25.
39 Ibid.
40 Above, Benthall, intro.
41 P.R.O., IR 29/29/55; IR 30/29/55; Trinder, *Ind. Rev. Salop.* 90, 143; Randall, *Broseley*, 238, 315–16; W.B.R., Q2/1/4. A planned monumental gateway to Willey Pk. (B.L. Add. MS. 36378, ff. 229–30) was prob. never built.
42 *V.C.H. Salop.* xi. 25; Blackwall, *Hist. Bridges of Salop.* 81–2; S.P.L., photos. 2542–5; *Arch. in Ironbridge 1985–6*, ed. M. Trueman (Ironbridge, 1986), 12–13, and erratum inside front cover; pl. 34.
43 Above, this section.
44 Trinder, *Ind. Rev. Salop.* 132.
45 S. Bagshaw, *Dir. Salop.* (1851), 558.
46 Randall, *Broseley*, 86–7.
47 S.R.O. 1313/149.
48 S.R.O. 1242, box XI, deeds *re* Tuckies ferry, 1860.
49 *P.O. Dir. Salop.* (1856), 24; C. Clark and J. Alfrey, *Jackfield and Broseley* (Nuffield Arch. Surv. [of Ironbridge Gorge] 4th Interim rep.; Ironbridge, 1988), 40.

the Werps ferry *c.* 1922 when the War Memorial footbridge opened.[50]

As local mining and industry grew during the 17th and 18th centuries they used the Severn as the cheapest route for coal and manufactures brought to the riverside wharves by a network of railways constructed from 1605 and used until the earlier 19th century.[51] Trows were carrying coal by 1606.[52] In 1674 garving (the cleaning and tarring of barge bottoms)[53] was controlled at Broseley.[54] In 1756, during a period when the number of boats increased to match the growth in the iron trade, there were 55 barge owners in the parish, most of them probably living in Jackfield. They owned 87 vessels and formed the largest community of Severn watermen between Welshpool and Gloucester. Two main types of vessel were operated: single-masted barges or frigates 12–18 m. long which carried 20–40 tons of coal; and multi-masted trows 18 m. long and 5–6 m. wide which had a crew of three or four and carried 40–80 tons of general cargo such as ore, iron, and bricks.[55]

In contrast to those on the opposite bank of the Severn, wharves at Ladywood, Calcutts, Lloyd Head, and the Tuckies seem to have been relatively insubstantial, although the river has scoured away much evidence.[56] One of the better constructed wharves may have been Willey wharf at the end of the Tarbatch dingle railway, from which the New Willey Co. shipped its products.[57] Boatmen remained an important part of the local economy until the railways arrived. Along the Severn bank ran the Coalbrookdale–Bewdley towpath, made *c.* 1800,[58] but from the later 18th century the Severn's navigable season gradually shortened. In 1862 many of the bargemen's houses were demolished when the Severn Valley Railway opened. By 1871 there were only five barge owners left in the Severn gorge; they carried mainly calcined ore from Broseley to the Black Country, bricks, and a few fine castings too valuable to be entrusted to the railways. All barge traffic had ceased by 1895.[59]

The Severn Valley line of the West Midland Railway (later G.W.R.), opened in 1862, followed the Broseley bank of the Severn.[60] Coalford, later Coalport West, station near Coalport bridge was open by 1870[61] and closed in 1963.[62] Jackfield halt, opened after 1928, was moved 400 yd. south in 1954 after a landslip, and closed in 1963.[63] The parish was also served from 1862 to 1963 by Ironbridge and Broseley station (in Benthall).[64] Several tile works had private sidings.[65]

GROWTH OF SETTLEMENT. In 1086 the recorded population of 'Bosle' was 9.[66] In the 13th century open-field land lay south of Broseley vill, while freehold farms, perhaps made as cultivation expanded, lay in the eastern half of the manor.[67] Riddings farm existed *c.* 1240,[68] Swinbatch by 1255,[69] and the Amies by 1327;[70] Rowton,[71] Woodhouse[72] and Woodlands[73] were probably also established by that time. Several of the farms' names suggest they originated as woodland assarts.[74]

By the 1550s cottages stood on Coalpit Hill[75] (so known by 1556)[76] and at Woodlands. Settlement grew rapidly during the late 16th century. James Clifford, lord of the manor, encouraged the immigration of miners, who were allowed to build cottages on irregular plots on the uninclosed commons and wastes north of the ancient village. In 1570 Broseley had a population of perhaps *c.* 125.[77] By *c.* 1620 there were *c.* 27 houses in Broseley village, with *c.* 33 scattered on Coalpit Hill and probably a similar number spread between Woodlands Green and the river.[78] The newcomers' settlements, lacking cohesion, were yet distinct from the ancient agricultural village of Broseley. Their segregation was emphasized by riots in the years 1605–7, when new cottagers were attacked by long-established substantial tenants resentful of the loss of common rights,[79] and in 1636 by the presentment of encroachments at Woodlands Green.[80]

During the early 17th century the wealth created by industry began to be displayed in substantial timber framed and brick houses. In 1672 ten of the 92 households taxed had five or more hearths.[81] Largest, with 14 hearths, was William Crompton's house. Others included John Geares's house (8 hearths) on the north side of Coalpit Hill, and Edward Eaves's (6 hearths) 500 m. north-west of it.[82] Adam Crompton's house (built 1654, 7 hearths in

50 W.B.R., Broseley dist. cttee. min. bk. 1906–13, pp. 355, 364; *V.C.H. Salop.* xi. 25; Clark and Alfrey, op. cit. 40.

51 D. M. Palliser, *Age of Eliz.: Eng. under later Tudors 1547–1603* (1983), 273; below, econ. hist. (industrial rlys.).

52 J. U. Nef, *Rise of Brit. Coal Ind.* (1932), i. 393. Cf. *V.C.H. Salop.* xi. 23.

53 *O.E.D.*

54 S.R.O. 1224/2/510, Bourton hund. ct. Apr. 1674.

55 *V.C.H. Salop.* i. 425–6; Trinder, *Ind. Rev. Salop.* 60–71; Randall, *Broseley*, 162–7; pl. 30.

56 Clark and Alfrey, *Jackfield and Broseley*, 41–3.

57 Below, econ. hist (industrial rlys.); Trinder, op. cit. 71.

58 Under 39 Geo. III, c. 8 (Local and Personal): C. Hadfield, *Canals of W. Midlands* (1969), 124.

59 Below, this section; Trinder, op. cit. 64–5, 68–9, 154.

60 Trinder, op. cit. 153; Sir G. Nabarro, *Severn Valley Steam* (1971), 35.

61 *P.O. Dir. Salop.* (1870), 26.

62 *T.S.A.S.* lxiv. 93.

63 Ibid. 68; *Shrews. Chron.* 26 Feb. 1954. Not on O.S. Map 6", LI. NE. (1928 edn.).

64 *V.C.H. Salop.* xi. 27.

65 O.S. Maps 6", XLIII. SW., LI. NE. (1903 edn.).

66 *V.C.H. Salop.* i. 338.

67 Below, econ. hist. (agric.).

68 Eyton, ii. 31–2.

69 *Rot. Hund.* (Rec. Com.), ii. 111.

70 *Cal. Pat.* 1327–30, 215.

71 Below, manor.

72 First known mention 1418–19: S.R.O. 1190/1, unlisted acct. r. 1417–27.

73 S.R.O. 1224/2/3.

74 Eyton, iii. 241; below, econ. hist. (agric.).

75 Below, econ. hist. (coal and ironstone; clay ind.); *T.S.A.S.* vi. 111.

76 *T.S.A.S.* vi. 111.

77 M. D. G. Wanklyn, 'Ind. Devt. in Ironbridge Gorge before Abraham Darby', *W. Midlands Studies*, xv. 4; idem, 'Rural Riots in 17th-cent. Salop.' in *Rural Social Change & Conflicts since 1500*, ed. A. Charlesworth [Hull, 1983], 11–12.

78 Charlesworth, *Rural Social Change*, 11–12; S.R.O. 1224/1/32; /7/2, pp. 45–6. The last group incl. *c.* 11 in Jackfield: below, this section.

79 Charlesworth, *Rural Social Change*, 11–13; below, econ. hist. (industrial rlys.).

80 S.R.O. 1224/2/356.

81 *Hearth Tax 1672* (Salop. Arch. Soc. 1949), 31–2.

82 S.R.O. 1224/1/21, 34.

1672)[83] stood at Coalford, close to another large house known later as the Old Hall. A sixth that can be identified is Rowton (7 hearths in 1672) in the east end of the parish near Gitchfield House.[84] Other large houses outside the main settlement included the Tuckies, Woodhouse Farm, and the Amies,[85] while Raddle Hall (1663)[86] and Wilcox's Farm stood near Broseley church.[87] Broseley village grew further, and by 1686 the streets later known as King Street, Duke Street, and Queen Street and connecting streets to the north end of the town had grown out of small strips of common that had survived between cottages built since the late 16th century.[88] Cottages continued to multiply in the later 17th century through natural increase rather than immigration,[89] and in 1681 there were probably over sixty cottages in the part of Broseley Wood that was in Marsh manor.[90]

As contemporaries recognized, Broseley was becoming one of the county's most considerable towns,[91] 'a place of great trade' in 1672.[92] In 1642 the Protestation was taken by 296 men in the parish, apparently none refusing.[93] By 1676 the number of adults was 793,[94] and *c.* 1690 Broseley Wood had become 'as a country town'.[95] Miners were most numerous but there were also watermen, potters, clay-pipe makers, and a wide range of service traders indicative of the town's new status and potential.[96]

By 1700 Broseley town had perhaps 2,000 inhabitants, and its population more than doubled again in the 18th century.[97] Brick, perhaps first used in Broseley in Raddle Hall (1663),[98] Church Street, came to be widely used both in major buildings such as Broseley and Jackfield churches (*c.* 1715 and 1759 respectively),[99] White Hall (early 18th century),[1] New House (later the Lawns, built in 1727 for Thomas Stephens, a local mine owner, and remodelled by John Wilkinson in the 1760s),[2] Broseley Hall (probably 1730s),[3] the market hall (1779),[4] and lesser buildings. The quality of some of the larger buildings was high, at least three having features designed by T. F. Pritchard.[5] One of the commonest types of cottage, exemplified by a small terraced row on Barratt's Hill, was of brick and of 1½ storey. The type probably first appeared in the early 18th century.[6] Subdivision of houses and infilling around them was widespread[7] and resulted in a denser rather than expanded settlement as the population grew. It is not clear who in general was responsible for cottage building, landlord or tenant. By 1800, however, houses were being built for workers at some of the larger industrial concerns such as Alexander Brodie's, and Banks & Onions's.[8] It was probably during the 18th century that High Street became the town's commercial centre, a northward shift emphasized and furthered in 1779 by the building of a new market hall at the end of High Street to replace the open site near the church.[9]

Two centuries of industrial prosperity ended *c.* 1800 as Broseley's coal ran out.[10] Broseley became the coalfield's most depressed area, and its population remained static throughout the earlier 19th century.[11] It was just over 4,800 in 1801 and 1841, having recovered from the loss of *c.* 500 workers following the closure of five blast furnaces before 1831. Thereafter it slowly declined, to 4,458 in 1881 and 3,037 in 1921. The town altered little throughout the 19th century; the street pattern of 1902 was hardly changed from that of the late 18th century, and few large buildings had been erected since the early 19th century. The names of the main mid 20th-century streets were in use by 1840 and some earlier still, Barratt's Hill being noted in 1790.[12] Improvements were generally small-scale and tardy. The town's paving and street drainage received attention in the 1840s,[13] street lighting was introduced from 1847, and iron street-name plates were first put up in 1880. There was no reliable public water supply, however, until the end of the century, and sewage disposal was primitive until the 1960s.[14]

Cottages and small terraced rows stood between larger houses in the confused tangle of streets and lanes between Broseley church and the north end of Broseley Wood. Different classes therefore lived side by side. Nevertheless there remained a group of large houses in Church Street, where John Onions, the ironmaster, lived at White Hall in 1851, while Broseley Wood was said in 1831 to contain the parish's filthiest and most dilapidated houses, some occupied by poor Irish. Many lanes and properties

83 Demolished 1939: *Shrews. Chron.* 24 Feb. 1939, with photo.
84 Randall, *Broseley*, 67–72, 84–5; *V.C.H. Salop.* i. 443.
85 Cf. e.g. S.R.O. 1224/1/32, 36; below, manor.
86 Date stone.
87 Below, manor.
88 Cf. S.R.O. 1224/1/21, 34; figs. 25–6.
89 *W. Midlands Studies*, xv. 4.
90 S.R.O. 1224/2/511, s.a.
91 *W. Midlands Studies*, xv. 4, which, however, overstates the rel. size of Broseley's pop. It was prob. less than Wellington's (*V.C.H. Salop.* xi. 205) or Oswestry's (*Hearth Tax 1672*, 251–3).
92 *T.S.A.S.* 4th ser. v. 306.
93 Ho. of Lords Papers 1641–2, Protestations Oxon. and Salop. f. 185.
94 *T.S.A.S.* 2nd ser. i. 90.
95 S.R.O. 1224, box 149, brief for Geo. Weld. For a discussion of settlement in Broseley Wood see C. Clark and J. Alfrey, *Benthall and Broseley Wood* (Nuffield Arch. Surv. [of Ironbridge Gorge] 3rd Interim Rep.; Ironbridge, 1987), 117–32.
96 Below, econ. hist. [intro.].
97 *W. Midlands Studies*, xv. 4; *V.C.H. Salop.* ii. 221. See also the discussion of Broseley in S. A. Lewis, 'Hist. and Geog. Study of Small Towns in Salop. 1600–1800' (Leic. Univ. Ph.D. thesis, 1991).
98 SA 11722.
99 Below, churches.
1 SA 11721.
2 *Jnl. Wilkinson Soc.* i [p. 6]; S.R.O. 1224/3/436–42.
3 SA 11720.
4 Below, econ. hist. (mkt. and fairs).
5 J. Harris, 'Pritchard redivivus', *Archit. Hist.* ii. 20–1 (Broseley Hall, the Lawns, and Woodhouse Fm.).
6 Clark and Alfrey, *Benthall and Broseley Wood*, 126–7.
7 Trinder, *Ind. Rev. Salop.* 186–8.
8 S.R.O. 515/4, pp. 236–7; /8, p. 232.
9 Pl. 21; below, econ. hist. (mkt. and fairs).
10 Below, econ. hist. (coal and ironstone).
11 Trinder, *Ind. Rev. Salop.* 146.
12 O.S. Map 6", SJ 60 SE. (1954 edn.); S.R.O. 1224/3/917–18; 1313/49.
13 *Amount of Money Expended in Repairing Highways in Par. of Broseley* (1848; copy in S.R.O. 1681/116/19). Cf. C. Hulbert, *Hist. and Descr. of Salop.* ii (1837), 342.
14 Below, public services; W.B.R., Broseley local bd. min. bk. 1876–86, pp. 155, 163.

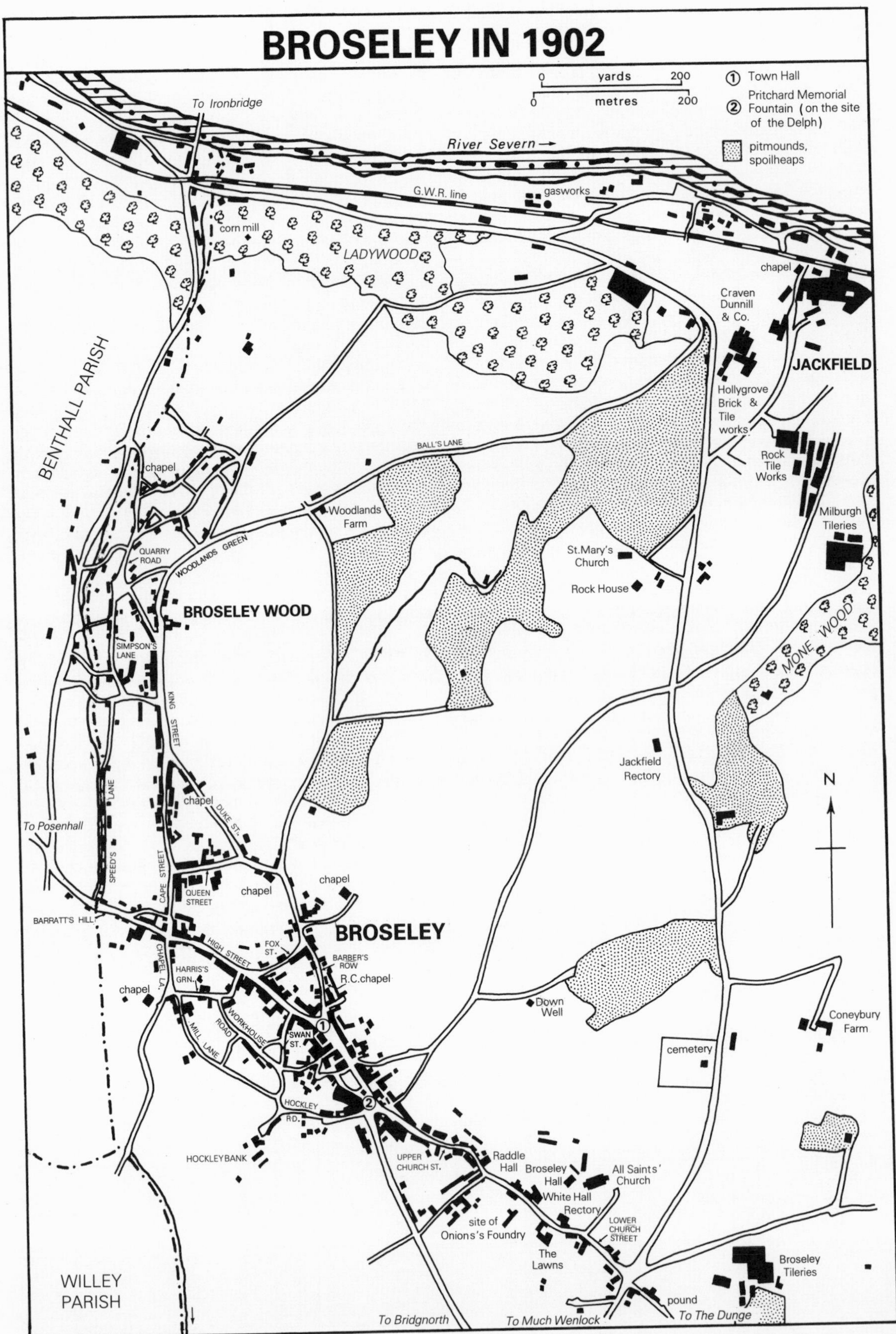
BROSELEY IN 1902
0 yards 200
0 metres 200
① Town Hall
② Pritchard Memorial Fountain (on the site of the Delph)
pitmounds, spoilheaps
To Ironbridge
River Severn
G.W.R. line
gasworks
corn mill
LADYWOOD
chapel
Craven Dunnill & Co.
JACKFIELD
Hollygrove Brick & Tile works
Rock Tile Works
Milburgh Tileries
BENTHALL PARISH
BALL'S LANE
Woodlands Farm
WOODLANDS GREEN
QUARRY ROAD
BROSELEY WOOD
SIMPSON'S LANE
KING STREET
St.Mary's Church
Rock House
MONE WOOD
Jackfield Rectory
N
To Posenhall
SPEED'S LANE
CAPE STREET
DUKE ST.
QUEEN STREET
BARRATT'S HILL
BROSELEY
FOX ST.
HIGH STREET
CHAPEL LA.
HARRIS'S GRN.
BARBER'S ROW
R.C.chapel
Down Well
WORKHOUSE ROAD
MILL LANE
SWAN ST.
cemetery
Coneybury Farm
HOCKLEY RD.
HOCKLEYBANK
UPPER CHURCH ST.
Raddle Hall
Broseley Hall
All Saints' Church
White Hall
Rectory
site of Onions's Foundry
LOWER CHURCH STREET
The Lawns
Broseley Tileries
WILLEY PARISH
pound
To Bridgnorth
To Much Wenlock
To The Dunge

Fig. 26

there were bounded by walls made of old saggars. The town's tradesmen and shopkeepers were widely dispersed, although High Street probably had the greatest concentration and Broseley Wood the least.[15]

In 1919 the standard of housing was low: only about six new houses had been built in the parish since 1899, and probably two thirds of houses had no more than two bedrooms. About 160 houses, mostly ruinous or substandard, stood empty.[16] Slum clearance began with the Addison programme in 1919 and the district committee agreed in principle to build 80 houses 'as and when required'.[17] In practice, however, building was even slower than in Madeley.[18] The first two pairs of houses, designed by Geo. Ridley & Sons of Wellington, were built in 1925 in King Street and New Road[19] and gradually added to. By 1936 there were 24 houses in King Street and 28 in New Road; they formed eight per cent of the housing stock.[20]

After the 1936 Housing Act[21] slum clearance continued and building schemes became larger. The 50-house Birch Meadow estate east of Broseley was begun in 1938[22] and extended between 1945 and 1947, when 48 houses were also added at New Road.[23] During the 1950s 46 more houses were built at New Road and 124 at King Street.[24] Other developments by the district committee in the 1950s and 1960s included 26 bungalows in High Street built in 1956;[25] Pritchard House, a block of six flats erected in the Square in 1959;[26] 50 houses, flats, and maisonettes constructed at Hockley Bank *c.* 1962;[27] and 123 houses and grouped dwellings begun at Church Street *c.* 1966.[28] Slum clearance remained a priority throughout.

From the start of the district committee's house-building programme until the 1960s there were no large speculative developments, and only a few private houses were put up, some on unsuitable ground.[29] Some small private estates were built in the earlier 1960s: eleven pairs of bungalows at the Rock *c.* 1960,[30] and *c.* 20 houses off Woodlands Road *c.* 1963.[31] Between the later 1960s and mid 1980s several big speculative estates were constructed, partly to accommodate commuters to Telford and the west midlands. To the south-east of Broseley the Tileries and two small associated schemes, in all *c.* 320 dwellings, were built between *c.* 1967 and 1985; north of Broseley an estate of *c.* 145 houses including Bramblewood and Underwood was constructed from 1974 onwards; north of Elizabeth Crescent the Cherrybrook estate of *c.* 90 homes was built 1976–9; and behind the Victoria Hall in High Street 15 flats were put up *c.* 1978. Following Bridgnorth district council's drafting of a district plan for Broseley in 1979 growth was checked and in 1985 no more major private schemes were foreseen. The only council building in the 1970s and early 1980s was for old people: 12 flats and bungalows south of Foundry Lane, completed *c.* 1980, and *c.* 28 dwellings off Park View, built 1984–5.[32]

The rising quality and number of houses reversed the long population decline. From its low point in the 1920s population rose gradually to 3,457 in 1951[33] and then more rapidly to *c.* 4,920 by 1981.[34]

Riverside settlement in Broseley always retained a separate identity and character. Between the later 16th and the 19th centuries watermen comprised a large part of the population, while in the 19th century brick and tile works came to dominate the community.[35] In 1963 the western portion of Jackfield was the only part of the parish to be included in Dawley (later Telford) new town.[36]

Jakes field, a pasture near the Severn, was mentioned in 1510–11.[37] Mining at the Tuckies began *c.* 1575[38] and the riverside settlement at Jackfield probably grew up at the same time. Jackfield, however, may only have come to be commonly used as the name of the whole Severnside area after it was made a separate ecclesiastical parish in 1862.[39] By *c.* 1620 *c.* 11 houses stood along the first 750 m. of river bank east of Benthall brook[40] and there were others further east at Calcutts.[41] By that time Jackfield had emerged as a notable river port.

As in Broseley, settlement at Jackfield both spread as new encroachments were made and increased in density through subdivision of plots and houses.[42] At Calcutts in 1730 single houses and some rows stood among 'mughouses' (pottery kilns), pits, and railway lines.[43] In 1767 blast furnaces were built there, and brick making probably started soon after.[44] From the start, however, bargemen had probably been the most

[15] S. Bagshaw, *Dir. Salop.* (1851), 562–4; S.R.O. 604, proc. Broseley bd. of health 1831–3, rep. 5 Dec. 1831; *Victorian Shrews.* ed. B. Trinder (Shrews. 1984), 98; *Arch. in Ironbridge 1985–6*, 22–7.

[16] W.B.R., B3/5/24.

[17] W.B.R., Broseley dist. cttee. min. bk. 1914–22, pp. 269, 276, 284, 287, 328, 332.

[18] *V.C.H. Salop.* xi. 30.

[19] W.B.R., Broseley dist. cttee. min. bk. 1922–30, pp. 98, 109, 156–7.

[20] Ibid. pp. 187, 191, 217–18, 243, 251, 281, 302; 1930–7, pp. 47, 77, 210, 258, 348.

[21] 26 Geo. V & 1 Edw. VIII, c. 51.

[22] W.B.R., Broseley dist. cttee. min. bk. 1937–42, pp. 21–3, 80, 176; O.S. Map 6", Salop. LI. NW. (1938 edn.).

[23] W.B.R., Broseley dist. cttee. min. bk. 1942–6, pp. 185–6, 247–8; 1946–52, pp. 35, 59–60.

[24] Ibid. 1946–52, pp. 212, 292, 334, 381–2; 1953–6, pp. 54, 64, 71, 80–1, 230.

[25] Ibid. 1953–6, p. 272.

[26] Ibid. 1959–62, pp. 182, 268.

[27] Ibid. p. 313; 1962–6, pp. 63, 85, 114.

[28] Ibid. 1962–6, pp. 195, 299, 355–6.

[29] W.B.R., Broseley dist. cttee. min. bks. *passim.*

[30] Ibid. 1957–61, p. 306.

[31] Ibid. 1962–6, p. 131.

[32] Inf. from Bridgnorth Dist. Council; Bridgnorth Dist. Council, *Broseley Dist. Plan: Plan Brief* (Nov. 1979; copy in S.P.L.).

[33] *V.C.H. Salop.* ii. 221, 229.

[34] *Census*, 1981, Small Area Statistics (adjusted for par. bdy. changes).

[35] Below, econ. hist. (clay ind.).

[36] Below, local govt.

[37] *L. & P. Hen. VIII*, xv, p. 468; S.R.O. 1224, box 342, Prior Gosnell's reg. f. 38v.

[38] Trinder, *Ind. Rev. Salop.* 6.

[39] A century after the building of a ch. there: Clark and Alfrey, *Jackfield and Broseley*, 9; below, churches.

[40] S.R.O. 1224/1/32.

[41] R. S. Smith, 'England's first rails', *Renaissance & Modern Studies*, iv. 127. Calcutts too first recorded (1464) as pasture: Birm. Univ. Libr., Mytton Papers, i. 198.

[42] Above, this section; Trinder, *Ind. Rev. Salop.* 186–8.

[43] B. Trinder, *Making of Ind. Landscape* (1982), 3.

[44] Below, econ. hist. (iron; clay ind.).

numerous class, and in 1793 there were 33 bargeowners in the parish.[45] Lodging houses, alehouses, and brothels were established at Jackfield for resident and passing watermen. By 1800 the river bank had a thriving community, where cottages and alehouses stood among ironstone mines, ironworks, brickworks, pottery kilns, clay-pipe manufactories, and a tar distillery.[46] Much of the river bank was lined with quays where trows and barges loaded cargoes, increasingly of ironstone rather than coal, from the railways which ran down from the higher ground to the south.[47]

During the 19th century Jackfield's economy and environment came to be dominated by brick and tile works and, from 1874, their tall chimneys.[48] Both Broseley and Jackfield had, besides brickmakers, many resident ceramic workers, some of whom in the late 18th and 19th centuries were talented artists employed at Coalport (reached by ferry or bridge) and Caughley.[49] In the later 19th century the arrival of the railway saw the end of river barge transport and Jackfield's 300-year role as a port.[50] The number of houses also began to drop, *c.* 50 being demolished *c.* 1862 to make way for the railway.[51] In 1870 Jackfield was described as a very poor bit of the 'fag end' of the world.[52] Prosperity returned, however, in the late 19th and early 20th century as the products of Maws' and Craven Dunnills' tile works gained international popularity. Although those works did not close until 1952, Jackfield's clay industries began to contract *c.* 1914.[53] By then many houses were already substandard and later more became so through increasing local poverty, neglect, and subsidence and slips, although the closure of brickworks reduced smoke pollution. In the 1930s Jackfield's population declined as people moved to new council houses around Broseley.[54] There were no council houses at Jackfield until 1946, when six were built in Calcutts Road;[55] 22 (St. Mary's Close) were added 1961–2,[56] and 10 (Lloyds Head) 1966 × 1974.[57] Private building in the 20th century comprised mainly single bungalows; the only larger speculation was ten bungalows at Chapel Road, built in 1937.[58]

SOCIAL AND CULTURAL ACTIVITIES. By 1681 many taverns and alehouses served Broseley's industrial communities: at least 8 in the Marsh manor part, most presumably in Broseley Wood, and 17 elsewhere in the parish.[59] Numbers remained fairly constant until the late 19th century, although many alehouses were short-lived.[60] There were 30–40 public houses between 1790 and 1810:[61] in 1835 19 public houses and 5 beer sellers in Broseley and 5 public houses and one beer seller in Jackfield;[62] and in 1879 22 public houses and alehouses in Broseley and 10 in Jackfield.[63] The principal 19th-century inn was the Red Lion, near the town hall.[64] In the 20th century the number of public houses fluctuated in Broseley from 17 in 1900 to 12 in 1922, to 7 in 1941, and 10 (plus 4 social and sporting clubs) in 1986; in Jackfield from 7 to 6, to 3, the same number as were open in 1986.[65]

Drunkenness was a regular feature of popular pastimes. On Whit Monday 1652 Morris dancers from Broseley with six 'sword bearers' and numerous followers visited Nordley in Astley Abbots and caused an affray at an alehouse.[66] Until the 1820s bulls were baited at the green in Broseley Wood and at Coalford (Jackfield) during Broseley's wake on St. Leonard's day (6 November). Bulldogs were also matched.[67] Cock fighting took place oftener and mains were arranged by colliers from Broseley and south Staffordshire.[68] By 1864 blood sports and insobriety at the wakes had greatly lessened.[69] In the later 19th century duck hunting with dogs was popular at Jackfield wakes, held at Coalport (in Madeley) as no suitable site existed at Jackfield.[70] A maypole still stood in Broseley Wood in 1879; though not used for dancing within living memory, it was occasionally garlanded.[71]

By the 1830s Broseley's fairs were largely for pleasure although pigs were sold.[72] The April fair ended some time between 1842 and 1856,[73] but by 1888 fair day was again the last Tuesday in April.[74] During the 20th century the fairground moved from a site off Bridgnorth Road to a site later occupied by Wilkinson Avenue,

45 Above, communications.

46 Trinder, *Ind. Rev. Salop.* 41, 65; below, econ. hist.

47 Above, communications; below, econ. hist. (industrial rlys.).

48 Below, econ. hist. (clay ind.); pl. 34.

49 Trinder, *Ind. Rev. Salop.* 214; above, communications.

50 Above, communications.

51 Clark and Alfrey, *Jackfield and Broseley*, 82.

52 *Ironbridge Weekly Jnl.* 26 Mar. 1870.

53 Below, econ. hist. (clay ind.).

54 Ibid.; W.B.R., B3/5/24; S.R.O. 4526/1, 2 Nov. 1937; /3, p. 97. For comment on ind. pollution (furnace smoke) in 1800 see S.R.O. 515/2, p. 100.

55 W.B.R., Broseley dist. cttee. min. bk. 1946–52, pp. 8, 29.

56 Ibid. 1962–6, pp. 1, 64, 174.

57 *Dawley U.D.C., A Story 1966–1974* (copy in S.R.O., DA 8/294).

58 Clark and Alfrey, *Jackfield and Broseley*, 108.

59 S.R.O. 1224/2/511, [p. 3].

60 Randall, *Broseley*, 326–8.

61 S.R.O. 2991/Misc/1. Cf. *'The Most Extraordinary District in the World': Ironbridge and Coalbrookdale*, ed. B. Trinder (1977), 39; W.B.R., Q1/11/2–10.

62 Pigot, *Nat. Com. Dir.* (1835), 351–2; cf. also S.R.O. 1681/48, 1 Oct. 1841 (innkeepers pd. for voters' entertainment).

63 Randall, *Broseley*, 247–8.

64 Hulbert, *Hist. Salop.* ii. 343; O.S. Map 1/2,500, Salop. LI. 2 (1882 edn.).

65 *Kelly's Dir. Salop.* (1900), 46–7, 111; (1922), 49–50, 118; (1941), 51–2, 123. A. J. Mugridge, *Brief Hist. of Jackfield* (Jackfield, priv. print. 1986), 9 (copy in S.P.L.); inf. from Miss Y. J. E. Staelens.

66 *Jnl. Wilkinson Soc.* iv. 13.

67 Trinder, *Ind. Rev. Salop.* 180–1; Randall, *Broseley*, 180–2; *V.C.H. Salop.* ii. 191; C. S. Burne, *Salop. Folk-Lore* (1883), 447; *Footprints on the Track of Time during 50 yrs.: Hist. of Birchmeadow Sun. Sch., Broseley, to its Jubilee, 1864* [1864], 14 (copy in S.P.L.).

68 Trinder, op. cit. 220; Randall, op. cit. 180; *Shrews. Chron.* 24 Feb. 1939, p. 6.

69 *Footprints on Track of Time*, 15.

70 *Wellington Jnl.* 2 Mar. 1957, p. 12; *Shropshire Jnl.* 21 Aug. 1970, p. 5.

71 Randall, *Broseley*, 182; P.R.O., IR 29/29/55; IR 30/29/55, field 467.

72 Below, econ. hist. (mkt. and fairs); S. Lewis, *Topog. Dict. Eng.* (1835).

73 Pigot, *Nat. Com. Dir.* (1842), 7; *P.O. Dir. Salop.* (1856), 23.

74 *Rep. R. Com. Mkt. Rights*, i [C. 5550], p. 196, H.C. (1888), liii.

and then *c.* 1920 to Dark Lane.[75] In the 1970s the October fair was moved to the late summer bank holiday.[76]

About 1793 there were six clubs or benefit societies in the parish each with *c.* 100 members.[77] There were eight friendly societies in the parish in 1794, all still active in 1857; there was one other society in 1857, others having formed and disbanded meanwhile:[78] in 1804 there had been a dozen societies with 1,003 members.[79] The Oddfellows had a Rose of Sharon lodge in Broseley from 1823 until 1977.[80]

In 1798 Broseley supplied a division of *c.* 50 men, under Cecil Forester of Willey, to the Wenlock Loyal Volunteers.[81] In 1804 its Broseley division numbered *c.* 130 and consisted of six companies.[82]

There was little organized political activity in Broseley, although before 1832 reform was a popular cause, and Chartists met in the town hall in 1842.[83] A Liberal and Labour Club met 1913–17.[84]

The town hall, opened as a market hall in 1779, was perhaps the 'assembly room' where John Wesley preached that year. In the mid 19th century it was used for social gatherings, such as concerts by the Broseley Philharmonic Society and demonstrations of conjuring and mesmerism.[85] In the earlier 20th century dances, wrestling, and lantern-slide shows were held there and it was a venue for both local and travelling theatrical companies.[86] The hall was demolished in the early 1960s.[87] About 1905 the Victoria Institute and Assembly Hall opened in the premises previously occupied as the Victoria Hall by the Plymouth Brethren. It was used for concerts and other social, non-sectarian, and public purposes.[88] Perhaps from the first it had billiards tables.[89] A prefabricated village hall was built in Jackfield *c.* 1950 on land belonging to the Severn Trow.[90]

The Broseley Literary Society established a news room and library next to the town hall in 1853. In 1856 the librarian was Isaac Burnet, a boot and shoe maker. The library had 1,000 volumes in 1891. It was probably moved to the newly opened Victoria Institute, where there was a library and reading room by 1909 and still in 1941. The Institute also offered a wide range of social and sporting activities.[91] George Maw, tile manufacturer and teetotaller, helped to found a reading room and workman's club at Calcutts House (1869); a working men's club and a British Workman at Broseley (1875, 1879); and a working men's club at Broseley Wood (1881).[92] County library book centres were opened in Jackfield in 1926–7 and Broseley in 1934.[93] From 1936 the Broseley district committee made a small annual grant to the 'public library',[94] probably the book centre. By 1958 there was a county library branch at the Victoria Hall; a new branch library opened in 1968.[95]

Broseley Social Club was formed *c.* 1922.[96] In 1983 its facilities included a bowling green. Bowling had been popular locally at least since the mid 18th century.[97] Among the various sports clubs that have existed in Broseley, two active in 1983 had long histories: the cricket club, formed in 1860,[98] and the lawn tennis club, formed *c.* 1890.[99] From its inception the cricket club played on the Stocking field, Broseley Wood, and from the 1920s well known professionals played for the club. A wooden pavilion was rebuilt *c.* 1930 and extended in 1973.[1] The Jackfield Association, a local football league, existed between 1908 and the 1930s.[2] In the late 19th and early 20th century many works had football and cricket teams.[3]

Notable among local musical groups[4] was the Jackfield Prize Silver Band (active 1986) which may have originated in the 18th century as a fife and drum band. By 1893 it was known as Jackfield Brass Band; it became a silver band in 1923.[5]

The Elite cinema opened during or after the Second World War in the former Birch Meadow Baptist chapel; it closed in 1959. After briefly being used by the Elite ballroom and the Cabaret Club, the building re-opened *c.* 1965 as the Bladen Club,[6] still going in 1986.

75 D. Mason, 'Memories of a Salop. Lad', 28–9 (TS., n.d., in I.G.M.T. Libr.).

76 Inf. from Dr. M. Stratton.

77 *'Most Extraordinary Dist.'* ed. Trinder, 39.

78 S.R.O., q. sess. rec. parcel 285, index to club articles; Registrar of Friendly Socs. *List of Friendly Socs. in Co. of Salop, 1793–1855* (H.M.S.O. 1857; copy in S.R.O. 119/27); S.R.O. 163/30; 1224/3/815–16.

79 *Poor Law Abstract*, H.C. 98, pp. 422–3 (1803–4), xiii.

80 Mason, 'Memories of a Salop. Lad', 35; inf. from Mrs. E. M. Matthews.

81 S.R.O. 1224/22/192–3, 197; below, M. Wenlock, social and cultural activities.

82 S.R.O. 1224/22/211; cf. Randall, *Broseley*, 237–8.

83 Trinder, *Ind. Rev. Salop.* (1981), 235.

84 *Kelly's Dir. Salop.* (1913), 50; (1917), 44.

85 J. Wesley, *Wks.* (Wesleyan Conference Office, 1872), iv. 146; S.R.O. 2118/37, extracts from Wiggins memo. bk.; F. H. Hartshorne, *Corresp. Public and Private, with Additional Remarks Upon the Pritchard Memorial and the Supply of Water in Broseley* (Birm. [1865]), 120; (copy in S.R.O. 2870/1); below, charities.

86 Mason, 'Memories of a Salop. Lad', 16–18; M. Stratton, *Broseley: Guide through an Early Ind. Town* (Broseley Soc. and I.G.M.T. 1981), p. [4].

87 Below, econ. hist. (mkt. and fairs).

88 Below, prot. nonconf.; *Kelly's Dir. Salop.* (1905), 46.

89 First mentioned 1909 (*Kelly's Dir. Salop.* (1909), 49) and perh. the large billiards hall of *c.* 1905 (I.G.M.T. Libr., photo. 1982.2144).

90 Clark and Alfrey, *Jackfield and Broseley*, 124.

91 *P.O. Dir. Salop.* (1856), 24–5; *Kelly's Dir. Salop.* (1891), 278; (1905), 47; (1909), 49; (1941), 50; S.R.O. 1681/116/11; S.P.L., Caradoc press cuttings, x. 21.

92 *Jnl. Tiles & Archit. Ceramics Soc.* iii. 7.

93 R.C. Elliott, 'Development of Public Libraries in Salop.' (Loughborough Univ. M.A. thesis, 1970; copy in co. libr.), 125, 127; Mugridge, *Hist. Jackfield*, 34.

94 W.B.R., Broseley dist. cttee. min. bk. 1930–7, p. 349.

95 Inf. from co. libr.

96 *Kelly's Dir. Salop.* (1922), 441.

97 Mason, 'Memories of a Salop. Lad', 90; S.P.L., Deeds 28 (field name).

98 *Shropshire Mag.* Mar. 1973, 16–17.

99 Cf. *Kelly's Dir. Salop.* (1885), 814; (1891), 279.

1 *Shropshire Mag.* Mar. 1973, 16–17; *Shropshire Star*, 3 Mar. 1981, p. 19.

2 *V.C.H. Salop.* ii. 220.

3 *Shropshire Mag.* Apr. 1977, 16. For sport see *Shrews. Chron.* 10 July 1936, p. 13.

4 I.G.M.T. Libr., photos. 1980.1759; 1982.2849.

5 'Jackfield (Ironbridge Gorge) Band: The first 250 years . . . or so' (TS.; copy in I.G.M.T. Libr., accession no. 1981.1555); *Shropshire Mag.* Dec. 1986, 50–1.

6 *Kelly's Dir. Salop.* (1941), 380 (no mention); F. Brown, *Silver Screen Memories* (Shrews. 1984), 10, 27; *Shropshire Mag.* July 1964, 46; G.P.O. *Telephone Dir.* (1965), sect. 72, p. 2024.

MANOR AND OTHER ESTATES. Evidently by 1198, and certainly by 1255, the manor of *BROSELEY* was held of the prior of Wenlock.[7] If Broseley may be identified with the 'Bosle' of Domesday Book,[8] then it had been held by Gethne before the Conquest and by 1086 was held by Helgot of Roger of Montgomery, earl of Shrewsbury and tenant in chief.[9] After 1086 'Bosle' is unrecorded, and Helgot and his heirs and successors as barons of Castle Holdgate are never found as lords of Broseley; moreover the earl's chief lordship of 'Bosle' must have been forfeited in 1102[10] so that there is no demonstrable tenurial continuity between 'Bosle' and Broseley,[11] although 'Bosle' could be a garbled[12] version of the early form of Broseley's name. In the 14th century Broseley was held of the prior by serjeanty service, sometimes described as that of sitting down once a year at the first dish in the prior's guesthouse, or of carving the main dish, or of acting as the prior's steward.[13] In the early 16th and early 17th centuries Broseley was said to be held in socage of the earl of Shrewsbury;[14] in 1503 and 1508, however, it was variously said to be held, for services unknown, of the earl of Arundel (1503) and of the Crown (1508).[15] That share of the demesne lordship which passed to Wenlock priory in 1363[16] was sold by the Crown in 1545 to be held in free burgage and common socage by fealty and for a small rent;[17] the tenure of the former priory share of the manor was thus distinguished from the tenure of the rest of the manor.[18] By the early 17th century the former priory estate was held in chief as 1/20 knight's fee[19] and had become known as the 'Priory land' or '*capite* land' as distinct from the rest of the manor, the 'socage land'.[20]

The Lorrainer Warin of Metz, ancestor of the FitzWarins, or his third son William probably obtained Broseley from Henry I, and indeed Warin may have been the demesne lord by *c.* 1115. William (fl. 1172), styled of Broseley by 1154,[21] was succeeded by Warin (II) of Broseley (d. 1212 × 1220), probably his son, and he in turn by his son Philip of Broseley. Philip died *c.* 1240 and was succeeded by his brother Roger of Broseley, who died in 1243. Philip's widow Emme was dowered in the manor 1259 × 1271, but in 1244 the fee had been divided between the three sisters of Philip and Roger: Mabel widow of Adam de Beysin, Alice probably widow of John Eaton, and Margery widow of John Bagot.[22]

Mabel Beysin, the eldest sister, died 1247 × 1255 and was succeeded in her share of the manor by her grandson Robert de Beysin, a minor.[23] Robert died *c.* 1267 and the share passed to Walter de Beysin, a minor and presumably Robert's son.[24] Walter enlarged his estate. At his death in 1309, in addition to his inherited share of the manor, he held a messuage and virgate from Richard of Pitchford, which had thus presumably been acquired from the share assigned to Margery Bagot in 1244. Walter also held a ninth of the manor[25] and so may be supposed to have acquired part of the share (presumably a third) in which Roger of Broseley's sister Alice had apparently been succeeded 1244 × 1256 by Roger of Eaton (fl. 1256–72), probably her younger son.[26] Roger Knighteleye, who held part of the manor in 1316,[27] perhaps held an interest in that share by the curtesy.

Walter de Beysin was succeeded by his sons Thomas (d. 1318 or 1319) and Walter in turn. At his death in 1344 the younger Walter, who held two thirds of the manor, owed service of 40*d.* a year to John 'de Eyton', probably for the share of the manor formerly the Eatons'. Walter's son John Beysin, a minor, succeeded in 1344[28] and died in 1360 holding Broseley jointly with his wife Anne. She married Sir Thomas Latimer (d. 1401) and retained two thirds of Broseley until her death in 1402. Under a settlement of 1377 the two thirds then passed to Agnes, sister of John Beysin and widow of John de Morehall.[29] Agnes obtained possession in 1402 and was later succeeded by their daughter Gillian, who had married first John Clopton and secondly (by 1389) Thomas Crewe. Gillian died in 1411 and Crewe retained a life interest in her estates until his death in 1418. Broseley then passed to

7 *Rot. Hund.* ii. 84.

8 As in Eyton ii. 1–2. Somewhat inconsistently, and inconclusively, Eyton (iii. 223–4) also calculated Broseley's 1 hide among the 20 M. Wenlock hides in Dom. Bk., although 'Bosle' was in a different hund.

9 *V.C.H. Salop.* i. 338.

10 Ibid. iii. 9–10.

11 Their identity is considered 'unlikely' in *Domesday Bk.: Salop.* ed. F. and C. Thorn (1986), n. 4.21.11; cf. *Salop. Domesday*, ed. A. Williams and R. W. H. Erskine (1988, 1990). Those sources evidently rely on the reasoning leading *P.N. Salop.* (E.P.N.S.), i, pp. xii, 63–4, not to adopt the identification, because 'Bosle' will not fit into the sequence of early forms of Broseley: inf. from Dr. M. Gelling. But early pronunciation of 'Burewardeslega' close to 'Bosle' is suggested by the existence of Bernard of 'Bosleie' (fl. 1204, attorney of Parnel of Willey: Eyton, ii. 2 n. 2) and has a Ches. analogy (*P.N. Ches.* (E.P.N.S.), iv. 93; v (1:i), p. xii); so it seems circumspect not to rule the identification out. The argument that the baron of Castle Holdgate lost 'Bosle' (i.e. Broseley) *temp.* Hen. I may receive support from his coeval losses of Millichope and Harley, for which see above, Lib. and Boro. of Wenlock (early est.); *V.C.H. Salop.* ii.40; iii. 38; viii. 87.

12 Allowed by Dr. Gelling.

13 Eyton, ii. 19; *Cal. Inq. p.m.* v, p. 125; vi, p. 98; x, p. 500.

14 *Cal. Inq. p.m. Hen. VII*, ii, pp. 268, 601; iii, p. 142; S.R.O. 1224/3/264, 302.

15 *Cal. Inq. p.m. Hen. VII*, iii, pp. 297, 543; cf. S.R.O. 1224/3/24.

16 Below, this section.

17 *L. & P. Hen. VIII*, xx (2), p. 227; *Cal. Pat.* 1548–9, 191.

18 S.R.O. 1224/3/105.

19 Ibid. /3/193, 215–16, 263; P.R.O., C 142/73, no. 80.

20 S.R.O. 1224/3/193, 258, 263–4.

21 Ibid. 1/17/2 (witnessed by Rog., earl of Heref.).

22 Para. based on Eyton, ii. 2–25; cf. above, Lib. and Boro. of Wenlock (early est.).

23 Eyton, ii. 12–13, 18–19. Rob.'s Broseley est. descended thereafter with Longnor and Water Eaton (Staffs.) until 1534: *V.C.H. Staffs.* iv. 80–1; v. 122.

24 Eyton, ii. 13, 19–21.

25 *Cal. Inq. p.m.* v, p. 125; P.R.O., C 134/18, no. 1. For Ric. of Pitchford see below, this section

26 Eyton, ii. 22–4.

27 *Feud. Aids*, iv. 228.

28 *V.C.H. Staffs.* iv. 81; *Cal. Inq. p.m.* vi, p. 98; viii, p. 359; P.R.O., CP 25/1/194/13, no. 33.

29 S.R.O. 1224/3/296; *Cal. Inq. p.m.* x, p. 500; xviii, pp. 140, 201; *Cal. Close*, 1360–4, 68; 1399–1402, 439, 550; K. B. McFarlane, *Lancastrian Kings and Lollard Kts.* (1972), 173; *S.H.C.* xi. 205–6; *T.S.A.S.* i. 289, 298–303; *V.C.H. Staffs.* iv. 80–1; *V.C.H. Warws.* iii. 190.

Gillian's son Sir William Clopton (d. 1419),[30] whose widow Joan still held the manor in 1426.[31] Their son Thomas died without issue and on Joan's death Broseley passed to his elder sister Agnes (d. 1453), wife first of Roger Harewell, of Wootton Wawen (Warws.), and secondly of Thomas Herbert. Agnes's son William Harewell[32] became lord *c.* 1462, died in 1500, and was succeeded by his son John (d. 1505), who left a son Thomas aged 11.[33] By 1511 Thomas had died a minor and without issue, and that year his grandmother (William's widow Agnes), dowered in Broseley, also died: Broseley thus passed to John's daughters, coheirs of their brother Thomas. The daughters surviving in 1534 partitioned their inheritance, and Broseley fell to James Clifford's wife Anne.[34] The Cliffords' grandson James Clifford bought the third of the manor that had belonged to Wenlock priory 1363–1540, thus reuniting the shares separated in 1244.[35]

The third of the manor which was alienated to Wenlock priory in 1363 was probably that allotted to the youngest Broseley coheir Margery Bagot in 1244. In 1248 Margery granted it to her daughter and son-in-law, Margery and Ralph of Coven. Ralph let it to Geoffrey of Pitchford *c.* 1260 and died soon after. Ralph and Margery's elder daughter Alice and her husband Robert de Pendeford later sold the fee of her parents' estate in Broseley to Pitchford, apparently disregarding Margery's dower rights. Lawsuits ensued between her and Alice, both of whom contracted later marriages. Pitchford's title, however, was secure by 1275. He was dead by 1299, and in 1312 his son Richard sold his estate in Broseley (presumably reduced from the share allotted to Margery Bagot by the messuage and virgate acquired by the Beysins) to Richard of Harley (d. 1316) and his wife Burga,[36] the heiress of Willey,[37] still alive in 1337.[38] The third descended to Burga's grandson Robert of Harley whose trustees conveyed it, with manorial rights, to the prior of Wenlock in 1363.[39] The priory retained the estate until its surrender in 1540, though at some time after 1379 it was incorporated in the priory's manor of Marsh.[40]

Robert of Harley may have retained some of the woodland and pasture belonging to his third of Broseley, so that it descended with the manor of Willey to the Lacons; Broseley presentments were heard at Willey court baron in 1460 and 1528.[41] In the 16th and 17th centuries the Upper Riddings and part of the Woodhouse estate probably descended with Swinney, belonging to the Lacons.[42] They had property in Broseley sometimes described as a manor,[43] probably with little justification. In 1615–16 Sir Francis Lacon mortgaged many of his estates to John Weld, who, in 1618, after Lacon's default and just as he was beginning to negotiate the purchase of other Broseley lands with William Porter, acquired the Lacons' mortgaged estates, a 'manor of Broseley' being mentioned in some of the conveyancing instruments.[44] Thereafter, however, the Welds' Broseley estate was incorporated in their manor of Marsh[45] and neither Weld nor his heirs claimed a manor in Broseley before George Forester bought the manor in 1795.[46]

The Broseley property formerly Wenlock priory's was sold by the Crown in 1545 to William and Elizabeth Pinnock.[47] The Pinnocks sold it to John Munslow in 1550, and in 1563 he sold it to Richard Cupper.[48] It was acquired from Cupper by James Clifford of Frampton on Severn (Glos.), who had inherited the other two thirds of the manor, and his wife Dorothy.[49]

James Clifford excepted the third of the manor he had bought (the '*capite* land' or 'Priory land') from settlements of 1598 and 1603 entailing his inherited two thirds on his daughter Mary and her husband Henry Clifford, of Boscombe East (Wilts.).[50] The 'Priory land' was excepted again in 1609, when James Clifford resettled the other two thirds after Mary and Henry had been divorced.[51] On James Clifford's death in 1613 the fee simple of the whole manor passed to Mary and her second husband John Cage.[52]

In 1620 the Cages sold the manor to Francis Langley of the Tuckies (d. 1650);[53] it was an estate much reduced by the Cages' previous sale of the 'socage land' freehold to William Porter (1618) and by Porter's acquisitions of long leaseholds of the 'Priory land';[54] Langley had nevertheless succeeded in preventing the sale of the 'Priory land' freehold.[55] The manor descend-

30 *Cal. Close*, 1399–1402, 551; *Cal. Fine R.* 1413–22, 264–5; *T.S.A.S.* i. 303–4; *V.C.H. Warws.* iii. 190; *Hist. Parl., Commons*, 1386–1421, 691–3.
31 S.R.O. 1224/3/191.
32 *T.S.A.S.* i. 309–10.
33 Birm. Univ. Libr., Mytton Papers, i. 198; *Cal. Inq. p.m. Hen VII*, ii, pp. 268, 601; iii, pp. 141–2, 297, 543; S.R.O. 1224/3/302.
34 P.R.O., C 142/27, no. 69; S.R.O. 1224/3/303; Dugdale, *Warws.* (1730), ii. 810; *V.C.H. Warws.* iii. 198.
35 Above and below, this section.
36 Eyton, ii. 27–31; S.R.O. 1224/3/189–90; above, this section.
37 *Visit. Salop. 1623*, ii. 304; *Feud. Aids*, iv. 228.
38 *Cal. Inq. p.m.* vii, pp. 495, 498; P.R.O., CP 25/1/194/11, no. 41; *V.C.H. Salop.* viii. 87.
39 *Cal. Pat.* 1361–4, 341, 393; P.R.O., C 143/349, no. 4; C 148/19.
40 P.R.O., SC 6/Hen. VIII/3021, m. 8; below, local govt.
41 Below, local govt.; Willey, manor. Wenlock priory, however, had a wood in Broseley in 1379: below, econ. hist. (agric.).
42 Above, Caughley, manors (Swinney). The Woodhouse was prob. partly 'socage land' and partly 'Priory land': cf. S.R.O. 1224/2/3, s.v. Broseley. The Lacons also owned the Woodlands: below, this section.
43 P.R.O., C 142/68, no. 7; C 142/312, no. 147; CP 25/2/261/32 Eliz. I East. [no. 12]; CP 25/2/342/7 Jas. I Trin. [no. 8]; S.R.O. 1224/3/159, 181; *T.S.A.S.* 2nd ser. v. 116.
44 S.R.O. 1224/3/160–84; P.R.O., CP 25/2/343/14 Jas. I Trin. [no. 15]; CP 25/2/343/16 Jas. I Trin. [no. 6]; below, this section.
45 Below, local govt.
46 Below, this section.
47 S.R.O. 1224/3/194; *L. & P. Hen. VIII*, xx (2), p. 227.
48 *Cal. Pat.* 1549–51, pp. 213–14; 1560–3, p. 551.
49 S.R.O. 1224/3/193.
50 Ibid. /3/195, 304–5; P.R.O., CP 43/62, rot. 9.
51 S.R.O. 1224/3/307–8 (correcting *V.C.H. Glos.* x. 145 n. 96).
52 P.R.O., C 142/73, no. 80; S.R.O. 1224/3/215–16.
53 S.R.O. 1224/2/528; /3/263–4, 323–7; Birm. Univ. Libr., Mytton Papers, i. 200; Langley, *Par. Regs. of Broseley*, i. 47.
54 Below, this section.
55 S.R.O. 1224/3/263, 323, 326; box 150, Exch. Chamber bill (Adams v. Porter *et al.* 1623).

ed to Langley's son John (d. 1693)[56] and probably to John's son Samuel (d. 1697).[57] Samuel's son Samuel (d.s.p. 1698) succeeded,[58] probably followed by his brother Mennes (d.s.p. 1699), whose heir was his cousin Herbert Langley (d. 1711).[59] Herbert's daughter Elizabeth succeeded, and by 1722 had married Edward Purcell (d. 1768) of Stafford.[60] She sold the manor in 1770 to Thomas Stephens (d. 1787) of Benthall.[61] His son John succeeded and sold the manor in 1795 to George Forester of Willey.[62] It descended thereafter with Willey, and Lord Forester was presumed to be lord in 1983.[63]

Roger of Eaton lived in Broseley in 1272[64] and Thomas de Beysin (d. *c.* 1319) had a manor house and dovecot there.[65] The house was worth nothing in 1363,[66] and in 1426 Lady Clopton let the site of the manor house, then built over with houses, to two Broseley yeomen, reserving only a gatehouse, which apparently had an upper chamber.[67] From the mid 16th century the manor house site was included in the property leased in survivorship to Rowland and Eleanor Wilcox and their son Richard (d. 1614).[68] It was near the church, forming the site of Wilcox's Farm, known as Broseley Hall in the 17th century and as the Old Hall in the 18th when a new Broseley Hall was built;[69] it was demolished in the mid or later 19th century.[70]

In the earlier 16th century a manor house on Wenlock priory's third of the manor was let to Roger and Joyce Wilcox.[71] James Clifford, who reunited the two parts of the manor by his purchase of the 'Priory land', was probably the first resident lord for centuries. He built the 'mansion' known *c.* 1620 as Priory House which stood in spacious grounds south of Broseley.[72]

James Clifford died in 1613[73] leaving the manor charged with family annuities and encumbered for payment of his debts. From 1612 William Porter, a Bristol attorney intent on speculating in Clifford's Broseley estate, gained possession of the land by acquiring the long leases and buying out the other interests created by Clifford's embarrassments.[74] In 1618 Porter also bought (from the Cages) the freehold of the 'socage land' ('Wilcox's farm'), some 574 a.,[75] selling almost all of it in 1620:[76] *c.* 224 a. to William Whitmore (kt. 1621),[77] 134 a. to Francis Adams of Cleeton,[78] and 119 a. to John Weld of Willey.[79] Next year Whitmore sold 57 a. on to Weld[80] and evidently the rest to Sir Edward Bromley.[81] Weld also bought *c.* 9 a. of Adams's purchase in 1621.[82] Porter had wished to buy the 'Priory land' freehold too, but Francis Langley had succeeded in having that conveyed to him with the manor in 1620.[83] In 1620–1 therefore, Porter, although he had undertaken to convey freehold estates from the 'Priory land',[84] could actually sell only long leaseholds: John Weld bought 177 a. including the 96-a. Upper farm and Priory House, some small properties let for lives, 22 cottages, and 29 a. of waste near the Benthall boundary; Francis Adams bought over 30 a. with Kynehill House; and Francis Old bought Prior's Hawksyard and Gitchfield.[85]

Porter retained the freehold of *c.* 70 a. around the *CALCUTTS* which in 1624 he sold to his cousin William Willett of Bristol, who still owned it in 1631.[86] Nevertheless under a lease of 1619 and a settlement of claims in 1628 possession of the Calcutts passed to Porter's creditor Alderman William Young and his heirs. In 1659 Richard Young, administrator of William Young's goods, assigned the lease to John Huxley of Broseley[87] and Stanley Hall (in Astley Abbots).[88] The Huxleys, who had long occupied the Calcutts estate and worked the coals,[89] still enjoyed it in 1685. The descent of the freehold is obscure and in 1685 William Porter's grandson James Porter, apparently unaware of the 1624 conveyance to Willett, requested 'plainer information' from John Huxley about the freehold.[90] It is possible that the freehold passed to, or was thought to belong to, the lord of the manor. Around 1696–1700, in connexion with a conveyance to him of the 'inheritance' of the 'Priory land' estate that his grandfather had

56 Ibid. /2/529; Langley, *Par. Regs. of Broseley*, i. 7, 125.
57 Langley, op. cit. i. 27, 133.
58 Ibid. 86, 134; S.R.O. 1224/3/336; S.P.L., MS. 4078, p. 1062.
59 Langley, op. cit. i. 98, 136; ii. 23; S.P.L., MS. 4078, pp. 1062–3; S.R.O. 1224/3/344.
60 Langley, op. cit. ii. 2; S.R.O. 1224/3/344; 2991/Rg/5, 5 May 1768.
61 S.R.O. 1224/3/370–2; 2991/Rg/5, 28 Nov. 1787.
62 S.R.O. 1224/3/383–4, 387–8.
63 *P.O. Dir. Salop.* (1856), 23; *Kelly's Dir. Salop.* (1941), 50; inf. from Ld. Forester; cf. below, Willey, manor.
64 Eyton, ii. 24.
65 P.R.O., C 134/61, no. 28.
66 Ibid. C 143/349, no. 4.
67 S.R.O. 1224/3/191.
68 Ibid. /3/214; box 342, Prior Gosnell's reg. f. 38v.; S.P.L., Deeds 11311; Birm. Univ. Libr., Mytton Papers, i. 198; Langley, *Par. Regs. of Broseley*, i. 14.
69 S.P.L., MS. 2366, p. 36; below, this section (Broseley Hall).
70 Cf. P.R.O., IR 29/29/55; IR 30/29/55, field 175; O.S. Map 1/2,500, Salop. LI. 2 (1882 edn.).
71 *L. & P. Hen. VIII*, xx (2), p. 227; S.R.O. 1224/3/192; P.R.O., E 303/14/Oxon./273.
72 S.R.O. 1224/1/32; /3/214, 262; below, this section (the Dunge and Ladywood).
73 Above, this section.
74 S.R.O. 840, box 43, survey of 1613–15, 'Mr. Porter's relation' [1622]; 1224/3/198, 202, 208–13, 219–20, 224–30, 239, 258, 276, 309–13, 319, 321–2; box 150, 'Instructions for Mr. Attorney to mediate' [1622], Exch. Chamber bill (Adams v. Porter *et al.* 1623) pp. 1, 9, 'Mr. Weld's reasons that Pester's money is no due debt'; Langley, *Par. Regs. of Broseley*, i. 12, 14.
75 S.R.O. 1224/3/235–7, 259; cf. ibid. /3/271–2. Wilcoxes occupied the 'Priory land' chief ho. in the earlier 16th cent. and the 'socage land' man. ho. in the later 16th cent.
76 S.R.O. 840, box 43, 'Mr. Porter's relation' [1622].
77 S.R.O. 1224/3/244–6; *T.S.A.S.* 4th ser. v. 54.
78 S.P.L., Deeds 12573.
79 S.R.O. 1224/3/241–3, 260.
80 Ibid. /3/244–6 (docketing), 256.
81 Ibid. /1/32; /3/244–6 (docketing). For Bromley see above, Caughley, manors (Swinney).
82 S.R.O. 1224/3/257, 266.
83 Ibid. /3/263; above, this section (manor).
84 S.R.O. 1224/3/263.
85 S.R.O. 840, box 43, 'Mr. Mic. Old's breviate concerning the Priory lands' [1658?]; 1224/1/32; /3/248–55, 262–3, 329, 572; Staffs. R.O., D. 1057/A/2/62; below, this section (for the acquisition of the freeholds of these purchases by Geo. Weld, the Cromptons, and Sam. Manning in the 1690s).
86 S.R.O. 840, box 43, deed 14 Sept. 1624 (copy).
87 Ibid. box 61, deed of 1659; 1224/3/271–3.
88 R. P. Tyrwhitt, *Notices and Remains of Fam. of Tyrwhitt* (priv. print. 1872), 84.
89 Below, econ. hist. (coal and ironstone).
90 S.R.O. 840, box 15, mining accts. 1683–4; box 43, list of 'Broseley leases expired', lease of Oct. 1677, mining accts. 1681–2, and mining agreement of June 1684; box 61, Jas. Porter to John Huxley, Dec. 1685.

bought leasehold, George Weld was suing Martin Eele (presumably for his costs in acquiring the freehold) as occupier of the Calcutts: Eele's possession presumably derived from the remaining term of the 1619 lease,[91] and a 1693 conveyance to Eele by Samuel Langley may indicate that Eele had then acquired the freehold.[92] In 1753 the Calcutts was owned by Francis Freeman of Bristol and in 1767 by his son-in-law Sir Onesiphorus Paul (d. 1774). It descended to the latter's son Sir George Onesiphorus Paul (d. 1820). The Calcutts ironworks was sold to James Foster *c.* 1831 but much of the estate remained in the hands of Paul's trustees *c.* 1840.[93] It was later[94] dispersed by sale.

The lands bought by John Weld and Francis Adams *c.* 1620–1 laid the foundations of what were, *c.* 1840, the two most considerable landed estates in the parish.[95] Weld (kt. 1642)[96] administered his Broseley estate as part of his manor of Marsh with which it descended thereafter.[97] The Weld (later Forester) estate was much the larger, though Weld's purchases were not added to for over 120 years (except for the freehold of his 'Priory land' estate, acquired in the 1690s), the major acquisitions being the Woodlands (1745); Upper and Lower Riddings and Swinney (1790); Gitchfield (1791); the manor (1795); the Amies and Swinbatch (1813); the Dunge (1818) and Ladywood (1820); and Rowton (1821).[98] The Forester estate in Broseley comprised 1,230 a. *c.* 1840,[99] and was further extended by the 2nd Lord Forester (succ. 1828, d. 1874) who bought many small properties.[1]

Sir Thomas Lacon passed an estate in Broseley called *THE WOODLANDS* or *CHILDS WOODLANDS* (so named after 14th-century tenants),[2] in which he had gained at least a part interest from Richard Clerke of the Marsh in 1512,[3] to his second son Edward.[4] In 1575 Edward's illegitimate son Lancelot Lacon sold half of the estate to his cousin Thomas Bromley (kt. 1579), who died a freeholder of the manor in 1587. Lancelot Lacon's son Silvanus bought it back from Bromley's son Sir Henry, of Holt (Worcs.), in 1594.[5] Thereafter the Woodlands descended in the Lacon[6] and (from 1720) Edwards families with West Coppice (in Buildwas) until George Weld bought the Woodlands in 1745.[7] Woodlands Farm stands on the northern edge of Broseley Wood; its core is perhaps 17th-century.

ROWTON was a freehold estate in the eastern part of the manor. Richard Old (d. 1626) owned it in 1605.[8] In 1620 Francis Old (perhaps Richard's son, d. 1622) bought *GITCHFIELD* (or *WITHIESFIELD HOUSE*) and *PRIOR'S HAWKSYARD* further east, parts of William Porter's leasehold 'Priory land'.[9] The brothers Francis (d. by 1678) and Michael (d. 1681) Old were described as 'of Rowton'. Michael left Rowton between his sons Samuel and John and Gitchfield to Samuel. Samuel was dead by 1685[10] and Rowton and Gitchfield had apparently passed to John's son, the Revd. Richard Old. In 1687 Richard settled Gitchfield on his aunt and uncle, Mary (*née* Old) and Richard Manning, a lawyer (d. 1719);[11] their son Samuel Manning bought the freehold from the lord of the manor in 1697,[12] and Gitchfield descended in the Manning family until George Forester bought it in 1791.[13] Rowton was left by Richard Old (d. 1692) to his brother John and sisters Jane, later wife of Richard Edwards of Chesterton (Hunts.), and Mary, wife of Nicholas Addenbrooke. In 1701 Richard Edwards acquired the whole estate, the minerals being divided between him and Addenbrooke.[14] In 1766 the Edwards estate was bought by Thomas Stephens of Broseley, whose son John, of Bridgnorth, conveyed it in part exchange to George Forester's trustees in 1822.[15] Rowton Farm appears to have been formed partly from a large brick barn, perhaps in the later 18th century. Its outbuildings include a later 16th-century timber framed barn and a dovecot built of clay lump, perhaps also of the later 18th century.[16]

THE AMIES, almost certainly named from preceding owners,[17] belonged to the Langleys, probably by the late 14th century, and descended from 1694 with the manor of Golding (in Cound).[18] The Amies remained in the Langleys' hands until 1717, when Thomas Langley sold it to Richard Littlehales, of Bridgnorth. Dr. John Littlehales (d. 1810) had the estate, then 56 a., in 1802, and his son Charles sold it to George

91 S.R.O. 1224/2/511, m. [22] and d.; above, this section.

92 S.R.O. 1037/21/52; cf. ibid. 1224/3/254 (endorsement of 1692). Langley was then selling the freeholds of leasehold estates created out of the 'Priory land' (above, this section).

93 S.R.O. 1037/21/53–6; P.R.O., IR 29/29/55; below, econ. hist. (iron). For the Pauls see *D.N.B.*; *V.C.H. Glos.* xi. 223–4, 300.

94 By 1910: S.R.O. 4044/90.

95 P.R.O., IR 29/29/55.

96 For Weld see M. D. G. Wanklyn, 'John Weld of Willey 1585–1665', *W. Midlands Studies*, iii. 88–99; idem, 'John Weld of Willey: est. management 1631–60', ibid. iv. 63–71; Trinder, *Ind. Rev. Salop.* 7.

97 Below, local govt.; cf. above, Barrow, manors; local govt.

98 Above and below, this section; above, Caughley, manors (Swinney).

99 P.R.O., IR 29/29/55.

1 S.R.O. 1224, boxes 48–58; Burke, *Peerage* (1949), 782; cf. *V.C.H. Salop.* iv. 205.

2 S.R.O. 1224/2/3.

3 *Cal. Chart. and Rolls in Bodl.* ed. W. H. Turner and H. O. Coxe (1878), p. 387.

4 S.R.O. 1224/3/489, 527–71; P.R.O., C 1/559, no. 50; C 1/844, no. 6; *T.S.A.S.* 3rd ser. ii. 312; *Hist. Parl., Commons*, 1509–58, ii. 487–8.

5 S.R.O. 840, box 1, Broseley ct. r. 1588; 1224/3/492–6; *Hist. Parl., Commons*, 1558–1603, i. 491–2; *Visit. Salop. 1623*, ii (Harl. Soc. xxix), 307.

6 Pedigree in S.P.L., MS. 2789, p. 366. Jas. Lacon was a principal partner in the Coalbrookdale iron and steel wks., his share going to Fra. Wolfe in 1667: P.R.O., C 104/22, pt. 1, assignment of 1667.

7 S.R.O. 1224/3/510–13; 2089/1/3/6–10, 12–13, 15–18, 20–22; cf. *S.P.R. Lich.* xiv (1), pp. v–vi; xiv (3), p. v.

8 S.R.O. 1224/3/306, f. [6], rental Mar. 1605; Randall, *Broseley*, 66–7; Langley, *Par. Regs. of Broseley*, i. 22.

9 Randall, op. cit. 66–73; S.R.O. 408/1, f. [14]; above, this section; deeds cited below, this section.

10 S.R.O. 1224/3/572–5, 593; Langley, *Par. Regs. of Broseley*, i. 100.

11 S.R.O. 408/1, f. [83v.]; 1224/3/576–9, 775.

12 S.R.O. 1224/3/580–1, 593.

13 Ibid. /3/582–96.

14 Ibid. /3/775–7; *Alum. Oxon. 1500–1714*, iii. 1087.

15 S.R.O. 1224/3/788–91, 800–4; 4791/1/4, p. 99; /5, p. 188.

16 *Trans. Anct. Monts. Soc.* xxxv. 136; inf. from Mrs. M. Moran.

17 Amyas fam.: *Cal. Pat.* 1327–30, 215.

18 *T.S.A.S.* 2nd ser. v. 127, 133–4; *V.C.H. Salop.* viii. 65.

Forester's trustees in 1813.[19] The Amies, 1 km. east of Broseley, was a large timber framed house, ruinous in 1879 and demolished soon afterwards. It is not known why in the 19th century it was considered the old manor house of Broseley. Possibly, however, the Amies may have been tenanted by Richard Eves at whose house the manor court was held in the 1650s. In 1661 John Langley left a life interest in the Amies house to his sister Elizabeth, widow of Robert Eves, and earlier the wife of William Langley, elder son of the purchaser of the manor in 1620.[20]

SWINBATCH farm was bought from the Revd. John Langley by George Forester's trustees in 1813.[21]

By 1608 John Huxley, soon thereafter tenant of Upper farm and the 'fair dwelling house' or mansion called Priory House[22] that James Clifford had built and recently lived in,[23] was apparently clerk of Clifford's coalworks[24] or perhaps acting more generally as bailiff, as he subsequently seems to have done for William Porter;[25] later he was steward of Marsh manor for John Weld.[26] In 1620 he was one of several mortgagees for Francis Langley, the new lord of the manor,[27] and in 1623–4 Langley sold him a freehold property.[28] The Huxleys, of Stanley Hall (in Astley Abbots) from *c.* 1658,[29] and their successors (from 1730) the Joneses[30] were freeholders in the manor,[31] with property around *THE DUNGE* and *LADYWOOD*. Edward Jones, of Windsor, sold what was evidently the Dunge property to R. C. Hartshorne,[32] and Jones's son Thomas (kt. 1760)[33] sold off the Ladywood property *c.* 1760. Both properties, or the greatest part of each, were bought up by George Forester's trustees in 1818 and 1820. The Dunge was put in the Forester farm to the north[34] run from a house that came to be called Dunge Farm.

THE TUCKIES belonged to the descendants of William Langley, younger son of William Langley of the Amies (fl. *c.* 1500);[35] one of them, Francis Langley of the Tuckies, bought the manor in 1620.[36] The Langleys mortgaged the Tuckies and their heirs the Purcells lost it in 1741.[37] The estate was gradually sold piecemeal thereafter,[38] the residue, with the house, being bought by Lord Forester in 1863.[39]

The Tuckies is a large **H** shaped building.[40] The north wing, probably 16th-century, is timber framed and once comprised part of a larger building. In the late 17th century 2½-storeyed central and south parlour ranges, of red brick on sandstone lower courses, were added to form a symmetrical front. The central hall range had a central door on its east side and a staircase with heavy turned balusters at its south end.

In 1787 the house was leased to Archibald Cochrane, earl of Dundonald, and in 1800 to his associate and fellow industrialist William Reynolds,[41] and it was probably at that time that a balcony (later removed) was added to the front of the house to command the magnificent views over the Severn Gorge. Shortly before 1860 the Tuckies was divided into 'two respectable dwelling houses';[42] it was perhaps then that alterations were made including refenestration, remodelling of the main staircase and some of the interior, and extension of the second storey over the east front in an overhang. Later still the house was divided into three tenements, as it was in 1986.

The *BROSELEY HALL* estate, so called by 1728,[43] derived mainly from that bought by Francis Adams of Cleeton from William Porter in 1620, including 134 a. of the 'socage land' (with the site of the medieval manor house) and 30 a. of the 'Priory land' (including Kynehill House).[44] Adams died in 1668[45] leaving a daughter and heiress Sarah,[46] the wife of William Crompton, and the estate (part of which Samuel Langley owned from 1670,[47] the freehold being presumably acquired from the Langleys in the 1690s)[48] eventually passed to their granddaughter Elizabeth Crompton.[49] Her uncle Henry Crompton had bought Woodhouse farm in 1710 and had sold small parts of it (to George

19 S.R.O. 515/4, pp. 315–16; 1224/1/36; /3/648–56; *Alum. Oxon. 1715–1886*, iii. 857.

20 Randall, *Broseley*, 81–3, and pl. facing 81; H. E. Forrest, *Old Hos. of Wenlock* (Shrews. 1914), 80, 92–3; *T.S.A.S.* 2nd ser. v. 115, 117, 121, 127.

21 S.R.O. 1224/3/675–82.

22 Site probably indicated by ho. platform (O.S. Nat. Grid SJ 679 012) NW. of Dunge Fm. Cf. S.R.O. 840, box 43, John Huxley's assignment of lease to Fra. Huxley 1639; 1224/1/32; /3/210–14, 234, 258, 260, 264; O.S. Map 6", SJ 60 SE. (1954 edn.).

23 S.R.O. 1224/3/202, 214. Huxley, the rector's s., marr. Mabel Clifford 1609: Langley, *Par. Regs. of Broseley*, i. 4, 11; cf. S.P.L., MS. 4360, p. 123.

24 S.R.O. 840, box 43, Jesse Whittingham's lease 1608 (copy).

25 Ibid. 'Mr. Porter's general aquittance' 1621.

26 Ibid. John Huxley's rental 1642, recording receipt of salary and other pmnts. for work done, etc., from Weld; S.R.O. 840, box 1, ct. r. of 1641.

27 S.R.O. 840, box 43, surrender of lands in Broseley 1620.

28 Reserving the minerals: ibid. deeds of 1623–4; S.R.O. 1224/3/741.

29 Tyrwhitt, *Notices and Remains of Fam. of Tyrwhitt*, 84.

30 Edw. Jones's purchase of the Huxleys' Broseley property evidently antedated his marr. to the Huxley coheir Mary. For the rest of this para. see S.R.O. 1224/3/712–68; J. B. Blakeway, *Sheriffs of Salop.* (Shrews. 1831), 194.

31 S.R.O. 1224/2/529.

32 Rector 1727–52 (below, churches) and husb. of the other Huxley coheir Eliz. (S.R.O. 1224/3/730).

33 W. A. Shaw, *Kts. of Eng.* (1906), ii. 289.

34 P.R.O., IR 29/29/55; IR 30/29/55.

35 *T.S.A.S.* 2nd ser. v. 114; R. Morris, *The Tuckies, Jackfield* (Ironbridge Arch. Ser. vi; Ironbridge, 1987).

36 *T.S.A.S.* 2nd ser. v. 114; above, this section.

37 S.R.O. 1224, box 61, Chancery decree of 1741 (copy).

38 Deeds in S.R.O. 1224, boxes 58–62; I.G.M.T. Libr., Maw & Co. Ltd. deeds.

39 S.R.O. 1224, box 62, corresp., covenant to produce title deeds, 1863; 1242, box XI, sale partic., etc.

40 W. G. Muter, *The Bldgs. of an Ind. Community: Coalbrookdale and Ironbridge* (1979), pls. 35, 93. Mr. Eric Mercer is thanked for draft hist. of bldg.

41 S.P.L., MS. 2366, deed 1 June 1787 (copy); below, econ. hist. (other ind.); Trinder, *Ind. Rev. Salop.* 55, 57, 105, 382, 384.

42 S.R.O. 1242, box 11, printed sale partic. 1860.

43 S.P.L., MSS. 2365–6.

44 S.P.L., Deeds 12573; S.R.O. 1224/3/329.

45 Langley, *Par. Regs. of Broseley*, i. 75.

46 S.P.L., MS. 4077, p. 40.

47 S.R.O. 840, box 43, Chancery bill 1673.

48 As were the freeholds of 'Priory land' estates belonging to the heirs of John Weld and Fra. Old.

49 S.P.L., MS. 4077, p. 40; MS. 4360, p. 130; Deeds 11130, 11241–2, 11361, 12610.

Weld) in 1717.[50] Henry's property passed *c.* 1725 to his niece Elizabeth Crompton[51] and descended thereafter with Broseley Hall.

Elizabeth Crompton died unmarried in 1747. The last of her family, she left her estates to Mary Browne, spinster daughter of Ralph Browne of Caughley.[52] Mary Browne, having built Jackfield church on part of Woodhouse farm,[53] died in 1763 and the Broseley Hall estate subsequently passed to her widowed sister-in-law Anne Browne (d. 1767),[54] to Anne's brother Francis Turner Blithe[55] (d. 1770), and to Francis's widow Jane Elizabeth (*née* Crawley) who married William Yelverton Davenport. In 1804 the bulk of the estate comprised the Hall, Coneybury, and Woodhouse farms. Mrs. Davenport died in 1811, her husband in 1832, when the estate passed to her grandson Francis Blithe Harries, who owned 374 a. in Broseley *c.* 1840. Harries's son Francis succeeded to the estate, and from 1848 it descended with Cruckton Hall in Pontesbury, passing to the Jenkins family in 1879.[56] In 1941 Maj. C. E. Jenkins, of Cruckton, remained the principal landowner in Broseley parish after Lord Forester.[57]

What became known as Broseley Old Hall[58] was superseded as the chief house by a new house, Broseley Hall, built nearby for Elizabeth Crompton[59] (d. 1747). The Hall is a five bayed, three storeyed house of brick with stone details. Between 1766 and 1770 various improvements were made inside the house to designs by T. F. Pritchard, who also designed a gothic temple or summerhouse for the garden and perhaps a gothic 3-seater boghouse.[60]

Coneybury and Woodhouse Farms are 18th-century brick buildings incorporating earlier cores.[61]

ECONOMIC HISTORY. Agriculture was the parish's mainstay until the late 16th or early 17th century when large-scale coal mining began, much coal being exported by river. Ironstone and local clays were also mined; iron and engineering industries developed, and tobacco pipes, bricks, and tiles were made from the 16th to the 20th century.[62]

Broseley became one of Shropshire's most considerable towns during the 18th century. In the late 17th century there were mercers[63] and a tailor there,[64] and in the early 18th a glazier,[65] and the surgeon Caesar Hawkins's move from Ludlow in 1688 signifies Broseley's increasing importance: he founded a dynasty of eminent surgeons and died rich in 1707.[66] The Wyke family were surgeons in Broseley in the 18th and 19th centuries.[67] In the later 18th century a market hall was built in High Street and a spring fair begun. As the town's trade increased local manufacturers and professional men joined in the provision of banking services. Edward Blakeway, owner of the former Thursfield pottery in Jackfield, was engaged in banking by the early 19th century,[68] and the attorney John Pritchard, moving from Ironbridge to Broseley in 1791, became agent for the Forester estate in 1794 and in 1799 a partner in the bankers Vickers, Son & Pritchard, with Broseley and Bridgnorth offices.[69]

In the mid 19th century the town retained marks of its former economic importance. After his death (1837) Pritchard's sons George (d. 1861) and John (d. 1891) had given up the law but stuck to their more gentlemanly occupation at the bank,[70] which was taken over by Lloyds Bank in 1888.[71] In 1851 the town remained fairly well supplied with tradesmen serving middle class needs.[72] The Pritchards, however, were attempting to gentrify themselves,[73] and the town's more substantial professional men had avocations elsewhere, especially in Madeley (superintendent registrar and county court clerk and high bailiff), whose county court had superseded Broseley's court of requests, and Much Wenlock (borough clerk of the peace and coroner).[74] In fact the town had declined in economic importance both relatively and absolutely in the earlier 19th century and the decline was not halted for over a century.[75] Nevertheless the parish derived some compensation from the thriving ceramic industries of Jackfield, whose encaustic decorated tiles were internationally renowned in the later 19th century.

AGRICULTURE. When Helgot, lord in 1086, obtained 'Bosle' it was waste. There were two ploughteams in 1086, but apparently little arable

50 The 1710 vendor was Ric. Richards, vicar of Longford, to whom it had passed in 1701 under the will of And. Langley (d. 1687): S.P.L., Deeds 11072, 11226; S.R.O. 1224/3/465; Langley, *Par. Regs. of Broseley*, i. 113.

51 S.R.O. 1224/3/486–7; *S.H.C.* new ser. xii. 109; S.P.L., MS. 4360, p. 130; Staffs. R.O., q. sess. rec., gamekeepers' depositions 1726.

52 B.L. Add. MS. 21237, p. 315; S.P.L., Deeds 11394.

53 Below, churches.

54 S.R.O. 1681/116/24; 2991/Rg/4, 13 May 1763.

55 Mayor of Shrews. 1744, high sheriff 1755: *T.S.A.S.* 2nd ser. ix. 202; 4th ser. iii. 12; iv. 91; Blakeway, *Sheriffs*, 192.

56 S.R.O. 515/5, pp. 234–53; 1681/62/1, partial abstr. (1830) of Davenport–Blithe marr. settlement 1771, dilapidations papers 1834, etc.; 1681/116/20; 2713, box 41, Davenport rental Lady Day 1773; 4044/90, pp. 3, 8–19, 25, 27–9, 71–3; P.R.O., IR 29/29/55; IR 30/29/55; S.P.L., MS. 2793, pp. 99–101; Burke, *Land. Gent.* (1914), 1044; *V.C.H. Salop.* viii. 274.

57 *Kelly's Dir. Salop.* (1941), 50.

58 S.P.L., MS. 2366, p. 36; above, this section (Broseley).

59 Crompton crest on rainwater heads: cf. *Fairbairn's Bk. of Crests* (4th edn.), i. 143.

60 'Broseley Hall' (n.d.; TS. in S.P.L.).

61 SA 11736; Forrest, *Old Hos. of Wenlock*, 91.

62 This and the next 2 paras. are based on details below, this section.

63 *T.S.A.S.* 4th ser. v. 306; H.W.R.O.(H.), Heref. dioc. rec., invs. of Thos. Crew, 1668; Rob. Hill, 1679; Thos. Oliver, 1692.

64 H.W.R.O.(H.), Heref. dioc. rec., inv. of Fra. Gears, 1692.

65 Ibid. inv. of Thos. Crowther, 1711.

66 *W. Midlands Studies*, xv. 5; *T.S.A.S.* 4th ser. vi. 108–20; *D.N.B.* s.v. Hawkins, Sir Caesar; Hawkins, Caesar Hen.; Hawkins, Fra. (d. 1877).

67 Above, this article, intro.; H.W.R.O.(H.), Heref. dioc. rec., inv. of Jacob Wyke, 1780.

68 *T.S.A.S.* lii. 72; below, this section (clay ind. [pottery]).

69 *T.S.A.S.* lviii. 224; S.P.L., Deeds 18054 (banknote).

70 *V.C.H. Salop.* iv. 212.

71 S.R.O. 1242, box XI, notice of taking over 1888.

72 S. Bagshaw, *Dir. Salop.* (1851), 562–4.

73 Serving as high sheriff, going into Parliament, etc.: W. Hughes, *The Sheriffs of Salop.* (Shrews. 1886), pp. vii, 53–4; *V.C.H. Salop.* iii. 311 n. 60, 316 n. 32, 334–5; iv. 211–12.

74 Bagshaw, op. cit. 562–4, 567, 581.

75 Above, this article, intro.

land, though the 4 bordars' share in one of the teams may imply that cultivation was then being expanded.[76] Broseley's open arable fields were referred to *c.* 1226–40, and by 1328 names of three fields around the village were recorded. South-west lay the field known in the 14th and 16th centuries as Polfield or Polefield,[77] in 1620 as West field,[78] and *c.* 1749 as Codbrook field.[79] South of the village lay the field generally known as South field[80] but referred to as Switfeld (*recte* Smitfeld?) *c.* 1230[81] and Smithfield in 1620. Eastwards lay the field known until the 17th century as East field[82] and thereafter usually as Amies field,[83] but in the 16th and early 17th century also as Strangemarsh field.[84] Lands were *c.* 150 m. long.[85] Locally dug marl was added to the soil *c.* 1270.[86] In the Middle Ages, however, relatively little of the parish was open arable land; in 1310 a third of the manor was said to comprise 60 a. arable, 10 a. wood, and meadow worth 18*d.* (probably *c.* 3 a.). In 1341 it was claimed that much of the parish lay uncultivated because of the tenants' poverty.[87] In ⅔ of the manor rent of demesne lands totalled £3 6*s.* 8*d.* 1417–18, while income from customary tenants totalled £6 13*s.* 3*d.*[88]

The name Broseley suggests extensive early medieval woodland.[89] Broseley was disafforested in 1301.[90] Despite assarting and the establishment of outlying farms extensive woodland reserves remained around the village at the end of the Middle Ages.[91] Rights of common were enjoyed in it,[92] and in 1379–80 nine men had 77 pigs in the prior's wood.[93] In 1407 among the pigs were 4 hogs owned by the bailiff of Cressage.[94] Much of the manorial woodland lay north of Broseley, covering the slopes and dingles down to the Severn.[95] Sales of wood from the demesne 'Astwood' produced £5 6*s.* 8*d.* in 1417–18.[96] Probably before the mid 16th century the land between Broseley and the river was divided by merestones into large blocks of common, and, despite encroachment by squatters, the divisions survived in the 17th century.[97] The surviving woodland lay in discrete blocks: Holly grove is first mentioned in 1510–11, Lady wood in the 1550s, and Mone wood in 1605.[98]

As well as the common woods and wastes the river was an important resource and during the Middle Ages there were fishponds and fish weirs on the Severn at Broseley.[99] In 1226 Buildwas abbey sold a weir at Swinney;[1] it was probably at Gitchfield[2] or Prior's Hawksyard.[3] There was a weir at Broseley in 1310,[4] and in the early 15th century John Fisher paid 32*s.* rent for a weir.[5] In 1575 there were three weirs.[6] James Clifford, lord of the manor, owned Robin's weir, probably that at Ladywood known in the early 17th century as Coppice or Upper weir,[7] and Lyed's weir, probably opposite the Lloyds in Madeley; the earl of Shrewsbury owned Swinney weir.

Reduction of the open fields by engrossment and inclosure was well advanced by *c.* 1620,[8] but the process was not complete until *c.* 1800.[9] Inclosure of arable and pasture was probably stimulated by the contraction of common grazing north of Broseley as squatters settled there in the late 16th century,[10] and by improvements to other former common land such as Riddings Lane east of Broseley.[11] Lime, burnt in coal-fired kilns, was being added to arable land by 1600.[12] By the end of the 18th century manuring, land drainage, and the floating of meadows were all commonplace.[13]

John Weld, who acquired much land in Broseley *c.* 1618–21 as he expanded his Willey estate, was an enterprising and energetic landowner.[14] In 1631, fearing for his health, he drew up instructions to his heirs for the management of his estates. He suggested that in Broseley rack rents should replace leases for lives, and that the landlord should have the option of taking his rent in corn from mills.[15] Weld, however, lived until 1666 and, while his rent income increased, he appears not to have tried to rack.[16] In 1634 heriots were demanded from both copyhold and freehold tenements, and also a relief of a year's rent on the latter.[17]

In 1609 Broseley manor comprised 600 a. of arable, 400 a. of pasture, 100 a. of heath, and 60 a. of wood, proportions similar to those of Childs Woodlands farm in 1594 (100 a. of arable, 100

76 *V.C.H. Salop.* i. 338; *Medieval Settlement*, ed. P. H. Sawyer (1976), 197–9; R. Lennard, *Rural Eng. 1086–1135* (1959), 356.
77 S.R.O. 1224/3/135, f. lv.; /3/292, 294.
78 Ibid. /3/242.
79 S.R.O. 1190/4/74.
80 Ibid.; S.R.O. 163/11; 1224/3/280, 294, 598, 828.
81 Ibid. 1224/3/279.
82 Ibid. /3/242, 294.
83 Ibid. /3/348–9, 536, 598.
84 Ibid. /3/135, f. lv.; H.W.R.O.(H.), HD 2/14/3.
85 S.R.O. 1224/2/528, s.a. 1634.
86 Eyton, ii. 20–1.
87 Ibid. 34; P.R.O., C 134/18, no. 1.
88 S.R.O. 1224/2/530.
89 Above, this article, intro.
90 *Cartulary of Shrews. Abbey*, ed. U. Rees (1975), ii, p. 251.
91 Eyton, iii. 241; above, growth of settlement.
92 Eyton, ii. 14, 16, 31–2.
93 W. F. Mumford, *Wenlock in the Middle Ages* (Shrews. 1977), 72.
94 S.R.O. 1190/1, unlisted acct. r. 1417–27 (ct. r. at end).
95 Randall, *Broseley*, 15; Eyton, ii. 14, 16, 31–2; S.R.O. 1224/2/3; /3/382.
96 S.R.O. 1224/2/530. Perh. near the modern Easthope coppice: O.S. Map 6", SJ 60 SE. (1954 edn.).
97 S.R.O. 1224/1/21, 32, 34. Note large areas of 'priory common'.
98 *T.S.A.S.* vi. 113; *L. & P. Hen. VIII*, xx (2), p. 227; S.R.O. 1224/3/306, [f.6], rental of 1605; 1224, box 342, Prior Gosnell's reg. f. 38v.
99 S.R.O. 1224/3/293, 390–1, 464; Eyton, ii. 23; S.P.L., MS. 2365, f. 8.
1 *T.S.A.S.* 3rd ser. vii. 383–4.
2 Randall, *Broseley*, 68.
3 S.R.O. 1224/3/572, 576–7, 595–6.
4 Ibid. /3/288.
5 S.R.O. 1190/1, unlisted acct. r. 1417–27; 1224/2/530.
6 See Hist. MSS. Com. 13, *10th Rep. IV*, *Gatacre*, p. 443.
7 S.R.O. 840, box 43, ct. r. of 1614 (copy), arts. of agreement (lease) of 1617; 1224/1/32; ibid. /3/306, f. [6], rental of 1605.
8 S.R.O. 1224/1/32; B.L. Lansd. MS. 1, f. 191.
9 S.R.O. 1224/3/598.
10 Above, growth of settlement.
11 S.R.O. 1224/3/207.
12 P.R.O., STAC 8/109/9, f. 4.
13 S.R.O. 1224/7/11.
14 Cf. esp. above, manor, and sources there cited; below, Willey, manor; econ. hist.
15 S.R.O. 1224, box 163, John Weld's bk. 1631, memo. *re* Willey.
16 S.R.O. 1224/3/387–8; *W. Midlands Studies*, iv. 68–9.
17 S.R.O. 1224/2/528, s.a.

TABLE XVI

BROSELEY: LAND USE, LIVESTOCK, AND CROPS

		1867	*1891*	*1938*	*1965*
Percentage of	grassland	66	77	89	72
	arable	34	23	11	28
Percentage of	cattle	12	26	30	48
	sheep	65	54	58	21
	pigs	23	20	12	31
Percentage of	wheat	54	45	71	42
	barley	21	36	13	52
	oats	25	19	16	5
	mixed corn & rye	0	0	0	1
Percentage of agricultural land growing roots and vegetables		11	10	4	0

Sources: P.R.O., MAF 68/143, no. 15; /1340, no. 5; /3880, Salop. no. 259; /4945, no. 259.

a. of pasture, 20 a. of meadow, 20 a. of wood), and Rowton farm in 1701 and 1766–7 (60 a. of arable, 60 a. of pasture, 20 a. of meadow, 8 a. of wood).[18] In the later 17th and early 18th century farms were mixed.[19] Clover was grown by 1660.[20] Dairy farming was relatively important, and some farmhouses had cheese chambers. Barley was grown to supply local alehouses with malt. Few farms had many sheep. Horses were replacing oxen as draught animals. Colliers and small tradesmen tended to keep one or two animals, especially pigs. On the Forester estate in Broseley in 1799 the two largest farms were 189 a. and 130 a. Five others were 40–85 a., and five 10–25 a.[21] In 1801 56 per cent of recorded cereal acreage in the parish was wheat, 32 per cent oats, and 12 per cent barley.[22] About 1840 there were 649 a. of arable, 940 a. of meadow and pasture, 202 a. of wood and waste, and 82 a. of gardens. The seven main farms then lay east of a line between Dean and Calcutts.[23] In the later 19th and early 20th century farmers turned increasingly to livestock farming, particularly cattle, and in 1938 pasture occupied ten times as much land as arable in the parish. After the Second World War there were more cattle than any other kind of stock as sheep farming declined; pig rearing also increased, and in 1964 the disused brickworks at Gitchfield was occupied by a model pig and poultry farm owned by Coalport Enterprises Ltd.[24]

MILLS. In 1188 Warin of Broseley was fined by the justices of the forest for building a mill,[25] most probably in Broseley. In 1312 there were two mills near the Dean,[26] south of Broseley, and a mill or mills remained on the site until the mid 19th century.[27] Two mills which had formerly belonged to Wenlock priory were mentioned in 1545 and 1550; one of them was at Birch batch.[28] In 1728 a water mill and mill house stood on a stream near Woodhouse Farm.[29] A watermill on the river bank at Calcutts was ruinous in 1788.[30] In 1793 and 1801 there were two water mills at Calcutts, south of the 1788 mill.[31] One of those, probably that called a colour mill *c.* 1840,[32] was a grinding mill for the Caughley porcelain works.[33] The other was demolished 1830 x 1840.[34]

There were two windmills in Broseley in 1776, worked by Leonard Jennings, an original shareholder in the Iron Bridge.[35] In 1801 windmills (perhaps those of 1776) stood at Syner's hill and Fernybank.[36] It was perhaps the remains of one of them which stood in 1983 west of Fox Lane. There was a miller in Church Street in 1870.[37]

COAL AND IRONSTONE. Coal was being got in Broseley by the early 15th century and intensive exploitation of the Coal Measures, which outcrop near the river, was the basis of Broseley's prosperity in the 17th and 18th centuries. The coal belonged to the lords of the manor and the owners (and sometimes the lessees) of freehold land. Access to seams and transport of coal required the co-operation of neighbouring landowners and their tenants; in the absence of agreements, or when they broke down, disputes were common and sometimes violent.[38]

In the two thirds of the manor owned by the Cloptons there was a mine for which John Hadyngton and John Horsley paid 20*s.* rent in 1417–18. Horsley had a lease for life in 1420–1 and he and Adam Collier paid 16*s.* 8*d.* for it in 1426–7. It was probably the mine which supplied the lord's household with 50 clods (*cledez*) of coal, worth 49*s.* 8*d.*, in 1418–19.[39] Wenlock priory had coal pits in Broseley in 1514–15 and

18 Ibid. /3/308, 495, 777, 790–1.

19 H.W.R.O.(H.), Heref. dioc. rec., invs. of Fra. Adams, 1668; Wm. Oakes, 1669; And. Langley, 1687; John Langley, 1693; John Ball, 1699; Ric. Roden, Edw. Edwards, 1723; Thos. Teece, 1727; Thos. Beddow, 1733. Dr. B. S. Trinder is thanked for lending transcripts.

20 S.R.O. 1224, box 163, ct. papers, Adams v. Williams.

21 Ibid. box 174, sched. of Geo. Forester's est. 1799.

22 P.R.O., HO 67/12/47.

23 P.R.O., IR 29/29/55; IR 30/29/55. For rest of para. see Table XVI.

24 Lloyd, *Wenlock Official Guide* (1964), 30–1.

25 Eyton, ii. 6.

26 S.R.O. 1224/3/190.

27 For later hist. cf. below, Willey, econ. hist. For poss. site cf. S.R.O. 1224/1/9–10, 'dry pool'.

28 *L. & P. Hen. VIII*, xx (2), p. 227; *Cal. Pat.* 1549–51, 213; S.R.O. 1224/3/8, f. 1v.

29 S.P.L., MS. 2366, ff. 6, 12.

30 Clark and Alfrey, *Jackfield and Broseley*, 122.

31 S.R.O. 1224/7/11, f. 12; 2991/Misc/1.

32 P.R.O., IR 29/29/55; IR 30/29/55.

33 Trinder, *Ind. Rev. Salop.* 126.

34 Clark and Alfrey, *Jackfield and Broseley*, 111, 117.

35 Trinder, op. cit. 107.

36 S.R.O. 2991/Misc/1. Poss. the 2 mills shown on R. Baugh, *Map of Salop.* (1808).

37 *P.O. Dir. Salop.* (1870), 26.

38 Above, this article, intro.; below, this section; Randall, *Broseley*, 126–33.

39 S.R.O. 1190/1, unlisted acct. r. 1417–27; 1224/2/530.

c. 1523, and also owned 'Coal meadow' near High Ridding.[40] In 1528 Robert Kirby and Alexander Wood, tenants of Sir Thomas Lacon, were mining for ironstone in the part of Broseley that belonged to Willey manor.[41] The priory received 1*s.* 4*d.* in 1540 from a coal work in its share of the manor;[42] it was perhaps the 'pit called a coal delf' that was held by William Hobson and William Adams in 1545 and thereafter descended with the share of the manor known as the 'Priory land'.[43]

About 1620 there were three parallel insetts or adit mines in the north-west corner of Broseley; they ran back from the Severn into the hillside near Ladywood. The easternmost mine was called the Priory insett; the other two were known as 'Mr. Cage's insetts'.[44] The insetts were perhaps then the longest-worked mines in Broseley, the group apparently reflecting the manorial divisions of 'Priory' or '*capite*' land (⅓) and 'socage land' (⅔).[45] In 1615 William Porter had noted that the Priory insett (then in Edward Pacie's occupation) yielded him only £40 a year, and he valued it at only £100. It was evidently the only mine on the 'Priory land' though Porter noted that more insetts might be made 'which will yield a great profit'. On the 'socage land' mines were more numerous and more valuable,[46] and large-scale mining dated from the 1570s. In 1575 James Clifford, lord of the manor, was found to have dumped large amounts of spoil into the Severn from a pit near the Tuckies.[47] Over the next thirty years Clifford encouraged immigrant miners to settle on the waste, and attempted to exploit coal not only under his own estate but also under the land of one of the main leaseholders in the manor. From *c.* 1588 there were mines at Calcutts on land leased to Richard Wilcox, which Wilcox allowed his landlord Clifford to open up and work. By 1605, however, when railways began to be laid, the agreement had broken down and there were violent disputes involving also Wilcox's undertenant William Wells.[48] In 1608 Clifford's mines in Yates's coppice (four insetts) were let to Jesse Whittingham, a Gloucester baker, for five years at a rent of £200 a year. In 1613, when William Porter was newly in possession,[49] the 'socage land' was said to contain 300 a. 'wherein there are two levels of coals very certain'. Every acre of coal was said to make £600 a year, £300 being allowed for charges and a like sum 'clear gain'. The clear annual profit of 'these coalmines lying on Severn side' was said to be £300 and upwards and their capital value 10 years' purchase, £3,000. The two insetts known before 1620 as Mr. Cage's doubtless accounted for part of the profit but more must have come from mines further down river opened by Clifford. Some of those lay in Calcutts, the 'great pasture ground where the coalmines are',[50] opened after Richard Wilcox had agreed to release the Calcutts to Clifford for the mining of 'stone coal or sea coal'. By 1615 they may have begun to repay a large capital investment. John Weld alleged in 1622 that £1,000 had been spent on them and that their clear annual profit was £100 and sometimes less. He had nevertheless considered the Calcutts mines adequate to indemnify him against encumbrances on the lands he bought from William Porter.[51] They were therefore probably the principal mines in the parish.

The Calcutts mines were managed in Clifford's and Porter's time by John Huxley,[52] and after 1620 the Huxleys evidently continued to manage them for the leaseholders interested in them. They acquired the leasehold for themselves in 1659 and were still working the mines in 1685.[53] In 1681–2 an average of 116 tons of coal a month was raised from Calcutts and Peartree croft (or close).[54]

Earliest recorded of the manor's freeholders to mine under their land were the owners of the Woodlands estate in 1578.[55] It was probably those mines which were at lease for £100 a year in 1607.[56] From 1620 Francis Adams worked mines on Coalpit hill and had a way to the Severn for his coal, probably across his own land and then over the Calcutts. He was still involved in mining when he died in 1668.[57] In the 1670s his widowed daughter Sarah Crompton owned adits running south from near the river to Cockshutt in Broseley Wood.[58] John Weld was the most substantial freeholder in the manor after 1620 and the leasehold 'Priory land' which he had bought included the Priory insett with wagons and access to the Severn. He became an important mine owner, and the extent of his interests enabled him to employ a variety of tactics in dealings with his local rivals. By 1631 he estimated that he had added £500 to the value of his lands in Broseley by persuading Silvanus Lacon of the Woodlands to allow him to run galleries beneath his land. At the same time he considered that Francis Adams might be hindered from taking his coal to the river if a lease of the Calcutts could be obtained from the Youngs. In 1634 he allowed Lawrence Benthall

40 S.R.O. 1224, box 342, Prior Gosnell's reg. f. 38v.; N.L.W., Wynnstay, RA 2.

41 S.R.O. 1224/2/538.

42 *V.C.H. Salop.* ii. 44; cf. S.R.O. 1224, box 342, Prior Gosnell's reg. f. 38v.

43 S.R.O. 1224/3/192; *L. & P. Hen. VIII*, xx (2), p. 227; above, manor.

44 At O.S. Nat. Grid SJ 6740 0334: S.R.O. 1224/1/32.

45 Above, manor.

46 S.R.O. 840, box 43, surv. of 1613–15; 1224/3/258.

47 *T.S.A.S.* xi. 426.

48 Above, growth of settlement; below, this section (industrial rlys.); P.R.O., STAC 8/109/9; STAC 8/294/25; Trinder, *Ind. Rev. Salop.* 6–7; *Renaissance & Modern Studies*, iv. 127; *T.S.A.S.* xi. 9–10.

49 S.R.O. 840, box 43, lease of 1608 (copy); 1224/3/208; /3/210, pp. 7–8.

50 S.R.O. 840, box 43, surv. of 1613–15.

51 S.R.O. 1224/3/200, esp. pp. 18–23; 1224, box 150, 'Instructions for Mr. Attorney to mediate' [1622]; above, this section.

52 S.R.O. 840, box 43, lease of 1608 (copy), 'Mr. Porter's general acquittance'; above, manor (the Dunge; Ladywood).

53 S.R.O. 1224, box 150, 'Instructions for Mr. Attorney to mediate' [1622]; above, manor (Calcutts).

54 S.R.O. 840, box 43, acct. of coal got in Calcutts 1681–2.

55 P.R.O., C 104/22, pt. 1, deed 7 Oct. 1578; CP 25/2/201/25 Eliz. I Trin. [no. 10]; cf. CP 25/2/344/21 Jas. I Mich. [no. 51]; SP 23/180, pp. 161–3, 165–6; S.R.O. 2089/1/3/6; above, manor.

56 S.R.O. 840, box 113, rental of 1607.

57 S.R.O. 1224/3/329; 3703/10; S.P.L., Deeds 12574.

58 S.R.O. 3703/10; H.W.R.O.(H.), Heref. dioc. rec., Fra. Adams's will 1667. For Cockshutt see P.R.O., IR 29/29/55.

of Benthall to mine under Woodlands Green via an insett from Benthall. Nevertheless Weld's experience of mining led him to warn his son in 1631 'not to be busy . . . in searching for coals nor in iron works' and to beware 'colliers or miners or projectors whose fair speech is but to get themselves money'. His own expense in 'seeking for coals' he listed as one of the reasons why his estate was not greater.[59]

Long-wall mining, whereby a network of galleries lead to a long working face, began in the area in the earlier 17th century;[60] investment costs could be high[61] and the dangers considerable.[62] Some coal was used locally, for instance in clay-pipe manufacture, but already Broseley coal was reaching Gloucester down the Severn. The importance of the parish's collieries was demonstrated by the Parliamentarians' seizure of them in 1645, along with those of Benthall and Stourbridge, to prevent passage of coal to royalist forces along the Severn.[63]

About 1700 extraction began on the Olds' Rowton estate, east of the earlier mines.[64] Nicholas Addenbrooke and Richard Edwards, husbands of Old coheirs, joined in partnership with Robert Evans, Richard Pearce, and Michael Stephens of the Amies. Coal, ironstone, and limestone were to be got in what was clearly a well capitalized venture, with the minerals being conveyed by railway across Gitchfield meadows to the Severn. In 1707 Thomas Sprott of the Marsh and Nicholas Harrison, master collier, of Broseley, lessees of Nicholas Addenbrooke's mineral moiety, agreed with Michael Stephens, lessee of Richard Edwards's moiety, to get coal from Tarbatch dingle. Stephens was to receive a royalty for the use of his Tarbatch dingle railway. By 1718 Stephens was also mining on the Woodhouse and Amies estates, allegedly gaining access by one of those pits to the Flint coal under Rowton. Stephens and Harrison remained lessees of the manorial coal rights in 1726.[65] Nicholas Harrison's son Thomas died in 1731 possessed of shares in mines including Rowton and Lower Ridding.[66] From 1731 or earlier Michael Stephens, with John Onions, also mined at Gitchfield east of Rowton.[67] In 1766 when Stephens's son, Thomas Stephens, bought Rowton the property included the Gitchfield coalwork.[68] Mines, probably near the south end of Corbatch Dingle, were bought in 1757 for £350 by Mary Browne of Broseley Hall from William Bromley.[69]

In the 18th century coal apparently remained the main product of Broseley's mines, although in 1717 and until the 1730s or later mines at Ladywood supplied ironstone to the Coalbrookdale furnaces.[70] In 1739 the commonest river freight at Bridgnorth was said to be Broseley coal,[71] and in 1758, when Henry Rainsford of Much Wenlock, a partner in the Madeley Wood Co., became lessee of the Broseley manorial mineral rights, an estimated 100,000 tons of coal a year were shipped from the Broseley and Madeley collieries. In the 1750s coal was sent to Willey Old furnace, and from 1757 to the New Willey Co.'s works.[72] By the 1760s Broseley's collieries, particularly those north of the town, were beginning to be worked out,[73] and in the next 50 years all the available clod coal, the only suitable Shropshire coal for coking, was exhausted.[74]

In the early 19th century ironstone replaced coal as the main product of the parish's mines and by 1810 was supplied to John Onion's Brierley Hill (Staffs.) Ironworks. As the production of Broseley's furnaces declined ore was sent increasingly to the Black Country, and by 1820 considerable amounts of calcined ironstone were reaching Brierley Hill. That trade, in which the Fosters were prominent, continued until the later 19th century.[75] About 1840 there were *c.* 126 people employed in Broseley's mines.[76] In 1870 the export of ore was one of Broseley's principal industries[77] but by 1881 nearly all the pits were closed and the two largest that remained were about to shut.[78] In the late 19th and early 20th century a few small mines continued to produce coal, but by then most pits in Broseley were for clay.[79]

IRON AND ENGINEERING. In 1767 George Matthews leased the riverside Calcutts estate from Sir Onesiphorus Paul.[80] Two furnaces were built: their bellows were operated by water wheels, the water being pumped back to a reservoir (later Mapps pool)[81] by a steam engine. By 1772 Calcutts pig iron was used in Stour Valley forges. In 1778 Matthews was in partnership with one of the Homfray family, and by 1786, when the leasehold was offered for sale, a partnership called Baille, Pocock & Co. operated Calcutts. It then included two blast furnaces each capable of producing 40 tons of iron a week, air furnaces, two bar iron forges, and three steam engines. By that time cannon were being manufactured and sold to the government.

59 S.R.O. 1224/3/260; 1224, box 163, John Weld's bk. 1631, lands and leases in Broseley; above, manor.
60 Trinder, *Ind. Rev. Salop.* 8.
61 Nef, *Rise of Brit. Coal Ind.* i. 378.
62 Firedamp hindered Weld at Willey: *W. Midlands Studies*, iv. 65.
63 Nef, op. cit. i. 121, 218, 288.
64 Acct. based on Randall, *Broseley*, 73–7. See ibid. 97, for list of other pits at that time.
65 Ibid. 59–60.
66 H.W.R.O.(H.), Heref. dioc. rec., Thos. Harrison's will 1731.
67 S.R.O. 3614, box 3, deed 20 Mar. 1730/1 and bdle. *re* Gitchfield coalwks. 1733–44.
68 Ibid. deed 28 Dec. 1765; above, manor. For pedigree S.P.L., MS. 4081, p. 2412.
69 W.B.R., M4/10.
70 Trinder, *Ind. Rev. Salop.* 15, 70.
71 *T.S.A.S.* ix. 197.
72 Trinder, op. cit. 54, 271; Randall, *Broseley*, 60; S.R.O. 1224, box 143, deeds 13 June 1757, 24 Sept. 1759.
73 S.P.L., MSS. 2365–6.
74 Trinder, op. cit. 146; S.R.O. 1224/7/28.
75 Trinder, op. cit. 146; S.R.O. 1224/1/45; 1681/47, pp. 287–8. N. Mutton, 'The Foster Fam.: a Study of a Midland Ind. Dynasty 1786–1899' (Lond. Univ. Ph.D. thesis, 1974), 106.
76 Bodl. MS. Top. Salop. c. 1, f. 117.
77 Trinder, op. cit. 143, 146.
78 W.B.R., Broseley local bd. min. bk. 1876–86, p. 207.
79 *Jnl. Wilkinson Soc.* viii. 3–6; I. J. Brown, *Mines of Salop.* (1976), pp. 51–5, 58-9; S.R.O. 1681/41, letters, deeds, etc., *re* Jackfield mines; Mugridge, *Hist. Jackfield*, 38; *Shrews. Chron.* 17 July 1936, p. 13; below, this section (clay ind.).
80 Acct. based on Trinder, *Ind. Rev. Salop.* 39–41; pl. 32. Cf. S.R.O. 686/1, f.7; ibid. /4.
81 *Salop. Mining Club Jnl.* (1973–4), 19–20.

The lease was bought in 1786 by Alexander Brodie, an inventive and enterprising Scottish blacksmith from London.[82] He soon closed the forge and concentrated on the foundry, whose main products were a ship's stove (patented by Brodie) and cannon. In 1796 32-pounder cannon were cast two at a time, and then bored up to eleven at a time in a steam-powered boring mill. Before 1796 Brodie, with James Glazebrook, a carpenter, had produced a steam blast engine for use at Calcutts. In the 1790s pig iron was sent to Lancashire.[83] In 1803 the two furnaces there in blast produced 29 and 15 tons a week; much was used on the premises in armaments production.[84] By *c.* 1804 there were four furnaces there including a 'snapper' worked at times of heavy demand,[85] and Brodie had set up a boring mill.[86] In 1811, when Brodie died, the works included two large blast engines, a steam-powered cannon-boring machine, a boring mill for cylinders, and a water-powered boring and turning mill.

Brodie was succeeded by his nephew Alexander Brodie (d. 1830).[87] The works suffered badly in the war years and were almost ruinous in 1815. About 1817, when two furnaces were in blast, the works was taken over by William Hazledine. In 1823 1,822 tons of iron were made there and production continued, albeit unprofitably, until the last furnace was blown out in 1828.[88] Broseley's population fell by 515 in the 1820s, largely owing to the closure of five blast furnaces.[89] James Foster acquired the works *c.* 1831, apparently to use its railway to take ore to the Severn. The foundry was demolished in 1836.[90]

A second ironworks, the Coneybury or Broseley Bottom Coal furnace, stood on the Broseley Hall estate, north-east of Broseley.[91] The works probably began to operate in 1786–7, and in 1788–9, when it was operated by Banks & Onions, it started to supply pig iron to the Stour Valley forges. By 1800 William Banks and John Onions operated the works, probably as Banks & Co., along with a foundry west of Church Street; in 1801 William Wilkinson described the products of Onions's new Broseley foundry as the neatest he had seen anywhere.[92] At that time the one furnace's make was 30–35 tons a week.[93] There in 1810 was produced the 50-ton *Victory*, one of the first iron boats.[94] Banks died in 1803 and Onions then bought out his son Christopher.[95] Onions died in 1819 and was succeeded by his son John (d. 1859), who in 1806 had married Frances, daughter of the local ironmaster John Guest. John Onions continued to trade as an ironfounder and brickmaker,[96] in 1810 as the Broseley Furnace Co.[97] The furnaces are said to have been blown out in 1823 but limited production continued for some time: 270 tons were made in 1830, and buildings still stood at the foundry site in 1844.[98]

Another furnace, built in 1806–7 by John Guest south-east of Broseley on the site of the later Broseley Tileries, was acquired by the Onions family soon after.[99] It was apparently blown out by 1840.[1]

John Wright and Joseph and Richard Jesson of West Bromwich (Staffs.), forgemasters and patentees in 1773 of a process to produce wrought iron with coke by heating pig in clay pots, took a lease of land in 1796 at Barnett's leasow,[2] above the Severn bank near the site of the later Free bridge.[3] In 1801 the company was called the Barnett's Leasow Co.[4] Two blast furnaces, blown by Watt engines, came into operation in 1797 and 1801, and pig was sent to the partners' Wrens Nest forges (in Astley Abbots and Linley) and to the Black Country.[5] In 1803 the joint make was *c.* 65 tons a week.[6] By 1815 Charles Phillips, probably an undertenant, had taken over, but in 1820 he and his partner William Parsons went bankrupt. James Foster took a new lease of the works from Lord Forester in 1821 and continued to produce iron there: 2,755 tons in 1823, and 1,316 tons in 1830. The furnaces went out of blast soon after 1830.[7]

W. H. Smith opened the Calcutts foundry on the former ironwork's site in the 1870s, specializing in the production of machinery for the local clay industries.[8] Smith's was taken over by Marshall Osborne & Co. Ltd., precision engineers, *c.* 1957, and had 185 employees in 1964. The foundry closed in 1982 when the firm moved to Stafford Park industrial estate, Telford.[9]

The Capacity Engineering Co. opened in King Street in 1914. Motor car accessories were made until after the Second World War when the firm, open in 1984, became general machin-

[82] Randall, *Broseley*, 120–22; pl. 25.
[83] Trinder, *Ind. Rev. Salop.* 49, 97.
[84] J. Randall, *The Wilkinsons* (Madeley, n.d.), 37 (copy in S.R.O. 245).
[85] Ibid. 35; *V.C.H. Salop.* i. 475; W. A. Smith, 'Swedish view of W. Midlands 1802–3', *W. Midlands Studies*, iii. 47–8, 58.
[86] S.R.O. 515/5, pp. 244–5.
[87] Randall, *Broseley*, 122.
[88] Ibid. 123; Trinder, *Ind. Rev. Salop.* 137, 143, 234.
[89] *V.C.H. Salop.* ii. 221, 230.
[90] Trinder, op. cit. 143; Calcutts sale partic. 1830 (in Apley Est. Office, Bridgnorth, in 1965). S.P.L., MS. 2366, loose plan of Calcutts ironwks. (dated *c.* 1800 by Trinder, op. cit. 41), is on paper watermarked 1831 and prob. depicts the wks. in Foster's time. See also Clark and Alfrey, *Jackfield and Broseley*, 72–3.
[91] Para. based on Trinder, op. cit. 40, 143; Randall, *Broseley*, 124–5; *V.C.H. Salop.* i. 475.
[92] Trinder, op. cit. 97; S.R.O. 515/4, p. 101.
[93] Randall, *Wilkinsons*, 38; H. Scrivenor, *Hist. of Iron Trade* (1854), 95.
[94] *V.C.H. Salop.* i. 474.
[95] S.R.O. 1190/4/251–6; inf. from Dr. H. S. Torrens.
[96] Trinder, *Ind. Rev. Salop.* 143; *Salopian Jnl.* 12 Feb. 1806, p. 2 (ref. owed to Dr. Torrens).
[97] S.R.O. 515/8, p. 4.
[98] S.R.O. 1190/4/530; P.R.O., IR 29/29/55; IR 30/29/55.
[99] Trinder, *Ind. Rev. Salop.* 40. Cf. Randall, *Broseley*, 125; *V.C.H. Salop.* i. 475; *Iron in the Making: Dowlais Iron Co. Letters 1782–1860*, ed. M. Elsas (1960), 238.
[1] Not on P.R.O., IR 29/30/55.
[2] Para. based on Trinder, op. cit. 40; Randall, op. cit. 124; W. K. V. Gale, *The Black Country Iron Ind.: A Tech. Hist.* (1966), 26.
[3] Clark and Alfrey, *Jackfield and Broseley*, 73.
[4] S.R.O. 515/4, pp. 117–24.
[5] Trinder, *Ind. Rev. Salop.* 40, 68; below, Linley, econ. hist.
[6] Randall, *Wilkinsons*, 38.
[7] Trinder, op. cit. 143; *Salopian Jnl.* 31 Jan. 1821; S.R.O. 7/66, 68; rentals in S.R.O. 1224, bdles. 188, 190; Apley Est. Office, Bridgnorth, Calcutts deeds, leases 25 Mar. 1821; *V.C.H. Staffs.* xvii. 38–9 (but cf. 39 against acct. above, this section).
[8] *P.O. Dir. Salop.* (1879), advts. p. 85.
[9] J. H. D. Madin & Partners, *Dawley New Town Rep. No. 2: Interim Proposals* (Sept. 1964), cap. 6, sect. 1, app. and map 14; inf. from the firm.

ists and toolmakers.[10] In 1964 Gaunt & Co. of Birmingham made metal buttons and badges.[11] C. H. R. (Development) Ltd. opened in King Street *c.* 1972, and moved to premises in an old malthouse in Queen Street *c.* 1978. The firm made domestic gas fires and employed thirteen people in 1984.[12]

CLAY INDUSTRIES. The production of goods from local clays was established by the early 17th century, and as industry developed around Broseley demand grew for bricks and tiles for shafts, furnaces, and houses. Mining exposed the abundant high-quality local clays, which were got along with coal and ironstone; by the 19th century, however, clay was mined separately as the local manufactories of clay goods expanded and began to supply a wide market.[13] In the later 19th century both Maws and Craven Dunnill gained international reputations for their encaustic tiles, but the brick and tile industries were badly hit by the slump in building during the First World War[14] and by the import of tiles from Belgium and France in the 1920s.[15] Many yards recovered to continue production until the Second World War, but on a much reduced scale and with increasing emphasis on the more profitable fireclay products.[16] Clay mining continued until the early 1950s.[17]

A 'tyle house' (kiln) adjoining a coal pit on the 'Priory land' was mentioned in 1545 and 1550.[18] Production of bricks and tiles probably increased as mining and population grew in the late 16th century, and during the 17th century many substantial houses in the parish were built at least partly of brick.[19] Between 1754 and 1756 large numbers of Broseley bricks were used at Horsehay in blast-furnace construction. By the later 18th century brick production was well established at Calcutts and Coalford[20] while durable blue roof tiles were made at Jackfield and traded via the Severn.[21] Bricks were also made on site for specific projects.[22] By 1835 Broseley fire bricks enjoyed a national reputation in furnace construction and were sent countrywide via the Severn.[23] After *c.* 1840 the local brick and roof tile industry boomed; new machines and processes became available, and the coming of the railway in 1862 allowed the local industry to reach wider markets.[24]

During the 19th century and until the First World War there were usually about nine firms in business. In the later 19th century roof tiles supplanted bricks as their main product, and the numbers employed increased dramatically as wider markets were reached. In 1851 there were *c.* 130 brickyard workers in Broseley and Benthall; by 1871 that number had trebled. In many brickyards production was concentrated in the summer months, when sub-contracted and, until the 1860s or later, child labour were extensively used.[25] Many businesses were long lived;[26] the Broseley Tileries Co. Ltd., which traded at the Dunge until 1940, claimed 1760 as its foundation date. By 1870 the firm produced tesselated and encaustic floor tiles as well as roof and plain floor tiles.[27] When incorporated in 1877 it had registered capital of £10,000. Not all the £20 shares, however, were taken up and the firm was in difficulties in the 1880s. The work force then numbered *c.* 40–50.[28] In the 1920s the works were combined with Milburgh and Wallace as the Prestage and Broseley Tileries Ltd.[29] Also at the Dunge between 1811 and *c.* 1903 was the Davies family's Dunge Works.[30] The younger John Onions, ironmaster, also made bricks and, in the 1840s, elaborate terracotta reliefs such as were used, for example, at Badger Hall and at Holland House, Kensington.[31] All the other main works were near the Severn, conveniently for river, and later rail, transport.

Most brick and tile works were concentrated around Jackfield. The Coalford works, which began in the late 18th century and was later known as the Excelsior Broseley Roofing Tile Works, was probably the largest brick and tile works in the east Shropshire coalfield, and exported goods abroad. It employed 80–90 men *c.* 1901. The firm closed in the 1930s.[32] The Hollygrove Red Brick and Tile Works operated from the late 18th century until 1895 or a little later, manufacture in the last 20 years concentrating on lighter-weight roof and floor tiles.[33] Nearby works included the Doughty family's, operating from before 1842 until 1939 on a site previously occupied by the Calcutts iron-

10 Inf. from the firm; *Kelly's Dir. Salop.* (1917–41).
11 Lloyd, *Wenlock Official Guide* (1964), 31.
12 Inf. from the firm.
13 e.g. *V.C.H. Glos.* iv. 136.
14 W.B.R., B3/5/24.
15 *Shrews. Chron.* 17 July 1936, p. 13.
16 *Salop. Mining Club Jnl.* (1973–4), 19–20.
17 *Guide to the Coalfields 1952* (Colliery Guardian Co. Ltd.), 292, 296.
18 *L. & P. Hen. VIII*, xx (2), p. 227; *Cal. Pat.* 1549–51, 213.
19 Above, growth of settlement; S.R.O. 1224/1/33, 'brick leasow' field name (*c.* 1658).
20 Trinder, *Ind. Rev. Salop.* 22, 59–60, 70; *Shropshire Mag.* Jan. 1959, 28.
21 J. Plymley, *Gen. View of Agric. of Salop.* (1803), 106; A. Young, *Tours in Eng. and Wales* (1932), 145.
22 S.R.O. 1190/4/56; 2991/Misc/1, f. 6.
23 Lewis, *Topog. Dict. Eng.* (1835).
24 P. Brown and D. N. Brown, 'Broseley—1851 and after', *Soc. for Clay Pipe Research Newsletter*, viii. 32.
25 Trinder, *Ind. Rev. Salop.* 240.
26 *Shrews. Chron.* 28 Oct. 1932, p. 10.
27 *P.O. Dir. Salop.* (1879), advt. p. 78; N. M. Dawes, 'Hist. of Brick and Tile Production on Coalbrookdale Coalfield' (n.d.; TS. in I.G.M.T. Libr.), 50, 52. At O.S. Nat. Grid SJ 682 015.
28 I. Gregory, 'E. Salop. Coalfield and the Gt. Depression" 1873–96' (Keele Univ. M.A. thesis, 1978), 107–11.
29 Clark and Alfrey, *Jackfield and Broseley*, 85.
30 Ibid. 88; Dawes, 'Brick and Tile Production', 52; *P.O. Dir. Salop.* (1879), advt. p. 54. Perh. at O.S. Nat. Grid SJ 682 013.
31 *Country Life*, 21 Apr. 1960, p. 879.
32 Dawes, op. cit. 51; Clark and Alfrey, op. cit. 86–7; *V.C.H. Salop.* i. 443; *Kelly's Dir. Salop.* (1929), 379; not in (1934), 398; *Wellington Jnl.* 1 July 1939, pp. 15–16; S.R.O. 2267/10. Perh. at O.S. Nat. Grid SJ 684 031.
33 Dawes, op. cit. 20–6; Clark and Alfrey, op. cit. 88–9; *V.C.H. Salop.* i. 443; *Shropshire Mag.* Jan. 1959, 27; Randall, *Broseley*, 149–51; S.R.O. 1242, box XI, memo. and sched. 1867, agreement 1884, and corresp. *c.* 1896 *re* tilewks. At O.S. Nat. Grid SJ 682 029.

works;[34] the Ladywood works, where various proprietors made red and white bricks between at least 1761 and 1939;[35] the works of William Exley & Sons, reputedly established at the Rock before 1840 and open until *c.* 1940, where in 1876 one of the coalfield's first down-draught chimneys was built;[36] Hargreaves & Craven, a tileworks operative under several partnerships in the 1860s;[37] Prestage & Co.'s Milburgh Tileries, open between 1870 and 1938, which specialized in exterior ornamentation for buildings and had *c.* 70 hands *c.* 1901;[38] and the Wallace Tileries, also operated by the Prestage family, which opened in 1889, had *c.* 25 hands *c.* 1901, and closed *c.* 1903.[39] About 1892 Exleys opened a large second factory, the Coalport Brick and Tile Works, at Gitchfield, soon among the largest roof-tile manufactories.[40] In 1949 the works was bought by G. W. Dickins who continued production for a time.[41] In 1879 and until at least 1900 Hopkins & Co. had a tile and terracotta works, the location of which in Jackfield is unknown.[42]

As well as these firms of local or regional importance two Broseley companies gained an international market in the late 19th century in decorative tiles. There had been at least two earlier attempts to make such tiles in the parish; 'Dutch tiles' were supposedly made at Jackfield by Maurice Thursfield *c.* 1750–60,[43] while *c.* 1835–45, under the guidance of the leading Coalport china modeller Peter Stephan (fl. in the Broseley area *c.* 1830–1860s), Exleys produced the first encaustic tiles in the district. Herbert Minton, a patentee of the process, threatened legal action, however, and production ceased.[44] Hargreaves, Craven & Dunnill, formed in 1870, occupied a tile works previously run by Hawse and Denny (in 1867), and by Hargreaves & Craven, who in 1867 made geometric tiles by the clay dust process. The resident managing partner was Henry Dunnill (d. 1895), since 1867 manager of Hargreaves & Craven.[45] A new factory, the Jackfield Encaustic Tile Works, designed by Charles Lynam of Stoke-upon-Trent, opened on a 4-a. site in 1874. In 1881, 53 men, 26 youths, and 16 women were employed there. Some of the impetus behind the new enterprise was provided by A. H. Brown, merchant banker and Liberal M.P. for Wenlock.[46] A profit-sharing scheme of 1870–2 was among benefits introduced for the workers. The factory's products, less diverse than those of Maws and primarily medieval-style encaustic floor tiles, were widely used in building and restoration work. By 1890 the product range had widened to include a variety of floor and wall, or furniture, tiles, both plain and mosaic, with painted, printed, and majolica decoration. These were widely exported. In the earlier 20th century considerable quantities of plain tiles and art deco friezes were produced. The firm closed in 1952, and the buildings were taken over and used until 1982 by Marshall Osborne & Co. Ltd., precision engineers. In 1984 the Ironbridge Gorge Museum Trust opened a tile museum there.

In 1883 Maw & Co. (Ltd. 1888) moved their works from Benthall to the new 5-a. 'Benthall' works at Jackfield,[47] also designed by Charles Lynam.[48] That move was already intended in 1862.[49] Maws had previously had an auxiliary branch of their Benthall factory here.[50] A wide range of tiles of frequently innovatory design continued to be produced, many for export, by a paternalistically managed firm: it introduced benefits such as a savings bank, and before 1887 it considered allowing workers to buy shares.[51] Maws was then the largest decorative tile factory in the world. In the early 1900s, in response to changing tastes, Maws' products became simpler, more like Craven Dunnill's. Maws' profits fell in the early 20th century. During the 1920s and 1930s bathroom and hearth tiles were the main products, although decorative friezes were also made. In 1961 Maws became part of the Campbell Brick & Tile Co. of Stoke-upon-Trent, itself bought out by the H. & R. Johnson–Richards Group in 1962. In 1964 the works had 224 employees. By then local clays were no longer used. Tile production ended in 1969. The works was partly demolished 1974–7, the remaining buildings being used for craft and residential units.[52]

In 1889 the area's leading manufacturers of roof tiles, which for some years had been known

34 Above, this section (iron); Dawes, op. cit. 52; Pigot, *Nat. Com. Dir.* (1842), 8. At O.S. Nat. Grid SJ 685 028.

35 Dawes, op. cit. 54; Clark and Alfrey, op. cit. 89; S.R.O. 1224, box 174, royalty acct. bk. 1815–34. At O.S. Nat. Grid SJ 697 031.

36 Dawes, op. cit. 59; Clark and Alfrey, op. cit. 90–1; Review Publishing Co. *Inds. of Salop. Business Review* [*c.* 1891], 46. At O.S. Nat. Grid SJ 683 027. Cf. above, Benthall, econ. hist. (ind.).

37 Inf. from Mr. A. T. Herbert. At O.S. Nat. Grid SJ 686 029.

38 Dawes, op. cit. 35–41; S.R.O. 1491/19, p. 466; 2267/1–9; *V.C.H. Salop.* i. 443–4; *Shropshire Mag.* Jan. 1959, 28. At O.S. Nat. Grid SJ 684 026.

39 Dawes, op. cit. 41–3; Clark and Alfrey, *Jackfield and Broseley*, 91; *V.C.H. Salop.* i. 443–4. At O.S. Nat. Grid SJ 688 027.

40 Dawes, op. cit. 59; Clark and Alfrey, op. cit. 87; Review Publishing Co. *Inds. of Salop.* 46; Gregory, 'E. Salop. Coalfield', 107.

41 S.P.L., SC2/10; S.R.O. 4965/1.

42 Clark and Alfrey, op. cit. 65.

43 Ll. Jewitt, *Ceramic Art of Gt. Brit.* (1883), 180.

44 Randall, *Broseley*, 153; *V.C.H. Salop.* i. 445; G. A. Godden, *Coalport and Coalbrookdale Porcelains* (1970), 127–8.

45 This section based on *Jnl. Tiles and Archit. Ceramics Soc.* iii. 3–10; *Ind. Arch. Rev.* iii. 146–52; Clark and Alfrey, *Jackfield and Broseley*, 65–7; T. A. Lockett, *Collecting Victorian Tiles* (1979), 55; Review Publishing Co. *Inds. of Salop.* 45; J. Randall, *Severn Valley* (Madeley, 1882), 310–13; Gregory, 'E. Salop. Coalfield', 116–17; *Ironbridge Weekly Jnl.* 2 July 1870; 21 Jan, 1 Apr. 1871; 5 Apr. 1873; 28 Feb. 1874; *Eddowes's Jnl.* 11 Mar. 1874, p. 6; *Shrews. Chron.* 4 Nov. 1932, p. 10; S.R.O. 1681/61, lot 26; inf. from Mr. Herbert. Thanks are due to Prof. J. Mordaunt Crook for comments on Lynam.

46 Randall, *Broseley*, 244; Jewitt, *Ceramic Art of Gt. Brit.* 182; fig. 27. Cf. S.R.O. 2076/2, 6; *Ironbridge Weekly Jnl.* 28 Feb. 1874; *Who Was Who*, 1916–28, 132; *V.C.H. Salop.* iii. 342, 346.

47 A. T. Herbert, *Jackfield Decorative Tile Ind.* (I.G.M.T. 1978); S.P.L., photo. neg. B. 119; Clark and Alfrey, op. cit. 67–9; above, Benthall, econ. hist. (ind.).

48 *Ironbridge Weekly Jnl.* 12 Aug. 1876.

49 Clark and Alfrey, op. cit. 68.

50 Jewitt, *Ceramic Art of Gt. Brit.* 189–90.

51 Gregory, 'E. Salop. Coalfield', 112–17; *Jnl. Tiles and Archit. Ceramics Soc.* iii. 5–6.

52 J. H. D. Madin & Partners, *Dawley New Town Rep. No. 2: Interim Proposals* (Sept. 1964), cap. 6, sect. 1, app. and map 14; A. Burton, 'Maws Tile Co.: their Contribution to Tile Manufacture and Design from 1850 to the turn of the Cent.' (TS., Dept. Ceramic Sculpture, N. Staffs. Polytechnic, 1981), 7–9 (copy in I.G.M.T. Libr.); Clark and Alfrey, *Jackfield and Broseley*, 67; Lloyd, *Wenlock Official Guide* (1964), 32; inf. from Mr. Herbert.

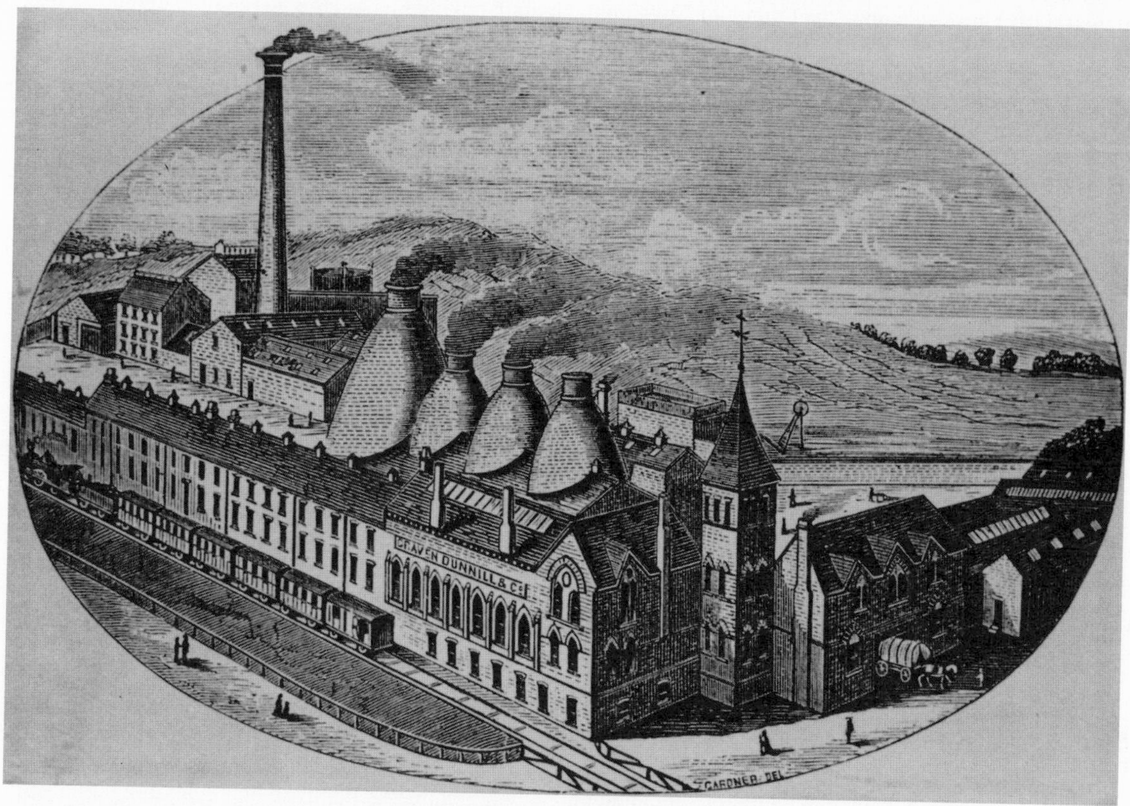

Fig. 27

by the generic name 'Broseley tiles', formed the Broseley Brick and Tile Manufacturers' Association.[53] Its objectives were to fix minimum prices, to curb over-production, to promote 'Broseley' tiles in the face of growing competition from Welsh slate, and to attempt to restrict the description 'Broseley tiles' to products of the Association's members; legal action was taken in 1892 against a Hanley firm producing 'Broseley' tiles, but it failed. The association remained in existence until roof-tile production ended in Broseley during the Second World War.

A mug dated 1634 is the first evidence of pottery production in Broseley, although there may have been earlier kilns.[54] In the 1720s the scale of the industry increased, and potters moved from Stoke-upon-Trent to Broseley potteries run by William Bird and Joseph Garner. Trade may have slumped in the 1730s when at least thirteen potters claimed poor relief.[55] As in other local potteries the main manufacture was coarse earthenware mugs (the usual drinking vessel in the Severnside inns or 'mughouses'), other products including pans, dishes, and horn-shaped drinking vessels known as 'tots'. Some wares were decorated with slip. Salt-glazed stoneware similar to contemporary Staffordshire wares was produced in Jackfield from the 1720s, perhaps at Salthouses by the immigrants from Stoke. By 1728 there were three 'mughouses' at Jackfield—rows of cottages with attached kilns—as well as a 'potworks' operated by Morris Thursfield.[56] In general in the 18th and 19th centuries there was much interaction between the Staffordshire and Jackfield industries.[57] In 1788, for instance, William Greatbatch, a leading potter at Etruria (Staffs.) then seeking to avoid creditors, came to Broseley to test a new kind of kiln to fire enamel with coal.[58]

About 1750 the Thursfield works, one of several in Jackfield, began the manufacture of Jackfield ware, a highly vitrified black-glazed earthenware. By the 1780s a range of good quality wares, including mugs and teapots, was being exported to America; most celebrated were the large jugs or 'black decanters'. The Jackfield industry consisted of several kilns built on the ends of cottages and, like much of the contemporary Staffordshire industry, was 'little more than a haphazard collection of family busi-

53 Clark and Alfrey, op. cit. 61–3; Dawes, 'Brick and Tile Production', 35–41, 47; Gregory, 'E. Salop. Coalfield', 111–12; S.R.O. 1681/191/9. Cf. *Salop. Mining Club Jnl.* (1973–4), 19–20.

54 Randall, *Broseley*, 133–4; *Shropshire Mag.* July 1983, 26. What follows is based on Trinder, *Ind. Rev. Salop.* 125–8.

55 Clark and Alfrey, op. cit. 44.

56 Ibid. 44–6, 49–50.

57 *Salop. Arch Soc. Newsletter*, xx. 3; J. Cotter, 'Potteries of Ironbridge Gorge', *Popular Arch.* Aug. 1985, p. 14; *T.S.A.S.* lxiv. 31; *W. Midlands Arch.* xxiv. 45–50.

58 D. Barker, *Wm. Greatbatch: a Staffs. Potter* (1991), 62–3.

nesses'.[59] Locating the various 18th-century potteries is difficult.[60]

After the death of W. M. Thursfield in 1783 the family's pottery passed to Edward Blakeway, ironmaster, entrepreneur, and a former (1755) mayor of Shrewsbury. He was joined *c.* 1793 by John Rose (b. 1772), a native of Barrow who had been apprenticed at the Caughley pottery. Black-glazed ware continued to be made at the works until *c.* 1800, although production of 'Jackfield ware' continued afterwards in Staffordshire.[61] Rose may also have made porcelain, and by 1800 Mocha wares, cream wares and blue transfer wares were all manufactured in Jackfield.[62]

By the mid 19th century it was more mundane goods that were made, such as yellow- and brown-glazed earthenwares and flower pots;[63] earthenware was still produced in Jackfield in the late 19th century.[64] A 'new' pottery was established by John Myatt in 1826, and in 1838 Myatt and Yates were making brown and yellow stonewares at the later Craven Dunnill site.[65] The business may have continued as the Ash Tree pottery (fl. 1845–6), which itself may have continued under the guise of the Ivanhoe pottery (fl. 1851–4). In 1851 that employed 27 men and boys. After 1854 a succession of Staffordshire partners ran the works, which closed *c.* 1865. In 1851 another earthenware pottery was run by William Exley at his brick-works. About 1930 the Benthall & Ironbridge Pottery Co. was making domestic pottery, including teapots, pancheons, and casseroles at William Southorn & Co's clay pipe works.[66]

By the time of their move to Jackfield in 1883 Maw & Co. were making decorative vases as well as tiles,[67] and art-pottery production continued after the First World War. Ashtrays were made in the 1950s. Craven Dunnill made similar products, including lustre wares, from about the same time as Maws.[68]

The manufacture of clay tobacco pipes probably began in Broseley *c.* 1630 using locally available white clays.[69] The well established industry seems to have expanded considerably *c.* 1680. Between then and 1700 there were probably more pipe makers active in the parish than at any time before the mid 19th century, and 'Broseley' became synonymous with clay pipes everywhere. Pipe making was largely a cottage industry, and from *c.* 1660 until the early 19th century both men and women makers stamped their own products. Like other local industries pipe making was conservative in its methods. Local clays were used until the early 18th century when the import of clay from Devon or Derbyshire[70] began; not until *c.* 1850 did Broseley pipes begin to be decorated.

In the 19th century several larger businesses were formed and, while few were long-lived, total production in the mid 19th century was considerable, and 'Broseley' remained a widely used term to denote any long-stemmed pipe.[71] About 50 people, mostly young women, were usually engaged in making clay pipes in Broseley in the later 19th century. William Southorn began making pipes in 1823, and William Southorn & Co. produced nationally distributed pipes in a factory at Legge's Hill. It had 36 employees in 1851. In the 1930s the firm moved to the Crown Pipeworks (Smithemans' 1881—1923), where it maintained production until *c.* 1960. 'Churchwarden', later a generic name for any long-stemmed pipe, probably originated as a Southorn trade name *c.* 1860.[72]

OTHER INDUSTRIES. About 1220 Philip of Broseley granted Buildwas abbey the right to quarry stone in his Broseley quarries, probably near the later Woodlands Green.[73] While there are small outcrops of limestone in the parish it was probably Carboniferous sandstone that was got there.[74] In 1631 John Weld noted that limestone could be got at the Dunge.[75] Later stone quarries included one of sandstone in Corbatch dingle, which supplied the stone *c.* 1843–5 for Broseley church.[76]

Salt may have been made on a small scale from before 1550 until the 18th century at Salthouses, Jackfield, using saline water from coalpits.[77]

59 Trinder, *Ind. Rev. Salop.* 126; Clark and Alfrey, *Jackfield and Broseley*, 53; S.R.O. 2713, box 41, rental, Lady Day 1773; H.W.R.O.(H.), Heref. dioc. rec., invs. of John Bell snr., 1793; John Poole, 1802; Thos. Evans, 1807; W. Bailey, *Bailey's Western and Midland Dir.* (1783), 365–6 (copy in S.P.L.). For wks. (*c.* O.S. Nat. Grid SJ 687 029) see S.P.L., MSS. 2365, f. 22; 2366, p. 26. The Bells, potters at Haybrook in Posenhall, perh. also had kilns in Broseley: S.R.O. 1224, box 140, deeds 20 June 1758, 5 Apr. 1793.

60 Clark and Alfrey, op. cit. 45–7.

61 M. F. Messenger, *Pottery and Tiles of the Severn Valley* (1979), pp. xi, 3–8; S. Smith, *View from the Iron Bridge* (I.G.M.T. 1979), pp. 33, 56; H. Owen and J. B. Blakeway, *Hist. Shrews.* (1825), i. 536.

62 Clark and Alfrey, op. cit. 45, 50–2.

63 Ibid. 45, 52–3; Messenger, op. cit. pp. xi, 3–8; Plymley, *Agric. of Salop.* 341; Tibnam & Co. *Salop. Dir.* (1828), 25, 31; Hulbert, *Hist. Salop.* ii. 344; S. Bagshaw, *Dir. Salop.* (1851), 564.

64 Jewitt, *Ceramic Art of Gt. Brit.* 158; S.R.O. 1681/189/37, agreement for occupn. of potwks., etc., at Jackfield 1861; S.R.O., dep. plan 349, partic. pt. 2 (no. 98).

65 For this and what follows see *Shropshire Mag.* Apr. 1984, 50–1; Bagshaw, op. cit. 557; *Salop. Arch. Soc. Newsletter*, xx. 3–4; L. Rimmell, 'Arch. and hist. study of 18th- and 19th-cent. pottery ind. at Jackfield' (Inst. Ind. Arch. dissertation, 1983), 21, 24, 29, 31–2 (copy in I.G.M.T. Libr.); Clark and Alfrey, op. cit. 47–9.

66 S.R.O. 1681/190/5; /190/17, Benthall & Ironbridge Pottery Co. Ltd. order form [1930s].

67 *Country Life*, 6 July 1978, 28–9; above, this section (bricks and tiles).

68 Inf. from Mr. Herbert.

69 Acct. based on D. R. Atkinson, *Tobacco Pipes of Broseley* (priv. print. 1975). Cf. also H.W.R.O.(H.), Heref. dioc. rec., invs. of Thos Roden, 1724; Thos. Taylor, 1739; Wm. Morris, 1756; Ric. Hartshorne, 1768; Wm. Harper, 1783; Ric. Legg, 1791; Sam. Roden, 1791; Sam. Roden, 1812.

70 Trinder, *Ind. Rev. Salop.* 8.

71 Ibid. 128; I. C. Walker, 'Churchwarden Clay Tobacco-Pipes and the Southorn Fam. of Broseley', *Post-Medieval Arch.* x. 142–9; Lloyd, *Wenlock Official Guide* (1964), 55.

72 Walker, op. cit.; inf. from I.G.M.T. Libr.; *Salopian Recorder*, xv. 2; 'The Clay Pipe Makers of Broseley' (1973; 16 mm. film in S.P.L.); S.R.O. 1681/190/17, headed corresp.; *Soc. for Clay Pipe Research Newsletter*, viii. 29–33; *Shrews. Chron.* 12 Aug. 1932, p. 11; 'Quaestor' [W. Byford-Jones], *Both Sides of the Severn* (1932), 81–5; fig. 28.

73 *V.C.H. Salop.* ii. 52, 56; Randall, *Broseley*, 14–15; above, communications.

74 Inst. Geol. Sciences Map 1/25,000, *Telford* (1978 edn.); Randall, op. cit. 14–15, 131–2.

75 S.R.O. 1224, box 163, John Weld's bk. 1631, lands and leases in Broseley.

76 Below, local govt.; churches; S.R.O. 515/5, pp. 62–3; Mugridge, *Hist. Jackfield*, 15. For use of brick cf. above, growth of settlement.

77 Plymley, *Agric. of Salop.* 71; Randall, *Broseley*, 94; Smith, *View from Iron Bridge*, p. 53; *Cal. Pat.* 1549–51, 213 ('saltemeadowe' field name).

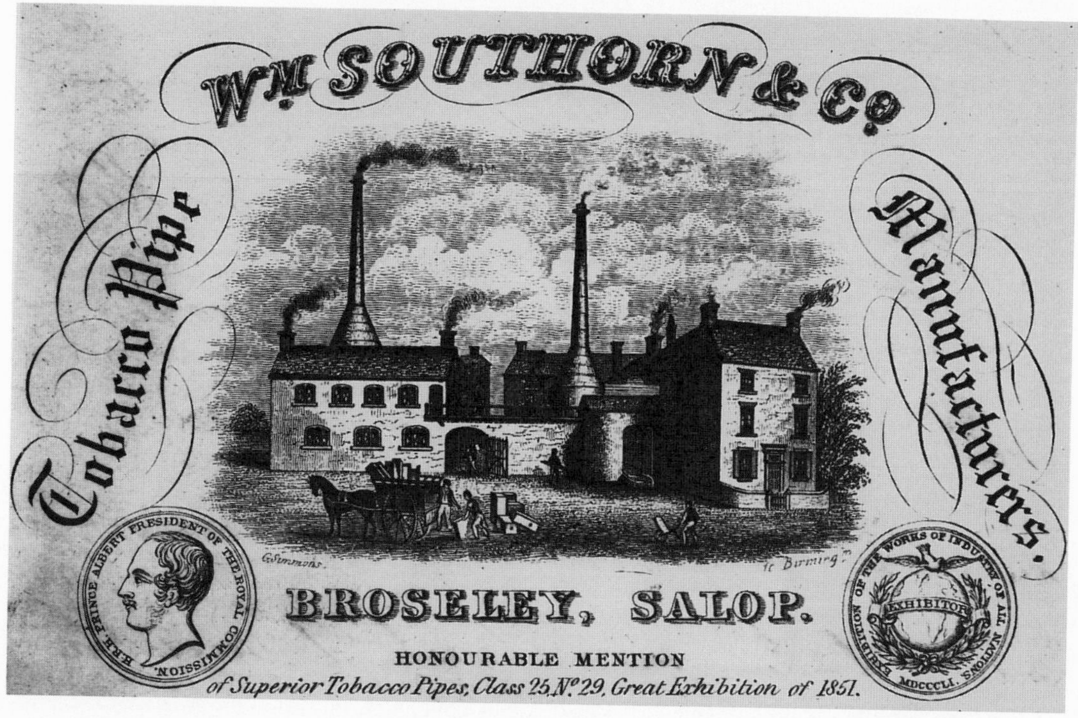

Fig. 28

BROSELEY WOOD: THE TOBACCO PIPE WORKS OF WILLIAM SOUTHORN & CO., KING STREET, PROBABLY IN THE LATER 19TH CENTURY

Lime was manufactured between the 17th and 19th centuries north of Broseley.[78]

Thomas Blakeway (fl. 1765, d. 1805), William Hartshorne (fl. 1793), and Peter (fl. 1760) and W. Onions (fl. 1790) were Broseley clock makers.[79]

In the early 17th century John Weld considered establishing a glass or soap works at Broseley; no action was taken.[80] Benjamin Batchelour, a glass maker from Amblecote (Staffs.), began to work a glasshouse north of Broseley *c.* 1730. Flint glass was probably made. By 1743 Batchelour had absconded to London in debt, leaving the premises ruinous.[81]

Barges were built, and rigging blocks made for the navy, in the parish in the mid 17th century.[82] There was a boat builder at Jackfield in the later 19th century.[83] Coracles were among the vessels built there.[84]

Local pitch was probably applied to barges at Broseley in 1674.[85] In the 1690s tar, pitch, and oil were extracted from bituminous shale at Jackfield under a patent granted to Martin Eele of Calcutts. The products remained flexible for longer than available alternatives and were especially used to caulk ships.[86] The works continued in 1711.[87] Tarbatch dingle was so called by 1707, and the products of bituminous wells there were reputed medicinal.[88] In 1711, perhaps not for the first time,[89] a 'burning well' was discovered, where carburetted hydrogen rose to the surface from the Coal Measures. It attracted much attention, as did a 'burning well' of 1750.[90] Lord Dundonald (d. 1831)[91] established a manufactory with 12 kilns or stoves at Calcutts in 1784–6 to distill pitch, tar, and oils by coking coal in closed vessels according to his patent of 1781. In 1794 there were 20 kilns there, but the works was not in use 'nor ever likely to be again'. Production, however, had restarted by 1803,[92] and as late as 1836 tar was collected there.[93]

In the earlier 18th century cloth was made and finished in the town.[94] There was a flax house in 1755.[95] In 1792 Messrs. Jennings, Latham, and

[78] *W. Midlands Studies*, iii. 46; xv. 5.

[79] D. J. Elliott, *Salop. Clock and Watchmakers* (1979), 33–4, 76, 102, 111; inf. from Mr. J. B. Lawson.

[80] Trinder, *Ind. Rev. Salop.* 7.

[81] *Jnl. Wilkinson Soc.* iv. 4–6; S.R.O. 1224, box 132, deed of 1743.

[82] *W. Midlands Studies*, xv. 5.

[83] P.R.O., BT 31/2076/9218.

[84] Mugridge, *Hist. Jackfield*, 29–30.

[85] Above, communications.

[86] C. Singer and others, *Hist. of Technology*, iii (1957), 688; Clark and Alfrey, *Jackfield and Broseley*, 75–6; cf. above, manor (Calcutts).

[87] *V.C.H. Salop.* i. 476.

[88] Randall, *Broseley*, 75, 90–1.

[89] Fields called 'fiery field' in 1840 were in an area called 'the old coal pit on fire' *c.* 1620: cf. P.R.O., IR 29/29/55; IR 30/29/55, fields 1130, 1133–4; S.R.O. 1224/1/32.

[90] Randall, op. cit. 92–3; Wesley, *Wks.* iii. 502; Camden, *Brit.* (1772), i. 472; *V.C.H. Salop.* i. 32; S. Bagshaw, *Dir. Salop.* (1851), 558.

[91] *D.N.B.* s.v. Cochrane, Archibald.

[92] Plymley, *Agric. of Salop.* 70; *V.C.H. Salop.* i. 475–6; Trinder, *Ind. Rev. Salop.* 55–8; *W. Midlands Studies*, iii. 48–9; B.L. Add. MS. 21237, p. 376; S.R.O. 515/2, pp. 195–6.

[93] Hulbert, *Hist. Salop.* ii. 344.

[94] H.W.R.O.(H.), Heref. dioc. rec., invs. of Sampson Bulkeley, 1711; Edw. Reynolds, 1742; Wm. Hall, 1758; Thos. Shaw, 1766; Wm. Hall, 1776.

[95] S.R.O. 1224, box 183, rental Mich. 1755.

Jennings had a textile warehouse in Broseley next to the 'cotton manufactory'. This otherwise unrecorded cotton mill is the only one known in the east Shropshire coalfield.[96]

The Burroughs family made rope at Ladywood, where they had a rope walk, from *c.* 1836 until *c.* 1900.[97] James Harrington operated as a rope and sail maker, probably also in Ladywood, in the 1830s and 1840s. There was a rope walk at Preens Eddy too.[98]

Thomas Mapp manufactured cement and ground colour at the old mill at Calcutts from *c.* 1850 until the 1870s. He had two employees.[99] In the 20th century concrete was made on the site of Doughty's tile works.[1]

There was a chemical works employing one labourer at the Werps in 1861 and 1881.[2]

Clogs were perhaps made in Jackfield in the late 19th century.[3]

The area's industrial buildings continued to be adapted to new uses in the later 20th century. Maws' tile works was divided into small craft and industrial units with attached housing. The remaining building at Doughty's tile works was used in 1988 by Westons Portable Buildings, and the site of the Rock tile works by the Rock Metal Co., who recycled waste metal. Hornsey Gates made aluminium gates on the site of the Milburgh Tileries. Previously the Coalport Brick and Tile Works had been used by the Wolverhampton Metal Co., afterwards by the Nuway Rubber Mat Co.[4]

INDUSTRIAL RAILWAYS. One of the country's first wagon railways, for carrying coal, was laid in Broseley in 1605 by Richard Wilcox and William Wells.[5] It ran north-east for over 1 km. from north of Broseley village via Birch batch to Calcutts and the Severn. The line crossed the land of James Clifford, lord of the manor and rival coalmaster; perhaps in anticipation of his opposition, Wilcox and Wells had sought a licence from the Privy Council for its construction. Within weeks Clifford's men had attacked and seriously damaged the railway. Apparently soon afterwards Clifford built his own railway from his mines near Calcutts to the river; those rails in turn were removed by Wilcox, and replacements of them by Wells. By 1608 Clifford had also laid rails from mines west of Calcutts,[6] and by the 1630s railways were an integral part of the local mining industry.[7]

In the later 17th century the main line was apparently still that down Birch batch, with branches from surrounding pits. Known later as 'Jackfield rails', the line continued in use well into the 19th century.[8] The parish's other main railway, along Tarbatch dingle, was begun either in 1702 by Richard Manning of Gitchfield and Lancelot Taylor or before 1707 by Michael Stephens, their successor as lessee of the Rowton mines. In 1757 the line was extended to the New Willey furnaces, giving them direct access to the Severn almost 4 km. away at Willey wharf, east of Swinney (in Caughley). In 1759 the amount of traffic necessitated the construction of a second line alongside the first.[9] By 1790 the line had been shortened and stopped *c.* 1 km. short of Willey furnaces,[10] but by 1827 the railway had been extended north-west to pits south-east of Broseley town. The line still led to the Severn in 1833, and perhaps did so until the opening of the Severn Valley line in 1862.[11] By 1882 its western termination was apparently at Broseley Tileries. In 1901 it still extended east as far as Upper Riddings Farm, with an extension to Turnersyard colliery in Caughley, but it closed before 1925.[12]

Other lines included one of the earlier 18th century which ran west of Corbatch dingle to the Tuckies,[13] and one which in 1827 ran along the riverside at Jackfield and connected several lines running to the river from the area east of the town.[14] By 1758 wagonways were in use underground in pits as well as in adits.[15] As mining and ironmaking declined so did the need for railways and by 1840, except for the Tarbatch dingle line, only short stretches survived.[16]

MARKET AND FAIRS. A Wednesday market begun without warrant in 1744 was short lived. Before 1779 a market was held in the yard of Whitehouse farm, near the rectory.[17] In that year a market hall, paid for by local charities, was erected by the vestry on the west side of High Street. It was a red-brick building of five bays with a pediment over the three central bays; over the ground floor concourse were upper rooms.[18] By 1826 the building was known as the town hall.[19] Until the later 1860s[20] Wednesday was market day, but the market was then discontinued owing to a lack of support already apparent in 1833. In 1872 the market was revived on Saturday outside the town hall.[21] In 1910 the

96 Trinder, *Ind. Rev. Salop.* 135.

97 Hulbert, *Hist. Salop.* ii. 343–4; Pigot, *Nat. Com. Dir.* (1842), 10; *Kelly's Dir. Salop.* (1900), 111; not ibid. (1905); O.S. Map 1/2,500, Salop. XLIII. 14 (1902 edn.).

98 Clark and Alfrey, *Jackfield and Broseley*, 77–8.

99 Ibid. 77; S. Bagshaw, *Dir. Salop.* (1851), 563; *P.O. Dir. Salop.* (1870), 28.

1 Clark and Alfrey, op. cit. 77.

2 Ibid. 77.

3 Ibid. 78.

4 Ibid.

5 Following paras. based on M. J. T. Lewis, *Early Wooden Rlys.* (1970), 95–108; R. S. Smith, 'England's first rails', *Renaissance & Modern Studies*, iv. 125–8.

6 S.R.O. 840, box 43, deed 22 Sept. 1608.

7 Poss. routes discussed in Clark and Alfrey, *Jackfield and Broseley*, 28–36; M. L. Brown, 'Broseley Wagonway Routes' (TS. in I.G.M.T. Libr., accession no. 1989.4220).

8 Lewis, op. cit. 235–6; S.P.L., MS. 2366, Woonhay map (loose).

9 Lewis, op. cit. 236–7, Randall, *Broseley*, 74–5; S.R.O. 604, plan of Riddings and Swinney est. 1790; 1190/4/40/1–8; 1224/3/537, 602.

10 S.R.O. 604, plan of Riddings and Swinney est. 1790; 1224/1/40.

11 C. & J. Greenwood, *Map of Salop.* (1827); O.S. Map 1", LXI. NE. (1833 edn.); above, communications.

12 O.S. Maps 1/2,500, Salop. LI. 2 (1882 and 1927 edns.); LI. 7 (1902 and 1927 edns.); S.R.O. 1224/1/48.

13 S.P.L., MS. 2366, p. 2.

14 Greenwood, *Map of Salop.*

15 Lewis, *Early Wooden Rlys.* 320.

16 O.S. Map 1", LXI. NE. (1833 edn.); P.R.O., IR 30/29/55. See discussion in Clark and Alfrey, *Jackfield and Broseley*, 33–5.

17 Randall, *Broseley*, 245; P.R.O., IR 29/29/55; N.L.W., Wynnstay, box 56/86. Perh. Whiteho. Fm. was the meeting ho. noted by Wesley in 1773: Wesley, *Wks.* iii. 502.

18 Above, social and cultural activities; below, charities; Pevsner, *Salop.* 87; Stratton, *Broseley*, p. [5].

19 Jackson, 'Madeley', bk. 3A, p. 18.

20 *P.O. Dir. Salop.* (1863), 661; (1870), 26.

21 Randall, *Broseley*, 245; Trinder, *Ind. Rev. Salop.* 198; Plymley, *Agric. of Salop.* 334; *Jnl. Tiles and Archit. Ceramics Soc.* iii. 7.

district committee asked the churchwardens to abate the nuisance caused by market stalls on Saturday evenings.[22] The town hall was sold by its trustees in 1960[23] and demolished soon after.[24]

Fairs perhaps began about the same time as the market. In 1792 Easter Monday was fair day. In 1803 and later fairs were held on the last Tuesday in April and on 28 October,[25] and by the 1830s were largely for pleasure.[26]

LOCAL GOVERNMENT. In 1568 Broseley township was said to be in Marsh manor—by which the leet jurisdiction of Marsh was probably meant, for Broseley was itself a manor.[27] Moreover only the 'Priory land'—⅓ of the manor—was in Marsh (which had absorbed it 1379 × 1540), for in the 17th century the 'socage land' (⅔ of the manor) owed suit to Bourton hundred.[28] Though the 'Priory land' was a scattered estate, its extent and bounds were familiar enough in the early 17th century for its inhabitants to be listed[29] and thus for suit to the Marsh leet to be exacted from them. The break-up of the manorial estate in and after 1620,[30] however, evidently blurred the old distinction between 'Priory land' and 'socage land', and by 1680[31] it appears that all the Welds' lands in Broseley, even those[32] bought from the 'socage land' sixty years earlier, were 'reputed Priory land'[33] and owed suit at Marsh leet;[34] 'socage land' owners other than the Welds owed suit to Bourton hundred.[35]

In the 1660s, 1670s, and earlier 1680s, when Bourton hundred court often met in Broseley,[36] offenders from the town against the assize of ale were regularly fined.[37] Other offences presented in the 1670s included grazing offences,[38] assault,[39] and making an affray.[40] Exaction of suit continued in the 1760s.[41] From 1634 many of the presentments being made at the twice-yearly leet of Marsh manor were presumably for the increasingly populous Broseley Wood area; they were mainly for breaking the assize of ale, maintaining cottages on the waste, and harbouring inmates;[42] other offences included affray and bloodshed.[43] In the 1670s and 1680s offences included assaulting the manorial bailiff,[44] getting stone at Woodlands Green,[45] pound breach, pulling down the parish butts, and coursing with a greyhound.[46] Cottagers were amerced in the 1820s and 1830s.[47]

The April and October courts leet for Broseley, held in the town hall in the 1830s, were probably those of the manor of Marsh, the Bourton leet and the Broseley court baron having lapsed. Four constables for Broseley were then appointed each October.[48] The constables were paid by the vestry until 1840[49] but not thereafter, the borough of Wenlock having begun to contribute to the new county police force.[50] Broseley had a police officer by 1845.[51] Formal appointment of constables charged with the duty of making presentments at the leet nevertheless continued, but after 1879 neither the leet (which used then to meet at the Lion inn)[52] nor the constables are heard of again.

Marsh manor (with its court leet) and Bourton hundred belonged to the Welds of Willey from 1620 and 1639 respectively.[53] In 1677 therefore the Welds opposed an attempt by the lord of Broseley, John Langley, to establish a title to a court leet with the right to take waifs, strays, and felons' goods.[54] In 1678 his son Samuel obtained a Crown grant of a twice-yearly leet with view of frankpledge for his own estate,[55] though nothing is known of any successful exercise of the jurisdiction.

In 1310 the pleas and perquisites of Broseley manor court were said to be worth nothing because the lord of the manor and his tenants made suit to the prior's court.[56] The prior held a court for his part of the manor in 1379, of which a record survives,[57] but before 1540 the prior's Broseley estate was in his manor of Marsh.[58] By 1418 the lord of the rest of Broseley manor had a court worth 8*s.* 10*d.* a year.[59] Rolls for that court survive for 1406–8, 1501, 1588, 1621–9, 1633–4, and 1657–63.[60] There is also record of a court of recognition of 1462 for William Harewell's tenants.[61] In the 17th century the court baron was usually held once a year but at no set time. By 1680 it may have been held less often.[62] Presentments for underletting

22 W.B.R., Broseley dist. cttee. min. bk. 1906–13, p. 230. Cf. below, charities.
23 Jackson, 'Madeley', bk. 3A, p. 132.
24 Stratton, *Broseley*, p. [5].
25 Plymley, *Agric. of Salop.* 336; *Rep. R. Com. Mkt. Rights*, i [C. 5550], p. 196, H.C. (1888), liii. *Thompson's Salop. Memorandum Bk.* (Ellesmere, 1836; copy in S.P.L., Deeds 17921), gives 29, not 28, Oct.
26 Above, social and cultural activities.
27 S.R.O. 1224/3/24.
28 Ibid. /2/16–133; /3/101; box 150, depositions in Weld *et al.* v. Langley 1680; below, this section.
29 S.R.O. 1224/3/261.
30 Above, manor.
31 S.R.O. 1224, box 150, depositions in Weld *et al.* v. Langley 1680.
32 e.g. Gt. Hurst, Rotherhurst, and pt. of Wilcox's fm.: cf. ibid. pp. 24, 47, 59; S.R.O. 1224/3/198, 208, 224–6, 244, 262.
33 See e.g. S.R.O. 1224, box 150, depositions in Weld *et al.* v. Langley 1680, pp. 41–2, 44, 59.
34 Ibid. pp. 59–61.
35 Ibid. pp. 9–10, 64–5, 100–1.
36 e.g. 1670 and 1671 (S.R.O. 1224/2/386–7); 1673–4 (ibid. /2/383–4); 1684 (ibid. /2/511, s.a.).
37 e.g. ibid. /2/370–1, 376–8.
38 Ibid. /2/384.
39 Ibid. /2/383.
40 Ibid. /2/511, s.a. 1683.
41 Ibid. /2/520–7.
42 Ibid. /2/353.
43 Ibid. /2/353–62, 364–8.
44 Ibid. /2/378–9.
45 Ibid. /2/380.
46 Ibid. /2/511, s.a. 1681–2.
47 Ibid. /2/325–35.
48 Pigot, *Nat. Com. Dir.* (1835), 349; Randall, *Broseley*, 33–4.
49 S.R.O. 2991/ChW/1, s.a.
50 *V.C.H. Salop.* iii. 157.
51 Bodl. MS. Top. Salop. c. 1, f. 482.
52 Randall, *Broseley*, 34.
53 Above, Lib. and Boro. of Wenlock (Lib.: Bourton hund.); Barrow, manors.
54 S.R.O. 1224/2/510, 3 Aug. 1677.
55 Ibid. /3/334; cf. above, manor (Broseley Hall).
56 S.R.O. 1224/3/288.
57 Ibid. /2/3 (the roll's chronological arrangement requires a date in Jan. 1380 for this entry, but the dating formula, though partly destroyed by rubbing, appears to make that impossible).
58 Ibid. /3/24, 81, 105.
59 Ibid. /2/530.
60 S.R.O. 840, box 1, ct. r. of 1501, 1588; 1190/1, unlisted Broseley acct. r. 1417–27 (ct. r. at end); 1224/2/528–9.
61 Birm. Univ. Libr., Mytton Papers, i. 198.
62 S.R.O. 1224/2/528–9; 1224, box 150, depositions in Weld *et al.* v. Langley 1680, p. 65.

or for encroaching on the waste were commonest, and those for petty agricultural offences and public disturbances were also frequent. Abandoned and unfilled coalpits were subjects of concern.[63] In 1795 it was stated that the manorial court was seldom held and that most of the court rolls were lost.[64] A pound south of Lower Church Street, there by *c.* 1620, survived into the 20th century.[65]

Presentments from Broseley (probably from Lacon tenants at Upper Riddings and the Woodhouse) were heard at Willey court baron in 1460 and 1528.[66]

There were two overseers in 1642, and in 1654 they paid small monthly doles to up to four people, usually widows. The money came from gifts, communion offerings, and fines collected by the constables, including one of 10*s.* on a Sunday tippler.[67] As in the other coalfield parishes various methods of poor relief were tried in the 18th and 19th centuries. Licence to build cottages for the poor at Harris's (or Harrison's) Green, the site of the later workhouse, was granted in 1734.[68] Between 1770 and 1793 the poor rate fell by half, and latterly between thirty and forty people relied on the parish. There was a workhouse, as contracting had proved oppressive.[69] It had 36 occupants 1803–4, *c.* 80 1812–14, and *c.* 50 in 1814–15. Rather more people usually received out relief.[70] During the winter of 1816–17, the worst period of distress following the French wars, 1,250 of the parish's 5,000 inhabitants received relief. The poor rate doubled and was paid by only 300 households.[71] By 1826 there was a select vestry and the poor were once again farmed, for £850.[72] Farming continued, at *c.* £1,000 a year, until 1835 when an assistant overseer was appointed at £50 a year.[73] The parish was in Madeley union 1836–1930.[74] The workhouse at Harris's Green, which had a garden south of Broseley, had three inmates in 1841.[75] It was probably where the Madeley union school was held between 1836 and 1851.[76]

Highway surveyors were appointed by 1714;[77] in the 19th century they were salaried.[78]

Broseley court of requests was formed in 1782[79] despite the opposition of Morgan Jones, rector of Willey and Barrow, who allegedly acted at the instigation of a Much Wenlock attorney.[80] Usually held on alternate Wednesdays, the court, for the recovery of debts under 40*s.*, had jurisdiction over the parishes of Barrow, Benthall, Broseley, Dawley, Linley, Madeley, Little Wenlock, and Willey. It consisted of a commissioner for each parish, and there was a serjeant or bailiff. According to the Act a ruinous building near the workhouse was to be converted to a gaol.[81] The court was abolished under the County Courts Act, 1846.[82]

Broseley was in Madeley rural sanitary district 1872–6.[83] In 1876 Broseley civil parish was formed into an urban sanitary district under a local board of health; it contained the districts of Broseley and Jackfield.[84] In 1879 the local board employed a medical officer, a collector and surveyor, and an inspector of nuisances.[85] By 1917 the offices of surveyor and rate collector (then under the district committee)[86] were separate.[87] Broseley U.S.D. was absorbed into the borough of Wenlock U.S.D. in 1889,[88] and thereafter formed one of the borough's four wards and sanitary divisions under a largely autonomous district committee until 1966.[89]

On the dissolution of Wenlock M.B. in 1966 the part of Jackfield in Dawley new town was transferred to Dawley U.D. and the thereby reduced civil parish of Broseley to Bridgnorth R.D.[90] In 1974 those respective parts of the old parish were assigned to the Wrekin and Bridgnorth districts.[91]

PUBLIC SERVICES. As population grew and more mines were sunk the water supply to Broseley town and Broseley Wood became more precarious. In the mid 17th century the main public supply was probably Down well, *c.* 300 m. north-east of the church,[92] while there may have been some private supplies via oak-lined channels.[93]

In the earlier 19th century Down well remained the town's main public supply, but demand, particularly in the summer, considerably exceeded supply. The only other public source was the Delph, an open pool in the Square, formed before 1728 from an infilled

63 S.R.O. 1224/2/529, s.a. Oct. 1658, 1660.

64 Ibid. /3/384.

65 Ibid. /1/32; O.S. Map 6", Salop. LI. NW. (1938 edn.).

66 S.R.O. 1224/2/537–8; cf. /2/536, 539, 546; above, Caughley, manors (Upper Riddings; the Woodhouse).

67 S.R.O. 4774/1; Ho. of Lords papers 1641–2, Protestations Oxon. and Salop. f. 185.

68 S.R.O., q. sess. order bk. 1726–41, ff. 95v.–96; below, this section. Cf. above, Benthall, local govt.; *V.C.H. Salop.* xi. 57, 88, 125–6, 165, 192, 234–5, 297, 317, 330.

69 Trinder, *Ind. Rev. Salop.* 207.

70 *Abstr. Rel. to Poor*, H.C. 98, pp. 422–3 (1803–4), xiii; H.C. 82, pp. 376–7 (1818), xix.

71 *Some Facts, shewing the Vast Burthen of the Poor's Rate in a particular District . . . , by a member of the Salop. Co. Cttee. for the employment of the poor destitute of work* (Holborn, 1817), 7 (copy in S.P.L.).

72 S.R.O. 2991/V/1, 28 Mar. 1826.

73 Ibid. *passim* to 21 Apr. 1834; ibid. 15 Apr. 1835.

74 V. J. Walsh, 'Admin. of Poor Laws in Salop. 1820–55' (Pennsylvania Univ. Ph.D. thesis, 1970), 148–50; *Kelly's Dir. Salop.* (1929), 51.

75 S.R.O. 2991/V/1, 13 Apr. 1829, 24 May 1830; *V.C.H. Salop.* ii. 231; P.R.O., IR 29/29/55; IR 30/29/55, fields 39, 1044.

76 Below, educ.; *V.C.H. Salop.* xi. 72–3.

77 *T.S.A.S.* lvi. 315, 322.

78 *Amount of Money Expended in Repairing Highways in Par. of Broseley* (1848; copy in S.R.O. 1681/116/19); *Shrews. Chron.* 19 June 1936, p. 13.

79 Broseley, etc., Small Debts Act, 1782, 22 Geo. III, c. 37.

80 *Bye-Gones*, v. 190, 210.

81 Lewis, *Topog. Dict. Eng.* (1835); Randall, *Broseley*, 239–40; idem, *Madeley*, 238–9; Pigot, *Nat. Com. Dir.* (1835), 349; 22 Geo. III, c. 37.

82 9 & 10 Vic. c. 95.

83 *V.C.H. Salop.* ii. 204.

84 S.R.O. 1242, box II, case for opinion *re* road at Jackfield, p. [1].

85 W.B.R., Broseley local bd. min. bk. 1876–86, pp. 9, 23–4; *Jnl. Tiles and Archit. Ceramics Hist. Soc.* iii. 8.

86 See below, this section.

87 W.B.R., Broseley dist. cttee. min. bk. 1914–22, p. 162.

88 *V.C.H. Salop.* ii. 221, 229; iii. 177 n. 48.

89 Local Govt. Bd.'s Prov. Order Conf. (No. 4) Act, 1889, 52 & 53 Vic. c. 22 (Local); S.R.O., DA 6/112/12–13.

90 *V.C.H. Salop.* ii. 237; above, this article, intro.

91 Sources cited in *V.C.H. Salop.* iii. 169 n. 29.

92 S.R.O. 1224/1/23; S.P.L., stereoscopic photo. 'Broseley Waterworks'.

93 Hartshorne, *Corresp. Upon Supply of Water in Broseley*, 9.

coalpit, and described in the 1860s as 'an open cesspool', green and bubbling.[94] There were apparently few private wells. Rainwater was sold, and in the mid 19th century a barrel of water from Wenlock made an acceptable gift.[95] Broseley Wood was better supplied from the Cob and Footroad wells and the 'mine spout' in Benthall. About 1840 a reservoir was built to store Down well water, largely at the expense of the banker George Pritchard, but it soon fractured owing to mining subsidence. In 1861 a local doctor, F. H. Hartshorne, found a good supply in his garden. At Pritchard's instigation it was made freely available to the public and the Delph was filled in. Pritchard's death in 1861 led to a dispute between Hartshorne and the local board over payment for the water. Hartshorne cut off his supply, but the board dug a deeper well nearby. At the same time the leaking reservoir was repaired and an ornate Pritchard memorial fountain, designed by Robert Griffiths,[96] was erected in the Square. The fountain was intended to provide water for the poor, but the water's high iron content rendered it unusable. The fountain was demolished in 1947.[97]

About 1885 Broseley local board built a storage tank at Down well[98] and in 1896–8 the district committee laid on piped supplies from bore holes at Posenhall and a spring adjoining Willey Hall.[99] About 1902 the Madeley & Broseley Water Works began to supply water from Harrington and *c.* 1946 Broseley also began to receive water from Beckbury.[1] Jackfield, where Severn water was still drunk in 1913, received water from Madeley via a main on the Free bridge by 1936.[2]

Sewage disposal, as in Madeley on the opposite bank of the Severn, remained inadequate until the late 1960s with large amounts of sewage discharged into the river.[3] Attempts between *c.* 1909 and *c.* 1914 to make the district committee adhere to the 1876 Rivers Pollution Prevention Act were fruitless.[4] Coalport sewage works at Gitchfield serving south Telford and Broseley opened in 1970.[5]

A board of health, including three local surgeons, operated during the cholera epidemic between 1831 and 1833 and Calcutts House became a hospital.[6] Wenlock Municipal Borough Small Pox Hospital opened in the parish in 1903 with eight beds.[7] It closed in the late 1920s.[8] The Lady Forester Memorial Hospital, opened in Church Street in 1907, was designed in a 'cottage' style, with timber framed and pebble dashed buildings. It had 24 beds and special wards for radium treatment; there were 30 beds in 1941.[9] In 1948 it became part of the National Health Service. In 1984 the hospital had fifteen beds, and the Lady Forester Trust continued to give grants for new equipment and improvements.[10]

Gas was supplied from 1844 by the Ironbridge Gas Light Co., and by 1847 street lighting in Broseley was well advanced.[11] In 1850 Wenlock borough council assumed the powers of lighting inspector for Broseley.[12] The Broseley Gas & Coke Co. was formed with local shareholders in 1872 when a gasworks was built at Ladywood and the existing network of pipes and appliances in Broseley parish was bought from the Ironbridge company.[13] The number of street lamps in Broseley and Jackfield rose from 21 in 1922, to 49 in 1932, and 68 in 1936.[14]

Electricity was available in Broseley by 1934, although parts of Jackfield remained unconnected in 1956.[15]

Broseley had a receiving house of the Shifnal–London fast horse mail by 1790.[16]

Fear of vagrants led to the construction of a parish lock-up at the Hole-in-the-Wall *c.* 1832, the cost being borne by subscribers and the poor rate. It was insecure and escapes were made via its closet and a sewer.[17]

Broseley Association for the Prosecution of Felons was formed in the later 18th century. Annual dinners ceased during the First World War, the last reward was paid in 1934, and the association was wound up in 1959.[18]

Broseley did not have a fire brigade until 1904. In 1905 it was uniformed and rented a room in the town hall, and covered the area encompassed by Broseley's water supply. A station at Jackfield closed in 1911, and that at Broseley was reduced to auxiliary status in 1938. The station finally closed in 1947 although the brigade agreed to continue as an unpaid 'rural fire party'.[19]

A mortuary chapel, probably designed by G. C. Haddon of Hereford, was built *c.* 1883[20] on

94 Para. based on ibid. 14 and *passim*; idem, *Supply of Water in Broseley and the Pritchard Memorial* (Birm. 1863), 4–6 and *passim* (copy in S.R.O. 2870/1); idem, *Letter to Geo. Maw Esq.* (1864) (copy in S.R.O. 2870/1); S.P.L., MS. 2366, pp. 43–4; S.R.O. 1190/4/529.

95 Cf. *Shrews. Chron.* 19 June 1936, p. 13.

96 *Kelly's Dir. Salop.* (1900), 45.

97 W.B.R., Broseley dist. cttee. min. bk. 1946–52, p. 65; pl. 21.

98 S.R.O. 1681/58/6.

99 Ibid. /41/39–55.

1 A. H. S. Waters, *Rep. on Water Supply* (S.C.C. 1946), 17–18; *V.C.H. Salop.* xi. 58; *Shropshire Mag.* July 1972, 23.

2 *Midland Evening News*, 5 June 1913; *Shrews. Chron.* 19 June 1936, p. 13.

3 S.R.O., DA 6/119/1, pp. 375–6; *V.C.H. Salop.* xi. 58–9.

4 39 & 40 Vic. c. 75; S.R.O. 119/82.

5 *V.C.H. Salop.* xi. 59; inf. from Severn–Trent Water Auth.

6 S.R.O. 604, box 19, proc. Broseley bd. of health 1831–3; Randall, *Broseley*, 236.

7 *Kelly's Dir. Salop.* (1913), 50.

8 Ibid. (1926), 50; not in (1929), 51.

9 Ibid. (1913), 50; (1941), 50.

10 Inf. from Salop. Health Auth.

11 S.R.O. 1491/15, 8 and 24 Nov. 1843; 7 Feb. 1845; 5 Feb. 1847.

12 W.B.R., B2/2/15.

13 S.R.O. 1349/20, 18 July, 1 Aug., 16 Aug. 1872; O.S. Map 6", Salop. XLIII. SW. (1903 edn.); Mugridge, *Hist. Jackfield*, 34.

14 W.B.R., Broseley dist. cttee. min. bk. 1922–30, p. 9; 1930–7, pp. 107, 373.

15 Ibid. 1930–7, p. 187; S.R.O., DA 6/112/12, 6 June 1956.

16 *Brit. Mailcoach*, xxix (June 1981), 3.

17 S.R.O. 2991/V/1, 27 Jan. 1831, 23 July 1832; Randall, *Broseley*, 239–40.

18 *Shropshire Mag.* Apr. 1963, pp. 22–3; *Jnl. Wilkinson Soc.* ix. 10–13.

19 W.B.R., Broseley dist. cttee. min. bk. 1897–1906, pp. 287, 291, 371, 412; 1906–13, p. 312; 1937–42, pp. 191–2; 1946–52, pp. 48, 58; *Shropshire Star*, 3 Mar. 1981, p. 19.

20 W.B.R., Broseley local bd. min. bk. 1876–86, pp. 248–9, 301, 360; cf. N. Pevsner, *Herefs.* (1963), 119, 128, 279, for probable identification of 'Mr. Haddon'.

land which the local board of health had bought for a cemetery *c.* 1881. The local board was constituted the burial board in 1884 and the cemetery opened in 1885.[21]

CHURCHES. A parson was serving Broseley chapel *c.* 1230, and there had probably been a chapel there since the 12th century or earlier.[22] In the Middle Ages the priest was sometimes called chaplain, sometimes rector. The benefice did not then include cure of souls. Broseley remained part of the parish of Holy Trinity, Much Wenlock, in 1332 and long after, and the chapel owed an annual pension to Wenlock priory in 1331. There was, however, presentation and institution to the living, usually described as a rectory.[23] The rectory was combined with Linley 1528–1930 and with Benthall from 1930.[24] Broseley's independence of Much Wenlock was probably achieved in 1595 with the grant of burial rights.[25]

The advowson descended with the manor by 1279, the coparceners exercising turns.[26] By 1359, and still in 1422, the patrons nominated the chaplain to the prior of Wenlock who then presented him to the bishop.[27] After 1363, when the priory acquired a third of the manor, the right of nomination to the prior remained with the holders of the other thirds.[28] For part of the 14th century the king held the priory's rights as those of an alien house.[29] After the priory's surrender in 1540[30] its right of presentation to the bishop seems to have lapsed to the owners of the manor and merged with the right of nomination to become a normal advowson. The two thirds of the advowson that had not belonged to the priory descended with the respective two thirds (later the whole) of the manor to John and Mary Cage.[31] In 1618 their right of advowson was included in the property that they sold to William Porter and that he sold to John Weld in 1620.[32] The other third of the advowson, formerly the priory's right of nomination, though it had lapsed after 1363, may have been the advowson claimed later by the Lacon family and bought by Weld in 1618.[33] Nevertheless there is no record of the Lacons having bought the third share of the advowson from the Crown since 1540, and the origin of their claim is as obscure as their claim to manorial rights in Broseley.[34] From 1620 the Weld (later Forester and Weld-Forester) family enjoyed an unchallenged right to the advowson,[35] and Lord Forester was patron in 1985.[36]

The rectory was worth £6 13*s.* 4*d.* in 1291[37] and £8 in 1379.[38] The gross value of Broseley and Linley combined was £8 5*s.* 8*d.* in 1535[39] and £7 18*s.* 8½*d. c.* 1708.[40] In the 17th and 18th centuries there were *c.* 11 a. of glebe scattered in Broseley and 1 a. in Linley.[41] In 1801 it was proposed to sell two houses to exonerate the living from the land tax.[42] The rector's glebe had been consolidated into three closes by 1840, and his tithes were commuted to £453.[43]

In the early 17th century the parsonage stood south-west of the church.[44] It was rebuilt in brick on the same site in the mid 19th century.

James, chaplain of Broseley (occ. *c.* 1240), was perhaps a stipendiary curate.[45] Medieval pluralists included Robert Turberville, incumbent *c.* 1290–1300, who was also rector of Wheathill and a prebendary of St. Mary's, Bridgnorth.[46] Richard of Pitchford, presumably a relative of one of the lords of Broseley, was rector *c.* 1300 and also held the cure of 'Covelham'.[47] He was succeeded in 1310 by his brother Geoffrey of Pitchford (d. by 1332), who also held a cure near Bray (Berks.).[48] Geoffrey was twice granted leave of absence; in 1314 to study for three years, and in 1320 to attend a baron of the Exchequer for two years.[49] Geoffrey's successor John Aaron was rector of Broseley until 1359 and of Madeley 1323–44.[50] Thomas Yate, rector 1414–22, apparently had a chaplain in 1416.[51] Edmund Mychell (d. 1555), first known rector of Broseley and Linley, was a former monk of Buildwas,[52] as was John Lee (or Lye) minister in 1560.[53] John Huxley, rector 1572–1616, left many local descendants.[54]

The first known graduate incumbent, Edmund Barton, instituted 1617,[55] was ejected 1642 × 1646 and Robert Ogdon, M.A., instituted.[56] In 1648, however, Barton as 'pastor of Broseley' signed *A Testimony of the Ministers in the Province of Salop*,[57] and he was minister in 1651.[58]

21 S.R.O. 1681/58/2; /116/22; Heref. Dioc. Regy., reg. 1883–1901, pp. 57–9.
22 Eyton, ii. 33–4.
23 Ibid. 34–6; Mumford, *Wenlock in Middle Ages*, 101; *Cal. Pat.* 1348–50, 189; below, this section.
24 *Reg. Bothe* (C.S.), 200; *Lond. Gaz.* 28 Feb. 1930, p. 1286; cf. below, Linley, church.
25 S.R.O. 322, box 6, grant of bur. rights. An appeal for bur. rights in 1542 had not succeeded: *T.S.A.S.* vi. 101, 116.
26 *Reg. Cantilupe* (C.S.), 237; *Reg. Swinfield* (C.S.), 539; T. F. Dukes, *Antiquities of Salop.* (1844), 263; cf. above, manor.
27 *Cal. Pat.* 1358–61, 264; S.R.O. 228/1; cf. above, Badger, church.
28 *Cal. Pat.* 1361–4, 393; S.R.O. 228/1; cf. above, manor.
29 *Cal. Pat.* 1358–61, 264; 1385–9, 26; *V.C.H. Salop.* ii. 42.
30 *V.C.H. Salop.* ii. 45.
31 *Dioc. of Heref. Institutions (1539–1900)*, ed. A. T. Bannister (Heref. 1923), 21, 28; H.W.R.O.(H.), Heref. dioc. rec. AL 19/16, f. 139; cf. above, manor.
32 S.R.O. 1224/3/234, 242; cf. above, manor.
33 H.W.R.O.(H.), Heref. dioc. rec. AL 19/16, f. 139; P.R.O., CP 25/2/343/16 Jas. I Trin. [no. 6]; cf. above, manor.
34 Above, manor.
35 Ibid. and sources there cited; Bannister *Heref. Institutions*, s.v. Broseley.
36 *Heref. Dioc. Yr. Bk.* (1985), 51.
37 *Tax. Eccl.* (Rec. Com.), 167.
38 Eyton, ii. 34.
39 Below, this section; *Valor Eccl.* (Rec. Com.), iii. 208.
40 J. Ecton, *Liber Valorum et Decimarum* (1711), 147.
41 S.R.O. 2991/Gl/1; 4427/T/1; H.W.R.O.(H), HD 2/14/13–14.
42 S.R.O. 515/4, p. 247.
43 P.R.O., IR 29/29/55; IR 30/29/55, fields 842, 852, 1082.
44 S.R.O. 1224/1/32–3.
45 Eyton, ii. 34 n.
46 Ibid. 35; *V.C.H. Salop.* ii. 125.
47 Eyton, ii. 35. 'Covelham' has not been identified.
48 Ibid.; *Reg. Swinfield* (C.S.), 539.
49 *Reg. Swinfield*, 546; *Reg. Orleton* (C.S.), 391.
50 Eyton, ii. 35; *Reg. Trillek* (C.S.), 48; *V.C.H. Salop.* xi. 61.
51 *Reg. Mascall* (C.S.), 180, 182; *Reg. Spofford* (C.S.), 350.
52 *T.S.A.S.* vi. 108, 110, 122.
53 Ibid. lx. 104.
54 Bannister, *Heref. Institutions*, 21, 28; Langley, *Par. Regs. of Broseley*, i. 16; above, manor.
55 *T.S.A.S.* 3rd ser. v. 361.
56 Ibid. 3rd ser. vii. 270; Bannister, op. cit. 28; S.R.O. 215/17; L. F. Peltor, *Linley (Broseley) Salop.: Short Acct. of Par., its Church and People* (1977), 15 (copy in S.P.L.).
57 *T.S.A.S.* 3rd ser. vii. 270; *Calamy Revised*, ed. A. G. Matthews, 33, 556.
58 P.R.O., E 339/1/5.

Ogdon later regained the living and held it until his death in 1680 probably with his nephew as curate from 1671. In the 1670s Ogdon also served as schoolmaster and was rector of Willey.[59] He was active against Quakers in Broseley, as was his successor John Crow, rector 1680–9.[60]

In 1716 there was an unlicensed curate and communion was celebrated at the main feasts.[61] By 1749 and until at least 1840 sacrament money was distributed among the poor. At first *c.* 4*d.* each was given to 10–15 people two or three times a year,[62] while in the year 1808–9 £14 17*s.* 6*d.* was distributed among many poor. In the 1830s fewer people received larger sums.[63]

R. C. Hartshorne, rector 1727–52, was also rector of Badger.[64] From the 18th century long incumbencies were usual in Broseley, notably those of Daniel Hemus, 1752–99,[65] and his successor Dr. Townshend Forester, brother of Cecil Forester (later Weld-Forester, cr. Baron Forester 1821). Forester held several other livings.[66] His curate 1817–18 was a bogus cleric, 'W. C. Gregory', actually Lawrence Hynes ('Henry') Halloran (1764–1831). Exposed, and convicted of forging a postal frank, Halloran was transported to Australia where he became a notable educational pioneer.[67] C. H. Hartshorne, the antiquary and a native of Broseley (d. 1865), was curate *c.* 1827–8.[68] Dr. Forester was succeeded by his nephew O. W. W. Weld-Forester, rector 1842–59,[69] author of tracts and sermons and eventually (1886) 4th Lord Forester; the church was rebuilt in his time.[70] On Census Sunday 1851 there was a morning congregation of 320 adults and 286 children, an afternoon one of 53 and 18 respectively, and an evening one of 490 adults.[71] Weld-Forester's successor R. H. Cobbold, rector 1859–73 and formerly archdeacon of Ning-po, published an ethnographic work, *Pictures of the Chinese Drawn by Themselves* (1860). During Cobbold's time and for the rest of the century there were morning and evening Sunday services with monthly communion. Communicants averaged *c.* 40 in 1859 and *c.* 30 in 1882. By 1926 there were three Sunday services and communion was weekly.[72]

A stipendiary curate was sometimes appointed to serve Linley in the later 19th century.[73]

All Saints' church hall opened in 1961.[74]

A mission church at Broseley Wood opened *c.* 1928 in the former Primitive Methodist chapel. There was weekly evensong and monthly communion 1931–46; communion was weekly or fortnightly from 1955 until the church closed in 1971.[75]

The church of *ST. LEONARD*, so known by *c.* 1740,[76] comprised a west tower, nave with south porch, and chancel; a north aisle was added *c.* 1618, apparently at the instigation of Richard Old,[77] and a timber framed eastward extension of the chancel was built in 1654. A three-decker pulpit with tester stood in the south-east corner of the nave, while pews occupied the nave, aisle, and chancel. In 1701 the font stood in the centre of the west end of the nave, and south doors pierced the west end of the nave, and the chancel.[78]

In 1707 a brief was issued for rebuilding[79] which began probably after 1710 and was complete by 1716.[80] The new, much larger church[81] retained the squat, two-stage, crenellated and pinnacled stone tower, probably partly refenestrated during the rebuilding.[82] New work consisted of a four bayed nave (53 ft. 4 in. long) and two bayed chancel (24 ft. 8 in. by 20 ft. 4 in.), both with south doors, and a south nave porch, all of brick with stone details, including rusticated quoins and a balustrade surmounting the porch. It was lit by round headed and circular windows. There was a west gallery.[83] A north gallery, largely for the poor, was added in 1749 by Mrs. Susanna Barrett, while the chancel was completely covered by a gallery built 1794–5.[84] By 1815 a large aisle and a north vestry had been added, and an organ had been put in the west gallery.[85] There was a well paid organist from 1835.[86] The church then had *c.* 782 kneelings; 168 were free but largely appropriated to Sunday school children.[87]

In 1841 the vestry decided to rebuild the church at an estimated cost of £3,000. It first intended to build nearer the main centre of population at Broseley Wood, but no stable site was found and the old one was retained.[88] *ALL SAINTS'*, built 1843–5 by William Exley & Sons to a design of Harvey Eginton,[89] was in a 'serious' Perpendicular style 'rather Somerset in

59 S.R.O. 2991/2, s.a. 1679; H.W.R.O.(H.), HD 5/2, bk. 23, s.v. Broseley; HD 7, Rob. Ogdon to bp.'s chaplain 1671; below, Willey, church.

60 *T.S.A.S.* 3rd ser. v. 374; 4th ser. ii. 76; v. 306–7; below, prot. nonconf.

61 H.W.R.O.(H.), HD 5/14/1/9.

62 S.R.O. 2991/P/1.

63 Ibid. /P/2.

64 Bannister, *Heref. Institutions*, 70, 89, 91.

65 *T.S.A.S.* 4th ser. ii. 106; vi. 328.

66 Ibid. 4th ser. vi. 328; *V.C.H. Salop.* xi. 90; Burke, *Peerage* (1938), 1035; *Rep. Com. Eccl. Revenues* [67], pp. 432–3, H.C. (1835), xxii.

67 K. Grose, 'Dr. Halloran—Pioneer Convict Schoolmaster in New S. Wales: Study of his Background', *Australian Jnl. Educ.* xiv. 303–24; *D.N.B.*

68 *D.N.B.*; E. Glasgow, *Hartshorne, Charles Henry* (pamph. issued with *The Eagle* (mag. of St. John's Coll. Camb.), East. 1984).

69 Bannister, *Heref. Institutions*, 158, 174.

70 B.M. *Gen. Cat. of Printed Bks. to 1955* (photolithographic edn. 1959–66), lxxv, col. 525; below, this section.

71 P.R.O., HO 129/358, no. 29.

72 S.R.O. 2991/SRg/1–2; *T.C.S.V.F.C.* x. 81.

73 Below, Linley, church.

74 Jackson, 'Madeley', bk. 3A, p. 138.

75 S.R.O. 2991/Mi/1–4; C. R. Jones, *Some Records of Broseley and Dist.* (Shrews. 1939), 6 (copy in S.P.L.).

76 B.L. Add. MS. 30316, f. 29v.

77 S.P.L., Deeds 14943; S.R.O. 1224/1/32; /3/575.

78 S.R.O. 163/5; 314/8–9; 1224/3/769–70.

79 *T.S.A.S.* x. 25; W. A. Bewes, *Ch. Briefs* (1896), 300.

80 S.R.O. 1224/3/771.

81 Ibid. /3/773.

82 For illustr. of church see S.P.L., MS. 3065, no. 32; MS. 372, vol. i, f. 116; J. H. Smith colln., nos. 35, 253; B.L. Add. MS. 21181, p. 14.

83 S.R.O. 314/11; 1224/3/772–4; Birm. Univ. Libr., Mytton Papers, i. 195–7.

84 S.R.O. 1681/116/2; 2991/Cy/1; B.L. Add. MS. 21181, p. 14.

85 B.L. Add. MS. 21181, p. 14; S.R.O. 1681/116/40, application for aid towards increasing accom. [in Broseley ch.] 18 Oct. 1842; 1681/116/5.

86 S.R.O. 2991/ChW/1, s.a.

87 S.R.O. 1681/116/40, printed pamph. *re* rebldg. n.d.

88 Ibid.; S.R.O. 2991/Ve/1, 4 June 1841; *Salopian Jnl.* 27 Apr. 1842, p. 3.

89 S.R.O. 1681/116/38–9; 2991/Ch/1, 18 Apr., 3 May 1842.

character'.[90] The actual cost was £9,474, raised mainly by subscriptions.[91] The church had chancel, clerestoried nave with north and south aisles, two storeyed south porch, south vestry, north, south, and west galleries, and a west tower containing six bells. The stone came from Corbatch dingle. Of the 1,240 seats 546 were rented.[92] During the rebuilding, when structural difficulties led to modification of Eginton's design, services were held in the town hall.[93] Choir stalls were fitted in 1890 when the church was reordered.[94] Glass by Kempe was installed about the same time. The tower pinnacles were removed *c.* 1950[95] and the north and south galleries taken down during a reordering in the late 1970s,[96] when a reredos by G. F. Bodley, formerly at Eardisley (Herefs.), was fitted.[97]

The graveyard was extended in 1840 and 1880.[98] The registers are complete from 1570.[99]

The church of *ST. MARY*, Jackfield, was built in 1759 as a chapel of ease to Broseley at Mary Browne's expense. Surplice fees were reserved to the rector of Broseley, and in 1766 Mrs. Anne Browne, of Benthall, endowed the curacy with £20 a year and the clerk with £2 10*s.* a year out of Woodhouse farm.[1] The curacy or perpetual curacy (as it was called in 1835) was in the gift of the owners of the Broseley Hall estate.[2] It was worth £40 in 1835, which was paid to the curate who served there.[3] In 1861 George Pritchard left £150 a year for the Jackfield curacy provided that Jackfield was constituted a separate ecclesiastical parish.[4] Jackfield parish was accordingly formed out of Broseley in 1862.[5] The patronage of the new living was divided between Francis Harries of Cruckton, owner of Broseley Hall, and the rector of Broseley, presenting alternately.[6] The patronage was conveyed to the bishop of Hereford in 1927.[7]

In 1851 attendance averaged 53 adults and 125 children in the morning, 110 adults and 50 children in the evening. Evening service was held in the National school at Calcutts,[8] as the church stood some distance from the riverside settlement.

A parish room opened in 1931.[9]

In 1863 the living was worth £104 derived from £1,000 given by George Pritchard together with a matching grant by the Ecclesiastical Commissioners, £20 from Queen Anne's Bounty, and £20 from Woodhouse farm, the latter a revision of the original endowment.[10] The income was augmented by £24 10*s.* in 1864 when the rectorial tithes arising from Jackfield were annexed to the living,[11] which became a rectory in 1866.[12] Following a benefaction and further endowments the living was worth £150 in 1871, £170 in 1900, and £348 in 1932.[13]

In 1851 the curate lived close to the church at Rock House;[14] in 1891 the rector resided at the Dunge in Broseley.[15] A parsonage, designed by Ewan Christian, was built in 1893 near Rock House. It stood 1 km. south-west of the new church.[16] The site, convenient for the old church, had been given in 1865 by W. O. Foster.[17]

Old St. Mary's, reputedly designed by T. F. Pritchard,[18] was of red brick with stone dressings and comprised nave, chancel, and west tower with flanking vestries.[19] Its details suggest the influence of Gibbs's *Book of Architecture* (1738).[20] It seated 188 adults, and 88 children in a gallery.[21] It had a graveyard which served Jackfield until at least 1879. In 1832 a cholera burial ground opened nearby.[22] The Pritchard Memorial, or new, church, built by subscription, opened at Calcutts in 1863 on land given by Francis Harries.[23] Annual services continued at the old church until the 1920s,[24] but it was demolished *c.* 1961, having been ruinous for several decades.[25] The new church, known by 1870 as St. Mary's,[26] was designed by Arthur Blomfield in the 'French pointed' style. Built of stone and locally made polychrome bricks and tiles, the church comprised nave, south porch, and polygonal apse. It seated 312 adults and 84 children.[27] A vestry was added in 1873–4.[28] In

90 Pevsner, *Salop.* 86.
91 S.R.O. 2991/Ch/1, abstr. of expenses.
92 S.R.O. 1681/116/5; H. B. Walters, *Ch. Bells of Salop.* (Oswestry, 1915), 65–6; inf. from Mr. J. D. Roberts.
93 S.R.O. 2991/Ch/1, 3 Jan. 1843; *Jnl. Wilkinson Soc.* ii. 3.
94 *Salopian Shreds & Patches*, ix. 271; Heref. Dioc. Regy., reg. 1883–1901, pp. 265–7.
95 *Jnl. Wilkinson Soc.* ii. 3.
96 Local inf.; Heref. Dioc. Regy., reg. 1969– (in use), pp. 254–5, 283, 311, 405.
97 Inf. from the late Mr. D. C. George.
98 S.R.O. 1681/116/20, 40 (bill *re* churchyd. consecration 8 July 1840).
99 S.R.O. 2991/Rg/1–11; /BRg/1–2; /MRg/1–7; regs. at ch.; Langley, *Par. Regs. of Broseley*.
1 S.R.O. 1681/116/23–4.
2 Ibid. /116/24; /116/27, case and opinion 27 June 1862; Lewis, *Topog. Dict. Eng.* (1835); above, manor.
3 *Rep. Com. Eccl. Revenues* [67], pp. 450–1, H.C. (1835), xxii.
4 S.R.O. 2991/Misc/2.
5 *Lond. Gaz.* 7 Feb. (pp. 651–3), 22 July (p. 3654) 1862.
6 Heref. Dioc. Regy., reg. 1857–69, pp. 209–10.
7 Ibid. reg. 1926–38, p. 47.
8 P.R.O., HO 129/358, no. 30; S.R.O. 1681/116/31, Potts & Son to T. Evans 20 July 1863.
9 *Kelly's Dir. Salop.* (1937), 124.
10 S.R.O. 1681/116/31, corresp. with Eccl. Com. *re* Jackfield 1861–3.
11 Ibid. Eccl. Com. to Potts & Son 14 May 1864; 1681/116/32, deed 7 June 1864; Heref. Dioc. Regy., reg. 1857–69, p. 403.
12 S.R.O. 1681/116/31, Eccl. Com. to Potts & Son 14 May 1864; *Lond. Gaz.* 13 Nov. 1866, p. 5998.
13 E. Cassey & Co. *Dir. Salop.* (1871), 93; *Kelly's Dir. Salop.* (1900), 111; *Crockford* (1932), 870; *Lond. Gaz.* 22 July 1862, p. 3654; 10 Jan. 1865, p. 121; 19 June 1868, p. 3442.
14 S. Bagshaw, *Dir. Salop.* (1851), 562; O.S. Map 1/2,500, Salop. LI. 2 (1882 edn.).
15 *Kelly's Dir. Salop.* (1891), 279.
16 S.R.O. 2337/5; O.S. Map 1/2,500, LI. 2 (1902 edn.).
17 Heref. Dioc. Regy., reg. 1857–69, pp. 486–8.
18 S.P.L., Deeds 18498. There is no doc. proof of Pritchard's involvement, but it is stylistically poss. Thanks are due to Mr. J. B. Lawson for comment.
19 J. H. Smith colln. nos. 113, 255; MS. 372, vol. iii, f. 64; pl. 28.
20 Cf. pls. 26–7 of that bk., depicting All Sts., Derby (ref. supplied by Dr. T. Friedman, who drew attention to the parallels).
21 S.R.O. 1681/116/30. 22 Randall, *Broseley*, 212–13.
23 S.R.O. 2991/Misc/2; Heref. Dioc. Regy., reg. 1857–69, pp. 357–9.
24 *Jnl. Wilkinson Soc.* ii. 4.
25 Pevsner, *Salop.* 158; S.P.L., photo. neg. B. 190; Heref. Dioc. Regy., reg. 1919–26, p. 28 (sale of fittings); 1953–68, pp. 340, 353 (demolition). 26 *P.O. Dir. Salop.* (1870), 26.
27 Pevsner, *Salop.* 158; S.R.O. 1681/116/30.
28 *Ch. Cal. Dioc. Heref.* (1875), 113.

1960 a reredos made of hand painted tiles was installed.[29]

ROMAN CATHOLICISM. Ten papists were listed in 1676[30] and 7 in 1767, including Edward Purcell, lord of the manor.[31] In 1869 Broseley became a preaching station; a house was used as a school and for mass. In 1888 an iron church opened on land whose purchase was assisted by Lord Acton. St. Winifred's, west of Barber Row, was served originally from Madeley but by 1900 from Shifnal; it closed in 1913.[32] In 1962 a temporary wooden church was built in Barber Row. That was replaced by a permanent building in 1979. Never a Catholic parish, Broseley was served between 1959 and 1978 from Much Wenlock and after 1981 from Dawley.[33]

PROTESTANT NONCONFORMITY. Quakers lived in Broseley by 1660, and by *c.* 1800 there were apparently flourishing Baptist and Wesleyan societies. Primitive and Independent Methodist societies began to meet in the 1830s when Broseley was considered to be fairly 'open', and on the evening of Census Sunday 1851 526 adult nonconformists worshipped in the parish as opposed to 601 Anglicans. There was not always harmony between Anglicans and nonconformists: in the earlier 1860s the Pritchards' bank engaged in a public correspondence against street preaching, and nonconformist meetings were not permitted in the town hall.[34] The Plymouth Brethren arrived in the 1860s, and the Broseley Brotherhood was established in the 1930s. This section treats the Quakers, Baptists, Methodists, Congregationalists, Plymouth Brethren, and Broseley Brotherhood in that order, the order of their establishment in the parish.

Quakers, present in the parish by 1660,[35] were distrained for unpaid tithes in 1673, and in 1676 there were three protestant nonconformists in the parish.[36] Particular meetings probably began *c.* 1684, whence births are recorded.[37] A meeting house was built off Duke Street in 1691–2[38] and land for a burial ground was bought in 1706.[39] The most prominent members of the meeting were the Darbys of Coalbrookdale, and Abraham Darby (I) was buried in Broseley in 1717. After the Coalbrookdale meeting house opened in 1741 the Friends ceased to meet at Broseley regularly. Nevertheless, the meeting house (possibly rebuilt in 1769) remained open until 1778.[40]

A chapel for Particular Baptists was built in 1741 and opened in 1742 in what became known as Chapel Lane. It was paid for by Isaac Wyke, a surgeon, who told neighbours he was building a 'house to cure mad people'; he may have constructed a baptism pool just over the Benthall boundary, perhaps representing it as a medicinal cold bath. By 1749 there were about fifteen members and their meeting became a church. At times in the 1770s there were over 150 worshippers. About 1801, following a dispute between the members, the Birch Meadow chapel was opened. The original membership, or Old Baptists, declined in numbers during the 19th century, from 66 in 1803, to 39 in 1827, and 17 in 1878.[41] Worshippers on the morning of Census Sunday 1851 included 96 adults.[42] The brick chapel, extended to the west in the mid 19th century, seated 300. Attached on the south were a schoolroom and manse, both of about the same date as the original chapel.[43] A detached schoolroom was added in 1949.[44] There was a membership of *c.* 20 in 1985.[45] The chapel possesses a two-handled silver communion cup presented in 1763.

Half the cost of the new Birch Meadow chapel was borne in 1801 by the ironmaster John Guest.[46] It had 100 free and 250 paid seats; on Census Sunday 1851 morning service was attended by 90 adults, evening service by 120, about 80 below average in the latter case.[47] As at the Old Baptist chapel numbers declined in the later 19th century, when Calvinism was preached, and there were 33 members in 1872.[48] The chapel, which had a burial ground, closed *c.* 1927.[49]

Wesleyan meetings in Madeley in the time of the Methodist vicar J. W. Fletcher (vicar 1760–85) were attended by people from Broseley parish.[50] John Wesley preached at Broseley in 1773, 1774, 1779, and 1781.[51] A Wesleyan chapel was reputedly first erected in Broseley in 1772; it apparently moved site at least once before 1811.[52] In the early 1800s the congregation sought to celebrate Holy Communion, and in 1815 Broseley was made the centre of a circuit covering most of the southern half of the coal-

29 Heref. Dioc. Regy., reg. 1953–68, p. 343.

30 *T.S.A.S.* 2nd ser. i. 90.

31 *Worcs. Recusant*, xxv. 30; S.R.O., q. sess. rec. parcel 281, reg. of papists' deeds 1717–88, p. 45; above, manor; *V.C.H. Staffs.* xvii. 240.

32 *Kelly's Dir. Salop.* (1885–1913); E. M. Abbott, *Hist. Dioc. Shrews. 1850–1986* [1987], 47–8.

33 W.B.R., Broseley dist. cttee. min. bk. 1902–6, pp. 74–5; *V.C.H. Salop.* xi. 67; Abbott, op. cit. 47–8; below, M. Wenlock, Rom. Cath.; inf. from the Revd. A. Elder.

34 Below, this section; Trinder, *Ind. Rev. Salop.* 161; Hartshorne, *Corresp. Upon Supply of Water in Broseley*, 25, 120.

35 S.R.O. 5709, Wenlock boro. q. sess. order bk. p. 4.

36 Above, churches; *T.S.A.S.* 2nd ser. i. 90; 4th ser. v. 306; Randall, *Broseley*, 219.

37 P.R.O., RG 6/1327.

38 H.W.R.O.(H.), Heref. dioc. rec. AL 19/20, f. 134v.; Friends' Ho. Libr., Yearly Meetings' Mins. i (1692), p. 298; H.W.R.O.(W.), ref. 898.2 BA 1204/21, pp. 15–16.

39 *T.S.A.S.* lix. 124; H.W.R.O.(W.), ref. 898.2 BA 1204/21, pp. 15–16.

40 *T.S.A.S.* lix. 126; *V.C.H. Salop.* xi. 68; H.W.R.O.(H.), HD 5/14/1/9; R.C.H.M.E. *Inv. of Nonconf. Chapels and Meeting-hos. in Central Eng.* (1986), 192–3.

41 Randall, *Broseley*, 222–6; R. F. Chambers, *Strict Baptist Chapels of Eng.* iv [?1963], 46; Dr. Williams's Libr., 'Prot. Dissenting Congregations' (MS.), iv. For Wyke see also above, this article, intro.; Benthall, nonconf.

42 P.R.O., HO 129/358, no. 32.

43 Randall, op. cit. 225; *Kelly's Dir. Salop.* (1905), 46; R.C.H.M.E. *Inv. Nonconf. Chapels in Central Eng.* 192.

44 Date stone.

45 Inf. from Mr. D. Oakley.

46 Trinder, *Ind. Rev. Salop.* 118. Another ironmaster, John Onions, was bur. there 1819: ibid. 118, 143.

47 P.R.O., HO 129/358, no. 56; fig. 29.

48 Trinder, op. cit. 176; Randall, *Broseley*, 226.

49 O.S. Map 1/2,500, Salop. LI. 2 (1882 edn.); *Kelly's Dir. Salop.* (1926), 50; not in (1929), 52.

50 J. Randall, *Hist. Madeley* (Madeley, 1880), 164; *V.C.H. Salop.* xi. 61–2.

51 Wesley, *Wks.* iii. 502; iv. 24–5, 146, 201.

52 Randall, *Broseley*, 227; S.R.O. 1224/3/641–2; Jones, *Records of Broseley*, 6.

Fig. 29

BROSELEY: BIRCH MEADOW SUNDAY SCHOOL IN 1864

field. Broseley chapel then had 96 members.[53] On Census Sunday 1851 there were 60 adults at the morning service and 160 at that in the evening.[54] The Duke Street chapel, seating 384 in 1940,[55] was in a classical style with pedimented porch and façade.[56] It was closed as unsafe in 1964.[57] A new chapel in blue brick replaced it in 1971.[58]

Wesleyan Methodists met regularly at Coalford by 1815[59] when there were 15 members, and a simple brick chapel opened in 1825. In 1851 it had 50 free and 60 paid seats; 30 adults attended afternoon service on Census Sunday and 35 the evening one.[60] The chapel closed in 1980.[61]

'Salthouse', presumably a meeting in Jackfield, came onto the Broseley Wesleyan circuit in 1826; it amalgamated with the Coalford meeting in 1832–3.[62]

In 1839 the Primitive Methodists opened a chapel in Broseley Wood. On Census Sunday the chapel, with 108 free and 84 paid seats, was attended by 37 adults in the afternoon and 91 in the evening. It closed *c.* 1920.[63]

Broseley was on the Dawley Green and Madeley New Connexion circuit in 1839,[64] and there was said to be a chapel in 1842.[65]

Congregationalists came to Broseley in 1837 thinking it to be a more open settlement than others in the area.[66] The disused Friends' meeting house and some adjacent land was bought, and *c.* 1841 a new chapel with 100 free and 210 rented seats was built; the meeting house became a schoolroom. The minister from 1842 to 1845 was Samuel Newth (1821–98), later professor of mathematics and ecclesiastical history and principal of New College, St. John's Wood. On Census Sunday attendance at chapel was below average: 92 adults in the morning and 120 in the evening.[67] The chapel closed in 1965 and had been demolished by 1978.[68]

The Plymouth Brethren built Gospel Rooms, later called the Victoria Hall, in High Street in 1867. Building was partly financed by the Maws.[69] About 1905 the Brethren moved to Broseley Wood, where they met until *c.* 1927.[70]

There was a Gospel Army mission room in

53 Trinder, *Ind. Rev. Salop.* 167; Shrews. Sch. Libr., Broseley circuit bk. 1815–41.
54 P.R.O., HO 129/358, no. 33.
55 Meth. Dept. for Chapel Affairs, *Meth. Church Bldgs.: Statistical Returns* (1940), 270.
56 Pl. 29; Stratton, *Broseley*, [7–8].
57 S.R.O. 4445/XVIII/1, 3 Dec. 1964.
58 O.N.S. (Birkdale), Worship Reg. no. 72683
59 Shrews. Sch. libr., Broseley circuit bk. 1815–41; Randall, *Broseley*, 84–5.
60 P.R.O., HO 129/358, no. 35.
61 S.R.O. 2533/114–15; Mugridge, *Hist. Jackfield*, 29; inf. from Mr. R. Miles.
62 Shrews. Sch. libr., Broseley circuit bk. 1815–1.
63 P.R.O., HO 129/358, no. 36; *Kelly's Dir. Salop.* (1917), 43; not in (1922), 49; above, churches.
64 Plan in S.P.L., class M 98.7 v.f.
65 Pigot, *Nat. Com. Dir.* (1842), 7.
66 Ironbridge, Shifnal, and M. Wenlock were the other places considered: Randall, *Broseley*, 229.
67 Ibid.; *Kelly's Dir. Salop.* (1905), 46; P.R.O., HO 129/358, no. 34; *D.N.B.*
68 S.R.O. 4950/1/10, T. E. Hunt to [W. T.] Hunter, 24 Nov. 1965; O.S. Map 1/10,000, SJ 60 SE. (1981 edn.).
69 Stratton, *Broseley*, p. [4]; O.S. Map 1/2,500, Salop. LI. 2 (1882 edn.); *Kelly's Dir. Salop.* (1900), 46.
70 Above, social and cultural activities; *Kelly's Dir. Salop.* (1905), 46; (1926), 50; not in (1929), 52.

Ferny Bank, Broseley Wood, in 1883. It had closed by 1896.[71]

In the 1930s the multi-denominational Broseley Brotherhood enjoyed success and was visited by nationally known speakers.[72]

EDUCATION. In the 1670s the rector was schoolmaster.[73] In 1716 a schoolmaster was teaching the catechism, and his pupils had to attend church services.[74] There was a schoolhouse in 1767,[75] and in 1770 there was one at Harris's Green and an old schoolhouse near the Delph.[76] For many years from the late 18th century a school was held in the former Quaker meeting house.[77] Schools were being kept in 1785, 1809, and 1817. The Misses Wyke kept another from 1816 to 1829 or later.[78] By 1819 there were 174–200 children attending day schools, and about the same number the Sunday school.[79]

In 1835 there were three day schools, all begun between 1823 and 1830, attended overall by 58 boys and 27 girls. Larger numbers went to the six Sunday schools. One was C.E., three (one with a lending library) were run by the Baptists, and the other two were Wesleyan. There were also four very small day and boarding schools.[80]

Until the 1890s there were usually at least two private schools in the parish.[81] Short lived were two nonconformist day schools: a Wesleyan one of *c.* 1842[82] and Broseley undenominational school (1871–4) founded by the Quaker industrialist George Maw.[83]

Madeley poor-law union school was held at Broseley, probably at the workhouse. Education given there from 1836 was very poor[84] and conditions were bad. In 1848 16 pupils under 11 were being taught by an infirm, crippled schoolmaster.[85] The matron acted as teacher from 1849[86] until 1851 when the children moved to the South-East Shropshire District school at Quatt.[87]

By 1837 there was a National school[88] which before 1843 was being held in a room, 61 × 21 ft., over the market hall.[89] In 1849 it had 205 places and attendance averaged 113; there were three pupil teachers.[90] A new National school, with three departments, was built in 1855 on a site south-west of the Square provided by Lord Forester;[91] a teacher's house adjoined. Built of blue brick to a design by Robert Griffiths in the Tudor style, the school cost £1,600; the National Society made a grant.[92] It was enlarged in 1876 to hold 550 pupils.[93] By 1852 the school was under inspection and earning pupil teachers' grants; by 1868 it also earned drawing grants and in the 1860s and 1870s night-school grants.[94] By 1878 there was a Standard VII.[95] Some pupils left to attend the undenominational school (1871–4) but returned when it closed.[96] The school was overcrowded in the 1870s and 1880s, with *c.* 400 pupils in 1885. Overcrowding became worse despite the opening of Broseley Wood C.E. Infant school in 1892, and attendance averaged *c.* 474 by 1913.[97] Seven head teachers served for long periods but assistants changed frequently.[98]

From 1939 to 1943 the school accommodated evacuees from Liverpool;[99] classes were held at the rectory[1] and the town hall.[2] Pupils aged 13 transferred to Madeley Modern school in 1950.[3] Next year the school became controlled;[4] the boys' and girls' departments amalgamated in 1952.[5] In 1958 it merged with the infant school.[6] Next year it became a primary school when 11 year-old pupils transferred to Madeley Modern school; in 1970 seniors began to attend the William Brookes Comprehensive school, Much Wenlock.[7] Accommodation had been reduced in 1937[8] and the successive schools were often overcrowded.[9] Moreover, despite improvements,[10] by the 1960s the building was outdated, inconvenient, and dreary; it had poor facilities.[11] In 1967 it was replaced by a new open-plan school in Dark Lane, with 400 places. Pupils

71 O.N.S. (Birkdale), Worship Reg. no. 27307.

72 *Shrews. Chron.* 10 July 1936; *Shropshire Star*, 3 Mar. 1981, p. 19.

73 Above, churches.

74 H.W.R.O.(H.), HD 5/14/1/9 (ref. supplied by Dr. R. Hume).

75 S.R.O. 1224/3/716.

76 Ibid. /3/370.

77 Randall, *Broseley*, 221; cf. above, prot. nonconf.

78 R. Hume, 'Changing Patterns of Educ. Devt. in Salop. 1660–1833' (Keele Univ. Ph.D. (Educ.) thesis, 1982), 170, 312–16.

79 *Educ. of Poor Digest*, H.C. 224, p. 747 (1819), ix (2).

80 *Educ. Enq. Abstract*, H.C. 62, p. 770 (1835), xlii; Bodl. MS. Top. Salop. c. 1, f. 117; *Footprints on the Track of Time during 50 yrs.: Hist. of Birchmeadow Sun. Sch., Broseley, to its Jubilee, 1864* [1864] (copy in S.P.L.).

81 Pigot, *Nat. Com. Dir.* (1835), 350; (1842), 8; *P.O. Dir. Salop.* (1856), 205; (1870), 258; *Kelly's Dir. Salop.* (1885), 1087; (1891), 577; (1895), 382; (1900), 46.

82 Pigot, *Nat. Com. Dir.* (1842), 8.

83 J. McFall, 'Educ. in Madeley Union of Salop. in 19th Cent.' (Keele Univ. M.A. (Educ.) thesis, 1973), 54–5.

84 Walsh, 'Admin. of Poor Laws', 207, 221, 239, 246–8; above, local govt.

85 *Mins. of Cttee. of Council on Educ., Schs. of Parochial Unions, 1847–9* [1111], pp. 230, 308–9, H.C. (1849), xlii.

86 Ibid. *1848–50* [1256], p. 169, H.C. (1850), xliii.

87 Ibid. *1850–2* [1532], pp. 300, 315, H.C. (1852), xxxix.

88 Hulbert, *Hist. Salop.* ii. 343.

89 McFall, 'Educ. in Madeley Union', 43; S. Bagshaw, *Dir. Salop.* (1851), 557; S.R.O. 1564/44.

90 *Mins. of Educ. Cttee. of Council, 1849–50* [1215], p. ccxxvii, H.C. (1850), xliii.

91 *P.O. Dir. Salop.* (1856), 23; *S.C.C. Mins. (Educ.)* 1966–7, 214.

92 McFall, 'Educ. in Madeley Union', 46–7, 144, 148; Stratton, *Broseley*, p. [4]; S.R.O. 1564/45–6.

93 *Kelly's Dir. Salop.* (1885), 814.

94 McFall, op. cit. 109, 113, 115, 117. The sch. was lit by gas by 1863: ibid. 164.

95 Ibid. 164.

96 Ibid. 54–5.

97 Ibid. 51, 134, 154; Broseley Nat. Inf. sch. log bk. (at Broseley C.E. (Contr.) Primary sch.), reps. 1900, 1914; *Kelly's Dir. Salop.* (1885), 814; (1905), 115; (1913), 50.

98 McFall, op. cit. 217; Broseley Nat. (later C.E.) sch. log bks. (at Broseley C.E. (Contr.) Primary sch.), *passim.*

99 Girls' sch. log bk. 11 Sept. 1939; 10 July 1942; 29 Jan. 1943; Boys' sch. log bk. 6 Jan. 1941.

1 Boys' sch. log bk. 30 May 1940.

2 Girls' sch. log bk. 1 Sept. 1941.

3 Ibid. 4 Sept. 1950.

4 Mixed sch. log bk. rep. 1955.

5 Ibid. 2 Sept. 1952.

6 Broseley C.E. (Contr.) Mixed and Inf. sch. log bk. (at Broseley C.E. (Contr.) Primary sch.), 7 Jan. 1958.

7 Broseley C.E. (Contr.) Primary sch. log bk. (at the sch.), 1 Sept. 1959; 24 June 1970.

8 Boys' sch. log bk. 7 Jan. 1937.

9 Log bks. *passim.*

10 Boys' sch. log bk. Christmas 1923; 31 July 1925; 12 Sept. 1932; 5 Sept. 1933; *S.C.C. Mins. (Educ.)* 1950–1, 26; Inf. sch. log bk. rep. 1952.

11 Log bks. (e.g. Boys' sch. rep. 1925; Girls' sch. reps. 1929, 1932, 1948; Inf. sch. reps. 1939, 1952; Mixed sch. rep. 1955; Primary sch. rep. 1965).

from the closed Broseley Wood C.E. (Controlled) Infant school were admitted.[12] Within two years the school was overcrowded.[13] The roll rose from 321 in 1967 to 438 in 1976[14] when the open-plan John Wilkinson County Primary school in Coalport Road, with 140 places, opened.[15] In 1982 the C.E. school roll was 244 and the county school's 174.[16]

In 1843 the rector opened a Sunday school and an infant school in Jackfield for 90 pupils in a small old building. It was demolished next year to provide a site for a schoolhouse and a new National school[17] with 88 places[18] in its schoolroom (55 × 22 ft.) and classroom (20 ft. sq.).[19] Planned and erected by Samuel Nevett of Ironbridge, the school cost £350, met by local subscribers and grants from the government and the National Society. It was enlarged for 250 pupils in 1870.[20] Income in 1848 came from subscriptions, collections, school pence, and Betton's Charity.[21] As early as 1852 the school was earning government grant and training pupil teachers.[22] By the 1890s, however, when industrial decline was affecting the parish, its managers were struggling to maintain it and to ward off a school board.[23]

The school had a separate infant department from 1903 to 1930.[24] In 1926 51 pupils transferred from the Lloyds school, which was then closed.[25] After senior pupils transferred to Madeley Senior Council school in 1939 the school became Jackfield C.E. Junior Mixed and Infant school.[26] Evacuees from Liverpool attended 1939–1942.[27] Long-serving and efficient teachers created a successful school despite its poor buildings and facilities.[28] The school was altered and improved after it became controlled in 1956[29] but the schoolhouse was demolished in 1972.[30]

The removal of families from Jackfield to new housing at Broseley in the 1930s[31] and after 1945,[32] the closure of local factories in the 1960s and 1970s,[33] and the opening of the John Wilkinson County Primary school at Broseley in 1976[34] resulted in a gradual decline in the roll at Jackfield school: from 195 in 1932 to 13 in 1981 when it closed.[35]

Broseley Wood C.E. Infant school, with 150 places, was built at Legge's Hill and opened in 1891.[36] The headmistress and pupils of the closed Benthall Parochial Mixed school[37] and 25 infants from the overcrowded Broseley National Infant school transferred to it.[38] Attendance averaged 117 in 1895.[39] In 1941 the roll comprised 33 local pupils and 18 Liverpool evacuees.[40] The school was controlled in 1949[41] and although scheduled to close was considerably renovated in 1956[42] to take the area's increasing school population.[43] The roll rose to 84 in 1958[44] but was only 45 when the school closed in 1967[45] and the pupils transferred to the newly built Broseley C.E. (Controlled) Primary school.[46]

In 1857 twenty Broseley artisans were attending an evening art class taught by the Coalbrookdale drawing school master.[47] County council classes were held in Broseley between 1891 and 1907, and an evening continuation school from 1894 to 1899. At Jackfield an art school master conducted well attended evening classes from 1893 to 1908; they enabled successful students to find employment in local tile and china works. Also well supported in Jackfield were ambulance classes from 1899 to 1902 and an evening continuation school from 1899 to 1903.[48] Evening classes were held in the Victoria Hall, Broseley, in the 1950s[49] and later in the schools.[50]

CHARITIES FOR THE POOR. In the later 17th century various legacies and gifts contributed to a stock for the poor amounting to £51 10*s*. Two of the benefactors were Langleys of the Amies, another was the lord of the manor, John Langley (d. 1693) of the Tuckies. The other benefactors seem to have been parishioners who died between 1666 and 1681 such as Mary Goodman (d. 1671), who left £3 for the stock.[51] Later there were larger legacies, amounting in all to £380. John Barrett of the Madeira Islands left £200, Mrs. Frances Morgan left £50, and in 1730 Mrs. Esther Hollyman left £20 to be added to the poor's stock. Also in 1730 Richard Edwards of Chesterton (Hunts.), owner of Rowton farm, left £110 to be laid out in land for poor

12 Primary sch. log bk. 9 Jan. 1967.
13 Ibid. 3 Sept. 1969.
14 Ibid. 9 Jan. 1967; 8 Jan. 1976.
15 Inf. from S.C.C. Educ. Dept.
16 S.C.C. Educ. Cttee. *Educ. Dir.* (1982), 4.
17 McFall, 'Educ. in Madeley Union', 43, 46, 50–1.
18 *Mins. of Educ. Cttee. of Council, 1849–50*, p. ccxxvii.
19 P.R.O., ED 7/103, ff. 143–4.
20 McFall, 'Educ. in Madeley Union', 46, 129, 143; S.R.O. 1564/155.
21 P.R.O., ED 7/103, ff. 143–4.
22 McFall, op. cit. 109, 117.
23 Ibid. 49.
24 S.R.O. 4526/2, pp. 1, 209.
25 Ibid. /1, p. 288; /2, p. 181; *V.C.H. Salop.* xi. 75.
26 S.R.O. 4526/1, p. 389.
27 Ibid. pp. 390, 407.
28 Ibid. /1–4.
29 Ibid. /3, pp. 149, 1166–7.
30 Ibid. /4, 14–15 Feb. 1972.
31 e.g. ibid. /1, p. 380; above, growth of settlement.
32 S.R.O. 4526/3, p. 97; above, growth of settlement.
33 Personal knowledge; above, econ. hist. (clay inds.).
34 S.R.O. 4526/4, 23 July 1976.
35 Ibid. /1, p. 339; /4, 27 Apr. 1981.
36 P.R.O., ED 7/103, ff. 147–8; *Kelly's Dir. Salop.* (1895), 45.
37 P.R.O., ED 7/103, ff. 147–8.
38 McFall, 'Educ. in Madeley Union', 51.
39 *Kelly's Dir. Salop.* (1895), 29.
40 Broseley Wood C.E. Inf. sch. log bk. (at Broseley C.E. (Contr.) Primary sch.), 10 Nov. 1941.
41 *S.C.C. Mins. (Educ.)* 1949–50, 100.
42 Log bk. 4 Sept. 1956.
43 Personal knowledge.
44 Log bk. 15 Apr. 1958.
45 Ibid. 9 Jan. 1967.
46 Ibid. 21 July 1967; Broseley C.E. (Contr.) Primary sch. log bk. (at the sch.), 5 Sept. 1967.
47 *Eddowes's Jnl.* 14 Jan. 1857, p. 3.
48 Organizing sec.'s ann. reps. to S.C.C. Intermediate Educ. Cttee. in *S.C.C. Mins.* 1892–1902; *S.C.C. Mins.* 1903–4, 98–103; reps. on work of Higher Educ. Dept. in *S.C.C. Mins. Educ.* 1904–5 sqq.
49 *S.C.C. Mins. (Educ.)* 1950–1, 249.
50 C.E. Primary sch. log bk. 28 Sept. 1971; S.C.C. Educ. Cttee. *Primary Sch. Surv. 1979*.
51 *3rd Rep. Com. Char.* H.C. 5, p. 304 (1820), iv. For prob. identifications cf. above, manor; Langley, *Par. Regs. of Broseley*, i. 70 (Eliz. Mivert), 73 (Thos. Edwards), 75–6 (Fra. Adams, John Huxley sr.), 82 (Mary Goodman), 100 (Mic. Old). Mary Ogden, widow, was presumably a relative of Rob. Ogden (or Ogdon), rector (d. 1680: ibid. 98); H.W.R.O.(H.), Heref. dioc. rec., will of Mary Goodman 15 Sept. 1671.

widows of the parish; in 1783 the parish acknowledged receipt of the sum, with interest, whereby the owner of the farm had discharged his estate. About 1777 the vestry borrowed the stock of £380 towards the building of a market hall and two shops; part of the income, not to exceed £18 a year, was earmarked for the poor. In 1802 the vestry resolved that £15 a year from the hall and shops be paid to the poor, with a further £3 a year to discharge a debt of £43, perhaps representing the stock accumulated in the late 17th century; though the debt was presumably discharged in 1816, £18 a year was still being paid in 1819.[52] In 1802 *c.* 100 beneficiaries received between 1*s.* 3*d.* and 2*s.* 6*d.*, and in 1836 the £18 was divided between *c.* 90 people.[53] By 1891 the charities' income had fallen to £9.[54] A scheme of 1961 reorganized the charities as the Broseley Town Hall Trust Fund, which in 1975 had an income of £36.[55]

Andrew Langley (d. 1687?) left a rent charge of 12*s.* on the Woodhouse estate, to be distributed to twelve widows.[56] The charity, known as Langley's bread charity, was still given in 1891.[57]

Charles Oare of Bridgnorth left £100 to provide men's clothing. In 1882 the charity had an income of £2 16*s.*[58]

In 1740 William Lewis granted a rent charge of £1 for distribution among twenty widows. The charity lapsed between 1820 and 1856.[59]

Mrs. Mary Cotton (d. 1838) left £300 stock, the income to be divided between forty widows.[60] In 1882 thirty widows received 4*s.* 6*d.* each.[61]

Four Pritchards made charitable benefactions during the 19th century. Mrs. Fanny Pritchard (d. 1839)[62] left £100 to be invested to provide warm clothing for widows. Ten women benefited in 1840 and 1882.[63] George Pritchard (d. 1861)[64] left the income on £100 for widows' clothing. Ten benefited in 1882.[65] Miss Mary Anne Pritchard (d. 1882) left £100 for charitable purposes; her brother John Pritchard added £100 more, and again the income was used to provide warm clothing for widows.[66] By 1891 the three legacies and John's gift were combined in Pritchards' charity, which provided 36 widows with clothing tickets.[67] In 1975 the charities of John Pritchard and others had an income of £20, and the George Pritchard Clothing Charity one of £3.[68]

DEUXHILL

DEUXHILL is 6.5 km. south-south-west of Bridgnorth.[69] The parish, conterminous with the manor[70] within boundaries recorded in 1838, is small (199 ha., 493 a.) and roughly lozenge shaped, somewhat irregular on the west. Crunells brook (a tributary of Borle brook) and its tributary Horsford brook define parts of the western and south-western boundaries and other tributaries of the Borle the north-eastern one. The southernmost part of the south-eastern boundary is marked by the parish's principal road.[71]

The name of the parish and the hamlet which crowns a hill at the centre are taken from the hill (138 m.), called after one Deowuc.[72] The hill forms the end of a spur of high land running down from the neighbourhood of Eudon Coppice 1.5 km. to the north-west; the hill is made more prominent by a saddle of lower land between it and the rest of the spur. The highest land is on the western edge where the road to Middleton Scriven crosses the spur of high land and the parish boundary at 139 m.; in the east and south-east, where streams drain out of the parish, the land falls below 91 m. The hill-top hamlet site and part of the northern extremity of the parish stand on an outlier of the coal measures to the east, beyond the Devonian Old Red Sandstone that underlies the rest of the parish and most of south-east Shropshire.[73]

The principal and only classified road through the parish runs south from Bridgnorth to Cleobury Mortimer crossing Crunells brook[74] by Horsford bridge, maintained by the county from 1820;[75] it was a turnpike 1762–1877.[76] A road runs west to Middleton Scriven; out of it a way north towards Eudon George and Chetton is a green lane as far as Tedstill and perhaps was so by the early 19th century.[77]

In 1793 there were 6 houses in the parish and there had been two or three more within memory.[78] Later there were never more than 8 or 9; a cottage on the Middleton Scriven boundary in the earlier 19th century had gone by 1883.[79] In

52 S.R.O. 1224/3/778, 793; 2991/Cy/1, p. 1; *3rd Rep. Com. Char.* 303–4; above, social and cultural activities; econ. hist. (mkt. and fairs).

53 S.R.O. 2991/Cy/1, s.a.

54 *Kelly's Dir. Salop.* (1891), 278.

55 *Review of Local Chars.* (S.C.C. 1975), 22.

56 *3rd Rep. Com. Char.* 305; S.R.O. 2991/Cy/1, p. 1. An And. Langley d. 1687: Langley, *Par. Regs. of Broseley*, i. 113.

57 *Salopian Shreds & Patches*, x. 9.

58 S.R.O. 2991/Cy/4, 9.

59 *3rd Rep. Com. Char.* 305; not in *P.O. Dir. Salop.* (1856).

60 S.R.O. 2991/Cy/2, p. 1; Randall *Broseley*, 194–5.

61 S.R.O. 2991/Cy/9.

62 Randall, op. cit. 192.

63 S.R.O. 2991/Cy/2, 9.

64 Randall, op. cit. 197.

65 S.R.O. 2991/Cy/3, 9.

66 Ibid. /2, 5–9.

67 *Salopian Shreds & Patches*, x. 9.

68 *Review of Local Chars.* 22.

69 *V.C.H. Salop.* i, map facing p. 23. This article was drafted in 1985 and later revised and amplified.

70 W.S.L. 350/3/40, Deuxhill p. [1]; Bodl. MS. Blakeway 10, f. 360e *verso.*

71 P.R.O., IR 30/29/106; O.S. *Area Bk.* (1883); O.S. Map 1/25,000, SO 68/78 (1982 edn.); fig. 30.

72 *P.N. Salop.* (E.P.N.S.), i. 108.

73 O.S. Maps 1/2,500, Salop. LXVI. 7 (1883 edn.); 1/25,000, SO 68/78 (1982 edn.); Geol. Surv. Map 1", sheet LXI. SE. (1868 edn.); *V.C.H. Salop.* i. 23–4, and map facing p. 1.

74 O.S. Map 1/25,000, SO 68/78 (1982 edn.).

75 *Abstr. Q. Sess. R. 1820–30*, ed. M. C. Hill (S.C.C. 1974), 283/192; S.R.O., dep. plan 223, draft contract 1825, plan, etc.

76 2 Geo. III, c. 79; Local Govt. Bd.'s (Highways) Prov. Orders Conf. (Dorset, &c.) Act, 1879, 42 & 43 Vic. c. 85 (Local); *Return of Turnpike Trusts Eng. and N. Wales*, H.C. 39, p. 12 (1860), lxi; S.R.O. 560/740–2.

77 S.R.O. 1931/5; P.R.O., IR 30/29/106.

78 S.P.L., MS. 6864, f. 43.

79 S.R.O. 1931/5; 2079/LXVI. 7, 11; 4044/11, f. 12v.; P.R.O., IR 29/29/106; IR 30/29/106; O.S. Maps 1/2,500, LXVI. 7, 11 (1883 edn.); 1/10,000, SO 68 NE., SO 78 NW. (1979 edn.). Cf. T. Rowley, *Salop. Landscape* (1972), 27.

80 Below, educ.

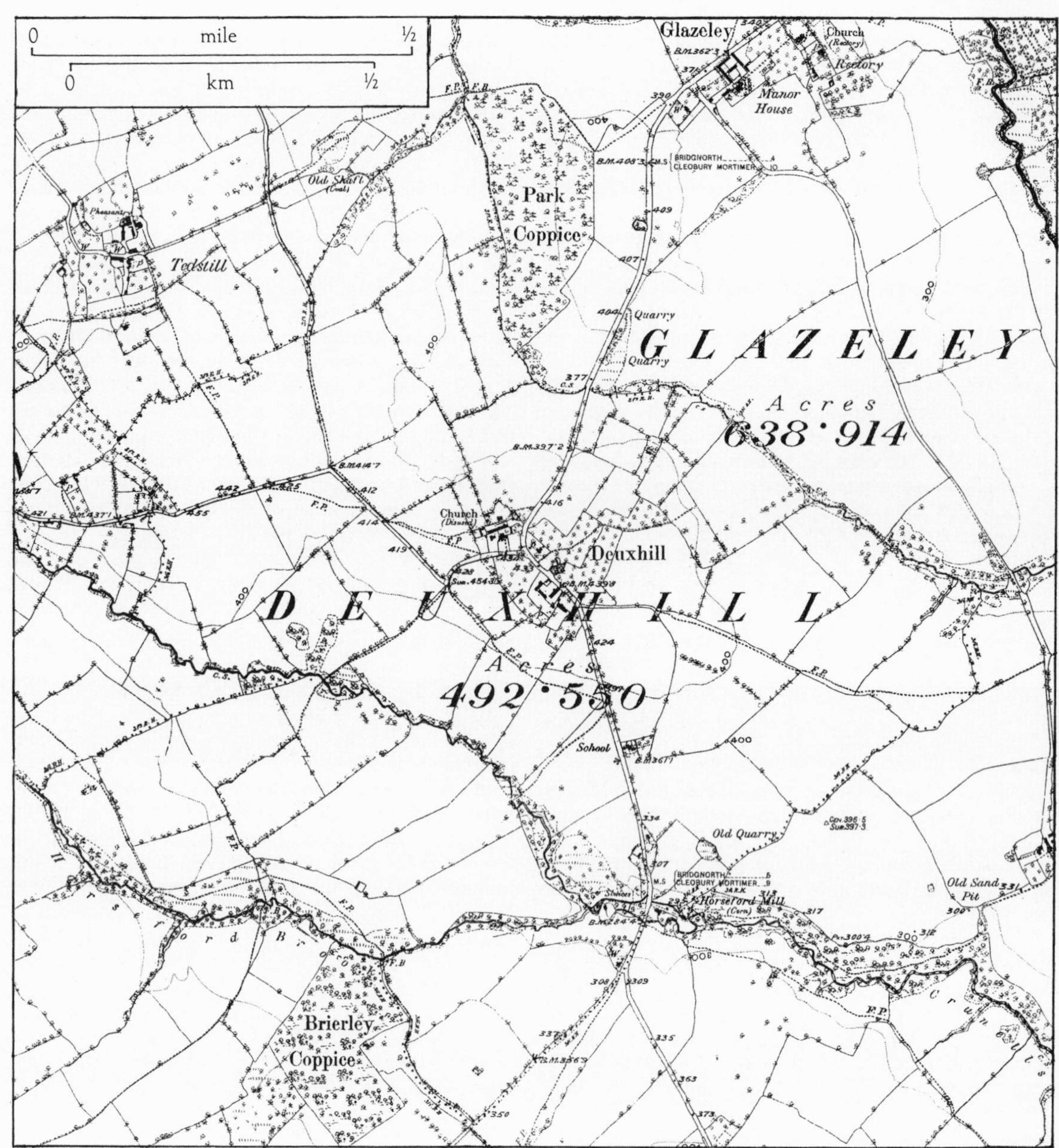

Fig. 30

DEUXHILL IN 1882

1985 the hamlet comprised Hall Farm, Church Farm, a cottage, and the fragments of the ruined church. It was the only settlement apart from five dwellings to the south along the Cleobury Mortimer road, including Horsford Mill and Old School House (1879),[80] the latter apparently the parish's newest house.

The recorded population was 4 in 1086.[81] In 1793 there were 22 inhabitants.[82] In the 19th and 20th centuries the population never varied much from a mean of 39, with a maximum of 55 (1831) and minimum of 19 (1981). Tending to increase up to 1901 (54), it fell thereafter.[83]

An ale-house was licensed in 1810.[84] There was no wake,[85] and in the 19th century few social activities were organized independently of those at the school or in neighbouring parishes[86] and nearby Bridgnorth.[87] In 1928, however, the

80 Below, educ.
81 *V.C.H. Salop.* i. 312.
82 S.P.L., MS. 6864, f. 43.
83 *V.C.H. Salop.* ii. 222; *Census*, 1971, *Co. Rep. Salop.* i. 3; 1981; Small Area Statistics: Salop.
84 W.B.R., Q1/11/1, s.a. 1810.
85 B.L. Add. MS. 30316, f. 9; Birm. Univ. Libr., Mytton papers, ii. 379.
86 S.R.O. 1158/7, pp. 306, 323, 358–9, 386–7, 395; /8, p. 198; 1484/Par/2.
87 S.R.O. 1158/7, pp. 129, 164, 309, 319.

county library opened a book centre,[88] and in 1963 the newly closed school was bought as a village hall for the surrounding district.[89]

MANOR. In 1066 St. Mildburg's church at Much Wenlock held *DEUXHILL*. Eardington (also held by the church in 1066)[90] and Deuxhill were probably the lands 'in the place called Chelmarsh' given to Mildburg before 704 by her half-brothers Merchelm and Mildfrith;[91] Chelmarsh, if reduced by their gift, yet remained a valuable royal estate[92] which in time became the earl of Mercia's.[93] St. Mildburg's church, refounded as the Cluniac priory of Wenlock *c.* 1080,[94] held Deuxhill as a demesne manor until its surrender in 1540.[95]

In 1543 James Leveson of Wolverhampton, a merchant of the staple, bought an estate in Deuxhill from the Crown[96] only to sell it a few weeks later to Thomas Grey of Whittington (Staffs.). Grey died in 1559–60 leaving a son John who came of age in 1561.[97] In 1586 John Grey, then of Enville (Staffs.), conveyed his Deuxhill property to his younger brother George, of Wolverhampton, and his wife Joyce (*née* Leveson). George Grey's purchase of other lands in Deuxhill from Sir John Lyttelton (d. 1590) probably brought the whole township or manor into his hands. In 1606 Grey sold the manor to John Sotherton of Glazeley,[98] a baron of the Exchequer,[99] and in 1611 Sotherton sold it to Thomas Hassold of Clerkenwell (Mdx.).[1]

The manor remained in the Hassold (or Hassall) family for over a century. After Edward Hassold's death in 1656 it seems to have passed to his widow Anne, probably the owner in 1672. Their son Timothy, born in 1657, evidently inherited. He died in 1710 and after the death of his widow Honor, *c.* 1721, the manor came to their surviving children Honor and Eliza, whose trustees sold it in 1728, either to the London glassman William Bowles[2] or to George Rider of Quatt who sold it on to Bowles, lord in the 1730s.[3] Bowles had bought the Burford estate, of which Deuxhill then became an outlier; he died childless in 1748[4] leaving the estate to his brother Humphry. Humphry (d. 1784) or his son George, who lived mainly at Wanstead Grove (Essex),[5] sold Deuxhill to John Lewis of Quatt, agent for the Dudmaston estate, and to another Mr. Lewis, a Bridgnorth attorney. The latter was bought out by John Lewis who by 1793 owned the whole parish except the rector's glebe and was lord of the manor.[6] John Lewis died in 1804,[7] and George Lewis was probably lord in 1805.[8]

Some time after 1805 the Lewis estate, consisting of one farm,[9] seems to have been split into two, the lordship of the manor apparently descending with Church farm.[10] By 1838 Church farm (224 a.) had been sold and belonged to Miss Sarah Pass (d. 1844), of the Square, Bridgnorth;[11] Mrs. Mary Deeton, of the same address, subsequently owned it. She died in 1860,[12] and Thomas Walker, of Studley Castle and Berkswell (Warws.), owned Church farm by 1863; he was described as lord of the manor in 1870, and from his time until 1919 the farm was part of the Middleton Scriven estate.[13] Walker died in 1887,[14] and by 1891 William Bunney (d. 1899), of Meole Brace, was lord. Bunney's trustees owned the manor in 1917, when it was last recorded,[15] and F. W. E. Bunney offered the farm (208 a.) for sale when the Middleton Scriven estate was broken up in 1919.[16]

Church Farm was probably where John Lewis lived in the 1790s and then called Deuxhill Hall;[17] it descended with the manor in the 19th and early 20th century. It is a 'handsome Georgian farmhouse' of brick with stone quoins and hipped roof.[18]

Hall farm (231 a.), with some smaller holdings, belonged to T. S. and R. H. Heptinstall and the Revd. A. B. Haden in 1838.[19] Haden (d. 1863) alone was named as owner in the 1850s

88 R.C. Elliot,'Development of Public Libraries in Salop.' (Loughborough Univ. M.A. thesis, 1970), 126.

89 S.C.C., Co. Sec.'s file VH/A/76.

90 *V.C.H. Salop.* i. 312, 318.

91 H. P. R. Finberg, *Early Charters of W. Midlands* (1972), pp. 203, 205.

92 The view that the church had 'lost' Chelmarsh by 1066 but 'still' held the 'two adjacent manors, Eardington and Deuxhill' (ibid. p. 148) needlessly elaborates what can be deduced from St. Mildburg's *Testament*.

93 *V.C.H. Salop.* i. 330. For the earl's est. in 1066 and its royal origins see C. P. Lewis, 'Eng. and Norman govt. and lordship in Welsh borders 1039–87' (Oxf. Univ. D.Phil. thesis, 1985), 60–1, 68–72.

94 *V.C.H. Salop.* ii. 38–9.

95 Ibid. 45; Eyton, i. 219–20; P.R.O., SC 6/Hen. VIII/3021, mm. 16d.–17.

96 *L. & P. Hen. VIII*, xviii (1), p. 535.

97 Bodl. MS. Blakeway 10, ff. 358, 359a; S. Shaw, *Hist. Staffs.* ii (1801), 268.

98 Bodl. MS. Blakeway 10, ff. 359a, 359d, 360a–c; P.R.O., C 2/Jas. I/S 7/33; C 3/271/6; cf. *V.C.H. Staffs.* xx. 97.

99 *D.N.B.*

1 Bodl. MS. Blakeway 10, f. 361a.

2 Ibid. ff. 360d *verso*, 361a–b; *Cal. S.P. Dom.* 1672, 578; *S.P.R. Heref.* v (5), 2, 4; W. H. Bowles, *Hist. of Vauxhall and Ratcliff Glass Hos. and their Owners 1670–1800* (priv. print. 1926), 34–9.

3 Birm. Univ. Libr., Mytton Papers, ii. 379.

4 W. H. Bowles, *Rec. of Bowles Fam.* (priv. print. 1918), 83–5 (wrongly stating that Bowles bought Deuxhill as part of the Burford est.), 87; *Hist. Parl., Commons*, 1715–54, i. 480.

5 S.R.O., q. sess. rec. box 260, reg. of gamekeepers 1742–79, 8 Oct. 1746, 5 May 1754; Bowles, *Bowles Fam.* pp. xvi, 88, 96 sqq. For the fam. cf. Burke, *Land. Gent.* (1921), 186–7.

6 S.P.L., MS. 6864, f. 43; cf. S.R.O., q. sess. rec. parcel 261, reg. of gamekeepers 1799–1807, ff. 11v.–12; 2922/14/8/4; *V.C.H. Salop.* iv. 203–4. The attorney was probably the man mentioned in S.R.O. 1190/3/734, pp. [2–3].

7 *S.P.R. Heref.* v (5), 16.

8 S.R.O., q. sess. rec. parcel 261, reg. of gamekeepers 1799–1807, ff. 124v.–125.

9 Below, econ. hist.

10 Church fm. is the modern name; others were used earlier. After Lewis's death the ldship. is next mentioned in 1870: below, this section.

11 P.R.O., IR 29/29/106; W.S.L. 350/3/40, Deuxhill p. [2]; S.R.O. 3662/BRg/1, p. 198 no. 1584.

12 S. Bagshaw, *Dir. Salop.* (1851), 644; *P.O. Dir. Salop.* (1856), 44; S.R.O. 3662/BRg/2, p. 134 no. 1068.

13 *P.O. Dir. Salop.* (1863), 682, 719; (1870), 313; M.I. in Middleton Scriven ch.

14 *S.P.R. Heref.* v (4), p. iii.

15 S.R.O. 1206/82, pp. 220–2; *Shrews. Chron.* 10 Nov. 1899, p. 8; *Kelly's Dir. Salop.* (1891), 307; (1895), 76–7; (1900), 79; (1917), 79.

16 S.R.O. 5586/5/8/21, esp. pp. 27–8.

17 Bodl. MS. Blakeway 10, f. 360e *verso*. Prob. referred to in *S.P.R. Heref.* v (5), 15, the ho. is less likely than Hall Fm. to have been the apparently ruinous farmho. of 1793: below, econ. hist.

18 Above, this section; cf. Pevsner, *Salop.* 120.

19 P.R.O., IR 29/29/106.

and early 1860s,[20] but by 1910 the 232 a. belonged to Agnes C. Hepinstall of Clevedon (Som.).[21]

Hall Farm, probably the original manor house,[22] is a 17th-century timber framed house, close panelled. Once a lobby-entrance type, perhaps contrived by adding to a pre-existing building (surviving at the house's north-west corner), the house was later extended on the east, and the south (parlour) wing is much altered. The west wall has been rebuilt in stone and brick.[23]

The two farms continued to be differently owned in the 20th century; neither was invariably owner occupied. By the 1980s a couple of other farms extended into the parish.[24]

ECONOMIC HISTORY. The manor, ½ hide, was worth 10*s.* in 1066 and 20*s.* in 1086. At the latter date there was 1 ploughteam on the demesne, and 2 bordars and a cottar had another team. There was also 1 *servus* in the manor.[25]

Rent from the priory's Deuxhill demesnes may have been owed at Ditton Priors in the late 14th century,[26] but in time Deuxhill may have become a separate bailiwick for in 1540 rents from other priory properties both near (the Pickthorn property and a weir at Quatt) and far[27] were owed to the Crown's minister there.[28]

There were freehold estates within the manor, but by the early 16th century Wenlock priory had probably acquired most of them[29] and probably owned most of the land in the parish apart from the rector's glebe. Nevertheless at least one hereditary estate seems to have survived: in 1540 John Pakington owed 3*s.* 4*d.* chief rent for a Deuxhill property[30] that he had acquired with the neighbouring manors of Glazeley and Wadeley in the later 1520s.[31]

For much of its recorded history since the early 16th century the manor evidently consisted of two substantial farms and some smaller holdings. In 1540 two copyhold farms and a copyhold cottage tenement were held of the priory; each was held for two named lives and had been granted at dates between 1506 or 1507 and 1532. Heriot and terciary were then,[32] and long had been, exacted from such tenants by the priory: in 1379,[33] when Agnes of Deuxhill died, her prosperous peasant farm owed a heriot of 1 ox and, as terciary at either a third or a half[34] of the live and dead stock, 2 more oxen, 1 cow, 1 bullock, 6 ewes, 2 geese, 18*s.* 10*d.*, shares of a salted ox and a salted hog, shares of corn in the barn and in the ground, 1 bu. of wheat, 2 bu. of beans, 1¼ qr. of peas, 1½ bu. of barley malt, 2 beehives, and 3 hens and a capon. Actually the priory took the cattle and sheep, 10 qr. of wheat (6 of them in lieu of the corn in the ground), and 3 qr. of oats, remitting the rest to Agnes's widower.

The west side of the manor, broken by the steep sided valleys of Crunells and Horsford brooks, probably consisted of rough pasture (perhaps once partly wooded) and meadow.[35] The open fields were on the east side of the manor.[36] Ridge and Reany piece, north of the hamlet, indicated the location of one, bounded on the east and north with rough moors, possibly once wooded;[37] the names and former shapes of fields south-east of the hamlet probably indicate the whereabouts of another that may have been called, in Shropshire fashion, the field towards Wadeley.[38] Probably between those two fields, where the glebe later lay, there was other open field land where inclosure was in progress by *c.* 1590: Parson's close, part of the glebe, had been all or mostly inclosed from an open field but still contained five ridges 'not being divided or mered from the residue of the said close' and which were claimed by the lord of the manor.[39]

There were no wood sales from the manor in 1540,[40] and any woodland that existed earlier may have been cleared by then. By the early 19th century there was very little wood, apparently only ¼ a. of managed woodland in 1838, but there were then woods in the Crunells brook valley which, with others along Horsford brook and here and there on the parish boundary, amounted to perhaps 8 scattered acres of spinneys in the 20th century. In the 19th and earlier 20th century the two farms had over 9 a. of orchards in the hamlet, but in the mid 20th century they were grubbed out.[41]

The land was said to be mostly arable in the 1730s. In the mid 18th century there were still two farmers and a few cottagers,[42] but by 1793 the farms had been made into one of 470 a. let for £300; one farmhouse, inhabited by a workman and probably Hall Farm, then looked

20 And later: cf. S. Bagshaw, *Dir. Salop.* (1851), 644; *P.O. Dir. Salop.* (1863), 682; (1879), 313; *Alum. Oxon. 1715–1886*, ii. 583.

21 S.R.O. 4044/11, f. 12v.

22 W.S.L. 350/3/40, Deuxhill p. [2].

23 E. Mercer, *Eng. Vernacular Hos.* (1975), 123 and n. 4; inf. from Mr. Mercer; cf. Pevsner, *Salop.* 120; S.R.O. 2479/63. The date 1601, on the ho., is a modern addition and probably too early.

24 *Kelly's Dir. Salop.* (1913–41); S.P.L., SC10/2–3; local inf.

25 *V.C.H. Salop.* i. 312.

26 Eyton, iii. 335.

27 Nantwich (Ches.), Bishopsgate (London), and Birdham (Suss.).

28 P.R.O., SC 6/Hen. VIII/3021, m. 17. Cf. 15th- and early 16th-cent. rentals in S.R.O. 1224, box 342, Prior Gosnell's reg. ff. 32v.–33; N.L.W., Wynnstay RA 2.

29 e.g. 1 virgate in 1342: P.R.O., C 143/263, no. 6; *Cal. Pat.* 1340–3, 529.

30 P.R.O., SC 6/Hen. VIII/3021, m. 16d.

31 Cf. ft. of fine Salop. 17 Hen. VIII East. now 'wanting' from P.R.O., CP 25/2/35/232; CP 25/2/35/233/22 Hen. VIII Mich. no. 12; *T.S.A.S.* lv. 33. For Pakington (d. 1560) see *D.N.B.*

32 P.R.O., SC 6/Hen. VIII/3021, m. 17; below, this section.

33 Rest of para. based on *T.S.A.S.* lviii. 69, 75 n. 19, 76.

34 Terciary was usually 1/3 of a deceased tenant's chattels (*V.C.H. Salop.* iv. 36), but on this occasion 1/2 may have been sought.

35 P.R.O., IR 29/29/106; IR 30/29/106; O.S. Map 1/25,000, SO 68/78 (1982 edn.).

36 Where J. Rocque, *Map of Salop.* (1752), shows arable land.

37 H. D. G. Foxall, *Salop. Field-Names* (Salop. Arch. Soc. 1980), 3, 8; P.R.O., IR 29/29/106; IR 30/29/106, field 3; cf. ibid. fields 1–2, 5.

38 P.R.O., IR 29/29/106; IR 30/29/106, fields 80, 82, 84–6.

39 P.R.O., C 3/271/6.

40 P.R.O., SC 6/Hen. VIII/3021, m. 17.

41 S.R.O. 1931/5; 5586/5/8/21, pp. 27–8 and map; S.P.L., SC10/2–3; P.R.O., IR 29/29/106; IR 30/29/106; O.S. Maps 1/10,000, SO 68 NE., SO 78 NW. (1979 edn.).

42 Birm. Univ. Libr., Mytton Papers, ii. 379; H.W.R.O.(H.), Heref. dioc. rec. AL 19/23, f. 53.

TABLE XVII

DEUXHILL: LAND USE, LIVESTOCK, AND CROPS

	1867	1891	1938	1962
Percentage of grassland	62	77	81	56
arable	38	23	19	44
Percentage of cattle	14	39	25	19
sheep	69	47	72	80
pigs	17	14	3	0
Percentage of wheat	54	44	53	56
barley	23	22	0	26
oats	23	33	47	18
mixed corn & rye	0	0	0	0
Percentage of agricultural land growing roots and vegetables	8	7	5	3

Sources: P.R.O., MAF 68/143, no. 9; /1340, no. 13; /3880, Salop. no. 198; /4792, no. 198. Deuxhill's returns were grossed with Glazeley's after 1962.

ruinous.[43] Division of the Lewis estate after 1805 separated the two farms again,[44] although in the mid 19th century their tenants were members of the same family, the Birkins.[45] In 1838, on land admittedly stiff and wet, farming was said to be slovenly; 233 a. were then arable, 205 a. pasture, and 45 a. meadow, and the usual four-year course, very similar to what had been followed over forty years earlier, was fallow, wheat, oats or clover (the latter partly mown, partly pastured), and oats or peas.[46]

In the later 19th century pastoral farming increased, with an emphasis on oats rather than wheat on the diminishing arable acreage and on cattle rather than sheep on the pastures; pig keeping fell steadily.[47] By 1905 permanent grass occupied 363 a., arable land only 101 a.; the proportions were similar on Church farm, a dairy and rearing farm, in 1919[48] and on Hall farm, a stock raising farm, in 1940. By 1951, however, nearly 40 per cent of Hall farm was under the plough[49] as arable farming revived in the mid century. Wheat (well suited to the heavy land) and barley became the main crops; on the grass there were more sheep, though in the 1980s there were dairy heifers on the parish's farms, in winter taken in to prevent poaching of the pastures.

By 1808 Horsford mill stood on Crunells brook, where it flowed out of the parish.[50] In the earlier 19th century, as well as the leat from the confluence of Crunells and Horsford brooks, there was a small pond and dam[51] higher up Crunells brook, and there may once have been 'water works' higher up Horsford brook. The mill was owned with Hall farm until some time between *c.* 1910 and 1940. A corn mill, it probably ceased working soon after 1900, but *c.* 1910 the Winwoods, the last millers, still occupied the *c.* 9 a. that had been let with it, and they may have worked them as a smallholding as late as 1929.[52]

In the 1730s it was recalled that 'formerly there was coal got' behind the church, evidently in Coalpit moors near the northern corner of the parish. The coal, however, proved very sulphurous, and the work was stopped 'upon account of the water'.[53]

There is an old quarry north-east of Horsford mill, and a nearby field was one of two in the parish called Limekiln leasow; the other was beside the road from Deuxhill to Middleton Scriven.[54]

LOCAL GOVERNMENT. Deuxhill owed suit to the prior of Wenlock's court of Bourton hundred from 1198 to 1763[55] or later.[56] There is evidence of Deuxhill manor court being held in the earlier 16th, and perhaps even the late 15th, century: it probably sat only occasionally, to renew copyholds and exact terciary and heriot. Perquisites of a Deuxhill court held in Ditton Priors in May 1540 amounted to 14*s.* in heriot and 46*s.* in terciary.[57]

Deuxhill was excluded from the municipal (though not the parliamentary) borough of Wenlock in 1836. The county magistrates then assigned it to the Bridgnorth petty sessional division of Brimstree hundred, evidently in ignorance of its whereabouts, but by January 1837 it was in the Chelmarsh division of Stottesdon hundred.[58]

Expenditure on 'occasional' relief of the poor was £3 a year 1812–14. It averaged £5 13*s.* a year 1814–17 and £24 19*s.* in 1818–19. Fluctuating somewhat in the 1820s and earlier 1830s, expenditure then averaged £16 3*s.*, lowest (£8 3*s.*) in 1827 and highest (£28) in 1831.[59]

43 S.P.L., MS. 6864, f. 43.
44 Above, manor.
45 P.R.O., HO 107/1986, ff. 52–3; S. Bagshaw, *Dir. Salop.* (1851), 644.
46 P.R.O., IR 18/8046. In 1793 wheat had been followed by peas or oats, oats by clover: S.P.L., MS. 6864, f. 43v.
47 Para. based on Table XVII; Salop. Agric. Returns, 1905; local inf.
48 S.R.O. 5586/5/8/21, pp. 27–8.
49 S.P.L., SC10/2–3.
50 R. Baugh, *Map of Salop.* (1808).
51 At O.S. Nat. Grid SO 6970 8668.
52 S.R.O. 1931/5; 2079/LXVI. 11; 4044/11, f. 12v.; S.P.L., SC10/2; P.R.O., IR 29/29/106; IR 30/29/106, fields 58a, 62–5, 74; RG 12/2093, f. 85v.; W.S.L. 350/3/40, Deuxhill p. [2]; O.S. Map 1/2,500, LXVI. 11 (1883 edn.); *Kelly's Dir. Salop.* (1900), 79 (last mention of mill); (1929), 90.
53 Birm. Univ. Libr., Mytton Papers, ii. 379; P.R.O., IR 29/29/106; IR 30/29/106, fields 5, 30, 44.
54 P.R.O., IR 29/29/106; IR 30/29/106, fields 17, 81; O.S. Map 1/2,500, LXVI. 11 (1883 edn.).
55 Above, Lib. and Boro. of Wenlock (Lib.: Bourton hund.); S.R.O. 1224/2/429.
56 Bodl. MS. Blakeway 10, f. 360e *verso*.
57 P.R.O., SC 6/Hen. VIII/3021, m. 17.
58 *V.C.H. Salop.* ii. 208, 211; iii. 310, 339; above, Lib. and Boro. of Wenlock (boro. 1836–89); S.R.O., q. sess. order bk. 1833–9, ff. 167v., 184v., 203.
59 *Poor Law Abstract*, H.C. 82, pp. 376–7 (1818), xix; *Poor Rate Returns*, H.C. 556, suppl. app. p. 144 (1822), v; H.C. 334, p. 179 (1825), iv; H.C. 219, p. 167 (1830–1), xi; H.C. 444, p. 162 (1835), xlvii.

Deuxhill was in Bridgnorth poor-law union 1836–1930,[60] Bridgnorth highway district 1863–95,[61] Bridgnorth rural sanitary district 1872–94, Bridgnorth rural district 1894–1974, and Bridgnorth district from 1974.[62] The civil parish had a joint parish council with Billingsley, Glazeley, and Middleton Scriven C.P.s by 1967.[63]

CHURCH. In the early 12th century Deuxhill was subject to a church at Glazeley, an estate which, like Deuxhill, may once have been a member of Chelmarsh since it lay between Chelmarsh and Deuxhill. Wenlock priory had probably founded a manorial chapel at Deuxhill by *c.* 1115 when it secured its independence from Glazeley church; some 12th-century fabric seems to have survived to the 19th century.[64] As the chaplain's tithes were not appropriated to the priory his benefice became a rectory, but because the parish was small the rectory was united during the Middle Ages with the rectorial chaplaincy of Middleton Priors,[65] on the nearest part of the priory's estate.

The advowson of the united rectory belonged to Wenlock priory.[66] Like the priory's other patronage it was exercised by the Crown during the Hundred Years' War[67] until denization in 1395[68] permitted the priory to resume its advowsons.[69] Deuxhill and Middleton Priors were still united in 1505, but in 1515 Peter Griffith was instituted as rector of Deuxhill alone,[70] and in 1521 the rector of Neenton was instituted to the adjoining Middleton Priors. The bishop was probably planning a measure of pastoral reorganization, for in 1530, when the rector of Glazeley (the nearest church to Deuxhill) resigned, the bishop sequestrated it and committed it to Griffith,[71] who, by 1535, was rector of both churches.[72] Wenlock priory evidently relinquished the advowson of Deuxhill, which by 1538 was united to Glazeley in the patronage of John Pakington,[73] who had recently acquired the manor and advowson of Glazeley and a small estate in Deuxhill.[74] The advowson of the united rectories[75] then descended with Glazeley manor until shortly after *c.* 1910,[76] although occasionally others acquired turns to present kinsmen.[77] Deuxhill with Glazeley was held with Chetton rectory (in the same patronage) 1716–50, but the informal union was interrupted, perhaps inadvertently, 1750–7; in 1759, however, a permanent union was made.[78] Three or four years after the death (1908) of the Bridgnorth carpet manufacturer T. M. Southwell his trustees sold the Glazeley estate, but they retained the advowson of Chetton with Glazeley and Deuxhill until R. B. Southwell, rector, died in 1953; it then passed to Lancing College (Suss.). From *c.* 1975 the Woodard Schools (Southern Division) Ltd. held it on the college's behalf. By 1985 a rector living at Sidbury held the united living in plurality with those of Billingsley with Sidbury, of Chelmarsh, and of Middleton Scriven, the patrons presenting jointly.[79]

Some medieval rectors bore local names.[80] Gilbert of Reigate (instituted in 1290) may have been a graduate,[81] but no other medieval rector of Deuxhill is known to have been. Hamon of Sandwich (1295) was much involved in ecclesiastical business, but his later career foundered through his neglect of his livings.[82] It may have been hard to achieve residence at Deuxhill.[83] During the Crown's exercise of the patronage one rector (instituted in 1358) was certainly a royal clerk[84] and others may have been: William of Burstall, rector 1349–58, may be the man who was master of the Rolls in the 1370s.[85] After the priory resumed its patronage Richard de Arderne became rector in 1399; he was also vicar of Ditton Priors and held other local livings.[86]

In 1291 Deuxhill and Middleton Priors together were worth less than £4 a year.[87] In 1535 Deuxhill and Glazeley were worth £4 5*s.* 4*d.* a year exclusive of an 8*s.* pension owed by the rector of Deuxhill to Wenlock priory;[88] about that time the tithes were leased and payment of

60 V. J. Walsh, 'Admin. of Poor Laws in Salop. 1820–55' (Pennsylvania Univ. Ph.D. thesis, 1970), 148–50; *Kelly's Dir. Salop.* (1929), 89.

61 *Lond. Gaz.* 27 Mar. 1863, p. 1767.

62 S.R.O. 4873/1, p. 297 (no. 117); *Rural Dist. Councillors Electn. Order, 1894* (Local Govt. Bd. order no. 31847); *V.C.H. Salop.* ii. 213; sources cited ibid. iii. 169 n. 29.

63 Inf. from Mrs. M. Roberts, clk.

64 Eyton, i. 217, 220; iii. 233; Cranage, x. 991; above, manor; Lib. and Boro. of Wenlock (early est.).

65 Above, Lib. and Boro. of Wenlock (early est.); *Reg. Cantilupe* (C.S.), 151; sources in notes to next para.

66 *Reg. Cantilupe,* 191; *Reg. Swinfield* (C.S.), 528, 530, 536, 544; *Reg. Orleton* (C.S.), 373–6.

67 *Cal. Pat.* 1343–5, 225, 245, 319; 1358–61, 64; 1385–9, 476; 1388–92, 94, 186; *Reg Trillek* (C.S.), 380, 390; *Reg. Gilbert* (C.S.), 122; *Reg. Trefnant* (C.S.), 174; Eyton, i. 221–2.

68 Eyton, i. 222; *V.C.H. Salop.* ii. 42.

69 *Reg. Trefnant,* 183; *Reg. Mascall* (C.S.), 171, 173; *Reg. Spofford* (C.S.), 351, 359.

70 *Reg. Mayew* (C.S.), 64, 283.

71 *Reg. Bothe* (C.S.), 244, 334; S.R.O. 1224, box 342, Prior Gosnell's reg. f. 19v.

72 *Valor Eccl.* (Rec. Com.), iii. 210.

73 The priory's 'gift' to Pakington (*Reg. Bothe,* 380 and n. 3) was probably a sale of the advowson. Cf. the sale of Ch. Preen in 1534: *T.S.A.S.* lxx. 191–3.

74 Above, econ. hist.

75 In 1554 the Crown mistakenly reserved the patronage of Deuxhill and Middleton Higford (*sic*) in a grant defective in other ways too: cf. *Cal. Pat.* 1553–4, 156; below, n. 89.

76 Cf. *T.S.A.S.* 4th ser. ii. 56; lv. 33–7; *Dioc. of Heref. Institutions (1539–1900)*, ed. A. T. Bannister (Heref. 1923), 35, 63, 99, 127, 166, 210, 216. Unnamed in institutions of 1554 and 1579 (ibid. 9, 25), Deuxhill was nevertheless then united with Glazeley: cf. Heref. D. & C. muniments, chapter act bk. 1512–66 (folio), f. 130.

77 Bannister, op. cit. 138, 175.

78 Ibid. 63, 66, 88, 92; *S.P.R. Heref.* v (5), pp. iii–iv; *T.S.A.S.* 4th ser. ii. 105; Heref. Dioc. Regy., reg. 1755–71, f. 53.

79 J. F. A. Mason, *Boro. of Bridgnorth 1157–1957* (Bridgnorth, 1957), 42–3, 51–2; S.R.O. 4044/11, f. 13v.; *T.S.A.S.* lv. 35; *Kelly's Dir. Salop.* (1913), 106; T. M. Southwell's will pr. 8 Dec. 1908; *Crockford* (1951–2), 1211; (1953–4), 1457; *Heref. Dioc. Yr. Bk.* (1985), 35; inf. from the provost, Woodard Schs. (S. Divn.) Ltd.

80 Rob. de Mudle (Myddle?) inst. 1278, Rob. of Easthope 1326, and Wm. of Ludlow 1344: *Reg. Cantilupe,* 191; *Reg. Orleton,* 373–6; *Cal. Pat.* 1343–5, 225.

81 Called 'magister' in 1321. See *Reg. Swinfield,* 528; *Reg. Orleton,* 200.

82 *Reg. Swinfield,* 338, 358, 377, 395, 439, 476, 530–2, 537, 540–1; *Reg. Orleton,* 96, 102–3, 116–18, 182, 386.

83 *Reg. Cantilupe,* 151.

84 *Cal. Pat.* 1358–61, 64.

85 *Reg. Trillek,* 380, 390; E. Foss, *Biog. Dict. of Judges of Eng.* (1870), 145.

86 *Reg. Trefnant,* 183–4, 191; below, Ditton Priors, manors (Middleton); churches.

87 *Tax. Eccl.* (Rec. Com.), 166, 175.

88 *Valor Eccl.* iii. 210, 216.

the pension fell to the rector's tenant.[89] By the mid 18th century Deuxhill and Glazeley together were worth less than £50 a year clear, insufficient to maintain a priest: thence the union with Chetton.[90]

In 1793 the rectory of Deuxhill had a barn and 17 a. of glebe 'lying well together' north of the hamlet and immediately east of the Bridgnorth road; it was worth £20 a year but was then in hand. The tithes were let for £35.[91] All the tithes belonged to the rector and in 1838 were commuted to £77 17*s*., including those of the glebe.[92] The rector's income from Deuxhill in 1851 was £108.[93] Deuxhill had more glebe than the other livings in the united benefice in 1887,[94] but no rectory house is recorded there, and most post-medieval rectors apparently lived at Glazeley[95] or, later, at Chetton.[96]

In 1553 Deuxhill and Glazeley shared a communion set.[97] Communion was celebrated six times a year in 1719,[98] presumably alternately in the two churches: that was the practice in 1793 when there were four celebrations a year (at the 'usual times'), two in Glazeley and two in Deuxhill. There were then very few communicants in Deuxhill, where the rector read morning service every other Sunday.[99] In 1851 the church had 93 sittings, 40 of them free. On Census Sunday that year the afternoon service was attended by 30 adults; the Sunday school was attended by 26 children, many from other parishes.[1]

The rubble stone church, of unknown dedication,[2] having lost its chancel by the 16th century, comprised in the 19th a nave and a south porch; an aisle mentioned in 1793 and 1856[3] was probably not structural.[4] The church was said in 1759 to be very ruinous but in 1793 and 1870 seems to have been in reasonable repair.[5] After 1875, however, parishioners resorted to the new church at Glazeley and their own, disused, was pulled down in 1886.[6]

In the 14th century, as in the following five centuries, the living was too poor to maintain the chancel effectively and the parishioners were too few to look after the nave properly. In 1318 an indulgence of 30 days was offered to all contributing to the repair and upkeep of the church and its bell turret (*campanile*).[7] As at Middleton Priors, however, the chancel was pulled down; that was done before the insertion of a late medieval window in the wall blocking a round chancel arch.[8]

A timber south porch seems to have been built in 1661 with the lady of the manor's aid,[9] and tablets were put up to commemorate Nathaniel Worthington (d. 1730), members of the Corfield family who died between 1730 and 1770, and the lord of the manor John Lewis (d. 1804) and his widow Frances (d. 1809).[10]

In 1793 an unrailed communion table stood against the east end of the aisle; there were also 9 irregular pews and 'a kind of pulpit', but no reading desk. The floor was then very bad,[11] but in 1837 the interior was described as 'very neat'.[12] The bell turret, which had had two bells (one broken) in the 1730s, contained one in 1851.[13] A font and clock were mentioned in 1856, when the church was said to be in 'good repair'.[14] The west end was lit by a single small window in the west wall, and the south wall contained just one square window. Only the north wall, buttressed at the west end, contained more than one window: it had three, probably all medieval. The westernmost one, 14th-century, in a short stretch of the wall, was all that survived in the 1980s. Wall footings then indicated the extent of the churchyard.

A single register was kept for Deuxhill and Glazeley. The earliest surviving volume covers the years 1655–68 and 1694–1720. The second begins in 1736, and the registers are complete thereafter.[15]

NONCONFORMITY. In 1672 Anne Hassold's house was licensed for Presbyterian worship,[16] and David Jenks, ejected from Bryngwyn (Radnors.) in 1661 but with local connexions,[17] was licensed to conduct Presbyterian worship. Shortly afterwards, however,

89 Consequent mention of the tenant in P.R.O., SC 6/Hen. VIII/3021, m. 17, was misinterpreted by speculators seeking to buy the tithes which they believed to be a Crown impropriation: *Cal. Pat.* 1553–4, 156.

90 H.W.R.O.(H.), Heref. dioc. rec. AL 19/23, f. 53.

91 S.P.L., MS. 6864, f. 43.

92 P.R.O., IR 29/29/106.

93 P.R.O., HO 129/356, no. 3.

94 Cf. *Return of Glebe Lands (Eng. and Wales)*, H.C. 307, p. 58 (1887), lxiv; *Kelly's Dir. Salop.* (1885), 821, 841, 856.

95 See e.g. S.P.L., MS. 6864, f. 45.

96 When Glazeley Rectory began to be used as a curate's ho.: see e.g. Heref. Dioc. Regy., reg. 1822–42, p. 81; 1926–38, p. 275.

97 *T.S.A.S.* 2nd ser. xii. 327.

98 H.W.R.O.(H.), HD 5/15, Deuxhill and Glazeley.

99 S.P.L., MS. 6864, f. 45.

1 P.R.O., HO 129/356, no. 3.

2 There was no wake (above, this article, intro.) to give a clue. Alleged dedication to St. Bartholomew (*Shropshire Mag.* Aug. 1961, 27) confuses it with Glazeley new ch.: cf. S.R.O. 1955/Misc/1; *T.S.A.S.* lv. 35.

3 S.P.L., MS. 6864, f. 45v.; *P.O. Dir. Salop.* (1856), 44.

4 Sources in n. 8 below.

5 H.W.R.O.(H.), Heref. dioc. rec. AL 19/23, f. 53; S.P.L., MS. 6864, f. 45v.; *P.O. Dir. Salop.* (1870), 49.

6 Heref. Dioc. Regy., reg. 1883–1901, pp. 173–5, 189–90; *P.O. Dir. Salop.* (1879), 313, 326; *Kelly's Dir. Salop.* (1885), 841; (1891), 307.

7 *Reg. T. de Cobham* (Worcs. Hist. Soc. 1930), 4; H.W.R.O.(H.), Heref. dioc. rec. AL 19/23, f. 53.

8 For the bldg. before demolition see S.P.L., MS. 372, vol. ii, p. 26; B.L. Add. MS. 21011, p. 66; Heref. Cath. Libr., R.13.6, drawings by Julia H. Purton; S.P.L., J. H. Smith colln. no. 67. Cf. Cranage, iv. 305; x. 991; Pevsner, *Salop.* 120.

9 B.L. Add. MS. 21011, p. 66, gives the initials A H and 1661, perh. a likelier date (being before the Act of Uniformity) than 1668 (S. Bagshaw, *Dir. Salop.* (1851), 644) in view of the lady's Presbyterian leanings (below, nonconf.).

10 B.L. Add. MS. 21237, f. 120; Bagshaw, op. cit. 644.

11 S.P.L., MS. 6864, f. 45v.

12 C. Hulbert, *Hist. and Descr. of Salop.* ii (1837), 344.

13 Birm. Univ. Libr., Mytton papers, ii. 379; S. Bagshaw, *Dir. Salop.* (1851), 644.

14 *P.O. Dir. Salop.* (1856), 44.

15 S.R.O. 1955/Rg/1–2; /MRg/1–2; current vols. at Glazeley ch. Cf. H.W.R.O.(H.), Heref. dioc. rec., transcripts for various yrs. from 1598; S.R.O. 4744/2. Cf. *S.P.R. Heref.* v (5); E. C. Peele and R. S. Clease, *Salop. Par. Doc.* (Shrews. [1903]), 170.

16 P.R.O., SP 44/38A, p. 244.

17 T. Rees, *Hist. of Prot. Nonconf. in Wales* (1861), 173; L.J.R.O., B/C/11, Thos. Jenks 8 Oct. 1684, showing David to be bro. of Thos., a Shrews. goldsmith, and therefore s. of Thos., vicar of Ditton Priors 1623–48: below, Ditton Priors, churches.

Jenks was licensed in Shrewsbury[18] where he normally lived,[19] and in 1676 no dissenter was recorded in Deuxhill.[20]

EDUCATION. In 1819 *c.* 5 pupils were taught in an unendowed day school at their parents' expense, but children of the poor, paying 1*d.* a week, could go *c.* 3 miles to a school 'on the new system'[21] in a neighbouring parish. A school, called a day and Sunday school in 1835 when there were 27 boys and 24 girls, was supported partly by the minister then and partly by subscribers in 1856 and 1871.[22] Like its successor it took most of its pupils from surrounding parishes.

Deuxhill was one of six parishes included in the united district of Chetton school board,[23] formed compulsorily in 1878. In 1879 one of the board's two schools[24] was built, centrally in the district, at Deuxhill; it opened in 1880 with 66 places in a schoolroom and classroom.[25] Inspected in its first year,[26] the school earned government grant, and from 1893 a drawing grant too.[27] Attendance was often high,[28] strikingly so[29] by the standards of rural schools; it averaged 59 in 1885.[30] As early as 1881 there were summonses for irregular attendance.[31] Fees were abolished in 1891.[32] The school, though a board school, was closely associated with the church and even had annual diocesan scripture examinations 1881–1904.[33] It was enlarged for 78 in 1895,[34] but in 1901 some pupils were transferred to the board's Chetton Down school.[35] In 1907–8 the school was enlarged for 100 and improved.[36] Attendance averaged 68 in 1896, 87 in 1905, and 96 in 1913.[37] Gardening was taught from *c.* 1916.[38]

The roll was 65 in 1924, 84 in 1933, and 70 in 1939 including 15 evacuees, 12 of them, with a teacher, from Liverpool. A teacher and 20 Wallasey evacuees were admitted in 1941. All evacuees had left by 1943. Building and facilities were improved in the 1940s, and in 1947 Deuxhill and Chetton Down schools were reorganized: Deuxhill temporarily became a senior and infant school, taking 16 senior pupils from Chetton Down and sending 11 juniors there. That year senior girls began attending Bridgnorth domestic science centre, and next year pupils aged 13–14 transferred to St. Mary's C.E. school, Bridgnorth. In 1950 there were 12 pupils aged 11–12 and 10 infants. When 11-year-olds went to St. Mary's in 1952 Deuxhill took 6 juniors from Chetton Down and became a primary school. The roll was 20 in 1952 but 14 by 1961 when the school closed, pupils transferring to Down County Primary school.[39]

County-council evening classes in wood carving (1895–8) and bee keeping, horticulture, and ambulance (1899–1902) were usually well attended[40] but those in drawing and elementary subjects (1904–6, 1926) less so.[41]

CHARITIES FOR THE POOR. Deuxhill, with Chetton and Glazeley parishes, shared in two of the three charities united in 1914 and known informally as the Chetton Ecclesiastical Charities. The combined annual income was £6 *c.* 1975: £4 from the charity left by Archdeacon Vickers (d. 1851) and £2 from Anne Vickers's charity, established 1864. Deuxhill was also one of seven parishes benefiting from the Glazeley and District Nursing Association, whose income of £70 was applicable, under a Scheme of 1975, to the relief of sick, disabled, or handicapped people.[42]

DITTON PRIORS

DITTON PRIORS is a large remote upland parish equidistant (*c.* 15 km.) from Bridgnorth to the east and Much Wenlock to the north.[43] As communications improved in the early 20th century its isolation was reduced, and by the later 20th century a high proportion of the working population commuted to Bridgnorth, Ludlow, or Kidderminster (Worcs.).[44]

In the 19th century the parish contained 5,566 a. (2,253 ha.)[45] and comprised the three townships of Ditton Priors, Middleton Priors (including Derrington), and Ashfield and

18 P.R.O., SP 44/38A, pp. 244, 269.

19 L.J.R.O., B/V/1/72, St. Chad's, Shrews. (1665); *Hearth Tax 1672* (Salop. Arch. Soc. 1949), 20.

20 *Compton Census*, ed. Whiteman, 257.

21 *Digest Educ. Poor*, H.C. 224, p. 750 (1819), ix (2).

22 *Educ. Enq. Abstract*, H.C. 62, p. 773 (1835), xlii; *P.O. Dir. Salop.* (1856), 44; E. Cassey & Co. *Dir. Salop.* (1871), 140.

23 With Billingsley, Chetton, Glazeley, Middleton Scriven, and Sidbury.

24 The other was Chetton Down sch., built at the same time.

25 *Sch. Bds. in Eng. and Wales, 1902* [Cd. 1038], p. 75 (1902), lxxix; P.R.O., ED 7/102, ff. 244–5; *Kelly's Dir. Salop.* (1885), 842; S.R.O. 1158/7, p. 86.

26 S.R.O. 1158/7, pp. 27, 29–30.

27 Ibid. pp. 125, 149, 259, 270–4, 279–80.

28 S.R.O. 1158/7–8 *passim*, esp. /7, p. 359; /8, p. 4.

29 Esp. in view of its wide catchment area: see e.g. ibid. /8, p. 182.

30 Ibid. /7, p. 149.

31 Ibid. p. 47 and *passim.*

32 Ibid. p. 223.

33 Ibid. *passim*. Clergy were sch. bd. members, sch. correspondents, and regular visitors.

34 Ibid. pp. 307, 313, 457.

35 Ibid. p. 387.

36 Ibid. pp. 384, 483, 498.

37 Ibid. pp. 329, 450; *Kelly's Dir. Salop.* (1913), 88.

38 S.R.O. 1158/8, pp. 68, 82, etc.

39 Ibid. p. 145; /9, pp. 77, 82, 84, 93, 105–6, 109, 127–8, 130, 185–7.

40 *S.C.C. Mins.* 1895–1902, organizing sec.'s ann. reps. to Intermediate Educ. Cttee.

41 S.C.C. *Higher Educ. Dept. Rep. 1904–5*, 12 (copy in S.R.O.); *S.C.C. Mins. (Educ.)* 1906–7, 52; S.R.O. 1158/8, pp. 201, 206.

42 S.C.C. Sec. and Solr.'s Dept., chars. index; *Review of Local Chars.* (S.C.C. 1975), 23–4; cf. *3rd Rep. Com. Char.* H.C. 5, p. 272 (1820), iv; *S.P.R. Heref.* v (5), p. iv.

43 This article was written in 1985–6 and later revised.

44 Below, this section; N. Smith, 'Changing Patterns in Salop.' (Wolverhampton Teacher Training Coll. dissertation, 1971), 82–4. Thanks are offered to the Revd. M. A. J. Harding for lending a copy of the dissertation and to the late Nancy Smith for permission to cite it.

45 O.S. *Area Bk.* (1884).

DITTON PRIORS IN THE LATE 19TH CENTURY
N
mile
km
0
½
1
To Bridgnorth
SIDNALL
Lightwood Farm
LIGHTWOOD
New Farm
GREAT HUDWICK
LOWER NETCHWOOD
To Little Hudwick and Monkhopton
Middleton North
Middleton Baggot
MIDDLETON
Middleton Priors
mill
To Neenton
To Cleobury North
Biches Farm
OAKWOOD
Oakwood Farm
To Cleobury North
To Monkhopton
To Weston
DERRINGTON
Rea Brook
Lower Ruthall
RUTHALL
Ruthall Manor
Ruthall Farm
To Great Oxenbold
DITTON PRIORS
vicarage
remnant open fields land boundaries
Hillside Farm
Ditton limeworks (disused)
BROWN CLEE HILL
ABDON BURF
POWKESMOOR COPPICE
Powkesmoor Farm
To Abdon
ASHFIELD
To Stanton Long
To Earnstrey Park and Tugford
chapel close (1841)
MIDDLETON NORTH
MIDDLETON BAGGOT
MIDDLETON
MIDDLETON PRIORS
Lodge
0 yards 100
0 metres 100
vicars well
Church Farm
school
church
Howard Arms P.H.
Ditton Farm
DITTON PRIORS
saw pit
Methodist chapel
Hall Farm
To the vicarage
saw pit
0 yards 100
0 metres 100

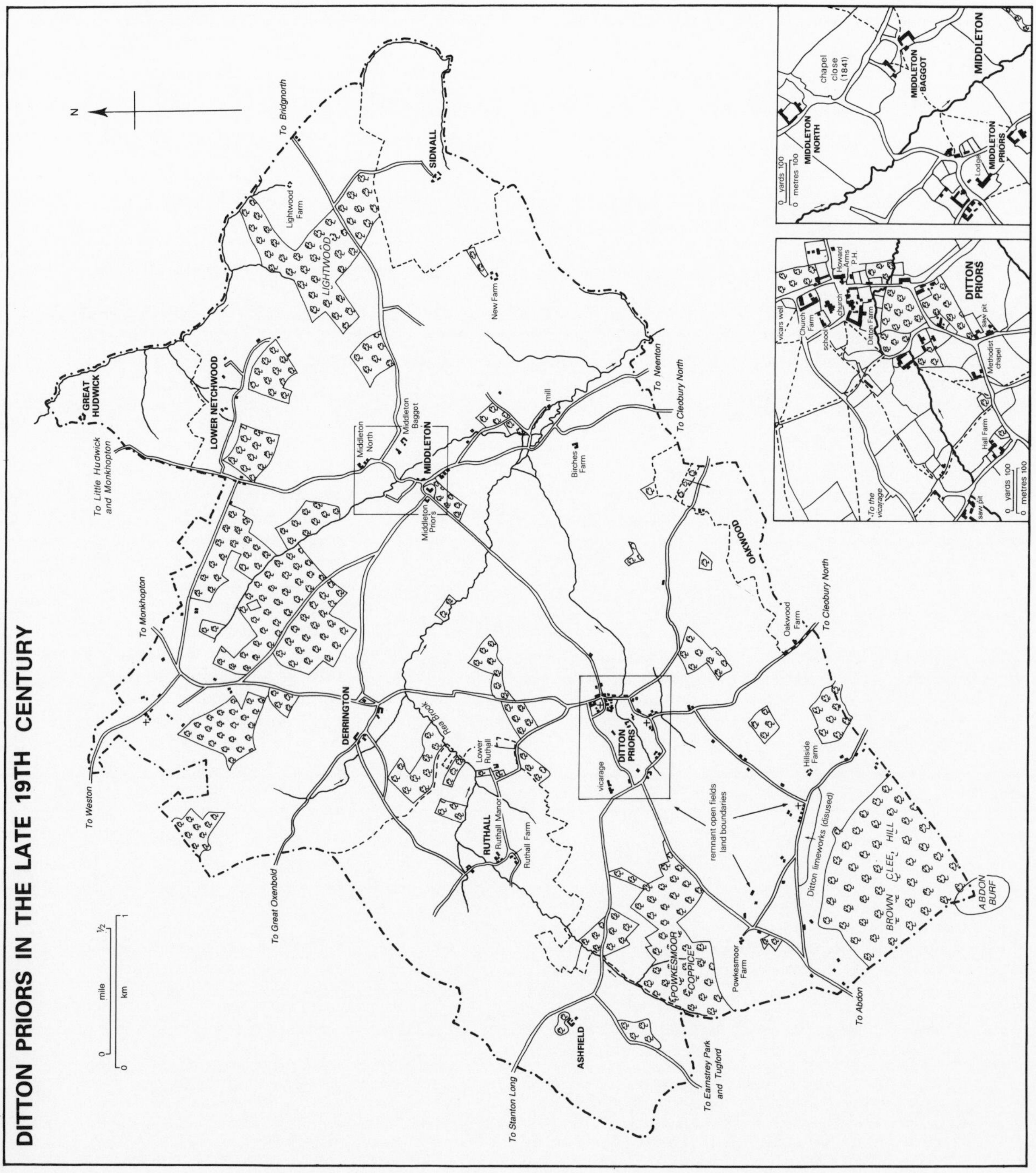

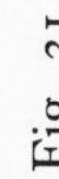

Fig. 31

Ruthall.[46] About 0.1 ha. beside the Ditton–Abdon road was transferred from Ditton Priors civil parish to Abdon C.P. in 1967.[47]

In places streams form the parish boundary, but only on the north-east side, where Beaconhill brook drains north down Park and Hudwick dingles, does that happen for any great distance. From the top of Park dingle the boundary runs south-east along the line of the former pale of Upton Cressett park, a manorial boundary in 1621.[48] The northern boundary, with Monkhopton, mostly follows the edge of the Clee Hills plateau but leaves the edge to exclude Little Hudwick and is in places defined by field boundaries.[49] The Brown Clee commons were divided probably in the earlier 17th century, and the boundary of Ditton's allotment later became that of the parish.[50] Elsewhere the boundary has a flowing line that suggests its definition by features such as the edges of woods.

Most of the parish lies at 200–250 m., falling below 140 m. only north of Great Hudwick where Beaconhill brook leaves the parish.[51] The parish includes the headwaters of the stream known, perhaps until the earlier 14th century, as the Neen (Nene) and thereafter as the Rea or South Rea;[52] anciently it probably divided Ditton from Middleton. Except for Ashfield the parish's settlements all stand on or near streams, principally the Rea and its tributaries.[53] South-west of Ditton village the ground rises steeply to Abdon Burf, highest point (1,790 ft., 545 m.) in the midlands[54] and the northern of the two peaks on Brown Clee hill. The hill is composed largely of Breconian Beds folded in a syncline with thin sheets of Coal Measures, capped overall by hard olivine dolerite. It is thought that Clee hill gained the description Brown (from the local soil colour) in the 15th century to distinguish it from Titterstone Clee 10 km. south. Apart from Brown Clee the parish lies on Lower Old Red Sandstone (Ditton Series), in which some cornstone appears.[55] Tufa formations in Hudwick dingle secured the designation of a site of special scientific interest in 1963.[56]

A probable Ditton–Wenlock 'Portway' by Ruthall (1327), Oxenbold coppice, and Weston (1256)[57] was superseded; later roads from Ditton ran north (via Derrington and Weston) and west (via Ashfield and Stanton Long) into the principal Corve Dale route from Ludlow forking near Shipton to Bridgnorth and Much Wenlock; by *c.* 1350 another ran south to Cleobury North[58] where it joined a Ludlow–Bridgnorth road running east of the Brown Clee. The direct road from Ditton to Bridgnorth, via Middleton, recorded in the mid 13th century,[59] was turnpiked in 1762 but was 'very bad' in 1794.[60] In 1825 the turnpike was extended to the foot of Brown Clee hill and separate districts for Ditton Priors and Cleobury North were created.[61] There were turnpike gates in Ditton village[62] and at Lightwood.[63]

From Middleton a road (now only a footpath) south to Cleobury North crossed the Rea by a bridge that was probably called Broad bridge in the 13th and 14th centuries;[64] other ways by then ran south-south-east to Neenton[65] and north-west to Derrington,[66] and 'Dodeley way' and 'Othleye (Overleye) way' were names for some of the roads from Middleton.[67]

Two roads running south-west from Ditton village to the base of Brown Clee hill perhaps originated as 'strake' (drift) roads to the common. The eastern one, settled by squatters, was called Bent Lane. In the early 17th century there were also strake roads to the hill from Ashfield and from Ruthall, only the former outlasting straking. The inclosure of Brown Clee and Netchwood in 1841 wrought minor changes to roads in Ditton and Middleton villages and in the Lightwood area.[68]

Cleobury Mortimer and Ditton Priors Light Railway was built in 1907–8 to carry stone from Abdon Burf quarry. Worked by the G.W.R., it ran from Ditton Priors to Cleobury Mortimer where it joined the line from Bewdley to Tenbury Wells. There was a passenger service from Ditton 1908–38, and the line served the Royal Naval Armaments Depot (near Ditton village) 1939–65.[69]

Flints and perhaps a basalt axe hammer have been found at Lightwood and Oakwood,[70] while the parish's southern extremity lies within Abdon Burf hill fort. Until largely destroyed by mining and quarrying in the early 20th century, it was one of Shropshire's most impressive Iron Age forts. Oval and probably univallate, it enclosed *c.* 7 ha. Of particular note were its apparently stone faced ramparts. Within it 44 possible hut circles of stone were visible in the earlier 19th century, and at the junction of the divisions of the common (the later parish boundaries) was a big stone with 'a cross and letters' on it.[71]

Ditton and Middleton were clearly the two

46 S. Bagshaw, *Dir. Salop.* (1851), 589; cf. S.P.L., MS. 6864, f. 47.

47 *Salop (No. 2) Order 1966* (Stat. Instr. 1966, no. 1529), map 43 (copy in S.R.O., DA 19/701/6).

48 S.R.O. 5460/4/1/6.

49 For the boundaries see O.S. Maps 6", Salop. LVII. SE., LVIII. SW., LXV. NW., VE , SE., LXVI. NW. (1903 edn.).

50 Below, econ. hist. (agric.); S.R.O. 1037/21/6.

51 O.S. Maps 1/25,000, SO 58–9, 68–9 (1956 edn.).

52 Ekwall, *Eng. Place-Names* (1960), 337; S.P.L., Deeds 6968; Nott. Univ. Libr. MSS. Dept., Mi. D. 3686/3; *V.C.H. Salop*. i. 57–8.

53 Fig. 31.

54 1,805 ft. before quarrying: *T.S.A.S.* 4th ser. xii. 87.

55 H. W. Ball, *Old Red Sandstone of Brown Clee Hill* (1961), 178; T. Rowley, *Landscape of Welsh Marches* (1986), 224; *T.S.A.S.* lviii. 48.

56 Inf. from Nature Conservancy Council.

57 Nott. Univ. Libr. MSS Dept., Mi.D. 3686/7; below, Monkhopton, intro. For this and the next two paras. cf. O.S. Map 1/50,000, sheet 138 (1988 edn.).

58 S.P.L., Deeds 6975, 6983.

59 Ibid. 6952, 6964.

60 2 Geo. III, c. 79; S.P.L., MS. 6864, f. 47.

61 6 Geo. IV, c. 49 (Local and Personal); S.R.O. 3419, turnpike papers.

62 R. Baugh, *Map of Salop.* (1808).

63 S.P.L., photo.

64 S.P.L., Deeds 6956–7, 6970.

65 Ibid. 6949, 6956, 6980.

66 Ibid. 6949–50, 6973.

67 Ibid. 6953, 6973.

68 *T.S.A.S.* lviii. 60–1; below, econ hist. (agric.); S.R.O. 990/2.

69 W. Smith and K. Beddoes, *Cleobury Mortimer and Ditton Priors Lt. Rly.* (1980), 9, 12, 16, 22, 29, 33, 44, 85, 101; M. Price, *Cleobury Mortimer and Ditton Priors Lt. Rly.* (Locomotion Papers xxii; Lingfield, 1983); *T.S.A.S.* lxiv. 93–4; below, this section; econ. hist. (ind.).

70 S.P.L., Chitty File 52/12–13; 158/1–17.

71 O.S. Map 1/2,500, Salop. LXV. 11 (1903 edn.); *V.C.H. Salop*. i. 197, 359, 371; S.R.O. 1037/21/6; *T.S.A.S.* 4th ser. xii. 85–96; C. H. Hartshorne, *Salopia Antiqua* (1841), 3–21; *Salop. N. & Q.* vi. 78–9, 107–8.

primary settlements. A possible interpretation of Ditton's name is 'place near a hill'.[72] Middleton's name seems to indicate its mid-way location between the townships of Ditton and Upton (Cressett)[73] but may possibly refer to its position between Rea brook and its tributary to the east.[74] By 1066 Middleton was probably one of Ditton's four berewicks (unnamed in 1086),[75] the others perhaps being the settlements to the north unnamed in 1086 but probably then in existence, Derrington and possibly Weston and Hopton.[76] Ruthall had probably once been a member of Ditton[77] but was manorially distinct by 1066.[78] Ditton, Middleton, and Ruthall (and perhaps Derrington) had open fields in the early 14th century.[79]

In Ditton Priors there were 12 tenements in 1510–11, fewer than in Middleton.[80] The only medieval timbers known in the parish are those re-used in the eastern half of Ditton Farm, which has a later 17th-century stair turret.[81] There is substantial 17th-century work in Church Farm,[82] which has traces of 17th-century wall painting on the gable of an upper chamber, and in Hall Farm (1693).[83] By the 1720s the manorial estate had some cottages and a dozen farmhouses in Ditton township,[84] probably most of them in or near the village. Also in the village, near the church, stood the vicarage and a public house, now the Howard Arms, one of the larger 18th-century buildings in the parish.[85] Alone among settlements in the parish Ditton grew in the 20th century. Between the 1920s and the 1940s more than 20 houses were built in and around the village: 16 in two rows near Hall Farm were for quarrymen, and there were 5 houses for county council smallholdings, built to accord to the national 'Type 2' but on a system using locally cast concrete panels and posts.[86] In 1955 an incongruous yellowish brick was used for 20 council houses in Brown Clee Road, off Station Road on the east side of the village.[87] The village was made a conservation area in 1982,[88] and in the mid 1980s houses there were increasing through refurbishments and barn conversions: Ditton Farm and its buildings, for instance, were made into 14 small dwellings.

In 1939 a Royal Naval Armaments Depot was established south-east of Ditton village and extending into Cleobury North and Neenton parishes on land made available by Lord Boyne.[89] After the Second World War the land was densely planted with Japanese larch.[90] The U.S. army used the depot as a temporary ammunition dump 1967–8, but by 1971 the adjoining land was available for agriculture again and some depot buildings had been sold for industrial use.

In the 1840s the lord of the manor piped water to Ditton village from a spring on Brown Clee hill and set up three or four public taps; one (1845) has an ornate arched stone surround.[91] In the 19th century 'parson's' or 'vicar's' well lay in Well meadow just north of Ditton;[92] it was perhaps a public well. In the 1940s the armaments depot and New Hall Farm were supplied by boreholes.[93] Ditton village received mains water in 1968,[94] electricity by 1979,[95] and a main sewer in 1985.[96]

Extensive earthworks in fields around Hyde Farm show that the nucleus of settlement at Middleton Priors was once considerably larger. In 1510–11 there were *c.* 15 tenements in Middleton and a church,[97] but in 1625 mention of Hither and Further Middleton[98] suggests that the settlement had already shrunk and lay dispersed, as in the 18th century. Hyde Farm is a stone and timber framed building of the 16th century and later[99] while Middleton Baggot, Middleton North, and the north range of Middleton Lodge are substantially 17th-century. In the Middleton half of the parish 20 of the houses that paid hearth tax in 1672 had one hearth, 7 had two, 2 had three, and the other 4 had four, five, six, and seven.[1] Middleton Lodge[2] is among the larger 18th-century buildings in the parish. By the 1720s the manorial estate included 10 farmhouses, some cottages, and a mill in Middleton Priors township.[3] Settlement continued to shrink in the 18th century. The chapel of ease closed *c.* 1780, and by the early 19th century the hamlet consisted of little more than the scattered Middleton Lodge, Hyde Farm, Middleton Baggot, and Middleton North.[4] Later in the century a school[5] and two or three cottages were built.

Derrington and Ruthall, north of Ditton, were minor settlements. Five men were described as 'of Ruthall' in 1312.[6] There were three tenements at Derrington in 1510–11[7] and three substantial

72 *P.N. Salop.* (E.P.N.S.), i. 106–7, 109–10. But cf. Ekwall, *Eng. Place-Names*, 146.

73 *P.N. Salop.* (E.P.N.S.), i, pp. xiv, 205, where Middleton Priors should be added to the examples. The three townships neatly cover the N. end of the Clee Hills plateau: O.S. Map 1", index to tithe survey, sheet LXI. SW., SE. [*c.* 1851].

74 Ekwall, op. cit. 325.

75 *V.C.H. Salop.* i. 317.

76 Eyton, iii. 329–30, suggests Derrington and Middleton and that the others might be two from Ashfield, Hudwick, Powkesmore, and Sidnall. Powkesmore seems unlikely. The early manorial and parochial connexions of Weston and Hopton are unknown.

77 As the par. topography and boundary suggest.

78 *V.C.H. Salop.* i. 339.

79 Below, econ. hist. (agric.).

80 Ibid.; below, this section.

81 SA 11825.

82 SA 11823.

83 SA 11826; below, manors.

84 S.P.L., Deeds 743, ff. 1–13; S.R.O., q. sess. rec. parcel 281, reg. of papists' deeds 1717–88, pp. 1–2, 188–9; J. Rocque, *Map of Salop.* (1752).

85 Below, churches; SA 11824.

86 Smith, 'Changing Patterns', 80; below, econ. hist. (ind.).

87 Inf. from Bridgnorth Dist. Council.

88 *Shropshire Star*, 10 Mar. 1981; inf. from S.C.C. Planning Dept.

89 Para. based on Smith and Beddoes, *Cleobury Mortimer and Ditton Priors Lt. Rly.* 85, 93–4; Smith, 'Changing Patterns', 78, 80; Price, *Cleobury Mortimer and Ditton Priors Lt. Rly.* 24–5; *Shropshire Star*, 4 July 1985, p. 8; O.S. Maps 1/25,000, SO 68 (1956 edn.), 78 (1958 edn.); 1/2,500, SO 6088/6188 (1973 edn.); below, econ. hist. (ind.).

90 Inf. from Mr. E. T. Edwards.

91 Inf. from Mr. Harding.

92 O.S. Map 6", Salop. LXV. NE. (1891 edn.); S.P.L., SC1/2, map, fields 245–6; S.R.O. 990/2.

93 A. H. S. Waters, *Rep. on Water Supply* (S.C.C. 1946), 46.

94 Smith, 'Changing Patterns', 82, 85.

95 Local inf.

96 Ditton smallholdings management file in S.C.C. County Valuer's and Land Agent's Dept., corresp. 22 May 1985, etc.

97 Below, econ. hist. (agric.); churches.

98 S.R.O. 3419, glebe terrier 1625.

99 SA 11817–18.

1 *Hearth Tax 1672* (Salop. Arch. Soc. 1949), 30; similar inf. for Ditton lost through damage to the MS.

2 SA 11819.

3 S.P.L., Deeds 734, ff. 24–32; S.R.O., q. sess. rec. parcel 281, reg. of papists' deeds 1717–88, pp. 1–2, 188–9; J. Rocque, *Map of Salop.* (1752).

4 Below, churches; O.S. Map 1", sheet LXI. SE. (1833 edn.).

5 Below, educ.

6 B.L. Harl. MS. 2063, f. 9.

7 Below, econ. hist. (agric.).

farmhouses there in the 1720s, Ruthall being about the same size.[8] By the end of the 19th century Derrington had shrunk to two farms,[9] but there were four at Ruthall in the 1980s, including Lower Ruthall 0.5 km. east of the others. The northern end of Derrington Manor Farm is 16th-century and it has a later 17th-century stair turret with the original staircase *in situ*.[10] Derrington Farm (formerly Derrington East) contains substantial 17th-century work[11] as do Ruthall Manor[12] and Upper Ruthall, a stone building mainly of *c.* 1800. Ruthall Farm was refronted and enlarged in the late 18th or early 19th century.

Ashfield, Great Hudwick, and Sidnall, respectively at the western, northern, and eastern extremities of the parish, were small in post-medieval times. At Ashfield and Sidnall, however, earthworks indicate bigger medieval settlements. In 1401 there were perhaps five farms at Ashfield,[13] and Sidnall's former earthworks[14] suggest that it may once have been of comparable size.[15] By 1510–11 the manorial estate included a single tenement in Hudwick and one in Sidnall,[16] and by the mid 18th century Ashfield also seems to have consisted of only one farm.[17] Great Hudwick was long uninhabited before 1986 when the remaining building, a barn, became a house.[18]

By the 1720s squatters had settled in the north at Netchwood and in the south around the bottom of Brown Clee; each area had *c.* 23 cottages.[19] At Netchwood in 1841 there were *c.* 28 cottages in two main concentrations, one at each end of the common, and by 1847 each had a Methodist chapel.[20] In the 20th century the western cluster was known as Upper Netchwood, the eastern as Lower Netchwood. In the later 19th[21] and the 20th century the number of cottages at Netchwood declined by about half. In the south the pattern was similar: in 1841 there were *c.* 18 cottages around the bottom of Brown Clee hill and *c.* 10 more along Bent Lane.[22] In the later 19th and early 20th century many were quarrymen's homes and some no more than wooden shacks with iron roofs.[23] Again the number has declined.[24]

Invariably the external walls of ancient farms in the parish (many containing substantial 17th-century work) are of the local dhu stone (dolerite) or sandstone, although internal walls are sometimes timber framed. Powkesmore brickyard was open by the early 19th century, but the ready availability of stone confined brick's use in the parish to the larger buildings (and often to their façades) like Ruthall Manor (*c.* 1820), the Vicarage (1828), Lower Ruthall, Sidnall, and Ashfield Farm (1878).[25] Clay roof tiles began to be commonly used in preference to stone slates in the late 19th century,[26] and brick and concrete were used in and around Ditton village in the 20th century.[27]

In 1086 Ditton's recorded population was 38, Ruthall's 5.[28] In Ditton 18 paid to the subsidy in 1327 and in Ashfield 4; Ruthall was then taxed with Easthope 5 km. to the north-west, the two places having a combined total of 10 taxpayers.[29] In 1542 ten men from Middleton were mustered, 9 from Ditton, and 3 each from Derrington and Ruthall.[30] The 1642 Protestation was taken by 118 men, with one refusal,[31] while in 1676 there were 424 parishioners, perhaps including children.[32] In 1672 hearth tax was paid by 29 householders in the Ditton half of the parish, 33 in the Middleton half.[33] The parish's population continued to grow, mostly, if not solely, in the squatter settlements. There were 608 inhabitants and 132 houses in 1794. For most of the 19th century the population fluctuated around 600–650, but, for reasons that are obscure but may have included the closure of the limeworks,[34] it fell sharply in the 1880s and 1890s, to 505 by 1901. In the 20th century it was usually just over 600, though the armaments depot was presumably responsible for increasing the population to a record 701 in 1951. In 1981 it was 547.[35]

After 1176 (and possibly before) the lord of Ditton did not reside, and in 1794 only two of the eleven landowners did—Elizabeth Onslow, owner of a small property at Ruthall,[36] and the vicar. In the 1790s there was often no borough magistrate nearer than Wenlock and even Ashfield and Ruthall (outside the borough) were far from a resident justice.[37] There was nevertheless some social life in the 18th century. Midsummer day wakes were held in 1733,[38] and in the 1780s an annual hunt was attended by local gentry and the more prosperous tenant farmers.[39] In the late 18th and early 19th century there were two alehouses in the parish.[40] In Ditton the Plough and the Canning Arms were open in 1851.[41] The Plough had closed by 1871, but there were two ale sellers at Netchwood in the 1870s.[42]

8 S.P.L., Deeds 734, ff. 21–3; S.R.O., q. sess. rec. parcel 281, reg. of papists' deeds 1717–88, pp. 1–2, 188–9; J. Rocque, *Map of Salop.* (1752); R. J. Ranford, *Hist. Ditton Priors* (Bridgnorth, 1936), 9–10 (copy in Bridgnorth branch libr.).
9 O.S. Map 6", Salop. LXV. NE. (1903 edn.).
10 SA 11821.
11 SA 11820.
12 SA 11828.
13 Below, manors (Ashfield); econ. hist. Cf. SA 1276.
14 Levelled *c.* 1980: inf. from Messrs. G. A. and G. S. Price.
15 SA 3371, and aerial photos. there cited; Rowley, *Landscape of Welsh Marches*, 172.
16 Below, econ. hist. (agric.).
17 Rocque, *Map of Salop.* (1752).
18 Below, manors (Gt. Hudwick).
19 S.P.L., Deeds 734, ff. 14–19v., 34–45.
20 S.R.O. 990/5; below, prot. nonconf.
21 S.P.L., SC1/2.
22 S.R.O. 990/3; Smith, 'Changing Patterns', 75.
23 Smith, op. cit. 78; *Shropshire Star*, 10 Feb. 1995, p. 13.
24 O.S. Maps 6", SJ 58 NE., 68 NW. (1954 edn.).
25 Below, manors (Sidnall; Ashfield; Ruthall); econ. hist. (ind.); churches.
26 S.R.O. 3419, Howard est. acct. bk. 1886–92, 7 Aug. 1890.
27 Above, this section.
28 *V.C.H. Salop.* i. 317, 339.
29 Below, econ hist. (agric.); *T.S.A.S.* 2nd ser. iv. 295, 319, 327. The reason for combining the tax records of the two places is not apparent.
30 *L. & P. Hen. VIII*, xvii, p. 508.
31 Ho. of Lords papers 1641–2, Protestations Oxon. and Salop. f. 192.
32 *Compton Census*, ed. Whiteman, 248, 257.
33 *Hearth Tax 1672*, 30–1.
34 Below, econ. hist. (ind.).
35 S.P.L., MS. 6864, f. 47; *V.C.H. Salop.* ii. 222; *Census*, 1971, *Co. Rep. Salop.* i. 3; *Census*, 1981, Small Area Statistics: Salop.
36 S.R.O. 515/4, p. 42; 1359, box 44, John Cheese's will 1789.
37 S.P.L., MS. 6864, f. 47v.
38 Birm. Univ. Libr., Mytton Papers, ii. 387.
39 *V.C.H. Salop.* ii. 166, implying a foxhunt; *Salop. N. & Q.* N.S. iii. 38, suggesting a hare coursing.
40 W.B.R., Q1/11/2.
41 S. Bagshaw, *Dir. Salop.* (1851), 590–1.
42 E. Cassey & Co. *Dir. Salop.* (1871), 284–5; (1874), 284–5; S.P.L., SC1/2, p. 6 (beerho. in or nr. field 90).

The Canning (from *c.* 1860 Howard)[43] Arms remained open. In the 19th century and until the First World War the high spots of the annual round of fêtes, sports, and 'club' events were perhaps Ditton's spring and autumn fairs, though Bridgnorth fair and regatta were outside attractions.[44] A cricket club formed in 1868 by the energetic vicar J. B. Wilkinson had 29 members in its first season and perhaps lasted into the early 20th century.[45]

The parish had a friendly society in the late 18th and early 19th century[46] and two a hundred years later; there was a mutual improvement society *c.* 1880–1920 and a lodge of the National United Order of Free Gardeners which paraded in 1894. A parish library was associated with the mutual improvement society, and in 1926 a county library book centre opened.[47] Other parish clubs and societies included a band (mentioned 1923)[48] and a Women's Institute (1924).[49] In 1967 the former armaments depot canteen was bought for a village hall. About 1980 land north of the church was bought as a recreation field for the village clubs and school; a pavilion was built there in 1983. Brown Clee was then increasingly used for recreation: a nature trail had opened *c.* 1970, at which time there was an annual sponsored race up the hill.[50]

MANORS AND OTHER ESTATES. In 1066 *DITTON* was held by Edwin, earl of Mercia (d. 1071), and in 1086 by Roger of Montgomery, cr. earl of Shrewsbury 1068.[51] Earl Roger's son Earl Robert forfeited his English estates in 1102,[52] and Ditton remained in the Crown's hands until granted to Hugh of Periers in 1154–5. Periers entered Wenlock priory and gave it the reversion of the manor after the death of his wife Alice de Cheney. When Periers died (1175 or early 1176) the king assigned the manor to the priory which, however, recognized Alice's interest and presumably compensated her. Alice remarried, and in 1180 her husband Geoffrey de Say obtained new terms from the priory: it was to pay 160 marks down to cover all Say's claim to the manor for eight years and after that an annuity to his wife. Wenlock retained the manor until its surrender in 1540.[53]

In 1544 the Crown sold the manor to Humphrey Pakington, a London mercer, to be held in chief as ¼ knight's fee for a reserved rent, sold by the Crown in 1550.[54] Humphrey was succeeded by his son John (d. 1578), of Chaddesley Corbett (Worcs.), and John by his son Humphrey, of Harvington Hall. Humphrey's recusancy led to the Crown's seizure of the manor and rectory in 1591, and the Crown then farmed it out.[55] Nevertheless Humphrey (d. 1631) settled the manor on his daughter Anne (d. 1642) and Sir Henry Audley (d. *c.* 1672) of Berechurch (Essex) when they married in 1628.

The Audleys' eldest surviving daughter Catherine married Robert Barker of Monkwick (Essex), who predeceased her. They left two sons Thomas (d. 1704) and Bestune (d. 1705) and the manor was later divided between their sister Apollonia (d. 1713), who married Francis Canning (d. 1734) of Foxcote (Warws.),[56] and their spinster aunt Mary Audley of Ramsden Heath (Essex). Mary's moiety was reunited with the Cannings' on her death in 1722,[57] and the manor descended from father to son until 1831: to Francis (d. 1766), Francis (d. 1806), and Francis (d. 1831). The last left no issue, and the manor passed first to his brother Robert (d. 1843) and then to their niece Eliza Minto Canning (d. 1865), who married P. H. Howard of Corby Castle (Cumb.).[58] Between 1874 and 1878 the estate passed to the Howards' son P. J. C. Howard, who in the 1880s sold *c.* 1,800 a. of it to G. R. Hamilton-Russell, Viscount Boyne, and died in 1934. His widow Mrs. A. C. Howard (d. 1941) was afterwards lady of the manor.[59]

Hall Farm, a **T** shaped stone building of two storeys and an attic, was built by Catherine Barker in 1693. Some windows have moulded labels, an unusual elaboration for the locality.[60]

When Hugh of Periers granted Ditton to Wenlock priory parts at least of *MIDDLETON* had been subinfeudated, and Periers safeguarded the rights of his tenants in fee there: Achilles, Walinger of Sidnall and his brother Aubrey, and Adam the butler (*pincerna*).[61] Adam

43 *P.O. Dir. Salop.* (1856), 105; (1863), 736.

44 Below, econ. hist. (fairs); Ranford, *Ditton Priors*, 15; Middleton Priors R.C. sch. log bk. (in possession of Mrs. P. H. Evans, Ditton Priors) refs. 1876–1924 (provided by Mrs. J. McFall). For the 'club' see next para.

45 Par. rec. (at the Vicarage 1984), par. log bk. i, s.a. 1868; ii, p. 7.

46 S.R.O., q. sess. rec. parcel 285, index to club articles, s.a. 1784.

47 Par. rec., par. log bk. i, s.a. 1894; ii, p. 35; R. C. Elliott, 'Development of Public Libraries in Salop.' (Loughborough Univ. M.A. thesis, 1970), 125 (copy in co. libr.).

48 Par. rec., par. log bk. ii, p. 39.

49 Middleton Priors R.C. sch. log bk. 23 Dec. 1924.

50 Smith, 'Changing Patterns', 80; *Shropshire Star*, 3 Jan. 1984, p. 21.

51 *V.C.H. Salop.* i. 317; iii. 7.

52 Ibid. iii. 10.

53 Eyton, iii. 330–5; *T.S.A.S.* v. 174; *V.C.H. Salop.* ii. 45.

54 Para. based on *L. & P. Hen. VIII*, xix (2), p. 81; *Cal. Pat.* 1549–51, p. 287; P.R.O., C 142/183, no. 76; C 142/466, no. 113; E 36/259, f. 305v.; Burke, *Peerage* (1949), 929–30; *V.C.H. Essex*, ix. 412; *V.C.H. Worcs.* iii. 36, 39–40; Warws. R.O., CR 1379, deeds *passim*.

55 *Recusant Roll*, i (Cath. Rec. Soc. xviii), 263–4; ii (Cath. Rec. Soc. lvii), 132; iii–iv (Cath. Rec. Soc. lxi), 76, 204; *Recusants in Pipe R. 1581–92* (Cath. Rec. Soc. lxxi), 130 (refs. provided by Mr. Michael Hodgetts).

56 W.S.L. 350/3/40, Ditton Priors pp. 1, 4; *V.C.H. Worcs.* iv. 367; Warws. R.O., CR 1379, box 4, deed 20 Nov. 1680, Cath. Barker's will; M.I.s in Ilmington ch. (Warws.), transcribed by Dr. Richard Hingley.

57 S.R.O., q. sess. rec. box 260, reg. of gamekeepers 1711–42, 13 Apr. 1717; parcel 281, reg. of papists' deeds 1717– 88, pp. 1–2; S.R.O. 1224, box 200, deed 30 Mar. 1700; Ranford, *Ditton Priors*, 11; Warws. R.O., CR 1379, box 4, Cath. Barker's will; Essex R.O., D/P 55/1/1, bur. 6 June 1722.

58 S.R.O., q. sess. rec. box 260, reg. of gamekeepers 1711–42, 2 June 1731, 2 June 1733; 1742–79, 2 Apr. 1765, 22 July 1766; parcel 261, reg. of gamekeepers 1799–1807, 5 Aug. 1799; parcel 281, reg. of papists' deeds 1717–88, pp. 188–9; S.P.L., Deeds 636, 2636; W.S.L. 350/3/40, Ditton Priors p. 1; inf. from Shakespeare Birthplace Trust R.O., Stratford-upon-Avon (citing DR 41/9).

59 Burke, *Land. Gent.* i (1846), 185–6, 598; S. Bagshaw, *Dir. Salop.* (1851), 589; E. Cassey & Co. *Dir. Salop.* (1874), 284; S.P.L., SC1/2; *Kelly's Dir. Salop.* (1885–1941); Burke, *Peerage* (1967), 1855; below, econ. hist. (agric.).

60 SA 11826; Ranford, *Ditton Priors*, 10. It is probably the bldg. whose rooms are listed in H.W.R.O.(H.), Heref. dioc. rec., inv. of Thos. Barker, 1704.

61 Eyton, iii. 331, 338.

was presumably Periers' butler,[62] and later landowners in Middleton, to judge from their surname Chamberlain, may have derived their estate from predecessors who served the lord of Ditton in a personal capacity. Stephen Chamberlain held an estate in Middleton of Wenlock priory and by 1256 had fallen behind with his rent of ½ mark;[63] he gave land to his daughter Agnes[64] and passed on the estate to his son William. William alienated many properties in Middleton,[65] thus perhaps breaking up his estate.

A sequence of personal names suggests a line of Middleton landowners descending from Adam the butler. William (fl. 1180) son of Adam[66] was probably the William Clerk of Middleton who, in the earlier 13th century, held 1 virgate in Middleton of Engelard of Acton for 5*s.* a year.[67] In the mid or later 13th century William Clerk's son Adam sold the virgate to Richard Clerk, son of the rector of Burwarton. Engelard of Acton's interest later seems to have passed to Wenlock priory.[68] There may have been a dynasty of clerks (later the Clerk family) serving the priory in various ways. Richard of Middleton (d. 1323 × 1329), clerk, perhaps the same as Richard Clerk, purchaser of the virgate, was also known as Richard of the farmery (i.e. infirmary). He left a widow and sons Richard and Roger le Clerk,[69] of Middleton. Roger may have been the Roger le Clerk who left a son John (fl. 1349),[70] possibly the John Clerk who was father of Gillian Low or Leye (fl. 1401–28).[71] The 1-virgate farm was known by 1510–11 as *HYGGS*[72] or *HYGGS YARD*.[73] Gillian Leye and her husband apparently sold it to John Page of Oxenbold in 1401 and later that year Page sold it to Richard de Arderne, the vicar. In 1418 Walter Arderne conveyed the farm to Thomas Hochekyns, but by 1428 it seems to have belonged to Richard de Arderne's nephew Richard Kynston of Ludlow. In 1443 Kynston sold it to Thomas Downe. William Clerk, esquire, bought the property from Downe's mortgagee in 1477,[74] and Thomas Clerk probably had it by 1510–11; he sold it in 1543 to John Taylor, who sold it to Richard Fewtrell in 1545.[75]

Wenlock priory had probably acquired most of the land in Middleton by the early 16th century,[76] leaving Hyggs Yard and Sidnall[77] as the only known lay estates. By 1230 it had bought 8½ virgates once Richard of Ruthall's and 1 virgate once William of Middleton's.[78] In the earlier 14th century much land in Middleton was sold[79] and it apparently passed ultimately to the priory.

The priory's land in Middleton evidently passed with Ditton manor to the Howards. In 1949 Mrs. A. C. Howard's only child Ursula, Lady Lawson (who became Mrs. Levin that year), sold Home farm, Middleton, the remnant of the Howard estate, to Joseph Bell, whose father had long been the family's agent. In 1950 Bell sold it to Mr. and Mrs. Albert Corfield, who had bought Middleton North in 1926 and Middleton Baggot in 1948.[80]

About 1945 the Howards' seat, Middleton Lodge, was bought from their estate by E. T. Rowlands.[81] Known in the 19th century as Middleton Hall, it is a large **L** shaped stone building of two and three storeys. Its core is perhaps 17th-century, but the building was greatly enlarged and refronted in the 18th century. There were also alterations in 1845, and then or later the house was divided into three dwellings.[82]

Hudwick was probably in Ditton manor in the Middle Ages. In 1510–11 John Marcus paid Wenlock priory £1 6*s.* 8*d.* a year for his tenement there.[83] The Crown separated what was evidently *GREAT HUDWICK* from Ditton manor, selling it in or before 1543, when Robert Burgoyne of London sold the farm there, occupied by Joan Markys, widow, to Matthew White of London.[84] In 1544 White sold it to Thomas Cressett (d. 1566),[85] who was succeeded by his son Francis.[86] Francis sold it in 1589 to Sir Rowland Hayward[87] (d. 1593) who in 1592 settled Hudwick manor or farm on his wife Catherine and their son George (kt. 1604, d. 1615), whose heir was his brother John (kt. 1619). Catherine survived in 1617,[88] but Sir George was lessor of the estate in 1612.[89]

Great Hudwick had passed to the Actons of Aldenham by 1662, when Sir Walter conveyed it to his brother Thomas (d. 1678). Thomas Acton's daughter Sarah owned it in 1682.[90] She afterwards married John Whitmore (d. 1715), of Ludstone (in Claverley), and in 1726 conveyed the manor to her son George (fl. 1737). In 1752 George Whitmore's sister Mary Osborne released her interest in Great Hudwick to her son Charles Osborne, who sold it that year to Edward Minton of Westminster.[91] It probably descended thereafter with the Coates (in Holdgate)[92] to

62 As the proximity of his est. to his ld.'s suggests: see J. F. A. Mason, 'Barons and their officials in the later 11th cent.' *Anglo-Norman Studies*, xiii. 253. Eyton (iii. 338) suggested that he was ld. of Middleton but evidence is lacking.

63 *Roll of Salop. Eyre 1256* (Selden Soc. xcvi), pp. 143–4.

64 Eyton, iii. 341; S.P.L., Deeds 6949–51.

65 Eyton, iii. 341–2, referring to Chamberlain's ct., which Eyton's source (S.P.L., Deeds 6952) does not. Cf. ibid. 6954.

66 Eyton, iii. 338.

67 As successor to Ernald le Fleming's dau. Emme, to whom Acton's predecessor Ric. de Eston had granted it in fee *c.* 1200: ibid. 338–9.

68 Ibid. 338–40; S.P.L., Deeds 6948.

69 Eyton, iii. 338–9; S.P.L., Deeds 6968–9.

70 S.P.L., Deeds 6967, 6980. Both sold selions in Middleton's fields which belonged to the virgate.

71 Ibid. 6984, 6993.

72 S.R.O. 1224, box 342, Prior Gosnell's reg. f. 37.

73 S.P.L., Deeds 7001.

74 Ibid. 6985, 6990, 6993–9.

75 Ibid. 7000–2; S.R.O. 1224, box 342, Prior Gosnell's reg. f. 37.

76 Eyton, iii. 338, 344; cf. e.g. P.R.O., C 143/263, no. 6; *Cal. Pat.* 1340–3, 529.

77 Below, this section.

78 Eyton, iii. 340–1; *T.S.A.S.* 3rd ser. vi. 174; S.R.O. 1224, box 342, Prior Gosnell's reg. f. 6.

79 Eyton, iii. 341–4; S.P.L., Deeds 6964–70, 6972–3.

80 Deeds in Mr. Corfield's possession; Burke, *Peerage* (1967), 1462; local inf.; below, econ. hist. (agric.).

81 Local inf.

82 SA 11819; S. Bagshaw, *Dir. Salop.* (1851), 590.

83 Eyton, iii. 334–5, 346; P.R.O., C 1/1316, no. 19.

84 *L. & P. Hen. VIII*, xviii (1), p. 449.

85 Ibid. xix (1), p. 506; *S.P.R. Heref.* iv (1), 5.

86 S.R.O. 563/1, 3; *T.S.A.S.* 4th ser. vi. 217–18.

87 S.R.O. 1037/21/174; Glam. R.O., CL/Deeds II, no. 10017.

88 P.R.O., C 142/363, no. 194; W. A. Shaw, *Kts. of Eng.* (1906), ii. 75, 135.

89 S.R.O. 563/3–4.

90 Glam. R.O., CL/Deeds I, Salop. nos. 57, 64.

91 Ibid. nos. 139–40; S.R.O. 2161/1; *S.P.R. Heref.* x. 222, 283; S.P.L., MS. 4080, pp. 1714–15.

92 S.P.L., Deeds 563; S.R.O. 515/2, p. 337; 1037/21/98; 3419, assessment on freeholders, 1810; cf. above, Holdgate, manors.

Edward Howells (d. *c.* 1830); his nephew Thomas[93] was in possession in the 1870s. George Howells was recorded as owner between 1881 and 1900, and in 1910 Elizabeth Howells owned the 125-a. property.[94] It later became part of the Burwarton estate.[95]

Hudwick House or Farm, long uninhabited, was demolished in the 1950s. In 1985–6 its barn was converted into a large new house.[96]

William Hide (d. 1792) left *OAKWOOD*, a 56-a. farm in 1799, to his son Thomas, on whose death (1805)[97] Oakwood, like Ruthall, passed to his brother William (d. 1807). William's son Thomas sold Oakwood in 1821 to his cousin's husband William Millward.[98] The property then comprised the house and 65 a.[99] Millward sold it to G. F. Hamilton-Russell, Viscount Boyne, in 1858,[1] and it remained part of the Burwarton estate.[2] Oakwood, a stone farmhouse, was probably built in the later 18th century.[3]

LITTLE HUDWICK remained in the Ditton Priors manorial estate until 1730.[4]

Hugh of Periers subinfeudated *SIDNALL*, and when he gave Ditton to Wenlock priory the tenant was Walinger of Sidnall (or of the Dykes, *des Diches*). Walinger and perhaps a namesake flourished 1176–1226.[5] Thomas of Sidnall was lord by 1301 and in 1323. William, perhaps Thomas's nephew, was lord in 1345–6.[6] In 1510 a chief rent was due from Sidnall to Wenlock priory.[7]

From 1519 or earlier Sidnall descended with Ashfield[8] until Thomas and Mary Smith sold the manor in 1561 to John Bullock (d. 1574), presumably a kinsman of Richard Bullock, Sidnall's lessee in 1510–11. John Bullock's son Nicholas (d. 1591) was next lord and was succeeded by his son John,[9] who was presumably dead by 1641 when his brother or nephew Edmund Bullock owned the manor.[10] By 1652 Sidnall had passed to John Careswell of Shifnal. His son Edward Careswell (d. 1689) included Sidnall in his 1,000-a. endowment of 18 exhibitions at Christ Church, Oxford.[11] Careswell's trustees sold Sidnall farm (*c.* 218 a.) in 1920 to Francis Myatt, a Wolverhampton brewer.[12] Sidnall Farm is an early 19th-century brick building.

There were other freehold estates in Sidnall in the late 16th[13] and early 17th century.[14]

ASHFIELD, presumably part of Ditton manor in 1086, was probably granted before 1155 to an ancestor of the Beysins. It was part of their serjeanty of keeping the king's hawks.[15] In 1198 Adam de Beysin was said to hold ¼ carucate in Ashfield.[16] About 1225 he gave his lands at Ashfield, then said to be 2 virgates, in marriage to his daughter Margery and Thomas of Badger (d. by 1246). Margery later apportioned Ashfield among her younger children: Henry Mauveysin received 1½ virgate *c.* 1252, Richard of Badger 1 virgate *c.* 1254, and Avice of Badger ½ virgate *c.* 1255.[17]

Henry Mauveysin (fl. 1255) was perhaps Margery's son-in-law. By 1292 his second son Thomas Mauveysin (or of Berwick, fl. *c.* 1285), to whom Ashfield had apparently passed, had died leaving a son and heir John of Berwick, a minor; Ashfield was held of John for life by his uncle Philip Mauveysin (or of Berwick).[18] Philip outlived John and acquired the fee. He died *c.* 1334 seised of a messuage and virgate in Ashfield held in chief by service of 4*s.* a year. Philip's heir was John's son John of Berwick,[19] who died in 1349 seised of ½ virgate in Ashfield held by knight service. John of Berwick's heir was his son Thomas aged 18.[20] Ashfield later passed to Philip of Berwick's kinsman and heir Richard Berwick of Berwick Maviston. By 1401 Richard had sold the estate, perhaps then 3 messuages, 4 virgates, and 10 a. of meadow, to John and Gillian Burley.[21]

Richard of Badger, who had received 1 virgate *c.* 1254, was said *c.* 1284 to hold Ashfield as ⅙ knight's fee of Walter de Beysin, the tenant in chief.[22] Richard died before 1292 and his heir was his son Roger (fl. 1320), but in 1292 the virgate was held by Richard's widow Margery. It was forfeited to the Crown as an unlicensed alienation from the Beysin serjeanty by 1304 when 1½ virgate and 3 a. in Ashfield, once Margery's, were in the king's hand. They remained so in 1345 but seem to have been restored to the Badgers by 1346, when Roger of Badger (fl. 1349), perhaps Margery's son of that name, granted a lease in Ashfield.[23] The later descent of Roger's estate has not been traced.

Richard of Badger enfeoffed Adam le King in a messuage and ½ virgate in Ashfield, said to be held in chief for 2*s.* 10*d.*, which Adam was to pay to Richard. Adam le King was succeeded by William le King (d. by 1319), whose heir was his son Nicholas (fl. 1320).[24] By 1346 the estate was probably that held by John King (or Carles) (d. by 1377), which was said to comprise 2 mes-

93 S.R.O. 757, box 50, Edw. Howells's will (extract).
94 E. Cassey & Co. *Dir. Salop.* (1871), 284; *P.O. Dir. Salop.* (1879), 387; *Kelly's Dir. Salop.* (1885–1900); S.R.O. 3419, Middleton est. sale cat. 1881, map; 4044/14, p. 5.
95 *Census*, 1851, 1881.
96 Inf. from Mrs. S. M. Knowles.
97 S.R.O. 515/4, p. 42; 1359, box 44, deeds 24 June 1783, 1 Jan. 1803, Wm. Hide's will pr. 5 July 1792; 5482/Rg/4, 19 Apr. 1792; /Rg/5, 6 May 1805.
98 S.R.O. 757/66/4; 1359, box 44, deed 1 Jan. 1803; 5482/Rg/5, 22 Apr. 1807; W.S.L. 350/3/40, Ditton Priors p. 2; below, this section (Ruthall).
99 S.R.O. 1359, box 44, deed 27 Oct. 1820.
1 S.R.O. 757/66/5.
2 Inf. from the tenant.
3 Not on J. Rocque, *Map of Salop.* (1752).
4 Below, Monkhopton, manors.
5 Eyton, iii. 345.
6 Ibid. 345–6; S.P.L., Deeds 6964–5, 6973, 6976.
7 Eyton, iii. 335, 346.
8 Below, this section; P.R.O., C 54/400, no. 17; CP 25/2/35/233, no. 5; CP 40/1137, Carte rot. 8; SP 1/4, f. 15; S.R.O. 757, box 69, deeds 4 Aug. 1544, 18 May 1559.
9 Eyton, iii. 335; P.R.O., C 142/248, no. 7; C 142/250, no. 22; CP 25/2/200/3 Eliz. I East. [no. 13].
10 S.P.L., MS. 4304, p. 72; P.R.O., CP 25/2/478/16 Chas. I Hil. [no. 6].
11 S.P.L., Deeds 6371; W.S.L. 350/3/40, Ditton Priors p. 2; *V.C.H. Salop.* ii. 164.
12 S.R.O. 4044/14, p. 5; 5016, min. bk. no. 1, p. 310.
13 P.R.O., CP 25/2/260/25 Eliz. I Trin. [no. 10]; DL 7/16, no. 2 (including impropriate tithes).
14 P.R.O., CP 25/2/477/6 Chas. I East. [no. 31].
15 Eyton, iii. 346, 348.
16 *Bk. of Fees*, i. 7.
17 Eyton, iii. 347.
18 Ibid. 350; vii. 397–8; ix. 88, 105–6.
19 *Cal. Inq. p.m.* vii, p. 399; *Cal. Fine R.* 1327–37, 435.
20 *Cal. Inq. Misc.* iii, p. 11.
21 *Cal. Pat.* 1399–1401, 427.
22 *Feud. Aids*, iv. 224 (for 'Ricardus' as tenant in chief presumably read 'Walterus').
23 *Cal. Fine R.* 1337–47, 419; Eyton, iii. 348–50.
24 Eyton, iii. 349.

suages, 1 virgate, and 6 a. of meadow in Ashfield. On John's death the estate passed to his kinsman and heir William son of Richard Herdewyk, who by 1401 had sold it to John Burley.[25] Burley thus held at least two of the three portions into which Ashfield had been divided *c.* 1255.[26]

The ½ virgate granted to Avice of Badger *c.* 1255 was held in 1292 by Thomas de la Cole.[27] It was perhaps later absorbed into the Kings' estate which was enlarged from ½ to 1 virgate between the later 13th century and 1377.[28]

By 1452 the estate, then reputed a manor, was apparently reunited under John Talbot, earl of Shrewsbury, and then descended with Aston (in Munslow) until 1542.[29] In 1559 Sir John Smith's son William conveyed Ashfield to his brother Thomas in return for a life annuity and discharge of his debts.[30] In 1561 Thomas Smith sold part of the estate, probably a moiety, to William Holland of Burwarton (d. 1590).[31] Another moiety of Ashfield manor belonged to Richard Hopton of Over Bitterley. In 1589 Hopton's son Thomas sold it to Jasper More of Larden.[32] Thomas Hopton's widow, with Thomas Hopton of Nether Bitterley, bought it back from More in 1599, and Hopton sold it in 1602 to Thomas Langley of the Amies (in Broseley).[33] In 1613 Langley sold the moiety to William Holland (d. 1642), who thus seems to have reunited the manor, a share of which his grandfather had bought in 1561.[34]

The manor then descended from father to son in the Holland family, the following being lords:[35] Thomas, William (d. 1699), Thomas (d. 1722), and William (d. 1736). William Holland's relict Anne Crump was in possession in 1748, and his son Bernard (d. 1803) had 220 a. there in 1799.[36] Bernard Holland was succeeded jointly by his sisters Elizabeth (d. 1822), wife of Benjamin Baugh (d. 1809) of Ludlow, and Margaret (d. unm. 1808).[37] The Baughs' daughter Harriet (d. 1854), wife of Gustavus Hamilton, Viscount Boyne (d. 1855), owned Ashfield in 1851.[38] In 1910 it belonged to the Boynes' great-grandson F. G. Hamilton-Russell.[39] Ashfield Farm was rebuilt in brick in 1878 after a fire. [40]

In 1066 Eskil (Oschil) held *RUTHALL*, and in 1086 Gerelm held it of Gerard of Tournai who held it of Earl Roger, the tenant in chief. Gerard probably forfeited his mesne lordship, and in 1102 Earl Robert forfeited the overlordship. By 1203 Ruthall was held in chief by Ralph Sandford of Sandford (in Prees), which had also been held of Gerard in 1086.[41] The Sandfords retained the overlordship until 1552 when George Sandford exchanged it with Richard Moreton of Haughton.[42] Moreton's granddaughter Anne married Humphrey Briggs (d. 1626), and the overlordship of Ruthall descended thereafter with Abdon.[43] In 1872 chief and fee-farm rents from Ruthall and Ditton were part of the Abdon estate of G. R. C. Herbert, earl of Pembroke and Montgomery.[44]

Philip of Ruthall, apparently as heir of his brother John of Ruthall (d. by 1203), was Ralph of Sandford's tenant in Ruthall by 1221.[45] John of Ruthall (fl. 1227) or others of that name were lords of Ruthall in 1255 and 1284.[46] William Bastard was lord in 1292 and 1316.[47] William's brother Edmund Bastard (d. 1332) had an estate in Ruthall, jointly with his wife Agnes and allegedly by grant from John Lengleys, perhaps a feoffee. Shortly before his death Edmund was outlawed and his land seized.[48]

Sir William Yonge (d. by 1505) had an estate in Ruthall.[49] His son Francis (d. 1533) was lord and was succeeded by his son William (d. 1565). William's heir was his brother Thomas (d. 1569), vicar of Bampton (Oxon.).[50]

In 1599 Edward Lacon and his wife conveyed Ruthall manor to Richard and Joan Churchman,[51] who in the same year conveyed half of it to Nicholas Hints (d. 1600). Hints settled the moiety on his second wife Alice who, after Nicholas's death, married John Smallman. In 1612 the Smallmans reunited the manor by buying the Churchmans' moiety.[52]

The manor may have passed, like John Smallman's estate at Norncott (in Stoke St. Milborough), to Nicholas Page (d. 1684).[53] In 1690 Alice Page, widow, with Ada and Elizabeth

25 Ibid. 349–50; *Cal. Pat.* 1399–1401, 427.
26 Above, this section.
27 Eyton, iii. 350.
28 Above, this section.
29 P.R.O., C 139/179, no. 58 (25); CP 40/1137, Carte rot. 8; SP 1/4, f. 15; *Cal. Inq. p.m. Hen. VII*, i, pp. 428–9. Cf. above, Munslow, manors.
30 S.R.O. 757, box 69, deed 18 May 1559.
31 Ibid. deed 10 Feb. 1560/1; 3962/Rg/1, s.a. 1590.
32 S.R.O. 757, box 69, deed 31 Oct. 1589.
33 Ibid. deeds 8 Mar. 1598/9, 14 Apr. 1602; above, Broseley, manor.
34 S.R.O. 757, box 69, deed 20 Oct. 1613; 3962/Rg/1, s.a. 1642; *Visit. Salop. 1623*, i. 250–1.
35 P.R.O., CP 25/2/476/5 Chas. I Trin. [no. 14]; CP 25/2/714/31 Chas. II Mich. [no. 3]; CP 25/2/1055/13 Geo. I Hil. [no. 3]; S.R.O. 757, box 69, deed 6 Jan. 1704/5; q. sess. rec. box 260, reg. of gamekeepers 1742–79, 13 Jan. 1747/8; W.S.L. 350/3/40, Ditton Priors pp. 2, 4. For Holland pedigrees see S.P.L., MSS. 2795, pp. 279–80; 4078, p. 747; *Visit. Salop. 1623*, i. 250–1.
36 S.R.O. 515/4, p. 42.
37 S.R.O., q. sess. rec. parcel 261, reg. of gamekeepers 1799–1807, f. 77; 3962/Rg/2, 15 Feb. 1735/6; /Rg/3, 31 Mar 1808.
38 W.S.L. 350/3/40, Ditton Priors p. 2; Burke, *Peerage* (1949), 240; Bagshaw, *Dir. Salop.* (1851), 590.
39 S.R.O. 4044/14, p. 11; Burke, *Peerage* (1949), 240.
40 Inf. from Mrs. M. A. Williams; date stone on fm. bldgs.
41 *V.C.H. Salop.* i. 339; iii. 10; Eyton, ii. 104; iv. 48.
42 *Feud. Aids*, iv. 223; *Cal. Inq. Misc.* ii, pp. 313, 332; S.R.O. 2/92–4, 96, 99; 5735/U/1/2, 4, 11; B.L. Harl. MS. 2063, f. 18; *Cal. Inq. p.m.* vii, p. 36.
43 *Visit. Salop. 1623*, ii (Harl. Soc. xxix), 368; S.P.L., MS. 4080, p. 2060; S.R.O. 1238/3, 14; Brigges Est. Act 1800, 39 & 40 Geo. III, c. 114 (Local and Personal); cf. above, Abdon, manor.
44 S.R.O. 1037/21/37.
45 Eyton, iv. 48–50; *Rolls of Justices in Eyre, 1221–2* (Selden Soc. lix), p. 507.
46 Eyton, iv. 49–50; B.L. Harl. MS. 2063, f. 8; S.P.L., Deeds 6952–3; *Feud. Aids*, iv. 223.
47 Nott. Univ. Libr. MSS. Dept., Mi. D. 3686/4; *Feud. Aids*, iv. 229.
48 *Cal. Inq. Misc.* ii, pp. 313, 332; S.R.O. 2/12.
49 S.R.O. 3365/165; Wedgwood, *Hist. Parl. 1439–1509: Biogs.* 983; *T.S.A.S.* 4th ser. xi. 26.
50 P.R.O., C 142/143, no. 35; ibid. E 150/854, no. 2; E. Yonge, *The Yonges of Caynton, Edgmond* (priv. print. 1969), 88, 90; *Ancestry of Bridget Yonge, First Wife of Governor Willys of Connecticut* (New Haven, 1903), 8, 23 (copy in S.P.L.).
51 P.R.O., CP 25/2/203/41 Eliz. I Trin. [no. 14].
52 P.R.O., C 142/477, no. 61; CP 25/2/203/41 & 42 Eliz. I Mich. [no. 16]; CP 25/2/343/10 Jas. I East. [no. 19].
53 Below, the Heath, manors.

Page, had Ruthall manor.[54] By 1706 moieties belonged to Ada (d. 1716) and Elizabeth (d. 1734) and their respective husbands Richard Langford (d. 1709) and Francis Milner (d. 1710).[55] Francis Milner, probably the son of Elizabeth and Francis,[56] seems to have been in sole possession by 1768[57] and probably sold it *c.* 1769.[58] Joseph Sparkes of Bridgnorth, lord by 1779,[59] sold it in 1784 to William Hide (d. 1792), of Oakwood,[60] who left Ruthall to his son Thomas.[61] Thomas, who had 150 a. there in 1799,[62] died in 1805, leaving the manor to his brother William (d. 1807), who left it to his son William until his other son Thomas (d. 1825) came of age and would succeed.[63] In 1826 or 1827 Thomas Hide's widow Sarah married William Gough of Bridgwalton (in Morville).[64] In 1835 trustees sold the manor with the manor house and 172 a. to Thomas Roberts of Broseley, lord in 1851.[65] In 1869 and 1881 Edward Rainforth owned the estate, then 172 a.[66] In 1909, when the estate was only 76 a., it was sold by George Robinson's trustees,[67] probably to Joseph Poole of Dawley, who owned 220 a. in Ruthall in 1910.[68]

Ruthall Manor is a stone building, probably 17th-century. It was refronted in brick and modernized *c.* 1820. Earthworks suggest that the medieval manorial buildings, which included the chief house and a dovecote *c.* 1330, stood east and north of it.[69]

By the 14th century there were several freeholds in Ruthall.[70] In 1334 Hugh Tyrel had freehold lands there.[71] They may have passed, with his Norncott lands, to William Burley (d. 1458), of Broncroft, for by 1499 they were descending with Burley's manor of Brockton.[72] In 1552 John de Vere, earl of Oxford, sold his moiety to John Stringfellow, whose son Richard had it *c.* 1560,[73] but the later descent of the Ruthall lands has not been traced.

Ankaret, Baroness Talbot (d. 1413), wife of Sir Richard Talbot, held lands in Ruthall of Nicholas Sandford.[74] They descended to her grandson John Talbot, earl of Shrewsbury (d. 1460); in 1468 his son John, 3rd earl (d. 1473), entered on the estate comprising 2½ messuages, 24 a., and 10*s.* of assize rent.[75] His uncle Sir Humphrey (d. 1493) had an estate in Ruthall,[76] which may thereafter have descended with Aston (in Munslow), for Sir John Smith owed a chief rent to the lord of Ruthall in 1544.[77]

William Benyon (d. 1610) held a house and 100 a. in Ruthall in chief by knight service.[78] Thomas Benyon sold it to William Cotton and his son William in 1637. In 1640 the younger William, with others interested in the estate, conveyed it to Edward and Anne Hassold (or Hassall) of Deuxhill. John Collins bought it from the Hassolds in 1649 to settle on his son William's marriage with Ann Corfield. In 1682 the Collinses' estate was bought by William Pinches (d. 1712), glover, of Longville. His nephew and namesake sold it, heavily mortgaged, to Josiah Miles in 1727, when Miles also bought two messuages in Ruthall from Sir John and Lady Astley. The Astleys', later Tankervilles', estate retained some interest in the parish in 1834.[79]

The *RECTORY* appropriated to Wenlock priory was worth £12 a year in 1291,[80] and £8 3*s.* 4*d.* in 1379.[81] The monks of Wenlock let some of their appropriated Ditton tithes to vicars before the Dissolution, and the great tithes of Middleton Priors evidently belonged to the vicar after Middleton was reunited to Ditton in the earlier 16th century.[82] The priory's appropriated tithes passed to the Crown in 1540 and in 1544 were bought by Humphrey Pakington with the manor,[83] thereafter descending with it.[84] In 1728 it was said that the lord of the manor's great tithes would be worth *c.* £80 a year when the fields were inclosed,[85] but he sold Ruthall and Oakwood tithes in 1803[86] and Ashfield's in 1807;[87] Sidnall's were sold about the same time to John Maddox, the occupier. The impropriate tithes were extinguished at inclosure in 1841 when lands were allotted in their stead to Robert Canning and the smaller impropriators, the more substantial of whom had property in Ashfield and Ruthall.[88]

ECONOMIC HISTORY. AGRICULTURE. Ditton was held with four berewicks in 1066. In 1086 there were 5 ploughteams and 10 *servi*

54 P.R.O., CP 25/2/867/2 Wm. & Mary Mich. [no. 8].
55 S.P.L., Deeds 9929; *S.P.R. Heref.* xiii. 570; S.R.O. 3571/Rg/2, bur. 23 June 1709, 21 Nov. 1716; 5482/Rg/1, 13 Sept. 1698; Morville par reg. (transcript in S.P.L.) bur. 4 July 1710; W.S.L. 350/3/40, Ditton Priors p. 4.
56 Birm. Univ. Libr., Mytton Papers, ii. 387; Morville par. reg. 20 June 1710.
57 P.R.O., CP 43/742, rot. 310.
58 S.P.L., MS. 6864, f. 47v.
59 S.R.O., q. sess. rec. box 260, reg. of gamekeepers 1742–79, 13 Mar. 1779.
60 S.R.O. 1359, box 44, deeds 24 June 1783, 25 Mar. 1784; above, this section.
61 S.R.O. 1359, box 44, Wm. Hide's will pr. 5 July 1792.
62 S.R.O. 515/4, p. 42.
63 S.R.O. 1359, box 44, administration of Thos. Hide's goods, Wm. Hide's will pr. 13 Oct. 1807.
64 Ibid. deed 22 Nov. 1826.
65 Ibid. deeds 3–5 Aug. 1835, 3 Aug. 1844; S. Bagshaw, *Dir. Salop.* (1851), 590.
66 S.R.O. 1359, box 44, deeds 2 Oct. 1869, 6 Mar. 1875; 3419, Middleton est. sale cat. 1881, map.
67 S.R.O. 2065/1.
68 S.R.O. 4044/14, p. 11.
69 SA 11828; S.R.O. 2/13.
70 For refs. to some, apart from those traced below, see *Cal. Inq. p.m.* x, pp. 296, 442; B.L. Harl. MS. 2063, ff. 11, 14.
71 *Cal. Chart. R.* 1327–41, 309.
72 *Cal. Inq. p.m. Hen. VII*, ii, p. 578; iii, pp. 127, 131; P.R.O., C 142/78, no. 140; cf. below, the Heath, manors; Shipton, manors.
73 S.R.O. 20/23/13; *Cal. Pat.* 1558–60, 349; *Visit. Hants 1622* (Harl. Soc. lxiv), 106.
74 *Cal. Inq. p.m.* xx, p. 37.
75 *Cal. Pat.* 1467–77, 134; Burke, *Peerage* (1949), 1830.
76 S.R.O. 3365/165.
77 B.L. Harl. MS. 2063, f. 18; cf. above, Munslow, manors (Aston).
78 P.R.O., C 142/317, no. 80.
79 S.R.O. 227/12; 1378/63; *V.C.H. Salop.* viii. 266. For Wm. Pinches (d. 1712) cf. J. H. Pinches, *Fam. of Pinches* (1981), 24–6, calling him yeoman, of Cardington.
80 *Tax. Eccl.* (Rec. Com.), 166.
81 B.L. Add. MS. 6164, pp. 386, 410.
82 Below, churches.
83 *L. & P. Hen. VIII*, xix (2), p. 81; above, this section.
84 P.R.O., C 142/183, no. 76; C 142/466, no. 113; S.P.L., Deeds 636, 2636; S.R.O. 515/4, p. 42.
85 S.P.L., Deeds 734, f. 52.
86 S.R.O. 1359, box 44, deed 1 Jan. 1803.
87 S.R.O. 757, box 69, deed 20 Sept. 1807.
88 S.R.O. 515/4, p. 42; S.R.O., incl. award A 18/51.

on the demesne, and 20 *villani* and 8 bordars had 6 teams; 13 more teams could have been employed.[89] The vill had a salt pan that rendered 2*s*. a year; it was at 'Wich', presumably Droitwich (Worcs.).[90] Ditton was worth £10 in 1066 and £11 in 1086; 12 hides there paid geld. At Ruthall, where ½ hide paid geld, there was enough land for 2 ploughteams, but only 2 half-teams were employed, one by 2 oxmen on the demesne, the other by 3 bordars; Ruthall was worth 6*s*. in 1066, 8*s*. in 1086.

Ditton, Middleton, and Ruthall were surrounded by open field land that was perhaps divided and regulated less formally, at least in the relatively well documented 13th and 14th centuries, than was usual in typical champaign English regions. Meadow, some of it common, flanked the Rea and its tributaries.[91] Around much of the edge of Ditton were woods and extensive tracts of common waste, their exploitation complicated by Ditton's inclusion in Clee forest.[92]

In the earlier 14th century most or all of Ditton's open field land lay in an arc west and south of the village, bounded in part by Powkesmore and Brown Clee hill. The land, whether or not divided formally into two or three fields, was in discrete *culturae* or divisions called 'Ardesley', near the road to Cleobury North, and 'Dykes', near the Cleobury North parish boundary.[93] Some or all of the demesne lay in a compact block in or near 'Ardesley'.[94] Middleton's open arable lay east, west, and south of the village, noted in the 13th century as in the fields towards Derrington and Neenton and in 'Cruftinge', 'Colverdale', 'Eddesley', and Bent fields, and in the 14th century as in the field or fields towards Ditton and 'Eddesley' and in Broadbridge field.[95] Other, apparently smaller, divisions of 'the field of Middleton' included furlongs, crofts, and 'Sevenacre'.[96] There was apparently an extensive area of strip cultivation divided by hedges, ditches, and roads into numerous enclosures, most in a nominal field. Selions were usually reckoned at ¼ a., but some as little as ⅛ a.[97] About 1300 Ruthall had open fields towards Ashfield, Ditton, and Weston;[98] the two last may be the fields towards the Clee and the park mentioned slightly later,[99] and there was an area that was a main field division or else a separate close in strips.[1]

The smaller enclosures that seem, along with large open fields, to have been components of the parish's field systems[2] probably often resulted from assarting,[3] encouraged by Wenlock priory in the 13th century. In 1232 the forester of Clee recognized the assarts made by Wenlock priory since the 1190s or earlier and the priory's right to inclose and plough 40 a. more on Powkesmore.[4] In 1262 the priory was allowed to bring 20 a. on Middleton's border with Sidnall into cultivation.[5] 'New land' was held separately from virgated holdings.[6] Inclosure of Powkesmore continued in the 15th century.[7]

Ditton Priors was the northernmost of the parishes that radiated from Brown Clee hill and were probably co-extensive with Clee forest or chase,[8] part of the estates (including Corfham) granted to Hugh of Periers in 1155. When Periers died *c*. 1175 Henry II gave his estates, except for Ditton but including Clee chase, to Walter of Clifford,[9] though the Crown retained, until the 14th century or later, at least the right to fallen branches and uprooted trees. In the 1230s the Cliffords' forester prevented Wenlock priory and its tenants from putting goats in certain demesne woods in the chase, including Ditton's. The priory's grazing rights, however, were established in 1232, when Walter of Clifford conceded free pasture throughout his chase,[10] and *c*. 1251 when he relinquished to Wenlock any right he had specifically in Ruthall, whose frith was mentioned *c*. 1300, and Oxenbold, whose 13th-century park may have extended into Derrington.[11] The Cliffords perhaps made up lost revenues in other ways: in the 1250s Walter of Clifford claimed a hen at Christmas and five eggs at Easter from every house in Clee chase and perhaps sheaves of wheat in autumn. Ditton's woods were still closely supervised in the 1270s,[12] but from the early 14th century, as the lord of Corfham concentrated his Clee chase interests on Earnstrey hay or park, Wenlock priory and its tenants perhaps had greater freedom to exploit their manorial woods.[13] They probably included Lightwood and Netchwood,[14] perhaps originally a belt of woodland *c*. 1 by 4 km. across the northern part of the parish, and Oakwood on the parish boundary south-east of Ditton village.[15] By the early 14th century Wenlock priory was employing John de Mora (d. by 1316), tenant of Middleton land, as its forester or woodward.[16]

Holly and willow still grew on Brown Clee hill in the later 16th century,[17] but the hill's main use was for grazing, and all the vills in the old chase had common rights there. Those some way from the hill, such as Ashfield and Ruthall,

89 Para. based on *V.C.H. Salop*. i. 317, 339.
90 Eyton, ii. 174 n. 1.
91 Nott. Univ. Libr. MSS. Dept., Mi. D. 6952–3.
92 Below, this section.
93 S.P.L., Deeds 6971, 6975–6, 6978, 6981, 6983.
94 Ibid. 6976.
95 Ibid. 6950, 6952, 6954, 6961–3, 6965, 6968, 6973, 6980. Broadbridge field also occ. 1625: S.R.O. 3419, glebe terrier 1625; cf. above, this article, intro. [communications].
96 S.P.L., Deeds 6949, 6952–3, 6963, 6973.
97 S.P.L., Deeds cited in preceding notes.
98 Nott. Univ. Libr. MSS. Dept., Mi. D. 3686/1.
99 Ibid. /5–7; B.L. Harl. MS. 2063, f. 9.
1 Nott. Univ. Libr. MSS. Dept., Mi. D. 3686/3.
2 Paralleled in other woodland areas: see e.g., for Salop., *V.C.H. Salop*. viii. 4, 182.
3 R. T. Rowley, 'Hist. S. Salop. Landscape' (Oxf. Univ. B.Litt. thesis, 1967), 63–4.
4 *T.S.A.S.* 4th ser. i. 391; *Pipe R.* 1190 (P.R.S. N.S. i), 127.
5 *Pipe R.* 1190 (P.R.S. N.S. i), 127; *Cal. Chart. R.* 1327–41, 488; *V.C.H. Salop*. ii. 46.
6 B.L. Add. Roll 67032 (grants to Thos. of Plowden and Thos. de Feelde, 1364); below, this section, for assart rents.
7 *E.H.R.* xcix. 538–9.
8 Para. based on *T.S.A.S.* lviii. 48–67; Eyton, v. 196–202.
9 Above, manors; *V.C.H. Salop*. i. 486 (corr. ibid. ii. 319).
10 *T.S.A.S.* 4th ser. i. 391–3.
11 Barnard MSS., Raby Castle, box 1, bdle. 16, nos. 1–2; Nott. Univ. Libr. MSS. Dept., Mi. D. 3686/5–6; below, Monkhopton, econ. hist.; S.P.L., SC1/2, map, fields 183, 185–6, 188–9.
12 *Rot. Hund.* ii. 83, 101.
13 *T.S.A.S.* lviii. 56–7.
14 *L. & P. Hen. VIII*, xix (2), p. 81.
15 Fig. 31.
16 Eyton, iii. 341–3.
17 Warws. R.O., CR 1379, e.g. ct. 12 Apr. 1570.

gained access to it by 'strake' roads, but generally strakers had fewer rights than did the inhabitants of immediately adjoining townships: strakers could turn out cattle and sheep but not have horses, pigs, goats, bees, or swans there, although fines show that such prohibitions were often ignored. There was a swainmote, and all commoners owed a small 'Clee rent', though by 1600 strakers often avoided payment.[18] The swainmote ceased to be held in the earlier 17th century, when straking was becoming less profitable, though even in the late 18th century some farmers, such as Edward Woof of Brookhampton (in Holdgate), still drove animals several miles to graze the hill. Nevertheless in the later 17th century the lord of Ditton, with the lords of other manors around the Brown Clee, had attempted to share out the commons and oust the jurisdiction of the lord of Clee chase. They were ultimately successful; nevertheless, when the Ditton part of Brown Clee was inclosed in 1841, 3 a. were allotted to the successor of the old lords of Clee chase.[19]

In the 14th century agricultural recession at first impoverished the peasants but later gave survivors of the Black Death the opportunity to rent the lord's demesne. In 1341 it was claimed that storms had destroyed the corn, 9 ruined tenants in the parish had left their holdings, and there were no sheep.[20] By the 1370s most of the lord of Ditton's income came from the rents of neifs and free tenants (over £9) and from a mill (6*s.* 8*d.*); 2 demesne carucates worked in a three-course rotation and 2 a. of meadow were valued at 22*s.* in 1369 but only 14*s.* by 1379.[21] In the 1380s the priory was granting leases of Ditton land and farms for one or two lives; entry fines were proportioned to the number of lives, and in the case of one lessee no heriot was due on his death as long as he was living with his co-tenant father. All lessees owed carriage service *inter alia*.[22]

About 1330 Ruthall's demesne comprised 40 a., some underwood, and a little meadow, together worth 13*s.*; assize rents amounted to 7*s.* 3¾*d.*[23] All Ruthall's tenants owed heriot as late as the 18th century and, allegedly, in 1851.[24] At Ashfield in 1401 there were two ½-virgate farms, three of 1 virgate or more, and 16 a. of meadow.[25]

In 1510–11 Wenlock priory's Ditton estate yielded £25 14*s.* 6*d.* a year, all in rents; some tenants paid small sums that had probably originated as assart rents and totalled 10*s.* 1½*d.* Fifteen holdings in Middleton were listed, 12 in Ditton, 3 in Derrington, 1 in Powkesmore, and 1 in Hudwick; there was also a chief rent from Sidnall. The largest holding was the manorial demesne let to William Smallman, who was converting arable to inclosed pasture.[26] The Smallmans probably occupied Ditton manorial demesne for most of the 16th and earlier 17th century: Prior Bayley leased it to William Smallman, his son, and grandsons (4 lives) in 1531,[27] and in 1563 John Pakington leased it to John Smallman and his two sons;[28] George Smallman held land in Ditton and Middleton in 1628 and 1641[29] but may have left the area by 1649.[30] In the 17th century the Audleys were granting three-life leases. By 1722, however, while two or three of the Cannings' tenants still had leases for lives granted by the Audleys, most held their farms at will.[31]

Livestock husbandry was prominent in the local mixed farming regime in the later 17th and early 18th century, though a discernible paucity of pigs may indicate that wood–pasture was no longer available. The better-off farmers were chiefly distinguished by their ownership of oxen, still preferred locally as plough and draught animals[32] (there was a working ox team on Middleton Hall farm as late as 1853),[33] and by the number of their other cattle. John Corfield (d. 1667), a Ruthall yeoman, had 6 oxen and 22 other cattle, worth in all £45 10*s.*; Arthur Lowe (d. 1700), a Middleton yeoman, had 4 oxen and 18 cattle worth £49; and Thomas Barker (d. 1704), lord of Ditton, 4 oxen and 7 cattle worth £30. Corfield apparently had no sheep, but Lowe had 15 worth £3 15*s.* and Barker a flock of 86 worth £10. Each probably had cereals in store worth as much as those they had growing; Corfield's cereals (partly hard corn and partly the less valuable lent grain) were worth £35 10*s.*, Lowe's £15, and Barker's £18. Only Corfield had hemp, worth £1 5*s.* and 'at the weaver's'; there were weavers in the parish.[34] Poorer men working on their own account apparently did no more than keep a few animals and till a croft: in 1706 William Pugh died owning only clothes worth £3 10*s.* and 8 sheep worth £1 4*s.*

In 1517 William Smallman, lessee of the Ditton demesne, had been accused of inclosing 20 a. arable for conversion to pasture.[35] Nevertheless open-field land, and in some cases whole fields, survived: in 1728 there were Little, Wildish, and Ditton fields in Ditton, the Field, the Great field, and the Little field in Middleton, and Upper Grounds, Dingle field, and the Yells in Derrington.[36] Inclosure by exchange and consolidation was then probably finishing off the old

18 *T.S.A.S.* 2nd ser. viii. 195–8; lviii. 58–67; S.R.O., incl. award B 21, Brown Clee swainmote rolls; Christ Ch., Oxf., mun. viii. a. 53, ff. 2–4; Rowley, *Landscape of Welsh Marches*, 225–6; *Countryside of Medieval Eng.* ed. G. Astill and A. Grant (1988), 134.

19 S.R.O., incl. awards A 18/51, B 21.

20 *Inq. Non.* (Rec. Com.), 190.

21 B.L. Add. MSS. 6164, pp. 384, 410; 6165, p. 99.

22 B.L. Add. Roll 67032.

23 S.R.O. 2/13, dated by Wm. of Caynton's terms as escheator (1328–9, 1330: *S.H.C.* 1912, 297).

24 Birm. Univ. Libr., Mytton Papers, ii. 387; S. Bagshaw, *Dir. Salop.* (1851), 590.

25 *Cal. Pat.* 1399–1401, 427.

26 S.R.O. 1224, box 342, Prior Gosnell's reg. f. 37 (arithmetic corrected); above, this section, for assarts.

27 S.P.L., MS. 2, f. 144v.; Warws. R.O., CR 1379, box 4, deed 24 Oct. 1531.

28 P.R.O., C 2/Jas. I/S 27/30, 48.

29 *T.S.A.S.* 4th ser. x. 267, 270, 272.

30 *Cal. Cttee. for Compounding*, iii. 2087.

31 S.R.O., q. sess. rec. parcel 281, reg. of papists' deeds 1717–88, pp. 188–9; cf. S.P.L., Deeds 734.

32 Para. based on H.W.R.O.(H.), Heref. dioc. rec., invs. of John Corfield, 1667; Thos. Hide, 1680/1; Art. Lowe, 1700; Hercules Hide, 1701; Thos. Barker, 1704; Ric. Smith, 1705; Wm. Pugh, 1706. None had more than 4 pigs or 4 horses.

33 *Eddowes's Jnl.* 16 Mar. 1853, p. [3].

34 H.W.R.O.(H.), Heref. dioc. rec., inv. of Ric. Morgan, 1689.

35 B.L. Lansd. MS. 1, f. 190v.

36 S.P.L., Deeds 734, ff. 5, 21–6, 28, 46.

arable fields;[37] traces of strips survived in the late 19th century south-west and south-east of Ditton village,[38] and in the 20th century field boundaries revealed the run of former strips.[39]

The open commons outlasted the open fields, but as straking had declined squatters had settled on Brown Clee hill. By 1722 there were 11 cottages on the manorial estate, each rented for *c.* 10*s.* a year. Other cottagers paid no rent but presumably a fine at the manor court.[40] Francis Canning seems to have regularized cottage tenancies on his Ditton estate in 1761, when he granted 27 leases for three lives.[41]

In 1794 it was said that a sixth of the parish remained uninclosed[42] and in 1813 that Brown Clee hill and Netchwood commons in the parish amounted to 410 a. In fact 600 a., about a ninth of the parish, was inclosed in 1841: 373 a. on Brown Clee and 227 at Netchwood. For his claimed 'seigniory' of Brown Clee common H. G. Mytton of Cleobury North received *c.* 3 a., and small freeholders received small allotments for their common rights, some also as impropriators, for simultaneously all tithes were extinguished. The vicar received most land after R. C. Canning who, as lord of Ditton manor and much the largest impropriator and for his common rights, received by far the greatest amount of land. Compensation of tithe owners and the making of exchanges meant that more land was reorganized than was inclosed from the common.[43]

R. C. Canning received almost all of the former common, an arrangement that helped to perpetuate the pattern of adjoining small holdings. In the early 19th century more than 60 of the lord of Ditton's tenants held 10 a. or less; their average holding was *c.* 3 a. and usually included land held on a life interest, some that was rack rented, and an encroachment on Brown Clee or at Netchwood.[44]

Farms were often large in the 18th and 19th centuries, and after the inclosure of 1841 further rationalization and consolidation was possible. On the Canning estate in 1728 Ditton farm was 448 a., although it, like other farms in the parish, included extensive tracts of common and rough grazing. There were also five farms of 200–299 a., nine of 100–199 a., and three of 25–99 a.[45] In 1768 there were two farms of more than 450 a., one of 300–399 a., five of 200–299 a., five of 100–199 a., and one of 25–99 a. On the same estate in 1828 the largest farm was 412 a., and there were three farms of 300–399 a., seven of 200–299 a., three of 100–199 a., and four of 25–99 a.[46] In 1910 the parish had three farms of 200–299 a., five of 100–199 a., and six of 25–99 a.[47]

In the mid 19th century the Ditton manorial estate was at its greatest extent, *c.* 4,000 a.[48] Between 1850 and 1867, however, P. H. Howard never visited it. His agent ran it and most of the main tenants were Roman Catholics.[49] In the early and mid 19th century farm leases for 8 or 11 years were used on the Cannings' estate, although yearly leases were known.[50] By 1870 and until 1919 or later Joseph Bell was the agent[51] and was probably the most important man in the parish for over 50 years.[52] Even before the agricultural depression of the late 1870s, which was especially severe around Bridgnorth,[53] the estate produced a poor return per acre.[54] At Lady Day 1878 Derrington farm was in hand,[55] and by February 1879 many rents were in arrears and several farms had been given up and re-let, if at all, for reduced rents. Until *c.* 1882 several farms were usually in hand at any one time. In 1879 regular rent reductions began, at first 5 per cent but in the 1880s 15 per cent.[56] A further remission of 10 per cent had to be made from 1889. Meanwhile from 1878 repeated attempts to sell all or parts of the estate failed until, in 1882, Lord Boyne bought *c.* 1,050 a. south of Bent Lane and the Ditton–Middleton road. In 1889 he bought 745 a. more, including Church and Powkesmore farms and much of Hill Side, all north of Bent Lane and the Ditton–Middleton road, so that Rea brook largely divided the two estates.[57]

In 1910 the Howard estate comprised 2,187 a. and the estate bought by Lord Boyne (then owned by F. G. Hamilton-Russell) 1,727 a. The only other private landowners with over 100 a. were Joseph Poole (220 a.) and George George (181 a.) at Ruthall and Elizabeth Howells (125 a.) at Great Hudwick.[58]

In 1919 and 1922 Hamilton-Russell offered much of his Burwarton estate for sale, including 721 a. in Ditton in 1919. Farms including Church farm (1919) and Derrington East (1922) were bought by their tenants,[59] while in 1919 the county council bought two farms north-east of Ditton, 111 a. in all, for ex-servicemen's smallholdings.[60] Five (10–38 a.) were created, those

37 Ibid. ff. 46–9.

38 O.S. Map 6", Salop. LXV. NE. (1891 edn.).

39 At O.S. Nat. Grid *c.* SO 600 881: O.S. Maps 1/2,500, Salop. LXV. 7 (1903 edn.), SO 5888/5988, 6088/6188 (1973 edn.).

40 S.R.O., q. sess. rec. parcel 281, reg. of papists' deeds 1717–88, pp. 188–9; incl. award B 21–2.

41 S.R.O. 3419, deeds and table of leases.

42 S.P.L., MS. 6864, f. 48.

43 Priors Ditton Incl. and Tithe Compensation Act, 1813, 53 Geo. III, c. 48 (Local and Personal, not printed); S.R.O., incl. award A 18/51; 990/1–5; 2707/1; S.P.L., SC1/2.

44 S.R.O. 3419, survs. n.d. and 1828.

45 S.P.L., Deeds 734.

46 S.R.O. 3419, surv. of Fra. Canning's Ditton est. 1768, 1828.

47 S.R.O. 4044/14. 48 S.P.L., SC1/2.

49 Ditton par. rec., par. log bk. i, newscuttings s.a. 1867.

50 S.R.O. 189/15–16; 886/3, 8.

51 *P.O. Dir. Salop.* (1870), 118; S.R.O. 3419, Howard est. acct. bks. 1874–1919.

52 Rivalled by the vicar J. B. Wilkinson: Ditton par. rec., par. log bk. i, s.a. 1867–8.

53 *V.C.H. Salop.* iv. 232–3.

54 Cf. income from Howard estates in other counties: J. Bateman, *Gt. Landowners of Gt. Brit. and Irel.* (1883), 230.

55 What follows is based on S.R.O. 3419, Howard est. acct. bks., Jos. Bell's ann. reps.

56 Cf. ibid. est. acct. bk. 1874–9, rental Mich. 1873; 1880–5, rental Lady Day 1880.

57 *Salopian Shreds & Patches*, iii. 63, 196; S.P.L., SC1/2; S.R.O. 757/67/20–1; 3419, Howard est. acct. bks. 1874–9 (16 Aug. 1879), 1880–5 (9 Aug. 1881, 2 Feb. 1882), 1886–92 (7 Feb., 10 Aug. 1889), Ditton est. sale cat. 1881.

58 Above, manors; S.R.O. 4044/14.

59 S.R.O. 4190/2, p. [6]; printed sale partic. of 1922 reported as in possession of Mrs. F. Smallman of Ditton Priors; inf. from the Misses F., I., and V. Childs (Derrington Fm.) and Mr. C. Thomas (Church Fm.).

60 Rest of para. based on smallholdings' management file in S.C.C. County Valuer and Land Agent's Dept. and inf. from Mr. C. W. Rowlands. See also *Salop. N.F.U. Jnl.* cx (Nov. 1960), 8–11 (copy in S.P.L.), and (for general background) *Ag. Hist. Eng.* viii. 137–9; *V.C.H. Salop.* iii. 197; iv. 263–5.

north of the Ditton–Middleton road being completed *c.* 1921. In 1969 and 1972 the council sold two of the houses and made a third into a cottage tenancy, adding land to the remaining two smallholdings. From 1990 the council offered daily work on a 30-a. smallholding to adults with learning difficulties.[61] More of the Howards' estate was sold after the First World War, including Middleton North in 1926. The last of the Howards' land in Ditton (Home farm, Middleton, and some woodland) was sold in 1948–9.[62]

The land was said in 1794 to be badly cultivated: the best course was wheat, peas or oats, and clover, but many sowed wheat, oats for two or three years afterwards, and then fallowed until the land could bear wheat again.[63] In 1801 there were 952 a. of arable: 49 per cent was growing wheat, 39 per cent oats, 3 per cent barley, 6 per cent peas, and 3 per cent roots.[64] The Cannings then required their tenants to follow a four-course rotation of fallow, wheat, a green crop such as vetches, and spring corn.[65] Hemp may still have been grown on butts at the edge of Ditton village.[66] About 1830 a rotation of wheat, oats, and fallow seems to have been usual.[67]

In the later 19th and early 20th century grassland gradually increased until, by 1938, *c.* 97 per cent of the parish's farm land was pasture.[68] Arable receded fastest on the smallholdings and smaller farms.[69] Sheep were much the commonest animal before the Second World War; later beef rearing became important. By 1965 arable was again gradually increasing.[70]

Woodland was carefully managed from the 18th century and in the last century at least was probably increased at the expense of marginal farm land. Perhaps following a survey of coppiceable land in 1728 Francis Canning planted extensive coppices, presumably intending to supply the nearby furnaces at Bouldon and Charlcotte with fuel and tanners with oak bark. In the 18th and 19th centuries oak fetched good prices; the estate had its own nursery, and both timber and bark were cropped.[71] The Cannings had over 200 a. of coppices by 1828,[72] 267 a. by 1878 mainly at Netchwood, Lightwood, and Powkesmore.[73] In the late 19th and early 20th century alder, ash, larch, oak, and poplar were regularly cut in plantations, coppices, and hedgerows. In 1907 the bark was still cropped and sold at Bridgnorth.[74] Lord Boyne planted trees on Brown Clee in 1884 to absorb recently abandoned farm land.[75] The parish was well wooded in the later 20th century, and oaks were managed as hedgerow timber. The Burwarton estate opened a timber treatment and preservation plant near Oakwood Farm *c.* 1972 and in 1985 moved the estate sawmill there from Burwarton.[76]

TABLE XVIII

DITTON PRIORS: LAND USE, LIVESTOCK, AND CROPS

	1867	*1891*	*1938*	*1965*
Percentage of grassland	68	86	97	78
arable	32	14	3	22
Percentage of cattle	18	28	44	18
sheep	69	63	51	78
pigs	13	9	5	4
Percentage of wheat	44	29	32	32
barley	15	24	3	54
oats	40	46	65	10
mixed corn & rye	1	1	0	4
Percentage of agricultural land growing roots and vegetables	6	3	1	3

Sources: P.R.O., MAF 68/143, no. 9; /1340, no. 13; /3880, Salop. no. 199; /4945, no. 199.

FAIRS. In Edward I's reign and George III's the lord of the manor petitioned the Crown for a fair. The later plea, that it was difficult to drive beasts 9 miles to the nearest market, requested fairs on 10 May and 25 October, and fairs were later held, remembered in the 1930s as high points of the year.[77] There was a cattle dealer at Ditton in 1851.[78] By 1907, on the eve of the railway's arrival, the St. Luke's fair livestock auction was one of four a year at Ditton, but the May fair auction seems not to have survived the First World War.[79] In the 1920s and until 1949 or later about six auctions a year were usual; 240 cattle and 480 sheep were sold in 1926, 500 and 5,400 in 1939, but only 49 and 701 in 1949.[80]

MILLS. In the early 14th century Upper mill adjoined Middleton's field towards Derrington. As Andrew Walker, a fuller, held land in Mid-

61 *The County Column* (S.C.C.) Sept. 1991, 5; inf. from S.C.C. Social Services Dept.
62 Inf. from Mr. and Mrs. A. Corfield; above, manors.
63 S.P.L., MS. 6864, f. 48.
64 P.R.O., HO 67/12/72.
65 S.R.O. 3419, lease of Derrington fm.
66 S.P.L., SC1/2, map; H. Green, 'Linen Ind. of Salop.' *Ind. Arch. Rev.* v. 114–18.
67 S.R.O. 3419, fm. surv. bk. (with maps).
68 Salop. Agric. Returns, 1905; Table XVIII.
69 S.R.O. 4190/2, pp. 95, 97–8, 104–6, 108–10, 112, 114.
70 Table XVIII.
71 S.R.O. 3419, C. Albot to F. Canning 29 May 1811; S.P.L., Deeds 735 (e.g. Lady Day 1781, 1783, 1792); cf. O. Rackham, *Ancient Woodland* (1980), 148, 154.
72 S.R.O. 3419, surv. of Fra. Canning's Ditton est. 1828.
73 S.P.L., SC1/2.
74 S.R.O. 3419, Howard est. acct. bks. 1874–1920.
75 Inf. from Mr. E. T. Edwards, Ld. Boyne's head forester from 1937, and Mr. A. Corfield.
76 Inf. from Mr. Edwards.
77 Ranford, *Ditton Priors*, 14–15.
78 S. Bagshaw, *Dir. Salop.* (1851), 590–1.
79 Smith and Beddoes, *Cleobury Mortimer and Ditton Priors Lt. Rly.* 18, 101.
80 W. M. Moisley, 'Mkts. of Salop.' (Lond. Univ. M.Sc. thesis, 1951), 45, 78–9; *Kelly's Dir. Salop.* (1926), 7, and later edns. (which descr. the auctions as monthly).

dleton's fields in 1319[81] the mill may not have been for corn. It perhaps stood 0.75 km. west of Middleton, on the Rea.[82] Ditton manor included a water corn mill in 1544[83] and the early 18th century, when it was in Middleton township.[84] In the 19th and 20th centuries the lord's mill at Middleton stood 1 km. south-south-east of the hamlet, and in 1878 it had two pairs of water-driven stones but also an engine;[85] it closed *c.* 1922.[86]

The vicar John Allen had a horse mill in the earlier 16th century,[87] and there was a water mill at Sidnall in 1592.[88]

Perhaps in 1845 a tower windmill was built south of Powkesmore Farm. It was disused by 1883 and, although later used as a house, had long been a ruinous stump by the 1980s.[89]

Netchwood mill existed in 1910[90] but its purpose and location are unknown.

INDUSTRY. Coal Measures lie near the surface of Brown Clee hill. Coal was probably got in the parish by the 1690s.[91] By the early 18th century many small mines were open on Brown Clee and, although the amount of coal got was declining by the end of the century, some was still mined there in the later 19th century.[92] Ironstone was got with the coal, and its extraction continued slightly longer.[93]

Dhu stone (dolerite) was widely quarried in the parish by the late 18th century when, as later, it was used as building stone, slates, flagstones, and grave stones.[94] Large-scale quarrying was begun in 1908 by the contractors building the light railway to Ditton, whose main purpose was to facilitate the extraction of dhu stone from the Burwarton estate.[95] Lord Boyne is said to have favoured the scheme as a relief of local unemployment.[96] The Abdon Clee Stone Quarry Co. built an 800-ft. inclined plane from the quarry on top of Brown Clee to Ditton, where 200 men were employed at a stone cutting and crushing works. At first the works' main product was tramway setts, demand for which fell in the 1920s. There was, however, still a good market for roadstone and railway ballast, and stone was also used in the company's concrete and tarmac works. Quarrymen were better paid than the farm labourers. By 1930 the hill's dhu stone cap had gone, and a large quarry was sunk on the hill top. By 1936 the stone works in Ditton had closed, but stone was still got for the company's other works.

Between 1914 and 1941 the company had a ferro-concrete works, developed by Hamish Cross, at the Ditton railway terminus. It employed 200 men casting panels and posts for sectional buildings. The components were used for housing in Neasden (Mdx.) and Wolverhampton (Staffs.) and in 1927, after a dam burst, at Dolgarrog (Caern.).[97]

The company also had an asphalt plant at Ditton station between *c.* 1914 and 1942. It produced asphalt 'carpet', a tar and dhu stone road surface.[98]

By the early 19th century bricks were made in the parish, and the Canning estate had a permanent brickworks at Powkesmore. Besides bricks, tiles, and pipes for the estate the works produced goods for sale.[99] In 1828, for instance, the new vicarage was built of Powkesmore bricks.[1] The works had closed by 1883.[2]

There was a limeworks in the early 18th century. In the 19th century the manorial estate had a large limeworks at the base of Brown Clee hill, which used locally dug cornstone and coal; it closed in the late 19th century.[3] There may also have been limekilns south and south-east of Middleton and at Sidnall.[4]

In 1971 the Ministry of Defence sold land attached to the former armaments depot, and it was later used for an industrial estate; by 1985 there were *c.* 10 small firms there, most of them concerned with light engineering.[5]

LOCAL GOVERNMENT. Records of Ditton manor court survive from the early 14th to the early 17th century. In the Middle Ages and in 1560 the court seems to have been simply a court baron dealing with agricultural and tenurial matters. By 1570, however, the lord had begun

81 S.P.L., Deeds 6962, 6966.
82 S.P.L., SC1/2, field 748 (old mills).
83 *L. & P. Hen. VIII*, xix (2), p. 81.
84 S.R.O., q. sess. rec. parcel 281, reg. of papists' deeds 1717–88, pp. 1–2; S.P.L., Deeds 734.
85 S.P.L., SC1/2, p. 5; O.S. Map 6", Salop. LXV. NE. (1903 edn.); S.R.O. 1634, deed 25 Apr. 1812; 3419, deed 25 Mar. 1801; W.S.L. 350/3/40, Ditton Priors p. 1; SA 15786.
86 S.R.O. 3756/147, pp. 39–40; N.B.R., photos. of mill.
87 P.R.O., C 1/1247, nos. 41–2; C 1/1255, nos. 43–4.
88 P.R.O., C 142/234, no. 78.
89 W. A. Seaby and A. C. Smith, *Windmills in Salop., Heref. and Worc.* (Stevenage Museum, 1984), 10, 18.
90 S.R.O. 4044/14, p. 10.
91 S.R.O. 5460/8/4/2 (Thos. Garbett of Ditton Priors, collier).
92 S.P.L., Deeds 734, p. 20; R. Baugh, *Map of Salop.* (1808); O.S. Map 1", sheet LXI. NE. (1833 edn.); 6", Salop. LXV. NE. (1883 edn.); Rowley, 'S. Salop. Landscape', 183; Birm. Univ. Libr., Mytton Papers, ii. 387.
93 S.P.L., Deeds 734; Birm. Univ. Libr., Mytton Papers, ii. 387; J. Rocque, *Map of Salop.* (1757); *V.C.H. Salop.* i. 34.
94 S.P.L., Deeds 735, accts. for 1798–1800; S.R.O. 3419, Howard est. acct. bk. 1892–7, 7 Aug. 1894, 17 Aug. 1896; acct. bk. 1914–20, 30 July 1918. Cf. O.S. Maps 6", Salop. LXV. NE., LXVI. NW., LXVII. SE. (1903 edn.).
95 Rest of para. based on Smith and Beddoes, *Cleobury Mortimer and Ditton Priors Lt. Rly.* 9, 22–23, 51, 72, 79–81; Price, *Cleobury Mortimer and Ditton Priors Lt. Rly.*; Rowley, 'S. Salop. Landscape', 183; S.R.O. 4044/14; S.P.L., photos. of inclined plane; Smith, 'Changing Patterns', 75.
96 Inf. from Mr. E. T. Edwards.
97 Smith, op. cit. 75; Smith and Beddoes, op. cit. 51, 75–6, 81, 84; S.P.L., photos.
98 Smith and Beddoes, op. cit. 76, 81, 84.
99 S.R.O. 3419, C. Albot to F. Canning 29 May 1811; Canning est. brick bks. 1814–23; poor-rate assessment 1816, for brick kiln; land tax bdle., printed advt. 1826; Warws. R.O., CR 1379, box 5, brickwks. acct. bk. 1830; O.S. Map 6", Salop. LXV. NE. (1891 edn.); S.P.L., SC1/2, map, fields 9–10.
1 S.R.O. 3419, land tax bdle., brickwks. acct. 1828.
2 O.S. Map 6", Salop. LXV. NE. (1891 edn.).
3 W.B.R., Q2/2/58–9; O.S. Maps 1", sheet LXI. SW. (1833 edn.); 6", Salop. LXV. NE. (1903 edn.); S.R.O. 3419, arts. of agreement 10 Sept. 1816; *V.C.H. Salop.* i. 24.
4 S.P.L., SC1/2, map, fields 659, 726; Christ Ch., Oxf., mun. viii. a. 53, f. 3.
5 Local inf.; Smith and Beddoes, *Cleobury Mortimer and Ditton Priors Lt. Rly.* 85.

to exercise leet jurisdiction: spring meetings of his court in 1570 and 1571 were described as a view of frankpledge with court baron and dealt with assaults, bloodshed, and breach of the assize of ale.[6]

There were manorial pounds at Ditton Priors and Middleton.[7]

No record of an Ashfield manor court is known. By 1263 Richard, king of the Romans, had compelled Ashfield to withdraw suit from Munslow hundred and attend the court of his barony of Castle Holdgate, even though Ashfield was held by a king's serjeant and so was not part of the feudal barony into whose liberty it was thus incorporated.[8] The suit may have been transferred during the shrievalty (1261–3) of James of Audley, a member of King Richard's household.[9] Ashfield was presenting at Holdgate leet in Henry VII's time and still in 1599[10] but apparently not by 1863.[11]

Pleas and perquisites of Ruthall's court were worth 6*d*. *c*. 1330.[12] A court of recognition called a view of frankpledge and court baron was held in 1706.[13]

By 1785 (probably by 1781) the parish was divided into Ditton end (Ditton and Ashfield and Ruthall) and Middleton end (Middleton and Derrington) for rating, separate accounts being kept for each until *c*. 1827, the year of the last account for Middleton.[14]

In 1737–8 the poor received cash, cloth, coal, and corn as out relief.[15] Ditton had a workhouse in the late 18th and early 19th century;[16] there were usually *c*. 8 paupers there 1812–15, when *c*. 30 received permanent out relief and 30 others occasional relief.[17] Annual expenditure on the poor peaked in 1818 at £552. In the later 1820s *c*. £250 was usual.[18]

The parish was in Bridgnorth poor-law union 1836–1930,[19] rural sanitary district 1872–94, and rural district 1894–1974, and in Bridgnorth district from 1974.[20] Ashfield and Ruthall formed a highway parish in Bridgnorth highway district 1867–95;[21] the rest of the civil parish, which ceased to be in Wenlock municipal borough in 1889,[22] probably continued to look after its own highways until 1895.

CHURCHES. Parts of Ditton church are 12th-century or perhaps earlier,[23] and Master Nicholas of Wolverhampton was incumbent in the later 1190s and until his death, probably in the mid 1220s when the living was appropriated to Wenlock priory; oddly Nicholas had been called 'vicar' when the appropriation was licensed in the later 1190s.[24] The priory had presumably acquired patronage of the living when Hugh of Periers granted it the manor *c*. 1175.[25] About 1196, however, St. Mary Magdalen's college, Bridgnorth, claimed the advowson, perhaps because Periers had acquired Ditton with Corfham (in Diddlebury) and Culmington, both of which owed tithes to St. Mary's.[26] The college's claim evidently failed, for the priory remained patron until its surrender in 1540. The Crown seized the priory as an alien house and presented to the living until the priory's denization in 1395.[27]

In 1544 the Crown sold the advowson with Ditton manor to Humphrey Pakington,[28] and it again descended with the manor.[29] From the 16th century the lords were Roman Catholics, and after 1605 others exercised their patronage; in the late 19th and earlier 20th century Cambridge university usually presented.[30] In 1964 P. J. C. Howard's trustees conveyed the advowson to the bishop of Hereford.[31]

Ditton was held in plurality with Neenton from 1952, the patrons presenting alternately. The incumbent also held Upton Cressett with Monkhopton 1955–62, living at Monkhopton from 1960 when Ditton Vicarage was sold.[32] Ditton Priors and Neenton were served 1963–6 by a priest-in-charge living at Neenton[33] but again from 1968 by an incumbent who lived at Ditton and from *c*. 1969 was also priest-in-charge of Aston Botterell with Wheathill and

[6] Warws. R.O., CR 1379, ct. r.; H.W.R.O.(H.), T 74, bdle. 359; S.R.O. 566/1; 1224/2/1, 3–9. Cf. *V.C.H. Salop*. iii. 53, for 'view of frankpledge'.

[7] S.P.L., SC1/2, p. 13 and map, field 540.

[8] *Rot. Hund.* (Rec. Com.), ii. 100; cf. Eyton, iii. 348.

[9] *V.C.H. Salop*. iii. 16; N. Denholm-Young, *Ric. of Cornwall* (1947), 90, 93; H. Wait, 'Household and Resources of the Ld. Edw. 1239–72' (Oxf. Univ. D.Phil. thesis, 1989), 298, 337.

[10] S.P.L., MS. 2, f. 146; *Salop. N. & Q*. i. 13, 47.

[11] S.P.L., Deeds 10194.

[12] S.R.O. 2/13.

[13] S.P.L., Deeds 9929.

[14] Par. rec., chwdns.' acct. bk. 1785–1857, with addns.; cf. S.P.L., Deeds 735, cottage acct. Lady Day 1781.

[15] S.R.O. 5709, Ditton Priors overseers' accts.

[16] S.P.L., Deeds 735, acct. for Lady Day 1803; SC1/2, field 555; S.R.O. 3419, poor rate assessment 1816; Ranford, *Ditton Priors*, 16.

[17] *Poor Law Abstract*, H.C. 82, pp. 376–7 (1818), xix.

[18] *Poor Rate Returns*, H.C. 556, suppl. app. p. 144 (1822), v; H.C. 334, p. 179 (1825), iv; H.C. 219, p. 167 (1830–1), xi; H.C. 444, p. 162 (1835), xlvii.

[19] V. J. Walsh, 'Admin. of Poor Laws in Salop. 1820–55' (Pennsylvania Univ. Ph.D. thesis, 1970), 148–50; *Kelly's Dir. Salop*. (1929), 196.

[20] *Rural Dist. Councillors Electn. Order, 1894* (Local Govt. Bd. order no. 31847); *V.C.H. Salop*. ii. 213; iii. 179, and sources cited ibid. 169 n. 29.

[21] *Orders of Q. Sess.* iv. 176–7; S.R.O., S.C.C. Local Govt., etc., Cttee. min. bk. 1894–1903, p. 29.

[22] Local Govt. Bd.'s Prov. Order Conf. (No. 4) Act, 1889, 52 & 53 Vic. c. 22 (Local).

[23] Below, this section.

[24] *Hereford 1079–1234*, ed. J. Barrow (Eng. Episcopal Acta, vii), pp. 169–70, 288–9.

[25] Above, manors.

[26] *V.C.H. Salop*. ii. 124; Eyton, iii. 330.

[27] *Reg. Trillek* (C.S.), 274, 405; *Cal. Pat.* 1354–8, 192, 276; *V.C.H. Salop*. ii. 42, 45.

[28] *L. & P. Hen. VIII*, xix (2), p. 81; P.R.O., E 36/259, f. 305v.

[29] H.W.R.O.(H.), Heref. dioc. rec. AL 19/17, pp. 289, 357–62; S.P.L., SC1/2, p. [1]; *P.O. Dir. Salop*. (1856), 105.

[30] Below, this section; Rom. Cath.; *Dioc. of Heref. Institutions (1539–1900)*, ed. A. T. Bannister (Heref. 1923), 83, 97, 121, 147, 176, 200; Warws. R.O., CR 1379, box 4, deed 15 Dec. 1781; S.P.L., MS. 6864, f. 49; Ranford, *Ditton Priors*, 11–12; Heref. Dioc. Regy., reg. 1902–19, pp. 26, 480, 619; 1926–38, pp. 202, 351; 1938–53, p. 182; cf. *Halsbury's Laws of Eng.* (4th edn.), xiv (1975), pp. 407–8.

[31] Heref. Dioc. Regy., reg. 1953–68, p. 452; above, manors.

[32] Heref. Dioc. Regy., reg. 1953–68, pp. 48–9, 95, 98–9, 255, 259, 268–9, 530; 1969–(in use), pp. 5, 263; *Heref. Dioc. Yr. Bk.* (1962–3), 29; *Crockford* (1961–2), 1118; S.R.O., reg. of electors, Ludlow (1961), p. 258; below, this section; inf. from dioc. registrar.

[33] *Crockford* (1965–6), 195; *Heref. Dioc. Yr. Bk.* (1964–5), 28; (1965–6), 29.

Loughton and of Burwarton with Cleobury North. In 1986 those benefices were united under an incumbent residing at Ditton, whose joint patrons included the bishop of Hereford.[34]

The vicarage was worth £4 6*s.* 8*d.* a year in 1291[35] and £3 6*s.* 8*d.* in 1379.[36] In 1401 Richard de Arderne, vicar, was a private landowner in the parish.[37] Before the Dissolution Wenlock priory let at least some of its appropriated tithes to the vicar,[38] and in 1532 John Allen, vicar 1492–*c.* 1542, held all or most of them for life.[39] Allen held other priory property too, a cottage in Ditton in 1510–11 and *c.* 1523 when he also held pasture on Powkesmore; at his death he held a priory farm in Sidnall.[40] In 1535 the net income of his benefice, after payment of a 10*s.* pension to Wenlock priory, was £5 15*s.* 8*d.* and seems by then to have included great tithes in Middleton Priors.[41]

Our Lady's service had no priest in 1548; its net income of 18*s.* 10*d.* came from two houses in Ditton and 7 a. in Ditton, Ruthall, and Monkhopton. In 1549 the lands were sold to speculators.[42]

In 1625 the vicar's glebe comprised three arable furlongs and an acre, meadow and pasture, and a couple of gardens and yards. The vicar owned all the small tithes and had 'custom money' for all tithe hay except that due from Ditton manor house; he also had the great tithes of Middleton and of all home closes in the parish except that of Ditton manor house. The tenant of Hither Middleton owed the service of carrying the vicar's tithes and also customarily paid him 12*s.* a year. In 1794 the vicar's glebe, *c.* 20 a., was scattered and barely worth 10*s.* an acre per annum.[43]

The living was worth £36 a year *c.* 1708.[44] It was augmented in 1827 with £600 from Queen Anne's Bounty to meet a joint benefaction of £400 by Francis Canning, patron, and Edward Ridsdale, vicar 1825–62.[45] The living was worth £147 in 1835. In 1841, at inclosure, the vicar's tithes were extinguished and he was allotted 219 a. as glebe: most of it lay together between Ditton village and the hamlets of Ashfield and Ruthall.[46] In 1878 the vicar was said to have 253 a. worth £300 a year, and the living's net value was claimed to be *c.* £304.[47] In 1960 the only glebe remaining, 61 a., was sold.[48]

During the latter years of Morgan Jones, vicar, who died in 1825 aged 89,[49] the vicarage house adjoining the churchyard[50] and the glebe fences became dilapidated. Jones's successor Edward Ridsdale built a new house in 1828, the old one being occupied by his farm servants. Designed by John Smallman the new vicarage just north-west of the village was built of local brick, a plain but imposing house of three bays and two storeys, with a central entrance and low hipped roof.[51] It was sold in 1960, and in 1967 a new vicarage was built across the road from the church.[52]

Master Nicholas of Wolverhampton, the first known incumbent, became archdeacon of Salop.[53] John of Skimblescott, vicar in the 1320s, killed a man in self defence.[54] In 1554 William Alcocke, who was also deacon of Holdgate, was deprived for marriage.[55] His successor Richard Sutton was also rector of Pitchford from 1563.[56] The first known graduate incumbent, apart from Nicholas of Wolverhampton, was Thomas Jenckes, 1623–48.[57]

In the 18th and 19th centuries vicars usually held the living, sometimes in plurality, for several decades and until death. George Osland, 1656–*c.* 1704, was a Presbyterian who conformed in 1662.[58] William Rutter (d. 1763), already vicar of Chelmarsh, was presented in 1743 by a relation.[59] His successor Joseph Ball (d. 1790)[60] closed Middleton chapel *c.* 1780.[61] In the later 18th and 19th centuries communion was celebrated at four times of the year. Ball's successor Morgan Jones (d. 1825) had a living in Radnorshire but lived at Ditton.[62]

During his absence in the early 1830s Edward Ridsdale, 1825–62, employed a curate. The church was then dilapidated[63] and church life at a low ebb. By 1851 attendance at nonconformist and Roman Catholic worship outstripped that at the parish church: the 149 rented and 19 free places were occupied by an average of 67 adults at morning service and just 7 in the afternoon.

34 *Crockford* (1969–70), 1003; *Heref. Dioc. Yr. Bk.* (1969–70), 28–9; (1970–1), 32–3; (1987), 34.

35 *Tax. Eccl.* (Rec. Com.), 166; cf. *Reg. Lacy* (C.S.), 78.

36 Eyton, iii. 337.

37 Above, manors (Hyggs Yd.). Hen. Ward's incumbency was shorter than recorded (1355–1405: *Cal. Pat.* 1354–8, 192; *Reg. Mascall* (C.S.), 168), the reason for the 1405 vacancy being wrongly registered.

38 Eyton, iii. 337; below, this section.

39 *Reg. Myllyng* (C.S.), 201; Bannister, *Heref. Institutions*, 2; Warws. R.O., CR 1379, box 4, deed in ct. r. bdle.

40 S.R.O. 1224, box 342, Prior Gosnell's reg. f. 37; N.L.W., Wynnstay, RA 2; *L. & P. Hen. VIII*, xix (2), p. 81.

41 *Valor Eccl.* (Rec. Com.), iii. 211; Eyton, iii. 337; below, this section.

42 *T.S.A.S.* 3rd ser. x. 363; *Cal. Pat.* 1548–9, 393; W.S.L. 350/3/40, Ditton Priors p. 3.

43 S.R.O. 3419, glebe terrier 1625; S.P.L., MS. 6864, ff. 47v., 49v.

44 J. Ecton, *Liber Valorum et Decimarum* (1711), 149.

45 C. Hodgson, *Q. Anne's Bounty* (2nd edn.), pp. ccviii, ccxx; Bannister, *Heref. Institutions*, 147, 176.

46 *Rep. Com. Eccl. Revenues* [67], pp. 436–7, H.C. (1835), xxii; S.R.O., incl. award A 18/51; above, econ. hist.

47 S.P.L., SC1/2, p. 30; cf. *Kelly's Dir. Salop.* (1885), 924.

48 *Crockford* (1951–2), 508; inf. from dioc. registrar.

49 S.R.O. 5482/BRg/1, 15 Sept. 1825.

50 S.R.O. 3419, glebe terrier; S.P.L., MS. 6864, f. 49.

51 S.R.O. 3698/5/1–6; Heref. Dioc. Regy., reg. 1822–42, p. 83; H.W.R.O.(H.), HD 8, box 31, plans; H. Colvin, *Biog. Dict. Brit. Architects, 1600–1840* (1978), 740.

52 Heref. Dioc. Regy., reg. 1953–68, pp. 554–5; inf. from dioc. registrar.

53 Eyton, iii. 336–7; A. B. Emden, *Biog. Reg. Univ. Oxf. to 1500*, iii. 2080.

54 *Reg. Orleton* (C.S.), 131, 255; Ranford, *Ditton Priors*, 6.

55 Heref. D. & C. mun., chapter act bk. 1512–66 (folio), f. 130 and v.

56 Bannister, *Heref. Institutions*, 9, 16; *T.S.A.S.* 3rd ser. i. 258; 4th ser. xii. 99.

57 H.W.R.O.(H.), Heref. dioc. rec. AL 19/17, pp. 362–3; B.L. Add. MS. 21237, f. 267; W.S.L. 350/3/40, Ditton Priors p. 4; *Alum. Oxon. 1500–1714*, ii. 807.

58 *Salop. N. & Q.* viii. 59; Bannister, op. cit. 59; R. F. Skinner, *Nonconf. in Salop.* (Shrews. 1964), 102.

59 Bannister, op. cit. 78, 83, 97; *S.P.R. Heref.* iii (4), p. v; Ranford, *Ditton Priors*, 11–12.

60 Bannister, op. cit. 97, 121; S.R.O. 3419, C. Albot to F. Canning 29 May 1811.

61 Below, this section.

62 Par. rec., chwdns.' acct. bk. 1785–1857, with addns.; S.P.L., MS. 6864, f. 49 and v.; S.R.O. 5482/BRg/1, 15 Sept. 1825.

63 S.P.L., MS. 6864, ff. 49v.–50v.; Bannister, *Heref. Institutions*, 147, 176; Heref. Dioc. Regy., reg. 1822–42, p. 201; *Rep. Com. Eccl. Revenues*, 436–7.

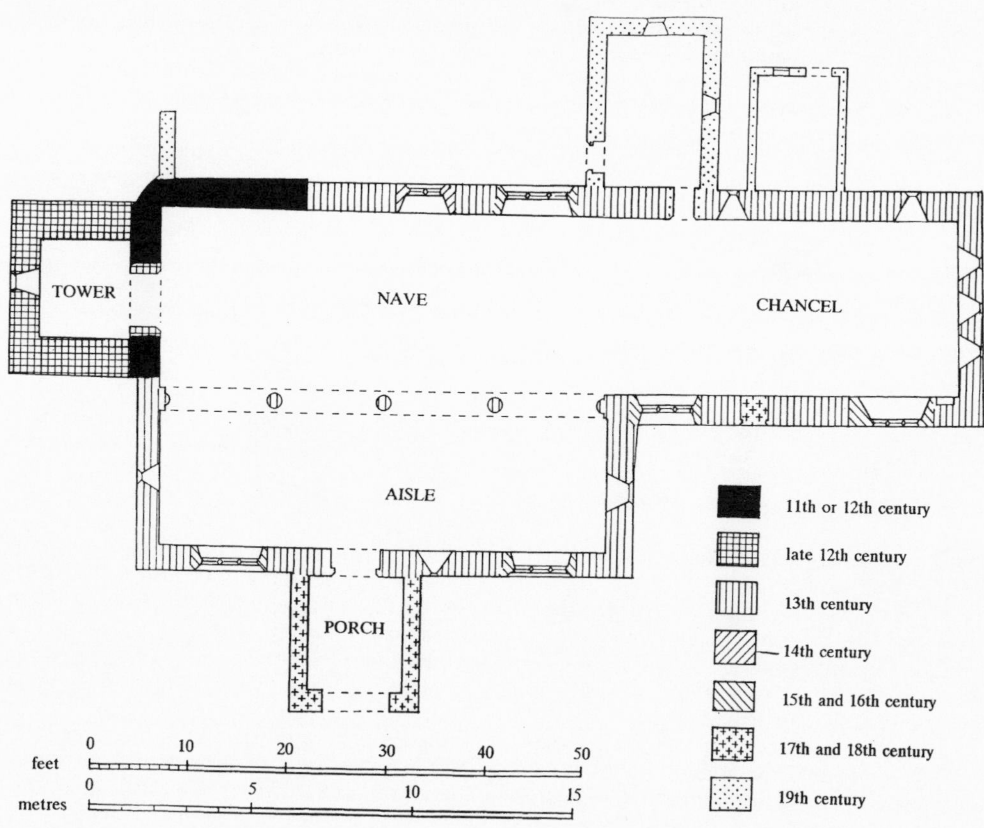

Fig. 32

DITTON PRIORS: THE CHURCH OF ST. JOHN THE BAPTIST

The choir was led by a double bass and a fife, played in the gallery where the poor sat. Latterly Ridsdale was ill and employed a curate, E. N. Stott, under whom church restoration began and a new school was built.[64] J. B. Wilkinson, vicar 1862–86 and minister at Shipton 1880–6,[65] completed the restoration and refounded the school. In his early years he vigorously promoted the church in the village and was particularly active against possible Romish influence exerted by the lord of the manor or his agent. Probably because of Catholic pressure no church rate was levied after the late 1850s, but Wilkinson introduced monthly offerings in 1863 and an annual thanksgiving and harvest home in 1864. In 1867 an unsalaried vestry clerkship was introduced; the man chosen, at a small meeting at which Catholics were in the majority, was a Catholic, and the post was quickly abolished by a larger meeting at which the Catholics were outvoted. By 1867 church attendance was improving, the choir more efficient, and the offertory yielding thrice what the church rate had last produced.[66]

By the early 15th century the church was dedicated to *ST. MARY THE VIRGIN*[67] but by 1831 to *ST. JOHN THE BAPTIST*.[68] The church, of rubble dhu stone and sandstone, consists of an undivided chancel and nave with north vestry, south aisle and porch, and a west tower topped by a shingled spire.[69] The north and west walls of the nave incorporate the oldest fabric, perhaps 12th-century or earlier. The slightly battered west tower, entered by a low arch, was added late in the 12th century. Early in the 13th century the church was almost rebuilt with the addition of a south aisle to the nave. The aisle has an irregular arcade of four bays and its original east and west lancets and one on the south survive; the chancel, rebuilt at or about the same time as the nave, has two lancets in the north wall, a group of three (badly restored) in the south wall, and a triple lancet east window. A blocked doorway in the south wall of the chancel may be contemporary with the rebuilding; one in the north wall probably gave access to an early vestry, perhaps that which existed in 1790. A two-light window was put into the north wall of the nave in the 14th century, and in the late 15th or early 16th century windows were put into the south wall of the chancel and the aisle and the north wall of the nave. The chancel

64 P.R.O., HO 129/356, no. 11 (cf. nos. 12–16); Ranford, *Ditton Priors*, 16; par. rec., par. log bk. s.a. 1863, 1871. For Stott cf. *Crockford* (1891), 1280.

65 Bannister, *Heref. Institutions*, 176, 200; *T.S.A.S.* 2nd ser. xi. 283–4.

66 Par. rec., par. log bk. i. For cessation of ch. rate, cf. chwdns.' acct. bk. 1785–1857, addns. at end.

67 *Reg. Mascall*, 168, 173.

68 W.S.L. 350/3/40, Ditton Priors p. 3.

69 Fig. 32. Descr. based on Cranage, iii. 191–3; Pevsner, *Salop.* 121; E. A. Gee, 'Hist. and arch. acct. of Wenlock priory and its dependent churches' (Birm. Univ. M.A. thesis, 1937), 245–50. For early illustr. of ch. see S.P.L., MS. 372, vol. ii, f. 45; S.P.L., photo. neg. B. 2107; Bodl. MS. Top. Salop. c. 2, f. 404.

screen is composed of panels of two 15th-century designs.[70] A screen across the centre of the aisle is presumably that which, in the 1830s, defined the chancel or chapel belonging to Ashfield manor.[71] The spire is probably of late medieval origin; the porch is probably post-medieval.

In the early 19th century the church had a gallery.[72] The spire was renewed *c.* 1832,[73] but the church was still partly clay floored and generally in a 'deplorable' state *c.* 1860 when restoration began under Stott. The work, completed *c.* 1871 in Wilkinson's time, included the construction of a new trussed rafter roof over both nave and aisle, and the church's reflooring, reseating, redecoration, and probably the restoration of many of the windows. It was probably then that the gallery was removed. Small grants for the work were received from the Hereford Diocesan Church Building Society in 1862 and 1866. A new vestry was built in 1894.[74] The spire was again renewed in 1978.[75] In 1983 a Lady chapel was made in that part of the aisle which had belonged to Ashfield manor. An oak communion table from Albrighton, near Shifnal, was acquired at the same time.[76]

Fragments of 15th-century woodwork, probably from a screen, are re-used in the pulpit and a desk front. The pulpit (with a reading pew) was moved in 1666 from an inconvenient position to the north-east corner of the nave, where it stood in the 20th century.[77] Two late medieval bench ends are re-used in the chancel, while the nave pews incorporate 17th- and 18th-century panelling, some dated 1666. Hangings include four 18th- and 19th-century commandment boards.[78] Two seats of *c.* 1714 and royal arms of 1814 were originally in Burwarton old church (closed 1877).[79] There are two chests, a wooden one of 1686 and an iron one of 1814 made by the Coalbrookdale Co. Memorials include an elaborate wall tablet with brass plate to Thomas Jenckes, vicar 1623–48, put up in 1667 by his son Thomas, a Shrewsbury goldsmith;[80] a fine iron floor slab to Ann (d. 1688) and Thomas (d. 1707) Hassall; and plain brasses of 1628 and 1733. There are hatchments for Gustavus Hamilton, Viscount Boyne (d. 1855), and Harriet his wife (d. 1854).

The church has a good range of fittings including four bells, one perhaps medieval and another of 1663 inscribed 'God save His Church Our King and Realm'.[81] The plate includes a secular Elizabethan cup given as a chalice in 1722–3.[82]

The parish register from 1583 survived in 1733, but by 1903 the registers were complete only from 1673.[83]

An additional burial ground west of the school was consecrated in 1932.[84]

There was a church or chapel at Middleton by the early 13th century;[85] its dedication is unknown but may possibly have been to St. Lawrence.[86] In the Middle Ages it was united with Deuxhill to form a rectorial benefice;[87] in 1277 the rector was accused of non-residence and his chaplain of failing to minister in the churches.[88] In 1291 Middleton and Deuxhill together were worth less than £4.[89] By 1331 Middleton chapel owed Wenlock priory an annual pension, apparently of 26*s.* from the great tithes, a due perhaps represented by an annual pension of 10*s.* owed to the priory from Middleton chapel *c.* 1523.[90] The union of Middleton chapel and Deuxhill, still in existence in 1505, was broken probably in 1515. The rector of Neenton was instituted to Middleton in 1521 but in 1532 the bishop reunited Middleton to Ditton Priors, in the patronage of Wenlock priory. About the same time Deuxhill was united to Glazeley rectory. Thus Middleton became, probably again, a chapel of ease to Ditton, whose vicar thus became responsible for the annual pension of 13*s.* 4*d.* to Wenlock priory.[91] In 1731 the vicar of Ditton was said to be endowed with Middleton chapel and the great tithes due to it from Middleton.[92]

In 1318 an indulgence of 30 days was offered to contributors to the fabric of the chapel and its bell turret (*campanile*).[93] The chapel stood at Middleton Baggot,[94] where a parcel of glebe was called Chapel close in 1841;[95] in 1625 the vicar's glebe had included the chapel yard at Middleton.[96] Last used for worship *c.* 1780, the chapel soon afterwards became a house. In its last years as a chapel it was a rectangular stone building with a small west bell turret and the scar of a chancel arch. By 1790 dormer windows (and so

70 There was a chancel screen in 1795: B.L. Add. MS. 21237, f. 267.

71 W.S.L. 350/3/40, Ditton Priors p. 3.

72 Above, this section.

73 For this para. see par. rec., par. log bk. i, s.a. 1863–71; *Rep. of Heref. Dioc. Ch. Bldg. Soc., Archd. of Salop 1869* (Ludlow, 1870); Ranford, *Ditton Priors*, 16; above, this section.

74 *Ch. Cal. Dioc. Heref.* (1894), 143.

75 *Bridgnorth Jnl.* 12 May 1978, p. 3.

76 Heref. Dioc. Regy., reg. 1969–(in use), p. 473.

77 H.W.R.O.(H.), HD 7, 1666/24.

78 W.S.L. 350/3/40, Ditton Priors p. 3; Heref. Dioc. Regy., reg. 1969–(in use), p. 278.

79 *Shropshire Mag.* June 1958, 32; Pevsner, *Salop.* 121; *T.S.A.S.* lxvi. 32.

80 Above, this section; B.L. Add. MS. 21237, f. 267; W.S.L. 350/3/40, Ditton Priors p. 4.

81 H. B. Walters, *Ch. Bells of Salop.* (Oswestry, 1915), 55–6.

82 D. L. Arkwright and B. W. Bourne, *Ch. Plate Archd. Ludlow* (Shrews. 1961), 27.

83 S.R.O. 5482/Rg/1–6; MRg/1–3; BRg/1; regs. at ch.;Birm. Univ. Libr., Mytton Papers, ii. 387; E. C. Peele and R. S. Clease, *Salop. Par. Doc.* (Shrews. [1903]), 152. Cf. bp.'s transcripts for 1638, 1660–71, etc., in H.W.R.O. (H.).

84 Heref. Dioc. Regy., reg. 1928–38, pp. 351–2.

85 Eyton, iii. 344.

86 The probable site (below, this section) was part of Lawrence meadow in 1878: S.P.L., SC1/2, p. 9, field 706.

87 Above, Lib. and Boro. of Wenlock (early est.).

88 *Reg. Cantilupe* (C.S.), 151.

89 Eyton, i. 220.

90 Ibid. iii. 337; *Cal. Pat.* 1348–50, 189; N.L.W., Wynnstay, RA 2.

91 *Valor Eccl.* iii. 210–11, 216; *Reg. Bothe* (C.S.), 248–50, 369; above, this section; Deuxhill, church; correcting the suggested date of 1537 (Eyton, iii. 344 n. 47).

92 W.S.L. 350/3/40, Ditton Priors p. 1.

93 *Reg. T. de Cobham* (Worcs. Hist. Soc. 1930), 4.

94 W.S.L. 350/3/40, Ditton Priors p. 1; Bannister, *Heref. Institutions*, 176.

95 At Nat. Grid ref. SO 626 906: S.R.O., incl. award A 18/51, map of exchanges; local inf.

96 S.R.O. 3419, glebe terrier (copy).

perhaps a second floor) had been inserted and a chimney had replaced the turret.[97] Two buildings stood near each other in Chapel close in 1841.[98] They were probably the former chapel and a dwelling house described in 1844 as adjoining it.[99] Both had gone by 1883.[1]

ROMAN CATHOLICISM. There were at least four recusants in the parish in the 1590s, and the lord of the manor was one.[2] One parishioner refused to take the Protestation in 1642,[3] and there were 3 papists in 1676, 6 recusants in 1693.[4] From the 16th century the lords of the manor adhered to the old faith,[5] as probably did the Smallmans, tenants of their demesne,[6] whose faith suggests a connexion with the Smalmans of Wilderhope.[7] Middleton became a mass centre and by 1824 was served from Madeley.[8] In 1851 the chapel of St. Michael the Archangel on the top floor of Middleton Lodge had 50 free sittings and was served fortnightly from Aldenham, the Dalberg-Actons' seat. On Census Sunday 1851 36 people worshipped in the morning, 20 in the afternoon; 53 and 46 were said to be the average numbers.[9] The chapel was served from Bridgnorth from 1855 to the late 1940s, and thereafter by the Montfort Fathers, first from Brockhurst (in Church Stretton) and later from Ludlow.[10] In 1948 *c.* 30 attended a 'romantic and bucolic' Easter mass.[11] Attendance later dwindled, and mass was discontinued in 1973.[12]

PROTESTANT NONCONFORMITY. William and Joyce Mayden and their servant were Anabaptists in 1663,[13] and in 1676 there were three protestant dissenters.[14]

By 1851 Methodism in the parish, with perhaps 200 or more people attending four meetings, had about thrice the adherents of the established church.

Wesleyans met in Ditton by 1801[15] and perhaps by 1795.[16] They opened a chapel in the village in 1816. It had 100 sittings in 1851, and an average attendance of 80 was claimed for the afternoon service. The stone chapel, seating 120, closed between 1955 and 1971.[17]

In 1816 Primitive Methodists built a small stone chapel at the south end of Bent Lane. In 1851 it had an average attendance of 20 in the morning and 60–80 in the afternoon. There was seating for 90. By then there was also a Primitive meeting at Lower Netchwood, in the steward's house where most of the 28 seats were said usually to be occupied. The brick chapel, seating 33 *c.* 1940,[18] was built in 1861.[19] The Bent Lane and Lower Netchwood chapels remained in use in 1984.

Wesleyans met in a house at Upper Netchwood in 1851, where 40 sittings were provided. An average of 25 then attended the morning service, 18 that in the evening. A small brick chapel seating 55 in pews was built *c.* 1865 and closed between 1940 and 1955.[20]

EDUCATION. Ditton Priors was one of the parishes whose boys, having attended grammar school and being natives of Shropshire, had preference in the award of Careswell exhibitions (endowed 1689) at Christ Church, Oxford.[21]

In 1719 there was a school whose pupils had to attend church and learn the catechism.[22] In 1794 there was no endowed school, but a schoolmaster and two or three women taught school.[23]

By 1819 there was a school with 10 pupils, for which the vestry agreed to build a room in 1821.[24] Another opened in 1833 and had 10 girls in 1835, when the earlier school had 8 boys and there was a Roman Catholic school at Middleton.[25]

The curate built a school on the glebe in 1862, and in 1876 a new C.E. school (evidently successor to the curate's) began there.[26] It had 80 places (100 after enlargement in 1889)[27] and was supported by voluntary contributions and school pence. Government grant was probably

97 W.S.L. 350/3/40, Ditton Priors p. 1; Bodl. MS. Top. Salop. c. 2, f. 404; S.P.L., MS. 372, vol. iii, ff. 83v., 100; par. rec., par. log bk. ii, p. 5.

98 S.R.O., incl. award A 18/51, map of exchanges.

99 T. F. Dukes, *Antiquities of Salop.* (1844), app. p. xii.

1 O.S. Map 1/2,500, Salop. LVII. 16 (1883 edn.); par. rec., par. log bk. ii, p. 5.

2 *Recusant R.* i (Cath. Rec. Soc. xviii), 263–4, 270; ii (Cath. Rec. Soc. lvii), pp. 132, 135; iii–iv (Cath. Rec. Soc. lxi), 76, 204; *Recusants in Pipe R. 1581–92* (Cath. Rec. Soc. lxxi), 130; above, manors (Ditton).

3 Ho. of Lords papers 1641–2, Protestations Oxon. and Salop. f. 192.

4 *Compton Census*, ed. Whiteman, 257; H.W.R.O.(H.), HD 7, presentment of 1693. Cf. S.R.O. 5709, Wenlock boro. q. sess. order bk. 1661–90, pp. 5, 15, 24, 34, etc.

5 Above, manors (Ditton); churches; S.R.O., q. sess. rec. parcel 281, reg. of papists' deeds 1717–88, pp. 1–2, 188–9.

6 For Geo. (fl. 1641–9) cf. *T.S.A.S.* 4th ser. x. 272; *Cal. Cttee. for Compounding*, iii. 2087; above, econ. hist. (agric.); for Anne (d. *c.* 1667), perh. his spinster sis., see S.R.O. 5709, Wenlock boro. q. sess. order bk. 1661–90, pp. 5, 57, 61.

7 Above, Rushbury, nonconf.

8 *V.C.H. Salop.* ii. 9 n. 26; xi. 67.

9 P.R.O., HO 129/356, no. 13; O.N.S. (Birkdale), Worship Reg. no. 66031. See also S.R.O. 3419, chapel, sch., and establishment acct. bks. 1886–1918.

10 E. M. Abbott, *Hist. Dioc. Shrews. 1850–1986* [1987], 77.

11 J. Lees-Milne, *Midway on the Waves* (1985), 29.

12 Abbott, op. cit. 77.

13 H.W.R.O.(H.), HD 7, presentment of 1663; S.R.O. 5709, Wenlock boro. q. sess. order bk. 1661–90, e.g. p. 38.

14 *Compton Census*, ed. Whiteman, 257.

15 *S.P.R. Noncont.* 314–16.

16 Heref. Dioc. Regy., reg. 1772–1802, f. 212.

17 P.R.O., HO 129/356, no. 12; *Methodist Church Bldgs.: Statistical Returns 1940* (Manchester, *c.* 1947), 271; inf. from Mr. J. H. Lenton and the Revd. M. A. J. Harding; O.N.S. (Birkdale), Worship Reg. no. 16864.

18 Inf. from Mr. Lenton; P.R.O., HO 129/356, nos. 14, 16; *Meth. Ch. Bldgs.: Statistical Returns 1940*, 271; O.N.S. (Birkdale), Worship Reg. no. 13129.

19 Date stone.

20 P.R.O., HO 129/356, no. 15; *Meth. Ch. Bldgs.: Statistical Returns 1940*, 271; inf. from Mr. Lenton; O.N.S. (Birkdale), Worship Reg. no. 16575.

21 *V.C.H. Salop.* ii. 164. This section was written *c.* 1982–3 and later revised.

22 H.W.R.O.(H.), HD 5/15, Ditton Priors (ref. supplied by Dr. R. Hume).

23 S.P.L., MS. 6864, ff. 47, 48v.

24 *Educ. of Poor Digest*, H.C. 224, p. 758 (1819), ix (2); R. Hume, 'Changing Patterns of Educ. Devt. in Salop. 1660–1833' (Keele Univ. Ph.D. (Educ.) thesis, 1982), 314; S.R.O. 3419, agreement to build sch. 4 June 1821.

25 *Educ. Enq. Abstract*, H.C. 62, p. 781 (1835), xlii; *P.O. Dir. Salop.* (1856), 105, 205; below, this section.

26 P.R.O., ED 7/102, ff. 250–1; par. rec., par. log bk. i, s.a. 1863, 1871, 1873; above, churches.

27 *Kelly's Dir. Salop.* (1885), 924; (1891), 396.

earned from 1878.[28] Attendance averaged 59 in 1885, 85 in 1895, and 75 in 1913.[29] The school accommodated Liverpool evacuees and their teacher 1939–41 and Wallasey evacuees with theirs (acting headmistress 1944) 1942–4.[30] Gardening was introduced in 1941 and art and craft lessons were held in the parish reading room.[31] The school was Controlled from 1949 and much improved.[32] Thirteen-year-old pupils went to Burwarton C.E. school from 1949 and 11-year-olds to Bridgnorth Boys' and Girls' Modern schools from 1958–9.[33] A demountable classroom was erected in 1967 and 10 pupils with their teacher were admitted from the closed Middleton Priors R.C. (Aided) Primary school.[34] Ten pupils from the closed Monkhopton C.E. (Aided) Primary school were admitted in 1983.[35] The roll was 63 in 1932, 35 in 1950, 71 in 1978, and 61 in 1985.[36]

Francis Canning started a Roman Catholic school at Middleton in 1829–30 and succeeding lords of the manor were the school's patrons. The slate-roofed stone school, with schoolroom, had *c.* 60 places and, in 1835, 23 pupils; a teacher's house adjoined.[37] The founder's widow Jane left an endowment in 1852;[38] it yielded £26 3*s.* in 1875, more than 70 per cent of the school's income, the rest coming as voluntary contributions and school pence. The patron then gave books and equipment.[39] Government grant was earned from 1875 and drawing grant from 1892.[40] There was a Standard VI by 1883 and a Standard VII by 1888.[41] Exceptionally for a small rural school there were middle class pupils; they usually went on to Catholic boarding schools.[42] The school earned good reports after 1882 and the building was improved in 1883 and 1894. Attendance averaged 30 (the number of places in 1905), but overcrowding necessitated the schoolroom's extension in 1912.[43] Catholic pupils were normally a small minority.[44]

Liverpool and Birmingham evacuees were admitted in 1939, others from Wallasey in 1941.[45] By 1951 the building was very substandard and the infants had to use the (unoccupied) teacher's house.[46] The school became Aided in 1958, and the building was improved, but the old threat of closure continued.[47] Pupils aged 13 had transferred to Burwarton C.E. school in 1953, and 11-year-olds transferred to Bridgnorth Boys' and Girls' Modern schools in 1958–9.[48] Two pupils left for Bridgnorth R.C. (Aided) Primary school in 1966,[49] and the school closed in 1967 when the teacher and 10 pupils went to Ditton Priors C.E. (Controlled) Primary school.[50]

Night school was held in 1876–7[51] and 1907–8[52] and county council classes in woodwork, horticulture, and livestock 1893– 1901.[53]

CHARITIES FOR THE POOR. By will proved 1700 Mrs. Catherine Barker left £5 a year charged on her estate;[54] in 1794 it was distributed in coal and bread but by 1820 in cash. By will dated 1723 Mrs. Dorothy Holland left £20 to be invested in land, the income to be spent on bread. In 1820 the income, 20*s.* a year, was distributed in cash with Mrs. Barker's charity.[55] In the later 19th and early 20th century the combined incomes, £6 a year, were usually distributed among *c.* 35 recipients,[56] but by 1975 they had not been received for several years.[57]

EATON-UNDER-HEYWOOD

EATON-UNDER-HEYWOOD parish lies in Ape Dale, dominated scenically by the wooded limestone scarp of Wenlock Edge. It is considerably smaller than it was in the early 19th century when it extended to 6,281 a. (2,542 ha.)[58] including a substantial detachment (1,496 a., 605 ha.) 4 km. to the north-east, which comprised Longville, Lushcott, and part of East Wall, treated separately.[59] The main part of the early 19th-century parish, treated here, comprised the

28 P.R.O., ED 7/102, ff. 250–1 (master willing to be examined).
29 *Kelly's Dir. Salop.* (1885), 924; (1895), 177; (1913), 197.
30 Ditton Priors C.E. sch. log bk. (at the sch. 1983), 6 Sept. 1939, 18 Dec. 1941, 5 Jan. 1942, 3 Apr., 21 Dec. 1944.
31 Ibid. 31 Mar., 2 Apr. 1941.
32 Ibid. rep. 1950.
33 Ibid. 13 Apr. 1949, 7 Jan. 1958; Ditton Priors C.E. (Contr.) sch. admissions bk. (at the sch. 1983); *S.C.C. Mins. (Educ.)*, 1959–60, 82.
34 Log bk. 10 Apr. 1967.
35 Inf. from the sch.
36 Log bk. 6 Jan. 1932; ibid. rep. 1950; S.C.C. Educ. Cttee. *Sch. List* (1978), 6; S.C.C. *Educ. Dir.* (1985), 5.
37 *Educ. Enq. Abstr.* ii. 781; P.R.O., ED 7/102, ff. 252–5; S. Bagshaw, *Dir. Salop.* (1851), 590; S.R.O. 3419, note of schoolrm. dimensions.
38 S.C.C. *Salop. Char. for Elem. Educ.* (1906), 32. Cf. Burke, *Commoners*, iii (1838), 262, 264; *V.C.H. Warws.* v. 99.
39 P.R.O., ED 7/102, ff. 254–5.
40 Middleton Priors R.C. sch. log bk. (in possession of Mrs. P. H. Evans, Ditton Priors) reps. 1875–6, 26 Sept. 1892.
41 Ibid. 19 Oct. 1883, 3 Feb. 1888.
42 Middleton Priors R.C. sch. admissions bk. 1875–1967 (in Mrs. Evans's possession).
43 Log bk. 23 Nov. 1911, 16 Oct. 1912, rep. 1912.
44 Log bks. religious instr. reps. 1923, 1936; ibid. 16 Jan. 1951, 10 Jan. 1953; ibid. reps. 1956–7; managers' min. bk. 1903–67 (in possession of the Revd. R. Luczka, Bridgnorth), 11 Apr. 1958, 1 Oct. 1964.
45 Log bk. 11 Sept. 1939, 7 July 1941.
46 Ibid. rep. 1951.
47 Managers' min. bk. 26 July 1910, 13 Mar. 1921, 5 June 1941, 11 Apr., 17 Oct. 1958, 9 Apr., 24 June, 14 July, 1 Sept. 1959; log bk. 30 June 1961, 4 Sept. 1962, 17 Oct. 1964.
48 Log bk. 28 July 1953, 25 July 1958, 1 Sept. 1959.
49 Inf. from Mr. C. J. Magner (1989).
50 Ditton Priors C.E. (Contr.) sch. log bk. 10 Apr. 1967.
51 P.R.O., ED 7/102, ff. 250–1.
52 *S.C.C. Mins. (Educ.)* 1908–9, 51.
53 Organizing sec.'s ann. reps. to Intermediate Educ. Cttee. in *S.C.C. Mins.* 1894–1901.
54 Copy will in Warws. R.O., CR 1379, box 4.
55 S.P.L., MS. 6864, f. 48v.; *3rd Rep. Com. Char.* H.C. 5, p. 305 (1820), iv.
56 Par. rec., par. log bk. i, s.a. 1865; ii, s.a. 1911.
57 *Review of Local Chars.* (S.C.C. 1975), 23.
58 Area calculated from O.S. *Area Bk.* (1884), adding the Longville, etc., detachment (below, Longville, etc., intro.) and deducting Topley (above, Munslow, intro.). This article was written 1989–90.
59 Below, Longville, etc.

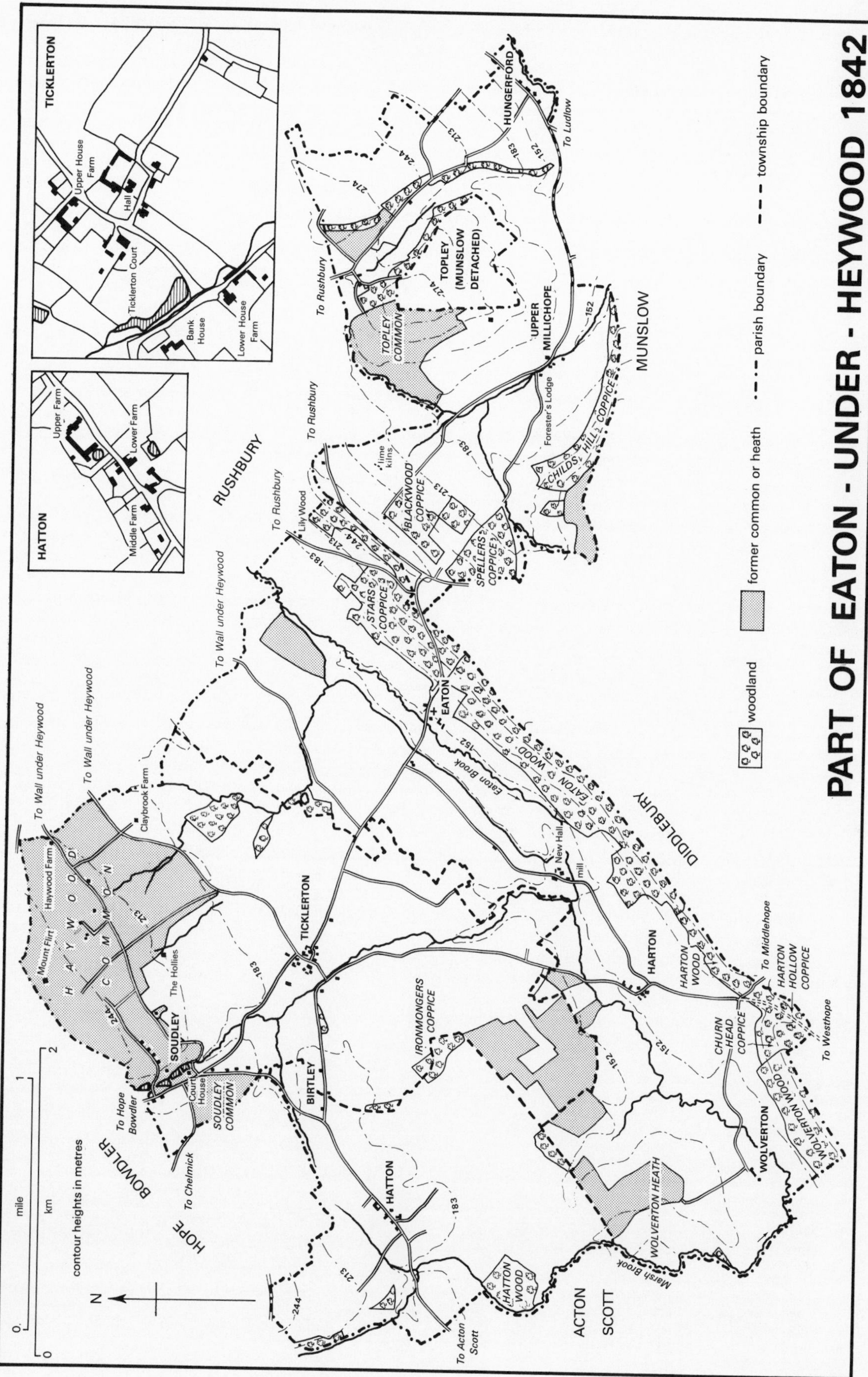
PART OF EATON - UNDER - HEYWOOD 1842
woodland
former common or heath
parish boundary
township boundary
contour heights in metres
mile
km
0
1
2
N
TICKLERTON
Upper House Farm
Hall
Ticklerton Court
Bank House
Lower House Farm
HATTON
Upper Farm
Lower Farm
Middle Farm
RUSHBURY
MUNSLOW
DIDDLEBURY
BOWDLER
HOPE
ACTON SCOTT
To Wall under Heywood
To Rushbury
To Ludlow
To Middlehope
To Westhope
To Acton Scott
To Chelmick
To Hope Bowdler
HUNGERFORD
TOPLEY (MUNSLOW DETACHED)
TOPLEY COMMON
UPPER MILLICHOPE
Forester's Lodge
CHILDS HILL COPPICE
lime kilns
BLACKWOOD COPPICE
SPELLERS COPPICE
Lily Wood
STARS COPPICE
EATON
EATON WOOD
Eaton Brook
New Hall
mill
HARTON
HARTON WOOD
HARTON HOLLOW COPPICE
CHURN HEAD COPPICE
WOLVERTON
WOLVERTON WOOD
WOLVERTON HEATH
Marsh Brook
HATTON WOOD
HATTON
BIRTLEY
IRONMONGERS COPPICE
TICKLERTON
SOUDLEY
Court House
SOUDLEY COMMON
The Hollies
Mount Flirt
Haywood Farm
Claybrook Farm
HAYWOOD COMMON

Fig. 33

townships of Eaton (including Harton and Wolverton), Hatton, and Ticklerton, and that which consisted of Upper Millichope and Hungerford,[60] hamlets beyond Wenlock Edge. Upper Millichope was excluded from Munslow parish *c.* 1115, an act which evidently led to its being united parochially to the Domesday manor of Ticklerton to form what became Eaton parish.[61] In 1883 the part of Topley hill that was a detachment of Lower Millichope (in Munslow parish), above Upper Millichope and Hungerford, was absorbed into Eaton civil parish,[62] but in 1967 Hungerford and Upper Millichope, with Topley hill, were transferred to Munslow C.P.[63] In 1987 Stone House farm and adjoining fields at Soudley were transferred to Hope Bowdler C.P.[64]

Before *c.* 1115 the main part of Ticklerton manor formed a 4-km.-long section of Ape Dale, bounded on the south-east by the crest of Wenlock Edge (*c.* 280 m.) and to the north-west by ground rising from the boulder clay drift of Ape Dale across mudstones, sandstones, and flagstones of the Llandovery and Caradoc Series towards Ragleth, Hazler, and Hope Bowdler hills.[65] Eaton's south-western boundary, with Acton Scott, was Mar (or Marsh) brook.[66] Minor streams also formed much of its north-eastern boundary, with Rushbury. When the parish boundary was defined on open ground is mostly unknown, though at Soudley it was perhaps in the earlier 13th century.[67] The hamlets of Eaton and Wolverton stand on a stream along the foot of Wenlock Edge, known as Eaton brook[68] or, formerly, Stree or Straw brook;[69] Harton stands near the brook but on higher ground which deflects its course.[70] That is the lowest land in the parish (*c.* 150 m.).[71] Clay brook, a tributary mentioned in 1756, gave its name to a farm.[72] Township boundaries, where known, mostly follow field edges.[73] That between Hatton and Ticklerton was fixed by 1237.[74]

The township including Upper Millichope and Hungerford is mainly on high ground (Topley hill reaching 300 m.) formed by Aymestry Group limestones rising between Hope Dale to the north-west and Corve Dale to the south-east. Hungerford hamlet is in Corve Dale just north of the Corve, while Upper Millichope is on a tributary of the Corve and a route between the two dales.[75] The part of Topley hill that was a detachment of Munslow parish until 1883 was presumably a share of the hill's common assigned to Lower Millichope after the two Millichope estates became distinct in the 12th century.[76]

The parish's 19th-century roads, all local and many bad, presumably represented old routes.[77] A road from the church to Upper Millichope climbed over Wenlock Edge in 1839,[78] but in 1882 its route above the Edge was represented only by nearby footpaths and sections of the abandoned trackway.[79] In 1765 the road to the Blackwood lime kilns from Wall under Heywood, via Rushbury, was turnpiked.[80] It was disturnpiked in 1875.[81] The road from Marshbrook, via Hatton and Ticklerton, to Wall's Bank was turnpiked under an Act of 1822;[82] a tollhouse was built at Birtley after 1842[83] and the road was disturnpiked in 1878.[84]

The Wenlock Railway Co.'s line from Buildwas to Craven Arms was opened across the parish in 1867. Harton (from 1881 Harton Road) station was open from 1867 to 1951, when the line south of Longville was closed.[85]

A polished Neolithic axe fragment from near Claybrook Farm[86] and possibly an enclosure near Upper Millichope[87] provide evidence of early man. A Roman villa with a mosaic floor was said in the 1830s to have been found at Hatton *c.* 1790.[88]

Ticklerton, as early forms of its name (e.g. 'Tikelewordin', 1221) reveal, was an enclosed settlement.[89] Though the name may not be earlier than the 8th century,[90] it was perhaps the area's primary settlement, still in 1086 the manorial vill, where a population of 16 was recorded.[91] It was fairly central to the priory's large manor, but Wenlock's acquisition of Millichope (1086 × 1094) and the confirmation of the priory's parochial rights over Upper Millichope (*c.* 1115) made Eaton more central to those estates and so perhaps the most eligible location for the church of a parish of widely scattered hamlets.[92] Ticklerton remained one of the parish's two larger settlements. The other four settlements in Ape Dale have the *tun* suffix and were probably named in the late Saxon period. In 1244 there were perhaps 11 households at Hatton,[93] and 12 free tenants were

60 S.P.L., MS. 6865, p. 82; fig. 33.

61 Below, manors.

62 *V.C.H. Salop.* ii. 225 note h (corr. below, Corrigenda).

63 By the *Salop (No. 2) Order 1966* (Stat. Instr. 1966, no. 1529); cf. ibid. maps 39, 42 (copies in S.R.O., DA 19/701/6).

64 *S. Salop. (Pars.) Order 1987* (Stat. Instr. 1987, no. 496).

65 Geol. Surv. Map 1", drift, sheet 166 (1967 edn.).

66 Above, Acton Scott, intro.; W.S.L. 350/5/40, Hope Bowdler p. 6.

67 Eyton, v. 116; xi. 350; above, Hope Bowdler, intro.

68 O.S. Maps 1/25,000, SO 48/58 (1983 edn.), 49/59 (1981 edn.).

69 Sixteenth and 18th cents.: S.P.L., MS. 2, ff. 144v.–145; 6741, pp. 107, 111; above, Rushbury, intro.

70 O.S. Map 1/25,000, SO 48/58 (1983 edn.).

71 Ibid. 1/50,000, sheet 137 (1985 edn.).

72 S.R.O. 783, box 79, acct. bk. 1756, 20 June.

73 S.R.O. 3315/Ti/1; fig. 33.

74 *T.S.A.S.* 4th ser. i. 396–7; Eyton, iii. 316.

75 Geol. Surv. Map 1", drift, sheet 166 (1967 edn.); O.S. Map 1/50,000, sheet 137 (1985 edn.).

76 Cf. below, manors (Millichope); econ. hist.

77 S.P.L., MS. 6865, p. 86; *T.C.S.V.F.C.* xi. 196–9.

78 P.R.O., IR 30/29/117.

79 O.S. Map 1/2,500, Salop. LXIV. 3, 4 (1884 edn.).

80 5 Geo. III, c. 86.

81 Ann. Turnpike Acts Continuance Act, 1873, 36 & 37 Vic. c. 90.

82 3 Geo. IV, c. 49.

83 A. Dakers, *Ticklerton Tales* (Ragdon, 1991), 75. Not on S.R.O. 3315/Ti/1.

84 Ann. Turnpike Acts Continuance Act, 1877, 40 & 41 Vic. c. 64.

85 *Railway Mag.* cxi. 376–7, 443–4; *T.S.A.S.* lxiv. 96.

86 S.P.L., Chitty File 55/72–85.

87 SA 2162.

88 W.S.L. 350/3/40, Eaton p. 8; 350/5/40, Acton Scott pp. 15–17.

89 *P.N. Salop.* (E.P.N.S.), i. 292; cf. *P.N. Elements* (E.P.N.S.), ii. 277.

90 B. Cox, 'Place-Names of Earliest Eng. Records', *Jnl. Eng. P.N. Soc.* viii. 66.

91 *V.C.H. Salop.* i. 312.

92 Below, manors (Millichope); church.

93 *T.S.A.S.* lviii. 71.

recorded there in the earlier 14th century.[94] In 1327 subsidy was paid by 17 in Eaton and 12 in Millichope,[95] and the parish's medieval population may have been substantial: each hamlet seems to have had open fields and access to extensive wood–pasture.[96] In the 16th century there may have been *c.* 10 houses at both Ticklerton and Hatton, and 5 each at Eaton, Harton, Wolverton, Upper Millichope, and Hungerford.[97] By 1544 there were houses at Birtley, west of Ticklerton.[98]

By the early 17th century the parish population was rising, and there were cottages in Hay wood.[99] The Protestation of 1642 was taken by 19 men from Hay wood and 6 from Soudley, a squatter settlement at its west end; 13 from Ticklerton took it, 9 each from Harton, Upper Millichope, and Hungerford, 8 from Hatton, 5 from Eaton, 4 from Wolverton, and 3 from New Hall.[1] In 1672 hearth tax was paid on 19 houses in Ticklerton (many of the 13 single-hearth dwellings presumably being Hay wood squatters' cottages), 10 houses in Eaton (probably including Harton, New Hall, and Wolverton), 4 in Hatton, and 15 in Hungerford and Millichope (Upper and Lower).[2] The numbers of adults and households in 1676 are comparable: 75 adults in 30 households in Ticklerton, 63 in 16 households in Eaton, Harton, Hatton, New Hall, and Wolverton, and 34 in 13 households in Hungerford and Upper Millichope.[3]

Upper Millichope Lodge is an exceptionally strong later 13th-century block perhaps built as a forester's lodge. Apart from that the parish's medieval buildings were probably timber framed. At least two late medieval houses, Lower Farm, Hatton, and Wolverton Manor, remain largely intact, and others retain some elements. Much 16th- and 17th-century timber framing survives, some cased in the local rubble stone used increasingly for building from the 18th century. Brick may not have been used until *c.* 1700 when it was employed in new wings and casing work at, for instance, Ticklerton Hall and Harton Manor.[4] When Millichope Court (later Upper Millichope Farm) was rebuilt *c.* 1730 it was stone that was used save for the façade (oddly facing away from the road), which was brick. As late as the mid 19th century stone was the usual material for cottages, such as Birtley tollhouse.

In 1793 there were said to be 35 farmhouses, 29 small tenements, and 35 cottages in the parish.[5] Most cottages were at Soudley and Hay wood,[6] although by *c.* 1730 there were also some around Black wood.[7] The parish's 19th-century population level was *c.* 550 until the 1870s when a steady decline began, to 328 in 1901 and 123 in 1961.[8] Much of the decline came as cottages were abandoned. A few small outlying farms were built in the mid to late 19th century, including Hattongrove Farm, the Saplings, and Whitefields Farm (originally called Eatonglebe),[9] but there was little new building in the parish in the 20th century. At Ticklerton Jacintha Buddicom designed Meadowbrook (built 1936–7) in a Tudor style for her aunt Lilian Hayward.[10] Four properties in Ticklerton were privately supplied with spring water by 1946[11] and *c.* 1952 two pairs of council houses were built there.[12] Several barns at Ticklerton were being converted into houses in 1990.

In the 18th century Eaton wake was on the Sunday after 15 August.[13] In 1793 there was no alehouse in the parish, although two or three houses that sold bread and cheese gave ale into the bargain.[14] The Blue Bell in Hatton was open *c.* 1830–60;[15] the Horseshoes and the Mason's Arms, both in Ticklerton, were open in the 1850s and the 1860s and 1870s respectively; the Pheasant, Birtley, was open *c.* 1850–80;[16] and the Buck's Head, Hungerford, was open by 1842 and closed *c.* 1957.[17] There were also beer sellers at Ticklerton in the later 19th century.[18]

In the 1790s some parishioners belonged to a benefit club at Condover, *c.* 20 km. away.[19] The county library opened a book centre in the parish in 1933,[20] and there was a village hall at Ticklerton by 1953.[21]

The writer George Orwell (Eric Arthur Blair, 1903–50) spent some boyhood holidays at Ticklerton Court.[22]

MANORS AND OTHER ESTATES. In 1066 the large manor of *TICKLERTON*, later *EATON-UNDER-HEYWOOD*, belonged to the church of Wenlock.[23] By 1255 Eaton, where there was a church by the 12th century, had replaced Ticklerton as the centre of the manor, held in demesne by Wenlock priory. The manor

94 S.R.O. 1224, box 342, Prior Gosnell's reg. f. 5v.
95 *T.S.A.S.* 2nd ser. iv. 326, 331.
96 Below, econ. hist.
97 *Cal. Pat.* 1550–3, 38–9; S.R.O. 1224, box 342, Prior Gosnell's reg. ff. 5v., 38v.; *L. & P. Hen. VIII*, xvii, p. 508. For two properties at Hungerford (Holloway and Muxhill) in Munslow par. see above, Munslow, manors.
98 *L. & P. Hen. VIII*, xix (1), p. 633.
99 S.R.O. 3651, box 101, deed 30 Dec. 1614.
1 Ho. of Lords papers 1641–2, Protestations Oxon. and Salop. f. 193. The vicar and par. officers, not listed by township, were also named.
2 *Hearth Tax 1672* (Salop. Arch. Soc. 1949), 38–9.
3 *Compton Census*, ed. Whiteman, 644–6.
4 Below, manors; pl. 16.
5 S.P.L., MS. 6865, p. 82.
6 S.R.O., incl. award B 14.
7 *S.P.R. Heref.* xix (3), 62–70, for pauper burials.
8 *V.C.H. Salop.* ii. 222.
9 S.R.O. 3315/Ti/1; O.S. Maps 6", Salop. LVI. SE., LXIV. NW. (1891 edn.).
10 Dakers, *Ticklerton Tales*, 83, 114; S.R.O. 3651, box 111, papers, bills, etc., *re* Meadowbrook's construction.
11 A. H. S. Waters, *Rep. on Water Supply* (S.C.C. 1946), 74.
12 Inf. from Mr. A. B. Dakers.
13 S.P.L., MS. 6741, p. 111; S.R.O. 3315/Ti/3, p. 3 at end.
14 S.P.L., MS. 6865, p. 85.
15 H. E. Forrest, *Old Hos. of Wenlock* (Shrews. 1914), 55; Dakers, *Ticklerton Tales*, 74.
16 Dakers, op. cit. 64–5, 68–9.
17 S.R.O. 3315/Ti/1–2, field 869; inf. from Mr. P. Bushell, clk. to Ludlow magistrates.
18 *P.O. Dir. Salop.* (1879), 316; *Kelly's Dir. Salop.* (1891), 312.
19 S.P.L., MS. 6865, p. 85.
20 R. C. Elliott, 'Development of Public Libraries in Salop.' (Loughborough Univ. M.A. thesis, 1970; copy in co. libr.), 127.
21 Dakers, *Ticklerton Tales*, 119.
22 B. Crick, *Geo. Orwell: A Life* (1980), 51, 65, 105; J. Buddicom, *Eric and Us: A Remembrance of Geo. Orwell* (1974), 58–69, 145.
23 *V.C.H. Salop.* i. 312; Eyton, iii. 311.

then comprised Eaton, Harton, Longville, Lushcott, Ticklerton, and Wolverton.[24] The priory surrendered in 1540,[25] and in 1544 the Crown sold the manor to John Pakington of Hampton Lovett (Worcs.).[26]

Pakington (kt. *c.* 1545) died in 1560, having settled the manor on his daughter and son-in-law Bridget and John Lyttelton[27] of Frankley (Worcs.). In 1562 Lyttelton and his son Gilbert sold Eaton to Richard Lutley (d. 1584).[28] Lutley's son John died in 1589 and the manor passed to John's sister Margaret, wife of George Jenkes, lord of Wolverton.[29] In 1600 George settled Eaton on his son Francis (d. 1627).[30] The manor then passed from father to son to Herbert (d. 1654), and Herbert (fl. 1696). The last named was a lunatic, whose heir was his brother Francis (fl. 1703).[31] Francis had three daughters, of whom Frances (fl. 1712), wife of Roger Williams, seems to have succeeded to Eaton. The couple were childless, and Eaton passed to Frances's cousin Philip Lutley.[32] Lutley (d. 1731) was succeeded by his son Jenkes (d. 1745) and Jenkes by his brother Bartholomew (d. 1783), who had assumed the surname Barneby in 1735 on his grandfather's death.[33] Bartholomew's son John Barneby sold the manor in 1789 to William Wainwright, who sold it in 1793 to Sir Jacob Wolff. Wolff sold it to Robert Bent in 1801, and in 1806 Bent was bankrupt and it was sold to John Beck.[34] Beck died in 1821 leaving his Eaton estate to his sister Maria, wife of the Shrewsbury banker John Eaton. She died in 1841, leaving the 640-a. property in trust for her daughters. Their trustees sold the property in the mid 1850s to W. H. Sparrow; the lordship then descended in his family[35] to A. B. H. Hanbury-Sparrow (d. 1936) of All Stretton.[36] His son Lt.-Col. A. A. H. Hanbury-Sparrow sold it in 1951 to C. E. Edwards of Mount Seifton (in Culmington). Soon after Edwards's death in 1954[37] it was bought from his representatives by the Revd. G. S. Hewins of Silvington, on whose death in 1975 it passed to his widow[38] Elsie V. Hewins.[39]

Eaton Manor is a late 18th-century brick farmhouse south-west of the church.[40] It may occupy the site of the medieval demesne farm.

New Hall, mid way between Eaton and Harton, was probably built in the 1590s for Francis Jenkes (d. 1627), later lord of Eaton and Wolverton manors.[41] It was later his son's home and possibly also his grandson's.[42] With its 191-a. farm it descended with Eaton manor until 1910 or later.[43]

New Hall, a large **H** shaped building of two storeys, is box framed but largely cased in brick. It may originally have had a smoke bay. In the main chamber a hunting scene of *c.* 1600 survives from more extensive wall painting.[44]

From the 17th century the Pinches family built up a considerable estate centred on *TICKLERTON COURT*. Thomas Lewes (fl. 1514) was succeeded in a Ticklerton property by his son John (fl. 1550), and he by his son Thomas. Thomas (d. 1598) bought a 174-a. farm from the Lytteltons in 1564, and in 1571 he settled the property on his daughter Margaret and her husband Fulk Pinches, son of John Pinches of Plaish (in Cardington).[45] Fulk and Margaret's son Richard died in 1639[46] and in 1674 his son William bought the grain tithes of his own property and others from Edward Palmer.[47] The estate then descended in the Pinches family, the following being owners: William's son Richard, Richard's son William (d. 1752), William's grandson William (d. 1818), and that William's son William (d. unmarried 1849).[48] The last named was a founder of the United Hunt and a keen naturalist, owner of what was then perhaps the finest specimen of the great auk. He was succeeded by his sister Elizabeth (d. 1859), second wife of the Revd. R. J. Buddicom, who succeeded her. In 1894 Buddicom (d. 1895) made over his Ticklerton property to his son W. S. Buddicom (d. 1922), who left it to his children R. A. Buddicom and Mrs. Lilian Hayward,[49] writers on the natural history of the area and

24 *Rot. Hund.* (Rec. Com.), ii. 85; below, church.

25 *V.C.H. Salop.* ii. 45.

26 *L. & P. Hen. VIII*, xix (1), p. 633; S.R.O. 551/9; *V.C.H. Worcs.* iii. 154–5.

27 *Cal. Pat.* 1550–3, 38–9; W. A. Shaw, *Kts. of Eng.* (1906), ii. 58.

28 *S.P.R. Heref.* xix (3), p. ii; H.W.R.O.(H.), LC, R 27/10908; S.P.L., Deeds 1503; P.R.O., C 142/204, no. 99.

29 *S.P.R. Heref.* xix (3), p. ii; below, this section; P.R.O., C 142/221, no. 121.

30 P.R.O., C 142/431, no. 102.

31 P.R.O., C 142/718, no. 144; *Dioc. of Heref. Institutions (1539–1900)*, ed. A. T. Bannister (Heref. 1923), 55, 58.

32 *S.P.R. Heref.* xix (3), p. ii; S.R.O. 1670/46, disproving that the manor passed to Phil.'s parents.

33 *S.P.R. Heref.* xix (3), p. ii; *T.S.A.S.* 4th ser. vi. 265–7; S.R.O. 1670/46.

34 S.P.L., MS. 6741, pp. 85, 109, 113; S.R.O. 515/5, pp. 193–205; 3651, box 109, abstr. of title 1806, p. 72. For Wolff see G.E.C. *Baronetage*, v. 142–3.

35 S.R.O. 3315/Ti/2; 3651, 'Jeffreys' box 5, vol. of 'Family wills', p. 71; *S.P.R. Heref.* xix (3), pp. ii–iii; S. Bagshaw, *Dir. Salop.* (1851), 536; S.P.L., Deeds 18611; ibid. MS. 6741, pp. 88, 90, and loose sheets *re* manor and Eaton fam. pedigree s.v. Eaton-under-Heywood; *Kelly's Dir. Salop.* (1885–1941).

36 For the Sparrows see *V.C.H. Salop.* iv. 211; viii. 126; above, Cardington, manors (Holt Preen); Rushbury, manors (Rushbury); *Kelly's Dir. Salop.* (1934), 68.

37 *Shrews. Chron.* 11 June 1954, p. 7; cf. *Kelly's Dir. Salop.* (1941), 85, 92, corr. by Burke, *Land. Gent.* (1952), 2366–7.

38 S.R.O., archivist's office file R 211, Hewins to co. archivist 19 Jan. 1955; G. S. Hewins's will pr. 15 Aug. 1975; M.I. in Cleeton ch.

39 Author of reminiscences (*Through the Yrs.* 1971) in which all the proper names are suppressed or disguised. She d. 1978: will pr. 3 Apr. 1979.

40 S.R.O. 515/5, pp. 199–200.

41 S.P.L., Deeds 1548; H.W.R.O.(H.), LC, R 27/10882. His and his wife's initials appear on a post. For the fam. see below, this section (Wolverton).

42 P.R.O., C 142/718, no. 144.

43 Sources cited above, this section; W.S.L. 350/3/40, Eaton p. 7; S.R.O. 4044/91, p. 27.

44 Inf. from Mr. Eric Mercer and Mrs. M. Moran; Forrest, *Old Hos. of Wenlock*, 55–6; S.P.L., MS. 6741, p. 84; P. A. Stamper, *'The Farmer Feeds Us All': Short Hist. of Salop. Agric.* (Shrews. 1989), 17.

45 P.R.O., C 142/287, no. 49; *Cal. Pat.* 1550–3, 39; S.R.O. 1224, box 342, Prior Gosnell's reg. f. 38v.; J. H. Pinches, *Fam. of Pinches* (1981), 12–13, 16, 20–3; W.S.L. 350/3/40, Eaton pp. 9–10; cf. Bodl. MS. Top. Salop. c. 1, f. 215.

46 P.R.O., C 142/619, no. 44.

47 S.R.O. 3651, box 109, abstr. of title 1860, p. 1. For Palmer see below, this section.

48 S.P.L., MS. 4360, p. 465; MS. 6741, Pinches pedigree loose s.v. Eaton-under-Heywood; S.R.O. 3651, box 109, abstr. of title 1860; 4066/13/6; *S.P.R. Heref.* xix (3), p. 174.

49 S.R.O. 3651, box 109, abstr. of title 1903; 4208/158; S.P.L, MS. 4360, p. 465; H. E. Forrest, *Fauna of Salop.* (1899), 26–7, and pl. facing p. 14; grave stone at Eaton; *S.P.R. Heref.* xix (3), p. v; inf. from Lady Brown, Ticklerton Cottage; '[Buddicom] Family Sketches', 218 (MS. in possession of Lady Brown).

local antiquarian matters.[50] In 1953 Mrs. Hayward and her nephew R. P. G. Buddicom sold the 1,147-a. Ticklerton estate to the Mercantile & General Reinsurance Co. Ltd.[51] About the same time Ticklerton Hall and Mount Flirt farms were sold to their tenants.[52] In 1988 653 a. of the Ticklerton estate, comprising Upper and Lower House farms, were sold to March Border Ltd.[53]

The late 16th-century Ticklerton Court was largely incorporated in 1824 in a three storeyed stone house with a hipped roof. The top storey was removed *c.* 1953.[54]

In the late 18th and early 19th century the Pinches family added to their Ticklerton estate properties formerly the Oxenbolds', the Barnebys', and William Cheney Hart's. Later, in the 19th and 20th centuries, their successors the Buddicoms added lands formerly owned by the Corfields and the Sparrows.

William Oxenbold had property at Ticklerton in 1514–15[55] as did he or a namesake in 1550.[56] Richard Oxenbold (d. 1589) enlarged the family holding by purchase from Richard Acton and his son Edward in 1585, the Actons having bought land from the Lytteltons in 1564. Richard Oxenbold was survived by his wife Alice and infant son Philip.[57] In 1704 Thomas Oxenbold, perhaps the man of that name who died in 1717, had what was presumably the estate enjoyed by earlier Oxenbolds. Thomas's son John (d. 1725) married Mary Meredith (d. 1769),[58] and when their son Richard died in 1798 the estate went to his brother's daughters Elizabeth Cook, Jane Nickson, and Mary Pinches. They sold their thirds in 1802 and 1805 to Robert Bent.[59] The Oxenbolds' farm, known by 1802 as *UPPER HOUSE* farm,[60] was bought in 1807 by William Pinches after Bent's bankruptcy.[61] It then descended with the Pinches family's Ticklerton estate.[62] Upper House Farm is a stone building of the 17th century and 1724.[63]

In 1576 Richard Lutley, lord of the manor of Eaton-under-Heywood, bought two farms in Ticklerton and associated tithes from the Crown.[64] In 1698 his descendants Sarah and Frances Jenkes sold part of that property to Richard Ward of Harton.[65] In 1712 Frances (Mrs. Williams) gave more of it to augment the living of Eaton-under-Heywood.[66] The family apparently retained property in Ticklerton, for in the late 18th century their descendants the Barnebys[67] owned properties, including their tithes, of 374 a. (principally the later *LOWER HOUSE* farm), 86 a., and 4 a. centred on the township.[68] John Barneby sold them in 1787 to the brothers William and Richard Pinches and their uncle Richard Oxenbold.[69] Richard Pinches (d. 1789)[70] left his share to his brother. Richard Oxenbold (d. 1798) left his to four nieces, and William Pinches bought three of their shares in 1799 and 1801; the fourth was left to his son William by the other niece Elizabeth Pinches (d. 1822) of Harton.[71] The reunited property then descended with the rest of the Pinches' Ticklerton estate.[72] Lower House Farm is a stone building of the later 16th and the 17th century.[73]

William Cheney Hart (d. 1819) owned 217 a. in Ticklerton comprising the Claybrook, Common, and Hollies farms, and the northern part of the later Upper House farm, all with tithes. In 1834 William Pinches bought the property, which then descended with his Ticklerton estate.[74]

In 1706 Thomas Bright of Little Stretton and his son Thomas settled an estate in Ticklerton on the marriage of the elder Thomas's daughter Mary to John Corfield of Whittingslow (in Wistanstow).[75] A branch of the Corfields had held land in Ticklerton in the 16th century.[76] That property, then comprising a farm in Ticklerton and 60 a. in several parcels, was owned in the late 18th century by Thomas Corfield and later by his son Thomas (d. 1815).[77] In 1841 John Griffiths had it.[78] Later the farm was split up, and the Revd. R. J. Buddicom bought some of it, though not the farmhouse,[79] Bank House, which stands west of Ticklerton Court.[80]

William Palmer held land in Ticklerton in 1551[81] and in 1563 bought the freehold from the Lytteltons.[82] Palmer or a namesake died in 1593,

50 Dakers, *Ticklerton Tales*, 108, 117–20; *S.P.R. Heref.* xix (3), p. viii; *V.C.H. Salop.* i. 99 n.; *T.S.A.S.* lvii. 272.

51 S.R.O. 3651, box 113, draft conveyance and sale partic.; Dakers, op. cit. 117; cf. *V.C.H. Salop.* iv. 256.

52 S.R.O. 3651, box 113, Mrs. Hayward to Mr. Sturton 25 Nov. 1952, sale partic. 1952; below, this section, for Ticklerton Hall fm.; inf. from Lady Brown.

53 S.P.L., SC25/3; local inf.

54 W.S.L. 350/3/40, Eaton p. 10; Dakers, *Ticklerton Tales*, 66–7; Buddicom, *Eric and Us*, 62–8, 164–5.

55 S.R.O. 1224, box 342, Prior Gosnell's reg. f. 38v.

56 *Cal. Pat.* 1550–3, 39.

57 P.R.O., C 142/226, no. 187; S.R.O. 1141, box 97, deed 20 Mar. 1585; 3925, box 9, deed 30 Jan. 1565/6; W.S.L. 350/3/40, Eaton p. 9.

58 S.R.O. 3651, box 109, abstr. of title 1860, p. 48; *T.S.A.S.* xliii, pp. *xvii*, *xix*; *S.P.R. Heref.* xix (3), p. 48.

59 S.R.O. 3651, box 103, Ric. Oxenbold's will, deeds 20 and 29 May 1802, 25 Mar. 1805; box 109, abstr. of title 1860, pp. 48 sqq.

60 S.R.O. 3651, box 103, deed 20 May 1802.

61 S.R.O. 4835/30, p. 4, field names; S.R.O. 3651, box 109, abstr. of title 1860, pp. 72, 80.

62 S.R.O. 3315/Ti/1–2; 3651, box 113, sale partic. 26 Sept. 1952; above, this section.

63 Date stone details (partly illegible 1990) in '[Buddicom] Family Sketches', 119.

64 S.R.O. 1037/21/103; S.P.L., MS. 2, f. 135.

65 S.P.L., MS. 6741, p. 92; S.R.O. 165/40.

66 S.R.O. 1670/46; below, church. 67 Above, this section.

68 S.R.O. 3651, box 109, abstr. of title 1860, p. 16; box 113, map schedule.

69 Ibid. box 109, abstr. of title 1860, p. 16. For relationships see below, this section; S.P.L., MS. 4360, p. 465.

70 S.P.L., MS. 4360, p. 465; S.R.O. 3651, box 103, case paper [1801] *re* Hay wood common.

71 S.R.O. 3651, box 109, abstr. of title 1860, pp. 20–4.

72 Ibid. box 113, sale partic. 1952; S.R.O. 3315/Ti/2.

73 Forrest, *Old Hos. of Wenlock*, 56.

74 S.R.O. 3651, box 100, map of est. 1827; box 103, sale partic. 1952; box 109, abstr. of title 1903; 4175/6. For Hart see above, Hope Bowdler, manors; A. Dakers, *Fordritishope: Hist. of a Salop. Par.* (Ragdon, 1986), 2.

75 S.R.O. 3651, box 98, deed 24 Apr. 1706.

76 e.g. *Cal. Pat.* 1550–3, 39; S.R.O. 1224, box 342, Prior Gosnell's reg. f. 38v.

77 S.R.O. 3651, box 98, map of Thos. Corfield's lands 1815; box 108, abstr. of title 1836; *S.P.R. Heref.* xix (3), 174.

78 S.R.O. 3315/Ti/1–2.

79 Cf. ibid. (John Griffiths's fm. and summary at end of /Ti/2); 3651, box 113, sale partic. 1952.

80 M. Carver *Out of Step* (1989), 11.

81 *Cal. Pat.* 1550–3, 39.

82 W.S.L. 350/3/40, Eaton pp. 9–10.

succeeded by a son Henry (d. 1597), whose relict Alice (d. 1633) was succeeded by their son Lancelot.[83] The estate may have passed to Edward Palmer (d. 1677).[84] Thomas Palmer (d. 1732) was followed by his son William (d. 1777).[85] The *TICKLERTON HALL* estate was sold *c.* 1778 to William Dyke, who sold it *c.* 1801 to Robert Bent.[86] In 1807 the 273-a. property was sold to Edward Downes. Downes's son Edward had it in 1842 but later sold it to a Mr. Dayus, probably Samuel Dayus of Longnor. In 1864 Dayus's grandsons, called Pryce, sold it to W. H. Sparrow,[87] lord of Eaton-under-Heywood, whose grandson A. B. H. Hanbury-Sparrow owned it in 1910.[88] It later passed to the Buddicoms and R. P. G. Buddicom kept it when the Ticklerton estate was sold in 1953.[89]

Ticklerton Hall, containing close studding of *c.* 1500, was enlarged *c.* 1580 and again *c.* 1660 to an **H** plan. It was cased in brick *c.* 1700 when perhaps the east wing was added.[90] The adjoining farm buildings are of *c.* 1800.[91]

HARTON was presumably part of Eaton-under-Heywood manor.[92] Edward Ward was a priory tenant there in 1514–15[93] and John Ward in 1538 and 1550.[94] John's son Edward bought the freehold from the Lytteltons in 1564. Harton then descended in the Ward family, and one of their two messuages in 1691 may have been that bought from the Crown by Richard English in 1586. Ann, *née* Ward, married Thomas Smith (fl. 1791–1819) of Bircher (Herefs.),[95] and their daughter Anne married Thomas Dunne of Gatley, who owned 412 a. there in 1842.[96] In the later 19th and early 20th century Harton formed part of the Warren family settled estate,[97] split up and sold after J. Loxdale Warren's death in 1909.[98]

Upper House and Lower House farms, presumably the Wards' two messuages of 1691, were mentioned in 1791[99] and are represented by two substantial timber framed farmhouses. Harton Manor comprises a hall and contemporary cross wing, evidently built by Richard Ward in 1615,[1] to which a brick parlour range on a stone plinth was added *c.* 1700. Harton Farm is a late 16th- or early 17th-century **T** shaped building on a stone plinth.[2]

An estate in *HATTON* was granted 1196 × 1215 by the prior of Wenlock to Robert of Hatton,[3] the name of one or more men who held the estate in 1227, 1237, and 1255.[4] In 1272 Robert of Hatton conveyed the manor to Malcolm of Harley (d. *c.* 1298).[5] Malcolm's brother Richard of Harley had it by 1302[6] and it descended with Harley.[7] In 1377 Joan of Harley settled the manor on William of Ightfield and Agnes his mother[8] and in 1380 on Roger of Ightfield, described as Joan's son and heir,[9] but by 1398 Joan and her husband John Darras were in possession.[10] About 1616 Sir Francis Lacon conveyed the manor, with Gretton (in Cardington and Rushbury), to Isaac and Edward Jones.[11] Edward Jones (d. 1648)[12] still had property in Hatton in 1645.[13]

The manor's descent over the next 150 years is unknown. Possibly the Hamonds were lords: a farm owned by Vincent Hamond (d. 1718) was bought by Thomas Powell of Bridgnorth, and he or his son Richard, rector of Munslow, was described as lord of Hatton and owner of 220 a. there in 1793. Thomas Powell may, however, have bought the lordship with Lower farm, reputedly once called the Manor. After Richard's death in 1806 the lordship was said to be his widow Elizabeth's. It afterwards descended in the Powell family from father to son, rectors of Munslow, until 1912 or later.[14] Later it was part of the Acton Scott estate until sold in 1921.[15]

In the mid 19th century the Powells had two farmhouses in Hatton. One, a 2½ storeyed **T** shaped stone building, was built in 1679, probably by Vincent Hamond, and was later at times a poor house and the Blue Bell public house.[16] The other was Lower Farm, whose earliest feature is a pair of late medieval cruck blades, which were once the central truss of an open hall. In the late 15th century those timbers were re-used in their present position as the

83 P.R.O., C 142/238, no. 59; C 142/263, no. 51; C 142/631, no. 53.
84 *S.P.R. Heref.* xix (3), 15.
85 Ibid. 64, 98; *T.S.A.S.* xliii, p. *xvi.*
86 S.R.O. 3651, box 109, abstr. of title 1860, p. 93; W.S.L. 350/3/40, Eaton p. 10.
87 S.P.L., MS. 6741, p. 90. See also S.R.O. 515/5; 4835/30, pp. 4–5; *P.O. Dir. Salop.* (1856), 68. For Bent's bankruptcy which occasioned the sale see above, this section.
88 S.R.O. 4044/91, p. 28.
89 S.R.O. 3651, box 113, draft sale partic. 1952; cf. above, this section (Ticklerton Ct.).
90 Inf. from Mrs. Moran.
91 S.R.O. 4835/30, p. 5.
92 S.R.O. 515/6, p. 193; 4835/30, p. 2.
93 S.R.O. 1224, box 342, Prior Gosnell's reg. f. 38v.
94 W.S.L. 350/3/40, Eaton p. 7; *Cal. Pat.* 1550–3, 39.
95 *Cal. Pat.* 1563–6, p. 49; W.S.L. 350/3/40, Eaton p. 7; S.P.L., Deeds 18449 (pedigree from docs. in S.R.O. 165, e.g. /71, 102, 104, 112, 125, 136, 141, 144); H.W.R.O.(H.), F 76/II/306, 308; ibid. LC, R 27/10907.
96 S.R.O. 3315/Ti/2, f. 59; *S.P.R. Heref.* xix (3), p. v.
97 S.R.O. 4044/91, p. 27; cf. above, Acton Scott, manors (Moat Fm.).
98 S.P.L., MS. 5365, pp. 146–7; *Shrews. Chron.* 23 and 30 Apr. 1909.
99 S.R.O. 165/170.
1 Date and initials 'RW' on two fireplaces.
2 Inf. from Mrs. Moran; Forrest, *Old Hos. of Wenlock*, 52.
3 Eyton, iii. 315 (Joybert's dates corr. from *V.C.H. Salop.* ii. 46); *Cur. Reg. R.* xiii. 35.
4 Eyton, iii. 315–16; *T.S.A.S.* 4th ser. i. 396–7; *Rot. Hund.* ii. 85.
5 Eyton, xi. 377, confusing Hatton with Acton Scott; *Cal. Pat.* 1292–1301, 342, 406.
6 *Cal. Pat.* 1292–1301, 191; *Cal. Chart. R.* 1300–26, 29.
7 *Cal. Chart. R.* 1300–26, 398; Eyton, iii. 317 n. 27; S.R.O. 840, box 41, deeds of 1364–1593 and valn. [*c.* 1608]; *Cal. Pat.* 1550–3, 38; *L. & P. Hen. VIII*, xix, p. 633; P.R.O., C 142/68, no. 7; cf. *V.C.H. Salop.* viii. 87–8.
8 S.R.O. 4032/2/12–13.
9 Glam. R.O., CL/Deeds I, Salop. 1380, 28 July.
10 P.R.O., CP 25/1/290/58 [no. 311].
11 P.R.O., CP 25/2/343/14 Jas. I Trin. [no. 13]; CP 43/138, rot. 12; S.R.O. 840, box 41, deeds of 1613–16; cf. above, Rushbury, manors (Gretton).
12 *V.C.H. Salop.* viii. 316.
13 S.R.O. 840, box 17, deed of 1645.
14 S.R.O. 515/5, p. 193; 1705/151; 4030/BRg/1, s.a. 1806; q. sess. rec. parcel 261, reg. of gamekeepers 1799–1807, f. 171; S.P.L., MS. 6865, p. 83; S. Bagshaw, *Dir. Salop.* (1851), 537; *S.P.R. Heref.* xv (2), pp. vii, 245; xix (3), p. iv; W.S.L. 350/3/40, Eaton p. 8; cf. above, Munslow, churches.
15 Laura Wood Acton's notes (in possession of Mrs. R. Acton).
16 *S.P.R. Heref.* xix (3), p. iv; Forrest, *Old Hos. of Wenlock*, 55; above, this article, intro.; below, local govt.

arch-braced collar of an open hall. In the mid to late 16th century the house was rebuilt as a timber framed hall range of 1½ storey with a cross wing. It was cased in stone *c.* 1800, and in the 19th century there was some internal reorganization.[17]

In 1635 Richard Wrednall, rector of Rushbury, bought a farm in Hatton from Edward Jones, lord of Hatton.[18] In 1681 Richard Wrednall of Downton (Herefs.) sold it to Bernard Hamond (d. 1736), a Ludlow apothecary.[19] Hamond's nephew John, a Somerset parson, sold the farm in 1753 to Edward Acton of Acton Scott.[20] In 1753 Acton bought a second farm in Hatton, formerly the Botfields' and the Baldwins'.[21] Both farms (*c.* 330 a. in all) descended with Acton Scott manor until sold *c.* 1960.[22] One of them had as its house Upper Farm, a two storeyed **L** shaped building.[23] Remains of a cruck framed truss indicate a late medieval core to a building refurbished in the early 17th century, with a house-place whose timbers displayed high quality detailing. A wing was added in the late 17th century, and the house was later cased in stone.[24] The farm buildings include a 10 bayed 17th-century barn with upper crucks and box-framed trusses, and a stone stable built by Edward Acton *c.* 1761. The other farmhouse, at the west end of the hamlet, was probably rebuilt in the 19th century.

In 1874 Augustus Wood of Acton Scott bought a 99-a. farm[25] which remained part of the Acton Scott estate until *c.* 1960.[26] Middle Farm is a mid 17th-century timber building later cased in stone.

In 1576 John and William Mershe, Londoners, bought land in Hatton once the Hospitallers'.[27]

WOLVERTON, part of Eaton-under-Heywood manor,[28] was subinfeudated by the prior of Wenlock before 1255, when John of Westhope was lord.[29] In 1623 the Jenkes family, for long lords of Wolverton, traced their ancestry back several generations before John ap Rees, or le Cambray (fl. 1323–4), the first head of the family said to be of Wolverton.[30] From his descendant Jenkyn Cambray (fl. 1400) son followed father, the following being lords: John Jenkes, Thomas Jenkes, John Jenkes, Rowland Jenkes (fl. 1497–1521),[31] John Jenkes, Thomas Jenkes, George Jenkes (fl. 1570–1600, granted arms 1584), Francis Jenkes (d. 1627),[32] and Herbert Jenkes (d. 1654). Wolverton apparently passed to Herbert Jenkes's daughter Margaret (d. 1674), who married Bartholomew Lutley (sheriff 1706,[33] d. 1716). The Lutleys' son Philip, next lord, also became lord of Eaton-under-Heywood, and the two manors descended together until the 1780s when John Barneby sold Wolverton to Peter Beck. Beck (d. 1798) was succeeded by his son Peter (d. 1824), a Shrewsbury banker, whose widow Hannah (d. 1859) had the 306-a. Wolverton farm in 1842.[34] In the later 19th and early 20th century Wolverton was part of the Warren family's settled estate,[35] which was split up and sold off after J. Loxdale Warren's death in 1909.[36]

Wolverton Manor comprises a long hall range of *c.* 1475 with an originally detached cross wing of *c.* 1581 at the south end. The two bayed open hall, separated by a screens passage from a two bayed service unit at its north end and possibly with a solar over the service end, may have been built against an existing structure later demolished. The hall employs two-tier crucks and has a spere truss whose aisle posts and other elements are moulded and trefoiled. In the later 16th century, when the cross wing was built, the hall's lower bay was converted to a smoke bay and a moulded ceiling was inserted in the hall's upper bay. About 1600 a link was built between hall and cross wing and a cellar was excavated beneath the cross wing. A stack was built in the smoke bay *c.* 1660, there was some reflooring, and a bay was added to the north end of the hall range.[37]

Gamel, a free man, held *MILLICHOPE* in 1066. In 1086 Helgot held it of Roger of Montgomery, earl of Shrewsbury (d. 1094), the tenant in chief,[38] who soon afterwards gave the manor to Wenlock priory.[39] Upper and Lower Millichope were separated parochially *c.* 1115 when Richard of Beaumais, justiciar of Shropshire, dismissed a claim that both Millichopes were in Munslow parish; his ruling assigned Lower Millichope to Munslow parish and confirmed Wenlock priory's parochial rights over Upper Millichope. Beaumais' reference to the 'two Millichopes' may indicate that already by *c.* 1115 they had been separately subinfeudated by the prior of Wenlock;[40] they evidently had by *c.* 1200, and each continued to be held of the priory until its surrender in 1540.[41]

The terre tenants of *UPPER MILLICHOPE*

17 N.M.R., R.C.H.M.E. hist. bldg. rep. (1991).
18 S.R.O. 2563/78; above, Rushbury, church.
19 S.R.O. 2563/79–81, 83, 85.
20 Ibid. /97–100.
21 Ibid. /86–90, 95–6.
22 Ibid. /1, ff. 1, 36–42; /2, p. 27; /34–5; S.P.L., MS 6741, p. 86; S.R.O. 3315/Ti/2; 4044/91, pp. 32–3; inf. from Mr. R. Acton.
23 Forrest, *Old Hos. of Wenlock*, 54–5.
24 Perh. in 1787: S.R.O. 1842/2.
25 S.R.O. 3315/Ti/2, f. 59; 3925, box 7, abstr. of title of Wm. Bristow 1874, decl. of John Morrall 1874, conveyance of Hatton fm. 1874.
26 S.R.O. 4044/91, p. 32; inf. from Mr. Acton.
27 *Cal. Pat.* 1575–8, p. 27. Presumably formerly property of Lydley preceptory: above, Cardington, manors.
28 Eyton, iii. 312, 317–18; *Cal. Pat.* 1550–3, 39; S.R.O. 515/5, p. 193; 4835/30.
29 Eyton, iii. 317; *Rot. Hund.* ii. 85.
30 For following pedigree see above, this section (Eaton); *Visit. Salop. 1623*, i. 275–7; S.P.L., MS. 6741, p. 92 and loose Jenkes pedigree; *S.P.R. Heref.* xix (3), p. ii.
31 S.R.O. 3365/165; Eyton, iii. 318 n. 31.
32 P.R.O., C 142/431, no. 102.
33 J. B. Blakeway, *Sheriffs of Salop.* (Shrews. 1831), 161; M. B. Colket, 'Jenkes fam. of Eng.' *New Eng. Hist. and Geneal. Reg.* cx. 247.
34 S.P.L., MSS. 4084, p. 4194; 6741, p. 92 and loose Jenkes and Eaton fam. pedigrees; 6865, pp. 83–4, 87; S.R.O. 515/5, p. 193; 3315/Ti/1–2; 4835/30, p. 5; W.S.L. 350/3/40, Eaton p. 7; *S.P.R. Heref.* xix (3), p. iii.
35 S.R.O. 4044/91, pp. 26, 60; *Shrews. Chron.* 23 and 30 Apr. 1909; S.P.L., MS. 5365, p. 146.
36 Cf. above, this section (Harton).
37 *T.S.A.S.* lxviii. 79–92; *V.C.H. Salop.* v (forthcoming); Forrest, *Old Hos. of Wenlock*, 52–3; *Vernacular Archit.* xxiv. 56, 58.
38 *V.C.H. Salop.* i. 337; iii. 7; Eyton, iv. 1–2.
39 Above, Lib. and Boro. of Wenlock (early est.).
40 Eyton, iii. 233; iv. 1–2.
41 Below, this section; *Rot. Hund.* ii. 85; *Cal. Inq. p.m.* x, p. 500; *V.C.H. Salop.* ii. 45.

also held in fee the office of royal forester of the Long Forest. Thomas of Millichope (fl. 1169–76) was perhaps the predecessor of Roger of Millichope, who succeeded his father as forester in 1199. Roger or a namesake (*alias* Roger Tosty) appears in the 1220s and died *c.* 1243. His daughter married Thomas de la Mare (fl. 1267), lord of Upper Millichope in 1255. Roger de la Mare was lord in 1300, Edmund de la Mare in 1316, and Roger de la Mare in 1322 and 1327.[42] By 1344 the manor had passed to Walter de Beysin,[43] and it descended with his share of Broseley[44] until 1534 when John Harewell's daughters divided their inheritance, Upper Millichope going to John Smith's wife Agnes.[45] From 1542 Upper Millichope descended with Sir John Smith's Aston estate until 1896 when E. C. Wright sold Upper Millichope to Capt. H. J. Beckwith.[46] Beckwith had 761 a. in the parish, mainly at Upper Millichope, in 1910[47] and remained a principal landowner until *c.* 1930.[48]

Upper Millichope Lodge is a stone building, apparently of the later 13th century, *c.* 10.4 by *c.* 5.5 m. internally, and with walls 2 m. thick. It has been suggested that it was built as a forester's lodge. It has a fine, well lit room on the first floor, above a basement lit by loops, which may have been the forester's prison. The original entrance to the first-floor room, probably his solar, was in the south gable wall. A two-light window, apparently original, with seats in the internal splays, survives in the north end of the room and a mutilated one in the east wall. Access to the basement was down a spiral stair in the south-west corner of the room. The building was substantially refurbished in the early 17th century when it was reroofed and partly refenestrated, a new staircase and a screen in the first-floor room were introduced, and a chimney was built on the east wall. The joists supporting the first floor, though massive and close set, are of *c.* 1633. It was perhaps also then that the first-floor entrance was blocked and a door made into the basement. The door head has re-used voussoirs carved with 14th-century ballflower ornament.[49] From the 17th century the basement served as the kitchen of the adjoining farmhouse, Millichope Court, rebuilt *c.* 1730.[50]

HUNGERFORD was presumably part of the Domesday manor of Millichope and was later reckoned a member of Upper Millichope.[51] Part or all of Hungerford (occasionally described as a manor) descended with Upper Millichope[52] and the Wrights apparently retained the lordship of Hungerford manor (unrecorded after the early 19th century)[53] after John Wright (d. 1792) sold his land there to Humphrey Wainwright (d. 1801). Wainwright's son William (d. 1829) was succeeded by his son, also William. In 1837 William Wainwright sold the 158-a. Hungerford estate to the Revd. R. N. Pemberton[54] of Millichope Park (in Munslow), whose family had had land at Hungerford since 1792 or earlier[55] and who had 194 a. there in 1842.[56] Those lands presumably formed a part of the Millichope Park sale of 1896 to Capt. H. J. Beckwith, principal or sole landowner at Hungerford in 1910.[57] The chief house at Hungerford, called Holloway (or the 'hall of Hungerford'), and a second substantial property, Muxhill, were in Munslow parish.[58]

In 1576 the Crown sold land in Hungerford once the Hospitallers' to John Dudley and John Ayscough.[59]

The *RECTORY*, appropriated to Wenlock priory, was worth £10 in 1291.[60] In 1495–6 the priory kitchen received £14 6*s.* 4*d.* in tithes from Eaton, Hatton, Millichope and Hungerford, Longville, and Lushcott.[61] In 1544 the Crown's sale of property in Eaton to John Pakington included some, perhaps most, of the parish's grain tithes.[62] The Lytteltons sold the grain tithes from 1,000 a. in Eaton and Upper Millichope, and perhaps other townships too, with the manor of Eaton to Richard Lutley in 1562.[63] Apart from some Ticklerton grain tithes, sold by Francis Jenkes in 1596,[64] those tithes descended intact with Eaton manor.[65]

The Lytteltons sold another large portion of the rectory to Richard Acton of Acton Scott in 1566.[66] On Acton's death in 1590 he owned half of the grain tithes of Eaton, Hatton, Harton, Ticklerton, and Wolverton townships,[67] although some tithes in Harton had already been disposed of.[68] In 1594 his son Edward Acton leased his tithes of Hatton to Thomas Chelmick for 1,000 years.[69] The lease later passed to the

42 Eyton, iv. 4–5; *T.S.A.S.* 2nd ser. iv. 331; *Feud. Aids*, iv. 228 (cf. Eyton, who gives a Ralph in 1316); *Cal. Pat.* 1321–4, 52.

43 P.R.O., CP 25/1/194/13, no. 33.

44 Above, Broseley, manor; P.R.O., CP 25/1/194/13, no. 33; *Cal. Fine R.* 1359–61, 144; 1413–22, 264–5; *Cal. Close*, 1399–1402, 551; *Cal. Inq. p.m.* x, p. 500; xiv, p. 258; xv, p. 41; xviii, p. 201; *Cal. Inq. p.m. Hen. VII*, iii, pp. 141–2.

45 Dugdale, *Warws.* (1730), ii. 810; *S.P.R. Heref.* xv (2), p. iv; xix (3), p. v.

46 P.R.O., C 142/132, no. 16; C 142/293, no. 70; S.R.O., q. sess. rec. parcel 261, reg. of gamekeepers 1799–1807, f. 12; parcel 281, reg. of papists' deeds 1717–88, pp. 199–203, 249–51; S. Bagshaw, *Dir. Salop.* (1851), 537; cf. above, Munslow, manors.

47 S.R.O. 4044/91, pp. 34–7.

48 *Kelly's Dir. Salop.* (1917–34).

49 Pl. 16. Descr. based on M. Moran and D. James, *The Forester's Lodge, Upper Millichope* (Ludlow [1986]); *V.C.H. Salop.* v (forthcoming); *Vernacular Archit.* xxvi. 70, 72.

50 W.S.L. 350/3/40, Eaton p. 5; above, this article, intro.

51 Eyton, iv. 2.

52 *Cal. Pat.* 1321–4, 52; *Cal. Inq. p.m. Hen. VII*, ii, p. 268; iii, p. 141; S.P.L., MS. 6741, p. 86; 6865, p. 87; W.S.L. 350/5/40, Munslow pp. 20–3; P.R.O., C 135/256, no. 10; C 142/35, no. 103; C 142/293, no. 70; CP 25/2/590/1652 Trin. no. 14; CP 40/1150, rot. 404.

53 S.R.O., q. sess. parcel 261, reg. of gamekeepers 1799–1807, f. 12; W.S.L. 350/5/40, Munslow pp. 10, 23.

54 S.R.O. 1011, box 244, deeds and papers *re* sale; *Bye-Gones*, N.S. xii. 21.

55 S.P.L., MS. 6865, p. 87. For Pemberton see *T.S.A.S.* xlii. 104–5; above, Munslow, manors.

56 S.R.O. 3315/Ti/2.

57 *T.S.A.S.* xlii. 105; S.R.O. 4044/91, pp. 34–7.

58 Above, Munslow, manors.

59 *Cal. Pat.* 1575–8, p. 180. Presumably formerly property of Lydley preceptory: above, Cardington, manors.

60 Below, church; *Tax. Eccl.* (Rec. Com.), 167.

61 S.R.O. 1224, box 342, Prior Gosnell's reg. f. 33.

62 *L. & P. Hen. VIII*, xix, p. 633.

63 P.R.O., C 142/204, no. 99; above, this section.

64 H.W.R.O.(H.), LC, R 27/10951.

65 P.R.O., C 142/431, no. 102; CP 25/2/203/42 Eliz. I Trin. no. 9; CP 25/2/477/6 Chas. I Mich. no. 11; S.P.L., MS. 6865, p. 90.

66 S.P.L., MS. 6741, p. 105; P.R.O., C 3/1/6; C 3/2/92.

67 P.R.O., C 142/228, no. 7.

68 S.R.O. 165/79.

69 S.R.O. 2563/77.

Wrednalls, owners of a farm there, with which it descended.[70]

The grain tithes of Upper Millichope and Hungerford were owned in the later 17th century by William Churchman of Thonglands (in Munslow). In 1722 his descendant James Tomkins sold them to Arthur Weaver of Bridgnorth.[71]

In 1842 most of the impropriate tithes were merged with their owners' land. The rest, payable to 12 impropriators, were commuted to £112 2*s*. 4*d*.[72]

ECONOMIC HISTORY. In 1086 the 10 hides of Ticklerton manor (corresponding to Eaton-under-Heywood parish north-west of Wenlock Edge) were relatively undeveloped: the tenants had five ploughteams and the lord one, but six more might have been employed. There were 6 *villani*, 6 bordars, 3 *servi*, and a radman in the manor, whose value, 50*s*., had halved since 1066.[73]

Eaton manorial demesne comprised 1 carucate and 2 a. meadow in 1369.[74] In 1237 the prior claimed, though unsuccessfully, a day's hay carrying from 10 men in respect of 1½ hide at Hatton.[75] In the 13th and 14th centuries tenants paid terciary to their lord, the prior of Wenlock.[76] The parish was probably affected by the economic setbacks of the early 14th century: in 1341 the small value of the tax collected was blamed on sheep murrain, storm damage to crops, and the abandonment of eight holdings.[77] In Hatton the demesne was farmed out and the rest was leased to free tenants for cash rents.[78]

Most hamlets probably had their own open-field land in the Middle Ages. Best recorded is Wolverton's, apparently in three fields: the Bruche field, probably also known as Marsh field, north and north-west of the hamlet,[79] Feltbatch (Feldbatch) field to the north-east, and the field under the Edge (or wood) to the south-east.[80] Some at least of Harton's open-field land lay east of that hamlet,[81] and field names suggest a west field too;[82] some may also have lain north of Eaton brook.[83] Some of Eaton's open-field land lay at the foot of the Edge[84] and some north-west of the hamlet, off the Ticklerton road.[85] The fields of Millichope were mentioned in 1256;[86] there were furlongs north and probably east of Upper Millichope.[87] Hungerford too had open-field land, north of the hamlet.[88] Hatton's fields lay east[89] and south[90] of it, and Ticklerton's probably both north and north-west of it[91] and to the south.[92]

In 1086 there was enough woodland for 60 swine.[93] The parish was in the Long forest until 1301[94] and there were two main areas of medieval woodland, neither of them in Hatton where the Harleys were granted free warren in 1302 and 1318.[95] One of the main wooded areas was along Wenlock Edge. In the 16th century, and probably for centuries before, the Edge wood was divided between the adjoining vills. Belonging to Eaton were Black wood[96] to the north-east and High wood, running south-west from the hamlet for *c*. 2 km.;[97] the latter was well warded in 1235.[98] Those woods, together with Longville wood and Hay wood,[99] remained part of the priory demesne in the later Middle Ages, the office of bailiff sometimes being farmed to the manorial lessee.[1] Black wood was at least partly inclosed in 1632.[2] South-west of High wood were Harton's wood and Wolverton's. The former, then called Harton's Edge, was inclosed by 1563.[3] In the later 18th and early 19th century Harton's wood, which was probably typical of the Wenlock Edge woods in the parish, was coppiced. Cord wood went to Bringewood forge (Herefs.), William Hazeldine's Shrewsbury ironworks, and Liverpool; bark went to Much Wenlock and huge numbers of faggots to local customers. Standards were left at 60 to the acre.[4] In the late 20th century conifers were fairly abundant in the plantations beneath the Edge, north-east from Harton wood to Stars coppice, and in Blackwood coppice and Childshill coppice near Upper Millichope.[5]

The other main area of medieval woodland was Hay wood, its name used to distinguish Eaton; it lay north of Ticklerton, its eastern part in Rushbury parish.[6] In 1235 the part in Eaton had oak and hazel but no underwood.[7] In Eaton parish the eastern end of Hay wood probably once extended south of its 19th-century limit,

70 S.R.O. 253/100; 1146/21; 2563/1, 82, 84–5; S.P.L., MS. 4647, p. 49.
71 S.R.O. 4023/1; *S.P.R. Heref.* xv (2), 112, 122, 129.
72 S.R.O. 3315/Ti/1.
73 *V.C.H. Salop.* i. 312.
74 B.L. Add. MS. 6165, p. 99.
75 *T.S.A.S.* 4th ser. i. 396.
76 Ibid. lvii. 68–74; Eyton, iii. 318; B.L. Add. Roll 67032.
77 *Inq. Non.* (Rec. Com.), 186.
78 S.R.O. 1224, box 342, Prior Gosnell's reg. f. 5v.
79 S.P.L., Deeds 1645–7. Field locations from inf. in deeds and from field names (mainly from S.R.O. 3315/Ti/1–2).
80 S.P.L., Deeds 1632, 1637, 1643, 1645, 1646–7.
81 H.W.R.O.(H.), LC, R 27/10907.
82 S.R.O. 3315/Ti/1–2, fields 492, 496.
83 H.W.R.O.(H.), LC, R 27/10922.
84 H.W.R.O.(H.), HD 2/14/20; S.R.O. 3315/Ti/1–2, fields 397–8.
85 S.R.O. 3315/Ti/1–2, field 344.
86 *Roll of Salop. Eyre 1256* (Selden Soc. xcvi), p. 239. It is not clear which Millichope was meant: cf. above, Munslow, econ. hist.
87 S.R.O. 3315/Ti/1–2, fields 769–70, 773, 785, 790–2.
88 Ibid. field 857; S.R.O. 837/49; 4260/1/6; SA 4310.
89 *T.S.A.S.* 4th ser. i. 397.
90 H.W.R.O.(H.), LC, R 27/10922.
91 S.R.O. 3315/Ti/1–2, fields 78, 88, 149, 158–9.
92 Ridge and furrow at O.S. Nat. Grid SO 486 906.
93 Including woods in the detached townships: see *V.C.H. Salop.* i. 312; below, Longville, etc., econ. hist.
94 *Cartulary of Shrews. Abbey*, ed. U. Rees (1975), ii, p. 250. See W.S.L. 350/3/40, Eaton p. 10, for claim that a forester's lodge stood at Soudley, but below, local govt., for a later ct. ho. there.
95 *Cal. Chart. R.* 1300–26, 29, 398.
96 *Cal. Pat.* 1550–3, 38–9.
97 Locations mainly from later maps, e.g. S.R.O. 3315/Ti/1–2.
98 *V.C.H. Salop.* i. 485.
99 Below, this section; Longville, etc., econ. hist.
1 Eyton, iii. 312; S.P.L., MS. 2, ff. 144v.–145; 6741, p. 107.
2 N.L.W., Dobell 1.
3 H.W.R.O.(H.), LC, R 27/10978. See also /10907.
4 S.R.O. 165/80–125, 129–44; 783, box 79, acct. bks.
5 O.S. Maps 1/10,000, SO 48 NE. (1980 edn.), 58 NW., 59 NW. (1978 edn.).
6 Above, Rushbury, econ. hist.
7 Eyton, vi. 338.

over land later occupied by Claybrook and Bentalls farms.[8] West of, and integral with, Hay wood was 'Suthleye' wood,[9] later Soudley common. By the mid 13th century there was assarting in the parish and goats were excluded from the commons.[10] In 1698 a farm at Ticklerton had a stint, in Hay wood and Soudley common, of 6 beasts, 6 pigs, and 20 sheep.[11]

In the early 16th century, when part of Hay wood in Rushbury was inclosed, common rights were claimed for vills in Eaton, Rushbury, Cardington, Hope Bowdler, Church Stretton, Hughley, and Church Preen parishes.[12] Parts of Soudley common and Hay wood were allotted *c.* 1563 in severalty to freeholders of Ticklerton and Chelmick (in Hope Bowdler), the latter in respect of part of Soudley. By the later 17th century little wood may have survived and then, as a century later, the commons were probably open pasture for sheep and cattle.[13] Some inclosures made in the previous century were thrown open by agreement *c.* 1674[14] and, while there were later inclosures and encroachments,[15] *c.* 300 a. remained open until Hay wood and Soudley common were inclosed, after long deliberation, in 1804.[16]

In the early Middle Ages the residue, at least, of a third large wood, 1 km. north to south by 2 km. east to west, divided Wolverton and Harton from Hatton. It extended south-east as far as the stream running from New Hall to Wolverton and south-west to an area called Espleys ('Aspen wood'), near the parish boundary.[17] Its northern boundary was marked by the north end of the later Ironmongers coppice, whence it probably extended into Ticklerton township as far as the Ticklerton–Harton road. With the wood was probably the heath where Hatton men were assarting in the earlier 14th century.[18] Clearance, however, may have begun much earlier, the name Hatton meaning a settlement on or near heath.[19] By 1531, when Hatton's heath was again recorded,[20] the remaining wood had probably been largely cleared and the resulting heath or pasture divided between Hatton, Harton, Ticklerton, and Wolverton.[21] Hatton also had a wood south-west of the hamlet, abutting the parish boundary[22] and surviving in part in 1989. Its hedges too supplied wood.[23]

Upper Millichope's woodland lay on the high ground west of Millichope Lodge. Childshill and the Spellers coppices, both surviving in 1989, were mentioned in 1761.[24] Hungerford's woodland included Rough wood, 1 km. north-west of the hamlet.[25] Adjoining to the west were Topley, a wooded detachment of Munslow parish,[26] and Topley common in Eaton parish.[27] Topley hill, until it was divided in that way, had probably been intercommoned by Upper and Lower Millichope.

TABLE XIX

EATON-UNDER-HEYWOOD: LAND USE, LIVESTOCK, AND CROPS

	1867	*1891*	*1938*	*1965*
Percentage of grassland	70	80	91	79
arable	30	20	9	21
Percentage of cattle	21	25	18	20
sheep	71	68	79	74
pigs	8	7	3	6
Percentage of wheat	59	34	30	33
barley	22	25	4	60
oats	19	41	62	7
mixed corn & rye	0	0	4	0
Percentage of agricultural land growing roots and vegetables	6	5	2	1

Sources: P.R.O., MAF 68/143, no. 15; /1340, no. 6; /3880, Salop. no. 224; /4945, no. 224.

In 1841 the woods were 'luxuriant'. Oak, hazel, ash, and hornbeam were said to grow well on the limestone and were cut at 10 to 15 years. Faggots had little value because of the costs and difficulties of carriage, but cordwood was burnt for charcoal and carried to forges near Bridgnorth.[28] Charcoal burning continued until the 1930s, and clogs were made.[29]

Inclosure of the open fields is unrecorded except at Harton, where it was done by agreement *c.* 1586.[30] The nature of the larger farms in the parish in the mid 17th century is indicated by the inventories of Edmund Philpott (d. 1664) of Eaton and Lawrence Palmer (d. 1666) of Ticklerton. Philpott owned 17 cattle worth £25 16*s.* 8*d.* and was storing butter and cheese worth £3. Other stock included 4 horses, 42 sheep, and 8 pigs. Crops were corn (£6), barley and peas (£2 10*s.*), and hemp and flax (3*s.* 4*d.*). Palmer had 6 oxen, 34 cattle, 6 horses, 8 sheep, 7 pigs,

8 Cf. 19th-cent. field names: S.R.O. 3315/Ti/1–2.
9 *Roll of Salop. Eyre 1256*, pp. 94–5.
10 S.R.O. 840/2/3/1; *T.S.A.S.* 4th ser. i. 397.
11 S.R.O. 165/40.
12 P.R.O., C 1/808, no. 47; above, Rushbury, econ. hist.
13 Bodl. MS. Top. Salop. c. 1, ff. 215–18; S.R.O. 3315/Ti/3, p. 6.
14 Bodl. MS. Top. Salop. c. 1, f. 216; H.W.R.O.(H.), LC, R 27/10882.
15 e.g. S.P.L., MS. 6865, p. 85.
16 S.R.O. 3651, box 103, case paper [1801] *re* Hay wood; 41 Geo. III, c. 114 (Local and Personal) (copy in S.R.O., incl. award B 14); S.P.L., MS. 6865, p. 84.
17 S.R.O. 3315/Ti/1–2, field names. For N. bdy. see also divn. betw. titheable and non-titheable lands in S.R.O. 1705/151 (fields identified from 3315/Ti/1–2).
18 S.R.O. 1224, box 342, Prior Gosnell's reg. f. 5v.
19 *P.N. Salop.* (E.P.N.S.), i. 145.
20 H.W.R.O.(H.), LC, R 27/10922.
21 Cf. Hatton–Harton boundary on S.R.O. 3315/Ti/2; Wolverton heath on O.S. Map 1", sheet LXI. SW. (1833 edn.).
22 S.R.O. 2563/41; 3315/Ti/1–2, field names.
23 S.R.O. 840, box 113, surv. of Gretton, etc., 1621.
24 O.S. Map 1/25,000, SO 48/58 (1983 edn.); S.R.O., q. sess. rec. parcel 281, reg. of papists' deeds 1717–88, p. 250.
25 S.R.O. 3315/Ti/1–2.
26 Above, this article, intro.; Munslow, intro.
27 B.L. Maps, O.S.D. 207. 28 P.R.O., IR 18/8063.
29 Dakers, *Ticklerton Tales*, 158.
30 H.W.R.O.(H.), LC, R 27/10907.

and corn worth £35.[31] In 1793 there were more rearing farms than arable in the parish.[32] Whitbach, an isolated top (or high) barn with cottage east of Topley, was probably built between 1817 and 1839 for Hungerford farm.[33] In 1841 wheat, oats, beans, and some rye and clover were said to be grown, although cultivation was 'precarious' where so much land was high, wet, and cold. Much of the higher grassland was used for young stock or as sheep walk. In several of the small valleys pasture was warmer, though liable to flood.[34] The percentage of farm land down to grass rose from 56 in 1842 to 91 in 1938; 79 per cent was still grass in 1965. Sheep were always the most numerous livestock.[35]

There were water mills at Eaton in the 13th and 14th centuries[36] and two in the parish in 1291.[37] In the 15th and 16th centuries there was one at Ticklerton, probably north-west of the hamlet.[38] A mill at Harton in the 14th and 16th centuries[39] was perhaps Clithes mill (1586), later called New Hall mill and last worked in 1925.[40] There was a medieval mill at Hatton[41] and probably one at Upper Millichope too.[42] There is said to have been a corn mill at Hungerford in the 19th century.[43] A windmill may have stood south of Ticklerton.[44]

Notable among several post-medieval fishponds were those at Soudley, from which, in the mid 18th century, fish were taken to a pool at Broncroft (in Diddlebury). Soudley pools were still stocked in the 20th century.[45]

In 1227 the prior of Wenlock was granted a Thursday market at Eaton;[46] no later evidence of it is known.

By the early 17th century and still in the 19th the Chatwall Sandstones were quarried near Soudley, supplying freestone and flags for roofs and floors.[47] Limestone was got and burnt at Blackwood north-west of Upper Millichope in the 18th and 19th centuries.[48] Bricks were probably made at Hatton *c.* 1607[49] and in the 18th century,[50] and bricks and tiles were produced at Claybrook in the 1850s and perhaps early 1860s.[51] In 1765 B. R. Barneby engaged colliers to bore for coal at Ticklerton.[52]

In the mid 17th century there was at least one tanner and glover at Soudley.[53] Later a tannery stood south of Ticklerton, but it had gone by 1842.[54] There is said to have been a tan yard at Hungerford in the 19th century.[55]

LOCAL GOVERNMENT. The prior of Wenlock was holding three or four courts a year for Eaton *c.* 1237.[56] Court records survive for the 14th and 15th centuries, and that of a court held for Wolverton by the prior in 1334.[57] Record also survives of a court of recognition held for the Harewells' tenants in Upper Millichope and Hungerford in 1464.[58] In the 1750s and 1760s annual courts were held at Soudley for the Barnebys, lords of Eaton and Wolverton manors.[59]

In the late 18th century each township had a constable.[60]

In 1737–8 clothing and cash were given as out-relief.[61] In 1792 the poor were sent to Church Stretton workhouse, but in 1793 the parish clerk farmed them, paying out-relief and occasional assistance to 93 people. Then, as usually for the next 40 years, a poorhouse was rented, variously at Hatton or Soudley. The poorhouse, however, usually accommodated fewer than six (for whom spinning materials were bought in 1819),[62] and out-relief was usual in the early 19th century.[63] Some children were apprenticed.[64] Expenditure rose from £106 in 1775–6 to £375 in 1802 and peaked at £667 in 1818–19.[65]

The parish was in Church Stretton poor-law union 1836–1930,[66] Church Stretton rural sanitary district 1872–94, Church Stretton rural district 1894–1934, Ludlow R.D. 1934–74, and South Shropshire district from 1974.[67] It had a

31 H.W.R.O.(H.), Heref. dioc. rec., invs. 19 Sept. 1664, 4 Sept. 1666.

32 S.P.L., MS. 6865, p. 84.

33 Not on B.L. Maps, O.S.D. 207; on P.R.O., IR 30/29/117.

34 P.R.O., IR 18/8063.

35 S.R.O. 3315/Ti/2; Table XIX. For late 19th- and 20th-cent. farming see Dakers, *Ticklerton Tales*, 154–8.

36 *Roll of Salop. Eyre 1256*, p. 122; P.R.O., C 143/206, no. 21; B.L. Add. MS. 6165, p. 99.

37 *Tax. Eccl.* 164.

38 Eyton, iii. 317; *L. & P. Hen. VIII*, xix (1), p. 633; S.R.O. 3315/Ti/1–2, field 150.

39 S.R.O. 566/1; Bodl. MS. Top. Salop. c. 1, ff. 215–18; P.R.O., C 142/204, no. 99.

40 H.W.R.O.(H.), LC, R 27/10907; 4835/30, p. 3; Dakers, *Ticklerton Tales*, 50–2; P. J. Madeley, 'Geog. descr. of area in par. of Rushbury' (Shenstone Coll., Bromsgrove, dissertation, 1967), 58.

41 S.R.O. 1224, box 342, Prior Gosnell's reg. f. 5v.

42 *T.S.A.S.* 3rd ser. vii. 130.

43 *Bye-Gones*, N.S. xii. 21.

44 Dakers, *Ticklerton Tales*, 52.

45 S.P.L., Deeds 1504; S.R.O. 783, box 79, acct. bks., e.g. 13, 29 May 1756, 9 Apr., 28 Nov. 1764; 3315/Ti/2; 3651, box 105, maps of Soudley; Dakers, op. cit. 83, 106.

46 *Cal. Chart. R.* 1226–57, 17.

47 S.R.O. 3315/Ch/1, s.a. 1822; 3651, box 108, deed 27 Nov. 1622; J. Plymley, *Gen. View of Agric. of Salop.* (1803), 68; *V.C.H. Salop.* i. 17; D. C. Greig and others, *Geol. of Country around Ch. Stretton, Craven Arms, Wenlock Edge and Brown Clee* (Mem. Geol. Surv. 1968), 129.

48 S.R.O., q. sess. rec. parcel 281, reg. of papists' deeds 1717–88, p. 200; 2563/33, 20 Jan. 1759; 3315/Ti/1–2, fields 688, 694, 696, 702, 718.

49 S.R.O. 840, box 113, rental.

50 S.R.O. 2563/32, s.a. 1753.

51 Dakers, *Ticklerton Tales*, 83, 85, 105; S.R.O. 3651, box 113, brickyd. acct. 1860. See also S.R.O. 783, box 79, acct. bk. 1763, 14 and 26 Nov.

52 S.R.O. 783, box 79, acct. bk. 1764, 2 May, 3 July; acct. bk. 1765, 5 Aug.

53 H.W.R.O.(H.), Heref. dioc. rec., inv. of Wm. Phifield, 1665.

54 S.R.O. 3315/Ti/1–2, field 236.

55 *Bye-Gones*, N.S. xii. 21.

56 Eyton, iii. 316.

57 S.R.O. 566/1; 1190/1, unlisted ct. r. 1403–4; 1224/2/1–2, 6–8.

58 Birm. Univ. Libr., Mytton Papers, i. 198.

59 S.R.O. 783, box 79, acct. bks., e.g. 15 Oct. 1756, 22 Nov. 1757, 7 Oct. 1763; 3315/Ti/1–2, field 124 (Court Ho.); above, manors (Eaton; Wolverton).

60 S.P.L., MS. 6865, p. 85.

61 S.R.O. 5709, Eaton overseers' accts.

62 S.P.L., MS. 6865, pp. 85–6; *Abstr. Rel. to Poor*, H.C. 98, pp. 422–3 (1803–4), xiii; H.C. 82, pp. 376–7 (1818); xix, S.R.O. 3315/P/3, s.a. 1817; 23 June 1819; s.a. 1835; Forrest, *Old Hos. of Wenlock*, 55.

63 S.R.O. 3315/P/1–3.

64 Ibid. /P/4–5; S.P.L., MS. 6865, p. 86.

65 *Abstr. Rel. to Poor* (1803–4), 422–3; (1818), 376–7; *Sel. Cttee. Poor Rate*, H.C. 556, suppl. app. p. 144 (1822), v.

66 V. J. Walsh, 'Admin. of Poor Laws in Salop. 1820–55' (Pennsylvania Univ. Ph.D. thesis, 1970), 148–50; *Kelly's Dir. Salop.* (1929), 94.

67 *V.C.H. Salop.* ii. 215, 217; iii. 178, and sources cited 169 n. 29.

joint parish council with Hope Bowdler from *c.* 1967.[68]

CHURCH. The confirmation of parochial rights over Upper Millichope to Wenlock priory *c.* 1115 may be related to the earliest evidence of a church at Eaton, its Norman fabric.[69] The rectory was appropriated to Wenlock priory between 1186 and 1198,[70] and Eaton remained a vicarage (in the priory's patronage until 1540)[71] until reconstituted a rectory in 1868.[72] After the Dissolution the advowson of the vicarage descended with Eaton manor[73] until sold *c.* 1784 to Thomas Gwynn of Ludlow. Between 1799 and 1805 the advowson passed to Henry and William Lloyd of Ludlow, and before 1831 Folliot Sandford of the Isle bought it for his son Richard.[74] The last resident rector resigned in 1960 and the parish had a curate in charge, the rector of Rushbury, until 1967.[75] The benefice having been united with that of Hope Bowdler in 1966,[76] the united benefice was held in plurality with Rushbury from 1967[77] and also with Cardington from 1980.[78] In 1987 Maj. Humphrey Sandford was a joint patron of Hope Bowdler with Eaton-under-Heywood.[79]

The vicarage was worth £4 6*s.* 8*d.* in 1291,[80] £6 13*s.* 4*d.* in 1379,[81] and £5 net in 1535.[82] In the later 16th century the vicar had 12 a. of glebe and the tithe sheaf of home closes and all other tithes except of grain.[83] In 1712 Frances Williams, a relation of the patron, augmented the vicarage with the gift of a farm,[84] and *c.* 1790 there were 140 a. of glebe.[85] Richard Sandford, the patron and vicar, rebuilt Eatonglebe (later Whitefields) Farm *c.* 1835.[86] In 1835 the vicar's net income was £280.[87] His tithes were commuted to £192 10*s.* in 1842.[88] The patron conveyed some impropriate tithe rent charges to the living and it became a rectory in 1868;[89] it was worth £350 in 1870.[90] Most of the glebe was sold in 1921, the rest in small parcels over the next 35 years.[91]

About 1600 the parsonage was a two bayed tiled mansion with a kitchen, barn, and stable.[92] As later, the house probably stood north-east of the church, and by 1654 a bridge over the intervening sunken lane connected them.[93] After augmentation of the living in 1712 the vicarage was rebuilt as a four bayed, two storeyed brick house with stone quoins, cornices, and plat bands; a surmounting bell turret was later removed.[94] Behind is a two storeyed brick tower with a first-floor dovecot. The house was sold in 1961.[95]

In 1345 the wardens of St. Mary's light were owed 4 qr. of wheat and oats, presumably to maintain the light.[96] Richard Clark, vicar in 1567 and 1587, was at first only a reader.[97] In the 18th century there were weekly services and occasional communion celebrated for small congregations.[98] In the later 18th and the 19th century resident curates were often employed.[99] Psalm singers were paid between 1817 and 1859.[1] During the incumbencies of Richard Sandford, 1831–60, and his son Holland, 1860–1900, the living was improved but not attendance,[2] with 30 at the one weekly service in 1851.[3] By 1878 there was an efficient choir, but the distance of the church from most of the hamlets was then a deterrent to good attendance,[4] as indeed it must always have been.

ST. EDITH'S, so dedicated by *c.* 1740,[5] is built of rubble and has a chancel with south tower and a nave with south porch.[6]

A small nave, forming the western part of the present church, was probably built in the 12th century. The present long chancel was built *c.* 1200; it is the same width as the nave and has three lancets in the east wall. About the same time the tower was built against the south side of the new chancel and a new north door was made in the nave. The tower, which has an open arch into the church and a south doorway with pointed head, has two-light round-headed windows in its upper stage. The windows in the north and south walls of the chancel were renewed at various dates in the 14th century and the west window is 15th- or early 16th-century. By the latter period, when the roofs were renewed, the division between nave and chancel had been moved to a point just east of the arch into the tower. There was no chancel arch, but

68 Inf. from the clk.

69 Eyton, iii. 233; below, this section.

70 Eyton, iii. 265, 313–14.

71 e.g. ibid. 315.

72 *Lond. Gaz.* 12 June 1868, p. 3306; Heref. Dioc. Regy., reg. 1857–69, pp. 606–7, 611.

73 *L. & P. Hen. VIII*, xix (1), p. 633; *Cal. Pat.* 1550–3, 38–9; 1572–5, p. 402; S.P.L., Deeds 1548; S.P.L., MS. 6741, p. 113; H.W.R.O.(H.), LC, R 27/10971.

74 S.P.L., MS. 6865, pp. 88–9, 93; S.R.O. 465/670; *S.P.R. Heref.* xix (3), pp. vi–vii.

75 S.R.O., reg. of electors, Ludlow const. (1960), p. 462; (1961), pp. 457–8; *Crockford* (1973–4), 182.

76 Heref. Dioc. Regy., reg. 1953-68, p. 513.

77 Ibid. pp. 527, 563; 1969– (in use), p. 50; *Crockford* (1973–4), 182; (1989–90), 39, 77.

78 Heref. Dioc. Regy., reg. 1969– (in use), pp. 354–5; *Crockford* (1989–90), 77.

79 *Dioc. Heref. Yr. Bk.* (1987), 40.

80 *Tax. Eccl.* 167.

81 B.L. Add. MS. 6164, p. 386.

82 *Valor Eccl.* iii. 210.

83 S.R.O. 3315/Ti/3, pp. 10–11 at end; *T.S.A.S.* xlvi. 44.

84 S.R.O. 1670/46; S.P.L., MS. 6741, p. 111.

85 S.R.O. 3315/Ti/3.

86 Dakers, *Ticklerton Tales*, 45, 83, confusing it with the vicarage: cf. S.R.O. 3315/Ti/1–2 (Wm. Bray, Eatonglebe tenant); /Ti/3, p. 68 (there called Bray Ho.).

87 *Rep. Com. Eccl. Revenues* [67], pp. 436–7, H.C. (1835), xxii.

88 S.R.O. 3315/Ti/2.

89 Heref. Dioc. Regy., reg. 1857–69, pp. 606–7.

90 *P.O. Dir. Salop.* (1870), 52.

91 Inf. from dioc. sec.

92 S.R.O. 3315/Ti/3; H.W.R.O.(H.), HD 2/14/21.

93 S.R.O. 4774/3.

94 S.P.L., MS. 6865, p. 89; Dept. of Environment, *List of Bldgs.: Ludlow R.D.* (1974), 73.

95 Inf. from dioc. sec.

96 S.R.O. 1224/2/1.

97 *T.S.A.S.* 4th ser. xi. 186; xlvi. 44.

98 H.W.R.O.(H.), HD 5/14/1/12; S.P.L., MS. 6865, p. 91.

99 Heref. Dioc. Regy., reg. 1847–56, p. 586; 1857–69, pp. 40, 111; S.P.L., MS. 6741, p. 97; S.R.O. 3315/Rg/2.

1 S.R.O. 3315/Ch/1.

2 *Dioc. of Heref. Institutions (1539–1900)*, ed. A. T. Bannister (Heref. 1923), 150, 174, 216; S.P.L., MS. 6741, p. 97.

3 P.R.O., HO 129/354, no. 23.

4 J. Randall, *Eaton-under-Haywood: its Townships, &c.* (Madeley, 1879), 11, 15 sqq.

5 B.L. Add. MS. 30316, f. 30.

6 Pl. 7. Following descr. based on S.P.L., MS. 6865, pp. 91–2; S.R.O. 3315/Ch/1, s.a. 1816–17; 3315/Ti/3, p. 5 at end; Birm. Univ. Libr., Mytton Papers, ii, f. 423; Soc. of Antiquaries, Ch. Com. plan of ch. 1845. Views of ch. include S.P.L., MS. 372, vol. ii, f. 92; J. H. Smith colln. no. 79. For descr. of ch. in 1830s see W.S.L. 350/3/40, Eaton p. 11.

a rood screen may have divided nave and chancel: there was a rood in the church in 1538, perhaps supported by the 'cross division wall between nave and chancel' removed *c.* 1650.[7] The chancel roof is low pitched and has intersecting moulded beams with a carved cornice and bosses decorated with foliage and grotesques. The small porch was probably of similar date and was originally of timber but its walls have been rebuilt in rubble.

The chancel was 'beautified' in 1743[8] by work not now identifiable. By 1793 the structure of the whole building was dangerous and substantial repairs were made to the tower and probably to the west end, while three large buttresses were built to the north. Inside, in a 'dark, foetid, and unwholesome' atmosphere, there were 'very irregular and somewhat ruinous' pews, three in the chancel and 28 in the nave. They seated *c.* 140, a west gallery, there by 1817, *c.* 30. The church was reseated *c.* 1845[9] and there were improvements in 1864–5.[10] It was perhaps then or in 1869 that the arms of the principal landowners were put up at the 'intersection' of nave and chancel.[11] In 1869[12] gallery, ceilings, and wall plaster were removed; the medieval east lancets were restored, and a later east window that had been cut into them was moved to the west end, where it was surmounted by a new wheel window; a square-headed three-light window was removed from the north wall of the nave and two Norman windows reopened there; other windows were renewed; and much stained glass and a communion table were introduced.[13] Later alterations were few.[14]

Early fittings include a tub font probably Norman (cover *c.* 1872),[15] a 14th-century wooden effigy in the chancel,[16] a late medieval chest,[17] and a three-decker pulpit assembled from parts of various dates, perhaps in 1670, the date on the sounding board.[18] The plate is 18th-century and later.[19] The three bells are of 1615, 1622, and 1869.[20]

The registers are complete from 1688.[21] The churchyard was largely walled in 1832; until then particular farms had been responsible for lengths of the fence.[22]

A chapel at Upper Millichope in 1331 had probably existed before 1281.[23] No record of it after the 14th century has been found. There was a ruinous chapel at Hatton, probably in the hamlet, in 1593.[24]

NONCONFORMITY. In the later 17th century there were a few papists in the parish, notably Bartholomew and Margaret Lutley, but only one was reported in 1676.[25]

Wesleyans met at Eaton in 1832,[26] Primitive Methodists at Haywood from 1837 to the 1850s,[27] and Methodists in a house at Soudley in the 1930s.[28]

EDUCATION. In 1793 a school at Hatton had 40–50 fee-paying pupils.[29] Children from Eaton parish were eligible to free places in Rushbury parochial school, endowed in 1820.[30] Between 1848 and the early 1850s the Primitive Methodists ran a Sunday school at Eaton; it had three teachers and *c.* 20 pupils.[31]

A parochial school, later called St. Edith's,[32] was built in 1863 by public subscription. An ill-lit brick building with teacher's house attached, it stood south-east of Ticklerton on the Eaton road. It had 60 places, later reduced to 35.[33] In the 1890s and until 1911 the building was much neglected and sometimes the school was poorly managed and equipped.[34] Until 1913 when a monitor was appointed, the teacher worked unassisted except by a sewing mistress.[35] Some pupils had to travel long distances.[36] Attendance averaged 35 in 1885 and 22 in 1900,[37] but the roll was only 20 in 1913 and 18 in 1919.[38] After severe gale damage in 1927 the school closed, its 13 pupils transferring to Rushbury and Hope Bowdler C.E. schools.[39]

CHARITIES FOR THE POOR. None known.

7 *S.P.R. Heref.* xix (3), p. i; W.S.L. 350/3/40, Eaton p. 11.
8 *T.S.A.S.* 4th ser. vi. 267.
9 *Eddowes's Jnl.* 11 Aug. 1869.
10 *Ch. Cal. Dioc. Heref.* (1866), 126.
11 Randall, *Eaton*, 18–19.
12 St. Deiniol's Libr., Hawarden, Sir Steph. Glynne's ch. notes, xc, f. 16; Birm. Univ. Libr., Mytton Papers, ii. 423.
13 *Ch. Cal. Dioc. Heref.* (1871), 155; *Eddowes's Jnl.* 11 Aug. 1869.
14 *S.P.R. Heref.* xix (3), p. vi; S.R.O. 3315/Ch/6–7; Heref. Dioc. Regy., reg. 1926–38, p. 544.
15 *Ch. Cal. Dioc. Heref.* (1872), 118.
16 Stamper, *'Farmer Feeds Us All'*, 22.
17 S.P.L., MS. 6767, no. 64.
18 Cranage, iii, pl. xxvi.
19 D. L. Arkwright and B. W. Bourne, *Ch. Plate Archd. Ludlow* (Shrews. 1961), 28.
20 H. B. Walters, *Ch. Bells of Salop.* (Oswestry, 1915), 91.
21 S.R.O. 3315/Rg/1–3; MRg/1–4; *S.P.R. Heref.* xix (3); regs. in ch. Earlier transcripts (for 1638, 1660, 1662–70, and 1672–88) survive in H.W.R.O.(H.).
22 S.R.O. 3315/Ch/1, s.a. 1832; /Ti/3, pp. 8–9 at end.
23 *Cal. Pat.* 1348–50, 136, 188.
24 S.R.O. 840, box 41, deed of 1593.
25 *Worcs. Recusant*, liii. 24, 27; H.W.R.O.(H.), HD 7, presentments of 1669, 1672, 1694; *Compton Census*, ed. Whiteman, 646.
26 Shrews. Sch. Libr., Broseley circuit bk. 1815–41, Oct. 1832.
27 S.R.O. 2138/48, p. [5]; /49; /56–62. Local inf. (via Mr. J. Madeley) suggests the ho. at O.S. Nat. Grid *c.* SO 486 923. Cf. Dakers, *Ticklerton Tales*, 85.
28 Dakers, op. cit. 81.
29 S.P.L., MS. 6865, p. 86.
30 Above, Rushbury, educ.
31 S.R.O. 2138/49, 56–62.
32 *S.C.C. Mins.* 1903–4, 119.
33 S.R.O. 3315/Sc/1; S.P.L., Deeds 18594; *Kelly's Dir. Salop.* (1885), 846; (1913), 92.
34 S.R.O. 262/3, pp. 11–12, 34–5, 51–2, 66, 71, 76–7, 92, 98, 112, 123, 132–4, 153, 166, 174, 182.
35 Ibid. pp. 58, 214, 271.
36 e.g. ibid. p. 68.
37 *Kelly's Dir. Salop.* (1885), 846; (1900), 83.
38 S.R.O. 262/3, pp. 206, 270.
39 *S.C.C. Mins. (Educ.)* 1927–8, 14, 33; Rushbury C.E. sch. log bk. (at Rushbury C.E. (Contr.) Primary sch. 1982), 31 Jan., 31 May 1927; inf. from Miss N. Sandells, the last headmistress.

LONGVILLE, LUSHCOTT, AND PART OF EAST WALL

THE TOWNSHIPS of Longville in the Dale and Lushcott, with part of East Wall (otherwise in Rushbury parish), formed a detached part (1,496 a., 605 ha.) of Eaton-under-Heywood parish[40] that was transferred to Rushbury civil parish in 1883.[41]

Longville stands on the watershed between Ape Dale, which drains south-west to the Onny, the whole of which seems to have been called Longfieldsdale in 1272,[42] and the dale that drains north-east by Plaish brook[43] to the Severn: neither the name Longville, meaning long open land,[44] nor the description 'in the Dale' is therefore wholly apt. The hamlet of Lushcott (Lussa's cot)[45] stands near the head of the north-east dale, East Wall near the head of Ape Dale. The upper parts of the two dales are bounded on the south-east by Wenlock Edge and in the opposite direction by the high land of Plaish (in Cardington) and Gretton (in Cardington and Rushbury).

Boundaries between the townships have not been ascertained, but the parish boundary surrounding them coincides on the west and south with the headwaters of Lakehouse brook, on the south-east with Wenlock Edge, and on part of the north with a tributary of Plaish brook; here and there field edges mark the boundary. The townships lie mainly on boulder clay, and north-west of Longville is an area of higher ground once wooded.[46]

No distinct medieval population figures are available for the townships, Longville and Lushcott probably being taxed with Millichope in 1327.[47] By 1256 there was at least one dwelling at the Lakehouse near East Wall.[48] In the earlier 16th century there seem to have been about eight farms in Longville and three in Lushcott,[49] presumably with cottages as well. In 1642 the Protestation was taken by 11 men in Longville and 8 in Lushcott.[50] In 1672 hearth tax was paid on 14 houses (the 3 biggest with three hearths each) in the two places,[51] and in 1676 there were 40 adults.[52] In 1805 there were at least 16 cottages.[53] The population was 97 in 1841 and 86 in 1891.[54] Longville hamlet is compactly built along both sides of the early 18th-century road from Church Stretton to Bridgnorth, where it ascends Wenlock Edge. Lushcott, at a junction of lanes, consists of little more than two farms.

The Stretton–Bridgnorth road was turnpiked in 1765,[55] and a new and easier route up the Edge, paid for by subscription, was made *c.* 1832.[56] Longville railway station on the Wenlock Railway Co.'s new line from Buildwas to Craven Arms (along the foot of Wenlock Edge) was opened in 1867. Passenger services ceased in 1951 but Longville, thereafter the southern terminus, retained freight traffic; the line closed in 1963.[57]

The Station Inn at Longville opened soon after the railway came and was renamed the Longville Hotel in the 1920s and the Longville Arms later.[58]

ESTATES. Longville and Lushcott were part of Wenlock priory's manor of Eaton-under-Heywood, and the priory had two farms at East Wall. The Crown sold the manor and the farms at East Wall in 1544 to John Pakington,[59] whose successors John and Gilbert Lyttelton sold most of Longville, Lushcott, and apparently the farms at East Wall.[60]

In 1563 the Lytteltons sold three farms (*c.* 430 a.) in *LONGVILLE* and Lushcott, with their great tithes, to John Adams of Harley, Thomas Adams of Acton Burnell, and Thomas Hill.[61] Hill (d. 1619) was succeeded by his daughter Alice, and she by her husband William Wilkes (d. 1636), whose heir was their son Thomas.[62] John Adams (d. by 1580) was succeeded by his spinster daughters Elizabeth and Dorothy, who sold their property that year to their sister Mary, also apparently unmarried.[63] Thomas Adams (d. 1593) left his estate to his wife with remainder to his daughters Joan Newnham and Avise Adams.[64] In 1625 Joan, to whom Avise's share had passed by 1623, settled a moiety on her son William, the rest to be his after her death. By will proved 1735 a later William Newnam left his estate, comprising three farms in Longville

40 O.S. Map 1/2,500, Salop. LVII. 5 (1883 edn.); O.S. *Area Bk.* Rushbury (1884), p. 10. This article was written 1989–90.

41 *V.C.H. Salop.* ii. 226 note c.

42 Eyton, xi. 377 (misinterpreting 'Hacton' as Acton rather than Hatton). For this para. see O.S. Map 1/25,000, SO 59 (1959 edn.); fig. 8.

43 *V.C.H. Salop.* iv. 9.

44 *P.N. Salop.* (E.P.N.S.), i. 75.

45 Ibid.; inf. from Dr. M. Gelling.

46 Geol. Surv. Map 1", drift, sheet 166 (1967 edn.); S.R.O. 3315/Ti/1–2, field names.

47 *T.S.A.S.* 2nd ser. iv. 331 (mention of Rog. of Longville). Growth of settlement at E. Wall is treated above, Rushbury, intro.

48 *Roll of Salop. Eyre 1256* (Selden Soc. xcvi), p. 227 (la Lak').

49 S.R.O. 1224, box 342, Prior Gosnell's reg. f. 38v.; *Cal. Pat.* 1550–3, 38–9.

50 Ho. of Lords papers 1641–2, Protestations Oxon. and Salop., ff. 194–5.

51 *Hearth Tax 1672* (Salop. Arch. Soc. 1949), 39.

52 *Compton Census*, ed. Whiteman, 645–6.

53 S.R.O. 515/5, p. 194; 4835/30, p. 7.

54 *V.C.H. Salop.* ii. 222 notes k–l. No later figs.

55 5 Geo. III, c. 86; O.S. Map 1", sheet LXI. SW. (1833 edn.); below, Shipton, intro.

56 *Shrews. Chron.* 18 Nov. 1831, p. 1; S.P.L., Deeds 13718. Cf. B.L. Maps, O.S.D. 207; S.R.O. 3315/Ti/1.

57 *Railway Mag.* cxi. 376–8, 440–4; *T.S.A.S.* lxiv. 98; below, M. Wenlock, communications.

58 *P.O. Dir. Salop.* (1870), 52; *Kelly's Dir. Salop.* (1929), 202; (1937), 211; O.S. Map 6", Salop. LVII. NW. (1928 edn.).

59 Above, Eaton, manors; Eyton, iii. 312; S.R.O. 515/5, p. 193; 1224, box 342, Prior Gosnell's reg. f. 38v.; 4835/30; *L. & P. Hen. VIII*, xix (1), p. 633; *Cal. Pat.* 1550–3, 39.

60 Above, Eaton, manors; below, this section.

61 S.R.O. 5001/4/2/1.

62 P.R.O., C 142/414, no. 63; C 142/636, no. 73.

63 S.R.O. 5001/4/2/2–3.

64 P.R.O., C 142/278, no. 142.

and their great tithes, to his wife. By 1746 the estate had recently been sold by his representatives to William Lutwyche of Lutwyche.[65]

Richard Corfield, grandson of Richard Corfield of Corfield, Chatwall, and Longville, had a son John (d. 1592). John had property in Longville, perhaps his great-grandfather's, and was succeeded in it by his son Thomas (d. 1598). At least some of the property was acquired by the Corfields' kinsmen, the Lutwyches, from 1590. Edward Lutwyche (d. 1614) held a messuage and 170 a.[66]

By 1567 one farm at Longville (108 a.) and its tithes had been sold to Ralph Corfield, brother of the younger Richard. From Ralph (d. 1573) the property passed to his wife Alice until their son William (d. 1661) was of age. William's grandson William Corfield sold his Longville property in 1710 to William Burroughs of Lincoln's Inn.[67]

In 1785 the part of the Lutwyches' estate that was offered for sale included 494 a. in Longville.[68] Soon afterwards a share of the family estate owned by Sarah Winford (*née* Lutwyche) was sold to Thomas Whitefoot, tenant of one of the farms, but much of the estate descended with Wilderhope (in Rushbury) and belonged to the Bensons of Lutwyche in 1910 and 1934.[69] In the 1980s the National Trust acquired Longville coppice.[70]

Sir H. W. Bayntun (d. 1840), to whom the Lutwyches' Wilderhope estate came, owned two farmhouses in Longville hamlet.[71] Fairly central was Longville Farm, a 1½ storeyed, timber framed, **T** plan building of the 17th century. The other house (later Station Farm), at the east end of the hamlet, is an 18th-century stone building with brick additions and a 19th-century gothic stone porch.

The Butchers owned over 300 a. around Longville in 1842 and 1910,[72] and their estate included two farmhouses in the hamlet: Home Farm (opposite Longville Farm), a 17th-century building refronted in the early 19th century, and what became the Station Inn, a three storeyed stone building of 1793.[73]

In 1563 the Lytteltons sold a farm at *LUSHCOTT*, with its tithes and share of Longville wood, to John Cock or Cox,[74] whose family had been tenants since 1515 or earlier.[75] Cock or a namesake sold the farm in 1596 to Edward Lutwyche.[76] In 1785 Lushcott farm (268 a.) and coppices (28 a.) were offered for sale with other Lutwyche family estates[77] but apparently descended with Wilderhope: Sir H. W. Bayntun had Lushcott farm and in 1851 his daughter Mrs. C. E. M. Boodé conveyed it to M. G. Benson (whose father Ralph had had 30 a. there in 1842) perhaps in exchange for other property.[78] With 462 a. R. B. Benson, of Lutwyche, was sole landowner in Lushcott in 1910.[79] In 1937 G. R. Benson sold Little Lushcott farm (60 a.) but failed to sell Lushcott farm (144 a.).[80]

Lushcott Farm contains some later 16th-century timber framing but is essentially an early 18th-century brick building of five bays and 2½ storeys. Alterations and additions were made in the later 19th century and *c.* 1960 a timber framed range to the rear was demolished.[81]

About 1564 the Lytteltons sold land and tithes in Longville and Lushcott to Richard Lawley (d. 1567) of Strensham (Worcs.). Lawley devised two thirds of the estate to his bastard son Francis Lawley or Cotterell and the rest was shared by Richard's five coheirs. Between 1570 and 1573 one of those, John Adys of Frampton on Severn (Glos.), bought up Francis Lawley's share and at least three of the other four shares.[82]

In 1577 Adys sold land and tithes in Longville and Lushcott to John More, rector of Great Comberton (Worcs.),[83] who had owned property in Lushcott since 1564 or earlier.[84] More (d. 1586) left his Longville and Lushcott estate to his nephew Thomas More (d. 1620)[85] and it descended with Lower Millichope to Thomas More (d. 1689).[86] More's property in Lushcott included Hockums house, later Oakham Farm.[87] That was perhaps sold *c.* 1686 by More's son Henry to Arthur Weaver (d. 1687). Weaver left lands that he had bought in Longville and Lushcott to his grandson Thomas Weaver,[88] whose property included Oakham farm.[89] That farm (129 a.) and another at Longville of 126 a. were probably among the property that Thomas's nephew Arthur Blayney (d. 1795) left to Henry Leigh Tracy, Viscount Tracy (d. 1797), husband of Blayney's late cousin. Lord Tracy's son-in-law Charles Hanbury-Tracy

65 S.P.L., Deeds 1096, 1353, 1946, 2867, 6390.

66 S.R.O. 4597/30–1; 5001/4/2/4–8; A. Sparrow, *Hist. of Ch. Preen* (priv. print. 1898), 47; *S.P.R. Heref.* xix (3), p. iii.

67 *Cal. Pat.* 1566–9, p. 113; P.R.O. C 142/167, no. 108; Sparrow, op. cit. 47–8; S.R.O. 1037/21/101; 4597/29–32; S.P.L., MS. 2, f. 135; ibid. Deeds 1095; *S.P.R. Heref.* xix (3), p. iii.

68 S.R.O. 4835/2, pp. 11–13.

69 Ibid. p. 11; S.P.L., MS. 4078, p. 994; S.R.O. 809, box 13, terrier and sched. 1934, pp. 103–4; 3315/Ti/1–2; 4044/91, p. 54; above, Rushbury, manors (Wilderhope; Lutwyche).

70 *Nat. Trust Handbk.* (1992), 184.

71 S.R.O. 3315/Ti/1–2.

72 Ibid.; 4044/91, pp. 53–4. Cf. W.S.L. 350/3/40, Eaton p. 2, for the fam.

73 S.R.O. 3315/Ti/1–2; Forrest, *Old Hos. of Wenlock*, 47; date stone 1793.

74 B.R.L., MS. 501889.

75 S.R.O. 1224, box 342, Prior Gosnell's reg. f. 38v.; *L. & P. Hen. VIII*, xix (1), p. 633; *Cal. Pat.* 1550–3, 38–9.

76 S.P.L., Deeds 1092.

77 S.R.O. 4835/2, p. 6.

78 S.R.O. 3315/Ti/1–2; New Ho. fm. (Shipton) deeds, abstr. of title (1909) of trustees of Mr. and Mrs. John Hippisley's marr. settlement (thanks are due to Mr. and Mrs. B. D. Williams, New Ho., for sight of this abstr.); S.R.O. 809, parcel 3, Lutwyche est. rental 1843–53; box 10, Lushcott, etc., ests., copy valn. and rep. *re* proposed exchange betw. M. G. Benson and Mrs. Lutwyche 1849; cf. above, Rushbury, manors (Wilderhope).

79 S.R.O. 4044/91, pp. 55–6.

80 *Shrews. Chron.* 1 Oct. 1937.

81 Forrest, *Old Hos. of Wenlock*, 47–8.

82 S.P.L., Deeds 364; Shrews. Sch. Libr., James Deed 65; S.R.O. 3320/21/1–3; *Cal. Pat.* 1575–8, p. 273.

83 S.R.O. 3320/21/4.

84 Ibid. /21/6.

85 S.P.L., Deeds 15685; *S.P.R. Heref.* xv (2), 29, 72.

86 S.R.O. 3320/21/9; S.P.L., MS. 4645, pp. 438–9; *S.P.R. Heref.* xv (2), 87. Cf. above, Munslow, manors (Lr. Millichope).

87 Glos. R.O., D2153/D/20–1, 23; /A/22.

88 *Mont. Colln.* xxii. 84–5. Hen. (d. 1689) still had fm. in 1686: Glos. R.O., D2153/A/22; S.P.L., MS. 4645, pp. 438–9.

89 Glos. R.O., D2153/D/27–8, 33–6, 38.

offered them for sale in 1805.[90] Oakham was owned by John Lowe's executors in 1842[91] and by R. B. Benson in 1910.[92] G. R. Benson put it up for sale in 1937.[93] The farmhouse is late 19th-century.

About 1565 Thomas and Anne Mynton sold lands and tithes in *EAST WALL* and Longville to Richard Lee (d. 1591).[94] The Lees of Langley already had interests in East Wall: Richard Lee had land in fee before 1517,[95] while Ralph Lee (perhaps Richard's brother) was tenant of one of the former priory's two farms in 1544 and 1550.[96] From Richard (d. 1591) the Lees' property, later East Wall farm, descended until 1819 with Acton Burnell.[97] In 1819 Sir E. J. Smythe offered a 167-a. farm in East Wall for sale.[98] In 1842 it was owned by the Lindops, the Hopwoods, Silvester James, and Elizabeth Gilbert.[99] Later it became part of Abraham Haworth's East Wall estate,[1] on the dispersal of which, in 1925, it was bought by the Hendersons, owners in 1990.[2] East Wall Farm, called New House Farm in the late 19th century,[3] is a big brick house of 1872.

Stone House farm presumably represents Wenlock priory's other East Wall farm,[4] and perhaps the 248 a. with tithes in Longville and East Wall which William Littleton conveyed to Adam Littleton in 1599. Adam (d. 1612), rector of Rushbury, was succeeded by his son Richard (d. 1654).[5] Richard's brother John (d. 1693)[6] probably followed him, and John's son Samuel was in possession in 1708. Samuel died in or before 1720[7] and the estate probably passed to his son John and later to the family of John's wife Anne Milner.[8] Edward Milner (d. 1803) of Shipton left a life interest in the farm to his wife Etheldra, with remainder to their son Richard (d. 1847). In 1858 Richard's illegitimate son Richard Childs (later Childs Milner) sold the 45-a. farm to John James, a Manchester tobacco merchant,[9] its owner in the 1870s.[10] It was later part of Abraham Haworth's East Wall estate, sold in 1925.[11] The farmhouse is a late 18th-century ashlar building of three bays and three storeys.

The Lakehouse was probably owned by Lawrence Ludlow (d. 1538).[12] Samuel Edwards (d. 1738) of West Coppice owned it, and it descended with Thonglands (in Munslow) until 1792 when Dudley Ackland sold the 30-a. farm to to John Davies, who sold it to Thomas Hamer in 1810. The Hamers owned it for a century or more.[13]

ECONOMIC HISTORY. In 1262 the prior of Wenlock had 19 a. of assarts in Longville and 35 a. in Lushcott,[14] and in 1384 a ½-virgate holding in Longville included an additional acre of 'new land'.[15] Locations of medieval arable lands are uncertain but there may have been some along the way from Lushcott to Oakham (Hoccum)[16] and south of Longville.[17] In the early to mid 16th century arable land, probably including open-field land, in Longville was put down to pasture.[18]

Until 1301 the townships were in the Long forest, and their stretch of the Edge wood (the wooded scarp of Wenlock Edge) was perhaps the 'Langsetewud' whose underwood and oaks were well kept in 1235.[19] Besides Edge wood,[20] commoners probably also had access to a large wood, indicated by the name Wood Farm, on the high ground north-west of Longville; nearer to Longville that high ground may have been heathland with some birches.[21] Commoners from the whole of Eaton-under-Heywood may have had access to Hargreaves, part of the Hay wood.[22] About 1563 the townships' stretch of the Edge wood was inclosed by agreement between the commoners,[23] but some access to Lower wood (in Easthope) may have remained for Lushcott tenants in 1785.[24] In the north land sloping down to the stream marking the Cardington parish boundary remained wooded in 1990.[25]

In 1785 the Lutwyche family estate included more than half of Longville and Lushcott, *c.* 830 a., of which *c.* 40 per cent was arable, 45 per cent grassland, and 15 per cent woodland.[26] In 1842 the percentages for the whole of the two and a half townships were 40, 56, and 4.[27] At one time flax or hemp had probably been grown extensively near Lushcott.[28]

A cattle market was laid out opposite the Longville Hotel in the early 20th century, and monthly sales of store cattle and sheep were held until *c.* 1945.[29]

90 *Mont. Colln.* xxii. 78–9, 91, 94–5; S.R.O. 4835/28; S.P.L., MS. 6865, p. 87; cf. above, Stanton Long, manors (Lower Ho. fm.).
91 S.R.O. 3315/Ti/1–2.
92 S.R.O. 4044/91, p. 55.
93 *Shrews. Chron.* 1 Oct. 1937.
94 *Cal. Pat.* 1563–6, p. 267; *V.C.H. Salop.* viii. 143.
95 B.L. Lansd. MS. 1, f. 191.
96 *L. & P. Hen. VIII*, xix (1), p. 633; *Cal. Pat.* 1550–3, 39.
97 P.R.O., CP 25/1/590/1653 Mich. no. 6; CP 43/412, rot. 12; *V.C.H. Salop.* viii. 8, 143; S.R.O. 3651, box 87, 'Sched. to which foregoing deed refers' [1812]; q. sess. rec. parcel 281, reg. of papists' deeds 1717–88, p. 123.
98 S.R.O. 4835/50.
99 S.R.O. 3315/Ti/1–2.
1 Ibid. /Ti/2, f. 59; 4044/91, p. 48.
2 Inf. from Rushbury & Dist. Record Trust; S.R.O. 5518, pp. 6–7.
3 Inf. from Mr. R. J. Henderson.
4 Above, this section.
5 P.R.O., C 142/330, no. 78.
6 *T.S.A.S.* 4th ser. iii. 305; *S.P.R. Heref.* xix (5), 49.
7 *S.P.R. Heref.* xix (5), p. x; *T.S.A.S.* 4th ser. iii. 327.
8 *S.P.R. Heref.* xvi (1), 18.
9 S.R.O. 1359, box 36, deeds, wills, etc.; 3315/Ti/1–2; *S.P.R. Heref.* i (1), 57, 59.
10 *P.O. Dir. Salop.* (1870), 52; (1879), 316.
11 S.R.O. 4044/91, p. 48; 5518, pp. 9–10.
12 P.R.O., C 3/109/35; below, Shipton, manors (Moorhouse).
13 S.R.O. 1224, box 101, deed 20 Feb. 1744/5; 1242, box 12, deeds; 4044/91, p. 49; *T.S.A.S.* xliii, p. *xvii*; above, Munslow, manors (Thonglands).
14 *Cal. Pat.* 1258–66, 207.
15 B.L. Add. Roll 67032.
16 S.R.O. 3315/Ti/1–2, fields 998, 1059–60, 1090.
17 Ibid. fields 951, 958, 960.
18 B.L. Lansd. MS. 1, f. 191; S.R.O. 5001/4/2/1.
19 Eyton, vi. 337; *Cartulary of Shrews. Abbey*, ed. U. Rees (1975), ii, p. 250; *V.C.H. Salop.* i. 485.
20 P.R.O., C 1/808/47; above, Eaton, econ. hist.
21 S.R.O. 3315/Ti/1–2, field names.
22 P.R.O., C 1/808/47; above, Rushbury, econ. hist.
23 B.R.L., MS. 501889; S.R.O. 3320/21/4; 5001/4/2/7; Shrews. Sch. Libr., James Deed 15.
24 S.R.O. 4835/2, p. 7.
25 Cf. O.S. Map 1/25,000, SO 49/59 (1981 edn.).
26 S.R.O. 4835/2, pp. 6–7, 11–13.
27 S.R.O. 3315/Ti/2.
28 Ibid. fields 1070–5; cf. H. D. G. Foxall, *Salop. Field-Names* (Salop. Arch. Soc. 1980), 31.
29 O.S. Map 1/2,500, LVII. 5 (1903 and 1926 edns.); P. J. Madeley, 'Geog. descr. of area in par. of Rushbury' (Shenstone Coll., Bromsgrove, dissertation, 1967), 49.

In 1666 Dr. Timothy Baldwyn (kt. 1670) had a 16-year lease of Lushcott's mineral rights from Edward Lutwyche;[30] it is not known if any minerals were worked. Limestone was later quarried from Wenlock Edge.[31]

Some time before 1842 there were brick kilns at East Wall and Lushcott.[32]

LOCAL GOVERNMENT. Longville and Lushcott formed part of Eaton-under-Heywood manor in the Middle Ages, being reckoned members of it in 1255.[33] There is no certain record that Wenlock priory had an interest in East Wall until 1514–15;[34] possibly it had an interest in the tithes there in 1495–6.[35]

Rushbury civil parish, to which the townships were transferred in 1883, was in the same poor-law union, highway district, rural (sanitary) district, and district as Eaton-under-Heywood C.P.[36]

CHAPEL OF EASE. Chapel field west of Lushcott, remotest of the parish's settlements from Eaton church, was so called in 1842[37] and may have been the site of a chapel.

NONCONFORMITY. There was a dissenters' meeting house at Longville in 1781.[38] Primitive Methodists met at East Wall and Lakehouse in the 1830s and 1840s[39] and a chapel was built at Lakehouse 1857–8.[40] The meeting apparently throve in the 1860s but usually had fewer than 10 members 1880–1910.[41] The chapel was sold in 1936.[42]

HUGHLEY

THE VILLAGE of Hughley stands *c.* 6 km. west-south-west of Much Wenlock. Its small rural parish (448 ha., 1,105 a.) is *c.* 3 km. from north-east to south-west and *c.* 1.5 km. wide.[43] Natural features mark only the two longer parish boundaries: Hughley brook, also known by other names,[44] divides Hughley from Church Preen and Kenley parishes to the west and north-west, and Wenlock Edge separates it from Presthope (in Much Wenlock parish) to the south-east. Harley (to the north-east) and Easthope (south-west) were formerly separated from Hughley by woods. In the late 20th century the boundary with Harley outside the remaining woodland coincided with field edges; that with Easthope ran across fields,[45] the parts of the fields in Easthope parish representing a strip of land belonging to Hughley manor that had paid tithe to the rector of Easthope by 1607.[46]

The whole parish is part of the South Shropshire hills area of outstanding natural beauty, designated in 1959.[47] From Hughley brook, at *c.* 100 m., the land slopes increasingly steeply up the scarp of Wenlock Edge to the top of the Edge almost 140 m. higher. It thus lies on the south-eastern side of the valley whose opposite slope there lies in Church Preen and Kenley parishes. The valley drains north-eastwards, from near Longville in the Dale to the Severn at Sheinton; most of the parish drains by a stream rising near Upper Hill Farm in the south and (after forming a short stretch of the north-east boundary) flowing into Hughley brook at the parish's northern extremity.[48]

The whole parish lies on the Silurian Wenlock Shales, grey silty mudstones with limestone bands; they are covered with boulder clay on the lower land but with a band of head above *c.* 130 m. in the north and *c.* 145 m. in the south. There is a small area of sand and gravel between the village and Upper Hill Farm, and one of peat stretching across the Easthope boundary. The Wenlock Shales are exposed just below the summit of Wenlock Edge where the Wenlock Limestone crops out.[49] The resulting soils, brown silt loams over silty clay loams, are more suited to forestry and pastoral farming than to arable cultivation.[50] Wenlock Edge supports tree and shrub species peculiar to the Silurian limestones and shale of the Welsh Marches, and a small area around the end of the old railway tunnel from Presthope became part of the Wenlock Edge site of special scientific interest, designated from 1954. There are alluvial deposits along Hughley brook and the mid course of its tributary stream, and the brook cuts through the Wenlock Shales where they contact underlying Llandovery Series shales: the richly fossiliferous rocks so exposed make the valley one of Britain's more important geological lo-

30 S.P.L., Deeds 985. For Baldwyn see *T.S.A.S.* 4th ser. ii. 340–3; *D.N.B.* s.v. Baldwin, Sir Tim.

31 e.g. quarries on O.S. Map 6", Salop. LVII. NW. (1890 edn.).

32 S.R.O. 3315/Ti/1–2, fields 909, 918–19, 1111.

33 *Rot. Hund.* (Rec. Com.), ii. 85.

34 S.R.O. 1224, box 342, Prior Gosnell's reg. f. 38v.

35 Eyton, iii. 314.

36 Above, Eaton, local govt.; V. J. Walsh, 'Admin. of Poor Laws in Salop. 1820–55' (Pennsylvania Univ. Ph.D. thesis, 1970), 148–50; *Kelly's Dir. Salop.* (1929), 4; *V.C.H. Salop.* ii. 215, 217; iii. 169, sources cited in n. 29.

37 S.R.O. 3315/Ti/1–2, field 1090.

38 S.R.O., q. sess. order bk. 1772–82, f. 254.

39 S.R.O. 2138/48, p. [6]; /49, 5 Mar. 1849.

40 Ibid. /66–9; O.S. Map 1/2,500, Salop. LVI. 12 (1903 edn.).

41 S.R.O. 3219/1, 4.

42 Ibid. /71, s.a. 1938.

43 O.S. *Area Bk.* (1883). Written in 1990, this article was later revised.

44 Ree or Plaish brook in 1607: H.W.R.O.(H.), HD 2/14/23; cf. *V.C.H. Salop.* iv. 9.

45 S.R.O. 1313/183; O.S. Map 1/25,000, SO 49/59 (1983 edn.); fields 1–7 in P.R.O., IR 29/29/146 and IR 30/29/146, for 'stocking', 'tree', and coppice names in Harley par.; above, Easthope, intro.; econ. hist.; below, econ. hist.

46 H.W.R.O.(H.), HD 2/14/23; S.R.O. 809, parcel 14, Easthope man. map 1732.

47 Land Use Consultants, *Salop. Hills Landscape* (Countryside Com. 1993), 4; *V.C.H. Salop.* iii. 220.

48 O.S. Map 1/25,000, SO 49/59 (1981 edn.); *V.C.H. Salop.* iv. 9; viii. 93, 124.

49 Geol. Surv. Map 1/25,000, *Wenlock Edge* (1969); *V.C.H. Salop.* i. 20 and map facing p. 1.

50 C. P. Burnham and D. Mackney, 'Soils of Salop.' *Field Studies*, ii (1), 92–3, 95; D. Mackney and C. P. Burnham, *Soils of Ch. Stretton Dist.* (Mem. Soil Surv. 1966), 93–4, 96, 189, 203–4, 228–9; *V.C.H. Salop.* iv. 9.

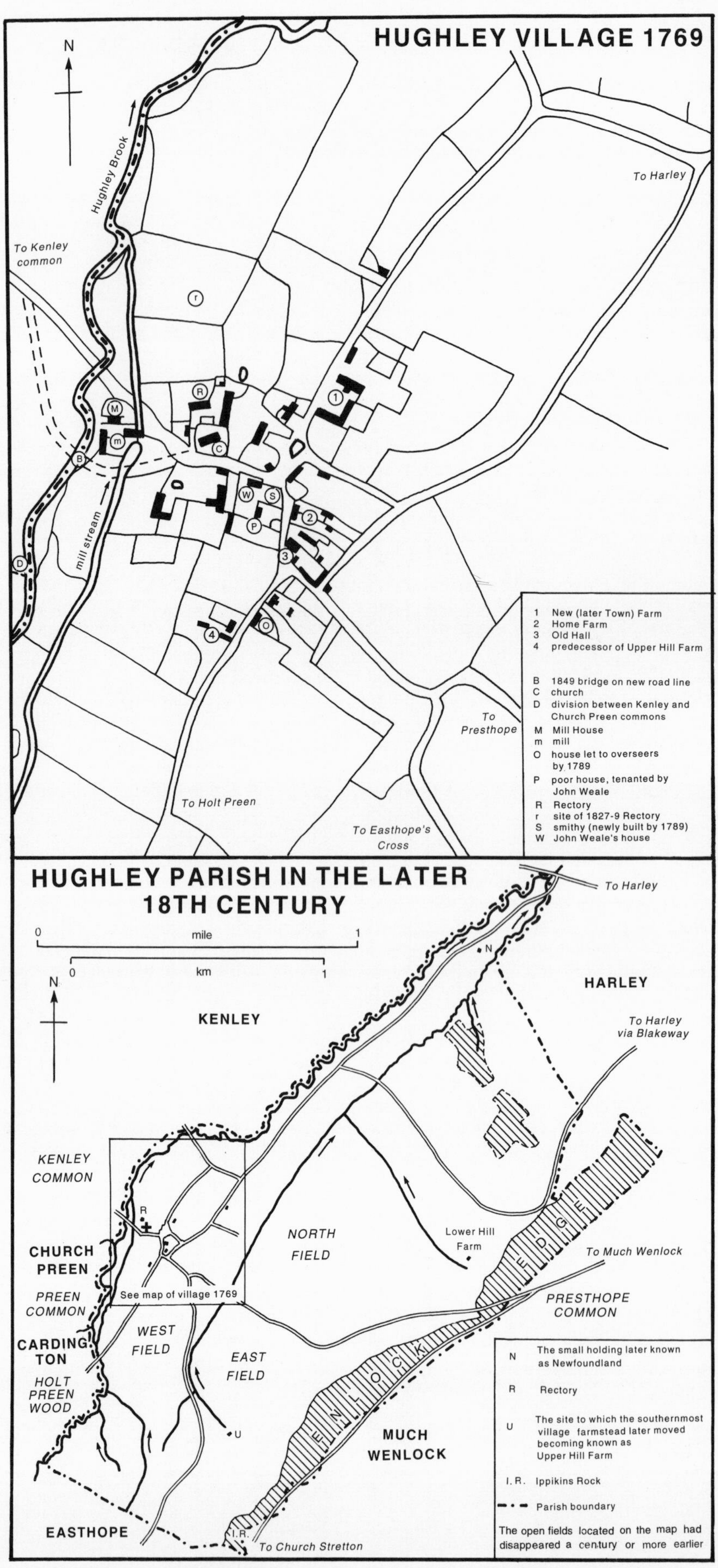

HUGHLEY VILLAGE 1769
N
Hughley Brook
To Kenley common
To Harley
mill stream
To Presthope
To Holt Preen
To Easthope's Cross
1 New (later Town) Farm
2 Home Farm
3 Old Hall
4 predecessor of Upper Hill Farm
B 1849 bridge on new road line
C church
D division between Kenley and Church Preen commons
M Mill House
m mill
O house let to overseers by 1789
P poor house, tenanted by John Weale
R Rectory
r site of 1827-9 Rectory
S smithy (newly built by 1789)
W John Weale's house
HUGHLEY PARISH IN THE LATER 18TH CENTURY
0 mile 1
0 km 1
N
To Harley
KENLEY
HARLEY
To Harley via Blakeway
KENLEY COMMON
CHURCH PREEN
PREEN COMMON
CARDINGTON
HOLT PREEN WOOD
EASTHOPE
NORTH FIELD
WEST FIELD
EAST FIELD
Lower Hill Farm
See map of village 1769
EDGE
WENLOCK
To Much Wenlock
PRESTHOPE COMMON
MUCH WENLOCK
To Church Stretton
I.R.
N The small holding later known as Newfoundland
R Rectory
U The site to which the southernmost village farmstead later moved becoming known as Upper Hill Farm
I. R. Ippikins Rock
Parish boundary
The open fields located on the map had disappeared a century or more earlier

Fig. 34 Hughley in the 18th Century

The woods (hatched) were earlier and later more extensive.

calities, designated a site of special scientific interest in 1985.[51]

Roads from Church Preen and Kenley (the latter by a new route of 1796)[52] converged from the west to ford Hughley brook north of the mill, where the valley was steep sided, and so to enter the parish and village. In 1849 the brook was bridged and the road rerouted southwards to achieve a gentler gradient.[53] Hughley's only thoroughfare, the road crosses the parish roughly eastwards and climbs the scarp of Wenlock Edge by a route shifted south in the late 18th or early 19th century; at the top, on the parish boundary where Presthope common was, it joins the road from Much Wenlock to Church Stretton.

In the mid 18th century there were other, if minor, thoroughfares. A lane beside the brook may once have led to Harley but by 1769 probably served only a smallholding at the north end of the parish. What in 1769 was still the road to Harley (via Blakeway) ran north-east from Hughley village, its two right-angled bends probably indicating the original extent of the wood (represented by Finnalls coppice) that it had to skirt; it was perhaps falling into disuse as a thoroughfare by the late 18th or early 19th century. Lanes from the village that had once led south-west via the West (or Middle) field, probably to common land in Holt Preen, and south to Easthope's Cross ('Colway') ceased to be thoroughfares probably between 1789 and 1817, when they apparently ran only to farms and fields. The former survived as a footpath, carried over the brook and into Holt Preen by a footbridge, one of several that may be successors to the 18th-century bridges thrown across the brook by farmers determined to get access to Preen and Kenley commons. The old lane to Easthope may have been replaced by a route from the Hughley–Presthope road along the foot of the Edge, though that (in existence by 1817) may have been only a private way to Upper Hill Farm, built after 1789.[54]

The railway from Much Wenlock to Craven Arms was constructed for *c.* 1.75 km. through the south-eastern edge of the parish *c.* 1865, entering it from Wenlock through a tunnel under the Edge; the nearest station was at Presthope. The line closed in 1963.[55]

Hughley village, in the 18th century the parish's only settlement apart from two or three farmsteads and perhaps a cottage near the brook, stands near the parish's western boundary on a northward spur of higher land east of Hughley brook.[56] Mill Farm and the church stand higher than the rest of the village, though not so high that

> The vane on Hughley steeple
> Veers bright, a far known sign,

for there never was a tall steeple.[57] To the west, where the land falls sharply to the brook, was the mill, but mill pool and leat were largely obliterated in the mid 20th century. The old rectory (called the Manor House from *c.* 1955)[58] and the rest of the village stand on ground falling gently north and east from the churchyard. The Old Hall near the south end of the village is 16th-century; it was presumably one of the two houses (both occupied by Corfields) taxed on 4 hearths in 1672 when four others had 2 hearths each and the rest 1.[59]

An intricate network of lanes in and around the village was progressively simplified from the late 18th century,[60] probably as two or three village farmsteads were replaced by new ones amid their fields: in the east Lower Hill Farm, tiled and timber framed, existed by 1769 as did a smallholding (known as Newfoundland by 1851)[61] in the northern tip of the parish. In the south, probably by 1817,[62] Upper Hill Farm had been built to replace a timber framed house at the south end of the village, which had been in disrepair in 1789. Most houses in the village were timber framed and thatched or tiled in 1789, but a new smithy had been built in brick and tile. In the 19th century a brick building that was possibly a Sunday school room was built a furlong out of the village on the Presthope road;[63] later it became a pheasantry or keeper's cottage.[64] The landlord rebuilt other farms and houses in locally made brick with tiled or slated roofs, and a new brick Rectory was built in 1827–9. Hughley thus acquired a distinctive appearance amid the area's stone built upland settlements.[65] By 1990 there were some modern houses and bungalows, and outbuildings near Church Farm were being converted to domestic premises that year; there were standings for mobile homes north of the old mill.[66]

Evidently by *c.* 1900 the parish was supplied with water piped by gravity from a source under Wenlock Edge.[67] A reservoir near Upper Hill Farm was made by 1972. Local residents own the system.[68]

The recorded Domesday population of Wen-

51 O.S. Map 1/25,000, SO 49/59 (1981 edn.); Geol. Surv. Map 1/25,000, *Wenlock Edge* (1969); inf. from S.C.C. Property and Planning Services Dept.

52 *V.C.H. Salop.* viii. 93.

53 By subscription: S.P.L., Watton press cuttings, vii. 46–7; date on bridge.

54 Fig. 34; S.P.L., Deeds 6232; Staffs. R.O., D. 1287 uncat., Jas. Bayles's plan 1769, Sam. Botham's plan 1789; B.L. Maps, O.S.D. 207; S.R.O. 2283/2/1; O.S. Maps 1", sheet LXI. SW. (1833 edn.); 6", Salop. L. SW. (1888 edn.); 1/25,000, SO 49/59 (1981 edn.); above, Easthope, intro.; below, this section; econ. hist.

55 Below, M. Wenlock, communications; *T.S.A.S.* lxiv. 101.

56 For this para. see Staffs. R.O., D. 1287 uncat., Bayles's plan 1769, Botham's plan 1789; O.S. Maps 1/10,000, SO 59 NE. (1977 edn.); 1/25,000, SO 49/59 (1981 edn.).

57 A. E. Housman, *A Shropshire Lad* (1896), no. 61.

58 Cf. S.R.O. 657/3, p. 233; 725/1, p. 239.

59 Below, manor; *Hearth Tax 1672* (Salop. Arch. Soc. 1949), 40.

60 For this para. cf. Staffs. R.O., D. 1287 uncat., Jas. Bayles's plan and field bk. 1769 (tracing and copy in S.R.O. 3657/2/7, 12), Botham's plan and survey bk. 1789; SA 18543; fig. 34; O.S. Map 1/2,500, Salop. L. 14 (1883 edn.).

61 P.R.O., HO 107/1990, f. 72v.

62 B.L. Maps, O.S.D. 207.

63 Below, educ.

64 O.S. Map 1/2,500, L. 14 (1902 edn.); S.R.O. 1313/183.

65 Mackney and Burnham, *Soils of Ch. Stretton Dist.* 36; below, econ. hist. (for 19th-cent. bricklayers and brickwks.); church.

66 Below, econ. hist.

67 Staffs. R.O., D. 1287 uncat., disbursements ledger 1, pp. 421, 465–6; S.P.L., SC30/162; A. H. S. Waters, *Rep. on Water Supply* (S.C.C. 1946), 36.

68 Local inf. Cf. O.S. Map 1/10,000, SO 59 NE. (1977 edn.).

lock priory's unnamed ½ hide, almost certainly at Hughley, was 1 *villanus*.[69] Seven people in Hughley paid to the subsidy of 1327,[70] 13 to the subsidy in 1524–5.[71] In 1672 hearth tax was paid by 17 households,[72] and in 1676 the adult population was 80.[73] There were 86 people in 15 households in 1793,[74] and over the next half century the population increased to a recorded peak of 127 in 1841. In the mid 19th century it was around 100, but after 1881 it fell for half a century and was 52 in 1931. Thereafter it was *c.* 60, the number of households increasing from 15 to 20 between 1971 and 1991.[75]

The parish wake was formerly held on the Sunday after the decollation of St. John the Baptist (29 August).[76] The parish is not known ever to have had a public house.[77] A men's social club, run by the curate, flourished briefly *c.* 1905.[78] Church Preen and Hughley village hall was built at Preen Common in 1934.[79]

The picturesque Ippikin's Rock on the parish boundary, jutting out from Wenlock Edge over a cave entered from Hughley woodland, generated folk tales of robber bands, buried treasure, and ghosts.[80] A distinct legend about the spot may be a garbled tradition of the death (1723) of Sir John Wolryche, the last of his family to own Hughley.[81]

MANOR. King Cenred of Mercia (reigned 704–9) gave an 8-hide estate at 'Lingen' to a nun called Feleburg and in the reign (709–16) of his successor Ceolred she gave it to St. Mildburg.[82] A suggestion that 'Lingen' is a 13th-century rendering of an earlier 'Lege' (or 'Lige') links it with ½ hide in Condover hundred held of Wenlock priory in 1086 by an unnamed son of Aelfric (Aluric). The son was perhaps the Eadric (Edric) of Wenlock who held Bourton of the priory in 1086, having inherited it from his father Aelfric; Eadric of Wenlock was the priory's only recorded tenant in fee in 1086[83] and may have been Edric the wild,[84] a leading Shropshire thegn of the Confessor's reign[85] last definitely mentioned in 1072.[86] The unnamed ½ hide is almost certainly to be identified with 'Legh' (or 'Leye'), later *HUGHLEY*, a manor held of the priory until it surrendered to the Crown in 1540.[87] Probably from 1548 it was held of the lord of Shipton by fealty and for 5*s.* a year[88] still owed in the earlier 18th century.[89]

The family which held Hughley and took its name (Lee) from the place is likely to have descended from Aelfric, for there is evidence that the family retained an interest at Bradeley, near Bourton, as late as 1281, when Sir Reynold of Lee gave a 24 *s.* rent at Bradeley to Limebrook priory (Herefs.).[90] Thomas of Lee, possibly a descendant of Ranulph of Lee (fl. 1120), probably held the manor before 1176 and probably died before 1200 to be succeeded by his son Sir Hugh of Lee (fl. 1203).[91] In the earlier 1220s Thomas of Lee was probably lord, and Hugh of Lee, perhaps Thomas's son, probably succeeded him *c.* 1225. Hugh, probably the lord by whose name the place was to be distinguished from the end of the 13th century,[92] was still alive in 1271 but was probably dead by 1283 when Sir Reynold of Lee, probably his grandson, was patron of the living and presumably lord.[93] He remained lord in 1316[94] and perhaps as late as 1337 or 1340, when the lord's name was the same.[95] He probably had a son Richard, for Richard of Lee's son Reynold of Lee occurred as lord 1369–73.[96] The latter may have left a male heir, for Roger of Hughley was patron of the living in 1391 and so probably lord of the manor.[97]

Probably after 1391 Hughley passed to the male issue of Joan, sister of Reynold (fl. 1369–73), and her husband and survivor Thomas of Gatacre,[98] lord of Gatacre (in Claverley) 1345–68:[99] they had sons William (fl. 1398–9), probably the elder dying without issue, and Thomas (fl. 1392),[1] possibly born *c.* 1327.[2] Hughley descended with Gatacre until the early 17th century.[3] Thomas Gatacre (fl. 1392) and his sons Thomas and John were alive in

69 *V.C.H. Salop.* i. 313. 70 *T.S.A.S.* 2nd ser. iv. 334.
71 P.R.O., E 179/166/130, 200.
72 *Hearth Tax 1672*, 40.
73 *Compton Census*, ed. Whiteman, 259.
74 S.P.L., MS. 6865, p. 113.
75 *V.C.H. Salop.* ii. 223; *Census* 1971, *Co. Rep. Salop.* i. 3; *Census*, 1981, Small Area Statistics: Salop.; S.C.C. Property and Planning Services Dept. inf. rep. C91/103.
76 Birm. Univ. Libr., Mytton Papers, iv. 767.
77 S.P.L., MS. 6865, f. 115.
78 *Kelly's Dir. Salop.* (1905), 111.
79 Also used by Kenley: inf. from Mr. A. Clews, clk. to Ch. Preen, Hughley, and Kenley par. council.
80 *Salop. Folk-Lore*, ed. C. S. Burne (1883), 14–15.
81 Ibid. 15; *T.S.A.S.* lv. 97–101; below, manor; M. Wenlock, manors (Presthope).
82 H. P. R. Finberg, *Early Charters of W. Midlands* (1972), pp. 139, 203, 206.
83 E. J. Dobson, *The Origins of the 'Ancrene Wisse'* (1976), 390–2; *V.C.H. Salop.* i. 313; Eyton, vi. 302; *T.S.A.S.* lv. 112–18; below, M. Wenlock, manors (Bourton).
84 A. Williams, *The English and the Norman Conquest* (1995), 91–3.
85 C. P. Lewis, 'Eng. and Norman govt. and lordship in Welsh borders 1039–87' (Oxf. Univ. D.Phil. thesis, 1985), 82–4, 97–8, 105–6. 86 Ibid. 169–76; *T.S.A.S.* lv. 113.
87 Eyton, vi. 303, 307.
88 *Cal. Pat.* 1560–3, 204; S.R.O. 566/8–49 (esp. 35), 54, 61, 63–5, 69; 637/1–8; P.R.O., C 142/345, no. 135; below, local govt.; church.
89 S.P.L., MS. 6865, doc. before p. 115.
90 *Cal. Pat.* 1272–81, 434; Dobson, *'Ancrene Wisse'*, 190–2.
91 Para. based on Eyton, vi. 303–7; W.S.L. 350/3/40, Hughley p. 1; S.P.L., MS. 2788, p. 265; S. Erdeswick, *Surv. of Staffs.* ed. T. Harwood (1844), 255–6.
92 *P.N. Salop.* (E.P.N.S.), i. 161.
93 *Reg. Swinfield* (C.S.), 524. It is not clear why Eyton (vi. 306) calls him Hugh's eldest son.
94 *Feud. Aids*, iv. 228.
95 Eyton, vi. 307; P.R.O., C 104/27, deed 16 June 1340.
96 *Reg. L. Charlton* (C.S.), 70; P.R.O., C 104/27, deed 7 July 1373. 97 *Reg. Trefnant* (C.S.), 175.
98 i.e. not to Joan and Thos. themselves, as the three pedigrees cited below, n. 1, assume.
99 *Cal. Inq. p.m.* xii, p. 187; *Abbrev. Rot. Orig.* (Rec. Com.), ii. 297.
1 Following S.P.L., MS. 2788, pp. 263 note b, 264. That pedigree makes them Joan's grandsons, but sources cited in *V.C.H. Salop.* viii. 41 nn. 95–6, imply that Joan and Alice were (as in S.P.L., MS. 4078, p. 593) successive wives of Thos. Gatacre (d. 1368), not wives of father and son namesakes. Both pedigrees probably introduce an unnecessary generation through following S.P.L., MS. 4645, p. 332, which, however, records Thos.'s two wives.
2 If he is the Thos. fl. 1374: *Cal. Inq. p.m.* xiv, p. 67.
3 For the rest of this para. see W.S.L. 350/3/40, Hughley pp. 1–2 (corr. and amplified by sources cited hereafter); S.P.L., MSS. 2788, p. 264; 4078, p. 593.

1404,[4] and the family estates, including Hughley, eventually came to John, presumably lord in 1426. He died in Henry VI's reign, and after him came his son John and grandson John. It is not certain which of these latter Johns was alive 1463–75 and in 1487, was lord in 1468, and was returned M.P. for Bridgnorth in 1470 and 1472. Possibly all those references[5] are to the third John[6] (d. 1499).[7] He may have settled Hughley, or an interest therein, on his second wife Eleanor, for after his son Robert's death in 1509 she and her husband Roger Vaughan made claims on it, against Robert's son William among others.[8] The manor was held by William (d. 1577) in 1560–1,[9] by his son Francis (d. 1599),[10] and by Francis's son William.[11] Francis was a recusant, and during his time the Crown confiscated the manor, leasing it to the Pigotts, probably Francis's relatives.[12]

William Gatacre was in debt to the Shrewsbury lawyer Thomas Harris[13] from 1607 when he mortgaged Hughley to him.[14] In 1611, as part of the ordering of Gatacre's affairs,[15] his brother-in-law Francis Wolryche[16] (d. 1614) of Dudmaston acquired Harris's interest.[17] Hughley then descended with Presthope until Godolphin Edwards of Frodesley sold it in 1745 to Orlando Bridgeman of Blodwel. Bridgeman (4th bt. 1747, d. 1764) bought Presthope in 1746 and the manors again descended together until Sir Henry Bridgeman sold Presthope in 1790.[18] He failed to sell Hughley[19] and until 1919 it remained with the Bridgemans,[20] of Weston under Lizard (Staffs.) since 1763,[21] Barons Bradford from 1794, and earls of Bradford from 1815.[22]

The estate included virtually all the parish (except the rector's glebe) in 1919 when it was sold, apparently without the manorial rights, of which no later mention is known. By 1922 some farmers owned their farms but Upper Hill farm, 206 a. at the south end of the parish, belonged to Maj. G. R. Benson of Lutwyche, who owned it until 1938[23] or later but not in 1947.[24]

The site of the house built in the early 1470s by the tenant of the demesne[25] was probably indicated by the remains of a moat, apparently near Hughley Old Hall, *c.* 1914.[26] The Old Hall near the south end of the village, described as the manor house *c.* 1830, is mainly of the later 16th century with later additions or alterations. No lord resided after the 14th century so it seems possible that the house was built for the lord's relatives the Pigotts, lessees of the manor in the late 16th century. The main range has three timber framed bays of two storeys with attics over and has a projecting central former entrance porch to full height and gabled. A two bayed gabled range to the right is probably earlier; a single-storey mid 19th-century range projecting forwards at right angles was demolished. Plaster work inside closely resembles work in Wilderhope Manor and other nearby houses; at Hughley and Wilderhope the same moulds appear to have been used, including one for a motif that has seemed to suggest recusancy at Wilderhope.[27] In 1769 Mr. Corfield—probably John (d. *c.* 1777), tenant since before 1743—occupied it as lessee of 244 a. for life,[28] and from *c.* 1778 it was held by Samuel Madeley with 193 a.[29] By 1839,[30] however, and probably for a century or more thereafter, it was divided into small dwellings and became increasingly dilapidated until its restoration, as one house again, in 1952–3.[31]

ECONOMIC HISTORY. If, as seems likely, the ½ hide in Condover hundred owned by Wenlock priory in 1086 was Hughley, it may represent a fragment of a much larger, 8-hide, estate called 'Lege' given to St. Mildburg in the early 8th century.[32] That perhaps comprised Hughley's three neighbouring manors of Harley, Kenley, and Preen, together amounting to 8

4 *Cart. Haughmond Abbey*, ed. U. Rees (1985), p. 50, supports S.P.L., MS. 2788, p. 264 (against MSS. 4078, p. 593; 4645, p. 332), in making Wm. (fl. 1398) uncle, rather than bro., of John and the younger Thos. (both fl. 1404).

5 *Visit. Salop. 1623*, i (Harl. Soc. xxviii), 197–8; *Reg. Spofford* (C.S.), 353; J. C. Wedgwood, *Hist. Parl.,Biogs. 1439–1509* (1936), 365; *T.S.A.S.* 4th ser. v. 39.

6 As assumed in S.P.L., MS. 4645, p. 332.

7 Ibid. Ld. 1493, 1497: P.R.O., C 116/213, m. 15; S.R.O. 3365/165.

8 P.R.O., STAC 2/19/229 (much damaged).

9 S.R.O. 566/54. See also *Hist. Parl., Commons*, 1509–58, ii. 196.

10 S.R.O. 566/54; 637/1; *S.P.R. Heref.* x, pp. iv, 38.

11 S.R.O. 566/54.

12 Below, nonconf.

13 *T.S.A.S.* 2nd ser. x. 77 sqq., for Harris. Cf. *V.C.H. Salop.* iii. 241 (corr. below, Corrigenda).

14 P.R.O., C 3/389/9; CP 25/2/342/5 Jas. I Trin. [no. 4].

15 P.R.O., C 3/389/9. The Gatacres kept Gatacre (*V.C.H. Salop.* iv. 27, 79, 255), Harris got Gt. Lyth (ibid. viii. 41), the Wolryches Hughley.

16 P.R.O., C 3/389/9; C 142/193, no. 39; A. E. C[orbet], *The Fam. of Corbet: its Life and Times*, ii [1918], 272–3.

17 S.P.L., Deeds 18106; P.R.O., C 142/345, no. 135.

18 W.S.L. 350/3/40, Hughley pp. 2–4 (some errors); S.P.L., Deeds 8772; MS. 6865, p. 115; *T.S.A.S.* 4th ser. ii. 90; S.R.O., q. sess. rec. box 260, reg. of gamekeepers 1711–42, 2 Nov. 1726, 20 Oct. 1733; 1742–79, 1 Feb. 1746/7, 20 Apr. 1748; Staffs. R.O., D. 1287 uncat., abstr. of Sir Hen. Bridgeman's title to Hughley and Presthope [*c.* 1790]; S.P.L., MS. 6865, doc. after p. 114; below, M. Wenlock, manors (Presthope).

19 Geo. Forester was interested: S.R.O. 7/25; S.P.L., MS. 6865, p. 114.

20 S.R.O., q. sess. rec. parcel 261, reg. of gamekeepers 1799–1807, f. 89; S.R.O. 2283/2/2/; 4044/92, pp. 1–4.

21 *V.C.H. Salop.* iv. 203.

22 Burke, *Peerage* (1949), 246–7.

23 S.P.L., SC30/162; S.R.O. 1313/183; *Kelly's Dir. Salop.* (1922), 115; S.R.O. 809, box 14, sale partic. 1938; *Wellington Jnl.* 26 Mar. 1938, p. 9.

24 S.R.O. 809, box 14, Herb. Smith & Co. to Lutwyche est. tenants 11 Nov. 1947.

25 Below, econ. hist.

26 H. E. Forrest, *Old Hos. of Wenlock* (Shrews. 1914), 39. SA 558 confuses the moat mentioned by Forrest with another earthwork, probably part of the mill and not (as suggested in *T.S.V.F.C.* v. 160) a moat.

27 W.S.L. 350/3/40, Hughley p. 10; S.P.L., SC30/162, p. 17; Dept. of Environment, *List of Bldgs. of Special Archit. or Hist. Interest: Shrews. and Atcham* [1986], 40; SA 521; above, Rushbury, manors (Wilderhope); below, econ. hist.; *Shropshire Mag.* Oct. 1953, 17–18, 35; June 1972, 32–3; cf. *T.S.A.S.* 3rd ser. iii, plates betw. pp. 16 and 17.

28 S.P.L., MS. 6865, doc. before p. 115; Staffs. R.O., D. 1287 uncat., Bayles's field bk. 1769, rentals and accts. Lady Day 1773–8 (s.v. Hughley).

29 Staffs. R.O., D. 1287 uncat., rentals and accts. Lady Day 1778 sqq. (s.v. Hughley), Botham's survey bk. 1789.

30 S.R.O. 2283/2/2, p. 2, field 89 (*recte* field 78: /2/1).

31 Forrest, *Old Hos. of Wenlock*, 39; S.P.L., SC30/162, p. 17; *Shropshire Mag.* Oct. 1953, 35; June 1972, 32–3.

32 Above, manor.

hides in 1086.[33] If so, ancient links between the four manors and the church of Wenlock may be detected in the property in Harley manor belonging to Wenlock priory and eventually incorporated in Holy Trinity parish, Much Wenlock,[34] and in the intercommoning of woods and wastes by Hughley with Kenley and Preen.[35]

In 1086 the ½ hide that was almost certainly Hughley was occupied by 1 *villanus* with 1 ploughteam, and there was room for another team.[36]

The three open fields were known as the West, East, and North fields in the late 16th century.[37] They lay near the village but probably beyond areas of meadow closer in:[38] acres in the West field (probably that known as the Middle field in 1607) touched the mill fleam;[39] the East field (probably the South field of 1607) presumably lay between 'Colway' and the road over the Edge to Much Wenlock;[40] and the North (probably Lower in 1607) field lay due east of the village.[41] The West field contained inclosed meadows in the late 16th century. By 1639 the fields may have been mostly or entirely inclosed.

No woodland was mentioned in 1086, but the manor was in the Long forest[42] until disafforestation in 1301.[43] Wenlock priory made an assart there, probably in the mid 13th century.[44] The slopes of Wenlock Edge, forming the manor's south-eastern margin, have probably always been wooded. The south-western and north-eastern ends of the manor, adjoining Easthope wood and Harley respectively, were evidently wooded in early times, the bends in the old way to Harley probably indicating the original extent of the wood later represented by Finnalls coppice.[45] Except perhaps when the whole property was leased (as to the Pigotts for 30 years in Elizabeth I's reign)[46] the lord probably kept the woods in hand.[47]

In the late 16th century the rector had common pasture in the fields and common for 6 beasts, a horse, sheep, and swine and 'other cattle'. Manorial tenants presumably enjoyed similar rights, which were perhaps being whittled away in the earlier 18th century when the lord was making them small allowances for excluding their animals from parts 'hayed up' to protect his coppices and timber.[48] Hughley was a small manor, and its tenants enjoyed common rights beyond its bounds. They intercommoned Haywood as late as the 1530s,[49] and the rector[50] and tenants certainly had rights on Kenley common.

The lord of Hughley's annual rights on Kenley common were defined in 1203 as 60 cartloads of dead wood, freedom from pannage dues for 60 pigs, and pasture rights for himself and his tenants; in return the Hughley tenants owed mowing services to the lord of Kenley. Goats which the Hughley tenants turned out on the common in 1231 were seized and kept by the Kenley men,[51] and Hughley's rights there were disputed in the 17th century.[52] It was presumably for intercommoning that the Hughley tenants owed wood hens at Christmas to the lord of Kenley, a due that had been commuted to 15*s*. a year by 1769.[53]

Hughley tenants also turned their animals out on Church Preen and Holt Preen commons, though not unchallenged in the 17th century, and they apparently pushed their claims when those two manors were in the hands of impoverished lords in the early 18th century. In return for access to Church Preen common the Church Preen demesne corn was ground free at Hughley mill and free use of a Hughley bull and boar was allowed. Even so Hughley claims on Church Preen common were strenuously resisted in the mid 18th century. In Holt Preen wood in the earlier 17th century the lord of Hughley had incited his tenants to throw open the lord of Holt Preen's attempted inclosures. Much common in Holt Preen, however, seems eventually to have been inclosed by Samuel Edwards (d. 1738); he was lord of Hughley too and, perhaps to avert opposition, added newly inclosed land to the leasehold of at least one of his principal Hughley tenants, John Corfield. Another of Edwards's tenants, the 'arbitrary' Lancelot Corfield, was an energetic leader in claims on Church Preen and other commons, carrying on the tradition of the 'Hughley Lions' who had broken open Church Preen cottagers' inclosures on the common when they would not work for the Hughley men at harvest or 'cringe and bend'.[54]

Kenley and Church Preen commons were inclosed in the 1780s. The lady of Church Preen, who had failed to inclose the common *c.* 1762, announced in 1779 that she intended to inclose it. She clearly succeeded, for in 1789 a Hughley farmer and seven smaller tenants held 140 a. in Church Preen and Holt Preen, at least 52 a. of which had evidently been allotted to their landlord; the lord of Hughley's allotments in Church Preen parish may have amounted to 70 a. In the same year two Hughley farmers held 57 a. that had been allotted to their landlord in Kenley. The rector of Hughley was allotted 3 a. in Kenley parish and 3 a. in Church Preen.[55]

33 *V.C.H. Salop.* viii. 88, 95, 126.
34 Ibid. 85; below, M. Wenlock, intro.
35 Below, this section.
36 *V.C.H. Salop.* i. 313; above, manor.
37 Para. based on H.W.R.O.(H.), HD 2/14/29, 30 (mentioning no open field 1639), 40.
38 S.R.O. 2283/2/1–2.
39 Cf. perh. ibid. field 43 (Great field).
40 Cf. S.R.O. 2283/2/1–2, field 35 (Long Butts); above, this article, intro.
41 Cf. S.R.O. 2283/2/1–2, fields 117a, 118, 140, 142 (Headland Stiles).
42 Eyton, vi. 336–7; *V.C.H. Salop.* iv. 45.
43 Mention of all the surrounding settlements but not of Hughley in Eyton, vi. 345–6; *Cartulary of Shrews. Abbey*, ed. U. Rees (1985), ii, pp. 250–1.
44 *Cal. Pat.* 1258–66, 207.
45 Fig. 34; above, this article, intro.; S.R.O. 2283/2/1–2, fields 173, 176.
46 Above, manor; below, nonconf.
47 Below, this section.
48 H.W.R.O.(H.), HD 2/14/29; S.P.L., MS. 6865, doc. before p. 115.
49 P.R.O., C 1/808, no. 47.
50 H.W.R.O.(H.), HD 2/14/31.
51 *V.C.H. Salop.* iv. 61; viii. 95.
52 S.R.O. 2922/1/3/1–43; /13/7/1–3.
53 S.P.L., Deeds 12459, receiver's acct. Mich. 1769, f. 12.
54 *V.C.H. Salop.* iv. 126; viii. 125, 127; S.P.L., Deeds 6232, esp. pp. 1–4, 6, 10; S.R.O. 1005/25–6; 2922/1/3/1–43; /13/7/1–3; above, Cardington, econ. hist.
55 *V.C.H. Salop.* viii. 95 (corr. below, Corrigenda), 125–126 (corr. below, Corrigenda); S.P.L., Deeds 12460, no. 8; Staffs. R.O., D. 1287 uncat., Botham's plan and survey bk. 1789; S.R.O. 1005/22–6; 1313/183 (locating allotments); below, church.

Hughley had no resident lord after the 14th century and in the early 1470s the demesne was let, the tenant being allowed 46*s.* 8*d.* to build a house and chamber.[56] There were usually half a dozen farms of 50–250 a. from the earlier 18th century, when at least three farms, including the two largest, were leased for lives. In 1769 there were six tenants holding less than 10 a. and one with 36 a. The farmsteads were almost all in the village, though in 1789 one had a hill barn and fold yard on the Edge near where Upper Hill Farm was later built. In 1789 nine tenants held less than 25 a., the two most substantial being the miller and the blacksmith. There was then little land on lease, and the landlord seems to have made changes to the holdings as tenants changed. There were, however, continuities: the Madeleys were farming in Hughley by 1772[57] and their descendant Frederick Hill continued to farm there until the late 19th century,[58] while from the early 16th century Corfields[59] were tenants,[60] though not continuously; they farmed there in the 1920s and at Lower Hill farm from 1948.[61]

Stone was evidently quarried in the 1460s.[62] There were fields called Coalpit field (1769) and Furnace piece (1839),[63] but the Hughley ironworks,[64] with which they were perhaps connected, was probably across the brook in Kenley parish.[65] Until the 20th century there were a few tradesmen: blacksmith, butcher, miller, and wheelwright, some of whom also held land. In the 1860s and 1870s there were carpenters and bricklayers, and a claypit and brick and tile works south of the road to Presthope at the bottom of the Edge, in existence by 1881, may date from then; it evidently closed well before 1901 when the site was wooded. By 1881, perhaps by 1872, there was a grocer's shop. Until just after the First World War successive shopkeepers combined their business with smallholding; in the 1930s the shop became a post office too, but it closed some time after 1941.[66] By the mid 1960s there was a caravan park north of the old mill, and by 1990 the development of a riding centre and 'holiday park', with caravan and tent pitches, on the 200-a. Mill farm represented a diversification of the local farming economy.[67]

Cattle were probably always of first importance: in 1747 the parish bought '3 papers upon the Distemper of Cattle', and much hay was grown.[68] In 1801 almost all the arable was under wheat and oats, about twice as much wheat as oats; small quantities of peas, barley, roots, and potatoes were also grown.[69] The arable area evidently increased and by 1839 amounted to almost half of the parish; after the mid 19th century, however, it declined.[70] Oats remained the second cereal to wheat during the 19th century, being displaced by barley in the 20th. Sheep were the main livestock in the 19th century, though significant numbers of cattle and pigs were also kept. With a local emphasis on dairying in the early 20th century cattle took first place, but pig keeping declined. Hughley was always mainly pastoral, even during the boom in arable farming after the Second World War: in the early 1960s Hughley had less arable than most of the surrounding parishes, though its pastures were perhaps less intensively stocked.[71]

TABLE XX

HUGHLEY: LAND USE, LIVESTOCK, AND CROPS

		1867	*1891*	*1938*	*1965*
Percentage of	grassland	64	80	91	67
	arable	36	20	9	33
Percentage of	cattle	22	34	69	50
	sheep	63	46	21	48
	pigs	15	20	10	2
Percentage of	wheat	52	41	45	51
	barley	10	20	19	49
	oats	38	39	26	0
	mixed corn & rye	0	0	10	0
Percentage of agricultural land growing roots and vegetables		5	4	2	2

Sources: P.R.O., MAF 68/143, no. 15; /1340, no. 5; /3880, Salop. no. 67; /4945, no. 67.

56 *V.C.H. Salop.* iv. 112.

57 S.P.L., MS. 6865, doc. before p. 115; Staffs. R.O., D. 1287 uncat., Bayles's plan and field bk. 1769, rentals and accts. Lady Day 1772 sqq. (s.v. Hughley), Botham's plan and survey bk. 1789.

58 N.L.W., Wynnstay, box 43/84 (13); S.R.O. 2283/2/1–2; P.R.O., HO 107/1990/10, ff. 71v.–72; RG 9/1861, f. 47v.; RG 11/2642, f. 38v.; *Kelly's Dir. Salop.* (1895), 105.

59 P.R.O., E 179/166/130, 200; J. J. Corfield, *The Corfields* (Rosanna, 1993), 217–18, 222–4, 226, 233, 236, 239–40; Forrest, *Old Hos. of Wenlock*, 39.

60 S.P.L., MS. 6865, doc. before p. 115; Staffs. R.O., D. 1287 uncat., Bayles's field bk. 1769, Botham's survey bk. 1789; N.L.W., Wynnstay, box 43/84 (13); S.R.O. 2283/2/2; P.R.O., HO 107/1990, f. 70v.

61 *Kelly's Dir. Salop.* (1922–9); S.R.O., reg. of electors, Shrews. const. (Oct. 1948), p. 85; S.P.L., SC9/52; Corfield, op. cit. 217, 239.

62 *V.C.H. Salop.* ii. 136.

63 Staffs. R.O., D. 1287 uncat., Bayles's plan and field bk. 1769; S.R.O. 2283/2/1–2, field 114.

64 *V.C.H. Salop.* i. 473, citing no source.

65 No ref. to a Kenley wks. ibid. 460–76; but see ibid. viii. 96; O.S. Map 1", sheet LXI. SW. (1833 edn.).

66 P.R.O., HO 107/928/10; HO 107/1990, ff. 70v.–73; RG 9/1861, ff. 47–9; RG 10/2762, ff. 12–13v.; RG 11/2642, ff. 38–40; O.S. Map 1/2,500, Salop. L. 14 (1883 and 1902 edns.); S.R.O. 1242, box 10, sale poster 1926; 1681/246/10; *Kelly's Dir. Salop.* (1885–1941).

67 Local inf.; inf. from S.C.C. Econ. Development Unit; O.S. Map 1/10,000, SO 59 NE. (1977 edn.).

68 S.R.O. 3903/Ch/1, s.a. 1747; below, church; cf. *V.C.H. Salop.* iv. 119.

69 *Home Office Acreage Returns Pt. II* (List & Index Soc. cxc), 181.

70 S.R.O. 2283/2/1–2.

71 Table XX; Salop. Agric. Returns, 1905; Mackney and Burnham, *Soils of Ch. Stretton Dist.* 29–31.

Woodland, *c.* 150 a. in the 18th, 19th, and 20th centuries, was mainly along the upper scarp of Wenlock Edge but with coppices in the north (Finnalls) and beside Hughley brook (Gwyn's).[72] By the later 18th century the coppices and hedgerows contained much good timber and the lord made *c.* £44 a year from coppice wood. In the early 18th century woodland 'a long mile in length', probably that along the Edge, was well stocked with game, and the lord employed a keeper;[73] the shooting, and indeed sporting rights over the whole estate, were let in the early 20th century.[74] Hughley brook was described as a good trout stream in the early 18th century.[75]

The village mill existed by the 16th century[76] and probably much earlier. In 1789, and probably 1834, its overshot wheel powered two sets of stones.[77] It ceased working *c.* 1920;[78] by 1952 the machinery had been demolished and one or two millstones were lying about.[79]

LOCAL GOVERNMENT. The lord of Hughley owed suit at Shipton court leet in the 16th and 17th centuries but seems usually to have defaulted.[80] His suit was perhaps personal because he held Hughley of the lord of Shipton,[81] and inquisitions and deeds which, at least until 1758, seem to represent Hughley as being within the leet of Shipton[82] are perhaps misleading, for the manor owed suit to the twice yearly leet of Bourton hundred from 1198[83] until as late as 1749, though rendering it with diminishing frequency in the earlier 18th century.[84]

The only known records of Hughley manor court baron are estreats of 1634–5[85] and presentments of 1676–7.[86]

The parish repaired the stocks in 1666, when it also made a pound which it later kept in repair.[87] The parish mended its bier in 1681 and bought a new one in 1840.[88]

From the late 17th century or earlier the vestry relieved the poor in a wide variety of ways, including grants in lieu of wages and for clothing, fuel, rent, house repair, sickness, and burial. Bastard children were maintained, and occasionally (as in 1686) a cottage was built for a poor family. A poor woman had her corn threshed on the rates in 1745. By 1694 and until 1762 there was a poor's stock of £2 out at interest. A poorhouse was rented in the mid and later 18th century, but whether continuously or not is uncertain.[89] One of two houses rented by the overseers was said in 1789 to be ripe for demolition. The other may have continued in use, for one was repaired *c.* 1815, but there was probably no house for some years before 1827 when the 'Old House' (apparently part of the village farmstead replaced by Upper Hill Farm) was taken and two male paupers ordered into it.[90] Eight adults received permanent outdoor relief and five occasional relief 1812–14; both figures increased by one in 1814–15. Expenditure on the poor averaged almost £39 between 1812 and 1834; it was above that in 1819, 1821–2, 1824–7 (peaking at almost £59 in 1824), and in the earlier 1830s.[91] There was normally one overseer, but two were appointed in 1816–17 and 1821–2.[92]

In the 18th century the vestry appointed a highway surveyor[93] and paid for road repairs out of the poor rate.[94] The vestry remained a highway authority, latterly under the 1835 Act,[95] until 1895.[96] From 1983 Hughley had a joint parish council with Kenley and Church Preen.[97]

Hughley formed part of Atcham poor-law union 1836–1930[98] and Atcham rural sanitary district from 1872.[99] When the borough of Wenlock acquired sanitary powers in 1889 Hughley was removed from it, remaining in Atcham R.S.D.[1] until 1894. It was in Atcham rural district 1894–1974 and from 1974 in the district (later that year borough) of Shrewsbury and Atcham.[2]

CHURCH. In the 1170s Peter de Leia (Lehe), prior of Wenlock, granted the chapel of Lee, i.e. Hughley, and its patronage to Thomas of Lee,

72 Staffs. R.O., D. 1287 uncat., Bayles's plan and field bk. 1769; S.R.O. 1313/183; 2283/2/2, p. 3; 4044/92, p. 3; Salop. Agric. Returns 1905; S.P.L., SC30/162; O.S. Map 1/25,000, SO 49/59 (1981 edn.).

73 S.P.L., MS. 6865, p. 114; S.R.O. 4572/6/2/56–7; regs. of gamekeepers cited above, nn. 18, 20.

74 S.R.O. 4044/92, p. 3 (pencilling); S.P.L., SC30/162.

75 S.R.O. 4572/6/2/56–7, s.v. Holt Preen.

76 P.R.O., CP 25/2/203/43 & 44 Eliz. I Mich. [no. 25]; H.W.R.O.(H.), HD 2/14/29.

77 Staffs. R.O., D. 1287 uncat., Botham's survey bk. 1789; S.P.L., MS. 201, ff. 37, 51.

78 *Kelly's Dir. Salop.* (1917), 108; (1922), 115.

79 S.R.O. 3756/147, no. 59.

80 Recorded regularly (but not invariably) in Shipton ct. rec.: S.R.O. 566/6–49, 54; 637/1–8.

81 Above, manor.

82 P.R.O., C 142/354, no. 95; C 142/374, no. 91; S.R.O. 566/63–5, 69.

83 When its suit of Condover hundred was withdrawn: *V.C.H. Salop.* viii. 1; *Rot. Hund.* (Rec. Com.), ii. 63, 85.

84 S.R.O. 1224/2/370, 390–8, 400, 404, 407–8, 410, 418–19, 500; above, Lib. and Boro. of Wenlock (Lib.: Bourton hund.).

85 P.R.O., C 116/220; C 116/221–2 (n.d., fragmentary), may also relate to Hughley.

86 In Staffs. R.O., D. 1287 uncat.

87 S.R.O. 3903/Ch/1, s.a. 1666, 1670.

88 Ibid. s.a. 1681; /Ch/2, s.a. 1839–40.

89 Ibid. /Ch/1, overseer's accts. 1665–1743; /P/1.

90 Ibid. /Ch/2 (at end), par. mtg. 10 May 1827; /P/1, s.a. 1814–15, 1815–16; 2283/2/1–2, no. 49a; Staffs. R.O., D. 1287 uncat., rentals and accts. 1772–1820, Botham's plan and survey bk. 1789. Wm. Taylor's tenancy suggests that W.S.L. 350/3/40, Hughley p. 10, is wrong in locating the poor ho. in the Old Hall.

91 *Poor Law Abstract*, H.C. 82, pp. 376–7 (1818), xix; *Poor Rate Returns*, H.C. 556, suppl. app. p. 144 (1822), v; H.C. 334, p. 179 (1825), iv; H.C. 83, p. 167 (1830–1), xi; H.C. 444, p. 162 (1835), xlvii.

92 S.R.O. 3903/P/1, s.a. 1816–17, 1821–2.

93 *T.S.A.S.* lvi. 315–16.

94 S.R.O. 3903/P/1, s.a. (e.g.) 1746, 1754, 1759, 1767, etc.

95 5 & 6 Wm. IV, c. 50: S.R.O. 3903/H/1.

96 S.R.O., S.C.C. Local Govt., etc., Cttee. min. bk. 1894–1903, p. 29; below, this section. It was not incl. in Condover highway dist. after 1889: S.R.O. 29/3.

97 Inf. from Mr. Clews, clk.

98 V. J. Walsh, 'Admin. of Poor Laws in Salop. 1820–55' (Pennsylvania Univ. Ph.D. thesis, 1970), 148–50; *Kelly's Dir. Salop.* (1929), 119.

99 *V.C.H. Salop.* ii. 212.

1 Local Govt. Bd.'s Provisional Order Conf. (No. 4) Act, 1889, 52 & 53 Vic. c. 22 (Local); above, Lib. and Boro. of Wenlock (boro. 1889–1966).

2 *V.C.H. Salop.* ii. 212; sources cited ibid. iii. 169 n. 29; Shrews. and Atcham charter 2 July 1974.

lord of the manor.[3] In early times the chapel may have been a dependency of Cound church,[4] but perhaps from the 12th century,[5] and until the later 16th century, it was in the parish of Holy Trinity, Much Wenlock.[6]

The patronage belonged to the lord of the manor.[7] In 1415 a turn was exercised by John Fitzpiers,[8] probably a lawyer or feoffee,[9] and the bishop collated by lapse in 1564 and 1580, when the patron, or perhaps the lessee of the advowson, was a recusant.[10] The lord sold his estate in 1919[11] and passed the advowson to the bishop of Hereford in 1926.[12] Next year the benefice was united with another in the bishop's patronage.[13]

Under the terms of Prior Peter's grant[14] the clerk presented was not to enjoy his benefice until he had sworn before the prior and convent to save for the mother church of Wenlock the mortuaries and other dues (*legata et cetera*) belonging to it and to pay 2*s.* a year to the priory sacrist; the clerk's own chaplain was similarly bound. The lord of the manor was to compel performance of their oaths if necessary and had to be at the priory at Christmas, on the translation of St. Mildburg (2 February),[15] at Easter and Whitsuntide, on St. John the Baptist's day (probably 29 August),[16] and on the invention of St. Mildburg (probably early November).[17] The 2*s.* pension was still paid when the priory surrendered in 1540, and in 1548 the Crown granted it with Shipton manor to Sir Thomas Palmer.[18]

Cure of souls in Hughley belonged not to the chaplain[19] or rector (as the incumbent was called by the 1350s)[20] but to the vicar of Much Wenlock, whose consent was required for solemnizing a marriage at Hughley in 1546.[21] Nevertheless Wenlock priory did not appropriate Hughley's tithes,[22] and apparently by 1576 the rector could bury.[23] The church was called parochial by 1592.[24] The rectory was united informally with the living of Church Preen 1851–74 and from 1891;[25] the union became formal in 1927.[26] Hughley was served from Frodesley 1943–65, from Harley 1965–73, and from Much Wenlock after 1973.[27] In 1981 the benefice of Hughley with Church Preen was merged in the Wenlock team ministry.[28]

The living was valued at less than £4 a year in 1291 and £4 7*s.* 8*d.* in 1536,[29] perhaps an underestimate: the benefice was worth £6 13*s.* 4*d.* in 1366 and £5 3*s.* 4*d.* in 1414; a rector retired with a pension of £4 in 1415, though that may have prevented his successor from residing.[30]

By the late 16th century the rector had something over 25 a. of glebe with common rights. By the late 18th century he received a 40*s.* modus for the tithe hay and clover of the whole parish, which, had it been taken in kind, would allegedly have equalled or surpassed all his other tithes, then worth *c.* £47 a year; in return for accepting the modus the rector was exempt from parochial taxes. His glebe was then almost 35 a. valued at just over £29 a year, and the lord of the manor paid the rector's land tax. At the inclosure of Church Preen and Kenley commons in the 1780s the rector was allotted 3 a. in each parish. In 1810 the parsonage grounds and glebe amounted to almost 37 a. For his tithes *c.* 1810 the rector took the eleventh wheatsheaf, the tenth cock of barley, oats, and peas, and the hay modus, then £1 18*s.* 10*d.*; clover mowed for seed was tithed as grain. The tenth fleece and the tenth lamb, pig, and goose belonged to the rector, and he took 20*d.* a score for over-wintered sheep, 6*d.* for a cow in calf, 1*d.* for a barren cow, 4*d.* for a swarm of bees, and 8*d.* for 'running of the mill'; he also tithed apples and potatoes.[31]

Worth £30 *c.* 1708, the rectory was augmented in 1724 with the aid of Queen Anne's Bounty.[32] The rector's annual income was £146 in 1835,[33] probably less than half of it in tithes, which yielded just over £56 a year 1829–35 on an 'exceedingly low' composition as they were no longer collected in kind;[34] they were commuted to £73 0*s.* 10*d.* in 1839.[35] In 1851 the living was worth £160 gross: besides the tithe rent charges there was £32 a year from glebe and £55 from other land,[36] presumably that bought by Queen Anne's Bounty and the Church Preen and Kenley allotments:[37] in 1887 the glebe, 88 a., included all that.[38]

3 S.R.O. 1224, box 342, Prior Gosnell's reg. f. 7v.; Eyton, vi. 303–4, 307; cf. *V.C.H. Salop.* ii. 46; A. B. Emden, *Biog. Reg. Univ. Oxf. to 1500*, iii. 2188.

4 e.g. of the arguments *re* Preen par. in *T.S.A.S.* lxx. 194.

5 i.e. before the 1170s grant to Thos. of Lee, and perh. from the time (*c.* 1110 x 1187) when Wigwig was taken into Holy Trinity par.: below, M. Wenlock, churches.

6 *T.S.A.S.* lxx. 199 n. 68; below, this section.

7 Eyton, vi. 307–8; *Reg. Trillek*, 386; *L. Charlton*, 70; *Spofford*, 353; *Stanbury* (C.S.), 185; *Bothe* (C.S.), 347; *Dioc. of Heref. Institutions (A.D. 1539–1900)*, ed. A. T. Bannister (Heref. 1923), 23, 44, 49, 60, 69, 84, 108–9, 131, 138, 147, 166, 202, 209 (sometimes confusing Hughley and Highley).

8 *Reg. Mascall* (C.S.), 181; cf. ibid. 174, 185.

9 e.g. of the earl of Arundel (d. 1415) and his kinsman Ld. Charlton (d. 1421): *Cal. Pat.* 1413–16, 336, 344; 1416–22, 63; *Cal. Fine R.* 1430–7, 77, 81; 1437–45, 165, 195; *V.C.H. Salop.* iii. 56.

10 Bannister, *Heref. Institutions*, 16, 26; below, nonconf.

11 Above, manor.

12 Heref. Dioc. Regy., reg. 1919–26, p. 427.

13 Below, this section.

14 Para. based on Eyton, vi. 303–4.

15 Rather than 26 May, as suggested in Eyton, vi. 304 n. 5–6: cf. *T.S.A.S.* lvii. 146.

16 Above, this article, intro., for date of par. wake.

17 The date of Wenlock's feast of relics: S.R.O. 1224/2/6.

18 Dugdale, *Mon.* v. 81; *Cal. Pat.* 1548–9, 14–15.

19 *Reg. S. Langham* (C. & Y.S.), 90.

20 Below, this section

21 *T.S.A.S.* vi. 118.

22 Eyton, vi. 307–8.

23 *S.P.R. Heref.* i (3), 1.

24 *Recusant Roll*, ii. 265.

25 Cf. *S.P.R. Heref.* i (3), p. iv; xvi (2), p. iv; *V.C.H. Salop.* viii. 127; S.R.O. 2283/1/1; 3903/SRg/1.

26 Heref. Dioc. Regy., reg. 1919–26, p. 442; 1926–38, p. 28; *V.C.H. Salop.* viii. 127.

27 *Crockford* (1969–70), 182 (s.v. Butler, C. E. M.); (1971–2), 667 (s.v. Morgan, J. A.); (1977–9), 3 (s.v. Acheson, R. R.); (1980–2), 1005 (s.v. Thomas, M.).

28 Heref. Dioc. Regy., reg. 1969– (in use), pp. 397–9.

29 *Tax. Eccl.* (Rec. Com.), 176; *Reg. Bothe*, 369; cf. *Valor Eccl.* (Rec. Com.), iii. 209.

30 *Reg. Langham*, 90; *Reg. Mascall*, 119, 182; *Reg. Lacy* (C.S.), 47.

31 H.W.R.O.(H.), HD 2/14/29–32, 40; S.P.L., MS. 6865, p. 117; S.R.O. 515/4, p. 231; *V.C.H. Salop.* viii. 125; above, econ. hist.

32 Heref. Dioc. Regy., reg. 1683–1709, f. 188v.; C. Hodgson, *Q. Anne's Bounty* (2nd edn.), pp. cxxxix, ccxc.

33 *Rep. Com. Eccl. Revs.* [67], pp. 440–1, H.C. (1835), xxii.

34 P.R.O., IR 18/8127.

35 S.R.O. 2283/2/2.

36 P.R.O., HO 129/359/6.

37 S.P.L., MS. 6865, p. 117.

38 *Return of Glebe Land, 1887*, H.C. 307, p. 59 (1887), lxiv.

Osbert, the chaplain who attested the prior's grant in the 1170s, may have been deputy to the incumbent of Hughley chapel.[39] Some of the 14th-century incumbents may have been related to their patron;[40] one, Master Philip of Lee, rector and pluralist in the 1350s and 1360s, was a civil lawyer.[41] From the 17th century[42] almost all rectors were graduates[43] and many held a living, mostly nearby, in plurality, Quatt 1695–1708,[44] Church Preen 1708–22, Easthope 1745–77,[45] Sheinton 1777–86, Little Wenlock 1786–1803,[46] Willey 1804–13,[47] Ospringe (Kent) 1815–26,[48] and Church Preen almost continuously after 1851.[49] Curates were employed at least some of the time.[50] W. H. Shields, 1903–7, was the last absentee rector,[51] C. E. B. Deacon, 1936–43, the last resident.[52]

Some pluralists resided in Hughley as did Jacob Littleford, his kinsman's curate there 1698–1708 and rector 1708–22.[53] He gave the third of the four new bells of 1701[54] and left charitable bequests for the parish.[55] The parsonage was said to be five bays including the barn in 1607 but four bays including a backhouse and excluding a barn of three bays in 1639.[56] It was rebuilt in brick 1711–23, Littleford's work being finished by his successor,[57] in whose time the patron gave a new silver chalice and paten (1725).[58] A new parsonage, designed by W. & J. Nicklin of Tipton (Staffs.), was built in 1827–8 by the first resident rector for fifty years; the patron gave £100.[59] The house was sold with 5¼ a. in 1953.[60]

In the early 18th century, and until 1777 or later, there were two Sunday services, one with a sermon. Communion was celebrated at Christmas, Easter, and Michaelmas.[61] By the 1790s there was communion four times a year, but congregations were small, with barely a dozen communicants. There were psalm singers *c.* 1806. In 1851, as in the 1790s, Sunday services were alternately morning and afternoon; on Census Sunday 60 adults and 22 children attended afternoon service.[62]

The church of *ST. JOHN THE BAPTIST*,[63] built of limestone rubble with sandstone ashlar dressings, has a structurally undivided nave and chancel with a timber south porch.[64] The thickness of the walls suggests that they may be 12th-century but the earliest datable features are two 13th-century lancet windows, with square-topped shouldered rear arches, in the north wall of the nave. All the other windows and the north and south nave doorways are 14th-century. The east and west windows are of three lights and have curvilinear, almost flamboyant, tracery, the east unusual in form and the west perhaps renewed; the east window contains fragments of late medieval glass. In the chancel there is a 14th-century pillar piscina against the south wall, and a 14th-century female corbel head in the east wall presumably served as an image bracket.[65] The porch (repaired in the 1680s and 1690s and in 1702 and 1900)[66] has sides containing continuous lights with 14th-century tracery. A late medieval rood screen displays a richness of decoration unparalleled in the county;[67] with others in the Welsh Marches it may have been made in or near Ludlow, perhaps *c.* 1500.[68] It intercepts a nave window on the south and a chancel window on the north but may originally have stood farther west; if so, it was presumably moved before 1786, when the present division of nave and chancel was already fixed.[69] A steeple or bell turret, timber with brick infill and formerly surmounted by a flèche, was erected in 1700[70] and contains a clock presented in 1893 by the patron to celebrate his colt Sir Hugo's win in the 1892 Derby.[71] The octagonal font looks 18th-century but apparently replaced an 'ancient circular' one, the 'clumsy workmanship of the village artist', that was in the church *c.* 1830.[72]

The church was restored and repaired in 1842 with aid from the Incorporated Church Building

39 Eyton, vi. 304, 308.

40 Hugh and Phil. of Lee, inst. 1313 and 1353, and Reynold of Hughley, inst. 1391: Eyton, vi. 308; *Reg. Trillek*, 386.

41 *Reg. Langham*, 90; Emden, *Biog. Reg. Oxf. to 1500*, ii. 1143.

42 Rest of para. based on *S.P.R. Heref.* i (3), pp. iii– iv; xvi (2), p. iv.

43 Cf. *T.S.A.S.* 3rd ser. viii. 47; 4th ser. ii. 71; *Alum. Cantab. 1752–1900*, iii. 605; *Crockford* (1940), 348, 833 (s.vv. Deacon, C. E. B., Lloyd, R. A.).

44 S.R.O. 4237/Rg/2, 12 Mar. 1707/8.

45 *S.P.R. Heref.* xix (4), p. vi, where 1744 should read 1745.

46 *T.S.A.S.* 4th ser. vi. 296, 299; *V.C.H. Salop.* xi. 90.

47 S.R.O. 3568/MRg/1; 3903/Rg/4–6.

48 *Alum. Cantab. 1752–1900*, iii. 605.

49 Above, this section.

50 *S.P.R. Heref.* i (3), p. iv; Heref. Dioc. Regy., reg. 1772–1802, ff. 34v., 51v.; 1791–1821, pp. 175, 241; 1822–42, p. 2; 1902–19, p. 125.

51 *S.P.R. Heref.* i (3), p. iv; Heref. Dioc. Regy., reg. 1902–19, pp. 125, 207; S.R.O. 3903/SRg/1.

52 *Crockford* (1969–70), 182, notes C. E. M. Butler as sequestrator 1943–65.

53 And perp. cur. of Ch. Preen (where there was no ho.) 1700–22: *S.P.R. Heref.* i (3), pp. iii, 27; xvi (2), p. iv; *V.C.H. Salop.* viii. 127; *Alum. Oxon.* 1500–1714, iii. 918.

54 H. B. Walters, *Ch. Bells of Salop.* (Oswestry, 1915), 94; S.R.O. 3903/Rg/2, note on back endpaper.

55 Below, educ.; charities.

56 H.W.R.O.(H.), HD 2/14/30, 40.

57 S.R.O. 3903/Rg/2, note on back endpaper; W.S.L. 350/3/40, Hughley p. 10.

58 D. L. Arkwright and D. W. Bourne, *Ch. Plate of Archd. of Ludlow* (Shrews. 1961), 35.

59 H.W.R.O.(H.), HD 8, boxes 31–2, plans, etc. (ref. supplied by Mr. C. J. Pickford); Heref. Dioc. Regy., reg. 1822– 42, pp. 82–4, 150; *S.P.R. Heref.* i (3), p. iv; W.S.L. 350/3/40, Hughley p. 10; SA 19942.

60 S.P.L., SC10/31.

61 H.W.R.O.(H.), HD 5/14/1/15A; 5/15, Hughley; S.P.L., MS. 6865, p. 117.

62 S.P.L., MS. 6865, p. 117; S.R.O. 3903/Ch/2, s.a. 1805– 6, 1806–7; P.R.O., HO 129/359, no. 6.

63 *T.S.A.S.* vi. 110; B.L. Add. MS. 30316, f. 30.

64 E. A. Gee, 'Hist. and arch. acct. of Wenlock priory and its dependent churches from earliest times to 1307' (Birm. Univ. M.A. thesis, 1937), plan facing p. 263.

65 Pevsner, *Salop.* 154–5 and pl. 28; Cranage, iii. 197– 9; St. Deiniol's Libr., Hawarden, Sir Steph. Glynne's ch. notes, xc. 23–4; S.P.L., J. H. Smith colln. no. 111 (a framed version in S.P.L. shows greater detail); MS. 372, vol. i, p. 15.

66 S.R.O. 3903/Ch/1, s.a. 1684, 1689, 1693, and 1702; Heref. Dioc. Regy., reg. 1883–1901, pp. 719–20.

67 Pl. 8; A. Vallance, *Eng. Ch. Screens* (1936), 44 and pl. 104; Pevsner, *Salop.* 154–5 and pl. 28.

68 F. H. Crossley and M. H. Ridgway, 'Screens, Lofts, and Stalls situated in Wales and Mon.: Pt. II', *Arch. Cambr.* cxi. 61–7, 85, and pl. IV(*b*).

69 S.P.L., MS. 372, vol. i, p. 15 (distinctive roofings).

70 B.L. Add. MS. 21237, f. 378v.; S.P.L., MS. 372, vol. i, p. 15.

71 *Ch. Cal. Dioc. of Heref.* (1894), 144; *Shropshire Mag.* Nov. 1973, p. 25; *Shrews. Chron.* 3 June 1892, pp. 3, 5.

72 W.S.L. 350/3/40, Hughley p. 11.

Society; the work included the repewing of the nave to add 39 sittings, 35 of them free. The new front pews met the screen whose bottom panels were evidently then preserved by being fixed to the east wall of the chancel as a sort of dado.[73] In the mid 19th century the screen, on which traces of original colour were visible in 1866, was painted 'oak'. Norman Shaw restored the trussed rafter roof in the 1870s, when, presumably, a 'modern stuccoed' ceiling (perhaps early 19th-century) was removed;[74] the boarding and most of the ribs and bosses are probably from that time. It was perhaps about then that the sunken boiler house was built against the north wall of the chancel.[75] Further restoration *c.* 1900 included repair of the east window jambs, repewing and reflooring of the nave, and removal from the nave 'gangways' of many 14th-century tiles[76] with incised decoration (including St. Mark's lion) and traces of original colouring; the tiles were reset on the chancel floor. It was probably then that part of the medieval altar slab was moved from the floor at the chancel entrance and fixed to the east wall north of the altar. The repewing enabled the chancel dado panels to be restored to the screen.[77] The chancel south window was glazed in memory of Lord Bradford (d. 1915).[78] Work done in 1927 included the provision of a raked floor west of the nave doors to receive a two-manual organ,[79] though in 1990 the church had only a harmonium, which stood against the screen next to a Jacobean pulpit in the north-east corner of the nave. A long plain oak chest stood beneath the west window.

In 1552–3 the church had a chalice and paten of silver and two bells.[80] New plate and four new bells by Rudhall of Gloucester were given in the early 18th century.[81]

The registers begin in 1576 and, save for the 20th-century loss[82] of the 1812–37 marriage register, are complete thereafter.[83]

The churchyard was extended north and northwest in 1923 and 1977.[84]

NONCONFORMITY. William and Francis Gatacre, successive lords of the manor and patrons of the rectory in Elizabeth I's reign, were recusants[85] but did not reside in Hughley. It is possible that their kinsmen the Pigotts, Crown lessees of the manor and advowson, were also unfriendly to protestantism, for the bishop collated by lapse in 1580.[86] There were no nonconformists in the parish in 1676 or 1716.[87]

Hughley was in the Broseley Wesleyan circuit in 1827–8[88] and Bishop's Castle Primitive Methodist circuit 1850–5.[89]

EDUCATION. Jacob Littleford, rector (d. 1722), left the parish 6*s.* a year to keep a poor child at school, but the money was misapplied in bread for the poor.[90] In 1819 the poor had no means of education, though they were 'very desirous' of it. A Sunday school begun in 1827 was supported by the rector in the 1830s and may still have existed in 1842 when a school room, possibly that a furlong south-east of the village, was mentioned.[91] By the 1880s children attended Church Preen National school opened in 1872.[92]

CHARITIES FOR THE POOR. Jacob Littleford left 4*s.* a year for the rector to distribute to the poor. With his legacy for the schooling of a poor child it was spent on bread doles.[93] In the early 20th century 10*s.* (12*s.* 6*d.* after the parish clerkship, to which Littleford had left 2*s.* 6*d.* a year, had lapsed *c.* 1917)[94] was distributed annually in gifts of 2*s.* 6*d.* or 5*s.*, but the annuity, charged on the Holt Preen estate, was lost in 1921.[95] By 1975 the only charity applicable to the parish was a share in Capt. S. H. Christy's, left in 1914 for poor widows in Cardington and neighbouring parishes.[96]

73 Heref. Dioc. Regy., reg. 1822–42, p. 654; S.R.O. 2283/3/1. Cf. Cranage, iii. 198–9; photo. in ch. showing altar slab and screen panels together (perh. briefly *c.* 1900) on E. wall.

74 S.P.L., MS. 6865, p. 118 (ceiling part wood, part plaster in 1790s); W.S.L. 350/3/40, Hughley p. 11; Glynne's ch. notes, xc. 23–4; Cranage, iii. 198.

75 Presumably contemporary with the heating system apparent in Cranage, iii, pl. facing p. 198.

76 Heref. Dioc. Regy., reg. 1883–1901, pp. 719–20; Glam. R.O., Cardiff, Deeds II, no. 6067.

77 Plate 8.

78 Cf. S.R.O. 2283/3/2–3.

79 Heref. Dioc. Regy., reg. 1926–38, p. 40.

80 *T.S.A.S.* 2nd ser. xii. 97, 311, 327.

81 Above, this section.

82 Cf. E. C. Peele and R. S. Clease, *Salop. Par. Doc.* (Shrews. [1903]), 192; S.R.O., archivist's office file P142.

83 S.R.O. 3903/Rg/1–6, 8; regs. in team rector's possession. Cf. *S.P.R. Heref.* i (3); H.W.R.O.(H.), bp.'s transcripts. There are many 16th- and 17th-cent. Hughley entries in Stanton Long reg.: S.R.O. 3901/Rg/1.

84 Heref. Dioc. Regy., reg. 1919–26, pp. 304–5; 1969– (in use), p. 261.

85 *Hist. Parl., Commons*, 1509–58, ii. 195–6; *Recusant Roll*, i (Cath. Rec. Soc. xviii), 265; ii (Cath. Rec. Soc. lvii), 132, 135; Bannister, *Heref. Institutions*, 23.

86 Bannister, *Heref. Institutions*, 23, 26; cf. above, manor [Old Hall]; econ. hist.

87 *Compton Census*, ed. Whiteman, 259; H.W.R.O.(H.), HD 5/14/1/15A.

88 Shrews. Sch. Libr., Broseley Wesleyan Meth. circuit bk. 1815–41.

89 S.R.O. 2138/58, 60–3; cf. *V.C.H. Salop.* ii. 15. No mention in P.R.O., HO 129/359.

90 *4th Rep. Com. Char.* H.C. 312, p. 268 (1820), v; *S.P.R. Heref.* i (3), pp. iii, 27.

91 *Digest Educ. Poor*, H.C. 224, p. 754 (1819), ix (2); *Educ. Enq. Abstract*, H.C. 62, p. 776 (1835), xlii; Heref. Dioc. Regy., reg. 1822–42, p. 654; O.S. Map 1/2,500, L. 14 (1883 edn.).

92 *Kelly's Dir. Salop.* (1885), 865; *V.C.H. Salop.* viii. 128.

93 *4th Rep. Com. Char.* 268.

94 *Kelly's Dir. Salop.* (1917), 108 (last mention).

95 Perh. through John Todd's dispersal of the former Sparrow est.: cf. S.R.O. 4693/91; *V.C.H. Salop.* viii. 126.

96 *Review of Local Chars.* (S.C.C. 1975), 43–4; above, Cardington, charities.

LINLEY

LINLEY was a small parish on the right bank of the Severn *c.* 4 km. south-east of Broseley. Its rural character was little altered by the enterprises of miners and ironmasters from the 17th to the early 19th century.[97]

The 19th-century parish comprised 643 a. (260 ha.). In 1934 the civil parish was enlarged by the addition of Caughley from Barrow C.P., but Linley C.P. was absorbed by Barrow C.P. in 1966.[98] This article treats the parish within its 19th-century boundary.

Linley's boundary was largely formed by water:[99] the Severn on the east, Dean brook[1] on the north, Linley brook on the south, and tributaries of Dean and Linley brooks on parts of the west. In 1639 the parish boundary north-east of Frog mill, which was on Linley brook, perhaps included fields on the right bank of Linley brook that were later in Astley Abbots.[2] The stream called Hifnal ('Issnall') brook in 1775 was probably the lowest, 0.75-km., length of Dean brook.[3]

From Linleygreen at *c.* 140 m. the land falls eastwards to the Severn at *c.* 34 m.; it also falls north and south to Dean and Linley brooks.[4] Geologically the parish divided into three: the eastern half was on Coalport Beds of the Upper Coal Measures; in the western half shales and sandstones of the Temeside Group of the Downtonian Series lay south of the church, while to the north were productive Middle Coal Measures consisting of shales, clays, and fireclays, with sandstones, and coal and ironstone seams. Some limestone occurs along Dean brook and near Frog mill on Linley brook.[5]

The Broseley–Bridgnorth road, locally called Linley Lane, ran north–south via Linleygreen and the church and was a turnpike 1756–1867.[6] In 1796 the owners of Preen's Eddy bridge (in Broseley) built a new straight section of 1 km. from Linleygreen to Lower Smithies, south-west of Linley church, in Willey and Astley Abbots; the old road, east of the new, survived as a drive to the Hall and church.[7] In 1639 a lane ran east from Linley Hall to Hifnal, an area in the north-east corner of the parish near the Severn. It survived as a bridleway in 1983. Another lane ran east from the Hem to the Severn, passing through the area of Colliersworks and of the fulling mill and crossing Linley brook to reach the Severn in Astley Abbots parish. By 1814 the eastern part had been diverted southwards via Frog mill; after 1949 the section from the Hem to the mill site disappeared, but the rest of that route survived as a track in 1983.[8]

The river was evidently the main outlet for Linley's industrial trade in the later 18th and early 19th century. In 1785 the lessees of mining rights had permission to lay a railway to a wharf on the Severn just in Astley Abbots parish.[9] Along the Severn bank ran the Coalbrookdale–Bewdley tow path, made *c.* 1800.[10] The Severn Valley line of the West Midland Railway (later G.W.R.), which opened in 1862, ran along the river bank, with Linley station in Astley Abbots parish.[11]

Linley's name, 'lime-tree wood',[12] attests its wooded character in the Saxon period. The earliest clearance was presumably in the area around Linley church and the Hall; church and manor were recorded in the 12th century.[13] By the 14th century there was settlement in the north at Darley, mainly in Caughley and Willey, where a few houses remained in the 20th century.[14] By the early 17th century the modern landscape had evolved.[15] Linley church stood isolated, while 200 m. south one or two cottages stood among the farm buildings around Linley Hall. To the north of Linley hamlet, near the Willey boundary, a few cottages clustered around Linleygreen, mentioned as a place of residence in 1538.[16] Probably the only substantial outlying farmhouse was the Hem, on the southern parish boundary.[17] The open fields had been inclosed. In the eastern half of the parish there was a coal works,[18] its site apparently covered by Colliersworks coppice by the early 19th century.[19] In 1729 Richard Lacon, lord of the manor, built Linley Villa[20] at Linleygreen, overlooking the Hall and church: of brick, its main element a central canted and embattled bay, the house was extended in the 18th and 19th centuries. The pattern of settlement hardly changed after 1800.

97 Below, econ. hist. This art. was written in 1984.

98 O.S. *Area Bk.* (1883); *V.C.H. Salop.* ii. 229 note u, 237; above, Barrow, intro.; Caughley, intro.

99 Fig 35; O.S. Map 1/25,000, SO 69 (1956 edn.); S.R.O. 4427/T/1.

1 So called 1609; S.R.O. 1224, box 75, Caughley map of 1609.

2 S.R.O. 4890.

3 S.R.O. 1224, box 111, deed 20 Sept. 1775; cf. O.S. Maps 6", Salop. LI. SE. (1888 edn.).

4 O.S. Maps 6", Salop. LI. SE., SW. (1888 edn.).

5 Geol. Surv. Map 1", drift, sheet 153 (1968 edn.); J. Randall, *Broseley and Its Surroundings* (Madeley, 1879), 324–6.

6 S.R.O. 1224/1/9–10, 16; 4427/H/1; S.P.L., plan 20; 29 Geo. II, c. 60.

7 R. Baugh, *Map of Salop.* (1808); S.P.L., MS. 2479; above, Broseley, communications.

8 S.R.O. 4890; B.L. Maps, O.S.D. 213; O.S. Maps 6", SO 69 NE. (1954 and 1978 edns.); 1/25,000, SO 69/79 (1983 edn.); below, econ. hist.

9 S.R.O. 3614/1/276; 4890 (for Lady leasow). There is no evid. that the rly. was built.

10 Under 39 Geo. III, c. 8 (Local and Personal): C. Hadfield, *Canals of W. Midlands* (1969), 124.

11 Above, Broseley, communications; O.S. Map 6", Salop. LI. SE. (1888 edn.); *T.S.A.S.* lxiv. 97.

12 *P.N. Salop.* (E.P.N.S.), i. 177.

13 Below, manor; church.

14 Above, Caughley, intro.; below, Willey, intro.

15 S.R.O. 1224/1/9–10, 16.

16 *T.S.A.S.* vi. 99.

17 Hem means border; Ekwall, *Eng. Place-Names* (1960), 233; H. D. G. Foxall, *Salop. Field-Names* (Salop. Arch. Soc. 1980), 22.

18 S.R.O. 4890.

19 B.L. Maps, O.S.D. 213; Baugh, *Map of Salop.*; C. & J. Greenwood, *Map of Salop.* (1827); S.R.O. 4427/T/1; O.S. Maps 6", Salop. LI. SE., SW. (1888 edn.).

20 Date stone.

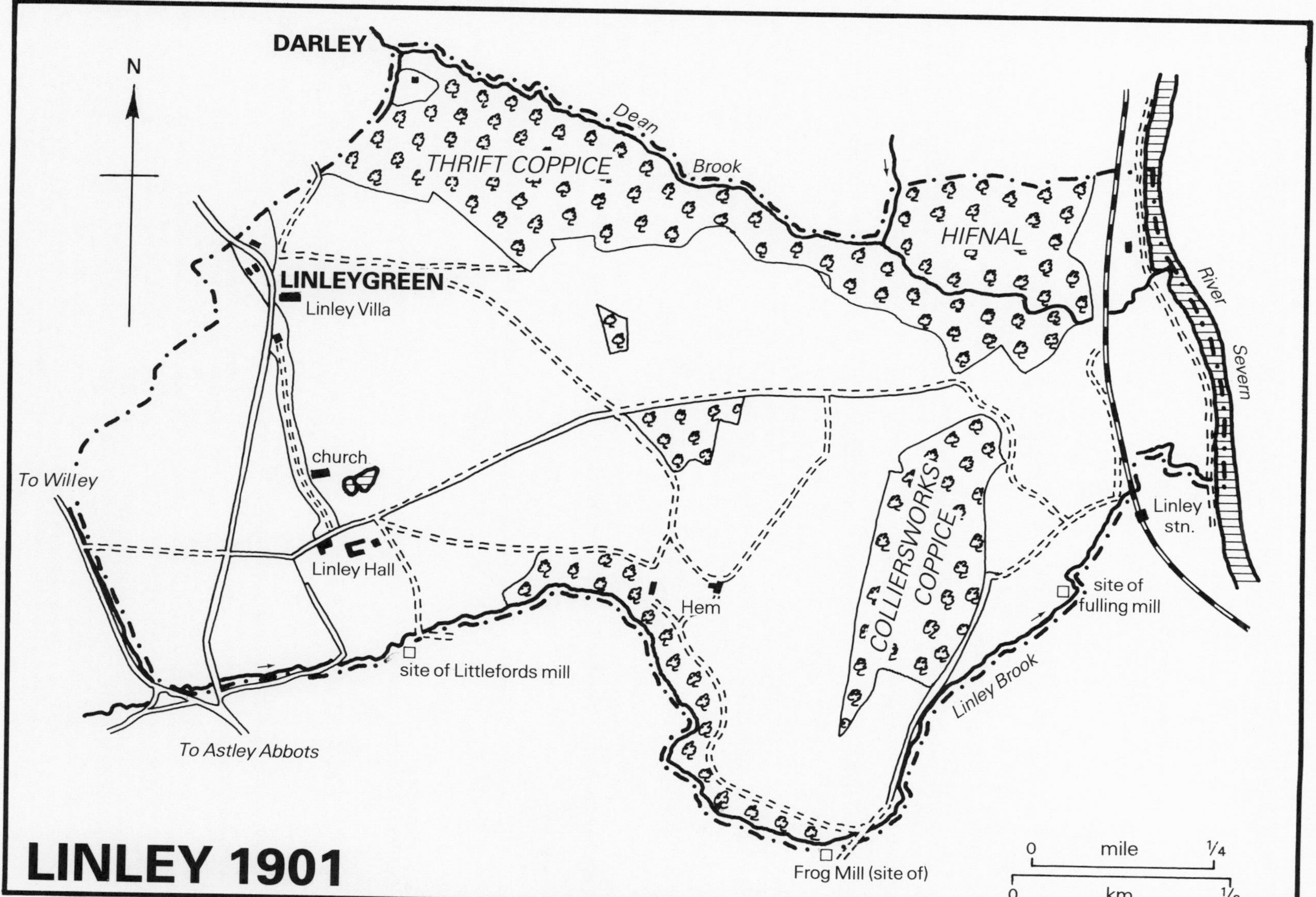
LINLEY 1901
DARLEY
N
Dean Brook
THRIFT COPPICE
HIFNAL
River Severn
LINLEYGREEN
Linley Villa
church
To Willey
Linley Hall
Hem
COLLIERSWORKS COPPICE
Linley stn.
site of fulling mill
site of Littlefords mill
Linley Brook
To Astley Abbots
Frog Mill (site of)
0
mile
1/4
0
km
1/2

Fig. 35

Eight people paid to the subsidy of 1327,[21] and 16 men were mustered in 1542.[22] By 1642 there were 20 men over 18 in the parish.[23] In 1672, apart from the Hall and the Hem, six houses paid tax on three hearths or fewer.[24] In the earlier 19th century the parish's population was usually *c.* 100, though reaching 131 in 1811. In 1851 there were 19 inhabited houses in the parish. The population declined in the later 19th century, particularly in the 1880s, to 55 in 1891, at which level it remained in 1931.[25]

Three alesellers were presented in 1666.[26] Between the later 18th and mid 19th century there were two inns in the parish: the Britannia, in the north-east corner of the parish near the Severn, and, at Linleygreen, that known in the 1850s as the Duke of Wellington.[27] Both had closed by 1882, the Britannia having become Wrensnest Farm.[28]

Linley Union friendly society was founded in 1802[29] but may have been dissolved by 1818.[30]

Rowland Hunt (d. 1943), M.P. for the Ludlow division 1903–18 and in 1917 a founder member of the National Party, lived at Linleygreen from 1925.[31]

MANOR AND OTHER ESTATES. Between the early 12th century and 1495 or later, *LINLEY* was held in socage of the prior of Wenlock.[32] In the later 1130s Richard of Linley, son of Baldwin, was lord,[33] and it was presumably Richard or members of his family who were mentioned later in the century: Richard and Ralph of Linley (*c.* 1150), Richard of Linley (1154–61), Walter of Linley (1177), and Richard of Linley (1180). Philip of Linley, lord in 1196 and 1200, was succeeded by two heiresses,[34] one who married William le Forcer (fl. 1216)[35] and Iseult, wife of Guy of Farlow (fl. 1221–*c.* 1235).[36] The manor was probably reunited by William's son Henry le Forcer, lord by 1255; he died in 1272 seised of a messuage and carucate charged with a rent due to the heirs of Guy of Farlow's son Philip.[37] Henry le Forcer's son William (kt. by 1310) died *c.* 1330 and was succeeded by Thomas le Forcer, presumably his son.[38] Later the manor was again divided, for in 1361 Ralph Darras (de Arras) was succeeded in a third of the manor by his son John, a minor.[39] John Darras had interests in the manor in 1395.[40]

The manor's further descent has not been traced with certainty [41] before 1460, when John Talbot, earl of Shrewsbury, died seised of half of the manor and leaving his son John as heir.[42] A moiety of Linley was held in dower by Margaret, countess of Shrewsbury (d. 1467), the 1st earl's widow, and passed to the 3rd earl in 1468.[43] He died in 1473,[44] and his uncle Sir Humphrey Talbot[45] died seised of the whole manor in 1493.[46] The manor then descended with Aston (in Munslow) until 1542 or later.[47]

Linley probably passed to Sir John Smith's son Edmund, whose daughter and heir Anne married William Powlett.[48] In 1581 Powlett sold his interest in Linley to Rowland Lacon.[49] Lacon settled the manor *c.* 1603 on his daughter-in-law Mary, with remainder to her husband Thomas Lacon and his heirs male.[50] Thomas died in 1640[51] and by 1649 Linley belonged to his son Richard.[52] Richard Lacon (d. 1676)[53] was succeeded by his son Thomas (d. 1725), and Thomas by his sons Richard (d. 1751)[54] and Rowland (d. 1756)[55] successively. Rowland was succeeded by his sons Richard (d. 1803) and Walter (d. 1814) in turn. Walter's son Thomas died unmarried in 1815 and Linley passed to Thomas's nephew Walter Lacon Atkinson[56] (Lacon from *c.* 1828),[57] a 'regular spendthrift'[58] who sold the encumbered estate to J. G. W. Weld-Forester, Lord Forester, in 1834.[59] Linley then descended with Willey[60] as part of the Forester estate.[61]

Linley Hall stands *c.* 150 m. south of Linley

21 *T.S.A.S.* 2nd ser. iv. 337.
22 *L. & P. Hen. VIII*, xvii, p. 508.
23 Ho. of Lords papers 1641–2, Protestations Oxon. and Salop. f. 191.
24 *Hearth Tax 1672* (Salop. Arch. Soc. 1949), 33–4.
25 *V.C.H. Salop.* ii. 224, 229; *Census*, 1851.
26 S.R.O. 1224/2/370, 383, 511.
27 S.R.O. 2992/1/2, p. 100; S.R.O., dep. plan 349; W.B.R., Q1/11/2; S. Bagshaw, *Dir. Salop.* (1851), 565; *P.O. Dir. Salop.* (1856), 66; E. Cassey & Co. *Dir. Salop.* (1871), 200 (no mention); R. F. J. Sawyer, *Short Acct. of Linley Par.* (1937), 12 (copy in S.R.O. 3756/43).
28 O.S. Maps 1/2,500, Salop. LI. 11, 15 (1883 edn.).
29 S.R.O., q. sess. rec. parcel 285, index to club articles.
30 No membership return in *Poor Law Abstract*, H.C. 82, p. 377 (1818), xix.
31 *V.C.H. Salop.* iii. 347–8, 354; W. D. Rubinstein, 'Hen. Page Croft and the National Party', *Jnl. of Contemp. Hist.* ix. 134; S.R.O., reg. of electors, Wrekin divn. (1925), p. 48; *Who Was Who, 1941–50*, 578.
32 Eyton, ii. 39; P.R.O., C 140/18, no. 16; *Cal. Inq. p.m. Hen. VII*, i, p. 428.
33 Eyton, ii. 39–40; *Cartulary of Shrews. Abbey*, ed. U. Rees (1975), i, pp. 21, 24, 28; ii, p. 259.
34 Eyton, ii. 40; S.R.O. 1/17/2 (witnessed by Rog., earl of Heref.).
35 Eyton, xi. 348 (dated ibid. xii. 92).
36 Ibid. ii. 40; iv. 192.
37 Ibid. ii. 40–1; iv. 192; *Cal. Inq. p.m.* i, pp. 268–9.
38 Eyton, ii. 41–2.
39 *Cal. Inq. p.m.* xi, p. 215.
40 Barnard MSS., Raby Castle, box 1, bdle. 29, nos. 23a–b.
41 T. F. Dukes, *Antiquities of Salop.* (1844), 264, mentions Thos., earl of Arundel, 1405–6 (citing no source and otherwise unreliable).
42 P.R.O., C 140/18, no. 16.
43 *Complete Peerage*, xi. 706; *Cal. Pat.* 1467–77, 134.
44 *Complete Peerage*, xi. 706.
45 Burke, *Peerage* (1967), 2278.
46 *Cal. Inq. p.m. Hen. VII*, i, pp. 428–9.
47 P.R.O., CP 25/2/35/233, no. 5; CP 40/1137, Carte rot. 8; SP 1/4, f. 15; Staffs. R.O., D. 593/B/5/1/6. Cf. above, Munslow, manors (Aston).
48 For pedigree see Burke, *Land. Gent.* (1925), 274.
49 P.R.O., CP 25/2/201/22 & 23 Eliz. I Mich. [no. 10]; CP 25/2/203/45 Eliz. I Hil. [no. 16]. For Lacon pedigree: S.P.L., MS. 2789, pp. 362–3.
50 S.R.O. 840, box 14, deed 31 Dec. 1602.
51 S.R.O. 3898/Rg/1, bur. 24 July 1640.
52 *Cal. Cttee. for Compounding*, iii. 1928.
53 S.R.O. 3898/Rg/2, bur. 22 Apr. 1676.
54 S.R.O., q. sess. rec. parcel 281, reg. of papists' deeds 1717–88, ff. 47–9, 195–6, 247; S.R.O. 3898/Rg/3, bur. 14 Nov. 1725; /Rg/4, bur. 31 Dec. 1751.
55 S.R.O. 2052, will pr. 1 Mar. 1756; 2991/Rg/4, bur. 9 Jan. 1756.
56 S.R.O. 1224, box 111, settlement 14 Mar. 1740/1; box 112, affidavit 12 Feb. 1827.
57 Ibid. box 112, deeds 1 June 1826, 16 Dec. 1828, 29 Aug. 1829, etc.
58 Randall, *Broseley*, 320–1.
59 S.R.O. 1224, box 111, deeds 9–10, 12 July 1834; box 112, mortgages; cf. parcel 192, rentals 1834; 1681/47, pp. 170–5 and *passim*; *T.S.A.S.* lix. 146.
60 S.R.O. 4044/89; *P.O. Dir. Salop.* (1879), 342; *Kelly's Dir. Salop.* (1941), 132.
61 Inf. from Ld. Forester.

church. The thick stone walls of the stair hall and the east wing may survive from the medieval house. That building was heightened and remodelled early in the 17th century, when the hall was part of an extensive group of buildings. The hall was extended south in the 18th century when it was given a brick front of three bays, the end bays being slightly recessed. About 1830 the south front was extended west by two bays and given a new centre of three bays surmounted by a pediment. About the same time the east elevation was cased in red brick; the interior was remodelled, a large stair hall being made within the area of the medieval hall; and a new service wing was added behind the stairs. The Roman Catholic Lacons had a chapel in an attic room lit by a gothick window at its north end.[62] North and west of the house is a courtyard surrounded by a wall reduced in height in the 20th century but retaining a base, possibly medieval, of large stone blocks and an upper section of early 17th-century red bricks decorated with lozenges of black headers. The former gardens, which in 1717 included a bowling green and a summer house,[63] are on the falling ground south of the house and are bounded on the west by a brick wall of the later 18th or early 19th century. A dovecot stood west of the church in 1639.[64] The farmhouse east of the Hall is early 19th-century.

By 1625 John Slaney, merchant tailor of London and brother of Richard Slaney (fl. 1603) of Linley,[65] apparently owned most of the southern half of Linley: *THE HEM* (164 a.) and Ruckleys farm (138 a.).[66] Richard's estate may have been acquired from the Lacons, some of whose lands lay interspersed among John Slaney's.[67] John (d. 1632) left the estate to Richard's son John[68] who sold it in 1652 to Michael Stephens, of Little Stretton. From Stephens (d. by 1680)[69] the property descended to his son Lancelot, probably the man who, as Lancelot Stephens the elder, of the Hem, died in 1711. His son Lancelot was probably the man of that name who died *c.* 1738, leaving the Hem to his son Peter.[70] In 1761 Peter Stephens, travelling in Italy, sold the property to his second cousin Thomas Stephens of Broseley, on whose death in 1787[71] it passed to his younger son John (d. 1830).[72] Another John Stephens was a principal landowner in the parish until, probably *c.* 1870, his property was sold to Lord Forester.[73]

The house is early 17th-century and timber framed.[74] The main range originally had two rooms on each floor, with a lower kitchen or hall wing behind its south end. The framing is of high quality, close studded on the ground floor and square framed above, and the west front is symmetrical. A detached building to the south, perhaps a dairy, was joined to the house in the later 17th century, possibly when a staircase was built into the southern rooms of the main range. Single-storeyed brick additions were made to the east in the 19th century.

In 1910 the only landowner besides Lord Forester was W. H. Foster of Apley Park, who had 104 a.[75]

ECONOMIC HISTORY. Linley was in Shirlett forest but was disafforested by 1301.[76] Woodland management was probably always part of the local economy; in 1717 49 oaks were sold from the Frith (or the Thrift), in the north-west corner of the parish, and in the 19th and 20th centuries the parish had large coppices[77] and was home to Lord Forester's head forester.[78] Thomas Barrett ran a small nursery 1828–44, growing fruit and other trees, shrubs, and plants for sale.[79]

The open fields, whose former existence is suggested by field names, were apparently inclosed by 1639.[80] Hemp butts then lay *c.* 0.5 km. east of the church, and further east, in the centre of the parish, there had formerly been a rabbit warren.[81] In 1910 Linley home farm comprised 223 a. and the Hem farm 135 a.[82]

Of the recorded arable acreage of 170 a. (a quarter of the parish) in 1801 about half was wheat, with barley, oats, and peas the other main crops.[83] In the late 19th and early 20th century the proportion of arable declined. It increased after the Second World War when more barley was grown. Pig keeping increased, and in the 1930s intensive poultry keeping was tried.[84]

In 1625 Littlefords mill was on Linley brook south of Linley hamlet and Frog mill was farther downstream.[85] Both were in Astley Abbots parish in 1842.[86] In 1639 a fulling mill, possibily inactive, stood downstream on the Linley side of the brook.[87] It was probably Doveys mill, which stood near fields called Walkmill leasow and closed before 1765.[88] In 1770 Needhams mill stood on the same side of Linley brook but nearer the Severn.[89]

In 1639 an area of 'colliers works' occupied

62 SA 11475; S.R.O. 4890; below, nonconf.
63 S.R.O., q. sess. rec. parcel 281, reg. of papists' deeds 1717–88, p. 48.
64 S.R.O. 4890.
65 S.R.O. 4077, p. 479.
66 S.R.O. 1224/1/16; 3614/1/260; 4890; S.P.L., plan 20.
67 S.R.O. 3614/1/267, abstracting the 1652 sale (below, this section) and unwarranted by the original (/1/263), states that it included half of the manor. The Lacons, selling much property in the early 17th cent. (*V.C.H. Salop.* iv. 133, 136), often described their properties in conveyancing docs. as manors.
68 P.R.O., PROB 11/161, ff. 326–7; *3rd Rep. Com. Char.* H.C. 5, pp. 300–1 (1820), iv; above, Barrow, educ.; charities.
69 S.P.L., MS. 4081, p. 2412.
70 S.R.O. 3614/1/151, 153, 267, 290, 355–7.
71 S.R.O. 2991/Rg/5, bur. 28 Nov. 1787.
72 S.R.O. 3614/1/265–9; S.P.L., MS. 4081, pp. 2411–12.
73 S.R.O. 4427/T/1; 5586/3/59, map of Albynes est.; *T.S.A.S.* lix. 146.
74 Perh. the ho. shown on S.R.O. 1224/1/16; 4890; cf. S.P.L., plan 20; SA 11476.
75 S.R.O. 4044/89.
76 Eyton, ii. 297; *Cart. Shrews.* ii, p. 251.
77 Above, this article, intro.; S.R.O. 1224, box 111, memo. 14 May 1717; O.S. Map 1/25,000, SO 69/79 (1983 edn.).
78 *Kelly's Dir. Salop.* (1917), 119; (1941), 132.
79 S.R.O. 1224, box 144, lease 1828, memo. 1844.
80 S.R.O. 3614/1/260; 4890.
81 S.R.O. 4890.
82 S.R.O. 4044/89.
83 P.R.O., HO 67/12/146.
84 Table XXI and sources there cited.
85 S.R.O. 1224/1/16.
86 P.R.O., IR 29/29/20; IR 30/29/20, fields 26, 66.
87 At O.S. Nat. Grid SO 703 983; S.R.O. 4890.
88 S.R.O. 3614/1/251–2.
89 Ibid.; S.R.O. 4890; Staffs. R.O., D. 845/4.

TABLE XXI

LINLEY: LAND USE, LIVESTOCK, AND CROPS

	1867	*1891*	*1938*	*1965*
Percentage of grassland	71	82	84	59
arable	29	18	16	41
Percentage of cattle	22	30	22	14
sheep	62	50	56	47
pigs	16	20	22	39
Percentage of wheat	50	41	57	42
barley	32	30	15	52
oats	6	29	28	6
mixed corn & rye	12	0	0	0
Percentage of agricultural land growing roots and vegetables	8	3	4	8

Sources: P.R.O., MAF 68/143, no. 15; /1340, no. 5; /3880, Salop. no. 262; /4945, no. 262.

the later site of Colliersworks coppice.[90] In the later 18th century coal and ironstone were mined on the Stephens estate in the eastern part of Linley.[91] There was opencast coalmining around Linleygreen *c.* 1948.[92]

Clay was dug to make bricks from the earlier 17th century or before,[93] and later some gravel was extracted.[94]

There were iron smithies along Linley brook before 1639.[95] In 1765 George Matthews, a Broseley ironmaster, took a lease of the former Doveys mill and in 1770 also had Needhams mill, previously let to the Madeley Wood Co., ironmasters. By 1770 Matthews had built a rolling and slitting mill and a forge, both in the area of Doveys mill,[96] and in 1775 Needhams mill was a boring mill. In 1775 the partners John Wright and Joseph and Richard Jesson, who had recently developed the 'Shropshire' method of producing wrought iron,[97] took over the premises with additional land on the south side of the brook near the Severn, in Astley Abbots parish, where they built a forge and ironworks called Wrens Nest forge.[98] In 1808 the sites along the lower Linley brook were collectively called Wrens Nest forges.[99] Two large ponds on the brook were associated with them, the upper in Linley parish, the lower mainly in Astley Abbots at the hamlet of Wrens Nest[1] (later Apley Forge). Pig iron doubtless came from Wright & Jesson's furnaces at Barnett's Leasow in Broseley, but other suppliers were Bishton & Onions's Snedshill furnaces (1799) and the Coalbrookdale Co.'s Horsehay furnaces (1801–3).[2] The forges perhaps fell victim to the depression in the iron trade after 1815.[3] A pair of cottages called Upper Forge remained in 1979 near Colliersworks coppice.[4]

In the earlier 1850s Edward Owen of Linley Villa was proprietor of Owen's pills and drops.[5]

LOCAL GOVERNMENT. Linley had a highway surveyor by 1722, and the parish was a highway authority until 1889 when that responsibility passed to the borough of Wenlock's Barrow district committee as urban sanitary authority.[6]

In the period 1812–15 there was no-one on permanent poor relief,[7] but expenditure on the poor rose from £93 in 1817 to £177 in 1818 before settling at its earlier level in the 1820s and 1830s.[8] The parish was in Madeley poor-law union 1836–1930[9] and Madeley rural sanitary district from 1872 until 1889 when it was included in the Barrow ward of Wenlock borough.[10] On the borough's dissolution in 1966 Linley, as part of Barrow civil parish, was transferred to Bridgnorth rural district,[11] and it was in Bridgnorth district from 1974.[12]

Linley was within the jurisdiction of the Broseley court of requests from 1782[13] until the court's abolition under the County Courts Act, 1846.[14]

CHURCH. Architectural evidence suggests that Linley chapel was built in the later 12th century; it provided sanctuary in 1203.

In the Middle Ages the chapel was in Holy Trinity parish, Much Wenlock,[15] but by 1528 it was considered a parish church and then became

90 S.R.O. 4890; cf. O.S. Map 6", Salop. LI. SE. (1888 edn.).
91 S.R.O. 3614/1/272, 276.
92 O.S. Map 1/25,000, SO 69 (1956 edn.); below, Willey, econ. hist. (coal and ironstone).
93 S.R.O. 3614/1/276; 4890, field name.
94 O.S. Map 6", Salop. LI. SE. (1888 edn.).
95 S.R.O. 3614/1/272, 'smithey' field names; 4890, field names; Randall, *Broseley*, 320.
96 S.R.O. 3614/1/251–2; cf. S.R.O. 4890.
97 Trinder, *Ind. Rev. Salop.* 35.
98 Staffs. R.O., D. 845/4; S.R.O. 1224, box 111, deed 20 Sept. 1775.
99 Baugh, *Map of Salop*.
1 B.L. Maps, O.S.D. 213; P.R.O., IR 30/29/20, fields 139, 160; S.R.O., dep. plan 341; J. Randall, *Broseley and Its Surroundings* (1879), 322.
2 Trinder, *Ind. Rev. Salop.* 40, 49; cf. *V.C.H. Salop.* i. 475; xi. 121, 293; above, Broseley, econ hist. (iron and engineering).
3 *Aris's Birm. Gaz.* 24 Apr. 1815; cf. Trinder, op. cit. 137, 143. B.L. Maps, O.S.D. 213, shows no forge.
4 O.S. Map 1/10,000, SO 79 NW. (1981 edn.).
5 S. Bagshaw, *Dir. Salop.* (1851), 565; *P.O. Dir. Salop.* (1856), 66 (descr. merely as farmer).
6 *T.S.A.S.* lvi. 315; S.R.O. 4427/H/1–18.
7 *Poor Law Abstract*, H.C. 82, pp. 376–7 (1818), xix.
8 *Poor Rate Returns*, H.C. 556, suppl. app. p. 144 (1822), v; H.C. 334, p. 179 (1825), iv; H.C. 219, p. 167 (1830–1), xi; H.C. 444, p. 162 (1835), xlvii.
9 V. J. Walsh, 'Admin. of Poor Laws in Salop. 1820–55' (Univ. of Pennsylvania Ph.D. thesis, 1970), 148–50; *Kelly's Dir. Salop.* (1929), 130.
10 *V.C.H. Salop.* ii. 215–16 (corr. below, Corrigenda).
11 Ibid. 205, 236–7 (corr. ibid. xi. 376); iii. 168.
12 Sources cited ibid. iii. 169 n. 29.
13 Broseley, etc., Small Debts Act, 1782, 22 Geo. III, c. 37.
14 9 & 10 Vic. c. 95. Cf. *V.C.H. Salop.* iii. 115, 165.
15 Below, this section; M. Wenlock, churches; Eyton, ii. 42.

united to Broseley rectory, although Broseley itself was not entirely independent of Holy Trinity until 1595.[16] In the 1920s, by arrangement with the rector of Broseley with Linley, the rector of Willey with Barrow took charge of the parish.[17] In 1930 the living of Linley was separated from that of Broseley and united to Astley Abbots rectory, the patrons of Astley Abbots becoming patrons of the united living.[18] From 1961 until that union was dissolved in 1976 Linley was served by priests in charge: the rector of Willey with Barrow 1961–72, the rector of Broseley 1972–6. [19] Linley remained an ecclesiastical parish until 1976 when the parish and benefice of Linley with Willey and Barrow were created[20] with Lord Forester as patron.[21]

Linley's tithes were appropriated to Wenlock priory, 2 marks a year being assigned from them to the priory kitchen. In 1274 the kitchen's portion and the demesne tithes were reserved when the priory granted the rest of the tithes to the vicar of Holy Trinity, Much Wenlock.[22] The chaplain of Linley mentioned in 1416,[23] and probably in 1343,[24] may have been endowed with the demesne tithes,[25] though by 1528 the living was too small to support a parish priest.[26]

By 1577 the Crown had seized Linley chapel, the chapel yard, and the tithes as concealed property, and in 1577 granted them on successive days to John Farnham and to Peter Grey and his son Edward.[27] They were probably recovered by Rowland Lacon (d. 1608),[28] lord of Linley and patron of Broseley.[29] In 1846 the rector of Broseley with Linley, who received moduses of £2 each for the tithes of the Weld-Forester and Stephens estates in Linley, had 1 a. of glebe there.[30] The glebe had gone by 1910.[31]

A monthly service was held by the rector in the 1730s, the rector of Willey was curate in 1797, and the curate of Broseley took the monthly service in the earlier 19th century.[32] About 1818 the church was said to be regularly repaired by two inhabitants 'of considerable property'.[33] In 1851 it drew an average congregation of 40.[34] A stipendiary curate was sometimes appointed to serve Linley in the later 19th century.[35] After the church was restored in 1858 there was a weekly service. That was due to the efforts of W. Layton Lowndes, the new, Anglo-Catholic, tenant of the Hall: he taught, trained, and led the singers, accompanying them at services on his concertina in place of 'the usual instrument'. Ascension Day, restored as a church festival, was also celebrated as a village holiday.[36] By 1883 the eucharist was evidently celebrated with a degree of Anglo-Catholic ceremonial.[37]

The small church, dedicated to *ST. NICHOLAS* in the 18th and early 19th century but to *ST. LEONARD* by 1856,[38] comprises chancel, nave, and west tower and is of local sandstone.[39] Chancel and nave are probably later 12th-century. The blocked north doorway has a tympanum displaying a green man. The south doorway, which may originally have been almost opposite that on the north, has a tympanum with zigzag decoration. The tower, externally as wide as the nave, was added late in the 12th century. It has pilaster buttresses, and the two-light windows in the upper stage are set in recessed fields on the north, south, and west faces. The south doorway may have been moved to the west end of the nave when the tower was built. In the 14th or 15th century new windows were put in the nave.

In the 1830s the church was poorly lit and seemed like a 'dungeon'.[40] It was restored in 1858, through Layton Lowndes's exertions and generosity, to designs of A. W. Blomfield. The nave windows were presumably restored then, those on the south being enlarged, and new lancets were put into the west end of the chancel whose east wall was rebuilt and provided with three round-headed lancets. The south door was blocked. The tower was restored and one of the two bells recast, while internally new ceilings were inserted, benches replaced the old pews (whose wood was used to panel the chancel), and the elaborate 12th-century font was moved from the east end of the nave to the tower.[41] In 1862 Layton Lowndes gave a new set of silver-gilt plate, receiving in exchange the old plate marked 'BL to Lindly Church'. The rector paid for glass by William Warrington for the east window.[42] An oak pulpit was brought from Monkhopton church in 1948.[43] The blocked north doorway of the nave contains a memorial slab to Francis Anderton (d. 1779) and George Johnson (d. 1803), monks of Douai who died at Linley while on the English mission.[44] The hatchment of Richard Lacon (d. 1803) hangs in the nave.

In the 1850s the church stood in a field near

[16] *Reg. Bothe* (C.S.), 200; cf. above, Broseley, churches.
[17] Sawyer, *Linley*, 1–2, 16.
[18] *Lond. Gaz.* 28 Feb. 1930, pp. 1286–7.
[19] *Crockford* (1977–9), 794, 1013.
[20] Heref. Dioc. Regy., reg. 1969– (in use), pp. 228–9.
[21] *Heref. Dioc. Yr. Bk.* (1976–7), 49.
[22] Eyton, ii. 42 n. 16; iii. 266.[23] *Reg. Mascall* (C.S.), 182.
[24] B.L. Add. MS. 50121, p. 7.
[25] Eyton, ii. 42 n. [26] *Reg. Bothe*, 200.
[27] *Cal. Pat.* 1575–8, pp. 309, 312.
[28] Cf. Cressage; *V.C.H. Salop.* viii. 77.
[29] Above, manor; Broseley, churches.
[30] S.R.O. 4427/T/1. [31] S.R.O. 4044/89.
[32] Birm. Univ. Libr., Mytton Papers, iv. 821; S.P.L., MS. 6865, p. 126; C. Hulbert, *Hist. and Descr. Salop.* (1837), ii. 345; S. Bagshaw, *Dir. Salop.* (1851), 565.
[33] *Poor Law Abstract*, H.C. 82, pp. 376–7 (1818), xix.
[34] P.R.O., HO 129/358, no. 37.
[35] Heref. Dioc. Regy., reg. 1847–56, p. 367; 1883–1901, pp. 206, 335.
[36] S.R.O. 4427/ChW/1, newscuttings Nov. 1858; *In Reverent Memory; Wm. Layton Lowndes* (Kelham, n.d.), 8–9, 11 (copy in S.P.L., class AL 91 v.f.); below, this section. For Lowndes cf. *V.C.H. Salop.* iii. 141–2, 144 n. 74, 145, 172, 173 n. 75, 360.
[37] S.R.O. 4427/ChW/1, inv. 1 Mar. 1883.
[38] B.L. Add. MS. 30316, f. 29v.; Lewis, *Topog. Dict. Eng.* (1835); *P.O. Dir. Salop.* (1856), 66.
[39] Descr. based on Cranage, iii. 202–4; x. 1028; B.L. Add. MS. 21181, p. 16; S.P.L., MS. 372, vol. i, f. 115; 3065, no. 98; J. H. Smith colln. no. 127; Salop. Librs. H.Q., Wm. Vickers, 'Drawings of Churches in Ludlow Archd.'; Birm. Univ. Libr., Mytton Papers, iv. 821; S.R.O. 4890.
[40] Hulbert, *Hist. Salop.* ii. 345.
[41] S.R.O. 4427/Ch/1–11; /ChW/1, 9 June 1858 sqq.; *In Reverent Memory*, 8–9; Eyton, ii, plates following p. 42; H. B. Walters, *Ch. Bells of Salop.* (Oswestry, 1915), 67.
[42] D. L. Arkwright and B. W. Bourne, *Ch. Plate Archd. Ludlow* (Shrews. 1961), 37; S.R.O. 4427/ChW/1, 23 Apr., 13 June, 1862.
[43] Heref. Dioc. Regy., reg. 1938–53, p. 389.
[44] For date of Johnson's d.: S.R.O. 2991/Rg/6, 20 Dec. 1803.

a 'venerable' yew, with no burial ground.[45] The iron fencing around the churchyard was put there in 1858.[46]

Baptisms and marriages at Linley were entered in the Broseley register, as were burials of Linley people.[47] Separate registers of baptisms and marriages at Linley were begun in 1859 and 1860,[48] though marriages and burials were said *c.* 1903 to take place at Broseley.[49]

NONCONFORMITY. Eleanor Ridley was a recusant in 1604.[50] Richard Lacon was one of two men in Linley who refused to take the Protestation in 1642,[51] and the Lacons were papists in the 1660s and 1680s. About 1685 Edward Lacon, priest, uncle of the lord of the manor who died in 1725, left money to endow a priest to assist at Linley and thereabouts; later there were other endowments, much disputed in the mid 18th century. The Lacons were a notable recusant family in 18th-century Shropshire, and from the attic chapel in Linley Hall a resident priest (sometimes a Douai monk on the English mission) served an area that extended as far as Beobridge (in Claverley).[52] In 1767 about half of the parish's Roman Catholics lived in the Hall.[53]

Wesleyans met at Linley in 1841.[54]

EDUCATION. By 1820 Linley children attended Barrow school.[55] Mrs. Jane Lowndes, of Linley Hall 1857–83,[56] kept a school for Linley children.[57] By the 1890s they attended Barrow or Broseley schools[58] and Miss C. Brown was then keeping a private preparatory school at Linley.[59]

CHARITIES FOR THE POOR. None known.

MONKHOPTON

MONKHOPTON village is 6.5 km. south of Much Wenlock. The townships that eventually formed Monkhopton parish were incorporated in Much Wenlock parish in the Middle Ages, having apparently been taken by Wenlock priory from neighbouring parishes such as Stanton Long (or Patton)[60] and possibly Ditton Priors.[61] Monk Hall and Weston, accounted separate townships in 1256, were one by 1522,[62] but by 1680 Monk Hall was included in Monkhopton township and the part of Oxenbold township that was not in Stanton Long parish was linked with Weston township.[63] Monkhopton parish came into existence between the 1550s and 1642,[64] perhaps in the earlier 17th century,[65] but no benefice was endowed until the mid 18th century.[66] The earliest certain evidence of the area of the parish is provided by the 1841 merger and commutation of the tithes of Little Hudwick, Monk Hall, Monkhopton, part of Oxenbold, and Weston;[67] that area was duly taken as the civil parish, which comprised 2,258 a. (914 ha.) until 1883 when Skimblescott (111 a., 45 ha.), a detachment of Shipton C.P., was added on the west.[68]

The parish, irregular in shape,[69] lies on and beneath the northern slope of the Clee Hills plateau and thus at the northern end of Corve Dale. In 1841 the parish's northern boundary towards the east followed brooks, but elsewhere, near Monk Hall and Weston, its angled line followed field edges. The eastern boundary followed both streams and artificial features, including the Monkhopton–Middleton road. The southern boundary, with Ditton Priors, broadly followed the edge of the Clee Hills plateau but in places was determined by fields;[70] it bore little resemblance to the corresponding part of the boundary of Much Wenlock parish, described in 1332, which followed roads and watercourses.[71] The western boundary followed Oxenbold brook as far north as Pool bridge, whence it took a tortuous course around fields.

45 S. Bagshaw, *Dir. Salop.* (1851), 565; St. Deiniol's Libr., Hawarden, Sir Steph. Glynne's ch. notes, xcvii, f. 57.

46 S.R.O. 4427/ChW/1, disbursements [1858].

47 *Par. Regs. of Broseley, 1570–1700*, ed. A. F. C. C. Langley (2 vols. 1889–90); above, Broseley, churches.

48 S.R.O. 4427/Rg/1; regs. at ch.; cf. banns 1860–78 in S.R.O. 4427/ChW/1.

49 *Salop. Par. Doc.* ed. E. C. Peele and R. S. Clease (Shrews. [1903]), 203. There seems to be no Linley reg. from 1700, as alleged by Cranage, iii. 204.

50 *Misc.* ii (Cath. Rec. Soc. ii), 295.

51 Ho. of Lords papers 1641–2, Protestations Oxon. and Salop. f. 191.

52 *Worcs. Recusant*, liv. 25; F. C. Husenbeth, *Life of Rt. Revd. John Milner* (1862), 93; Sawyer, *Linley*, 6; S.R.O. 1224, box 110, Ric. Lacon's will 25 Jan. 1800 (mentioning chap.); 5709, Wenlock boro. q. sess. order bk. pp. 13–15; B.A.A., A 30, 91, 203b, 257–8, 261–2, 266–7, 345, 500, 762; C 382, 665, 667, 1426; W.A.A., Old Brotherhood 1693; above, church. Some refs. above were provided by Dr. M. Rowlands.

53 *Worcs. Recusant*, xxv. 34–5.

54 Shrews. Sch. Libr., Broseley circuit bk. 1815–41, June 1841.

55 R. Hume, 'Changing Patterns of Educ. Devt. in Salop. 1660–1833' (Keele Univ. Ph.D. (Educ.) thesis, 1982), 226.

56 *In Reverent Memory*, 4, 7; S.R.O. 4427/ChW/1, newscutting Nov. 1858.

57 Sawyer, *Linley*, 6; M.I. in ch.

58 *Kelly's Dir. Salop.* (1891), 382; (1895), 115.

59 Ibid. (1895), 115 (and later edns.); personal knowledge.

60 Below, church; cf. above, Stanton Long. This article was written in 1987 but includes later additions.

61 Lit. Hudwick may have been part of Ditton Priors par. and man. until after, possibly long after, the Dissolution (below, manors) and is not known to have been in Monkhopton par. and tns. before 1718 (below, church). For the suggestion that some of Ditton's unnamed late 11th-cent. berewicks should perhaps be sought in the later area of Monkhopton par. see above, Ditton Priors, intro.

62 *Roll of Salop. Eyre 1256* (Selden Soc. xcvi), pp. 216, 239, 316–17; S.R.O. 566/2.

63 S.R.O. 5709, Wenlock boro. q. sess. order bk. 1661–90, p. 121; *T.S.A.S.* lvi. 315, 324.

64 Ho. of Lords papers 1641–2, Protestations Oxon. and Salop. f. 196; below, church.

65 Cf. above, Barrow, church (independent of M. Wenlock by 1611); below, Willey, church (1661).

66 Below, church.

67 P.R.O., IR 29/29/222.

68 *Census*, 1881, ii. 333; 1891, ii. 543, 652.

69 Fig. 36.

70 P.R.O., IR 30/29/222.

71 S.R.O. 1224/2/11, bdy. of Holy Trin. par., M. Wenlock, with Ditton Priors.

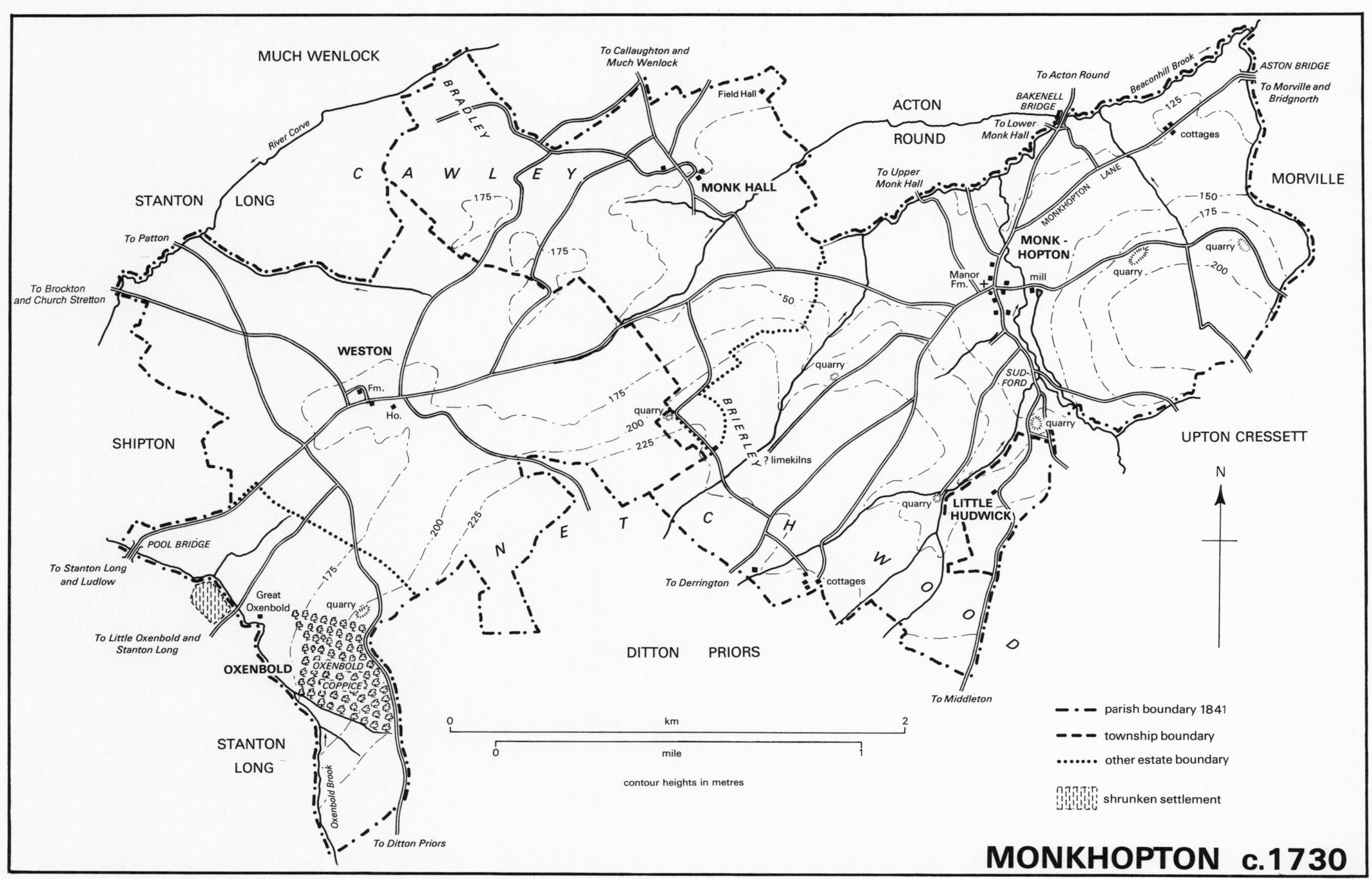
MONKHOPTON c.1730
parish boundary 1841
township boundary
other estate boundary
shrunken settlement
N
0 km 2
0 mile 1
contour heights in metres
MUCH WENLOCK
MORVILLE
UPTON CRESSETT
ACTON ROUND
DITTON PRIORS
STANTON LONG
SHIPTON
STANTON LONG
MONK-HOPTON
MONK HALL
WESTON
LITTLE HUDWICK
OXENBOLD
OXENBOLD COPPICE
BRADLEY
CAWLEY
BRIERLEY
NETCHWOOD
ASTON BRIDGE
BAKENELL BRIDGE
POOL BRIDGE
SUDFORD
MONKHOPTON LANE
To Morville and Bridgnorth
To Acton Round
To Lower Monk Hall
To Upper Monk Hall
To Callaughton and Much Wenlock
To Patton
To Brockton and Church Stretton
To Stanton Long and Ludlow
To Little Oxenbold and Stanton Long
To Ditton Priors
To Derrington
To Middleton
Beaconhill Brook
River Corve
Oxenbold Brook
Field Hall
Manor Fm.
mill
cottages
quarry
? limekilns
Great Oxenbold
Fm.
Ho.

Fig. 36

The parish lies on strata of the Lower Old Red Sandstone, tilted down to the south-east. The northern and western parts are on the Ledbury Group of the Downton Series, consisting of red marls with sandstone bands; the other, higher, parts are on the Ditton Series, comprising red marls with sandstones, cornstone conglomerates, and cornstones. At the junction of the two series are narrow bands of '*Psammosteus*' Limestones.[72] The soils are red-brown loams, mostly well drained.[73]

The land rises to a steep southern escarpment, which ascends to plateaux at Highclear and Netchwood; the name Netchwood perhaps derives from OE. 'atten ecg' ('at the edge').[74] The eastern half of the parish, including Monkhopton village and Monk Hall, drains north by Beaconhill brook (called Hopton brook in 1628)[75] and its tributaries. Weston and Oxenbold drain north-west towards the Corve.

Evidence for prehistoric occupation is confined to a Neolithic flint axe found near Woolshope[76] and small flints found near there and at Monkhopton village. A sherd of Samian ware found near Woolshope suggests a Roman presence nearby.[77]

By the Middle Ages almost all settlement was on the lower land. Hopton village (by 1292 Monkhopton) was probably settled well before the Conquest: its name (from OE. *hop*, 'valley')[78] describes its situation at the foot of converging valleys in the escarpment.[79] Twenty-eight men of Monkhopton township took the Protestation in 1642.[80] In 1731 five farmhouses (not counting the mill) stood within 150 m. of the church, near the junction of the main road with the road to Middleton and Ditton.[81] In the 1830s, however, the village was reduced and settlement became less compact, three farmsteads being demolished in favour of isolated ones in the fields,[82] though their loss was compensated by the building of a teacher's house and a vicarage in the 1840s.[83] The village was probably less frequented from the 1840s when the main road was diverted.[84] The village changed little thereafter. From the early 20th century it was supplied with spring water by a private scheme using a wind pump at Highclear. Thence a supply was laid to four council houses[85] for farm workers built near the main road east of Monkhopton *c.* 1945: six more were added in 1955. The three Vicarage Bungalows, privately built at the north end of the village, were completed in 1963.[86]

In 1731 there were few cottages outside Monkhopton village.[87] Three on the main road near Aston bridge were perhaps those recorded in 1667.[88] The rest were near the southern boundary of Monkhopton township, one at the edge of Brierley, the others at the margin of Netchwood. By 1817 there were four more roadside cottages between Monkhopton and Aston bridge and six between Monkhopton and Weston.[89] Most of them disappeared between 1841 and 1882,[90] the parish having lost a third of its population 1831–71.[91]

Monk Hall, called Far Monk Hall in 1817,[92] stands 1.5 km. north-west of Monkhopton village. It is the most southerly of a group of settlements of that name, the rest being in Acton Round parish. The name, recorded as 'Muggehal' in 1182 and 'Mughale'in 1227,[93] and possibly as 'Buchehale' in 1086,[94] derives from OE. *halh*, denoting the valley around which the settlements lay.[95] Probably they were always small and scattered. In 1545 there were two farms at Monk Hall in Monkhopton,[96] one of them called Harper's Monk Hall by 1361.[97] There may once have been a third, for in 1731 there was an isolated house called Field Hall[98] between Monk Hall and Upper Monk Hall (in Acton Round); it stood until the early 20th century.[99] Four Monkhopton parishioners in Monk Hall took the 1642 Protestation.[1] The two farmhouses stood on opposite sides of the lane in 1731.[2] The eastern remained as Monk Hall in 1990. It was two storeyed, probably 17th-century and timber framed, but later cased in brick, and much altered in the mid 20th century. A cottage on its west side was demolished before 1841. By then amalgamation of the farms had reduced the western farmhouse to a cottage,[3] there in 1990.

West of the prior of Wenlock's house at Great Oxenbold there are earthworks in Stanton Long parish indicating an abandoned street and house sites.[4] In 1642 seven men in Great Oxenbold took the Protestation.[5] Great Oxenbold was the only farm in the Monkhopton part of Oxenbold by 1747[6] and the only house there by 1841.[7]

Weston, mentioned *c.* 1230[8] and presumably named before the Conquest from its geographical

72 Geol. Surv. Map 1", solid, sheet 166 (1974 edn.); Inst. Geol. Sciences Map 1/25,000, SO 59 *Wenlock Edge* (1969 edn.); D. C. Greig and others, *Geol. of Country around Ch. Stretton, Craven Arms, Wenlock Edge, and Brown Clee* (Mem. Geol. Surv. 1968).

73 Soil Surv. Map 1", sheet 166 (1972 edn.).

74 Cf. H. D. G. Foxall, *Salop. Field-Names* (Salop. Arch. Soc. 1980), 22.

75 S.R.O. 5460/10/2.

76 SA 3766.

77 *Salop. Newsletter*, xlv. 12–13.

78 *P.N. Salop.* (E.P.N.S.), i. 209.

79 Cf. above, Bouldon; Tugford.

80 Ho. of Lords papers 1641–2, Protestations Oxon. and Salop. f. 196.

81 S.R.O. 3765/2; fig. 36.

82 Below, econ. hist.

83 Below, church; educ.

84 Below, this section.

85 O.S. Map 1/2,500, Salop. LVIII. 5 (1927 edn.); A. H. S. Waters, *Rep. on Water Supply* (S.C.C. 1946), 48.

86 S.R.O., DA 17/516/1D, ff. 105–7; /516/13, f. 107; /516/27, f. 121; /516/35, f. 213.

87 S.R.O. 3765/2; fig. 36.

88 *Salop. N. & Q.* i–ii. 25.

89 B.L. Maps, O.S.D. 207. The sites are shown in greater detail on S.R.O., dep. plan 248.

90 P.R.O., IR 30/29/222; O.S. Maps 6", Salop. LVII. NE., SE. (1891 edn.); LVIII. NW. (1892 edn.).

91 *V.C.H. Salop.* ii. 224.

92 B.L. Maps, O.S.D. 207.

93 *Pipe R.* 1182 (P.R.S. xxxi), 23; Dugdale, *Mon.* v. 74 n.

94 Below, manors (Buchehale).

95 M. Gelling, *Place-Names in the Landscape* (1984), 104.

96 S.R.O. 566/5.

97 S.R.O. 1037/3/54. A John Harper fl. 1327: *T.S.A.S.* 2nd ser. iv. 328.

98 S.R.O. 1093, parcel 115, rental of 1841; 3765/2; P.R.O., IR 29/29/222; IR 30/29/222, fields 38–40; fig. 36.

99 At O.S. Nat. Grid SO 616 943: O.S. Map 1/2,500, Salop. LVII. 8 (1902 and 1926 edns.).

1 Ho. of Lords papers 1641–2, Protestations Oxon. and Salop. f. 196.

2 S.R.O. 3765/2; fig. 36.

3 P.R.O., IR 29/29/222; IR 30/29/222, field 27; below, econ. hist.

4 SA 364

5 Ho. of Lords papers 1641–2, Protestations Oxon. and Salop. f. 196. Earlier records do not distinguish Gt. Oxenbold (mainly in Monkhopton par.) from the rest of Oxenbold tns. (in Stanton Long).

6 S.R.O. 168/2, f. 93; below, manors.

7 P.R.O., HO 107/928/9, f. 6v.

8 Eyton, iv. 44.

relationship to Hopton (which had Aston Eyre a similar distance to the east), stood on a knoll on the main road with at least five houses in 1545.[9] Ten men of Weston took the Protestation in 1642,[10] and in 1747 there were three farms. Between 1783 and 1841 the farms were reduced to two, later called Weston House farm and Weston farm, with houses on opposite sides of the road; the third farmhouse served thereafter as cottages.[11] A few other houses were added in the 20th century, including four council houses in 1946.[12]

The parish as a whole had 212 inhabitants in 1801. The total was only 168 by 1821, but by 1831 stood at 208. Thereafter it tended to fall, markedly so in the 1860s and 1890s, reaching 140 in 1921. Population rose in the 1940s and 1950s, to 206 by 1961, but fell somewhat in the 1970s, to stand at 179 in 1991.[13]

A supposed Roman road, believed to run from Greensforge (Staffs.) to central Wales, crossed the parish from east to west.[14] It was the Bridgnorth–Munslow road *c.* 1575.[15] By the early 18th century, as the Bridgnorth–Ludlow road, it entered the parish over Aston bridge (mentioned in 1522)[16] and curved south to pass through Monkhopton village before resuming its Roman alignment.[17] It then passed through Weston hamlet and left the parish by Pool bridge,[18] mentioned in 1747.[19] At Monkhopton it was called Monkhopton Lane.[20] In 1839 the road was turnpiked from Morville to Shipton[21] and by 1841 had been straightened by the building of two long new stretches, one west of Aston Eyre and passing south of Aston bridge, the other passing north of Monkhopton village.[22] Disturnpiked in 1872, it became a main road in 1878.[23]

From Weston a north-westward branch of the Bridgnorth–Ludlow road ran through Brockton to Church Stretton.[24] Turnpiked to Easthope's Cross with the main road in 1839, it was likewise disturnpiked in 1872.[25] Near Weston a northward branch from it ran to Patton,[26] perhaps the 'Patton way' mentioned in 1332.[27] In 1256 there was a highway from Weston to Much Wenlock.[28] One such road seems to have run north-east by way of Monk Hall, Upper Monk Hall (in Acton Round), Spoonhill wood, and Callaughton (in Much Wenlock);[29] another appears to have run directly from Weston to Upper Monk Hall.[30] There was also a lane from Weston to Netchwood,[31] possibly the way from Weston to Ditton Priors that passed near Brierley in 1262[32] and perhaps the Wood Lane mentioned in 1747.[33] On the Bridgnorth–Ludlow road between Weston and Pool bridge a more direct lane to Ditton branched south and skirted the probable eastern edge of the park at Great Oxenbold.[34]

North of Monkhopton a branch from the Bridgnorth–Ludlow road led north over Beaconhill brook to Acton Round, by a bridge called Baknall (later Bakenell) bridge in 1540,[35] and to Lower Monk Hall (in Acton Round).[36] Another ran south from Monkhopton through Sudford (perhaps 'south ford') and by Little Hudwick and Middleton to Ditton Priors.[37] A road from Much Wenlock to Ditton, which branched south from the Much Wenlock to Weston road at Upper Monk Hall, seems to have entered Monkhopton village on the west side of the church; it ran thence south-west to Ditton by Netchwood and Derrington.[38]

The late 20th-century metalled roads were the main road, the branches from Monkhopton to Acton Round, Bourton, and Ditton (one by Little Hudwick, the other by Netchwood), and those from Weston to Easthope's Cross and to Netchwood.

On a Sunday in 1547 Richard Lawley directed a *communis ludus* at Monkhopton;[39] whatever its nature, the event was evidently unusual, and it seems that the inhabitants were always too few and dispersed for organized social activities. There was one alehouse in 1667 and 1790;[40] Richard Davis kept an inn in 1763.[41] By 1839 the Wenlock Arms, formerly a farm called Brook House, stood on the main road east of Monkhopton village;[42] it closed *c.* 1860 and reverted to its original name.[43] In 1906 the parish joined the Diocese of Hereford Circulating Parish Library and *c.* 1927 was provided with a county library centre.[44] In the mid 20th century parishioners found social opportunities in Morville, Bridgnorth, and other nearby places.[45]

MANORS AND OTHER ESTATES. In 1066 Eadric (Edric) and Siward held *OXENBOLD* as two manors and were free. In 1086 Roger of Montgomery, earl of Shrewsbury, held the manor in chief, and Helgot held of him.[46] Thereafter the tenancy in chief is presumed to have

9 *L. & P. Hen. VIII*, xx (1), p. 223.
10 Ho. of Lords papers 1641–2, Protestations Oxon. and Salop. f. 196.
11 Below, econ. hist.; P.R.O., HO 107/928/9, f. 6 and v.
12 S.R.O., DA 17/516/15, f. 107.
13 *V.C.H. Salop.* ii. 224; *Census*, 1981, Small Area Statistics: Salop.; S.C.C. Property and Planning Services Dept. inf. rep. C91/103.
14 *T.S.A.S.* lvi. 233–43.
15 S.R.O. 356, box 327, surv. *c.* 1575, p. 161.
16 S.R.O. 566/2.
17 S.R.O. 3765/2; fig. 36.
18 S.R.O., dep. plan 249.
19 S.R.O. 168/2, f. 89
20 P.R.O., HO 107/928/9, ff. 3v., 5.
21 2 Vic. c. 30 (Local and Personal); S.R.O., dep. plan 249.
22 A. Blackwall, *Historic Bridges of Salop.* (Shrews. 1985), 72; O.S. Maps 6", Salop. LVII. NE. (1891 edn.); LVIII. NW. (1892 edn.).
23 Ann. Turnpike Acts Continuance Act, 1871, 34 & 35 Vic. c. 115; Highways and Locomotives (Amendment) Act, 1878, 41 & 42 Vic. c. 77.
24 Below, Shipton, intro.
25 Above, this section.
26 B.L. Maps, O.S.D. 207.
27 S.R.O. 1224/2/11.
28 *Roll of Salop. Eyre 1256* (Selden Soc. xcvi), pp. 138–9.
29 B.L. Maps, O.S.D. 207; S.R.O., dep. plan 249; S.R.O. 1093/2; *Roll of Salop. Eyre 1256*, pp. 138–9; Hull Univ., Brynmor Jones Libr., DDFA/26/120; Callaughton map of 1796 (in possession of Mr. J. R. Craig).
30 S.R.O. 1093/2.
31 B.L. Maps, O.S.D. 207; S.R.O., dep. plan 249.
32 *Cal. Chart. R.* 1327–41, 488.
33 S.R.O. 168/2, f. 89.
34 P.R.O., IR 30/29/222; B.L. Maps, O.S.D. 207.
35 P.R.O., SC 6/Hen. VIII/3021, m. 9; S.R.O., O.S. Map 6", Salop. LVII. NE. (1891 edn. annotated in S.C.C. Co. Surveyor's dept.).
36 S.R.O. 1093/2; 3765/2; fig. 36.
37 S.R.O. 3765/2; P.R.O., IR 30/29/222; fig. 36.
38 S.R.O. 1093/2; 3765/2; B.L. Maps, O.S.D. 207; fig. 36.
39 *Salop.* (R.E.E.D.), i. 115; ii. 649–50.
40 *Salop. N. & Q.* i–ii. 25; W.B.R., Q1/11/2.
41 Hull Univ., Brynmor Jones Libr., DDFA(2)/15/15.
42 S.R.O., dep. plan 249.
43 *P.O. Dir. Salop.* (1856), 84; (1863), 720; below, econ. hist.
44 R. C. Elliott, 'Development of Public Libraries in Salop.' (Loughborough Univ. M.A. thesis, 1970; copy in co. libr.), 46, 125.
45 e.g. par. newsletter (1987) in ch.; S.R.O. 4598/1, pp. 12–13, 15, 25; local inf.
46 *V.C.H. Salop.* i. 337.

followed the descent of Castle Holdgate until 1256.[47]

The terre tenancy belonged to Robert de Girros (d. 1190×1191)[48] and descended to another Robert de Girros,[49] presumably his son. Robert gave Oxenbold manor to Wenlock priory in 1244 to support three monks,[50] and in 1256 William Mauduit, lord of Castle Holdgate, relinquished his overlordship to the priory.[51] In 1522 the priory leased the demesnes at Oxenbold to William Lee as the 'manor' of Oxenbold; the manor to which they belonged was soon renamed Shipton (Shipton having become one of its constituents by 1344)[52] and in 1540 passed to the Crown.[53]

In 1544 the Crown sold part of the former manor of Oxenbold, under that name, to John Jennyns to hold in chief by knight service. He sold it a few weeks later to Thomas Bromley (kt. by 1546).[54] At Bromley's death in 1555 Oxenbold passed to his daughter Margaret and her husband Richard Newport[55] (kt. 1560, d. 1570). On Lady Newport's death in 1598 it passed to their son Francis (kt. 1603)[56] and thereafter followed the descent of Harley.[57] In 1919 Lord Barnard sold Great Oxenbold farm (220 a., including 91 a. in Stanton Long parish) and Great Oxenbold coppice (61 a.). The farm was sold to Herbert Barker, in whose family it remained in 1990, and the coppice to R. Groom, Sons & Co.,[58] Wellington timber merchants.[59] The rest of Oxenbold manorial estate seems to have been sold about that time to sitting tenants.[60]

In 1205 the canons of Holdgate were said to be tenants in part of the manorial estate.[61]

Buildings at Great Oxenbold incorporate considerable remains of a medieval house, but their interpretation is uncertain.[62] The earliest fabric may be that of the main rubble-built east–west block, which apparently dates from the 1240s.[63] Sited on a gentle slope, it may represent an open hall and was built on a solid earth-filled plinth, in part of which was a cellar. Lit originally by two pairs of lights in each wall, the main block was entered near the east end by a north doorway set above ground level, over the cellar, and reached by external steps. A vice in a turret at the north-east angle of the block led down to the cellar. In the 13th century a building was added to the east end and blocked the windows there. It too was built on a solid platform and had lancet windows north and south; access was by a doorway in the east wall of the main block.[64] A later piscina and aumbry within the east block indicate eventual use as a chapel. In the 14th or 15th century a broad external doorway to the cellar was made, directly underneath the doorway of the main block and partly below ground level. The main doorway was apparently reached then by retractable wooden steps pivoted at the top on a horizontal beam, which lay parallel to the threshold and revolved at either end in stone sockets, one of which remained *in situ* in 1990. Prior Gosnell had the 'great hall' paved in 1521–2 and glazed in 1522–3. In 1522–3 he provided a chimney for the kitchen,[65] evidently a detached building. The main block seems to have been reroofed in the earlier 16th century.[66] Both blocks were divided into two storeys, perhaps by that time; the vice of the main block was built up to reach the first floor; and the chapel block's original floor was lowered by excavation. At about the same time an axial stack was inserted in the main block, dividing it into two compartments, and a single-storeyed extension was built along the south side of the chapel block. A single roof was then placed over the chapel block and its extension.

The architectural evidence suggests that the main block at Great Oxenbold was built by Prior Humbert (or Imbert) shortly after he acquired the manor; his park was licensed in 1251.[67] Humbert was a royal servant and an ambitious builder.[68] He entertained the king at the priory in the 1230s and 1240s[69] and may afterwards have wished for a retreat fit to receive important guests: Bishop Swinfield stayed at Oxenbold in 1290.[70]

In or after 1066 Almaer (Elmer) held *BUCHEHALE*, and by 1086 William Pantulf held it of Roger of Montgomery, earl of Shrewsbury.[71] Since 'Buchehale' was in Patton hundred it was possibly the later Monk Hall ('Muggehal' in 1182),[72] part of which, like most of Patton hundred, was in the liberty of Wenlock by 1255.[73] A resemblance between the name 'Buchehale' (1086) and those of 'Bacundale' (1380), 'Baknall' (1540), and 'Bakenell' (1910), which were on the boundary between Monkhopton and the part of Monk Hall in Acton Round, may nevertheless be fortuitous.[74] In 1255 two thirds of Monk Hall belonged, as did some manors in south Shropshire, formerly Pantulf's, to John FitzAlan; they were part of FitzAlan's

47 Below, this section; cf. above, Holdgate, manor.
48 *Pipe R.* 1190 (P.R.S. N.S. i), 124; 1191 & 92 (P.R.S. N.S. ii), 78; 1195 (P.R.S. N.S. vi), 42. Cf. Eyton, iv. 20.
49 *Rot. de Ob. et Fin.* (Rec. Com.), 209.
50 Barnard MSS., Raby Castle, abstr. of writings, pt. 1, f. 43; *T.S.A.S.* 4th ser. vi. 183–4.
51 *Roll of Salop. Eyre 1256*, pp. 12–13; cf. *Rot. Hund.* (Rec. Com.), ii. 85.
52 P.R.O., C 1/878, no. 17 (cf. C 1/936, no. 35); SC 6/Hen. VIII/3021, mm. 6d.–8, 18; S.R.O. 566/5. Cf. below, Shipton, manors.
53 *V.C.H. Salop.* ii. 45.
54 Barnard MSS., Raby Castle, abstr. of writings, pt. 1, ff. 44–5. Cf. W. A. Shaw, *Kts. of Eng.* (1906), ii. 58; *Hist. Parl., Commons*, 1509–58, i. 508.
55 P.R.O., C 142/104, no. 94; SC 2/197/118.
56 P.R.O., C 142/256, no. 7; *T.S.A.S.* 4th ser. xi. 155.
57 P.R.O., C 142/402, no. 146; S.R.O. 659/1; q. sess. rec. box 260, reg. of gamekeepers 1742–79, 1 Dec. 1743, 18 [Oct.] 1764; parcel 261, reg. of gamekeepers 1799–1807, ff. 15, 126. Cf. *V.C.H. Salop.* viii. 88 (corr. ibid. xi. 377).
58 S.P.L., SC1/13 (lots 5, 22).
59 *V.C.H. Salop.* xi. 230.
60 S.P.L., SC1/13 (lot 8); *Shrews. Chron.* 28 Nov. 1919.
61 *Cur. Reg. R.* iv, p. 45.
62 Thanks are due to Mrs. M. Moran, Mr. Eric Mercer, and Dr. M. C. Horton for advice on aspects of the ho.
63 *Vernacular Archit.* xxiv. 57.
64 Moulded jamb temporarily uncovered in 1990.
65 S.R.O. 1224, box 342, Prior Gosnell's reg. f. 22v.
66 *Vernacular Archit.* xxiv. 57.
67 Eyton, iv. 24; *Close R.* 1247–51, 567; *Cal. Chart. R.* 1226–57, 369.
68 *V.C.H. Salop.* ii. 41.
69 W. F. Mumford, *Wenlock in the Middle Ages* (Shrews. 1977), 18–19.
70 *Household Roll of Bp. Swinfield* (Camd. Soc. [1st ser.], lix), 77.
71 *V.C.H. Salop.* i. 333.
72 *Pipe R.* 1182 (P.R.S. xxxi), 23.
73 *Rot. Hund.* ii. 85.
74 S.R.O. 1224/2/5; 4044/1, Monkhopton, no. 224; P.R.O., IR 29/29/4; IR 30/29/4, fields 153–4, 156, 159; SC 6/Hen. VIII/3021, m. 9. Dr. M. Gelling is thanked for comment on the place-name evidence.

manor of Acton Round. The rest belonged in 1255 to Wenlock priory.[75]

Wenlock priory's demesne manor of *WESTON* included Monkhopton and Monk Hall by 1255[76] and by 1334 was treated as a member of Oxenbold.[77] In 1545 the Crown sold the five farms then in Weston to Thomas Ireland.[78] He conveyed them that year to Thomas Bromley,[79] who added them to his Oxenbold manorial estate.

In 1545 the Crown sold *HOPTON* and *MONK HALL*, formerly members of Oxenbold, to the brothers Richard and Thomas Lawley to hold in chief by knight service as one manor;[80] later deeds usually described it as two. Richard died in sole possession in 1569.[81] The manor then descended with Bourton (in Much Wenlock) until the death of Beilby Richard Lawley, Lord Wenlock, in 1880.[82] By 1885 it had passed to Wenlock's second son R. T. Lawley,[83] 4th baron 1912. The manor descended with the barony until the death in 1932 of Arthur Lawley, the last baron,[84] from whom it passed to his sister Mrs. Caroline Elizabeth Molyneux (d. 1934) and then to a nephew Yvo Richard Vesey, Viscount De Vesci.[85] De Vesci sold the estate in 1947 to Lt.-Col. H. R. ('Peter') Marsh, who passed it in 1968 to his son J. R. N. Marsh, owner in 1990.[86] Manor Farm (renamed St. Peter's House *c.* 1989) is presumed to have been the chief house. It has a timber framed gable dated 1715, perhaps of an added wing, but was otherwise thoroughly remodelled in brick and stone in the 19th century, probably by Sir Francis Lawley (d. 1851).

In 1634 Ferrars Gresley sold a freehold estate in Monkhopton to William Barklam of Woolstaston. It was absorbed by the manorial estate in 1738 when Thomas Barklam sold it to Sir Robert Lawley.[87]

Francis Canning severed *LITTLE HUDWICK* from Ditton Priors manorial estate in 1730 by selling it to Hugh Lowe of Meadowley (in Morville).[88] In 1807 George Lowe sold it to Edward Palmer,[89] who sold it to Benjamin Tipton, his wife's brother-in-law, in 1811.[90] Tipton's daughter and son-in-law Elizabeth and Edward Farmer sold it to Sir Francis Lawley in 1847,[91] and Little Hudwick was thus added to the Hopton and Monk Hall manorial estate.

In the Middle Ages the *RECTORIAL TITHES* of the area which became the parish of Monkhopton, with the possible exception of those of Little Hudwick, belonged to the church of Holy Trinity, Much Wenlock, appropriated to Wenlock priory.[92]

In 1548 the Crown sold the great tithes of Monkhopton, Weston, and Monk Hall to Sir Thomas Palmer[93] but in 1553 resumed them on his attainder for high treason.[94] In 1608 James I sold them to Francis Phelipps and Richard Moore, who immediately resold them to John Lutwyche.[95] They descended thereafter with Shipton manor[96] until 1783, when Thomas Mytton sold them to Benjamin Mountford.[97] They yielded *c.* £60 a year in 1793.[98] By 1841 those tithes had been divided. Mountford's son Richard had sold part in 1834 to William Butcher,[99] whose brother John owned that part in 1841. The rest were in the hands of Richard's widow Mary, his daughter Alice Palmer, and his granddaughter's husband Edward Farmer.[1]

From 1544 those great tithes of Oxenbold that were formerly the priory's (and thus within the later parish of Monkhopton) apparently descended with Oxenbold manor and belonged in 1841 to the duke of Cleveland.[2]

At commutation in 1841 the impropriate tithes were merged in the freehold lands wherever possible, the rest, variously owned, being commuted to £115 18*s.*[3]

ECONOMIC HISTORY. In 1086 Oxenbold manor was worth only 8*s.* and rated at 1 hide. The demesne had an oxman and ½ ploughteam; a *villanus*, a bordar, and a Frenchman had 1½ ploughteam, but there was said to be land for 4 teams.[4] In Oxenbold township Robert de Girros had a park by 1244,[5] and in 1251 Wenlock priory was licensed to inclose a new one.[6] Oxenbold manor lay in Clee chase, then held by Walter of Clifford,[7] who allowed the area of the new park to be disafforested.[8] At the same time William of Corfield's son Roger exchanged the pasture rights that he had enjoyed in the old park for new ones (excluding swine and goats) over the manor's fallow lands outside the prior's woods and meadows.[9]

The prior's park probably included the southward projection of the parish, on the slopes south-east of Great Oxenbold; the projection's eastern boundary was marked in 1987 by a ditch and the remains of an internal bank, *c.* 1.5 m. high in places. The park evidently included woodland, for in 1431 swine were being pannaged

75 *Rot. Hund.* ii. 71, 85. Cf. Eyton, iv. 27; xi. 296–7.
76 *Rot. Hund.* ii. 85.
77 S.R.O. 566/1.
78 *L. & P. Hen. VIII*, xx (1), p. 223.
79 Barnard MSS., Raby Castle, abstr. of writings, pt. 1, f. 50.
80 *L. & P. Hen. VIII*, xx (2), p. 222; S.R.O. 1037/20/134.
81 P.R.O., C 142/152, no. 162.
82 P.R.O., C 142/201, no. 115; Hull Univ., Brynmor Jones Libr., DDFA/26/9–10, 20, 35, 40–1, 78, 80; S. Bagshaw, *Dir. Salop.* (1851), 579; *P.O. Dir. Salop.* (1856), 84; (1879), 363. Cf. below, M. Wenlock, manors (Bourton).
83 *Kelly's Dir. Salop.* (1885), 897.
84 Ibid. (1922), 155; L. G. Pine, *New Extinct Peerage* (1972), 292. For the pedigree after 1880 see also *Complete Peerage*, xii (2), 487–8.
85 *Kelly's Dir. Salop.* (1934), 163; (1937), 164. On De Vesci see J. Lees-Milne, *Midway on the Waves* (1985), 39.
86 Inf. from Mr. Marsh.
87 Hull Univ., Brynmor Jones Libr., DDFA/26/12, 50.
88 S.R.O., q. sess. rec. parcel 281, reg. of papists' deeds 1717–88, pp. 2, 190; 2482/153–4. Cf. above, Ditton Priors, manors.
89 S.R.O. 2482/158–9.
90 S.R.O. 2623/178.
91 Ibid. /126.
92 Below, M. Wenlock, manors (rectory).
93 *Cal. Pat.* 1548–9, 15.
94 S.R.O. 1037/16/8; *D.N.B.*
95 S.R.O. 1037/20/4.
96 Ibid. /20/70, 72, 74, 77, 131; 2482/162. Cf. below, Shipton, manors.
97 S.R.O. 2623/181, ff. 1–4.
98 S.P.L., MS. 6865, p. 145.
99 S.R.O. 2623/181, ff. 13–15.
1 P.R.O., IR 29/29/222. For the fam. connexions see S.R.O. 2623/126, 178, 181.
2 P.R.O., C 142/256, no. 7; C 142/402, no. 146; CP 25/2/714/32 & 33 Chas. II Hil. no. 10; IR 29/29/222.
3 P.R.O., IR 29/29/222.
4 *V.C.H. Salop.* i. 337.
5 Eyton, iv. 24. For its poss. site see above, Stanton Long, intro.; econ. hist.
6 Eyton, iv. 24; *Close R.* 1247–51, 567; *Cal. Chart. R.* 1226–57, 369.
7 Eyton, v. 196–7.
8 Barnard MSS., Raby Castle, abstr. of writings, pt. 1, f. 43.
9 Eyton, iv. 24.

there,[10] and in 1817 a large part of the supposed area was covered by Oxenbold coppice.[11]

It seems that in the Middle Ages open-field arable was virtually confined to land below 200 m., roughly the northern and western sides of the 19th-century parish, where the main settlements also stood. Weston had its own three fields,[12] of which the Lower field was mentioned in 1566;[13] so presumably did Monk Hall, where inclosures called Weston field were mapped in 1731, and Monkhopton. Above 200 m. much woodland and pasture adjoined Ditton Priors and Upton Cressett, which probably intercommoned them until boundaries were defined. Each main settlement had its own meadows: Monkhopton's, for example, were concentrated immediately north-west of the village, bordering a tributary of Beaconhill brook, and Monk Hall's were immediately south and west of the farmsteads.[14]

In the 13th century the area ploughed and grazed was being extended. Assarting was mentioned at Weston in 1262,[15] and 'new' land was recorded there in 1322.[16] The Middle Ages saw much clearance of woodland on the high ground towards Upton Cressett, for arable, and at Netchwood, towards Ditton Priors, apparently for pasture. The New Leasow, some 75 a. of pasture on high ground below Netchwood, was also presumably reclaimed from woodland. The names Brierley (recorded 1262)[17] and Cawley, for large areas towards the Ditton Priors and Stanton Long parish boundaries, probably denoted other woods, as did the Brydleys and the Stockings at Weston.[18] By 1322 Brierley and Cawley were arable areas outside the open fields.[19] There were evidently extensive pastures at Oxenbold *c.* 1327, when Philip de Cheyne had at least 400 sheep there.[20] The manor's meadow lands, probably restricted to the proximity of water, barely sufficed by 1390 to sustain its working animals.[21]

In the open fields mixed husbandry was practised. A three-course rotation was followed in the later 14th century,[22] and tenants were penalized for failing to fence the growing crops, for allowing their animals into the common fields thus fenced, and for unauthorized grazing of the fallows.[23] At his death in late February 1379 Richard of Weston, one of the prior's customary tenants there, had stores of oats, vetches, and wheat (*bladum*), and livestock including an ox, a bullock, a ram or boar (*hogetus*), a mare and foal, and poultry. Other animals were presumably slaughtered earlier that winter. Richard's buildings included a granary and a barn;[24] in 1404 a tenant elsewhere had a covered sheepfold, and another in 1449 had a wainhouse.[25]

In the early 14th century the usual open-field holding seems to have been a virgate or half-virgate, held by copy for life and subject to the usual exactions of 'varneth', heriot, and terciary.[26] Most labour services may have been commuted by then,[27] but carrying services (*averagium*) persisted.[28] Free tenants were recorded by 1369.[29] There was at least one isolated arable farm, called the 'Brochous' in 1322 and comprising a ¼-virgate at the 'Broks'.[30] It was presumably represented in 1987 by Brook House (a 26-a. farm in 1841)[31] near Beaconhill brook north-east of Monkhopton village. In the early 16th century the vicar of Stanton Long reported that at Great Oxenbold 'the prior of Wenlock doth keep husbandry . . . now better than I knew before'.[32]

In 1545,[33] and still in 1731, Monkhopton village had six farms including the mill,[34] and Monk Hall had two.[35] Weston had five farms, occupied as four, in 1545.[36] Little Hudwick consisted of one farm in 1730.[37] At Weston the farms had been reduced to three by 1747 and there was only one at Great Oxenbold, about half of which lay in Stanton Long parish.[38] The Monkhopton farms and three of those at Weston were copyholds in 1545, but the Monk Hall farms were leaseholds for long terms of years granted by the priory in 1518 and 1534.[39] Great Oxenbold, too, was subject to a long lease of 1536.[40]

Inclosure of open-field arable at Weston was reported in 1517.[41] By the mid 18th century the whole parish was inclosed.[42] It was noted in 1793 that some former smallholdings had been absorbed by other farms, and their houses reduced to labourers' cottages. The labourers, unless they kept a pig, lived mainly on bread and potatoes.[43] Between 1834 and 1841 the six farms of Monkhopton village were reduced to two, later called Manor farm (then rebuilt) and Home farm, and three new farms were created, with houses set amidst their fields: Highclear, Netchwood, and Woolshope. By 1841 the parish's Monk Hall farms had been amalgamated. Field boundaries on the Lawley estate were extensively altered before 1834 and the woods had been taken into the lord's hand by 1841.[44] Many of the changes were among Sir Francis Lawley's rapid and thorough estate improvements begun after 1834, which required new buildings,

10 S.R.O. 1224/2/8.
11 B.L. Maps, O.S.D. 207.
12 Barnard MSS., Raby Castle, box 1, bdle. 17, no. 12.
13 P.R.O., SC 2/197/118.
14 Field names of 1731 in S.R.O. 3765/2.
15 *Cal. Chart. R.* 1327–41, 488.
16 S.R.O. 1037/19/1.
17 *Cal. Chart. R.* 1327–41, 488.
18 S.R.O. 168/2, ff. 89, 90, 91; 3765/2. Cf. M. Gelling, *Place-Names in the Landscape* (1984), 199.
19 S.R.O. 1037/19/1.
20 *Cal. Pat.* 1327–30, 78.
21 S.R.O. 1224, box 342, Prior Gosnell's reg. f. 35v.
22 B.L. Add. MS. 6165, p. 98.
23 S.R.O. 1224/2/1, 4–5.
24 Ibid. /2/15.
25 S.R.O. 1190/1, unlisted ct. r. 1403–4; 1224/2/9.
26 S.R.O. 1093/19/1; 1224/2/8, 15. For 'varneth' cf. *V.C.H. Salop.* xi. 43, 82. On terciary see *T.S.A.S.* lviii. 68–76.
27 They were assigned a cash value in 1291: *Tax. Eccl.* (Rec. Com.), 164.
28 S.R.O. 566/1; 1224/2/1.
29 B.L. Add. MS. 6165, p. 98.
30 S.R.O. 1037/19/1.
31 P.R.O., IR 29/29/222; IR 30/29/222, field 252.
32 Heref. D. & C. mun. 4575.
33 *L. & P. Hen. VIII*, xx (2), p. 222.
34 S.R.O. 3765/2.
35 S.R.O. 566/5.
36 *L. & P. Hen. VIII*, xx (1), p. 223.
37 S.R.O. 2482/153–4.
38 S.R.O. 168/2, ff. 89–93; P.R.O., IR 29/29/297; IR 30/29/297.
39 S.R.O. 566/5; *L. & P. Hen. VIII*, xx (1), p. 223.
40 P.R.O., SC 6/Hen. VIII/3021, m. 18.
41 P.R.O., C 104/26, comrs.' return.
42 S.R.O. 168/2, ff. 89–93; 3765/2; Birm. Univ. Libr., Mytton Papers, iv. 764.
43 S.P.L., MS. 6865, pp. 141, 143.
44 S.R.O., dep. plan 246; B.L. Maps, O.S.D. 207; P.R.O., IR 29/29/222; IR 30/29/222.

TABLE XXII

MONKHOPTON: LAND USE, LIVESTOCK, AND CROPS

		1867	*1891*	*1938*	*1965*
Percentage of	grassland	56	78	90	66
	arable	44	22	10	34
Percentage of	cattle	12	30	23	14
	sheep	80	61	71	81
	pigs	8	9	6	5
Percentage of	wheat	42	28	45	61
	barley	19	37	4	29
	oats	39	35	51	7
	mixed corn & rye	0	0	0	3
Percentage of agricultural land growing roots and vegetables		11	7	2	3

Sources: P.R.O., MAF 68/143, no. 10; /1340, no. 13; /3880, Salop. no. 204; /4945, no. 204.

draining, and the introduction of more efficient husbandry.[45] At Weston two of the farms were amalgamated before 1834 as the later Weston House, and the third, later called Weston (or Little Weston) farm, had been sold.[46] The woodland at Oxenbold and Weston had all been taken in hand by 1911.[47]

About 1730 the parish was said to contain as much arable as pasture,[48] and in 1841 there were equal acreages of arable and grass on the Lawley estate.[49] In 1793 the soil was 'cold, wet, and stiff'. A rotation of wheat, oats, clover, and fallow was usual, though clover was sometimes followed by oats again. Bad roads made it very difficult to carry manure to outlying land, which was therefore not ploughed.[50] In the parish as a whole grass exceeded arable by 5 to 4 in 1867 and most of the arable was turned over to grass during the late 19th and early 20th century.[51] During that period sheep were the predominant livestock but cattle were increasingly kept, especially for beef. In 1801 the main cereal crops had been wheat and oats. The same was true in 1867, but the proportion of barley was then also considerable and by 1891 had doubled, mainly at the expense of wheat. By 1938, however, barley growing had dwindled greatly, its former proportion of cereal acreage having been taken over equally by wheat and oats. In the mid 20th century there was a move towards arable, especially for wheat and to a lesser extent barley. On the grassland, which remained predominant, more sheep and fewer cattle were kept.

A mill of Oxenbold manor was mentioned in 1291.[52] By 1731 Monkhopton mill stood in the village on a leat on the east side of Beaconhill brook.[53] It continued working until *c.* 1950.[54]

In the mid 19th century there were small and scattered quarries for limestone and cornstone,[55] evidently not continuously worked; only two quarrymen lived in the parish in 1841.[56] Stone from the parish was used for road mending in the early 18th century,[57] and was evidently burnt for lime before 1731, when Limekiln leasow was recorded near Netchwood;[58] there were no commercial limeburners in 1841.[59] Clay, perhaps for brick making, was dug before 1883 in the north-east corner of the parish.[60]

In 1841 the parish included a shoemaker, a cooper, and a blacksmith.[61] The smithy, built *c.* 1763,[62] was at the northern entrance to Monkhopton village in the 1840s[63] and moved before 1883 to a site on the main road east of the village.[64] In 1987 it was a garage and general store.

LOCAL GOVERNMENT. Weston, a separate manor including Monk Hall and Monkhopton in 1255,[65] was part of Oxenbold by 1334.[66] Before 1544 Oxenbold manor also included parts of Shipton and Stanton Long parishes. Records of its manor court survive for 1333–4, 1344–5, 1379–80, 1403–4, 1411–12, 1420–1, 1431, 1449, 1522, and 1566.[67] In the 14th century the court seems to have met four times a year, but in the 15th century sometimes only once or twice. The meeting place in May 1540 was at Oxenbold.[68] Officers included a bailiff,[69] aletasters, a woodward, and, for each of the townships, one or more constables. The business was mainly that of a court baron but breaches of the assize of bread and of ale were also dealt with.

Leet jurisdiction was granted to the lord of Oxenbold in 1544[70] and to the lords of Hopton

45 *V.C.H. Salop.* iv. 214.
46 S.R.O., dep. plan 246.
47 S.R.O. 4011/1, no. 207.
48 Birm. Univ. Libr., Mytton Papers, iv. 764.
49 P.R.O., IR 29/29/222.
50 S.P.L., MS. 6865, p. 143.
51 Rest of para. based on Table XXII.
52 *Tax. Eccl.* 164. For a mill nr. Gt. Oxenbold see above, Stanton Long, econ. hist.
53 S.R.O. 3765/2; fig. 36.
54 S.R.O. 3756/147, pp. 39–40.
55 P.R.O., IR 29/29/222; IR 30/29/222, fields 37, 182, 281, 304; *P.O. Dir. Salop.* (1856), 84; O.S. Maps 6", Salop. LVII. NE., SE. (1891 edn.); LVIII. NW. (1892 edn.); Greig, *Geol. of Country around Ch. Stretton*, 230–1, 236.
56 P.R.O., HO 107/928/9, ff. 4, 5.
57 *T.S.A.S.* lvi. 324.
58 S.R.O. 3765/2; fig. 36.
59 P.R.O., HO 107/928/9, ff. 3v.–7.
60 Brickwks. nearby in Morville par.: O.S. Map 1/2,500, Salop. LVIII. 5 (1883 edn.).
61 P.R.O., HO 107/928/9, ff. 3v., 4v., 6.
62 S.R.O. 3765/2 (not shown); Hull Univ., Brynmor Jones Libr., DDFA(2)/15/15.
63 P.R.O., IR 29/29/222; IR 30/29/222, field 243.
64 O.S. Map 1/2,500, Salop. LVII. 8 (1884 edn.).
65 *Rot. Hund.* (Rec. Com.), ii. 85.
66 S.R.O. 566/1.
67 Ibid. /1–2; 1190/1, unlisted ct. r. 1403–4; 1224/2/1–9; P.R.O., SC 2/197/118; cf. above, Stanton Long, local govt.; below, Shipton, local govt. Rest of para. based on the rolls.
68 S.R.O. 1037/16/15.
69 *T.S.A.S.* lviii. 73.
70 Barnard MSS., Raby Castle, abstr. of writings, pt. 1, p. 44.

and Monk Hall in 1545.[71] In the early 18th century the division between the manors coincided with that between two of Wenlock borough's townships, Oxenbold (or Weston and Oxenbold) and Monkhopton, each of which had a constable[72] and a highway surveyor.[73] There was a pinfold near Monkhopton church in 1731.[74] In the period 1821–43 an Oxenbold court was being summoned every three years in October.[75]

In 1714 the parish had two overseers of the poor[76] but in the 19th century only one; in 1828–9 he was a small farmer and administered the rates personally.[77] Expenditure on the poor 1775–6 was £30, but in 1802–3 was £97 or about 6*s*. per head of population. Fourteen adults and four children then received regular relief. In the peak year 1814–15 expenditure per head was about 8*s*. and 29 adults had regular relief.[78] By the early 1820s expenditure had fallen markedly but thereafter rose to another peak, *c*. 9*s*. per head, in 1828–9,[79] presumably related to the parish's large but short-lived population rise of the 1820s.[80]

The civil parish (enlarged in 1883 by the addition of Skimblescott)[81] was in Bridgnorth poor-law union 1836–1930,[82] Bridgnorth rural sanitary district 1872–94, Bridgnorth rural district 1894–1974, and Bridgnorth district from 1974.[83] The parish, which ceased to be in Wenlock municipal borough in 1889,[84] probably remained a highway authority until 1895.[85]

CHURCH. The earliest fabric of Monkhopton church is 12th-century and a chaplain was mentioned *c*. 1180.[86]

By 1331, and probably long before, the chapel depended on Holy Trinity church, Much Wenlock,[87] to whose parish Weston, Monkhopton, and (since 1244) part of Oxenbold belonged,[88] their tithes having presumably been annexed to Holy Trinity after Wenlock priory acquired lands there.[89] The whole of Oxenbold had probably paid tithe to the rector of Stanton Long, who was suing the prior for tithes in 1270,[90] and part of Oxenbold remained in Stanton Long. Monk Hall was probably always in Holy Trinity parish until parts were included in Acton Round and Monkhopton parishes when they were formed in post-medieval times.[91] From 1274 the inhabitants of Monkhopton, Weston, and Monk Hall had to pay the vicar of Much Wenlock an annual amount of grain and money called 'shrift corn' for their confessions.[92] Wenlock priory, as appropriator of Holy Trinity, Much Wenlock, received dues worth 73*s*. 4*d*. from Monkhopton chapel in 1369.[93] The chapel had no burial rights in the 1550s: they belonged to Holy Trinity, Much Wenlock.[94] In the 16th and 17th centuries Oxenbold and Weston often, perhaps usually, buried at Stanton Long.[95] By 1701, however, Monkhopton church had burial rights and marriages were solemnized there.[96] Little Hudwick was part of the parish by 1718.[97]

The chaplain or curate in 1587 received a stipend of £5 13*s*. 4*d*.,[98] but from whom is not known; in 1694 the inhabitants paid it,[99] and *c*. 1730 they 'hired' the minister.[1] Following the first of several benefactions from Queen Anne's Bounty in 1747[2] the living became a perpetual curacy, in Sir Robert Lawley's gift by 1759; the advowson descended thereafter with Hopton and Monk Hall manor.[3] Occasionally by 1820 and regularly from 1869 the curates were styled vicars.[4] In 1927 the vicarage was united with Upton Cressett rectory and the patrons presented alternately.[5] From 1955 the bishop allowed the united benefice to be held in plurality with those of Ditton Priors and Neenton, and from 1958 presentation to all three was ordered to be exercised in a series of four turns by the respective patrons.[6] In 1962, however, the patronage rights were suspended and the vicar of Acton Round and of Morville with Aston Eyre was appointed curate-in-charge of Upton Cressett with Monkhopton.[7] Monkhopton and Upton Cressett ecclesiastical parishes were united as Upton Cressett with Monkhopton in 1970, with one church at Monkhopton.[8] From the late 1970s that parish, with that of Morville with Aston Eyre, was in the pastoral care of a non-stipendiary minister living in Bridgnorth.

71 S.R.O. 1037/20/134.
72 *Salop. N. & Q.* i–ii. 25; Birm. Univ. Libr., Mytton Papers, vii. 1523.
73 *T.S.A.S.* lvi. 315–16, 322, 324–5.
74 S.R.O. 3765/2.
75 S.R.O. 248/35.
76 W.B.R., Q1/13/151.
77 S.R.O. 1634, box 40, case for counsel's opinion; S.R.O. 3894/Ch/1, 27 Mar. 1856.
78 *Poor Law Abstract*, H.C. 175, pp. 422–3 (1803–4), xiii; H.C. 82, pp. 376–7 (1818), xix.
79 *Poor Rate Returns*, H.C. 556, suppl. app. p. 144 (1822), v; H.C. 334, p. 179 (1825), iv; H.C. 219, p. 167 (1830–1), xi; H.C. 444, p. 162 (1835), xlvii.
80 *V.C.H. Salop*. ii. 224.
81 Above, this article, intro.
82 V. J. Walsh, 'Admin. of Poor Laws in Salop. 1820–55' (Pennsylvania Univ. Ph.D. thesis, 1970), 150; *Kelly's Dir. Salop*. (1929), 159.
83 *Rural Dist. Councillors Electn. Order, 1894* (Local Govt. Bd. order no. 31847); *V.C.H. Salop*. ii. 213; iii. 179, and sources cited ibid. 169 n. 29.
84 Local Govt. Bd.'s Prov. Order Conf. (No. 4) Act, 1889, 52 & 53 Vic. c. 22 (Local).
85 *Lond. Gaz*. 27 Mar. 1863, p. 1769; S.R.O., S.C.C. Local Govt., etc., Cttee. min. bk. 1894–1903, p. 29.
86 Eyton, iv. 112.
87 Ibid. 29.
88 S.R.O. 1224/2/11. It is not clear whether Lit. Hudwick (later in Monkhopton par.) was at that time in M. Wenlock or in Ditton Priors par.
89 Above, manors.
90 Birm. Univ. Libr., Mytton Papers, v. 1209.
91 Above, this article, intro.
92 Eyton, iii. 266; iv. 112.
93 S.R.O. 1224, box 342, Prior Gosnell's reg. f. 36.
94 *T.S.A.S.* vi. 99, 103, 107, 111, 121.
95 S.R.O. 3901/Rg/1.
96 H.W.R.O.(H.), Heref. dioc. rec., bp.'s transcripts, Monkhopton; S.R.O. 3894/Rg/1.
97 S.R.O., q. sess. rec. parcel 281, reg. of papists' deeds 1717–88, p. 2.
98 Heref. Cath. Libr., M.R. 6.A.iv, f. 7v.
99 H.W.R.O.(H.), HD 7, chwdns. to registrar 18 June 1694.
1 Birm. Univ. Libr., Mytton Papers, iv. 764.
2 C. Hodgson, *Q. Anne's Bounty* (2nd edn.), p. ccxc.
3 *Dioc. of Heref. Institutions (1539–1900)*, ed. A. T. Bannister (Heref. 1923), 94, 136, 143, 157, 182, 190, 197; *Crockford, passim*. Cf. above, manors.
4 Bannister, op. cit. 143; Heref. Dioc. Regy., reg. 1857–69, pp. 639, 684.
5 Heref. Dioc. Regy., reg. 1926–38, pp. 44, 298.
6 Ibid. 1953–68, pp. 95, 98–9, 255, 268–9.
7 *Crockford* (1975–6), 469.
8 Heref. Dioc. Regy., reg. 1969– (in use), pp. 66–7.

The curacy had no endowment until the 18th century and no glebe house in 1716.[9] By 1793, however, the minister had £11 6*s.* from tithe.[10] Queen Anne's Bounty made grants in 1747, 1769, 1786, 1809, and 1825,[11] and the curate's net income was £56 by 1835.[12] Glebe was bought at Clee Stanton in 1782[13] and there was glebe worth £25 a year by 1842;[14] it included 7½ a. at Clee Stanton,[15] which were sold in 1863.[16] In 1887 the glebe comprised 20 a., mostly at Redmarley D'Abitot (Worcs., later Glos.) and Stottesdon.[17] In the later 18th century the parishioners were contributing to the curate's stipend by unlawful annual payments out of church rates.[18] In 1844 two benefactions from Sir Francis Lawley, matched by Queen Anne's Bounty, increased the stipend by £33,[19] and in 1845 the payments from rates were stopped.[20] About 1840 Sir Francis built a large house in spacious grounds for his nephew, the new perpetual curate.[21] It remained Sir Francis's property and in 1869, when a non-resident vicar was appointed, became a private house.[22] A resident vicar was appointed in 1877 and the diocese then provided a smaller house in the village, used as a vicarage until 1954 and during 1960–2.[23]

The curate resided in 1587[24] but by the later 17th century the poverty of the curacy was such that it was often, perhaps regularly, filled by non-resident pluralists. William Hotchkiss (d. 1674), John Farmer (fl. 1677), and Richard Ellis (fl. 1685) were ministers of Acton Round, and the curacy seems to have been held continuously by ministers of Acton Round from 1726 to 1798,[25] two of whom lived at Cleobury Mortimer.[26] The minister of Upton Cressett held the curacy *c.* 1698–1719 and the vicar of Stanton Long 1719–26.[27] From 1810 to 1841 it was held by the assistant curate (from 1835 the vicar) of Much Wenlock.[28] The first resident minister in modern times was R. W. Dayrell, the patron's nephew, instituted in 1841.[29] Except for the period 1869–77 the incumbent was normally resident until 1954,[30] though Samuel Boot abandoned the parish in 1880 and resigned in 1884,[31] and S. G. Hayward held successive livings in plurality with Monkhopton 1887–1927.[32] Since 1955, except during 1960–2, the cure has been exercised by non-residents.[33] Until 1841 services were often taken by assistant clergy,[34] who were themselves frequently incumbents or assistant curates of nearby parishes.[35]

In 1716 there was an afternoon service every other Sunday and communion three or four times a year.[36] In the mid 18th century, however, services were irregular and infrequent until the parishioners began to supplement the minister's stipend.[37] In 1793 there was a service every Sunday and communion four times a year.[38] Communion was celebrated five times 1830–1[39] and six times 1863–4.[40] In 1851 congregations averaged 30 morning and afternoon.[41] In the late 19th century there were two services every Sunday, and monthly communion. Easter communicants averaged *c.* 22.[42] The vicar adopted the surplice in 1894.[43] In 1987 services were much less frequent but congregations of *c.* 20 were usual.[44]

The small church of *ST. PETER*, so dedicated by 1546,[45] is built of sandstone rubble with ashlar quoins and consists of chancel, with north organ chamber, and nave, with south porch, north vestry, and west bell turret.[46] The small churchyard is rectangular.

Chancel and nave were built in the 12th century. Surviving features of that period are a splayed window on the north side of the chancel,

9 H.W.R.O.(H.), HD 5/14/1/17.
10 S.P.L., MS. 6865, pp. 2, 142.
11 Hodgson, *Q. Anne's Bounty* (2nd edn.), p. ccxc.
12 *Rep. Com. Eccl. Rev.* [67], p. 447, H.C. (1835), xxii.
13 Downton Hall muniments, deed.
14 Lewis, *Topog. Dict. Eng.* (1842), ii. 505.
15 P.R.O., IR 29/29/84, fields 1–2.
16 Downton Hall muniments, deed.
17 *Return of Glebe Land, 1887*, H.C. 307, p. 59 (1887), lxiv.
18 S.P.L., MS. 6865, p. 145; S.R.O. 3894/Ch/1, 27 Mar. 1845.
19 Hodgson, *Q. Anne's Bounty* (2nd edn.), pp. ccxxxiv, ccxc.
20 S.R.O. 3894/Ch/1, 27 Mar. 1845.
21 *Rep. Com. Eccl. Rev.* p. 447; P.R.O., IR 29/29/222; IR 30/29/222, field 332; below, this section.
22 E. Cassey & Co. *Dir. Salop.* (1871), 237.
23 Heref. Dioc. Regy., reg. 1867–83, p. 658; S.R.O. 2079/LVII. 8; 4044/1 (no. 231); *Crockford* (1953–4), 1196; (1955–6), 371, 1187; (1959–60), 1091; (1961–2), 1118; (1971–2), 458; S.R.O., reg. of electors, Ludlow const. (1955), 255–6; (1956), 254; (1960), 256; (1961), 258; (1963), 259–60; (1964), 266; cf. above, Ditton Priors, churches.
24 Heref. Cath. Libr., M.R. 6.A.iv, f. 7v.
25 S.R.O. 3894/Rg/1–3; 3898/Rg/5, bur. 23 May 1759; 5482/Rg/1, bur. 8 Sept. 1674; S.P.L., Acton Round par. reg. transcript; H.W.R.O.(H.), Heref. dioc. rec., bp.'s transcripts, Monkhopton; Bannister, *Heref. Institutions*, 94; *S.P.R. Heref.* iii (3); ix (1), 314.
26 S.P.L., MS. 6865, p. 145; *T.S.A.S.* ii. 59, 67.
27 H.W.R.O.(H.), Heref. dioc. rec., bp.'s transcripts, Monkhopton; S.R.O. 3894/Rg/1. For their Upton Cressett and Stanton Long incumbencies see *S.P.R. Heref.* xxii. 9, 15; S.R.O. 3901/Rg/1.
28 Bannister, *Heref. Institutions*, 136, 143, 157; S.R.O. 3898/Rg/8, 18 Mar. 1841. For M. Wenlock clergy see Bannister, op. cit. 153; Heref. Dioc. Regy., reg. 1822–42, p. 8; S.R.O. 3898/Rg/8, 18 Mar. 1841.
29 *Eddowes's Jnl.* 21 June 1843; Bannister, op. cit. 157.
30 P.R.O., IR 29/29/222, field 332; *P.O. Dir. Salop.* (1856), 84; Bannister, op. cit. 169 (s.v. Acton Round), 182, 190; E. Cassey & Co. *Dir. Salop.* (1871), 46; *Kelly's Dir. Salop.* (1885 and later edns.); *Crockford* (1947), 746; (1953–4), 131; (1955–6), 1187.
31 S.R.O. 3894/Rg/5; Heref. Dioc. Regy., reg. 1867–83, pp. 724, 726; 1883–1901, pp. 14–16; Bannister, *Heref. Institutions*, 197.
32 *Crockford* (1935), 590.
33 Heref. Dioc. Regy., reg. 1953–68, pp. 95, 255, 268–9; *Crockford* (1955–6), 371, and later edns.; above, this section; inf. from the Revd. H. J. Patterson.
34 H.W.R.O.(H.), Heref. dioc. rec., bp.'s transcripts, Monkhopton; S.R.O. 3894/Rg/3; *S.P.R. Heref.* iii (3); Heref. Dioc. Regy., reg. 1772–1802, f. 217v.; 1791–1821, ff. 36v., 130; 1822–42, p. 421.
35 S.P.L., Acton Round par. reg. transcript; *S.P.R. Heref.* i (6); xxiii.
36 H.W.R.O.(H.), HD 5/14/1/17.
37 S.R.O. 3894/Ch/1, 27 Mar. 1845.
38 S.P.L., MS. 6865, p. 146.
39 S.R.O. 3894/Ch/1, 27 Mar. 1845.
40 Ibid. 1863–4.
41 P.R.O., HO 129/356, no. 121.
42 S.R.O. 3894/Rg/5.
43 Ibid. Easter Day 1894.
44 Inf. from Mr. Patterson.
45 *T.S.A.S.* vi. 118.
46 Descr. based on S.P.L., MS. 372, vol. i, f. 106; S.P.L., J. H. Smith colln. no. 140; B.L. Add. MS. 21237, f. 291; Cranage, iii. 207; E. A. Gee, 'Hist. and arch. acct. of Wenlock priory and its dependent churches' (Birm. Univ. M.A. thesis, 1937), 243–4; Pevsner, *Salop.* 202.

two similar windows in the nave on the north and south sides, and the south doorway of the nave, which has a chevron-moulded arch. In 1795 the doorway also had a tympanum with geometrical carving. The south window of the chancel has three orders of heavy 12th-century moulding internally, a chain between two rows of chevrons. The arch, perhaps originally that of a doorway, was evidently introduced from elsewhere before 1793.[47] A priest's doorway, its hoodmould decorated with dog tooth, was inserted on the south side of the chancel in the earlier 13th century, and in the late 13th or early 14th century a two-light traceried window was inserted in the nave's south wall near the east end. In 1795 the chancel's east window had remains of painted glass representing the Crucifixion, and above the chancel arch was a painted wooden canopy, perhaps medieval and designed for a statue. The nave roof, apparently medieval, is of three bays, the trusses having collar beams and arched braces.

About 1840 the church was restored throughout at Sir Francis Lawley's expense.[48] The nave's 12th-century windows were blocked; three new windows were inserted on the north side and one on the south, all copied from the medieval traceried window in the south wall. An embattled brick or stone turret replaced the former timber framed west bell turret and was supported by a brick wall built across the nave near the west end. A new porch was made. Medieval mouldings were extensively renewed and the whole exterior was rendered, with incised lines to imitate ashlar joints.

Later in the 19th century, perhaps in 1885, a new three-light east window was inserted and a vestry was added on the north side of the chancel.[49] The plain hexagonal font, benches, wooden chancel screen, and brass and wood communion rail are all 19th-century.

The vestry became an organ chamber, perhaps in 1911.[50] In the 20th century the blocked 12th-century north window of the nave was opened up and fitted with heraldic glass in memory of R. T. Lawley, Lord Wenlock (d. 1918). A new north vestry at the west end of the nave was dedicated in 1938. At the same time the chancel was furnished with an 'English' altar.[51] A plain oak pulpit was given *c.* 1946 by Lady De Vesci[52] and the former pulpit was given to Linley church.[53]

A brass commemorating Jane Cressett (d. 1640) and signed by Francis Grigs was removed to Monkhopton from Upton Cressett church before 1970 and hangs in the nave. About the same time four panels of 16th- or 17th-century German or Flemish glass depicting Passion scenes were taken from the east window of Upton Cressett church and inserted in the west window at Monkhopton.[54]

In 1552 the church had two bells in what was called a steeple,[55] presumably the timber-clad west bell turret recorded in 1789.[56] One of two bells in 1915 was dated 1727.[57] By 1961 the plate included a chalice and paten of 1575, a pewter plate of 1721, and a chalice and paten of 1911;[58] a paten hallmarked for 1781 evidently came from another church.[59]

The registers survive from 1698 and there are transcripts 1638–9 and from 1660.[60]

NONCONFORMITY. Henry Maurice, an Independent minister, preached at 'Hopton', probably Monkhopton, on 18 August 1672,[61] but no other reference to Dissent is known.

EDUCATION. P. B. Lawley-Thompson, Lord Wenlock, built a National school and teacher's house in 1849; the schoolroom had 48 places. Wenlock's family supported the school until 1905 or later.[62] The school was under inspection from *c.* 1877.[63] The roll was *c.* 40 in 1851, and attendance averaged 21 in 1875, 48 in 1885, and 31 in 1913.[64]

By 1953 senior girls attended weekly domestic science classes in Bridgnorth.[65] The school became aided in 1954,[66] and next year 11-year-old pupils went to St. Mary's C.E. (Aided) school, Bridgnorth.[67] The roll was 29 in 1957.[68] Closure, periodically threatened from 1959, was resisted by the headmistress,[69] and a class was accommodated in the teacher's house 1962–4 until a new demountable classroom was added.[70] The roll was 42 in 1979[71] but only 27 in 1983 when the school closed: the building reverted to Lord Wenlock's heirs and the pupils went to Morville and Ditton Priors C.E. (Controlled) Primary schools.[72]

CHARITIES FOR THE POOR. None known.

47 S.P.L., MS. 6865, p. 146.
48 Lewis, *Topog. Dict. Eng.* (1840), ii. 460; ibid. (1842), ii. 505.
49 Heref. City Libr., Beddoe Colln. i, p. 92; S.R.O. 3894/Rg/5, 26 July 1885.
50 *Kelly's Dir. Salop.* (1913), 160.
51 Heref. Dioc. Regy., reg. 1926–38, p. 542; notice in vestry.
52 Heref. Dioc. Regy., reg. 1938–53, p. 298; inscr. on pulpit.
53 Above, Linley, church.
54 Inf. from Council for the Care of Churches.
55 *T.S.A.S.* 2nd ser. xii. 94.
56 S.P.L., MS. 372, vol. i, f. 106.
57 H. B. Walters, *Ch. Bells of Salop.* (Oswestry, 1915), 69.
58 D. L. Arkwright and B. W. Bourne, *Ch. Plate Archd. Ludlow* (Shrews. 1961), 45–6.
59 Possibly Sutton, nr. Shrews. The paten is inscr. 'Henricus Burton, Rector', with the date 1921: ibid. 46. *Crockford* lists no-one of that name *c.* 1921, but Hen. Burton was rector of Sutton in 1797 (*T.S.A.S.* 4th ser. vi. 326) and Sutton's communion plate was in lay custody in 1895 (ibid. v. 146).
60 S.R.O. 3894/Rg/1–4; regs. (bap. and bur. from 1813, marr. from 1839) at ch.; transcripts at H.W.R.O.(H.).
61 Maurice's diary (MS. in possession of the late Dr. A. B. Cottle, Bristol Univ., who supplied a transcript).
62 P.R.O., ED 7/102, ff. 434–5; *Kelly's Dir. Salop.* (1900), 150; (1905), 154. This section was written 1982–3 and later revised.
63 S.R.O. 3898/Sc/6, p. 20.
64 S. Bagshaw, *Dir. Salop.* (1851), 579; P.R.O., ED 7/102, ff. 434–5; *Kelly's Dir. Salop.* (1885), 897; (1913), 160.
65 S.R.O. 4598/1, p. 16.
66 Ibid. p. 36; *S.C.C. Mins. (Educ.)* 1954–5, 66.
67 S.R.O. 4598/1, pp. 32–3, 39–40.
68 Ibid. p. 92.
69 Mrs. B. M. Stoves, 1955–82: ibid. pp. 126–8, 133–4, etc.; inf. from Mrs. Stoves; personal knowledge.
70 S.R.O. 4598/1, pp. 164, 182, 187–8, 195, 203–4.
71 S.C.C. Educ. Cttee. *Sch. List* (1979), 7.
72 S.R.O. 4598/2, 22 July 1983; *Bridgnorth Jnl.* 11 Feb. 1983, p. 3; *Shropshire Star*, 23 July 1983, p. 14.

POSENHALL

POSENHALL, a small extra-parochial place, represents part of a former chapelry and township in Much Wenlock parish; it lies between Barrow, Benthall, and Willey, *c.* 4 km. north-east of Much Wenlock. It was entirely agricultural save during the 18th and 19th centuries when there were extractive and pottery industries.[73] Anciently it probably included land which by 1844 formed the south-western excrescence of Benthall parish:[74] in 1618 land west of the road to Broseley (including Posenhall green) was reckoned part of Posenhall, but it was later in Benthall.[75] Part of the township, probably representing the former priory demesne, evidently owed no tithes, and the chapel disappeared before 1618.[76] The untithed part of the township became extra-parochial, and in the 19th century, maintaining its own poor, duly became a civil parish.[77] It then comprised 345 a. (140 ha.) including 51 a. (21 ha.) in a rectangular detachment to the south-east surrounded by Barrow parish.[78] The detachment, unpopulated, was transferred in 1883 to Barrow C.P.,[79] which absorbed the rest of Posenhall C.P. in 1966.[80]

In the south-west the boundary touched the 213-m. contour, and in the north-east the land is over 180 m. From all parts the land falls to Hay (formerly Cheese)[81] brook which, rising in Benthall, drains through Posenhall into Dean brook in Willey. Between Posenhall hamlet and Marsh Head, Hay brook flows through Colley's dingle, narrow there but opening out to the south.[82] The name Posenhall perhaps means a hollow shaped like a bag[83] or purse.[84] The 19th-century boundary followed the Broseley road in the north-west but elsewhere field edges, some coinciding with the line of the medieval park pale of Willey.[85] Posenhall lies almost entirely on boulder clay.[86]

Posenhall was larger in the Middle Ages than it was later and, to judge from the existence of a chapel there,[87] it was perhaps more populous, but there are no medieval figures.[88] As in 1618 settlement probably flanked the Broseley road, on whose east side stood the chapel, mentioned in the early 14th century. The settlement was probably largely surrounded by open-field land, although there was common around the township's northern edge and woodland probably in the south.[89] In 1618 four farms lay around Posenhall green, one to the west, the others to the east. Just to the north, in Benthall, was Purse well, a main water source.[90]

North and south of Posenhall green there were lanes out of the Broseley road north to Benthall and south-west to Arlescott (in Barrow). A little farther south the road forked, one way to Much Wenlock (via the Marsh), the other to Barrow. The Broseley–Wenlock road, whose width was set at 41 ft. in 1637,[91] was turnpiked in 1756 and disturnpiked in 1867.[92]

By the 1830s settlement had contracted; only two of the four farmhouses of 1618 remained and the green had been inclosed. The Benthall parish boundary then ran along the east side of the former green; Little Posenhall Farm, occupied in 1618 by Rowland Haynes, was thus in Benthall parish in the 1830s. It is a substantial **T** shaped building. One wing, of two storeys and an attic, is of stone and probably late 16th-century. Its large lateral stack is topped by elaborate brick chimneys of similar date. The abutting brick wing, *c.* 1750, probably replaced a timber framed predecessor. Abutting to the north-east is a brick malthouse and pigeon house, also *c.* 1750. To the east stood what in 1618 had been Roger Moane's farmhouse, a late 16th-century building much altered in the 18th century; its service end was burnt down in the mid 1960s. In the 1830s a few cottages were scattered around the farmhouses.[93] In the 19th and earlier 20th century the population was *c.* 20, as it had probably been from the 17th.[94]

MANOR AND OTHER ESTATES. In 1086 *POSENHALL* was probably part of Much Wenlock manor.[95] By the 1140s Uchtred held it of the prior, for 10*s.* a year. On his death *c.* 1150 Prior Reynold granted the estate in fee for 12*s.* a year to Uchtred's son Gregory.[96] Gregory had the whole of Posenhall, which was later divided between at least two estates.

One was evidently held by Alan son of Berengar, or of Buildwas (fl. 1176, d. by 1226), who was succeeded by another Alan of Buildwas (fl. 1228, d. by 1230) and he by another (fl. 1230–67).[97] In 1255 Alan of Buildwas and Andrew of Willey were joint lords of Posenhall, holding of the prior of Wenlock and paying 22*s.* between

73 This article was written in 1984.
74 Below, chapel of ease; above, Benthall, church.
75 S.R.O. 1224/1/9; 3956. 76 Below, chapel of ease.
77 Cf. ibid.; *V.C.H. Salop.* ii. 205.
78 O.S. *Area Bk.* (1883); above, fig. 20.
79 Divided Parishes Act, 1882, 45 & 46 Vic. c. 58, s. 2; O.S. *Area Bk.* Barrow (1883).
80 *V.C.H. Salop.* ii. 236–7.
81 S.R.O. 1224/3/109 (Chesebroke, 1455, located by Cheese field, 1618: ibid. /1/9); S.P.L., Deeds 18120.
82 O.S. Map 1/25,000, SJ 60 (1958 edn.).
83 *P.N. Salop.* (E.P.N.S.), i. 239.
84 Cf. next para. for Purse well.
85 *T.S.A.S.* lxv. 70–2; above, fig. 20.
86 Inst. Geol. Sciences Map 1/25,000, *Telford* (1978).
87 Below, manor; chapel of ease.
88 Unmentioned in e.g. Dom. Bk., the township was taxed with Barrow and Benthall in 1327: *T.S.A.S.* 2nd ser. iv. 331–3.
89 Below, econ. hist.
90 S.R.O. 1224/1/9; 3956.
91 S.R.O. 1224/1/9; /1/16; S.P.L., Deeds 18120.
92 Below, M. Wenlock, communications.
93 H. E. Forrest, *Old Hos. of Wenlock* (Shrews. 1914), 83; S.R.O. 3956; O.S. Map 1", index to tithe survey, sheet LXI. NE. [*c.* 1851]; S.R.O. 294/2.
94 *L. & P. Hen. VIII*, xvii, p. 508; *Hearth Tax 1672* (Salop. Arch. Soc. 1949), 34; *V.C.H. Salop.* ii. 226, 229.
95 Eyton, iii. 223.
96 Ibid. 284–5.
97 Ibid. 285–7; vii. 320–2; *T.S.A.S.* 3rd ser. vii. 385; *Roll of Salop. Eyre 1256* (Selden Soc. xcvi), p. 87.

them.[98] The third Alan also held land in Willey[99] and may have been related to its lords.[1]

In 1292 Alan of Buildwas's daughter and heir Alice apparently held his share of Posenhall, as she and her husband Edmund de Leynham did in 1302.[2] The later descent of the Leynhams' estate has not been traced, but it may have reverted to the priory. A farm at Posenhall owed suit by 1321 to the prior's demesne manor of Bradley, which was absorbed by Marsh manor in the 1380s.[3] In the 15th and 16th centuries two farms (Childe's and Haynes's) which had belonged to the priory's manor of Marsh also owed rent or suit to the Lacons and their court at Willey.[4]

In the early 17th century most of the land in Posenhall was acquired by John Weld. In 1618 John Slaney, lord of Marsh, and his brother Humphrey sold Haynes's and Childe's farms to Weld,[5] who was already the owner of the largest farm in Posenhall, Moane's farm,[6] and so the largest landowner in the township. Weld bought Willey manor in 1618 and Marsh manor in 1620,[7] and Posenhall descended with them,[8] remaining part of the Willey estate in 1984.[9]

In 1455 Isabel, widow of William Horseley of Posenhall, conveyed a small farm in Posenhall to William Bastard whose son and heir William conveyed it in 1475 to Joan Robinson, daughter of Walter Childe of Posenhall.[10] In 1518 Thomas Lacon leased the farm to Thomas Childe[11] and in 1618 it was sold, with Haynes's, to John Weld.[12]

Before 1518 John Robinson granted 16*s*. rent from the farm to Our Lady's service in Much Wenlock parish church.[13] The rent that Thomas Clarke of Posenhall paid to that service in 1547–8[14] was probably the 16*s*. rent that the Crown leased in 1573 and sold (to London speculators) in 1576;[15] the tenant of Childe's farm paid 16*s*. 'chantry rent' to Thomas Lawley's heirs in 1631.[16]

In 1576 Stephen and Margaret Hadnall sold lands in Benthall, Posenhall, and Wyke to Lawrence Benthall. The property was probably incorporated into Benthall manor.[17]

In 1554 the Crown granted impropriate *TITHES* in Posenhall, formerly owned by Wenlock priory, to Stephen Hadnall for life, and in 1581 sold them to Edmund Downing and Peter Ashton.[18] They descended thereafter with the great tithes of Barrow until 1631 or later.[19] Like the Posenhall small tithes, they were afterwards added to the tithes of neighbouring parishes.[20]

ECONOMIC HISTORY. Uchtred, who held Posenhall in the earlier 12th century, had Posenhall's share of a wood that evidently extended south towards Barrow and east into Willey. In a resolution of a dispute with Wenlock priory and its tenants in Barrow concerning part of the wood, Uchtred, with his son Gregory, partitioned the disputed part of the wood with them; the undisputed part, which lay partly in Willey and partly in Posenhall, remained in the respective hands of the priory and of Uchtred and Gregory. Gregory later allowed the priory's tenants in Barrow to have firebote and hedgebote and pannage and other pasture rights in his wood, though he reserved timber and the right to make assarts.[21] What was probably the wood retained by Gregory seems still to have been in existence in the mid 13th century.[22] Posenhall was in Shirlett forest until the disafforestation of 1301.[23]

In 1637 John Weld and Lawrence Benthall divided the extensive area of common along the Posenhall–Benthall boundary, Weld receiving Posenhall green and Marsh Head while Benthall took Posenhall common and Benthall Marsh.[24]

Much of medieval Posenhall was probably occupied by open fields. In 1455 selions lay in at least six separate fields and were being engrossed.[25] In 1517 William Childe was said to have inclosed 20 a. of arable and converted it to pasture.[26] By 1618, when no open fields were left, the main farms were Roger Moane's (155 a.), Rowland Haynes's (87 a.), and Richard Childe's (50 a.). By 1620 Rowland Haynes's farm and other land had apparently passed to Richard and Thomas Haynes who farmed 79 a. and 49 a. respectively.[27]

About 1585 leases for lives specified the maximum numbers of animals a farmer could keep,[28] and in the 16th and 17th centuries, as later, farming was mixed, perhaps with an emphasis on dairying. Some yeomen added other trades to farming, as did John (d. *c*. 1686) and Anne (d. *c*. 1691) Bowen, who were also skinners and glovers.[29] Richard Colley (d. *c*. 1684) was a particularly prosperous farmer. His livestock comprised a bull, 8 oxen and 33 other cattle, 2 mares, 72 sheep, and 13 pigs, altogether worth £128 5*s*. He had corn, grain, and malt (worth £70), hay (£30), and hemp and flax (£3). His farm's pastoral bias is clear from the presence in the farmhouse of a milk house, a cheese press room, two butteries, and what was probably over

98 *Rot. Hund.* (Rec. Com.), ii. 84.
99 S.R.O. 1224/3/150, no. 4.
1 If the first Alan of Buildwas was the Alan of Willey to whom Warner of Willey granted land in Willey 1180 x *c*. 1212: ibid. no. 3.
2 Eyton, vii. 322–3.
3 Below, local govt.
4 S.R.O. 1224/2/535–8, 546; /3/109–15, 135; cf. P.R.O., C 1/839/27–8. Willey descended with Harley: cf. below, Willey, manor; *V.C.H. Salop.* viii. 88.
5 S.R.O. 1224/1/135, pp. 14, 20; /3/131–3.
6 Ibid. /1/9; /7/1, ff. 21–5; box 163, Mr. Weld's memo. bk. 1619/20, f. 1.
7 Above, Barrow, manors (Marsh); below, Willey, manor.
8 S.R.O. 1224, boxes and parcels 183–93, rentals.
9 Inf. from Ld. Forester.
10 S.R.O. 1224/3/109–10.
11 S.R.O. 1224/3/112.
12 Above, this section.
13 *T.S.A.S.* vi. 103 (stating in error that he gave the farm itself); S.R.O. 1224/3/112; cf. below, M. Wenlock, churches.
14 S.R.O. 1224/3/8, ff. 9–10 (which gives the rent as 17*s*.).
15 S.R.O. 1224/3/114–15; *Cal. Pat.* 1575–8, p. 30.
16 S.R.O. 1224, box 163, John Weld's bk. 1631, f. 3, nos. 25, 29.
17 *Cal. Pat.* 1575–8, p. 164.
18 *Cal. Pat.* 1554–5, 22; 1580–2, p. 5.
19 S.R.O. 1224, box 163, John Weld's bk. 1631, f. 8; cf. above, Barrow, manors (tithes).
20 Below, chapel of ease.
21 Eyton, iii. 285.
22 S.R.O. 1224/3/150, no. 7.
23 Eyton, iii. 297–8; *V.C.H. Salop.* i. 488; iv. 45; *Select Pleas of Forest* (Selden Soc. xiii), p. 8; *Cartulary of Shrews. Abbey*, ed. U. Rees (1975), ii, p. 250.
24 S.P.L., Deeds 18120; cf. above, Benthall, econ. hist. (agric.).
25 S.R.O. 1224/1/9; /3/109, 150 (nos. 5, 13); *V.C.H. Salop.* iv. 84 (corr. below, Corrigenda).
26 B.L. Lansd. MS. 1, f. 191.
27 S.R.O. 1224/1/9; /3/136–7; /7/1, ff. 21–5.
28 Ibid. /3/136–7.
29 H.W.R.O.(H.), Heref. dioc. rec., invs. of Wm. Evans, 1680; John Bowen, 1685/6; Thos. Neale, 1687; Anne Bowen 1691; Jos. Reynolds, 1712. Mr. S. P. Mullins is thanked for the loan of transcripts.

a ton of cheese, worth £17 10s.[30] Oxen were still used as draught animals in 1712.[31]

In the later 18th century there was just one farm, of 289 a.; in 1793 it was roughly half pastoral (118 a. pasture, 24 a. meadow), half arable (139 a. cereals, 7 a. turnips). There were also two smallholdings.[32]

In 1808 a windmill stood on the north-western edge of Posenhall hamlet.[33]

In 1631 John Weld noted coal and ironstone in Posenhall,[34] and in the 18th century Posenhall was one of the places where the tenants of Willey ironworks had the right to get ironstone.[35]

Clay was probably cut and sold from Posenhall in the mid 17th century.[36] In 1742[37] or before[38] John Thursfield (d. 1760) established the Haybrook Pottery south of the road from Broseley to Much Wenlock on the northern boundary of Posenhall.[39] It produced earthenwares; unlike the Thursfield family's other works it did not later produce Jackfield ware.[40] Thursfield was succeeded by his son John (d. 1789) and perhaps also by his son William (also known as Morris, d. 1783). In 1770 the younger John leased four pothouses at Posenhall; two years later he built a new pottery on the north (Benthall) side of the road.[41] Soon afterwards John Thursfield probably gave up the Haybrook Pottery, for by 1776 it was leased to John Bell (d. 1799), who was succeeded by his son William, tenant until 1824 when Poole & Lloyd (or John Lloyd & Co.) became lessees. Until *c.* 1845 a series of partnerships held Haybrook: Poole & Lloyd 1824–33, Lloyd, Jones & Bathurst 1833–5, Jones & Bathurst 1835–7, Easthope, Jones & Bathurst 1837–43, and Jones & Bathurst who reunited the Haybrook and Benthall potteries *c.* 1845. Thenceforward the two works were always run together, although in the early 1850s W. T. Jones may have been responsible for the Haybrook works, which employed six men in 1851.[42]

In the 19th century a clay-pipe kiln stood south-east of Haybrook Pottery.[43]

LOCAL GOVERNMENT. What property Wenlock priory had in Posenhall[44] seems to have been administered through a court at Bradley grange by 1321[45] and later through the court of Marsh manor. Posenhall was still presenting at the Marsh court when it ceased to be held in the late 19th century.[46] Posenhall tenants, however, also owed suit to Willey manor court in the Middle Ages and the later 17th century,[47] presumably in respect of lands outside the prior's demesne.

In 1622 Posenhall was fined in Marsh manor court for not keeping up shooting butts,[48] and in 1663 the pound and stocks were in disrepair.[49]

Posenhall had a highway surveyor in the 1720s[50] and remained a highway authority until 1889.[51] Posenhall's expenditure on its poor averaged *c.* £30 a year 1812–19, peaking at £40 in 1814–15 when there were 6 recipients of permanent out-relief and 10 relieved occasionally. Expenditure averaged *c.* £11 a year 1820– 34.[52]

Posenhall was in Madeley poor-law union 1836–1930,[53] and Madeley rural sanitary district from 1872 until 1889 when it was transferred to the Barrow ward of Wenlock borough.[54] After the dissolution of Wenlock borough in 1966 Posenhall was transferred to Barrow civil parish, and was thus in Bridgnorth rural district 1966–74[55] and Bridgnorth district from 1974.[56]

Posenhall was within the jurisdiction of Broseley court of requests from 1782[57] until the court's abolition in 1846.[58]

CHAPEL OF EASE. In 1331 Posenhall chapel was confirmed to Wenlock priory as a dependency of Holy Trinity parish church, Much Wenlock.[59] The chaplaincies of Posenhall and Barrow were then linked; indeed the chapel at Posenhall may have gone, for in 1321 Hamon Corn, chaplain, had been granted all the lands of Barrow chapel in Barrow and Posenhall and obliged to keep the glebe buildings in Posenhall (where no chapel was mentioned) and Barrow in repair.[60]

Certainly there was no chapel by 1618, only

30 Ibid. inv. of 1684; cf. *Yeomen and Colliers in Telford*, ed. B. Trinder and J. Cox (1980), p. 78.

31 S.R.O. 1224/2/538.

32 Ibid. /7/11 (ff. 2–3), 18; box 174, sched. of Geo. Forester's est. in Posenhall 12 Mar. 1799; box 183, rental Lady Day 1755; 4791/1/2, p. 274.

33 Above, Benthall, econ. hist. (agric.).

34 S.R.O. 1224, box 163, John Weld's bk. 1631, f. 7.

35 Ibid. box 140, deed 16 Oct. 1711; below, Willey, econ. hist. (coal and ironstone).

36 S.R.O. 1224/2/545.

37 *T.S.A.S.* lv. 160.

38 J. Randall, *Severn Valley* (Madeley, 1882), 309, says 1729.

39 At O.S. Nat. Grid SJ 663 019: Trinder, *Ind. Rev. Salop.* 125.

40 Ibid.; J. Randall, *Clay Inds. on Banks of Severn* (Madeley, 1877), 21.

41 *T.S.A.S.* lv. 160–1; S.R.O. 1224/1/51.

42 S.R.O. 1224, box 140, deed 1 Feb. 1799; box 174, sched. of Geo. Forester's est. 1799; bdles. 185–93, Posenhall rentals 1776–1846; 2979/3, s.v. W. T. Jones; Pigot, *Nat. Com. Dir.* (1835), 351; C. Hulbert, *Hist. and Descr. of Salop.* ii (1837), 342; S. Bagshaw, *Dir. Salop.* (1851), 556. For wks. after 1845 see above, Benthall, econ. hist. (ind.).

43 SA 17175.

44 Above, manor.

45 Eyton, iii. 287; W. F. Mumford, *Wenlock in the Middle Ages* (Shrews. 1977), 157–8.

46 B.L. Add. MS. 6164, p. 383; S.R.O. 1224/2/16; above, Barrow, local govt.; below, M. Wenlock, local govt.; J. Randall, *Broseley and its Surroundings* (Madeley, 1879), 34.

47 S.R.O. 840, box 1, Lacon ct. r. of 1438; 1224/2/537–8, 541, 544, 546; /3/111–12; box 163, Mr. Weld's memo. bk. 1619/20, ff. 3 (26–7), 13; above, manor.

48 S.R.O. 1224/2/347.

49 Ibid. /2/111.

50 *T.S.A.S.* lvi. 315.

51 Local Govt. Bd.'s Prov. Order Conf. (No. 4) Act, 1889, 52 & 53 Vic. c. 22 (Local).

52 *Poor Law Abstract*, H.C. 82, pp. 376–7 (1818), xix; *Poor Rate Returns*, H.C. 556, suppl. app. p. 144 (1822), v; H.C. 334, p. 179 (1825), iv; H.C. 219, p. 167 (1830–1), xi; H.C. 444, p. 162 (1835), xlvii.

53 V. J. Walsh, 'Admin. of Poor Laws in Salop. 1820–55' (Univ. of Pennsylvania Ph.D. thesis, 1970), 148–50; *Kelly's Dir. Salop.* (1929), 130.

54 *V.C.H. Salop.* ii. 215–16 (corr. below, Corrigenda).

55 Ibid. 205, 236–7 (corr. ibid. xi. 376); iii. 168.

56 Sources cited ibid. iii. 169 n. 29.

57 Broseley, etc., Small Debts Act, 1782, 22 Geo. III, c. 37.

58 9 & 10 Vic. c. 95. Cf. *V.C.H. Salop.* iii. 115, 165.

59 *Cal. Pat.* 1348–50, 188; Eyton, iii. 287–8.

60 Above, Barrow, church.

a site east of Posenhall green marked by fields called Chapel yard.[61] The extra-parochial status of part of Posenhall township by the 19th century suggests that that part had been the priory's demesne (the former Leynham fee), and was therefore tithe-free.[62] It was presumably the rest of Posenhall that owed tithes to the vicar of Much Wenlock in 1640,[63] and they presumably passed later to one or more of the parishes created out of Much Wenlock and adjoining Posenhall, namely Barrow, Benthall, and Willey.[64] By the 17th century Posenhall's inhabitants attended Barrow church and made payments to the minister there.[65]

NONCONFORMITY. None known.

EDUCATION. Children went to school in Barrow.[66]

CHARITIES FOR THE POOR. None known.

SHIPTON

SHIPTON, a small rural parish, lies in Corve Dale *c.* 10 km. south-west of Much Wenlock. From 1844, when the boundary with Stanton Long was settled,[67] its main part contained 1,753 a. (709 ha.).[68] It comprised the townships of Shipton and Larden, and part of Brockton township, which lay partly in Stanton Long. A detached area, Skimblescott (111 a., 45 ha.), was transferred to Monkhopton civil parish in 1883.[69] The main part is compact and regular in shape. The long south-eastern boundary lies mostly along the river Corve, the north-western along the limestone ridge of Mogg Forest. The land slopes evenly from *c.* 280 m. at the ridge to *c.* 145 m. on the Corve, and is cut by the valleys of streams running down to the river.[70]

The underlying strata dip down from north-west to south-east.[71] The higher part of the parish is on Aymestry Group limestone; several small quarries there yielded building stone in the 18th century.[72] Lower down, towards the Wenlock–Ludlow road, the rocks are mainly Upper Ludlow Shales. Along the road and east of it occur rocks of the Ledbury and Temeside groups of the Downton Series of the Lower Old Red Sandstone. At Shipton a search for lead near the road in the 1790s failed to find commercial quantities.[73] South and east of the Moorhouse is a covering drift of head, with boulder clay north-east of it; alluvial soils cover both deposits.

Neolithic tools have been found on high ground west of Shipton village and a Bronze Age cremation above Brockton, towards the Ditches.[74] The Ditches, or Larden Ditches, a circular triple-ditched Iron Age hill fort,[75] partly in Rushbury parish, was called Wylleburi or Bileburie in the 13th century[76] and Wynbury Castle in the 16th.[77] It seems that most of the parish, including what later reverted to woodland as Mogg Forest,[78] was occupied in the Iron Age and Roman periods. Ditched enclosures, presumed to be Iron Age or Romano-British, lie on the north-western ridge and below, near the Wenlock–Ludlow road.[79] Romano-British pottery has been found at the Ditches and elsewhere.[80]

In the Middle Ages each of three or four valleys descending to the Corve contained one of the parish's main settlements: Shipton, Nether Larden (on Moorhouse brook), Brockton (on Brockton, or Easthope, brook), and perhaps, if it was at Upper Barn, the deserted Over Larden.[81] In 1676 the parish had 90 adult inhabitants.[82] By 1793 there were 145 inhabitants[83] but by 1801 only 119. There was some growth before 1851 but a decline from the 1880s to a population of 91 in 1931. After the Second World War numbers stabilized at *c.* 130 until the 1980s, when they fell to 117.[84] By the 17th century the changes were mainly in Shipton and Brockton villages; earlier shrinkage at Over and Nether Larden is presumed but the Moorhouse and Skimblescott are unlikely ever to have had more than one or two houses.

Shipton ('sheep estate') was so called by 1086. In 1272 there was a Little Shipton, but no later reference to it is known.[85] Shipton township had at least 11 houses in 1540.[86] Henry Mytton, lord 1688–1731, stopped letting smaller farmhouses when they fell vacant but dwellings remained in view of the Hall across the road[87] until they were demolished in the later 18th century.[88] In the

61 S.R.O. 1224/1/9; /7/1, f. 21. *Salop. News Letter*, xxxvi. 7–8, wrongly locates the chap. *c.* 300 m. to the SW.
62 Above, manor; cf. S.R.O. 294/3, 7.
63 H.W.R.O.(H.), HD 2/14/49.
64 Cf. below, M. Wenlock, churches.
65 S.R.O. 1224/3/130; box 163, Inf. of parishioners of Barrow to commissioners [etc.]; above, Barrow, church.
66 Above, Barrow, educ.
67 S.R.O. 1681/76/21–2. This article was written in 1990.
68 O.S. *Area Bk.* (1884).
69 Above, Monkhopton, intro.
70 Fig. 12.
71 Geol. descr. based on Inst. Geol. Sciences Map 1/25,000, SO 59 *Wenlock Edge* (1969 edn.).
72 O.S. Maps 6", Salop. LVII. NW., SW. (1903 edn.); S.R.O. 4572/6/2/56.
73 S.P.L., MS. 6831, p. 173; J. Plymley, *Gen. View of Agric. of Salop.* (1803), 51–2. Cf. *Salop. Caving and Mining Club Jnl.* (1980), 15–19.
74 SA 360, 641, 2751.
75 SA 357; *V.C.H. Salop.* i. 377.
76 Staffs. R.O., D. 938/671; S.P.L., Deeds 421; S.R.O. 1037/3/3. Cf. ibid. /3/48.
77 S.R.O. 1037/3/118; /16/12.
78 Below, econ. hist.
79 R. Whimster, *The Emerging Past* (R.C.H.M.E. 1989), 56–7.
80 SA 357, 626.
81 Below, manors (Over Larden).
82 *Compton Census*, ed. Whiteman, 259 n.
83 S.P.L., MS. 6831, p. 172.
84 *V.C.H. Salop.* ii. 227; *Census*, 1971, *Co. Rep. Salop.* i. 4; *Census*, 1981, Small Area Statistics: Salop.; S.C.C. Property and Planning Services Dept. inf. rep. C91/103.
85 *P.N. Salop.* (E.P.N.S.), i. 265.
86 P.R.O., SC 6/Hen. VIII/3021, mm. 6d.–7.
87 S.R.O. 4572/3/30; J. Rocque, *Map of Salop.* (1752); R. Baugh, *Map of Salop.* (1808); B.L. Maps, O.S.D. 207.
88 S.P.L., MS. 6831, p. 172. Earthworks remain: R.C.H.M.E., draft field rep. (1985).

19th century Shipton village consisted of the Hall, the Grange, the Bull's Head, and a few old cottages;[89] buildings were of stone or stone and timber framing. Shipton Hall Cottages (two) were added in 1937, Shipton Grange Cottages (two) in 1946, and six council houses *c.* 1956.[90] New House, an isolated farm at the parish's southern tip, was standing in the 17th century.[91] Barn farm (*c.* 118 a.) was amalgamated with it in the 1790s; its isolated house, later represented by Upper Barn, stood near Mogg Forest west of Shipton village.[92]

There was a settlement at Brockton by 1086, named from the brook that flows through it.[93] In 1404 Brockton township included 6 messuages, 2 cottages, the mill, and *c.* 14, mostly vacant, tofts or house plots.[94] Most of the dwellings presumably stood near the site of the castle, of which some earthworks remain.[95] The township had at least 10 houses in 1525 including the mill,[96] and at least 12 in 1581.[97] By 1591 there were cottages on Highley common in Stanton Long parish[98] and in the later 17th and early 18th century at least three cottages were built on the manorial waste.[99] Thomas More, lord 1780–1804, was probably the builder or improver of Larden Cottage (renamed Brockton Grange *c.* 1990), a villa set in grounds inclosed from Mogg Forest; in 1793 he had it in hand, and the grounds were newly planted with forest trees.[1] It was much embellished in the 19th century and by 1834[2] overlooked Cottage Pool, an ornamental lake created by a massive dam on Brockton brook. In 1805 the village had two farmhouses, the Feathers public house, a smithy, a wheelwright's shop, and 10 cottages, mostly old, stone-built or timber framed, and thatched.[3] The larger houses were grouped at a crossroads on the Wenlock–Ludlow road while several of the cottages stood by the northward road on the Mogg Forest and Easthope side of the village.[4] There was little change thereafter.

The parish had other cottages in or near Mogg Forest. Evan Robert of Mogg Forest was a tenant of Shipton manor in 1636.[5] In 1718 permission was sought for a cottage near the Ditches,[6] and in 1817 Larden had at least two cottages towards the Forest;[7] two, stone-built, were standing in 1944.[8]

Larden (formerly Nether Larden) consisted in 1817 of the Hall and the nearby farmhouse. About 1830 the farmhouse was rebuilt *c.* 500 m. to the north as Larden Grange.[9] The Hall grounds, 17 a. in 1805,[10] had been enlarged by 1833 and again, to 65 a., by 1869.[11] Earthworks and ponds near the Hall are probably those of the former farm buildings and of 19th-century landscaping.[12]

By 1752 the Moorhouse, associated with early medieval assarting, and Moorhouse Farm stood either side of Moorhouse brook.[13] A cottage was built for the Moorhouse *c.* 1782,[14] and a few others have been added nearby.

The Wenlock–Ludlow road, elsewhere called St. Mildburg Way,[15] was mentioned in Shipton parish in the 13th century.[16] It was turnpiked through the parish in 1756, disturnpiked in 1867, and declared a main road in 1879. In 1839 a new road, part of the Morville–Shipton turnpike, was authorized between Corfield Cross (in Stanton Long) and the Wenlock–Ludlow turnpike at Shipton. It was disturnpiked in 1872 and mained in 1878.[17]

In the early 18th century the road from Church Stretton to Bridgnorth (mentioned in 1675) went via Longville (in Eaton-under-Heywood), passed over Mogg Forest near the Ditches,[18] descended along the parish boundary to cross the Wenlock–Ludlow road at Brockton's Cross,[19] and continued thence through Weston, Monkhopton, and Morville.[20] By the mid 18th century a route via Easthope was evidently preferred;[21] it was turnpiked from Easthope's Cross to Brockton and Weston in 1839 and disturnpiked in 1872.[22] The Mogg Forest route was disused by 1827.[23]

In 1717 the road from Stanton Long to Shipton was allegedly part of the only road from Cleobury Mortimer to Shrewsbury,[24] presumably via Ashfield (in Ditton Priors).

In the Middle Ages local ways linked Nether Larden to Brockton mill and Shipton church,[25] and Brockton to Skimblescott[26] (crossing the river by Skimblescott bridge, mentioned in

89 O.S. Maps 1/2,500, Salop. LVII. 10 (1883 edn.), 14 (1884 edn.).
90 S.R.O., DA 17/516/16, f. 247; /516/28, f. 232; /518/2, f. 238.
91 Below, manors.
92 S.R.O. 515/2, pp. 364–5; 5555; inf. from the late Mr. J. D. Williams.
93 *P.N. Salop.* (E.P.N.S.), i. 265.
94 P.R.O., C 116/207, extent of 1403–4. Cf. below, econ hist.
95 Below, manors (Brockton).
96 P.R.O., E 179/166/127, m. 4; above, Stanton Long, econ. hist.
97 P.R.O., C 142/216, no. 16.
98 S.R.O. 3901/Rg/1, 14 Feb. 1590/1, etc.; for Highley see below, econ. hist.
99 S.R.O., q. sess. order bk. 1709–26, p. 51; *Orders of Q. Sess.* i. 159, 217.
1 S.P.L., MS. 6865, p. 179.
2 S.R.O., dep. plan 246.
3 S.R.O. 515/5, pp. 304–14.
4 B.L. Maps, O.S.D. 207.
5 S.R.O. 566/38.
6 S.R.O. 4572/3/30.
7 B.L. Maps, O.S.D. 207. Three shown in O.S. Map 1", sheet LXI. SW. (1833 edn.); S.R.O. 1242, box 15, sale partic. of 1895.
8 S.R.O. 5236/B15/10/20.
9 Rocque, *Map of Salop.*; B.L. Maps, O.S.D. 207; C. & J. Greenwood, *Map of Salop.* (1827); O.S. Map 1", sheet LXI. SW. (1833 edn.).
10 S.R.O. 515/5, p. 304.
11 O.S. Map 1", sheet LXI. SW. (1833 edn.); S.R.O. 1681/76/29.
12 R.C.H.M.E., draft field rep. (1986).
13 Rocque, *Map of Salop.*; below, econ. hist.
14 S.R.O. 1037/21/182; 2997/6/3.
15 Above, Stanton Long, intro.
16 S.R.O. 3195/1, f. 31.
17 Above, Stanton Long, intro.
18 S.R.O. 4572/3/29–30; Ogilby, *Britannia* (1675).
19 Mentioned 1409: S.R.O. 1037/3/82.
20 Baugh, *Map of Salop.*
21 Rocque, *Map of Salop.*
22 2 Vic. c. 30 (Local and Personal); S.R.O., dep. plan 249; Ann. Turnpike Acts Continuance Act, 1871, 34 &35 Vic. c. 115.
23 Greenwood, *Map of Salop.*
24 S.R.O. 1037/26/301.
25 S.R.O. 3195/1, ff. 62, 113.
26 P.R.O., IR 30/29/288; O.S. Map 1/25,000, SO 49/59 (1981 edn.).

1545)[27] and Stanton Long.[28] None was metalled in 1990.

St. Mildburg's well, presumably a medieval holy well, was recorded at Brockton in 1573.[29]

Shuffleboard was played at Shipton in 1639.[30] Brockton common was considered a 'fine hunting ground' *c.* 1740.[31] The parish had no alehouse in 1793,[32] but the Bull's Head, Shipton, opened before 1846.[33] It may have closed as an alehouse *c.* 1880.[34] It was a temperance house in 1895 but may have closed soon afterwards.[35] Brockton had the Feathers public house, in Stanton Long parish.[36] The Easthope Memorial Hall opened at Shipton *c.* 1955.[37]

MANORS AND OTHER ESTATES. *SHIPTON* was probably among the lands by the river Corve that Merchelm and Mildfrith gave to their half-sister St. Mildburg before 704.[38] In 1066 and 1086 Shipton belonged to St. Mildburg's church of Wenlock, and it remained with Wenlock priory until the house surrendered to the Crown in 1540.[39] By 1344, and probably by 1334, it was in the priory's manor of Oxenbold,[40] which was renamed Shipton after 1522.[41]

The Crown dismembered that manor in the 1540s;[42] the remnant, called Shipton manor, was granted in 1548 to Sir Thomas Palmer.[43] After his attainder for high treason in 1553[44] the Crown sold it in 1557 to Thomas Reve and Anthony Rotsey, who immediately conveyed it to John Swyfte.[45] Swyfte sold it in 1560 to Edward Gilbert who sold it next year to John Molyneux.[46] John Lutwyche bought the manor from Molyneux in 1580.[47]

Dying without issue in 1615, John Lutwyche left it to his kinsman Edward Mytton of Worcester (d. 1620),[48] and it descended from father to son through Henry (d. 1663),[49] Henry (d. 1688),[50] and Henry[51] who died unmarried in 1731. The manor then passed to the last Henry's brother Thomas (d. 1752). Thomas left it to his son Henry (d. 1757), who was succeeded by his son Thomas (d. 1787).[52] Thomas left it to his widow Mary[53] (d. 1830), who left it to their grandson Thomas Mytton. At Thomas's death childless in 1874 the manor passed successively to his cousin the Revd. R. H. G. More of Larden (d. 1880) and the latter's nephew R. J. More of Linley.[54]

Fig. 37

SHIPTON HALL

In 1896 R. J. More sold the Shipton estate (503 a.) to Charles Bishop of Darlaston (Staffs.),[55] whose family had farmed at Little Oxenbold (in Stanton Long).[56] When Bishop died in 1913 the estate passed successively to his sons the Revd. Thomas Bishop[57] (d. 1930) and F. C. Bishop. The latter settled it *c.* 1940 on his son Maj. C. R. N. Bishop,[58] who settled it in 1967 on his son J. N. R. N. Bishop, the owner in 1990.

Shipton Hall was built *c.* 1598.[59] The architect may have been Walter Hancox (d. 1599) of Much Wenlock.[60] The owner, John Lutwyche, had been responsible for some building work at Lincoln's Inn.[61] The house is built of stone on an **H** plan, facing south-east. The hall block has two and a half storeys and a lateral rear chimney stack. The hall has opposing doorways at the lower end, the front doorway covered by a west-facing four storeyed porch tower in the angle between hall and east wing; the tower had crenellation and a cupola *c.* 1730. A two storeyed canted bay window lit the upper end of the hall block.[62] Access to the first floor was apparently a stair-

27 S.R.O. 1037/9/84.
28 Above, Stanton Long, intro.
29 P.R.O., C 116/207.
30 S.R.O. 566/32.
31 S.R.O. 4572/6/2/56.
32 S.P.L., MS. 6831, p. 173.
33 P.R.O., IR 18/8274.
34 *P.O. Dir. Salop.* (1879), 397; *Kelly's Dir. Salop.* (1885), 936 (no mention).
35 S.R.O. 1242, box 15, sale partic.
36 Above, Stanton Long, intro.
37 S.R.O., DA 17/516/27, f. 289.
38 H. P. R. Finberg, *Early Charters of W. Midlands* (1972), pp. 147–8, 203.
39 *V.C.H. Salop.* i. 312; ii. 45; P.R.O., SC 6/Hen. VIII/3021, mm. 6d.–8.
40 S.R.O. 566/1; 1224/2/1.
41 Above, Monkhopton, manors.
42 Ibid.; above, Stanton Long, manors (Patton).
43 *Cal. Pat.* 1548–9, 13–14.
44 *D.N.B.*
45 *Cal. Pat.* 1555–7, 406–7; S.R.O. 1037/15/1.
46 S.R.O. 1037/15/3–4, 6.
47 *Cal. Pat.* 1578–8, p. 245; S.R.O. 1037/15/7.
48 P.R.O., C 142/354, no. 95; C 142/374, no. 91; *S.P.R. Heref.* i (1), 22; S.R.O. 566/27.
49 P.R.O., C 3/366/10; *S.P.R. Heref.* i (1), 30; B.L. Add. MS. 21237, f. 52v.
50 S.R.O. 566/41; *S.P.R. Heref.* i (1), 34.
51 S.R.O. 1037/15/29; B.L. Add. MS. 21237, f. 52v.
52 *S.P.R. Heref.* i (1), 43, 47, 53; S.P.L., Deeds 676.
53 S.R.O. 1037/17/42, f. 9.
54 S.R.O. 5321/A60.
55 Ibid. /A61, A64.
56 S.R.O. 3901/Rg/4, 18 Feb. 1816, 5 June 1853; /BRg/1, 28 Jan. 1885. Rest of para. based on inf. from Mr. J. N. R. N. Bishop.
57 Cf. *Kelly's Dir. Salop.* (1917), 199.
58 Cf. S.R.O. 5321/A64.
59 Glazing contract with Thos. Showsmith of Worc. 20 Aug. 1598 cited in W.S.L. 350/3/40, Shipton p. 8.
60 J. Summerson, *Archit. in Brit. 1530 to 1830* (1977), 76; below, M. Wenlock, econ. hist.
61 *Hist. Parl., Commons,* 1558–1603, ii. 502.
62 Birm. Univ. Libr., Mytton Papers, v. 1187; fig. 37.

case turret projecting at the rear, perhaps in the angle between hall block and west wing.[63]

About 1700, perhaps in 1670,[64] a two storeyed rear addition was built, apparently parallel to the hall block and abutting the stair turret.[65] In the mid 18th century it was partly replaced by a projecting two storeyed rear wing, which included a first-floor library reached by a new staircase on the site of the stair turret; the wing's parapet and cornice resemble those of the detached stable block of 1756–7. The house was extended east by a stone service block 1757–9. Work on the library was in progress between 1760 and 1767.[66] Its rococo overmantel, designed in the later 1760s by T. F. Pritchard of Shrewsbury, is similar in style to work in the hall. The iron grate in the hall was also designed by Pritchard,[67] and rococo plaster work there has been attributed to Francesco or John Vassalli,[68] of whom John seems to have worked with Pritchard at Hatton Grange (in Shifnal) 1767–8.[69] It was probably at the same period that the timbers of the original hall ceiling were taken down to form the roof of the cellar below,[70] and the original panelling was removed to bedrooms above. A rainwater head of 1769 in the angle formerly occupied by the bay window seems to show that the bay window was removed then or a little earlier; the walling in its place resembles that of the stable block. An undated drawing shows a central front doorway to the hall, perhaps opened when the hall was redecorated.[71] The gothick plaster work over the main staircase and gothick windows at the rear of the house are presumably later 18th-century. By the 1830s the hall had no central doorway.[72]

A circular stone dovecot stands to the north-east. It was surmounted by an 18th-century wooden louvre[73] until the roof collapsed in the early 20th century; a new roof and louvre were made in 1962.[74]

In the earlier 12th century the prior of Wenlock enfeoffed Edric (Hedricus) with ½ virgate and a croft in Shipton.[75] It may have passed later to William Powke (fl. 1393).[76] *POWKE'S HOUSE*, with land near Shipton cross,[77] belonged in 1521 to John Paramore.[78] In 1581–2 William Paramore sold the greater part to the lord of Shipton manor and the rest to Maurice Ludlow of the Moorhouse.[79]

NEW HOUSE, a farm of 368 a. in Shipton manor,[80] was sold to a Mr. Stanley in 1796.[81] The two storeyed house of Aymestry limestone had two symmetrical wings at the rear and perhaps dated from *c.* 1700.[82] Soon after the sale it was remodelled inside and out. The front was heightened at the eaves, rendered, refenestrated, and given a classical stone doorway. The farm belonged to William Downes in 1846,[83] and later passed through the Hippisley, Burnett, Hide, and Farmer families to the Williamses.[84]

By 1255 Hugh le Gyrros (or Hugh of Larden) was lord of *NETHER LARDEN*, later called simply *LARDEN*, which he held of Wenlock priory. His son Alan[85] succeeded,[86] and Roger son of Alan was lord by 1280.[87] Roger was succeeded after 1292[88] by his son Henry de la Halle (fl. 1310–49).[89] John Broadstone (fl. 1418)[90] was lord of Nether Larden by 1377[91] and held land there in right of his wife Isabel (fl. 1400–1),[92] presumably Isabel de la Halle who received rent in Nether Larden in 1393 and 1415[93] and in widowhood conveyed the lordship in 1423 to William Bailly of Brockton.[94]

Bailly sold it in 1434[95] to his brother-in- law[96] Richard More of Nether Larden, who settled the manor house in 1463 on his grandson Richard More, also of Nether Larden. Richard More's brother William (fl. 1477–1505)[97] had lands there by 1489,[98] and the estate passed from father to son, through William's son Edward (d. *c.* 1554),[99] to Thomas (d. 1567),[1] and Jasper,[2] at whose death in 1614[3] Larden passed to his kinsman and son-in-law Samuel More of Linley.[4] In 1622 Samuel, after divorce from Jasper's daughter and the consignment of her bastard children to the *Mayflower*,[5] sold the lordship to his father Richard, of Linley.[6] At Richard's

63 *Soc. Archit. Historians Gt. Brit. Ann. Conference, 1988*, 42 (copy in S.P.L.).

64 *Building News*, 14 Aug. 1891, 216.

65 *Soc. Archit. Historians Ann. Conf.* 42.

66 H. E. Forrest, *Old Hos. of Wenlock* (Shrews. 1914), 63; H. B. Walters, *Ch. Bells of Salop.* (Oswestry, 1915), 99.

67 Undated drawings in Washington, D.C., American Inst. of Architects, Pritchard album (copy in S.R.O. 1559/1); J. Harris, 'Pritchard redivivus', *Archit. Hist.* ii. 20–3.

68 *Shropshire Mag.* May 1970, 28. The painted arms on the overmantle were added after 1910: *Country Life*, 19 Mar. 1910, 417, 421.

69 *Country Life*, 29 Feb. 1968, 469.

70 Cf. W.S.L. 350/3/40, Shipton pp. 8–9.

71 Bodl. MS. Top. Salop. c. 2, f. 435; S.P.L., MS. 3065, no. 302; *Soc. Archit. Historians Ann. Conf.* 42.

72 W.S.L. 350/3/40, Shipton p. 8.

73 Photo. in F. Moss, *Pilgrimages to Old Homes, mostly on the Welsh Border* (1903), 360.

74 *Shropshire Mag.* Aug. 1964, 20.

75 Bodl. MS. Gough Salop. 11, f. 94.

76 S.R.O. 3195/1, f. 122.

77 S.R.O. 566/2.

78 S.R.O. 1037/17/1.

79 Ibid. /17/10–11.

80 S.R.O. 515/2, pp. 364–5.

81 S.R.O. 1037/25/36.

82 Cf. *Bldgs. of the Countryside, 1500–1750*, ed. M. W. Barley (1990), 121, 134.

83 P.R.O., IR 29/29/288; IR 30/29/288.

84 *P.O. Dir. Salop.* (1856), 113; *Kelly's Dir. Salop.* (1891), 409; (1917), 199; (1922), 207; deeds in possession of the late Mr. J. D. Williams, New Ho.; inf. from Mr. Williams.

85 P.R.O., C 104/27, undated deed (Hamon to Wm. son of Herb.); *Rot. Hund.* (Rec. Com.), ii. 85.

86 P.R.O., C 104/26, undated deed (Agnes of Larden to Wm. of Larden).

87 S.R.O. 3195/1, f. 40.

88 P.R.O., C 104/27, deed.

89 S.R.O. 1037/3/49; 3195/1, ff. 64, 70.

90 S.R.O. 1037/3/85.

91 *Reg. Gilbert* (C.S.), 181; Birm. Univ. Libr., Mytton Papers, v. 1193.

92 S.R.O. 1037/3/77; *Cal. Close*, 1399–1402, 380.

93 S.R.O. 3195/1, f. 122; 4032/2/28.

94 S.R.O. 1037/3/88–9, 107 (for surname); S.P.L., MS. 2342, nos. 12878, 12881.

95 S.P.L., MS. 2342, no. 12892.

96 S.R.O. 1037/3/74; /3/121, deed of 1415.

97 Ibid. /3/107–8; N.L.W., Dobell 1, deed of 1505.

98 S.P.L., MS. 2342, nos. 12920–1.

99 Eyton, iii. 309; Burke, *Land. Gent.* (1952), 1819; P.R.O., C 116/207.

1 P.R.O., C 142/152, no. 163; *S.P.R. Heref.* i (1), 9.

2 Under a settlement of 1543: P.R.O., C 142/152, no. 163. In possession 1569: S.R.O. 1037/3/113.

3 *S.P.R. Heref.* i (1), 20.

4 S.R.O. 1037/10/3, 8–9; Burke, *Land. Gent.* (1952), 1819; *D.N.B.* s.v. More, Sam.

5 A. R. Wagner, 'Origin of the *Mayflower* children: Jasper, Ric. and Ellen More', *New Eng. Hist. and Genealogical Reg.* cxiv. 163–8; D. F. Harris, 'The More children of the *Mayflower*', *Mayflower Descendant*, xliii. 123–32; xliv. 11–20, 109–18.

6 S.R.O. 1037/10/10–12, 15.

death in 1643[7] it reverted to Samuel, who settled it in 1650 on his son Richard.[8] When Richard died without legitimate issue in 1698[9] it passed successively to his brother Robert (d. 1719)[10] and Robert's son Robert (d. 1780).[11] Robert left Larden to his illegitimate son Thomas Willes[12] (d. 1804), who changed his name to More and left the manor to his son R. H. G. More.[13] The Revd. R. H. G. More (d. 1880) left it to his nephew R. J. More of Linley,[14] who sold the estate in separate lots in 1895.[15]

Larden Hall, in 70 a. of grounds, was bought by Charles Bishop, purchaser of the Shipton estate,[16] and sold *c.* 1897[17] to Col. F. A. Wolryche-Whitmore (d. 1927), whose widow gave it to their son J. E. A. Wolryche-Whitmore in 1931.[18] The son sold it in 1938 to Jasper More, R. J. More's grandson, who sold it in 1944 to T. F. M. Corrie. Corrie had just acquired the Moorhouse and in 1945 added the Poplars (in Stanton Long) and Larden Grange, thus creating a new Larden Hall estate of 805 a., which he sold in 1947 to Albert Curry of Theddingworth (Leics.). Curry sold the Moorhouse in 1951, the Poplars in 1952,[19] and Larden Grange *c.* 1958[20] but remained at Larden Hall in 1990.

Larden Hall incorporated a late 16th-century two storeyed timber framed range. In 1607 Jasper More added a three storeyed stone wing at right angles.[21] The ground floor comprised a hall, parlour, and kitchen in 1614.[22] The house was demolished in 1968, the timbers intended for export to the United States of America.[23] A smaller brick house designed by Graham Goatley was built on the site in 1969.[24]

Hamon of Larden (fl. *c.* 1245)[25] was lord of *OVER LARDEN*,[26] which he held of Wenlock priory. His son William (fl. 1274) succeeded before 1255.[27] By 1306 the estate, or part of it, seems to have been annexed to the Moorhouse: Richard, son of Richard of the Moorhouse, was then the priory's tenant of lands in Larden.[28] Roger More (fl. 1346–78) of the Moorhouse, chaplain, had property in Over Larden,[29] apparently including a chief house that he leased out in 1360.[30] William Moorhouse had a freehold in Over Larden in 1409.[31] So did Thomas Ludlow of the Moorhouse in 1540[32] and George Ludlow in 1632;[33] the Ludlows' property at Over Larden included a house in 1581.[34] By 1801[35] the Moorhouse estate included land that lay in 1919 as a detached and compact area of 134 a. (54 ha.) adjoining the grounds of Larden Hall and centred on buildings called Upper Barn,[36] the possible site of Over Larden's chief house. That land, severed from the Moorhouse in 1951, was sold in 1953 by Albert Curry of Larden to Maj. C. R. N. Bishop of Shipton.[37]

In 1199 Otes of Larden held ¼ virgate at 'la More',[38] which adjoined the fields of Brockton *c.* 1300.[39] The *MOORHOUSE*, mentioned in the late 13th century,[40] was presumably named from that area. Thomas of the Moorhouse was mentioned in 1305[41] and Richard (fl. 1322), son of Richard of the Moorhouse, was Wenlock priory's tenant there in 1306.[42] Roger of the Moorhouse or de la More (fl. 1355) was mentioned in 1320. A chaplain called Roger of the Moorhouse or More (fl. 1346–78), probably Roger's son, was living at the Moorhouse in 1375. He was succeeded by William Moorhouse or More (fl. 1352–1422), son of Isabel de Knoville, who was probably the chaplain's sister.[43]

It seems to have been William Moorhouse's son Richard More (fl. 1409–22),[44] who bought the lordship of Nether Larden in 1434,[45] but the further descent of the Moorhouse is uncertain before 1518. In 1505 Maurice Ludlow and his daughter Joan Walwen confirmed their estate at the Moorhouse to Maurice's son Lawrence.[46] In 1518 John Godfrey's daughter and coheir Agnes quitclaimed the reputed manor of the Moorhouse to Lawrence.[47] At his death in 1538 Lawrence Ludlow held it of Wenlock priory in fee. He was followed successively by his sons Thomas[48] (d. 1581), Maurice (d. 1595),[49] and presumably Rowland.[50] Rowland's son Thomas succeeded, and in 1626 Thomas's sister and heir

7 *D.N.B.*
8 S.R.O. 1037/10/18, 23.
9 S.R.O. 4134/4/31; *S.P.R. Heref.* ii (3), 43.
10 S.R.O. 1037/10/23, 38; *S.P.R. Heref.* ii (3), 51.
11 S.R.O. 4572/4/11–12; *D.N.B.* s.v. More, Sam.; Burke, *Land. Gent.* (1952), 1819–20.
12 Loton Hall MSS., Sir B. Leighton's diary 20 Sept. 1865; 23 Sept. 1869.
13 S.R.O. 1681/76/25.
14 S.R.O. 1242, box 15, abstr. of title.
15 Ibid. sale partic.; *Shrews. Chron.* 26 July 1895.
16 *Kelly's Dir. Salop.* (1900), 199; above, this section (Shipton).
17 G. C. Wolryche-Whitmore, 'Notes on Dudmaston Est.' (TS. n.d. in S.P.L., class qOQ 22.3), 26.
18 S.R.O. 5321/A70.
19 Ibid. /A73.
20 S.R.O., DA 17/516/30, f. 235.
21 Forrest, *Old Hos. of Wenlock*, 61–2; E. Mercer, *Eng. Vernacular Hos.* (R.C.H.M.E. 1975), 196–7; date stone in M. Wenlock museum.
22 S.R.O. 1037/10/42.
23 *Shropshire Mag.* Dec. 1968, 3; *Bridgnorth Jnl.* 22 Nov. 1968.
24 *Shropshire Mag.* Dec. 1969, 36–7.
25 Eyton, iii. 307.
26 P.R.O., C 104/27, undated deed (Hamon to Wm. son of Herb.).
27 *Rot. Hund.* ii. 85, 110.
28 P.R.O., C 104/26, deed; cf. below, this section (the Moorhouse).
29 S.R.O. 1037/3/106.
30 Ibid. /3/52, 55; 3195/1, f. 103.
31 P.R.O., C 104/24, pt. 1, deed.
32 P.R.O., SC 6/Hen. VIII/3021, m. 6d.
33 P.R.O., CP 25/2/477/8 Chas. I Hil. no. 23.
34 P.R.O., C 142/216, no. 16.
35 S.R.O. 2997/6/3.
36 S.R.O. 1037/21/184. For acreage see O.S. Maps 1/2,500, Salop. LVII. 9 (1903 edn.), 10 (1902 edn.). Name recorded 1882: ibid. LVII. 9 (1883 edn.).
37 S.R.O. 5321/A73. Cf. above, this section (Shipton; Nether Larden).
38 *T.S.A.S.* 2nd ser. x. 312.
39 S.R.O. 1037/3/2; 3195/1, f. 31.
40 S.R.O. 1037/3/3.
41 Eyton, iii. 309.
42 P.R.O., C 104/26, deed. Eyton, iii. 309, wrongly gives the father's name as Hen.
43 P.R.O., C 104/27, deed of 1352; S.R.O. 1037/3/58, 61, 67–8, 71, 75–6, 120; S.R.O. 3195/1, ff. 69, 91, 101, 105–6, 175; S.P.L., MS. 2342, no. 12855; J. B. Blakeway, *Sheriffs of Salop.* (Shrews. 1831), 215. It is been assumed that Isabel (fl. 1355) dau. of Rog. of the Moorhouse, Isabel (fl. 1399–1400) dau. of Rog. de la More, and Isabel de Knoville (fl. 1352) were the same.
44 S.R.O. 1037/3/82, 120.
45 Above, this section (Nether Larden).
46 P.R.O., C 104/25, deed; *Visit. Salop. 1623*, ii (Harl. Soc. xxix), 342–3.
47 P.R.O., C 104/25, deed.
48 P.R.O., E 150/858, no. 3; ibid. SC 6/Hen. VIII/3021, m. 6d.
49 P.R.O., C 142/216, no. 16; *S.P.R. Heref.* i (1), 15.
50 He succ. Maurice at Easthope: P.R.O., C 104/23, pt. 2, memo. [early 17th century?].

Jane, with her husband James Hall, conveyed the Moorhouse to Thomas's son George (d. 1670),[51] who was followed by his son George.[52] George Ludlow died in 1677[53] leaving his daughters Anne, Katherine, Elizabeth, and Frances as coheirs. In 1684 Anne settled her share on her husband John Holloway, who bought Frances Ludlow's share in 1691. The share of Elizabeth (Mrs. Baugh) was divided at her death, before 1721, between John Holloway and his daughter Elizabeth. Katherine (Mrs. Rawlins) left her share, by will dated 1716, to a trustee; it apparently passed before 1721 to John Holloway's daughter Dame Anne Oxenden, for she then, with her father and sister Elizabeth Holloway, sold the reputed manor to Samuel Edwards (d. 1738).[54]

Samuel Edwards's trustees sold the estate in 1745 to Thomas Mytton, lord of Shipton (d. 1752), who left it to his daughters Amy (d. 1763)[55] and Anne. In 1779 Anne conveyed it to trustees, who sold it in 1782 to Maj. Richard Grant of Shrewsbury (d. 1788).[56] His son Richard sold the Moorhouse in 1802 to Richard Corser of Aston Munslow. At Corser's death in 1824 it passed to his son Richard (d. 1825)[57] who left it to his brother John.[58] At John's death in 1874 the estate passed successively to his son W. R. Corser[59] (d. 1894) and grandson J. S. Corser, who sold the Moorhouse in 1920 to Jonathan Roberts of Sarn (in Whittington). In 1941 Roberts sold it (311 a.) to Count P. A. W. Münster, who conveyed it in 1942 to his wife. In 1944 Countess Münster sold it to T. F. M. Corrie, who incorporated it into the Larden Hall estate, with which the Moorhouse then descended until bought by G. M. Stokes in 1951. Stokes sold it in 1969 to E. G. Jones of Brockton, who sold the house *c.* 1973 but retained the land in 1990.[60]

The present house, renamed Moor (later More) Hall in the early 20th century,[61] was built of rubble on an **H** plan facing west. The central range, whose walls may be medieval, contained the hall, which had a cross passage at the lower end and a stack against the rear wall. The two storeyed north wing, which contained two parlours, may have been built or rebuilt in 1571;[62] its north wall has two chimney stacks which are partly of diaper-patterned brick. A rear staircase wing was built at the same time, in the angle between hall and north wing. Both it and the north wing have roll mouldings at the quoins and in the jambs of a first- floor doorway linking the two.[63] A date stone of 1626 on the north wing may refer to later alterations, perhaps including the added garderobe tower on the north. There is much early 17th-century panelling in the house. That on the first floor of the central range may have been moved from the floor below, but that in the room over the former 'little' parlour incorporates an heraldic overmantel dated 1652 and may be in its original location. In the 18th century the external doorways of the cross passage were closed and a new doorway was made in the centre of the range. The southern part of the lower floor of the range was probably partitioned off at the same time to form a separate room and the northern part became an entrance hall with a stone flagged floor and reduced fireplace. Early in the 19th century a new staircase was put into the hall and the south wing was demolished, new windows being put into the exposed end wall of the central range.[64]

An outbuilding south-west of the house is probably of 17th-century origin. It may have been used as a malthouse. A stable with rooms or chambers over it and a mount in the garden were mentioned in 1664.[65]

In 1255 *SKIMBLESCOTT* belonged to Wenlock priory.[66] It became part of the priory's manor of Oxenbold (called Shipton after 1522),[67] and in 1548 was presumably conveyed to Sir Thomas Palmer with Shipton manor,[68] to which it belonged in 1651 and 1783.[69]

In or after 1230 the terre tenant was called William. His son[70] Roger of Skimblescott had succeeded by 1255.[71] Roger's son Roger (fl. 1325)[72] probably succeeded, perhaps followed by Walter of Skimblescott (fl. 1330–9).[73] Thomas Clerke of Much Wenlock was the prior's freehold tenant *c.* 1496[74] and was followed by his son Edward.[75] Thomas Lacon of Willey (d. 1536)[76] held the freehold by 1521[77] and his son Edward succeeded.[78] On Edward's death in 1564[79] it passed to his brother Lancelot (fl. 1567),[80] of Kenley,[81] whose son Christopher was in possession in 1576.[82] Christopher's brother Edward, who had succeeded by 1577,[83] sold the freehold in 1595 to Francis Newport,[84] who succeeded in 1598 to Oxenbold manor,[85] with which Skimble-

51 *Visit. Salop. 1623*, ii. 343; S.P.L., MS. 4360, p. 299; S.R.O. 1037/21/180; *S.P.R. Heref.* i (1), 32.
52 S.R.O. 1037/21/180.
53 B.L. Add. MS. 21237, f. 52v. For descent 1677–1825 see S.R.O. 1037/21/180–3.
54 *Hist. Parl.,Commons*, 1715–54, ii. 5.
55 *S.P.R. Heref.* i (1), 47, 49.
56 *S.P.R. Lich.* xiv (2), 124.
57 S.R.O. 3902/Rg/2, p. 4.
58 S. Bagshaw, *Dir. Salop.* (1851), 550.
59 S.R.O. 3902/Rg/1, p. 22; /Rg/2, p. 31; *P.O. Dir. Salop.* (1879), 417.
60 S.R.O. 5321/A73; inf. from Mr. E. G. Jones.
61 O.S. Map 1/2,500, Salop. LVII. 10 (1902 and 1927 edns.).
62 Birm. Univ. Libr., Mytton Papers, v. 1193. Inscr. '1571 TL' formerly in gt. parlour: ibid.
63 Cf. similar mouldings on porch at Wilderhope Man. *c.* 1590.
64 Cf. *Salop. N. & Q.* 3rd ser. iii. 39.
65 P.R.O., C 104/22, pt. 2, deed.
66 *Rot. Hund.* ii. 85.
67 P.R.O., SC 6/Hen. VIII/3021, m. 6d.; above, Monkhopton, manors.
68 Above, this section (Shipton).
69 S.R.O. 566/48; S.P.L., Deeds 1361, f. 7.
70 P.R.O., C 104/27, undated deed (Ric. son of Bernard to Agnes dau. of Rob.) witnessed by Hugh, ld. of Patton. Hugh succ. in or after 1230: above, Stanton Long, manors (Patton).
71 *Rot. Hund.* ii. 85.
72 S.R.O. 1037/3/7; 3195/1, f. 71.
73 S.R.O. 1037/3/23, 34.
74 S.R.O. 3365/165.
75 S.R.O. 1224, box 342, Prior Gosnell's reg. f. 9v. The son is called Edm. in P.R.O., C 1/17, no. 211.
76 P.R.O., C 142/58, no. 60.
77 S.R.O. 1224, box 342, Prior Gosnell's reg. f. 39.
78 P.R.O., SC 6/Hen. VIII/3021, m. 6d. For pedigree see *Visit. Salop. 1623*, ii. 307.
79 *Hist. Parl., Commons*, 1509–58, ii. 488.
80 S.R.O. 566/54.
81 S.P.L., MS. 2789, p. 367.
82 S.R.O. 566/10.
83 Ibid. /54.
84 P.R.O., CP 25/2/203/37 Eliz. Trin. [no. 6].
85 Above, Monkhopton, manors.

scott descended until the early 20th century.[86] Lord Barnard probably sold Skimblescott when Oxenbold was broken up *c.* 1919.[87]

Three free men, Saemaer (Semaer), Algeard (Eliard), and Edwin, held *BROCKTON* in 1066. Earl Roger held it in chief in 1086 and Reynold of Bailleul had a mesne lordship,[88] which is presumed to have become a tenancy in chief in 1102 on the forfeiture of Earl Robert, and to have passed a few years later, with Reynold's other Shropshire estates, to Alan son of Flaald and thus to the FitzAlans,[89] overlords *c.* 1243[90] and still in 1507, when Brockton was held (as in 1404)[91] of their manor of Acton Round.[92] The overlordship belonged by 1615 to Thomas Howard, earl of Suffolk,[93] having presumably been among the forfeited estates of his half-brother Philip Howard, earl of Arundel, grandson of the last FitzAlan earl.[94] In 1581, however, Brockton was said to be held of Sir Rowland Hayward as lord of Acton Round,[95] and Sir George Hayward granted a lease in Brockton in 1613.[96]

The terre tenant in 1086 was Richard.[97] Nicholas of Brockton, a tenant of the FitzAlans in 1166,[98] is presumed to have been lord, as are Robert son of Nicholas (fl. *c.* 1180) and William son of Robert (fl. 1203).[99] A William of Brockton, presumably the last named, held land at Brockton in 1203,[1] as did Hugh of Brockton (fl. 1227)[2] in 1221.[3] A lord called John was mentioned in the earlier 13th century.[4] Robert of Brockton was lord *c.* 1243[5] and his son Thomas of Brockton (d. 1273 × 1280)[6] in 1255.[7] A John, perhaps Thomas's son of that name,[8] was lord in 1280[9] and for over a century the manor was held, perhaps continuously, by lords called John,[10] among whom were John of Aston or le Fourches (fl. 1335–48),[11] nephew of John of Bromfield,[12] and John Walford (fl. 1358–81).[13] Thomas Cotes, however, was described as lord in 1378.[14] John, son of Sir John Ludlow, was lord in 1395,[15] and John Burley (d. *c.* 1415) by 1397.[16] Burley's son William was in possession by 1428.[17] After William's death without sons in 1458[18] the manor was held for life by Margaret Walwen, related to his brother-in-law Reynold, Lord Grey of Wilton.[19] At Margaret's death in 1491 it was divided between Edward Trussell, grandson and heir of William's daughter Elizabeth, and Joan Lyttelton, William's other daughter.[20]

When Edward Trussell died in 1499 his moiety passed successively to his son John, who died the same year, and daughter Elizabeth.[21] Elizabeth predeceased her husband John de Vere, earl of Oxford, at whose death in 1540[22] their son John, earl of Oxford, had livery of their estates.[23] In 1552 the earl sold the moiety to John Stringfellow,[24] whose son Richard sold it in 1559 to Thomas Spragges.[25] Spragges sold it in 1563 to Thomas Ludlow of the Moorhouse.[26]

Joan Lyttelton died in 1504. Her moiety passed to her son Sir William (d. 1507) and then to his son John[27] (d. 1532), who left it to his son John.[28] That John sold it in 1546 to Thomas Gower[29] of Oxenbold and in 1553 Thomas conveyed it to his son Lawrence.[30] Lawrence Gower sold it to Thomas Ludlow in 1573.[31]

Ludlow thus owned the whole manor of Brockton at his death in 1581[32] and it descended thereafter with the Moorhouse until 1745 when Samuel Edwards's trustees sold the Moorhouse.[33] They sold Brockton manor in 1746 to Robert More of Larden, whose ancestors had been freeholders in Brockton since the Middle Ages.[34] The manor descended with Larden[35] until Brockton and Larden were dismembered in 1895–6.[36] Lower Brockton Farm (with 327 a.),[37] probably the chief house,[38] was sold to

86 S.R.O. 168/2, f. 100; 566/35, 48; 4044/1, no. 188; S.P.L., Deeds 1361, f. 6; P.R.O., IR 29/29/288. Cf. above, Monkhopton, manors.

87 Above, Monkhopton, manors; S.R.O., DA 17/517/1, f. 106.

88 *V.C.H. Salop.* i. 320.

89 Ibid. iii. 10–11.

90 *Bk. of Fees*, ii. 963.

91 P.R.O., C 116/207.

92 *Cal. Inq. p.m. Hen. VII*, iii, p. 332.

93 *T.S.A.S.* 4th ser. iii. 2.

94 *Complete Peerage*, i. 254. Cf. *V.C.H. Salop.* iv. 133–4.

95 P.R.O., C 142/216, no. 16.

96 P.R.O., C 116/210.

97 *V.C.H. Salop.* i. 320.

98 *Red Bk. Exch.* (Rolls Ser.), i. 273.

99 Eyton, iv. 111–12.

1 Ibid. 109.

2 Dugdale, *Mon.* v. 74 n.

3 *Rolls of Justices in Eyre, 1221–2* (Selden Soc. lix), p. 430.

4 P.R.O., C 104/27, undated deed (Thos. son of Nic. to Rob. of Skimblescott).

5 *Bk. of Fees*, ii. 963.

6 *Roll of Salop. Eyre 1256* (Selden Soc. xcvi), p. 28; *Rot. Hund.* ii. 101; S.R.O. 3195/1, f. 40.

7 *Rot. Hund.* ii. 71.

8 S.R.O. 1037/3/121, s.vv. Brockton and Larden.

9 S.R.O. 3195/1, f. 40.

10 Ibid. ff. 70, 77, 79; *Feud. Aids*, iv. 223, 229; S.R.O. 1037/3/23/27, 46, 49.

11 P.R.O., C 104/26, deed of 1335; S.R.O. 1037/3/28, 43; *Feud. Aids*, iv. 244.

12 P.R.O., C 104/25, deed of 1326.

13 P.R.O., C 104/25, deed of 1358; C 104/26, deed of 1381.

14 S.R.O. 1037/3/61.

15 P.R.O., C 104/25, deed.

16 *T.S.A.S.* 4th ser. vi. 230–1; *Cal. Inq. Misc.* vi, p. 114.

17 *Feud. Aids*, iv. 249.

18 *T.S.A.S.* lvi. 272.

19 *Cal. Inq. p.m. Hen. VII*, i, p. 303; *T.S.A.S.* lvi. 264; *Complete Peerage*, vi. 180.

20 *Cal. Inq. p.m. Hen. VII*, i, p. 303; ii, p. 210.

21 *Cal. Inq. p.m. Hen. VII*, ii, p. 210; P.R.O., C 142/20, no. 12.

22 *Complete Peerage*, x. 247.

23 *L. & P. Hen. VIII*, xv, p. 148.

24 S.R.O. 20/23/13; *Visit. Hants, 1622* (Harl. Soc. lxiv), 106.

25 P.R.O., C 104/27, deed.

26 P.R.O., C 104/26, deed.

27 *Cal. Inq. p.m. Hen. VII*, ii, p. 577; iii, pp. 305, 331–2.

28 P.R.O., C 142/54, no. 137.

29 P.R.O., C 104/26, deed of 1546.

30 Ibid. deed of 1553.

31 P.R.O., C 104/23, pt. 1, deed; CP 25/2/200/15 Eliz. East. [no. 13].

32 P.R.O., C 142/216, no. 16.

33 Ibid.; N.L.W., Dobell 1, deed of 1627; S.R.O. 1037/21/180–1; 4572/6/2/60; *Orders of Q. Sess.* i. 159, 217; above, this section (the Moorhouse).

34 S.R.O. 1037/3/1, 11, 17, 58–60, 82, 92; /9/71, 80, 82–3; 3195/1, f. 103; S.P.L., Deeds 1751, 1759; MS. 2342, nos. 12855, 12905, 12920–1, 12954.

35 S.R.O. 1681/76/20; above, this section (Nether Larden).

36 S.R.O. 1242, box 15, sale partic. of 1895; *Shrews. Chron.* 26 July 1895, p. 8; above, this section (Nether Larden; the Moorhouse).

37 S.R.O. 1242, box 15, sale partic. of 1895 (lot 3).

38 Below, this section.

Robert Morgan in 1896.[39] After Morgan's death in 1938[40] it passed to David Thomas,[41] who was succeeded in 1942 by B. G. Thomas,[42] from whom it passed in 1944 to E. G. Jones,[43] the owner in 1990. Jones also bought Larden Grange *c.* 1958[44] and the Moorhouse in 1969.[45] Lower Brockton Farm, renamed the Manor House *c.* 1989, is built of Aymestry limestone, has two storeys and two symmetrical wings projecting from the rear, and perhaps dates from *c.* 1700.[46] The space between the wings was later filled in.

There are remains of a small oval flat-topped medieval motte 200 m. east of the Manor House, with a water-filled ditch fed from the adjoining brook and indications of a bailey on the west side.[47] In 1895 the site belonged to Lower Brockton farm.[48]

Between 1256 and 1269 Nicholas, son of Robert of Walton, gave 5*s.* rent from Brockton to the sacristy of Wenlock priory.[49] Still payable at the Dissolution,[50] it was claimed by the Crown in 1567[51] and granted in 1568 to George Darcye and James Glasier.[52]

Before the Dissolution all the *TITHES*, great and small, of Shipton, Larden, the Moorhouse, Skimblescott, and (under the name 'St. Mildburg's tithes')[53] of part of Brockton[54] belonged to Wenlock priory.[55] Having passed to the Crown in 1540, the grain and hay tithes of those places were conveyed with Shipton manor to Sir Thomas Palmer in 1548[56] and resumed by the Crown at his attainder in 1553. They were granted in 1582 to Sir Christopher Hatton,[57] who sold them next year to John Lutwyche, lord of Shipton.[58] In 1586 the Crown granted the small tithes to Hatton, who conveyed them immediately to Lutwyche.[59] All the tithes then seem to have followed the descent of Shipton manor[60] until after 1823, when all belonged to Mrs. Mary Mytton,[61] but by 1846 those of the Moorhouse, New House, Larden, Brockton (in Shipton parish), and Skimblescott had been variously alienated. By 1849 all the tithes except those of Skimblescott had recently been merged.[62]

ECONOMIC HISTORY. The parish's highest ground, the ridge that formed its north-western boundary, was occupied in the Middle Ages by Mogg or Monk Forest,[63] a belt of woodland pasture that extended into Easthope and Rushbury parishes and was intercommoned. In 1530 a boundary was set between the common of Wilderhope (in Rushbury) and that of Shipton, Larden, and the Moorhouse,[64] and by 1588 Brockton's inhabitants were excluded from the recently inclosed Lutwyche coppices (in Rushbury). By the late 16th century Mogg Forest in Shipton parish had been divided into Shipton, Larden, and Brockton woods; the Moorhouse used Larden wood;[65] Skimblescott had no share but in the 13th century had been allowed common of pasture on Brockton's meadows and open fields.[66] In the 16th century Brockton also had a common woodland pasture, called Highley; it evidently occupied rising ground in Stanton Long parish between Brockton brook and Natal common[67] and was called Brockton common in the early 18th century.[68] Another waste, 'la More', on low ground south of Brockton, included 'Dademore', 'Frythemore', and the Marsh. Assarting began there in or before the 12th century; ¼ virgate of arable was mentioned in 1199.[69]

Open-field arable occupied the sloping ground below Mogg Forest.[70] Shipton had Middle (or Mynde) field towards the Forest, Barn field towards the Moorhouse, and Corve field.[71] Larden had Low field towards Shipton,[72] Wood field towards the Forest, and a field towards Brockton.[73] Brockton had South, North, and East fields.[74] In 1306 the tenant of the Moorhouse was permitted to get marl in Shipton's fields.[75]

Meadows occupied the lowest ground, along the river Corve.[76] Common meadows included Town meadow, Long doles, and the 'Pecadolls'.[77]

Shipton manor was worth 30*s.* 4*d.* a year in 1086. Arable, with 10 ploughteams,[78] was probably complemented by sheep farming, which had given the main settlement its name.[79] In 1291 labour services were still owed, but nearly half of Wenlock priory's revenue of £4 9*s.* from Shipton consisted of assize rents.[80] In 1340 it was claimed that the parish had no sheep, much of

39 S.R.O. 1681/177/34. 40 S.R.O. 3902/Rg/2, p. 46.
41 *Kelly's Dir. Salop.* (1941), 220.
42 S.R.O., DA 17/516/9, f. 247.
43 Ibid. /516/12, f. 246. 44 Ibid. /516/30, f. 235.
45 Inf. from Mr. Jones.
46 Cf. Barley, *Bldgs. of Countryside*, 121, 134. Former date stone '1760' reported by Mr. Jones.
47 *V.C.H. Salop.* i. 398; S.P.L., Chitty file 414/65; D. J. Cathcart King, *Castellarium Anglicanum* (1983), ii. 429; SA 358.
48 S.R.O. 1242, box 15, sale partic. (lot 3).
49 Eyton, iv. 111.
50 S.R.O. 1037/16/15; 1224, box 342, Prior Gosnell's reg. f. 31v.
51 P.R.O., E 178/1879, m. [2].
52 *Cal. Pat.* 1566–9, p. 163. 53 S.R.O. 1037/9/70.
54 Heref. D. & C. mun. 4836 (xlviii).
55 Below, M. Wenlock, churches.
56 *Cal. Pat.* 1548–9, 14–15.
57 P.R.O., C 66/1213, mm. 18–22.
58 S.R.O. 1037/17/29; above, this section (Shipton).
59 S.R.O. 1037/17/4, 30.
60 Ibid. /17/5, 23; S.R.O. 566/66; 3385/1/1; Heref. D. & C. mun. 4836 (xlviii); S.P.L., MS. 6831, p. 172; 6865, p. 176; above, this section (Shipton).
61 S.R.O. 1037/17/32. 62 P.R.O., IR 29/29/288.
63 Names interchangeable in 1588: S.R.O. 566/11.
64 S.R.O. 840, box 42, memo. of agreement.
65 S.R.O. 566/11; 1037/3/118; /16/12. The wood of Larden had been mentioned 1387: S.R.O. 1037/3/65.
66 *Roll of Salop. Eyre 1256*, p. 28.
67 P.R.O., C 116/207; above, Stanton Long, econ. hist.
68 S.R.O. 809, parcel 14, map of 1732.
69 S.R.O. 1037/3/2; 3195/1, f. 31; *T.S.A.S.* 2nd ser. x. 312.
70 Birm. Univ. Libr., Mytton Papers, v. 1186.
71 S.R.O. 566/29; 637/1; 1037/16/17.
72 S.R.O. 3195/1, ff. 40, 62, 117.
73 S.R.O. 1037/3/3, 8. For other names, apparently of Larden open fields or furlongs, see S.R.O. 1037/3/29; 3195/1, f. 40; P.R.O., C 104/26, undated deed (Thos. de la Lake to Rog. son of Rog.).
74 P.R.O., C 104/24, pt. 1, terrier of 1545.
75 Eyton, iii. 309.
76 Birm. Univ. Libr., Mytton Papers, v. 1186.
77 S.R.O. 566/9, 10; 1037/17/19.
78 *V.C.H. Salop.* i. 312.
79 *P.N. Salop.* (E.P.N.S), i. 265.
80 *Tax. Eccl.* (Rec. Com.), 164.

the cereal crop had perished, and a third of the arable was uncultivated for want of tenants.[81] By 1370 the priory had stopped cultivating the Shipton demesne, having apparently let it off in small lots; assize rents totalled £10 10*s*., other income only 13*s*.[82] In 1540 the priory's gross rental from lands comprised £10 8*s*. 10*d*. from Shipton, £1 8*s*. 3*d*. from Larden and the Moorhouse, and 13*s*. 4*d*. from Skimblescott.[83]

Brockton manor was worth 28*s*. a year in 1066. Later 'waste', it was worth 15*s*. by 1086. There was then 1½ ploughteam but room for 4 more,[84] and there were assarts by the late 13th century.[85] Rents totalled *c*. £10 in 1404. The chief house and 2 carucates of the demesne were then on lease to John Broadstone, lord of Nether Larden,[86] but the lord of Brockton had ½ virgate in hand. There were five other ½-virgate holdings and another of 1 virgate, all held at will and with houses in Brockton. There were a few small assarts, mostly held by non-residents, and a larger assart held with one of the ½ virgates. Several vacant tofts[87] were held at will by a small resident freeholder. In 1573 rents totalled little more than in 1404 but holdings were larger on average, that of the chief house having been reduced.[88]

Wheat, barley, peas, and oats were grown in the 1370s.[89] The chaplain who died in 1521 had wheat and oats, oxen, a few cows, pigs, and poultry, and more than 100 sheep.[90] Some arable had recently been inclosed and converted to pasture at Brockton and Nether and Over Larden,[91] and there was evidently some pressure on available pastures later in the 16th century; sheep and other animals were stinted on the common by 1553, and in 1567 the inhabitants of Brockton, the Moorhouse, and Larden and of townships in neighbouring parishes were warned against grazing over Shipton's fields.[92] At Larden in March 1614 Jasper More had 62 cattle, including 12 draught oxen and 20 cows, 10 horses, 178 sheep, and 80 swine; he grew corn, barley, and oats.[93]

Mogg Forest was gradually inclosed, for example by Thomas More *c*. 1550,[94] Maurice Ludlow and Jasper More *c*. 1580,[95] and Thomas Mytton *c*. 1736.[96] Though some of the earlier inclosures were for coppicing,[97] New House and Barn farms, near the parish's south-western boundary, may have been created by clearance in the 16th century,[98] and in 1772 Thomas Mytton's grandson owned at least 60 a. of arable inclosed from the forest.[99] Part of the common remained open in 1793[1] but that may have gone by 1801 when the Moorhouse had 27 a. called Mogg Forest new inclosure.[2] By 1817 the former forest had virtually no trees in Shipton parish except at the Ditches.[3]

Inclosure of the open fields, gradual in the 17th century,[4] seems to have been complete by the late 18th.[5] Over the same period Shipton and Larden halls ceased to be farmhouses, and other farms were amalgamated. Shipton township had eight farms in 1540, two cottage holdings, and the mill.[6] Under Henry Mytton, lord of Shipton manor 1688–1731, small farms were absorbed when they fell vacant.[7] In Shipton township by the early 19th century the farms were those of Shipton Grange (329 a., including two other houses), New House (370 a.), and the Bull's Head (41 a.), besides two cottage holdings; Shipton Hall retained only 23 a.[8] In the rest of the parish each township had had, probably for centuries, only one or two large farms; in the early 19th they were Larden Grange,[9] the Moorhouse,[10] Moorhouse farm,[11] Lower Brockton,[12] and Skimblescott.[13] Larden Hall then had only 17 a.[14]

At Shipton Grange progressive methods and meticulous accounting were practised *c*. 1770. Sheep farming was secondary to dairying, and in 1771–2 the farmer sold 5,220 lb. of cheese and 798 lb. of butter. Cattle were usually bought locally but the sheep included Leicesters and others bought at Ashbourne (Derb.). Horses, bought in Leicestershire and elsewhere, included a mare from Robert Bakewell. Apart from the usual cereals and beans, potatoes were produced in quantity for sale and as pig food. Turnip and clover seeds were bought, and lime.[15] Isolated barns, set by 1833 on the slopes above Shipton and Larden,[16] are further evidence of improved farming.

In 1846 the parish had equal proportions of arable and grass.[17] Grass predominated increasingly until the mid 20th century, especially for beef cattle, though sheep remained important.[18] Lower Brockton, a prize-winning stock farm in 1884, kept Herefords for beef and milk. Its arable used no strict rotation. The local climate was 'backward', late harvests making wheat an economic risk;[19] in the parish as a whole wheat declined in relation to barley and oats in the late 19th century but recovered in the 20th.[20]

Shipton mill, mentioned in the 13th century,[21]

81 *Inq. Non.* (Rec. Com.), 187.
82 B.L. Add. MS. 6165, p. 98; Add. Roll 67032.
83 P.R.O., SC 6/Hen. VIII/3021, mm. 6d.–7.
84 *V.C.H. Salop.* i. 320.
85 P.R.O., C 104/27, undated deed (John, ld. of Brockton, to John, ld. of Easthope).
86 Above, manors.
87 Above, this article, intro.
88 P.R.O., C 116/207, extent of 1403–4, ct. r. of 1573.
89 S.R.O. 1224/2/15.
90 S.R.O. 566/2.
91 B.L. Lansd. MS. 1, f. 191; P.R.O., C 104/26, return of 1517.
92 S.R.O. 566/6, 8.
93 S.R.O. 1037/10/42.
94 Ibid. /16/12, ff. 15–16.
95 S.R.O. 637/1.
96 S.R.O. 4572/6/2/59.
97 e.g. S.R.O. 566/16.
98 Above, this article, intro.; manors.
99 S.R.O. 3385/5/1.
1 S.P.L., MS. 6831, p. 173.
2 S.R.O. 2997/6/3.
3 B.L. Maps, O.S.D. 207.
4 S.R.O. 1037/17/19.
5 S.R.O. 515/2; /5, pp. 304–14; 2997/6/3; 3385/5/1.
6 P.R.O., SC 6/Hen. VIII/3021, mm. 6d.–7.
7 S.R.O. 4572/3/30.
8 P.R.O., IR 18/8274; S.R.O. 5321/A53.
9 S.R.O. 515/9, p. 61.
10 S.R.O. 2997/6/3.
11 S.R.O. 5321/A53.
12 S.R.O. 515/5, pp. 306–8.
13 S.R.O. 168/2, f. 100.
14 S.R.O. 515/9, p. 61.
15 S.R.O. 2547.
16 O.S. Map 1", sheet LXI. SW. (1833 edn.).
17 P.R.O., IR 18/8274.
18 Table XXIII and sources there cited.
19 *Jnl. R. Agric. Soc. Eng.* 2nd ser. xx (2), 555–8.
20 Table XXIII.
21 S.R.O. 3195/1, f. 52.

TABLE XXIII

SHIPTON: LAND USE, LIVESTOCK, AND CROPS

		1867	1891[a]	1938[a]	1965[a]
Percentage of grassland		65	69	79	49
	arable	35	31	21	51
Percentage of cattle		9	13	17	19
	sheep	87	85	81	65
	pigs	4	2	1	16
Percentage of wheat		49	22	32	44
	barley	31	44	12	35
	oats	20	34	56	20
	mixed corn & rye	0	0	0	1
Percentage of agricultural land growing roots and vegetables		9	5	5	8

[a] Excluding Skimblescott.

Sources: P.R.O., MAF 68/143, no. 15; /1340, no. 5; /3880, Salop. no. 226; /4945, no. 226.

stood near the Corve[22] on a 'flem' (leat) running by Flem meadow and Flem yard.[23] The mill ground malt and grain in the early 17th century.[24] By 1655 the flem was clogged and the mill ruined,[25] but it was mentioned as late as 1707.[26]

Brockton mill, mentioned in 1256,[27] rebuilt *c.* 1400,[28] and surviving in the later 17th century,[29] stood in Stanton Long parish, just upstream of Brockton village near Mill bank.[30] There had evidently been fulling at Brockton in or before the 16th century; Walkmill green was mentioned in 1565.[31]

A market at Shipton may have been granted by Henry III.[32] An 'indifferent' Tuesday market at Shipton was mentioned in 1673 but no other certain record is known.[33]

LOCAL GOVERNMENT. Shipton township was part of Wenlock priory's demesne manor of Oxenbold by the mid 14th century[34] and had two constables in 1522;[35] Skimblescott, and probably Larden, also went into Oxenbold manor before 1540.[36] After the dismemberment of Shipton (formerly Oxenbold) manor in the 1540s[37] jurisdiction over Patton and Corve passed (by 1566) to the new Oxenbold leet (cr. 1544), though their suit was still claimed by Shipton.[38] Its court appointed two constables,[39] one for Shipton, the other for Patton and Shipton manor's other 'out hamlets'.[40] In the 16th and 17th centuries Shipton court baron met twice yearly. Court rolls, drafts, or estreats survive for much of the period 1553–1664.[41] The court claimed leet jurisdiction by 1553;[42] beatings, affrays, and bloodshed were presented,[43] as were breaches of the assize of bread and of ale.[44]

Brockton manor had one constable in 1413.[45] Rolls of Brockton court baron survive for several dates 1552–1627,[46] and Thomas More held a court baron for Brockton in 1784.[47] The court was concerned solely with agrarian and tenurial matters.

In the early 17th century highway labour was enforced by Shipton manor court.[48] Shipton, the Moorhouse, and Larden were each liable by custom for their own highways in 1707.[49] Shipton and Brockton had a surveyor each in 1716.[50]

The parish had no workhouse,[51] and was put in Church Stretton poor-law union in 1836,[52] in which it remained until 1930.[53] The parish was in Church Stretton highway district 1863–95 except for Skimblescott, which was put in Bridgnorth highway district.[54] From 1872 the parish was in Church Stretton rural sanitary district,[55] with which Church Stretton highway district was held to coincide by 1878.[56] In 1883 Skimblescott, since 1836 the only part of the parish in Wenlock municipal borough,[57] was added to Monkhopton civil parish and thus to Bridgnorth union and rural sanitary district.[58]

Shipton C.P. was in Church Stretton rural district 1894–1934, Bridgnorth R.D. 1934–74, and Bridgnorth district from 1974.[59] In 1970 a joint parish council was formed for Easthope, Shipton, and Stanton Long.[60]

22 S.R.O. 1037/2/121.
23 So called 1848: S.R.O. 5321/A53.
24 S.R.O. 1037/17/21.
25 S.R.O. 566/42, 49.
26 S.R.O. 5709, Shipton land tax assessment.
27 *Roll of Salop. Eyre 1256*, p. 28.
28 P.R.O., C 116/207.
29 S.R.O., q. sess. order bk. no. 3, 23 Apr. 1661; S.R.O. 3901/Rg/1, 5 Oct. 1671.
30 *Shropshire Mag.* Sept. 1974, 27; P.R.O., IR 29/29/297; IR 30/29/297, field 76.
31 P.R.O., C 116/207.
32 *R. Com. Mkt. Rights* [C. 5550], p. 111, H.C. (1888), liii.
33 R. Blome, *Britannia* (1673), 193 (ref. supplied by Mr. D. J. Lloyd).
34 Above, manors; Monkhopton, local govt.
35 S.R.O. 566/2.
36 P.R.O., SC 6/Hen. VIII/3021, m. 6d.
37 Above, Monkhopton, manors.
38 Above, Stanton Long, local govt.; Monkhopton, local govt.
39 S.R.O. 566/18 and later rolls.
40 Ibid. /47–8;: above, Stanton Long, local govt.
41 S.R.O. 566/6–11, 13–14, 16, 18, 20–37, 41–3, 45, 47–9; 637/1, 3, 5–8; 1037/16/19. Lost ct. r. listed in S.R.O. 566/54.
42 S.R.O. 566/6.
43 Ibid. /25, 30, 43; 637/3.
44 S.R.O. 566/35–6, 43, 45.
45 P.R.O., JUST 1/753, m. 32.
46 P.R.O., C 116/207, 210.
47 S.R.O. 1011, box 167, ct. r.
48 S.R.O. 566/23–4.
49 S.R.O. 4572/3/29.
50 S.R.O. 566/59 (dated by *Orders of Q. Sess.* ii. 25); *T.S.A.S.* lvi. 321.
51 *Poor Law Abstract*, H.C. 175, pp. 422–3 (1803–4), xiii; H.C. 82, pp. 376–7 (1818), xix.
52 V. J. Walsh, 'Admin. of Poor Laws in Salop. 1820–55' (Pennsylvania Univ. Ph.D. thesis, 1970), 150.
53 *Kelly's Dir. Salop.* (1929), 212.
54 *Lond. Gaz.* 27 Mar. 1863, p. 1769; S.R.O., S.C.C. Local Govt., etc., Cttee. min. bk. 1894–1903, p. 29.
55 *V.C.H. Salop.* ii. 217.
56 S.R.O. 560/769.
57 *V.C.H. Salop.* ii. 211.
58 Above, Monkhopton, local govt.
59 *Rural Dist. Councillors Electn. Order, 1894* (Local Govt. Bd. order no. 31847); *V.C.H. Salop.* ii. 213, 217; iii. 179, and sources cited ibid. 169 n. 29.
60 *Easthope, Shipton and Stanton Long Combined Par. Council Order 1970* (copy in S.R.O. 4873/1/205).

CHURCH. Shipton, Larden, Brockton, and Skimblescott may have been parts of the minster parish of Much Wenlock in St. Mildburg's time. Brockton may have been attached to Stanton Long parish by *c.* 1200, whence part of Brockton may have been reunited with Holy Trinity parish, Much Wenlock, *c.* 1271.[61] Such changes would account for the geographical isolation of Shipton, Larden, and the part of Brockton not in Stanton Long from the rest of Much Wenlock parish. Parts of Shipton church are 12th-century.[62] A certain Grenta's claim that Shipton was a separate parish from Much Wenlock was dismissed *c.* 1110,[63] but Roger Owayn was called parson of Shipton in the mid 13th century.[64] In 1275 a chaplain was instituted on the prior of Wenlock's presentation,[65] but the archbishop ruled in 1282[66] that he occupied the chapel unlawfully, and in 1284 the bishop required future chaplains to be appointed by the prior and merely presented to the bishop's official (evidently without institution or induction) and to pay 2*s.* a year to the vicar of Holy Trinity, Much Wenlock.[67] No institution or induction was recorded until 1909.[68] By 1539 weddings and burials were regularly performed;[69] the vicar of Much Wenlock's claims to exclusive burial rights were ineffective.[70] In or before 1425 land was charged with maintenance of a lamp in Shipton church for ever.[71]

In 1535 the prior appointed Alan Clyffe chaplain for life, with a stipend of £2 13*s.* 4*d.* and all the tithes of Skimblescott.[72] Clyffe was still chaplain in 1548 when the grant of great tithes to Sir Thomas Palmer required the impropriator to appoint and maintain a chaplain in perpetuity.[73] The patronage was later with the Crown,[74] presumably from Palmer's attainder in 1553[75] until it was granted to Sir Christopher Hatton in 1586.[76] Meanwhile the stipend remained payable by the impropriators: the Crown until 1582,[77] Hatton 1582–3, and John Lutwyche from 1583.[78] Lutwyche acquired the advowson in 1586[79] and it descended thereafter with Shipton manor.[80] After R. J. More sold the manorial estate in 1896[81] the advowson was said to belong to the purchaser Charles Bishop.[82] The benefice, a donative chaplaincy, became presentative in 1899 and was called a vicarage from the first institution (1909).[83] By 1905 the advowson belonged to More's son T. J. M. More (d. 1947).[84] Mrs. Gladys Lyon had it in 1949 when she transferred it to More's son Jasper (kt. 1979).[85] The patronage was suspended from 1975 until 1981 when Shipton was included in the new benefice of Wenlock, with Sir Jasper (d. 1987) a member of its patronage board.[86]

The chaplain William Scaltoke (d. 1521) occupied a well stocked farm at the prior's will.[87] In the later 16th century the 'curate's house' stood in the churchyard;[88] 6 a. of arable and 1 a. of meadow belonged to it.[89] The queen granted the house to Sir Christopher Hatton with the advowson in 1586.[90] By 1588, however, the chaplain was usually non-resident,[91] and in 1615 the site was no more than a 'croft or waste place'.[92] There was no glebe in 1793 and Thomas Mytton (d. 1787) refused an augmentation from Queen Anne's Bounty.[93] In 1879 there was still no glebe and the chaplain's stipend remained £2 13*s.* 4*d.*, reputedly the smallest living in England,[94] but Miss Frances Holland (d. 1883), a relative of the Myttons, left endowments that in 1887 yielded £115 a year for the living.[95]

Alan Clyffe, chaplain from 1535, was a former monk of Wenlock. Later, as vicar of Kinlet,[96] his duties at Shipton were presumably done by deputy, as his indenture of appointment allowed.[97] No chaplain is known to have lived in the parish after Richard Churchman, chaplain *c.* 1563–1621, became vicar of Stanton Long in 1572;[98] he did not live at Shipton in 1588[99] and was buried at Stanton.[1] Until 1826 many of his successors[2] are known to have been clergy of Stanton Long or nearby parishes,[3] where some certainly lived.[4] John Gough, however, was bur-

61 Fig. 12; above, Stanton Long, church.
62 Below, this section.
63 Eyton, iii. 232–3.
64 P.R.O., C 104/27, undated deed (Hamon of Larden to Wm. son of Herb.).
65 *Reg. Cantilupe* (C.S.), 9, 28.
66 *Reg. Epist. Fr. J. Peckham* (Rolls Ser.), ii. 500–1.
67 *Cal. Pat.* 1348–50, 187–8.
68 Heref. Dioc. Regy., reg. 1902–19, p. 370.
69 *S.P.R. Heref.* i (1), 3.
70 *T.S.A.S.* vi. 104, 119.
71 S.R.O. 1037/3/92; *T.S.A.S.* 3rd ser. x. 373.
72 S.R.O. 1037/17/2.
73 Ibid. /16/3; above, manors (tithes).
74 The queen was (wrongly) returned as patron in 1589: H.W.R.O.(H.), HD 2/14/54.
75 Above, manors (Shipton).
76 S.R.O. 1037/17/30.
77 Ibid. /17/4; *Cal. Pat.* 1578–80, p. 195.
78 *Cal. Pat.* 1580–2, p. 185; S.R.O. 1037/17/29.
79 S.R.O. 1037/17/4; *T.S.A.S.* xlvi. 45.
80 S.P.L., MS. 6865, pp. 176–7; W.S.L. 350/3/40, Shipton p. 26; *Rep. Com. Eccl. Rev.* [67], p. 450, H.C. (1835), xxii.
81 Above, manors.
82 *Kelly's Dir. Salop.* (1900), 199.
83 Benefices Act, 1898, 61 & 62 Vic. c. 48, s. 12; S.R.O. 3902/Rg/2, 20 Feb. 1901, 15 Nov. 1909; Heref. Dioc. Regy., reg. 1883–1901, p. 323; 1902–19, p. 370.
84 *Kelly's Dir. Salop.* (1905), 205. Cf. Burke, *Land. Gent.* (1952), 1819–20.
85 Heref. Dioc. Regy., reg. 1938–53, p. 415; *Who's Who* (1988), 1251.
86 Heref. Dioc. Regy., reg. 1969– (in use), pp. 206, 397–9; *Crockford* (1977–9), 3.
87 S.R.O. 566/2; *T.S.A.S.* vi. 119.
88 S.R.O. 1037/17/4. W.S.L. 350/3/40, Shipton p. 26, places the ho. on the E. side of the chyd.; Forrest, *Old Hos. of Wenlock*, 63, at the NW. corner, according to Revd. R. H. G. More.
89 H.W.R.O.(H.), HD 2/14/54.
90 S.R.O. 1037/17/30.
91 Below, this section.
92 P.R.O., C 142/374, no. 91.
93 S.P.L., MS. 6865, pp. 175–6.
94 *P.O. Dir. Salop.* (1879), 397; *Return of Glebe Land, 1887*, H.C. 307, p. 61 (1887), lxiv.
95 Inf. from Ch. of Eng. Record Centre; Burke, *Land. Gent.* ii (1847), 911.
96 *T.S.A.S.* vi. 102.
97 S.R.O. 1037/17/2.
98 *S.P.R. Heref.* i (1), 3; *Dioc. of Heref. Institutions (1539–1900)*, ed. A. T. Bannister (Heref. 1923), 21.
99 *T.S.A.S.* xlvi. 45.
1 S.R.O. 3901/Rg/1, Aug. 1621.
2 Names and dates from *S.P.R. Heref.* i (1), *passim*; S.R.O. 3902/Rg/1–3, *passim*; Ho. of Lords papers 1641–2, Protestations Oxon. and Salop. f. 179; *Compton Census*, ed. Whiteman, 259 n.
3 *S.P.R. Heref.* i (3), 9; Bannister, *Heref. Institutions*, 36, 44, 49, 77, 85, 111–12, 121, 141; S.R.O. 3901/Rg/1, 13 Mar. 1716/17; /Rg/3, flyleaf; 4131/Rg/3, 27 Nov. 1764; /Rg/5, 9 May 1775; 4132/Rg/2, 4 Feb. 1798; 29 Dec. 1809.
4 *Hearth Tax 1672* (Salop. Arch. Soc. 1949), 179; S.R.O. 3901/Rg/1, 13 Mar. 1716/17; /Rg/3, 29 Jan. 1780; S.P.L., MS. 6865, pp. 102, 175.

ied at Shipton in 1639.[5] Ambrose Phillips, ejected from Westbury in 1646, later ministered at Shipton briefly.[6]

In 1716 services were weekly.[7] The stipend was probably insufficient to attract a chaplain. Instead the Myttons paid fees to local clergy to take the services. By the 1790s, however, the Myttons could afford only a service every three weeks in summer and every month in winter, performed by the rector of Willey (living at Much Wenlock) at ½ guinea a time.[8] R. H. G. More, chaplain 1826–80,[9] presumably required no stipend or fees because he had a private estate in the parish, on which he lived.[10] There was a service every Sunday by 1851.[11] His successors until 1975 were incumbents of nearby parishes[12] and lived outside Shipton.[13] Weekly services were maintained in the 1920s and 1930s.[14] The church was served 1975–81 by clergy of Much Wenlock with Bourton parish[15] and thereafter by the Wenlock team ministry.[16] There were two services a month in 1987.[17]

The small church of *ST. JAMES*, so dedicated by 1535,[18] consists of chancel, nave with south porch, and west tower. It is built of coursed rubble with tiled roofs. The nave and tower are rendered externally, as in 1789.[19] The chancel arch dates from the 12th century; in the nave a blocked south window, a north doorway, and the plain font bowl may be of the same period. The south doorway is an unmoulded rectangular opening of unknown date, its lintel a massive block of rough-hewn stone. The tower was added *c.* 1200 or a little later. The timber framed belfry stage was presumably added before 1552, when the 'steeple' contained three bells.[20] About 1300 a two-light window was inserted in the south wall of the nave and two cusped lancets in the north, one of them in place of the north doorway, then blocked. A blocked opening high on the north side of the chancel arch, and a central stone bracket above the arch on the west, indicate a medieval rood loft. Squints of unknown date flank the chancel arch. A plain chest with medieval ironwork remained in 1990 but the attached carvings of *c.* 1600 and panelled lid, recorded in 1952,[21] were gone.

The chancel was in 'great ruin' by 1553.[22] It was demolished and replaced at John Lutwyche's expense in 1589.[23] Medieval floor tiles in the nave may be from the old chancel. Lutwyche's chancel is probably a copy of its predecessor; the asymmetrical placing of its southern openings and its mixture of styles seem inconsistent with a fresh design of the late 16th century. The two-light south window resembles that of the nave, and the three-light east window also uses a style of *c.* 1300; the medieval chancel may therefore have been refenestrated with the nave. The chancel's embattled parapet and priest's doorway, square headed, may have copied alterations made to the former chancel in the 15th century. Lutwyche furnished the chancel with glass depicting Elizabeth I's arms and badges; much of it remains in the east window. His trussed-rafter roof also remains. The south porch is contemporary with his chancel but has a round arch of Renaissance pattern.

A communion rail, originally round three sides of the table, and a reading desk and a pulpit were added in the 17th century. The nave had pews of the same period, one inscribed 'AP 1640'; there were also pews in the chancel. The nave roof seems to be 17th- or 18th-century. There are many 17th-century and later memorials to the Myttons and Mores. A west gallery was built after 1789. To light it a medieval south lancet was heightened above the eaves and capped with a dormer. The gallery entrance was a plain external doorway high in the north wall. A barrel organ stood in the gallery by the 1830s. Other 18th- and early 19th-century additions were the funeral hatchment of Thomas More (d. 1804), the royal arms of 1816–37 in front of the gallery, the Commandments and Creed on large canvasses flanking the east window, and a small pedestal font, the ancient one having been abandoned outside.

In the Victorian period the communion rail was altered to span the chancel, a harmonium and choir stalls were provided, the ancient font bowl was reinstated on a new base, and stained glass was fitted in some windows. The character of the nave was much altered 1905–6 when the gallery was removed, the walls stripped of internal plaster, and the pews dismantled to make benches.[24] The Commandments and Creed were taken down during a general restoration of 1954–5.[25]

The three bells are of the 1550s, 1694 (by Ellis Hughes), and 1875.[26] In 1961 the plate consisted of a silver chalice and cover, perhaps of the 1620s, a plated flagon and paten, and a Norwegian silver tankard given in 1909.[27] The registers begin in 1539[28] and are virtually complete.

Brockton chapel, with land belonging to it,

5 *S.P.R. Heref.* i (1), 26.
6 *Walker Revised*, ed. A. G. Matthews, 307.
7 H.W.R.O.(H.), HD 5/14/1/23.
8 S.P.L., MS. 6865, p. 175.
9 Plaque in ch.
10 S.P.L., MS. 6865, p. 177; Pigot, *Nat. Com. Dir.* (1835), 385; (1842), 51; *P.O. Dir. Salop.* (1870), 147; (1879), 417; above, manors (Nether Larden).
11 P.R.O., HO 129/354, no. 72.
12 *Kelly's Dir. Salop.* (1885), 936; *Crockford* (1935), 590; Heref. Dioc. Regy., reg. 1883–1901, p. 323; 1902–19, p. 370; 1919–26, p. 448; 1926–38, p. 97; 1953–68, pp. 12, 30–1, 184; 1969– (in use), p. 206.
13 *Kelly's Dir. Salop.* (1885), 936; (1891), 367; (1895), 101; (1913), 213; (1922), 207; (1929), 93; S.R.O., reg. of electors, Ludlow const. (1955), 271; (1958), 269.
14 S.R.O. 3901/SRg/2.
15 S.R.O. 3902/Rg/1–2; *Crockford* (1977–9), 3, 405, 1070.
16 Heref. Dioc. Regy., reg. 1969– (in use), pp. 397–9.
17 Local inf.
18 S.R.O. 1037/17/2.
19 Pl. 5. Archit. descr. based on S.P.L., MS. 372, vol. i, f. 99; W.S.L. 350/3/40, Shipton p. 27; Cranage, iii. 208–11; S.R.O. 3902/Ch/1; Pevsner, *Salop.* 246.
20 *T.S.A.S.* 2nd ser. xii. 94.
21 S.P.L., MS. 6767, no. 58.
22 S.R.O. 566/6.
23 Contemp. brass plate in chancel.
24 *Kelly's Dir. Salop.* (1909), 209; S.R.O. 2610/1.
25 Local inf.; S.R.O. 3902/Rg/1, memo. at end. Cf. S.P.L., photo. by S. A. Jeavons (1949).
26 H. B. Walters, *Ch. Bells of Salop.* (Oswestry, 1915), 99, 468.
27 D. L. Arkwright and B. W. Bourne, *Ch. Plate Archd. Ludlow* (Shrews. 1961), 54.
28 *S.P.R. Heref.* i (1); S.R.O. 390/Rg/1–4; regs. from 1970s at ch.

was mentioned in the earlier 13th century[29] and in the 16th century a 'Lady acre' was said to have once supported a service of the Blessed Virgin Mary in Brockton 'church'.[30] Brockton chapel was the lord's personal property in 1552. It was then disused but still stood in 1627.[31] The attached chapel yard,[32] mentioned in 1812,[33] was presumably represented by the later Chapel field immediately south of the castle site.[34]

NONCONFORMITY. The Independent minister Henry Maurice visited Shipton in 1672 and 'taught a little in the family',[35] but no papists or dissenters were reported in 1676.[36]

Mogg Forest was put on the Hopton Bank Primitive Methodist circuit in 1831[37] and the sect had several members in the parish in the late 19th century.[38] A Convent of the Sacred Heart occupied Larden Cottage 1940–5.[39] From 1947 to 1951 weekly mass was said at Shipton Hall by Montfort Fathers from Brockhurst (in Church Stretton).[40]

EDUCATION. Ambrose Phillips had a private school *c.* 1650[41] and a master was keeping school in 1678–9,[42] but there was none by 1716.[43] A school that opened in 1824 was still active in 1835, when there were 58 pupils; 30 of the poorest were taught at the Revd. R. H. G. More's expense; he also supplied books.[44] From 1845 children attended Brockton National school.[45]

CHARITIES FOR THE POOR. None known.

STOKE ST. MILBOROUGH

STOKE ST. MILBOROUGH village is 9 km. north-east of Ludlow.[46] The parish was Wenlock borough's most southerly detachment. Wholly agricultural and little frequented, it comprises Stoke village and a scattering of farms and ancient hamlets, and the main part was divided into the townships of Stoke, Downton, and Stanton.

A detached part of the parish 3 km. to the north comprised the Heath and Norncott and constituted the Heath civil parish from 1884. The Scirmidge was an extra-parochial place, amounting to less than 1 a., where Cold Weston, Hopton Cangeford, and Stoke St. Milborough parishes met. The origin of its extra-parochial status is unknown, but in the 1780s and 1790s the stone cottage at the Scirmidge seems to have been the home of a midwife to whom women resorted (or were sent) to be delivered of illegitimate children, who thus had no settlement in the surrounding parishes.[47] It seems to have been annexed to Stoke St. Milborough civil parish in 1868.[48] This article treats the large, nearly rectangular area (4,990 a., 2,019 ha.) that constituted Stoke St. Milborough C.P. from 1884.[49]

The eastern half of the parish is occupied by the rising slopes, which reach 500 and 400 m. respectively, of the Brown and Titterstone Clees and of the high ground between them; the north-west quarter by the rising slopes, which reach 300 m., of Weston hill and the Thrift. The streams thus drain south-west. An east–west ridge divides them into a northern system converging on Ledwyche brook and a southern one converging on Dogditch brook.

Most of the parish lies on the Ditton Series of the Lower Old Red Sandstone.[50] On Brown Clee that is overlain by Lower Old Red Sandstone of the Clee Group, which is covered at the summit by the Middle and Lower Coal Measures, capped by dolerite. Narrow bands of the Upper and Lower Abdon limestones occur on the lower slopes of Brown Clee and on Weston hill. The parish's south-western quarter lies on the Ledbury Group of the Downton Series of Lower Old Red Sandstone. Narrow bands of '*Psammosteus*' Limestones occur where that series meets the overlying Ditton Series, around the base of Titterstone Clee and along the south side of the parish's east–west watershed. The soils are mainly red-brown loams, with alluvium in the lower lying south-west.[51]

Clee Burf and Titterstone Clee were each crowned in the Iron Age by a fortified enclosure of unknown purpose, each formed by a single earth and rubble rampart.[52] The rampart of Clee Burf was badly damaged by coal digging before 1841,[53] and both have since been nearly destroyed by quarrying. A few isolated finds of

29 P.R.O., C 104/27, undated deed (Thos. son of Nic. to Rob. of Skimblescott).
30 P.R.O., E 178/1879, m. [2].
31 P.R.O., C 116/207, 210.
32 P.R.O., C 116/207.
33 S.R.O. 1681/76/24, tenancy agreement.
34 Ibid. /76/11. The acreage matches that of field 39 on O.S. Map 1/2,500, Salop. LVII. 6 (1902 edn.).
35 Maurice's diary (MS. in possession of the late Dr. A. B. Cottle, Bristol Univ.), 19 Aug. 1672.
36 *Compton Census*, ed. Whiteman, 259.
37 S.R.O. 2941/2/2, 21 Mar. 1831.
38 S.R.O. 2612/17, pp. 41, 69, 95.
39 S.R.O., DA 17/516/4, f. 134; /516/13, f. 134.
40 E. M. Abbott, *Hist. Dioc. Shrews. 1850–1986* [1987], 26.
41 *Walker Revised*, ed. A. G. Matthews, 307.
42 H.W.R.O.(H.), HD 7, chwdns.' presentment (ref. provided by Dr. R. Hume).
43 H.W.R.O.(H.), HD 5/14/1/21.
44 *Educ. Enq. Abstract*, H.C. 62, p. 782 (1835), xlii.
45 P.R.O., ED 7/103, ff. 67–8. Cf. above, Stanton Long, educ.
46 This article was written 1991–2.
47 *T.S.A.S.* liii. 293–5.
48 P.R.O., RG 10/2727, f. 51v. (presumably under the Poor Law Amendment Act, 1868, 31 & 32 Vic. c. 122, s. 27: no q. sess. order under the Extra-Parochial Places Act, 1857, 20 Vic. c. 19, s. 4).
49 O.S. *Area Bk.* (1885); fig. 38. The history of the Heath C.P. follows below.
50 Para. based on Geol. Surv. Map 1", solid, sheet 166 (1974 edn.).
51 Soil Surv. Map 1", sheet 166 (1972 edn.).
52 *Arch. Cambrensis*, lxxxix. 83–111.
53 C. H. Hartshorne, *Salopia Antiqua* (1841), 21.

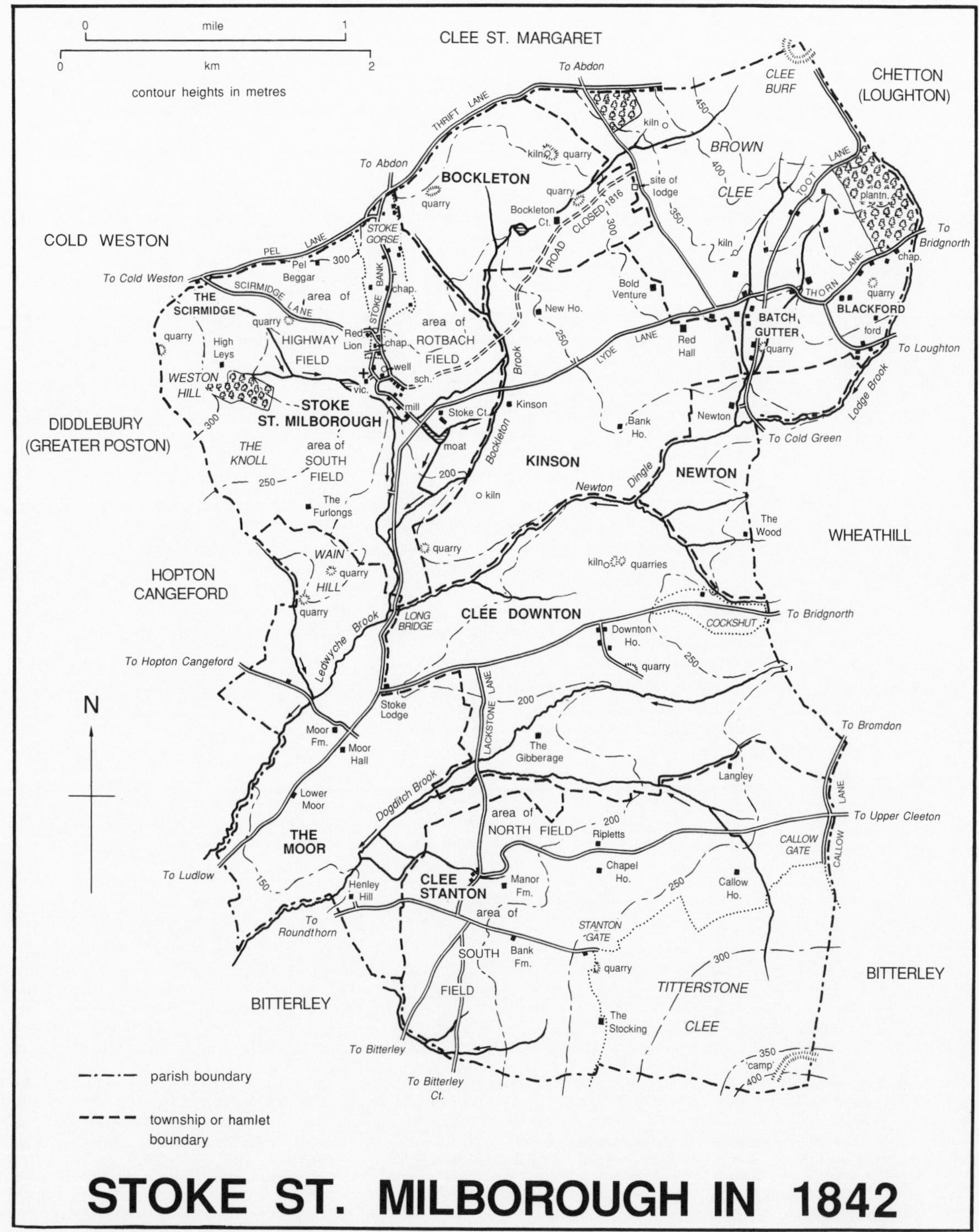

Fig. 38

The edge of Brown Clee common coincided with the eastern and northern boundaries of Bockleton, Kinson, and Newton.

prehistoric artefacts[54] are the only other evidence of human activity in the parish before the Anglo-Saxon period.

Except in the south-west quarter the parish boundaries are straight or gently sinuous and tend to follow high ground; they were probably defined mostly in the 13th century across wastes previously intercommoned with neighbouring townships. Brown Clee's upper slopes, however, were not so divided until the 17th century,[55] and the township divisions across Titterstone Clee common were presumably late too. In the low lying south-west the parish boundary is angular and so may have been defined by fields.

Stoke and Stanton manors were settled by 1086, though Stanton had only one recorded inhabitant.[56] Other *tun* names, Downton, Kinson ('Ekinestaneston'), and Newton, all recorded by 1255,[57] were given to what were presumably subsidiary settlements. The Moor, cultivated by 1291,[58] may have been reclaimed from marshy waste. Earthworks at Kinson,[59] Newton, the Moor,[60] and Stanton[61] indicate hamlets there; Bockleton and Downton were probably hamlets too. Like Stoke, each hamlet stood just below the head of a valley except for Downton and the Moor, which stood on the central watershed. The hamlets probably shrank in the earlier 14th century; 11 farms in the parish were abandoned by 1340.[62]

When recovery came[63] settlement did not return to the old hamlets; indeed conversion of open-field arable to inclosed pasture *c.* 1500 caused further shrinkage at Bockleton, Downton, Kinson, the Moor, Newton, and Stanton.[64] In the whole parish, however, the number of households increased from *c.* 33 in 1524[65] to over 43 by 1672,[66] and 218 adults and children were listed for the 1660 poll tax.[67] Much of the new settlement took the form of single farmhouses, away from the old hamlets and in new fields.[68] In addition, seven cottages were reported on the wastes of Stoke manor in 1654; a group at Blackford, on Brown Clee, existed in 1752.[69] There were 89 households by 1801[70] but, of the ancient settlements, only Stoke was a village; in 1815 Stoke had 16 houses (9 of them cottages), while Downton and Stanton had 4 houses each, the Moor 3, Kinson 2, and Bockleton and Newton one.[71] The older houses in Stoke village are mostly built of rubble. Elsewhere in the parish some are of rubble, some are timber framed.

In 1815 there were 11 cottages on Stoke Gorse and 24 on Brown Clee,[72] grouped at Mount Flirt, Blackford, and Batch Gutter; many were less than 25 years old.[73] The parish's population grew rapidly and stood at 554 in 1821; it then remained steady until 1871 or later.[74] In 1841 the cottagers on Brown Clee were mostly farm labourers, colliers, and widows.[75] Between 1871, when the population was 548, and 1891 there was a steep decline; cottages on Brown Clee diminished from 43 in 1871 to 30 (6 of them empty) by 1891.[76] There was another steep fall in population in the mid 20th century, to 215 by 1971.[77] By 1991 it had risen again to 300,[78] chiefly increased by commuters and the retired. Without much new building, houses were made by converting old buildings like Stoke school and mill and Stanton Methodist chapel, and especially by restoring cottages on Brown Clee.[79]

The Bridgnorth–Ludlow road crossed the parish from east to south-west. A turnpike road 1756–1873, declared a main road in 1878,[80] it was the parish's only classified road in 1992. A ridgeway called Thrift (or Frith) Lane[81] ran north-east, along or parallel to the parish's northern boundary, to Brown Clee; near Pel Beggar it was called Pel Lane.[82] In the early 17th century it was the Cold Weston strakers' route to Brown Clee.[83]

Neither of those roads served Stoke village directly, and both may therefore have been more ancient.[84] The village was connected to the Bridgnorth–Ludlow road by two lanes. One led south towards Ludlow.[85] The other ran east through Kinson and via Lydall (or Lyde) Lane[86] towards Bridgnorth;[87] near Blackford it was called Thorn Lane.[88] Stoke village was joined to Thrift Lane by the westward Scirmidge Lane and the northward Stoke Bank,[89] which crossed Stoke Gorse common and also led, across Thrift

54 SA 572, 3513, 3906, 4498.
55 Above, Abdon, econ. hist.
56 *V.C.H. Salop.* i. 312–13.
57 *Rot. Hund.* (Rec. Com.), ii. 85.
58 *Cal. Chart. R.* 1257–1300, 406.
59 R.C.H.M.E., draft field rep. (1985).
60 O.S. field reps. (copies in S.P.L.).
61 R.C.H.M.E., draft field rep. (1987).
62 *Inq. Non.* (Rec. Com.), 188.
63 Below, econ. hist.
64 B.L. Lansd. MS. 1, f. 190 and v.; P.R.O., C 104/26, comrs.' return of 1517.
65 P.R.O., E 179/166/200 (including Norncott). Cf. (for Stoke man.) S.R.O. 1224, box 342, Prior Gosnell's reg. f. 40v.; T. F. Dukes, *Antiquities of Salop.* (1844), 86–9.
66 *Hearth Tax 1672* (Salop. Arch. Soc. 1949), 40–1 (including Norncott).
67 P.R.O., E 179/168/219, mm. 10–11 (including Norncott).
68 Below, econ. hist.
69 Dukes, *Antiquities of Salop.* 79; J. Rocque, *Map of Salop.* (1752).
70 S.P.L., MS. 6862, f. 119 (including Norncott).
71 S.R.O. 4366/Pa/1.
72 Ibid. fields Q 7, 9–25, 27–32, 34–43.
73 S.R.O., incl. award B 21, Wm. Kidson to Jos. Loxdale 12 Nov. 1809. Cf. above, Abdon, econ. hist.
74 *V.C.H. Salop.* ii. 227.
75 P.R.O., HO 107/913/13, ff. 17v.–19v.
76 *V.C.H. Salop.* ii. 227; P.R.O., RG 10/2727, ff. 62–64v., 66v.; RG 12/2083, ff. 12 and v., 13v.–14v., 16. Cf. above, Abdon, intro.
77 *V.C.H. Salop.* ii. 227; *Census*, 1971, *Co. Rep. Salop.* i. 5. Cf. above, Abdon, intro.
78 S.C.C. Property and Planning Services Dept. inf. rep. C91/103.
79 M. Thom and M. Pearce, *A Quart in a Pint Pot: the story of Stoke St. Milborough Par.* (Stoke St. Milborough, 1986), 32, 39.
80 Ludlow Turnpike Act, 1756, 29 Geo. II, c. 59; Ann. Turnpike Acts Continuance Act, 1872, 35 & 36 Vic. c. 85; Highways and Locomotives (Amendment) Act, 1878, 41 & 42 Vic. c. 77.
81 *T.S.A.S.* liii. 293; S.R.O. 757, box 11, deed of 1810.
82 O.S. Map 6", Salop. LXXII. NW. (1891 edn.).
83 *T.S.A.S.* 2nd ser. viii. 197; cf. S.R.O., incl. award B 33.
84 Para. based on B.L. Maps, O.S.D. 206.
85 S.R.O. 757, box 10, deed of 1839.
86 Ibid. box 26, deed of 1681; box 31, deed of 1768; box 27, agreement of 1814; order of 1816.
87 S.R.O., incl. award B 33.
88 O.S. Map 1/25,000, SO 48/58 (1983 edn.).
89 O.S. Map 6", Salop. LXXII. NW. (1891 edn.).

Lane, to Clee St. Margaret and Abdon. From Stoke a north-eastward lane, accessible also from Kinson, led through Bockleton to Brown Clee common; it was stopped up in 1816 after the common was inclosed.[90]

A lane crossing Lydall Lane led from Newton to the summit of Clee Burf, climbing the hill as Toot Lane.[91] By the early 19th century it was the route from the Batch Gutter cottages up to the coal pits.[92]

From the Bridgnorth–Ludlow road Lackstone (or Hackston) Lane led south to Stanton hamlet and on through Bitterley to Ludlow.[93] Just south of Stanton it was crossed by a lane from Roundthorn, on the turnpike road, to Stanton gate, the hamlet's main point of access to Titterstone Clee common. Ludlow could be reached from Stanton via Roundthorn, but the most direct route was south by a lane through Bitterley. An eastward lane from Stanton led to Upper Cleeton.[94]

St. Mildburg's (or St. Milburgha's) well, a spring with an old stone basin, on the east side of Stoke village, was mentioned in 1321.[95] It was later a common clothes-washing place. Stories of a miraculous origin were recorded in the mid 19th century, when the water was said to be good for sore eyes. It was 'covered in and altered' *c.* 1873 and altered again in 1906.[96] By 1945 its water was piped to six houses.[97]

A play was performed at Stoke Gorse in 1615.[98] The parish wake was traditionally on the Sunday after 25 June, the reputed anniversary of St. Mildburg's death;[99] by the 1730s it was the Sunday after Midsummer Day (24 June).[1] It was customary then to deck the graves with evergreens[2] and make merry in the churchyard, a practice suppressed *c.* 1820.[3] By 1790 the parish had an alehouse,[4] probably that which stood in 1813 on the south side of Scirmidge Lane at the edge of Stoke Gorse.[5] Called the Red Lion by 1851, it closed in the 1860s and was later called Upper House. Oddfellows were said to have met there, and later a Men's Friendly Society.[6] At Clee Downton the Holly Bush inn had opened by 1851, when a Friendly Benefit Society met there;[7] it too seems to have closed in the 1860s.[8] Stoke village had a variety of social organizations and events in the early 20th century, many of which used the school.[9] The parish belonged 1900–6 to the Diocese of Hereford Circulating Library and from 1926 had a county library book centre.[10] In 1922 an army hut was re-erected near Kinson as the parish hall.[11] Organized social activities dwindled after the Second World War, but by the 1980s newcomers had revived them.[12] Clee Stanton people, however, were attracted to Bitterley rather than Stoke.[13]

Sir Thomas Littleton (1647–1710), speaker of the House of Commons 1698–1700,[14] was a native of the parish.[15]

MANORS AND OTHER ESTATES. *STOKE ST. MILBOROUGH* was probably part of lands about the Clee hills said to have been given to St. Mildburg before 704 by her half-brothers Merchelm and Mildfrith.[16] In 1086 the manor rightfully belonged to Wenlock priory but had been given by Earl Roger to his chaplains.[17] It was restored to the priory,[18] which held it until 1540.[19]

The Crown granted the manor to the see of Canterbury in 1542[20] but resumed it in 1559[21] and sold it in 1574 to John Smith of Little Baddow (Essex) in fee farm.[22] Smith (kt. 1576)[23] and his brother Clement sold the manor in 1584 to Oliver Briggs[24] (d. 1596). Briggs was succeeded by his son Humphrey, who bought Abdon manor in 1598.[25] Stoke manor thereafter descended with Abdon[26] until 1873, when G. R. C. Herbert, earl of Pembroke and Montgomery, sold it to G. R. Hamilton-Russell, Viscount Boyne[27] (d. 1907). Boyne left all his Shropshire estate, including Stoke manor, to his second surviving son F. G. Hamilton-Russell, who was still lord in 1917. The manorial title was not sold with his Stoke St. Milborough estate in 1919 and has not been traced since.[28]

In 1581 Sir John and Clement Smith sold the chief house, *STOKE COURT*, and the demesne

90 S.R.O. 757, box 27, order of 1816; below, econ. hist.
91 Thom and Pearce, *Quart in Pint Pot*, map inside front cover.
92 S.R.O., incl. award B 33.
93 O.S. Map 6", Salop. LXXII. SW. (1891 and 1904 edns.). Para. based on B.L. Maps, O.S.D. 206.
94 S.R.O. 757, box 21, deed of 1740.
95 S.R.O. 1037/19/1.
96 C. S. Burne, *Salop. Folk-Lore* (1883), 417; Eyton, iv. 6; Thom and Pearce, *Quart in Pint Pot*, facing p. 11.
97 A. H. S. Waters, *Rep. on Water Supply* (S.C.C. 1946), 80.
98 *Salop.* (R.E.E.D.), i. 325–6.
99 C. S. Burne, *Salop. Folk-Lore* (1888), 440.
1 Birm. Univ. Libr., Mytton Papers, v. 1224.
2 Thom and Pearce, *Quart in Pint Pot*, 26.
3 Burne, *Salop. Folk-Lore*, 339–40.
4 W.B.R., Q1/11/2.
5 S.R.O., incl. award B 33.
6 S. Bagshaw, *Dir. Salop.* (1851), 551; *P.O. Dir. Salop.* (1863), 762; (1870), 148; Thom and Pearce, *Quart in Pint Pot*, 28, 30.
7 Registrar of Friendly Socs. *List of Friendly Socs. in Co. of Salop, 1793–1855* (H.M.S.O. 1857; copy in S.R.O. 119/27), 5.
8 P.R.O., RG 9/1838, f. 53v.; RG 10/2727, ff. 53–66v.
9 Thom and Pearce, *Quart in Pint Pot*, 24, 30.
10 R. C. Elliott, 'Development of Public Libraries in Salop.' (Loughborough Univ. M.A. thesis, 1970; copy in co. libr.), 46, 125.
11 Thom and Pearce, op. cit. 28.
12 Ibid. 32.
13 *Shropshire Star*, 24 Oct. 1979, p. 10.
14 *D.N.B.*; G.E.C. *Baronetage*, ii. 204.
15 *S.P.R. Heref.* xix (5), p. x (citing the MS. now S.P.L., MS. 14, p. 118).
16 H. P. R. Finberg, *Early Charters of W. Midlands* (1972), pp. 147–8, 203.
17 *V.C.H. Salop.* i. 312.
18 *Rot. Hund.* ii. 85.
19 *Valor Eccl.* (Rec. Com.), iii. 215.
20 *L. & P. Hen. VIII*, xvii, p. 256.
21 Under 1 Eliz. I, c. 4: *Cal. Pat.* 1558–60, 31.
22 *Cal. Pat.* 1572–5, pp. 197, 546.
23 W. A. Shaw, *Kts. of Eng.* (1906), ii. 77.
24 S.R.O. 933, box 16, case [of 1823], mm. 7–12.
25 P.R.O., C 142/253, no. 68; above, Abdon, manor.
26 P.R.O., C 142/424, no. 86; S.R.O., q. sess. rec. box 260, reg. of gamekeepers 1742–79, 22 Dec. 1760, 20 Jan. 1770, 17 Sept. 1771; Brigges Estates Act, 1800, 39 & 40 Geo. III, c. 114 (Local and Personal); S.R.O. 933, box 16, case [of 1823]; Fitzwilliam Estates Act, 1833, 3 & 4 Wm. IV, c. 26 (Priv. Act). Cf. above, Abdon, manor.
27 S.R.O. 757, box 22, deed.
28 Below, this section; *Kelly's Dir. Salop.* (1917), 253.

lands to Thomas Littleton and Rowland Bishop.[29] Littleton was in sole possession of Stoke Court at his death in 1622[30] and was succeeded by his son Adam[31] (cr. bt. 1642), after whose death in 1647[32] it belonged to his son Sir Thomas Littleton (or Poyntz).[33] In 1652 Sir Thomas sold the estate to Henry Bernard, who sold it in 1671 to George Lee[34] (d. 1673) of the Moor.[35] Lee's heir was his daughter Mary, who afterwards married John Conyers (d. 1725). Their son Edward sold Stoke Court to William Hall in 1727.[36] Hall (d. by 1732) was succeeded by his sister Elizabeth, wife of Wredenhall Pearce of Downton Hall. On her death in 1762 the estate passed to their son William, who took the additional surname Hall. The estate, a reputed manor by 1772, passed on his death to his brother Charles Pearce Hall, who died childless in 1795. It then passed to the representatives of their three sisters. The estate was partitioned in 1809 and Stoke Court was allotted to the representatives of Ann Thomson (formerly Pearce). They sold it in 1813 to John Wall (d. 1817), who became vicar of Stoke St. Milborough that year. Wall's trustees conveyed it in 1825 to William Bright, who immediately vested part, including Stoke Court, in a trustee. In 1834 the trustee sold it back to Wall's trustees, who conveyed it in 1839 to Wall's widow Elizabeth (d. 1843). She was succeeded by her son C. L. Wall, who sold the estate and reputed manor (740 a.) to Lord Boyne (d. 1872) in 1867.[37] At the sale of F. G. Hamilton-Russell's Stoke St. Milborough estate in 1919 Stoke Court was bought by J. B. Whiteman,[38] in whose family it remained in 1992.

The medieval house, called the Court by 1322,[39] is reputed to have stood within a rectangular moat,[40] substantial parts of which remain. A later house, north of the moat, dates from *c.* 1600 and its original two storeyed stone range contains a hall and parlour with a stack in each gable end. The main doorway has a carved stone surround and the parlour, formerly wainscotted,[41] has a carved wooden overmantel of *c.* 1600.[42] The former moat, fed from Bockleton brook, may have become a garden feature at that time; near or within it is a mount. In the later 18th century the front of the house was faced in brick.

In 1799 Joseph Owen of Albrighton married Ann Corne, who had inherited Bold Venture farm and Upper House, Kinson.[43] Owen bought the Brookhouse, Kinson, in 1808[44] and Lower House farm, Clee Downton,[45] and died in 1816 leaving the whole to his son F. C. Owen (d. 1819), whose coheirs were his brothers George Owen (d. 1830), Herbert Owen, and Edmund Hemming Owen. E. H. Owen bought part of the Stoke Court estate in 1825[46] and in the 1840s built a villa on it,[47] *STOKE ST. MILBOROUGH LODGE.* He had bought Herbert's share of their father's estate in 1832 and bought another farm at Clee Downton in 1843.[48] He sold the whole estate (633 a.) to Lord Boyne in 1867.[49]

In 1580 Sir John and Clement Smith sold a chief house at *THE MOOR* to William Adams.[50] It passed to Richard Adams, whose son William died in 1637.[51] The estate then seems to have passed to William's widow Elizabeth, who married George Lucy (d. 1658) of Middleton Higford[52] and died in 1667. Her heir was her daughter Elizabeth Lucy, wife of George Lee (d. 1673).[53] Lee bought Stoke Court, and the Moor seems to have descended with it until 1809[54] when, on the partition of the Stoke Court estate, Upper and Lower Moor farms were allotted to Catherine, daughter of Thomas and Catherine Browne (*née* Pearce), and her husband Lt.-Col. John Edwards[55] (cr. bt. 1838), who survived her and died in 1850.[56] The estate then passed to their nephew Thomas Browne Browne (formerly Jones) who sold it (299 a.) to Lord Boyne in 1867.[57] Upper Moor (later Moor) Farm was probably the estate's chief house[58] and dates from *c.* 1600. It has a two storeyed hall range with a contemporary 2½ storeyed cross wing at each end. The lower end of the hall range has a through passage; the upper end has a large axial stack serving both the hall and the great parlour in the adjoining cross wing, which had a little parlour too. The lower cross wing seems to have contained a kitchen and dairy and has a lateral stack. In 1667 a drawing room and a study were mentioned.[59]

Edward Bishop (d. 1625)[60] owned *MOOR HALL* and was succeeded by his son George (d. 1668),[61] whose son the Revd. William sold it in 1710 to William Lucas (d. 1731).[62] Lucas's

29 B.L. Add. MS. 31932, f. 223.
30 *T.S.A.S.* 4th ser. iii. 316.
31 H.W.R.O.(H.), Heref. dioc. rec. AL 19/16(ii), pp. 469–70.
32 G.E.C. *Baronetage*, ii. 204.
33 Glam. R.O., CL/Deeds I, Salop. 16 July 1650.
34 Downton Hall muniments.
35 *S.P.R. Heref.* xix (5), 14. Cf. below, this section.
36 *Hist. Parl., Commons*, 1715–54, i. 572; S.R.O. 1037/27/36; 2589/R/1.
37 Act for Vesting Ests. of Eliz. Pearce and Wm. Hall, 1772, 12 Geo. III, c. 95 (Priv. Act); S.R.O. 757, box 35, deeds of 1809, 1813; box 9, deeds of 1825; box 10, deeds of 1834, 1839, 1867. For explanation of the descent 1813–34 see *Salopian and W. Midland Monthly Illustr. Jnl.* July 1876, 75.
38 Below, this section; *Shrews. Chron.* 19 Sept. 1919, p. [3].
39 S.R.O. 1037/19/1.
40 *Salopian and W. Midland Monthly Illustr. Jnl.* July 1876, 75.
41 W.S.L. 350/3/40, Stoke St. Milborough p. 1.
42 Descr. based on inf. from Mrs. M. Moran.
43 Para. based on S.R.O. 1671/5, abstr. of title of E. H. Owen 1866.
44 S.R.O. 757, box 12, deed.
45 S.R.O. 4366/Pa/1; P.R.O., IR 29/29/84; IR 30/29/84, field 292.
46 S.R.O. 757, box 12, decl. of J. S. Bright.
47 P.R.O., IR 30/29/84 (not shown); S. Bagshaw, *Dir. Salop.* (1851), 551; S.R.O. 757, box 12, deed of 1867.
48 S.R.O. 757, box 12, decl. of J. S. Bright.
49 Ibid. deed.
50 S.R.O. 933, box 16, case [of 1823], m. 6.
51 Birm. Univ. Libr., Mytton Papers, v. 1223.
52 *S.P.R. Heref.* iv (2), 239.
53 Ibid. xix (5), 14; M.I. of Eliz. Lucy in ch.
54 Above, this section; S.R.O. 1037/27/36; 12 Geo. III, c. 95 (Priv. Act).
55 S.R.O. 757, box 35, deed of 1809.
56 Ibid. box 20, decl. of T. J. Griffiths; *Dict. Welsh Biog.* 189.
57 S.R.O. 757, box 20, Cath. Edwards's will, sched. of deeds, deed of 1867.
58 Geo. Lee said to have lived there: W.S.L. 350/3/40, Stoke St. Milborough p. 3.
59 Descr. based on inf. from Mrs. Moran; H.W.R.O.(H.), Heref. dioc. rec., inv. of Eliz. Lucy, 1667.
60 *S.P.R. Heref.* xix (5), p. x.
61 Ibid. 13; S.R.O. 933, box 16, case [of 1823], m. 12.
62 S.R.O. 757, box 17, deed; *S.P.R. Heref.* xix (5), 3, 58.

widow Margaret and son William succeeded; on William's death in 1760[63] his interest passed to his brother John. In 1763 Margaret and John sold the estate to John's brother Benjamin (d. by 1793). John Lucas sold it in 1793 to William Walcot of Bitterley (d. 1807), who was succeeded by his son William (d. 1860), from whose coheirs Lord Boyne bought it (349 a.) in 1871.[64] The house, a stuccoed villa, was probably built by William Walcot *c.* 1793.[65]

In 1581 Sir John Smith sold an estate at Clee Downton to Thomas Wall,[66] which remained with Wall's descendants until 1869. It was called 'the farm in Clee Downton' by 1766,[67] Downton House by 1815, and *EAST FARM* by 1919.[68] To it were added Kitchen's (or Clee Downton, later West) farm, part in 1772 and the rest in 1800,[69] and the Gibberage farm in 1812. The whole estate, including the Knapp farm (80 a.) in Wheathill, descended to Martha Wall, who sold it (454 a.) to Lord Boyne in 1869.[70] East Farm is a two storeyed stone range of two units with axial stack, and was probably built in the 16th or 17th century. Projecting wings were added later to front and rear, so making a cruciform plan.[71]

John Smith sold *BOCKLETON* to John Jenkes in 1576. In 1608 Jenkes settled it on his son-in-law Charles Foxe of Greete, who sold it in 1633 to Samuel Martyn, John Clarke, and Bryan Wotton, all of the Charterhouse, London. In 1647 Clarke, the foundation's former receiver, conveyed Bockleton to the governors.[72] The Charterhouse sold it *c.* 1800 to Samuel Sneade, rector of Bedstone, who sold it in 1806 to Robert Tench. Tench sold it in 1811 to William Smith of Maerdynewydd (in Llancarfan, Glam.).[73] Smith died in 1819 leaving the estate to Mary, daughter of his servants John and Anna Smith, who married John Patrick and died in 1857. The Patricks' son W. S. Patrick sold the estate and reputed manor (439 a.) to Lord Boyne in 1874.[74] Bockleton Court seems to have been built *c.* 1500 as a two storeyed timber framed farmhouse, jettied on three sides. In the earlier 17th century it was extended, heightened, and reroofed, and the front cased in stone. At the same time two three storeyed gabled projections were added at the front, one of them incorporating a porch.[75]

In 1579 Sir John Smith sold *NEWTON* to Edward Hopton of Bitterley.[76] Hopton's son Thomas sold it *c.* 1605 to George Bishop, a London stationer. In 1607 Bishop leased it to the Stationers' Company for 500 years after the deaths of himself and his wife, at a peppercorn rent, the company to pay annual sums out of the profits to Christ's Hospital, to preachers at Paul's Cross, and in loans to young freemen of the company. When he died *c.* 1610 his widow conveyed her life interest to the company.[77] Benjamin Robinson, who may have bought the estate in 1774,[78] sold it *c.* 1789.[79] George Creighton acquired Newton and left it to his nephew George Creighton, who left it to his son John. John Creighton's trustees sold it in 1846 to Benjamin Pitt of Ludlow (d. 1853), who left it to his son Thomas. Thomas Pitt sold Newton farm (133 a.) to Lord Boyne in 1875.[80] The house includes a two storeyed stone range of two units with end stacks and an integral byre at the south end. The house's upper floor gave access to the byre's so that cattle could be fed from above. The byre also had a central through passage for feeding. The house was later extended north by another bay and east to add a kitchen.[81]

In 1796 *THE SCIRMIDGE*, consisting of a house and garden, was conveyed by Thomas Burton to his daughter and son-in-law Rachel and Thomas Powell. The Powells sold it in 1812 to Thomas Wheelwright, whose mortgagee sold it in 1866 to Thomas Millichap. Lord Boyne bought it from him in 1868.[82]

Lord Boyne (d. 1907)[83] thus owned almost the whole parish outside Clee Stanton. He left the estate to his son, F. G. Hamilton-Russell,[84] who sold it in separate lots in 1919.[85]

CLEE STANTON, probably another part of the lands said to have been given to St. Mildburg around the Clee hills,[86] belonged to the church of Wenlock in 1066 and to Wenlock priory in 1086.[87] It was subinfeudated by *c.* 1200 when Ives de Clinton (fl. 1194)[88] was lord. Clinton's son Hugh succeeded by 1203.[89] Philip de Clinton (fl. 1274) had the manor by 1255,[90] Ives de Clinton (fl. 1301) by 1291,[91] and John de Clinton (fl. 1341) by 1316.[92] He or his son of that name had it in 1348,[93] but by 1352 it belonged to John Bryce (d. 1377).[94] John Rowsley (fl. 1435) was lord by 1431, and had a son John.[95] Henry

63 *S.P.R. Heref.* xix (5), 70.
64 S.R.O. 757, box 19, deeds of 1760, 1763; box 20, deeds of 1793, 1871, bill of complaint 1871.
65 S.P.L., MS. 6862, f. 119v.
66 S.R.O. 933, box 16, case [of 1823], m. 7.
67 S.R.O. 757, box 15, deed of 1832; 1141, box 49, deed of 1869.
68 S.R.O. 4366/Pa/1, field P 1; S.R.O. 4190/2, lot 59.
69 S.R.O. 757, box 14, deed of 1772; box 15, deed of 1800; P.R.O., IR 29/29/84, field 261; S.R.O. 4190/2, lot 61.
70 S.R.O. 1141, box 49, deed of 1869.
71 Descr. based on inf. from Mrs. Moran.
72 London Metropolitan Archives, Acc. 1876/D 6/326, 329–30, 332–3; Sutton's Hosp., Charterhouse, assembly order bk. B, ff. 76v.–77.
73 Sutton's Hosp., Charterhouse, assembly order bk. I, p. 96; S.R.O. 757, box 27, deed of 1811; *Dioc. of Heref. Institutions (1539–1900)*, ed. A. T. Bannister (Heref. 1923), 105, 135.
74 S.R.O. 757, box 27, Wm. Smith's will, marr., bur., and bapt. certifs., deed of 1874.
75 Descr. based on inf. from Mrs. Moran.
76 S.R.O. 933, box 16, case [of 1823], mm. 5–6.
77 P.R.O., C 2/Jas. I/S 39/4; Barnard MSS., Raby Castle, bdle. 3, no. 3.
78 S.P.L., MS. 6862, f. 122.
79 S.R.O. 515/1, p. 35.
80 S.R.O. 757, box 25, Geo. Creighton's will, deeds of 1819, 1837, 1846, 1875.
81 Descr. based on inf. from Mrs. Moran.
82 S.R.O. 757, box 29, deeds.
83 *Complete Peerage*, ii. 269.
84 S.R.O. 5236/A/49, abstr. of title.
85 S.R.O. 4190/2; *Shrews. Chron.* 19 and 26 Sept. 1919.
86 Finberg, *Early Charters of W. Midlands*, pp. 148, 203.
87 *V.C.H. Salop.* i. 313.
88 *Rot. Cur. Reg.* (Rec. Com.), i. 136.
89 S.R.O. 1224, box 342, Prior Gosnell's reg. f. 5v.
90 *Rot. Hund.* ii. 85; *Cal. Inq. p.m.* ii, p. 59.
91 *Cal. Chart. R.* 1257–1300, 406; *Cartulary of Shrews. Abbey*, ed. U. Rees (1975), ii, p. 246.
92 *Feud. Aids*, iv. 228; P.R.O., CP 25/1/194/13, no. 1.
93 S.P.L., Deeds 5441.
94 Ibid. 5237; *T.S.A.S.* lviii. 74.
95 *Feud. Aids*, iv. 269; S.P.L., Deeds 5238.

Rowsley (fl. 1492) was lord by 1489[96] and John Rowsley *c.* 1497.[97] That John or a namesake, lord in 1541, died in 1561 and was succeeded by his daughter Maud, who afterwards married William Knyfton.[98] Maud and William sold the manor in 1591 to Thomas Littleton of Stoke Court and Edward Sheppard of Tugford (fl. 1608) as tenants in common.[99]

Sheppard's son Edward, of Abcott, conveyed his moiety in 1614 to John Sheppard of Hilluppencott (d. 1631), who was succeeded by his grandson John Sheppard. That John sold his moiety in 1650 to John Sheppard of Crowleasows,[1] his cousin.[2] Littleton's grandson Sir Thomas Littleton (or Poyntz)[3] sold his moiety in 1653 to Henry Bernard, who bought John Sheppard's share in 1662.[4]

Bernard (kt. 1677) died in 1680.[5] The manor passed to his daughter Elizabeth and her husband James Brydges, Lord Chandos (d. 1714), and in 1715 she sold it to their daughter's brother-in-law Humphrey Walcot (d. 1743) of Bitterley.[6] Walcot's widow Anna (d. 1755) succeeded,[7] followed by their son the Revd. Humphrey Walcot. In 1768 Walcot's trustees[8] sold it to William Pearce Hall.[9] Hall's heir was his daughter Catherine (d. 1808), wife of C. W. Boughton-Rouse (later Rouse-Boughton, cr. bt. 1791, succ. as 9th bt. 1794, d. 1821), lord by 1793.[10] The manor is presumed to have descended with the baronetcies:[11] Mary F. Rouse-Boughton (d. 1991),[12] only child of the last baronet (d. 1963),[13] claimed to be lady of the manor in 1970.[14] The manorial estate, two small farms (90 a.) in 1815, had three farms (138 a.) by 1842, and four (608 a.) by 1911.[15] Langley farm was sold in 1919 and the rest in separate lots in 1920.[16]

In 1589 William Knyfton sold the chief house and demesne lands, then called *WALKER'S FARM* or the farm of Clee Stanton, to Richard Walker. House and land descended in the Walker family until 1830 when Robert Head bought them. In 1839 Head settled them on George Bradley (d. 1868) and his wife Sarah (d. 1864). The Bradleys' representatives sold the estate to the lord of the manor in 1869.[17] The house, later called Manor Farm, was probably on or near the site of the medieval chief house: Gatehouse meadow[18] adjoined it on the west. Manor Farm is a mid 18th-century red brick farmhouse with a symmetrical three bayed main block and a lower, narrower service wing. It stands on a plinth of re-used rubble which includes ashlar blocks. The joinery, of oak, includes panelled doors and a staircase.

The appropriated *RECTORY* seems to have descended with Stoke St. Milborough manor until 1650[19] when Sir Humphrey Briggs sold the rectorial tithes to Edward Baldwin.[20] During the 1650s Baldwin sold portions of them to the freeholders[21] and by *c.* 1764 there were 18 impropriators.[22] In 1842 those rectorial tithes that had not passed to the vicar were merged in the freeholds, except those of Sir John Edwards, which were commuted to £30 2*s.*[23]

ECONOMIC HISTORY. By 1086 the land immediately surrounding Stoke St. Milborough and some of the other settlements was evidently arable; Stoke manor had 11 ploughteams and Clee Stanton one.[24] The outer and higher parts of the parish, which had presumably been covered with ancient woodland,[25] may have been partly cleared and settled; the presence of bordars on Stoke manor suggests that possibility.[26] Nevertheless 19 more teams could have been employed in Stoke manor and 6 in Stanton.

By the early 13th century increased grazing, inclosure, and reclamation of woods and wastes brought neighbouring lords into conflict. In 1231 the prior of Wenlock disputed the boundary between Stoke and Wheathill manors with Walter Haket,[27] and in 1232 the prior, in return for accepting Walter of Clifford's right to enforce the conservation laws of Clee chase within Stoke manor, was allowed to inclose any part of the manor's woods as ox pasture and, for himself and the manorial tenants, to graze freely over the uninclosed parts of Brown Clee.[28] The names Newton (recorded in 1255) and the Moor (1292)[29] suggest reclaimed areas, presumably during the period of comparatively unregulated clearance that seems to have preceded the agreement of 1232. The field name Stocking, found in Downton, Kinson, and Stanton townships, indicates woodland clearance there too.[30]

96 *Cal. Fine R.* 1485–1509, pp. 101, 158.
97 S.R.O. 3365/165.
98 Dukes, *Antiquities of Salop.* 91; P.R.O., C 142/183, no. 52.
99 S.P.L., Deeds 3299, 3346.
1 Ibid. 3299, 3301, 3305–6.
2 P.R.O., C 142/475, no. 128.
3 G.E.C. *Baronetage*, ii. 204.
4 P.R.O., CP 25/2/590/1653 East. no. 14; CP 25/2/712/14 Chas. II East. no. 9.
5 Shaw, *Kts. of Eng.* ii. 252; S.P.L., MS. 4360, p. 31.
6 S.P.L., Deeds 6234.
7 S.R.O., q. sess. rec. box 260, reg. of gamekeepers 1742–79, 17 Dec. 1747.
8 S.R.O. 807/78–9. For relationships and dates of death 1680–1755 see *Complete Peerage*, iii. 128–9; Burke, *Ext. Peerage* (1846), 91; Burke, *Land. Gent.* (1937), 2341; *S.P.R. Heref.* iv (2), 341.
9 Downton Hall muniments.
10 S.P.L., MS. 6862, f. 119v.
11 For which see Burke, *Peerage* (1959), 264.
12 *Shropshire Star*, 30 Dec. 1991, p. 5.
13 *Who Was Who, 1961–70*, 118.
14 S.C.C. Ch. Exec.'s Dept., file CL(A) 933, Benson & Rogers-Coltman to clk. 17 July 1970.
15 P.R.O., IR 29/29/84; S.R.O. 4011/39, nos. 255–7, 263, 265–6, 324; 4366/Pa/1.
16 *Shrews. Chron.* 22 Aug. 1919, p. [5]; H.W.R.O.(H.), T 74/825.
17 Downton Hall muniments.
18 So called in 1815: S.R.O. 4366/Pa/1, field G 13. Located from P.R.O., IR 29/29/84; IR 30/29/84, field 71.
19 *Cal. Pat.* 1572–5, p. 546; P.R.O., C 142/253, no. 68; CP 43/262, rot. 30.
20 P.R.O., CP 25/2/590/1650 East. no. 31.
21 S.R.O. 933, box 16, case [of 1823], mm. 12–14, 17.
22 Heref. D. & C. mun. 5299.
23 P.R.O., IR 29/29/84; IR 29/29/154; below, church.
24 Para. based on *V.C.H. Salop.* i. 312–13.
25 *T.S.A.S.* 2nd ser. viii. 196; 4th ser. i. 391–3; field names in P.R.O., IR 29/29/84; IR 30/29/84.
26 *V.C.H. Salop.* iv. 43–4.
27 *Cur. Reg. R.* xiv. 248; *Bracton's Note Bk.* ed. Maitland, ii, p. 455.
28 *T.S.A.S.* 4th ser. i. 391–3.
29 *Rot. Hund.* ii. 85; *Cal. Chart. R.* 1257–1300, 406.
30 P.R.O., IR 29/29/84; IR 30/29/84, fields 42, 301; S.R.O. 757, box 31, deed of 1768; J. Field, *Eng. Field-Names: A Dictionary* (1989), 220.

Wool and woollen cloth seem to have been important products of the parish in the 14th century. Walter the fuller was mentioned in 1322, and a weaver in 1334;[31] in 1345 cloths made in Stoke manor had to be taken to the prior's fulling mill.[32] In 1377 the lord of Stanton had 300 sheep and lambs, though he also had 15 oxen and two ploughs and grew wheat and oats.[33] In Stoke manor the prior's demesnes included 6 carucates of arable in 1291, valued at a mark each, and the manor was worth £21 14*s*. 8*d*. a year gross.[34] In 1340 it was alleged that the parish's crops had been devastated by storms, that flocks had dwindled, and that 11 tenants had abandoned their holdings, which lay fallow.[35] In 1369 the manor was worth only £9 4*s*. 6*d*. and the demesne arable had been reduced to 3 carucates, worth only 10*s*. each;[36] they were worth 3*s*. each ten years later.[37] There was evidently a recovery during the 15th century, for by 1535 the manor's gross rental was £22 10*s*. 8*d*.[38] By that time the prior's demesnes, which had only 2 virgates of arable, were leased to a farmer.[39]

The open fields of Stoke village, of which there were three in 1321,[40] were Rotbach (east, near 'Brodward' brook), Highway (north-west), and South fields in 1607, with stinted common grazing at the Over Knoll (on Weston hill), on Stoke Gorse, and on Brown Clee.[41] Stanton's open fields included North (or Cross) and South fields in 1620,[42] with common grazing on Titterstone Clee.[43] The parish's other hamlets presumably had open fields too, and grazing on Brown Clee; Downton also had grazing on Cockshut common.[44]

In the early 16th century farmers in Bockleton, Downton, Kinson, the Moor, Newton, and Stanton were converting arable to inclosed pasture,[45] and in 1581 the lord of Stoke reserved the right to let parts of the commons in severalty for pasture;[46] the Knoll waste had been inclosed and divided by 1654.[47] All the land of Bockleton and Newton hamlets may have been inclosed early (by 1655 at Bockleton);[48] they had one tenant each in the early 16th century.[49] Other hamlets, where agreement between tenants was necessary, may not have been fully inclosed before the late 18th century, by gradual exchange and consolidation of open-field lands;[50] only part of Stoke's South field was open in 1654.[51]

Inclosure was accompanied, from the 16th century if not earlier, by the formation of many outlying farms, probably on inclosed wastes at first, then on land severed from the open fields. Those established before 1700 included High Leys at Stoke;[52] Red Hall and Bold Venture at Kinson;[53] the Gibberage at Downton;[54] and Henley Hill at the Moor.[55] The process was continuing *c*. 1750 when a house was first built on land at Ripletts in Stanton township.[56]

In the later 17th and earlier 18th century the farms were much concerned with livestock; each usually had a herd of cattle and a less valuable flock of sheep. Some small farmers kept mainly sheep. Each farm usually had a significant cereal acreage too.[57] Stoke Court had an attached malthouse, perhaps built in the 17th century,[58] and *c*. 1720 another was built at Lower House, Stanton, where hops were grown.[59] In May 1708 Bockleton Court, an exceptionally large and compact farm (*c*. 250 a.),[60] had 45 cattle (excluding oxen) and *c*. 400 sheep, produced cheese in commercial quantities, and had a malt mill.[61]

Large areas of common grazing remained, especially on the Clees; in 1777 Bockleton Court was summering more than 300 sheep on Brown Clee.[62] Animals were evidently wintered on the farms. In 1813 Stoke Gorse, Cockshut common, and Stoke common (part of Brown Clee) were inclosed,[63] but Titterstone Clee (2,208 a.) remained common. Though inclosed in 1813, 80 a. of the former Stoke common on Brown Clee were registered as a common in 1968.[64]

Little barley was grown by the 1790s, when a frequently used rotation was fallow, wheat, oats (two years), long ley, and oats (two years); there was some use of peas and turnips by 1801.[65] Since the parish was not controlled by any large estate before the late 19th century, improvements were not concerted. At Bockleton Court a meadow was 'part watered' by 1777; in 1805 the wet parts of the farm were being drained and much of its permanent grass could be 'floated' through recently dug channels; and the farm's field boundaries were regularized between the 1770s and 1840s.[66] Pel Beggar farm was claimed in 1819 to be 'lately much improved'.[67] On the

31 S.R.O. 566/1, ct. r.; 1037/19/1.
32 S.R.O. 1224/2/1, ct. r.
33 *T.S.A.S.* lviii. 74.
34 *Tax. Eccl.* (Rec. Com.), 164.
35 *Inq. Non.* 188 (figs. include the Heath and Norncott).
36 B.L. Add. MS. 6165, p. 99.
37 Ibid. 6164, p. 384.
38 *Valor Eccl.* iii. 215.
39 Dukes, *Antiquities of Salop*. 88.
40 S.R.O. 1037/19/1.
41 H.W.R.O.(H.), HD 2/10/33; *T.S.A.S.* 2nd ser. viii. 198. Rotbach and Highway fields located from P.R.O., IR 29/29/84; IR 30/29/84, fields 386, 494.
42 S.R.O. 1146/16.
43 S.R.O. 757, box 21, deed of 1740.
44 S.R.O., incl. award B 21, John Wheelwright's claim 11 Aug. 1809.
45 B.L. Lansd. MS. 1, f. 190 and v.; P.R.O., C 104/26, comrs.' return of 1517.
46 B.L. Add. MS. 31932, f. 223.
47 S.R.O. 757, box 28, deed.
48 London Metropolitan Archives, Acc. 1876/M.P. 6/38.
49 S.R.O. 1224, box 342, Prior Gosnell's reg. f. 40v.
50 e.g. S.R.O. 1146/16 (deed of 1620).
51 S.R.O. 757, box 28, deed.
52 Downton Hall muniments, lease of 1691.
53 S.R.O. 757, box 26, deed of 1681; 1671/5, sched. of deeds.
54 S.R.O. 1141, box 51, deed of 1650; abstr. of title.
55 S.R.O. 757, box 17, deed.
56 Ibid. box 21, deeds of 1740, 1753.
57 Para. based on H.W.R.O.(H.), Heref. dioc. rec., prob. invs. Transcripts were lent by Dr. B. S. Trinder.
58 SA 11381.
59 S.R.O. 757, box 19, deed of 1729/30.
60 London Metropolitan Archives, Acc. 1876/M.P. 6/38; /D 6/342.
61 H.W.R.O.(H.), Heref. dioc. rec., inv. of Geo. Wood, 1708.
62 London Metropolitan Archives, Acc. 1876/D 6/342.
63 Abdon and Stoke St. Milborough Incl. Act, 1809, 49 Geo. III, c. 109 (Local and Personal); S.R.O., incl. award B 33.
64 S.C.C. Ch. Exec.'s Dept., commons reg., reg. unit nos. CL 12 (partly in other pars.), CL 72.
65 S.P.L., MS. 6862, f. 120v.; P.R.O., HO 67/12, no. 216.
66 London Metropolitan Archives, Acc. 1876/D 6/342; S.R.O. 515/6, p. 17; 4366/Pa/1; P.R.O., IR 29/29/84; IR 30/29/84.
67 *Shrews. Chron.* 9 July 1819, p. [1].

Table XXIV

Stoke St. Milborough: Land use, livestock, and crops

		1867	*1891*	*1938*[a]	*1965*[a]
Percentage of	grassland	74	86	96	87
	arable	26	14	4	13
Percentage of	cattle	19	23	19	15
	sheep	75	72	77	81
	pigs	6	5	4	4
Percentage of	wheat	46	30	28	29
	barley	28	24	7	56
	oats	26	45	64	13
	mixed corn & rye	0	1	1	2
Percentage of agricultural land growing roots and vegetables		6	3	1	3

[a] Excluding the Heath and Norncott.

Sources: P.R.O., MAF 68/143, no. 21; /1340, nos. 7–8; /3880, Salop. no. 117; /4945, no. 117.

Stoke Lodge estate (633 a.), formed in the earlier 19th century, only Bold Venture farm could boast any modern buildings in 1866.[68] There was no marked tendency in the 19th century for farms to be permanently enlarged, or for their field boundaries to be rationalized.[69] John Patrick of Bockleton Court, however, held a group of farms (800 a.) in 1851, within which labourers occupied the former farmhouses at Newton, Red Hall, and Bold Venture.[70] The number of lesser smallholdings (6–20 a.) increased in the earlier 19th century; in the later 19th century greater smallholdings (21–40 a.) increased in number, while cottage holdings (1–5 a.) decreased markedly.[71] A few smallholdings survived in the 1980s.[72]

In 1840 there was about half as much arable as grass.[73] During the later 19th century the proportion fell to a sixth and in the early 20th century to a twentieth, mostly growing oats. It did not increase until the Second World War, when pastures were ploughed to provide more rotation grass and fodder crops. In 1919 there were a few mixed farms; most, however, were for rearing cattle and sheep, and some were suited to dairying or feeding.[74] Dairying gradually superseded beef production, especially after the Second World War. Barley was the chief cereal crop by 1965.

There was a mill at Stoke by 1334.[75] By the 19th century its pond was fed by a leat from Bockleton brook and by water from the Stoke Court moat.[76] The mill was re-equipped in 1871[77] and served a large area in 1919.[78] It was working in 1929 but had closed by 1953.[79] A mill at the Moor was mentioned in 1321.[80]

The site of the prior's fulling mill mentioned in 1345[81] is unknown, but fulling mills were listed among the appurtenances of Stoke Court in 1652.[82]

In 1581 the lord of Stoke reserved to himself any mines on the waste,[83] and in 1637 he had mines of ironstone and limestone, which he was alleged to let to poor people at dear rates.[84]

The only coal and ironstone within the parish boundary were at its northern tip, on Clee Burf;[85] there were disused shafts there in 1883.[86] Close by, in Loughton township (in Chetton), there was a group of active pits in 1813,[87] and some Stoke parishioners evidently worked there; in 1793 five householders were colliers or miners. Many of the farm labourers also worked then as colliers or 'limers', or kept horses to carry lime and coal; their condition was better than that of the ordinary farm hands, some of whom needed constant poor relief.[88] Coal and ironstone mining on Brown Clee declined in the later 19th century.[89] Six coal miners lived in the parish in 1861 but none in 1871.[90]

Limestone was being quarried in Stoke manor in 1637.[91] Any commercial working is likely to have been at the parish's two concentrations of quarries and kilns around the bases of Brown Clee and Titterstone Clee;[92] there were limekilns at Bockleton before 1655[93] and field names indicate limeburning in Stanton township too.[94] Isolated kilns such as that at the Moor, still in use *c.* 1900,[95] may have been worked by farmers to supply themselves.[96] A lime maker who lived at Batch Gutter in 1841 was described in 1851

68 S.R.O. 1671/5, valn. of E. H. Owen's est.; above, manors (Stoke St. Milborough Lodge).
69 S.R.O. 4011/39; 4366/Pa/1; P.R.O., IR 29/29/84; O.S. Maps 6", Salop. LXV. SE., SW. (1903 edn.); LXXII. NE., NW., SE. (1903 edn.), SW. (1904 edn.).
70 P.R.O., HO 107/1982, ff. 491v.–492v.
71 S.R.O. 4011/39; 4366/Pa/1; P.R.O., IR 29/29/84.
72 Thom and Pearce, *Quart in Pint Pot*, 39.
73 P.R.O., IR 29/29/84. Para. based on Table XXIV and R. Dumont, *Types of Rural Economy* (1957), 384–6.
74 S.R.O. 4190/2.
75 S.R.O. 566/1, ct. r.
76 S.R.O. 757, box 10, deed of 1839 (with map); O.S. Map 1/2,500, Salop. LXXII. 6 (1884 edn.).
77 S.R.O. 3756/174, no. 75.
78 S.R.O. 4190/2, lot 7.
79 *Kelly's Dir. Salop.* (1929), 275; S.R.O. 3756/174, no. 75.
80 S.R.O. 1037/19/1.
81 S.R.O. 1224/2/1, ct. r.
82 Downton Hall muniments, deed.
83 B.L. Add. MS. 31932, f. 223.
84 *Cal. S.P. Dom.* 1637, 445.
85 Geol. Surv. Map 1", solid, sheet 166 (1974 edn.).
86 O.S. Map 1/2,500, Salop. LXV. 15 (1884 edn.).
87 S.R.O., incl. award B 33.
88 S.P.L., MS. 6862, ff. 119v., 121.
89 G. L. A. Price, 'Coal mining in the Clee Hills', *Birm. Enterprise Club Trans.* ii. 15 (copy in S.P.L.).
90 P.R.O., RG 9/1838, ff. 52v., 61v., 63v.–64v; RG 10/2727, ff. 53–58v., 62–66v.
91 *Cal. S.P. Dom.* 1637, 445.
92 O.S. Maps 1/2,500, Salop. LXXII. 2, 3, 6, 11, 14 (1884 edn.); D. C. Greig and others, *Geol. of Country around Ch. Stretton, Craven Arms, Wenlock Edge and Brown Clee* (Mem. Geol. Surv. 1968), 226, 244.
93 London Metropolitan Archives, Acc. 1876/M.P. 6/38.
94 S.R.O. 4366/Pa/1, fields B 27, D 22.
95 Greig, *Geol. around Ch. Stretton*, 227; Thom and Pearce, *Quart in Pint Pot*, 33.
96 S.P.L., MS. 6862, f. 120v.

as a retired labourer,[97] and Richard Childs of Green Tump was a collier, smallholder, and limeburner in the 1840s.[98] They were among the last to burn lime for a living.

Several stone masons lived in the parish near Brown Clee during the 19th century,[99] and a few of the many small sandstone quarries remained in use until *c.* 1900.[1] On Clee Burf a small roadstone quarry opened in the early 20th century and extended into the parish, but it closed *c.* 1939.[2]

LOCAL GOVERNMENT. Records of Stoke manor court survive for 1334, 1345, 1379–80, 1403–4, 1411–12, 1420, 1431, and 1449,[3] and an estreat for 1565.[4] In the 14th and early 15th century courts were held thrice yearly. The business was usually that of a court baron, but breaches of the assize of ale were also heard. Two reeves, two aletasters, and a hayward were elected. In the mid 15th century courts may have been less frequent, and in 1581 the lord reserved the right to hold his court once a year in the hall of Stoke Court.[5] In 1811 the court baron was amercing unlicensed cottagers.[6] A court baron for Stanton was mentioned in 1678.[7]

In the early 17th century Stoke and Stanton manors comprised three constablewicks within Bourton hundred: Stoke (including Bockleton, Kinson, and Newton), Downton (including the Moor), and Stanton. By the later 17th century Stanton, Downton, and the Moor formed a single constablewick.[8]

The inhabitants of Stoke manor were also subject, in the 16th century, to the swainmote of Clee chase.[9] One of the four chasekeepers' lodges[10] stood in 1655 at the edge of the common, near the main point of access from Stoke village,[11] but had gone by 1777.[12] It was said that in the late 17th century, after the swainmote lapsed, cottagers on the wastes of Stoke manor used to owe suit and amercements to the manor court of Earnstrey Park, and after 1709 to that of Abdon; if so, they had ceased to do so by 1744.[13] Bourton hundred amerced two of them in 1670,[14] but in the 1690s failed to establish a new claim to the suit of all cottagers on the wastes of Stoke manor.[15]

The parish was divided into three highway townships by 1724: Stoke (including Bockleton, Kinson, and Newton), Downton (including the Moor), and Stanton. Each had its own surveyor and rates.[16] Those divisions remained in the 1850s.[17] For poor-law purposes there were no divisions in the 18th and early 19th century.[18] The vestry arranged to send paupers to workhouses at Madeley (from 1774) and Church Stretton (from 1783) and planned its own workhouse in 1784.[19] From 1786, however, and still in 1793, the master of Ludlow workhouse was paid to take in paupers from the parish and give out-relief.[20] By 1812 the overseers had resumed relief.[21]

The parish was in Ludlow poor-law union 1836–1930,[22] Ludlow highway district 1863–95,[23] Ludlow rural sanitary district 1872–94, Ludlow rural district 1894–1974, and South Shropshire district from 1974.[24] From 1953 the civil parish had a joint council with Hopton Cangeford.[25]

CHURCH. There was a church at Stoke *c.* 1200, and it seems to have incorporated vestiges of an earlier one.[26] In 1291 the rector owed an annual portion to Wenlock priory.[27] In 1344 the rectory was appropriated to the priory and a vicarage ordained.[28]

The advowson of the rectory, and of the vicarage from 1344, belonged to Wenlock priory by 1272 and descended with Stoke manor until 1575,[29] except that it was in the king's hands by 1342 and until the priory's denization in 1395,[30] and was not held by the see of Canterbury 1542–59.[31] In 1575 John Smith sold the advowson to Richard Hopton, still patron in 1588;[32] George Hopton was patron in 1621.[33] The advowson passed to Charles Foxe of Greete, who

97 P.R.O., HO 107/913/13, f. 18; HO 107/1982, f. 491.

98 P.R.O., HO 107/1982, f. 488v.; S.R.O. 4366/Rg/5, 18 Mar. 1846, 31 Jan. 1848.

99 S.R.O. 4366/Rg/5, 20 May 1821; P.R.O., HO 107/1982, ff. 487v.–488; RG 12/2083, ff. 4v., 5v., 12 and v., 13v.

1 O.S. Maps 1/2,500, Salop. LXXII. 2, 3, 5, 6, 11 (1884 and 1903 edns.); Greig, *Geol. around Ch. Stretton*, 227, 235.

2 O.S. Map 1/2,500, Salop. LXV. 15 (1903 edn.) (not shown); Thom and Pearce, *Quart in Pint Pot*, 19–20; B. E. Simmonds, *Brown Clee Liberty and Clee St. Margaret* ([Clee St. Margaret] 1992), 71–2 (copy in S.P.L.).

3 S.R.O. 566/1; 1190/1, unlisted ct. r. 1403–4; 1224/2/1–9.

4 P.R.O., SC 2/197/146.

5 B.L. Add. MS. 31932, f. 223.

6 S.R.O., incl. award B 21, J. Powell and others to Jos. Loxdale 28 Mar. 1811.

7 Downton Hall muniments, abstr. of title of Wm. Pearce Hall.

8 S.R.O. 1224/2/370, 377–9, 389–94, 398, 400, 403–7, 418–30, 432, 515–27.

9 S.R.O., incl. award B 21, memo. of Brown Clee drift, 1553; swainmote ct. r. (copies); S.R.O. 1037/21/1.

10 *T.S.A.S.* lviii. 58.

11 O.S. Nat. Grid SO 582 834: London Metropolitan Archives, Acc. 1876/M.P. 6/38.

12 Ibid. Acc. 1876/D 6/342.

13 S.R.O. 1037/21/10; above, Abdon, local govt.

14 S.R.O. 1224/2/389.

15 S.R.O. 1037/21/10.

16 *T.S.A.S.* lvi. 315–16, 322.

17 S. Bagshaw, *Dir. Salop.* (1851), 550.

18 W.B.R., Q1/13/151; S.R.O. 53/74; 5709, overseers' acct. 1737–8.

19 S.R.O. 53/74, 20 July 1774, 21 May 1783, 29 Feb. 1784.

20 Ibid. 8 June 1786, 4 Mar. 1790; S.P.L., MS. 6862, f. 121.

21 S.R.O. 53/74, overseers' accts. from 1812.

22 V. J. Walsh, 'Admin. of Poor Laws in Salop. 1820–55' (Pennsylvania Univ. Ph.D. thesis, 1970), 150 (copy in S.R.O.); *Kelly's Dir. Salop.* (1929), 275.

23 *Lond. Gaz.* 27 Mar. 1863, p. 1772; S.R.O., S.C.C. Local Govt., etc., cttee. min. bk. 1894–1903, p. 29.

24 *Rural Dist. Councillors Electn. Order, 1894* (Local Govt. Bd. order no. 31847); *V.C.H. Salop.* ii. 215; iii. 179, and sources cited ibid. 169 n. 29.

25 Inf. from the clk., Hopton Cangeford and Stoke St. Milborough par. council.

26 Archit. evidence below, this section.

27 *Tax. Eccl.* 166. There is no evidence that the par. was formed out of Holy Trin., Much Wenlock, as suggested in *Minsters and Par. Churches*, ed. J. Blair (1988), 73.

28 Below, this section.

29 *Cal. Pat.* 1266–72, 710; 1572–5, p. 197. Cf. above, manors.

30 *Cal. Pat.* 1340–3, 473; 1348–50, 400, 461, 496; 1388–92, 116, 233, 323; 1391–6, 514. Cf. *V.C.H. Salop.* ii. 42.

31 *L. & P. Hen. VIII*, xvii, p. 256.

32 S.R.O. 933, box 16, case [of 1823], m. 11; *T.S.A.S.* xlvi. 32.

33 H.W.R.O.(H.), Heref. dioc. rec. AL 19/16, f. 295.

sold it in 1631 to Adam Littleton of Stoke Court;[34] Littleton's mother-in-law Jane Docwra had presented in 1630.[35] It seems to have descended with Stoke Court[36] until 1819 when the trustees of John Wall, former patron and vicar, sold it to George Morgan (d. 1866).[37] Morgan presented himself as vicar, as did the next two patrons, George de Gruchy (d. 1893) and T. J. Smith (d. 1901), the latter through an intermediary.[38]

In 1903 Smith's widow transferred the advowson to Sir C. H. Rouse-Boughton. In 1908 Sir W. St. A. Rouse-Boughton transferred it to the vicar's father-in-law, the Revd. Daniel Vawdrey (d. 1934), whose daughter Mrs. C. M. Chandos Burton inherited it.[39] The patronage was suspended 1954–7 after which the benefice was held in plurality with that of Abdon with Clee St. Margaret and that of Cold Weston. In 1962 Mrs. Burton gave the advowson to the diocesan patronage board.[40] From the next vacancy, in 1972, the parish was served by priests or curates in charge until 1983 when the united benefice of Bitterley with Middleton, Hopton Cangeford, Stoke St. Milborough with the Heath, Clee St. Margaret, and Cold Weston was formed, with the diocesan patronage board as one of the joint patrons. The ecclesiastical parish of Stoke St. Milborough with the Heath absorbed that of Hopton Cangeford in 1985.[41]

In 1291 the rectory was valued at £13 13*s.* 4*d.* a year, of which £3 was payable annually to Wenlock priory.[42] In 1344, when the rectory was appropriated, the small tithes and oblations were assigned to the vicarage, together with the former rectory house and some land at Stoke St. Milborough and the Heath; the vicar was to pay 6*s.* 8*d.* a year to Hereford cathedral choristers.[43] The vicarage was worth £6 13*s.* 4*d.* in 1370[44] and 1535; in 1535 glebe yielded 10*s.* a year and tithes the rest.[45] By 1793 the vicar had some of the great tithes and let all his tithes for £105 a year. The glebe was let for £63; that at the Heath formed Peckledy farm.[46] In 1810 there were 77½ a.[47] The vicar's net income in 1835 was £474.[48] Between 1841 and 1846 his tithes, a payment for hay tithes called hay silver, and other moduses were commuted to £423 19*s.* 8*d.*[49] In 1887 his glebe was let for £75 a year.[50] Peckledy was sold in 1921.[51]

In 1607 the vicarage house had three bays, containing 'house', parlour, and kitchen. A combined barn and cowhouse, of three bays, stood nearby with garden, fold, and 'pool yard'.[52] The house, of sandstone rubble, was built or greatly altered, probably in 1764, for John Pearce.[53] The main staircase is of that period, and the grounds were also improved then.[54] In the early 19th century the building was heightened, remodelled, and stuccoed to create a polite villa of three bays and 2½ storeys; that was probably *c.* 1813, when the vicar resumed residence.[55] In 1827 a south wing contained the kitchens and other offices, with stables, coach house, and beast house nearby. The wing and outbuildings were demolished shortly afterwards and replaced by an east wing with nearby stables and coach house; the garden and drive were then laid out with shrubberies, fountain, and grotto.[56] Lawns led down to a large fishpond, apparently an ornamental feature of the 18th or early 19th century.[57] The incumbents stopped living there in 1972.[58]

In 1344 the rector was assisted by a resident chaplain Henry of Larden,[59] perhaps related to a previous rector Richard of Larden (fl. 1312–28).[60] Another chaplain was assisting the vicar in 1348.[61] From 1534 or earlier vicars were usually resident.[62] Notable exceptions were Roger Stedman, 1588–1630, who lived at Munslow,[63] and John Phillipps, 1772–1812, who lived at Eaton Bishop (Herefs.);[64] both employed resident curates.[65] In 1719 there was a morning and evening service every Sunday, and communion monthly from Easter to November as well as at festivals.[66] By 1793, however, no Sunday evening congregation could be 'procured', probably because the parish had many small remote settlements. Communion was then celebrated only six times

34 Downton Hall muniments, deed.
35 *T.S.A.S.* 3rd ser. v. 358; 4th ser. iii. 321–2, 324.
36 W.S.L. 350/3/40, Stoke St. Milborough p. 3; *Dioc. of Heref. Institutions (1539–1900)*, ed. A. T. Bannister (Heref. 1923), 49, 77, 91, 105, 137, 141; *T.S.A.S.* 4th ser. ii. 109; S.P.L., MS. 6862, f. 123. Cf. above, manors (Stoke Ct.).
37 S.R.O. 757, box 11, deed of 1832 (copy); *Gent. Mag.* ccxxii (N.S. iii), 253. Rest of para. based on Bannister, op cit. 137, 141, 143, 180, 208.
38 *Shrews. Chron.* 28 July 1893, p. 8; 1 Sept. 1893, p. 7; 8 Feb. 1901, p. 5; *Crockford* (1897), 1249.
39 S.R.O. 5985, vestry min. bk. 1834–1920, 15 Apr. 1901; Heref. Dioc. Regy., reg. 1902–19, pp. 50, 271; 1926–38, p. 427; Burke, *Land. Gent.* (1937), 2329, 2341.
40 Heref. Dioc. Regy., reg. 1953–68, pp. 58, 196, 416; *Crockford* (1955–6), 1653; (1957–8), 1654.
41 Heref. Dioc. Regy., reg. 1969– (in use), pp. 127, 299, 457–8, 507; *Crockford* (1977–9), 616; (1989–90), 557.
42 *Tax. Eccl.* 166.
43 B.L. Add. MS. 50121, pp. 21–2.
44 Ibid. 6164, p. 410.
45 *Valor Eccl.* iii. 201.
46 S.P.L., MS. 6862, ff. 73, 120, 123v.
47 S.R.O. 515/8, pp. 151–3.
48 *Rep. Com. Eccl. Rev.* [67], p. 451, H.C. (1835), xxii.
49 P.R.O., IR 29/29/84; IR 29/29/154.
50 *Return of Glebe Land, 1887*, H.C. 307, p. 61 (1887), lxiv.
51 Dumont, *Types of Rural Economy*, 396 n.
52 H.W.R.O.(H.), HD 2/10/33.
53 S.P.L., MS. 6862, f. 123; detached date stone 'IP 1764' preserved in gdn. wall. The work was later attributed to C. Pearce Hall's mother Eliz. Pearce, d. 1762: S.P.L., MS. 6862, f. 123; above, manors (Stoke Ct.). She was also John's mother and patron: *S.P.R. Heref.* xix (5), p. viii; Bannister, *Heref. Institutions*, 93. Pt. of ho. visible on a drawing of 1791: S.P.L., MS. 372, vol. iii, f. 30.
54 H.W.R.O.(H.), Heref. dioc. rec. AL 19/23, f. 20v.; S.R.O., q. sess. order bk. 1757–72, f. 105 and v.
55 Below, this section.
56 H.W.R.O.(H.), HD 8, box 31, faculty papers and drawings (ref. supplied by Mr. C. J. Pickford).
57 P.R.O., IR 29/29/84; IR 30/29/84, fields 489–90; O.S. Map 1/2,500, Salop. LXXII. 2 (1884 edn.).
58 S.R.O., reg. of electors, Ludlow const. (1973), 472; (1974), 474; above, this section.
59 Eyton, iv. 12; S.R.O. 1224/2/1, Stoke ct. r.
60 *Reg. Swinfield* (C.S.), 541; S.R.O. 1037/3/121, deed of 1328.
61 S.P.L., Deeds 5236.
62 *T.S.A.S.* 4th ser. x. 210; *S.P.R. Heref.* xix (5), pp. x, 19, 35–7, 41–2, 53, 65, 80; S.R.O. 4366/MRg/1; /Rg/5; S.P.L., MS. 6862, f. 73v.; *P.O. Dir. Salop.* (1856–79); *Kelly's Dir. Salop.* (1885–1941); S.R.O., reg. of electors, Ludlow const. (1951), 478; (1953), 473; (1958), 482.
63 *S.P.R. Heref.* xv (2), 74; xix (5), p. x; *T.S.A.S.* xlvi. 32, 44; ibid. 3rd ser. v. 358.
64 Bannister, *Heref. Institutions*, 105, 137; Burke, *Land. Gent.* (1952), 2024; S.P.L., MS. 6862, f. 123.
65 *S.P.R. Heref.* xix (5), pp. x, 116–20; S.P.L., MS. 6862, f. 73v.
66 H.W.R.O.(H.), HD 5/15, Stoke St. Milborough.

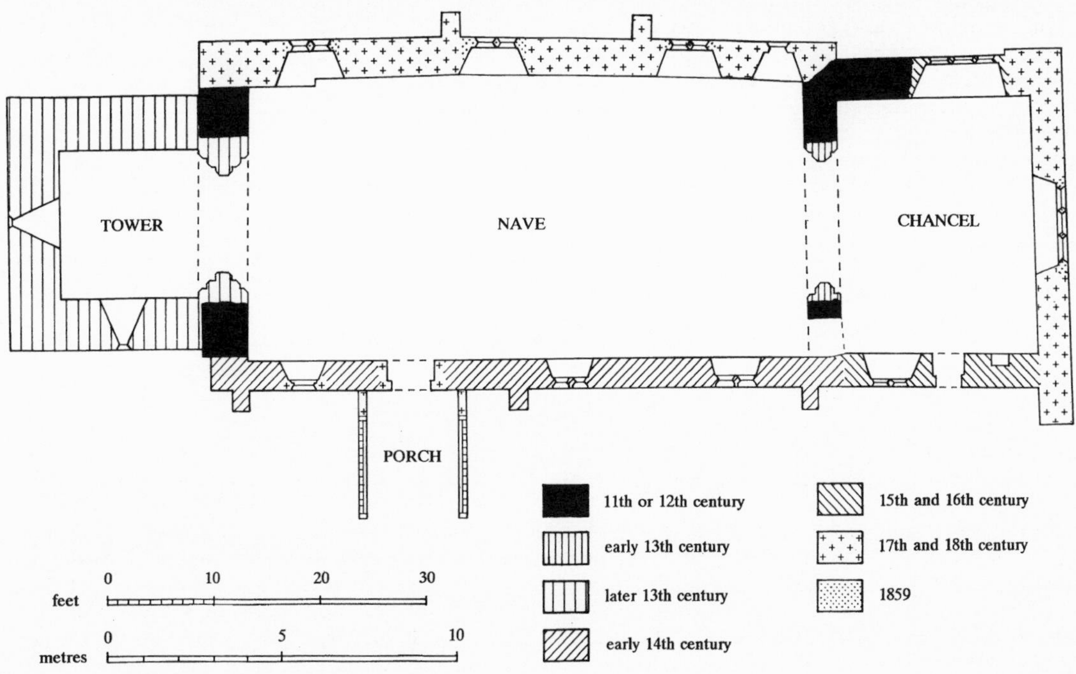

Fig. 39

Stoke St. Milborough: the Church of St. Milborough

a year, with 30 or 40 communicants at Easter. Evening prayer was limited to Lent and Wake Sunday in late June.[67] By 1851 Evening prayer was weekly but few attended.[68] Cottage services in the early 20th century reached some of the remoter inhabitants, and the church sustained a Sunday school, choir, and men's bible class.[69] In 1992 there was communion or Evensong every week and a monthly family service.[70]

The church of *ST. MILBOROUGH*, so dedicated by 1740[71] and perhaps by the 1270s,[72] is built of rubble with ashlar dressings and has a chancel, nave with south porch, and west tower.[73] The fabric shows signs of several partial rebuildings, not all of them datable or clearly defined.

The corners of an earlier and narrower nave survive in the angles between the tower and the west wall of the nave. The thick north wall of the chancel, which is aligned on the north-west corner of the earlier nave, is probably late 11th- or 12th-century. The chancel arch has early 13th-century capitals but may have been cut into an older wall. A low tower was added in the later 13th century. Its corbel table, which survives on all four sides, suggests that it may have had a pyramidal roof. The nave was probably widened in the early 14th century, the apparent date of its south windows; the south wall of the chancel is later, and has a mid 14th-century window, perhaps reset. In the 15th century the tower was heightened by one stage and a new window was put into the north wall of the chancel; indulgence was offered in 1424 to those who contributed to repair of the church fabric.[74] There was formerly a rood screen and loft, which was perhaps reached by a wooden stair in the opening south of the chancel arch. Traces of medieval painting remain over the arch.

There were extensive repairs and alterations *c.* 1700. The north wall of the nave and the top of the tower[75] were rebuilt, a new south doorway was put in, and the roof was renewed.[76] The cruck framed porch appears to be later but may be nearly contemporary. The west gallery and the south lancet that lighted the space under it may also have been of that time. In the 17th or 18th century the east wall of the chancel was rebuilt, perhaps farther west than its medieval predecessor. By the late 18th century the communion table was railed on three sides and the chancel contained wall monuments to the Botterell, Lee, Lucy, and Wall families. George II's arms, painted on canvas by James Smallwood in 1741, replaced cast iron arms apparently purporting to be those of William III.[77] Four

67 S.P.L., MS. 6862, f. 123v.; above, this article, intro.
68 P.R.O., HO 129/352, no. 46.
69 Thom and Pearce, *Quart in Pint Pot*, 27.
70 Local inf.
71 B.L. Add. MS. 30316, f. 29.
72 *P.N. Salop.* (E.P.N.S.), i. 283.
73 Fig. 39. Descr. based on P. Klein, *Guide to Stoke St. Milborough Par. Church* ([Stoke St. Milborough] 1992). Thanks are due to Mr. Klein for discussions about the fabric.
74 *Reg. Spofford* (C.S.), 49.
75 Beam dated 1698, parapets 1711.
76 Truss dated 1707.
77 Earlier arms in tower in 1992. Before the casting was made, the 'C' of the wooden pattern, which represented Chas. II's arms, was changed to 'G', probably for 'Gulielmus' (Wm. III) but conceivably for 'Georgius', the arms themselves remaining unaltered.

Commandment tables on sheet zinc were set up in the earlier 19th century.[78]

There was a general restoration in 1859 when the gallery, box pews, and Commandment tables were removed; a window, with glass by David Evans,[79] was put into the east wall of the chancel; choir stalls and a straight communion rail were made; and new windows of 14th-century character were put into the north wall of the nave. Some of that work, including the raised floor of the chancel, was removed at a further general restoration in 1911.

One bell (1622) was by William Clibury of Wellington, the other three (1637) by Thomas Clibury.[80] There was a silver paten of 1720 and an undated 18th-century silver chalice and paten.[81] The registers begin in 1654, earlier registers (since 1588) having been lost since the early 19th century.[82]

The churchyard, roughly rectangular, was extended north in 1898 and 1962.[83]

In 1719 there were two chapels, each with a monthly service.[84] That at the Heath survives;[85] the other, at Clee Stanton in Chapel yard, was later converted to a house and demolished by 1830.[86]

NONCONFORMITY. The Parrs were Baptists in the 1670s and 1680s.[87] Chapel House, Clee Stanton, so called by 1815, may have been an early meeting place.[88]

In Stoke village Wesleyan Methodists were preaching by 1834[89] and licensed a new chapel in 1842. In 1851 attendance averaged 30 in the afternoon and 15 in the evening.[90] The chapel closed in 1922[91] when one at Stanton opened. Wesleyans had begun to meet at Stanton in 1841.[92] In 1851 they had a separate room attached to a house, and on Census Sunday there were 50 worshippers in the afternoon and 20 in the evening.[93] The room closed in 1922 when a disused brick Wesleyan chapel from Leamoor Common (in Wistanstow) was re-erected near Stanton Farm.[94] It seated 60[95] but closed in 1970.[96]

Edward Bytheway's house was licensed for Primitive Methodist worship in 1822.[97] It may have been at Shortwood, near Blackford, where he had bought land in 1815 and had a house by 1842.[98] In 1823, however, a new chapel seating 75 was built next to a pair of cottages at Blackford. On Census Sunday 1851 10 people attended in the morning, 60 in the afternoon, and 30 in the evening.[99] Known as the iron chapel in 1851, it closed in 1869 when a new stone chapel was built nearby,[1] which had a fortnightly service in 1992.[2] Stoke was put on the Hopton Bank Primitive Methodist preaching plan in 1835[3] and a chapel there was licensed in 1842. In 1851 attendance averaged 40 in the afternoon and 50 in the evening.[4] Perhaps rebuilt in the 1870s,[5] it closed in 1972.[6]

EDUCATION. A schoolhouse was built in Stoke St. Milborough village *c.* 1760 by subscribers.[7] The master received a £5 rent charge given *c.* 1760 by Mrs. Elizabeth Pearce and another of £3 paid from *c.* 1754 by successive vicars.[8] By 1793 only the latter sum was paid. The curate, then master, taught poor children chosen by the vicar and churchwardens, and *c.* 20 paying pupils.[9] The £3 salary lapsed before 1819, when there were six pupils,[10] and the school had closed by 1820.[11] It was revived before 1835, when 21 fee-paying children were taught, and was a National school in 1851.[12] It was taught 'under great difficulties' by a 'village dame' and her daughter.[13]

A new school was built by subscription in 1856.[14] A stone building with gothic details, designed by James Cranston, it comprised a schoolroom and classroom; the schoolroom was enlarged *c.* 1870.[15] School pence varied between 1*d.* and 2*d.* according to writing proficiency.[16]

78 Stored at W. end in 1992.

79 *Eddowes's Jnl.* 12 Oct. 1859, p. 7 (ref. supplied by Mr. Klein).

80 H. B. Walters, *Ch. Bells of Salop.* (Oswestry, 1915), 159–60, 417.

81 D. L. Arkwright and B. W. Bourne, *Ch. Plate Archd. Ludlow* (Shrews. 1961), 57.

82 *S.P.R. Heref.* xix (5), esp. p. x; S.R.O. 4366/Rg/5; /MRg/2; 5985; regs. at ch.

83 Heref. Dioc. Regy., reg. 1883–1901, pp. 637–8; 1953–68, p. 396.

84 H.W.R.O.(H.), HD 5/15, Stoke St. Milborough.

85 Below, the Heath, chapel of ease.

86 P.R.O., IR 29/29/84; IR 30/29/84, field 76; Downton Hall muniments, deed of 1830 (Edw. Walker to Rob. Head).

87 *Compton Census*, ed. Whiteman, 255; *Worcs. Recusant*, liv. 35.

88 S.R.O. 4366/Pa/1. There was no Wesleyan mtg. at Stanton then: S.R.O. 5630/1/1. The medieval chapel was *c.* 1 km. W. of Chapel Ho.

89 S.R.O. 5166/3/1/1.

90 S.R.O. 1141, box 45, deed of 1842; P.R.O., HO 129/352, no. 50.

91 S.R.O. 3544/7/2, p. 25; /7/3, 24 July 1922.

92 S.R.O. 2612/11, June 1841.

93 P.R.O., HO 129/352, no. 51.

94 S.R.O. 3544/7/3, 2 Jan., 21 Aug. 1922.

95 *Methodist Church Bldgs.: Statistical Returns 1940* (Manchester *c.* 1947), 271.

96 S.R.O. 5166/1/2/1/2, pp. 228–9.

97 P.R.O., HO 129/352, no. 48; Heref. Dioc. Regy., reg. 1822–42, p. 11.

98 S.R.O. 5236/A/49, deed; P.R.O., IR 29/29/84; IR 30/29/84, field 736.

99 Thom and Pearce, *Quart in Pint Pot*, 37; P.R.O., HO 129/352, no. 48; IR 29/29/84; IR 30/29/84, field 722; S.R.O. 5236/A/49, Succession Duty acct. of 1856.

1 P.R.O. HO 107/1982, f. 489; Thom and Pearce, op. cit. 37–8.

2 *West of the Clee*, x (11), 2 (copy in S.P.L., class QK 97 v.f.).

3 S.R.O. 2941/2/2, 21 Dec. 1835.

4 P.R.O., HO 129/352, no. 49.

5 O.N.S. (Birkdale), Worship Reg. no. 9913 (de-registration of Prim. Meth. chap. at Stoke 1880 on revision of official list).

6 S.R.O. 3212/8/1, p. 171.

7 S.R.O. 53/74, vestry mins. 1759–60. At O.S. Nat. Grid SO 568 822: P.R.O., IR 29/29/84; IR 30/29/84, field 397.

8 S.R.O. 53/74, vestry min. 19 Jan. 1760; *3rd Rep. Com. Char.* H.C. 5, pp. 307–8 (1820), iv.

9 S.P.L., MS. 6862, f. 121v.

10 *Digest Educ. Poor*, H.C. 224, p. 762 (1819), ix (2).

11 *3rd Rep. Com. Char.* 307.

12 *Educ. Enq. Abstract*, ii, H.C. 62, p. 784 (1835), xlii; S. Bagshaw, *Dir. Salop.* (1851), 551.

13 *Mins. of Educ. Cttee. of Council* [1624], p. 511, H.C. (1852–3), lxxx (1).

14 *Salopian and W. Midland Monthly Illustr. Jnl.* July 1876, 75; P.R.O., ED 7/103, ff. 83–4.

15 S.R.O. 1564/351, 352–4 (watermarked 1870).

16 P.R.O., ED 7/103, ff. 83–4.

Some pupils travelled from outlying hills.[17] Children from the upper part of Blackford went to school at Loughton,[18] and others, from Clee Stanton, went to Bitterley.[19]

In the later 1930s the master and his wife produced school meals.[20] Attendance averaged *c.* 67 in 1885 and *c.* 77 in 1909.[21] The roll fell to *c.* 47 in 1916, and to *c.* 42 in 1939.[22] In 1941 the school admitted 15 evacuees from Liverpool.[23] Senior pupils received no practical instruction, except gardening *c.* 1914–45.[24] In 1950, when the roll was 26, children aged 14, and in 1952 those aged 12, transferred to Burwarton C.E. school.[25] The building was much improved after the school became Aided in 1955.[26] In 1958 pupils aged 11 transferred to Ludlow C.E. Modern school.[27] In 1968 the roll was 18[28] and the school closed in 1969.[29]

A small private school is said to have been kept at Blackford in the earlier 19th century.[30]

Evening classes in mathematics, drawing, and horticulture were held in 1893–4 and free but ill attended continuation evening classes 1893–9.[31]

CHARITY FOR THE POOR. In 1846 George Morgan, vicar, gave £400 to endow monthly bread doles.[32] The income, estimated at £10–£25 in 1965,[33] was still designated for bread in 1975.[34]

THE HEATH

THE HEATH (641 a., 259 ha.) and Norncott (209 a., 85 ha.) formed a northern detachment of Stoke St. Milborough parish in 1831 and from 1884 constituted the Heath civil parish, the area treated in this article.[35] The area, formerly divided between the townships of the Heath and Norncott and *c.* 12 km. north-east of Ludlow, has always been agricultural. It has only one through road for wheeled traffic and there are few visitors except those coming to see the Norman chapel.[36]

The civil parish lies on the Clee plateau and is bounded on the west by the plateau's edge, on the north by Norncott (or Tugford) brook, and on the south by Clee (or Pye) brook. The northern part, a dome rising to 268 m., is bounded on the south-east by a straight line, probably drawn in the Middle Ages across land formerly intercommoned by Norncott and Clee St. Margaret. The other part falls to the south. It is defined on the east by a stream that flows down Lea Batch, so called by 1529,[37] and it is cut by the valleys of two other tributaries of Clee brook, one of which was by 1652 called Weston's brook.[38]

The parish lies on the Ditton Series of the Lower Old Red Sandstone, except for a small outcrop of the underlying '*Psammosteus*' Limestones on the west boundary.[39] The soils are mostly freely drained loams, but are less well drained in the higher northern part.[40]

By the mid 12th century, when the chapel was built,[41] there was a settlement at the south-west edge of the heath from which by 1236 it had been named.[42] Earthworks show it to have been closely grouped between the heads of two valleys.[43] In 1301 the hamlet consisted of the chief house, the chapel, and four farmhouses; cottages, if any, were not recorded.[44] One of the farmsteads was abandoned in or before the 16th century,[45] probably that which stood immediately east of the chapel.[46] Of the other four house sites, three were abandoned in the 18th or early 19th century (two of them *c.* 1810) following farm amalgamations; only Heath House was left. In the same period, however, new farmsteads were established at a distance from the old centre, at Upper Heath, New House, and Peckledy.[47]

By 1771 there was a group of cottages by the lane east of the Heath hamlet, near the boundary with Clee St. Margaret parish;[48] there were three in 1833, called Lane Houses (or Cottages).[49] One of them became Heath Cottage (later Farm), and in 1846 the other two belonged to it;[50] both of them remained in 1913 but only one in 1982.[51] Weir (or Perry Green) Cottage stood by 1841 isolated on part of the glebe near the west boundary.[52] It was abandoned in the late 19th century.[53] A pair of cottages was built in Sally Coppice Lane, south of the Heath hamlet, in the

17 S.R.O. 2251/1, p. 85.
18 Thom and Pearce, *Quart in Pint Pot*, 23.
19 S.R.O., DA 22/100/7, p. 343.
20 *Shropshire Mag.* Dec. 1979, 29, 49.
21 *Kelly's Dir. Salop.* (1885), 964; (1909), 260.
22 S.R.O. 2251/1, pp. 26, 148.
23 Ibid. p. 154.
24 Ibid. pp. 10, 174, 209.
25 Ibid. pp. 206, 219.
26 Ibid. p. 242.
27 Ibid. pp. 247, 251.
28 S.C.C. Educ. Cttee. *Sch. List* (1968), 8.
29 R. J. Phillips, *Church and State: Heref. Diocesan Schs.* [1987], 97.
30 Thom and Pearce, *Quart in Pint Pot*, 37.
31 *S.C.C. Mins.* 1894–9, Intermediate Educ. Cttee. reps.
32 Board in church. Modified by deed of 1859: S.C.C. Ch. Exec.'s Dept., chars. index.
33 S.C.C. Ch. Exec.'s Dept., chars. index.
34 *Review of Local Chars.* (S.C.C. 1975), 60.
35 Below, local govt. Acreages from O.S. *Area Bk.* (1884). A map of the Heath and Norncott forms part of fig. 15 above. This article was written in 1992.
36 J. Piper and J. Betjeman, *Salop.* (Shell Guide, 1951), 31.
37 Bodl., Craven dep. 3.
38 Ibid. 19, f. 3. Cf. P.R.O., IR 29/29/154; IR 30/29/154, field 59.
39 Geol. Surv. Map 1", solid, sheet 166 (1974 edn.).
40 Soil Surv. Map 1", sheet 166 (1972 edn.).
41 Below, chapel of ease.
42 P.R.O., IR 29/29/154; IR 30/29/154, field 24; below, econ. hist.; *T.S.A.S.* 4th ser. iv. 172.
43 Medieval Village Research Group, *Ann. Rep.* xxix. 9–10; R.C.H.M.E., draft field rep. (1985).
44 *Two Est. Surveys of the FitzAlan Earls of Arundel* (Suss. Rec. Soc. lxvii), 88.
45 Below, econ. hist.
46 Only that site, vacant by 1771 (S.P.L., MS. 2481, map X), is otherwise unaccounted for.
47 Below, manors; econ. hist.
48 S.P.L., MS. 2481, map X.
49 O.S. Maps 1", sheet LXI. SW. (1833 edn.); 1/2,500, Salop. LXV. 14 (1884 edn.).
50 P.R.O., IR 29/29/154; IR 30/29/154, fields 30–1, 35.
51 S.R.O. 2079/LXV. 14; 4011/39, nos. 191, 193; O.S. Map 1/25,000, SO 48/58 (1983 edn.).
52 P.R.O., HO 107/913/20, f. 3; HO 107/1982, f. 497; IR 29/29/154; IR 30/29/154, fields 126–7.
53 O.S. Map 1/2,500, Salop. LXV. 13 (1884 and 1903 edns.)

1870s[54] and belonged in 1913 to Heath House.[55] North of the hamlet, the medieval park lodge, later a farmhouse, was abandoned in the late 17th or early 18th century, and buildings on the presumed site were later called Heath Barns.[56] A new farmstead, Harp Farm, was created there *c.* 1952.[57]

Norncott ('Normonnechot' in 1255)[58] lay on the north-eastern side of the heath, where settlement was confined to a strip of suitable land between the heath and a steep downward slope. The surviving farmsteads at Upper and Lower Norncott, 0.7 km. apart, were there in the 17th century.[59] Earthworks midway between them suggest a close group of houses there, along one side of a north–south hollow way. That site was last occupied in the 18th century.[60] By the 1840s part of it was within Lower Norncott farm and part within Lower House farm, Abdon.[61]

The population of the Heath and Norncott was 40–50 for most of the 19th century. There was a short-lived rise after 1831 and another after 1891,[62] and then a slow decrease until 1981. The population rose from 22 in 1981 to 31 in 1991.[63]

A road north-east from Bouldon (in Holdgate) skirted the north side of the Heath hamlet[64] and continued by Upper Norncott and Abdon to Bridgnorth,[65] probably via Marsh gate and Ditton Priors.[66] It still led to Bridgnorth in 1738.[67] A road from Bouldon via Peckledy Cross to Clee St. Margaret crossed the parish's southern edge.[68] Near Bouldon mill, just outside the parish's western boundary, a branch climbed north-east to the centre of the Heath hamlet[69] and continued via Cockshutford to the common at Clee Liberty.[70] By 1771 the Bouldon–Bridgnorth road had been abandoned east of the Heath and had been diverted through the hamlet to join the Bouldon–Cockshutford road, which between Bouldon and the Heath consequently declined to a bridleway. The road from Bouldon through Peckledy to Clee St. Margaret, from which it branched, deteriorated west of Peckledy in the 19th century. The new Bouldon–Cockshutford route was the parish's only metalled thoroughfare in 1992.

From the Heath hamlet a road led north to Tugford, skirting the park. It dwindled to a bridleway during the 19th century. Another road, later called Sally Cop[71] (or Sally Coppice) Lane, ran south over Hunger hill to Peckledy Cross;[72] it was the 'road to the barn' in 1771.[73] South of New House it had become a mere footpath by the late 19th century. A path from it was the shortest way from the Heath to Clee St. Margaret in 1590.[74]

A road from Tugford south to Clee St. Margaret, via Upper Cross Lanes, passed near Lower Norncott. A branch ran through Norncott's deserted settlement[75] to Upper Norncott and on towards Cockshutford; it was probably the road used in the early 17th century by Tugford's and Norncott's strakers[76] but was merely a footpath by 1833. During the 19th century the part from Tugford to Lower Norncott also fell into disuse, but the southward part to Upper Cross Lanes remained the occupation road for Lower and Upper Norncott, the latter by way of a short stretch of the former Bouldon–Bridgnorth road.

MANORS AND OTHER ESTATES. In 1086 *THE HEATH* was presumably part of Wenlock priory's manor of Stoke St. Milborough; it was included in that manor's 20 hides in 1255.[77] The priory claimed to have been overlord since the 1190s or earlier,[78] and by 1255 the baron of Castle Holdgate held the Heath from the priory in fee farm.[79] He owed the farm to the priory until 1540 and thereafter to the Crown, but by 1267, and still in the 17th century, the farm was paid for him by the terre tenant.[80] The lord of Holdgate was still entitled to chief rents from the Heath in 1800.[81]

The Heath had been further subinfeudated by 1236 when Peter son of Reynold quitclaimed it to William son of John, of Castle Holdgate,[82] who held it of the lord of Holdgate in 1255.[83] William son of John had been succeeded by 1263 by his son John (fl. 1267),[84] whose son John had succeeded by 1272.[85] As John of the Heath (fl. 1337) he and his wife Iseult had an estate at the

54 P.R.O., RG 11/2617, f. 62 and v.
55 S.R.O. 2079/LXV. 13; 4011/39, no. 182.
56 O.S. Map 1", sheet LXI. SW. (1833 edn.); below, econ. hist.
57 S.R.O., reg. of electors, Ludlow const. (1952), p. 403 (no mention); (1953), p. 401.
58 *Rot. Hund.* (Rec. Com.), ii. 85.
59 Above, manors.
60 Medieval Village Research Group, *Ann. Rep.* xxix. 10; R.C.H.M.E., draft field rep. (1986); SA 3363; B.L. Maps, O.S.D. 206 (not shown).
61 P.R.O., IR 29/29/84; IR 30/29/84, fields 786, 788. Cf. IR 29/29/1; IR 30/29/1, field 198.
62 *V.C.H. Salop.* ii. 223, 227, s.v. the Heath, adjusted by ref. to P.R.O., HO 107/913/20, ff. 2v.–3v.; HO 107/1982, ff. 496–7; RG 9/1838, ff. 50v.–1, 60v.; RG 10/2727, ff. 66v.–68; RG 11/2617, ff. 61v.–62v.
63 *V.C.H. Salop.* ii. 223; *Census*, 1971, *Co. Rep. Salop.* i. 5; *Census*, 1981, Small Area Statistics: Salop.; S.C.C. Property and Planning Services Dept. inf. rep. C91/103.
64 R.C.H.M.E., draft field rep. (1985). Descr. of roads based hereafter on S.P.L., MS. 2481, ff. 51–2 and map X; B.L. Maps, O.S.D. 206; O.S. Maps 1", sheet LXI. SW. (1833 edn.); 6", Salop. LXV. SW. (1891 edn.); P.R.O., IR 29/29/154; IR 30/29/154.
65 By 1652: Bodl., Craven dep. 19, f. 3.
66 Above, Abdon, intro.; Ditton Priors, intro.
67 S.P.L., Deeds 10389.
68 By 1590: H.W.R.O.(H.), HD 2/10/31.
69 R.C.H.M.E., draft field rep. (1985).
70 By 1652: Bodl., Craven dep. 19, f. 3. Cf. below, econ. hist.
71 S.R.O., reg. of electors, Ludlow divn. (1929), p. 408.
72 By 1562: S.P.L., Deeds 7146, ct. r.
73 S.P.L., MS. 2481, f. 52, field 48.
74 H.W.R.O.(H.), HD 2/10/31.
75 R.C.H.M.E., draft field rep. (1986).
76 *T.S.A.S.* 2nd ser. viii. 197. Cf. above, Tugford, econ. hist.; below, econ. hist.
77 *Rot. Hund.* (Rec. Com), ii. 85.
78 *Roll of Salop. Eyre 1256* (Selden Soc. xcvi), p. 47.
79 *Rot. Hund.* ii. 85. Cf. above, Holdgate, manor.
80 *Cal. Inq. p.m.* i, p. 216; S.P.L., Deeds 7451, 9742, 9749; S.R.O. 1224, box 342, Prior Gosnell's reg. f. 39; Dugdale, *Mon.* v. 81; P.R.O., LR 2/184, f. 67; Bodl., Craven dep. 19, f. 9.
81 S.P.L., Deeds 10195.
82 *T.S.A.S.* 4th ser. iv. 172; *Roll of Salop. Eyre 1256*, p. 47.
83 *Rot. Hund.* ii. 85.
84 *Cal. Inq. p.m.* i, p. 216; below, this section.
85 Eyton, iv. 17.

Heath in 1320;[86] and he was probably the John Gorri whose wife Iseult had an estate there, formerly William of Castle Holdgate's, in 1348.[87] By 1428 it had reverted to the lord of Holdgate.[88]

By 1263 John, son of William son of John, had subinfeudated the Heath to John FitzAlan (d. 1267),[89] who was succeeded by his son John (d. 1272)[90] and then by John's son Richard, later earl of Arundel.[91] Between 1292 and 1295 it may have passed to Earl Richard's brother John of Arundel,[92] but it was Richard's again by 1301.[93] It belonged by 1345 to Richard's grandson Richard FitzAlan, earl of Arundel and Surrey (d. 1376),[94] whose son Earl Richard succeeded. After his forfeiture in 1397 the manor was in the king's hands[95] until restored in 1400 to his son Earl Thomas.[96] The manor descended with the earldom of Arundel until 1560[97] when Earl Henry sold it to Rowland Hayward, lord of Tugford.[98] Hayward annexed the Heath to that manor, in which it seems to have remained.[99] Parliament confiscated Lord Craven's Shropshire estates in 1651[1] and sold the Heath in 1653 to Samuel Hill;[2] Craven regained it at the Restoration.[3] In 1846 the manorial estate consisted principally of Upper Heath farm (189 a.) and Heath park (119 a.).[4] C. O. Childe-Pemberton sold Upper Heath and part of the park in 1874,[5] and H. J. Beckwith's representatives sold the rest of the park, called Heath (later Harp) farm, in the 1930s.[6]

The medieval chief house presumably occupied the moated site immediately north-west of the chapel.[7] The house had gone by 1771, replaced by the timber framed Heath House Farm nearby;[8] that was probably the house which consisted in 1652 of ground-floor hall, parlour, kitchen, and buttery, and three chambers above and was occupied by the Millichap family, as in 1771.[9] That too was demolished between 1790 and 1833[10] and was replaced on a different site by the new Heath (later Upper House or Upper Heath) Farm, which is a red brick farmhouse of *c.* 1810 with a central pediment on brick pilasters, accompanied by model farm buildings.

William Rawlyns had a freehold in 1567[11] as did John Rawlyns (fl. 1584) in 1590.[12] It belonged by 1609 to Thomas Botterell (fl. 1616).[13] Edward Botterell (fl. 1651) had succeeded by 1620.[14] The estate descended to his sons Thomas (d. 1669) and Edward (d. 1684) in turn and then from father to son through Edward (d. 1728), John (d. 1752), Edward (d. 1782), and Thomas (d. 1786) to Edward (d. 1834).[15] The last Edward's heir was his sister Drusilla (d. 1847), wife of Edward Price.[16] Edward Turner had most of the estate (180 a.) by 1846,[17] T. R. C. Downes by 1874,[18] his son Sir A. H. Downes by 1913,[19] C. D. Morgan (d. 1943) by 1921,[20] and his son-in-law K. W. Deakin in 1992, but Price (fl. 1861) retained 20 a. with Heath Cottage (later Farm),[21] which belonged in 1913 to Charles Jones.[22]

Thomas le Clerk, a freeholder of ½ virgate in 1256,[23] was perhaps the man of that name who had ½ virgate in 1301.[24] The estate was probably that held in 1567 by Richard Wicke and later by his widow Amy.[25] William Stoke had it by 1584[26] and Richard Stoke (fl. 1616) by 1609.[27] John Stoke (fl. 1664) owned the estate in 1631[28] and Thomas Stoke (fl. 1682) sold it in 1717 to John Botterell.[29] Botterell succeeded to his father's estate in 1728, and Stoke's farm was consequently united with it.[30] The Stokes' house was apparently the later *HEATH HOUSE*, where an outbuilding has a reset stone dated 1684, inscribed 'IS' (probably John Stoke) and 'TSS' (probably Thomas and Sarah Stoke).[31] The Botterells had probably occupied a house *c.* 100 m. south of the chapel.[32] After 1728, however, John Botterell seems to have remained at Heath House, *c.* 150 m. to the west, which he is said to have rebuilt;[33] it was his successors' chief house in 1846, when only 'buildings' remained

86 S.R.O. 356/MT/1188; *T.S.A.S.* vi. 331.
87 *Feud. Aids*, iv. 245.
88 Ibid. 250. Cf. above, Holdgate, manor.
89 Eyton, iv. 17; *Cal. Inq. p.m.* i, p. 216; *Complete Peerage*, i. 240.
90 *Close R.* 1268–72, pp. 505, 507.
91 *Feud. Aids*, iv. 224; *Complete Peerage*, i. 240–1.
92 *Cal. Inq. p.m.* iii, p. 124; Eyton, iv. 18; *Cartulary of Haughmond Abbey*, ed. U. Rees (1985), p. 227.
93 *Two Est. Surveys of the FitzAlan Earls of Arundel* (Suss. Rec. Soc. lxvii), 88–9.
94 *Cal. Pat.* 1343–5, 488; *Complete Peerage*, i. 242–4.
95 *Cal. Pat.* 1396–9, 278; *Complete Peerage*, i. 245.
96 *Cal. Inq. p.m.* (Rec. Com), iv. 26; *Complete Peerage*, i. 246.
97 *Cal. Fine R.* 1413–22, 165; S.P.L., Deeds 9749; *Cal. Inq. p.m.* (Rec. Com.), iv. 197; S.R.O. 1224, box 342, Prior Gosnell's reg. f. 39; 567, box 30, acct. r. of 1528–9; *L. & P. Hen. VIII*, xx (2), p. 414. Cf. *Complete Peerage*, i. 247–52.
98 P.R.O., CP 25/2/200/2 Eliz. I East. no. [13]; above, Tugford, manors.
99 S.P.L., Deeds 7146, 7527 (ct. r. of 1598), 10400, 10462, 10944, 10962, 13056. Cf. above, Tugford, manors.
1 *Cal. Cttee. for Compounding*, ii, p. 1617.
2 P.R.O., C 54/3764, mm. 10–12.
3 S.P.L., Deeds 9718.
4 P.R.O., IR 29/29/154; IR 30/29/154. Cf. S.P.L., MS. 2481, ff. 51–2 and map X.
5 S.R.O. 3651, box 18B, deed (copy).
6 S.R.O. 2030/6/83, 126; 4011/39, no. 179.
7 R.C.H.M.E., draft field rep. (1985).
8 S.P.L., MS. 2481, f. 52 and map X, field 39. Named in P.R.O., IR 29/29/154, award. Drawing in S.P.L., MS. 372, vol. ii, f. 36.
9 Bodl., Craven dep. 19, f. 3.
10 S.P.L., MS. 372, vol. ii, f. 36; O.S. Map 1", sheet LXI. SW. (1833 edn.).
11 S.P.L., Deeds 8384.
12 Ibid. 7467; H.W.R.O.(H.), HD 2/10/31.
13 S.P.L., Deeds 7145, rental; 7451.
14 For pedigree see W.S.L. 350/3/40, Stoke St. Milborough p. 15; *T.S.A.S.* xlvi. 73–4; *S.P.R. Heref.* xix (5), pp. v, 14, 19. For descent of est. 1620–1782 see W.S.L. 350/3/40, Stoke St. Milborough pp. 13–15; Bodl., Craven dep. 19, f. 9.
15 S.P.L., Deeds 485.
16 *S.P.R. Heref.* xix (5), p. v.
17 P.R.O., IR 29/29/154.
18 S.R.O., reg. of electors, Southern divn. (1874), p. 114.
19 S.R.O. 4011/39, no. 182; *Who Was Who, 1929–40*, 381.
20 S.R.O. 2030/6/39; gravestone at Holdgate.
21 P.R.O., IR 29/29/154; RG 9/1838, f. 51.
22 S.R.O. 4011/39, no. 192.
23 *Roll of Salop. Eyre 1256*, pp. 33–4.
24 *Two Est. Surveys of Earls of Arundel*, 88.
25 S.P.L., Deeds 8384; H.W.R.O.(H.), HD 2/10/31.
26 S.P.L., Deeds 7467.
27 Ibid. 7145, rental (same chief rent as in 1301); 7451.
28 Bodl., Craven dep. 19, f. 9; S.P.L., Deeds 7548, Tugford rent r.
29 W.S.L. 350/3/40, Stoke St. Milborough pp. 14–15.
30 S.P.L., Deeds 485; above, this section.
31 R.C.M.H.E., draft field rep. (1985). For Sarah see *S.P.R. Heref.* xix (5), 26.
32 S.P.L., MS. 2481, map X (Edw. Botterell's property).
33 *T.S.A.S.* xlvi. 74.

on the probable site of the old Botterell house.[34] Heath House is mid 18th-century, with a symmetrical three bayed main block and a pair of rear wings, all of sandstone rubble, but its present appearance results from an exterior remodelling of the early 19th century when it was reroofed, the back court was filled in, a circular hall and a stone staircase were added to the front, and the main rooms were redecorated.

A freehold belonged in 1771 to William Millichap (d. 1786)[35] and in 1787 to Thomas Millichap.[36] Edward Millichap (fl. 1851) had *NEW HOUSE* (20 a.) by the 1830s[37] and E. H. Millichap (fl. 1941) by 1913.[38] By 1881 the house was also called Sally Coppice.[39]

NORNCOTT is assumed to have been part of Wenlock priory's manor of Stoke St. Milborough in 1086; it was included in that manor's 20 hides in 1255.[40] The priory remained tenant in chief until its surrender.[41]

Norncott had been subinfeudated by 1255 when Sir Richard Tyrel held all but 1 virgate of the priory; the virgate was held by Richard of Thonglands, and under him by the heirs of one Thomas.[42] Sir Roger Tyrel (fl. 1268–1306)[43] presumably succeeded Sir Richard Tyrel, for Sir Roger's son Hugh was in possession by 1334.[44] He died in 1343, and his son and heir John died in possession in 1360. John's heir was his brother Hugh.[45] By 1453 William Burley owned Norncott.[46] It descended thereafter with Brockton until the mid 16th century.[47] John de Vere, earl of Oxford, sold his moiety in 1552 to John Stringfellow,[48] who sold it next year to Thomas Barker.[49] John Lyttelton's moiety was perhaps represented in 1569 by the Norncott estate of Nicholas Heathe.[50] The later descent of the moieties has not been traced.

John Smallman of Oxenbold (fl. 1624) was a freeholder at Norncott.[51] A farm formerly held by him belonged in 1641 to Nicholas Page (d. 1684).[52] By 1652 *UPPER NORNCOTT* had been acquired by John Browne of Sowbach.[53] It descended thereafter with the Stanton Long demesne until 1753[54] when Thomas Tomkys sold Upper Norncott to Edward Botterell.[55] It then descended with Heath House until 1844,[56] when Charles Head bought it.[57] By 1913 it belonged to the Bradley family,[58] with whom it remained in 1992. The oldest part of the house has an L plan formed by a timber framed cross wing and a truncated hall range with a large stack between them. While the cross wing has a tall attic first floor, the hall has an inaccessible upper part and may have been an open hall. In the cross wing the principal room is a parlour which has panelling throughout, most of it apparently *in situ*, dated 1595 above the fireplace. The truncation of the hall, perhaps in the 18th century, probably coincided with the rebuilding of its walls in rubble and the addition of a service range against its south side. The thatch on the roof was replaced by corrugated iron and the plaster in the panels of the cross wing was replaced by brick nogging in the mid 20th century.

Richard Wall (d. 1707) had *LOWER NORNCOTT* by 1686. By 1730 Thomas Reynolds had bought it.[59] Before 1746 he sold it to Thomas Tasker the elder (d. 1782).[60] Tasker's nephew[61] Francis Hudson (d. 1811) had it by 1809.[62] Elizabeth Hudson owned it in 1842,[63] Miss M. H. Southern in 1913,[64] and Thomas Norgrove in 1921.[65] Norgrove's family remained in possession in 1992.[66] The house is timber framed, originally of two bays, and was later cased in brick, perhaps by Thomas Tasker.[67]

ECONOMIC HISTORY. The heath which gave a name to one of the townships evidently occupied the high ground between the Heath and Norncott, and was presumably intercommoned before a boundary was drawn between them. Clee St. Margaret probably intercommoned there too until Norncott's eastern boundary was drawn.[68] By the early 15th century most of the Heath's part of the heath had been imparked. It then consisted of timber and pasture, and the grazing was let to the lord of Broncroft (in Diddlebury).[69] In the 16th century the heath was no larger than the park,[70] but it

34 P.R.O., IR 29/29/154; IR 30/29/154, fields 56–7.
35 S.P.L., MS. 2481, map X; *S.P.R. Heref.* xix (5), 84.
36 S.R.O. 1359, box 20, land tax assessment.
37 W.S.L. 350/3/40, Stoke St. Milborough p. 3; P.R.O., IR 29/29/154; HO 107/198, f. 497.
38 S.R.O. 4011/39, no. 189; *Kelly's Dir. Salop.* (1941), 262.
39 P.R.O., RG 11/2617, f. 62.
40 *Rot. Hund.* ii. 85.
41 *Cal. Inq. p.m.* x, p. 484; *Cal. Inq. p.m. Hen. VII*, ii, pp. 211, 578; iii, pp. 128, 332; S.R.O. 1224, box 342, Prior Gosnell's reg. f. 39; Dugdale, *Mon.* v. 81.
42 *Rot. Hund.* ii. 85.
43 Eyton, v. 166; P.R.O., C 104/26, deed 13 July 1306.
44 *Cal. Chart. R.* 1327–41, 309; *Cal. Inq. p.m.* viii, p. 353.
45 *Cal. Inq. p.m.* viii, p. 297; x, p. 484; xi, p. 418.
46 P.R.O., CP 25/1/195/22, no. 41.
47 *Cal. Inq. p.m. Hen. VII*, ii, pp. 211, 427, 578; iii, pp. 128, 332; S.R.O. 1224, box 342, Prior Gosnell's reg. f. 39; P.R.O., SC 6/Hen. VIII/3021, m. 18d. Cf. above, Shipton, manors (Brockton).
48 S.R.O. 20/23/13.
49 P.R.O., CP 40/1156, rot. 13.
50 S.P.L., Deeds 587.
51 S.P.L., MS. 2, f. 153v.; S.R.O. 3901/Rg/1, 31 July 1624.
52 S.P.L., Deeds 469; *S.P.R. Heref.* xix (1), 29.
53 Bodl., Craven dep. 19, ff. 2–3, 5.
54 S.R.O. 1037/21/105A; S.P.L., Deeds 10389. Cf. above, Stanton Long, manors.
55 W.S.L. 350/3/40, Stoke St. Milborough p. 3.
56 Abstr. of title in Miss B. E. Bradley's possession; P.R.O., IR 29/29/84; IR 30/29/84, field 751. Cf. above, this section.
57 Chancery deposition in Miss Bradley's possession.
58 S.R.O. 4011/39, no. 178.
59 S.P.L., Deeds 698; *S.P.R. Heref.* xix (5), 53.
60 S.R.O., incl. award B 21–2, cross-examination of Thos. Powell, May 1810; H.W.R.O.(H.), Heref. dioc. rec., bp.'s transcripts, Tugford, bur. 13 Dec. 1746; S.P.L., Deeds 701; *S.P.R. Heref.* xix (1), 71.
61 S.R.O. 3901/Rg/3, bap. 11 Sept. 1757; 4131/Rg/2, bap. 24 July 1732, 19 Aug. 1739; 4131/Rg/5, marr. 29 Mar. 1765.
62 S.R.O., incl. award B 21–2, claim of Fra. and Ann Hudson; cross-examination of Thos. Powell, May 1810; S.R.O. 3901/Rg/3, bur. 14 July 1811.
63 P.R.O., IR 29/29/84.
64 S.R.O. 4011/39, no. 196.
65 S.R.O. 2030/6/3.
66 Local inf.
67 SA 14402. Tasker 'built a ho.' at Norncott: S.R.O., incl. award B 21–2, cross-examination of Thos. Powell, May 1810.
68 Above, this article, intro.
69 S.P.L., Deeds 9742; cf. *T.S.A.S.* 4th ser. vi. 229.
70 S.R.O. 567, box 30, acct. r.; S.P.L., Deeds 8429.

had earlier extended farther south.[71] The inhabitants of the Heath and Norncott had summer grazing rights, as 'strakers', on the part of Brown Clee called Clee Liberty, in Clee St. Margaret parish,[72] and common woods probably stood where the Heath bordered Tugford and Bouldon[73] and on Hunger hill.[74] The Heath had three open fields in 1529: Leabatch (south-east of the hamlet), Weston (presumably south, towards Cold Weston), and Wynett (west).[75]

The Heath manor had 2 carucates of demesne arable in the late 13th century, worth 20*s.*,[76] and gardens, meadow land, and a 'grove' (*grava*) were worth 8*s.* 8*d.* in 1301. Outside the demesne, another 2¾ virgates were in the hands of four resident tenants in 1301, whose rents totalled 24*s.* 2½*d.*[77] By 1408 the demesne and park were also rented out, and rent income 1407–8 was 65*s.* 7*d.*; a further 2*s.* came from the manor court and 66*s.* 10*d.* from wood sales.[78] Rents in the 16th century were much the same (62*s.* ½*d.* in 1528–9, 61*s.* in 1566–7), but in 1567 holdings outside the demesne and park were only two freeholds and a copyhold.[79]

Inclosure of open-field arable for pasture was reported at Norncott in 1517,[80] but by 1590 had made little progress on the glebe of Stoke St. Milborough at the Heath.[81] Change at the Heath was more rapid in the 17th century. Most arable on the manorial estate was inclosed by 1631 and all by 1652.[82] From 1610 the park was let as a farm,[83] the house (mentioned 1631) being presumably a former lodge; by 1631 part of the farm had been ploughed, and the farm lay in four divisions by 1652. The park timber, which included many good oaks, was then valued at £30.[84] More than a third of it was felled by Samuel Hill in the Interregnum,[85] but in the 18th century the lord's timber was carefully managed and much remained in 1771 in the former park and on Hunger hill.[86]

The copyhold farm at the Heath was a leasehold by 1611.[87] It was amalgamated with the former park in the late 17th or early 18th century,[88] and with the demesne *c.* 1805, to form Heath (later Upper Heath) farm.[89] The two other holdings were combined in the 18th century to form Heath House farm.[90] Between the late 17th and early 19th centuries the Heath's five farms thus became two, and land exchanges in or after the late 18th, including one in 1815, made them more compact.[91] Two small additional farms were created, New House by 1771[92] and Peckledy by 1793; the latter was the Stoke St. Milborough glebe, still centred on an isolated barn in 1771.[93] Norncott had only two farms by 1815.[94]

Farm rents on the Heath manorial estate were doubled *c.* 1610,[95] but fell well below real annual values (put at £69 in 1631 and £134 in 1771)[96] and were not increased again until the early 19th century.[97] The lord preferred to take substantial entry fines,[98] but the owner of the Heath House estate let it for an economic rent in 1788.[99]

Farming was mixed in the 17th[1] and early 18th century. In January 1708 the Heath demesne farm (80 a.) had 23 cattle, including 4 oxen and 6 cows, sheep worth £8, and £10 worth of corn in the ground.[2] In the 1770s Edward Botterell, who owned and occupied the Heath House estate (*c.* 200 a.)[3] and rented the former park (118 a.) and another farm (92 a.), had 300–500 sheep.[4] The former dairy at Heath House contains a 19th-century cheese press. Upper Heath was built by the lord *c.* 1810[5] as a model farm.

In 1846 there was twice as much grass as arable,[6] but in 1938 more than ten times as much. Beef cattle and sheep were then predominant, and the arable was mostly under oats. More land was taken under the plough during and after the war, and in 1965 barley and wheat were the main cereals.[7] In 1950, however, Peckledy remained wholly pastoral.[8] In 1992 Heath House farm and Upper Norncott were mainly pastoral but Upper Heath was arable.

The nearest known mill to the Heath hamlet was at Bouldon. In 1267 the lord of the Heath was receiving ½*d.* a year from a mill[9] and in 1301 the ½ virgate held by Hugh of Bouldon, probably lord of Bouldon, at the Heath yielded 5*s.* a year

71 S.P.L., MS. 2481, f. 52 and map X, field 46.
72 S.P.L., Deeds 8429; *T.S.A.S.* 2nd ser. viii. 196–7 (for the 'king's shield' see S.R.O. 1037/21/6); S.R.O., incl. award B 21–2, brief of [1810], ff. 7–9v.
73 S.P.L., MS. 2481, map X.
74 'Hongerell' in 1631: Bodl., Craven dep. 40, p. 96. Probably from OE. *hongra* 'wood on a steep hillside': H. D. G. Foxall, *Salop. Field-Names* (Salop. Arch. Soc. 1980), 38.
75 Bodl., Craven dep. 3. Cf. P.R.O., IR 29/29/83; IR 30/29/83, fields 16–17, 68, 304–5; S.P.L., MS. 2481, map X.
76 P.R.O., C 132/35, no. 18; Eyton, iv. 18.
77 *Two Est. Surveys of Earls of Arundel*, 88. Another fm., of 6 a. (ibid. 89), was probably in Clee St. Margaret par.: Bodl. Craven dep. 40, p. 94.
78 S.P.L., Deeds 9742.
79 S.R.O. 567, box 30, acct. r. of 1528–9 (perh. including 3*s.* from Clee St. Margaret), 1566–7 (rent from Clee St. Margaret not recorded). For the freeholds see above, manors.
80 B.L. Lansd. MS. 1, f. 190v.
81 H.W.R.O.(H.), HD 2/10/31.
82 Bodl., Craven dep. 19, ff. 1–10; 40, pp. 94–6.
83 S.P.L., Deeds 8429.
84 Bodl., Craven dep. 19, ff. 2, 10; 40, p. 94.
85 S.P.L., Deeds 9718, Heath ct. r.
86 Ibid. 10946; S.P.L., MS. 2481, map X.
87 S.P.L., Deeds 8422.
88 Ibid. 10863, 10944, 10961–2. Cf. S.P.L., MS. 2481, f. 51 and map X, field 2.
89 Above, manors. Cf. S.P.L., MS. 2481, ff. 51–2 and map X.
90 By 1788: S.P.L., Deeds 485. Cf. above, manors.
91 S.P.L., MS. 2481, ff. 51–2 and map X; P.R.O., IR 29/29/154; IR 30/29/154; S.R.O. 3651, parcel 17C, p. 154.
92 Above, manors.
93 S.P.L., MS. 2481, f. 52 and map X, field 48; 6862, f. 73; P.R.O., IR 29/29/154; IR 30/29/154, field 117.
94 S.R.O. 4366/Pa/1.
95 S.P.L., Deeds 7145 (rental of 1609), 7451, 8422–3, 8429.
96 Bodl., Craven dep. 40, pp. 94–6; S.P.L., MS. 2481, ff. 51–2. The Clee St. Margaret fm. is not counted here.
97 S.P.L., Deeds 9868; MS. 2510.
98 e.g. S.P.L., Deeds 10400, 10462, 10944, 10961–2, 13056.
99 Ibid. 485.
1 Bodl., Craven dep. 19, ff. 2–8; 40, pp. 94–6.
2 S.P.L., Deeds 10400; H.W.R.O.(H.), Heref. dioc. rec., inv. of John Millerchap.
3 In 1846: P.R.O., IR 29/29/154.
4 S.R.O., incl. award B 21–2, brief of [1810], f. 7 and v.; S.P.L., Deeds 10462, 10944; above, manors.
5 Above, manors.
6 P.R.O., IR 29/29/154 (excludes Norncott).
7 P.R.O., MAF 68/3880, Salop. no. 107; MAF 68/4945, no. 107.
8 R. Dumont, *Types of Rural Economy* (1957), 396–8 (fm. identified from *Kelly's Dir. Salop.* (1937), 265).
9 P.R.O., C 132/35, no. 18.

rent, 'which is owed to him for a mill'.[10] Neither reference implies a mill at the Heath, and the latter suggests that Bouldon mill was used. Earthworks of a pond and dam remain 130 m. west of the former moated house at the Heath and could have served a mill but may indicate a fishpond.[11] A Pool yard was mentioned in 1408.[12] There may have been a mill at Lower Norncott, on the site later used for ironworks; a little beyond the brook, in Abdon parish, lay Mill field and Mill furlong in 1642.[13] Over 1 km. upstream lay Floodgate meadow.[14]

The ironworks at Lower Norncott was on the west bank of the brook,[15] where masonry, slag, and charcoal have been reported.[16] On the facing bank, in Abdon parish, lay Furnace meadow and Furnace leasow; Furnace Lane, so called by 1692, approached the works from Abdon.[17]

A large limestone quarry lay on the boundary with Bouldon in 1846,[18] and a mason lived at Weir Cottage in the 1860s and 1870s.[19] A small sandstone quarry lay *c.* 175 m. east of the chapel by 1846 and remained open in 1901.[20] A mason was living at one of the Lane Cottages in 1841.[21] There was a limekiln in the former park in 1833, but no evidence of commercial production.[22]

LOCAL GOVERNMENT. The Heath presented at the court leet of Castle Holdgate barony by 1422 and still in 1551. Norncott was in the liberty (and the borough) of Wenlock.[23]

The Heath had a court baron. In the early 15th century it met infrequently, and in some years not at all.[24] From 1560 until the mid 18th century or later, the Heath was usually subject to Tugford manor court,[25] but a court baron was sometimes held for the Heath in the late 16th century[26] and perhaps during the Heath's separation from Tugford 1653–60; in 1652 courts baron were said to be held at the will of the lord,[27] and one was held in 1660 immediately after Lord Craven regained possession.[28]

The Heath chapelry raised and spent its own poor rate by 1698[29] and in 1793 was also raising its own church rate for repair of the chapel.[30] Norncott was subject to Stoke St. Milborough vestry until joined with the Heath in 1884.[31] The Heath and Norncott were in Ludlow poor-law union 1836–1930,[32] Ludlow highway district 1863–95,[33] Ludlow rural sanitary district 1872–94, Ludlow rural district 1894–1974, and South Shropshire district from 1974.[34] In 1992 the Heath had a joint parish council with Abdon.[35]

CHAPEL OF EASE. A chapel was built in the 12th century and was dependent in the mid 14th on Stoke St. Milborough church.[36] It had no separate advowson or endowment and was not licensed for weddings until 1922.[37] A weathered medieval grave slab from the chapel yard is the only evidence of burials before the consecration of an adjoining graveyard in 1938.[38] Families of the Heath seem to have buried previously at Stoke,[39] while those of Norncott often buried and baptized at Abdon.[40]

There may have been a resident priest in the Middle Ages; an isolated plot of glebe, next to the chapel and moated site, was called Priest yard,[41] but there was no priest's house in 1590.[42] The chapel was served by Stoke St. Milborough's clergy in the 18th century and until 1922,[43] when the vicar of Clee St. Margaret was appointed curate in charge of the Heath. That arrangement lasted until *c.* 1933.[44] The rector of Diddlebury with Bouldon and Munslow was curate in charge 1973–5 and 1977–82.[45] From 1983 the chapel was served by clergy of the united benefice created that year.[46]

Services were monthly in 1719[47] and remained so until the late 19th century or beyond.[48] In 1793 the congregation numbered 15–20, and when there was no service worshippers some-

10 *Two Est. Surveys of Earls of Arundel*, 88; above, Bouldon, manor. 11 R.C.H.M.E., draft field rep. (1985).

12 S.P.L., Deeds 9742.

13 Bodl. MS. Gough Salop. 11, ff. 51v.–52; P.R.O., IR 29/29/1; IR 30/29/1, fields 23–4, 29.

14 Bodl. MS. Gough Salop. 11, f. 54; P.R.O., IR 29/29/1; IR 30/29/1, field 212.

15 O.S. Nat. Grid SO 567 867.

16 S.R.O. 5403/7/4/1; R. T. Rowley, 'Hist. of S. Salop. Landscape' (Oxf. Univ. B.Litt. thesis, 1967), 169–70; *Post-Medieval Arch.* i. 120–1; S.P.L., Heath photos. neg. B. 3784 (sketch plan).

17 P.R.O., IR 29/29/1; IR 30/29/1, fields 35–6; *S.P.R. Heref.* xix (1), p. vi.

18 P.R.O., IR 29/29/154; IR 30/29/154, field 76. Cf. above, Bouldon, econ. hist.

19 P.R.O., RG 9/1838, f. 50v.; RG 10/2727, f. 67v. Cottage located from P.R.O., HO 107/913/20, f. 3; IR 29/29/154; IR 30/29/154, field 127.

20 P.R.O., IR 29/29/154; IR 30/29/154, field 25; O.S. Map 1/2,500, Salop. LXV. 9 (1903 edn.).

21 P.R.O., HO 107/913/20, f. 3.

22 O.S. Map 1", sheet LXI. SW. (1833 edn.); P.R.O., IR 29/29/154; IR 30/29/154, field 5.

23 S.P.L., MS. 2, f. 146 and v.; cf. above, Holdgate, local govt.; fig. 16.

24 S.P.L., Deeds 9742, 9744–9; S.R.O. 567, box 30, accts. of 1528–9.

25 S.P.L., Deeds 7146, 10462. Cf. above, manors.

26 S.P.L., Deeds 7141, 7467, 7527.

27 Bodl., Craven dep. 19, f. 9.

28 S.P.L., Deeds 9718, ct. r.; 10960–1. Cf. above, manors.

29 *Orders of Q. Sess.* i. 171; S.P.L., MS. 6862, f. 73.

30 S.P.L., MS. 6862, f. 73.

31 *V.C.H. Salop.* ii. 227 n.

32 V. J. Walsh, 'Admin. of Poor Laws in Salop 1820–55' (Pennsylvania Univ. Ph.D. thesis, 1970), 150; *Kelly's Dir. Salop.* (1929), 275.

33 *Lond. Gaz.* 27 Mar. 1863, p. 1772; S.R.O., S.C.C. Local Govt., etc., Cttee. min. bk. 1894–1903, p. 29.

34 *Rural Dist. Councillors Electn. Order, 1894* (Local Govt. Bd. order no. 31847); *V.C.H. Salop.* ii. 215; iii. 179, and sources cited ibid. 169 n. 29.

35 Local inf. 36 B.L. Add. MS. 50121, p. 21.

37 Heref. Dioc. Regy., reg. 1919–26, p. 239.

38 P. Klein, *Guide to the Heath Chap.* (1990), 11; Heref. Dioc. Regy., reg. 1926–38, pp. 589–91; S.R.O. 4208/140.

39 *S.P.R. Heref.* xix (5), 80, 84, 98–101, 103, 105–8, 110–11, and index s.v. Bottrell.

40 Ibid. (1), 16–17, 22–3, 25–6, 29–31, 33, 40, 42, 52, 56, 71–2, 82.

41 In 1846: P.R.O., IR 29/29/154; IR 30/29/154, field 52.

42 H.W.R.O.(H.), HD 2/10/31.

43 S.P.L., MS. 6862, f. 73v.; P.R.O., HO 129/352, no. 47.

44 Heref. Dioc. Regy., reg. 1919–26, p. 222; *Crockford* (1930), 749; (1940), 653.

45 *Crockford* (1977–9), 504, 707; (1989–90), 321, 441.

46 Heref. Dioc. Regy., reg. 1969– (in use), pp. 457–8; above, Stoke St. Milborough, church.

47 H.W.R.O.(H.), HD 5/15, Stoke St. Milborough.

48 S.P.L., MS. 6862, f. 73; W.S.L. 350/3/40, Stoke St. Milborough p. 4; S. Bagshaw, *Dir. Salop.* (1851), 552; *P.O. Dir. Salop.* (1879), 418.

times went to Stoke.[49] In the later 20th century services were twice monthly.[50] Four families attended regularly in 1965.[51]

The mid 12th-century chapel, of no known dedication, is a 'perfect example of a small Norman church'.[52] It consists of a rectangular chancel and a nave with south doorway, each of two bays. The walls are of grey siltstone rubble with ashlar dressings of yellowish sandstone; the contrasting colours were formerly disguised by rendering and whitewash, which was mostly removed by 1790 but traces of which remained *c.* 1900.[53] Masons' marks occur on some of the dressed stones. The only external decoration is on the doorway, where there are chevron mouldings on the arch and hoodmould and incised abstract patterns on the capitals; on the inner west capital they seem to form a face.[54] On the tympanum faint 'incised cross lines' were reported in the 1890s.[55] The two iron hinge straps on the door may be 12th-century. Two small lights in the west gable presumably lit an upper compartment or gallery within. Such a feature at the west end may explain why the south doorway was sited so far east that the middle buttress of the south wall is east of its northern counterpart. A ledge over the chancel arch probably supported the nave roof's eastern tiebeam. The chancel arch, of three plain orders, has scalloped capitals. A plain rectangular recess in the chancel south wall may represent a former piscina but has no drain hole. The cylindrical tub font is plain but for shallow incised arcading round part of the top; lines in a spandrel on the north side seem to form a face. The font stood by 1852 on one square stone platform set diagonally upon another.[56]

In the later Middle Ages the upper walls were covered with paintings; St. George is recognizable on the south nave wall. There was a chancel screen: a crested and moulded beam has been re-used as a sill beneath pews in the nave and chancel. The hoodmould over the chancel arch has been interrupted at the top, as if to accommodate a vertical timber. Plain bench ends at the west end of the nave seem to be medieval or of medieval materials.

In the 16th or 17th century the nave roof was renewed, perhaps completely. A flat plaster ceiling was made in the chancel. In chancel and nave medieval paintings were whitewashed over and texts were painted, at least on the lower walls; they included the Commandments and Creed in the nave, and were themselves later whitewashed over. In the 17th century a rail was placed on three sides of the communion table. A pew incorporating medieval materials, including a beam from the former chancel screen and a crude tulip shaped finial, was introduced on the south side of the chancel, facing the pulpit; the chancel had three pews in 1793.[57] The pulpit is a 17th-century two-decker in the north-east angle of the nave, lit by an original north window enlarged in the 17th century to a square opening. Nave pews, some carved to match the pulpit, were introduced at the same time.

A small vertical opening was made at the top of the west gable, evidently for a small bell that hung inside by the 1730s.[58] One window had a little ancient stained glass in 1863. In 1870 flags were laid and the shafts of the doorway were replaced. The door lost one of its three hinge straps in the later 19th century.[59] In 1912 the chancel ceiling was removed and a new chancel roof built; the remaining chancel pew was moved to the north side to make it face the altar;[60] and some of the wall paintings were exposed.

The plate consists of an unmarked Elizabethan silver chalice and a silver paten of 1720.[61] A marriage register, the only register kept at the Heath chapel, begins in 1922.[62]

CHARITY FOR THE POOR. The Heath shared in George Morgan's charity.[63]

MUCH WENLOCK

CENTRED on a very small market town, 18 km. south-east of Shrewsbury and 11 km. north-west of Bridgnorth, Much Wenlock parish is rural in character.[64] Formerly the administrative centre of an ancient borough,[65] the town has not grown much since the 17th century and, though it has not stagnated, Much Wenlock has given nostalgic visitors the impression that it 'belongs in spirit wholly to the past'.[66]

49 S.P.L., MS. 6862, f. 73.

50 *Shrews. Chron.* 28 Aug. 1959, p. [1]; *The Lectern* (Summer 1990), 13 (copy in S.P.L., class Q 97 v.f.).

51 S.R.O. 3756/95, Revd. E. E. Lewis to L. C. Lloyd 5 June 1965.

52 Pevsner, *Salop.* 147; pl. 9. Following descr. based on Klein, *Heath Chap.*

53 S.P.L., MS. 372, vol. ii, f. 36; S.P.L., 2 photos. of S. doorway, Cranage, ii, pl. XVI.

54 S.P.L., 2 photos. of S. doorway (pre-1912). Carvings since decayed.

55 *Woolhope Trans.* (1893–4), 9.

56 T. Wright, *Hist. Ludlow* (1852), 100.

57 S.P.L., MS. 6862, f. 73v.

58 Birm. Univ. Libr., Mytton Papers, iv. 734. Prob. that descr. in H. B. Walters, *Ch. Bells of Salop.* (Oswestry, 1915), 110.

59 Wright, *Hist. Ludlow*, 100; Cranage, ii, pl. XVI.

60 'The Heath', *West of the Clee*, v (7), 6–7 (copy in S.P.L., class QK 97 v.f.).

61 D. L. Arkwright and B. W. Bourne, *Ch. Plate Archd. Ludlow* (Shrews. 1961), 32. For paten cf. Stoke St. Milborough's: ibid. 57.

62 At the chapel.

63 Above, Stoke St. Milborough, charity.

64 This article was written 1985–7 and revised in 1993.

65 Above, Lib. and Boro. of Wenlock.

66 *Country Life*, 7 Apr. 1977, p. 830.

The parish of *c.* 1831, the subject of this article, was aligned south-west to north-east. It was the remnant of a much larger parish, from which chapelries had been lost when severed to become distinct parishes.[67] The parish boundary of *c.* 1831 enclosed 8,770 a.[68] (3,590 ha.) and seven townships: Atterley and Walton; Bourton; Callaughton; Farley, Wyke, and Bradley; Harley (part), Wigwig, and Homer; Presthope; and Much Wenlock.[69] That part of the parish in Harley, Wigwig, and Homer township included 20 small detachments intermingled with Harley parish,[70] to which the detachments, 111 a. (45 ha.), were transferred in 1883, when Much Wenlock gained *c.* 1 a. from Benthall civil parish;[71] there were no changes thereafter.

The townships approximated to drainage basins. Harley brook enters the Severn at Sheinton. Farley brook, rising at Westwood and there called the Rhe in the 16th century,[72] flows through the town to the Severn at Buildwas. Wyke's Arnegreave brook[73] flows through Hunger Dale to the Severn. Callaughton drains, by means of Callaughton brook and its tributaries, towards Mor brook, as do Atterley and Walton by means of Beggarhill and Walton brooks respectively. Presthope and Bourton drain through several streams to the Corve.

The parish lies on sedimentary strata tilted slightly down from north-west to south-east.[74] On the north-west the Wenlock Limestone outcrops as Wenlock Edge, a continuous ridge parallel to the parish boundary in the townships of Presthope, Much Wenlock, and Farley, Wyke, and Bradley; there is a smaller outcrop immediately north of the town. The deep overlying Lower Ludlow Shales form both the extensive lower ground immediately east of Wenlock Edge and the upward slope of the Downs towards Shirlett, and thus cover most of the remaining parts of the townships just mentioned. There is a drift deposit of boulder clay over much of the Lower Ludlow Shales. The shales are overlain by the Aymestry Group (siltstones and limestone), which outcrops as a watershed east of, and parallel to, Wenlock Edge; it thus broadly divides Atterley and Walton, Bourton, and Callaughton townships from the rest of the parish. South-east of the watershed, on the south-facing slopes of those townships, the strata overlying the Aymestry Group appear successively from north-west to south-east. They are the Upper Ludlow Shales, which occur in Bourton and Much Wenlock townships; the shallow Temeside Shales around Walton; and the Ledbury Group (marls with sandstone bands) in Atterley, Callaughton, and Bradeley. Homer and Wigwig, isolated west of and below Wenlock Edge, lie over Wenlock Shale, covered with drift deposits of boulder clay and sand and gravel and, at the foot of the Edge, a head of sandy, silty clay. The parish's soils, mainly acid loams,[75] were mostly graded 2 and 3 in the 1970s, grade 3 predominating north of the town.[76]

Finds of Neolithic and Bronze Age implements[77] indicate early settlement and long-distance contacts, and it appears that the area enjoyed some prosperity in the Roman period. A bronze brooch[78] and a hoard of more than 3,000 coins, apparently deposited in the late 3rd century,[79] have been found on the south-eastern slope of Henmoor hill near Westwood Farm. The land attached to a villa[80] at Yarchester (in Harley) presumably included the neighbouring part of Wigwig called Harchester.[81] There may have been a pre-Christian religious site at Much Wenlock. Its Christian holy wells[82] may represent a former pagan water cult,[83] and a Romano-British sculpture of a Celtic deity was stored with medieval sculpture fragments on the site of Wenlock priory in 1911.[84]

A room (believed to be of Romano-British type)[85] on the site of the priory church[86] seems to have been part of a continuous range, possibly also Romano-British.[87] The room's eastward orientation, and the veneration implied when a medieval church was built centrally over it, support the suggestion that it was used by Romano-British Christians within the large house that the range would imply.[88] If there was a large Romano-British house, it could have been the centre of the estate that was conveyed to St. Mildburg in the late 7th century under the name 'Wininicas'.[89] Burials provisionally dated to the 3rd–5th and 5th–7th centuries have been found south of Barrow Street;[90] an unfurnished grave, oriented east–west and aligned upon a pot and two bowls that may have been Romano-British, was found in 1855 in the centre of the priory's Lady chapel;[91] and a sherd of Samian pottery of the 1st or 2nd century was found in 1993 in excavations immediately south of the Raven inn in Barrow Street.[92]

67 Below, churches.
68 O.S. *Area Bk.* (1883).
69 S.R.O. 294/1, 3–7; fig. 43.
70 O.S. *Area Bk.* (1883), 13–23. The whole of Harley is treated in *V.C.H. Salop.* viii. 85–92.
71 Divided Parishes and Poor Law Amendment Act, 1882, 45 & 46 Vic. c. 58; O.S. *Area Bk.* (1883; with amendment slip).
72 Leland, *Itin.* ed. Toulmin Smith, ii. 84.
73 So called 1592: S.R.O. 1224/3/117.
74 Para. based on Geol. Surv. Maps 1", drift, sheets 152 (1932 edn.), 166 (1967 edn.); Inst. Geol. Sciences Maps 1/25,000, *Telford* (1978 edn.); SO 59 *Wenlock Edge* (1969 edn.)
75 Soil Surv. Map 1", sheet 166 (1964 edn.).
76 Min. of Ag. Fish. and Food, Agric. Land Classificn. Maps 1", sheets 118 (1971 edn.), 129 (1973 edn.).
77 SA 923, 2755, 2966, 3576.
78 *Jnl. Roman Studies*, xxi. 226.
79 *Salop. News Sheet*, ix. 6.
80 *Salop. Newsletter*, ii. 1–2; iv. 1–2; *T.C.S.V.F.C.* xvi. 53, 70; *Shropshire Mag.* July 1962, 24–5; G. Webster, *The Cornovii* (1991), 98–9.
81 S.R.O. 294/5, fields 1351–2, 1354; 1709/55/1.
82 Below, this section.
83 Dr. M. C. Horton's suggestion.
84 S.P.L., Frith neg. 34. It was in M. Wenlock Mus. by 1990.
85 E. Fernie, *Archit. of Ang.-Saxons* (1983), 64–5, 72; *Med. Arch.* xxvii. 203; xxix. 237.
86 Reported in *T.S.A.S.* 3rd ser. ii. 407–8; *Archaeologia*, lxxii. 107–8 (which recognized its affinity with the 'Roman apse tradition' but suggested a 7th-cent. date).
87 *Med. Arch.* xxvii. 203; H. M. Woods, 'Excavations at Wenlock priory, 1981–6', *Jnl. Brit. Arch. Assoc.* cxl. 58–65; cf. ibid. cxli. 178–81.
88 Fig. 41; cf. C. Thomas, *Christianity in Roman Brit.* (1981), 104–6, 158, 166, 180–3.
89 Below, manors.
90 *T.S.A.S.* lxiv. 111–13; *Jnl. Brit. Arch. Assoc.* cxl. 38–9.
91 *Arch. Cambrensis*, 4th ser. iv. 374–81.
92 *Bridgnorth Jnl.* 12 Nov. 1993, p. 7.

St. Mildburg's well was mentioned in Barrow Street in the 13th century[93] and was said *c.* 1730 to be 'in a little narrow lane turning out of Barrow Street'.[94] It was possibly that mapped in 1882 as 'St. Milburga's well'[95] in the lane once called Rowsell (later St. Milburga's Row);[96] the well-head may be partly medieval.[97] In 1897, however, the traditional name of that well was said to be Wimperis well.[98] Another well in Barrow Street[99] has a medieval roof[1] and is named 'St. Milburga's well' on a stone placed over it in 1897.[2] St. Mildburg's well was venerated at Rogationtide by the monks of Wenlock in the early 16th century.[3] St. Owen's well[4] was mentioned in Mardol Lane in 1546.[5] Steps led down to the spring. Closed in the 19th century, it was reopened and restored in 1897.[6] It seems likely that the dedicatee was St. Ouen (d. 684), adviser to St. Baldhild, foundress of the convent at Chelles (Seine-et-Marne)[7] in which St. Mildburg was probably educated.[8] It was reported in 1905 that on Maundy Thursday young men used to carry branches round the town, stopping at St. Mildburg's well, where girls would throw in pins and wish for sweethearts while the youths drank beer brewed from water off the church roof. The well water was also believed to cure sore eyes,[9] as was that of the Shady well, which stood in 1897 among bushes by Shadwell quarry near the railway.[10]

James I was said to have stayed at the Talbot and touched for the King's Evil.[11] Charles I, *en route* from Shrewsbury to Bridgnorth, reached Much Wenlock on 12 October 1642[12] and is said to have slept at Ashfield Hall.[13] Royalist cavalry under Sir William Vaughan was reported to have beaten Parliamentarian cavalry at Much Wenlock on 9 May 1645.[14] Later that year the rearguard of the royal army, going to Bridgnorth, spent the night of 30 September at Much Wenlock.[15] Thomas Smalman, a Royalist officer, was said to have escaped his enemies by leaping on horseback over a precipice near Stretton Westwood, called Major Smallman's Leap by the 1830s.[16] Ann ('Nanny') Morgan (d. 1857)[17] of Westwood was feared as a witch; after she was killed by a lodger her books and papers were burnt on the mayor's order.[18] In 1949 local people participated in the filming in south Shropshire of *Gone to Earth*,[19] directed by Michael Powell and Emeric Pressburger,[20] an event vividly remembered in Much Wenlock 40 years later.

Distinguished natives include Walter of Wenlock, abbot of Westminster 1283–1307,[21] and John Bill (1576–1630), one of the king's printers 1617–30.[22] Dr. William Penny Brookes (1809–95), a native and lifelong resident, campaigned for compulsory physical education in schools and contributed to the international Olympic movement.[23] In Much Wenlock he was a leading figure in the formation of the gas, railway, and market companies and of the library and museum.[24] W. W. Hull (1794–1873), liturgical writer and hymnologist, lived at Tickwood Hall from 1846,[25] and the novelist and poet Mary Webb (1881–1927), *née* Meredith, lived at the Grange 1882–96.[26]

COMMUNICATIONS. One of the principal medieval roads from London to Shrewsbury, by Worcester and Bridgnorth, crossed the parish and passed the edge of the town.[27] The Bridgnorth–Shrewsbury section was also part of the Bristol–Chester road *c.* 1360[28] and in 1480,[29] and

93 Nott. Univ. Libr. MSS. Dept., Mi. D. 3705.
94 Birm. Univ. Libr., Mytton Papers, vii. 1524.
95 At O.S. Nat. Grid SO 6253 9983: O.S. Map, 1/2,500, Salop. L. 8 (1882 edn.).
96 S.P.L., MS. 4131, 'Names and position[s] of places in M. Wenlock'.
97 SA 325.
98 S.P.L., MS. 4131.
99 At O.S. Nat. Grid SO 6243 9990.
1 Inf. from Dr. Horton.
2 C. G. Milnes Gaskell's est. diary, p. 110 (in private hands; Mr. W. M. Motley kindly arranged access).
3 *Shropshire Mag.* Sept. 1969, 28.
4 O.S. Nat. Grid SO 6228 9998.
5 *T.S.A.S.* vi. 105.
6 C. G. Milnes Gaskell's est. diary, p. 110.
7 D. H. Farmer, *Oxf. Dict. of Saints* (1978), 32, 308. For other poss. dedicatees see T. Kerslake, 'St. Ewen, Bristol, and the Welsh border', *Jnl. Brit. Arch. Assoc.* xxxi. 154–7; Bede, *Hist. Eccl.* ed. B. Colgrave and R. A. B. Mynors (1969), 338.
8 H. P. R. Finberg, *Early Charters of W. Midlands* (1972), pp. 207–9, 220.
9 C. Milnes Gaskell, *Spring in a Salop. Abbey* (1905), 61–2.
10 S.P.L., MS. 4131.
11 H. E. Forrest, *Old Hos. of Wenlock* (Shrews. 1914), 27.
12 H. Owen and J. B. Blakeway, *Hist. Shrews.* (1825), i. 430.
13 [J. Randall], *Randall's Tourist's Guide to Wenlock* ([Madeley], 1875), 12 (citing docs. in possession of earl of Dudley); *T.S.A.S.* 3rd ser. v, p. *x* (citing boro. rec. seen by W. P. Brookes). Elsewhere Chas.'s stay at Ashfield Hall is dated *c.* 1630: *P.O. Dir. Salop.* (1879), 434. Derivation of the name Audience meadow at Tickwood from a supposed audience given by Chas. I (*Kelly's Dir. Salop.* (1900), 272) is groundless: Over and Nether Auden existed there by 1592 (S.R.O. 1224/3/135).
14 *T.S.A.S.* 4th ser. ii. 283.
15 *Diary of Marches of Royal Army* (Camd. Soc. [1st ser.], lxxiv), 244.
16 At O.S. Nat. Grid SO 593 985: *Salop. Folk-Lore*, ed. C. S. Burne (1883), 14; *T.S.A.S.* 3rd ser. iii. 4–6; *Shropshire Mag.* Jan. 1955, 16–17; Apr. 1955, 23.
17 S.R.O. 3597/37, 17 Sept. 1857 (ref. supplied by Mr. O. G. McDonald).
18 Burne, *Salop. Folk-Lore*, 160–2; C. Milnes Gaskell, 'Old Wenlock and its folklore', *Nineteenth Cent.* xxv (1894), 264–5.
19 Fred. Brown, *Silver Screen Memories* (Shrews. 1984), 10.
20 M. Powell, *A Life in Movies* (1986), 32; idem, *Million-Dollar Movie* (1992), 65–74.
21 E. H. Pearce, *Wal. de Wenlok, abbot of Westminster* (1920), 49–50, 62–3.
22 *Dict. of Printers and Booksellers in Eng., Scot. and Irel. 1557–1640*, ed. R. B. McKerrow (1910), 31–3; *N. & Q.* 8th ser. xi. 282–3.
23 C. R. Hill, *Olympic Politics* (1992), 9–15; D. C. Young, *The Modern Olympics: a Struggle for Revival* (1996). Mr. McDonald is thanked for drawing attention to these sources.
24 *Shrews. Chron.* 13 Dec. 1895, p. 6; *V.C.H. Salop.* i. 54; pl. 36; below, communications; socal and cultural activities; econ. hist. (mkts. and fairs); public services.
25 *D.N.B.*
26 G. M. Coles, *The Flower of Light: biog. of Mary Webb* (1978), 19–38.
27 B. P. Hindle, 'Road network of medieval Eng. and Wales', *Jnl. of Hist. Geog.* ii. 220; J. Ogilby, *Britannia*, i (1675), pl. 50; fig. 43.
28 *Map of Gt. Brit. known as the Gough Map*, ed. E. J. S. Parsons (1970), 36.
29 Wm. Worcestre, *Itin.* ed. Harvey, 331; *V.C.H. Salop.* iv. 71.

may have been the Bridgnorth–Shrewsbury route used in 1102.[30] It crossed Wenlock Edge at Harley hill (called Wenlock Pitch in 1675),[31] which was already noted *c.* 1190 as a difficult gradient.[32] It was probably in the early Middle Ages, when the town came into existence,[33] that the road, as it approached from Shrewsbury, was diverted into the main street. Thereafter the ancient continuation to Bridgnorth had the appearance of a side road until the earlier 20th century, when a remodelling of the junction, next to the Gaskell Arms, restored its priority.[34] The Bridgnorth–Shrewsbury road had presumably been eclipsed as a London–Shrewsbury route in 1726, when the Shifnal–Wellington–Shrewsbury road was turnpiked,[35] but it remained the principal Bath–Worcester–Shrewsbury road[36] and was turnpiked in 1752.[37]

Other early thoroughfares radiated from Much Wenlock market place. One of them ran north along Sheinton Street to Lawleys Cross[38] and thence[39] over the Severn by Buildwas bridge to Little Wenlock, Madeley, and Shifnal.[40] It was turnpiked to Strethill Farm (in Madeley) in 1756.[41]

The Iron Bridge, opened in 1780, provided a Bridgnorth–Shrewsbury route that passed through Broseley instead of by Much Wenlock.[42] The Much Wenlock trustees, however, anticipated the bridge in 1779[43] by turnpiking the lane from their Buildwas bridge road at Gleedon hill through Sheinton to the road between Much Wenlock and Shrewsbury at Cressage;[44] that route avoided Harley hill but without diverting Shrewsbury traffic from Much Wenlock. The ensuing rivalry between the Iron Bridge and Much Wenlock coaching routes was not resolved before coaching itself declined.[45]

An early road ran east from the market place along Barrow Street to the Marsh (in Barrow), whence two branches led to Broseley, one through Posenhall and the main one through Barrow. Another branch led from the Marsh through Hangstree Gate (in Barrow) to Swinney ferry on the Severn near Caughley,[46] and another, the way to Aldenham in 1262,[47] led from the Marsh through Shirlett to Bridgnorth.[48]

The route from Much Wenlock to Broseley via Posenhall was turnpiked in 1756. At the same time the Marsh–Bridgnorth road was turnpiked, not on its earlier line but through Hangstree Gate and Willey to the Broseley–Bridgnorth road.[49] Before 1808 the turnpiked route between the Marsh and Willey was altered to go through Barrow.[50] By 1827 the section of that road between Barrow and Nordley common was disturnpiked. The Barrow–Broseley road, however, was by then newly turnpiked and thus provided an alternative turnpike from Much Wenlock to Broseley.[51]

An early road led south-west from the market place along Spittle Street to Bourton[52] and thence ran the length of Corve Dale. It was the road to Ludlow by the 13th century.[53] It was called St. Mildburg Way south of Bourton in 1332,[54] perhaps from the monks' annual Whitsun procession into the countryside, carrying St. Mildburg's relics.[55] In Much Wenlock it was called Bourton Lane by 1736.[56] In 1756 it was turnpiked as far as the borough boundary at Beambridge (in Munslow).[57]

Parallel roads, mentioned in 1262,[58] led south-west along Wenlock Edge to Presthope from the road between Much Wenlock and Shrewsbury at the Bank. Called Upper and Lower Green Lane,[59] they converged on Presthope common, whence a road continued along the Edge[60] past Easthope.[61] In 1765 the Lower Green Lane was turnpiked to Presthope with its continuation thence to the Shrewsbury–Ludlow turnpike at Church Stretton.[62]

Settlements not on the main thoroughfares were mostly served by their own lanes from the town centre. The way to Wyke and Bradley was called Wyke (or Bradley) Lane in 1652.[63] Atterley and Walton were reached by Atterley Way.[64] St. Mary Way[65] or Mary Lane[66] (later St. Mary's Lane and Racecourse Road), continued by Callaughton Lane,[67] led to Callaughton.[68] In 1715 there was a 'church way' from Wigwig to Much Wenlock;[69] but by 1847 the usual road to Wigwig was over Homer common from the Buildwas bridge road.[70] In the 18th century Bradeley was accessible through Bourton.[71]

Other lanes helped to link settlements to outlying resources. Westwood common was

30 *Eccl. Hist. of Orderic Vitalis*, ed. M. Chibnall, vi. 28.
31 J. Ogilby, *Britannia*, i (1675), p. 100 and pl. 50.
32 *Giraldi Cambrensis Opera* (Rolls Ser.), vi. 146.
33 Below, growth of settlement.
34 O.S. Maps 1/2,500, Salop. L. 12 (1926 edn.); 6", SO 69 NW. (1954 edn.).
35 12 Geo. I, c. 9.
36 N. Cossons and B. Trinder, *The Iron Bridge* (1979), 40.
37 25 Geo. II, c. 49.
38 S.R.O. 1224/1/19; N.L.W., Wynnstay, MS. Plans 1.
39 The way to Buildwas *c.* 1540: N.L.W., Wynnstay, RA 5.
40 *V.C.H. Salop.* xi. 24–5, 77, 81.
41 29 Geo. II, c. 60.
42 Cossons and Trinder, *Iron Bridge*, 39.
43 *Shrews. Chron.* 28 Aug. 1779.
44 Under 18 Geo. III, c. 89.
45 Cossons and Trinder, *Iron Bridge*, 39–40.
46 S.R.O. 1224/1/10, 14.
47 P.R.O., C 143/2, no. 16.
48 S.R.O. 1224/1/14.
49 29 Geo. II, c. 60.
50 R. Baugh, *Map of Salop.* (1808).
51 C. & J. Greenwood, *Map of Salop.* (1827).
52 Nott. Univ. Libr. MSS. Dept., Mi. D. 3740.
53 S.R.O. 3195/1, f. 31.
54 S.R.O. 1224/2/11.
55 Recorded *c.* 1163: *Jnl. Brit. Arch. Assoc.* 3rd ser. iv. 124.
56 N.L.W., Wynnstay, box 43/86.
57 29 Geo. II, c. 60.
58 P.R.O., C 143/2, no. 16.
59 N.L.W., Wynnstay, box 56/6.
60 S.R.O. 3657/1.
61 N.L.W., Wynnstay, L 1306, 28 Apr. 1726.
62 5 Geo. III, c. 86.
63 S.R.O. 840, box 1, ct. r. 21 Oct. 1652; *T.S.A.S.* vi. 122; N.L.W., Wynnstay, MS. Plans 1.
64 N.L.W., Wynnstay, box 43/3; S.R.O. 775/86; 1093, parcel 161, Atterley and Walton map of 1722; 1224/2/104.
65 S.R.O. 1037/19/1.
66 *T.S.A.S.* vi. 118, 125.
67 Nott. Univ. Libr. MSS. Dept., Mi. D. 3760; S.R.O., q. sess. rec. parcel 283, reg. of enrolled incl. awards, p. 26.
68 Ogilby, *Britannia*, i, pl. 50; Callaughton map of 1796 (in Mr. J. R. Craig's possession).
69 S.R.O. 1224/2/161.
70 S.R.O. 294/5.
71 W.B.R., M10/22.

reached from Much Wenlock by Westwood Lane, mentioned in 1554,[72] and from Bourton over Henmoor hill. Bourton[73] and Callaughton[74] were linked to Spoonhill wood, Atterley and Walton to Shirlett (in Barrow),[75] and Wyke to Tickwood.[76]

The parish's turnpike roads were disturnpiked in 1867 except for the Bridgnorth–Shrewsbury road, which was disturnpiked in 1875[77] and declared a main road in 1878.[78] Within the civil parish and beyond the town's streets the rest, except the Posenhall and Sheinton roads, were declared main in 1889;[79] where they formed streets they were declared main in 1893.[80] Only the Bridgnorth–Shrewsbury road was a Ministry of Transport class A road.[81]

In 1862[82] the locally promoted Much Wenlock & Severn Junction Railway Co. opened a single-track line from Much Wenlock to the Severn Valley Railway at Buildwas, with a short spur beyond it to the Severn.[83] From Buildwas Much Wenlock limestone could be carried on the Severn Valley line towards ironworks in the west midlands[84] or by river to local ironworks.

Meanwhile in 1861 the Wenlock Railway Co., also promoted locally,[85] was incorporated to extend the line at both ends:[86] northwards across the Severn to Coalbrookdale, whence the G.W.R. would continue it to a junction (in Madeley) with its own Madeley branch and with the Wellington & Severn Junction Railway, and southwards through Presthope to Craven Arms (in Stokesay) via a junction with the Shrewsbury & Hereford Railway at Marsh Farm (in Wistanstow).[87] The extensions would not only ease the transport of local limestone to the east Shropshire coalfield but also, it was claimed, connect Much Wenlock with South Wales, Staffordshire, and Birmingham.[88] The extensions opened in 1864, but the southward line reached only to Presthope until its continuation to Marsh Farm opened in 1867.[89]

There were stations at Much Wenlock and Presthope.[90] Lack of a direct connexion with the eastern part of the coalfield,[91] and a falling demand for fluxing limestone,[92] prevented the line from fulfilling its promoters' highest hopes. In 1896 ownership passed to the G.W.R. To meet road competition halts were added at Farley (1934) and Westwood (1935). Passenger services ceased between Much Wenlock and Craven Arms in 1951 and between Much Wenlock and Buildwas in 1962. Freight services between Buildwas and Longville (in Eaton-under-Heywood) ended in 1963 when the line closed.[93]

GROWTH OF SETTLEMENT. Much Wenlock was the parish's only large settlement. Elsewhere only Bourton and Callaughton, and later Farley and Homer, ever comprised more than a handful of dwellings; several settlements shrank after the 17th century. In the 16th century settlements were usually nucleated but with outlying farms or cottages, especially near large woods, and were normally sited between 135 m. and 185 m. and near streams; they often avoided the highest and lowest ground. The two main periods of post-medieval cottage building on common wastes were in the 17th and in the late 18th and 19th centuries. Farley, Homer, and Wenlock Bank were settled almost entirely in that way.

MUCH WENLOCK TOWN. The three main streets from the Middle Ages onwards were Spittle[94] (later High[95] or Hospital) Street, Barrow[96] (formerly Southpool)[97] Street, and Wilmore[98] (continued northwards as Sheinton)[99] Street. They formed a **T**, its junction at an entrance (the 'churchyard stile')[1] to Holy Trinity churchyard; the main streets seem unrelated to the site of the 11th-century priory.[2] It is likely that before the Conquest the people of the district were using worship at Holy Trinity as an opportunity for weekly trade; Sunday was market day until 1224.[3] The building of permanent shops on the approaches to the churchyard set the medieval street pattern and made the beginnings of a town.

72 P.R.O., SC 2/197/148, m. 6; N.L.W., Wynnstay, box 43/139; box 56/6 (marking it incorrectly as the Ch. Stretton turnpike); S.R.O., q. sess. rec. parcel 283, reg. of enrolled incl. awards, p. 33.
73 W.B.R., M10/22.
74 Hull Univ., Brynmor Jones Libr., DDFA/26/120; Callaughton map of 1796 (in Mr. J. R. Craig's possession).
75 S.R.O. 1093, parcel 161, Atterley and Walton map of 1722; 1224/1/10, 14.
76 The 'way in Alden' 1611 (S.R.O. 1224/3/127–8), located from S.R.O. 294/4, fields 1675–6.
77 Ann. Turnpike Acts Continuance Acts, 1867, 30 & 31 Vic. c. 121; 1873, 36 & 37 Vic. c. 90.
78 Highways & Locomotives (Amendment) Act, 1878, 41 & 42 Vic. c. 77.
79 *S.C.C. Mins.* Main Roads and Bridges Cttee. rep. 27 Apr. 1889; S.R.O., S.C.C. min. bk. 1889–93, pp. 28–9.
80 W.B.R., B3/5/97.
81 O.S. Maps 1/25,000, SJ 60 (1958 edn.); SO 69 (1956 edn.).
82 P.R.O., RAIL 502/2, p. 82.
83 M. Wenlock & Severn Junction Rly. Act, 1859, 22 & 23 Vic. c. 26 (Local and Personal); S.R.O., dep. plan 375.
84 P.R.O., RAIL 502/2, p. 161.
85 S.R.O. 809, box 12, proof of John Fowler.
86 Wenlock Rly. Act, 1861, 24 & 25 Vic. c. 189 (Local and Personal); S.R.O., dep. plan 385.
87 G.W.R. (Lightmoor to Coalbrookdale, &c.) Act, 1861, 24 & 25 Vic. c. 204 (Local and Personal); S.R.O. dep. plan 386; *Eddowes's Jnl.* 25 July 1860.
88 S.R.O. 809, box 12, prospectus of 1860.
89 E. T. MacDermot, *Hist. of G.W.R.* ed. C. R. Clinker, ii (1964), 308.
90 J. M. Tolson, 'In the Tracks of the Iron Masters', *Railway Mag.* cxi. 375.
91 H.L.R.O., Bks. of Evid. 'Mins. of Evid. Sel. Cttee. on M. Wenlock & Severn Junction Rly. Bill' (1873), 20 June, pp. 10, 13, 114, 132.
92 Below, econ. hist. (quarries).
93 *Railway Mag.* cxi. 377, 440, 444; above, Longville, etc., intro.
94 By 1316: Nott. Univ. Libr. MSS. Dept., Mi. D. 3727.
95 By 1736: N.L.W., Wynnstay, M 2530 (transcript provided by the late Mr. V. H. Deacon).
96 By 1355: Nott. Univ. Libr. MSS. Dept., Mi. D. 3767.
97 By *c.* 1300: ibid. 3705. Identified with Barrow St. by comparison of deeds of 1444, 1496, and 1602 in S.R.O. 3614, box 11. Evid. of a pool on the N. side of the street at the far end was found by excavation in 1994: inf. from Dr. P. A. Stamper.
98 By 1488: N.L.W., Wynnstay, RA 1.
99 By 1444: S.R.O. 3614, box 11, deed.
1 So called 1558: *T.S.A.S.* vi. 111. Perh. the 'scala cimiterii' mentioned 1386: Nott. Univ. Libr. MSS. Dept., Mi. D. 3809.
2 Figs. 40, 43; pls. 2, 22.
3 *Rot. Litt. Claus.* (Rec. Com.), i. 622.

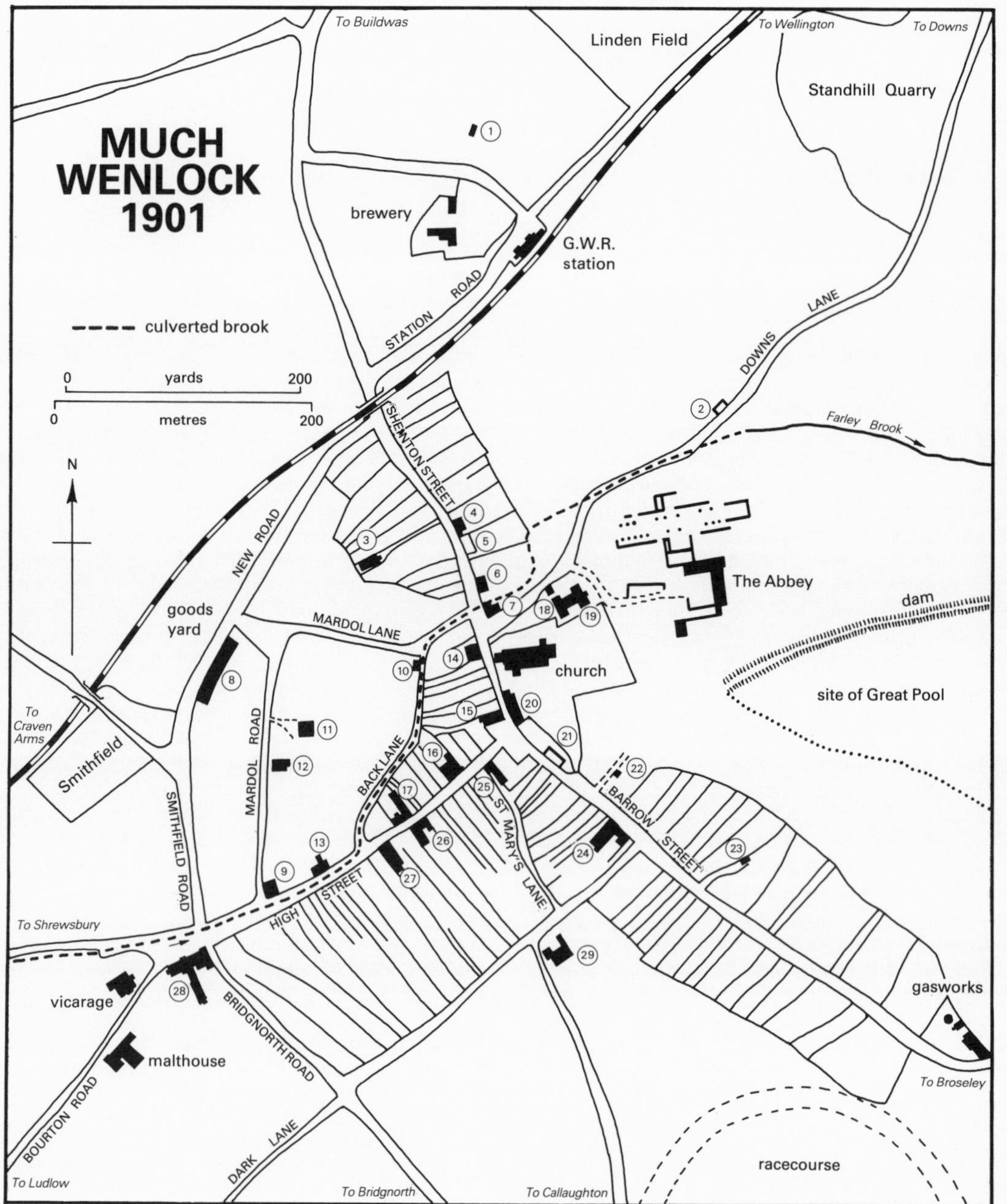

Fig. 40

KEY TO BUILDINGS

1. Pumping station for water.
2. Site of parish workhouse.
3. Wesleyan Methodist chapel.
4. Almshouses.
5. Probable site of Bastard's Hall.
6. Police station.
7. Teacher's house (formerly savings bank).
8. Mardol Terrace.
9. The Wheatland Fox.
10. St. Owen's well.
11. Mardol House.
12. Primitive Methodist chapel.
13. Ashfield Hall (likely site of St. John's hospital).
14. The Stork.
15. Market Hall (on site of glebe houses).
16. Corn Exchange.
17. Reynalds Mansion (formerly White Hart).
18. Tower in priory wall.
19. National school.
20. Guildhall.
21. Site of medieval almshouses.
22. St Mildburg's well (reputed).
23. St. Mildburg's well (reputed).
24. The Raven.
25. The George and Dragon.
26. The Talbot (formerly Abbot's Hall).
27. The Swan & Falcon.
28. The Gaskell Arms.
29. Wenlock Villa.

Encroachment of marketing on the churchyard was apparently followed by the demarcation[4] of distinct market places, the Bull Ring to the north[5] and the junction of Barrow and Wilmore streets to the west. The latter space seems to have been cigar shaped,[6] but by the early 16th century had been narrowed by buildings that encroached on its east side:[7] a house was built *c.* 1421 on part of the horse market, then in the king's highway,[8] and other encroachments included the almshouses (by 1485)[9] and guildhall (begun *c.* 1540).[10] The Bull Ring was likewise narrowed in the 15th or 16th century by encroachment of a row of houses on the south side and, it seems likely, of houses on the north. The principal market place in 1558 was 'at the churchyard stile' before the 'court hall' (guildhall);[11] the pavement next to the hall was the 'heart of the market' in 1624;[12] and in 1671 the 'market house' and adjoining street were the site of the corn market.[13] At that time the markets and fairs were small by Shropshire standards[14] and presumably took up little room.

The borough guildhall[15] had been built *c.* 1540 by the carpenter Richard Dawley[16] over a ground floor then open on all sides and which served as a covered market. In 1577 the building was extended north over the nearby stone gaol by the addition of a smaller second chamber[17] partly supported, like the main hall, on posts. About 1707 the posts under the east and south sides of the building were replaced in brick;[18] under the main hall those brick supports, in their turn, were replaced *c.* 1719[19] by a blind brick arcade (pierced by windows) along the east side and, on the south side, by a brick wall with an arch through it.[20] In 1868 the building was extended south by the addition of a first-floor retiring room, built over a passageway that preserved the site and function of the 'churchyard stile'.[21] The east arcade was later extended north to enclose the basement of the smaller (or council) chamber. The large (or court) room displays the royal arms (1589) on wood, a board commemorating 'this work' in 1678,[22] and a board of that date with Latin motto,[23] none necessarily in its original setting.

The manor's many bordars in 1086[24] probably included town dwellers.[25] By 1247 Much Wenlock town was called a borough. There were 8 free men, 39 burgesses, and a number of customary tenants (*vilani*).[26] There were 32 taxpayers in 1327,[27] about the same number as in Newport and Wellington.[28] In the 19th century long plots ran back from the main streets;[29] they were the remains of medieval burgages. A plot in Southpool Street measured 45 by 174 ft. in 1442.[30] If the traditional siting of St. John's hospital[31] marked the town's western limit, Spittle Street had no houses west of the junction with Back Lane in the early 13th century. Expansion seems to have paused there. Remains of late medieval houses farther west,[32] however, indicate that by *c.* 1500 the south side of Spittle Street was built up as far as the Bridgnorth–Shrewsbury road; west of the traditional hospital site the street is both wider and on a different alignment. The 19th-century pattern of house plots[33] suggests that by *c.* 1500 Barrow and Sheinton streets were built up for as great a length as Spittle Street. Barrow Street, however, seems to have had none of the medieval town's named halls.[34] The plots in Barrow Street east of the Raven are especially uniform and may therefore represent a discrete scheme of planned expansion;[35] pottery unearthed near its east end suggests that it was built up by 1300.[36] Medieval lanes off the main streets included Mary Lane,[37] Mardol Lane,[38] 'Revelone',[39] and 'Wyvelleslone'.[40]

The later medieval houses, of which there are many vestiges,[41] sometimes stood parallel to the street. They were timber framed, of good quality, and usually began as open halls. Other plans

4 A ditch dividing the chyd. from the Bull Ring was found in 1991 by Dr. M. C. Horton.

5 Burials found in the Bull Ring (SA 2919, 3767; *Shropshire Star* (First edn.), 9 Nov. 1983, p. 12) show that at least pt. of it previously occupied pt. of a graveyard.

6 J. N. Croom, 'Topographical analysis of medieval town plans', *Midland Hist.* xvii. 22.

7 Ibid. 31; S. P. Mullins, *M. Wenlock: Hist. Guide* (Salop. Co. Museums inf. sheet 6), [4] (copy in S.P.L., class M 66 v.f.).

8 S.R.O. 1224/2/7.

9 Below, charities.

10 Below, this section.

11 *T.S.A.S.* vi. 111.

12 W.B.R., B3/1/1, p. 537.

13 Ibid. /1/2, f. 18.

14 *V.C.H. Salop.* iv. 162 n.; below, econ. hist. (mkts. and fairs).

15 Pl. 38. So called by 1596: W.B.R., B3/1/1, p. 318. The following descr. owes much to F. W. B. Charles, *Conservation of Timber Bldgs.* (1984), 172–92, but interprets the evid. differently.

16 W.B.R., B3/1/1, p. 144. He may have been the carpenter of that name who d. 1594: S.R.O. 3898/Rg/1, 4 Feb. 1593/4.

17 *T.S.A.S.* xi. 5; pl. 41.

18 W.B.R., B3/1/2, bailiff's acct. 1706–7. One brick pillar remains beneath the SE. corner of the smaller chamber.

19 Ibid. 1719–20.

20 Undated watercolour (copy in M. Wenlock Mus., MW 183) repr. in S. Mullins, *The British Olympians: Wm. Penny Brookes and the Wenlock Games* (Brit. Olympic Assoc. 1986), 11.

21 W.B.R., corpn. min. bk. 1810–74, 3 Feb., 3 Aug. 1868.

22 Probably a ref. to the 'pentice' then erected along the E. side of the bldg. (W.B.R., B3/1/2, f. 34 and bailiff's acct. 1677–8) and since removed.

23 On the motto see *N. & Q.* [1st ser.] ix. 552.

24 *V.C.H. Salop.* i. 312.

25 *Studies in Medieval Hist. presented to R. H. C. Davis*, ed. H. Mayr-Harting and R. I. Moore (1985), 103.

26 *T.S.A.S.* lxvi. 60–2.

27 Ibid. 2nd ser. iv. 325.

28 *T.S.A.S.* i. 173–4.

29 S.R.O. 1931/1.

30 S.R.O. 3614, box 11, deed.

31 Below, charities.

32 Nos. 26–32 (SA 11939) and 48 (SA 11949) High St.

33 S.R.O. 1931/1.

34 Below, this section.

35 Dr. T. R. Slater's suggestion.

36 Inf. from Dr. Horton.

37 By 1322: S.R.O. 1037/19/1. St. Mary's La. by 1791: N.L.W., Wynnstay, box F/1A.

38 By 1321: S.R.O. 1037/19/1. Part later Fox La. (S.R.O. 1242, box 9, draft deed of 1879) or Mardol Rd. (P.R.O., RG 11/2640, ff. 18–19) and later King St. (cf. O.S. Map 1/2,500, Salop. L. 8 (1882 edn.)); other part later Queen St. (S.R.O., reg. of electors, Southern divn. (1904), 530 (no. 510); (1910), 599 (no. 467)).

39 By 1322: S.R.O. 1037/19/1.

40 By 1392: Nott. Univ. Libr. MSS. Dept., Mi. D. 3813.

41 e.g. SA 11908, 11931–2, 11934, 11939, 11949, 11951, 11967, 14307, 15554. Nos. 5–6 Queen St. (SA 11958) date from *c.* 1416: *Vernacular Archit.* xxv. 32, 34. Pt. of no. 15 High St. (SA 11933) was probably built *c.* 1408: ibid. xxiv. 57. Thanks are due to Mrs. M. Moran for much advice on M. Wenlock vernacular archit. during preparation of this section.

occurred. A 15th-century house in Spittle Street[42] may have had shops beneath a first-floor hall; a 13th-century house in Sheinton Street had a service wing parallel to the street and a hall at right angles to it.[43] In the centre, where there was probably pressure on frontage space and a consequent subdivision of plots, no. 23 Barrow Street, built *c.* 1330,[44] and Brook House Farm, Sheinton Street, also had only a short wing parallel to the street, the main hall being at right-angles down the plot.[45] Among the more important medieval houses were Abbot's Hall[46] (later the Talbot),[47] Ashfield Hall,[48] Rindleford Hall (probably the later Gaskell Arms),[49] and Spittle Hall,[50] all in Spittle Street; Basford Hall,[51] probably in the Bull Ring;[52] and Bastard's Hall[53] (unusual in being a stone house)[54] and Doggyns Hall[55] in Sheinton Street. Shops (*selde*) were mentioned in 1329,[56] and two late medieval terraces of uniform cottages or shops are known: one in Barrow Street[57] and a probable one in the Bull Ring,[58] both fronting medieval market places.

By 1284 a weeping cross,[59] called Jilote cross in 1322[60] and later Hamon Weal's cross (then made of wood), stood in Callaughton Lane; it was gone by 1556.[61] The Spital cross was mentioned in the 1520s.[62]

In 1524 Much Wenlock township had 58 taxpayers, perhaps representing a population of 200–400.[63] By 1642, when 206 took the Protestation, the total may be estimated at 600–700.[64] By 1695 it had grown to 1,138.[65] The town's great population increase in the 16th and 17th centuries, and the success of its diverse trades,[66] were reflected by the adaptation and replacement of old houses and by the building of cottages at the ends of the main streets, in back lanes,[67] and in clusters outside the town.

By the early 18th century most houses other than cottages had four to eight rooms, with two to four chambers, and were necessarily two storeyed.[68] Several 17th-century staircases survive.[69] About a fifth of houses had more than eight rooms, and at least a tenth had acquired garrets by insertion of a second floor. Barrow Street, wide and away from the open sewer, then contained houses larger than average, though it never became socially exclusive.[70] The White Hart in Spittle Street,[71] held by John Raynolds, had seven ground-floor rooms, six chambers, and four garrets. It was also called Reynolds Tenement (and later Raynalds Mansion). Formerly a 15th-century hall, it had been enlarged by 1682.[72] Though it was one of the town's largest timber framed houses and had one of the more elaborate façades, its size and embellishments did not rival those of the greater houses in Bridgnorth, Ludlow, or Shrewsbury. The decorative timbering, if of 1682, is a crude and late example of a style already abandoned in more fashionable towns.

By the early 18th century there were many cottages at the north end of Sheinton Street[73] and the west end of Spittle Street. Most had at least two rooms; single storeyed cottages were evidently being converted by the insertion of attic floors.[74] Other groups of cottages were at Westwood common and the Bank. Westwood had 22 cottages in 1736[75] and 29 in 1841, when nearly all inhabitants were farm labourers.[76] At New Town at the Bank, west of the medieval town, cottages clustered around quarries and junctions on the Shrewsbury road, whence lanes branched up to Wenlock Edge.[77] In 1736 there were 49 cottages at New Town, 9 in Bourton Lane, and 8 in nearby Westwood Lane.[78] Agricultural labour and lime burning were the commonest trades among a variety there in 1841.[79]

During the 18th century the town's economy stagnated[80] and its population stopped increasing.[81] Visitors were contemptuous. In 1735 it was called 'a very paltry, dirty town'.[82] In 1769

42 Nos. 55–6 (SA 11961), later Raynalds Mansion.

43 Nos. 55–7 (SA 11967), perh. to be identified with Bastard's Hall: below, this section; *Vernacular Archit.* xxv. 32, 34.

44 *Vernacular Archit.* xxiv. 57.

45 SA 14307; *Shropshire Mag.* July 1984, 23–4; inf. from Mrs. Moran.

46 Mentioned 1391: Nott. Univ. Libr. MSS. Dept., Mi. D. 3812. In Spittle St.: N.L.W., Wynnstay, box 43/2.

47 *T.S.A.S.* vi. 126.

48 Below, manors (M. Wenlock).

49 Ibid.

50 In Spittle St. *c.* 1730: Birm. Univ. Libr., Mytton Papers, vii. 1524.

51 Ibid. 1525 (an addendum that claims it was on the site of the Boar, Spittle St.).

52 In 1700 'Basfords house' lay between the brook and the E. end of the par. ch.: S.R.O. 3898/Rg/2, memo. at end.

53 Mentioned 1530: S.R.O. 1514/369. In Sheinton St.: *T.S.A.S.* vi. 118. Bastard fam. mentioned 1379: S.R.O. 1224/2/2.

54 *T.S.A.S.* vi. 118.

55 Mentioned 1539: N.L.W., Wynnstay, box 43/2. In Sheinton St.: P.R.O., LR 2/184, ff. 79v., 83.

56 *Cal. Pat.* 1327–30, 473.

57 M. Moran, 'A Terrace of Crucks at M. Wenlock', *Vernacular Archit.* xxiii. 10–14; cf. ibid. xxv. 32, 34.

58 Mr. P. J. Drury's suggestion.

59 *Cal. Inq. Misc.* i, p. 605.

60 S.R.O. 1037/19/1.

61 *T.S.A.S.* vi. 125.

62 S.R.O. 1224, box 342, Prior Gosnell's reg. f. 39v.

63 P.R.O., E 179/166/200; cf. *T.S.A.S.* lxiv. 36–8.

64 Ho. of Lords papers 1641–2, Protestations Oxon. and Salop. ff. 197–8; cf. *Compton Census*, ed. Whiteman, p. lxvii.

65 *T.S.A.S.* xi. 55.

66 Below, econ. hist.

67 e.g. surviving examples in King St., St. Mary's La., and Smithfield Rd. (formerly Powke La.: S.R.O. 1242, box 9, draft deed of 1885).

68 Para. based on N.L.W., Wynnstay, box E/62 (surv. of Sir John Wynn's M. Wenlock properties, 1714).

69 e.g. at nos. 12–13 (the Talbot), 15 (the Swan & Falcon, later Barclays Bank), 48, 55–6 (Raynalds Mansion), 61 High St. (SA 11931, 11933, 11949, 11951, 11954); Brook Ho. Fm., Queen St. (SA 15554); 20 (the Manor Ho.), 24 Sheinton St. (SA 11963–4).

70 e.g. P.R.O., HO 107/928/19, ff. 13v.–18.

71 To be distinguished from a later White Hart, which became the Gaskell Arms: below, social and cultural activities.

72 Nos. 55–6 High St. (SA 11951). Earlier 15th-cent. date from dendrochronology: inf. from Mr. D. H. Miles.

73 N.L.W., Wynnstay, L 1306, 10 Oct. 1723; surviving examples.

74 N.L.W., Wynnstay, box E/62; surviving examples.

75 N.L.W., Wynnstay, M. 2530.

76 P.R.O., HO 107/928/18, ff. 40v.–42v.

77 S.R.O. 294/7; surviving examples.

78 N.L.W., Wynnstay, M. 2530.

79 P.R.O., HO 107/928/18, ff. 43v.–50v.

80 Below, econ. hist.

81 S.P.L., MS. 6965, p. 206. It may be estimated at *c.* 1,300 in 1801, i.e. 65 per cent of the par. total (1,981: *V.C.H. Salop.* ii. 229) as in 1695 (*T.S.A.S.* xi. 55) and 1841 (*V.C.H. Salop.* ii. 229).

82 B.L. Add. MS. 5842, f. 132.

it had 'two ill-built streets, and standing low, is so dirty, that strangers, by way of derision, call it Muck Wenlock'.[83] The houses were then mostly old, timber framed, and thatched. Many incorporated limestone rubble or were clad with it, and some cottages were wholly of rubble. A few houses still had roofs of 'slate',[84] probably the flaggy calcareous sandstone called Harnage slate, a fine local material once used to sumptuous effect on the prior's lodging but old fashioned by 1769.[85] Some brick and tile had begun to be used, but a row[86] of three 'handsome well-built' houses with shops, of brick with stone dressings, tiled roof, and sash windows, erected in Barrow Street after 1736, was conspicuously modern in 1769.[87] No improvement was detectable in 1793,[88] when the town seemed 'sunk'.[89]

The parish's population, 1,981 in 1801, increased by 22 per cent to 2,424 by 1831 (having grown 10 per cent in the 1820s alone),[90] a rate of growth not equalled thereafter.[91] The stimulus presumably came from limestone quarrying, itself linked to the then buoyant iron trade.[92] There was much refurbishment and new building on existing sites in the early 19th century, especially in the town centre. By 1817[93] Robert Tovey had built a 'fancy villa' in the 'cottage style', Hoarley Grange[94] (later the Grange), southwest of the town, and in 1823 Wenlock Villa (later Maryway House) was built in St. Mary's Lane.[95] By 1837 the town was 'far from deserving the reproach which has been heaped upon it'.[96]

The parish's population grew little after 1831, however, and between 1871 and 1921 fell 21 per cent (from 2,531 to 1,991),[97] probably a reflection of agricultural and industrial recession.[98] One visitor claimed 'a more somnolent habitation we never saw'.[99] Among the few later 19th-century houses in the town were Mardol House, a detached villa off Fox Lane, built *c.* 1870 for a local ironmonger,[1] and Mardol Terrace, 12 brick cottages built in New Road in 1870.[2] By 1900 the town's lack of modern development was being commended by admirers of the quaint and 'historical',[3] and in the 1980s Much Wenlock was prominent among Shropshire towns for its surviving wealth of medieval domestic timber framing.

Between 1921 and 1951 the parish's population increased 19 per cent to 2,369.[4] The borough council's Wenlock district committee completed the town's first 16 council houses, the Crescent, in 1927,[5] and 98 more had been built by 1939;[6] a further 38 were finished in 1947[7] but many more were needed.[8] The population grew only 9 per cent (to 2,578) 1951–91 but much new building reduced its density.[9] Eighty council houses and flats were completed at Much Wenlock between 1953 and 1964,[10] some designed for old people.[11] Bridgnorth rural district council completed High Causeway (43 houses) in 1972;[12] the few other council houses provided after 1970[13] were for the old.[14] Large-scale private building at Much Wenlock began in the early 1960s with Oakfield Park (59 houses),[15] then Walton Hills (50 houses);[16] Swan Meadow (26 houses) and Sytche Close (13 houses) followed in the 1970s.[17] Twentieth-century housing estates were all at the edges of the town; the picturesque street frontages were preserved, and in 1970 the town centre was designated a conservation area.[18]

THE MONASTIC PRECINCT.[19] The priory's main gateway faced the Bull Ring.[20] The Abbey Gate inhabited in 1662[21] may have been that part of the gateway remaining in 1775[22] and the north-facing gateway mapped in 1820 at the eastern end of the Bull Ring.[23] A 'singular building . . . apparently one of the fortified gates of the priory close' fell down *c.* 1845.[24] In Wilmore Street,[25] probably near the priory gateway, the almonry remained in 1785.[26] It was perhaps part of the large building that was nearly opposite the house called the Priory[27] and was demolished in or after 1847.[28] A plain square medieval tower, mentioned in 1550[29] and used as a pigeon house by 1700,[30]

83 *Descr. of Eng. and Wales*, viii (London, 1769), 54.
84 N.L.W., Wynnstay, L 1288.
85 *T.S.A.S.* lxiv. 116–18. 86 Nos. 19–21 (SA 11905).
87 N.L.W., Wynnstay, L 1288.
88 S.P.L., MS. 6865, p. 206.
89 *Torrington Diaries*, ed. C. Bruyn Andrews, iii. 228.
90 *V.C.H. Salop.* ii. 229.
91 Ibid.; below, this section.
92 *V.C.H. Salop.* xi, *passim*; below, econ. hist. (quarries).
93 B.L. Maps, O.S.D. 207.
94 *Gent. Mag.* c (2), 285; C. Hulbert, *Hist. and Descr. of Salop.* ii (1837), 355.
95 Clwyd R.O. (Ruthin), DD/WY/4471.
96 Hulbert, op. cit. ii. 352.
97 *V.C.H. Salop.* ii. 229. 98 Below, econ. hist.
99 Wal. White, *All Round the Wrekin* (1860), 120.
1 S.R.O. 1242, box 9, draft deed of 1869; draft abstr. of title of R. T. Haynes.
2 Date stone.
3 *Randall's Guide to Wenlock*, 5; H. James, *Eng. Hours* (1905), 217. 4 *V.C.H. Salop.* ii. 229.
5 S.R.O., reg. of electors, Wrekin divn. (1927), 674–92. In this para. hos. are identified as council-built (to 1964) from S.R.O., DA 6/516/26, and (from 1964) from inf. supplied by Bridgnorth Dist. Council.
6 Reg. of electors, Wrekin divn. (1939), 894–918.
7 Ibid. (1947), 386.
8 Boro. of Wenlock, 'Review of Co. Dist. Bdys,' (TS. 1948), 3 (copy in S.R.O. 5112/6/1).
9 *V.C.H. Salop.* ii. 229; *Census*, 1971, *Co. Rep. Salop.* i. 4; *Census*, 1981, Small Area Statistics: Salop.; S.C.C. Property and Planning Services Dept. inf. rep. C91/103.
10 S.R.O., reg. of electors, Ludlow const. (1954), p. 151; (1965), pp. 157–65.
11 Inf. from Bridgnorth Dist. Council.
12 S.R.O., reg. of electors, Ludlow const. (1973), p. 187.
13 Ibid. Bridgnorth dist. (1983), sect. 2CQ, pp. 2–3.
14 Inf. from Bridgnorth Dist. Council.
15 S.R.O., reg. of electors, Ludlow const. (1963), p. 155; (1970), p. 190. 16 Ibid. (1969), pp. 169–70.
17 Ibid. Bridgnorth dist. (1979), p. 186; (1980), sect. 2CQ, p. 4.
18 Under the Civic Amenities Act, 1967, c. 69: *S.C.C. Mins.* 1969–70, 368; 1970–1, 15.
19 Fig. 41. 20 P.R.O., SC 6/Hen. VIII/3021, m. 13.
21 *T.S.A.S.* xi. 39.
22 F. Grose, *Antiquities of Eng. and Wales*, iii (1775), s.v. 'Wenlock monastery'.
23 B.L. Add. MS. 36378, f. 212 (at O.S. Nat. Grid SJ 6240 0006, near the modern entrance to Wenlock Abbey's front drive). 24 *Arch. Jnl.* ii. 87.
25 N.L.W., Wynnstay, RA 5; ibid. box E/62, p. 11. The name was interchangeable with that of the Bull Ring: P.R.O., SC 6/Hen. VIII/3021, m. 13.
26 N.L.W., Wynnstay, RA 19, f. 1.
27 B.L. Add. MS. 36378, f. 212; S.R.O. 1931/1, no. 154. Rowland Littlehales, who held the former almonry in 1785 (N.L.W., Wynnstay, RA 19, f. 1), also held a maltho. (ibid. R 64/9, R 70/12, R 80/9) on the later Nat. sch. site (ibid. L 1288; S.R.O. 1634, box 16, draft deed of 1847).
28 S.R.O. 294/7. 29 P.R.O., LR 2/184, f. 151.
30 *T.S.A.S.* xi. 57; N.L.W., Wynnstay, MS. Plans 1.

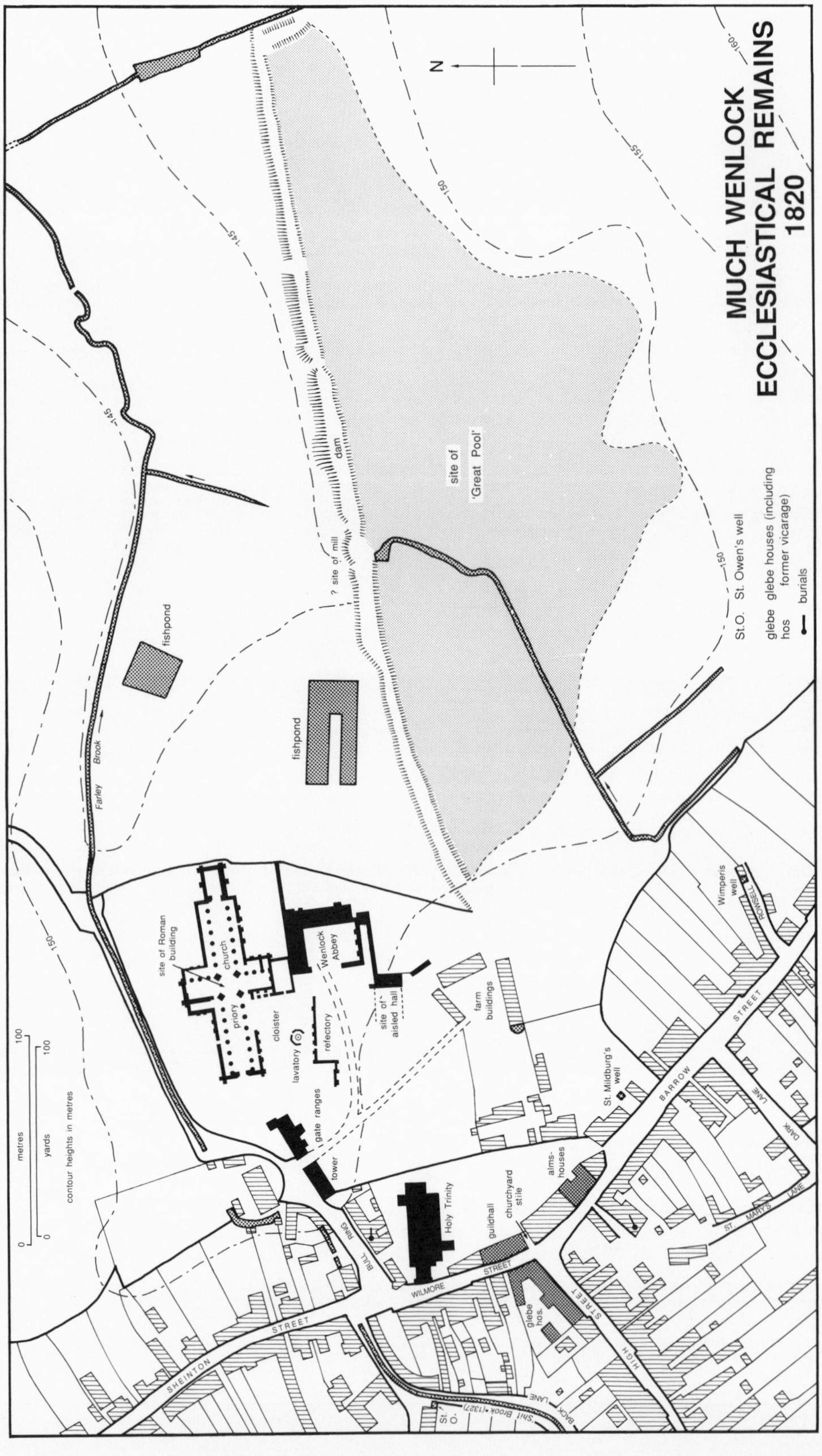
MUCH WENLOCK
ECCLESIASTICAL REMAINS
1820
N
St.O. St. Owen's well
glebe hos glebe houses (including former vicarage)
burials
metres
yards
contour heights in metres
site of 'Great Pool'
dam
? site of mill
fishpond
fishpond
Farley Brook
site of Roman building
church
priory
cloister
lavatory
refectory
Wenlock Abbey
site of aisled hall
farm buildings
gate ranges
tower
Holy Trinity
guildhall
churchyard stile
alms-houses
St. Milburg's well
Wimperis well
glebe hos.
SHEINTON STREET
WILMORE STREET
BULL RING
HIGH STREET
BARROW STREET
BACK LANE
ST. MARY'S LANE
DARK LANE
'Shit Brook' (1327)

Fig. 41

stands *c.* 12 m. south-west of the main gateway, to which it was formerly connected by an intervening range.[31] It was a corner tower in the monastic precinct wall[32] and probably dates from the mid 13th century.[33] The wall was mentioned *c.* 1200.[34]

The 11th-century priory church stood close to the northern edge of the monastic precinct.[35] It is not clear whether it was built before the Conquest as a new minster church,[36] perhaps with the assistance of Earl Leofric (d. 1057),[37] or after.[38] The new church was built over earlier walls,[39] which seem to have belonged to a Christian building and are suspected by some archaeologists to be of Romano-British origin;[40] the earlier building had perhaps been one of the churches (by then abandoned) of St. Mildburg's double monastery.[41] The new church was aisled and had triple apses at the east end. The length of the nave is not known but its plan may have been followed in the 13th-century rebuilding. It has been inferred that, unlike the major Cluniac monastic churches in England, it did not have transepts, but the position of the chapter house, south of the centre of the east wall of the cloister, suggests that there was a range of substance between it and the south aisle. The chapter house, which has a square east end, is of the later 12th century and its inner walls are richly decorated with rows of intersecting blind arches. The re-used shafting and springing for the three bayed vault is also 12th-century but appears to have been added after the decoration of the walls. The 12th-century dormitory range stood south of the chapter house and ended at the reredorter. An elaborate free-standing lavatory in the south-west corner of the cloister garth appears to be of two dates: an early central column which supported a spouted system was encircled by later masonry, faced in part with late 12th-century sculptural panels on which rested a circular trough.

The rebuilding of the priory church was begun in the late 12th century and probably completed, at the west end, *c.* 1240. It has an aisled nave of eight bays and a presbytery of the same length but only seven bays. Both transepts had eastern aisles of three bays. To the west of the south transept, and opening from it, was a narrow room arcaded to the cloister, which may have been a library, sacristy,[42] or vestry.[43] A wider room to the west of the north transept had an undercroft beneath, and it has been suggested that it was a vestry over a bone hole. The west range of the cloister survives only at foundation level, but above the three western bays of the south aisle of the nave there is a vaulted room which was presumably a chapel for the early prior's lodging in the adjacent range.

The 13th-century vaulted refectory was on the south side of the cloister. Its lack of alignment with the other claustral buildings, in which respect it resembled the 12th-century refectory of Worcester cathedral priory,[44] and its closer relationship to the parish church's alignment, have given rise to the suggestion that it may preserve elements of the plan of St. Mildburg's

---

Fig. 41 (*opposite*)

Medieval and later changes obscure the source of the monastery's original water supply. Almost certainly it could not have been Farley brook, flowing round the north side of the precinct and in medieval times known, where it ran through the town, as Shit brook. So water was probably supplied from the south. Three nearby springs are contained within medieval stonework, and two were named after 7th-century saints connected with the beginning of the claustral life at Wenlock.

The churchyard was perhaps separated from the priory precinct *c.* 1100 when Holy Trinity became the parish church. The Bull Ring and Wilmore Street with the north end of Barrow Street were market places encroaching on the churchyard and later themselves encroached upon by buildings. The house known after the Dissolution as Wenlock Abbey consisted of the prior's lodging (east range) and the north range adjoining; the farm buildings to the south adjoining may represent the priory's home farm.

The alignment of the refectory, different from that of the priory church and cloister, is somewhat nearer to that of Holy Trinity. If the 7th-century double monastery had two churches of which Holy Trinity represents one, the refectory may have been built on the site of the other.

For burials in Barrow Street see the introduction of this article, for those near the Bull Ring see the account of growth of settlement.

31 B.L. Add. MS. 36378, f. 212.

32 Views in Bodl. MS. Top. Salop. c. 2, ff. 552 (from SE.), 546 (from SW.), showing south-running high wall attached, dividing churchyard from Abbey grounds. In 1855 the churchyard had an 'ancient stone wall, in which is a square turret': St. Deiniol's Libr., Hawarden, Sir Steph. Glynne's ch. notes, xcvi, f. 13.

33 The N. doorway has a shouldered arch, as do the N. transept and the service block (*c.* 1250) S. of the cloister.

34 Hist. MSS. Com. 69, *Middleton*, p. 50.

35 For the priory see also *V.C.H. Salop.* ii. 38–50; *Jnl. Brit. Arch. Assoc.* cxl, plan facing p. 40.

36 As suggested by A. W. Clapham (*Archaeologia*, lxxii. 108, 132) and agreed by E. D. C. Jackson and E. Fletcher after further excavation (*Jnl. Brit. Arch. Assoc.* 3rd ser. xxviii. 34– 5). Further remains, unexcavated, were recorded from the air in 1976: *Salop. News Sheet*, v. 5–6.

37 He gave *ornamenta* to a Wenlock *coenobium*: 'Florence of Worc.', *Chron. ex Chronicis* (Eng. Hist. Soc.), i. 216. Wm. of Malmesbury, perhaps inaccurately paraphrasing 'Florence' (as Finberg believed: *Early Charters of W. Midlands*, p. 198), recorded a refoundation by Leofric: *Gesta Regum* (Rolls Ser.), i. 237.

38 Cranage's dating of the remains as 11th-cent. Norman (*T.S.A.S.* 3rd ser. ii. 407–8; *Archaeologia*, lxxii. 108) seems to have depended on Wm. of Malmesbury's mention of a Norman rebuilding (*Gesta Pontif.* (Rolls Ser.), 306); but Wm. was in fact referring to repairs at Holy Trin. (*T.S.A.S.* lvii. 144–5). Mr. H. M. Woods, however, cites new archaeol. evid. for a Norman date: *Jnl. Brit. Arch. Assoc.* cxl. 61–2.

39 *Archaeologia*, lxxii. 107–8.

40 Above, this article, intro.

41 *T.S.A.S.* lvii. 141. Evid. that it was a double foundation is in *Monumenta Germaniae Historica, Epistolae Selectae*, i. 8; P. H. Sawyer, *A.-S. Charters* (1968), no. 221; A. J. M. Edwards, 'Odo of Ostia's Hist. of the Translation of St. Milburga' (Lond. Univ. M.A. thesis, 1960), 86; cf. Finberg, *Early Charters of W. Midlands*, pp. 197–8; P. Sims-Williams, *Religion and Literature in Western Eng.* (1990), 120, 243.

42 The M. Wenlock 'sextry' was nr. the chapter ho.: A. Sparrow, *Hist. of Ch. Preen* (priv. print. 1898), 95.

43 Cf. the identically sited 'vestry' at Peterborough abbey: *V.C.H. Northants.* ii. 445, and plan facing p. 440.

44 Sited over high-status graves of the 6th or 7th cents.: *Med. Arch.* xviii. 146–51.

Fig. 42

WENLOCK ABBEY: THE HALL IN 1820

monastery.[45] A building surviving *c.* 1101 only a 'stone's throw' from Holy Trinity was then believed to be St. Mildburg's oratory (*oratorium*),[46] a cell (*cubiculum*) in which she had slept and prayed, within or near her monastery.[47]

Adjacent to the south west corner of the reredorter is the two storeyed service block for an aisled hall of *c.* 1250 which stood to the west.[48] It may have been the infirmary. That use has also been suggested for a 12th-century building which abutted the south side of the chapter house and ran for some distance to the east. The two storeyed range of lodgings at right-angles to its east end also has some 12th-century fabric; the doorway of the first-floor hall was originally round headed, and the same wall has a blocked round headed opening in the next room south. The hall had a central open hearth supported from the ground floor by a stone column. The range was remodelled *c.* 1425[49] and later, and provides four rooms on each floor. Each room has a fireplace and some have garderobes. The northern room on the ground floor is a chapel. A stone gallery of two storeys with continuous fenestration was built along the west side of the range and gave access to the first-floor rooms.[50] Wall paintings visible in the early 19th century on the south wall of the first-floor hall[51] were perhaps those said in 1786 to be of the Seven Champions and 'over the cloister'.[52] The east end of the church required considerable repair in the time of Prior Richard Wenlock (*c.* 1486–1521). He added or rebuilt the Lady chapel and added flying buttresses to the presbytery.

The priory's 'grange'[53] and other working buildings seem to have stood south-west of its church and claustral ranges, and due south of the main gateway.[54]

Between 1540 and the early 18th century the monastic buildings, except the prior's lodging, were robbed for their materials. Sir Watkin Williams Wynn (d. 1749) halted the spoliation[55]

45 *Jnl. Brit. Arch. Assoc.* cxl. 39, 61.

46 *T.S.A.S.* lvii. 139.

47 Edwards, 'Odo of Ostia's Hist.' 77, 81–2.

48 Descr. in *Arch. Jnl.* cxv. 167 (plan), 169. For date see upper E. windows, which closely resemble those at Gt. Oxenbold: above, Monkhopton, manors.

49 *Vernacular Archit.* xxv. 32, 34.

50 Cf. Bablake Sch., Coventry: *V.C.H. Warws.* viii. 140. For post-Dissolution hist. of prior's lodging see below, manors (M. Wenlock).

51 Fig. 42.

52 R. Gough, *Sepulchral Monuments in Gt. Brit.* i (1), p. cxxvi n. 1.

53 Mentioned 1532: P.R.O., E 303/14/Salop./269.

54 A lane from the presumed gateway site gave access to that area in the mid 19th cent.: S.R.O. 1931/1.

55 Grose, *Antiquities of Eng. and Wales*, iii, s.v. 'Wenlock monastery'.

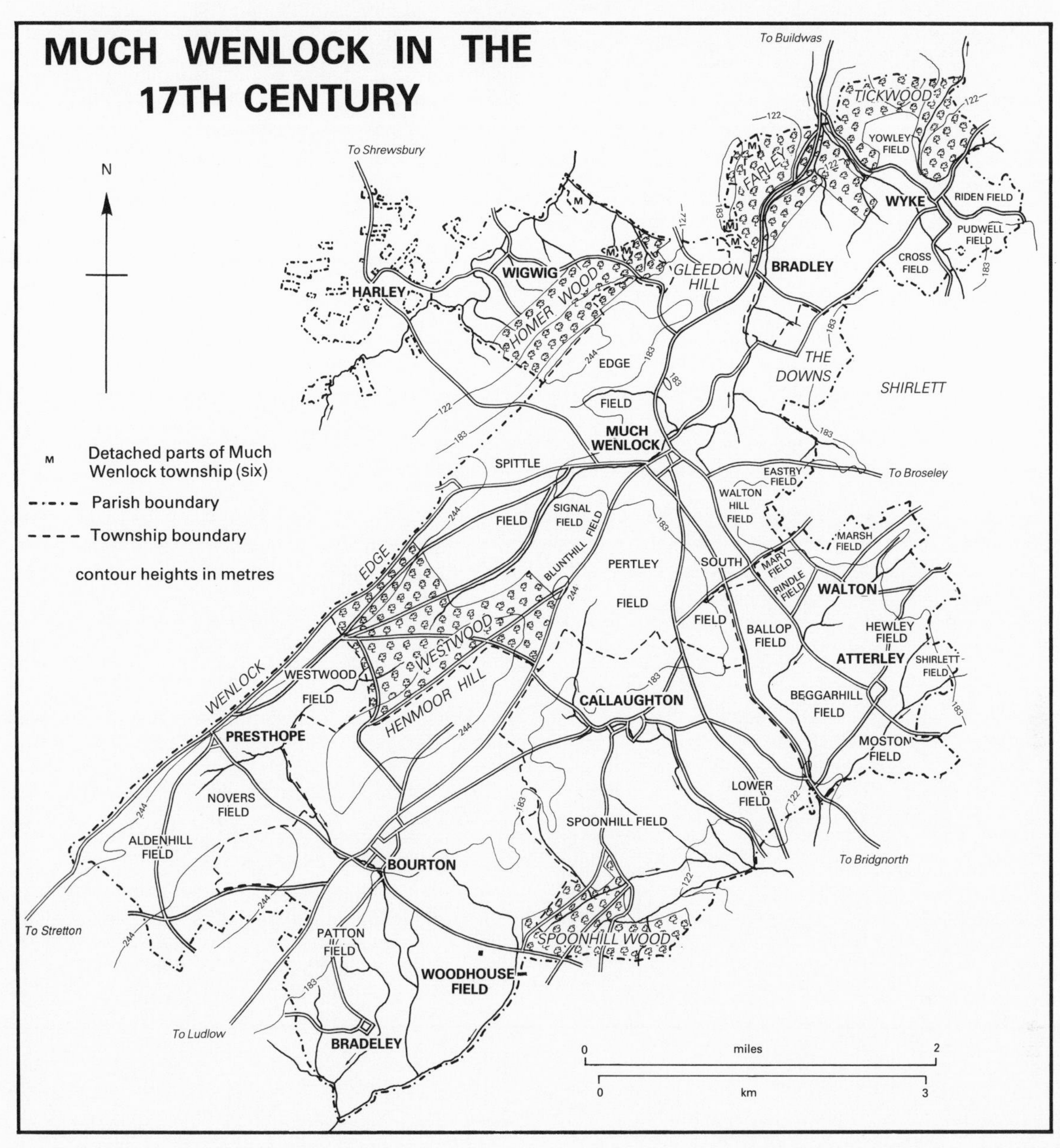

Fig. 43

and subsequent losses have been small.[56] In Herefordshire John Leland was told that the body of St. Mildburg's father Merewalh was found 'in a wall' in the 'old church of Wenlock', but Leominster priory (Herefs.)[57] and Repton church (Derb.)[58] were also reputed to have his remains.

RURAL SETTLEMENTS.[59] Bourton was the largest of the parish's outlying settlements. Its name indicates that in the Anglo-Saxon period it occupied or adjoined a *burh* ('fortified place'),[60] perhaps on the high ground occupied by the medieval chapel[61] and chief house.[62] The manor had a recorded population of 12 in 1086,[63] probably representing a total population of *c.* 50–60. The township had 6 taxpayers in 1327[64] and 14 in 1524.[65] By 1642, when 48 took the Protestation,[66] the township's total population may have been above 150. It was 181 in 1695[67] and about the same in 1841[68] and 1881.[69] In the 18th century the village's farms and cottages stood both on the high ground and either side of the brook that ran below it.[70] By the late 19th century there were few houses on the high ground and the surroundings of Lord Wenlock's house, the Cottage, were correspondingly more spacious and

56 There has been little change since the engraved view (1731) of S. and N. Buck. 57 Leland, *Itin.* ed. Toulmin Smith, ii. 74.
58 Finberg, *Early Charters of W. Midlands*, p. 218.
59 Fig. 43. 60 *P.N. Salop.* (E.P.N.S.), i. 55.
61 Below, churches. 62 Below, manors.
63 *V.C.H. Salop.* i. 312.
64 *T.S.A.S.* 2nd ser. iv. 328. 65 P.R.O., E 179/166/200.
66 Ho. of Lords papers 1641–2, Protestations Oxon. and Salop. f. 199 (including Bradeley total).
67 *T.S.A.S.* xi. 55.
68 P.R.O., HO 107/928/18, ff. 29v.–32v., 34.
69 P.R.O., RG 11/2640, ff. 45–49v.
70 S.R.O. 3765/1; Bourton map of 1795 (in Mr. J. R. Craig's possession).

private,[71] but the settlement pattern in 1986 had otherwise changed little in two centuries.

Bourton township included two other ancient settlements, Bradeley and Woodhousefield. The former was mentioned in 1194.[72] Its mill became disused in the 15th century.[73] In 1642 the Protestation was taken by six inhabitants,[74] but there were only three houses in the 18th century.[75] One of them was uninhabited by 1841,[76] and only a single farm remained forty years later.[77] Woodhousefield was a moated house near Spoonhill wood.[78] Later re-sited outside the moat, it stood alone[79] until the 19th century when a few cottages were added.[80]

Callaughton, mentioned in 1224,[81] had 10 taxpayers, four more than Bourton, in 1327[82] and 13, one fewer, in 1524.[83] Earthworks east of the mill[84] suggest houses abandoned, perhaps in the later Middle Ages. Callaughton grew less markedly than Bourton in the 16th and 17th centuries. The 1642 Protestation was taken by 28,[85] probably representing a township population of *c.* 100, and in 1695 there were 92 inhabitants,[86] presumably including some at Spoonhill and Beggarhill Brook. In the late 18th century the village and its mill stood in a hollow about the Callaughton brook.[87] It had 17 houses in 1841 and *c.* 120 inhabitants.[88] In 1881, though 15 houses remained, only 75 people lived there.[89] In 1986 the settlement pattern had hardly changed since the 18th century.

Callaughton township had two large outlying houses, Spoonhill, built in the 16th century,[90] and Beggarhill Brook Farm (formerly Bradley's Tenement), standing by 1695.[91] Except for associated cottages they remained isolated.

Atterley and Walton were treated as one township for some purposes by 1524. Together they then had nine taxpayers,[92] probably representing a population fewer than 60. The total had increased markedly by 1642, when 33 took the Protestation,[93] and stood at 104 in 1695.[94] Cottages at the edge of Shirlett may have housed at least some of the additional people. Ballop mill closed in the 18th century[95] and by 1841 the population was down to 58.[96] In 1986 Atterley and Walton each consisted of little more than a farmhouse.

Atterley, mentioned in 1255,[97] had 11 householders in 1635[98] and 14 manorial suitors in 1775.[99] In 1722 Atterley hamlet consisted of four farm houses and two cottages, grouped above a hollow watered by Beggarhill brook; in isolated positions at the edge of the township, next to Shirlett, were six cottages.[1] Farm amalgamations reduced the hamlet to three farmhouses by 1847[2] and two by 1882.[3] Four of the cottages were standing in 1925.[4] Of the two farmhouses one had been empty for some years by 1986.

Walton, whose name suggests a pre-Conquest settlement,[5] was mentioned in 1255.[6] Walton had seven householders in 1635[7] and eight manorial suitors in 1775.[8] In 1722 the hamlet consisted of four farmhouses and two cottages, fronting a lane that descended to Walton brook; there were also two isolated cottages at the edge of Shirlett.[9] Hummocks and protruding masonry in pasture immediately south of Walton Farm may mark the sites of houses abandoned before the 17th century. Amalgamations reduced the hamlet to two farms and two cottages by 1841,[10] and by 1882 to one farm and a cottage,[11] which both remained in 1986. The cottages by Shirlett were gone before 1847.[12]

Wyke and Bradley were treated as one township for some purposes by 1524 when there were eight taxpayers.[13] Only at Wyke was there a nucleated settlement, and that was eclipsed from the late 18th century by a cluster of new cottages at Farley.

Wyke, mentioned in 1221,[14] stood on a spur between two brooks. It had four farmhouses in 1611 and in 1820.[15] By 1849, however, amalgamation had reduced the hamlet to two farmhouses and five cottages,[16] of which all but one cottage remained in 1986. The outlying Newhouse and Wood House were probably established in the Middle Ages.[17] By 1796 an isolated holding called the Vineyards (probably the Wyniattes of 1592)[18] lay at the north-east edge of the township.[19] There were two cottages there in 1841,[20] next to a limestone quarry.[21]

Bradley, mentioned in 1255,[22] had two farms from the 16th century to the 19th,[23] on opposite sides of Farley brook.[24] A few cottages were built on Farley common in the 17th century.[25]

The population of Wyke and Bradley township rose 1695–1841, from 81 to 150.[26] New housing was almost all at Farley, which had 15 houses in 1841[27] and 19 in 1881,[28] mostly along the margin between the Buildwas road and the

71 O.S. Map 1/2,500, Salop. LVII. 3 (1883 edn.).
72 Eyton, iii. 271.
73 Below, econ. hist. (mills).
74 Ho. of Lords papers 1641–2, Protestations Oxon. and Salop. f. 199.
75 S.R.O. 3765/1; Bourton map of 1795 (in Mr. J. R. Craig's possession).
76 P.R.O., HO 107/928/18, f. 32 and v.
77 P.R.O., RG 11/2640, f. 45v.
78 Below, manors.
79 S.R.O. 294/3.
80 P.R.O., HO 107/928/18, f. 32v.; RG 11/2640, f. 46.
81 Eyton, iii. 288.
82 *T.S.A.S.* 2nd ser. iv. 329.
83 P.R.O., E 179/166/200.
84 Inf. from Dr. M. C. Horton.
85 Ho. of Lords papers 1641–2, Protestations Oxon. and Salop. f. 199.
86 *T.S.A.S.* xi. 55.
87 Callaughton map of 1796 (in Mr. J. R. Craig's possession).
88 P.R.O., HO 107/928/18, ff. 21–22v.
89 P.R.O., RG 11/2640, ff. 39–40v.
90 Below, manors.
91 Hull Univ., Brynmor Jones Libr., DDFA/26/27, 57; S.R.O. 924/570.
92 P.R.O., E 179/166/200.
93 Ho. of Lords papers 1641–2, Protestations Oxon. and Salop. f. 198.
94 *T.S.A.S.* xi. 55.
95 Below, econ. hist. (mills).
96 P.R.O., HO 107/928/18, ff. 18v.–19v.
97 *Rot. Hund.* (Rec. Com.), ii. 84.
98 S.R.O. 1224/2/69.
99 S.R.O. 775/102.
1 S.R.O. 1093, parcel 161, Atterley and Walton map; 3507/1.
2 S.R.O. 294/1, fields 1829, 1831, 1837.
3 O.S. Map 1/2,500, Salop. LI. 13 (1883 edn.).
4 Ibid. 9, 13 (1927 edn.).
5 *P.N. Salop.* (E.P.N.S.), i. 299.
6 *Rot. Hund.* ii. 84.
7 S.R.O. 1224/2/69.
8 S.R.O. 775/102.
9 S.R.O. 1093, parcel 161, Atterley and Walton map.
10 P.R.O., HO 107/928/18, f. 18v.; S.R.O. 294/1, fields 1774, 1870.
11 P.R.O., RG 11/2640, ff. 62v.–63; O.S. Map 1/2,500, Salop. LI. 9 (1883 edn.).
12 S.R.O. 294/1.
13 P.R.O., E 179/166/200.
14 Eyton, iii. 284.
15 Below, manors.
16 S.R.O. 294/4.
17 Below, manors.
18 S.R.O. 1224/3/135.
19 S.R.O. 1224, box 88, abstr. of title of 1813.
20 P.R.O., HO 107/928/18, f. 11v.
21 S.R.O. 294/4, fields 1697–8.
22 *Rot. Hund.* ii. 84.
23 S.R.O. 1224/3/136; below, manors.
24 S.R.O. 294/4, fields 1511, 1581.
25 S.R.O. 1224/2/75, 87, 122.
26 *T.S.A.S.* xi. 55; P.R.O., HO 107/928/18, ff. 9–12.
27 P.R.O., HO 107/928/18, ff. 1–10v.
28 P.R.O., RG 11/2640, ff. 59–61.

brook.[29] Farley emerged as a settlement (called New Farley in 1811)[30] because of an extension of limestone quarrying nearby in the late 18th and 19th centuries.[31] Farley's single largest occupation in 1841 was that of road wagoner, presumably for hauling stone to the Severn; there was work for four blacksmiths and two wheelwrights.[32] In 1983 Farley had 10 occupied houses.[33]

Wigwig township comprised few houses until the 17th century, when cottages began to proliferate on Homer common. In 1086 Wigwig manor had seven recorded inhabitants.[34] Wigwig had two farms and a mill in 1540[35] and two ratepayers in 1632.[36] By 1841, and in 1986, Wigwig consisted of the former mill house and, close together on a spur above Wigwig brook, two farmhouses.[37]

On Homer common, still called Homer wood in the early 17th century, there were three unlicensed cottages in 1636.[38] By 1671 there were 12[39] and in 1675 a number of 'extravagant and idle persons', some of them strangers, had recently settled on the common and were 'daily' making new inclosures.[40] By 1708 there were 23 cottages,[41] and traditions of a rapid settlement by 'gypsies' remained *c.* 1900.[42] There was little further growth, however, before the end of the 18th century.[43] There were 28 dwellings in 1841[44] and 40 by 1881.[45] The 19th-century growth was connected with an extension of quarrying nearby;[46] most of the inhabitants in 1841 were farm labourers or quarrymen.[47] Homer was nicknamed 'Donkeyland' from the animals kept.[48] By 1945 only *c.* 30 houses remained,[49] but Homer was later a favoured setting for new private houses, many of them bought by commuters,[50] and by 1983 there were about 80 homes,[51] old and new.

Presthope, mentioned in 1167,[52] had five taxpayers in 1327[53] and four in 1524.[54] There were 57 inhabitants in 1695.[55] In the 18th century the few farms were spaced along the upper dip slope behind Wenlock Edge, at the head of a valley (OE. *hop*)[56] that descended to Bourton.[57] Thirteen cottages were built *c.* 1800 on the small common,[58] presumably for limestone workers;[59] they included a row known as the Five Chimneys.[60] In the later 19th and earlier 20th century Presthope had thus some focus as a settlement, and its own railway station. All coherence, however, was lost in the 1960s and 1970s. The station closed in 1963.[61] The Five Chimneys were demolished in the 1960s[62] and the ancient farmhouses were abandoned[63] as quarrying advanced.[64] Afterwards there remained only Black Barn Farm, near Bourton, the Plough (later the Wenlock Edge) inn at the Easthope boundary, and two cottages.[65]

SOCIAL AND CULTURAL ACTIVITIES.

All the townships had alesellers in the 17th century. Much Wenlock township had 21 in 1614;[66] even Wyke had three in 1621[67] and Homer two in 1681.[68] In Much Wenlock township 41 licences were granted in 1800.[69] Uproarious drinking was a favourite amusement of the younger gentry and farmers in the earlier 19th century.[70] By mid century, however, the town's licensed houses had diminished by half.[71] Twelve were listed in 1879[72] and eight in 1984.[73] Outside the town there were no alehouses by 1793.[74] Those that opened later were mostly near quarries. At Presthope an alehouse opened *c.* 1800.[75] The Plough inn, licensed there from 1862,[76] moved to Hilltop in the early 20th century[77] and remained, as the Wenlock Edge inn, in 1990. There were two public houses at Farley in 1841[78] and one in 1901; the Rock House had opened next to Bradley Rock quarry in 1834[79] and remained in 1986. At Bourton the Talbot, open by 1841, had gone by 1882.[80]

By the 18th century the town's principal inns were the Swan & Falcon,[81] the Talbot,[82] and the White Hart[83] in Spittle Street, and the Fox and the Raven in Barrow Street.[84] The county quarter sessions met by adjournment at the Talbot in 1697,[85] and 'regular courts' sat at the Raven in 1803.[86] The George & Dragon[87] in Spittle Street had a 'market room'.[88] Locals assumed that a gentleman would stay at the Swan & Falcon or the Raven, though the latter had little

29 S.R.O. 294/4. 30 Glam. R.O., CL/Deeds II, nos. 7030–1.
31 Below, econ. hist. (quarries).
32 P.R.O., HO 107/928/18, ff. 9–10v.
33 S.R.O., reg. of electors, Bridgnorth dist. (1983), sect. 2CQ, p. 1. 34 *V.C.H. Salop.* i. 335.
35 S.R.O. 1224/3/8, ff. 2 and v., 4; below, econ. hist. (mills). 36 W.B.R., Q1/13/167.
37 P.R.O., HO 107/928/18, f. 5v.; S.R.O. 294/5.
38 S.R.O. 1224/2/73. 39 S.R.O. 840, box 1, ct. r.
40 S.R.O. 1224/2/116. 41 Ibid. /2/120, 129, 147.
42 Gaskell, *Spring in a Salop. Abbey*, 85.
43 S.R.O. 1224/2/260, 278, 433, 437, 455, 469, 477.
44 P.R.O., HO 107/928/18, ff. 5v.–8v.
45 P.R.O., RG 11/2640, 54–58v.
46 Below, econ. hist. (quarries).
47 P.R.O., HO 107/928/18, ff. 5v.–8v.
48 Gaskell, *Spring in a Salop. Abbey*, 85.
49 S.R.O., reg. of electors, Wrekin divn., civilian (Oct. 1945), pp. 361–70. 50 *Birm. Post*, 27 Nov. 1971, p. 10.
51 S.R.O., reg. of electors, Bridgnorth dist. (1983), sect. 2CQ, p. 2. 52 Eyton, iii. 290.
53 *T.S.A.S.* 2nd ser. iv. 334.
54 P.R.O., E 179/166/200. 55 *T.S.A.S.* xi. 55.
56 *P.N. Salop.* (E.P.N.S.), i. 156.
57 S.R.O. 3657/1. 58 S.R.O. 4175/1, sale partic. of 1802.
59 Below, econ. hist. (quarries).
60 S.R.O. 294/6; photo. in *Shropshire Mag.* Jan. 1955, 5.
61 Above, communications.
62 *Wenlock Herald*, Jan. 1960 (set in S.R.O. 3898/Pr); S.R.O. 1038/1, p. 153; 2320/1, p. 190.
63 S.R.O. 1969/1, p. 147; 2128/1, p. 165; 3084/1, pp. 190–1; 3523/1, p. 192. 64 Below, econ. hist. (quarries).
65 S.R.O. 3523/1, p. 192.
66 N.L.W., Wynnstay, box E/139.
67 S.R.O. 1224/2/50. 68 Ibid. /2/511, f. [3v.].
69 W.B.R., Q1/11/2. 70 *Nineteenth Cent.* xxv. 261–2.
71 W.B.R., P8/2/7; S. Bagshaw, *Dir. Salop.* (1851), 587–8.
72 *P.O. Dir. Salop.* (1879), 435–6.
73 *M. Wenlock: an Historic Town* (M. Wenlock and Dist. Tourist Assoc. 1984; copy in S.P.L., class M 66 v.f.).
74 S.P.L., MS. 6865, p. 211. 75 W.B.R., Q1/11/2.
76 Co. of Salop, *Return of Licensed Hos. 1901* (copy in S.P.L., accession 6117), p. 343.
77 S.R.O. 2079/L. 14; 4044/92, f. 35 (no. 315); O.S. Map 1/2,500, Salop. LVII. 2 (1926 edn.).
78 P.R.O., HO 107/928/18, ff. 9, 10.
79 *Return of Licensed Hos. 1901*, p. 362.
80 P.R.O., HO 107/928/18, f. 32; S. Bagshaw, *Dir. Salop.* (1851), 588; O.S. Map 1/2,500, Salop. LVII. 3 (1883 edn.).
81 Mentioned 1736: N.L.W., Wynnstay, M 2530.
82 Mentioned 1550: P.R.O., LR 2/184, f. 152v.
83 Mentioned 1714: N.L.W., Wynnstay, box E/62, f. 34.
84 Both mentioned 1736: N.L.W., Wynnstay, M 2530.
85 *Orders of Q. Sess.* i. 165. 86 S.R.O. 1224/7/20.
87 Mentioned 1488: N.L.W., Wynnstay, RA 1.
88 *Wenlock Herald*, Sept. 1960.

to offer the refined guest in 1793.[89] By 1769 (apparently between 1714 and *c.* 1730)[90] the White Hart (later the Wynnstay Arms)[91] sign had moved west to the Bridgnorth–Shrewsbury road,[92] turnpiked in 1752,[93] and there took most of the coaching trade.[94] In or before 1805 the Fox (later the Wheatland Fox) had moved to the west end of High Street,[95] probably with the same object. The Stork hotel opened in Wilmore Street *c.* 1860[96] and was the nearest inn to the railway station. The Swan & Falcon closed *c.* 1920,[97] but the other principal inns remained in 1986.

By 1900 the Gaskell (formerly Wynnstay) Arms, the Raven, and the Stork had assembly rooms.[98] The Stork Room was still used for social events *c.* 1960.[99] The guildhall and, from 1900,[1] the Corn Exchange were public halls, and in 1921 the Market Hall was converted into a Memorial Hall, little used by 1963.[2] In 1983 the former National school became the Priory Hall.[3] In the early 20th century fun fairs, circuses, and small events were held on the 'fair' field north of Ashfield Hall.[4]

Late night playing of knucklebones was a nuisance at Much Wenlock in 1420,[5] and gaming was commonplace at alehouses in the early 17th century.[6] In the early 18th century there was a bowling green at the Blue Bridge.[7] Cock fighting was carefully arranged;[8] fights were held at the Shoulder of Mutton, Barrow Street,[9] and elsewhere,[10] and in the early 19th century a main of cocks regularly accompanied the races.[11]

Minstrels (*ystriones*) performed for the abbot of Westminster at Much Wenlock in 1290,[12] and professional entertainers in the 16th and 17th centuries included Robert Eyr, a minstrel buried in 1593,[13] and William Aldersene, a wandering minstrel whose son was born at Bourton in 1614.[14] Abraham Lloyd, a fiddler, lived in the parish in 1649.[15] By 1880, and until the 1930s or later, local morris men, usually quarrymen, entertained the district at Christmas in order to supplement their wages.[16]

Before the mid 18th century the larger social gatherings had been incidental to more serious occasions: church festivals,[17] livestock fairs, local-government and law sittings, rent audits, and harvests. By 1733 there was also a two-day flat race meeting in July[18] on Westwood common.[19] About 1770 the course was a straight mile.[20] The common was inclosed in 1814[21] and the races were revived in 1820[22] as a one-day meeting.[23] The elliptical course ran a mile over fields south of the town;[24] a permanent grandstand and enclosure were provided *c.* 1870,[25] but the last meeting was in 1876.[26] A separate steeplechase meeting was held there 1872–1939.[27]

By the early 17th century the annual bailiff's feast marked his successor's election.[28] It continued, as the mayoral banquet, until *c.* 1936[29] and was revived as a dinner-dance or charity ball after the Second World War.[30] The races were followed by a ball in the 19th century,[31] and another annual ball was mentioned 1835 and 1853.[32] A 'jubilee', perhaps annual,[33] took place on Trinity Sunday 1810.[34] In the later 19th century the May fair was an annual pleasure fair.[35]

The Much Wenlock Friendly Society, formed in 1757, flourished in 1823.[36] The Royal Society began in 1770 and still existed in 1814. In 1802–3 there were four societies, with 310 members.[37] The Wenlock Improved Provident Society, formed in 1818,[38] survived until 1883.[39] The Waterloo Benevolent Society, started in 1835, was still active in 1856. The Fountain of Friendship lodge of Odd Fellows (Manchester Unity) began in 1841;[40] by 1897 the Gaskell Club was formed by secession from it.[41] In 1901 the Loyal St. Milburga Odd Fellows' lodge (Manchester Unity) was established;[42] it had 50 members in 1906. The Albert Edward court of Foresters, begun in 1862, had 281 members in 1906 and *c.* 100 in 1984.[43] In 1907 a Much Wenlock Medical Aid Society served the town and an area 3 miles around.[44]

The Wenlock Loyal Volunteers were recruited

89 *Torrington Diaries*, ed. Andrews, iii. 227–31.
90 Below, manors (M. Wenlock).
91 Pigot, *Nat. Com. Dir.* (1842), 51.
92 N.L.W., Wynnstay, box 43/3.
93 Above, communications.
94 Tibnam & Co. *Salop. Dir.* (1828), 132.
95 *Return of Licensed Hos. 1901*, p. 336; S.R.O. 1931/1; W.B.R., P8/2/7, no. 513.
96 *Return of Licensed Hos. 1901*, p. 346.
97 *Kelly's Dir. Salop.* (1917), 280; (1922), 289–90.
98 Ibid. (1900), advt. pp. 34, 37–8.
99 *Wenlock Herald*, Mar. 1960.
1 Below, this section.
2 *Kelly's Dir. Salop.* (1922), 287; *Wenlock Herald*, Nov. 1963.
3 S.C.C. Ch. Exec.'s Dept., chars. index.
4 *M. Wenlock Monthly Mag.* Aug. 1902 (colln. in S.R.O. 3898/Pr); *Wenlock Herald*, Sept. 1962.
5 S.R.O. 1224/2/7, ct. r.
6 Ibid. /2/50.
7 Hull Univ., Brynmor Jones Libr., DDFA(2)/15/10.
8 *V.C.H. Salop.* ii. 190 n.
9 *Salop. N. & Q.* 3rd ser. ii. 91.
10 *Nineteenth Cent.* xxv. 259.
11 *Salopian Jnl.* 29 June 1825.
12 *Docs. illustr. rule of Wal. de Wenlok* (Camd. 4th ser. ii), p. 187.
13 S.R.O. 3898/Rg/1, 7 Sept. 1593.
14 Ibid. 25 Mar. 1614.
15 Ibid. /Rg/2, 17 May 1649.
16 *Shrews. Chron.* 5 Apr. 1935; E. C. Cawte, 'The Morris Dance in Herefs., Salop., and Worcs.' *Jnl. Eng. Folk Dance and Song Soc.* ix. 202; Salop. Co. Mus. Service, Oral Hist. Colln. no. 137; inf. from Mr. G. C. Ashman.
17 For church ales (mentioned 1543) see below, churches.
18 J. Cheny, *Hist. List of Horse-matches, 1733*, 91.
19 The 'starting post' mentioned 1736: N.L.W., Wynnstay, M 2530.
20 N.L.W., Wynnstay, box 56/6 (map).
21 Below, econ. hist. (agric.).
22 *Shrews. Chron.* 27 Oct. 1820.
23 *V.C.H. Salop.* ii. 181.
24 C. & J. Greenwood, *Map of Salop.* (1827).
25 *Eddowes's Jnl.* 24 Feb. 1875, suppl. p. 2.
26 Ibid. 9 Aug. 1876, p. 7 (last known rep.).
27 Ibid. 10 Apr. 1872; *Racing Calendar (Steeplechases)*, 1938–9, 777; *V.C.H. Salop.* ii. 183.
28 W.B.R., B3/1/1, p. 477.
29 *Salopian Jnl.* 7 Oct. 1835; 16 Nov. 1836; *Shrews. Chron.* 15 Nov. 1935, p. 5; 13 Nov. 1936, p. 5.
30 e.g. *Shropshire Mag.* Dec. 1965, 33; *Bridgnorth Jnl.* 14 Apr. 1978.
31 *Shrews. Chron.* 13 Oct. 1820.
32 Brookes fam. letter bk. pp. 5, 55 (in private hands; Mr. W. M. Motley kindly arranged access).
33 As Wellington's: *V.C.H. Salop.* xi. 212.
34 W.B.R., P4/5/4, 24 June 1810.
35 Below, econ. hist. (mkts. and fairs).
36 Rest of para. based on S.R.O., q. sess. rec. parcel 285, index to club articles; Registrar of Friendly Socs. *List of Friendly Socs. in Co. of Salop, 1793–1855* (H.M.S.O. 1857; copy in S.R.O. 119/27).
37 *Abstr. Rel. to Poor*, H.C. 175, p. 423 (1803–4), xiii.
38 W.B.R., Q2/5/1.
39 S.R.O. 2724, papers in Boak v. the soc.
40 W.B.R., Q2/5/2.
41 *Shrews. Chron.* 29 Jan. 1897, p. 8.
42 Ibid. 16 Aug. 1901, p. 8; *M. Wenlock Monthly Mag.* Aug. 1902.
43 *M. Wenlock Monthly Mag.* June 1906; *Wenlock Herald*, Mar.–Apr. 1984.
44 *M. Wenlock Monthly Mag.* Feb. 1907.

in 1799 and served until 1802. They had Broseley, Madeley, and Wenlock divisions. The corps was re-formed in 1803, with an establishment of officers and 320 privates, in four divisions.[45] It became part of the local militia in 1808 and was disbanded in 1816.[46] An Air Training Corps squadron was formed in 1941,[47] and a Royal Observer Corps branch by 1966.[48]

In the earlier 19th century there were occasional theatrical performances in the town,[49] and amateur musical concerts.[50] There was nevertheless a want of polite society. The nearest great house was at Willey.[51] In 1848 a lady resident noted that Much Wenlock 'if possible is duller than ever, for I hear of no visiting whatever'; the town recalled Goldsmith's *Deserted Village*.[52]

A small theological library, left by a vicar for the clergy's use, had been taken over in 1798 by the Associates of Dr. Bray as a parochial lending library and remained in 1835.[53] In 1841[54] the brothers W. P. and A. G. Brookes[55] began the Wenlock Agricultural Reading Society for farmers and the lower classes. It formed a small museum and a library, which had *c.* 1,500 volumes by 1851.[56] Few working men subscribed. In 1852 the society moved to a new stone building in Hospital Street, designed by S. Pountney Smith. The arcaded Corn Market occupied the ground floor and a library, reading room, and museum the first.[57] The building was enlarged *c.* 1856 by addition of a working men's library and reading room on the ground floor and a combined museum and classroom on the first.[58] In 1858 the lending library had 87 subscribers, the reading room 40. The working men's branch had 30 members.[59] The society's philharmonic class was formed by 1855[60] and met weekly to practise singing.[61] W. P. Brookes founded a boys' drum and fife band[62] before 1860.[63]

The society's most successful class was the Olympian (later the Wenlock Olympian Society).[64] It had 305 subscribers in 1858.[65] Its annual games were held from 1850 to 1931 and intermittently from the end of the Second World War.[66] By 1875 the society used the 7-a. Linden Field, which included a bowling green, cricket pitch, and running track.[67] C. G. Milnes Gaskell leased it to the borough council in 1898 as a park and recreation ground for the parish,[68] and his widow gave it to the council in 1935.[69] In 1973 it was merged with the adjoining William Brookes school's playing field and swimming pool, for joint school and public use.[70] A sports hall was added in 1975.[71] By 1984 the Olympian Society's activities included not only athletics but also mountaineering and hill climbing, five-a-side football, short tennis, an annual arts festival (begun 1979), and an annual art, handicraft, and produce show.[72]

The reading society was defunct by 1900, when its building (then called the Corn Exchange) and the contents were vested in the borough council. Most of the books were afterwards sold or lost; *c.* 740 remained in 1986. The museum remained until the 1920s.[73] It was revived in 1968 and moved in 1970 to the former Memorial Hall, where it passed to the county council in 1974.[74]

In other ways too the reading society's aims survived its demise. There was a commercial circulating library in 1902[75] and the county library opened a 'centre' in the parish room *c.* 1927.[76] It became a part-time branch library in 1955[77] and moved to the Corn Exchange in 1962.[78] A lending library in Homer school house was mentioned in 1902,[79] and a county library centre opened at Bourton in 1928.[80]

In 1900 a working men's club was formed at the Corn Exchange.[81] It lapsed in the 1950s, was revived,[82] but by 1960 was failing again.[83] Its role may have passed to the local British Legion branch, formed in 1931,[84] which had a hall in Smithfield Road. Part of the hall, used also by other organizations, was converted *c.* 1980 for the Royal British Legion Club.[85] In 1903 J. H. A. Whitley built a working men's club and reading room at Bourton, attached to his house.[86] The club room had closed by 1985.[87] The Callaughton mission room was also used as a club room in 1964.[88]

A town brass band began in 1900[89] and survived until the Second World War.[90] A choral society was formed in 1902,[91] and men's and

45 G. A. Parfitt, *Salop. Militia and Volunteers* (Hist. of Corps of King's Salop. Light Inf. iv [1970]), 203, 210, 439–40; S.R.O. 1224/22/97, 100, 197; pl. 26.
46 Hist. Note in *Freedom of Wenlock to K.S.L.I.* (1965; copy supplied by the late Mr. G. A. Parfitt).
47 *Wenlock Herald*, May 1962.
48 *Bridgnorth Jnl.* 15 Apr. 1966.
49 W.B.R., M8/23a (playbill 1831).
50 Brookes fam. letter bk. p. 46 (1 Feb. 1850).
51 Below, Willey.
52 Brookes fam. letter bk. p. 45.
53 S.R.O. 3898/Pr/1, bookplate; Lewis, *Topog. Dict. Eng.* (1835), iv, s.v.
54 Rest of para. based on E. B. Higgs, 'Wenlock Agric. Reading Soc. Librs.' (TS. [*c.* 1980] in M. Wenlock town clk.'s office).
55 Brookes fam. letter bk. p. 18.
56 S. Bagshaw, *Dir. Salop.* (1851), 582; *V.C.H. Salop.* iv. 217.
57 *Kelly's Dir. Salop.* (1900), 271; pl. 22.
58 *Shrews. Chron.* 26 Oct. 1855. Mus. contents descr. in *Randall's Guide to Wenlock*, 7–8.
59 *Shrews. Chron.* 29 Oct. 1858, p. 6.
60 Higgs, 'Wenlock Agric. Reading Soc. Librs.' 3.
61 *Shrews. Chron.* 29 Oct. 1858, p. 6.
62 M. E. R. Jackson, 'Notes on Hist. of Madeley' (microfilm in S.P.L.), bk. 3A, p. 95.
63 Brookes fam. letter bk. p. 74.
64 *V.C.H. Salop.* ii. 192; Mullins, *Brit. Olympians.*
65 *Shrews. Chron.* 29 Oct. 1858, p. 6.
66 M. Wenlock Mus., MW 51/84/44 (programme of 1948); *Shropshire Star*, 17 July 1978, p. 15; pl. 36.
67 *Randall's Guide to Wenlock*, 10.
68 S.R.O. 1242, box 7, deed.
69 *Shrews. Chron.* 14 June 1935, p. 6; inscr. on Linden Lodge.
70 *S.C.C. Mins. (Educ.)* 1971–2, 357–62; 1972–3, 129–30, 304; 1973–4, 175–6; 1974–5, 88.
71 Ibid. *1975–6,* 190.
72 Wenlock Olympian Soc. *Ann. Olympian Games, 1984* (programme; copy in M. Wenlock Mus.).
73 *Kelly's Dir. Salop.* (1922), 287, 290; (1926), 307, 310.
74 S.R.O. 3814/1, 17 Dec. 1973, pp. 4–5.
75 *M. Wenlock Monthly Mag.* Dec. 1902.
76 S.R.O. 3898/PCC/2, 13 Dec. 1926.
77 *S.C.C. Mins. (Educ.)* 1953–4, 232; 1954–5, 91, 94.
78 Ibid. 1961–2, 206.
79 *M. Wenlock Monthly Mag.* Nov. 1902.
80 R. C. Elliott, 'Development of Public Libraries in Salop.' (Loughborough Univ. M.A. thesis, 1970; copy in Co. Libr.), 126.
81 *Shrews. Chron.* 12 Oct. 1900, p. 8.
82 L. C. Lloyd, *Boro. of Wenlock Official Guide* (1955), 64 (copy in S.P.L., class M 66 v.f.); Jackson, 'Madeley', bk. 3A, p. 126.
83 *Wenlock Herald*, Oct. 1960.
84 Ibid. July–Aug. 1972.
85 Local inf.; P.O. *Telephone Dir.* (1980), sect. 303, p. 46.
86 *M. Wenlock Monthly Mag.* Jan. 1904.
87 Local inf. It was still used in 1960: *Wenlock Herald*, Oct. 1960.
88 Lloyd, *Wenlock Official Guide* (1964), 64 (copy in S.P.L., class M 66 v.f.); local inf.
89 *Shrews. Chron.* 31 Aug. 1900, p. 7.
90 Ibid. 25 May 1956, p. 6.
91 *M. Wenlock Monthly Mag.* Nov. 1902.

women's choirs flourished in 1985.[92] A Literary and Debating Society was formed in 1906,[93] but in 1930 the Social and Literary Society failed for lack of support; cinema, wireless, and the county library were blamed.[94] In the earlier 20th century films were shown in the Corn Exchange,[95] and in 1935 the Wenlock Cinema opened in the Memorial Hall.[96] It closed in 1961.[97]

There had been a cricket team by 1841,[98] and in 1902 there were also clubs for bowls, football, and tennis. A Bourton cricket club began in 1902.[99] The Ancient Order of Foresters held annual sports at Much Wenlock before the First World War.[1] A golf club, with a nine-hole course on the north side of the town, flourished *c.* 1907–*c.* 1920.[2] A horticultural society that expired *c.* 1890 was revived in 1909[3] and held annual shows before the First World War, but was defunct by 1922.[4] Bourton had a flower show with rural sports by 1903.[5]

In the mid 20th century Much Wenlock had sports and gardening clubs and branches of the usual women's, welfare, and youth organizations.[6] Within Wenlock borough's civic society a Much Wenlock group was formed in 1960[7] and revived in 1984 as the Much Wenlock and District Society.[8] In 1959 the vicar began the *Wenlock Herald*, a monthly newspaper with emphasis on the churches, which later became a free magazine.[9] An annual 'charter day fair' began in 1971 and regularly attracted 2,000–3,000 visitors,[10] but it expired before 1986.[11]

MANORS AND OTHER ESTATES. The earliest estates of St. Mildburg's church formerly belonged to the ruling house of the people called the West 'Hani' or West 'Hecani'.[12] In the late 7th century their ruler Merewalh sold to Aethelheah, abbot of Iken (Suff.), an estate of 97 *manentes* at 'Wininicas', which Aethelheah and Abbess Liobsynd afterwards governed. Before 690 Merewalh's daughter Mildburg gave 60 *manentes* at 'Homtun' to the abbot and abbess in exchange for 'Wininicas'.[13] In 1066 *MUCH WENLOCK* (assumed to be included in 'Wininicas') belonged to the church of St. Mildburg and before 1086 passed to its successor the Cluniac priory of Wenlock,[14] which surrendered to the Crown in 1540.[15]

In 1545 Thomas Lawley (d. 1559) bought the priory site and demesne lands in Much Wenlock from the royal physician Agostino Agostini,[16] who had bought them from the Crown earlier that year.[17] Thomas, descended from a long line of Much Wenlock freeholders, was younger brother of Richard Lawley of Spoonhill, the purchaser of Bourton and Callaughton.[18] Thomas lived at the priory in buildings that included the prior's lodging.[19] That house probably passed from his widow to his son Thomas in 1571,[20] was then called the Abbey,[21] and was afterwards regarded as Much Wenlock manor house.[22]

In 1600 the Crown sold the manor to Thomas and his brother Robert,[23] who at the same time together bought almost the whole estate of the former service of Our Lady in the parish church.[24] Thomas, in sole possession by 1614,[25] died in 1622 and was succeeded by his son Sir Edward[26] (d. 1623), whose daughter and heir Ursula[27] married Sir Roger Bertie. She died (as Lady Penruddock) *c.* 1681 and was succeeded by her son Robert Bertie (d. 1698), who left the manor to Thomas Gage,[28] son of his half-sister Elizabeth (*née* Penruddock). Gage (cr. Viscount Gage 1720),[29] sold the manor in 1714 to Sir John Wynn,[30] a kinsman of the Berties. Wynn died in 1719, leaving the manor to his cousin Watkin Williams (2nd bt. 1740, d. 1749), who then added the surname Wynn. The manor descended with the Williams Wynn baronetcy[31] until 1858 when it was bought by Sir Watkin's niece's husband, James Milnes Gaskell[32] of Thornes House (Yorks. W.R.).[33] The Abbey had become a decayed farmhouse,[34] but Gaskell (d. 1873), followed by his son C. G. Milnes Gaskell[35] (d. 1919), restored it as a gentleman's country house.[36] There C. G. Milnes Gaskell and his wife Lady Catherine received guests who included Thomas Hardy, Henry James, Sir H. M. Stanley, and Philip Webb.[37] Lady Catherine (d. 1935) owned the manor from 1919 and their

92 Local inf.
93 *M. Wenlock Monthly Mag.* Mar. 1906.
94 *Wenlock Herald*, Aug. 1960.
95 Ibid. Sept. 1962.
96 Ibid. Feb. 1960.
97 Ibid. Dec. 1961 (last advt.).
98 *Shrews. News & Cambrian Reporter*, 16 Oct. 1841.
99 *M. Wenlock Monthly Mag.* Apr.–June and Oct. 1902.
1 M. Wenlock C.E. Mixed sch. log bk. 16 July 1913.
2 *Kelly's Dir. Salop.* (1909), 285, 288; (1917), 277, 280; (1922), 287, 290 (no mention); local inf.
3 *Shrews. Chron.* 13 Aug. 1909, p. 6.
4 *Kelly's Dir. Salop.* (1909), 285; (1922), 290.
5 M. Wenlock C.E. Mixed sch. log bk. 5 Aug. 1903.
6 *Wenlock Herald*, Sept. 1962 and *passim*.
7 Ibid. Oct. 1960.
8 *M. Wenlock and Dist. Soc. Newsletter*, i (1985; copy kindly supplied by hon. sec.).
9 *Bridgnorth Jnl.* 9 Dec. 1977.
10 *Shropshire Star*, 24 June 1978, p. 1.
11 *Wenlock Herald*, Sept.–Oct. 1986.
12 On the ruling fam. see Finberg, *Early Charters of W. Midlands*), pp. 217–24. Identification of the W. 'Hani' or 'Hecani' with the later Magonsaete (assumed in *V.C.H. Salop.* ii. 39) is debatable: *Origins of A.- S. Kingdoms*, ed. S. Bassett (1989), 171–83; P. Sims-Williams, *Religion and Literature in Western Eng.* (1990), 40–2.
13 Finberg, op. cit. pp. 201–2, 209; for the identity of Iken see *Proc. Suff. Inst. Arch. and Nat. Hist.* xviii. 31–2; on 'Wininicas' in preference to 'Wimnicas' see Finberg, op. cit. pp. 239–40; for poss. meanings of 'Wininicas' and 'Wenlock' see Bassett, *A.-S. Kgms.* 192–3.
14 *V.C.H. Salop.* i. 312.
15 Ibid. ii. 45.
16 *L. & P. Hen. VIII*, xx (2), p. 124.
17 Ibid. (1), pp. 666–7.
18 Below, this section.
19 *T.S.A.S.* vi. 110; *V.C.H. Salop.* ii. 45.
20 *T.S.A.S.* 3rd ser. ii. 317.
21 S.R.O. 3898/Rg/1, 18 July 1570.
22 For archit. descr. see above, growth of settlement; *Country Life*, 1 Dec. 1960, 1282–5; 8 Dec. 1960, 1432–5.
23 *T.S.A.S.* 3rd ser. ii. 309, 317.
24 S.R.O. 1224/3/8, f. 9 and v.
25 N.L.W., Wynnstay, box 43/139.
26 Ibid. /5.
27 *T.S.A.S.* 3rd ser. ii. 323.
28 N.L.W., Wynnstay, box 43/83; box 56/109–10.
29 Burke, *Peerage* (1938), 1058–9.
30 P.R.O., CP 25/2/960/13 Anne East. [no. 6].
31 N.L.W., Wynnstay, box 56/91; Burke, *Peerage* (1938), 2635–7.
32 S.R.O., q. sess. rec. box 260, reg. of gamekeepers 1742–79, 18 Nov. 1766; N.L.W., Wynnstay, box 43/14; box F/3bb. For Gaskell pedigree see Burke, *Land. Gent.* i (1965), 302.
33 S.R.O. 1224, box 108, deed 22 Mar. 1858.
34 F. Leach, *Co. Seats of Salop.* (1891), 341; *Archaeologia*, lxxii. 131.
35 *P.O. Dir. Salop.* (1879), 434.
36 Leach, op. cit. 341.
37 Visitors' bk. (privately owned; Mr. W. M. Motley arranged access).

daughter Mrs. Mary Ward succeeded her.[38] In 1953 Mrs. Ward settled the estate in trust for the children of her niece Mrs. Mary Juliana Motley (b. 1906).[39] Nothing was known of the manorial lordship in 1985.[40] In 1983 the Abbey was bought by Louis de Wet, a painter, and his wife Gabrielle Drake, an actress.[41] He began an extensive internal restoration and redecoration.[42]

William Ashfield was living at Much Wenlock in 1396.[43] John Ashfield (d. 1506), who held five messuages and 70 a. of arable there, was succeeded by his son Christopher; they also held Bradeley,[44] with which their Much Wenlock estate thereafter descended.[45] William Ashfield's house in Spittle Street, mentioned in 1421,[46] was presumably Ashfield Hall, parts of which date from the 15th century or earlier;[47] it later belonged, like Ashfield's estate, to the Lawleys of Spoonhill.[48] Dr. W. P. Brookes bought it *c.* 1853.[49]

The Almoner's Ground in Much Wenlock township,[50] appropriated to the priory's almonry,[51] belonged to the Crown in 1576,[52] but by 1634 Silvanus Lacon held it of the king in socage.[53] James Lacon sold it in 1720 to Samuel Edwards (d. 1738),[54] whose trustees sold it in 1745 to Thomas More. More's son-in-law Col. (later Gen.) Dudley Ackland sold the estate (117 a. including Coates farm) in 1790 to George Forester.[55]

A freehold said in 1714 to belong to the relict of Thomas Sprott[56] seems to have descended with the Marsh chief house (in Barrow). Comprising 85 a. in 1808,[57] it was acquired before 1848 by the Foresters.[58]

Lord Forester owned only 194 a. of land in Much Wenlock township in 1848, but in 1858 he bought 827 a. more, over half of the Much Wenlock manorial estate, from Sir Watkin Williams Wynn by agreement with J. M. Gaskell, who was buying the lordship of the manor and the rest of the estate.[59] Much of the Forester estate in Much Wenlock township was sold in the 20th century.[60]

An estate in Much Wenlock belonging to Richard Wenlock (born *c.* 1304) passed to his daughter Joan and her husband Nicholas Wyvell. Wyvell's grandson in the male line, Sir John Wenlock, owned the estate in 1448, when it comprised 16 messuages and 80 a. Wenlock (cr. Baron Wenlock of Someries 1461) died in 1471 when the estate passed to his kinsman and heir Thomas Lawley (fl. 1477).[61] It subsequently descended to Thomas's great-grandson[62] Richard Lawley, whose younger brother Thomas bought the priory site.[63] Before buying Callaughton and building Spoonhill in the mid 16th century,[64] the Lawleys may have lived in Rindleford Hall in Spittle Street, a house that belonged to the Lawleys of Spoonhill in 1700 and was also called Sir Thomas Lawley's Hall.[65] By *c.* 1730 the White Hart was said to have been built on its site.[66] If so, it was evidently the later White Hart, which became the Gaskell Arms,[67] parts of which date from the 16th century.

CALLAUGHTON is presumed to have been part of Much Wenlock manor in 1086[68] and was so in 1255.[69] As one of the manor's rural townships, it was probably subject to a leet in the priory liberty.[70] Some time before 1540 Callaughton acquired a court baron.[71] Richard Lawley bought Callaughton from the Crown in 1543.[72] It descended thereafter with Bourton[73] but remained a separate manor.[74] The chief house was let to the Francis family from the 15th century to the 18th.[75] Meanwhile Richard Lawley is presumed to have built Spoonhill House, in Callaughton township; his widow was living at Spoonhill in 1569.[76] The Lawleys seem rarely to have lived there after the mid 17th century[77] when Sir Francis bought Canwell Priory (Staffs.).[78] The west-facing house was of stone with tiled roofs and some timber framing.[79] It had eight hearths in 1672.[80] Sir Robert demolished it in the 1730s.[81] At that time an avenue, the Walk, extended *c.* 200 m. east from the house, and a chain of large ponds lay along a stream *c.* 300 m. to the south-west.[82]

By 1272 William, son of Hugh of Clun and later apparently a clerk of Walter of Wenlock, abbot of Westminster, had a freehold at Bourton,[83] and in

38 *Kelly's Dir. Salop.* (1922), 287; (1937), 296; local inf.
39 *Country Life*, 8 Dec. 1960, 1435.
40 Inf. from Mr. W. M. Motley.
41 *Shrews. Chron.* 15 July 1983, p. 34.
42 *Shropshire Mag.* Jan. 1985, 29, 31.
43 *Cal. Close*, 1392–6, 460.
44 *Cal. Inq. p.m. Hen. VII*, iii, p. 260.
45 Hull Univ., Brynmor Jones Libr., DDFA/26/1–2, 4, 9, 20, 41, 80; N.L.W., Wynnstay, box 56/81; S.R.O. 294/7; 2079/L. 11, 15; 4044/92, ff. 39–40; cf. below, this section (Bradeley).
46 Nott. Univ. Libr. MSS. Dept., Mi. D. 3827.
47 SA 323; *Shrews. Chron.* 25 Apr. 1986, p. 17.
48 *T.S.A.S.* vi. 123; Hull Univ., Brynmor Jones Libr., DDFA/26/46.
49 'Historicus', *Ancestral Homes of Salop.: the Lawleys*, 9 (copy in S.P.L.).
50 Nott. Univ. Libr. MSS. Dept., Mi. D. 3759.
51 S.R.O. 2089/1/3/7.
52 *Cal. Pat.* 1575–8, p. 104. 53 S.R.O. 2089/1/3/7.
54 Ibid. /1/3/20; *V.C.H. Salop.* viii. 82.
55 S.R.O. 1224, box 101, abstr. of title; 1224/7/7.
56 N.L.W., Wynnstay, box E/62, p. 6 (where 'relict' may be a mistake for 'daughter': cf. above, Barrow, manors (Marsh)).
57 Ibid. box 43/3; /7, ff. 9–10; box 56/81; above, Barrow, manors. 58 S.R.O. 294/7.
59 Ibid.; S.R.O. 1224, box 108, deeds.
60 e.g. Westwood Cott. (S.R.O. 1681/42/16), Perkley, Lower and Upper Westwood (S.P.L., SC2/3).
61 *Complete Peerage*, xii (2), 479–85.
62 L. G. Pine, *New Extinct Peerage* (1972), 291.
63 Above, this section.
64 Below, this section.
65 Hull Univ., Brynmor Jones Libr., DDFA/26/29.
66 Birm. Univ. Libr., Mytton Papers, vii. 1524. There had been an earlier White Hart in Spittle St. but in 1672 and 1714 it was on the manorial, not the Lawley, est.: N.L.W., Wynnstay, box E/62, f. 34.
67 Above, social and cultural activities.
68 Eyton, iii. 223–4. 69 *Rot. Hund.* (Rec. Com.), ii. 84.
70 Bourton hund. or Marsh.
71 P.R.O., SC 6/Hen. VIII/3021, m. 14d.
72 *L. & P. Hen. VIII*, xviii (2), p. 239.
73 P.R.O., C 142/152, no. 162; C 142/201, no. 115; C 142/431, no. 98; Hull Univ., Brynmor Jones Libr., DDFA/26/5, 9, 20, 35, 40–1, 80; DDFA(2)/15/1; S.R.O. 294/3; 924/570; S. Bagshaw, *Dir. Salop.* (1851), 588; *P.O. Dir. Salop.* (1856), 86; *Kelly's Dir. Salop.* (1900), 272; (1905), 282; (1937), 296; (1941), 292; below, this section.
74 e.g. P.R.O., C 142/152, no. 162; Hull Univ., Brynmor Jones Libr., DDFA/26/9; /42/1, 12.
75 S.R.O. 1224, box 342, Prior Gosnell's reg. f. 32v.; P.R.O., SC 6/Hen. VIII/3021, m. 14d.; Hull Univ., Brynmor Jones Libr., DDFA/26/32.
76 Hull Univ., Brynmor Jones Libr., DDFA/26/5.
77 *S.H.C.* 1923, 241; *Hearth Tax 1672* (Salop. Arch. Soc. 1949), 37. 78 S. Shaw, *Hist. Staffs.* ii (1801), 22.
79 Forrest, *Old Hos. of Wenlock*, 78–9 and pl. facing p. 76; Hull Univ., Brynmor Jones Libr., DDFA/26/120.
80 *Hearth Tax 1672*, 37.
81 Birm. Univ. Libr., Mytton Papers, vii. 1524.
82 Hull Univ., Brynmor Jones Libr., DDFA/26/120.
83 Eyton, iii. 272–3.

1290 he sold a freehold at Spoonhill, in Callaughton or Bourton, to the abbot's mother Agnes Spicer (fl. 1298) of Much Wenlock.[84]

ATTERLEY and *WENLOCK WALTON* are believed to have been in Much Wenlock manor in 1086,[85] in which they lay in 1255.[86] Walton was in Marsh manor by 1322,[87] and Atterley and Walton were in Marsh grange in 1369.[88] They continued in Marsh manor immediately after the Dissolution.[89] In 1544 William Whorwood, the attorney general, bought much of both townships, together with the manorial rights, from the Crown.[90] The rights descended thereafter with those of Barrow,[91] with which Atterley and Walton formed a single manor by the later 16th century.[92]

Atterley House, the chief house,[93] is a late 16th- or early 17th-century timber framed house consisting of a central range and two rear cross wings. By 1986 it had been empty some years.

Before the Reformation Our Lady's service in the parish church owned an estate in Walton;[94] in the early 18th century the estate allegedly had manorial rights including a court.[95] In 1599 two London speculators bought it from the Crown to hold in socage; they sold it that year to Lancelot Taylor of Walton.[96] In 1733 Thomas Creswell sold it to George Weld of Willey,[97] whose descendant Cecil Weld-Forester exchanged it (112 a.) in 1814 with the manorial estate for other land, some in Walton.[98] The chief house,[99] known as Walton Farm in 1986, and its buildings are in mid 18th-century brick.

In the 13th and 14th centuries the Burnells, priory tenants in Benthall, held 24 a. in Atterley of the priory.[1] Lawrence Benthall claimed in 1636 that some of Walter Acton's lands in Atterley were subject to Benthall manor,[2] and Benthall's successor Elizabeth Browne had interests in Atterley in 1737.[3]

In 1602 Sir Thomas Whorwood, lord of the manor, sold a freehold estate in Atterley to Ralph Deyos, clerk, of Acton Round;[4] it comprised 119 a. in 1773.[5] Most of it belonged by 1814 to Cecil Weld-Forester, who then exchanged it with the manorial estate for other land, some in Walton.[6] In 1819 George Forester's trustees bought the rest from Francis Ash, descendant of Ralph Deyos.[7]

In 1610 Whorwood sold a freehold in Walton to Bryan Richards, a Bridgnorth mercer. Richards's descendants sold it back to the manorial estate in 1739.[8]

In 1847 Sir John Acton owned all Atterley and Walton except for 73 a., mostly Lord Forester's.[9] Forester acquired the manorial estate *c.* 1855[10] and C. T. Weld-Forester, the 5th baron, owned virtually all the land in those townships in 1910.[11]

WYKE and *BRADLEY* (also called Bradley under Down or Buttermilk Bradley)[12] were presumably part of Much Wenlock manor in 1086[13] and were so in 1255.[14] They were probably in Bradley manor by 1321 and therefore in Marsh manor by 1390.[15] At least some of Farley was in Much Wenlock manor in 1431,[16] and Much Wenlock township had rights in Farley wood in the 16th century.[17] In 1554, however, Farley was reckoned in Marsh manor.[18] Farley was considered part of Bradley in the 17th century.[19]

After the Dissolution the lords of Marsh manor divided up Wyke and Bradley into small estates, which were mostly reunited by the Lords Forester in the 19th and 20th centuries.

In 1611 John Slaney, lord of Marsh, sold a freehold in Wyke to Lucy Bowdler, with remainder to her son by her first marriage, Michael Stephens. It remained in the Stephens family until sold as Wyke farm (90 a.) to Dr. Townshend Forester in 1820.[20] Wyke (or Lower Wyke) Farm[21] is a timber framed **T** shaped house of the earlier 17th century, cased in brick before 1700.

In 1592 Hampden Powlett, lord of Marsh, created four 4,000-year leaseholds in Wyke. Edward Alcox's was held by his descendants until 1666; John Chilton bought an assignment from their successors in 1670, and in 1820 Chilton's descendant Richard Jabet assigned it to Dr. Forester as Wood House and Lower House farms (130 a.).[22] Wood House, dated *c.* 1605,[23] is a **T** shaped timber framed building later cased in stone.

Another of the leaseholds in Wyke was granted to William Powlett and others, who assigned it in 1598 to Ralph Littlehales. The presumed farmhouse in Wyke, which belonged to Ralph's great-grandson Richard Littlehales in 1688, was later called the Stone House, Upper Farm, or Manor Farm.[24] A mid 17th-century timber framed building, with a stair turret added *c.* 1700,[25] it was rebuilt with stone in the earlier 18th century.

A third leasehold at Wyke, probably Newhouse

84 *Docs. illustr. rule of Wal. de Wenlok*, pp. 176–7, 246.
85 Eyton, iii. 223–4.
86 *Rot. Hund.* ii. 84.
87 Eyton, iii. 283. Cf. above, Barrow, manors; local govt.
88 B.L. Add. MS. 6165, p. 97.
89 S.R.O. 1224/3/8, ff. 1, 2v.–3.
90 *L. & P. Hen. VIII*, xix (1), p. 638.
91 P.R.O., C 142/104, no. 89; C 142/496, no. 120a; S.R.O. 775/80, 91, 95, 107, 138; 1976/1, f. 44 and v.; cf. above, Barrow, manors.
92 S.R.O. 1175/1.
93 S.R.O. 1093, parcel 110, leases reg. f. 31v.; parcel 161, Atterley and Walton map of 1722; S.R.O., reg. of electors, Bridgnorth dist. (1979), p. 181; (1980), sect. 1CQ, p. 1.
94 S.R.O. 1224, box 91, deed of 1518.
95 Ibid. box 68, partic. of Walton demesnes [*c.* 1725].
96 Ibid. deeds of 1575, 1599.
97 Ibid. deed.
98 S.R.O., incl. award B 38.
99 S.R.O. 1093, parcel 161, Atterley and Walton map of 1722, field 9.
1 *Cal. Inq. p.m.* iii, p. 122; xi, p. 373; xv, p. 289; cf. above, Benthall, manor.
2 S.R.O. 1224, box 66, answer of Lawr. Benthall, ff. 9–10.
3 Deed in late Sir Paul Benthall's possession (summary in S.R.O., archivist's office file 'Benthall').
4 S.R.O. 1093/2/466.
5 S.R.O. 1093, parcel 161, Atterley and Walton map of 1722; 3507/1.
6 S.R.O., incl. award B 38.
7 S.R.O. 1224, box 95, deed, abstr. of title of Fra. Ash.
8 S.R.O. 1093/2/468, 477.
9 S.R.O. 294/1.
10 S. Bagshaw, *Dir. Salop.* (1851), 588; *P.O. Dir. Salop.* (1856), 86.
11 S.R.O. 4044/92, ff. 36–7.
12 S.R.O. 1224, box 342, Prior Gosnell's reg. f. 16v.; N.L.W., Wynnstay, box 43/102.
13 Eyton, iii. 223–4.
14 *Rot. Hund.* ii. 84.
15 Below, econ. hist. (agric.); local govt.
16 S.R.O. 1224/2/8, ct. r.
17 Ibid. /3/8, f. 8.
18 P.R.O., SC 2/197/148, m. 9.
19 S.R.O. 1224, box 144, undated draft deed.
20 Ibid. box 88, abstr. of title, deed of 1820.
21 S.R.O., reg. of electors, Bridgnorth dist. (1983), sect. 2CQ, p. 5; O.S. Map 1/10,000, SJ 60 SW. (1978 edn.).
22 S.R.O. 1224, box 86A, sale plan; abstr. of title; deed of 1820.
23 Date stone formerly visible: local inf.
24 Forrest, *Old Hos. of Wenlock*, 83–4; SA 11979; S.R.O. 4044/92, f. 42; O.S. Map 1/10,000, SJ 60 SW. (1978 edn.).
25 Date board of 1688 attached to stair turret.

farm, was granted to Richard Adams; he assigned it in 1606 to Robert Phillips, who assigned it in 1610 to Richard Littlehales. Newhouse, a timber framed 17th-century building, was rebuilt in brick in the early 19th century.

Both of those leaseholds held by the Littlehales family eventually descended to Charles Littlehales; he assigned Newhouse farm (103 a.) to Charles Guest in 1813[26] and the rest (220 a.) to Dr. Forester in 1820.[27]

Forester's acquisitions of 1820 in Wyke created the *TICKWOOD ESTATE* on which, by 1828,[28] he had built a brick mansion of two storeys and three bays, Tickwood House (later Hall).[29] He acquired Newhouse farm from Guest in 1828[30] and added it to the estate. In 1839 Forester conveyed the Tickwood estate to his nephew J. G. W. Weld-Forester, Lord Forester,[31] lord of Marsh, and its 4,000-year leases thus terminated. Tickwood Hall remained part of the Forester estate in 1910[32] but was sold before 1941 to Capt. E. H. Villiers.[33] John R. S. Dugdale (kt. and d. 1994) bought it in 1956.[34] There were 284 a. attached in 1975. The house was extended in the mid 19th century and a servants' wing added in the 20th.[35]

The fourth lease of 1592 at Wyke, to William Powlett and others, was assigned by them to John Wossolde in 1594. In 1627 Richard Littlehales held it[36] and in 1657 his widow's husband Rowland Habberley. In 1674 Samuel Bowdler bought it.[37] It passed to his descendants through the Sprott, Ashwood, and Hawley families[38] until 1845 when Sir Joseph Henry Hawley[39] sold it (112 a.) to Lord Forester.[40]

About 1576 Stephen Hadnall, lord of Marsh, sold lands in Wyke to Lawrence Benthall,[41] lord of Benthall, who died in 1603 holding them of the king in socage as of Bourton hundred.[42] In 1737 his successor at Benthall, Elizabeth Browne, had interests in Wyke,[43] but by 1848 the Benthall family's lands at Wyke had passed to the Forester estate, which then comprised 679 a. in Wyke and Farley.[44]

In 1592 Hampden Powlett leased two farms in Bradley and Farley, with other premises, for 4,000 years to William Powlett and others. The estate eventually passed to Thomas Stephens (d. 1747), whose executrix assigned it in 1750 to John Windsor. In 1773 Windsor's widow Sarah assigned Bradley farm to Thomas Pitt, whose son Francis assigned it in 1827 to Abraham Darby (IV);[45] it comprised 142 a. in 1848.[46] The timber framed house was built in the 17th century and cased in stone *c.* 1800. In 1777 Sarah Windsor assigned Farley farm[47] to the ironmaster Richard Reynolds; it was augmented by 38 a. at the inclosure of Farley common in 1818[48] and comprised 102 a. in 1848.[49] In 1774 she assigned Birdbach (or Farley) mills to William Jeffreys, and his grandson's widow assigned them to Thomas Harper in 1824.[50] In 1858 Harper's son Caleb bought the woodland[51] that Cecil Weld-Forester had received at the inclosure of Farley common[52] and in 1889 and 1891 acquired the Darby and Reynolds leaseholds.[53] He died in 1905 leaving more than 260 a. in Bradley and Farley to his nephew R. H. Trevor[54] (d. 1916), who left the estate in trust for his son Hubert (d. 1918) and widow Edith Mary, who married Edward Williamson.[55] Lord Forester bought it in 1930.[56]

PRESTHOPE, the 'priests' valley', probably belonged to the pre-Conquest minster at Much Wenlock[57] and was presumably in Much Wenlock manor in 1086.[58]

By 1167 part of Presthope was subinfeudated. Ralph of Presthope and his son Roger (fl. *c.* 1200–*c.* 1230) were presumably lords of that part, for Roger's son Ralph (fl. *c.* 1245–1262) certainly was.[59] John of Presthope (fl. 1272) may have been the lord of that name mentioned in 1316 and 1331. John's son Thomas[60] was probably the Thomas of Presthope named as lord in 1348,[61] from whom the manor passed in or before 1377 to Philip of Willey (fl. 1370–1402).[62] Philip's sister and coheir Margaret is said to have married Roger Wolryche (d. 1392 × 1402)[63] and the manor is presumed to have descended through their son William (fl. 1402–31),[64] his son Andrew[65] (fl. 1470), and his son Thomas (d. by 1507), to Thomas's son Humphrey (d. 1533),[66] lord in 1522.[67] The manor passed to Humphrey's son John (d. 1537) and to John's widow Mary, who married Richard Dauntsey and died in 1549. Her son William Wolryche (d. 1566) succeeded to the estate, followed by his widow Dorothy[68] (d. *c.* 1604), who married Jerome Corbet.[69] The estate had passed by 1604 to her son Francis Wolryche[70] (d. 1614), who was followed by his son Thomas (cr. bt. 1641, d. 1668). Sir Thomas left the estate to a younger son John (d. 1685) and thereafter to John's son Thomas (3rd bt. 1689, d. 1701). That Sir

26 S.R.O. 1224, box 88, deed of 1813.
27 Ibid. box 86C, deed.
28 Ibid. box 88, deed of 1828.
29 SA 11982.
30 S.R.O. 1224, box 88, deed.
31 Ibid. box 103, deed.
32 S.R.O. 4044/92, f. 42.
33 *Kelly's Dir. Salop.* (1941), 292–3.
34 *The Times*, 31 Dec. 1994, p. 21.
35 *Shropshire Mag.* June 1975, 37.
36 S.R.O. 1224, box 87, decl.; 1224/2/515.
37 Lincs. Archives Office, 2 Hawley 1/G/73–4.
38 S.R.O. 1224, box 97, abstr. of title.
39 *D.N.B.*
40 S.R.O. 1224, box 97, deed.
41 *Cal. Pat.* 1575–8, p. 164.
42 P.R.O., C 142/299, no. 130; cf. above, Benthall, manor.
43 Deed in late Sir Paul Benthall's possession (summary in S.R.O., archivist's office file 'Benthall'); cf. above, Benthall, manor.
44 S.R.O. 294/4.
45 S.R.O. 1224, box 104, abstr. of title of Abr. Darby (IV); 3898/Rg/4, bur. 2 Mar. 1746/7.
46 S.R.O. 294/4.
47 S.R.O. 1359, box 26, decl. of 1891.
48 S.R.O. 1681/144/2.
49 S.R.O. 294/4.
50 S.R.O. 1359, box 26, deed of 1824.
51 Ibid. deed.
52 S.R.O. 1681/144/2.
53 S.R.O. 1359, box 27, deed of 1889; 1681/145/16.
54 *Standard*, 4 Aug. 1905; S.R.O. 1681/244/1, will and codicil; /245/1, valn.
55 S.R.O. 1206/99, p. 184; 1681/244/1, deed of 1922.
56 Local inf.
57 Below, churches.
58 Eyton, iii. 223–4.
59 Ibid. 290–2; *Rot. Hund.* ii. 85.
60 *Feud. Aids*, iv. 228; Eyton, iii. 292; S.R.O. 3195/1, f. 79.
61 Barnard MSS., Raby Castle, box 1, bdle. 18, nos. 5a–6.
62 S.R.O. 1093/2/482, 507–8.
63 J. B. Blakeway, *Sheriffs of Salop.* (Shrews. 1831), 169; H. Owen and J. B. Blakeway, *Hist. Shrews.* (1825), ii. 455; S.P.L., MS. 2793, p. 190.
64 S.P.L., MS. 2793, p. 190; S.R.O. 2922/3/6.
65 S.R.O. 2922/3/6.
66 S.P.L., MS. 2793, pp. 190, 195; P.R.O., C 142/56, no. 61.
67 S.R.O. 1224, box 342, Prior Gosnell's reg. f. 39.
68 P.R.O., C 142/56, no. 54; C 142/89, no. 149; C 142/193, no. 39.
69 A. E. C[orbet], *The Fam. of Corbet: its Life and Times*, ii [1918], 272–3.
70 S.R.O. 2922/1/4/1.

Thomas's son Sir John[71] sold the Presthope estate in 1716 to Richard Newport, earl of Bradford, who sold it in 1718 to Samuel Edwards of Frodesley (d. 1738).[72] Edwards left Presthope to trustees for the repayment of debts, with remainder to his son Godolphin.[73] In 1746 the manor, but not the chief house, was bought from Godolphin Edwards by Bradford's son-in-law Orlando Bridgeman[74] (4th bt. 1747, d. 1764); Bridgeman's son Sir Henry sold it in 1790 to John Wheeler of Upton Magna, an ironmaster[75] who had bought the chief house from the Edwards trustees in 1787.[76] Wheeler went bankrupt *c.* 1804; in 1815 his assignees sold the manor to Ralph Benson (d. 1845), and it thereafter descended with Lutwyche.[77] R. B. Benson sold Lea farm (245 a.) *c.* 1909.[78] G. R. Benson sold 361 a. in 1938[79] and Accumulated Investments Ltd., his successors at Lutwyche, sold 124 a. in 1952.[80] Nothing was known of any manorial rights in 1987.[81]

The chief house,[82] a 'substantial' stone house in 1802,[83] was the Plough inn from 1862 and later Plough Farm;[84] it was demolished *c.* 1974.[85]

The part of Presthope not subinfeudated by the priory was evidently in Marsh manor before the Dissolution,[86] and appears to have remained with the lord of Marsh afterwards. Presthope presented at Marsh manor court in 1548,[87] and in 1578 Stephen Hadnall, lord of Marsh, sold to John Ball the younger the freehold of Presthope lands[88] of which Ball's family had been copyholders.[89] In 1639 Ball's son John bought a Presthope freehold from John Lee,[90] to whom it had descended from Edward More of Larden (fl. 1543).[91] The Balls' Presthope estate remained with them in 1710[92] but had been alienated by 1783.[93]

The small manor of *PETELIE*, which belonged to Wenlock priory in 1086[94] and was called a vill *c.* 1102,[95] is probably to be located near Perkley, a farm in Much Wenlock township towards Callaughton. An assart in 'Purteley' was mentioned in the late 12th century.[96] There was an open field called 'Putlee' in 1221,[97] 'Pertley' in 1736.[98] Petelie was probably absorbed by Much Wenlock manor before 1255.[99]

BOURTON was perhaps one of the estates 'by the Corve' which St. Mildburg's half brothers gave to her before 704:[1] it belonged to St. Mildburg's church in 1066. Aelfric (Aluric) was then the tenant, and by 1086 his son Eadric (Edric) of Wenlock[2] had succeeded.[3] Before 1255 Wenlock priory resumed the demesne lordship,[4] though Eadric's descendants may have retained land at Bradeley as late as 1281.[5] The tenants *c.* 1302 were William Glazier (*le verrour*) and his wife,[6] possible relatives of Walter of Wenlock, abbot of Westminster.[7] Bourton had a court baron by 1333.[8]

In 1543 Richard Lawley of Tipton (Staffs.), the purchaser of Callaughton,[9] bought most of Bourton from the Crown.[10] In 1545 he bought more land in Bourton with the reputed manor of Bradeley.[11] At his death in 1569 he held Bourton in chief by knight service.[12] It then passed successively to his son Francis (d. 1583), and to Francis's son Richard (d. 1624), from whom the manor passed to Richard's brother Thomas (cr. bt. 1641, d. 1646).[13] Thereafter it descended from father to son until 1834, the following being lords:[14] Sir Francis (d. 1696), Sir Thomas (d. 1729), Sir Robert (d. 1779),[15] Sir Robert (d. 1793),[16] and Sir Robert (cr. Baron Wenlock 1831, d. 1834).[17] The manor passed successively to Lord Wenlock's brothers Sir Francis Lawley[18] (d. 1851) and Paul Beilby Lawley-Thompson, Baron Wenlock (d. 1852).[19] Lord Wenlock was succeeded by his son Beilby Richard Lawley, 2nd baron (d. 1880),[20] whose son Beilby, 3rd baron,[21] sold the manor in 1901 to J. H. A. Whitley (d. 1940).[22] His widow Mrs. S. I. B. Whitley died as lady of the manor in 1941,[23] leaving a life interest to her niece the

71 P.R.O., C 142/345, no. 135; *T.S.A.S.* 4th ser. iv. 108, 111, 116–17, 130, 139, 144–6; S.P.L., Deeds 3360.

72 W.S.L. 350/3/40, Hughley p. 3; S.R.O., q. sess. rec. box 260, reg. of gamekeepers 1711–42, 2 Nov. 1726. For Edwards pedigree see *V.C.H. Salop.* viii. 82.

73 S.R.O. 2089/9/2/11.

74 Staffs. R.O., D. 1287, add misc., abstr. of Sir Hen. Bridgeman's title to Hughley and Presthope [*c.* 1790]; S.R.O., q. sess. rec. box 260, reg. of gamekeepers 1711–42, 20 Oct. 1733; 1742–79, 1 Feb. 1746/7.

75 S.R.O. 809, box 1, draft deed of 1815, f. 4; 3657/2/7.

76 N.L.W., Wynnstay, box 43/105; box 56/6; S.R.O. 809, box 1, draft deed of 1815, f. 2.

77 S.R.O. 294/6; 809, box 1, draft deed of 1815; Burke, *Land. Gent.* ii (1969), 40–2; *P.O. Dir. Salop.* (1879), 434; *Kelly's Dir. Salop.* (1891), 467; (1913), 294; above, Rushbury, manors (Lutwyche).

78 S.R.O. 809, box 13, H. Thursby to R. [B. Benson] 1 Feb. 1909; 2079/L. 15; 4044/92, f. 32.

79 S.R.O. 809, box 14, sale partic.

80 Ibid. box 2, sale partic.

81 Inf. from Capt. Ralph Benson, Minton Ho.

82 Identified from S.R.O. 3657/2/12 (not shown); 4175/1 (no. C 39). 83 S.R.O. 4175/1, sale partic.

84 *Return of Licensed Hos. 1901*, p. 343; O.S. Map 1/2,500, Salop. L. 14 (1883 edn.); S.R.O. 809, box 13, surv. of 1934, p. 97.

85 S.R.O., reg. of electors, Ludlow const. (1974), p. 190 (called Presthope Fm.); O.S. Map 1/10,000, SO 59 NE. (1977 edn.).

86 Below, local govt.; cf. above, Barrow, manors; local govt. The priory had no ct. for Presthope 1333–1450 (S.R.O. 566/1; 1190/1, unlisted ct. r. 1403–4; 1224/2/1–5, 7, 9) and Presthope was in Marsh 'parish' in 1540 (P.R.O., SC 6/Hen. VIII/3021, m. 8). Presthope, however, was not separately represented at Marsh man. ct., at least from 1477 to 1530: S.R.O. 1224/2/1–5, 7, 9. 87 P.R.O., SC 2/197, no. 117.

88 S.P.L., Deeds 2912. 89 S.R.O. 1224/3/8, f. 3v.

90 S.P.L., Deeds 3210.

91 S.P.L., MS. 2342, no. 12949; ibid. Deeds 15686.

92 Ibid. Deeds 2913–20.

93 N.L.W., Wynnstay, box 43/84 (4).

94 *V.C.H. Salop.* i. 312.

95 *T.S.A.S.* lvii. 146. 96 Eyton, iii. 294.

97 *Rolls of Justices in Eyre, 1221–2* (Selden Soc. lix), p. 500.

98 N.L.W., Wynnstay, box 43/86 (dated from box 56/81).

99 Not mentioned in *Rot. Hund.* ii.

1 Finberg, *Early Charters of W. Midlands*, p. 148.

2 *T.S.A.S.* lv. 112–18. 3 *V.C.H. Salop.* i. 312.

4 *Rot. Hund.* ii. 85. 5 Above, Hughley, manor.

6 *Cal. Pat.* 1301–7, 94.

7 *Docs. illustr. rule of Wal. de Wenlok*, pp. 30, 246–7.

8 S.R.O. 566/1. 9 Above, this section.

10 *L. & P. Hen. VIII*, xviii (2), p. 239.

11 Below, this section. 12 P.R.O., C 142/152, no. 162.

13 Hull Univ., Brynmor Jones Libr., DDFA/26/5, 9–11; DDFA(2)/15/1; P.R.O., C 142/201, no. 15; C 142/431, no. 98.

14 For pedigree see Pine, *New Extinct Peerage*, 291–2.

15 Hull Univ., Brynmor Jones Libr., DDFA/26/20, 35, 40–1. Sir Rob. owned all Bourton tns. in 1731: S.R.O. 3765/1.

16 N.L.W., Wynnstay, box 43/84 (16).

17 Hull Univ., Brynmor Jones Libr., DDFA/26/80.

18 S.R.O. 294/3. 19 S. Bagshaw, *Dir. Salop.* (1851), 588.

20 *P.O. Dir. Salop.* (1856), 86.

21 *Kelly's Dir. Salop.* (1900), 272.

22 Ibid. (1905), 282; S.R.O. 3898/Sc/6, pp. 331–2; gravestone at Bourton; cf. C. Penn, *Staffs. and Salop. at Opening of 20th Cent.* (1907), 203; D. H. S. Cranage, *Not Only a Dean* (1952), 70; inf. from Capt. Micklethwait.

23 *Kelly's Dir. Salop.* (1941), 292; gravestone at Bourton.

Hon. Mrs. H. E. D. Field, who relinquished it in 1972. The estate then passed in accordance with Mrs. Whitley's will to Capt. R. M. Micklethwait, the owner in 1986.[24] After the Second World War some of the farms were sold.[25] Nothing was known of the manorial lordship by 1986.[26]

The court, Eadric of Wenlock's manor house, was mentioned in 1086[27] and the name Bourton suggests that it was or had been fortified.[28] By 1550 and in 1695 the demesne had two houses, one on the site of the modern Grange, the other next to it.[29] Only the Grange, the manor's home farm by 1906,[30] remained in 1847.[31] It is a 19th-century brick house, perhaps one of those rebuilt by Sir Francis Lawley.[32]

By 1819 the Lawleys lived occasionally at Bourton Cottage near the church.[33] In 1874 Norman Shaw greatly enlarged it in a Tudor style, mainly in stone, and it was later named Bourton Manor. The interior was redecorated about the time of Whitley's purchase in 1901.[34]

In 1522 William Gatacre held an estate at *WOODHOUSEFIELD* of Wenlock priory;[35] it was between Bourton and Acton Round. In 1608 William Gatacre of Gatacre conveyed the freehold to Richard Acton of Aldenham, who conveyed it to his brother Walter in 1628.[36] The Actons had it in 1747,[37] but it passed before 1795 to John Cleobury,[38] who still owned it (130 a.) in 1808.[39] By 1848 Woodhousefield belonged to Sir Francis Lawley and was reckoned part of Bourton township.[40] In 1980 there were remains of a rectangular moat at the homestead site.[41] An inclosed pasture at Woodhousefield, in Acton Round township in 1523,[42] was let by Wenlock priory in 1536 as a copyhold of Marsh manor.[43] It was presumably the freehold at Woodhousefield, within Marsh leet jurisdiction, held in 1634 by Thomas Lawley.[44]

BRADELEY, formerly Goose (or West) Bradeley, was held of Wenlock priory in 1255 by Robert de Beysin, lord of Broseley,[45] though descendants of Eadric of Wenlock, lord of Bourton in 1086, seem to have had an interest there in the late 13th century.[46] John Easthope, lord of Easthope, had property in West Bradeley in 1427, which his feoffees conveyed in 1440 to John Ashfield of Much Wenlock.[47] In 1443 Ashfield (d. *c.* 1455) held the reputed manor of Bradeley,[48] and John Ashfield (d. 1506) held it of John Harewell, lord of Broseley. Ashfield was succeeded by his son Christopher,[49] who sold Bradeley to John Leveson in 1544.[50] A year later Leveson sold it to Richard Lawley, purchaser of Bourton and Callaughton.[51] The estate descended thereafter with Bourton.[52] A connexion with Broseley remained in 1620.[53] Still reputed a manor in 1799,[54] Bradeley seems later to have been absorbed into Bourton manor.[55]

In 1281 a rent of 24*s.* in Bradeley was given to Limebrook priory (Herefs.) by Sir Reynold of Lee,[56] and the priory seems to have retained it until its surrender in 1539.[57]

In 1066 *WIGWIG*, which evidently included Homer, was held by Aelmer (or Elmar). Turold of Verley held it of Earl Roger by 1086[58] and presumably held it in chief after Earl Robert's forfeiture in 1102.[59] Between 1108 and 1121 Turold's son Robert gave Wigwig to Shrewsbury abbey,[60] and before 1187[61] the abbey conveyed it to Wenlock priory. The vill was a member of Much Wenlock manor by 1255[62] but by 1345 was part of Marsh manor.[63] By 1369 it was reckoned in Bradley manor,[64] and thus by 1390 was in Marsh manor again.[65] In 1847 Lord Forester, lord of Marsh, owned 54 a. in Homer,[66] and in 1920 the 6th Lord Forester sold 68 a. there in small lots.[67] The 7th Lord Forester sold manorial rights in Homer *c.* 1956 to E. W. Hill.[68]

In 1545 the Crown sold the farm held by Joan Sprott at Wigwig to George Tresham and Edmund Twynyho.[69] By 1584 Richard Sprott owned it.[70] Called the Pall in 1624,[71] it had a chief house known in 1670 as Wigwig Hall (or Farm).[72] William Icke of Leegomery bought nearly all the estate over the period 1692–1706[73] and the Ickes' estate at Wigwig comprised 85 a. in 1801.[74] It passed *c.* 1850 to the Meire family,[75] which owned it as Mill farm in 1910.[76] Lord Forester was the owner in 1986.[77] By 1847 the late 18th-century mill house was also the farm house.[78] The site of Wigwig Hall is unknown.

24 Will of Mrs. S. I. B. Whitley, pr. 17 Dec. 1942; inf. from Capt. Micklethwait.
25 Local inf.
26 Inf. from the Hon. Mrs. Field and Capt. Micklethwait.
27 *V.C.H. Salop.* i. 312.
28 *P.N. Salop.* (E.P.N.S.), i. 55.
29 P.R.O., LR 2/184, f. 148v.; S.R.O. 1037/19/7; 3765/1.
30 *Estate Mag.* vi. 415.
31 S.R.O. 294/3.
32 S. Bagshaw, *Dir. Salop.* (1851), 588.
33 S.R.O. 294/3; 4791/1/10, p. 554; cf. *Shropshire Mag.* Jan. 1963, 27 (contemp. picture).
34 Forrest, *Old Hos. of Wenlock*, 59; A. Saint, *Ric. Norman Shaw* (1977), 409.
35 S.R.O. 1224, box 342, Prior Gosnell's reg. f. 39.
36 S.R.O. 1093/2/484, 487; P.R.O., C 142/496, no. 120a.
37 S.R.O. 1093/2/489–98.
38 Bourton map of 1795 (in Mr. J. R. Craig's possession).
39 N.L.W., Wynnstay, box 43/7, f. 13.
40 S.R.O. 294/3.
41 SA 327.
42 N.L.W., Wynnstay, RA 2.
43 S.R.O. 1224/3/8, f. 4; cf. above, Barrow, manors.
44 S.R.O. 1224/2/65.
45 *Rot. Hund.* ii. 84.
46 Above, this section (Bourton); Hughley, manor.
47 P.R.O., C 104/27, deeds of 1427, 1440.
48 Ibid. E 40/6016; *T.S.A.S.* vi. 321.
49 *Cal. Inq. p.m. Hen. VII*, iii, pp. 141–2, 260, 297.
50 Hull Univ., Brynmor Jones Libr., DDFA/26/1.
51 Above, this section.
52 Hull Univ., Brynmor Jones Libr., DDFA/26/2, 5, 9, 20, 35, 40–1, 80; DDFA(2)/15/1; P.R.O., C 142/201, no. 115; C 142/431, no. 98.
53 Above, Broseley, manor; S.R.O. 840, box 43, Mr. Mic. Old's breviate concerning the priory lands [?1658].
54 Hull Univ., Brynmor Jones Libr., DDFA/26/90.
55 S.R.O. 294/3.
56 *Cal. Pat.* 1272–81, 434; cf. above, Hughley, manor.
57 P.R.O., SC 2/197/148, m. 6; cf. D. Knowles and R. N. Hadcock, *Medieval Religious Hos.: Eng. and Wales* (1971), 281.
58 *V.C.H. Salop.* i. 335.
59 Ibid. iii. 10; *Cartulary of Shrews. Abbey*, ed. U. Rees (1975), ii, p. 262.
60 *Cart. Shrews.* i, pp. 34, 39; ii, p. 262.
61 Ibid. ii, p. 300.
62 *Rot. Hund.* ii. 84.
63 S.R.O. 1224/2/1. For Marsh see above, Barrow, manors.
64 B.L. Add. MS. 6165, p. 98.
65 Below, local govt.
66 S.R.O. 294/5.
67 S.P.L., SC2/34.
68 Local inf.
69 *L. & P. Hen. VIII*, xx (1), pp. 415–16.
70 S.R.O. 1224/3/136.
71 Ibid. /2/514.
72 S.R.O. 1709/55/1.
73 Ibid. /55/7, 9, 15, 17, 19–20, 22.
74 N.L.W., Wynnstay, box 43/7, f. 18.
75 S.R.O. 294/5; S. Bagshaw, *Dir. Salop.* (1851), 589.
76 S.R.O. 4044/92, f. 35 (no. 320).
77 Local inf.
78 S.R.O. 294/5.

In 1545 Tresham and Twynyho also bought the farm held by Thomas Taylor in Wigwig.[79] It passed to Thomas Harnage (d. *c.* 1562) of Belswardine,[80] and by 1808 the Harnages' estate included New House (or Wigwig) farm,[81] Red House farm at Wigwig, and Homer farm.[82] Red House farm belonged to the Revd. Samuel Minton by 1847[83] and passed to R. F. M. Wood before 1910.[84] In 1888 Sir Henry George Harnage's trustees had sold the rest to Wood,[85] who sold the whole (292 a.) in 1919.[86] The estate's later descent has not been traced.

The *RECTORY* was formally appropriated to Wenlock priory 1186 × 1198.[87] From 1274 its income consisted mainly of corn tithes.[88] It was valued at £34 13*s*.4*d*. in 1291,[89] £35.4*s*. in 1535,[90] and *c*. £100 in 1587.[91] In the late 16th and early 17th century the Crown sold the rectorial tithes of the townships separately , often to speculators from whom local landowners soon bought them.[92] At commutation between 1847 and 1849 they were deemed to consist of corn and grain tithes only, except in Farley, Wyke, and Bradley, where they also included hay tithes.[93] The former priory's reputed desmesne lands, all in Much Wenlock and Callaughton, were declared prescriptively tithe free. There were then 15 impropriators, of whom Sir John Dalberg-Acton, Lord Forester, and Sir Francis Lawley had tithes from their property alone, whilst Sir George Harnage and Sir Watkin Williams Wynn also had tithes from other people's. The owners of the Harnage, Lawley and Williams Wynn estates merged their tithes in their freeholds, and the rest of the tithes were commuted to £329 10*s*. 7*d*.

ECONOMIC HISTORY. Outside the town agriculture has been the main economic activity in the parish. Limestone was plentiful and quarrying the parish's most enduring industry from medieval times. The town, endowed with markets and fairs by the 12th and 13th centuries, had some concentration of manufactures, crafts, trades, and eventually professions, and it thus came to fill the modest role of supplier of goods and services to a small agricultural area.

AGRICULTURE. Names like Atterley, Bradeley, Bradley, Farley, and 'Petelie' suggest woodland clearance, probably in Anglo-Saxon times. Much Wenlock manor had woodland for 300 swine in 1086[94] but then included places outside the parish.[95] Other woods belonged to Wigwig and 'Petelie'; the latter's included a hay.[96] In the 13th century assarting was reported in Atterley, Callaughton, Walton, Much Wenlock, and Wigwig.[97]

The later medieval woods separated townships[98] and were presumably intercommoned until boundaries were fixed. Westwood covered at least 350 a. of high ground between Much Wenlock, Bourton, Callaughton, Presthope, and Hughley[99] but by 1235 had long been reduced to underwood and thorns.[1] Presthope used woods adjoining Harley,[2] and Bourton shared Spoonhill wood with Callaughton and Acton Round; Acton Round's boundary within it was defined in 1256.[3] Peat was dug at Spoonhill in the early 15th century.[4] Homer wood, between Much Wenlock and Wigwig, was probably the wood for 50 swine attributed to Wigwig in 1086.[5] By the 16th century it included 23 a. of 'thin-set trees with small oaks'. Farley wood was between Bradley, Buildwas, and Much Wenlock. Poorly managed by the 16th century, it then had 20 a. of hazel and thorn, with old pollard oaks, 'part timber cropped and stubbed'.[6] Homer and Farley woods included areas of common waste.[7] At Wyke woodland adjoined Benthall and Buildwas; by 1332 a ditch divided the priory's wood from Buildwas abbey's.[8] Lawleys cross, at the parish boundary in 1542,[9] stood on the Wenlock–Buildwas road[10] and was said to mark the end of the prior's estate.[11] By the 16th century Wyke monopolized Arnegreave and Tickwood coppice woods[12] and Thorlyes, Tickwood bank, and Nathole woods.[13] Oak and ash grew in Arnegreave and Tickwood,[14] and elm, holly, and lime in Thorlyes.[15] Thorlyes and Tickwood bank were partly waste.[16] Atterley and Walton depended on rights in Shirlett,[17] outside the parish,[18] where Much Wenlock[19] and Wyke[20] also had rights. Bourton men made unlawful depredations in Shirlett.[21]

Almost the only permanent common pastures were in woodlands and former woodlands. Westwood was the largest. Much Wenlock,[22] Atterley,[23] Callaughton,[24] and Wyke[25] townships, and presumably the others too, had common meadows. By the 16th century, however, many meadows and pastures were held in severalty.[26]

79 *L. & P. Hen. VIII*, xx (1), pp. 415–16.
80 S.R.O. 1224/2/23.
81 S.R.O. 1709, box 206, deed of 1821.
82 N.L.W., Wynnstay, box 43/7, f. 18.
83 S.R.O. 294/5. 84 S.R.O. 4044/92, f. 35 (no. 321).
85 S.R.O. 1709, box 207, Sir H. G. Harnage's will (copy); 3651, box 33, corresp. 86 S.P.L., SC1/12.
87 *Cal. Pat.* 1348–50, 186. For date see Eyton, iii. 265.
88 Eyton, iii. 266. 89 *Tax. Eccl.* (Rec. Com.), 167.
90 *Valor Eccl.* (Rec. Com.), iii. 216.
91 Heref. Cath. Libr., M.R. 6.A.iv, f. 7.
92 *Cal. Pat.* 1575–8, pp. 487, 490; *T.S.A.S.* xvlii. 29; Hull Univ., Brynmor Jones Libr., DDFA/26/14; P.R.O., C 66/1354, mm. 13–14; C 142/393, no. 142; SC 12/32/32; S.R.O. 1224, box 81, letters patent of 1581 (copy); 1976/1, f. 45; W.B.R., Q1/13/167.
93 S.R.O. 3898/Ti/1. Rest of para. based on S.R.O. 294/1, 3–7. 94 *V.C.H. Salop.* i. 312.
95 Eyton, iii. 223–4. 96 *V.C.H. Salop.* i. 312, 335.
97 *Cal. Pat.* 1258–66, 207; *Cal. Chart. R.* 1327–41, 488.
98 S.R.O. 1224/2/11; field names in S.R.O. 294/1, 3–7; fig. 40.
99 N.L.W., Wynnstay, box 56/6. 1 Eyton, iii. 297.
2 *V.C.H. Salop.* viii. 85–6.
3 *Roll of Salop. Eyre 1256* (Selden Soc. xcvi), pp. 138–9.
4 S.R.O. 1224/2/6. 5 *V.C.H. Salop.* i. 335.
6 S.R.O. 1224/3/8, f. 8. 7 Ibid. /1/19; /2/47; /3/135.
8 Ibid. /2/11. 9 *T.S.A.S.* vi. 102.
10 P.R.O., IR 29/29/125; IR 30/29/125, field 1565.
11 *Randall's Guide to Wenlock*, 104.
12 S.R.O. 1224/3/136. 13 Ibid. /1/19; /2/49; /3/127.
14 Ibid. /2/31; /3/39. 15 Ibid. /2/31, 531–2.
16 Ibid. /2/49; /3/135.
17 Ibid. /3/136; S.R.O. 1175/1.
18 Above, Barrow, econ. hist.
19 *L. & P. Hen. VIII*, xx (1), p. 667; S.R.O. 1224/3/8, f. 8.
20 S.R.O. 1224/2/531. 21 Ibid. /2/21.
22 B.L. Add. MS. 6165, p. 97.
23 S.R.O. 2228/1, ff. 39, 41 and v., 43v.
24 P.R.O., E 303/14/Salop./267.
25 S.R.O. 1224/3/135.
26 e.g. ibid.; ibid. /2/31; /3/8, f. 2v.; 2228/1, ff. 39, 41 and v., 42v., 43v.

Open-field arable lay around the chief settlements in the later Middle Ages. Much Wenlock town had four large fields:[27] Spittle,[28] Edge (or West)[29], South,[30] and Pertley.[31] Smaller fields included Blunthill, Knightstree (or Eastry),[32] Signal, and Walton Hill.[33] At Wyke there were Cross, Pudwell, Riden, and Yowley fields.[34] Atterley's fields were Beggarhill, Hewley, Moston, and Shirlett,[35] and Walton had Mary (or Little)[36] field, Marsh,[37] Ballop, and Rindle[38] fields.[39] The fields at Presthope were Aldenhill, Westwood, and Novers.[40] At Bourton there were Harp, Patton, and Routhers fields.[41] Bradeley had a field towards Patton.[42] There were 'common' fields in Bradley.[43] Callaughton had Spoonhill, Lower, and Pertley fields,[44] the latter shared with Much Wenlock. An open field at Wigwig was mentioned in 1262.[45]

By the late 13th century Wenlock priory's large manor of Much Wenlock was divided into separately run estates. Bradley and Wyke, with Benthall and Posenhall, seem to have been managed as one estate, called Bradley;[46] by 1369, with Wigwig and Harley added, it was called Bradley grange.[47] Atterley and Walton, with Barrow, were apparently administered together by 1291 as Marsh,[48] called Marsh grange by 1369. The granges' revenues consisted mostly of rents from free tenants.[49] Between 1379 and 1390, perhaps in response to agricultural recession, Marsh grange absorbed that of Bradley.[50] In 1291 Callaughton's revenues had long been assigned to the priory kitchen.[51]

In 1086 Much Wenlock manor, which then included (outside the later parish) Barrow, Benthall, Posenhall, and perhaps other places,[52] had 46 bordars in a recorded population of 58. It was an unusually high proportion, and there were only 9 *villani*.[53] Many of the bordars were probably small tenants who also worked on the demesnes and as servants in the monastery; others perhaps occupied marginal lands.[54] In 1247 the prior's immediate tenants in Much Wenlock township were 8 free men and 39 burgesses, all owing cash rents. Beneath them were undertenants and villeins. Though able to plead in the king's court, the free men and burgesses owed terciary and, in one case, labour services.[55] Most townships in the 13th and 14th centuries had free tenants paying cash rents; at Bourton neifs too paid cash in 1369.[56] By the early 16th century tenants were usually leaseholders for terms of years or copyholders for lives; in the town there were also tenants at will.[57]

In the later Middle Ages mixed farming was usual.[58] Winter corn, lent grain, and fallow were rotated in the open fields.[59] On the priory demesnes, and probably elsewhere, livestock was also important. In 1291 the prior had 25 cows, 19 mares, and 976 sheep for wool, of which 209 were breeding ewes,[60] and a Callaughton tenant had at least 70 sheep in 1274.[61] A tenant at Atterley paid for 19 swine in the lord's wood in 1431.[62] In Wyke and Bradley the seven farms *c.* 1580 had common stints totalling 36 oxen, 54 kine, 460 sheep, and 17 horses.[63] Some commoners of Wyke in 1587 forged neighbours' earmarks,[64] and in 1584 foreign pigs, bullocks, and sheep were pastured in Farley wood.[65]

Adam atte (or de la) Home of Much Wenlock (fl. 1338–45) was a merchant who bought wool from Wales and the Marches and exported it through London and Hull.[66] He evidently invested in land; his son Richard del Home (fl. 1354) and grandson Peter del Home (fl. 1373) owned land in several townships in Much Wenlock and Shipton parishes.[67]

In the general economic crises of the earlier 14th century the parish's arable and meadow fell sharply in value and, at least in Bradley grange and Bourton, in extent. By 1341 bad weather and sheep disease were afflicting the parish.[68] Wenlock priory had let out some of its demesne by 1390,[69] and by 1540 the only demesne in hand was *c.* 460 a. in Much Wenlock township, whose pasture (some of it former arable)[70] and meadow were inclosed. The parish's agricultural value in 1540 had increased since the 14th century.[71]

In the later Middle Ages some isolated farms were formed, both by inclosure of open-field

27 S.R.O., q. sess. rec. parcel 283, reg. of enrolled incl. awards, pp. 2–49.

28 Ibid. Unless otherwise stated, fields mentioned in this para. without self-descriptive names are located by S.R.O. 294/1, 3–7.

29 P.R.O., LR 2/184, f. 61v.

30 Nott. Univ. Libr. MSS. Dept., Mi. D. 3702.

31 Ibid. 3679. Wheat field (60 a.) was mentioned in 1541: Dugdale, *Mon.* v. 82.

32 S.R.O., q. sess. rec. parcel 283, reg. of enrolled incl. awards, pp. 2–49.

33 Nott. Univ. Libr. MSS. Dept., Mi. D. 3745, 3759, 3761, 3836.

34 S.R.O. 1224/3/127–8, 135.

35 S.R.O. 2228/1, f. 39 and v.

36 Ibid. f. 42v.

37 S.R.O. 1224, box 68, undated surv.

38 Ibid. estreat of ct. r. of 1564.

39 Locations: S.R.O. 1093, parcel 161, Atterley and Walton map.

40 N.L.W., Wynnstay, RA 2.

41 Hull Univ., Brynmor Jones Libr., DDFA/26/34.

42 Barnard MSS., Raby Castle, box 1, bdle. 17, no. 11.

43 S.R.O. 1224/3/135.

44 S.R.O. 3614, box 11, deed of 1748.

45 P.R.O., C 143/2, no. 16.

46 *Tax. Eccl.* (Rec. Com.), 164.

47 B.L. Add. MS. 6165, p. 98.

48 *Tax. Eccl.* 164.

49 B.L. Add. MS. 6165, pp. 97–8.

50 Ibid. 6164, p. 383; S.R.O. 1224, box 342, Prior Gosnell's reg. ff. 35v., 40; cf. below, this section.

51 *Tax. Eccl.* 164; S.R.O. 1224, box 342, Prior Gosnell's reg. f. 32v.

52 Eyton, iii. 223–4; cf. above, pp. 191, 226 n. 8.

53 *V.C.H. Salop.* i. 312.

54 *Medieval Settlement*, ed. P. H. Sawyer (1976), 197–9; *Studies in Medieval Hist. presented to R. H. C. Davis*, 103.

55 B.L. Harl. Ch. 45 A 33. On terciary see *T.S.A.S.* lviii. 68–76.

56 *Tax. Eccl.* 164; B.L. Add. MS. 6165, pp. 98–9.

57 P.R.O., SC 6/Hen. VIII/3021, mm. 1–14d.

58 Ibid.; *Tax. Eccl.* 164; B.L. Add. MS. 6165, pp. 97–9.

59 B.L. Add. MS. 6165, pp. 97–9; S.R.O. 775/77; 1224/2/7, 16.

60 *Tax. Eccl.* 164.

61 *Rot. Hund.* ii. 101.

62 S.R.O. 1224/2/8.

63 Ibid. /3/136.

64 Ibid. /2/534.

65 Ibid. /2/531.

66 *Cal. Close*, 1337–9, 434; 1341–3, 81; *Cal. Pat.* 1340–3, 59, 103, 159; 1343–5, 585.

67 P.R.O., C 104/26, deeds of 1354, 1373.

68 *Inq. Non.* (Rec. Com.), 186.

69 S.R.O. 1224, box 342, Prior Gosnell's reg. f. 35v.

70 Ridge-and-furrow observed 1985: R.C.H.M.E., draft field rep. (1985).

71 B.L. Add. MS. 6165, pp. 97–9; Dugdale, *Mon.* v. 80–2; *V.C.H. Salop.* iv. 86.

arable and presumably, as the names suggest, by assarting. Newhouse and Wood House near Wyke existed by 1540[72] and probably by 1477.[73] John Oswald, presumably of Wood House,[74] was accused in 1517 of inclosing arable at Bradley to make pasture. William Wilcokes was similarly accused in Bourton.[75] Wood House was wholly inclosed by 1592.[76] Woodhousefield, next to Spoonhill wood near Bourton, had inclosed pastures by 1536.[77]

In the late 16th and earlier 17th century agriculture was evidently thriving, for many farmhouses were then wholly rebuilt.[78] Most of their timber frames were later cased in brick or stone.

In the 17th and 18th centuries inclosure was completed and estates were consolidated by exchanges, such as those at Wyke *c.* 1600[79] and at Atterley in 1724.[80] Bourton and Bradeley, under single ownership, were wholly inclosed by 1731.[81] Atterley and Walton, with three substantial freeholders, still had much open-field land in 1722,[82] as did Callaughton in 1748.[83] In Much Wenlock township, with many freeholders and some large estates, the parish's last open-field land, 551 a., had to await inclosure by Act of Parliament in 1777.[84]

The Atterley and Walton commoners' rights in Shirlett were extinguished in 1775 by Act of Parliament.[85] Two large commons then remained: Westwood (327 a.), which Much Wenlock, Presthope,[86] and Callaughton[87] manors still intercommoned, was inclosed in 1814[88] and Farley (58 a., including 19 a. of wood) in 1818.[89] Presthope common, probably the 'green' grazed by oxen in 1584,[90] consisted of 14 a. next to Wenlock Edge in 1769[91] and was inclosed by 1846.[92] By 1986 the only common left in the parish[93] was the remnant, 2.3 ha., of Homer common.[94]

Isolated farms were created in the later 17th or earlier 18th century. The Downs, mentioned in 1714,[95] was formed after 1647[96] from demesne lands in Much Wenlock township. Coates farm, mentioned in 1724,[97] was created after 1634 from part of the Almoner's Ground.[98]

Copyholds seem to have been replaced in the earlier 17th century, sometimes by freeholds,[99] but usually by leaseholds.[1] A late survival in 1641 was the Lewes family's copyhold in Atterley, granted in 1597.[2] By the early 17th century leases were usually for three lives.[3] The Lawleys continued to grant such leases until the later 18th century,[4] but on other estates the policy changed in the early 18th century. On the Much Wenlock manorial estate tenancies at will were substituted for expiring leases after Robert Bertie died in 1698.[5] In 1726, however, Watkin Williams began to offer 99-year chattel leases; many were made in the late 1720s[6] and some presumably lasted until the 1820s. By contrast the Actons' policy in the mid 18th century was to grant 21-year leases at high rents.[7] By the early 18th century holdings could be accumulations of tenancies and undertenancies, not all held of one landlord; they might also have undertenants and be part freehold.[8]

Cereals remained the basic produce in the 17th and 18th centuries,[9] with wheat and spring-sown mixed grains the usual crops. Oats and barley were grown, with some peas, vetches, and beans. Most cereal farmers kept horses, and a minority kept oxen or bullocks too; some, however, had no plough beasts and presumably used their neighbours'.

On Much Wenlock manorial estate in 1714 permanent pasture, including Westwood common, accounted for half of all agricultural land; a sixth of the rest was meadow.[10] In the 17th and 18th centuries most farmers in the parish had cattle, particularly cows; herds of adult cows or heifers averaged about four, and the largest known comprised 17. Commercial cheese making, however, was rarer than around the nearby east Shropshire coalfield.[11] Hay was the usual winter fodder, and clover hay was mentioned in 1671.[12] There were some cattle dealers: in the early 17th century Thomas Chirbury, Thomas Cliveley, and Lewis Heighway were frequent buyers at Shrewsbury fairs.[13] Sheep were often kept, more

72 For their descents from 1592 see above, manors (Wyke and Bradley) and sources there cited. The tenants in 1540 were John Adams and Joan Oswald: S.R.O. 1224/3/8, f. 3 and v.
73 The tenants may have been Wm. Adams (in 1475: S.R.O. 1224/3/110) and John Oswald (in 1477: ibid. /2/16).
74 Ibid. /2/16.
75 I. S. Leadam, 'Inquisition of 1517: Inclosures and Evictions', *Trans. R.H.S.* N.S. viii. 319–20.
76 S.R.O. 1224/3/135.
77 Ibid. /3/8, f. 4.
78 e.g. Atterley Ho., Bourton Hall, Bradley Fm., Manor Fm. (Wyke), Newhouse (Wyke), Wyke Fm., and Wood Ho. (Wyke).
79 S.R.O. 1224/3/139, dated from signature of Evan Davies (vicar 1594–1613: *T.S.A.S.* 3rd ser. viii. 40, 45).
80 S.R.O. 3614/1/270.
81 S.R.O. 3765/1.
82 S.R.O. 1093, parcel 161, map.
83 S.R.O. 3614, box 11, deed.
84 *V.C.H. Salop.* iv. 173.
85 13 Geo. III, c. 105 (Priv. Act); S.R.O. 163/100.
86 S.R.O. 4175/1, sale partic. of 1802.
87 S.R.O. 3614, box 11, deed of 1748.
88 Under 47 Geo. III, Sess. 1, c. 22 (Local and Personal, not printed): S.R.O., incl. award B 38.
89 By private agreement: S.R.O. 1681/144/2.
90 *T.S.A.S.* iii. 298.
91 S.R.O. 3657/2/7, 12.
92 S.R.O. 294/6.
93 Ibid. /5, field 1472.
94 S.C.C. Ch. Exec.'s Dept., commons reg., reg. unit no. CL 102.
95 N.L.W., Wynnstay, box E/62, p. 2.
96 Ibid. box 43/147.
97 H.W.R.O.(H.), Heref. dioc. rec., inv. of Thos. Smith (transcript supplied by Mr. S. P. Mullins).
98 S.R.O. 2089/1/3/7.
99 Above, manors (Atterley and Wenlock Walton; Wigwig; Wyke and Bradley).
1 See e.g. S.R.O. 775/77.
2 S.R.O. 2228/1, f. 39.
3 Ibid. ff. 41 and v., 42v., 53; N.L.W., Wynnstay, box E/62; Hull Univ., Brynmor Jones Libr., DDFA(2)/15/2.
4 Hull Univ., Brynmor Jones Libr., DDFA/26/27, 31–2, 34, 36, 39, 51, 57; DDFA(2)/15/8; S.P.L., Deeds 1384, 1864.
5 N.L.W., Wynnstay, box E/62.
6 Ibid. /92; box F/13–29; cf. *V.C.H. Salop.* iv. 213.
7 S.R.O. 1093, parcel 112, farms reg.; 775/220.
8 N.L.W., Wynnstay, box E/62.
9 This para. and the next based on Mr. Mullins's transcripts of 233 M. Wenlock probate invs. 1649–1764; all but two of the invs. (P.R.O., PROB 4/9606; PROB 4/12439) are in H.W.R.O.(H.), Heref. dioc. rec.
10 N.L.W., Wynnstay, box E/62; Westwood acreage derived from S.R.O., incl. award B 38.
11 For agric. nr. the coalfield see *Yeomen and Colliers in Telford*, ed. B. Trinder and J. Cox (1980), pp. 72–90; *V.C.H. Salop.* iv. 142, 151.
12 H.W.R.O.(H.), Heref. dioc. rec., inv. of Ralph Littlehales; cf. *V.C.H. Salop.* iv. 153.
13 P. R. Edwards, 'Cattle trade of Salop. in late 16th and 17th cents.' *Midland Hist.* v. 79.

so than near the coalfield and in larger flocks, averaging *c.* 35; the largest known flock had 147.[14] Some farmers had fairly small flocks of sheep without cattle.

Farmhouses stood in all the main streets of the town in the early 18th century.[15] Several had only a barn as an outbuilding. A stable was not unusual, sometimes combined with the barn. Cow or beast houses were rare and carthouses unusual.

Farms were of all sizes, and outside the town several exceeded 100 a. in the early 18th century.[16] Tradesmen usually occupied the smallest: for example in February 1663 a Much Wenlock shoemaker had 2 a. of corn, small stores of corn, vetches, peas, and hay, 2 cows, and 9 sheep.[17] In July 1731 one of the largest holdings, at Presthope, comprised 74 a. under crops, 71 cattle, 147 sheep, 11 horses, 36 swine, and poultry; there were 80 cheeses in store.[18]

In the 18th century larger farms absorbed smaller ones. On the Wynn estate, holdings over 25 a. fell from sixteen in 1714[19] to nine by 1808, increasing greatly in size.[20] Plans to reduce the number of farms had existed by 1769, in expectation of Much Wenlock's inclosure Act.[21] In Callaughton amalgamation reduced the ten holdings of 1783[22] to six by 1799.[23] In Atterley and Walton the Actons' farms over 25 a. fell from four to three between 1724[24] and 1808.[25] After the inclosure of Westwood common in 1814,[26] however, some new farms were created there: Lower Westwood on the Williams Wynn estate and Westwood and Westwood Cottage (later Cottage farm) on the Lawley estate.[27] More large farms were created during the century, including Black Barn in Presthope, Perkley and Walton Grange in Much Wenlock, Callaughton farm, and Callaughton House.[28]

Near the town in the 19th and the early 20th century there were smallholdings[29] on land unsuitable for larger farms.[30] Until after 1945 several of the urban smallholders were cowkeepers[31] supplying milk locally. A small early 19th-century cowhouse and dairy was standing in 1987 at 24 Barrow Street.[32] In 1960 the parish's smaller farms produced milk and eggs, while many of the larger were concerned with grain, roots, and beef cattle. Much of the milk was then sent to London.[33] In the 20th century farm sizes continued to increase.[34]

Increased cereal production, one of the objects of 18th-century improvements, was stimulated by high prices and rents during the Napoleonic wars.[35] In 1793 arable predominated over grass. There were some grazing farms, but mixed husbandry was more common.[36] In 1801 wheat far exceeded barley and oats as the main cash crop.[37] In Presthope arable increased from 38 per cent of agricultural land in 1802[38] to 60 per cent by 1820.[39] In Much Wenlock township arable formed 60 per cent of the manorial estate's farmland by 1813.[40] Pasture was ploughed up 'indiscriminately', and the arable over-cropped. After the wars much arable was returned to pasture and slowly recovered fertility. It was then ready to be ploughed again,[41] and in the late 1840s arable formed 60 per cent of the land on farms over 25 a.[42] A ten-year depression, a 'frightful ordeal', lasted until the mid 1850s.[43] The result seems to have been a new move towards livestock. In 1867 grass exceeded arable by 3 to 2, and it predominated increasingly until the Second World War. In 1965 grass still

TABLE XXV

MUCH WENLOCK: LAND USE, LIVESTOCK, AND CROPS

	1867	*1891*	*1938*	*1965*
Percentage of grassland	61	73	81	59
arable	39	27	19	41
Percentage of cattle	13	21	23	29
sheep	75	72	64	63
pigs	12	7	13	8
Percentage of wheat	51	34	54	43
barley	38	38	9	51
oats	11	28	35	6
mixed corn & rye	0	0	2	0
Percentage of agricultural land growing roots and vegetables	8	6	5	4

Sources: P.R.O., MAF 68/143, no. 15; /1340, no. 5; /3880, Salop. no. 265; /4945, no. 265.

14 H.W.R.O.(H.), Heref. dioc. rec., inv. of Ric. Francis, 1731.
15 N.L.W., Wynnstay, box E/62.
16 Ibid.; S.R.O. 836/23.
17 H.W.R.O.(H.), Heref. dioc. rec., inv. of Geo. Patten.
18 Ibid. inv. of Ric. Francis. His fm. identified from S.R.O. 809, box 1, deed of 1815 (copy); 4175/1, sale partic. (B on plan).
19 N.L.W., Wynnstay, box E/62.
20 Ibid. box 43/7, ff. 1–7.
21 Ibid. /3.
22 Ibid. /84 (15).
23 S.R.O., q. sess. rec. parcel 262, land tax assessment.
24 S.R.O. 836/23, ff. 32–6.
25 N.L.W., Wynnstay, box 43/7, f. 15.
26 S.R.O., incl. award B 38.
27 S.R.O. 294/7, fields 961, 1002, 1043.
28 Ibid. /3, 6–7; Callaughton map of 1796 (in Mr. J. R. Craig's possession); B.L. Maps, O.S.D. 207; O.S. Maps 1/2,500, Salop. L. 12, 16; LVII. 2 (1902 edn.).
29 S.R.O. 294/7; 4044/92.
30 S.R.O. 1224/7/50.
31 *Kelly's Dir. Salop.* (1891), 469; (1900), 274–5; local inf. collected by Mr. O. G. McDonald and deposited in W.B.R.
32 Inf. from Mrs. M. Moran.
33 *Wenlock Herald*, Jan. 1960.
34 P.R.O., MAF 68/3880, Salop. no. 265; MAF 68/4945, no. 265.
35 T. H. Thursfield, *Wenlock Farmers' Club 1842–1902* [*c.* 1902], 9 (copy in S.P.L., class M 22).
36 S.P.L., MS. 6865, p. 209.
37 *List & Index Soc.* cxc. 390, 393.
38 S.R.O. 4175/1, sale partic.
39 S.R.O. 809, box 8, surv. of 1820, ff. 12–15.
40 N.L.W., Wynnstay, box 43/85, ff. 27–9.
41 Thursfield, *Wenlock Farmers' Club*, 9–10.
42 S.R.O. 294/1, 4–7.
43 Thursfield, op. cit. 17–19.

occupied nearly 60 per cent of agricultural land.[44] Before the development of motor transport dairy farming was limited by distribution difficulties, and beef rearing predominated, usually of Herefords. 'High' feeding in covered yards was widely practised by 1906; the high pitched 'Cundy' roof of spaced wooden boards, combining ventilation with shelter, was much favoured.[45]

Notable herds of cattle in the 20th century included Herefords at Callaughton farm[46] (later at Callaughton House),[47] Ayrshires at the Downs,[48] and Jerseys at Tickwood Hall.[49] At Callaughton the Milners bred nationally reputed shire horses.[50] In the century from 1867 sheep became relatively less important than cattle.[51] The Shropshire Down was considered the best breed for the Wenlock area by 1851[52] and in 1906,[53] but it was less popular later. In 1883 there were flocks of Shropshires at Bourton Grange and Callaughton farms[54] but none by 1920.[55]

Practice varied considerably in the 19th and 20th centuries.[56] In Presthope, for example, arable continued to predominate over grass *c.* 1890.[57] A diversity of aims, methods, and resources accentuated differences between neighbouring farms, not always reflected in their arable–grass ratios. In Presthope in 1938 Plough farm (63 per cent grass in 1934) was a stock rearing enterprise, but Lower Presthope (70 per cent grass) was called a mixed farm and Black Barn (43 per cent grass) a stock and grain farm.[58]

The Wenlock Farmers' Club, begun in 1842, was the foremost in Shropshire. Its members were informed, articulate, and independent.[59] In the later 19th century farmers' interests were espoused politically by the 2nd and 3rd Lords Wenlock and C. G. Milnes Gaskell.[60] In 1884, however, Gaskell's wife could still dream of a social order in which farming families had few aspirations; agricultural depression, she believed, was linked with the farmer's taste for culture and recreation.[61] In 1906 local farmers were judged to have survived the depression well, and without complete sacrifice of social pleasures. Tradesmen were prepared to give them long term credit, and J. H. A. Whitley failed to convince his tenants of the alternative merits of co-operative bulk buying for ready money.[62]

Wheat and barley were the predominant cash crops in 1867, but wheat lost ground to oats in the late 19th century. In 1906 a five-course rotation was usual: turnips; swedes, mangolds, or potatoes; barley; clover or mixed seeds for two years; and wheat or oats. Barley was then thought too speculative for extensive sowing, and gave way to wheat before 1939. By 1965, however, barley had overtaken wheat, mainly at the expense of oats.[63] In 1960 most of the grain went to Liverpool and Manchester.[64]

QUARRIES. On Wenlock Edge Silurian limestone[65] lies near the surface in abundance and has been quarried for building, iron fluxing, aggregate, and conversion to lime for building, tanning, and agriculture.

In the Middle Ages the stone was used in the priory and nearby churches.[66] One early source was Standhill,[67] immediately north of the town.[68] There was also a cluster of quarries immediately west of the town, near the Bank.[69] In 1399–1400 quantities of building lime were supplied to Caus castle *c.* 30 km. away,[70] and 16 loads for Shrewsbury school in 1594.[71] Much Wenlock was 'famous' for limestone by 1607,[72] and quarries and kilns were scattered all over the Edge.[73] There were also two kilns at Wyke in 1523.[74] There were self-employed lime 'carriers' (perhaps producers as well as distributors) in the 16th and 17th centuries,[75] and several lime burners flourished in the earlier 18th century.[76] Unauthorized digging on the commons[77] and the erection of noxious kilns[78] were penalized, and in 1778 the Williams Wynn estate required royalties on lime burnt and the reinstatement of land after digging.[79] On that estate 13 lime burners produced 3,503 wagon-

44 Table XXV; *Estate Mag.* vi. 411.

45 *Estate Mag.* vi. 411–12.

46 *Shrews. Chron.* 27 Apr. 1928, 7; *Farmers Weekly*, 8 July 1949, 36.

47 S.R.O. 2584/8; *Bridgnorth Jnl.* 18 May 1979; E. Heath-Agnew, *Hist. of Heref. Cattle* (1983), 181–3, 253, 288, 308, 315.

48 *Wenlock Herald*, Sept. 1961.

49 *Jnl. Welsh & Salop. Jersey Breeders' Assoc.* [1963], 38 (copy in S.P.L., class C 22.5 v.f.).

50 *Estate Mag.* vi. 412; *Shrews. Chron.* 27 Apr. 1928, 7; *Farmers Weekly*, 8 July 1949, 36; *Cent. of Progress 1875–1975: Salop. & W. Midlands Agric. Soc.* ed. R. Kenney (Shrews. 1975), 32, 51.

51 See Table XXV.

52 Thursfield, *Wenlock Farmers' Club*, 17.

53 *Estate Mag.* vi. 412.

54 Shropshire Sheep Breeders' Assoc. *Flock Bk. of Shropshire Sheep*, i. 8, 128.

55 Ibid. vol. xx.

56 G. W. Robinson, *Surv. of Soils and Agric. of Salop.* (Shrews. 1912), 59.

57 S.R.O. 809, box 8, scheds. (identified and dated from *Kelly's Dir. Salop.* (1885), 984; (1891), 469).

58 S.R.O. 809, box 13, surv. of 1934, pp. 93–7; box 14, sale partic. of 1938, lots 11, 14, 19.

59 Thursfield, *Wenlock Farmers' Club, passim*; *V.C.H. Salop.* iv. 215, 217–19.

60 *V.C.H. Salop.* iii. 316, 342–3.

61 C. M. Gaskell, 'A farm that pays', *Nineteenth Cent.* xvi (1884), 568–75; *V.C.H. Salop.* iv. 217

62 *Estate Mag.* vi. 410–11, 414.

63 Ibid. 411; Table XXV.

64 *Wenlock Herald*, Jan. 1960.

65 Geol. Surv. Maps 1", solid, sheets 152 (1962 edn.), 166 (1967 edn.).

66 E. A. Gee, 'Hist. and arch. acct. of Wenlock priory and its dependent churches' (Birm. Univ. M.A. thesis, 1937), 177–8.

67 H. D. G. Foxall, *Salop. Field-Names* (Salop. Arch. Soc. 1980), 42; cf. P.R.O., SC 6/Hen. VIII/3021, m. 1.

68 N.L.W., Wynnstay, MS. Plans 1.

69 S.R.O., q. sess. rec. parcel 283, reg. of enrolled incl. awards, pp. 28, 33, 43; N.L.W., Wynnstay, box 43/85; P.R.O., HO 107/928/18, ff. 44–50; S.R.O. 294/7, fields 1153, 1161, 1165, 1170, 1210–11, 1213, 1225, 1231; S.R.O. 1224, box 144, deed of 1740.

70 S.R.O. 279/131.

71 *Salop. N. & Q.* N.S. ii. 32.

72 Camden, *Brit.* (1695), col. 543.

73 S.R.O. 294/4, fields 1566, 1700, 1703, 1725; /6, fields 2568, 2575–6, 2628, 2673–4, 2676; /7, fields 202, 342, 1057, 1137, 1143. An hist. gazetteer of quarry sites is given in J. Glyn Williams, *The Wenlock Limestone Ind.: an Historical Note* (M. Wenlock, 1990; copy in S.P.L.).

74 N.L.W., Wynnstay, RA 2.

75 S.R.O. 3898/Rg/1, 24 Aug. 1584, 15 Dec. 1595, 27 Apr. 1634; /Rg/2, 4 Apr. 1654.

76 N.L.W., Wynnstay, RA 19, f. [10]; box E/62, p. 6; Mr. Mullins's transcripts of H.W.R.O.(H.), Heref. dioc. rec., invs. of Jos. Smith, 1722; Thos. Owen, 1728; Fra. Southern, 1730; Edw. Frances, 1752.

77 S.R.O. 1224/2/36, 53, 133.

78 Ibid. /2/116.

79 N.L.W., Wynnstay, RA 19, f. 8.

loads in 1789–90.[80] Agricultural tenants were allowed to get stone and make lime for their own use.[81]

In the early 18th century Abraham Darby (I) bought Wenlock stone for iron smelting.[82] As the local iron industry expanded, quarries between the town and the Severn were acquired by ironmasters operating in the southern part of the coalfield. The Wenlock–Buildwas road led to a wharf on the Severn downstream of Buildwas bridge,[83] whence supplies were carried down river towards the ironworks. The ironmaster Richard Reynolds bought Farley farm in 1777.[84] In 1780 William Ferriday and his partners at Lightmoor took a 21-year lease of stone near Gleedon hill and the Coalbrookdale Co. took a similar lease of a quarry nearby. Both paid royalties, and the Coalbrookdale Co. undertook to get at least 1,500 tons a year.[85] In 1789–90 the Lightmoor Co. paid royalties on 1,200 tons.[86] Joseph and Richard Jesson and Richard Wright took a lease of stone under Wyke farm in 1797,[87] presumably for the Wrens Nest works.[88] By 1800 Alexander Brodie occupied nearby quarries to supply his Calcutts works.[89] In 1800 William Reynolds and his partners took a lease of stone under 61 a. at Tickwood and Wyke,[90] whence a railway was built north-east,[91] probably to a Severnside wharf on the Buildwas–Benthall boundary.[92] John Wheeler's purchases at Presthope in 1787 and 1790[93] were presumably intended to yield fluxing stone.

In the early 19th century the Madeley Wood Co. succeeded to the Wenlock quarries of Richard and William Reynolds and the Coalbrookdale Co.,[94] and between 1824 and 1833[95] built a railway north from Gleedon hill to a Severnside wharf about 1½ km. above Buildwas bridge.[96] The Wyke railway had gone by 1833.[97] Thomas and William Botfield bought quarries on Gleedon hill in 1826,[98] and in 1839, with their nephew Beriah, bought the former Coalbrookdale Co. site nearby.[99] Abraham Darby (IV) bought Bradley farm in 1827,[1] and Bradley Rock quarry became the sole source for Dawley Castle and Lightmoor.[2] In 1831 the parish's quarries employed *c.* 130 men.[3] In 1849 Francis and John Yates of Ironbridge[4] took a 14-year lease of a new quarry in Windmill Hill field, later called Shadwell Rock; they expected to get at least 9,000 tons a year.[5]

It was mainly to improve transport of limestone to the Severn, and of coal thence to the Wenlock kilns,[6] that a railway was opened from Buildwas to Much Wenlock in 1862 and extended to Presthope in 1864.[7] It immediately stimulated quarrying, especially south of the town where the industry was less developed.

The South Wales & Cannock Chase Coal & Coke Co. became lessees of Shadwell Rock.[8] The fluxing stone, *c.* 22,500 tons in 1873, was all sent beyond Stourbridge (Worcs.). Bradley Rock was then yielding *c.* 20,000 tons a year for the Coalbrookdale Co. At Westwood the Madeley Wood Co. was getting 8,000–9,000 tons a year for Blists Hill.[9]

At Presthope Lord Granville, a principal shareholder in the Lilleshall Co.,[10] took a lease of limestone under 28½ a. in 1862,[11] and in 1864 William Field, a Shrewsbury merchant and railway contractor,[12] took a lease of the stone under an adjoining 10 a.,[13] to supply ironworks in Shropshire and Staffordshire. By 1873 neither quarry had been profitable and Field's had closed;[14] Granville's rent was halved in 1876.[15] Lack of direct rail access to the eastern part of the coalfield made Presthope stone uncompetitive with imports from north Wales.[16]

The late 19th-century decline of Shropshire's iron industry[17] further curtailed demand for Wenlock stone. The Coalbrookdale Co. sold Bradley Rock in 1889,[18] Gleedon Hill quarries closed between 1882 and 1901,[19] and Shadwell Rock closed *c.* 1911.[20] The Lilleshall Co. (which succeeded to Granville's lease)[21] had its rent reduced twice[22] but closed its quarry *c.* 1915.[23]

During the iron industry's prosperity lime for agriculture and building continued to be pro-

80 Ibid. R 54/24.
81 S.R.O. 1224/2/531.
82 Trinder, *Ind. Rev. Salop.* 15.
83 S.R.O. 1671, Buildwas est. map and surv. of 1837, field 227.
84 Above, manors (Wyke and Bradley).
85 N.L.W., Wynnstay, RA 19, f. 9.
86 Ibid. R 54/24.
87 S.R.O. 1224, box 88, deed.
88 Above, Linley, econ. hist.
89 S.R.O. 1224, box 86A, deed.
90 Ibid. box 86C, deed.
91 Ibid. box 86A, deed of 1800; Lincs. Archives Office, 2 Hawley 5/F/3; B.L. Maps, O.S.D. 207.
92 At O.S. Nat. Grid SJ 661 036: S.R.O. 1671, Buildwas est. map and surv. of 1837, field 199.
93 Above, manors (Presthope).
94 N.L.W., Wynnstay, box 43/7, f. 16; S.R.O. 1681/184/1–4.
95 B.L. Maps, O.S.D. 207 (not shown); S.R.O. 1681/184/1; O.S. Map 1", sheet LXI. NE. (1833 edn.).
96 At O.S. Nat. Grid SJ 633 040: S.R.O. 1671, Buildwas est. map and surv. of 1837, field 298.
97 O.S. Map 1", sheet LXI. NE. (1833 edn.).
98 S.R.O. 1150/817.
99 S.R.O. 1359, box 26, deed.
1 Above, manors (Wyke and Bradley).
2 Ho. of Lords R.O., Bks. of Evid. 'Mins. of Evid. Sel. Cttee. on M. Wenlock & Severn Junction Rly. Bill' (1873), 20 June, pp. 68, 73.
3 *Census*, 1831, i. 527.
4 See *V.C.H. Salop.* xi. 38, 44.
5 Clwyd R.O. (Ruthin), DD/WY/5370. No quarry mentioned there 1848: S.R.O. 294/7, field 259.
6 H.L.R.O., 'Mins. of Evid. on M. Wenlock & Severn Junct. Rly. Bill', 20 June, pp. 2, 4.
7 Above, communications.
8 S.R.O. 2079/L. 8; 4044/92, f. 41 (no. 363).
9 H.L.R.O., 'Mins. of Evid. on M. Wenlock & Severn Junct. Rly. Bill', 20 June, pp. 45, 49, 64–5, 68; 25 June, p. 134.
10 W. K. V. Gale and C. R. Nicholls, *The Lilleshall Co. Ltd.: a Hist. 1764–1964* (1979), 42.
11 S.R.O. 809, parcel 7, deed.
12 *P.O. Dir. Salop.* (1863), 751.
13 S.R.O. 809, parcel 7, deed.
14 H.L.R.O., 'Mins. of Evid. on M. Wenlock & Severn Junct. Rly. Bill', 20 June, pp. 23–4; 25 June, pp. 116–20, 139, 147.
15 S.R.O. 809, parcel 7, deed.
16 H.L.R.O., 'Mins. of Evid. on M. Wenlock & Severn Junct. Rly. Bill', 20 June, pp. 132, 135; 25 June, pp. 118, 121.
17 Trinder, *Ind. Rev. Salop.* 239.
18 S.R.O. 1359, box 27, deed.
19 O.S. Maps 1/2,500, Salop. L. 4, 8 (1882 and 1901 edns.).
20 S.R.O. 2079/L. 8; 4044/92, f. 41 (no. 363); *Kelly's Dir. Salop.* (1913), 296 (no mention).
21 S.R.O. 809, box 13, rental 1879–98, f. 36.
22 Ibid. box 1, deed of 1896 and endorsement.
23 *Kelly's Dir. Salop.* (1913), 296; (1917), 280.

duced by small operators[24] as well as at the iron companies' quarries,[25] and that trade managed to survive the iron industry's decline.[26]

In the mid 20th century, and especially after 1945, limestone quarrying revived to supply the construction industry with aggregates, while improvements in road transport eased distribution. Crushing plant was installed and, for agriculture, ground limestone supplanted the more expensive burnt lime. Quarries were opened or revived at Farley and Shadwell, north of the town, and Lea, Knowle, Coates, and Hayes on the road from Presthope to Much Wenlock. Demand increased after the designation of Dawley new town in 1963, and the old Lilleshall Co. quarry reopened *c.* 1966. Annual production in the parish, 600,000 tonnes in 1970, had doubled by 1974 but fell to 800,000 tonnes by 1980. In 1977 *c.* 80 per cent went for aggregate and *c.* 8 per cent for agricultural lime. About 10 per cent went for concrete and concrete goods, and on the Presthope to Much Wenlock road there were three works making concrete products. The quarries sent about half of their output to Staffordshire and the west midland conurbation; about a fifth was used in Telford and the rest elsewhere in Shropshire. Wenlock was the main source of agricultural lime for 30 miles around. The limestone industry was believed to account directly for about a third of all jobs in the Much Wenlock area.[27]

In 1978 the county council decided that, for environmental reasons, quarrying on Wenlock Edge should cease when existing sites were worked out.[28] By 1984, however, the council accepted that new starts might be needed to provide jobs or if other Shropshire sources of comparable stone proved inadequate.[29]

Prospectors failed to find useful quantities of other minerals. James Miner, of Derbyshire, had permission in 1397 to mine copper and silver on Wenlock priory's demesnes,[30] but there were no such mines in 1540.[31] In the later 16th century Robert Acton paid for rights to ironstone in Presthope.[32] John Wase of Broseley agreed in 1733 to extract coal from the Lawleys' estate.[33] Elsewhere Coalpit leasow lay near Downs Farm in 1848 and Coalpit meadow near Perkley.[34]

MARKETS AND FAIRS. In 1138 King Stephen granted Wenlock priory a three-day fair 23–5 June.[35] Before 1224 weekly markets were held at Much Wenlock on Sundays. In that year Henry III granted the priory instead a weekly Monday market,[36] apparently of little account by the 1550s.[37] In 1468 the rights were vested in the borough corporation,[38] and in 1873 in the local board of health.[39] The corporation resumed them at the board's dissolution in 1889[40] and they passed in 1966 to the rural borough council.[41]

In 1631 a fair on 5–7 October was granted.[42] In the 1630s additional fairs were occasionally held outside the appointed dates.[43] Two more fairs were granted in 1720, on 1 May and 23 November.[44] The calendar reform of 1752 shifted the fair days to 12 May, 5 July, 17 October, and 4 December.[45] Another fair, on the second Monday (later the second Tuesday) in March,[46] was added in the 1820s.[47] The July fair ceased in the 1840s.[48]

Until 1852 the only covered area was under the guildhall, for butter[49] and corn.[50] The covered Corn Market, 'long wanted',[51] was then opened in Hospital Street by subscription.[52] In 1879 the local board built the Market Hall at the corner of Hospital and Sheinton streets, on the site of the glebe houses;[53] it was designed by S. Pountney Smith in a 'half-timbered' style[54] to match the nearby guildhall. There was an open market space in front, and the board provided another small market place, the Square, on the opposite corner of Hospital Street.[55] About that time the Corn Market was renamed the Corn Exchange.[56] The Market Hall closed *c.* 1920,[57] allegedly with the connivance of shopkeepers.[58] In 1938, however, weekly auctions of farm produce were being held at the Fox.[59] In 1960 the borough council opened a small general market at the Corn Exchange,[60] which later occupied additional space under the guildhall.

The ancient fairs were of only local impor-

24 N.L.W., Wynnstay, box 43/7, ff. 1, 3–4, 7–9, 12; *P.O. Dir. Salop.* (1856), 194–5; (1879), 511.

25 Gleedon Hill: N.L.W., Wynnstay, RA 19, f. 9. Lilleshall Quarry, Presthope: O.S. Map 1/2,500, Salop. L. 14 (1883 edn.). Shadwell: *P.O. Dir. Salop.* (1879), 511.

26 *Kelly's Dir. Salop.* (1922), 418; *Shrews. Chron.* 6 Nov. 1935, p. 16.

27 *Mineral Extraction on Wenlock Edge: Discussion Paper and Rep. of Surv.* (S.C.C. 1979); *Mineral Extraction on Wenlock Edge: Updating Rep. of Surv.* (S.C.C. 1981); *Shropshire Star* (First edn.), 13 Dec. 1982, p. 18.

28 *Salop Co. Structure Plan: Written Statement* (S.C.C. 1978), p. 76; *Mineral Extraction on Wenlock Edge: Subject Plan: Written Statement* (S.C.C. 1983), p. 8.

29 *Salop. Co. Structure Plan: Alteration No. 1: Explanatory Memo.* (S.C.C. 1984), pp. 106–7.

30 *Cal. Close*, 1396–9, 128.

31 P.R.O., SC 6/Hen. VIII/3021.

32 S.R.O. 1224/2/513.

33 Hull Univ., Brynmor Jones Libr., DDFA/26/44.

34 S.R.O. 294/7, fields 180, 851.

35 *T.S.A.S.* lxvi. 56–8.

36 *Rot. Litt. Claus.* (Rec. Com.), i. 622.

37 *V.C.H. Salop.* iv. 162 n.

38 *Cal. Chart. R.* 1427–1516, 229–30.

39 Under the Local Govt. Act, 1858, 21 & 22 Vic. c. 98, s. 50: *Lond. Gaz.* 15 Apr. 1873, p. 1976.

40 Local Govt. Bd.'s Prov. Order Conf. (No. 4) Act, 1889, 52 & 53 Vic. c. 22 (Local).

41 *Salop Order 1966* (Stat. Instr. 1966, no. 8).

42 W.B.R., B1/2.

43 Ibid. B3/6/80.

44 Ibid. B1/3.

45 *Descr. of Eng. and Wales*, viii (London, Newbery & Carnan, 1769), 55.

46 S. Bagshaw, *Dir. Salop.* (1851), 580.

47 Pigot, *London and Provincial New Com. Dir.* (1822), 380; Tibnam & Co. *Salop. Dir.* (1828), 3.

48 S. Bagshaw, *Dir. Salop.* (1851), 580.

49 W.B.R., B3/1/2, f. 33.

50 Ibid. f. 18. For sites of street mkts. see above, growth of settlement.

51 *Salopian Jnl.* 8 May 1839.

52 *Kelly's Dir. Salop.* (1900), 271; above, social and cultural activities.

53 *Kelly's Dir. Salop.* (1900), 271; S.R.O. 1242, box 5, draft deed of 1877.

54 *Kelly's Dir. Salop.* (1900), 271; pl. 38.

55 S.R.O. 1242, box 5, draft deeds of 1876, 1884.

56 *P.O. Dir. Salop.* (1870), 164; (1879), 433.

57 *Kelly's Dir. Salop.* (1917), 277; (1922), 287.

58 *Wenlock Herald*, Sept. 1960.

59 Wilding & Son Ltd. *M. Wenlock Official Illustr. Guide* (1938), advt. at end.

60 *Wenlock Herald*, Dec. 1960.

tance in the 1630s, when sellers came almost exclusively from within the borough; buyers came from a slightly wider area, including Bridgnorth, Wistanstow, and Wrockwardine. The greatest trade was at the June fair, where cattle and horses preponderated, but sales rarely exceeded 20 animals. Sheep appeared mainly in October.[61] In 1769 they appeared at all fairs, especially in July; swine appeared especially in October.[62] In the late 18th century the October fair attracted Leicestershire and Northamptonshire graziers buying oxen.[63] By 1835 the May fair was a hiring fair,[64] and by 1868 had become a pleasure fair,[65] held mainly in Barrow and High streets.[66]

In 1862 the corporation substituted new livestock fairs, on the Monday after the first Shrewsbury fair in alternate months.[67] That year the new Wenlock Smithfield Co. opened a railside smithfield in Powke Lane managed by a firm of auctioneers; street sales of livestock ceased.[68] There were fortnightly sales of fatstock and stores, and occasional horse sales by the 1880s;[69] people attended from as far as Birmingham, Wolverhampton, and West Bromwich.[70] Seventeen sales took place in 1890; in Shropshire only Cleobury Mortimer had fewer.[71] The company sold the smithfield to the auctioneer in 1890.[72] In 1925–6 *c.* 9,600 animals passed through but by 1939 sales were almost non-existent. That year, however, Much Wenlock was designated a fatstock grading centre and survived solely as a fatstock market. In 1950 some 9,800 animals were sold, from upper Ape Dale and part of upper Corve Dale.[73] As road transport developed, however, producers preferred larger centres, and the smithfield closed in 1954.[74]

MANUFACTURES, CRAFTS, AND PROFESSIONS. Sparse early references to crafts and trades suggest that the ubiquitous cloth and leather trades were among the first to be established locally. A William Weaver (*le webbe*) and Walter Shearer (*le sherar*) lived in Much Wenlock manor in 1327.[75] Adam Tailor (*le tailur*) lived at Much Wenlock in the late 13th century,[76] and a tailor was mentioned in Much Wenlock township in 1413.[77] Plentiful lime and bark encouraged tanning. Ithenard the tanner held 3 a. in Much Wenlock in 1221,[78] and Alexander, John, Roger, and Thomas le Barker were mentioned in the manor in 1345.[79] Specialized leather craft is indicated by the presence of Hugh Glover (*cirothecarius*) in the manor in 1327.[80] A shoemaker was mentioned in 1448.[81]

From the 16th century evidence is more abundant for the leather and cloth trades and for a wider variety of other trades and manufactures. Generations of the Bradeley[82] and Morrall[83] families were involved in tanning in the 16th and 17th centuries. Richard Bradeley lived at Presthope in 1588,[84] but Ralph was in Barrow Street by 1605.[85] Christopher Morrall (d. 1594) also lived in Barrow Street,[86] where a tannery was held by Josiah Morrall (d. 1694).[87] By 1717 the tannery was held of the Morralls by Thomas Mason (d. 1732).[88] After him came Thomas Mason (d. 1757),[89] Richard Corbett (d. 1770),[90] and probably Thomas Corbet (fl. 1785–1805).[91]

A tannery on the north side of Spittle Street, leased to Edward Hancocks in 1684,[92] passed to Anne Hancocks (d. 1710).[93] It was held in 1714 by Humphrey Hinton and Richard Parsons[94] and by John Hinton 1769–85.[95] It had probably closed by 1800, by which time a new tannery had opened at the north end of Sheinton Street,[96] occupied by Edward Howells.[97] In 1808 Howells also held the Barrow Street tanyard.[98] In 1830 he left the Sheinton Street premises to his nephew George Adney (d. 1875), whose son Thomas continued the business[99] until *c.* 1890.[1] The Barrow Street site,[2] also held by George, closed before 1872.[3]

There were many shoemakers in the parish in the 16th century and at least four glovers 1558–1608.[4] John How (fl. 1600)[5] and Joseph Crowther (d. 1667)[6] were saddlers. Such trades, like tanning, long survived. William James was

61 W.B.R., B3/6/80.
62 *Descr. of Eng. & Wales*, viii. 55.
63 J. Plymley, *Gen. View of Agric. of Salop.* (1803), 257.
64 Pigot, *Nat. Com. Dir.* (1835), 385.
65 Slater, *Dir. Salop. and Wales* (1868), 53; above, social and cultural activities.
66 Brookes fam. letter bk. p. 77.
67 Thursfield, *Wenlock Farmers' Club*, 21.
68 S.R.O. 1242, box 9, abstr. of title of 1890; *P.O. Dir. Salop.* (1879), 469; *Kelly's Dir. Salop.* (1909), 287; (1913), 357; (1941), 370.
69 S.R.O. 1242, box 9, C. E. Ainsworth to Cooper & Haslewood 7 Aug. 1890 (letterhead).
70 *Salopian and W. Midland Monthly Illustr. Jnl.* July 1875 (copy in S.P.L.), [11].
71 W. M. Moisley, 'Mkts. of Salop.' (Lond. Univ. M.Sc. thesis, 1951), 40.
72 S.R.O. 1242, box 9, deeds of 1890–1.
73 Moisley, op. cit. 44–5, 75.
74 Inf. from Nock, Deighton & Son.
75 *T.S.A.S.* 2nd ser. iv. 325.
76 S.R.O. 1514/168.
77 *E.H.R.* xcix. 548.
78 *Rolls of Justices in Eyre 1221–2* (Selden Soc. lix), p. 508.
79 S.R.O. 1224/2/1.
80 *T.S.A.S.* 2nd ser. iv. 325.
81 S.R.O. 3614, box 11, ct. r.
82 S.R.O. 3898/Rg/1, 6 Aug. 1559; 3 Feb. 1599/1600; 7 Nov. 1619; /Rg/2, 24 Jan. 1649/50; P.R.O., LR 2/184, f. 79v.; W.B.R., B3/1/1, p. 109.
83 S.R.O. 3898/Rg/1, 11 Dec. 1594; 2 July 1598; P.R. E 179/168/214; N.L.W., Wynnstay, box E/62, f. 25.
84 S.R.O. 3898/Rg/1, 4 Feb. 1587/8.
85 Ibid. 29 Sept. 1605.
86 Ibid. 11 Dec. 1594.
87 Ibid. /Rg/2, 12 May 1694; N.L.W., Wynnstay, box E/62, f. 30; H.W.R.O.(H.), Heref. dioc. rec., inv. of 1694.
88 S.R.O. 1224, box 89, deed; 3898/Rg/4, 4 Mar. 1731/2.
89 S.R.O. 3898/Rg/5, bur. 18 Apr. 1757.
90 Ibid. bur. 2 June 1770; N.L.W., Wynnstay, L 1288, s.v. Barrow St.
91 N.L.W., Wynnstay, RA 19, f. 6; S.R.O. 1681/158/7.
92 N.L.W., Wynnstay, box E/62, f. 28.
93 S.R.O. 3898/Rg/3, 6 Feb. 1709/10; H.W.R.O.(H.), Heref. dioc. rec., inv. of 1710.
94 N.L.W., Wynnstay, box E/62, f. 28.
95 N.L.W., Wynnstay, L 1288; RA 19, f. 6.
96 S.R.O. 1242, box 7, sale partic. of 1891.
97 *Univ. Brit. Dir.* iv [*c.* 1798], 720.
98 N.L.W., Wynnstay, box 43/7, ff. 4, 8.
99 S.R.O. 1242, box 7, abstr. of title.
1 *Kelly's Dir. Salop.* (1885), 984; (1891), 468 (no mention).
2 O.S. Nat. Grid SO 624 999: S.R.O. 1931/1; W.B.R., P8/2/7, no. 27.
3 'Wenlock Abbey', f. 39 (MS. privately owned; Mr. W. M. Motley arranged access).
4 S.R.O. 3898/Rg/1.
5 Ibid. 16 Nov. 1600.
6 Ibid. /Rg/2, 9 Apr. 1650, 5 May 1667; H.W.R.O.(H.), Heref. dioc. rec., inv. of 1667.

a glover in 1774,[7] but none was recorded *c.* 1798 or later.[8] There were 25 shoemakers living in the town in 1841 and one each living in Atterley, Bourton, and Farley.[9] Saddlers too were found in the 19th century: there were at least three *c.* 1851.[10]

Cloth was the town's chief manufacture in the 16th century[11] and also a significant trade. A haberdasher was mentioned in 1586[12] and mercers from 1592 onwards;[13] there were at least four mercers in 1661,[14] and another issued one of the town's 17th-century tokens.[15] The parish had many tailors in the 16th century[16] and two cappers were mentioned in the late 16th century,[17] a hatter in 1616,[18] and a feltmaker in 1661.[19] Weavers were mentioned in the later 18th century.[20] In 1841 fifteen men of the town, and three of Bourton, worked at tailoring. There remained two 'clothmakers' living in High Street and a wool carder in Barrow Street. There was also a weaver living at Westwood, and ten people worked as drapers, including two living at Atterley.[21]

Fulling was found outside the town: it had ceased at Wigwig mill by 1695,[22] but walkmills in Wyke and Bradley township were mentioned in 1743.[23]

The building trades seem to have flourished before and after the Dissolution. William the carpenter was mentioned in 1386,[24] and under Prior Singer (d. 1521) Walter Wilcock was carpenter to Wenlock priory,[25] and Clement Mason was mason there.[26] Richard Dawley, who framed the borough's 'court house' (the guildhall) 1539–40,[27] and his family were carpenters until 1636[28] or later. Walter Hancox (d. 1599), mason, architect, and sculptor, enjoyed a regional reputation.[29]

Thomas Simons was a pewterer in 1578,[30] and John Bridde was a nailer in the late 16th century.[31] Nailing continued in a small way into the 19th century:[32] in 1808 Randle Peck owned two nail shops,[33] and in 1841 five people living in Sheinton Street worked at nailing.[34] The trade had ceased by 1900.[35] Needle making is believed to have spread to Much Wenlock from the west midlands in the 17th century.[36] Adam Clun (d. 1642) was one of the earliest makers.[37] Moses Meredith was one by 1654[38] and lived in Barrow Street.[39] John Meredith (d. 1713)[40] followed the same trade.[41] Meanwhile Michael Adams (d. *c.* 1684) made needles at Walton.[42] There was a needle mill at Bradley in 1763,[43] and Thomas Cliveley was a needle maker in 1782,[44] but the trade was not mentioned *c.* 1798[45] or later.[46] Richard Byrd (fl. 1642–59) was a clockmaker,[47] and Edward Jeffries made clocks and watches in 1778.[48] There were two watchmakers *c.* 1798.[49] Farley had a plating forge in 1777,[50] together with a frying-pan shop by 1790.[51] There was a pump maker living at Wenlock Bank in 1841.[52]

Paper manufacture was carried on outside the town, where water power was available. In 1635 a paper mill stood beyond two pastures north-east of the Abbey.[53] It was probably the same as Masons (or Mayres) mill, whose occupant Francis Selman made paper *c.* 1702.[54] John Clarke of Wyke was a paper maker in 1661,[55] perhaps at the Farley paper mill mentioned 1733–43.[56]

The town had at least four malthouses in 1714[57] and 11 in 1808.[58] In 1769 Thomas Littlehales, in the Bull Ring, was making *c.* 2,000 bushels a season.[59] Six maltsters were recorded in 1842[60] but by 1900 only one.[61] Richard Canlin (d. 1757)[62] and his descendants were maltsters in High Street until the 1840s[63] and had another

7 S.R.O. 3898/Rg/5, bur. 5 Mar. 1774.
8 e.g. P.R.O., HO 107/928/18–19.
9 Ibid.
10 S. Bagshaw, *Dir. Salop.* (1851), 588–9.
11 S.R.O. 3898/Rg/1.
12 Ibid. 22 May 1586.
13 Ibid. 10 Nov. 1592, 24 Nov. 1605; S.R.O. 1224, box 89, deeds of 1678, 1720; box 97, deed of 1708; H.W.R.O.(H.), Heref. dioc. rec., invs. of John Carver 1683; Wm. Donne, 1725; N.L.W., Wynnstay, box E/62, f. 26.
14 P.R.O., E 179/168/214.
15 G. C. Williamson, *Trade Tokens Issued in 17th Cent.* (1967), ii. 960.
16 S.R.O. 3898/Rg/1.
17 Ibid. 6 Feb. 1568/9, 10 Feb. 1579/80.
18 Ibid. 17 Nov. 1616.
19 P.R.O., E 179/168/214.
20 S.R.O. 3898/Rg/5, bur. 17 July 1760; bur. 25 Nov. 1789.
21 P.R.O., HO 107/928/18, ff. 19v., 30, 31, 41v., 47, 52 and v.; HO 107/928/19, ff. 6, 9v., 12 and v., 13v., 14v., 15v., 22v.
22 Below, this section (mills).
23 W.B.R., Q2/2/157.
24 Heref. D. & C. mun. 569.
25 *T.S.A.S.* vi. 107.
26 Ibid. 121.
27 W.B.R., B3/1/1, p. 144.
28 S.R.O. 3898/Rg/1, 4 Feb. 1593/4; 10 June 1623; 7 July 1636; *T.S.A.S.* 2nd ser. vi. 270.
29 S.R.O. 3898/Rg/1, 16 Sept. 1599; *Mont. Colln.* lix. 138–40; *Arch. Jnl.* cxxxviii. 35; *S. Staffs. Arch. and Hist. Soc. Trans.* xxvi. 69.
30 S.R.O. 3898/Rg/1, 1 May 1578.
31 Ibid. 31 Jan. 1573/4; *T.S.A.S.* 2nd ser. vi. 270.
32 e.g. S.R.O. 1224, box 97, deed of 1708; W.B.R., Q2/2/107.
33 N.L.W., Wynnstay, box 43/7, f. 10.
34 P.R.O., HO 107/928/19, ff. 4v.–5, 6.
35 *Kelly's Dir. Salop.* (1900), 274–5.
36 *Econ. H.R.* xxxi. 355.
37 S.R.O. 3898/Rg/2, 23 Oct. 1642.
38 Ibid. 22 Mar. 1653/4.
39 *Hearth Tax 1672*, 29.
40 S.R.O. 3898/Rg/3, 11 Aug. 1713.
41 H.W.R.O.(H.), Heref. dioc. rec., inv. of John Meredith, 1713.
42 Ibid. inv. of Mic. Adams, 1684.
43 *Aris's Birm. Gaz.* 21 Feb. 1763.
44 S.R.O. 3898/Rg/5, bur. 5 Sept. 1782.
45 *Univ. Brit. Dir.* iv. 720.
46 P.R.O., HO 107/928/18–19.
47 D. J. Elliott, *Salop. Clock and Watchmakers* (1979), 42.
48 Ibid. 85.
49 *Univ. Brit. Dir.* iv. 720.
50 S.R.O. 1681/144/1.
51 S.P.L., MS. 6865, p. 214.
52 P.R.O., HO 107/928/18, f. 49.
53 N.L.W., Wynnstay, box F/31.
54 S.R.O., q. sess. rec. box 34, recognizance bk. 1700–9, loose sheet after East. 1702 entries, dated by *Orders of Q. Sess.* i. 203; below, this section (mills).
55 P.R.O., E 179/168/214.
56 S.R.O. 1359, box 26, deed of 1733; W.B.R., Q2/2/157.
57 N.L.W., Wynnstay, box E/62, p. 8, ff. 30, 34.
58 Ibid. box 43/7, ff. 2, 4–5, 8, 10–12.
59 N.L.W., Wynnstay, L 1288.
60 Pigot, *Nat. Com. Dir.* (1842), 51.
61 *Kelly's Dir. Salop.* (1900), 274.
62 S.R.O. 3898/Rg/5, bur. 19 Oct. 1757; H.W.R.O.(H.), Heref. dioc. rec., inv. of Ric. Canlin, 1757.
63 Pigot, *Nat. Com. Dir.* (1842), 51.

malthouse in Bourton Lane by 1797,[64] which William Canlin (d. 1864) left to his nephew Richard Cooper[65] (d. 1891).[66] Cooper's executors let it to C. E. Ainsworth *c.* 1892,[67] and it closed *c.* 1911.[68] Ralph Patson was brewer to Wenlock priory in 1539,[69] but large scale commercial brewing did not begin until George Lloyd bought the former Sheinton Street tannery in 1894[70] and converted it to the Wheatland Brewery.[71] It closed *c.* 1924.[72]

Clay tobacco pipes were being made by Robert Lumas and Samuel Deacon in the mid 1650s; Deacon lived in Spittle Street,[73] and the town had many pipemakers in the later 17th and earlier 18th century,[74] though John Kidson (d. *c.* 1726) worked at Wyke.[75] In 1675 pipes were the town's chief manufacture,[76] and there was still a pipemaker's shop in Mary Lane in 1769;[77] later, however, the trade centred on Broseley.[78]

Early brickmaking is indicated by the names Brick yard near Atterley,[79] Brick leasow near Bourton,[80] and Brickkiln piece near Presthope.[81] William Fletcher (fl. 1777) was a brickmaker.[82] A small brick and drainpipe works opened at Woodhousefield by 1841[83] and closed *c.* 1903.[84] By 1974[85] A. & J. Mucklow Ltd. made bricks and concrete blocks at Presthope, and in 1979 employed *c.* 60 there and at its Coates quarry works.[86]

About 1800 the main surviving industries were tanning and malting which, like the smaller scale nailmaking, were carried on mainly in the town. Weavers, tailors, drapers, shoemakers, and saddlers, crafts and trades associated with cloth and leather, were found in the parish too. Some compensation for the loss of other urban manufactures, clay pipes, needles, and clocks and watches, can be discerned in the growth of professions and services concentrated in the town. There had been surgeons and apothecaries since the early 18th century.[87] By 1798 there were two attorneys,[88] and in 1828 a partnership of three.[89] In 1811 there was a bank belonging to Richard Collins, Francis Pitt, and Edward Howells,[90] and in 1822[91] C. & J. H. Cooper of Bridgnorth[92] opened a bank in Barrow Street,[93] which moved to Hospital Street in 1876.[94] The Wenlock Franchise Savings Bank, in existence by 1826,[95] took a lease of premises in the Bull Ring in 1829.[96] It had, together with the Ironbridge branch,[97] 1,909 investors in 1850[98] but closed *c.* 1870.[99] Coopers' bank became, in due course (1914), a branch of the Midland Bank,[1] and branches of Lloyds Bank and of a precursor of Barclays were established in 1889 and *c.* 1907 respectively.[2]

A printing press was set up in Wilmore Street by Thomas Lawley in 1835.[3] William Lawley ran it until *c.* 1898, when it passed to A. E. Trevor,[4] and it closed *c.* 1903.[5] T. H. Thompson was a stationer and printer in 1903.[6] About 1950 the Old Mint Press moved to Smithfield Road from Shrewsbury.[7]

MILLS. In 1086 Much Wenlock manor had two mills 'serving the monks' and there was another at Bourton.[8] By 1400 there were at least eight mills in the parish. After 1600 the number declined, and only three survived until the early 20th century.

In 1540 the mill on the Much Wenlock demesne[9] stood at the Great pool,[10] which was retained by a dam over 400 m. long on a tributary of Farley brook.[11] The manor also included Green mill, mentioned in the 13th century,[12] perhaps that serving the town in 1535.[13] Green

64 S.R.O. 4791/1/3, p. 413.
65 S.R.O. 1206/16, pp. 785–6; 1242, box 10, deeds sched. of 1896.
66 S.R.O. 1242, box 10, will of Ric. Cooper (copy).
67 Ibid. undated draft deed.
68 *Kelly's Dir. Salop.* (1909), 287; (1913), 295 (no mention).
69 *T.S.A.S.* vi. 98.
70 S.R.O. 1242, box 7, deed of 1894.
71 *Kelly's Dir. Salop.* (1900), 274.
72 Ibid. (1922), 290; S.R.O. 1681/166/5–6 (lot 6).
73 S.R.O. 3898/Rg/2, 31 Dec. 1654; 20 Feb. 1673/4; H.W.R.O.(H.), Heref. dioc. rec., inv. of Sam. Deacon, 1673.
74 H.W.R.O.(H.), Heref. dioc. rec., invs. of Thos. Edwards, 1668; Sam. Browne, 1668; Morris Vaughan, 1671; Griffith Powell, 1673; Wm. Savage, 1686; Alice Deacon, 1691; Thos. Dawley, 1714; Ric. Roberts, 1716; Wm. Wilkinson, 1728; Sam. Hughes, 1730; Wm. Bryan, 1731; S.R.O. 1224, box 89, deed of 1726; box 97, deeds of 1708, 1729; N.L.W., Wynnstay, box E/62, f. 26; *T.S.A.S.* 3rd ser. vii. 163.
75 H.W.R.O.(H.), Heref. dioc. rec., inv. of John Kidson, 1726.
76 J. Ogilby, *Britannia*, i (1675), p. 100.
77 N.L.W., Wynnstay, L 1288.
78 Above, Benthall, econ. hist. (ind.); Broseley, econ. hist. (clay inds.); *Univ. Brit. Dir.* iv. 720 (no mention in M. Wenlock).
79 S.R.O. 1093, parcel 161, Atterley and Walton map of 1722.
80 S.R.O. 3765/1.
81 S.R.O. 294/6, field 2552.
82 S.R.O., QR 107/9.
83 P.R.O., HO 107/928/18, f. 32v.; O.S. Map 1/2,500, Salop. LVII. 3 (1883 edn.).
84 *Kelly's Dir. Salop.* (1900), 275; (1905), 285 (no mention).
85 P.O. *Telephone Dir.* (1975), sect. 303, p. 229.
86 *Mineral Extraction on Wenlock Edge: Discussion Paper and Rep. of Surv.* (S.C.C. 1979), 49–50.
87 *Woolhope Trans.* xxxiv (2), 137; S.R.O. 3898/Rg/3, 26 Sept. 1723; H.W.R.O.(H.), Heref. dioc. rec., will of Edm. Parkes, pr. 1723; inv. of John Phillips, 1724; S.R.O. 1224, box 89, deed of 1726; N.L.W., Wynnstay, L 1288, s.v. Spittle St.
88 *Univ. Brit. Dir.* iv [*c.* 1798], 720.
89 Tibnam & Co. *Salop. Dir.* (1828), 131.
90 S.R.O. 2623/178.
91 *Bridgnorth Jnl.* 25 June 1976.
92 W. F. Crick and J. E. Wadsworth, *Hundred Yrs. of Joint Stock Banking* (1936), 78.
93 Tibnam & Co. *Salop. Dir.* (1828), 131; Pigot, *Nat. Com. Dir.* (1835), 386.
94 *Bridgnorth Jnl.* 25 June 1976.
95 W.B.R., Q2/6/1.
96 S.R.O. 1242, box 7, deed (abstr.).
97 *V.C.H. Salop.* xi. 59.
98 S. Bagshaw, *Dir. Salop.* (1851), 582.
99 S.R.O. 1242, box 7, trustees' min. 1 Aug. 1870 (copy).
1 Crick and Wadsworth, *Hundred Yrs.* 44, 78.
2 R. S. Sayers, *Lloyd's Bank in the Hist. of Eng. Banking* (1957), 313; *Kelly's Dir. Salop.* (1909), 289; (1913), 296; (1917), 280.
3 W.B.R., Q2/6/2.
4 *Kelly's Dir. Salop.* (1895), 258; (1900), 275.
5 Ibid. (1900), 275; (1905), 285.
6 *Bourton Flower Show and Fête* (notice; copy in M. Wenlock Mus., MW 41/84).
7 Local inf.
8 *V.C.H. Salop.* i. 312.
9 N.L.W., Wynnstay, box 43/96.
10 P.R.O., SC 6/Hen. VIII/3021, m. 1.
11 R.C.H.M.E., draft field rep. (1985).
12 P.R.O., C 104/27, undated deed (Rog. le Kinch to Wenlock priory).
13 N.L.W., Wynnstay, box 43/96.

mill stood in 1553[14] at the site on Farley brook later called Wenlock[15] (or the Town, or Downs)[16] mill, *c.* 1 km. downstream of the priory. Downs mill, worked until the early 20th century,[17] may have been the 'lower' mill of 1321.[18]

Also at Much Wenlock was Masons mill, mentioned in 1534[19] and comprising a pair of mills in 1583.[20] In the earlier 16th century it was held by the Mayre family with the Almoners barn[21] and may therefore have been the same as the Mayres (or Mayors) mill mentioned 1522–1731:[22] that was separated from the barn by the Almoners croft[23] north-east of the priory.[24] No mill worked there by the 1840s.[25]

There was a windmill at Much Wenlock by 1321.[26] One stood *c.* 1 km. north of the town in 1714.[27] Still working in 1815,[28] it was wrecked by lightning *c.* 1850.[29] The 18th-century stone tower stood in 1986. The mill may have been the malt mill mentioned 1622–47.[30]

Farley (formerly Birdbach) mill on Farley brook[31] was mentioned in 1321.[32] In 1774 it consisted of two mills.[33] They were rebuilt in 1791–2, one with a 28-ft. overshot wheel.[34] By 1844 they used both water and steam power.[35] Still working in 1925,[36] they had closed by 1953.[37]

Just downstream of Farley mills were three mill ponds in 1849, all belonging to Jeremiah Aston,[38] a miller in 1841.[39] Unoccupied mills remained at two of them in 1849.[40] The pond nearest to Farley mills was perhaps that of the paper mill, later a plating forge,[41] mentioned 1733–77[42] and assigned to Richard Reynolds of Ketley in 1777.[43] The other two mills were presumably those owned in 1799 by Serjant Roden of Benthall,[44] one of which was called the Upper mill in 1806,[45] and probably those sold in 1826, one of which was then newly built.[46]

Bradley mill, mentioned in 1412,[47] was also called Samsons (or Nether Masons) mill in the 16th century.[48] In 1598 Thomas Lawley bought the residue of a 4,000-year lease.[49] His successor in title, Sir Watkin Williams Wynn,[50] had a mill in 1808,[51] possibly the same, but it became derelict *c.* 1820.[52] It stood on Farley brook near Lawleys Cross.[53] Samsons mill was held by the Mayres in the mid 16th century[54] and so may have been the Mairs (or Mayrs) mill in Wyke and Bradley township in the 18th.[55]

In 1321 Walton township included Ballop mill[56] on Walton brook below a sluice visible in 1882.[57] By 1339 it was a freehold of William de Walleye.[58] In 1542 Edward Twynyho, a speculator, sold it to Richard Dawley.[59] Lancelot Taylor acquired it by marriage to Dawley's great-granddaughter in 1593,[60] and from 1599 it descended with Taylor's chief house.[61] The mill seems to have closed *c.* 1760.[62]

In 1329 Adam de Aynho gave a freehold water mill in Callaughton to Wenlock priory.[63] The Crown sold it to Richard Lawley in 1543[64] and it became part of the Callaughton estate.[65] The mill stood on Callaughton brook[66] and closed in the later 1920s.[67]

Bourton had a mill by 1086.[68] Richard Lawley bought it from the Crown in 1543[69] and it presumably became part of the Bourton estate.[70] It seems to have closed before 1653,[71] perhaps superseded by a windmill on Henmoor hill[72] standing *c.* 1717.[73] Two large ponds remaining in 1731[74] were dry by 1795;[75] the upper was

14 *T.S.A.S.* vi. 122.
15 S.R.O. 4791/1/10, p. 25.
16 N.L.W., Wynnstay, R 70/12; W.B.R., P4/5/4, 13 Jan. 1853; B.L. Maps, O.S.D. 207.
17 O.S. Map 1/2,500, Salop. L. 8 (1902 and 1926 edns.).
18 S.R.O. 1037/19/1.
19 P.R.O., SC 6/Hen. VIII/3021, m. 12d.
20 N.L.W., Wynnstay, box E/70.
21 P.R.O., SC 6/Hen. VIII/3021, m. 12d.
22 N.L.W., Wynnstay, box 43/1; *T.S.A.S.* xi. 50; H.W.R.O.(H.), Heref. dioc. rec., inv. of Jos. Hughes, 1731.
23 P.R.O., LR 2/184, f. 61.
24 N.L.W., Wynnstay, MS. Plans 1. O.S. Nat. Grid SJ 629 003 was a reputed mill site: local inf.
25 S.R.O. 1931/1; W.B.R., P8/2/7.
26 S.R.O. 1037/19/1.
27 N.L.W., Wynnstay, MS. Plans 1.
28 S.R.O. 4791/1/10, p. 25.
29 N.L.W., Wynnstay, RA 27, s.a. 1850, 1858 (ref. supplied by Mr. O. G. McDonald).
30 N.L.W., Wynnstay, box 43/5, 147.
31 S.R.O. 1224/1/19; 1359, box 26, deed of 1844.
32 S.R.O. 1037/19/1.
33 S.R.O. 1359, box 26, deed of 1824.
34 S.P.L., MS. 6865, p. 214.
35 S.R.O. 1359, box 26, deed.
36 O.S. Map 1/2,500, Salop. L. 4 (1926 edn.).
37 S.R.O. 3756/147, pp. 9–10.
38 S.R.O. 294/4, fields 1544, 1548, 1554.
39 P.R.O., HO 107/928/18, f. 10.
40 S.R.O. 294/4, fields 1546, 1555.
41 S.P.L., MS. 6865, p. 214.
42 S.R.O. 1359, box 26, deed of 1824; 1681/144/1.
43 S.R.O. 1681/144/1.
44 S.R.O. 1359, box 26, land tax redemption certif.
45 S.R.O. 1634, box 20, deed.
46 *Wolverhampton Chron.* 19 Apr. 1826.
47 S.R.O. 1224/2/6.
48 Ibid /3/8, m. 5d.; /3/13/1; /3/123; P.R.O., LR 2/184, f. 140.
49 S.R.O. 1224/3/123.
50 Above, manors (M. Wenlock).
51 N.L.W., Wynnstay, box 43/7, f. 16.
52 N.L.W., Wynnstay, R 75/10; R 80/9.
53 S.R.O. 294/4, fields 1561–6. A Mill meadow lay just over the par. bdy. in 1837: S.R.O. 1671, Buildwas est. map.
54 S.R.O. 1224/3/8, m. 5d.; /3/123.
55 W.B.R., Q2/2/154, 157.
56 S.R.O. 1037/19/1.
57 At O.S. Nat. Grid SO 632 978: S.R.O. 1093, parcel 161, Atterley and Walton map of 1722; O.S. Map 1/2,500, Salop. L. 16 (1883 edn.).
58 N.L.W., Wynnstay, box E/72, deed.
59 S.R.O. 1224, box 91, deed of 1625.
60 Ibid. deed of 1593; S.R.O. 3898/Rg/1, marr. 25. Nov. 1593.
61 S.R.O. 1224, box 68, deed of 1733; box 91, deeds of 1625–1749; cf. above, manors (Atterley and Wenlock Walton).
62 S.R.O. 1224, box 183, Lady Day rental of 1760, f. 9; Mich. rental of 1760, f. 9. Thos. Howells (named therein) held the former Taylor est. in 1783: N.L.W., Wynnstay, box 43/84 (7).
63 *Cal. Pat.* 1327–30, 473–4.
64 *L. & P. Hen. VIII*, xviii (2), p. 239.
65 Hull Univ., Brynmor Jones Libr., DDFA(2)/15/2, 6–7, 9; N.L.W., Wynnstay, box 43/7, f. 14; /84 (15); S.R.O. 294/3; 2079/L. 16; 4044/92, f. 37 (no. 334). Cf. above, manors.
66 O.S. Map 1/2,500, Salop. L. 16 (1926 edn.).
67 *Kelly's Dir. Salop.* (1926), 311; (1929), 305; S.R.O. 3756/147, pp. 13–14.
68 *V.C.H. Salop.* i. 312.
69 *L. & P. Hen. VIII*, xviii (2), p. 239.
70 S.R.O. 3765/1; cf. above, manors.
71 A 1653 lease of the site mentioned no mill: Hull Univ., Brynmor Jones Libr., DDFA(2)/15/2, 9.
72 At O.S. Nat. Grid SO 602 974: S.R.O. 3765/1.
73 S.R.O., q. sess. rec. parcel 281, reg. of papists' deeds 1717–88, p. 148.
74 At O.S. Nat. Grid SO 593 963: S.R.O. 3765/1.
75 Bourton map of 1795 (in Mr. J. R. Craig's possession).

flooded again before 1882,[76] apparently to power a saw mill.[77]

Bradeley mill farther downstream[78] was in complete decay in 1421, and by 1427 the 'mill land' was let at a reduced rent.[79] A Mill hill between Bradeley and Patton was mentioned in 1307.[80]

Wigwig mill on Harley brook[81] was mentioned in 1291.[82] After the Dissolution it seems to have descended with Mill farm.[83] It consisted in 1670 of two mills, presumably in one building.[84] It was a fulling mill, perhaps in the 17th century,[85] but in 1695 was a corn mill.[86] It seems to have closed in the earlier 19th century.[87]

LOCAL GOVERNMENT. Much Wenlock manor had great (leet) and small (baron) courts, probably by 1272.[88] Their jurisdiction embraced the township of Much Wenlock and perhaps other areas too, and the great court's leet jurisdiction may have extended farther. Other manors had, or came under, other small courts: Bourton had one,[89] Bradley had one for the estates within Bradley grange[90] (including, by 1369, Bradley, Wyke, part of Harley, and Wigwig),[91] and Marsh (in Barrow) had a court for the estates of Marsh grange (including Atterley and Walton).[92] Between 1379 and 1390 Marsh's court absorbed Bradley's, perhaps for economic reasons,[93] and by 1540 it seems to have had jurisdiction over the demesne part of Presthope.[94] Bradeley presumably came under the lord of Broseley's court baron by the 15th century[95] and Callaughton, some time before 1540, acquired its own court baron.[96] The subinfeudated part of Presthope had a court baron in 1697.[97]

Records of Bourton manor court survive for 1333–4, 1344–5, 1379–80, 1404, 1420–1, 1431, and 1449 and of Much Wenlock small court for those dates and 1403, 1411–12, 1432, and 1450.[98] In the 14th century Bourton manor court seems to have been held two or three times a year; in the 15th and the early 16th century it usually met only once a year.[99] It dealt mainly with agricultural matters but also amerced breaches of the assize of ale. Trespasses in Spoonhill wood were presented there in the 16th century,[1] and in 1522 Patton (in Stanton Long) elected to appear thenceforth at Bourton's court baron instead of Oxenbold's.[2]

Much Wenlock small court usually met on Saturday. It was held only four times 1344–5, but 15 times 1379–80, 17 times 1403–4, 13 times 1420–1, and eight times 1449–50. The court had much more commercial than agrarian business.

Records of Much Wenlock's great court survive for 1344–5, 1379–80, 1403–4, 1412, 1420–1, 1431, and 1449–50. In the 14th and 15th centuries it met twice yearly to deal with breaches of the peace and of the assize of bread and of ale and with nuisances and trespasses. Officers included two constables in 1404 and two aletasters in 1344.[3]

By 1247 the town had a distinct class of burgesses paying a uniform rent of 1*s.*[4] The burgesses enjoyed trading privileges, for in 1333 a mercer of Willey paid the prior an annual tenser rent to live in the liberty and trade in the town.[5] Although the town had no autonomy, the freemen and burgesses were able in 1247 to assert their interests so far as to secure, from a jury summoned under royal writ, a verdict defining their tenurial obligations in the face of the prior's arbitrary exactions.[6]

After 1468 the small court of Much Wenlock manor probably lost much of its commercial business to the borough bailiff's court,[7] and by 1550 the manor's small and great courts were united. Rolls survive for 1550, 1554, and 1719–33,[8] an estreat of fines for 1614,[9] and many other records 1722–1857.[10] In 1614 the manor court was still punishing affrays and minor bloodsheds. By 1719, however, it had virtually ceased to deal with public order offences[11] or assize breaches. The biannual meetings were mainly concerned with abuses of the open fields, commons, streets, watercourses, and weights and measures, and routine amercements of tanners, shoemakers, unlicensed cottagers, and keepers of unringed pigs. Unusually, scolds were fined in 1730.[12] Meetings were in the guildhall by 1786.[13] Until the later 1790s manorial officers included two clerks of the market, a searcher and sealer of leather, and a pig ringer.[14] Two constables were appointed until 1857[15] or later. The manorial lock-up was at a house in Sheinton

76 O.S. Map 1/2,500, Salop. LVII. 3 (1883 edn.).
77 *Estate Mag.* vi. 415.
78 At O.S. Nat. Grid SO 598 955: S.R.O. 3765/1.
79 S.R.O. 1190/1, unlisted acct. r. of 1420–1, 1426–7.
80 Barnard MSS., Raby Castle, box 1, bdle. 17, no. 11.
81 At O.S. Nat. Grid SJ 609 018: field names in S.R.O. 294/5, fields 1382–3.
82 *Tax. Eccl.* 164.
83 S.R.O. 1709/55/15; N.L.W., Wynnstay, box 43/7, f. 18; cf. above, manors.
84 S.R.O. 1709/55/1.
85 Ibid. /55/4, 6–9.
86 Ibid. /55/23.
87 N.L.W., Wynnstay, box 43/7, f. 18; S.R.O. 294/5 (no mention).
88 The tns. was separately represented at the 1272 eyre: P.R.O., JUST 1/736, m. 24.
89 By 1333: S.R.O. 566/1.
90 By 1321: Eyton, iii. 287; cf. above, econ. hist. (agric.).
91 B.L. Add. MS. 6165, p. 98.
92 Cf. above, econ. hist. (agric.); Barrow, local govt.
93 B.L. Add. MS. 6164, p. 383; S.R.O. 1224, box 342, Prior Gosnell's reg. f. 35v.; S.R.O. 1224/2/16; cf. above, econ. hist. (agric.).
94 Above, manors (Presthope).
95 S.R.O. 1190/1, unlisted acct. r. of 1421–2; cf. above, manors (Bradeley); Broseley, local govt.
96 P.R.O., SC 6/Hen. VIII/3021, m. 14d.
97 S.P.L., Deeds 3360.
98 S.R.O. 566/1; 1190/1, unlisted ct. r. 1403–4; 1224/2/1–9, on which this para. is based.
99 S.R.O. 566/2.
1 P.R.O., LR 2/184, f. 148v.
2 S.R.O. 566/2.
3 S.R.O. 1190/1, unlisted ct. r. 1403–4; 1224/2/1–2, 6–9.
4 *T.S.A.S.* lxvi. 60–2.
5 S.R.O. 566/1, 27 Nov. 1333; above, Lib. and Boro. of Wenlock (Lib.: Bourton hund.).
6 *T.S.A.S.* lxvi. 60–2.
7 Above, Lib. and Boro. of Wenlock (boro. 1468–1836).
8 P.R.O., SC 2/197/148, m. 6; SC 2/197/152, mm. 1–2d.; N.L.W., Wynnstay, L 1306.
9 N.L.W., Wynnstay, box 43/139.
10 Ibid. /9, 12–54, 93–5; box 56/87, 93–4; box E/14–32; box F/1–3; L 140; M 2518–27; W.B.R., M/9/1.
11 Only one was recorded 1719–33: N.L.W., Wynnstay, L 1306, 20 Oct. 1721.
12 Ibid. 16 Apr. 1730.
13 N.L.W., Wynnstay, box 56/87.
14 Ibid. box 43/26, 30.
15 Ibid. box E/32.

Street,[16] later called retrospectively the 'old gaol'.[17]

Soon after William Whorwood bought the manorial rights over Atterley and Walton in 1544,[18] he withdrew those townships from Marsh manor and placed them, with Barrow, under a new court.[19] Rolls survive for 1626, 1717, 1740, 1765, and 1786,[20] and many other records 1676–1836.[21] The court was peripatetic at first[22] but from the 17th century usually met at Atterley.[23]

In each township the main manorial officer was the constable. Bourton, Callaughton,[24] and Much Wenlock[25] had two each, the other townships one.[26] In the 17th century the constables of Wyke and Bradley, Atterley, and Walton were appointed from the principal houses in rotation.[27] In 1719 the Much Wenlock constables' duties included repairing the gates of the open fields.[28] In 1730 they had a 'grublestool' (cucking stool).[29] Each township was expected to have stocks, archery butts, and a pound, and in the 17th century several did.[30] An old pound remained at Presthope in 1882.[31] Much Wenlock pound in Victoria Road[32] remained in 1986.

In 1775 the vestry met monthly after evensong to fix the poor rate. The Easter Monday vestry appointed churchwardens and nominated overseers. Other, mostly poor-law, business was discussed at special meetings after morning service or on Monday afternoon.[33] A poor-law committee was elected in 1786.[34] From the early 19th century the vestry normally met on weekdays.[35]

In 1712–13 expenditure on the poor was £112, including monthly pay to 31 people. By 1731 the parish rented a workhouse,[36] managed by trustees. It was a stone building[37] on the north side of Downs Lane.[38] In 1731–2 it cost £31 to run, generating only 15*s.* 3*d.* income. Monthly out-relief, for *c.* 8 children, cost £17 19*s.*, and £46 3*s.* was given out as 'necessity money'.[39]

Average annual expenditure on the poor rose from £80 *c.* 1760 to £350 *c.* 1790.[40] Some years all the poor were farmed,[41] but often a salaried assistant overseer was resident workhouse master.[42] In 1781 the vestry considered establishing a 'manufactory' at the house. A vestryman had to visit daily and the overseers at least thrice weekly. The vestry had begun renting a house for poor families in 1777,[43] and a house at the Bank was repaired for the parish in 1813.[44] From 1780 the vestry subscribed to the Salop Infirmary, and in 1788 an apothecary was retained for the workhouse. The house had room for Morville paupers taken in in 1787.[45] In 1793 all 27 inmates were women or children. Older children were usually apprenticed in Lancashire cotton mills.[46]

In 1802–3 the workhouse had only nine inmates, but by 1812–13 there were 38 adults besides children. During the same period regular out-relief to adults also increased.[47] From 1826 the vestry retained a surgeon to attend all the poor, except midwifery cases, within 5 miles of the town.[48] In 1834 the house contained 6 men, 6 women, and 8 children; the men worked at roadmending.[49] Weekly out-relief was 1*s.* 6*d.* a head and each workhouse inmate cost 5*s.* a week. About 300 families a year received out-relief, which was withheld from able-bodied men: instead they too were sometimes paid for roadmending.[50] In 1836 the parish became part of Madeley poor-law union,[51] and the workhouse soon closed.[52]

By the 1720s Much Wenlock township had two highway surveyors, the other townships one each. The borough magistrates appointed them annually.[53] In 1730 the Much Wenlock township surveyors were liable to amercement in the manor court.[54] The vestry began to nominate the surveyors for that township in 1822[55] and by 1840 appointed a salaried highway surveyor for it.[56]

During an epidemic of 'malignant disease' in 1845 the vestry established a temporary board of health.[57] The parish was in Madeley rural sanitary district 1872–3,[58] but in 1873 a local board of health for the parish was formed,[59] with an urban sanitary authority's powers.[60] Its elliptical seal, 31 mm. × 25 mm., bore the town's rebus (WEN and a fetterlock) and was inscribed (Roman) MUCH WENLOCK LOCAL GOVERNMENT BOARD at the circumference.[61] From 1873 the

16 S.R.O. 2584/8, undated newscutting.
17 *T.S.A.S.* 3rd ser. v, p. *xi*.
18 Above, manors.
19 S.R.O. 1175/1.
20 S.R.O. 775/77, 92, 95, 97, 106.
21 Ibid. /78–91, 93–4, 96, 98–105, 107–50.
22 S.R.O. 1175/1.
23 Above, Barrow, local govt.
24 W.B.R., q. sess. files, summons 6 Mar. 1599/1600.
25 N.L.W., Wynnstay, box 43/139.
26 S.R.O. 1224/2/16, 53, 66; W.B.R., q. sess. files, summons 6 Mar. 1599/1600.
27 S.R.O. 840, box 2, ct. r. of 1644; 1224/2/58, 126.
28 N.L.W., Wynnstay, L 1306, 14 Oct. 1719.
29 Ibid. 16 Apr. 1730.
30 N.L.W., Wynnstay, box 43/139; S.R.O. 840/1/73; 1224/2/66, 69, 73, 87.
31 O.S. Map 1/2,500, Salop. L. 14 (1883 edn.).
32 S.R.O. 1931/1; W.B.R., P8/2/7, no. 618.
33 W.B.R., P4/5/3.
34 Ibid. 8 May 1786, 17 Apr. 1792.
35 W.B.R., P4/5/4–5.
36 Ibid. Q1/13/132–3.
37 N.L.W., Wynnstay, L 1288, s.v. Bullring St.
38 Ibid.; S.R.O. 1931/1; W.B.R., P8/2/7, no. 209.
39 W.B.R., Q1/13/133.
40 S.P.L., MS. 6865, p. 211.
41 e.g. W.B.R., P4/5/1, 21 July 1762; /5/3, 15 May 1786.
42 Ibid. /5/1, 28 Sept. 1775, 2 June 1777; /5/3, *passim*.
43 Ibid. /5/3, 12 Jan. 1777, 22 Apr. 1781, 20 May 1787.
44 Ibid. /5/4, 31 Jan. 1813.
45 Ibid. /5/3, 2 May 1780, 4 June 1787, 19 May 1788.
46 S.P.L., MS. 6865, p. 211.
47 *Poor Law Abstract*, H.C. 175, p. 423 (1803–4), xiii; H.C. 82, p. 377 (1818), xix.
48 W.B.R., P4/5/4, 4 May 1826; Tibnam & Co. *Salop. Dir.* (1828), 131.
49 *Rep. Poor Law Com.* H.C. 44, p. 199*g* (1834), xxxv.
50 Ibid. p. 199*h* (1834), xxxvi.
51 S.R.O. 134/1, pp. 1–2.
52 W.B.R., P8/2/7, no. 209.
53 W.B.R., Q1/2/5, 18, 20, 25, 57, 63, 73, 78, 81, 85; cf. *T.S.A.S.* lvi. 314–27.
54 N.L.W., Wynnstay, L 1306, 16 Apr. 1730.
55 W.B.R., P4/5/4, 22 Sept. 1822.
56 Under the Highway Act, 1835, 5 & 6 Wm. IV, c. 50: W.B.R., P4/5/4, 26 Mar. 1840.
57 Ibid. 27 Mar. 1845.
58 Public Health Act, 1872, 35 & 36 Vic. c. 79.
59 Under the Local Govt. Act, 1858, 21 & 22 Vic. c. 98: *Lond. Gaz.* 15 Apr. 1873, p. 1976.
60 Public Health Act, 1872, 35 & 36 Vic. c. 79.
61 Impression in W.B.R., M. Wenlock local bd. min. bk. 1873–89, p. 6.

board appointed the highway surveyor.[62] In 1889 the board was abolished, its powers passing to the Wenlock district committee of the borough council, sanitary authority for the borough's Wenlock ward, which coincided with Much Wenlock civil parish.[63] In 1888 the vestry had appointed the local board as the civil parish's burial board,[64] but in 1890, after the local board had been dissolved, the vestry appointed a burial board that was differently constituted.[65]

By 1900 the vestry met only twice yearly, once to nominate overseers and once, at Easter, to appoint churchwardens, sidesmen, and the burial board and to receive the wardens' and board's accounts.[66] The borough council was empowered to appoint parish overseers and assistant overseers in 1923 (shortly before those offices were abolished everywhere).[67] After the vestry relinquished the burial board's powers to the borough council in 1948,[68] its only function was to elect churchwardens.[69]

When the municipal borough was dissolved in 1966 the civil parish was constituted a rural borough[70] and put in Bridgnorth rural district.[71] When Bridgnorth district absorbed the rural district in 1974, the rural borough council became a town council with a town mayor.[72]

PUBLIC SERVICES. In 1403 St. Mildburg's well was a public water supply.[73] In the 17th and 18th centuries there were common wells at Atterley,[74] Homer,[75] and Wyke, [76] and presumably throughout the parish. In 1900–1 the borough council provided the town with mains water from a borehole near the railway station via a reservoir.[77] A second borehole, near the gasworks, was added in 1925.[78] In Bourton and Callaughton the landlord provided mains water by 1906[79] and still in 1986.[80] The rest of the parish had no piped supply until after 1945.[81]

The brook flowing through the town was called 'Schittebrok' by 1321[82] and was the main sewer[83] until the 20th century. By 1849 a sewer laid along part of Barrow Street discharged into it,[84] and in 1866 an improved sewerage scheme was prepared.[85] Mapped as an open watercourse in the 1840s, the brook had been culverted through the town by 1882.[86] In 1913 the borough council sewered the town[87] to new disposal works near Downs mill.[88] The rest of the parish was without main drainage until after 1945.[89]

By 1790 the town was served by a local penny post operating from Shifnal and by 1834 from Ironbridge.[90] The town has had only a sub post office since. At Bourton a sub post office opened before 1870.[91]

By 1808 the parish maintained a fire engine,[92] and did so until *c.* 1880.[93] In 1901–2 Wenlock district committee formed a fire brigade.[94] It passed to the National Fire Service in 1941 and to the county council in 1948.[95] The fire station was then in Bridgnorth Road.[96] A newly built station opened in Smithfield Road in 1956.[97]

The parish was policed under the watch committee of the borough's Wenlock ward 1836–40 and thereafter by the county constabulary.[98] In 1856 there was one officer, stationed under the guildhall.[99] In 1865[1] a newly built police station opened in Sheinton Street; it was replaced by one in Smithfield Road in 1966.[2]

In 1840 the borough council adopted the Lighting and Watching Act, 1833,[3] for the town only,[4] and by 1846 the streets were gas-lit.[5] In 1856 the Wenlock Gas Co. was formed under the chairmanship of Dr. W. P. Brookes, and a works site in Barrow Street was bought in 1857.[6] The company was wound up in 1890[7] and the undertaking sold to the tenant William Lawley.[8] It was bought in 1900 by the borough council,[9] which sold it in 1937 to the Iron Bridge & District Gas Co. Ltd., a subsidiary of the Severn Valley Gas Corporation Ltd.[10] The works closed

62 Ibid. pp. 8, 10.
63 Local Govt. Bd.'s Prov. Order Conf. (No. 4) Act, 1889, 52 & 53 Vic. c. 22 (Local).
64 Under the Public Health Act, 1875, 38 & 39 Vic. c. 55, s. 343: W.B.R., P4/5/5, 18 Oct. 1888.
65 Under the Burial Act, 1853, 16 & 17 Vic. c. 134: ibid. 17 Jan. 1890.
66 Ibid. 22 Mar., 19 Apr. 1900.
67 W.B.R., boro. council min. bk. 1911–28, p. 378; Rating and Valuation Act, 1925, 15 & 16 Geo. V, c. 90.
68 38 & 39 Vic. c. 55, s. 343: W.B.R., P4/5/5, 30 Mar. 1948.
69 e.g. *Wenlock Herald*, Apr. 1960 (copy in S.R.O. 3898/Pr/12).
70 Local Govt. Act, 1958, 6 & 7 Eliz. II, c. 55, s. 28.
71 *Salop Order 1966* (Stat. Instr. 1966, no. 8).
72 Under the Local Govt. Act, 1972, c. 70.
73 S.R.O. 1190/1, unlisted ct. r. 1403–4.
74 S.R.O. 775/92.
75 S.R.O. 1224/2/169.
76 Ibid. /2/111.
77 S.R.O. 1242, box 2, circular 13 Nov. 1900; O.S. Map 1/2,500, Salop. L. 8 (1902 edn.); *Kelly's Dir. Salop.* (1909), 285.
78 *Kelly's Dir. Salop.* (1929), 302; R. W. Pocock and others, *Shrews. Dist.* (Mem. Geol. Surv. 1938), 226.
79 *Estate Mag.* vi. 416; *Shropshire Star*, 11 Jan. 1986, p. 25.
80 Local inf.
81 A. H. S. Waters, *Rep. on Water Supply* (S.C.C. 1946), 18.
82 S.R.O. 1037/19/1.
83 W.B.R., M. Wenlock local bd. min. bk. 1873–89, p. 335.
84 W.B.R., P4/5/4, 29 Mar. 1849.
85 Ibid. /5/5, 16 Aug. 1866.
86 S.R.O. 1931/1; O.S. Maps 1/2,500, Salop. L. 8, 12 (1882 edn.). The culvert's fabric, however, looks older than 19th-cent.: inf. from Mr. P. A. Kennedy, land drainage officer, S.C.C.
87 *Kelly's Dir. Salop.* (1917), 277.
88 O.S. Map 1/2,500, Salop. L. 8 (1926 edn.).
89 Local inf.
90 D. Salt, 'Shifnal and Ironbridge Penny Posts', *Brit. Mailcoach*, xxix (June 1981), 3–8.
91 *P.O. Dir. Salop.* (1870), 166.
92 W.B.R., P4/5/1, 27 July 1808.
93 *Shrews. Chron.* 2 Aug. 1901, p. 8.
94 W.B.R., Wenlock dist. cttee. min. bk. 1900–8, pp. 81, 87, 94.
95 *V.C.H. Salop.* iii. 221.
96 S.R.O., S.C.C. Fire Brigade Cttee. min. bk. 1947–51, p. 25.
97 *S.C.C. Mins.* 1956–7, 22.
98 Above, Lib. and Boro. of Wenlock (boro. 1836–89).
99 *P.O. Dir. Salop.* (1856), 88.
1 S.R.O., q. sess. Const. Cttee. rep. bk. 1854–65, f. 239.
2 S.R.O. 2452/2, rep. of Co. Architect (facing p. 78).
3 3 & 4 Wm. IV, c. 90.
4 W.B.R., boro. council min. bk. 1835–65, 9 Nov. 1840.
5 W.B.R., B2/2/26.
6 S.R.O. 1242, box 6, draft decl. of W. P. Brookes; O.S. Map 1/2,500, Salop. L. 12 (1882 edn.).
7 *Lond. Gaz.* 18 July 1890, p. 3998.
8 *Wellington Jnl.* 14 June 1890, p. 1; S.R.O. 1242, box 6, draft min. of directors' mtg. 7 July 1890.
9 Local Govt. Bd.'s Prov. Orders Conf. (Gas) Act, 1898, 61 & 62 Vic. c. 97; S.R.O. 1242, box 6, draft deed.
10 *Iron Bridge and Dist. Gas Order 1937* (Stat. Rules & Orders, 1937, no. 708).

in the 1950s.[11] Electric street lighting was introduced in 1945.[12]

The burial board's cemetery in Bridgnorth Road, consecrated with a chapel in 1891,[13] was extended in 1943[14] and 1975.[15]

In 1901 the district committee opened an isolation hospital in a rented cottage at Bell Hole.[16] North of the town the Lady Forester Memorial Hospital, built and endowed under the will of Lady Forester (d. 1893), opened with 16 beds in 1903; it was designed by E. B. I'Anson.[17] It passed to the National Health Service in 1948.[18]

CHURCHES. If St. Mildburg's double monastery[19] had two churches, Mildburg (fl. 727) was presumably buried in the women's.[20] The alleged discovery of her bones in Holy Trinity church in 1101[21] seems, however, to be contradicted by reports that her remains were known at Much Wenlock *c.* 1031[22] and that a reliquary, though empty of recognizable relics, was extant *c.* 1080.[23] Whatever the truth about St. Mildburg's remains, Holy Trinity may have been the survivor of a pair of churches and was presumably the minster that existed in 901[24] and probably came to be served by secular priests;[25] Holy Trinity was called a minster *c.* 1101.[26] It may have become redundant in the 11th century when a new minster church was built north-east of it;[27] St. Mildburg's nunnery was said to be deserted by *c.* 1080,[28] and in 1101 Holy Trinity was dilapidated and under repair.[29] The reconstitution of the new minster as a Cluniac priory probably led in the early 12th century to the reinstatement of Holy Trinity as a parish church[30] and to its complete rebuilding.

About 1110[31] Richard of Beaumais, bishop of London and justiciar of Shropshire, declared the priory's estates to be one parish, a ruling confirmed by the bishop of Hereford *c.* 1190 and by the king in 1348.[32] Wigwig, which may have been in Cound parish *c.* 1110,[33] was probably included in that of Much Wenlock by 1187.[34] In the early 14th century Holy Trinity parish was in practice less extensive than the priory estate, though it included what later became the parishes of Acton Round, Barrow, Benthall, Broseley, Hughley, Linley, Monkhopton, Shipton, and Willey, the chapelry of Bourton, and the extra-parochial Posenhall.[35] Afterwards those places became ecclesiastically separate in varying degrees and by 1716 the parishioners believed Holy Trinity to have only one dependent chapel, Bourton.[36] Much Wenlock and Bourton benefices were united in 1926 and the ecclesiastical parish was renamed Much Wenlock with Bourton.[37] Over the period 1969–76 the vicar was put in charge of the benefices of Hughley with Church Preen, Harley, Kenley, Stanton Long with Easthope, and Shipton.[38] In 1981 they and Much Wenlock with Bourton were united to form Wenlock united benefice; the constituent ecclesiastical parishes remained distinct. A team ministry of rector and two vicars was set up, with the vicar of Much Wenlock with Bourton as first rector. The advowson of the rectory was vested in a board comprising the patrons of the constituent livings and chaired by the bishop. Future team vicars were to be appointed by the bishop and rector jointly. Much Wenlock vicarage became the rectory house.[39]

After the formal appropriation of the rectory between 1186 and 1198 a vicarage was established. The advowson of the vicarage descended with the rectory, passing in 1540 to the Crown,[40] which sold it to Henry Bromley with the rectorial tithes of Much Wenlock township in 1590;[41] Bromley's cousin was the wife of Thomas Lawley (d. 1622),[42] to whom the advowson (by 1616) and the tithes passed.[43] Lawley's successors as lords of the manor and impropriators of Much Wenlock thereafter owned the advowson.[44] In 1705 the patron, a papist,[45] presented Hugh Pugh,[46] rector of Tugford.[47] The parishioners petitioned against his institution,[48] and in 1706 the bishop collated their nominee instead.[49]

A minimum income of £13 13*s.* 4*d.* was intended for the vicar by an agreement of 1274. He was assigned the small tithes of the townships that became the modern parish, and all the tithes of Benthall and Linley. The hay tithes of Much Wenlock township were excluded, and all tithes

11 *Wenlock Herald*, Oct. 1960.
12 W.B.R., Wenlock dist. cttee. min. bk. 1941–6, pp. 281, 287.
13 Heref. Dioc. Regy., reg. 1883–1901, pp. 304–6; *Kelly's Dir. Salop.* (1900), 271.
14 Heref. Dioc. Regy., reg. 1938–53, pp. 212–13.
15 Ibid. reg. 1969– (in use), pp. 212–13.
16 W.B.R., Wenlock dist. cttee. min. bk. 1900–8, pp. 45, 140; *S.C.C. Mins.* Sanitary Cttee. rep. 3 May 1902, 4.
17 *Kelly's Dir. Salop.* (1905), 282.
18 Inf. from Salop. Health Auth.
19 Above, growth of settlement.
20 As suggested in *T.S.A.S.* lvii. 141.
21 Ibid. 145.
22 *A.-S. Eng.* vii. 68, 89.
23 *T.S.A.S.* lvii. 144.
24 Sawyer, *A.-S. Charters*, no. 221.
25 Finberg, *Early Charters of W. Midlands*, p. 198.
26 *T.S.A.S.* lvii. 144.
27 As suggested in *Jnl. Brit. Arch. Assoc.* 3rd ser. xxviii. 35. On that church and its precinct see above, growth of settlement.
28 *Gesta Pontif.* (Rolls Ser.), 306; *Gesta Regum* (Rolls Ser.), i. 268.
29 *T.S.A.S.* lvii. 144–5.
30 As suggested in Eyton, iii. 265.
31 Ibid. 232.
32 *Cal. Pat.* 1348–50, 186.
33 *Jnl. Brit. Arch. Assoc.* cxlv. 8.
34 Above, manors (Wigwig).
35 *Cal. Pat.* 1348–50, 188; S.R.O. 1224/2/11.
36 H.W.R.O.(H.), HD 5/14/1/25.
37 Heref. Dioc. Regy., reg. 1926–38, p. 4.
38 *Crockford* (1977–9), 3 (s.v. Acheson).
39 Heref. Dioc. Regy., reg. 1969– (in use), pp. 397–9.
40 *Reg. Swinfield* (C.S.), 529; *Reg. Orleton* (C.S.), 386; *Reg. Spofford* (C.S.), 357; *Reg. Boulers* (C.S.), 22; *Reg. Stanbury* (C.S.), 191; *Dioc. of Heref. Institutions (1539–1900)*, ed. A. T. Bannister (Heref. 1923), 16. For the rectory see above, manors.
41 P.R.O., C 66/1354, mm. 13–14.
42 *Visit. Salop. 1623* (Harl. Soc. xxviii–xxix), i. 77–8; ii. 373–4.
43 P.R.O., C 142/393, no. 142; Bannister, *Heref. Institutions*, 28.
44 Bannister, op cit. 34, 46, 89, 122, 157, 185; P.R.O., CP 25/2/960/13 Anne East. [no. 6]; *P.O. Dir. Salop.* (1879), 433; Heref. Dioc. Regy., reg. 1902–19, p. 264; 1919–26, p. 325; 1938–53, p. 224; 1953–68, p. 521; 1969– (in use), p. 336.
45 *Complete Peerage*, v. 596 n.
46 N.L.W., Plas-yn-Cefn 2693.
47 S.R.O. 4132/Ch/1, s.a. 1705–6.
48 N.L.W., Plas-yn-Cefn 2693, 2708, 2716, 2730.
49 Bannister, *Heref. Institutions*, 60.

from the priory's demesne. He was to receive 30 thraves of wheat and oats from Bourton and a customary corn payment from Monkhopton. Fees and offerings were assigned as well as 'shrift corn' payable at confessions. His glebe was to be property in Much Wenlock worth 13*s*. a year and 30 a. in Benthall;[50] there was a vicarage house by 1300.[51] In 1284 the bishop added pensions of 2*s*. each from the chaplains of Acton Round, Barrow, and Shipton.[52] In 1379, however, the vicar's income was only £10.[53] By 1535 tithes from Sutton, near Shrewsbury, had been added, bringing his net income to £12 9*s*. 8*d*.[54] In 1536 the vicar hoped to supplement that by taking a lease of Bourton rectorial tithes.[55]

In the 16th century the glebe in Much Wenlock consisted mainly of houses on the corner of Spittle and Wilmore streets. One housed the vicar, another his curate, and the rest were let.[56] The 30 a. in Benthall were seized by the Crown *c*. 1562 as alleged chantry lands and sold.[57] Woodland under Benthall Edge in 1551, anciently called the 'vicar of Wenlock's dole of wood',[58] was not mentioned in 1607 or later. The only other glebe was ½ a. in Gleedon Hill field and three small pieces of meadow in Callaughton and Walton;[59] the Gleedon hill land included a profitable stone quarry.[60] In 1646 George Penruddock, the lady of the manor's husband,[61] settled the corn tithes of Much Wenlock township on the living, augmenting it by £40;[62] that arrangement presumably ceased at the Restoration. The living was valued at £45 *c*. 1708.[63]

On the eve of commutation the vicarial tithes were deemed[64] to consist of small tithes except in Farley, Wyke, and Bradley, where only some of the small tithes and no hay tithes were vicarial. Large acreages were prescriptively free of vicarial tithe in Much Wenlock, Bourton, and Callaughton, and moduses were payable from considerable portions of Atterley, Harley, Homer, and Wigwig. Between 1847 and 1849 the vicar's tithes and moduses were commuted to £342 7*s*. 2*d*., to which was added 18*s*. 5*d*. from Callaughton in lieu of fees and Easter offerings.[65]

The vicar, as patron of Bourton,[66] could hold the perpetual curacy himself and did so 1788–1833[67] and from 1870 until the benefices were united in 1926.[68] As patron of Benthall he could also hold that living, and did so 1842–58 and 1899–1902;[69] that was hardly profitable, however, for he had to pay a curate to serve Benthall.[70]

The vicarage house, which had a study and three chambers in 1664,[71] was in good repair in 1716, but the vicar stopped using it about then.[72] The glebe houses thereafter decayed and by 1835 there was no fit benefice house.[73] Evan Morris, vicar 1786–93, lived elsewhere in the town,[74] and by 1845 the patron rented a large house at the west end of High Street to the vicar.[75] By the 1870s the glebe houses were mostly untenantable, but they occupied a valuable site and were sold in 1874 for £710,[76] presumably to augment the living. The vicars occupied the High Street house until *c*. 1944 and then lived at Priory Cottage in the Bull Ring until *c*. 1969 when a vicarage was built in New Road.[77]

On the eve of the Reformation the clergy of the parish were well educated and the liturgy was carefully observed. Between 1521 and 1523 the vicar John Bacheler, M.A., was involved in a disputation with Prior Gosnell on Duns Scotus's *quaestio* 'De sacramento altaris'.[78] Thomas Butler, vicar 1524–62,[79] owned a copy of the pseudo-Aristotelian *Secreta Secretorum*[80] and kept a journal recording contemporary religious changes.[81] Assistant clergy included, besides Our Lady's chaplain, a married deacon or clerk; he instructed schoolboys in plainsong and 'prick song' so that the church was 'well served',[82] and bought a processional.[83] The boys perhaps used the pre-Reformation west gallery.[84] Mass was celebrated daily, but the parishioners communicated only at Easter.[85] Pre-Reformation ornaments included a silk banner bearing a representation of the Trinity.[86] Church ales were mentioned in 1543.[87]

A service of the Blessed Virgin Mary was founded before 1376.[88] The Lady chapel's fabric suggests an origin in the late 13th or early 14th century,[89] but the service was reconstituted by Sir Edmund Dudley[90] (d. *c*. 1485),[91] whose family were patrons of Wenlock's dependent

50 Eyton, iii. 266.
51 Nott. Univ. Libr. MSS. Dept., Mi. D. 3716.
52 *Cal. Pat.* 1348–50, 187–8.
53 B.L. Add. MS. 6164, p. 386.
54 *Valor Eccl.* (Rec. Com.), iii. 209.
55 S.R.O. 1037/19/4.
56 *T.S.A.S.* vi. 105, 118; H.W.R.O.(H.), HD 2/14/46–7.
57 *Cal. Pat.* 1560–3, 257; H.W.R.O.(H.), HD 2/14/46, 48.
58 *T.S.A.S.* vi. 121.
59 H.W.R.O.(H.), HD 2/14/47–9.
60 S.P.L., MS. 6865, p. 216.
61 N.L.W., Wynnstay, box 56/110.
62 S.R.O. 3898/Ti/1, comrs.' opinion of 1839; *T.S.A.S.* 3rd ser. vii. 277.
63 J. Ecton, *Liber Valorum et Decimarum* (1711), 148.
64 From weak and confused evid.: S.R.O. 3898/Ti/1.
65 S.R.O. 294/1, 3–7.
66 Below, this section.
67 Bannister, *Heref. Institutions*, 119, 122, 152.
68 Ibid. 183, 186, 189; Heref. Dioc. Regy., reg. 1902–19, p. 339; 1919–26, p. 336; 1926–38, p. 4.
69 Bannister, op. cit. 158–9, 173, 214; *Kelly's Dir. Salop.* (1929), 34.
70 S.R.O. 4774/15; Cranage, *Not Only a Dean*, 67, 71.
71 H.W.R.O.(H.), Heref. dioc. rec., inv. of Wm. Amyes, 1664.
72 H.W.R.O.(H.), HD 5/14/1/25; cf. S.P.L., MS. 6865, p. 216.
73 *Rep. Com. Eccl. Rev.* [67], p. 455, H.C. (1835), xxii.
74 Bannister, *Heref. Institutions*, 118; S.P.L., MS. 6865, pp. 215–16.
75 Heref. Dioc. Regy., reg. 1842–6, p. 224; S.R.O. 294/7, field 630.
76 S.R.O. 1242, box V, surv. of 1873, abstr. of title of 1891.
77 S.R.O., reg. of electors, Wrekin divn. (1939), p. 905; Wrekin const., civilian (May 1945), p. 368; Ludlow const. (1969), p. 162; (1970), p. 191.
78 *L. & P. Hen. VIII*, iv (1), p. 413; *Reg. Bothe* (C.S.), 337. For the date see *V.C.H. Salop.* ii. 44–5.
79 *Reg. Bothe*, 337; *T.S.A.S.* vi. 130; Bannister, *Heref. Institutions*, 15.
80 *E.H.R.* xciv. 274–5.
81 *T.S.A.S.* vi. 93–132.
82 Ibid. 102–3, 117–18.
83 Stonyhurst Coll., MS. 41: N. R. Ker and A. J. Piper, *Medieval MSS. in Brit. Librs.* iv (1992), pp. 421–2.
84 Below, this section.
85 S.R.O. 1037/19/4.
86 *T.S.A.S.* vi. 103.
87 Ibid. 116.
88 Nott. Univ. Libr. MSS. Dept., Mi. D. 3794.
89 Below, this section.
90 *T.S.A.S.* 3rd ser. x. 365.
91 *Complete Peerage*, iv. 480.

priory at Dudley.[92] A guild was mentioned in 1539.[93] Two wardens administered its property,[94] which lay mainly in Much Wenlock township[95] and yielded £6 5*s.* 10*d.* a year. In 1548 a stipendiary priest had £3 15*s.* 10*d.* a year[96] and two houses next to St. Owen's well,[97] presumably the two cruck framed bays of *c.* 1416 standing in 1985.[98] Our Lady's priest 1543–6 was William Corfill (or Wenlock), formerly subprior of the monastery, a noted craftsman, organ builder, and bell founder.[99] There was a pre-Reformation light of the Holy Trinity endowed with land.[1]

Post-Reformation vicars until 1752 probably all resided,[2] and most stayed long[3] or until death.[4] Most were graduates,[5] and at least some were Shropshire natives.[6] From 1605 the borough corporation paid the vicar 20*s.* a year to read prayers daily at 6 a.m.[7] In 1646 it instituted an annual sermon to be preached three days before the bailiff's election; only burgesses who attended the sermon could vote.[8] George Adney, instituted in 1616,[9] was a presbyterian minister by 1647[10] and a 'painful, laborious, and most zealous pastor'; he died in office in 1655.[11] His successor William Amyes conformed in 1662.[12] He owned a valuable collection of books, as did John Parsons (d. *c.* 1705).[13] During Thomas Baker's incumbency, 1706–*c.* 1752,[14] there were two sermons every Sunday and communion monthly and at Easter, Whitsun, and Christmas.[15] There was no assistant curate in 1677,[16] but one was mentioned in 1716 and 1747.[17]

The vicars, pluralists 1752–86 and 1793–1841,[18] were absentees until 1835[19] when the appointment of a resident vicar evoked popular rejoicing.[20] In Dr. Maurice Wynn's time (1793–1835)[21] there had been only one Sunday service, but under his successor Edward Tellet there were again two.[22] The curates in charge of the parish 1752–86 and 1793–1835[23] were often themselves pluralists.[24]

There were psalm singers by 1760, with a salaried master from 1782. Young people were encouraged to join the choir,[25] and in the early 19th century the girls wore special gowns.[26] Anthems were sung[27] and until 1851[28] instruments, including clarinets and a bass viol, accompanied the singers.[29] At festivals the church was decked with branches.[30]

On Census Sunday 1851 there were 201 adults at morning prayer and 190 at evensong,[31] but at Easter 1874 only 66 communicants.[32] By the end of F. R. Ellis's incumbency, 1875–1907, there were usually 150–200 Easter communicants,[33] but regular communicants averaged *c.* 25.[34] The choir moved to the chancel in 1881 and wore surplices from 1892.[35] Dr. E. B. Bartleet, Ellis's successor, had raised the number of confirmed parishioners to *c.* 500 by 1913,[36] but regular communicants did not increase significantly[37] until E. W. R. David, vicar 1959–65[38] and an Anglo-Catholic,[39] almost doubled them[40] and ventured to suggest a daily celebration.[41] In 1985 communion was celebrated weekly[42] and houseling cloths were still used.[43] Curates were employed continuously from the early 19th century until the First World War, but thereafter less regularly.[44] In 1985 the clergy were assisted by a deaconess.[45]

92 *V.C.H. Worcs.* ii. 160–1.
93 N.L.W., Wynnstay, box 43/2.
94 T. F. Dukes, *Antiquities of Salop.* (1844), 94; S.R.O. 1224/3/111–12; 1224, box 91, deed of 1518.
95 N.L.W., Wynnstay, RA 7; S.R.O. 1224/3/8, m. 10 and d.
96 *T.S.A.S.* 3rd ser. x. 365.
97 *T.S.A.S.* vi. 105.
98 Nos. 5–6 Queen St.: Forrest, *Old Hos. of Wenlock*, 34–5; *Vernacular Archit.* xxv. 32, 34.
99 *V.C.H. Salop.* ii. 44–5; *T.S.A.S.* 3rd ser. vi. 22; lx. 101.
1 P.R.O., E 178/1879, m. [2].
2 Vicars bur. in par.: S.R.O. 3898/Rg/1, p. 80; /Rg/2, 16 June 1655, 31 Jan. 1663/4. Handwriting changes in regs.: /Rg/1, bap. 2 Jan. 1613/14, 29 Mar. 1616; /Rg/2, bur. 22 Feb. 1663/4. Residence affirmed: H.W.R.O.(H.), HD 5/14/1/25.
3 *T.S.A.S.* 3rd ser. viii. 40; S.R.O. 3898/Rg/1, marr. 16 Dec. 1613, bur. 28 Jan. 1615/16; Bannister, *Heref. Institutions*, 46, 60.
4 S.R.O. 3898/Rg/1, p. 80; /Rg/2, bur. 16 June 1655, 31 Jan. 1663/4; Bannister, op. cit. 46, 89.
5 *T.S.A.S.* 3rd ser. viii. 40; *Alum. Oxon. 1500–1714*, i. 22 (Wm. Ames), 59 (Thos. Baker), 256 (Jonas Chalener); ii. 1123 (John Parsons; no degree recorded); *Alum. Cantab. to 1751*, i. 128 (Josias Bell).
6 S.R.O. 3898/Rg/1, p. 10; *Alum. Cantab. to 1751*, i. 128; *Alum. Oxon. 1500–1714*, i. 59; ii. 1123. Chris. Terne (Bannister, op. cit. 16) had a local surname.
7 Hist. MSS. Com. 13, *10th Rep. IV, Wenlock*, p. 422; *T.S.A.S.* 2nd ser. vi. 278.
8 *T.S.A.S.* 2nd ser. vi. 280.
9 Bannister, *Heref. Institutions*, 28.
10 *T.S.A.S.* 3rd ser. vii. 266.
11 S.R.O. 3898/Rg/2, bur. 16 June 1655.
12 R. F. Skinner, *Nonconf. in Salop.* (Shrews. 1964), 102.
13 H.W.R.O.(H.), Heref. dioc. rec., invs. of Wm. Amyes, 1664; John Parsons, 1705.
14 Bannister, *Heref. Institutions*, 60, 89.
15 H.W.R.O.(H.), HD 5/14/1/25.
16 Ibid. HD 7, Jos. Bell to registrar 5 Mar. 1696/7 [*recte* 1676/7].
17 Ibid. HD 5/14/1/25; B.L. Add. MS. 21011, f. 146.
18 Bannister, *Heref. Institutions*, 89, 118, 122, 143, 153; *S.P.R. Lich.* xiv (1), 54, 76; S.P.L., MS. 6865, p. 215; *Alum. Oxon. 1715–1886*, ii. 1622; S.R.O. 3898/Rg/8, 18 Mar. 1841.
19 *S.P.R. Lich.* xiv (1), 54, 66, 76, 79; S.R.O. 3898/Ti/1, comrs.' opinion of 1839.
20 Brookes fam. letter bk. p. 3.
21 Bannister, *Heref. Institutions*, 122, 153; *Alum. Oxon. 1715–1886*, ii. 1622.
22 Brookes fam. letter bk. pp. 3, 15.
23 S.R.O. 3898/Rg/8–11; H.W.R.O.(H.), Heref. dioc. rec. AL 19/23.
24 *S.P.R. Lich.* xiv (1), 54, 79; Bannister, *Heref. Institutions*, 104, 111, 136, 143.
25 W.B.R., P4/5/1, acct. of 1759–60; /5/3, 17 Feb. 1782, 29 Apr. 1792.
26 W.B.R., P4/1/10, Wilkin's bill of 1823; /1/18, Bright's bill of 1831.
27 Ibid. /5/1, accts. 12 Apr. 1784, 5 Aug. 1823.
28 Ibid. /5/4, 24 Apr. 1851.
29 Ibid. /5/1, 4 Aug. 1823, 30 Oct. 1835; /1/4, Hartshorn's bill of 1811–13.
30 Ibid. /5/3, 24 Mar. 1788.
31 P.R.O., HO 129/358, no. 42.
32 S.R.O. 3898/Rg/17.
33 *M. Wenlock Monthly Mag.* Apr. 1907.
34 Ibid. Jan. and May 1902; S.R.O. 3898/Rg/23.
35 W.B.R., P4/5/5, 3 Aug. 1881, 21 Apr. 1892.
36 *M. Wenlock Monthly Mag.* Apr.–May 1913.
37 S.R.O. 3898/Rg/24–7.
38 Heref. Dioc. Regy., reg. 1953–68, pp. 298, 504.
39 S.R.O. 3898/Rg/27, 19 Jan. 1963.
40 Ibid. *passim.*
41 *Wenlock Herald*, July 1963.
42 Ibid. Apr.–May 1985.
43 Notes in ch.
44 Heref. Dioc. Regy., regs. from 1822.
45 *Wenlock Herald*, Apr.–May 1985.

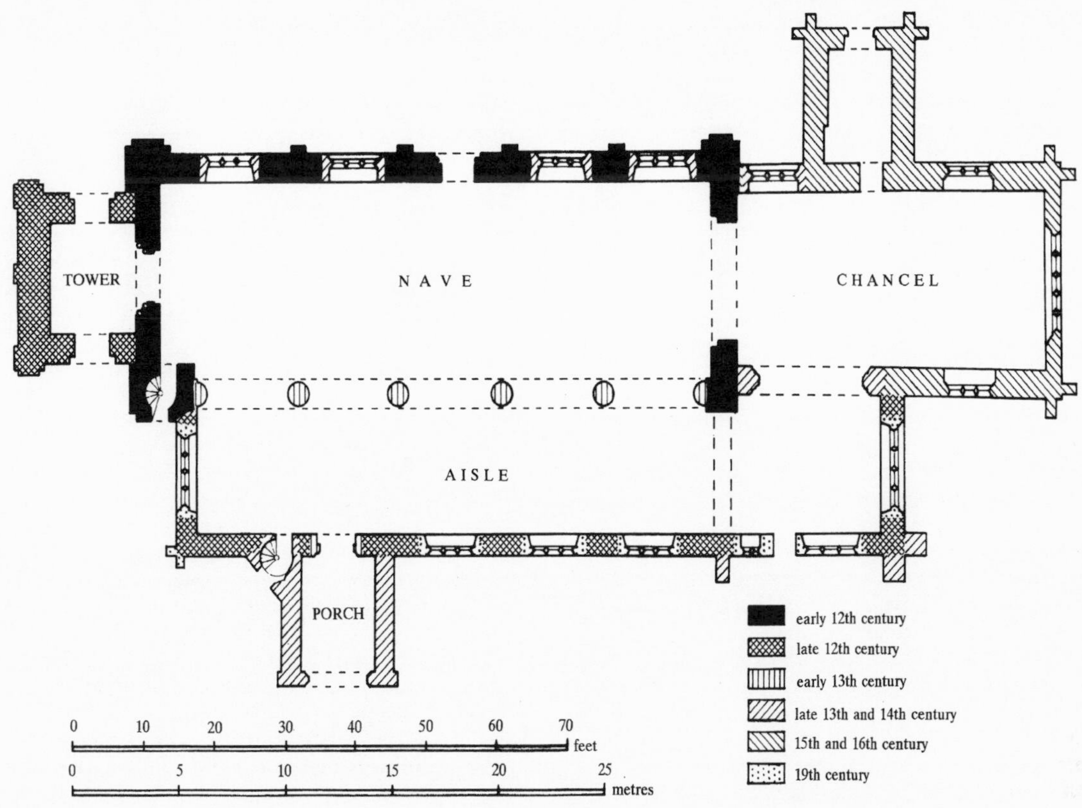

Fig. 44

MUCH WENLOCK: THE CHURCH OF HOLY TRINITY

A room in the former savings bank served as a parish room *c.* 1870–*c.* 1955.[46] It was reinstated in 1961[47] but closed *c.* 1967 when the building was sold.[48]

In the 17th and 18th centuries Wigwig people used Harley church nearby.[49] Some winter services were provided in a mission room next to Callaughton mill until *c.* 1963 and in Homer schoolroom until the 1970s.[50]

The spacious parish church of the *HOLY TRINITY* replaced a church so dedicated by 1101.[51] That building had a high altar and an altar of St. George.[52] The present church, built mainly of limestone rubble with sandstone dressings,[53] has a chancel with north vestry and south Lady chapel, a nave with south aisle and south porch, and a west tower. It began in the early 12th century as an aisleless nave of five bays with a chancel of one bay. The nave had a central north doorway, a larger west doorway, and presumably a south doorway too. The gabled west front, with three tiers of blind arcading above a central window, was more impressive than any of that period now surviving in the county.[54] A turret at the south-west angle of the nave gave access, by a doorway in the nave, a spiral stair, and steps in the thickness of the nave west wall, to a doorway high in the east face of that wall. The doorway opened into the space over a flat nave ceiling,[55] and a corresponding doorway pierced the nave east wall above the chancel arch. The nave roof was steeply pitched.

A west tower of four stages incorporating a porch with north and south doorways was added in the later 12th century, hiding the west front and filling the space between it and the street; the doorways allowed access between the north and south parts of the churchyard. At the same period a low south aisle and a chapel east of it seem to have been added to the nave and chancel respectively, the nave's south windows being preserved as a clerestory. The aisle roof is presumed to have met the nave wall at a height still marked by a quarter-round corbel. Apparently of the same build as the aisle, the chapel was about the same height as the chancel. Its

46 S.R.O. 1242, box 7, trustees' min. 1 Aug. 1870 (copy); *S.C.C. Mins. (Educ.)* 1954–5, 91; local inf.; and e.g. *Shrews. Chron.* 28 Sept. 1900, p. 8; S.R.O. 3898/PCC/1–2.

47 *Wenlock Herald*, Sept. 1961; above, social and cultural activities.

48 Local inf.

49 *T.S.A.S.* iv. 336–8.

50 *M. Wenlock Monthly Mag.* Jan. 1902, Apr. 1913; *Wenlock Herald*, Oct. 1960; local inf.

51 *T.S.A.S.* lvii. 144.

52 A. J. M. Edwards, 'Odo of Ostia's Hist.' (Lond. Univ. M.A. thesis, 1960), 89, 159 n.

53 Descr. based on Cranage, iii. 215–30; E. A. Gee, 'Hist. and arch. acct. of Wenlock priory and its dependent churches' (Birm. Univ. M.A. thesis, 1937), 192–220; Pevsner, *Salop.* 211–12; D. C. Cox and M. D. Watson, 'Holy Trinity Ch., M. Wenlock: a Reassessment', *Jnl. Brit. Arch. Assoc.* cxl. 76–87 and pl. IX–X; figs. 44–5.

54 *T.S.A.S.* lxvi. 20–9.

55 Cf. Tixover ch. (*V.C.H. Rut.* ii. 229), discussed in D. Parsons, *Churches and Chapels* (Council for Brit. Arch. 1989), 35. For pre-Conquest examples see H. M. Taylor, *A.-S. Archit.* iii (1978), 827, 1017–19.

roof met the chancel south wall on an inserted string course incorporating a corbel.

In the earlier 13th century the present nave arcade was built. It cut into the nave south windows, the remains of which were accordingly blocked. The aisle roof was then made steeply pitched, to meet the nave wall above the arcade. The south doorway of the aisle may also belong to that phase. The door and its fittings are partly medieval but of uncertain date.[56] The south doorway of the chapel had 13th-century mouldings and shafts.

In the later 13th or earlier 14th century new arches were built on the chapel's north and west sides. The north arch has an integral niche in its east jamb, which held a statue of the Virgin in 1544, when a screen divided the chapel, then a Lady chapel, from the chancel.[57] Soon afterwards the aisle south wall was doubled in height to take three large new windows. The new and higher part of the wall was divided into five equal compartments, corresponding to the nave bays, by four vertical strips of squared blocks, probably for reinforcement. When the wall was raised the aisle roof became almost flat. The chapel received a south window of the same design as those in the aisle and, about the same time, an east window of three lights and intersected tracery.

It may have been about that period that the nave walls were heightened to permit a north clerestory. The new and higher part of the north wall is divided externally by broad vertical strips, similar to those of the aisle, and has a small internally splayed window in each bay. The heightened nave received a new roof. It rose from wall posts resting on stone corbels set internally in the side walls at the level of the former eaves. The corbels have half-octagonal abaci and are mostly in the form of crowned heads, but one of them consists of three human faces.

In the earlier 14th century large north windows with reticulated tracery were inserted in the nave and chancel. A 'high cross' in the nave was mentioned in 1367.[58] The large square window high in the east end of the nave's north wall may have been inserted to light it.

A south porch of three storeys was added to the aisle in the 14th century. On the first floor was a living room with an altar, fireplace, large window into the aisle, a squint towards the Lady altar, and possibly a garderobe; the second floor was probably a bedroom. The accommodation was perhaps for Our Lady's priest. On the ground floor were stone seats, and a large stoup was later inserted to the right of the doorway into the aisle.

Later pre-Reformation changes suggest elaboration of the calendar and liturgy and more assistant clergy.[59] Side chapels, not architecturally distinct, included those of St. Clement, in the south aisle, and St. James. There was a pulpit in the nave, and nearby a statue of Our Lady of Pity. Elsewhere stood a statue of St. Christopher.[60] In the 15th century the chancel was heightened and doubled in length by a lavish extension, which had sedilia on the south and a large aumbry on the north. Statue niches were made either side of the altar and there were spiked brackets on the side walls, probably for suspending a lenten veil. A little later a north vestry or sacristy was added, entered from the chancel. A screen divided chancel from nave.[61] At the west end of the nave a gallery was built, reached by a doorway inserted in the stair turret. A crenellated parapet was added to the tower, as was a wooden spire, perhaps the 'steeple' of 1545[62] and certainly standing by 1675.[63] A 15th-century panelled chest was observed in 1821.[64]

At the Reformation the statues were destroyed,[65] the side altars abolished, and most of the plate confiscated. The Lady altar was briefly reinstated under Mary I[66] and its chapel was afterwards the 'little chancel'.[67] It contained a table in 1793[68] and was used as a court at visitations; there was then a gallery over the archway from the nave.[69] The porch roof was lowered and the upper rooms made into one. A new pulpit was made in the later 16th or earlier 17th century. Nave seating in the 16th and 17th centuries consisted of both pews and benches.[70] There was also a singers' pew.[71] Modest wall monuments were erected, including small brasses to Margaret Deyos (d. 1578), Richard Ridley (d. 1593), John Burd (d. 1600), and Robert Thorne (d. 1646).[72] In 1661 or 1662 a gallery was built across the chancel arch, as part of a screen; it contained four private pews in 1778.[73] In 1746 there were also seats under that gallery.[74] In the chancel the communion table was enclosed on three sides by a rail.[75]

In the 16th century rectorial responsibility for chancel repairs was assigned in various ways,[76] but by 1745 the impropriator of Much Wenlock township was regarded as having sole responsibility for chancel repairs,[77] an arrangement that endured in the 20th century.[78]

In 1736 a restoration was planned.[79] Those parts of the scheme carried out were probably completed in 1748.[80] The church was almost wholly reroofed[81]

56 Inf. from Dr. J. Geddes.

57 *T.S.A.S.* vi. 102.

58 Hist. MSS. Com. 13, *10th Rep. IV, Wenlock*, p. 423.

59 Above, this section.

60 *T.S.A.S.* vi. 101, 118, 129.

61 Ibid. 99. In 1839 the ch. had 'some scanty remnants of Gothic woodwork, the basement of a screen': ibid. iii. 388.

62 Ibid. vi. 118.

63 J. Ogilby, *Britannia*, i (1675), pl. 50.

64 B.L. Add. MS. 36378, f. 224v.

65 *T.S.A.S.* 2nd ser. xii. 92–3, 311–12.

66 *T.S.A.S.* vi. 109.

67 S.R.O. 1224, box 68, Walton est. partic. of *c.* 1600; W.B.R., P4/5/1, acct. of 1759–60.

68 B.L. Add. MS. 21237, f. 7v.

69 S.P.L., MS. 6865, p. 219.

70 *T.S.A.S.* vi. 118; S.R.O. 1224, box 68, Walton est. partic. of *c.* 1600; W.B.R., Q1/13/160.

71 W.B.R., P4/1/8, Hewlett's acct. of 1817–18 ('old singing pew').

72 Birm. Univ. Libr., Mytton Papers, vii. 1528–9; B.L. Add. MS. 21237, f. 2; Cranage, iii. 218.

73 B.L. Add. MS. 21237, f. 7v.; Heref. Dioc. Regy., reg. 1772–1802, f. 78v.

74 H.W.R.O.(H.), Heref. dioc. rec. AL 19/22, ff. 105v.–106.

75 S.R.O. 3898/Ch/8.

76 S.R.O. 1037/19/4; *Cal. S.P. Dom.* 1547–80, 566; *Cal. Pat.* 1569–72, p. 284.

77 Hist. MSS. Com. 43, *15th Rep. VII, Puleston*, p. 332.

78 *M. Wenlock Monthly Mag.* Jan. 1902.

79 S.R.O., q. sess. files, 1/72; *Orders of Q. Sess.* ii. 91.

80 *T.S.A.S.* xi. 292; Cranage, iii. 229; Hist. MSS. Com. 43, *15th Rep. VII, Puleston*, p. 332; B.L. Add. MS. 21237, f. 8.

81 Cranage, x. 1012–13.

Fig. 45

MUCH WENLOCK: HOLY TRINITY CHURCH IN 1820

and repewed;[82] nave and chancel received plaster ceilings;[83] brick parapets were built on the exterior walls; and doors were fitted to the outer archway of the porch. About 1760 a 'Grecian' altarpiece, carrying the Creed, Lord's Prayer, and Commandments, was set up.[84] A singers' gallery was built at the west end of the nave *c.* 1803.[85]

In 1814 the chancel arch gallery was removed.[86] The west window of the aisle was replaced in 1843 to a design of S. Pountney Smith.[87] In 1851 the church was repewed to Pountney Smith's designs and the west gallery enlarged,[88] apparently to provide free sittings;[89] shortly afterwards an organ was installed there.[90] The south windows of the aisle, designed by a Mr. Hewitt, were inserted 1862–3[91] and fitted with stained glass by Hardman & Co. in 1877;[92] in 1866 a south window of similar design was inserted in the former Lady chapel[93] and given stained glass.[94] In 1877 the Lady chapel received a new east window by Philip Webb.[95] The organ was moved there in 1881 and the gallery taken down.[96] By 1884 the communion rail had been altered to span the chancel from wall to wall.[97] The 18th-century ceilings were removed *c.* 1900.[98] A gothic font in Caen stone, inlaid with ceramic plaques, had been given in 1875;[99] it remained in the church after its plain Norman predecessor was brought inside *c.* 1920.[1] The spire was dismantled in 1930.[2] In 1958[3] the westernmost north window of the nave received new tracery,[4] the original having been lost. The organ was replaced by a smaller instrument in 1961, and in 1973 the Lady chapel was reinstated to designs by J. K. Maggs, with an altar and other new furnishings.[5]

The plate consisted in 1552 of a chalice and paten, a pyx, and two crosses.[6] Some of the plate was stolen in 1778[7] and a new chalice, two

82 H.W.R.O.(H.), Heref. dioc. rec. AL 19/22, ff. 107v–109. Presumably the pews were those drawn *c.* 1842: S.R.O. 3898/Ch/8.
83 Presumably those photographed in 1892: S.P.L., photo. neg. B. 764.
84 W.B.R., P4/5/1, 21 July 1760.
85 Ibid. 11 Apr. 1803. It remained for singers' use *c.* 1842: S.R.O. 3898/Ch/8.
86 W.B.R., P4/5/1, acct. 10 Oct. 1814 ('Smith's gallery', identified from S.R.O. 1681/158/2).
87 S.P.L., photo. neg. B. 2129; W.B.R., P4/5/1, acct. of 1843.
88 W.B.R., P4/5/4, 27 June 1850, 19 Apr. 1851; Brookes fam. letter bk. p. 49.
89 S.R.O. 3898/Ch/5. 90 *P.O. Dir. Salop.* (1856), 86.
91 W.B.R., P4/5/2, 19 Apr., 11 June 1862, 23 Feb., 23 Nov. 1863; /5/5, 7 May 1863.
92 *Salopian Shreds & Patches*, ii. 158.
93 W.B.R., P4/5/2, 24 Apr. 1866.
94 Ibid. /5/5, 10 May 1866.
95 'Wenlock Abbey' (MS. privately owned), f. 39.
96 W.B.R., P4/5/5, 3 Aug. 1881.
97 S.R.O. 3898/Ch/13–15.
98 Cranage, x. 1012. 99 W.B.R., P4/5/5, 1 Apr. 1875.
1 S.R.O. 3898/PCC/1, 19 Oct. 1920.
2 Ibid. /PCC/2, 7 July, 9 Dec. 1930.
3 Inscr. in ch.
4 Heref. Dioc. Regy., reg. 1953–68, p. 218.
5 S.R.O. 3898/Ch/17.
6 *T.S.A.S.* 2nd ser. xii. 92–3.
7 S. A. Jeavons, *Ch. Plate Archd. Salop* (Shrews. 1964), p. 18.

patens, and a ewer were bought in 1780; in 1961 only a silver paten of 1723 and some pewter pieces remained of the pre-1778 plate.[8] There were four bells in 1552, including a 'clock' bell.[9] By 1654 there were five bells and a chiming clock.[10] Six bells by Abraham Rudhall replaced the old ones in 1729,[11] and in 1931 two more bells, by Taylor of Loughborough, were given.[12] The royal arms of 1801–15, repainted in 1831, are on a large canvas and hang in the aisle.

The late medieval churchyard contained a cross and, near the west end of the church, a charnel house mentioned in 1556.[13] Before the Reformation the wardens of Our Lady's service were responsible for fencing part of the churchyard.[14] It was enlarged on the east by ¾ a. *c.* 1850.[15] Most of the gravestones were removed *c.* 1949.[16]

The registers begin in 1558 and are complete thereafter.[17]

The chapel of the *HOLY TRINITY*, Bourton, so dedicated by 1897,[18] was never assigned a separate district. Bradeley people were baptized there by the 14th century,[19] a wedding was allowed in 1538,[20] and burials were made by 1673,[21] but no baptism or burial registers were kept until 1841[22] and there was no licence for weddings until 1955.[23] A service of Our Lady, endowed with land at Bradeley, was said to have existed before the Reformation.[24]

A 'parson' was mentioned in 1556,[25] but the separate benefice dated from 1770 when endowments of £200 each were provided by the Revd. Francis Southern, Sir Robert Lawley, and Queen Anne's Bounty. In 1771 Queen Anne's Bounty gave £400 more to meet the Southern and Lawley benefactions,[26] and that year the living was recorded as a perpetual curacy in the vicar's gift.[27] Its value was £40 in 1793.[28] Queen Anne's Bounty gave another £200 in 1826.[29] In 1851 the endowment included Black House farm (in Bettws-y-crwyn)[30] worth £50 a year, while £6 a year came from the Bounty.[31] The vicar himself held the curacy 1788–1833 and 1870–1926.[32] R. H. G. More, minister of Shipton,[33] served the cure unpaid 1833–69[34] assigning the income to an assistant curate,[35] a practice adopted by the vicar after 1870[36] but discontinued before 1898.[37]

In 1716 there was a weekly service, with sermon.[38] In 1851 there were two Sunday services in summer and one in winter. Morning attendance averaged 95 adults, afternoon 25.[39] Congregations at the end of the 19th century 'represented all classes'.[40]

The small plain chapel stands on a hill above the village. It is built of sandstone and limestone rubble and has a chancel with north vestry and a nave with south porch, north aisle, and timber-clad west bell turret.[41] The nave seems from its south doorway (integral with the nave plinth) to have been built in the 12th century. The plain cylindrical font seems contemporary with it. The upper part of the nave south wall was rebuilt later in the Middle Ages; there was formerly a square-headed window east of the porch.[42] The porch is later than the rebuilt south wall. The chancel was heightened, probably in the later Middle Ages; there was a late 13th- or early 14th-century square-headed window, since blocked, in its south wall, and the head of another remains in the east wall over a 19th-century gothic window. In 1844 a Norman aisle was added to the nave at Lady Lawley's expense,[43] presumably with the chancel arch and two nave windows, which are in the same style. A north vestry was added to the chancel later in the century.

A large ornate wooden pulpit dates from the later 16th or earlier 17th century, and panels of the same period are used in the 19th-century reading desk, lectern, and dado. The communion rail is earlier 18th-century. There were two bells in 1552;[44] four new ones were cast by Thomas Rudhall in 1770.[45] The plate consisted in 1961 of a silver chalice, paten, and flagon, all dated 1774, and a silver paten of 1885.[46] The funeral hatchment of Lord Wenlock (d. 1834) hangs in the aisle. The pews are of 1844[47] and so, probably, is the west gallery, which has a stair from the aisle. The only stained glass, in the chancel east window, was dedicated in 1955.[48] The communion table dates from *c.* 1972.[49]

8 W.B.R., P4/5/1, acct. of 1780–1; /5/3, 30 July 1780; D. L. Arkwright and B. W. Bourne, *Ch. Plate Archd. Ludlow* (Shrews. 1961), 60.
9 *T.S.A.S.* 2nd ser. xii. 93.
10 W.B.R., Q1/13/159, 163.
11 H. B. Walters, *Ch. Bells of Salop.* (Oswestry, 1915), 70–2.
12 S.R.O. 3898/PCC/2, 16 Dec. 1929, 20 Apr. 1931; *Shropshire Mag.* June 1952, 21.
13 *T.S.A.S.* vi. 125.
14 N.L.W., Wynnstay, RA 1.
15 W.B.R., P4/5/4, 2 Oct. 1849; S. Bagshaw, *Dir. Salop.* (1851), 582.
16 Heref. Dioc. Regy., reg. 1938–53, p. 414.
17 S.R.O. 3898/Rg/1–14; regs. at church.
18 Cranage, iii. 189.
19 *Cal. Inq. p.m.* xv, p. 184.
20 *T.S.A.S.* vi. 99.
21 Ibid. xi. 45.
22 E. C. Peele and R. S. Clease, *Salop. Par. Doc.* (Shrews. [1903]), 37; regs. at church.
23 Heref. Dioc. Regy., reg. 1953–68, p. 115; reg. at church.
24 *Cal. Pat.* 1560–3, 257.
25 *T.S.A.S.* vi. 125.
26 C. Hodgson, *Q. Anne's Bounty* (2nd edn.), pp. clxix, cclxxxix.
27 Bannister, *Heref. Institutions*, 104.
28 S.P.L., MS. 6865, p. 216.
29 Hodgson, *Q. Anne's Bounty*, p. cclxxxix.
30 Heref. dioc. regy., reg. 1869–83, p. 308.
31 P.R.O., HO 129/358, no. 41A.
32 Above, this section.
33 *T.S.A.S.* 2nd ser. xi. 283.
34 Plaque in Shipton ch.
35 e.g. Heref. Dioc. Regy., reg. 1822–42, p. 238; 1842–6, p. 182; 1847–56, p. 297; 1857–69, pp. 83, 443.
36 W.B.R., P4/1/28, acct. of 1871.
37 Cranage, *Not Only a Dean*, 67.
38 H.W.R.O.(H.), HD 5/14/1/25.
39 P.R.O., HO 129/358, no. 41A.
40 Cranage, *Not Only a Dean*, 74.
41 Descr. based on Cranage, iii. 189; Gee, 'Hist. and arch. acct.' 233–4.
42 S.P.L., MS. 372, vol. i, f. 102.
43 *Kelly's Dir. Salop.* (1900), 272.
44 *T.S.A.S.* 3rd ser. xii. 96.
45 Walters, *Ch. Bells of Salop.* 65.
46 Arkwright and Bourne, *Ch. Plate Archd. Ludlow*, 10.
47 *Ch. Cal. Dioc. Heref.* (1871), 155.
48 Inscr. in chancel.
49 Heref. Dioc. Regy., reg. 1969– (in use), p. 114.

ROMAN CATHOLICISM. In the 1590s Elizabeth, wife of Thomas Lawley (d. 1622) of the Abbey, was a recusant.[50] Anne Grindle of Wyke was a papist in 1657[51] and the only one in the parish in 1676.[52] By 1682 she had been joined at Wyke by Margaret King.[53] Thomas Gage, lord of Much Wenlock 1698–1714,[54] was also a papist.[55] There were a few in the 1750s[56] but only one family in 1767[57] and 1793.[58]

In the later 18th century the priest of Acton Burnell sometimes baptized at Much Wenlock,[59] and a baptism there by the Madeley priest was recorded in 1824.[60] From 1849 to 1852 mass was celebrated regularly at Much Wenlock by the Aldenham priest,[61] and adult attendances averaged 80 in 1851;[62] they presumably included the 32 resident Irish.[63] Until the 1940s, however, provision remained intermittent. In 1935 a malthouse in Sheinton Street was adapted as a chapel,[64] and in 1955 the church of St. Mary Magdalen was opened in Barrow Street; it is a small brick building with carved stone dressings. The first resident priest came in 1959, and Much Wenlock was separated from Madeley R.C. parish in 1978.[65] Two Sisters of St. Louis lived at Much Wenlock 1972–8 and did social work in Telford.[66]

PROTESTANT NONCONFORMITY. Although the borough corporation and the parish church had a puritan complexion in the earlier 17th century,[67] only about four dissenters were reported in 1676[68] and three in 1716.[69] In 1851, however, protestant nonconformists accounted for a quarter of total adult attendances recorded on Census Sunday.[70]

Two houses were licensed for meetings of Independents in 1672: one in Barrow Street[71] occupied by Edmund King,[72] mercer,[73] and another occupied by Henry Maurice, formerly rector of Church Stretton.[74] Maurice also preached and taught at King's house.[75] Mrs. Margaret Clively's house in Spittle Street[76] was licensed for dissenters in 1692.[77] Two Anabaptists and a Quaker were the only nonconformists recorded in 1716.[78] Several meeting houses were registered in the 1750s: in Powke Lane and at Bradeley in 1754, in Spittle Street in 1755, and in Bourton Lane in 1757.[79]

Samuel Sankey's house on Homer common was licensed for Particular Baptists in 1811.[80] In the same year dissenters registered a building in Mardol Lane, Much Wenlock.[81] By 1843 Baptists worshipped in Much Wenlock, where attendance in 1851 averaged 40.[82] They bought land in Mardol Lane in 1846, presumably for a chapel, but sold it again in 1870.[83]

There was regular Wesleyan preaching at Much Wenlock by 1813.[84] The society had only 10 members in 1815 but in 1819 bought a site in Sheinton Street and by 1825 had built a plain stone chapel there. Wesleyan worship began at Bourton in 1831 and at Homer in 1833.[85] On Census Sunday 1851 Sheinton Street chapel was attended by 28 adults in the afternoon and 46 in the evening.[86] Another Wesleyan society had been formed at Farley by 1875.[87] It was supported by R. H. Trevor[88] (d. 1916), grandson of Thomas Harper,[89] an original trustee of the Sheinton Street chapel.[90] It met in a separate room in a house[91] and continued until *c.* 1938.[92]

Hopton Bank Primitive Methodist circuit started a mission to the Much Wenlock area in 1833.[93] Regular preaching began at the Presthope and Westwood quarrying settlements, and in 1834 at Much Wenlock. The circuit created a Much Wenlock branch in 1835.[94] The mission and the branch were continually troubled by internal wrangling, much of it blamed on Thomas Haynes of Brookhampton (in Holdgate).[95] The branch became a separate circuit in 1843[96] but in 1847, its affairs in disorder,[97] was absorbed by Wrockwardine Wood circuit.[98]

50 *Recusant R. 1592–3* (Cath. Rec. Soc. xviii), p. 270.
51 S.R.O. 840/1/73, Wyke and Bradley presentment.
52 *Compton Census*, ed. Whiteman, 259 n.
53 *Wenlock, 1468–1968*, ed. L. C. Lloyd (M. Wenlock, 1968), 32–3.
54 Above, manors.
55 *Complete Peerage*, v. 596 n.
56 S.R.O. 3898/Rg/5, bur. 29 May 1756, 7 Nov. 1758, 23 Mar. 1760.
57 *Worcs. Recusant*, xxv. 41.
58 S.P.L., MS. 6831, p. 218.
59 *S.P.R. Rom. Cath.* 63–4, 66.
60 Madeley Rom. Cath. reg. 1784–1826 (copy in S.R.O. 2266/1), 29 Apr. 1824.
61 Rest of para. based on E. M. Abbott, *Hist. of Dioc. of Shrews. 1850–1986* [1987], 79.
62 P.R.O., HO 129/358, no. 44.
63 P.R.O., HO 107/1989, ff. 533v.–576v.
64 Inf. from Mr. O. G. McDonald; H. Gow, 'The chapel in an oast house', *Catholic Fireside*, 9 Dec. 1938, 743–4.
65 M. E. R. Jackson, 'Notes on Hist. of Madeley' (microfilm in S.P.L.), bk. 3A, p. 99; *V.C.H. Salop.* xi. 67.
66 Abbott, *Hist. Dioc. Shrews.* 104.
67 Above, churches.
68 *Compton Census*, ed. Whiteman, 259 n.
69 H.W.R.O.(H.), HD 5/14/1/25.
70 P.R.O., HO 129/358, nos. 41A–47.
71 *Hearth Tax 1672*, 29.
72 *Orig. Rec. of Early Nonconf.* ed. G. Lyon Turner, ii. 741 (gives forename as Edw.).
73 H.W.R.O.(H.), HD 7, chwdns.' presentment of 1672.
74 Turner, op. cit. ii. 741; above, Ch. Stretton, prot. nonconf.
75 Maurice's diary (MS. in possession of the late Dr. A. B. Cottle, Bristol Univ., who supplied a transcript), 10–12 and 20 Aug. 1672.
76 *Hearth Tax 1672*, 28; N.L.W., Wynnstay, box E/62, f. 19.
77 S.R.O., q. sess. order bk. 6, 12 Jan. 1691/2.
78 H.W.R.O.(H.), HD 5/14/1/25.
79 S.R.O., q. sess. order bk. 1741–57, ff. 213 and v., 235v.; 1757–72, ff. 13v.–14.
80 S.R.O., q. sess. file 10/217; *Orders of Q. Sess.* iii. 172.
81 Heref. Dioc. Regy., reg. 1791–1821, f. 96 and v.
82 P.R.O., HO 129/358, no. 46.
83 S.R.O. 1242, box IX, receipts 7 Apr. 1879, 11 Oct. 1889; draft deed 7 Apr. 1879.
84 Shrews. circuit plan (copy in S.P.L., C 98.7 v.f.).
85 Shrews. Sch. Libr., Broseley circuit bk. 1815–41; S.R.O. 1242, box VII, deed of 1874 (abstr.).
86 P.R.O., HO 129/358, no. 45.
87 S.R.O. 3027/3/1, 27 Mar. 1876.
88 Ibid. /3/45.
89 Above, manors.
90 S.R.O. 1242, box 7, deed of 1874.
91 D. E. Woodford, *Methodism in M. Wenlock* (Edgmond, 1994), 26 and frontispiece (copy in S.P.L.).
92 Ibid. 72.
93 S.R.O. 2941/2/1, 15 May 1833.
94 Ibid. /2/2, 26 Dec. 1833, 24 Mar. 1834, 15 June 1835.
95 Ibid. /2/1, 2 Sept. 1834, 18 Mar. 1840; /2/2, 23 June 1834, 20 Mar. 1837, 17 Dec. 1838, 24 Mar. 1840.
96 *Primitive Methodist Min.* (1843), 6.
97 S.R.O. 1861/4.
98 S.R.O. 3605/1, p. 185; *Prim. Meth. Min.* (1847), 5.

The Much Wenlock society used a room on the Bank by 1845,[99] and in 1851 on Census Sunday 32 adults attended in the afternoon and 52 in the evening.[1] A small brick chapel opened in Mardol Lane in 1862.[2] At Stretton Westwood a small brick chapel was built *c.* 1878;[3] it closed *c.* 1973.[4]

Relations between the two Much Wenlock Methodist societies were poor in 1957,[5] but in 1960 the Sheinton Street chapel closed and they united.[6] In 1993 there were *c.* 30 members.[7]

EDUCATION. There was a schoolmaster in 1404,[8] and schoolboys sang at parish church services, and perhaps in the priory church, in the early 16th century.[9] By 1654 the parish maintained a school house,[10] apparently let by 1677 as a private grammar school to Robert Ogdon, rector of Broseley and Willey,[11] who employed a master.[12] The Revd. Francis Southern, by will proved 1778, left endowments for the teaching of 10 poor boys and to buy Bibles and expositions;[13] by 1793 his legacy was being applied to the school, then held in the room over the church porch.[14] In 1819 the master taught the free boys and 26 paying pupils, employing an usher.[15] Still over the porch in 1828,[16] the free school moved in the later 1830s to a room at the White Hart.[17]

About 1710 the vicar and others built a school east of the churchyard on land belonging to the lord of the manor,[18] who was to nominate the master.[19] A legacy of Anne Minshall (d. 1752)[20] for the education of poor children was applied to the school by 1793[21] but lost by *c.* 1800,[22] and the school had no places for the poor by 1819.[23] As a private day school it remained on that site, rented in 1837 and still in 1845 to George Crowther, who also had a boarding school in Sheinton Street[24] until 1856[25] or later.

The vestry founded a Sunday school in 1787.[26] It closed between 1821 and 1835.[27]

The parish had several petty schools in 1793[28] and at least three private schools (in addition to the free school) in the 1830s, four in the 1850s, three in the 1870s, one or more in the 1880s, and two in the 1890s (one still open in 1922); some took boarders.[29] The survivor of two later schools,[30] Abbey Mews, Bourton Road, closed in 1946.[31]

A National school was built *c.* 1847 on a small site north of the churchyard, let free by the lord of the manor while the school lasted.[32] Designed by S. Pountney Smith in local stone with Norman details, the school had two rooms[33] and 276 places in mixed and infant departments.[34] Southern's endowment reduced poor pupils' fees,[35] but normal fees were above average for the area; fees were abolished in 1891.[36] The school was earning government grant and training pupil teachers by 1852. In 1853 a commercial school in the town merged with it to 'good effect'. Taught from 1857 by an art master from Coalbrookdale Drawing School[37] (the later Art and Scientific Institution), boys were earning drawing grant by 1863. By 1870, and until 1880 or later, girls were examined too, and in 1880 there were as many as 174 examinees, the highest number from any Shropshire school. Between 1861 and 1878 the mixed school was unsurpassed by any known to H.M. Inspector: older pupils stayed on, and 25 of 103 presented in 1867 were in Standards V–VI; 29 of 173 in 1878 were in Standards V–VII.[38] Grammar, history, and geography were taught in 1870, gymnastics and drill (at the instigation of Dr. W. P. Brookes, a long-serving manager)[39] in 1871, and algebra in 1876.[40] In 1870 the greater part of the former savings bank was taken as a teacher's house.[41] The school was overcrowded in the 1870s and again, despite the addition *c.* 1873 of a classroom designed by Pountney Smith,[42] from the 1890s.[43]

99 N.L.W., Wynnstay, R 100/1 (no. 107); *P.O. Dir. Salop.* (1856), 88.

1 P.R.O., HO 129/358, no. 47.

2 Date stone.

3 Deeds sched. in possession of supt. minister, Telford South Meth. circuit (who supplied a copy).

4 Inf. from supt. minister, Telford South Meth. circuit; sale authorization 22 May 1974, in possession of supt. minister.

5 S.R.O. 2533/133, 6 Sept. 1957.

6 S.R.O. 4445/X/2, 30 Dec. 1959; *Wenlock Herald*, Feb. 1960.

7 Woodford, *Methodism in M. Wenlock*, 9.

8 S.R.O. 1190/1, unlisted ct. r. 1403–4.

9 *T.S.A.S.* vi. 103; lx. 105.

10 W.B.R., Q1/13/163.

11 Above, Broseley, churches; below, Willey, church.

12 H.W.R.O.(H.), HD 7, Ogdon to registrar 20 May 1677; ibid. petition of M. Wenlock inhabs. [1677].

13 S.C.C. *Salop. Char. for Elem. Educ.* (1906), addenda (*c.* 1912), 112–13.

14 S.P.L., MS. 6865, p. 212.

15 J. McFall, 'Educ. in Madeley Union of Salop. in 19th Cent.' (Keele Univ. M.A. (Educ.) thesis, 1973), 37–8.

16 S.R.O. 1634, box 16, acct. bk. 'Revd. Dr. Wynne', front endpaper and acct. loose in front.

17 Pigot, *Nat. Com. Dir.* (1835), 386; (1842), 51; S.R.O. 1172/41; 1931/1; W.B.R., P8/2/7, no. 656.

18 Bannister, *Heref. Institutions*, 60; N.L.W., Wynnstay, box E/62, p. 3; C. Hulbert, *Hist. and Descr. of Salop.* ii (1837), 354; S.R.O. 1931/1; W.B.R., P8/2/7, no. 20; Bodl. MS. Top. Salop. c. 2, f. 546.

19 S.P.L., MS. 6865, p. 213.

20 S.R.O. 3898/Rg/4, bur. 15 Mar. 1752.

21 S.P.L., MS. 6865, p. 213.

22 *24th Rep. Com. Char.* H.C. 231, p. 480 (1831), xi.

23 *Digest Educ. Poor*, H.C. 224, p. 763 (1819), ix (2).

24 Hulbert, *Hist. Salop.* ii. 354; P.R.O., HO 107/928/19, f. 9; Pigot, *Nat. Com. Dir.* (1842), 51; N.L.W., Wynnstay, R 100/1 (no. 25).

25 *P.O. Dir. Salop.* (1856), 87.

26 W.B.R., P4/5/3, 30 Apr., 6 May, 15 July 1787.

27 Ibid. /5/4, 16 Jan. 1821; *Educ. Enq. Abstract*, H.C. 62, p. 786 (1835), xlii (no mention).

28 S.P.L., MS. 6865, p. 213.

29 *Educ. Enq. Abstract*, 786; S. Bagshaw, *Dir. Salop.* (1851), 587; *P.O. Dir. Salop.* (1856), 205; *Kelly's Dir. Salop.* (1870), 258, and later edns.; *Wellington Jnl.* 24 Feb. 1883, p. 4.

30 Inf. from Miss N. Sandells, headmistress of Barrow C.E. sch. 1938–59.

31 S.R.O. 3898/Sc/5, pp. 21–2.

32 McFall, 'Educ. in Madeley Union', 38, 47, 142, 149.

33 S.R.O. 1564/387, 390; M. Wenlock Nat. Mixed sch. log bk. 26 July 1928.

34 *Mins. of Educ. Cttee. of Council 1849–50* [1215], p. ccxxviii, H.C. (1850), xliii.

35 McFall, 'Educ. in Madeley Union', 37; P.R.O., ED 7/103, ff. 176–7.

36 McFall, op cit. 119, 124–5. Rest of this para. based on ibid. 63, 109, 115–117, 145, 173, 198, 205–6.

37 *Eddowes's Jnl.* 14 Jan. 1857, p. 3; cf. *V.C.H. Salop.* xi. 33, 73.

38 Mixed sch. log bk. 13 Feb. 1867; 5 Feb. 1878.

39 For him cf. above, this article, intro.; *V.C.H. Salop.* ii. 192–3.

40 Mixed sch. log bk. 13 Mar. 1876.

41 S.R.O. 1242, box VII, extract from bank trustees' mins. 1 Aug. 1870; 3898/Sc/1, 13 July 1895, 27 Jan. 1903; McFall, op. cit. 145; inf. from Mr. H. P. Barber, headmaster, who bought the ho. *c.* 1967.

42 S.R.O. 1564/388, 390; 3398/Sc/1, 5 Apr. 1872–27 Jan. 1873.

43 Mixed sch. log bk. reps. 1878–9, 1883, 1901, 1907–9; ibid. 12 Mar. 1895, 8 Mar. 1899, 1 Feb. 1904.

The building was altered in 1894 and improved again in 1900 and 1903.[44] Mixed pupils' attendance averaged *c.* 120 in 1866, *c.* 183 in 1877, 260 in 1885, 250 in 1900 and 140 in 1910.[45] Infant attendance averaged 50 in 1885, and the roll was *c.* 100 in 1900 and *c.* 122 in 1910.[46] Annual treats at the Abbey[47] and Lady Catherine Milnes Gaskell's ha'penny dinners of soup and bread between 1891 and 1912 encouraged attendance.[48] The school was understaffed from *c.* 1895 to 1914, critically so in 1912 and 1914.[49]

The buildings were substandard in the 1920s and 1930s.[50] Staff changes and admission of *c.* 50 boys from Dr. Barnardo's home, opened in Corris House, Southfield Road, in 1930,[51] created great problems: pupils aged 5–9 were taught in the infant room, the rest in the other two rooms.[52] Some evacuees from St. Alban's R.C. school, Liverpool, were accommodated 1939–42,[53] double shifts being worked in 1939–40.[54] The parish room and King Street Methodist Sunday school were used 1940–2,[55] the parish room again from 1945, and Red House, Linden Avenue, in 1947 to relieve serious overcrowding.[56]

Gardening was taught by 1918,[57] and from 1936 senior pupils attended a domestic-science and woodwork centre at the Raven Hotel hut in St. Mary's Lane; the woodwork centre, closed in 1940, had reopened by 1947.[58] Pupils aged 13 went to Madeley Modern school in 1947, but some returned in 1949 and, with 13-year-olds from Much Wenlock and seven village schools,[59] were taught in Station Drive where new H.O.R.S.A. huts provided two classrooms, science, domestic-science, and woodwork rooms.[60] The infants' roll was *c.* 81 in 1920, *c.* 90 in 1935, *c.* 111 in 1946, and *c.* 103 in 1952; the mixed department's roll was *c.* 170 in 1920, *c.* 143 (including 33 Barnardo's boys) in 1935, *c.* 162 in 1945, and *c.* 215 in 1952.[61] The school closed in December 1952, pupils going next month to two new schools.[62]

Much Wenlock County Primary school opened in 1953 with 215 pupils in six classes in the extended and adapted H.O.R.S.A. huts.[63] Often overcrowded,[64] it used nearby youth-club premises from 1971.[65] The roll was 253 in 1957 and 225 in 1973.[66] The huts were replaced in 1973 by an open-plan school on the S.C.O.L.A. system, opened in Racecourse Lane with 240 places and 213 on roll.[67] By 1985 the roll was only 162;[68] the Barnardo's home had closed in 1979.[69]

Much Wenlock Modern school opened in 1953 with 240 places[70] and took seniors from 10 primary schools[71] and later from four more.[72] Gradually during the 1950s and 1960s numbers rose (to 384 by 1971) and the school was considerably extended.[73] As William Brookes school it became comprehensive for pupils aged 11–16 in 1970[74] but acquired a sixth form in 1974.[75] The roll was 851 in 1985 but 688 in 1987.[76] A swimming pool for local schools and the public was built in 1966, partly by subscription, and a sports hall added in 1975.[77]

The only schools outside the town were at Bourton and Homer. An early National school in Shropshire,[78] sometimes called Bourton Charity school, was built in 1819 by P. B. Lawley. Owners of the Bourton estate maintained it until 1903,[79] meeting deficits in the 1870s.[80] The brick-floored schoolroom[81] adjoined the teacher's house;[82] with a classroom added in 1885[83] the school had 100 places.[84] The school earned government grant from 1874 and drawing grant from 1892.[85] Despite understaffing[86] the school was usually efficient. Grammar, history, and geography were being taught in 1874, English literature, mechanics, and domestic economy in 1879, but only grammar and geography in 1880.[87] There was a Standard VI by 1880 and a Standard VII by 1884.[88] An assistant teacher was appointed in 1885,[89] but the school was inefficient thereafter until 1899.[90] In 1893 only two pupils were presented above Standard

44 Ibid. 24 Sept. 1894, 11 Jan. 1901, 21 Sept. 1903.
45 Ibid. 15 June 1866, 27 July 1877, 31 Jan. 1911; *Kelly's Dir. Salop.* (1885), 983; (1900), 273.
46 *Kelly's Dir. Salop.* (1885), 983; Inf. sch. log bk. (at M. Wenlock Co. Primary sch.) 2 Jan. 1900, 2 Dec. 1910.
47 Log bks. *passim.*
48 Ibid. 24 Jan. 1912, 14, 19, and 24 Mar. 1912.
49 Ibid. *passim*, esp. reps. 1912, 1914.
50 *S.C.C. Mins. (Educ.)* 1925–6, 81; 1931–2, 14; 1937–8, 17, 19; Mixed sch. log bk. rep. 1936.
51 *Kelly's Dir. Salop.* (1934), 314; *Wenlock Herald*, Feb. 1960.
52 Mixed sch. log bk. reps. 1931–2, 1935.
53 Ibid. 11 Sept. 1939, 28 Feb. 1942; cf. *V.C.H. Salop.* xi. 75.
54 Mixed sch. log bk. 18 Sept. 1939, 14 May 1940.
55 Ibid. 22 Jan., 2 Sept. 1940, 28 Feb. 1942.
56 Ibid. 10 Oct. 1945, 14 Apr. 1947.
57 Mixed sch. log bk. 27 May 1919.
58 Ibid. 9 and 23 Nov. 1936; *S.C.C. Mins. (Educ.)* 1936–7, 27; Barrow C.E. sch. log bk. (at the sch. 1983) 13 May 1947; inf. from Mr. W. F. R. Miles, woodwk. master 1936–40.
59 Barrow, Bourton, Brockton, Cressage, Harley, Ch. Preen, and Sheinton.
60 Mixed sch. log bk. 25 July 1947, 5 Sept. 1949.
61 Log bks. *passim.*
62 Mixed sch. log bk. 19 Dec. 1952.
63 M. Wenlock Co. Primary sch. log bk. (at the sch. 1983), 13 Jan. 1953.
64 Ibid. *passim.*
65 Ibid. 7 Sept. 1951.
66 Ibid. 30 Apr. 1957, 1 May 1973.
67 Inf. from the headmaster; S.C.C. Educ. Cttee. *Sch. List* (1973), 7.
68 S.C.C. Educ. Cttee. *Educ. Dir.* (1985), 6.
69 *Shropshire Star*, 12 May 1979.
70 Inf. from S.C.C. Educ. Dept.
71 Barrow, Bourton, Brockton, Cressage, Eaton Constantine, Harley, Ch. Preen, Sheinton, M. Wenlock, and Wroxeter: *S.C.C. Mins. (Educ.)* 1952–3, 24.
72 Acton Burnell, Berrington, Cound, and Pitchford: ibid. 1953–4, 45.
73 Personal knowledge; S.R.O. 2782/50; *Sch. List* (1971), 1.
74 *S.C.C. Mins. (Educ.)* 1970–1, 139.
75 Ibid. 1973–4, 71.
76 *Educ. Dir.* (1985), 2; (1987), 2.
77 Personal knowledge; *S.C.C. Mins. (Educ.)* 1971–2, 357–9; 1975–6, 190; above, social and cultural activities.
78 The eighth acc. to Dr. R. Hume.
79 S.R.O. 3898/Sc/6, p. 1 and facing; above, manors; below, this section.
80 P.R.O., ED 7/103, ff. 141–2.
81 McFall, 'Educ. in Madeley Union', 152.
82 Inf. from Mr. D. G. Attwood, Bourton sch. ho.
83 McFall, 'Educ. in Madeley Union', 153.
84 Ibid. 282.
85 S.R.O. 3898/Sc/6, pp. 2, 175.
86 Ibid. pp. 8, 52–3.
87 Ibid. pp. 2, 39–40, 49–50.
88 Ibid. pp. 49–50, 85.
89 Ibid. p. 96.
90 Ibid. reps. 1885–99.

IV.[91] Beilby Lawley, Lord Wenlock (d. 1912), gave annual treats, prizes for attendance, and in the 1890s hot soup in winter.[92] Attendance averaged 65 in 1874,[93] 55 in 1884, and 73 in 1900.[94]

The school building was condemned[95] and in 1901 Lord Wenlock built a new brick and tile one nearby; it had 112 places[96] in a schoolroom and classroom.[97] That year it passed with the Bourton estate to J. H. A. Whitley, who let it to the borough from 1903 at a nominal rent[98] and required children from Bourton to attend it rather than Much Wenlock National school.[99] The old school became part of the master's house.[1] The school earned very good reports 1899–1957 despite frequent changes of assistant teachers, unqualified till 1943.[2] Attendance averaged 82 in 1910.[3] Gardening was introduced that year,[4] and seniors attended the woodwork and domestic-science centre from 1936.[5] In 1939 the school admitted 17 Liverpool evacuees and their teacher[6] and from the 1940s several Much Wenlock children.[7] Thirteen-year-olds went to Much Wenlock C.E. school in 1949[8] and 11-year-olds to Much Wenlock Modern school in 1953.[9] Attendance averaged *c.* 52 in 1928, 47 in 1942, and 34 in 1956, but the roll was only 15 in 1967 when the school, aided since 1957, closed.[10] Pupils went to Brockton C.E. (Controlled) or Much Wenlock County primary schools.[11]

Homer Infant school, with 30 places[12] for pupils aged 3–8 years,[13] was built by private subscription[14] before 1874,[15] when it was affiliated to Much Wenlock National school and then called Homer Church Infant school.[16] The schoolroom[17] was part of the purpose-built stone school house. Pupils played on a patch of common nearby.[18] The school was inspected from 1875.[19] Fees were introduced in 1876.[20] Lady Harnage was a benevolent regular visitor 1874–1899,[21] and the mistresses were efficient from 1888.[22] The roll exceeded 19 in 1874 and was 29 in 1890 but only 16 in 1909 and 8 in 1917, when the school closed.[23]

Artisans' drawing classes affiliated to Coalbrookdale Drawing School were begun at Much Wenlock National school in 1856,[24] and a school of art and science began in the town in 1858, probably over the Corn Market.[25] County-council classes in drawing, cookery, dairy instruction, stock management, horticulture, agricultural chemistry, and hygiene were held 1891–1902, evening continuation classes in 1893–4 and 1901–2,[26] and a university extension course in 1903–4.[27] Attendance at a night school at Bourton for reading, writing, and arithmetic, held in 1903–4, mainly for adults who had failed to acquire a sufficient grounding at elementary school, averaged 12.[28]

County-council evening classes were held in the 1920s and 1930s[29] at the C.E. school,[30] from 1949 in the H.O.R.S.A. huts,[31] and from 1953 at the Modern school.[32] Student hours increased from *c.* 3,186 in 1953–4 to *c.* 8,500 in 1954–5.[33]

CHARITIES FOR THE POOR. St. John's hospital, with a master and brethren, mentioned in 1267,[34] supported 'lost and naked beggars'. Impoverished in 1275,[35] the hospital had perhaps closed by *c.* 1328 when Nicholas the chaplain conveyed the freehold of the premises to Wenlock priory.[36] The house had given its name to Spittle Street by 1316.[37] If, like hospitals elsewhere, St. John's stood at the edge of the town, it may have been at or near Ashfield Hall.[38]

Before 1485 the chaplain and wardens of Our Lady's service in the parish church had maintained four almshouses in Barrow Street, on the southern edge of the churchyard.[39] That year, however, and in 1488 Hugh Wolmer was maintaining the houses and paying the wardens a nominal rent. His will provided for continuance of the payment, so that the almspeople should say the psalter of Our Lady weekly and pray for the souls of himself and his family.[40] The almshouses eventually became private property.

91 Ibid. p. 189.
92 Ibid. /Sc/6–7, *passim.*
93 P.R.O., ED 7/103, ff. 141–2.
94 S.R.O. 3898/Sc/6, pp. 88, 202, 301.
95 Ibid. /Sc/7, note (30 May 1910) at front.
96 *Kelly's Dir. Salop.* (1909), 287.
97 S.R.O. 3898/Sc/6, p. 324.
98 Ibid. /Sc/7, note (30 May 1910) at front.
99 M. Wenlock Nat. Mixed sch. log bk. (at M. Wenlock Co. Primary sch.), 6 Jan. 1902.
1 Inf. from Mr. Attwood.
2 S.R.O. 3898/Sc/6–9, *passim.*
3 Ibid. /Sc/6, p. 495.
4 Ibid. /Sc/12, 19 July 1910.
5 Inf. from Mr. Miles. Dom. science centre opened 1936: M. Wenlock C.E. sch. log bk. 23 Nov. 1936; S.R.O. 3898/Sc/9–10 *passim.*
6 S.R.O. 3898/Sc/8, pp. 199–200.
7 See e.g. ibid. /Sc/5, p. 21.
8 M. Wenlock C.E. sch. log bk. 5 Sept. 1949.
9 *S.C.C. Mins. (Educ.)* 1952–3, 24, 121.
10 Ibid. 1956–7, 205; S.R.O. 3898/Sc/8, pp. 5, 120, 237; /Sc/9, pp. 206, 282. The bldg. reverted to the Bourton est.: ibid. /Sc/12, 6 July 1957; *Bridgnorth Jnl.* 13 Mar. 1981.
11 S.R.O. 3898/Sc/9, p. 282.
12 *Kelly's Dir. Salop.* (1895), 258.
13 Homer Ch. Inf. sch. log bk. (at M. Wenlock Co. Primary sch. 1982) e.g. 19 Apr. 1875, 17 Aug. 1892.
14 Inf. (1968) from the late E. W. Hill, Homer. Stone was carted from Shadwell quarry.
15 Log bk. started 4 Feb. 1874.
16 S.R.O. 3898/Sc/1, 31 Jan. 1874; log bk. title.
17 Log bk.
18 Inf. from Mr. Hill.
19 Log bk. rep. 1875.
20 Ibid. 13 Jan. 1876.
21 Ibid. *passim.*
22 Ibid. reps. 1888–1909.
23 Ibid. 4 Feb. 1874, 28 July 1890, 30 Apr. 1909, 31 Oct. 1917.
24 *Eddowes's Jnl.* 14 Jan. 1857, p. 3.
25 *P.O. Dir. Salop.* (1870), 165.
26 *S.C.C. Mins.* 1891–1902, organizing sec.'s ann. reps. to Intermediate Educ. Cttee.; Mixed sch. log bk. 21 Sept. 1893, 25 July 1894.
27 Mixed sch. log bk. 21 Jan. 1903, 17 Mar. 1904.
28 S.C.C. *Higher Educ. Dept. Rep. 1903–4* (copy in S.R.O.), 30, 39.
29 *S.C.C. Mins. (Educ.)* 1924–32, *passim.*
30 S.C.C. *Tech. and Evg. Classes, 1924–5: 21st Ann. Rep.* 5, 7; S.C.C. *Tech. and Evg. Classes, 1925–6,* 6–7.
31 M. Wenlock C.E. sch. log bk. 26 Sept. 1949.
32 *S.C.C. Mins. (Educ.)* 1950–1, 77.
33 Ibid. 1954–5, 117.
34 *Cal. Pat.* 1266–72, 99.
35 Ibid. 1272–81, 114.
36 P.R.O., C 143/206, no. 21; *Cal. Pat.* 1327–30, 473.
37 Nott. Univ. Libr. MSS. Dept., Mi. D. 3727.
38 The reputed site in 1856: S.P.L., prints and engravings, W47; Eyton, iii. 271. The later suggestion of the Corn Exchange site, in *Randall's Guide to Wenlock*, 11–12, and Forrest, *Old Hos. of Wenlock*, 26, repeated in *V.C.H. Salop.* ii. 22, seems groundless.
39 O.S. Nat. Grid SO 6238 9991 (17–18 Barrow St.): *T.S.A.S.* vi. 119; N.L.W., Wynnstay, M 2530; S.R.O. 1242, box V, abstr. of title of Edw. Richards's reps. ff. 24, 30; 1931/1; W.B.R., P8/2/7, nos. 4–5.
40 Dukes, *Antiquities of Salop.* 94; N.L.W., Wynnstay, RA 1.

From Samuel Bowdler (d. 1704) they descended with Arlescott (in Barrow), to be left by Samuel Yate Sprott (d. 1802) to William Moseley (d. 1869).[41] Moseley demolished the houses as unfit *c.* 1810 and replaced them *c.* 1819 with a row of four brick cottages in Sheinton Street, which he owned in 1830. He and the Sprotts had nominated the almspeople. For some time widows had been invariably chosen,[42] but in earlier times men too had been admitted.[43] By 1841 the vicar and churchwardens were the owners.[44] The almshouses and residents were maintained by the parish, aided by charitable endowments[45] that yielded £1,330 a year in 1975. Eligibility was extended to the whole of Harley civil parish in 1973.[46]

Bequests dating from 1587[47] or earlier may have contributed to the poor's stock, which amounted to £72 in 1641[48] and £241 in 1820, when the income, £7 4*s.*, was distributed in bread.[49]

John Skett by will dated 1728 left a rent charge of 10*s.* for bread.[50] John Littlehales (d. 1761)[51] left a rent charge of 30*s.* for bread for the aged.

There were many small gifts of money, the interest to be used for bread, clothing, coals, or cash doles. Ten remained in 1985: (i) that of John Morrall (d. 1769) for church attenders; (ii) that of Francis Southern, vicar of Cardington,[52] left by will proved 1778, for six widows or old men, church attenders, with preference for his relations; (iii) that of Edward Hughes left by will proved 1859; (iv) that of Richard Patten left by will proved 1860; (v) that of Andrew Dodd, left between 1820 and 1872;[53] (vi) that of Anne Cliveley given 1895; (vii) that of Annie Ada Instone left by will proved 1903; (viii) that of Elizabeth, Lady Harnage, left by will proved 1918, for Homer residents; (ix) that of Sophia Wayne, left by will proved 1926, for two old or infirm people; and (x) that of Gertrude Greatrex, left by will proved 1950, for old people.

By 1975 the poor's stock and the 12 foregoing charities were administered jointly, with an income of £44.[54]

After the savings bank closed *c.* 1870,[55] the trustees used rent from the building for charitable purposes.[56] In 1967 sale of the building endowed the Franchise Savings Bank Fund, whose annual income, £140 in 1975,[57] was used to benefit residents of the civil parish.[58]

Thomas Cooke, by will proved 1932, left £1,000,[59] which yielded £33 in 1975.[60]

Lost endowments include £10 from George Carver (d. 1729), perpetual curate of Kenley,[61] £5 for bread for widows or widowers from Thomas Baker, vicar 1706–*c.* 1752,[62] and £10 10*s.* for bread for widows and housekeepers from Mrs. Mary Smyth by will proved 1781.[63]

WILLEY

WILLEY was a small parish on the edge of the east Shropshire coalfield, 4 km. east of Much Wenlock and south-west of Broseley which it adjoined.[64] At various times coal and ironstone were mined and iron was smelted and worked on streams bordering the parish, but the industrial activity was not on a scale that altered the parish's essentially rural character. In the mid 19th century Willey was said to be a 'simple, prosperous village, almost feudal in its customs',[65] and in the 1980s Willey remained closely dependent on the Weld-Foresters, lords of the manor for over 350 years. From the Middle Ages the lords' parks, one medieval (the 'old park'), another 17th-century, and a third 19th-century, occupied a significant portion of the parish.

The parish was bounded on the west and south partly by Linley brook;[66] in 1620 the brook's western length was apparently known as Atherwell brook,[67] after the spring of that name, and in 1684 its southern part was called Smithy brook.[68] Willey was bounded on the east largely by Dean brook.[69] The northern part of the parish, occupied by the 13th century and until the 18th century by a park,[70] had no natural boundary; tributaries of Dean brook, the northernmost known as Hay brook,[71] cross it.

In the earlier 19th century the parish covered 1,397 a.[72] (566 ha.) and extended *c.* 4 km. from north to south and *c.* 2 km. from west to east. The highest ground, over 600 ft. (183 m.), is on the northern parish boundary and in the centre of the parish north of Willey Hall. The land falls to the streams on the south, west, and east, the lowest land, under 300 ft. (91 m.), lying near the site of Lower Smithies hamlet.[73]

41 S.R.O. 1242, box V, abstr. of title of Edw. Richard's reps.; *24th Rep. Com. Char.* H.C. 231, p. 480 (1831), xi; *V.C.H. Staffs.* xx. 70; cf. above, Barrow, manors (Arlescott; Marsh).

42 S.R.O. 1634, box 16, deed of 1819; *24th Rep. Com. Char.* 480.

43 *T.S.A.S.* vi. 102.

44 W.B.R., P8/2/7, no. 233.

45 *24th Rep. Com. Char.* 480; S.R.O. 4693/195, acct. for 1929; *Shropshire Mag.* Nov. 1951, 40.

46 *Review of Local Chars.* (S.C.C. 1975), 24.

47 S.P.L., Deeds 15685; Birm. Univ. Libr., Mytton Papers, vii. 1525.

48 W.B.R., Q1/13/47.

49 *3rd Rep. Com. Char.* H.C. 5, pp. 309–10 (1820), iv.

50 Rest of this section based on *Char. Don. 1786–8*, ii, H.C. 511, pp. 1040–1 (1816), xvi (2); *3rd Rep. Com. Char.* 308–11; S.C.C. Ch. Exec.'s Dept., chars. index.

51 B.L. Add. MS. 21237, f. 7v.

52 *T.S.A.S.* 4th ser. ii. 93.

53 S.R.O. 3898/Cy/1.

54 *Review of Local Chars.* (S.C.C. 1975), 25.

55 Above, econ. hist.

56 Local inf.

57 *Rev. of Local Chars.* 25.

58 Inf. from the rector.

59 Inscr. in guildhall.

60 *Rev. of Local Chars.* 25.

61 *24th Rep. Com. Char.* 480; Birm. Univ. Libr., Mytton Papers, vii. 1529.

62 *T.S.A.S.* 4th ser. ii. 83, 105.

63 S.R.O. 3898/Cy/1.

64 This article was written in 1984.

65 *The Old Tower: a Salop. Quarterly Mag.* ii (1879), 346 (copy in S.P.L.).

66 O.S. Map 6", SO 69 NE. (1954 edn.).

67 S.R.O. 1224/1/9; /2/541.

68 Ibid. /2/544.

69 Ibid. box 75, Caughley map of 1609.

70 Below, econ. hist. (agric.).

71 By 1637; above, Posenhall, intro.

72 O.S. *Area Bk.* (1883).

73 O.S. Maps 1/25,000, SJ 60 (1958 edn.); SO 69 (1956 edn.); fig. 46.

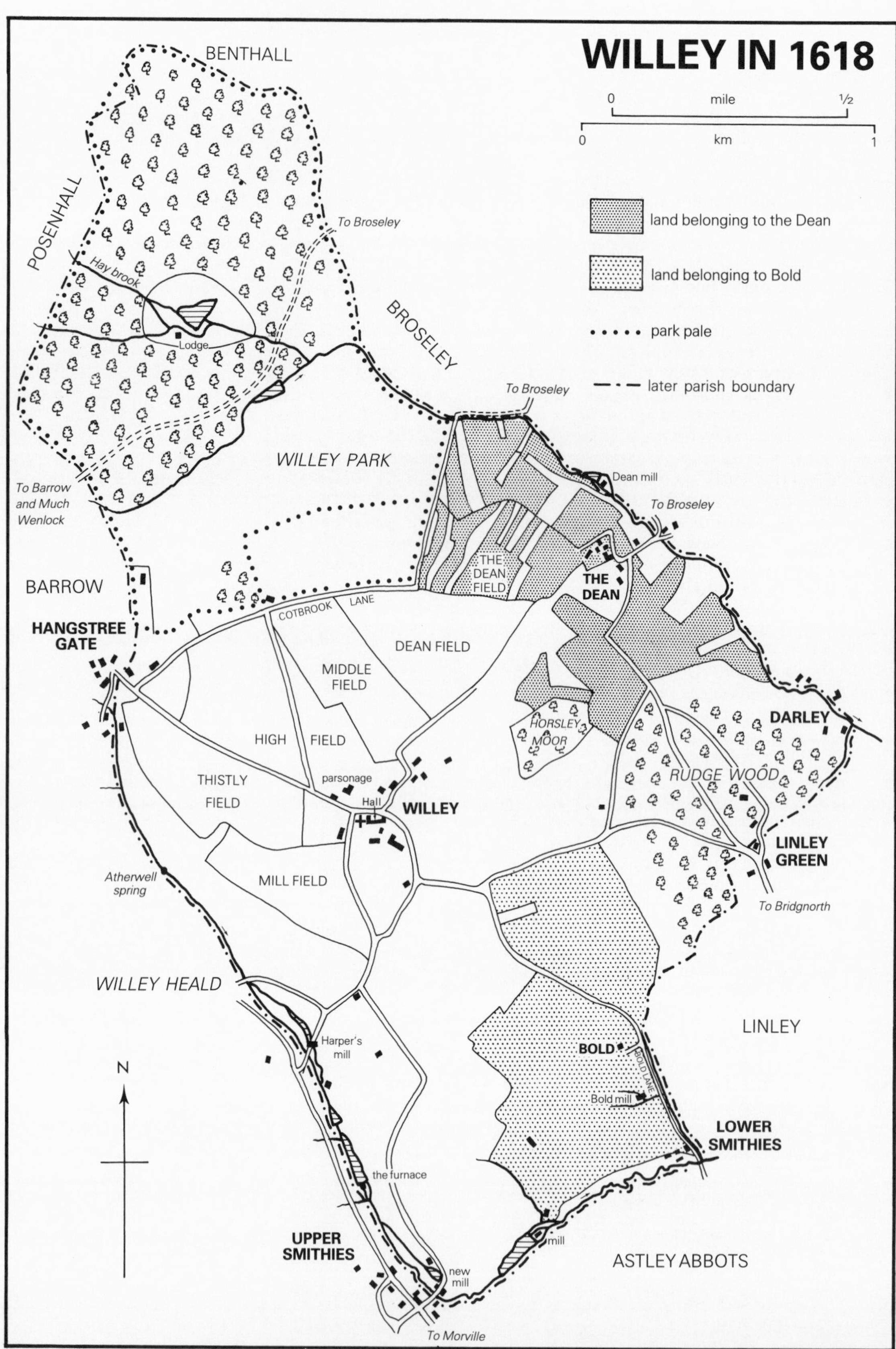
WILLEY IN 1618
0
mile
½
0
km
1
land belonging to the Dean
land belonging to Bold
park pale
later parish boundary
BENTHALL
POSENHALL
BROSELEY
To Broseley
Hay brook
Lodge
WILLEY PARK
To Barrow and Much Wenlock
BARROW
HANGSTREE GATE
To Broseley
Dean mill
To Broseley
THE DEAN FIELD
THE DEAN
COTBROOK LANE
DEAN FIELD
MIDDLE FIELD
HIGH
FIELD
THISTLY FIELD
parsonage
Hall
WILLEY
HORSLEY MOOR
DARLEY
RUDGE WOOD
LINLEY GREEN
To Bridgnorth
MILL FIELD
Atherwell spring
WILLEY HEALD
LINLEY
Harper's mill
BOLD
BOLD LANE
Bold mill
LOWER SMITHIES
N
the furnace
UPPER SMITHIES
mill
ASTLEY ABBOTS
new mill
To Morville

Fig. 46

ern boundary of Willey old park,[74] where extensive outcrops of the Lower Coal Measures are overlain by spreads of sand, gravel, and boulder clay. Between the two faults shales and sandstone occur, shale also appearing south of the Willey fault.[75]

The highway from Bold to Willey was mentioned in 1316.[76] In 1618 the principal roads across Willey were those from Broseley via Barrow to Much Wenlock, which bisected Willey park, and from Broseley to Bridgnorth via the Dean and Linleygreen.[77] By *c.* 1680 the lord of the manor had closed the old Wenlock road[78] and made Cotbrook Lane the main Broseley–Barrow–Wenlock road; in 1618 that road, bounding the park, had been the bridle way to Swinney wharf on the Severn.[79] Its status was disputed in 1728.[80] In 1756 the road from Hangstree Gate, through Willey, to Bold, was turnpiked as part of a new route from Wenlock to Bridgnorth. By 1808 the road from Hangstree Gate to Broseley along Cotbrook Lane had been superseded by a new road on the north, turnpiked by 1827. The turnpike road ran partly on the line of the early 17th-century road from Broseley to Barrow and Wenlock and passed by the recently blown out Willey furnaces along a causeway across New Furnace pool.[81] The Round House, a crenellated brick tollhouse on that road, just inside Broseley parish, was perhaps built in the late 18th century as an estate lodge.[82] Soon after, when a new park was made, several roads were closed as highways and some of them abandoned: Cotbrook Lane, the road from Willey to Hangstree Gate, the road connecting this latter road to Cotbrook Lane, and the road running south from just west of Willey church.[83] The road leading south to the new mill in 1618 had probably gone long before 1838.[84]

Although no woodland was recorded in 1086,[85] later evidence suggests a well wooded, only partly cleared, estate. By 1300 the main elements of the later medieval landscape were present. The northern part of the manor was occupied by a park, while Rudge (or Ridge) wood covered much of the south-east.[86] Open fields occupied the centre, west side, and south end of the parish. Within them or on their edges were the small settlements of Willey, with the Hall and church in the centre of the manor, the Dean and Bold on freehold estates along the eastern and south-eastern boundaries, and Horsley east of Willey.[87] Other hamlets straddled the boundary, Hangstree Gate on the west,[88] Darley and perhaps Linleygreen on the east.[89]

The Black Death greatly reduced the hamlet of Willey[90] and possibly led to the desertion of Horsley and the incorporation of its open fields into others.[91] In the mid 15th century there were apparently hamlets at Willey, Bold, and the Dean,[92] but by 1618,[93] when Willey had about eight dwellings and the Dean four, there was only a chief house and mill at Bold. Darley, Linleygreen, and Hangstree Gate each had some houses in Willey in 1618, and new hamlets had appeared, perhaps in the 16th century, on Linley brook: Upper or Over Smithies, with about a dozen houses, stood at the south-west corner of the parish, with Willey furnace immediately north of it, and most of the houses there were on Shirlett common (in Barrow); Lower, Nether, or Willow Smithies, with about five houses, stood *c.* 1 km. east. Inhabitants of the Smithies hamlets presumably included coalminers and iron workers.[94] There were also a few isolated dwellings by 1618.[95]

Settlements at the Smithies declined after 1618. In 1805 several lettable houses remained there,[96] but by 1838 little trace of earlier settlement at the Smithies survived in Willey, although there were houses scattered over the adjoining part of Astley Abbots parish.[97] Hangstree Gate was cleared *c.* 1818 when the new Willey Hall and its park were constructed.[98] In 1838[99] there was no settlement in the parish of more than about three houses and by the earlier 1980s only isolated houses and farms.

There were 2 *villani* and 2 bordars in 1086.[1] In 1327 the lady of the manor and 8 other householders paid to the subsidy.[2] After the sharp decline of the mid 14th century[3] the population had recovered by the mid 16th, when 18 men were mustered in 1542, and increased in the later 16th; the 1642 Protestation was taken by all 47 adult male parishioners (besides the curate and two churchwardens).[4] In 1676 the adult population was 90.[5] The parish had 163 inhabitants in 1801 and the number fluctuated little between then and 1951 when there were 136.[6]

George Forester (d. 1811) and his whipper-in

74 Fig. 46.

75 Inst. Geol. Sciences Map 1/25,000, *Telford* (1978); *V.C.H. Salop.* i. 45 and map facing p. 1.

76 S.R.O. 1224/3/150 (no. 10).

77 Ibid. /1/9–10; fig. 46.

78 S.R.O. 1224/1/12.

79 Ibid. /1/9–10.

80 Ibid. box 147, depositions 7 Oct. 1728.

81 Cf. ibid. /1/23–4 and O.S. Map 1/2,500, Salop. LI. 6 (1927 edn.); 29 Geo. II, c. 60; R. Baugh, *Map of Salop.* (1808); C. & J. Greenwood, *Map of Salop.* (1827); Trinder, *Ind. Rev. Salop.* 88; below, econ. hist. (agric.; iron); above, M. Wenlock, communications.

82 A. Winkworth and others, *Willey Round Ho.; Bldg. Survey* (Ironbridge Arch. Ser. x, Ironbridge, 1987).

83 *T.S.A.S.* lxv. 70–4.

84 Cf. fig. 46; P.R.O., IR 29/29/350; IR 30/29/350. For pk. see below, growth of settlement; econ. hist. (agric.).

85 *V.C.H. Salop.* i. 335.

86 Below, econ. hist. (agric.). For the name Ridge wood see e.g. S.R.O. 1224/1/9–10.

87 S.R.O. 1093/2/499, 502; below, econ. hist. (agric.).

88 Fig. 46; above, Barrow, intro.

89 Above, Caughley, intro.; Linley, intro.; fig. 46.

90 *Cal. Inq. p.m.* ix, p. 186.

91 Below, econ. hist. (agric.). Field of Horsley last mentioned 1436; S.R.O. 840, box 1, Willey ct. r. of 1436.

92 S.R.O. 1224/2/536.

93 Ibid. /1/9–10.

94 Ibid. box 163, Willey surv. of 1618, p. 17; below, econ. hist. (coal and ironstone; iron); above, Barrow, intro.

95 S.R.O. 1224/1/9–10.

96 Ibid. /7/22.

97 P.R.O., IR 29/29/350; IR 30/29/350; S.R.O. 3375/54.

98 Below, econ. hist. (agric.); above, Barrow, educ.; charities.

99 P.R.O., IR 29/29/350; IR 30/29/350.

1 *V.C.H. Salop.* i. 335.

2 *T.S.A.S.* 2nd ser. iv. 336.

3 *Cal. Inq. p.m.* ix, p. 186.

4 *L. & P. Hen. VIII*, xvii, p. 508; Ho. of Lords papers 1641–2, Protestations Oxon. and Salop. f. 201.

5 *Compton Census*, ed. Whiteman, 248, 258.

6 *V.C.H. Salop.* ii. 229. No separate figures available after 1951.

from *c.* 1776, Tom Moody (d. 1796), made Willey famous in hunting circles. A pack was kept at kennels west of the Hall and at others at Kennel Bank (in Barrow) until Forester's death.[7]

Morris men danced locally in the mid 18th century.[8] No public house has been identified in Willey hamlet; in the later 18th and early 19th century there were alehouses at Hangstree Gate[9] and the Smithies.[10] In the 1930s the Foresters allowed the public to skate on Willey pools.[11] Willey and district village hall opened in 1948.[12]

MANOR AND OTHER ESTATES. Hunning (Hunnit) held Willey in 1066 and 1086. By the latter date he held it of Turold of Verley, who in turn held it of Roger of Montgomery, earl of Shrewsbury.[13] The earl's chief lordship was presumably forfeited by his son Earl Robert in 1102.[14] Turold's mesne lordship, like ten other of his estates, passed from his heirs to the fee held by the Chetwynd family under the FitzAlans' barony of Oswestry.[15] The FitzAlans' chief lordship and the Chetwynds' mesne lordship were last recorded in 1256,[16] and already in 1255 Willey was said to be held of the prior of Wenlock.[17] In 1338 Robert of Harley acknowledged that he held Willey by the service *inter alia* of carrying the prior's frock in Parliament,[18] a serjeanty that must have been invented when the prior was first summoned.[19]

Warner was perhaps lord *c.* 1115 and, if so, had probably been succeeded by 1120 by Hugh of Willey.[20] In 1180 Warner of Willey was lord. A leading figure in county government and undersheriff 1198–1200, Warner had been succeeded by his son Nicholas by 1231; Nicholas, similarly prominent in county government, was undersheriff in 1241 and dead by 1255.[21] He was succeeded by his son Andrew, a minor. Andrew died at the battle of Evesham in 1265; his estate was forfeited, and only in 1276[22] was seisin delivered to William of Stapleton, whose son Philip had married Andrew's infant daughter and heir Burga. By 1283, however, Burga had married Richard of Harley (d. 1316), and thenceforward until 1618 Willey descended with Harley[23] (of which, with Willey, Joan of Harley was evidently still lady in 1410);[24] Willey, however, did not belong to the lord's son and heir 1462–75.[25]

In 1618 Sir Francis Lacon sold almost the whole manor or estate of Willey[26] to John Weld.[27] Willey formed the centre of a group of estates bought by Weld (kt. 1642, d. 1666), a rich town clerk of London.[28] His son John Weld the younger (kt. 1642, d. 1681), who like his father had to compound for his estates,[29] was succeeded by his son George (d. 1701) and George by his son, another George. The younger George (d. 1748) left the manor and estate to trustees for George Forester, son of his daughter Elizabeth, wife of Brooke Forester of Dothill; Elizabeth (d. 1753) was to have the profits during her lifetime. In 1774 George Forester (d. 1811) inherited Little Wenlock, and Willey descended thereafter with it and from 1821 with the Forester peerage.[30] G. C. B. Weld-Forester, Baron Forester, owned Willey in the early 1980s.[31]

In the Middle Ages the manor house probably occupied the same site as it did in 1618, just east of the church.[32] To it may have belonged a gatehouse that was in disrepair in 1438.[33] In 1618 the Hall, on a site terraced into the hillside, had three ranges around a courtyard open to the north. The central range was entered from the south by a two storeyed porch rising the full height of the building. Before the south side of the house was a walled court with a small construction, perhaps a conduit, at its centre and an early 16th-century octagonal brick building, probably a dovecot, on its east side. Another detached building, the day house (dairy), stood to the south-west, and the farm buildings were to the south-east. North of the house, on rising ground, was a small garden reached by a bridge over the road.[34]

Among works proposed by Weld in 1619 was the construction of a dovehouse and a new stable.[35] The dovehouse was perhaps that which

7 J. Randall, *Old Sports and Sportsmen* (1875), *passim*; *V.C.H. Salop.* ii. 175; O.S. Map 6", SO 69 NE. (1954 edn.).

8 M. Moulder, *Salop.* (Shell Guide, 1973), 147.

9 Randall, *Broseley*, 271. Perh. the 'Ring of Bells': ibid. 274.

10 S.R.O. 1224, box 162, valuation of 1793, f. 11.

11 *Shropshire Star*, 3 Mar. 1981, p. 18.

12 Date on bldg.

13 *V.C.H. Salop.* i. 299, 335.

14 Ibid. iii. 9–10.

15 Eyton, ii. 46–9; viii. 82.

16 *Roll of Salop. Eyre 1256* (Selden Soc. xcvi), p. 53.

17 *Rot. Hund.* (Rec. Com.), ii. 85.

18 *V.C.H. Salop.* ii. 43.

19 His only known summons, in 1341 (*Reps. from Lords Cttees. touching the Dignity of a Peer* (1829), iv. 533; *Cal. Close*, 1341–3, 113–14), was evidently not his first: writs to abbots and priors are incompletely recorded (D. Knowles, *Religious Orders in Eng.* ii (1961), 300–1) before the stereotype of 1364–5 (ibid. 304), leaving Wenlock out.

20 Descent to 1300 based on Eyton, ii. 50–8.

21 *V.C.H. Salop.* iii. 12, 15; *Rot. Hund.* ii. 85; *Roll of Salop. Eyre 1256*, p. 239.

22 *Cal. Fine R.* 1272–1307, 76.

23 P.R.O., C 142/58, no. 60; C 142/68, no. 7; C 142/312, no. 147; S.R.O. 1224/3/152, 159; *Cal. Inq. p.m.* ix, p. 186; *Cal. Inq. p.m. Hen. VII*, iii, p. 543; cf. *V.C.H. Salop.* viii. 87–8, not noting Sir Ric. Lacon's son and heir Ric., ld. of Willey (and presumably of Harley) in 1446, afterwards dying s.p. to be succ. by his bro. Wm.: S.R.O. 1224/2/536; *Cal. Close* 1441–7, 435–6; *Visit. Salop. 1623*, ii (Harl. Soc. xxix), 306.

24 *Reg. Mascall* (C.S.), 176.

25 *V.C.H. Salop.* viii. 88 (corr. below, Corrigenda) and source there cited; *T.S.A.S.* 4th ser. xi. 22.

26 Sir Edw. Bromley bought a small property; above, Broseley, manor.

27 P.R.O., CP 25/2/343/14 Jas. I Trin. [no. 4]; CP 25/2/343/16 Jas. I Trin. [no. 1]; Barnard MSS., Raby Castle, box 1, bdle. 29, nos. 38, 40–5, 52–3; S.R.O. 1224/3/162–3, 165–72, 174–80, 182–4.

28 M. D. G. Wanklyn, 'John Weld of Willey 1585–1665', *W. Midlands Studies*, iii. 88–99, esp. p. 89; *V.C.H. Salop.* iv. 136; above, Broseley, manor.

29 *Cal. Cttee. for Compounding*, ii. 978, 1202–3.

30 *V.C.H. Salop.* iv. 205; Burke, *Peerage* (1938), 1035–6; S.R.O. 1224, box 155, will of Geo. Weld, 1748; 1681/36/22; *Shropshire Star*, 6 Jan. 1977; cf. *V.C.H. Salop.* xi. 80. For the Foresters see S.R.O. 1224, bdle. 385, pedigree roll, for the Welds *T.S.A.S.* 3rd ser. i. 185–212; cf. (for the Foresters of Willey) Randall, *Broseley*, 267–8, 275–89.

31 Inf. from Ld. Forester.

32 S.R.O. 1224/3/141.

33 S.R.O. 840, box 1, Willey ct. r. of 1438.

34 Acct. of ho. in 17th cent. based on S.R.O. 1224/1/9–11; fig. 47; cf. (for bridge) ibid. box 163, Mr. Weld's memo. bk. 1619/20, f. [23].

35 Ibid. box 163, Mr. Weld's memo. bk. 1619/20, f. 3.

Fig. 47
WILLEY: THE HALL AND CHURCH IN 1674

stood south-west of the church in the early 19th century.[36] The stable may have been the gabled stone building adjoining the south side of the octagonal brick building in 1984. By 1674 a second walled court lay west of the stables and there was a small formal garden south of the church. In the 17th century a long brick stable range was built south of the stone stables, and in the 18th century a five bayed carriage house was added on the opposite side of what had by then become a stable court. The west (parlour) wing and perhaps other parts of the house were rebuilt or encased in brick in the earlier 18th century,[37] and the gardens were probably extended during that century.[38]

Following Cecil Weld-Forester's succession to the estate in 1811 a new house was built. The old Hall was demolished by November 1812,[39] though its service and stable blocks survived and were later converted to residential use.[40] Work began on the new site, 0.5 km. to the west, in 1812, and payments to the building workers ceased in 1820.[41] In 1822 the Hall was 'lately finished'.[42] The architect, Lewis Wyatt, had probably left supervision to a clerk of works.[43] The house stands on level ground overlooking the steep sided valley containing Willey pools and was enhanced by the creation of a new park. The gardens were improved in the early 19th century by the building of more walls and hothouses.[44] In the 1860s elaborate formal gardens designed by W. A. Nesfield were laid out around the Hall.[45]

The main part of Willey Hall is of Grinshill stone with a *porte cochère* on the north-west, a central bow with detached columns on the south-west, and an integral conservatory on the south-east. A lower service wing of sandstone joins the north-east side and beyond it there is a small service court. The principal rooms are arranged around a central two storeyed hall which has a double stair at one end and an open gallery round the first floor.[46]

Additions of 1874 were a billiard room on the east side of the house, an extension of the kitchens, and a detached game larder; the first two were demolished *c.* 1970.[47] The Hall had a gas plant by 1883[48] and an electricity generator by 1910.[49]

There were two compact freehold estates on the southern and eastern edges of the manor. In 1566 Hugh Bayly, probably by descent from George Bayly (fl. 1493),[50] had a freehold in *BOLD*, which he left to his son Thomas Bayly[51] (or Baylis), who held it of the manor as 1/40 knight's fee in 1592 and 1620.[52] In 1610 the freehold comprised 127 a.[53] Baylis was probably succeeded by Richard Baylis, from whom Bold passed before 1628 to Walter Acton (d. 1641), whose son and heir was Edward Acton (bt. 1644, d. 1659). In 1661 Thomas Acton of Aldenham, Sir Edward's second surviving son (d. 1678), owned Bold, and Thomas's widow (d. 1684) held it for life.[54] Their eldest son Edward (d.s.p. 1707) probably held it and later his brother Thomas (d. 1734) had a 2/3 share. By 1755 that Thomas's son Edward (d. 1767) seems to have owned the whole. Edward's executors had it until 1780 or later.[55] Bold became part of the Forester estate in the later 19th or early 20th century.[56] Bold Farm is a 1½ storeyed building, perhaps 17th-century, cased in brick in the 18th and 19th centuries.

Possible owners of *THE DEAN* are recorded

36 *S.P.R. Heref.* xvi (5), p. ii; P.R.O., IR 29/29/350; IR 30/29/350, field 67.

37 Bodl. MS. Top. Salop. c. 2, f. 524; H. E. Forrest, *Old Hos. of Wenlock* (Shrews. 1914), 96; *S.P.R. Heref.* xvi (5), p. ii; SA 613, 11470.

38 S.R.O. 1224/1/22.

39 Ibid. box 165, case for Mr. Butler's opinion Nov. 1812.

40 *P.O. Dir. Salop.* (1856), 148; (1879), 444; *Kelly's Dir. Salop.* (1900), 228.

41 S.R.O. 1224, bdle. 170, Willey Hall bldg. acct. bk.; box 174, bp. of Ely to C. Weld-Forester 31 Aug. 1815; 4791/1/10, p. 124 (Hall insured 1816).

42 S.R.O. 1066/127, ff. 43–4.

43 H. Colvin, *Biog. Dict. Brit. Architects, 1600–1840* (1978), 954; J. M. Robinson, *The Wyatts* (1979), 144, 148, and pl. VI; Willey Hall, letters *re* bldg. work, Wyatt's plans.

44 S.R.O. 1224, bdle. 170, Willey Hall bldg. acct. bk., final summary; P.R.O., IR 30/29/350; S.R.O. 1224/1/23–4; above, this article, intro.; below, econ. hist. (agric.).

45 Willey Hall, plans by Nesfield (exhibited at Univ. of Durham 1994); *D.N.B.* The supposition that Nesfield altered the park (*T.S.A.S.* lxv. 73) is wrong.

46 Fig. 48.

47 Inf. from Ld. Forester; Willey Hall, plans of the Hall (list in S.R.O.).

48 O.S. Map 6", Salop. LI. SW. (1883 edn.).

49 S.R.O. 4044/89, p. 28.

50 P.R.O., C 116/213, m. 15; S.R.O. 3365/165.

51 S.R.O. 1093/2/511.

52 S.R.O. 1224/1/9; /2/541; /3/156; /7/1; S.P.L., Deeds 12974.

53 Below, econ. hist. (agric.).

54 P.R.O., C 142/611, no. 120 (1); Burke, *Peerage* (1938), 77; F. and F. E. Acton, *Genealogia degli Acton* (Naples, 1969), tables IV, XVII; S.P.L., Deeds 1083; S.R.O. 1224/2/544; *S.P.R. Heref.* i (6), 14–15.

55 N.L.W., Hawarden Deeds, no. 1032; S.R.O. 1224, box 183, rental Mich. 1755, chief rents; bdle. 185, rental Mich. 1780, f. 12; Acton, op. cit. table XVII.

56 Cf. S.R.O. 1224, parcel 193, rental Mich. 1863 (no mention); S.R.O. 4044/89, p. 29.

Fig. 48
WILLEY PARK IN 1825

from *c.* 1230.[57] Thomas Corbet of the Dean died in 1538.[58] In 1618 the then freeholder, John Corbet, owned 104 a. there.[59] He or a namesake was dead in 1653,[60] and Richard Corbet of the Dean died in 1684.[61] Richard's son-in-law Richard Hartshorne (d. 1697), rector of Willey from 1687,[62] held the Dean, as did his son the Revd. R. C. Hartshorne (d. *c.* 1752). The son left his estates to Elizabeth Garrett, who married Jonathan Key in 1765.[63] In 1792 property comprising 99 a. at the Dean and a 15-a. allotment in Shirlett was said to belong to Keay & Co. Jonathan Key died in 1805 and in 1809 his widow Elizabeth and son John sold the Dean to Penelope Cartwright.[64] After Henry Cartwright's death in 1876 the Dean passed to his daughter Mrs. Elizabeth Penelope Ireland, who married John Hillman in 1879 and died in 1880. In 1910 the Dean (67 a.) belonged to her widowed daughter Mrs. Sarah Elizabeth Sidebotham (*née* Ireland).[65] The house, called Little Dean Farm by 1966, when G. W. Chatham owned it,[66] is a timber framed 2½ storeyed building, presumably that described as new in 1631.[67]

Wenlock priory had *c.* 60 a. of demesne land in Willey park called 'Prior's Tongue', which was sold to Richard Lacon in 1537.[68] A chantry in Holy Trinity church, Much Wenlock, owned *c.* 6 a. in Willey.[69]

ECONOMIC HISTORY. AGRICULTURE. In 1086 there were 2 *villani* and 2 bordars at Willey, with 2 ploughteams;[70] the small numbers suggest that relatively little of the later arable land was then exploited.

In the Middle Ages there were at least four areas of open-field land, each associated with a separate settlement. Dean[71] and Bold[72] fields adjoined those settlements, while at least part of the open-field land of Willey hamlet lay south-east of the hamlet. Horsley fields lay between Willey field, Rudge wood, and the road from Bold to Willey.[73] Bold may have had its own fields in 1384; 2 virgates were mentioned.[74]

57 Eyton, ii. 38.
58 *T.S.A.S.* vi. 99.
59 S.R.O. 1224/1/9–10; /2/98; /7/1, f. 20; box 163, Mr. Weld's memo. bk. 1619/20, f. 18.
60 *S.P.R. Heref.* xvi (5), p. 27.
61 Ibid. pp. x, 27.
62 Ibid. pp. ix, 6; Forrest, *Old Hos. of Wenlock*, 94.
63 S.R.O. 1224, box 83, abstr. of title, with addns., 1847; above, Barrow, manors; *Dioc. of Heref. Institutions (1539–1900)*, ed. A. T. Bannister (Heref. 1923), 89.
64 S.R.O. 515/1, pp. 151–2; 1224/7/10; box 83, abstr. of title, 1847.
65 S.R.O. 1681/248/2, statement of claim (1880) in Ireland *v.* Edge; /249/2, legacy receipt of 1876; /249/3, draft marr. settlement of 1879; /250/22, draft will of Hen. Cartwright 13 Apr. 1852; 4044/89.
66 S.R.O., DA 17/516/39, p. 255.
67 Forrest, *Old Hos. of Wenlock*, 94, and pl. facing 93; S.R.O. 1224, box 163, John Weld's bk. 1631, f. 2.
68 S.R.O. 160/4; 1224/3/151; *Cal. Pat.* 1554–5, 22; Dugdale, *Mon.* v. 81; below, econ. hist. (agric.); cf. *T.S.A.S.* lxx. 190–3.
69 S.R.O. 1224/3/8, f. 10v.; box 163, Mr. Weld's memo. bk. 1619/20, f. 15v., no. 8.
70 *V.C.H. Salop.* i. 335.
71 S.R.O. 1093/2/499; 1224/3/143, 150 (no. 14).
72 S.R.O. 1224/3/142, 150 (no. 17).
73 Ibid. /142, 150 (nos. 10, 14–16).
74 Ibid. /147.

Meadow, some divided into strips,[75] was presumably concentrated on the streams bordering the manor. Horsley moor, mentioned in 1316,[76] was perhaps common for that settlement. In 1379–80 the lady of the manor paid pannage at Marsh manor court for 40 pigs.[77]

In 1446 the manor included 8½ virgates held by 8 tenants, while 15 minor tenants held *c.* 1½ virgate between them. The manor also had a tenant of 2½ virgates at Bold and another of 1 virgate at the Dean.[78] In 1587 tenements at Bold were held of the lord of Willey for rents and labour services, suit of court, and heriot.[79] All tenants of the manor were required to keep a dog in 1649.[80] A heriot of the best beast remained payable in 1684.[81]

By 1262 the prior of Wenlock had assarted 4½ a. in Willey.[82] The manor was in Shirlett forest until disafforestation in 1301,[83] and next year and in 1318 the Harleys were granted free warren there, evidently in amplification of a grant of 1283.[84] By the early 14th century there were two large woods in the manor, Rudge wood in the south-east[85] and, evidently, a wood in Willey park in the north.[86]

The park, mentioned in 1291,[87] was probably that denoted by nearby field names in 1426–7.[88] In 1537 Richard Lacon bought Prior's Tongue (*c.* 60 a.), Wenlock priory's demesne land within the park,[89] adding the land to his own part. By 1618 the park comprised 432 a. and occupied the northern third of the township. It contained two fishponds, the larger of them in the northern, heavily wooded part which also contained an inclosure around a lodge. John Weld, anxious to improve the park's profitability, noted in 1619 that stocks of deer, swans, fish, and bees might be obtained and horses bred there. Attention was also paid to the park's 3,300 timber trees. The lodge was rebuilt or enlarged in 1630.[90] By *c.* 1680 the park had shrunk, been largely cleared of wood, and divided into closes.[91]

In 1618,[92] besides the park (432 a.), the Willey estate included 391 a. of demesne in Willey and land at the Dean (70 a.), Rudge wood (62 a.), Willey Heald or Hill[93] (284 a.) in Barrow parish, the Upper Riddings and Swinney in Broseley and Barrow parishes,[94] and Posenhall (292 a.). Bold and the Dean freeholds were respectively 127 a. and 104 a., while 5 tenants in Willey each held an average of 33 a., and 15 smallholders had 22 a. between them. Apart from the glebe (*c.* 27 a.) and the Dean's fields, the open fields were largely inclosed by 1618,[95] but John Weld was still promoting inclosure *c.* 1620.[96] Willey had five fields: Mill field to the south-west, with Dean, Middle, High, and Thistly fields ranging east–west in a line north of the village. Farther east were Dean and Mill fields belonging to the Dean. Bold's fields had been inclosed, perhaps having absorbed Horsley's fields.[97] More open-field land had probably once lain south of Willey's Mill field.[98] A fourth part of the common of Rudge wood belonged to the Dean.[99] At least some hemp and flax was grown,[1] and bees were kept.[2] Cattle were commoned on Willey Heald, probably until the 1650s or later,[3] and in Rudge wood.[4] Inhabitants of the manor could fish Atherwell brook, but only in Rogation week.[5] In 1808 the 50-a. Rudge wood, where the freeholder and manorial tenants of the Dean continued to enjoy grazing rights, was inclosed by agreement.[6]

When Shirlett, including Willey Heald, was divided and allotted in 1625, John Weld, lord of Willey, received 410 a., and the freeholders and copyholders of Bold, the Dean, and Willey 300 a.[7] Weld inclosed much of his allotment in a new park, together with the former Thistly and Mill fields west of Willey. He also made more fishponds in his parks; they were managed at least until the mid 18th century.[8] Weld limed and manured his demesnes. Among other improvements which he considered in 1619 and 1631 (but may not have effected) were the irrigation of large parts of Willey's meadow and coppice land, the creation of a warren, sale of hay, rack renting, and the purchase of freeholds. Also in 1631 he considered letting out more demesne, which he found unprofitable in hand.[9]

The 17th-century contraction of the old park (as it became known) was perhaps partly due to John Weld's inclosure of a new park, probably between 1625 (when Shirlett was allotted) and 1631. The new park, *c.* 400 a., extended west from Willey church into Shirlett (in Barrow

75 Ibid. /142, 147, 150 (no. 8).
76 Ibid. /142.
77 Ibid. /2/3.
78 Ibid. /2/536; /3/155.
79 Ibid. /3/156.
80 Ibid. /2/547; cf. *V.C.H. Salop.* xi. 32.
81 S.R.O. 1224/2/544.
82 *Cal. Pat.* 1258–66, 207.
83 Eyton, iii. 297; *V.C.H. Salop.* i. 488; *Cartulary of Shrews. Abbey*, ed. U. Rees (1975), ii, p. 251.
84 S.R.O. 840, box 41, charter of 1283; *Cal. Chart. R.* 1300–26, 29, 398.
85 S.R.O. 1224/3/150 (no. 16); cf. ibid. /1/9; *Cal. Inq. p.m.* (Rec. Com.), i. 88 ('Rugwey' wood 1284–5).
86 Next para.
87 *Cal. Close*, 1288–96, 184. For a fuller acct. of Willey's successive pks. see *T.S.A.S.* lxv. 70–4.
88 S.R.O. 1190/1, unlisted Broseley acct. r. 1417–27; cf. P.R.O., IR 29/29/55; IR 30/29/55, fields 1115–16.
89 Above, manor.
90 S.R.O. 1224/1/9–10; /7/1, ff. 4, 26; box 163, Mr. Weld's memo. bk. 1619/20; SA 675.
91 S.R.O. 1224/1/12.
92 Para. based on ibid. /1/9–10; /7/1.
93 For Willey Heald see above, Barrow, econ. hist.
94 S.R.O. 1224, box 163, Mr. Weld's memo. bk. 1619/20, f. 13.
95 S.R.O. 1224/1/9.
96 S.R.O. 1224, box 163, Mr. Weld's memo. bk. 1619/20, f. 18 (for date cf. ibid. f. 17).
97 Cf. above, this article, intro.
98 S.R.O. 1224/1/9, Peas furlong.
99 Ibid. /7/1, f. 20; box 163, John Weld's bk. 1631, f. 2v.
1 S.R.O. 1224/7/1, f. 13; cf. also /2/542.
2 Ibid. /2/541.
3 Ibid. /2/99.
4 S.R.O. 1224, box 75, deposition *re* Caughley 1651.
5 Ibid. /2/541.
6 Ibid. box 83, deeds 10 Oct. 1805 and 21 July 1808, map of Dean fm. and Rudge wood.
7 S.R.O. 163/47; above, Barrow, econ. hist. (agric.).
8 S.R.O. 604, deed, 13 June 1757; 1224, box 163, Mr. Weld's memo. bk. 1619/20; box 174, acct. of 1698–9 and Wm. Onslow's acct. 22 May 1700; box 176, receipt from Edw. Hodgkis 18 Mar. 1744/5.
9 S.R.O. 1224, box 163, Mr. Weld's memo. bk. 1619/20 (ff. 3, 4 and v., 13, 15), John Weld's bk. 1631 (f. 4 and v.), copy of terriers 1707 (f. 5).

parish) where most of it lay;[10] it was at least partly walled with stone by the 1740s.[11]

Clover was sown on the Willey demesne by 1699.[12] In 1702 the demesne livestock comprised 12 cows, 110 sheep, 34 pigs, and 15 horses. Threshed crops comprised 60 bu. of wheat and rye, 5 of clean wheat, and 2 of white peas, worth £12 14*s.* altogether, while unthreshed corn and tithes were valued at £74.[13] Animals were kept in similar proportions on Bank farm in 1747: 20 horned cattle, 92 sheep, 10 pigs, and 5 horses. Seed and grain stock was then 200 bu. of wheat, 240 of barley, 150 of oats, and 140 of peas, and 7 cwt. of seed clover.[14]

On George Weld's death in 1748 the Willey estate, long mismanaged, was *c.* £22,250 in debt:[15] there was no account book, though over £1,000 was owed to servants, labourers, and tradesmen; there was no rent roll, and many tenants were badly in arrears, some holding land without a formally agreed rent. Rents totalled £342 a year, while 861 a. was in hand. Large sums were owed on bonds. Weld's agents had in some cases been lax or dishonest, for instance in the management of Willey's coal resources.[16] Economies were made, tenants in arrears distrained, and the estate improved by the investment of the maternal inheritance of Weld's son-in-law Brooke Forester (d. 1774).[17]

In the 18th century the old park was further altered: in 1757 the south-eastern part was let to the New Willey Co. for an ironworks. The lodge kept something of its original character: a dower house in 1758, it perhaps became the place where George Forester had his kennels.[18] Both the new park and the walk to the lodge probably survived until *c.* 1815 to be replaced by yet another park, 270 a. around the new Willey Hall,[19] which brought about some conversion of farm land.[20]

In 1828 the parish's farms other than Willey home farm, Bold, and the Dean, were Lodge farm (185 a.), Bank farm (144 a.), Dean Common farm (127 a.), and Dean farm (53 a.).[21] By 1810, as on much of the Forester estate, yearly renewable leases were in use; they included detailed land management clauses.[22] In 1831 Lodge farm lacked drainage and was overrun by the landlord's game,[23] and from the 19th century the Weld-Foresters carefully preserved the game on their estate.[24] In 1910 there were three farms of *c.* 160 a., three of *c.* 95 a., with twelve more holdings averaging 25 a.[25] The home farm and park grounds were kept in hand, and in 1922 Lord Forester and his son formed the Willey Estates Co., owned by them, to run the estate.[26]

Table XXVI

Willey: Land use, livestock, and crops

	1867	*1891*	*1938*	*1965*
Percentage of grassland	65	81	89	77
arable	35	19	11	23
Percentage of cattle	11	21	24	48
sheep	79	73	58	31
pigs	10	6	18	21
Percentage of wheat	47	39	75	63
barley	32	25	10	37
oats	21	36	15	0
mixed corn & rye	0	0	0	0
Percentage of agricultural land growing roots and vegetables	12	2	4	3

Sources: P.R.O., MAF 68/143, no. 15; /1340, no. 5; /3880, Salop. no. 266; /4945, no. 266.

In 1801 *c.* 28 per cent of the parish was arable, of which 46 per cent was under wheat, 27 per cent under oats, and 18 per cent under barley; there were also small amounts (in descending order) of peas, potatoes, turnips or rape, and beans.[27] In 1838 two fifths of the parish was arable, two fifths meadow or pasture, and one fifth woodland.[28] By 1867 there was about twice as much grassland as arable and the proportion later increased. The amount of woodland altered little. In the later 19th and earlier 20th century the proportions of wheat and barley increased at the expense of oats. Over the same period cattle and pigs increased steadily, and sheep declined sharply. Before the Second World War there was some intensive poultry keeping.

Mills. There was a mill in Willey manor by

10 Ibid. John Weld's bk. 1631, ff. 1, 3v., 4 and v.; S.R.O. 1224/1/11–12.

11 S.R.O. 1224, box 171, 'concerning repairs', bk. *re* Mr. Weld's affairs (p. 9); box 176, bdle. 'Weld 1741–3', e.g. acct. 3 Sept. 1742.

12 Ibid. box 174, Wm. Onslow's acct. 1698–9; 1224/1/22, Clovergrass field.

13 Ibid. box 164, inv. of goods 19 Sept. 1702.

14 Ibid. box 177, bdle. 'Weld 1744', stock on Bank fm. 22 Nov. 1747; cf. also box 171, acct. Willey fm. 11 Nov. 1748 and inv. of Geo. Weld's goods, etc., of 1748.

15 Ibid. box 171, memos. *re* condition of est. on d. of Geo. Weld, bk. of the state of Weld's affairs, valuation of lands in hand, rent r. of late Geo. Weld's est.

16 Below, this section (coal and ironstone).

17 S.R.O. 1224, box 171, acct. Willey fm. 11 Nov. 1748, memo. *re* 6 actions to be taken to reduce est.'s debt; box 183, rental Lady Day 1755; *V.C.H. Salop.* iv. 205.

18 S.R.O. 1224/1/23–4, 31; box 155, Madame Weld's will 1758; box 183, rental Lady Day 1759; above, this article, intro.; this section; Randall, *Broseley*, 267–82.

19 Above, manor; S.R.O. 314/28; 1224/1/13.

20 S.R.O. 314/28; cf. S.R.O. 1224/1/23–4.

21 S.R.O. 1224/7/44.

22 Ibid. box 140, deed 10 July 1810 (Bank fm.); cf. ibid. deeds 10 July 1810, 12 Aug. 1818 (Posenhall fm.); *V.C.H. Salop.* xi. 84, 225.

23 S.R.O. 1224/7/47.

24 S. Bagshaw, *Dir. Salop.* (1851), 554; *V.C.H. Salop.* iv. 220; Randall, *Broseley*, 287; S.R.O. 1681/43/11, 13–15, 18; /47, pp. 148–9; /48, abstr. of pmnts. 1842, and *passim* (for rabbit money).

25 S.R.O. 4044/89.

26 S.R.O. 1681/43/24.

27 P.R.O., HO 67/12, no. 245.

28 S.R.O. 160/4. Rest of para. based on Table XXVI and Salop. Agric. Returns, 1905.

1421,[29] perhaps the water mill mentioned in 1561.[30]

By the late 18th century there were Upper and Lower water mills at the Smithies, on Linley brook, originally used for grinding corn. In 1793 the Upper mill was let to Thomas Turner and used in connexion with his Caughley porcelain factory.[31] The mills were let to Blakeway, Rose & Co. from *c.* 1800 to 1822, to James Pearce 1822–4, and to John Rose & Co. 1824–42.[32] At least one of them stood immediately south of Bank Farm, at the southern tip of the parish, and was used in the late 19th and early 20th century as a sawmill. Before 1956 the sawmill moved to new premises south of Willey hamlet.[33]

There were two mills at the Dean in 1312.[34] There was a water mill at the Dean in the 17th century[35] and a windmill belonging to it by 1755.[36] Dean mill last ran as a corn mill *c.* 1757 when the New Willey Co.'s ironworks was built nearby.[37]

There were several water mills in 1618 apart from that at the Dean,[38] but few lasted long. Harper's mill stood on Linley brook north of Upper Smithies; it was in disrepair in 1684[39] but perhaps worked in 1711.[40] South of Upper Smithies stood the 'new' mill, also mentioned in 1631[41] and perhaps converted to a cottage by 1654.[42] South of Bold Farm stood Bold mill, mentioned in 1557, while another mill stood on the southern boundary of the manor, at the Hammer in Astley Abbots. White mill, working in the late 17th century, has not been located.[43]

COAL AND IRONSTONE MINING. In 1446 four men, one occupying a virgate in Willey, held a pit each (paying 6*s.* 8*d.* a year each) in Willey coal mine.[44] Sir John Weld (d. 1666) sought to exploit Willey's minerals, particularly those under the old park and Rudge wood, and to send them out via the Severn: by 1631 he had begun to bore, dig pits, and make wagonways there. He was equally concerned to prevent John Corbet from getting coal at the Dean and carrying it away.[45] Coal was dug at Dean Corner, 1 km. west of the Dean, in the late 17th and early 18th century[46] and was probably the old park coalworks that produced 1,081 wagonloads of coal in 15 months in 1728–9.[47] In 1730 coal from the old park was sent out via the Benthall and Hill rails.[48]

Richard Knight's lease of Willey furnace from 1714 included the right to mine ironstone for it on Weld's estate in and around Willey.[49] Under an agreement of 1757 the New Willey Co. was to be supplied for 41 years with 5,000 tons of clod coal and 1,880 dozen of ironstone a year from the Foresters' pits in Willey, Barrow, Broseley, and Posenhall.[50] Under a new agreement of 1759 the company undertook the mining itself; in Willey the park (presumably the new one) and the area 500 yd. round Willey Hall were excluded from the lease.[51] Presumably also excluded was Dean Corner, where John Bell and John Thursfield had leased the coal from George Forester in 1758.[52]

In 1804 the New Willey ironworks closed and the company ceased mining on the Forester estate.[53] In 1813 a partnership called Jones & Mytton (by 1814 Jones, Pott, & Mytton) began to mine coal on Forester land.[54] Mining continued in the northern part of Willey until the mid 19th century or later, but after the closure of the New Willey works it was probably on a very limited scale.[55] In the 1940s there was opencast coalmining at Rudgewood, Willeypark Wood, and Horsleymoor. Further opencast mining, primarily for fireclay, by Coalmoor Refractories (Horsehay) Ltd., began west of the Deerleap, at the northern tip of the parish, in the late 1950s or 1960s. Mining there was taken over in 1983 by Coal Contractors Ltd.[56]

IRON. It was probably in Willey that John Forest held a forge in 1503–4 for 26*s.* 8*d.*,[57] and the smith pool was mentioned in 1537 and 1553.[58] Some ironworking took place in Willey park,[59] but bloomeries were probably concentrated on Linley brook where, in 1618, stood the settlements of Upper and Lower Smithies and their cinder heaps.[60] Generally there seems to have been much ironmaking in the area by the mid 16th century.[61]

Before John Weld bought the manor in 1618,

29 S.R.O. 840, box 1, Willey ct. r. of 1421.

30 S.R.O. 1224/2/155.

31 Ibid. box 162, partic. and valn. of est. of Geo. Forester 1793, f. 12. In 1992 porcelain, incl. wasters, was recovered at site of Upper Smithies blast furnace (SO 6716 9806).

32 Ibid. box 140, deeds 24 Dec. 1800, 13 Apr. 1824; bdle. 188, rental no. 20; bdle. 190, rentals 25 Mar., 29 Sept. 1822, 25 Mar. 1824; bdle. 193, rentals 25 Mar., 29 Sept. 1842; /7/6, 16, 27; P.R.O., IR 29/29/350; IR 30/29/350, field 34; Trinder, *Ind. Rev. Salop.* 126; G. A. Godden, *Coalport and Coalbrookdale Porcelains* (1970), 25–6.

33 O.S. Maps 1/2,500, Salop. LI. 14 (1883, 1902, and 1927 edns.); 6", SO 69 NE. (1956 edn.).

34 S.R.O. 1224/3/190.

35 Ibid. /1/9; /3/221, 463–4.

36 S.R.O. 604, deed 13 June 1757; 1224, box 183, rental Mich. 1755, s.v. Broseley.

37 W.B.R., M4/14; below, this section (iron).

38 S.R.O. 1224/1/9–10.

39 Ibid. /2/544.

40 Ibid. box 140, deed 16 Oct. 1711.

41 Ibid. /2/542.

42 Ibid. /2/99.

43 Ibid. box 147, depositions 7 Oct. 1728, f. 5; S.R.O. 1093/2/511.

44 S.R.O. 1224/2/536.

45 Ibid. box 163, Mr. Weld's memo. bk. 1619/20, f. 1, 2v., 3; John Weld's bk. 1631, at end; Trinder, *Ind. Rev. Salop.* 7; above, manor.

46 S.R.O. 1224/10/510, s.a. 1699–1702.

47 Ibid. box 176, bdle. marked 'cf. for coalwks.', acct. of coals 30 Mar. 1728–28 June 1729.

48 Ibid. box 174, acct. old pk. coal wks. 31 Oct.–24 Dec. 1730.

49 Ibid. box 140, deed 16 Oct. 1711.

50 Ibid. box 143, deed 13 June 1757; cf. box 171, inv. of Geo. Weld's goods, etc., of 1748, pp. 27 sqq.; box 173, coal accts.

51 Ibid. box 143, deed 24 Sept. 1759; S.R.O. 2228/1, p. 53.

52 S.R.O. 1224, box 140, deed 20 June 1758.

53 Cf. ibid. bdle. 188, rentals nos. 26–7.

54 Ibid. nos. 41–4.

55 S.R.O. 1244, box 174, royalty acct. bk.; bdles. 188–91, rentals; *Salop. Mining Club Jnl.* (1973–4), 21.

56 Inf. from S.C.C. Planning Dept.

57 S.R.O. 1224/2/546.

58 *L. & P. Hen. VIII*, xxi (1), p. 766; *Cal. Pat.* 1553, 121–2.

59 S.R.O. 1224, box 163, John Weld's bk. 1631, f. 3v.

60 Ibid. /1/9–10; box 163, Mr. Weld's memo. bk. 1619/20, f. 17; *W. Midlands Studies*, iii. 96.

61 Leland, *Itin.* ed. Toulmin Smith, v. 18; above, Barrow, econ. hist. (ind.); Caughley, econ. hist. (ind.).

and perhaps *c.* 1594,[62] the bloomeries were probably largely, if not entirely, superseded by a blast furnace on Linley brook, north of Upper Smithies. It stood below two ponds, the upper *c.* 200 m. long. In 1618 the furnace was held by John Slaney,[63] who had been making iron in Morville since 1599 or earlier;[64] he had probably left the Willey furnace by 1620.[65] Before 1631 Weld had rebuilt it.[66]

In 1673 it was let to Philip Foley for 21 years, but next year Foley assigned his lease to Lord Newport (as guardian of his son Thomas Newport) and three other partners. In 1681 a new partnership was formed between Thomas Newport and others.[67] Some pig iron from Willey was sent to Wytheford forge (on the Roden) in 1687–8.[68] In 1696 the partners in Willey furnace were also partners in ironworks at Leighton, Longnor, Sheinton, and Upton Magna.[69] Richard Baldwin had the furnace in 1710, when he bought the crop of a coppice in Ruckley and 500 more cords from Sir Edward Smythe, the wood to be cut in 1711.[70] In 1711 George Weld undertook to lease the furnace for 14 years from 1714 to Richard Knight.[71]

Before 1733 the furnace was again let to Richard Baldwin. That year Richard Ford and Thomas Goldney, the senior Coalbrookdale partners, took over the lease, perhaps because the expiry of Newcomen's patent allowed them to respond to an increasing demand for ironwork.[72] Ford died in 1745 and his son Edmund took the furnace.[73] From 1733 the furnace was coke-fired and used Willey coal, 762 tons in 1752 and 1,002 tons in 1753. Among its products was pig iron for the Bristol market.[74] At times the water supply may have been inadequate, and in 1757, when the iron trade was depressed, Ford and Goldney did not renew their lease of the furnace, then in disrepair.[75]

In 1757 the New Willey Co. was formed by Brooke Forester, who had four of the ten £1,600 shares; another partner was the ironmaster John Wilkinson. Although the company took over the old furnace and works and was to use them until 1774, it immediately began to build the New Willey works 2.5 km. to the north, on Dean brook, near four fishponds that the company was allowed to use;[76] much of the timber for the works came from Willey.[77] Warehouses were built[78] and railways laid. In 1757 the Tarbatch dingle railway in Broseley was extended to link the New Willey Co.'s works with the Severn. In 1759 a second track was laid alongside the first, and the lines continued to serve the works until the late 18th century.[79] The works also had access to the river via the Benthall and Hill rails and rail links to mines.[80] Probably from the start a Newcomen engine returned water to pools above the works.[81]

By 1759 the company was supplying pig iron to the Stour Valley forges, and by the end of the century Willey itself had one of the country's principal forges. From the outset armaments were an important product: in 1759 shot and swivel guns were made, and in 1761 shells, shot, cannon, and pig iron worth £8,000 awaited sale in London. Joseph Hateley, engineer, was demonstrating a steam engine at the works in 1761, and by 1762 steam engine parts were being made.[82]

Wilkinson gradually gained a controlling interest in the company and by 1774 was sole lessee of the works.[83] Pig iron from Horsehay was then used there.[84] In 1774 Wilkinson patented a machine for boring cannon, in which the solid casting rotated round a stationary boring head. A similar one was already in use at Woolwich Arsenal and Wilkinson's patent was revoked in 1779 after a challenge by the Board of Trade. In 1776, however, Wilkinson adapted his machine to bore cylinders for Boulton & Watt's new engines. The second engine so produced was installed at Willey in 1776; it was the first ever to blow a blast furnace directly.[85] There were then apparently two furnaces at Willey, each making over 20 tons of pig iron a week.[86] A second Boulton & Watt engine, perhaps converted from the Newcomen engine of 1757, was installed in 1777 to return used water to the pools. In 1788, without Boulton & Watt's licence, Wilkinson built a third, rotative, steam engine at the works to power the boring mill.[87]

Wilkinson introduced iron boats on the Severn. The first, a barge-type vessel, was made at Willey in 1787. Apparently, however, there were problems with the design, and most Severn

62 Inf. from Mr. J. B. Lawson, who is thanked for reading this subsection in draft.

63 At O.S. Nat. Grid SO 673 978. See S.R.O. 1224/1/9–10; /3/187–8.

64 Trinder, *Ind. Rev. Salop.* 10.

65 S.R.O. 1224, box 163, Mr. Weld's memo. bk. 1619/20, f. 17.

66 Ibid. John Weld's bk. 1631, f. 1.

67 S.P.L., Deeds 3100. This para. corrects P. Riden, *Gaz. of Charcoal-fired Blast Furnaces in Gt. Brit. in use since 1660* (1993), 62–3.

68 Trinder, *Ind. Rev. Salop.* 11.

69 S.P.L., Deeds 3230.

70 S.R.O. 1514/2/18.

71 S.R.O. 1224, box 140, deed 16 Oct. 1711.

72 *V.C.H. Salop.* i. 462, 473; A. Raistrick, *Dynasty of Iron Founders: the Darbys and Coalbrookdale* (1953), 148; Trinder, *Ind. Rev. Salop.* 18, 24.

73 Trinder, op. cit. 19; Raistrick, op. cit. 67; S.R.O. 1224, box 171, 'Yearly roll of late Geo. Weld's est.'

74 Trinder, op. cit. 18, 54; Raistrick, op. cit. 148; *Trans. Newcomen Soc.* lviii. 53.

75 Trinder, op. cit. 24, 37; S.R.O. 1224, box 183, Geo. Forester rental Lady Day 1757.

76 Trinder, op. cit. 24, 37, 271–2; S.R.O. 604, deed 13 June 1757; 1224/1/23–4; box 143, deeds 13 June, 22 Aug. 1757; R.C.H.M.E., draft field rep. (1985).

77 S.R.O. 1224, box 183, Geo. Forester rentals Lady Day 1757 (s.v. Willey), Lady Day 1760.

78 SA 653.

79 Above, Broseley, communications; S.R.O. 1224, box 183, Geo. Forester rental Lady Day 1759; SA 653.

80 Trinder, *Ind. Rev. Salop.* 26, 73; above, Benthall, intro.

81 Trinder, op. cit. 95; *Jnl. Wilkinson Soc.* vii. 10. For layout of wks. see S.R.O. 1224/1/23–4, 26; *Jnl. Wilkinson Soc.* ix. 3–9; SA 653–5, 11718–19, 12864.

82 Trinder, op. cit. 26, 39, 53, 95; *V.C.H. Salop.* i. 473; S.R.O. 1987, box 20, bdle. 'Bankruptcy Abraham and Ric. Ford', acct. between Willey Co. and Thos. Goldney 1757–64; *Aris's Birm. Gaz.* 16, 23, 30 Mar. 1761.

83 Trinder, op. cit. 37, 122–3; *Jnl. Wilkinson Soc.* i. [3–4]; *T.S.A.S.* lvi. 79.

84 Trinder, op. cit. 70–1.

85 Ibid. 95–6; idem, *Making of Ind. Landscape* (1982), 70, 73; *Ind. Arch. Rev.* iii. 31, 33; *Trans. Newcomen Soc.* lviii. 53–5.

86 *T.S.A.S.* lvi. 79.

87 Trinder, *Ind. Rev. Salop.* 38, 96, 99; *Jnl. Wilkinson Soc.* vii. 10–11. See also *J. Rennie's Diary of Journey Through N. Eng. 1784*, ed. R. B. Matkin (E. Kent Marine Trust Hist. Study ii), 23–4.

barges continued to be of wood.[88] Iron piping, some for export to France, was made in the late 18th century.[89] Production was probably in decline *c.* 1799; by 1796 and still in 1803 only one furnace was in blast, and Wilkinson gave up the works in 1804. The forge at least was later worked by the Foresters until the 1820s.[90]

OTHER INDUSTRIES. From before 1618 until the later 18th century or later clay was dug and bricks and tiles were made in the parish;[91] many were used in Willey Hall, the lodge, and the Foresters' other estate buildings.[92] From the 1740s or earlier to the 1770s or later pipe clay and potting clay were dug in the old park, probably for use in pipe works and potteries at Benthall and Broseley.[93]

Before 1631 John Weld unsuccessfully dug for limestone in Willey.[94] In the late 18th century there were probably coke ovens at the New Willey works, and oil or tar may have been a by-product.[95] In the early 18th century trades in the parish included those of wheelwright, ship's carpenter, and cooper, attesting the continued role of woodland in the local economy.[96]

LOCAL GOVERNMENT. Willey owed suit to Bourton hundred in 1369[97] and probably in 1568,[98] but in 1634 the lord of Bourton hundred agreed that Willey should be subject to John Weld's court leet of Marsh (in Barrow),[99] and Willey afterwards presented there regularly. The commonest presentments were for assize breaking and for erecting cottages on the waste. In the 1630s there were pound, stocks, and butts;[1] the stocks were mentioned again in 1712.[2]

Records of Willey court baron survive for a dozen or more years scattered between 1421 and 1684.[3] Some 15th-century courts were called 'great'.[4] Suitors included some from Broseley (probably Upper Riddings and the Woodhouse), Posenhall, and Swinney (in Barrow).[5]

Willey had highway surveyors *c.* 1595,[6] and by 1658 a constable, a surveyor, an overseer of the poor, and a churchwarden; their appointments were reported to the Marsh court, where the first two were sworn in.[7] Willey remained a highway authority until 1889.[8]

Out relief was given in 1737–8.[9] In 1812–13 £128 was spent on permanent out relief for 17 adults; in the next two years just over £100 a year was spent relieving 11 poor.[10] In 1828 the Willey overseers were tenants of a cottage to house paupers.[11]

The parish was in Madeley poor-law union 1836–1930,[12] Madeley rural sanitary district 1872–89, and the Barrow ward of Wenlock municipal borough 1889–1966.[13] On the dissolution of Wenlock M.B. in 1966 Willey civil parish was absorbed into Barrow C.P., in Bridgnorth rural district 1966–74[14] and Bridgnorth district from 1974.[15]

Willey was within the jurisdiction of the Broseley court of requests from 1782[16] until its abolition under the County Courts Act, 1846.[17]

CHURCH. Willey church's earliest fabric appears to be 12th-century,[18] and it was probably in the early 12th century that its status as a chapel in Holy Trinity parish, Much Wenlock, was reasserted.[19] The vicar of Holy Trinity had cure of souls in Willey in 1324,[20] and Willey's great tithes belonged to Wenlock priory as appropriator of Holy Trinity. They may have made up most of the value at which Willey church was assessed, which was £5 6*s.* 8*d.* in 1291 and 1535 and £6 13*s.* 4*d.* in 1379.[21] An annual pension of 7*s.* was payable to the priory from Willey church by 1323.[22] After the Dissolution the great tithes passed to the lord of the manor, who in the 1630s gave them to the incumbent as an endowment.[23]

The lord of the manor's advowson of the chapel was challenged by the prior of Wenlock in 1214 and 1233.[24] The lord presented in 1304,[25] but perhaps not alone, for by 1323 the lord presented first to the prior, who then presented to the bishop.[26] The prior's advowson was exercised by the king between 1337 and 1395, while the priory was in his hands as an alien house,[27]

88 Trinder, op. cit. 71; *V.C.H. Salop.* i. 474; *Jnl. Wilkinson Soc.* xiii. 4–11; xv, *passim.*
89 *Jnl. Wilkinson Soc.* vii. 11.
90 Ibid. ix. 3; *V.C.H. Salop.* i. 476; J. Randall, *The Wilkinsons* (Madeley, n.d.), 38 (copy in S.R.O. 245); S.R.O. 1224/1/26; cf. bdle. 188, rentals nos. 26–7; W.B.R., M4/14.
91 S.R.O. 1224/1/9–10, field names; P.R.O., IR 29/29/350; IR 30/29/350, fields 41, 108, 173.
92 S.R.O. 1224/2/545; box 183, rental Mich. 1755, Geo. Forester rental Lady Day 1760.
93 S.R.O. 1224, box 177, bdles. 'Weld 1742–3' (acct. 27 Dec. 1742), 'Weld 1744–8' (acct. 1 May 1748); bdle. 185, rental Mich. 1776.
94 Ibid. box 163, John Weld's bk. 1631, f. 2v.
95 Trinder, *Ind. Rev. Salop.* 57–8.
96 *S.P.R. Heref.* xvi (5), pp. 6–7.
97 B.L. Add. MS. 6165, p. 100.
98 S.R.O. 1224/3/24.
99 Ibid. /2/65.
1 Marsh ct. r. cited above, Barrow, local govt.
2 S.R.O. 1224/2/394.
3 Ibid. /2/535–45; S.R.O. 840, box 1, ct. r. of 1421, 1436, 1438.
4 S.R.O. 1224/2/535–6.
5 Ibid. /2/537–8, 541, 544; 840, box 1, ct. r. 1438; cf. above, Caughley, manors (Swinney; Upper Riddings; the Woodhouse); Posenhall, manor.
6 *T.S.A.S.* lix. 291.
7 S.R.O. 1224/2/104/1.
8 Local Govt. Bd.'s Prov. Order Conf. (No. 4) Act, 1889, 52 & 53 Vic. c. 22 (Local).
9 S.R.O. 5709, overseers' accts.
10 *Poor Law Abstract,* H.C. 82, pp. 376–7 (1818), xix.
11 S.R.O. 1224/7/44.
12 V. J. Walsh, 'Admin. of Poor Laws in Salop. 1820–55' (Pennsylvania Univ. Ph.D. thesis, 1970), 148–50; *P.O. Dir. Salop.* (1856), 148; *Kelly's Dir. Salop.* (1929), 319.
13 *V.C.H. Salop.* ii. 215–16.
14 Ibid. 235, 237; above, Barrow, local govt.
15 Sources cited *V.C.H. Salop.* iii. 169 n. 29.
16 Broseley, etc., Small Debts Act, 1782, 22 Geo. III, c. 37.
17 8 & 10 Vic. c. 95.
18 Below, this section.
19 Above, Lib. and Boro. of Wenlock (early est.).
20 *Reg. Orleton* (C.S.), 278–9, 281; S.R.O. 1224/3/150, no. 11.
21 *Tax. Eccl.* (Rec. Com.), 167; *Valor Eccl.* (Rec. Com.), iii. 209; Eyton, ii. 60.
22 Eyton, ii. 59; S.R.O. 1224/3/150.
23 S.R.O. 1224, box 163, memo. of Feb. 1638/9.
24 Eyton, ii. 59.
25 *Reg. Swinfield* (C.S.), 536.
26 S.R.O. 1224/3/150; cf. above, Badger, church.
27 *Cal. Pat.* 1348–50, 189; 1354–8, 608, 628; 1358–61, 190, 344; 1377–81, 74; 1381–5, 297, 311, 374; 1385–9, 54, 96, 375; 1388–92, 423; 1391–6, 211; *V.C.H. Salop.* ii. 42.

and was last mentioned in 1412.[28] The lord's advowson continued during that period[29] and remained in being after the surrender of the priory in 1540.[30] The chaplains, though sometimes styled rector before the Reformation, had only small tithes in 1535.[31] Following the gift of tithes in the 1630s the living became a rectory, but the church remained dependent on Holy Trinity until 1661 when burial rights, which the vicar of Much Wenlock refused in 1547[32] and for which John Weld had hoped in 1619,[33] were conceded.[34] In 1822 the rectory was united with the perpetual curacy of Barrow,[35] which rectors of Willey had served since the late 17th century.[36] In 1976 the church was declared redundant and was appropriated to Lord Forester as a private chapel, and at the same time the parish and benefice of Linley with Willey and Barrow were created.[37]

The rectory was worth £44 *c.* 1708.[38] In 1755 the tithes, at least of the Foresters' demesne, were compounded for.[39] By 1801 the rectory had 26 a. of glebe in Willey, a 5-a. allotment in Shirlett (in Barrow), common in Rudge wood, and Easter dues and all tithes.[40] In 1818 it was worth £120.[41] In 1838 the rector's tithes and Easter dues were commuted to £252 10*s.*; 60 a. in Willey old deer park, said to be the land bought from Wenlock priory by Richard Lacon in 1537, was then claimed to be tithe free.[42] The combined living was worth £311 2*s.* 6*d.* in 1851, comprising £274 from tithes, £37 from the glebe, and 2*s.* 6*d.* fees.[43] Most of the *c.* 30 a. of glebe was sold in 1947.[44]

In 1618 and 1674 the glebe house stood north of the church.[45] In 1736 George Weld built a new brick rectory south of the village.[46] Enlarged to plans by Griffin & Weller of Wolverhampton *c.* 1859,[47] it remained in use until 1972. It was occupied by St. Aidan's College, a centre for religious studies, from *c.* 1973 to 1976 and was sold to Lord Forester in 1977.[48]

Medieval chaplains may not have resided at Willey as the benefice did not have cure of souls. The first known incumbent was Adam of Wheathill, acolyte, inducted in 1276.[49] Philip of Harley, incumbent between 1324 and *c.* 1357, was a son of the lord of the manor. He became steward of Wenlock priory's manors *c.* 1344, and in 1352, when he was also vicar of Eaton-under-Heywood, was placed in joint charge of the priory during war with France.[50] While Wenlock priory was in the king's hands only two chaplains continued for five years or more: Hugh le Yonge (1360– 77), a royal clerk and prebendary of St. Mary's, Shrewsbury,[51] and his successor John Hervy (1377–83).[52] Between 1383 and 1392 there were eight chaplains.[53] The only known graduate before the Reformation was Richard Talbot (1411–12),[54] brother of Lord Furnivalle and later archbishop of Dublin and chancellor of Ireland.[55]

In 1547 land in Willey worth 2*s.* a year, given for lights in the church, passed to the Crown.[56]

In the 1680s the rector of Willey began to hold Barrow in plurality. Long incumbencies were common.[57] Robert Ogdon (d. 1680) was also rector of Broseley.[58] In 1662 he travelled thence to preach every third Sunday at Willey.[59] Francis Wheeler, rector 1680–*c.* 1686, became archdeacon of Salop in 1684.[60] Joseph Barney, 1698–1727, lived at Barrow school in 1716. There were then two Sunday services, one with a sermon, and communion five times a year.[61] Dr. John Fayle, rector 1740–78 and rector of Beckbury from 1754, employed curates for Willey.[62] Morgan Jones, rector 1778–1817, was also rector of Hughley 1804–13. He employed curates for Willey, and was described by George Forester as a saucy 'black Tom'.[63] In 1801 there was a midday service, with sermon, every Sunday and communion on five feast days.[64] Michael Pye Stephens, 1817–22, was a sporting parson and also a magistrate and amateur medical practitioner.[65]

28 *Reg. Mascall* (C.S.), 177.

29 Ibid. 176; *Reg. Trillek* (C.S.), 302, 356, 368, 385, 394; S.R.O. 1224/3/145, 149, 152 (no. 4).

30 S.R.O. 1224/3/152 (no. 1); Bannister, *Heref. Institutions*, 12, 16, 20, 44, 49, 55, 72, 81, 111, 141, 145, 165, 191; *T.S.A.S.* 3rd ser. v. 362, 376; 4th ser. ii. 75, 79, 91, 99; vi. 316; *Kelly's Dir. Salop.* (1905–41); cf. above, manor. H.W.R.O.(H.), Heref. dioc. rec. AL 19/16, f. 297, mentions Rowland Lacon as patron in 1631, presumably in ignorance of John Weld's purchase of man. and adv. in 1618.

31 *Reg. Swinfield*, 520; *Reg. Orleton*, 281; *Valor Eccl.* iii. 209.

32 *T.S.A.S.* vi. 106, 119–20.

33 S.R.O. 1224, box 163, Mr. Weld's memo. bk. 1619/20, f. 15v., no. 12.

34 Ibid. box 82, deed 4 Dec. 1661.

35 Heref. Dioc. Regy., reg. 1822–42, pp. 12–13.

36 Above, Barrow, church.

37 Heref. Dioc. Regy., reg. 1969– (in use), pp. 228–9.

38 J. Ecton, *Liber Valorum et Decimarum* (1711), 147.

39 S.R.O. 1224, box 183, rental Mich. 1755.

40 H.W.R.O.(H.), HD 2/14/59.

41 Ibid. HD 9, diocese bk.

42 S.R.O. 160/4; above, manor.

43 P.R.O., HO 129/358, no. 38.

44 Inf. from dioc. registrar; cf. *P.O. Dir. Salop.* (1856), 148; *Kelly's Dir. Salop* (1941), 309.

45 S.R.O. 1224/1/9–11.

46 L. F. Peltor, *Pars. of Willey and Barrow, Salop* (Glouc. 1966), 8, 11 (copy in S.P.L.).

47 H.W.R.O.(H.), Heref. dioc. rec. AA 58, plans, etc., of 1859.

48 Inf. from the Revd. L. F. Peltor and dioc. registrar; *St. Aidan's Coll.* (pamph. in S.P.L.); S.C.C. chars. index; *Bridgnorth Jnl.* 10 Aug. 1973, 2 Apr. 1976, 7 Jan. 1977.

49 *Reg. Cantilupe* (C.S.), 82.

50 *Reg. Orleton*, 272–3, 278–9, 281; *Reg. Trillek*, 356, 368, 390, 394; above, manor; W. F. Mumford, *Wenlock in the Middle Ages* (Shrews. 1977), 64–5; *T.S.A.S.* lx. 110.

51 *Cal. Pat.* 1358–61, 344; 1377–81, 74; R. A. Griffiths, *Principality of Wales in Later Middle Ages*, i (1972), 177–8.

52 *Cal. Pat.* 1377–81, 74; 1381–5, 297.

53 Ibid. 1381–5, 297, 311, 374; 1385–9, 54, 96, 375; 1388–92, 423; 1391–6, 211; *Reg. Gilbert* (C.S.), 117, 119, 121; *Reg. Trefnant* (C.S.), 176.

54 *Reg. Mascall*, 176–7.

55 A. B. Emden, *Biog. Reg. Univ. Oxf. to 1500*, iii. 1845–6; *D.N.B.*

56 *S.P.R. Heref.* xvi (5), p. vii; *Cal. Pat.* 1549–51, 82; S.R.O. 1224/3/154; box 163, Mr. Weld's memo. bk. 1619/20, f. 13v.

57 Bannister, *Heref. Institutions*; *S.P.R. Heref.* xvi (5), pp. viii–x.

58 Bannister, op. cit. 44; above, Broseley, churches.

59 H.W.R.O.(H.), HD 7, Broseley presentment of 1662; cf. *Par. Regs. of Broseley*, ed. A. F. C. C. Langley, i (1889), 51.

60 Bannister, op. cit. 44, 49; *S.P.R. Heref.* xvi (5), p. ix.

61 Bannister, op. cit. 55, 72; H.W.R.O.(H.), HD 5/14/1/4.

62 Bannister, op. cit. 81, 111; *S.P.R. Heref.* xvi (5), 1, 31–2.

63 Bannister, op. cit. 111, 131, 138, 141; *S.P.R. Heref.* xvi (5), 33–4; Randall, *Broseley*, 300.

64 H.W.R.O.(H.), HD 2/14/59.

65 Bannister, op. cit. 141, 145; Randall, *Broseley*, 292–7; J. Randall, *Severn Valley* (Madeley, 1882), 339–43; *V.C.H. Salop.* xi. 90.

In 1851 the church had 85 seats, 25 of them free; 70 people attended the fortnightly service.[66] G. T. O. Bridgeman, antiquary, writer, and second son of the 2nd earl of Bradford, was rector 1852–3.[67] His successor Dr. Thomas Rowley, rector 1854–77 after a distinguished headmastership of Bridgnorth grammar school, employed curates.[68] During W. H. Wayne's long incumbency (1878–1921) the church was restored and a new burial ground for Willey and Barrow consecrated at Barrow in 1881.[69]

The church of *ST. JOHN THE BAPTIST*, so known by *c.* 1740,[70] is built of rubble and ashlar and has a chancel with north organ chamber and south chapel, an aisled nave, and a west tower entered by a west door.

Nave and chancel are 12th-century and windows (possibly reset) of that period survive in the south wall of the chancel and north wall of the nave. The broken bowl of a possibly Norman font lies in the churchyard. There is a late medieval window in the north wall of the chancel and there were others of similar date in the north wall of the nave.[71]

By the 17th century a south chapel had been added at the junction of chancel and nave; it may have been built for the Welds, whose pew it was by 1736.[72] The tower was rebuilt in 1712;[73] its shape and diagonal buttresses suggest that it is modelled on a 14th-century predecessor. In 1716 the church was said to be in good repair.[74] Extensive repairs were probably undertaken *c.* 1777.[75] By 1821 the south chapel had been replaced by one parallel to the nave which was entered from the south and served as Lord Forester's pew. There was then a west gallery.[76]

In 1880 A. W. Blomfield restored the church at the expense of Alexandrina, widow of J. G. W. Weld-Forester, Lord Forester (d. 1874).[77] Blomfield's main additions were north and south aisles, each incorporating a quasi-transept. The more elaborate south aisle has a memorial chapel to Lord Forester (d. 1874) at its east end and a raised pew for Lord Forester's family in the quasi-transept at the west. At the east end of the north aisle is an organ chamber. A west gallery was removed from the nave and a west window inserted in the tower. Plaster was stripped from the walls inside and out and ceilings removed. The largely 17th-century pulpit, reading desk, sanctuary chair, pews, and panelling were incorporated into new furniture. A possibly 18th-century communion table is encased in the altar frame. In the sill of a mullioned two-light window in the western part of the south wall of the nave is an oval bowl hollowed out as a font or piscina; it has a wooden cover, possibly 18th-century. There is another font, perhaps an 18th-century composition of medieval fragments. There are several memorials to the Welds and Foresters, the earliest to Sir John Weld (d. 1666) and his wife (d. 1668). At the west end of the nave are Queen Victoria's arms carved in wood.

There were few alterations in the century after 1880, though the east window was made by Morris & Co. in 1933. A paten given in 1895 was added to plate of the 17th and 18th centuries. Two bells were added in 1880 to two of 1618 and a third of 1726.

The registers are complete from 1644, though containing only baptisms until 1665.[78] The churchyard is small and occupies the same area as it did in 1618.[79]

NONCONFORMITY. There was at least one papist in the 1660s.[80] No dissenters were noted in 1676 or 1716.[81] In 1767 a family of three papists was recorded.[82]

EDUCATION. Children have attended Barrow school since the 19th century or earlier.[83] Anne Wright kept school at the Dean *c.* 1670.[84] A day school begun in 1831 had 10 boys and 13 girls in 1835.[85] In 1869 there were two private schools.[86]

CHARITIES. The poor's stock, begun by 1668, stood at £60 in 1777 when £40 of it was lent to the parish for church repairs, the interest to be paid to the poor.[87] The interest, never distributed, was in 1802 consolidated with the principal. Again the interest seems not to have been distributed, and the whole stock was lost by 1820, when there was nevertheless a long-standing annual distribution of £5-worth of corn by the farmers.

Benefactions of £10 by Dorothy Weld (d. 1674)[88] and Catherine Strange (d. 1730)[89] had by 1801 been lost or absorbed into the poor's stock.[90]

66 P.R.O., HO 129/358, no. 38.

67 *S.P.R. Heref.* xvi (5), p. x; *T.S.A.S.* 2nd ser. viii. 191–4.

68 *S.P.R. Heref.* xvi (5), p. x; S.R.O. 4363, p. 46; Heref. Dioc. Regy., reg. 1847–56, p. 548; 1869–83, p. 369; cf. [J. G.] Brighton, 'Memoir of Revd. Dr. Rowley', *The Old Tower: a Salop. Quarterly Mag.* ii (1879), 74–87, 179–88, 338–55 (copy in S.P.L.); *V.C.H. Salop.* ii. 143.

69 Peltor, *Willey and Barrow*, 25; below, this section; S.R.O. 1224, box 82, bdle. *re* burial ground 1881.

70 B.L. Add. MS. 30316, f. 29v.

71 Bodl. MS. Top. Salop. c. 2, f. 524.

72 S.R.O. 1224/1/9–11; Birm. Univ. Libr., Mytton Papers, vii. 1577.

73 *3rd Rep. Com. Char.* H.C. 5, p. 312 (1820), iv.

74 H.W.R.O.(H.), HD 5/14/1/4.

75 *3rd Rep. Com. Char.* 312.

76 B.L. Add. MS. 21013, p. 46.

77 Heref. Dioc. Regy., reg. 1869–83, pp. 532–4; *Ch. Cal. Dioc. Heref.* (1881), 129. Following descr. based on *Kelly's Dir. Salop.* (1891), 478–9; (1900), 287; SA 614, citing Council for Care of Churches, 'Willey (P.M. 320)' (TS. 1973).

78 S.R.O. 3568/Rg/1–11; /MRg/1–7; /BRg/1–2; regs. at Broseley Rectory; cf. *S.P.R. Heref.* xvi (5); H.W.R.O.(H.), bp.'s transcripts for nine yrs. betw. (and incl.) 1600 and 1640.

79 S.R.O. 1224/1/9.

80 H.W.R.O.(H.), HD 7, presentment of 1669; S.R.O. 5709, Wenlock boro. q. sess. order bk., p. 19.

81 H.W.R.O.(H.), HD 5/14/1/4; *Compton Census*, ed. Whiteman, 258.

82 *Worcs. Recusant*, xxvi. 23.

83 *3rd Rep. Com. Char.* 303; P.R.O., ED 7/103, ff. 139–40; above, Barrow, educ.

84 S.R.O. 1224, box 147, depositions 7 Oct. 1728, f. 4.

85 *Educ. Enq. Abstract*, H.C. 62, p. 787 (1835), xlii.

86 S.R.O. 4365, p. 12.

87 Section based on *3rd Rep. Com. Char.* 311–12.

88 *S.P.R. Heref.* xvi (5), 27.

89 Ibid. 29.

90 H.W.R.O.(H.), HD 2/14/59.

By will proved 1687[91] Francis Wheeler, rector, left 10*s*. a year to be paid by the ministers of the two Bridgnorth churches and distributed in bread or cash. The charity survived in 1975.[92]

In 1707 Robert Evans of the Dean left 10*s*. a year to be given in bread. The charity remained in 1820 but has not been traced thereafter.

91 *S.P.R. Heref.* xvi (5), p. ix.

92 *Review of Local Chars.* (S.C.C. 1975), 21.

INDEX

NOTE. Page numbers in bold-face type indicate main references. A page number followed by *n* is a reference only to the footnotes on that page.

INDEX

CORRIGENDA TO VOLUMES I–IV, VIII

Earlier corrigenda to Volumes I–III were published in Volumes II–IV. In references to pages printed in more than one column *'a'*, *'b'*, and *'c'* following a page number denote the first, second, and third column.

Vol. I, page 285, line 9, *for* 'Patton . . . 1½' *read* 'Patton . . . 1' *and after entry* 'Patton' *add new entry* ''Petelie' . . . ½'

,, ,, 319*b*, lines 54–5, *move* 'fol. 254*b*.' *to follow* 'geld.'

,, ,, 334, note 84, *for existing note read* 'Perhaps in one of the 11 town(ship)s, of which 5 were in Ruyton parish, 6 in West Felton.'

,, ,, 336*b*, line 37, *for* 'Minton' *read* '? Menutton'

,, ,, 411, line 17, *delete* 'Nills'

,, ,, 431*b*, line 30, *for* 'county' *read* 'country'

,, ,, 489, line 13, *for* 'La Cleye' *read* 'la Clye'

,, ,, 493, line 37, *for* 'Stoke St. Milborough' *read* 'Stokesay' *and for* 'north' *read* 'north-west'

Vol. II, page 3, line 15, *after* 'Milson' *delete asterisk*

,, ,, 3, line 17, *before* 'Llanfair' *add* 'Leintwardine'

,, ,, 3, line 27, *after* 'Billingsley' *delete asterisk*

,, ,, 3, line 31, *before* 'Badger' *add* 'Acton Scott,'

,, ,, 3, line 33, *after* 'Linley,' *delete asterisk*

,, ,, 3, line 34, *after* 'Madeley,' *delete asterisk*

,, ,, 3, line 35, *for* 'Lacy' *read* 'Long'

,, ,, 3, note 48, *for* 'Abbots, Aston Eyre, and Billingsley' *read* 'Abbots and Aston Eyre'

,, ,, 3, note 49, *for* 'a chapelry of' *read* 'united to', *for* 'Madeley and Woolstaston, also' *read* 'Woolstaston,', *for* 'occur' *read* 'occurs', *and for* '17th' *read* '16th'

,, ,, 4, line 25, *after* 'Boningale,' *delete asterisk*

,, ,, 4, line 34, *before* 'Kenley' *add* 'Isombridge,'

,, ,, 5, note 70, *after* 'other.' *add* 'Up Rossall was included in 1291 but omitted in 1535.'

,, ,, 9, line 4, *for* 'was a public chapel at' *read* 'were public chapels at Madeley and' *and for* 'seven' *read* 'six'

,, ,, 21, line 41, *for* 'its . . . but' *read* 'some of its estates passed to the Hospitallers, some'

,, ,, 22, note 6, *for* 'no foundation for the' *read* 'a'

,, ,, 24, *Wenlock deanery boundary to include Acton Scott*

,, ,, 43*a*, line 18, *for* 'Bradley' *read* 'Bradeley'

,, ,, 43*a*, line 21, *for* 'Heath' *read* 'Stoke St. Milborough'

,, ,, 43*a*, line 28, *for* 'third' *read* 'share'

,, ,, 45*b*, line 28, *for* 'pre-conquest' *read* 'earliest'

,, ,, 45*b*, lines 29–30, *for* 'The . . . century;' *read* 'Of the late Saxon (or Norman) church'

,, ,, 85*a*, line 29, *for* 'apparently' *read* 'may have'

,, ,, 85*b*, line 16, *after* 'country' *add* 'east and'

,, ,, 85, note 7, *for* 'south-west of' *read* 'near'

,, ,, 86*b*, line 39, *after* 'house' *add* ', perhaps'

,, ,, 86*b*, line 43, *after* 'structures' *add* ', though it stands on earlier stone building (now a basement)'

,, ,, 139*b*, line 28, *for* 'Hugene' *read* 'Lingen'

,, ,, 170*b*, line 54, *for* 'waters' *read* 'Waters'

,, ,, 172*b*, line 31, *for* 'Dunwaters of Plaish' *read* 'Dun-Waters'

,, ,, 172*b*, lines 34, 43, 45, *for* 'Dunwaters' *read* 'Dun-Waters'

,, ,, 173*a*, lines 6, 31, *for* 'Dunwaters' *read* 'Dun-Waters'

,, ,, 173*a*, line 8, *for* 'waters' *read* 'Waters'

176*a*, lines 18 and 24, *for* 'Dunwaters' *read* 'Dun-Waters'

,, ,, 176*a*, line 22, *for* 'waters' *read* 'Waters'

,, ,, 177*a*, line 26, *delete* 'first'

,, ,, 204, line 34, *for* ', Shrewsbury, and Wenlock' *read* 'and Shrewsbury', *for* 'Borough' *read* 'Boroughs', *and after* 'Ludlow' *add* 'and Wenlock'

,, ,, 207, line 5, after '1831' *add* 'corrected, where necessary, from other sources'

,, ,, 207, line 9, *for 'North' read '(North Division)'*

,, ,, 207, *s.v.* 'Bradford (North Division)', col. 2, *after* 'Wem' *delete* '5'

,, ,, 207, line 22, *for* 'North Hundred' *read* 'Hundred (North)'

,, ,, 207, line 25, *for 'South' read '(South Division)'*

,, ,, 207, note 4, *for* 'North Hundred' *read* 'Hundred (North)'

,, ,, 207, *delete note 5*

,, ,, 208, lines 15–16, *for* 'dissolution' *read* 'dismemberment' *and for* 'Liberties' (*twice*) *read* 'Borough'

,, ,, 208, line 32, *after* 'In' *add* '1835, upon the dismemberment of the Borough of Wenlock, its detached parts in Much Wenlock parish passed into Condover Hundred. In'

,, ,, 208, note 12, *for* 'Not given' *read* 'Population returned with Donington'

,, ,, 208, note 19, *before* 'Q.' *add* '5 & 6 Wm. IV, c. 76, ss. 7–8;'

,, ,, 208, note 21, *before* 'Little' *add* 'The population of', *delete* 'under Great Hanwood in 1811, but', *and for* ', 1821–41' *read* '(separately) in 1811 and 1841'

,, ,, 209, *s.v.* '*Munslow*', col. 2, *after* 'Munslow' *add* '(part of)[26a]' *and delete* 'Scirmidge[28]'

,, ,, 209, line 17, *for* 'dissolution' *read* 'dismemberment', *for* 'Liberties' *read* 'Borough', *and before* 'Shipton' *add* 'part of Munslow, the greater part of'

,, ,, 209, line 20, *before* 'Shipton' *add* 'the greater part of'

,, ,, 209, note 25, *for* 'Liberties' *read* 'Borough'

,, ,, 209, *after note 26 add new note* '[26a] Partly in the Borough of Wenlock until 1836.'

,, ,, 209, *delete note 28*

,, ,, 209, note 29, *for* 'Liberties' *read* 'Borough'

,, ,, 209, note 40, *for* 'North Hundred' *read* 'Hundred (North)'

,, ,, 210, line 5, *after* '*Purslow*' *add* '*and Clun*'

,, ,, 210, *s.v.* '*Purslow and Clun*', col. 1, *after* 'Horderley Hall' *add* 'Leintwardine (part of)[43a]'

,, ,, 210, line 18, *for* 'Stow' *read* 'Stowe'

,, ,, 210, *s.v.* 'Stottesdon', col. 2, *for* 'from' *read* 'by'

,, ,, 210, *after note 43 add new note* '[43a] i.e. Heath and Jay, whose population was returned under Herefs. 1801–71.'

,, ,, 210, note 53, *for* 'Not' *read* 'Population not'

,, ,, 210, note 54, *for* 'Liberties' *read* 'Borough'

,, ,, 211, line 33, *delete* '*and Liberties*'

,, ,, 211, *s.v.* '*Borough of Wenlock*', col. 2, *after* 'Monkhopton' *add* 'Munslow (part of)[66a]' *and after* 'Posenhall[67]' *add* 'Scirmidge[67a]'

,, ,, 211, line 43, *for* 'Liberties' *read* 'Borough', *for* 'were dissolved' *read* 'was dismembered', *and after* 'In' *add* '1835[68a] its detached parts in Much Wenlock parish passed into Condover Hundred. In'

,, ,, 211, line 45, *before* 'the' *add* 'Munslow (part of),'

,, ,, 211, line 46, *for* 'liberties' *read* 'borough'

,, ,, 211, note 64, *for* 'North Hundred' *read* 'Hundred (North)'

,, ,, 211, *after note 66 add new note* '[66a] i.e. Lower Millichope. Remainder in Munslow Hundred.'

,, ,, 211, *after note 67 add new note* '[67a] Not given 1801–21.'

,, ,, 211, *after note 68 add new note* '[68a] 5 & 6 Wm. IV, c. 76, ss. 7–8.'

,, ,, 216, *s.v.* '*Madeley R.D.*' col. 1, *below* 'Benthall' *add* 'Broseley—constituted an U.S.D. 1876' *and below* 'Buildwas' *add* 'Dawley—constituted an U.S.D. 1876'

,, ,, 216, *s.v.* '*Madeley R.D.*', col. 1, *above* 'Posenhall' *add* 'Madeley—constituted an U.S.D. 1880'

,, ,, 216, *s.v.* '*Madeley R.D.*', col. 2, *below* 'Wenlock, Little' *add* 'Wenlock, Much—constituted an U.S.D. 1873'

,, ,, 222, second note l, *for* '1882' *read* '1883'

,, ,, 223, notes p and w, *for* '1882' *read* '1883'

,, ,, 225, note h, *for* '1882' *read* '1883'

,, ,, 227, note j, *for* '1882' *read* '1883'

,, ,, 229, line 3, *delete* 'and libs.'

,, ,, 229, first note q, *for* 'Dissolved' *read* 'Dismembered'

,, ,, 238*a*, *s.v.* '*Aitone* (unidentified)', *delete* ', 323' *and after that entry add new entry* '*Aitone* (? the Isle, in Shrewsbury St. Chad), 323'

,, ,, 239*a*, *before entry* '*Bosle*' *add new entry* 'Boreton (*Burtune*, Bourton) in Condover, 312'

,, ,, 239*a*, *after entry* 'Bouldon' *add new entry* 'Bourton, in Condover, *see* Boreton'

,, ,, 239*a*, *s.v.* 'Brockton (*Broctune*)', *before* 'Stanton' *add* 'Shipton and'

,, ,, 239*b*, *s.v.* '*Burtone* (*Burtune*)', *after* '*see*' *add* 'Boreton; Bourton;'

,, ,, 241*b*, *before entry* 'Isombridge' *add new entry* 'Isle, the, in Shrewsbury St. Chad, *see Aitone*'

,, ,, 242*a*, *before entry* 'Meole, Crow' *add new entry* 'Menutton, in Clun, *see Munetune*'

,, ,, 242*a*, *s.v.* 'Millichope', *before* 'Munslow' *add* 'Eaton-under-Heywood and'

,, ,, 242*a*, *s.v.* 'Minton', delete '336,'

,, ,, 242*b*, *after entry* '*Munete*' *add new entry* '*Munetune* (? Menutton, in Clun), 336'

,, ,, 242*b*, *s.v.* 'Osbern Fitz Richard', *delete* '339,'

,, ,, 245*a*, *before entry* 'Womerton' *add new entry* 'Wolverley (*Ulwardelege*) in Wem, 331'

,, ,, 246*a*, *s.v.* 'Abdon', *delete* 'Abdon Burf;'

,, ,, 246*a*, *s.v.* 'Abdon Burf', *delete* 'Abdon,' *and before* 'and' *add* 'Diddlebury,'

,, ,, 246*b*, *s.v.* 'Acton Scott', *before* '209' *add* '3,'

,, ,, 249*c*, *s.v.* 'Barrow', *after subentry* 'geol.' *add new subentry* 'Marsh Farm, i. 442'

,, ,, 253*a*, *after entry* 'Bradburn' *add new entry* 'Bradeley, in Much Wenlock, ii. 43'

,, ,, 254*b*, *s.v.* 'Brimstree Hundred', *delete* '210 *n*,'

,, ,, 255*a*, *s.v.* 'Broseley, C.P.', *after* '213,' *add* '216,'

,, ,, 255*a*, *s.v.* 'Broseley, U.S.D', *after* 'ii.' *add* '216,'

,, ,, 255*b*, *s.v.* 'Brown Clee Hill', *after* 'Cleobury North,' *add* 'Diddlebury,'

,, ,, 259*b*, *s.v.* 'Clee', *for* 'Cleye' *read* 'Clye'

,, ,, 259*c*, *delete entry* 'Cleye, La'

,, ,, 260*b*, *after entry* 'Clwyd' *add new entry* 'Clye, la, *see* Clee, Chase or Forest of'

,, ,, 263*a*, *s.v.* 'Dawley, C.P.', *after* 'ii.' *add* '216,'

„ „ 263*a*, *s.v.* 'Dawley, U.S.D.', *after* 'ii.' *add* '216,'
„ „ 263*c*, *s.v.* 'Diddlebury', *for* 'Broncroft' *read* 'Abdon Burf; Broncroft; Brown Clee Hill'
„ „ 265*a*, *s.v.* 'Dunwaters', *for* 'Dunwaters' *read* 'Dun-Waters' *and move entry to precede entry* 'Dunbar'
„ „ 265*b*, *s.v.* 'Eaton-under-Heywood', *after* 'Dale;' *add* 'Millichope;'
„ „ 267*b*, *s.v.* 'Felton, West', *before* 'ii' *add* 'i. 334 *n*;'
„ „ 270*a*, *s.v.* 'Grindle Nills Hill', *delete* 'Nills'
„ „ 271*a*, *s.v.* 'Hanwood, Great', *delete* 'and *n*'
„ „ 274c, *delete entry* 'Hugene'
„ „ 278*a*, *s.v.* 'Lee, Ric.', *for* '1500' *read* '1498'
„ „ 278*b*, *s.v.* 'Leintwardine', *after* 'ii.' *add* '3,'
„ „ 279*c*, *s.v.* 'Lingen', *after subentry* 'Margery' *insert new subentry* 'Phil., Warden of the Ludlow Palmers' Guild, ii. 139'
„ „ 281*b*, *after entry* 'Lower Melverley' *add new entry* 'Lower Millichope, *see* Millichope (Lower Millichope)'
„ „ 283*a*, *s.v.* 'Madeley, C.P.', *after* 'ii.' *add* '216,'
„ „ 283*a*, *s.v.* 'Madeley, Rom. Cath.', *after* '9' *add* 'and'
„ „ 283*a*, *s.v.* 'Madeley, U.S.D.', *after* 'ii.' *add* '216,'
„ „ 283*c*, *s.v.* 'Marsh Farm', *for* 'Posenhall' *read* 'Barrow'
„ „ 285*a*, *s.v.* 'Millichope, in Munslow', *after* 'in' *add* 'Eaton-under-Heywood and' *and after* '40,' *delete* '43,'
„ „ 285*a*, *s.v.* 'Millichope, in Eaton-under-Heywood and Munslow', *for subentry* 'pop.' *substitute new main entry* 'Millichope (Lower Millichope), in Munslow, ii. 43, 211 *n*, 225 *n*'
„ „ 286*c*, *s.v.* 'Munslow', *before* 'Poston' *add* 'Millichope (Lower Millichope);'
„ „ 291*b*, *s.v.* ''Petelie'', *after* 'i.' *add* '285,'
„ „ 291*c*, *s.v.* 'Pimley', *for* 'St. Mary's, Shrewsbury' *read* 'Uffington'
„ „ 292*a*, *s.v.* 'Plaish', *after* 'Cardington' *for* ', ii. 172' *read* ':'
„ „ 292*b*, *s.v.* 'Posenhall', *delete subentry* 'Marsh Farm'
„ „ 295*b*, *s.v.* 'Rossall, Up', *before* '211' *add* '5 *n*,'
„ „ 297*a*, *s.v.* 'Scirmidge', *for* '209' *read* '211'
„ „ 300*c*, *s.v.* 'Shrewsbury, St. Mary's par.', *after* 'Newton;' *delete* 'Pimley; Shelton and Oxon;'
„ „ 302*a*, *s.v.* 'Sleap, in Myddle . . .', *for* '228' *read* '227'
„ „ 303*a*, *s.v.* 'Stanton Long', *before* '39' *add* '3,'
„ „ 303*c*, *s.v.* 'Stoke St. Milborough', *delete subentry* 'park'
„ „ 304*a*, *s.v.* 'Stokesay', *after subentry* 'man.' *add new subentry* 'park, i. 493'
„ „ 304*b*, *s.v.* 'Stretton, Little', *for* 'Grindle Nills Hill' *read* 'Grindle Hill'
„ „ 306c, *s.v.* 'Uffington', *after* 'Hill' *add* '; Pimley'
„ „ 309*c*, *s.v.* 'Wenlock, Much', *before* '211' *add* '208,'
„ „ 309*c*, *s.v.* 'Wenlock, Much, C.P.', *after* '213,' *add* '216,'
„ „ 309*c*, *s.v.* 'Wenlock, Much, U.S.D.', *after* 'ii.' *add* '216,'
„ „ 309*c*, *s.v.* 'Wenlock, Much, *and see*', *before* 'Bradley' *add* 'Bradeley;'

Vol. III, page 40, *Wenlock boro. to include Lower Millichope and Norncott*
„ „ 76, note 35, *for* 'Cotes' *read* 'Coats'
„ „ 96, line 6, *for* 'Cotes' *read* 'Coates'
„ „ 113, line 10, *for* 'Cotes' *read* 'Coates'
„ „ 118, note 58, *for* '117' *read* '98'
„ „ 168, line 31, *after* 'year' *add* 'and early next'
„ „ 241, note 19, line 7, *before* 'M.P.' *add* 'probably' *and for* 'Harries' *read* 'Harris'
„ „ 241, note 19, line 8, *for* 'Cruckton: ibid.' *read* 'Cornworthy, Devon'
„ „ 364*a*, *s.v.* 'Arlescott', *for* 'Posenhall' *read* 'Barrow'
„ „ 364*b*, *s.v.* 'Baldwyn, Chas.', *for* '1707' *read* '1706'
„ „ 364*c*, *s.v.* 'Barrow', *before* 'Shirlett' *add* 'Arlescott;'
„ „ 369*a*, *before entry* 'Coats' *add new entry* 'Coates, in Holdgate, 96, 113'
„ „ 369*a*, *s.v.* 'Coats', *for* '76, 96, 113' *read* '76 *n*'
„ „ 370*a*, *before entry* 'coroners' *add new entry* 'Cornworthy (Devon), 241 *n*'
„ „ 370*c*, *s.v.* 'Cressett', *delete subentry* 'fam., 76 *n*'
„ „ 371*a*, *s.v.* 'Cruckton', *after* '241' *add* '*n*'
„ „ 371*b*, *s.v.* 'Devon', *before* 'Okehampton' *add* 'Cornworthy;'
„ „ 374*c*, *s.v.* 'Grey, Edw.', *for* '1604' *read* '1602'
„ „ 375*b*, *s.v.* 'Harris', *before subentry* 'Sir Thos.' *add new subentry* 'Thos. (fl. 1586), 241 *n*'
„ „ 376*c*, *after entry* 'Holdgate' *add new entry* 'Holdgate, *see* Coates'
„ „ 377*b*, *s.v.* 'hundreds, reorganization', *before* '11,' *add* '6,'
„ „ 379*a*, *s.v.* 'Le Strange, John', *for* '1269' *read* '*c.* 1269'
„ „ 379*b*, *s.v.* 'Leighton, fam.', *before* '233' *add* '76 *n*,'
„ „ 386*b*, *s.v.* 'Posenhall', *delete* '; *and see* Arlescott'
„ „ 394*c*, *s.v.* 'Warin the bald', *for* '11' *read* '9–11'

Vol. IV, page 5, note 31, *for* 'Greigg' *read* 'Greig'
„ „ 43, line 25, *for* 'Condover' *read* 'Cound'
„ „ 68, line 21, *delete* '1251–3 and' *and for* 'charters' *read* 'a charter'
„ „ 68, note 48, *delete* '–2; *Close R.* 1251–3, 321' *and for* '/1–3' *read* '/1–2'
„ „ 84, line 28, *for* '1445' *read* '1455'

” ” 84, note 53, *for* '2/9' *read* '1/9'
” ” 127, note 60, *for* 'Goodwin' *read* 'Goodman'
” ” 135, note 1, *for* '1911–18' *read* '1911–47'
” ” 169, line 13, *for* 'foot and mouth disease' *read* 'cattle plague'
” ” 212, note 86, *after* 'Moore)' *add* ', 28 Aug. 1891, p. 6'
” ” 270*a*, *s.v.* 'Abdon', *delete* 'Abdon Burf;'
” ” 270*a*, *s.v.* 'Abdon Burf', *before* 'Cleobury' *delete* 'Abdon,' *and before* 'and' *add* 'Diddlebury,'
” ” 270*b*, *s.v.* 'animal diseases, cattle', *after* '92' *add* ', 119, 169'
” ” 272*b*, *s.v.* 'Brown Clee Hill', *before* 'Ditton' *add* 'Diddlebury,'
” ” 274*a*, *s.v.* 'Condover', *delete subentry* 'pk., 43'
” ” 274*b*, *s.v.* 'Cound', *after subentry* 'Bullhill' *add new subentry* 'pk., 43'
” ” 275*c*, *s.v.* 'Diddlebury', *for* 'Broncroft' *read* 'Abdon Burf; Broncroft; Brown Clee Hill'
” ” 277*b*, *s.v.* 'foot and mouth disease', *before* '233' *delete* '169,'
” ” 288*b*, *s.v.* 'Stretton, Church, marketing', *before* '164' *and* '70' *add* '68,'
” ” 288*b*, *s.v.* 'Stretton, Church', *after subentry* 'Stretton, All' *add new subentry* 'Stretton, Little, *q.v.*'
” ” 288*b*, *s.v.* 'Stretton, Little', *after* 'Little' *add* '(in Church Stretton)'
Vol. VIII, page xv, line 6, *for* '1960' *read* '1959'
” ” xvii*a*, *s.v.* 'C 142', *for* '2 Hen.' *read* 'Hen.'
” ” xviii*b*, *s.v.* '840', *for* 'Tyrrwhit' *read* 'Tyrwhitt'
” ” xix, *s.v.* 'Cranage', *for* '1901–12' *read* '1894–1912'
” ” xix, *s.v.* '*Salop. Peace Roll*', *for '1404' (twice) read '1400'*
” ” [xx], *for* '1840' *read* '1831' *and correct the western boundary of Leighton parish (to exclude Eaton Constantine parish) and the boundary of Harley parish (to show Much Wenlock parish detachments)*
” ” 1, line 1, *for* 'south-east' *read* 'south'
” ” 1, line 2, *for* 'north' *read* 'north-east'
” ” 1, line 27, *for* 'when' *read* 'after'
” ” 1, lines 28–9, *delete* 'The tenants . . . 13th century.[9]'
” ” 1, lines 31–2, *after* 'Abbey,' *add* '[9]', *before* 'annexed' *add* 'later', *and after* 'Bradford' *delete* 'South after the Dissolution'
” ” 1, note 8, *after* '129' *add* '; *Rot. Hund.* (Rec. Com.), ii. 63, 84–5, 91'
” ” 1, *delete note 9, renumber note 10 as* '[9]', *and add new note* '[10] P.R.O., J.I. 1/1589; Eyton, vii. 320, 322.'
” ” 2, note 28, *after* 'townships' *add* '(except Oaks)'
” ” 4, *reposition* 'HARLITH' *south-west of hamlet 58*
” ” 5*b*, line 6, *for* 'Radnor' *read* 'Radnal'
” ” 8*a*, line 7, *for* '1617 to' *read* '1622 to Sir'
” ” 8, note 37, *for existing note read* 'S.R.O. 1514/46.'
” ” 8, notes 54 and 55, *for* 'E.' *read* 'N.'
” ” 10*b*, line 38, *for* 'Thereafter' *read* 'From 1622'
” ” 10*b*, line 42, *for* 'Sergeantson' *read* 'Serjeantson'
” ” 10, note 67, *for* 'Sergeantson' *read* 'Serjeantson'
” ” 12*a*, line 20, *before* 'Richard' *delete* 'Sir'
” ” 12*a*, line 26, *after* 'Bath.' *delete* '[4]'
” ” 12*a*, line 27, *for* '1552' *read* '1553'
” ” 12, note 4, *for* '100' *read* '303'
” ” 13*a*, line 42, *after* 'Abbots,' *add* 'Betton Strange,'
” ” 14*a*, line 10, *for* 'northern' *read* 'eastern'
” ” 14*a*, line 15, *for* 'The north-eastern' *read* 'There the'
” ” 14*a*, line 37, *for* 'western' *read* 'northern'
” ” 14*a*, line 41, *for* 'east' *read* 'west'
” ” 14*b*, line 11, *for* 'east' *read* 'north and north-west'
” ” 14, note 10, *for* '59' *read* '60'
” ” 15, note 59, *for* 'Lloyd' *read* 'LLoyd'
” ” 18*b*, line 2, *for* '1136' *read* '1121'
” ” 18*b*, line 13, *for* 'Phillip' *(twice) read* 'Philip'
” ” 19*a*, line 18, *for* 'Phillip' *read* 'Philip' *and for* 'Richard's' *read* 'Philip's'
” ” 19*a*, line 21, *delete* 'de'
” ” 19*b*, line 9, *for* '1588' *read* '1589'
” ” 19*b*, line 13, *for* '–15' *read* '–16'
” ” 19*b*, line 14, *for* '1715' *read* '1716'
” ” 19, note 9, *for* '746' *read* '1743'
” ” 19, note 21, *for* '1588' *read* '1589'
” ” 19, note 24, *for* 'settlement, 1715' *read* 'deed, 1716'
” ” 20*b*, line 43, *for* '1346' *read* '1348'
” ” 22*b*, line 35, *for* '1½' *read* '½'
” ” 22*b*, line 36, *before* 'the mill' *add* 'in the early 13th'
” ” 22*b*, line 36, *for* '½ virgate' *read* 'selion'
” ” 22, note 84, *after* 'Ibid.' *add* 'deed, 1653.'
” ” 23*a*, line 5, *for* 'some 30 a.' *read* 'land'

CORRIGENDA

” ” 23, note 89, *for* ‘1571’ *read* ‘1575’
” ” 25*a*, line 37, *for* ‘them . . . were’ *read* ‘a portion of them to Joseph Sparkes,[13] which was’
” ” 25*a*, line 38, *delete* ‘Sir’
” ” 25*b*, line 9, *delete* ‘Noel’
” ” 25*b*, line 30, *for* ‘Richard Noel Hill’ *read* ‘Richard Hill, later Noel-Hill’
” ” 26, notes 47 and 49, *for* ‘1680–1830’ *read* ‘1830–1966’
” ” 32*b*, line 2, *after* ‘opened’ *add* ‘to the parish’
” ” 32*b*, lines 27–8, *for* ‘end . . . Hill’ *read* ‘end.[56] Trenches on the summit of Lyth Hill are not ancient’
” ” 33*a*, line 2, *for* ‘eastern’ *read* ‘western’
” ” 33*a*, line 13, *for* ‘The Revd.’ *read* ‘Miss’
” ” 33*a*, line 13, *for* ‘his’ *read* ‘her’
” ” 36*a*, line 28, *delete* ‘Farm’
” ” 36*a*, line 32, *for* ‘The farm-house’ *read* ‘Wheathall Farm’
” ” 37*b*, line 7, *delete* ‘A house on the site of’
” ” 38*b*, lines 6–8, *for* ‘On . . . tail’ *read* ‘After Mary’s death the same year,[65a] Vynar was in sole possession’
” ” 38*b*, line 12, *for* ‘leased’ *read* ‘assigned’
” ” 38*b*, line 12, *after* ‘1567,[68]’ *add* ‘died in 1575, and Walter Lee [68a]’
” ” 38, note 63, *for* ‘(1)’ *read* ‘(2)’
” ” 38, *after note 65 add new note* ‘[65a] *T.S.A.S.* 2nd ser. xi. 193.’
” ” 38, *after note 68 add new note* ‘[68a] Ex inf. Mr. F. J. Jackson-Baylis.’
” ” 39*a*, line 1, *for* ‘latter’ *read* ‘former’
” ” 39*a*, line 3, *after* ‘who’ *add* ‘then took the name Owen and’
” ” 39, note 89, *after* ‘19’ *add* ‘; Burke, *Land. Gent.* (1952), 436’
” ” 42*a*, lines 14–15, *for* ‘Edwards’ *(twice) read* ‘Edmunds’
” ” 42*b*, lines 31–2, *delete* ‘a house on the site of’
” ” 42*b*, line 50, *for* ‘Harrop’ *read* ‘Hulton-Harrop’
” ” 42, note 18, *for* ‘ii’ *read* ‘11’
” ” 43*a*, line 23, *for* ‘Edwards’ *read* ‘Edmunds’
” ” 48*b*, lines 19–23, *after* ‘given’ *for rest of sentence read* ‘a mill-stank before 1160.[48]’
” ” 55*a*, line 41, *for* ‘Cholmondeley’ *read* ‘Owen (formerly Cholmondeley)’
” ” 55*b*, line 49, *for* ‘Randall’ *read* ‘Randal’
” ” 60*b*, line 27, *for* ‘Cresset’ *read* ‘Cressett’
” ” 63*b*, lines 40, 41, 45, 47, *for* ‘Cresset’ *read* ‘Cressett’
” ” 63, note 79, *for* ‘(4)’ *read* ‘(5)’
” ” 64*a*, line 21, *for* ‘Cresset’ *read* ‘Cressett’
” ” 65*a*, line 12, *delete* ‘Sir’
” ” 65*b*, line 2, *for* ‘Richard’ *read* ‘William Whalley’
” ” 65*b*, line 4, *for* ‘Richard’ *read* ‘William’
” ” 65*b*, line 25, *for* ‘Hope-’ *read* ‘Hope’
” ” 65*b*, line 27, *for* ‘Edwards’ *read* ‘Edwardes’
” ” 66*a*, line 32, *for* ‘Cresset’ *read* ‘Cressett’
” ” 67*a*, line 13, *for* ‘Cresset’ *read* ‘Cressett’
” ” 68, note 80, *for* ‘(4)’ *read* ‘(5)’
” ” 70*b*, lines 5–6, *for* ‘early-13th-century grant’ *read* ‘early grant or grants’
” ” 70*b*, line 35, *before* ‘1609’ *add* ‘?’
” ” 70*b*, lines 36, 38, 43, *for* ‘Cresset’ *read* ‘Cressett’
” ” 70, notes 68, 70, 73, *for* ‘(4)’ *read* ‘(5)’
” ” 71*a*, line 9, *for* ‘his successor Richard Wood’ *read* ‘Richard Wood, instituted in 1609,’
” ” 71*a*, line 10, *for* ‘Cresset’ *read* ‘Cressett’
” ” 71, note 87, *for* ‘(4)’ *read* ‘(5)’
” ” 72*a*, line 10, *for* ‘Cresset’ *read* ‘Cressett’
” ” 72, notes 29 and 38, *for* ‘(4)’ *read* ‘(5)’
” ” 73, note 22, *delete* ‘*Salop.*’
” ” 75*a*, line 6, *for* ‘Ralph’ *read* ‘Ranulph’
” ” 75*b*, line 12, *for* ‘1508’ *(twice) read* ‘1507’
” ” 75*b*, line 13, *for* ‘Littleton’ *read* ‘Lyttelton’
” ” 75*b*, line 26, *after* ‘trustees’ *add* ‘and reversioners’
” ” 75*b*, line 28, *for* ‘trustee . . . Pulteney.[22] On’ *read* ‘reversioner, William Pulteney (5th bt. 1794).[22] After’
” ” 77*a*, line 37, *delete* ‘in 1578’
” ” 77*a*, line 38, *after* ‘Farnham’ *add* ‘in 1577’
” ” 77*a*, lines 38–9, *for* ‘the following year’ *read* ‘1578–9’
” ” 77*a*, line 40, *for* ‘1595’ *read* ‘1587–8’
” ” 77, note 97, *delete* ‘2nd ser.’
” ” 81*b*, line 25, *for* ‘in 1248’ *read* ‘*c.* 1247’
” ” 82, notes 19 (second occurrence) –21, *renumber as 20–2*
” ” 85*a*, line 23, *delete* ‘a’ *and for* ‘part’ *read* ‘parts’
” ” 85*a*, line 40, *for* ‘part’ *read* ‘parts’

,, ,, 85*a*, line 43, *for* 'It was not' *read* 'They may not have been'
,, ,, 85*a*, line 44, *for* 'part' *read* 'parts'
,, ,, 85*b*, line 24, *for* 'it seems' *read* 'they seem'
,, ,, 85*b*, line 25, *for* 'part' *read* 'parts'
,, ,, 86*a*, line 32, *for* 'part' *read* 'parts'
,, ,, 86, note 20, *for* '1752' *read* '1808'
,, ,, 87, note 42, *for* 'has . . . 1859' *read* 'was remade 1858–61'
,, ,, 88*a*, line 12, *after* 'passed' *add* ', usually'
,, ,, 88*a*, line 12, *after* 'son' *add* ','
,, ,, 88*b*, line 9, *for* '1619' *read* '1620'
,, ,, 88*b*, line 27, *for* 'Priory' *read* 'Abbey'
,, ,, 88, note 95, *for* 'Ibid.' *read* '*Feud. Aids*, iv. 256.'
,, ,, 88, note 1, *for* '312/7' *read* '312/147', *for* 'until 1567' *read* 'in 1546', *and for* 'xiii' *read* 'xxi'
,, ,, 88, note 34, *for* 'Priory' *read* 'Abbey'
,, ,, 89*a*, line 7, *for* 'part' *read* 'parts'
,, ,, 90*b*, line 42, *for* 'part' *read* 'parts'
,, ,, 93*a*, line 8, *for* 'but . . . east' *read* 'as does a short stretch of the eastern, which otherwise'
,, ,, 93*b*, line 8, *for* '1793' *read* 'the 1780s.'
,, ,, 94*b*, line 39, *for* '1254' *read* '1255'
,, ,, 95*a*, lines 37–8, *for* '1793, when 52' *read* 'the 1780s, when 57' *and delete* 'Earl of Bradford as'
,, ,, 95*b*, line 42, *for* 'On' *read* 'After'
,, ,, 95*b*, line 43, *for* '1793' *read* 'the 1780s.'
,, ,, 95, note 97, *for existing note read* 'Staffs. R.O., D. 1287 uncat., Sam. Botham's plan and survey bk. 1789.'
,, ,, 97*a*, line 4, *for* 'Until the 19th century' *read* 'In the 17th and 18th centuries'
,, ,, 97*a*, line 5, *for* 'held by the impropriator' *read* 'owned by the patron'
,, ,, 99*b*, line 16, *for* 'Since' *read* 'Probably since'
,, ,, 99, note 42, *after* 'Cart.' *rest of note to read* 'f. 134, however, seems not to refer to the churchyard.'
,, ,, 101*b*, line 11, *for* 'Wolryche-Whitmore' *read* 'Wolryche Whitmore'
,, ,, 101*b*, line 34, *for the first* 'in' *read* 'by'
,, ,, 104*b*, line 30, *before* 'when' *add* 'as was shown'
,, ,, 104*b*, line 33, *delete* 'and Lichfield'
,, ,, 110*a*, line 24, *for* '48;' *read* '30;'
,, ,, 110*a*, line 25, *for* '1948' *read* '1930'
,, ,, 110, note 30, *after* 'Ibid.' *insert* '; ex inf. Mr. D. H. G. Salt.'
,, ,, 111*a*, line 16, *for* '1624' *read* '1623'
,, ,, 111, note 51, *for* '1624' *read* '1623'
,, ,, 115*b*, line 30, *for* 'west' *read* 'east'
,, ,, 116*b*, line 46, *for* 'westwards' *read* 'eastwards'
,, ,, 119*a*, line 12, *for* '22' *read* '23'
,, ,, 119*a*, line 13, *for* '1622' *read* '1623'
,, ,, 119, note 29, *after* '370' *add* '; *S.P.R Lich.* i (2), 54'
,, ,, 124*a*, line 35, *for* '13th' *read* '16th'
,, ,, 124, note 2, *for* 'See p. 127' *read* 'S.R.O. 1224/2/11; P.R.O., E 178/3075; E 315/214, f. 117'
,, ,, 125*a*, line 29, *for* 'but' *read* 'and' *and delete* 'not'
,, ,, 125*a*, line 30, *for* 'until' *read* 'in' *and for* '1790s' *read* '1780s'
,, ,, 125, note 36, *after* '62' *add* ', 91'
,, ,, 126*a*, line 8, *for* 'surrendered' *read* 'sold'
,, ,, 126*a*, line 9, *for* 'the Crown' *read* 'Giles Covert' *and for* 'The' *read* 'Although the'
,, ,, 126*a*, line 10, *for* 'still' *read* 'said to be'
,, ,, 126*a*, lines 10–11, *for* 'but was shortly afterwards granted to Giles Covert' *read* 'it remained with the Covert family'
,, ,, 126*a*, line 11, *for* 'Covert was' *read* 'Covert's son and namesake was'
,, ,, 126*a*, line 12, *for* '1559' *read* '1557'
,, ,, 126*a*, lines 13–14, *for* 'the following year' *read* '1560'
,, ,, 126*b*, line 35, *for* 'him as' *read* 'the'
,, ,, 126, note 44, *for existing source substitute* 'P.R.O., C.P. 40/1083, rot. 441.'
,, ,, 126, note 45, *delete* 'ii.'
,, ,, 126, note 46, *add* 'P.R.O., E 302/1/5/116;' *at the beginning*
,, ,, 126, note 47, *for existing source substitute* 'P.R.O., C 142/114/32.'
,, ,, 127*b*, lines 5–6, *for* 'presumably . . . parishes' *read* 'that may have been a recent arrangement'
,, ,, 127*b*, lines 11–12, *for* 'Since . . . perpetual' *read* 'Some time after *c.* 1587 the living became a'
,, ,, 127*b*, line 13, *for* '1869' *read* '1868'
,, ,, 127*b*, lines 20–1, *for* 'manor until 1926, when' *read* 'manor; in 1926'
,, ,, 127*b*, line 38, *delete* 'perpetual'
,, ,, 127*b*, line 41, *for* 'Willis' *read* 'Wilkes', *and for* '98' *read* '*c.* 1698'
,, ,, 127, notes 27 and 31, *for* '(1)' *read* '(2)'
,, ,, 128, note 45, *for* '(1)' *read* '(2)'

CORRIGENDA

,, ,, 129*a*, line 27, *before* 'in Ratlinghope' *add* 'the rest of which was'
,, ,, 129, note 1, *for* 'SO 30' *read* 'SJ 30'
,, ,, 134*b*, line 29, *before* 'descendant' *add* 'perhaps a'
,, ,, 134*b*, line 35, *for* '1265' *read* '1255'
,, ,, 135*a*, lines 34–7, *for* 'from . . . Lee' *read* 'successively to his son, grandson, [50] and great-granddaughter, who held it in 1419. From her it passed to her daughter Joan, wife of John Walker of Lee'
,, ,, 135*a*, lines 40–1, *delete* 'his grandson'
,, ,, 135, note 50, *for* '*T.S.A.S.* liv. 32' *read* 'S.P.L., Deeds 6904'
,, ,, 141*b*, line 18, *for* 'still' *read* 'probably'
,, ,, 141*b*, line 20, *for* 'accounted part of' *read* 'disputed with'
,, ,, 141*b*, line 21, *for* 'at' *read* 'near'
,, ,, 141*b*, line 22, *for* 'lord' *read* 'chapel'
,, ,, 142, note 50, *for existing note read* 'See pp. 144–5.'
,, ,, 143*a*, line 43, *for* '1500' *read* '98'
,, ,, 143*a*, line 44, *for* '1500–16' *read* '1498–1516', *for* '–74' *read* '–61', *and for* '1574' *read* '1561'
,, ,, 143*a*, line 45, *for* '1617' *read* '1622'
,, ,, 143, note 96, *after* '17' *add* '; S.R.O. 1514/140'
,, ,, 144*b*, line 11, *for* '1785' *read* '1782'
,, ,, 144, notes 39 and 43, *for* '1785' *read* '1782'
,, ,, 145*a*, line 1, *for* '1785,[61] was still' *read* '1782,[61] may have been that'
,, ,, 145*b*, line 37, *for* 'north-east' *read* 'north-west'
,, ,, 145, note 61, *for* '1785' *read* '1782'
,, ,, 146, note 2, *for* '153' *read* '133'
,, ,, 152*a*, line 20, *for* '1227, when' *read* '1231, before which date'
,, ,, 152*b*, lines 12–13, *for* '[2] and . . . Philip' *read* ',[2] his nephew Philip (son of his brother Roger),[3] Margery's grandson,[4]'
,, ,, 152*b*, line 41, *delete* 'in 1919'
,, ,, 156*b*, line 34, *for* '13th' *read* '14th'
,, ,, 158*b*, line 38, *for* '1612–53' *read* '?1612–1653'
,, ,, 158, notes 60, 62, 66, 68, *for* '(2)' *read* '(3)'
,, ,, 158, note 66, *before* '115' *add* '109,'
,, ,, 159, notes 70, 72, 75, 94, *for* '(2)' *read* '(3)'
,, ,, 160, notes 10, 26, 48, *for* '(2)' *read* '(3)'
,, ,, 160, note 13, *for* '176' *read* '76'
,, ,, 164, note 37, *for* 'vi' *read* 'v'
,, ,, 165*a*, line 4, *for* 'son H. W. Powys' *read* 'grandson H. W. Feilding (later Powys)'
,, ,, 165*a*, line 5, *delete* 'great-'
,, ,, 165*b*, line 2, *before* 'wife' *add* 'later the'
,, ,, 165*b*, line 10, *after* 'the' *add* 'widow 1872–94, and' *and for* 'brothers and sisters' *read* 'sons and daughters'
,, ,, 165*b*, line 11, *for* '1871' *read* '1894'
,, ,, 165*b*, line 12, *for* 'Jasper, 1899–1917' *read* 'James, 1899–1919'
,, ,, 165*b*, line 13, *after* '1919–27' *add* '; Anne, 1927'
165*b*, line 20, *for 's'* (*twice*) *read 'd'*
,, ,, 165*b*, note 85, *add* '; Hope-Edwardes MSS., Linley Hall, will of T. H. Hope-Edwardes; *Shrews. Chron.* 13 May 1927, p. 7.'
,, ,, 165*b*, note 86, *for* 'Ibid' *read* 'Burke, *Land. Gent.* (1952), p. 1820.'
,, ,, 170*a*, line 8, *for* 'western' *read* 'eastern'
,, ,, 171*a*, lines 21–7, *delete* 'The early 13th . . . the existing road.'
,, ,, 171*a*, line 28, *before* 'when' *add* 'even'
,, ,, 171, *delete note 28*
,, ,, 171, notes 35, 46, *for* 'ff. 134–5' *read* 'f. 134'
,, ,, 174*a*, line 32, *delete* 'then'
,, ,, 174*a*, line 33, *after* '69 a.' *add* 'in 1795[68a]'
,, 174*a*, line 34, *for* '1782' *read* '1805'
,, ,, 174, *after note 68 add new note* '[68a] Ibid. valuation.'
,, ,, 176*b*, last line, *for* 'Wolryche-Whitmore' *read* 'Wolryche Whitmore'
,, ,, 179, *Upper Stanford (the area arrowed into Wales) to be defined by the hundred and national boundaries*
,, ,, 179, *in Ratlinghope parish transpose the names* 'Stitt' *and* 'Gatten'
,, ,, 179, *for* '1840' *read* '1831'
,, ,, 180, line 5, *delete* 'Gatten (in Ratlinghope parish),'
,, ,, 180, line 6, *after* ')' *delete* ','
,, ,, 180, line 7, *after* 'Worthen,' *add* 'with the township of Gatten (in Ratlinghope parish), as a possible member of the Domesday manor of Wentnor,[14a]'
,, ,, 180, *after note 14 add new note* '[14a] Eyton, xi. 52 n., 190.'
,, ,, 181*a*, line 6, *before* 'Trefnant' *add* 'Lower Stanford,'
,, ,, 181*a*, line 9, *for* '371' *read* '381', *delete* 'a', *and for* 'part' *read* 'parts'
,, ,,

181*a*, line 10, *for* 'within Cardeston parish.[2] The' *read* 'civil parish within, or beyond, Cardeston civil parish after the'
,, ,, 181*a*, lines 11–12, *for* ', all now civil parishes, have' *read* 'became separate civil parishes. They had'
,, ,, 181*a*, line 13, *after* 'and' *add* '(except for Upper Stanford, a former detachment of Bausley)'
,, ,, 181*a*, line 14, *delete* 'of the parish'
,, ,, 181*a*, line 24, *for* '.[5] The latter' *read* 'and, with a detachment of Bausley civil parish (65 a. at Upper Stanford, simultaneously transferred from Montg.), went to form Alberbury-with-Cardeston civil parish.[5] Cardeston parish had'
,, ,, 181*b*, line 4, *for* 'eastern' *read* 'western'
,, ,, 181, note 2, *after* '188' *add* ', which does not show the smaller Alberbury detachment (near Upper Stanford)'
,, ,, 181, note 5, *after* '1891' *add* '; *16th Ann. Rep. Local Govt. Bd.* [C. 5131], pp. lxiv, 325, 332, 334, H.C. (1886–7), xxxvi. The O.S. shows the Upper Stanford detachment of Bausley township (later civil parish) in Montg. *c.* 1851 but (wrongly) not in 1882: O.S. Map 1", index to tithe survey, sheet LX.NE. [*c.* 1851]; 1/2,500, Salop. XXXII.8, 12 (1882 edn.)'
,, ,, 181, note 7, *for* 'Horedon' *read* 'Hovenden'
,, ,, 183*a*, line 5, *for* 'transferred to Alberbury' *read* ', as has been seen, included in Alberbury-with-Cardeston'
,, ,, 183, notes 22, 26, 28, *for* 'Horedon' *read* 'Hovenden'
,, ,, 184*a*, line 26, *for* 'west' *read* 'east'
,, ,, 184*a*, line 31, *for* 'east' *read* 'west'
,, ,, 184, notes 31 and 49, *for* 'Horedon' *read* 'Hovenden'
,, ,, 185, note 81, *for* '166' *read* '171'
,, ,, 185, note 87, *for* 'Horedon' *read* 'Hovenden'
,, ,, 186, note 98, *for* '166' *read* '171'
,, ,, 187, notes 13, 22, 26, *for* 'Horedon' *read* 'Hovenden'
,, ,, 188, in title, *for* 'ALBERBURY-WITH-CARDESTON' *read* 'PARISHES OF ALBERBURY (PART) AND CARDESTON'
,, ,, 188, *Upper Stanford should be shown as a detachment of Bausley (as on page 179)*
,, ,, 188, *Lower Stanford should not be surrounded by a township boundary and shown as a detachment of Alberbury township*
,, ,, 188, in underline, *for* 'Based' *read* 'The bold pecked line defines the external boundary of Alberbury-with-Cardeston civil parish, created 1886, and Wollaston civil parish. The fine pecked lines are township boundaries, based'
,, ,, 189*b*, line 53, *delete* 'Sir' *and for* '1780 and 1783' *read* '1777 and *c.* 1780'
,, ,, 189, notes 53 and 56, *for* 'Horedon' *read* 'Hovenden'
,, ,, 190, notes 73 and 86, *for* 'Horedon' *read* 'Hovenden'
,, ,, 191, notes 13, 15, 24, *for* 'Horedon' *read* 'Hovenden'
,, ,, 192, note 56, *for* '166' *read* '171'
,, ,, 192, note 61, *for* 'Horedon' *read* 'Hovenden'
,, ,, 194*a*, line 43, *for* 'west' *read* 'east'
,, ,, 194, notes 91, 94, 4, 12, 13, 17, *for* '166' *read* '171'
,, ,, 195, notes 26 and 28, *for* '166' *read* '171'
,, ,, 195, notes 37 and 39, *for* 'Horedon' *read* 'Hovenden'
,, ,, 196*a*, line 24, *for* '1347' *read* '1348'
,, ,, 196*b*, line 12, *for* '80;' *read* '73;[93a]'
,, ,, 196*b*, line 13, *for* '1780–4' *read* '1773–84'
,, ,, 196*b*, line 14, *for* '28;' *read* '27;[93b]' *and for* '1828' *read* '1827'
,, ,, 196, note 84, *for* '1500' *read* '1500–1'
,, ,, 196, note 85, line 3, *for* '25,' *read* 'x. 25; ibid. xi.'
,, ,, 196, *after note 93 add new notes* '[93a] Loton Hall MSS., TS. hist. of Leighton fam. to 1871, pp. 15, 24–5, 58 (2nd nos.).' *and* '[93b] Ibid.'
,, ,, 201*b*, lines 29–30, *for* 'made the estate over in 1880 to' *read* 'died in 1889 and was succeeded by'
,, ,, 201*b*, line 30, *delete* 'Sir' *and for* 'Lowry Corry' *read* 'Lowry-Corry'
,, ,, 201*b*, line 31, *for* 'was' *read* 'had been' *and for* 'the same year' *read* '1880'
,, ,, 201*b*, line 34, *for* 'Lowry Corry' *read* 'Lowry-Corry'
,, ,, 201, note 72, *after* '202' *add* '; *Complete Peerage*, xi 214 n'
,, ,, 202*b*, line 16, *for* 'Alreton' *read* 'Alretone'
,, ,, 203*a*, lines 21 and 24, *for* '1346' *read* '1348'
,, ,, 203, notes 28 and 37, *for* '166' *read* '171'
,, ,, 206*b*, line 29, *after* 'and' *add* 'whose trustee'
,, ,, 207*a*, line 47, *for* 'Hill' *read* 'Noel-Hill'
,, ,, 208*a*, line 50, *for* 'this was sold in 1855' *read* 'in 1855 this was intended to be sold'
,, ,, 208, notes 4, 12, 17, *for* '166' *read* '171'
,, ,, 208, note 26, *for* '58' *read* '62'
,, ,, 210, notes 93 and 95, *for* '166' *read* '171'
,, ,, 210, notes 1 and 6, *for* 'Horedon' *read* 'Hovenden'
,, ,, 214*a*, line 18, *for* 'Rector' *read* 'Vicar'
,, ,, 214, note 19, *delete* 'i.'

" " 215, note 47, *delete* 'i.'
" " 218, note 62, *after* 'vi' *add* '–vii'
" " 219, notes 88 and 93, *for* '166' *read* '171'
" " 222*a*, lines 28–31, *for* 'on . . . house' *read* 'in 1794[14] on the other side of the road, with master's house attached. In 1845 a new school was built next to it'
" " 222, note 29, *for* '166' *read* '171'
" " 223*a*, line 48, *for* 'Tithes' *read* 'Rectorial tithes'
" " 223*a*, line 49, *before* 'Ford' *add* 'the impropriator of'
" " 223*a*, line 52, *after* 'due' *add* 'in lieu of rectorial tithes'
" " 223*b*, line 45, *before* 'Ford' *add* 'the impropriator of'
" " 223*b*, line 49, *after* 'Alberbury' *add* 'and owed small tithes to its vicar'
" " 223, note 6, *after* 'Ibid.' *add* '; ibid.'
" " 224*a*, line 52, *delete* 'Inn'
" " 225*a*, line 55, *delete* 'section of the latter road north of the'
" " 227*a*, line 20, *delete* 'inns,'
" " 227*a*, lines 24 and 43, *delete* 'Inn'
" " 227*a*, line 29, *for* 'inn' *read* 'building'
" " 227*a*, line 36, *delete* 'original'
" " 227*a*, line 43, *for* '1660' *read* '1670'
" " 230*a*, line 17, *for* 'Gray' *read* 'Grey'
" " 230*b*, line 1, *for* 'tenant' *read* 'manorial tenants'
" " 232*a*, line 55, *for* 'on' *read* 'after' *and after* 'passed to' *add* 'the representatives of'
" " 233, note 79, *for* '1775' *read* '1785'
" " 234*a*, line 29, *for* 'chaplain' *read* 'warden'
" " 234*b*, line 4, *for* 'early' *read* 'mid'
" " 234*b*, line 16, *after* 'chapel' *add* 'to its appropriator'
" " 234*b*, line 19, *for* 'its appropriation' *read* 'the appropriation of St. Michael's in the Castle'
" " 234*b*, lines 20–3, *after* 'Battlefield' *rest of sentence to read* 'College Ford tithes passed to the College and in 1548, as has been seen, to the Crown.[14]'
" " 234*b*, line 39, *for* 'chaplain of Ford' *read* 'incumbent of St. Michael's in the Castle'
" " 234*b*, line 45, *for* 'by the College's' *read* 'for 999 years by the College and its'
" " 234, note 88, *for* '384' *read* '354'
" " 234, note 14, *for* 'See p. 237' *read* 'Above'
" " 234, note 25, *for* '1314–15, 280' *read* '1343–5, 280–1'
" " 235*b*, line 10, *before* 'served' *add* 'probably' *and after* 'by' *delete* 'the'
" " 235*b*, line 11, *for* 'of' *read* 'appointed from' *and for* 'Michael' *read* 'Michael's'
" " 235*b*, lines 11–16, *for* 'At . . . parish' *read* 'Ford'
" " 235*b*, line 16, *after* 'appears' *add* 'sometimes'
" " 235, *delete notes 49 and 50*
" " 238*a*, line 36, *for* 'Pontesford' *read* 'Pontesbury'
" " 238*b*, line 28, *for* 'up' *read* 'down'
" " 239*b*, line 48, *delete* 'in that year' *and for* 'The' *read* 'In 1347 the'
" " 240*a*, line 31, *for* '1888' *read* '1887'
" " 240*a*, line 48, *after* 'was' *add* 'said to have been'
" " 240*b*, line 14, *for* 'in the early 17th century' *read* 'probably in 1593'
" " 241*b*, line 35, *for* 'jupping' *read* 'supping'
" " 242, note 62, *delete* 'ii.'
" " 244*a*, line 39, *after* '1884' *add* 'and 1885'
" " 244*b*, line 24, *for* 'township' *read* 'and Cruckton townships'
" " 245*a*, line 9, *for* 'east' *read* 'west'
" " 248*a*, line 3, *for* 'Londgen' *read* 'Longden'
" " 258*b*, line 21, *after* 'colonnade' *add* 'dates from 1800' *and after* 'portico' *add* 'formerly'
" " 258*b*, line 22, *for* 'were' *read* 'was'
" " 258, note 75, *after* 'Head' *add* 'and Mr. P. D. Miles'
" " 259, note 83, *for* '358' *read* '258'
" " 259, note 84, *for* '360' *read* '258'
" " 261*b*, line 11, *before* 'the' *add* 'beneath'
" " 261*b*, line 12, *for* 'valley' *read* 'hill' *and delete* 'of'
" " 264*b*, line 12, *for* '1346' *read* '1348'
" " 266, note 78, *for* 'D 141/2/17' *read* 'C 141/2/19'
" " 267*a*, line 1, *for* 'brother' *read* 'son'
" " 267*a*, line 4, *for* 'nephew' *read* 'brother'
" " 269*b*, line 4, *after* 'Berrington' *add* '(later Berington)'
" " 269*b*, lines 10 and 11, *for* 'Berrington' *read* 'Berington'
" " 270*b*, line 25, *for* '54' *read* '51'
" " 270*b*, line 26, *for* '1754' *read* '1751'
" " 270*b*, line 28, *for* '1771' *read* '1770'

” ” 270, note 51, *for* ‘*1404*’ *read* ‘*1400*’
” ” 271*b*, line 3 *for* ‘uncle’ *read* ‘brother’
” ” 272, note 34, *for* ‘*1404*’ *read* ‘*1400*’
” ” 274*a*, lines 40–1, *for* ‘Church and’ *read* ‘Church, and in 1783 he’
” ” 277, note 30, *for* ‘*1404*’ *read* ‘*1400*’
” ” 279*a*, line 32, *for* ‘1860’ *read* ‘*c.* 1862’
” ” 280*a*, line 1, *for* ‘1802’ *read* ‘1805’
” ” 280, note 21, *for* ‘1802’ *read* ‘1805’
” ” 282*b*, line 41, *for* ‘assistant’ *read* ‘deputy’
” ” 283*a*, line 32, *for* ‘adoption’ *read* ‘introduction’
” ” 289*b*, line 30, *for* ‘1636’ *read* ‘1637’
” ” 289*b*, lines 40–2, *for* ‘These . . . again recast’ *read* ‘A sixth was added’
” ” 289, *delete note 37*
” ” 290*b*, line 1, for ‘Meredith-Warter’ *read* ‘Warter Meredith’ *and for* ‘Randall’ *read* ‘Randal’
” ” 300*a*, line 3, *before* ‘east’ *add* ‘north-’
” ” 300, note 57, *delete* ‘(priv. act)’
” ” 301, notes 74 *and* 75, *delete* ‘(priv. act)’
” ” 307*a*, line 22, *delete* ‘south-’
” ” 307, note 10, *for* ‘E.’ *read* ‘T.’
” ” 311*b*, line 39, *after* ‘sold’ *add* ‘by Lord Bath’
” ” 312*b*, line 16, *for* ‘William’ (*twice*) *read* ‘Edward’
” ” 312, note 17, *for* ‘27–29’ *read* ‘278–80’
” ” 313*b*, line 31, *for* ‘Whitton to Dr.’ *read* ‘their Whitton estate to the Revd. William Severne, and it later passed to his nephew’
” ” 313*b*, line 42, *for* ‘1346’ *read* ‘1348’
” ” 313, note 77, *for* ‘1586’ *read* ‘1508’
” ” 315*a*, line 20, *for* ‘1346’ *read* ‘1348’
” ” 315*b*, line 34, *for* ‘A. A.’ *read* ‘A. S.’
” ” 316*a*, lines 33 *and* 35, *for* ‘Tyrrwhit’ *read* ‘Tyrwhitt’
” ” 326, note 81, *for* ‘*Botha*’ *read* ‘*Bothe*’
” ” 327*a*, line 35, *for* ‘74’ *read* ‘72’
” ” 327*b*, lines 33–4, *for* ‘continuously after 1776’ *read* ‘intermittently from 1768’
” ” 333*b*, *s.v.* ‘Adderbury’, *for* ‘Ric.’ *read* ‘John’
” ” 333*c*, *s.v.* ‘Alberbury’, *before* ‘Whitfield’ *add* ‘Wattlesborough;’
” ” 333*c*, *s.v.* ‘Alreton’, *for* ‘Alreton’ *read* ‘Alretone’
” ” 334*a*, *s.v.* ‘Apley’, *delete* ‘95,’ *and add new entry* ‘Apley, in Wellington, 95’
” ” 334*b*, *s.v.* ‘architects’, *for* ‘Randall’ *read* ‘Randal’
” ” 334*b*, *s.v.* ‘Auden’, *for* ‘Revd. H.’ *read* ‘H.’
” ” 334*c*, *s.v.* ‘Bausley’, *before* ‘183’ *add* ‘181,’
” ” 335*a*, *s.v.* ‘Berington’, *after* ‘John (d. 1892), 269;’ *add* ‘Phil., 269; Thos., 269;’ *and after* ‘Wm., 269;’ *add* ‘fam., 269;’
” ” 335*a*, *s.v.* ‘Berrington’ (*surname*), *delete* ‘Phil., 269;’ *and* ‘Thos. (d. 1811), 269;’ *and after* ‘fam., 44, 263,’ *add* ‘269,’
” ” 335*a*, *s.v.* ‘Berrington, boundaries’, *delete* ‘, 48’
” ” 335*b*, *s.v.* ‘Biggs, Lucy’, *for* ‘(dau. of last-named)’ *read* ‘, m. Ric. Oakley’
” ” 335*b*, *s.v.* ‘Biggs, Sarah’, *before* ‘232’ *add* ‘m. Geo. Smythe,’
” ” 335*c*, *s.v.* ‘Bradford, Earls of’, *for* ‘95’ *read* ‘126’
” ” 335*c*, *s.v.* ‘Bradford South’, *delete* ‘South’
” ” 336*b*, *s.v.* ‘Buildwas Abbey’, *for* ‘Richard’ *read* ‘Whalley’
” ” 337*b*, *s.v.* ‘Cholmondeley’, *after* ‘Thos.’ *add* ‘(later Owen)’
” ” 337*c*, *s.v.* ‘Coldwell’, *after* ‘Coldwell’ *add* ‘(later Hope-Edwardes)’
” ” 337*c*, *s.v.* ‘Condover, Bulridges’, *delete* ‘, 48’
” ” 338*a*, *s.v.* ‘Corbet’, *for* ‘John (d. 1347), 203, 239’ *read* ‘John (d. by 1347), 239; John (fl. 1348), 203’
” ” 338*c*, *s.v.* ‘Covert’, *for* ‘Giles, 126’ *read* ‘Giles (fl. 1534), 126; Giles (d. 1557, another), 126’ *and at end add* ‘; fam., 126’
” ” 338*c*–339*a*, *s.v.* ‘Cresset’, *for* ‘Cresset’ *read* ‘Cressett (Cresset)’ *and for* ‘Cresset Pelham’ *read* ‘Cressett Pelham’
” ” 339*a*, *s.v.* ‘Cresset Pelham’, *for* ‘Cresset’ *read* ‘Cressett’ *and after see for* ‘Cresset’ *read* ‘Cressett’
” ” 339*a*, *s.v.* ‘Cruckmeole’, *before* ‘Pontesbury’ *add* ‘Ford, Great Hanwood, Meole Brace, and’ *and before* ‘264’ *add* ‘244,’
” ” 339*a*, *s.v.* ‘Cruckton’, *before* ‘Pontesbury’ *add* ‘Great Hanwood and’ *and before* ‘264’ *add* ‘244,’
” ” 339*c*, *s.v.* ‘Edmunds’, *before* ‘Morris’ *add* ‘H. A., 42–3; L. E., 42;’
” ” 340*a*, *s.v.* ‘Edwardes’, *before* ‘Revd. Sir John’ *add* ‘Sir Hen. Hope, bt., 65;’ *and before* ‘Smitheman’ *add* ‘Hope-Edwardes;’
” ” 340*a*, *s.v.* ‘Edwards’, *delete* ‘H. A., 42, 43;’ *and* ‘L. E., 42;’
” ” 340*c*, *s.v.* ‘Ford’, *at end of entry add* ‘; *and see* Cruckmeole’
” ” 341*a*, *s.v.* ‘Gatten’, *delete* ‘in Ratlinghope,’
” ” 342*a*, *s.v.* ‘Hanwood, Great’, *before* ‘Gadbridge’ *add* ‘Cruckmeole; Cruckton;’

" " 342*a*, *s.v.* 'Hanwood, Little', *before* '282' *add* '280,'
" " 342*c*, *s.v.* 'Harrop', *delete entry*
" " 343*a*, *s.v.* 'Hill', *for* 'Ric., Lord Berwick' *read* '(later Noel-Hill), Ric. Noel, Lord Berwick' *and for* 'Revd. Ric. Noel' *read* '(later Noel-Hill), Revd. Ric.' *and transpose the two subentries*
" " 343*a*, *s.v.* 'Hill', *delete* 'Thos. Hen., Lord Berwick (d. 1947), 19, 24;' *and for* 'Revd. Thos. Hen. Noel' *read* '(later Noel-Hill), Revd. Thos. Hen.'
" " 343*a*, *s.v.* 'Hill', *delete* 'Revd. Thos. Noel (d. 1888), 25;' *and before* 'Wm., Lord Berwick' *add* '(later Noel-Hill),'
" " 343*a*, *s.v.* 'Hill', *for* 'fam., 16, 19, 207,' *read* 'fam., 17, 19' *and after* 'Hulle' *add* '; Noel-Hill'
" " 343*b*, *s.v.* 'Hope', *before* 'John' *add* '(later Hope-Edwardes), Anne, 165; (later Hope-Edwardes), Ellen, 165; (later Hope-Edwardes), Lt.-Col. H. J., 65, 165;' *and before* 'Ric.' *add* '(later Hope-Edwardes), Julia, 165;'
" " 343*b*, *s.v.* 'Hope', *before* 'Thos. Hen.' *add* 'St. Leger Fred, 165; (later Hope-Edwardes),' *and before* 'fam.' *add* '(later Hope-Edwardes), Mrs., 57, 165;'
" " 343*b*, *s.v.* 'Hope-Edwardes', *for existing entry substitute new entry* 'Hope-Edwardes, Anne, *see* Hope; Clare, *see* Coldwell; Ellen, *see* Hope; Lt.-Col. H. J., *see* Hope; Julia, *see* Hope; St. Leger Fred., *see* Hope; Thos. Hen., *see* Hope; Mrs., *see* Hope; fam., 34, 53, 55; *and see* Edwardes; Hope'
" " 343*c*, *s.v.* 'Hulle', *after* 'Hill' *add* ';Noel-Hill'
" " 343*c*, before entry 'Humphreston', *add new entry* 'Hulton-Harrop (formerly Hulton), Wm., 42; fam., 43'
" " 343*c*, *s.v.* 'Hundreds', *delete* 'South'
" " 344*a*, after entry 'Johnson', *add new entry* 'Johnstone (later Pulteney), (Sir) Wm., bt., 75, 88'
" " 344*a*, *s.v.* 'Jones', *for* 'Tyrrwhit' *read* 'Tyrwhitt'
" " 344*b*, *s.v.* 'La Zouche' *delete* 'de' *(twice)*.
" " 344*c*, *s.v.* 'Langley, in Ruckley and Langley: chap.', *for* '142' *read* '142–3'
" " 344*c*, before entry 'Lea Cross', *add new entry* 'Lea, in Church Pulverbatch, *see* Lee'
" " 344*c*, *s.v.* 'Lee' (*surname*), *for* 'Ric. (d. 1500)' *read* 'Ric. (d. 1498)', *before* 'Ric. (d. 1591)' *delete* 'Sir', *for* 'Thos. (d. 1574)' *read* 'Thos. (d. 1561)', *and before* 'fam.' *add* 'Wal., 38;'
" " 344*c*, *s.v.* 'Lee' (*place name*), *after* 'Lee' *add* '(?Lea, in Church Pulverbatch)'
" " 345*a*, *s.v.* 'Leighton', *for* 'Sir Baldwin, bt. (d. 1828)' *read* 'Sir Baldwin, bt. (d. 1827)'
" " 345*b*, *s.v.* 'Lingen', *before* 'Eliz.' *add* 'Edw., 312;'
" " 345*b*, *s.v.* 'Lingen', *delete* 'Wm. (d. 1636), 312;'
" " 345*b*, *s.v.* 'Lisle' *delete* 'of'
" " 345*b*, *s.v.* 'Littleton', *for* 'Lyttleton' *read* 'Lyttelton'
" " 346*a*, *s.v.* 'Lyttleton', *for* 'Lyttleton' *read* 'Lyttelton'
" " 346*c*, *s.v.* 'Meole Brace', *before* 'Edgbold' *add* 'Cruckmeole;'
" " 346*c*, *s.v.* 'Meredith', *after* 'Warter' *add* '; Warter Meredith'
" " 347*a*, *s.v.* 'Montgomery', *for* 'A. A.' *read* 'A. S.'
" " 347*b*, *s.v.* 'Nag's Head Colliery', *before* '280' *add* '255,'
" " 347*c*, after entry 'Nock', *add new entry* 'Noel-Hill, Revd. Ric., Lord Berwick, *see* Hill; Ric. Noel, Lord Berwick, *see* Hill; Thos. Hen., Lord Berwick, 19, 24; Revd. Thos. Hen., *see* Hill; Revd. Thos., 25; fam., 207; *and see* Hill; Hulle'
" " 347*c*, *s.v.* 'Oakley', *before* 'Wm.' *add* 'Lucy, *see* Biggs;'
" " 348*a*, *s.v.* 'Ottley', *for* 'Thos. (d. 1622), 119; Thos. (d. 1636)' *read* 'Thos. (d. 1623), 119; Thos. (d. 1637)'
" " 348*a*, *s.v.* 'Owen', *before* 'Ursula' *add* 'Thos. (d. 1864), *see* Cholmondeley;'
" " 348*b*, *s.v.* 'Peverel' *for* 'Ralph' *read* 'Ranulph'
" " 349*b*, *s.v.* 'Pontesbury', *after* 'Polmere;' *add* 'Pontesbury Hill;'
" " 349*b*, before entry 'Pontesford, Hugh de', *add new entry* 'Pontesbury Hill, 238, 245–6, 251–4, 272, 277, 281, 292'
" " 350*a*, *s.v.* 'Pulteney', *for* '75, 88' *read* '88; *and see* Johnstone'
" " 350*a*, *s.v.* 'Pulverbatch, Church', *after* 'Cothercott;' *add* 'Lee;' *and before* 'Walleybourne' *add* 'Stitt and Gatten;'
" " 350*b*, *s.v.* 'Randall', *for* 'Randall' *read* 'Randal'
" " 350*b*, *s.v.* 'Richard, Abbot of Buildwas', *delete entry*
" " 351*b*, *s.v.* 'Sergeantson', *for* 'Sergeantson' *read* 'Serjeantson'
" " 351*b*, *s.v.* 'Severne', *delete* 'Dr.' *and before* 'fam.' *add* 'Revd. Wm., 313;'
" " 352*a*, *s.v.* 'Smythe', *before* 'Wm.' *add* 'Sarah, *see* Biggs;'
" " 352*b*, *s.v.* 'Stanford, Lower', *for* '182' *read* '181, 182, 212'
" " 352*b*, *s.v.* 'Stanford, Upper', *before '182' add* '181,'
" " 352*c*, *s.v.* 'Stitt and Gatten', *before* 'Ratlinghope' *add* 'Church Pulverbatch and'
" " 352*c*, *s.v.* "Stokes", *delete* ', 200' *and before* '204' *add* '200,'
" " 353*a*, *s.v.* 'Stretch', *for* '283' *read* '282'
" " 353*a*, *s.v.* 'Tatham', *before* 'Mary' *add* 'Hen. de Grey Warter, 230, 267; (later Tatham Warter),'
" " 353*a*, *s.v.* 'Tatham Warter', *for* '230, 267' *read* '*see* Tatham' *and before 'and' add* 'Mary Eliza, *see* Warter;'
" " 353*b*, *s.v.* 'Topp', *delete* 'A. C., 332;' *and for* 'Agatha, 313' *read* 'Agatha C., 313, 332'
" " 353*c*, *s.v.* 'Tyrrwhit', *for* 'Tyrrwhit' (*twice*) *read* 'Tyrwhitt'
" " 353*c*, *s.v.* 'Tyrrwhit-Jones', *for* 'Tyrrwhit' (*twice*) *read* 'Tyrwhitt'
" " 354*a*, *s.v.* 'Walker', *before* '; Job' *delete* ', *and see* Walleybourne' *and for* 'Lea (d. by 1470)' *read* 'Lee (d. by 1470) and his w. Joan'

„ „ 354*b*, *s.v.* 'Walleybourne', *delete* 'Joan . . . John de, 135' *and after* 'Rob. de' *add* 'and his gt.-granddau.'

„ „ 354*b*, *s.v.* 'Warter, Hen. (d. 1879)' *delete* '290,' *and after* 'Meredith; Tatham Warter' *add* '; Warter Meredith'

„ „ 354*b*, after entry 'Warter', *add new entry* 'Warter Meredith, Hen. (d. 1879), *see* Warter; Hen. (d. 1901), 290; *and see* Meredith; Tatham Warter; Warter'

„ „ 354*c*, *s.v.* 'Wattlesborough', *before* 'Cardeston' *add* 'Alberbury and'

„ „ 354*c*, after entry 'Weniet', *add new entry* 'Wenlock Abbey estate, 88; *and see* Wenlock Priory'

„ „ 354*c*, *s.v.* 'Wenlock Priory', *after* '*Dictum of*' *add* ';Wenlock Abbey estate'

„ „ 354*c*, *s.v.* 'Wentnor', *before* '*see*' *add* '180; *and*'

„ „ 355*a*, *s.v.* 'Weymouth', *delete* 'of'

„ „ 355*a*, after entry 'Weymouth', *add new entry* 'Whalley, Wm., Abbot of Buildwas, 65'

„ „ 355*a*, *s.v.* 'Whitmore', *before* 'fam.' *add* 'Wm. Wolryche, 101, 176;'

„ „ 355*b*, *s.v.* 'Wilkes', *before* 'Revd.' *add* 'Revd. Hen., 127;'

„ „ 355*c*, *s.v.* 'Willis', *delete entry*

„ „ 356*a*, *s.v.* 'Wolryche-Whitmore', *delete* 'Wm., 101, 176;'

„ „ 356*c*, at end, *add new entry* 'Zouche, *see* La Zouche'